*Population Growth
and Socioeconomic Change
in West Africa*

# Population Growth and Socioeconomic Change in West Africa

Edited by
## JOHN C. CALDWELL

with the collaboration of

N. O. ADDO          A. IGUN
S. K. GAISIE          P. O. OLUSANYA

Published for the Population Council, New York

*New York and London*          *Columbia University Press*     •     *1975*

**Library of Congress Cataloging in Publication Data**
Main entry under title:

Population growth and socioeconomic change in West Africa.

   1. Africa, West—Population. 2. Africa, French-speaking West—
Population. I. Caldwell, John Charles, ed. II. Addo, N. O., ed.
HB3665.P66      301.32'9'66     74-17409
ISBN 0-231-23732-5

# Contributors

**N. O. Addo** is Senior Research Fellow in Demography and Director of the Population Dynamics Programme at the University of Ghana. He has published articles and monographs in the fields of population, migration, and urbanization.

**Eugene Benjamin** is Deputy Director at the Central Statistics Office in Freetown, Sierra Leone and has contributed articles to a number of statistical and geographical journals.

**Christian Bouquet** is head of the Geography Department of the University of Chad and head of the Demography Division of the Tchadien Institut pour les Sciences Humaines. He is the author of a number of articles on the geography and demography of Chad, and of a forthcoming regional study.

**Joseph Boute** is the head of the Department of Demography at the National University of Zaïre. He has been head of Research at the Office National de la Recherche et du Développement. He is the author of *La Démographie de la Branche Indo-Pakistanaise d'Afrique* and has contributed widely to books and journals.

**John C. Caldwell** is Professor of Demography at the Australian National University and has been a demographer at the Universities of Ghana, Ife, Ibadan, Nigeria (Nsukka) and Nairobi, and Regional Demographic Director for Africa with the Population Council. He is the author of *Population Growth and Family Change in Africa: The New Urban Elite in Ghana*, and *African Rural-Urban Migration: The Movement to Ghana's Towns;* co-author of *A Manual for Surveys of Fertility and Family Planning;* the major author of the second volume of *A Study of Contemporary Ghana;* co-editor of *The Population of Tropical Africa;* and has written many articles on West African population questions.

**Pierre Cantrelle** is Director of Research in the Demography Section of ORSTOM in Paris. From 1954 to 1969 he was engaged in medical and demographic research in francophone Africa. His publications include *La moyenne vallée du Sénégal* and *Etude démographique dans la région de Sine-Saloum (Sénégal).*

**André Courel** is engaged in demographic research in Upper Volta. He has conducted economic and statistical surveys and has written a number of papers.

**Issaka Dankoussou**, a sociologist particularly interested in languages and literature, has been Executive Secretary of the Regional Center of Documentation on Oral Tradition at Niamey since 1969. He is the author of *History of Dawra* and of *History of Katsina*, as well as a number of works on music, theater, and linguistics.

**Souleymane Diarra** is with the Geography Department of the University of Dakar.

**Thomas E. Dow** is Associate Professor of Sociology at the State University of New York. His research includes a national demographic survey in Sierra Leone, where he was Resident Adviser in Demography and Sociology at Fourah Bay College. He has written for *Demography* and other journals.

**Charles N. Ejiogu** is the United Nations Population Affairs Officer for English-speaking Africa and some Far East Asian countries at the United Nations Population Division, New York. He has lectured in demography at the University of Nairobi, Kenya, and has done work in census analysis and evaluation in Nigeria. He has chapters on population in Africa included in several books and is co-editor of *Population Growth and Economic Development in Africa.*

**Michel Francois** is attached to INSEE: he has directed the Bureau des Enquêtes Statistiques et de la Démographie in Gabon from 1961 to 1971 and founded the UDEAC Bureau Technique Régional for demography in the Central African Republic where he worked during 1971–1973.

**S. K. Gaisie** is Senior Lecturer in Demography in the United NationsR egional Institute for Population Studies at the University of Ghana. He directed the 1968–69 National Demographic Sample Survey of Ghana. His writings include *Dynamics of Population Growth in Ghana* as well as a number of contributions to demographic books and journals.

**M. F. Ganon** is attached to INSEE and is permanent expert of FAC. He has been active in demographic research in francophone Africa since 1952. He has written extensively on the demography of Zaïre.

**A. D. Goddard** is Computer Officer in the University of Liverpool and is associated with its African Population Mobility Project. He was earlier with the Rural Economy Research Unit, Ahmadu Bello University. He has published papers on Nigeria and Uganda.

**Davidson R. Gwatkin** is Program Adviser in Population for the New Delhi, India, Office of the Ford Foundation. He previously served in the same capacity in the Ford Foundation's West Africa Office.

**William A. Hance** is Professor of Economic Geography, Department of Geography, Columbia University, where he is also a member of the Institute of African Studies. He is the author of *African Economic Development*, *The Geography of Modern Africa*, and *Population, Migration and Urbanization in Africa*.

**Barbara Harrell-Bond** is a research fellow at the Afrika-Studiecentrum, Leiden, Holland. She is the author of *Modern Marriage in Sierra Leone: A Study of the Professional Group*, and has recently completed a study of family law in Sierra Leone.

**Milton F. Harvey** was the head of the Department of Geography of Fourah Bay College, Sierra Leone, and is now Professor of Geography, Kent State University.

**Adenole A. Igun** is Professor of Demography and Director of the Institute of Population and Manpower Studies at the University of Ife, Nigeria. He is co-author of *Demographic Statistics in Nigeria* and *Surveys of Fertility, Family, and Family Planning in Nigeria*. He has written a number of articles on data collection methods and other aspects of demography.

**S. B. Jones** is Executive Director, Ghana Manpower Board, Ministry of Economic Planning, and helped to produce the Ghana White Paper on population policy. He has written papers and articles on population policies and family planning.

**Wesner Joseph** was a demographer with the Liberian Department of Statistics and is now with the United Nations Development Program in Cameroon.

**Tom K. Kumekpor,** sociologist and demographer, is a lecturer in sociology on leave of absence from the University of Ghana. He is at present the Assistant Regional Secretary in Charge of the IPPF Africa Regional Sub-Office in West Africa. He has carried out many sociodemographic surveys and written many articles on West Africa, particularly on Ghana, Togo, and the Ivory Coast.

**B. Lacombe** is in the demographic section of ORSTOM and has undertaken sociological and demographic research in Senegal and Madagascar. He is the author of books and articles on African demography. At present he is attached to the National Statistical Institute of Tunisia.

**B. Lamy** was attached to the Dakar-Hann office of ORSTOM in Senegal, and is now working on agricultural economics in France.

**Dioulde Laya** is Director of CNRSH and Secretary-General of the *Commission Nationale* of UNESCO. He is the author of a number of articles on African sociological research.

**Akin L. Mabogunje** is Professor of Geography, head of the Department of Geography, and co-director of the Planning Studies Programme of the University of Ibadan. He is author of *Yoruba Towns, Urbanization in Nigeria, Regional Mobility and Resource Development in West Africa*, and *Cities and Social Order*.

**Robert W. Morgan** was Principal Investigator of the Lagos Family Health Project during 1965–1973 and the Sokoto Family Health Project during 1972–73, and was previously a research associate at the Nigerian Institute for Social and Economic Research, Ibadan. He is now a member of the Department of Population Sciences, Harvard School of Public Health.

**M. J. Mortimore** is Reader in Geography at Ahmadu Bello University, Nigeria. He is a member of the Population Studies Group of the Institute of British Geographers and has carried out demographic research in the Kano Close-Settled Zone. He is the author of several papers on Nigerian Demography.

**D. W. Norman** is Professor of Agricultural Economics and head of the Department of Agricultural Economics of Ahmadu Bello University, Nigeria. He has written extensively on agricultural economics.

**P. O. Ohadike** is chief of the Fertility Studies Section of the Population Programme Centre of the United Nations Economic Commission for Africa. He has had considerable experience in demographic work in Africa. He contributed to *The Population of Tropical Africa* (Caldwell and Okonjo, eds.) and has written two monographs and a book, *The Population of Zambia*, and numerous other articles and papers on Africa.

**Francis Olu. Okediji** is Professor of Sociology, University of Ibadan, Nigeria. He has undertaken research on a broad field of social problems in Nigeria. With O. O. Okediji he co-edited *The Sociology of the Yoruba;* with J. Comhaire-Sylvain, de Fernand Bezy, and P. O. van den Berghe, *Le Nouveau Dossier Afrique;* and edited *Population Dynamics Research in Africa*.

**P. O. Olusanya** is Senior Lecturer in the Department of Sociology and Anthropology at the University of Ife, Nigeria. He has written articles on various aspects of Nigerian demography.

**Hilary Page** was a sociologist at Princeton University and is now Regional Corepresentative for West Africa of the Demographic Division of the Population Council. She worked for two years in the Geography Department of University College Dar es Salaam, and has written papers and articles on African fertility and mortality.

**André Podlewski** is Maître de Recherches Principal at ORSTOM in Paris. Between 1959 and 1970 he carried out extensive demographic research in the Cameroons. He is the author of *La Dynamique des principales populations du Nord Cameroun* and many articles on regional studies and demographic methodology.

**D. Ian Pool** is Associate Professor in the Department of Sociology at Carleton University, Ottawa. He has directed surveys in Ghana, Upper Volta and Niger and has published many articles on Africa, New Zealand, and Canada.

**S. P. Reyna** is Assistant Professor of Anthropology at the University of New Hampshire. He has lectured in Social Anthropology at the University of Ife in Nigeria, and conducted research in Chad, Cameroons, and Mauritania. He is the author of a number of papers in population anthropology.

**Louis Roussel** is Maître de Conferences at the University of Paris (X) and is Director of Studies at the Institut National d'Etudes Démographiques. He has worked for the Planning Ministry of Abidjan, Ivory Coast. He has written a number of articles on the population of Ivory Coast.

**Barbara Thompson** is a sociologist with the Medical Research Council, University of Aberdeen, Scotland. She has contributed numerous articles to medical journals, and from 1961 to 1964 she carried out socio-medical field work in a Gambian village.

**Jean Trevor** is a sociologist with Exeter University School of Education. She has been involved since 1952 in education and demographic research in northern Nigeria.

**Reuben K. Udo** is Professor of Geography at the University of Ibadan, Nigeria. He has contributed to a number of journals and is the author of *Migrant Tenant Farmers of Nigeria* and *Geographical Regions of Nigeria*.

**Etienne van de Walle** is Professor of Demography and member of the Population Studies Center of the University of Pennsylvania. From 1957 to 1961 he was engaged in demographic fieldwork in Rwanda and Burundi as research associate with IRSAC. He is a co-author of *The Demography of Tropical Africa*.

**J. Vaugelade** is in charge of research in the Economic-Demographic section of ORSTOM in Dakar, Senegal.

# Contents

# *Figures*

# Preface

THE PAPERS published in this book were especially commissioned for it. The intention was to cover the whole region of West Africa, both in terms of regional change and of its national subdivisions, and to find the person best qualified for each task. Nearly all those chosen initially to write for the book accepted.

Because such cooperation was achieved the book has retained the balance originally envisaged. It provides the first English language report on population trends and research in many francophone countries. In its approximately equal balance of African and foreign authors, it both provides evidence of the growth of African demography and ensures that population phenomena will be interpreted by those who have been participants.

The "West Africa" referred to in the title and regional chapters means here the western or Atlantic side of the whole of tropical Africa and covers nearly all the continent described in United Nations documents as "West Africa" and "Middle Africa." Thus it spans 4,000 miles from Mauritania to southeast Zaïre, an area which, in 1970, probably contained over 140 million persons forming two-fifths of the inhabitants of the whole continent and about two-thirds of those of tropical Africa. To the south and east it excludes Angola, Zambia, Rwanda and Burundi, and to the north the Arab world.

The editors were drawn from the two original demography units attached to West African universities. N. O. Addo and S. K. Gaisie were staff members of the Demographic Unit (and Department of Sociology)

of the University of Ghana; this Unit was the final product of the demography program at the University of Ghana which dated back to 1960. A. Igun and P. O. Oluṣanya were staff members of the Demographic Training and Research Unit (and the Department of Demography and Sociology) of the University of Ife in Nigeria. I was a member of the staff of the former program in 1962–64 and of the latter in 1969.

The project received generous financial assistance from the West African Office of the Ford Foundation, and administrative and other encouragement from the Population Council. The Australian National University also helped in numerous ways.

Among the many people who helped formulate ideas for this book and subsequently to keep the whole project moving several stand out. Haldore Hanson, then living in Lagos, argued the need for it. My wife, Pat Caldwell, took on much of the strain of the work in both Africa and Australia. Others who worked long hours on tasks which ranged from correspondence and day-to-day editing to typing and proof-reading were Wendy Cosford, Dorothy Campbell, Helen Ware, Wendy Redgrave, and Susan Robbins.

The book represents an attempt by those most involved in estimating the effects of population change to report on the position in the early 1970s.

JOHN C. CALDWELL.
*Canberra, Australia*
January 1975

*Population Growth
and Socioeconomic Change
in West Africa*

# PART
# ONE

*The
Regional
Analysis*

# CHAPTER ONE

# Introduction
## Some Important Issues

JOHN C. CALDWELL

BOTH population growth and socioeconomic change have become increasingly rapid in tropical Africa in the course of the present century. Each affects the other, sometimes in obvious ways and sometimes in the more subtle ways examined in this book.

Some demographers doubt whether the region's population was growing at all until the present century, but evidence of any type is almost nonexistent. However, by the 1960s, West Africa,[1] in common with other parts of the continent, appeared to have achieved an annual growth rate of about 2½ percent[2] with its guarantee that, if unchecked, each generation would be succeeded by one twice its size. This rate is as high as that of most Asian countries, which have been deeply concerned by the impact of such unprecendently high population growth rates upon attempts to raise individual incomes and consumption, and which have, for the most part, organized large programs to attempt to curb population growth.

Africa's economic backwardness, the current difficulties of many countries in reaching economic growth targets, and the apparent timelessness of much of its partly subsistence rural sector often obscure the rapidity of its social and economic change. Most West Africans have had to make greater adjustments in outlook in their lifetimes than have other peoples in the world. During the course of a century the areas of traditional religion have been deeply penetrated by Christianity and Islam and by the "Western" and "Middle-Eastern" values brought with them. Over a considerably shorter period, cash-cropping, traders, roads, trucks, and a vast rise in the levels of exports and imports have meant that the market (and global) economy has loomed ever larger in importance for nearly the whole population. In the last decade, independence has increased interest and local involvement in development planning

[1] That is, the whole region as defined in this book.
[2] R. K. Som, "Some Demographic Indicators for Africa," in John C. Caldwell and Chukuka Okonjo, eds., *The Population of Tropical Africa* (London: Longmans, Green & Company, and New York: Columbia University Press, 1968), 193–94.

and more recently in the implications of rapid population growth for the success of the plans.

Yet, West Africa's demographic position is far from simple. The basic reason is that, prior to the present century, the climate probably made it the most unhealthy major region in the world. Death rates were almost certainly the world's highest (presumably close to 50 per thousand with expectations of life at birth under 20 years), and population numbers were sustained only by equally high birth rates, achieved by placing great cultural and social stress on high-fertility values. Thus, current high rates of population growth have been attained by widening the gulf between continued very high birth rates and death rates which, although declining, are still undeniably substantial. It is this relatively high death rate—probably still well over 20 per thousand for the region as a whole— which makes West Africa unique, and which has made many people wonder whether fertility decline should be encouraged. In terms of attitudes to population growth, another element emerges quite clearly from this book: Attitudes vary (although probably not as much now as a few years ago) between ex-British and ex-French areas, more because of differences in historical experience and current thinking between English- and French-speaking areas outside Africa than between those within (Sudan may have had as much influence on population policy in Ivory Coast as have the housing problems of Abidjan).

This introduction will not attempt to summarize the population picture presented in the various chapters. This was necessary a few years ago,[3] but the increase in published material on the demography of tropical Africa has produced a framework within which they can easily be understood. The passage of time has tended to throw light on some of the questions on fertility and mortality levels and trends, and has thereby isolated a series of demographic and policy issues, which will be examined here.

[3] That is, in Caldwell and Okonjo, *The Population of Tropical Africa.*

## MAJOR ISSUES: DEMOGRAPHIC AND ECONOMIC INFORMATION

### DEMOGRAPHIC-ECONOMIC INTERRELATIONS.

The post-World War II concern with population growth has centered on growth rates rather than on the present or eventual total population achieved. The period has witnessed a considerable number of countries—some of them in West Africa—attaining annual population growth rates of 3 percent per annum or more. Such rates are much higher than has been the usual historical experience, except in areas of overseas European settlement during the periods of frontier expansion. Industrialization has usually been accomplished with growth rates under $1\frac{1}{2}$ percent per annum, even in the so-called population boom in Europe during the nineteenth century, and higher growth rates may inhibit industrialization in most countries.

The reasons that fast population growth may hinder economic development, and especially the improvement of individual welfare, have been set out elsewhere both with regard to developing countries as a whole and with specific attention to tropical Africa.[4] At every stage of development one problem is that the provision of duplicated facilities for the increase in population (extra housing, schools, roads, production facilities, and so on) uses up savings which could otherwise be used for increasing the capital investment per worker and so raising productivity. Another is that a fast-growing population is characterized by an age structure which contains a relatively small proportion of persons in the main occupational age span (15–64 years of age) and a high proportion of dependent population (mostly children who either do not work or do so less efficiently relative to their consumption needs); hence the same per capita

[4] Ansley J. Coale and Edgar M. Hoover, *Population Growth and Economic Development in Low-Income Countries: A Case Study of India's Prospects* (Princeton, N.J., Princeton University Press, 1958); Advisory Mission of the Population Council, "The Importance of a Population Programme to the Republic of Kenya," in Ministry of Economic Planning and Development, *Family Planning in Kenya* (Nairobi, 1967), pp. 2–9.

earnings as in a more slowly growing population mean relatively lower per capita consumption (and also lower per capita savings). Ultimately, faster population growth may also press harder upon available resources either in terms of their absolute amounts or the rate at which new resources can be made available.

One of the reasons for encouraging the studies in this book was to secure evidence about such demographic-economic inter-relations in West Africa. Some of the evidence obtained is employed later in this chapter. Nevertheless, the main impression resulting from this part of the effort, and the impression given by a seminar held at the Nairobi University College on the same theme in 1969, is that surprisingly little good research and adequate measurement has been applied to such problems in West Africa.

It is clear that many governments are embarrassed, and are likely to become more so, by an increase in the numbers of school children at such a rate as to mock the inten-tion to achieve universal schooling in the near future. Similarly, urban housing and other facilities are being strained by the rate of growth of town population, and urban unemployment is worryingly high in many countries; but this is a product of both urban natural increase and rural-urban migration (though such migration is likely to be greater when the rate of rural natural increase is higher). But it is less certain what such population growth means for rural invest-ment and production, especially in the subsistence sector.

It is also clear that the population change has been affected by social and economic factors. Urbanization is of itself a form of both social and economic change and its rate usually is affected by the rate of change of the economy. Mortality decline in nineteenth-century Europe was, to a very considerable degree, a measure of increasing prosperity; in West Africa it has owed more to the import of free or relatively cheap modern medical technology, but the continued spread of medical personnel and facilities into rural areas may depend increasingly on the health

of the economy. Fertility in the West eventually declined with increasing pros-perity as a result almost solely of personal initiatives. However, West Africa is faced by a question Europe did not have to answer: whether birth rates of 50 per thousand and growth rates around 3 percent per annum will slow economic growth to the point where the date at which declining fertility will come to the economic rescue will be postponed for a very long time. The fundamental question is whether an optimum path can be plotted and followed whereby economic growth and fertility decline interact so as to come closest to maximizing each.

THE VALUE OF THE NEW DEMOGRAPHIC EVIDENCE. Our knowledge of West African demography has been greatly extended in the last few years by the publication of analyses done at Princeton University employing stable population methods and the Brass techniques[5] and in Paris by various French organizations which have collaborated with francophone African governments.[6] Some work has also been undertaken in West African research institutes using the new techniques.[7]

However, the sophistication of the tech-niques may well lead to a too confident acceptance of results which have often unfortunately, but necessarily, been built on the shakiest of foundations. Users of these data might note some of the problems out-lined below.

All methods have to use data collected by census or survey enumerators with imperfect

[5] William Brass et al., *The Demography of Tropical Africa*, (Princeton, N.J., Princeton University Press, 1968), pp. 88–150; Hilary J. Page and Ansley J. Coale, "Estimates of Fertility and Child Mortality in Africa South of the Sahara," Seminar on Population Growth and Economic Development, University College Nairobi, 14th–22nd December, 1969; chapter 2 in this book.

[6] Mostly published in the series of documents issued by INSEE Service de Coopération, Ministère de la Co-opération of the French Government in collaboration with various African governments.

[7] See for example S. K. Gaisie, *Dynamics of Population Growth in Ghana*, (Accra-Tema: Ghana Publishing Corporation, 1969).

education, training, and often understanding of what is being done. Sometimes there is resistance taking the form of deliberate dishonesty by those being enumerated (see Chapter 11 in which Olusanya claims that no Nigerian growth rates based on the comparison of two censuses mean anything). More often the resistance springs from cultural problems in providing certain answers. Joseph (Chapter 25) and Morgan (Chapter 9) and Trevor (Chapter 10) all emphasize the fear of providing exact numbers about persons. Trevor, somewhat discouragingly, points out the chances of being given wrong information about wives and children in harems and the likelihood of pregnant women lying about dead children so as not to bring ill luck upon the fetus. Coupled with these fears may be a more justified apprehension of further taxation (Joseph in Chapter 25).

Age errors are made on a vast scale and are usually partly systematic, thus diminishing the value of smoothing, which is sometimes carried out on the francophone data with the implication that the smoothed data, obviously at a glance still highly distorted, is somewhere close to the truth. Age errors arise almost entirely from ignorance of age, and better enumeration methods cannot extract the truth out of the respondents. It may be possible to use age sets to determine age (although Thompson in Chapter 24 points out that the *kafo* in Gambia apparently spans about three years) or to determine for individual communities correction factors for systematic errors (a recent attempt in the Ife Division of Nigeria[8] was not very successful). One can substitute a stable population structure, as the Princeton group tend to do (and as Caldwell does in Chapter 24), but success depends on three factors, all of which are difficult to test. (1) The matching model population must be chosen by securing agreement about the enumerated and model cumulated population by age to a *certain exact age* where it is believed that the net

movement of misstated enumerated ages across that age is zero. (2) The fertility and mortality schedules of the model population must approximate those of the real population (the fertility schedule has been held to be the most important in determining age structure, but, as explained below, there may be unusual problems in West Africa because of relatively high child mortality). (3) Fertility, and, to a lesser extent, mortality, must have been approximately constant. As discussed below, there may be quite dramatic local annual fluctuations in the birth rate, but the regional level and the longer-term levels have probably been fairly constant, thus generating age structures of the stable type as observed in the Fakao area of Senegal which has had an adequate registration system for over 30 years (Chapter 33).

Certain other types of census data are often more inaccurate than age data but excite less comment from demographers because they are not employed (except perhaps indirectly for correcting or explaining age structures) in determining fertility and mortality. Van de Walle claims (in this book) that African censuses are still not collecting meaningful data on employment, education, and migration among other things. Part of the reason is undoubtedly that the census officials have not been exposed to as much demand and advice in these areas as they have on age, fertility, and mortality statement. In Gambia, Thompson (in this book) concluded from a study of a particular area that the 1963 census was less—probably very much less—than 5 percent off in the total head count, but was 95 percent off in the determination of immigrants as judged by place of birth and possibly equally in error on tribal definition.

In terms of the total population count (which affects fertility and mortality estimates in that they tend to be estimated so that the rate of natural increase agrees with that calculated from intercensal population growth), the evidence is that most censuses are reasonably good, and better than the pre-World War II population counts. However, most enumeration still is carried out over a considerable period because of staff

[8] John C. Caldwell and Adenola A. Igun, "An Experiment with Census-Type Age Enumeration in Nigeria," *Population Studies*, XXV, 2 (July 1971).

and equipment shortages (even the 1960 Ghana census, frequently described as simultaneous, took two weeks), thus raising problems of overcounting or undercounting mobile population. Varying the census date from one count to the next can also mean enumerating very different numbers of seasonal workers (Chapter 35).

The usual way of estimating total populations and annual population change in the francophone areas has been by the *administrative census* which is the national total of populations registered by local administrative officers. Van de Walle believes that these have deteriorated since independence but may be worth improving again. In fact, Niger has decided to do this from 1970 and to collate all the material centrally (Chapter 33). Most chapters on ex-French areas in this book also point to large errors in the earlier period and cast doubt on the use of such "censuses" for demographic purposes. The interest of governments in using them for tax purposes has led the enumerators to concentrate unduly on adult males, who sometimes also tried to avoid the count for this reason (Chapters 26, 27, 30, 34, 35, and 37); when used for other purposes, such as the distribution of groundnuts in Senegal, they overcounted the groups who would benefit most from these purposes. Surveys proved undercounts in administrative censuses ranging from 10 to 25 percent in Dahomey, Cameroon, Ivory Coast, and Upper Volta for the final period of French rule; while, in independent Chad, the 1968 administrative census produced a total population smaller than that estimated from the 1964 sample survey. Furthermore, administrative surveys are most effective in areas of traditional residence: in both Dahomey and Upper Volta they were shown to be much more defective in urban areas than in rural ones.

The sample surveys, which have been such a feature of the francophone areas, and which have been the major source of data for the Brass analyses, have had problems similar to the census in collecting the usual census-type data (Podlewski says that in Cameroon and elsewhere female fertility was employed in determining age, thus introducing serious problems into the analysis of fertility by age). The sample designs, based on the administrative censuses, often made the inflation of survey figures to give national totals highly suspect, and in Senegal the figures have been regarded as useless (see Chapter 35). Another weakness was the failure to organize follow-up, post-enumeration checks.

Unlike most West African censuses, the surveys attempted to collect potentially very valuable retrospective data on fertility and mortality over fixed periods and also over open past periods. Three major problems have been encountered. The first is a degree of underreporting greater than that encountered with most census data (the Brass methods attempt to correct this but the analysis obviously becomes more likely to err as the basic data become worse). Some of the problems in collecting fertility data are illuminated by various comments in this book: Harrell-Bond indicated that in Freetown males probably reported only a fraction of their fertility outside marriage and that female fertility also was underreported; in Nigeria, Morgan stated that it was regarded by women as bringing bad luck to say how many had died, while Trevor reported that such fears are greater among pregnant women whose underreporting is the highest of all. In Senegal, Cantrelle reported relative understatement of child mortality in retrospective surveys compared with continuous registration in two areas ranging from 15–47 percent for infants and up to 31 percent for 1–4 year olds. The Institut National de la Statistique et des Etudes Economiques (INSEE) report comparing data for all these surveys concluded that the mortality data were probably unusable. The second problem is that the reference periods for which respondents provide data apparently often average lengths very different from those asked by the survey organizers (again the Brass techniques provide corrections but the possibility of error certainly rises with increasingly poor data). The third point, which can be very serious in countries where mortality estimates rest on a single survey period, is that mortality, and even fertility, vary enormously from year to year or one period to another (Chapters 4, 11, 24, and 35). Epidemics or famines can in one year double or triple infant mortality rates over what they had been the previous year, at least in limited areas. Perhaps more unexpectedly, Gambian research (see Chapter 24) has shown that, in such areas, the birth rate can double in a year following high infant mortality; this is a remarkable self-adjusting demographic phenomenon, but it can play havoc with fertility estimates. Also, retrospective data for the fixed period can be strangely incomparable with that for the open period; van de Walle (in Chapter 30) remarks that the 1961 Dahomey survey produced sex ratios of 95 male births per 100 female births in the former and 105 per 100 in the latter.

The various analyses in this book bring out clearly two problems in some of the past stable population estimates of fertility. The first is the use of the proportion of either females or the total population under 15 years of age. This age has the advantage that it includes only relatively recent births while coming close to dichotomizing the population and hence producing a large fraction unlikely to be subject to very great proportional variation. But, especially when the analysis is confined to females (in some countries the disadvantage of employing males is that their age structure is more affected by international migration), this may well deflate fertility estimates because of a frequently noted tendency for a net movement of females from the 10–14 to the 15–19 age groups. Analyses in this book show that this proportion often produced the lowest fertility estimates of any age proportion (Chapters 11, 21–24, but for a contrary view see van de Walle, Chapter 30). The Princeton group has recently been experimenting with the use of proportions of the combined sexes[9] and median results from the use of several proportions.[10] The second

problem is that African mortality may be so high in the 1–4 age group that none of the model life tables at present in use may be suitable. The Princeton group has recently begun using the tables for these tropical African analyses from the second birthday instead of from birth or the first birthday (that is, from $l_2$ instead of from $l_0$ or $l_1$) but it may well be that the fifth birthday ($l_5$) should be employed until sets of life tables based on actual African experience are available. This does not mean that projected natural increase for the immediate future will necessarily be wrong. It may well mean that the surviving population over 5 years of age is a product of considerably higher birth rates and 0–4 mortality rates than has been suggested. Hence, with mortality decline, the potential for population growth may be greater than most current analyses indicate.

The Brass techniques[11] will remain of great value in West Africa until adequate registration schemes can be evolved. It is, therefore, surprising how little has been done to test the various assumptions by employing a mix of continuous registration and retrospective surveys in experimental areas. The fertility technique assumes that the reporting by younger women is reasonably correct, which seems plausible and may well prove to be the case; yet, if it is true that the most reluctant respondents are pregnant women (and the incidence of pregnancy is higher among younger women), such a conclusion may have to be modified. The technique also assumes that apparent increasing discrepancies with age between average live births reported and those calculated by cumulating to that age the fertility claimed for the previous 12 months are entirely attributable to increasing memory lapse with age. However, the discussion below shows that there is a possibility that fertility has risen in at least some areas with modernization (because of the relaxation of various taboos on sexual intercourse, but possibly also with improved health). There is also a possibility that the reference period varies with age (the young tend to be better educated and probably

[9] Page and Coale, "Estimates of Fertility and Child Mortality."

[10] Etienne van de Walle and Hilary Page, "Some New Estimates of Fertility and Mortality in Africa," *Population Index*, XXXV, 1 (January–March 1969), 3–17.

[11] Brass et al., *Demography of Tropical Africa*, pp. 88–150.

more accurate), but any errors would be limited because of the small proportion of all fertility attributable to the older women. The whole theory of memory lapse in tropical Africa may need experimental re-examination; van de Walle reports that the 1961 Dahomey survey data did not evidence it (Chapter 30), and Thompson indicates that the Gambian data yielded little evidence, and none that could not be explained biologically (see Chapter 24). One fundamental source of disquiet with all techniques must remain the age data. Experience in Nigeria suggests to the writer that the data may be so bad as to vitiate analysis techniques which assume (as they inevitably must) certain consistent or definable relationships between stated and real age. The mortality technique includes two assumptions which may well result in an underestimate of mortality: first, that as high a proportion of live children are forgotten as dead children (an assumption that several chapters imply is probably not the case in West Africa); and second, that the ability or willingness to recall dead children does not decline faster with age than does the recall of live children.

Certainly, the different techniques, and the same techniques with variations, have given significantly different fertility and mortality estimates and can be made to yield even larger differences (Chapters 24 and 30). While all estimates indicate the general order of fertility, their variability makes it impossible to distinguish limited changes in fertility and can make the estimate of natural increase vary most significantly.

The alternative to such methods is not likely to be vital registration data, at least on a national scale, for many years. Some chapters report capitals nearing complete coverage (see Chapters 24 and 30 and Cantrelle reporting on Dakar, Chapter 4), but other capital cities still have a long way to go (Chapter 37 where underregistration of births in Ouagadougou is reported to be 30–34 percent). The problems in rural areas are enormous, although Nigeria and Ghana have decided that they will attempt to implement the Economic Commission for Africa's recommendation of full, national vital registration.

One danger in West Africa has been the basing of too many conclusions or policy decisions on a single census or survey. Gabon has accepted the 1960–1961 survey as proving that birth rates at the time were scarcely at replacement level, and that the situation may not have changed much by 1971 (Chapter 31). The findings of a decade ago appear to be strangely at variance with those of the other coastal countries, and the predictions for the 1970s anomalous when it is realized that the country's schooling levels and per capita incomes (admittedly a good deal of the income goes to mining companies) are West Africa's highest, and the health coverage well above average. It may well be that the next population count will lead to a revision of beliefs not only about the current demographic situation but about that of 1960–1961.

MORTALITY TRENDS. The most needed, and most elusive, demographic information is that on the trend in the death rate (and hence the trend in natural increase as long as fertility remains largely unchanged). Recent work, as exemplified by the reports in this book, has yielded less than might have been hoped. The 1970 Zaïre census enumerated a larger population than had been anticipated, suggesting that mortality had long been lower than had been thought to be the case and had been declining (Chapter 29). The result may have been affected by some underenumeration in 1955–1957 and some overenumeration in 1970, as well as an underestimate of the influx of refugees. Nevertheless, the impression remains that the disorders of the 1960s had little effect in slowing down a mortality decline resulting from a complex of social and economic changes which can be described as modernization. Olusanya (Chapter 11) has argued from the evidence that the Nigerian crude death rate seems to have fallen by about half a point per annum between the 1952–1953 and 1963 censuses, and Gaisie (Chapter 20) that the Ghanaian rate fell one point per annum between 1960 and 1968 reaching 15 per thousand by the latter date. In each case the evidence was good enough to convince one that a decline had been under way, without carrying the same assurance about the actual magnitude of the change. In at least some areas, mortality change has been fast enough to be apparent to the population: Morgan's survey recorded that two-thirds of the Lagos respondents believed that a larger proportion of children was now surviving and attributed this to modern medicine and health education (Chapter 9). It should be noted that all this evidence comes from coastal countries which have clearly experienced considerable social and economic change in the last 15 years; it cannot be assumed that parallel movements have been taking place in the poor, and wholly inland, savanna countries of West Africa.

Most population projections certainly assume declining mortality to the extent that the expectation of life at birth rises by about half a year every year and that the crude death rate falls by about one point every $2\frac{1}{2}$ years (Chapters 24, 26, 32, 35, and Gaisie's projections for Ghana[12]), but such assumptions probably have little stronger demographic basis than the pre-World War II experience of developing countries in other continents which is incorporated in the United Nations and Princeton model life tables.[13]

The justification for borrowing the experience of other continents is twofold: health measures are expanding and very considerable socioeconomic changes are taking place. Although van de Walle reports that it is not clear that the 1960s have witnessed an advance in Dahomey's health services (in Chapter 30) and elsewhere he has applied these fears more broadly,[14] this does

not appear to be the view held by most of the writers in this book who cite considerable public health expenditures and mass inoculation campaigns. Compared with most of Asia, West Africa's public health expenditures are high, averaging about 10 percent of budgets, although admittedly in most countries this is little more than U.S.$1 per head (Chapter 8). A good deal of hope now is expressed for the success of the mass programs against measles (a major cause of death in West Africa). On the debit side is a continued savage urban-rural differential in public and private health services (Chapters 21–23 and 33): of Niger's 50 doctors, 30 are found in Niamey which has no more than one-fiftieth of the country's population. As Okediji so well demonstrates, even the urban facilities are often nearly monopolized by the elite, and the failure of the poor to make use of them is by no means an irrational response (Chapter 12). Nevertheless, the destruction of the traditional society in rural areas, with the inroads of commerce, money, and more scientific ways of coping with illness, may also have had a very marked effect in reducing mortality levels. It is clear that work in Cameroon has shown mortality in areas of traditional culture and religion to be relatively greater than in areas of predominantly Christian or Islamic influence to an extent that cannot be explained merely on economic or public health grounds (Chapter 25); one is forced to conclude that it must be explained partly by a difference in fatalistic acceptance of illness.

Data, particularly from research in francophone areas, now lead one to believe that Africa has long been marked by relatively enormously high toddler mortality (Chapters 4 and 24, and an earlier study by Clairin).[15] This might well make any external life tables unusable and might have considerable implications for family planning programs (see below). Deaths in the age range 1–4 in much of rural tropical Africa, and perhaps all of

---

[12] Gaisie, *Dynamics of Population Growth*, pp. 96–115.

[13] United Nations, *Age and Sex Patterns of Mortality*, Population Studies No. 22 (New York, 1955); Ansley J. Coale and Paul Demeny, *Regional Model Life Tables and Stable Populations* (Princeton, N.J., Princeton University Press).

[14] See Pierre Pradervand, *Family Planning Programs in Africa*, Organization for Economic Cooperation and Development (Paris, 1970), p. 17, quoting Etienne van de Walle, "The Population of Tropical Africa in the 1980s," *Symposium on Africa in the 1980s*, April 14th–18th, 1969, University of Chicago.

[15] Rémy Clairin, "The Assessment of Infant and Child Mortality from the Data Available in Africa," in Caldwell and Okonjo, *Population of Tropical Africa*, pp. 199–213.

tropical Africa in the past, equal or exceed those under one year of age. In the Princeton "West" tables at these mortality levels the former are half the latter, and, even in the "North" tables, the fraction rises only to two-thirds. The cause lies partly in the types of health problems prevalent: malaria, measles, parasites and malnutrition. Nevertheless, it is hard to avoid the conclusion that social factors play a role: for example, children are fed at meals last, and given the worst and often the least food; also, much farm work is done by mothers accompanied by babies but not by toddlers. It is probable, but not satisfactorily proven, that this pattern is changing in the towns and other areas of modernization. It is a pattern that may change with public health education programs and certainly should be a major target for them.

URBAN FERTILITY TRENDS. There is little belief, or data to support a belief, that secular change in rural fertility levels is occurring. But a vigorous debate has begun on the subject of urban fertility.[16] Urban fertility is definitely lower than rural fertility in Ghana and may have been so for at least half a century.[17] This also appears to be true at present in Ivory Coast, Upper Volta, Niger, Chad, Dahomey, and Sierra Leone (see Chapters 32, 37, 34, 27, 30, 21–23). On the other hand, there is equally strong evidence of higher urban fertility in Zaïre and Gabon (Chapters 27 and 31) and more debatable evidence for it in Nigeria[18] (Chapters 11 and 9). One is almost tempted to distinguish an east West African pattern from a west West African one.

The position seems to be that urban residence does affect behavior patterns which

determine fertility in various ways. Fertility rises or falls according to the balance of these forces, a balance which may be influenced by the rate of urbanization, the length of the urban tradition, the urban-rural differential in behavior patterns and possibly in health levels, and the rural fertility and marriage patterns.

One depressant of urban fertility is undoubtedly delayed female marriage in the towns. Wherever urban-rural differentials in female age at marriage have been examined (Ghana,[19] and, in this book, Cameroon, Chad, Niger, and Upper Volta), the average age at marriage has been shown to be later in the towns. Furthermore, there may be fairly rapid change: in Ouagadougou (Chapter 37) the proportion of 15–19-year-old females never married rose from 35 percent in 1962 to 56 percent in 1968, the kind of phenomenon which was witnessed (at a slower rate) in the early years of the Western fertility transition. There are educational and social differentials in age at marriage and these partly explain the urban-rural one.[20] In most traditional areas there is no social role for unmarried females over about 15 years of age, but this is certainly not the case in the larger towns. Late urban marriage may be a less important phenomenon when rural marriage also is delayed, a significant observation in the case of Lagos if Morgan is correct in his claim that the average age of female marriage in Yoruba areas (admittedly highly urbanized) is nearly 20 years or 5 years above the level in northern Nigeria. Pool has argued that lower urban fertility in Ghana is explained also by greater urban marital instability and by a more persistent attempt to restrict fertility.[21]

The most powerful force tending to raise urban fertility is the much greater tendency to reduce the period of the postnatal taboo on

[16] A. Romaniuk, "Fertility Trends in Africa," *Proceedings of the International Population Conference, London, 1969*, I, Liège, pp. 739–47.

[17] John C. Caldwell, "Fertility Differentials as Evidence of Incipient Fertility Decline in a Developing Country; the Case of Ghana," *Population Studies*, XXI (July 1967), 5–7.

[18] See also P. O. Olusanya, "Modernization and the Level of Fertility in Western Nigeria," *Proceedings of the International Population Conference*, pp. 812–25.

[19] Dov Friedlander and Raymond T. Smith, "Fertility, Mortality and Family Structure in Ghanaian Communities; a Preliminary Report," (1963); Caldwell, "Fertility Differentials," 11–16.

[20] *Ibid.*

[21] D. I. Pool, "Conjugal Patterns in Ghana," *The Canadian Review of Sociology and Anthropology*, V, 4 (November 1968), 241–52.

sexual relations or to abandon it altogether, a phenomenon which appears to be almost universal in the larger centers. Boute (Chapter 29) describes the full cycle. Women in rural areas are more likely to observe the taboo and to direct the husbands' sexual interests elsewhere, especially to other wives in polygynous marriages. In the town, where polygyny is much less likely to be practiced (partly because of housing and other financial difficulties), wives in monogamous marriages, separated from most of their relatives, are much more apt to struggle to keep their marriages together by relaxing the taboo. This willingness to break with tradition is encouraged by the anonymous and innovating urban setting, away from the ridicule and scorn likely to be the lot of the lactating village woman who becomes pregnant (Thompson, Chapter 24). More frequent pregnancies result, leading in Kinshasa, Boute believes, to a fairly widespread desire for adequate contraceptive methods. It is also possible that fertility may increase in towns because of better health services, although towns may encourage venereal disease as well as providing for its cure (Chapters 9 and 32), and that rural fertility in some areas may be depressed by very young mothers having their reproductive capacities injured by too early childbirth (Chapter 10 and a substantial body of evidence on the point from India).

West African countries may have other potentials for rising fertility. The evidence appears indisputable that the fertility of nomads is lower than that of sedentary populations, and, on balance, appears to suggest that it is lower in polygynous than monogamous marriages. As the proportion of nomads and polygamously married women appears to be declining, there may be marginally significant rises in fertility from these causes too.

Perhaps one could summarize by arguing that fertility may well rise in many, but by no means all, African urban centers. But this will almost certainly be the prelude (as indeed greater proportions of surviving children, regardless of fertility trends, probably will be everywhere) to the more widespread practice of family planning and ultimately to declining fertility.

THE IMPETUS OF POPULATION GROWTH. Discussions of family planning programs in West Africa and elsewhere often become confused with such issues as whether population growth should as yet be slowed down or whether rural population densities are sufficiently great. Cameroon, for instance, with about 6 million people, has announced that it will take no steps to limit fertility until its population reaches 15 million (Chapter 8). There is undoubtedly a tendency here to underestimate the present potential for population growth even with an improbably rapid decline in fertility, for the mothers of the next generation are already born and in much of the region are twice as numerous as their mothers were. High fertility populations have a much greater potential for continued growth than did Europe, for instance, in the late nineteenth century. The real struggle in West Africa over the years immediately ahead may be to hold the population growth rate from climbing higher as mortality falls (the aim now adopted by Ghana; see Chapter 20).

What is the built-in capacity for growth? First one can look at the extreme, and, in West Africa, the ludicrous case, of age-specific birth rates dropping immediately to bare replacement level as the population stabilizes. Keyfitz has calculated the general formula and has shown that various Latin American populations would still increase by about 50 percent before stabilizing in contrast to a continued growth of under 25 percent in the United States.[22] West Africa has higher birth rates, but these do not compensate for its much higher death rates. Thus, while current demographic evidence would indicate Ghana's population increasing by almost 50 percent, the rise in Nigeria might not be above 25 percent, and Mali would apparently stabilize at its present population level.

[22] Nathan Keyfitz, "On the Momentum of Population Growth," Demography, VII, 1 (February 1971), 71–80.

However, no population would actually decline.

But the truth about what will happen is far from this. Birth rates will, at the most, decline slowly, and death rates will continue to fall. For most coastal countries the likely range of experience is probably contained in the projections for two countries summarized in Table 1.1. In 1970 Gambia was probably

TABLE 1.1
Population multiplication from 1970 according to projections for Gambia and Ghana

| | | Multiplication | |
| Country | Projection | by Year 2000 | By the Time a Stationary Population Is Reached[a] |
|---|---|---|---|
| Gambia[b] | High[c] | 2.3 | 3.5 |
| | Medium | 1.9 | 2.5 |
| | Low | 1.8 | 1.9 |
| Ghana | High[b] | 2.8 | 4.9 |
| | Low | 2.4 | 3.3 |

SOURCES: Gambia projections—see chapter 24. Ghana projections—S. K. Gaisie, *Dynamics of Population Growth in Ghana*, University of Ghana (Legon, 1969).
[a] That is, if age-specific birth rates fall to replacement level in year 2000.
[b] Employing the projections which assume that mortality is not independent of fertility.
[c] Constant fertility.

still, by West African standards, a high mortality and moderate fertility country (estimates employed in projections: expectation of life at birth = $37\frac{1}{2}$ years, crude birth rate = 46) while Ghana was a high fertility and low mortality country (estimates employed in projections: expectation of life at birth = 44 years, crude birth rate = 51).

What the projections mean is that even coastal countries which begin family planning programs now (and the medium and low Gambian and Ghanaian projections assume this) are likely to come close to doubling their populations by the end of the century if their present fertility-mortality gap is relatively small (i.e., a rate of natural increase of about 2 percent per annum as is estimated for Gambia) or close to multiplying their numbers by $2\frac{1}{2}$ if it is relatively large (a rate of natural increase of about 3 percent per annum as is estimated for Ghana). This

means that Nigeria, which probably has a fertility level similar to Ghana's and a mortality level more like that of Gambia, would be likely, even with a national family planning program, to increase from a possible 60 million in 1970[23] to at least 120 million by the end of the century. Even if the most vigorous measures were then taken, resulting in only replacement birth rates, the population would not be likely to level off under about 160 million—or a greater density of population than that of contemporary India.

Similarly vigorous measures would stabilize some of the savanna countries' populations at considerably lower levels. But national family planning programs in them (as distinct from their larger urban areas) would be likely to begin to be effective only as their mortality levels become lower. The kind of discussion above on coastal countries might be held some years ahead in the inland countries with perhaps similar predictions being made then.

A range of population projections has been constructed for Ghana[24] to show the effects of achieving sustained and constant declines in fertility until levels are reached which would ultimately mean a stationary population (i.e., the net reproduction rate reaches one). If Ghana could do this in (1) 30 years, (2) 50 years, or (3) 70 years, it would have to reduce fertility (as measured by the average annual drop in the gross reproduction rate) at, in the case of (1), the rate Japan did between 1950 and 1960, but for three times the period; in the case of (3) something faster than did England and Wales from 1881 to 1931. The magnitude of the postulated change can be seen from the fact that we have used the periods of maximum decline for the non-African countries in the comparison. It might also be noted that projections (1), (2), and (3) postulate fertility declines nine, six, and four-and-a-half times faster than that averaged by

[23] For a discussion of this figure see John C. Caldwell and Adenola Igun, "The Population Outlook in Nigeria," *Proceedings of an Expert Group Meeting Held at the Development Centre, O.E.C.D., Paris, 6th–8th April, 1970.*
[24] Projection construction by Tomas Frejka, Demographic Division, The Population Council, 1971.

France from 1851 to 1931. Yet the projections show Ghana not achieving stationary population before 25.5, 38.5, or 60.3 million for projections (1), (2), and (3) respectively with a multiplication of 1970 population of almost three, five, and seven times. In none of the populations would growth become particularly slow even when a net reproduction rate of one was first reached. A growth rate of 1 percent per annum, the highest rate most northwestern European countries have ever known for any sustained period, would not be attained until about the years 2018, 2032, and 2046 respectively, or half a century, two-thirds of a century, and three-quarters of a century respectively from now. In no case would growth cease until the end of the twenty-first century. The actual number of persons added to the population each year would not fall below that experienced in the second half of the 1960s (and regarded then as large) for another 50, 80, or 100 years respectively.

THE ROLE OF FAMILY PLANNING PROGRAMS IN FERTILITY DECLINE. The possibility of alternative population paths is suggested in African population programs on the assumption that governments can contribute to fertility decline. The United Nations' Economic Commission for Africa has published population projections, not under the usual headings of "high," "medium," and "low," but described as "demographic strategy" (unquestionably governmental strategy is implied here): "neutral," "moderately effective," and "highly effective."[25] The decision to try to restrict fertility is undoubtedly primarily a product of socioeconomic change. But the effective carrying out of that decision almost certainly owes something to whether suitable, and perhaps cheap, contraceptives can be supplied. This may be especially true in West Africa where retail outlets and supply channels for imported pharmaceuticals are limited, and where much of the population is very poor and accustomed to receiving

health services (if at all) freely or cheaply through government facilities. It is also almost certainly true that government information services can convince some persons who would like to limit their families' sizes that they can in fact do so.

It is fairly clear that birth rates have fallen faster in recent years in South Korea, Taiwan, Hong Kong and Singapore than would have occurred had not government or private organizations been making contraceptives easily available. This has also been the case in an increasing number of countries in terms of the supply of legal or illegal abortion services (e.g., legal services in eastern Europe and Japan and illegal but easily available services in Korea). Family planning services are likely to work only where there is some demand for the limiting of family size. Much of West Africa has been shown by surveys to have a lower level of demand than possibly any region outside tropical Africa.[26] Chapter 3 on "Fertility Control" suggests that, for at least a decade, family planning programs in West Africa would be likely to be reasonably successful only in coastal countries, and that even there much of the demand will be concentrated in the towns. Nevertheless, the meeting of that demand would have some effect on population growth and would lay the needed base for the effective national services that will subsequently be necessary nearly everywhere. One of the existing bases for the spread of modern contraceptive use into family life, at least in the cities, is provided by the situation observed by Harrell-Bond in Freetown, where a high proportion of males report the use of some form of contraception in sexual relations outside marriage. Another is the reported increase in medically induced abortion in the large towns (Chapters on Nigeria, Ghana, and Gabon).

CHANGE IN WEST AFRICA. The fundamental issue is the magnitude of social change (and the economic change which partly causes it) and whether this is sufficiently great to induce

[25] United Nations Economic Commission for Africa, "Recent Demographic Levels and Trends in Africa," *Economic Bulletin for Africa*, V (January 1965), 78.

[26] John C. Caldwell, "The Control of Family Size in Tropical Africa," *Demography*, V, 2 (1968), 598–619.

any substantial shift in fertility attitudes and practices.

Recent change in West Africa has been greater than various indices, such as the per capita incomes attained, might at first suggest. All the chapters discuss the transformation of traditional ways of life. Chapter 29 points to the importance in Zaïre of the "non-traditional" population, that is, those living outside the lands which they can work by the inherited rights of their ethnic subgroups. By 1959 almost one-quarter of the total population was of this type; perhaps by 1970 (judging from an indirect calculation based on the movement of other data already released) the proportion was close to half. Some areas are changing more rapidly and more obviously than others: e.g., "benign" Chad in contrast to "austere" Chad (Chapter 27). Yet, even in the remotest areas, life is very different from what it was in the past. Ganon (Chapter 34) shows that the Niger nomads are to some extent becoming sedentary, but, more importantly, that the cash economy has invaded most aspects of their economic life. Morgan describes a city life which he says is not industrialized, but which is affected deeply by the infusion of the artifacts and ideas of industrialization; Addo describes how aspects, perhaps diluted, of this city life are spread through the country by the cyclic nature of internal migration.

Perhaps the two most significant changes are those in the levels of education and urbanization. The reports on education in the various chapters of this book bring out several points very clearly. First, most countries in the region recorded huge increases in the proportion of children receiving some schooling in the course of the 1950s and 1960s. Second, the increases were often greatest in the more advanced regions so that there are a substantial number of urban areas and richer cash-cropping or mining areas around the coast (especially from Ivory Coast to Zaïre) where most children now go to school at some time—a proportion that may well be ten times greater than that recorded by their parents. Third, the gap between the education of boys and girls is probably declining (partly, in countries like Ghana and Gabon, because of deliberate government action to hasten modernization by educating the next generation's mothers). Fourth, by the late 1960s emphasis was passing from further expanding schooling to secondary and tertiary education. Fifth, the cost of schooling to both governments and parents (and other relatives) had become so burdensome in many areas that it was not likely to continue rising rapidly; in Dahomey it had reached about one-quarter of the national budget and was regarded as being at its ceiling (Chapter 30). Nevertheless, in these areas the changes are now irreversible, and a high proportion of the young parents (especially the fathers) or potential parents of the latter 1970s and 1980s will have been to school. Already rural schooling is the cause of increased rural-urban migration, as can be shown clearly in Ivory Coast (Chapter 32) and Ghana.[27]

Tropical Africa is still the least urbanized part of the world, but, as measured by the rate of growth of urban population, it is the most rapidly urbanizing, a fact which more than any other gives African peoples the feeling that they are modernizing. The censuses of the 1930s showed no West African town outside Nigeria with a population over about 60,000; by 1970, Accra, Dakar, and Abidjan were all past the half-million mark and Lagos, Kinshasa, and Ibadan have probably reached 1 million. In centers of this size, many aspects of traditional life dissolve rapidly, although, as Morgan points out in Chapter 9, modern and traditional behavior patterns can often exist together to a surprising degree. Studies in Ivory Coast (Chapter 32) and Ghana[28] show that the urban cultural patterns persist

[27] John C. Caldwell, *African Rural-Urban Migration: The Movement to Ghana's Towns* (Canberra: Australian National University Press, 1969) pp. 60–69; John C. Caldwell, "Determinants of Rural-Urban Migration in Ghana," *Population Studies*, XXXI, 3 (November 1968), 361–77.

[28] John C. Caldwell, "Fertility Attitudes in Three Economically Contrasting Rural Regions of Ghana," *Economic Development and Cultural Change*, XV, 2 (January 1967), 217–38.

to a considerable degree into the cash-cropping areas; and in one area of this type in Dahomey it was shown that the residents visited the towns surprisingly frequently (Chapter 30 on the Mono survey). By 1970, over half the population of Nigeria's Western State, where populations have long been nucleated, were living in centers with over 20,000 inhabitants; by less rigorous criteria of urbanization, it has been estimated that the urban proportions of the populations of both Ghana [29] and Ivory Coast (Chapter 32) will reach two-fifths by about 1975.

Such levels of urbanization will certainly have important demographic repercussions. According to all evidence, urban residence and two characteristics associated with urbanization—higher levels of education and of nonagricultural employment—yield lower mortality levels, lower desired family sizes, and a greater tendency to attempt some form of family planning. Towns are the places where ideas change, where there are "increasing expectations" (see Chapter 13), and where one encounters more than anywhere else what Roussel writes about Ivory Coast: "the dominant feeling, especially in the young people, is an impatient longing for progress and modernity."

Government demand for fertility decline is likely to be associated closely with urbanization and education, both of which are proving to be embarrassingly costly. With regard to the towns, the reason is that governments feel the need to spend money on housing and other facilities while these are largely the product of individual or communal effort in the villages. Many West African governments are also increasingly worried by urban unemployment which they tend to link with rapid population growth.[30]

## MAJOR ISSUES: FERTILITY DECLINE

ARE MORTALITY LEVELS TOO HIGH TO ALLOW FERTILITY DECLINE? The single most important issue in terms of predicting fertility decline, the desirability of introducing family planning programs, and the likely market for the services of such programs is the impact of mortality, especially infant and child mortality. What might be described as the pessimistic view has probably been put most forcefully by Pradervand in a paper admittedly confined to francophone Africa (although not described that way on the cover or title page of the published booklet):

. . . one is never going to convince women to adopt contraception on a large scale as long as mortality levels are so high. The rare countries where family planning programs seem to have a slight effect on fertility all have among the lowest death rates in the world. There is no example of a successful large-scale family planning program in any country with death rates above 12 per thousand. In the majority of countries of West Africa, death rates are well over 200 percent higher, and sometimes almost 300 percent higher than this figure. It should thus not surprise the reader that we conclude that high mortality is undoubtedly the single most important obstacle to the adoption of contraception on a large scale in Africa today.[31]

Some of this comment seems to confuse fertility decline or the potential for fertility decline in parts of a community with the success of national family planning programs. Other parts are questionable. The use of the crude death rate is unfortunate, especially when comparing countries with slow and rapid fertility declines, but, if we are going to use it, it should be noted that by the early 1960s the rate had apparently fallen below 24 per thousand in Senegal and Zaïre, as well as, in anglophone Africa, in Ghana. For comparison, it fell below this level in France and England in the mid-nineteenth century after fertility decline had begun in the former but not in the latter, and when the two

---

[29] John C. Caldwell, "Migration and Urbanization," in Walter Birmingham, I. Neustadt, and E. M. Omaboe, eds., *A Study of Contemporary Ghana*, II, *Some Aspects of Social Structure* (London: George Allen and Unwin, and Evanston: Northwestern University Press, 1967), p. 190.

[30] Government of Ghana, *Population Planning for National Progress and Prosperity*, White Paper (March 1969).

[31] Pradervand, *Family Planning Programs*, p. 18.

countries exhibited birth rates in the low 20s and low 30s respectively.[32] The organized availability of contraceptives has almost certainly had more than a slight effect on the fertility of Singapore, Hong Kong, Taiwan, and South Korea, and had begun to have this effect in the latter when the death rate was still well over 12. Large family planning programs have been organized in countries with death rates well over 20: India, Pakistan, Indonesia, and Iran for example.

There are two basic problems, which will be treated separately here. The first is whether fertility decline is likely to endanger national or individual family numbers. The second is whether family planning programs would be likely to attract enough customers to justify them.

National populations are certainly not in danger. By 1970 they were probably all increasing at an annual rate exceeding 2 percent with the possible exceptions of Gabon and Chad and thus tending to double in less than 35 years; in all of them this rate is almost certainly climbing, perhaps quite steeply. More importantly, fertility decline is likely to come latest in countries which still have very high mortality levels. Fertility rates began to fall in western Europe when the rate of natural increase was closer to 1 percent.

The really important consideration, in a region where the old look to the young for support in old age or other adversity, is the risk, with lower birth rates, of having no one to give such support. There is no risk of children not exceeding parents in total numbers; even with successful family planning programs, rates of natural increase are likely to remain above 2 percent everywhere and above 3 percent in some countries for a considerable time. Thus, each succeeding generation is likely to be double its predecessor, a very different position from traditional West Africa, for among populations at the turn of the century, growing slowly with death rates not far below birth rates, total surviving children probably exceeded total

parents by less than one-seventh.[33]

The important question is whether a demographic transition starting from a position of very high birth and death rates is likely to leave more aged parents without support than a transition starting from moderate birth and death rates. The following discussion examines the probability of having surviving children. In fact the West African position is usually more complex than this, with support (sometimes the main support) coming from nephews and nieces as well, and sometimes younger siblings or other relatives or even nonrelatives one has helped. There is indeed a theoretical case in some areas for couples wishing to maximize their ultimate economic return by reducing their own fertility while encouraging that of their siblings. The more widespread support is, the less the risk of lack of support for individual families, and the greater the proportion of aged who will receive support at a given ratio of the size of the succeeding generation to the one before it in the whole society. Support is more widespread again for the polygamist.

However, let us examine the relationship for monogamous parents and their children. This was the subject of a letter from two members of the staff of Makerere University Medical School to *The Lancet* in 1968.[34] It was argued that the major aim is to secure one surviving son, and that, with only three-quarters of males surviving to age 15 (equivalent to an expectation of life at birth for males of 47 years in the Coale and Demeny North life tables), parents are likely to aim at having three sons (and six children) to give themselves a 98.4 percent chance of one surviving to 15. They further argued that this explains a fertility level characterized by completed fertility of about six live births and that the potential market for family planning

---

[32] Data from Nathan Keyfitz and Wilhelm Flieger, *World Population, An Analysis of Vital Data* (Chicago: University of Chicago Press, 1968).

[33] J. C. Caldwell, "The Demographic Victory: Population Change, 1880-1935," in A. Boahene, ed., *General History of Africa*, Vol. VII (Paris: UNESCO, 1975).
[34] M. A. Gumbi and S. A. Hall, Department of Preventive Medicine, Makerere University College Medical School, "Attitudes of Rural Workers in the Tropics to Family Planning," letter to the editor of *The Lancet* (August 31, 1968), 508-9.

services are those families which have attained three male births with fewer than six births of both sexes.

This may be an explanation for sustaining an average of six births when the only anti-natal measures are unaffected by the number of surviving children (for example, the observance of the postnatal taboo on sexual relations for a fixed period after each birth). The guarantee needed that one son will survive seems to be extraordinarily high: not only much higher than in Europe when fertility began to decline (where admittedly the need for a son may have been much less strongly felt) but also much higher than it must have been at this fertility level in Africa until recent times. With the kind of mortality that probably prevailed in tropical Africa at the beginning of this century,[35] the birth of three sons would have provided only an 82 percent chance of one surviving to age 15; to reach 98 percent a couple would have needed seven sons or an average of 14 children. Yet there is no evidence of declining fertility, and the mortality, assumed above to represent contemporary mortality, would

provide a 94 percent chance of one out of two sons reaching age 15, a much higher guarantee than was the experience of the traditional society with three or four sons.

However, this kind of calculation has little relevance for couples actually planning their families to any extent with the aid of contraception. The reason is that a woman can decide to have a second or third son if the first dies during the perilous younger years. Take the position of women who have reached the end of their fecund years, or the end of the years during which they are prepared to be fertile, at 40 years of age (and employing the same measure of mortality as above which is equal to the best West African national levels, and also higher mortality similar to that now found in the West African savanna countries and the wetter countries of the far southwest). Table 1.2 sets out some of the possibilities. These could be regarded as the same probabilities for a woman who had reached the end of her fecund years by having a sterilizing operation.

Table 1.2 is a model which approximates the real position. Its greatest departure from reality is probably in part A in that it

[35] Coale and Demeny, *Regional Model Life Tables*, North Set, Level 2.

TABLE 1.2
Position of contracepting women with regard to male survivors at the end of their fecund period by level of mortality

| Male Survivorship Position | Mortality | Probability that a Son Will Reach 15 Years | Past History of Survival Percentage of women who had following number of live male births | | | | | Average Live Male Births |
|---|---|---|---|---|---|---|---|---|
| | | | 1 | 2 | 3 | 4 | 5+ | |
| A. One son has reached 15 years of age | Low | 1.00 | 75 | 19 | 5 | 1 | — | 1.3 |
| | High | 1.00 | 57 | 25 | 10 | 5 | 3 | 1.7 |
| B. One son has reached 10 years of age | Low | 0.98 | 77 | 18 | 4 | 1 | — | 1.3 |
| | High | 0.96 | 60 | 24 | 10 | 4 | 2 | 1.7 |
| C. One son has reached 5 years of age | Low | 0.94 | 80 | 16 | 3 | 1 | — | 1.3 |
| | High | 0.89 | 64 | 23 | 8 | 3 | 2 | 1.6 |

SOURCE: Coale and Demeny "North" Life Tables.
NOTE: Low = Level 13, male expectation of life at birth, 46.7 years; High = Level 7, male expectation of life at birth, 32.0 years.

TABLE 1.3

Probabilities of one male child surviving to 15 and 25 years of age by composition of family and level of mortality

| Composition of Family by Sex | | Percentage of All Families of this type[a] | Percentage of Families Where at Least One Son Will Survive to 15 Years | | Percentage of Families Where at Least One Son Will Survive to 25 Years | |
|---|---|---|---|---|---|---|
| Males | Females | | High mortality[b] | Low mortality[b] | High mortality[b] | Low mortality[b] |
| 4 | 0 | 6.25 | 97 | 99.9 | 95 | 99 |
| 3 | 1 | 25 | 92 | 99.6 | 89 | 98 |
| 2 | 2 | 37.5 | 82 | 98 | 77 | 92 |
| 1 | 3 | 25 | 57 | 94 | 52 | 71 |
| 0 | 4 | 6.25 | — | — | — | — |

[a] We assume that the sex ratio at birth is at parity, which may be close to the truth in West Africa.
[b] As in Table 1.2.

assumes an original cohort of women successfully replacing each dead son by another if necessary. For the few who have to replace several sons, or where the son dies at a comparatively advanced age, or where the attempt to replace the son is for a time frustrated by a succession of daughters, it may be impossible to have a 15-year-old son by 40 years of age; in this case the gradient in part A would be steeper (that is, a higher proportion would have had one male birth and a lower proportion three or four) and the surplus women would be found in part B or part C (there would be some steepening in the gradients here as well).

These qualifications do very little to alter the essential picture. Even in the high mortality areas, family size averaging 3.4 or 3.3 (depending on the sex ratio at birth), smaller where males came early and did not die (and in fact with a somewhat smaller average because families of this type might desist from having another daughter), would provide a much better chance than did the traditional society of rearing a son to adulthood. In fact, even highly successful African family planning programs are unlikely to reduce average family size below four for a long time to come, and hence the probable fate of the four-child family is analyzed in Table 1.3 according to the mortality levels employed in Table 1.2. It might be noted that fertility and mortality levels of this magnitude would yield a population (even without further falls in mortality) growing at 0.2 and 1.2 percent per annum for high and low mortality respectively when stabilized.

The probability of having one son survive to 25 years is around 90 percent or higher for the 69 percent of low mortality families with two to four sons and the 31 percent of high mortality families with three to four sons. The other 31 percent of families in the low mortality conditions and 69 percent in the high mortality conditions might well be the majority which move toward becoming five-child and even six-child families. This will not necessarily raise the average size of all families, for those which already are dominated by sons before four are reached, may stop short of four. To take the extreme example, $12\frac{1}{2}$ percent of families will start off by having three sons (half of them potential four-son families and half potential three-sons-and-one-daughter families) and these families may well have no more children; they already have the chances of survival for sons shown in Table 1.3 for the three-sons-and-one-daughter families.

There are, of course, all kinds of qualifications which should be added. The life tables do not exactly fit West African conditions, and, for the same expectation of life at birth as is given by the tables, the chance of survival to age 15 (especially in the high mortality societies) may be somewhat lower; however, a continuing decline in mortality will probably outweigh this, especially as family planning clinics may also provide child health services. Smaller families, better looked after and probably better educated, may well have higher than average chances of survival and even of yielding greater support for parents or other older relatives.[36] National fertility decline may hasten mortality decline, especially among children (Chapter 24). In spite of the emphasis here on sons (partly in accordance with the emphasis in the letter to *The Lancet*), West African society does not place very great emphasis on the need for sons. However, a widespread argument for the very large family is that in a society where "white-collar" urban incomes are very many times greater than urban laborers' or most rural incomes, a large family will have a greater chance of producing one exceptional child, in whom funds for education can be invested and from whom support can later be received. The contrary argument is that ability is often hard to identify at an early stage and that the small family has a greater chance of keeping all children at school until scholastic success can be predicted. Finally, for comparison, it might be noted that in France of 1850, after fertility had been declining for at least half a century, and in England and Wales of 1880, just as steep fertility decline was about to occur, a family of two boys and two girls (significantly larger than average at that time in France and slightly larger than in England) would have had (at the mortality rates of that date) an 82 percent and a 91 percent chance respectively of one son surviving to age 25.

Perhaps, however, these figures overemphasize the danger that children might not survive, for the clientele of family planning programs are to a very high degree self-selective, and determined as well by where family planning facilities are located. The great majority of the clientele will tend to come (as is assumed in Chapter 3) from areas of lower than average mortality—the towns or the mining and cash-cropping areas. Even here (and elsewhere) they tend to be from socioeconomic groups with lower than average mortality, and to a considerable extent from individuals tending to have above average fertility.

If a completed family size of four live births

were achieved, this would mean for most countries a decline in fertility of over one-third and in the rate of population growth of two-thirds with a fair chance of achieving a rate near 1 percent per annum unless mortality decline accelerated.

ARE PRONATALIST ATTITUDES TOO DEEPLY EMBEDDED TO ALLOW FERTILITY DECLINE? West Africa, largely as a result of social and economic change this century, is by no means a monolithic, proextreme fertility region. When asked about the case for the large family, half of urban elites and a substantial proportion of all population now tend to answer that there is no case. This is especially so when the respondents have had some schooling. In a region where completed family size is most commonly six to seven live births (that is, half of all women have a greater number), and where the average number surviving childhood among the residents of major towns and all persons with schooling beyond the elementary level is in most coastal countries probably nearing five, it is highly significant that one-third to one-half of metropolitan populations surveyed do not want a fifth child. It is in fact the possibility of preventing the birth of the fifth surviving child that holds most promise for any attempt to restrict African fertility. By the standards of many countries the desire for four surviving children is pronatalism indeed. But in the lower mortality areas in West Africa, the towns and major cash-cropping and mining areas, it could mean an ultimate drop in the birth rate of one-fifth and in the rate of natural increase of between one-quarter and one-third, even if fertility ideals do not sink lower.

Perhaps the more important point to make is that an increasing proportion of West Africa's population is by no means unqualifiedly in favor of unlimited fertility. That proportion will inevitably grow not only with modernization and education but also with the spread of ideas and examples.

IS THE REGION TOO SPARSELY POPULATED FOR FAMILY PLANNING PROGRAMS TO BE IN THE NATIONAL INTEREST? Population density is

[36] John C. Caldwell, "The Erosion of the Family: A Study of the Fate of the Family in Ghana," *Population Studies*, XX, 1 (July 1966), 5–26.

a relative term and can only really be measured in comparison with available resources. Much of the governmental talk in West Africa of underpopulation comes from the savanna lands of the interior. Judging by national density figures, these countries are indeed more sparsely settled than their neighbors on the coast. Yet these are precisely the areas classified by Hance as experiencing population pressure.[37] To an American (Hance) or an Australian (Caldwell) these areas are reminiscent of great stretches of land in their own countries which are less densely settled still and which are believed to be deservedly so. Hance (in Chapter 5) describes the soils and even the mineral wealth as being unfavorable compared with those of much of the world.

West African densities outside the arid regions are closer to those found in most of the world. Already 35–40 million people in all West Africa probably live in areas seriously affected by population pressure (Hance, Chapter 5). Niger may be an extreme example, but some perspective is given by the calculation that the population density is 8 per square mile for the whole country, 35 per square mile for that part of it outside the desert, and 200 per square mile in arable areas (Chapter 34). The degree to which the savanna people migrate is a meaningful measure of relatively deficient resources at home.

It is true that the denser areas in West Africa can often be explained by their histories: the centers of powerful kingdoms, positions away from the tracts of disease along rivers, and, increasingly in recent decades, the places with the best communications. However, it is increasingly difficult to regard the more thinly populated areas in between as anything but *lebensraum* for the inevitable population growth which will take place even if family planning programs become widespread.

There is little evidence of population growth in specific areas bringing individual

benefits, although there are examples of the development of resources encouraging population growth partly by immigration. It is said that soil fertility is deteriorating in some of the older areas of dense settlement (Chapter 32), and that in such areas land holdings have declined in size and land prices have inflated (Chapter 15). A more contentious issue is that of raising productivity in cash-cropping areas; Roussel and Udo (Chapters 32 and 13) believe that this can only be done with tree crops by creating larger holdings worked by fewer people.

There is relatively little satisfactory evidence comparing the welfare of persons in adjacent or similar areas with very different population densities. What there is does not support the idea that welfare is greater in the denser regions. Where such comparisons have been attempted in Senegal, the denser areas appear to be characterized by less land per capita, a lower per capita diet, and a higher infant mortality rate (Chapters 4 and 35). Higher rates of out-migration can be shown for the most densely populated areas in Nigeria, Cameroon, and Upper Volta, with, in the latter, increasing evidence of soil exhaustion in the Mossi heartland. However, in southern Dahomey (Chapter 30) a study of the Mono area does not show soil deterioration with population growth but does reveal pressure on incomes because a greater proportion of the cash crops is being eaten locally. In most areas greater population densities do not seem to mean a mere movement of the settlement frontier into unoccupied land.

There is little evidence, then, to suggest that West Africa would benefit from either greater population densities or higher rates of population growth than those which will certainly now take place even with the most energetic measures to reduce fertility. In terms of producing satisfactory rural incomes, there may be a case in much of the forest for aggregating farms as more capital becomes available (for transport and cultivation) and in the more arid parts of the savanna for encouraging emigration to the richer cash-cropping areas or to the towns. Van de Walle

[37] William A. Hance, *Population, Migration and Urbanization in West Africa* (New York: Columbia University Press, 1970), p. 17.

argues that the world market for tree crops is unlikely to grow as fast as the West African rural population, a sobering statistic even if we assume no rise in productivity.

ARE CHILDREN TOO GREAT AN ECONOMIC ASSET AND INSUFFICIENTLY AN ECONOMIC DISADVANTAGE TO MAKE FERTILITY DECLINE PROBABLE? A specific study in Ghana,[38] together with the evidence from various chapters in this book, suggests the following conclusions. Children, in traditional farming areas, enter the labor force at 4–6 years of age. They are partly economic and partly social assets in that they perform such labor as looking after animals, carrying messages, transporting water and kindling, and, in the case of girls, acting as nursemaids for the toddlers, tasks which adults find inconvenient or beneath their dignity. Nevertheless, they are not very efficient, and there is no clear evidence of family prosperity, as distinct from prestige, being demonstrably higher in very large families. However, a man with several wives may till more land and may be clearly more prosperous, although it is frequently his prosperity which has enabled him to take more wives.

The position is different in tree-crop areas. Roussel believes that the ethnic division of labor which has been established and the role played by migrant labor restricts the work that the farmers' children can do. In Ghana and Nigeria, it is quite clear that tree-crop incomes have permitted the education of children to the point where both they and their parents feel that it is preferable for them to do nothing rather than work on the farms.

In the towns, the large family can be a major problem in that the children almost inevitably go to school. This is directly costly in terms of fees, books, and better clothes and indirectly expensive in that educated children develop more wants and are more effective in demanding the satisfaction of these wants.

To some degree, the problems listed above for the urban parent face parents in any village where a school has appeared. It has been suggested before that it may have been

[38] Caldwell, "Fertility Attitudes," pp. 217–38.

no accident in northwestern Europe that fertility began to decline during the same decade that compulsory schooling was enforced, and not a generation later when educated parents became universal.

A fair summary might be that the economic advantage of children for present production is nowhere, outside the most traditional farming areas, as great an encouragement for high fertility as is the desire for future production so as to provide security in old age, or in sickness. In contrast, the very large family is an increasing economic burden in the towns and certain other modernized areas. West Africans have intensified this burden by the fervor, which is widespread, for educating their children as much as possible. Harrell-Bond (Chapter 23) describes the pressures on the Freetown elite to reduce fertility because of the expenses arising from cars, large houses, Western clothing, imported foods, and school fees. She adds, however, that there is still some motivation to higher fertility, not because of any economic advantages posed by children, but because of the prestige accruing to the head of a large family.

DO EXTENDED FAMILY OBLIGATIONS REDUCE ANY GAINS MADE BY LOWERING INDIVIDUAL FERTILITY? West Africans feel obligations toward a much wider circle of relatives than their nuclear families and these obligations are inevitably exacted to a greater extent from those who are in a better position to provide. Hence, it is a plausible argument that no great saving can be made when parents restrict their own fertility. The matter has not been thoroughly tested in a large population. A study at the University of Ghana in 1963 showed that most students would expect to make substantial personal savings by reducing fertility, but, significantly, the margin of savings which could be kept within the nuclear family was believed to be smaller by those students who had already worked for a living.[39] Harrell-Bond believes

[39] John C. Caldwell, "Extended Family Obligations and Education: A Study of an Aspect of Demographic Transition among Ghanaian University Students," *Population Studies*, XIX, 2 (November 1965), 183–99.

that extended family obligations reduce the motivation to restrict fertility among the Freetown elites, but that it is not a decisive determinant (Chapter 23). Much the same viewpoint commonly is expressed in discussions by the better-off urban population.

IS THE REGION TOO RURAL AND TOO UN-EDUCATED FOR SIGNIFICANT FERTILITY DE-CLINE TO OCCUR? Pradervand claims that significant fertility decline cannot occur, and he is probably correct with regard to a considerable area. However, there are very great differences between areas. When describing Chad (Chapter 27), Reyna and Bouquet drew attention to the contrast between "benign Chad" and "austere Chad": the former, being non-Moslem, was entered by missionaries who have exerted a strong Westernizing influence, and it now has about one-third of 6–14-year olds in school; the latter, admittedly with a much poorer economic base, has only 1 in 18 children at school. They point to a tendency for the differential in development to become wider with differential schooling as the main mechanism. Roussel draws similar contrasts, at a different level, in the much more developed Ivory Coast (Chapter 32). In Abidjan, one-third of the population is literate in contrast to only 1 in 12 in rural areas. In all the towns, only 5 percent of the population claim adherence to the traditional religions, compared with a much higher fraction in rural areas.

Thus, there are certainly areas where Pradervand's description no longer holds true; this is the case in much of West Africa among the young and will soon be so among young adults. In terms of the potential for fertility restrictions the period is not long, for West African women have half their live births within about a dozen years of leaving middle school or its equivalent (about 15 years of age). Furthermore, where the people and the governments can afford it, the average period of education is likely to become longer for the reason that Roussel distinguishes in Ivory Coast: educational advance itself has led to a devaluing in the labor market of the educational certificate awarded at the end of elementary school.

IS THE ROLE AND EDUCATION OF WOMEN TOO INFERIOR FOR WIDESPREAD FAMILY PLANNING? Pradervand is inclined to think that the status of women in the francophone countries will preclude widespread family planning, but it is probable that he should have confined these remarks to the Moslem inland savanna. In much of West Africa, women enjoy a substantial degree of independence, partly because of the extent to which they remain members of their ancestral families in contrast to their conjugal families, and partly because they are largely responsible for their own and their children's support. Gaisie found evidence that, even in the modern sector of Ghana's economy, female activity rates climbed faster than male ones during the 1960s.

There has been a sex differential in education, but in most coastal countries it has not been as severe as that found in south and southwest Asia. The West African evidence seems to be that it is lessening partly because of government action and partly because of changing family attitudes. Roussel says that, in Ivory Coast, the latter change is especially marked in the towns. There is evidence that the educated girls marry later and are less fertile in the younger age groups even when not still going to school: in Niger, 15–19 year olds are 40 percent less fertile if they have been to school than if they have not (Chapter 34).

Harrell-Bond is almost certainly correct when she concludes from her study of a group where social change has probably gone furthest (the Creole elite of Freetown) that fertility decline is ensured only when the role of women changes to the point where considerable emphasis is put on the sexual relationship within marriage in contrast to that on reproduction and motherhood. She argues convincingly that a male's interest in the female partner's enjoyment of sex is part of modernization and that films, magazines, and books have taught it. She also adds that females play a role in this change, and that they are only likely to play it if they have been educated, presumably either because this changes their feelings about themselves or men's feelings about them, or more likely the interaction of both. Certainly, the attention given by demographers during the 1960s to the possibility of a family planning revolution in developing countries paid too little notice to the broader sexual revolution (evidenced among the urban elites of West Africa by a greatly increased discussion of sexual relations in their periodic reading matter and exhibited films) which may have been the necessary vehicle.

IS LIFE TOO CAPRICIOUS AND FATALISM TOO GREAT? Traditionally West Africa has been dominated by the belief that such important matters as being born and dying were largely outside man's control, which indeed they were. Such conditions tend to produce not only an acceptance of fate (which may or may not be an integral part of religious belief) but also a fear of interfering with its course. Trevor says that the fear of modern contraception in northern Nigeria is fundamentally based on the suspicion that it really works.

Sometimes the reply that "it is up to God" or that "fate will decide" to questions such as whether more children are desired merely means that the matter is not important and that the decision of luck will be accepted. However, it is instructive to note that, in the Sierra Leone survey, the proportion of respondents stating that "it is up to God", when asked whether they wanted another child, declined with the number of children already possessed.

It is highly significant that, in KAP (studies of fertility and knowledge of, attitudes toward, and practice of family planning) surveys, fatalistic responses decline with urbanization, education, and higher incomes—that is, precisely among those groups who do have some control over the demographic factors in their lives. Unqualified fatalism is found only among those groups least likely to practice family planning, least likely to need to do so, and least likely to

find themselves near government or other facilities dispensing contraceptives.

IS FAMILY PLANNING A SIMPLE REACTION TO DEVELOPMENT OR IS IT ALSO THE SPREAD OF AN IDEA? Family planning information services sometimes are described as if the failure to practice contraception merely arose from lack of knowledge. In contrast, it has been argued that the appearance given in European fertility transition of precepts and practices flowing from urban to rural areas was entirely misleading, and that the truth was that conditions in urban areas merely meant that smaller families were needed there sooner and, at any given time, by a bigger proportion of the population.[40]

Nigerian research suggests that West African contraceptive use is likely to be a compound of need and knowledge.[41] Among those who know enough about contraception to be able to use it, urban residents are much more likely to do so than rural residents. However, even among groups potentially likely to want to practice contraception, most claim only to have achieved sufficient knowledge and to have applied that knowledge during the unprecedented spate of information and (in Lagos) contraceptive availability in the 1960s (Chapter 3).

Certainly, the press takes up aspects of family life and the need for changes in traditional patterns. Even far inland in Niamey (Chapter 33), the press is given to debating bride price, polygyny, and the rights of women. Harrell-Bond (Chapter 23) reports the position among the Freetown elite to be very similar to that reported earlier by the author among the Ghanaian urban elite:[42] The Western nucleated small-family system is regarded as a good thing; the

---

[40] Gösta Carlsson, "The Decline of Fertility: Innovation or Adjustment Process," *Population Studies*, XX, 2 (November 1966), 149–74.

[41] John C. Caldwell and Adenola A. Igun, "The Spread of Anti-natal Knowledge and Practice in Nigeria," *Population Studies*, XXIV, 1 (March 1970), 21–34.

[42] John C. Caldwell, *Population Growth and Family Change in Africa: The New Urban Elite in Ghana* (Canberra: Australian National University Press, 1968).

criticism of the Western family centers on its failure to retain a mechanism for guaranteeing family care and attention to the aged.

Certainly, all chapters in this book report a flow of ideas which are believed to be affecting family planning and other behavior patterns. Freetown and Lagos are pointed to as the paramount importers of cultural change into their countries, and Morgan would go further and claim this role for Lagos with regard to much of West Africa. Harrell-Bond believes that the metropolitan elite form the original channel for these new ideas and describes them in the first place as providing a beachhead for their relatives to the modern world.

THE PROBLEMS OF INNOVATION. Some sections of the population, especially rural ones, have less social and economic inducement to restrict fertility than do other groups. Nevertheless, the very low level of antinatal practice among the most traditional elements of the population arises also partly from lesser capacity for coping with rapid change. In general, the writer's description of the position in 1963 among Ghana's urban elite still holds:

There is considerable evidence, among the elite at least, that a smaller incidence of family planning among the less educated, the rural-born and the first generation members of the elite is not indicative of a desire for relatively large families but of greater general problems in coping with social and technological innovation, and with—another case of innovation itself—communication about innovation. Most of the individual respondents in these groups show almost as much desire to prevent pregnancy as do their counterparts in the complementary groups, but are likely to do so only if contraceptive methods are simple enough and presented to them in an easy enough fashion to reduce to a minimal level the problems of coping with innovation and if public acceptance is sufficiently widespread or sufficiently publicized to reduce their problems of communicating with their spouses and doctors.[43]

Some West African societies appear to value innovational behavior more than others.

[43] Ibid., p. 188.

The Wolof of Senegal and the Ibos of Nigeria are examples. It is possible that they will also be more willing than average to reduce family size.

POTENTIAL LEADING GROUPS IN FERTILITY CHANGE. All West African KAP surveys agree on the types of people among whom family planning is first likely to be common and among whom fertility decline may begin. These were distinguished in the Sierra Leone survey by ascertaining marked differentials (always more than 15 percent) from their complementary groups: those who had been to school rather than those who had not (the widest of all differentials); the literate rather than the illiterate; those with wide knowledge of things outside their own society rather than those with lesser knowledge; Christians rather than Moslems (although this may be largely a measure of an associated differential in Western schooling). Fertility declines will almost certainly start first in the more developed areas, partly because their wealth has allowed them to train and attract more educated persons, partly because economic progress induces urbanization and nonagricultural employment (both of which pose problems for the large family), but partly also because they have more social welfare services so that the old do not have to turn exclusively to their younger relatives.

MAJOR ISSUES: THE ADOPTION OF FAMILY PLANNING PROGRAMS

GOVERNMENTAL ATTITUDES. Population policies and family planning programs have been slower to develop in West Africa than in Asia, probably partly because of West Africa's higher mortality levels and partly because of its lower settlement densities. Nevertheless, Gwatkin is undoubtedly right when he asserts that the policy changes which occurred in the 1969–1971 period could not have been foreseen two years earlier. The major events included the adoption of a population policy and the beginning of the establishment of a network of family planning facilities by Ghana and the announced intention to set up a family planning program by Nigeria. The same period also witnessed introspection about the effects of rapid population growth in Dahomey and Gambia and the requests by both for expert missions to advise on the position. It might be noted that the Nigerian decision was preceded by that of the Lagos City Council in the mid-1960s to allow the use of some of its health clinics for family planning. On the other hand, rapid population growth was still being encouraged in Cameroon and Gabon and was desired in Ivory Coast.

These contrasts will not necessarily be long lasting. As late as 1964, Ghana (under the Nkrumah government) stopped the import and sale of contraceptives and discussed the provision of penal sanctions against contraceptive practice. Nevertheless, the present Ghana population policy originated in the findings of the 1960 census and in various demographic analyses during the following decade.[44] Olusanya (in Chapter 11) believes that the Nigerian population policy decision followed inevitably the marked rise in official interest in population matters stemming basically from the 1963 census results. It is far from impossible that the 1970 census round will have the same effect in some francophone countries.

The reasons for government interest are given by van de Walle and others in various chapters as a concern with the effect of high rates of population growth in frustrating the reaching of economic targets and specific concern with urban and educational problems. Against this is a general apprehension about running counter to African traditions and Catholic beliefs and that intellectual tradition which holds Africa (and possibly France) to be underpopulated. Questions have also been raised as to why fertility decline in Africa might need to be hastened by government intervention when this was not necessary in Europe. The simple answer

[44] S. K. Gaisie, S. B. Jones, John C. Caldwell, and Gordon W. Perkin, "Ghana," *Country Profiles*, The Population Council and the International Institute for the Study of Human Reproduction, Columbia University (New York, October 1970).

is that West Africa's high rates of population growth do not provide it with the time that Europe had. But there are also other supplementary answers. The poverty of Africa has made government intervention in the form of health services and mass vaccination campaigns the chief vehicle for reducing mortality; and it is unlikely that national fertility can be reduced anywhere in the immediate future without similar intervention. It is possible also that the publicizing of official viewpoints will do something to undermine the high fertility tradition.

IS THE PUBLIC HEALTH FRAMEWORK SUFFICIENT TO SUPPORT NATIONAL FAMILY PLANNING PROGRAMS? Pradervand, referring to the francophone countries, has claimed that national family planning programs cannot be supported by public health services. The writer feels that, while this may be true of abortion programs (which are not currently being promoted), it is a more doubtful claim in the case of contraceptive programs. Health facilities are reasonably widespread in urban areas and in the richer rural areas of the coastal countries. Olusanya has reported that the recent division of Nigeria into 12 states has speeded up the establishment of rural services. It is the existence of such facilities which has made the present rate of population growth possible.

Nevertheless, there will be strains. Family planning programs in West Africa will have to depend heavily on auxiliary medical personnel rather than on doctors, as the rural public health services already do. It may well be that the coupling of family planning with maternal and child health services will mean that family planning programs help to carry child care programs to many areas considerably earlier than would otherwise be the case.

POSSIBLE GAINS FROM FAMILY PLANNING PROGRAMS. It is clear that the implementation of national family planning programs will endanger neither national nor family survival. The reason is that the individual clients are self-selected in terms both of surviving children and of the chances of those children continuing to survive. The same kinds of criteria determine which countries are likely to adopt programs first, how vigorously they will pursue them, and which parts of the country such programs will cater to most intensively.

However, Chapter 3 in this book makes it clear that no West African country is likely to achieve the degree of fertility control during the coming decade that has already been gained in parts of East Asia. It is, then, pertinent to ask whether the gains which could be made during the 1970s in West Africa would be worth the governmental effort and expenditure.

There is little doubt that, for every country likely to introduce a major family planning program, the answer is yes. From the national viewpoint, there would be a reduction of pressure on schooling and urban facilities among other things which might well be disproportionately greater than the fertility decline, because the families restricting fertility are more likely to be those which keep their children longer at school and which live in urban areas. From the individual point of view there will be the benefit of being able to control fertility easily by utilizing facilities not previously available.

But the major gains may well be elsewhere. The building of such infrastructure during the 1970s might mean a success in fertility control during the 1980s which could not otherwise have been achieved to the same extent. In the meantime, the ability of an increasing number of families to control fertility might mean an advance toward the kind of responsible society of individual decision making which is necessary for economic modernization. Ultimately, modernization may depend to a considerable extent on the ever greater concentration of parents on the education and other aspects of training of a comparatively small number of children. This is most likely when it is thought almost certain that each will grow up. The path to this position passes inevitably through both mortality and fertility decline. These may in West Africa be not successive phases but interrelated ones, especially if family planning clinics also undertake maternal and child health.

CAN THE PROGRAMS WORK? The responsibility for making the programs work depends upon two factors: government and individual acceptance.

As Gwatkin makes clear in Chapter 8, the likelihood of governments announcing population policies aimed at reducing the birth rate seems much greater now than it did two or three years ago. It is probable that in the 1970s such policies will spread across West Africa in much the same way as they spread across Asia in the 1960s.

The kind of evidence on family planning change examined in Chapter 3 suggests that there is some demand for contraceptive (and even abortion) services and that the satisfaction of this might well give rise to further demand. The process is almost certainly self-sustaining, although the exact pace of such a chain reaction is more debatable.

## OTHER ISSUES

EDUCATION AND URBANIZATION. A major demographic issue in West Africa, second only to that of population growth, is urbanization. The chapters on Ivory Coast and Ghana document a position that has been outlined in earlier research[45] and surmise, namely that the rural exodus to the towns is gaining pace and is influenced by levels of rural education to perhaps a greater degree than anywhere else in the world. The road to economic modernization and high per capita incomes undoubtedly lies through urbanization, industrialization, and universal education. However, the process is a long one and governments tend to be more worried about the immediate problems. It is probable that West African governments have tended to react suspiciously to the rapid growth of city populations, partly because urban misery is more visible than rural distress (although the latter in West Africa can often be horrifyingly greater) and partly because governments do spend more per head on urban populations.

[45] Caldwell, *African Rural-Urban Migration*.

At the same time, it is clear that most rural children with post primary education, and many with only primary schooling, feel that they have been fitted solely for urban employment. Thus, they either go to the towns and stay there or form an unemployed group in the farming areas.

It is inevitable that governments will be tempted to think in terms of discouraging new residents in the towns, increasing investment in manufacturing industries in rural areas, and slowing down the expansion of rural schooling. All three decisions could, in the long run, be harmful. Manufacturing industry in West Africa is likely to suffer severely from the high cost of production for many years to come. As much of it will depend to a very considerable degree on imported materials, and on the production of a small number of other factories within the country, such costs can probably be held down only by a concentration of industrialization. Inevitably this will have to be in the large urban areas and, in those countries bordering the sea, in one or two large ports.

At the same time a good deal more introspection is needed on the issue of rural production and desired levels of efficiency in the rural sector. This sector will inevitably experience a very great rise in population over the next generation and might well benefit from exporting some of its population to the towns even if these are the youngest and most educated persons.

DATA COLLECTION AND RESEARCH. Population growth will probably remain the most important variable in West African economic planning, partly because economic growth rates are, for the whole region, relatively low compared with most other world regions, while the same cannot be said of population growth. Many countries are still unsure whether their total numbers are likely to increase by less than one-tenth or more than one-sixth in a five-year period.

There is, then, a continuing need for census and survey demographic data. At the same time, there is often a reluctance to spend as much on a census as on a single new road. Undoubtedly this arises in many countries from the methods of financing censuses, which often are regarded as an additional special item to be considered by the government for inclusion in the budget as a kind of extra. The writer believes that they are a developmental expenditure and should be shown as such in the forecast expenditures in the economic plan.

The time has probably also come for further experiments with vital registration systems although it might be noted that there is as yet no West African experience to provide confidence that such systems will work well enough to justify their cost.

Finally, population data are most valuable, often only valuable, when they are competently analyzed. It is also important that enough of this analysis should be done within the country to give administrative confidence that the local scene is understood and, probably more importantly, to provide administrators and politicians with experts they can consult easily.

By the beginning of the 1970s West African universities were more likely to have some teaching and some research in demography than were the universities in any other major region outside tropical Africa. Nevertheless, many of these demographic programs need strengthening and enlargement as well as an increasing concern with academic standards and technical expertise.

IN RECENT United Nations' estimates of birth rates for major world regions,[1] the figure of 49 births per thousand population for the Western African region (defined as extending from Mauritania to Nigeria) exceeds all others, and that of 44 per thousand for the Middle Africa region (from Chad through Zaïre to Angola) is third highest among the remaining 23 regions. Clearly West Africa includes some of the world's highest fertility populations. But fertility is not high throughout the area; in certain parts, notably in sections of the Central African Republic and Zaïre, fertility is currently at such low levels as to scarcely, if at all, ensure replacement of the present population.

Despite recent advances in the collection and analysis of demographic data from tropical Africa, estimation and interpretation of fertility patterns is a hazardous undertaking, for the primary data are both limited and defective. Data amenable to serious demographic analysis were collected in very few countries prior to the 1950s. Twenty years later there is a small quantity of information available for almost all areas of West Africa, but a country with data referring to more than a single point in time is still a rarity; in some cases the only information available is now well over ten years old and surely is outdated. At the national level, reliable data providing direct evidence of fertility levels (such as are yielded by comprehensive and efficient vital registration systems) are nonexistent over most of the region. One is forced to rely instead on materials from census and sample survey sources that provide only more or less indirect and fragmentary evidence of vital rates. These materials are, moreover, subject to grievous omissions and misreporting. For comparative analysis, additional problems are introduced by the use of noncomparable definitions and data-collection procedures in the different countries. At the local level, small-scale intensive studies are capable of providing more accurate data on fertility, but they are not free of other weaknesses. Many

[1] United Nations, *Demographic Yearbook*, 1969 (New York, 1970), p. 115.

# CHAPTER TWO

# *Fertility Levels*

## *Patterns and Trends*

HILARY PAGE

of the studies conducted so far have been more of anthropological or medical than of strictly demographic orientation, and the fertility data they include have not always been suitable for demographic analysis. Most small studies have been subject to the same limitations as the large-scale investigations with respect to the limited time period they cover. They are generally subject to even greater restrictions with regard to comparability, because of their use of concepts and procedures specifically tailored to fit a particular culture. Finally it should be noted that extrapolation of their findings to larger populations is often prevented by reason of the purposive selection of a study population and by the rather small size of the sample observed.

None of the available raw materials for a study of fertility levels can be accepted uncritically at face value. However, considerable progress has been made within the last decade or so in the development of comparatively sophisticated methods of analyzing large-scale data from the area; it is largely the results of this work that are brought together in summary form here. We have drawn very heavily on the methods and results of two recent publications, first, *The Demography of Tropical Africa* (1968) prepared at Princeton University, and second, *Afrique Noire, Madagascar, Comores: Démographie Comparée* (1967) compiled by the French *Institut National de la Statistique et des Etudes Economiques* and *Institut National d'Etudes Démographiques*.[2] As far as possible, the results have been updated to include data available as of early 1970.

The very modest scope of this chapter in relation to its subject matter should be stressed at the outset. Our intention is to delineate in general terms the approximate levels of fertility and the patterns and some possible correlates of fertility differentials in the region; it is also to provide a broad frame of reference for statements on fertility levels

that are included in subsequent chapters. The bulk of the sources used consists of large-scale census and sample survey results (which are listed in the appendix to this chapter); critical evaluation of the detailed local sources and of the wealth of anthropological literature available is left to the authors of the area studies, who are more familiar with local conditions and with the peculiarities of the data. Because of the uncertainty attached to both the existing data and estimation procedures, the present chapter includes some discussion of their characteristic defects and limitations. However, since the major emphasis here lies in the actual fertility patterns rather than in methodological issues, consideration of points that are treated quite fully elsewhere is skeletal.

The chapter is divided into four parts according to the following plan. We shall first outline the availability of different forms of fertility data, their potential uses, and their weaknesses. The second section is devoted to the regional pattern of fertility differentials; estimates of birth rates and total fertility rates are presented and their plausibility is discussed. We have not attempted here to examine the pattern of fertility differentials by ethnic unit; the very large number of tribes in West Africa and the uneven quality of the fertility data published by tribe make a thorough comparative analysis beyond the scope of a short summary chapter. Ethnic differentials of particular consequence may be included in the more detailed area chapters. The third section considers nuptiality patterns as a major determinant of fertility levels, and surveys some of the data relating to the impact of different marriage patterns on fertility. The final section turns to the question of fertility trends, concentrating primarily on evidence of current fertility differentials associated with levels of modernization.

## FERTILITY DATA IN WEST AFRICA

VITAL REGISTRATION. Vital registration data in the area are very scanty. Only Zaïre during the 1950s had a system anywhere near

[2] William Brass et al., *The Demography of Tropical Africa*, (Princeton N.J.: Princeton University Press, 1968); INSEE, *Afrique noire, Madagascar, Comores: Démographie comparée* (Paris, 1967).

approaching full, nationwide registration: approximately 83 percent of the births reported in the demographic survey (conducted from 1955–1957) as having occurred in the preceding 12 months had been properly registered.[3] Elsewhere compulsory registration has existed and has been fairly effective within only limited areas, usually urban locations that can scarcely be taken as representative of wider areas. These registration records can be examined for internal consistency to reveal particular shortcomings of the registration system, or for certain characteristics such as seasonality of birth registration;[4] but they have little value in the estimation of fertility levels in the areas they cover since the size of the base population responsible for the vital events they record is rarely known with sufficient accuracy.

RETROSPECTIVE FERTILITY DATA FROM SINGLE-ROUND INQUIRIES. Information about past vital events has been gathered in the French-aided demographic surveys in the region, in Zaïre, and in the sample postenumeration survey of the 1960 Ghana census; limited information was also obtained in Guinea (Bissau) in the 1950 census.[5] Similar information was scheduled for collection in connection with the 1962 census of Nigeria, but with the abandonment of that census on the grounds of gross procedural irregularities leading to major distortions and with the hasty scheduling of a repeat enumeration in 1963, the scheme to collect and publish such detailed information was not realized.

Single-round surveys have been used to elicit information about fertility with reference to two distinct time periods. The first covers the total fertility experience to date of each adult woman, summarized in the total number of children she has ever borne (parity); the second concerns current fertility experience (usually births within the 12 months preceding the survey). Average values for both types of data are tabulated by age of women for all the detailed surveys in the area, except for Guinea (Bissau) for which only the first type are available. In some cases they are also tabulated in more detail giving the parity distributions for each age group of women, or giving parity and/or current fertility data classified by the marital situation or history of the woman or by the sex of the children.

Use of the age-specific parity data is jeopardized by both age misreporting and omissions. The former occurs over the entire age range and bedevils all attempts at demographic analysis, but is likely to be particularly severe around certain critical ages. Systematic distortions are particularly common among women in their teens and early twenties, where an age estimate is often made on the basis of observed marital status and fertility history. The classic official comment on the prevalence of such systematic age misstatement is probably that made in the report on the Central African Republic demographic survey, to the effect that interviewers followed too rigidly ". . . the rule of two years between each birth . . . calculation of the age of a woman with children thus becomes simple arithmetic: $14 + 2 \times$ number of children."[6] Age-specific marital status and fertility data may well represent the interviewer's preconceptions rather than reality under these conditions. The problem of omissions in reporting of total number of children ever born is apparently more serious for the older than for the younger women. Reported parity rarely rises steeply enough beyond the first two or three fertile age groups to be consistent with the contemporary age pattern of fertility

[3] République du Congo, Bureau de la Démographie, *Tableau général de la démographie congolaise: Enquête démographique par sondage, 1955–57: Analyse générale des résultats statistiques* (Léopoldville, 1961), p. 47.

[4] For example, G. M. K. Kpedekpo, *Studies on Vital Registration Data from the Compulsory Registration Areas of Ghana, 1962–67*, University of Ghana, Institute of Statistical, Social and Economic Research, Technical Publications Series (Legon, 1970).

[5] For a more detailed discussion of the data than can be attempted here see Etienne van de Walle, "Characteristics of African Demographic Data," in Brass et al., *Demography of Tropical Africa*.

[6] République Centrafricaine, Mission Socio-économique Centre-Oubangui; France, Secrétariat d'État aux Rélations avec les États de la Communauté, *Enquête démographique Centre-Oubangui, 1959: Méthodologie, résultats provisoires* (Paris, 1969), p. 13.

as reported in current fertility data; sometimes the sequence actually declines from around age 45. An increasing propensity to omit children (especially those who are dead or absent) with advancing age is doubtless largely responsible for this characteristic: In this case, the reported children-ever-born to women just completing their reproductive period cannot be used to approximate the size of completed families as it will be an underestimate. Even comparisons of relative levels reported by these women from different areas or tribes may be misleading, because of the possibility of differential levels of misreporting. In view of these two types of defect and the possibility that survival prospects may vary with parity, the parity data cannot be used without extreme caution.

Limited indications of fertility levels and, more particularly, of trends can be gleaned from scrutiny of the data in a few instances. First, irregularities in the sequence of average parity values by age of the woman may suggest some recent change in fertility levels, unless differential survival of women of different parities or a particularly marked pattern of misreporting has been operating. Thus in some of the apparently low fertility areas of Middle Africa, women recorded in the very oldest age groups report higher

parity than those recorded in age groups that have only recently completed their reproductive span. Examples of these distributions are given in Table 2.1, together with examples of the more usual sequences of constant or declining reported parity for comparison. The anomalous parity sequences reported here for Southeast and North Cameroon and for parts of the Central African Republic may be taken as slight (though far from conclusive) indications that some fertility decline may have occurred over the experience of the cohorts involved. Second, other indications of fertility trends can occasionally be gained through examination of the detailed parity distributions by age, a technique used by Romaniuk with data on childlessness from Zaïre. Table 2.2 reproduces a set of some irregular sequences of proportions childless by age in those districts where childlessness had been high for several decades. For three of the six districts (Equateur, Haut-Uélé, and Maniéma) the sequences are striking in that women in their twenties report a smaller proportion childless than women over thirty, quite a good indication that some reduction in the level of sterility had occurred quite recently in these districts.

The current fertility data are subject not only to similar defects of age misreporting as

TABLE 2.1
Reported parity above age 45 for selected areas

| Area | Age Group | | | | | |
|---|---|---|---|---|---|---|
| | 45–49 | 50–54 | 55–59 | 60–64 | 65–69 | 70+ |
| Central African Republic | 4.1 | 4.1 | 4.3 | 4.3 | 4.4 | 3.7 |
| Center | 3.7 | 3.9 | 4.0 | 4.3 | 4.0 | 3.8 |
| River | 3.4 | 3.4 | 3.8 | 3.6 | 3.4 | 4.1 |
| West | 4.5 | 4.6 | 4.6 | 4.4 | 4.5 | 3.4 |
| North Cameroon | 4.3 | 4.6 | 4.6 | | 4.8 | |
| North Bénoué | 4.6 | 4.9 | 4.9 | | 5.0 | |
| South Bénoué | 3.0 | 3.2 | 3.3 | | 3.8 | |
| Southeast Cameroon | 3.4 | 3.8 | 3.8 | 4.2 | 4.3 | |
| Niger | 5.8 | 5.7 | 5.6 | 5.5 | 5.5 | |
| Upper Volta | 5.3 | 5.4 | 5.4 | 5.3 | 5.4 | |
| Mali (central Niger Delta) | 5.5 | 5.4 | 5.4 | 5.2 | 5.4 | |
| Senegal (middle Senegal Valley) | 5.3 | 5.1 | 5.3 | 5.3 | 5.2 | |

SOURCES: See appendix to this chapter.

TABLE 2.2

Proportion childless among ever-married women, by age: selected low fertility districts of Zaïre (1955–1957 survey)

| District | Age Group | | | | | | |
|---|---|---|---|---|---|---|---|
| | 15–19 | 20–24 | 25–29 | 30–34 | 35–44 | 45–54 | 55+ |
| Equateur | 0.60 | 0.40 | 0.38 | 0.38 | 0.41 | 0.40 | 0.28 |
| Tshuapa | 0.75 | 0.51 | 0.44 | 0.40 | 0.38 | 0.33 | 0.25 |
| Bas-Uélé | 0.60 | 0.47 | 0.50 | 0.49 | 0.45 | 0.37 | 0.26 |
| Haut-Uélé | 0.54 | 0.42 | 0.46 | 0.46 | 0.44 | 0.37 | 0.28 |
| Stanleyville | 0.46 | 0.32 | 0.34 | 0.34 | 0.29 | 0.23 | 0.20 |
| Maniéma | 0.27 | 0.26 | 0.27 | 0.26 | 0.27 | 0.24 | 0.34 |

SOURCE: A. Romaniuk, *La fécondité des populations congolaises* (Paris, 1967), p. 148.

the parity data and to omissions, but also to the possibility of misperception of the reference period. This additional source of possible distortion may or may not be related to the age or other characteristics of the respondent. The use of a short time period raises another problem: further uncertainty in the reported fertility levels is introduced by the sampling variability of the observed number of births. The sampling variability of the number of children ever born is considerably lower than that of current fertility because of the larger number of births involved, and is rarely likely to cause difficulties. Some idea of the size of sample required to obtain a reasonably small sampling variation for fertility estimates based on the number of births occurring in a population over a given time period can be obtained from Table 2.3. Overall birth rates are much less variable than age-specific fertility rates. These figures refer to simple random samples; for cluster sampling, which must almost invariably be adopted in such surveys, observations on intracluster correlations available from a few West African surveys suggest that the sample size should be increased by 50 percent or more to obtain the same confidence limits on the birth rate estimate and by correspondingly greater amounts for age-specific fertility estimates.[7] Clearly a number of the smaller-scale surveys have been of insufficient size for reliable estimation, especially of age-specific fertility rates or subsequently derived indices. For all but the smallest samples, however, it is quite probable that nonsampling errors have exceeded sampling variability.

The procedure developed by Brass to estimate total births by combining the more reliable sections of the age-specific parity and current fertility data is frequently used.[8] Essentially the procedure assumes that the reported age-specific fertility rates are approximately correct in age structure though not necessarily in overall level, and that the average parity reported for younger women is accurate. Any error in the overall level of reported current fertility resulting from common levels of omission or misperception of the reference period is corrected by means of an adjustment factor that is obtained by comparing the average parity reported for younger women with the cumulative-fertility they would have reported, on the average, if they had experienced the reported age-specific fertility rates.

Application of the Brass procedure unfortunately suffers from several drawbacks. Theoretically, there are some grounds for questioning the assumption underlying the derivation of the particular adjustment factors developed by Brass. These factors were derived from a standard age-specific fertility

[7] United Nations Economic Commission for Africa, "Demographic Objectives and Required Sample Size for Vital Rate Surveys" (paper prepared for United Nations *Inter-Regional Workshop on Methodology of Demographic Sample Surveys*, Copenhagen, 1969), p. 13.

[8] The method is described fully in William Brass and Ansley J. Coale, "Methods of Analysis and Estimation," in Brass et al., *Demography of Tropical Africa*.

TABLE 2.3

95 percent confidence limits for selected fertility estimates derived from simple random samples, by size of sample

(a) Crude Birth Rate Estimates (for population crude birth rate of 45 per 1,000)

| Sample Size (person-years) | $2\sigma$ |
|---|---|
| 25,000 | ∓2.6 |
| 50,000 | ∓1.9 |
| 75,000 | ∓1.5 |
| 100,000 | ∓1.3 |

(b) Age-Specific Fertility Rates and Mean Age of Fertility Estimates

| | Age Group | | | | | | | |
|---|---|---|---|---|---|---|---|---|
| | 15–19 | 20–24 | 25–29 | 30–34 | 35–39 | 40–44 | 45–49 | 15–49 |
| Assumed proportion of total population | 0.052 | 0.044 | 0.037 | 0.031 | 0.026 | 0.022 | 0.018 | mean age of fertility |
| Assumed fertility rate (per 1,000) | 110 | 280 | 290 | 240 | 180 | 080 | 020 | $\bar{m} = 29.4$ |

| Sample Size (person-years) | $2\sigma$ | | | | | | | |
|---|---|---|---|---|---|---|---|---|
| 50,000 | ∓12.3 | ∓19.3 | ∓21.1 | ∓21.7 | ∓21.3 | ∓16.4 | ∓9.3 | ∓1.29 |
| 100,000 | ∓8.7 | ∓13.5 | ∓14.8 | ∓15.3 | ∓15.1 | ∓11.6 | ∓6.6 | ∓0.91 |
| 150,000 | ∓7.1 | ∓11.0 | ∓12.2 | ∓12.5 | ∓12.3 | ∓9.4 | ∓5.4 | ∓0.75 |
| 200,000 | ∓6.2 | ∓9.6 | ∓10.5 | ∓10.8 | ∓10.7 | ∓8.2 | ∓4.6 | ∓0.68 |

SOURCE: United Nations, Economic Commission for Africa, "Demographic Objectives and Required Sample Size for Vital Rate Surveys" (Paper prepared for United Nations *Inter-Regional Workshop on Methodology of Demographic Sample Surveys*, Copenhagen, 1969), Tables 1, 4, and 5.

schedule that was allowed to vary only in its starting age and overall scale; but it seems likely that the early portion of the age structure of fertility varies in its form as well as in its starting point and that the simpler approximation may be slightly unrealistic. The rising portion of an age-specific fertility schedule is affected strongly by the age pattern of entry into regular cohabitation. Coale has shown that the age patterns of proportions ever married for a number of diverse societies are well approximated by a standard curve that varies not only in its starting point but also in the steepness with which it rises.[9] This suggests that the latter characteristic would also be needed to

describe the early portion of the age structure of fertility. Any biases introduced by using the simpler approximation are probably quite trivial, however, compared with those arising from the weaknesses of the raw data. The assumption that any error in the reported age-specific fertility rates is uniform throughout the entire fertile age range may be unwarranted, for example. The most serious drawback to the method is its sensitivity to forms of age misreporting that are linked to current fertility or parity status.[10] It is not appropriate in those cases where the age-specific fertility or parity schedules are implausible (for example, the Ghanaian age-specific fertility schedule exhibits implausibly high fertility at older ages relative to that at younger ages

[9] Ansley J. Coale, "Age Patterns of Marriage," *Population Studies*, XXV, 2 (July 1971), pp. 193–214. None of the societies considered by Coale was from Africa, but it seems plausible that somewhat similar patterns would prevail.

[10] Etienne van de Walle, "A Note of the Effect of Age Misreporting."in Brass et al., *Demography of Tropical Africa*.

and hence is not directly amenable to the Brass procedure,[11] or where the sequence of ratios of reported parity to cumulated current fertility is very erratic in the younger ages. In those cases where the reported age structures of current fertility and parity appear plausible and where the parity/cumulative-fertility ratios are consistent, it is reasonable to use the Brass method to adjust the total number of births reported for the preceding year. It does not always follow that total fertility rates can be adjusted in the same way; because of the widespread tendency to inflate the number of women in the childbearing ages through age misstatement, such estimates are likely to be deflated. It should also be noted that the method is not applicable at all in circumstances where fertility has declined, since the theoretical correspondence between age-specific fertility rates and parity levels breaks down under these circumstances.

AGE DISTRIBUTION DATA FROM SINGLE-ROUND INQUIRIES. Since the age distribution of any population closed to migration depends only on its recent history of mortality and fertility, one can infer fertility levels from the population age distribution, given information about mortality conditions. The development of stable population theory and the tabulation of stable age distributions and associated population parameters for a range of fertility and mortality conditions permit the rapid estimation of fertility levels wherever the assumption of constant fertility and mortality levels is tenable.[12] For quasi-stable situations, in which mortality has recently declined, methods of adjusting the stable population estimates have been detailed and the necessary adjustment factors tabulated.[13] Reported age distributions are available for almost all of West Africa, and an index of recent mortality

levels can be obtained for the countries of French expression, Zaïre, Ghana, and Guinea (Bissau). Since birth rate estimates derived from model stable populations are comparatively insensitive to fairly small differences in mortality levels, it is sometimes possible to use a rough guess as to the level of mortality where data on this are lacking. It is rarely possible to make adjustments for quasi-stability, because of the lack of data on the duration and intensity of mortality declines. It is necessary, therefore, to use an index of the age composition that is not very sensitive to the effects of declining mortality.

Birth rate estimates derived from stable population models can vary greatly. The assumption of stability (or a conjecture regarding the extent of any departure from stability) introduces the first uncertainty. Choice of an appropriate model life table on the basis of fragmentary and defective mortality data introduces the second; slight variations in birth rate estimates result from different choices. Wide variations can occur depending on which of the several possible indices of the age distribution is chosen as being the least distorted by misreporting (and instability). A distorted age composition yields many conflicting estimates of the birth rate, some of which may be grossly at variance with each other; selection of the "best" can be an uncertain affair. Yet more possibilities for error exist in the estimation of total fertility than in estimation of the birth rate, since this requires an additional data input in the form of an estimate or conjecture of the mean age of fertility. We have already seen that the sampling variability of this index is quite high (Table 2.3); the effects of fertility-related age misstatement on it may well be even greater.

For many areas, the reported age distribution is the sole indication of fertility levels available; stable population estimates are then Hobson's choice. Where retrospective fertility data exist, the stable population methods provide alternative, and in some cases less dubious, estimates compared with the Brass method. The stable population procedures have definite advantages in those

[11] S. K. Gaisie, *Dynamics of Population Growth in Ghana*, (Accra-Tema: Ghana Publishing Corporation, 1969). Gaisie attempts an adjustment of the reported data.

[12] Ansley J. Coale and Paul Demeny, *Regional Model Life Tables and Stable Populations* (Princeton, N.J.: Princeton University Press, 1966).

[13] United Nations, *Manual IV, Methods of Estimating Basic Demographic Measures from Incomplete Data* (New York, 1967).

instances where reported age-specific fertility data are especially suspect, either because of age misreporting or because of the small size of the sample (for example, in detailed breakdowns by local area or ethnic units).

MULTIROUND SURVEYS. The difficulties inherent in the analysis of retrospective fertility reports and in attempts to assign model stable, or quasi-stable, population parameters to a population on the basis of a reported age distribution that is known to be defective have led some demographers to despair of achieving meaningful results through these operations and to focus their attention on alternative strategies of data collection. Specifically, there is a trend toward advocacy of the use of multiround surveys in which the same population is surveyed at regular intervals. The main objective is to improve upon the single-round survey's catch of the vital events that have occurred, partly through a reduction in the reference period and partly through the technique of identifying new elements in the population (births and immigrants) and departures from it (deaths and emigrants) by comparing the population records of earlier with those of later visits. Such surveys could open up the possibility of providing additional detailed forms of information not easily obtained from conventional vital registration or single-round surveys. Unfortunately, just as the potential of multiround surveys is large, so too are the practical problems of realizing this potential; these greatly exceed the problems associated with single-round surveys. The core difficulties include those of nominal reidentification of the population at each round, of continuing effectiveness, and of reconciliation of the need for data quality (which requires intensive procedures using well-trained field workers who conduct frequent visits) with the requirements of a sufficiently large sample. The results of multiround surveys to date have been somewhat disappointing. The 1962 Gabon survey results were never published; the Nigerian rural survey of 1965–1966 produced data so patently deficient that almost one-third of the sampling units were

rejected for fertility estimation.[14] Results of the Senegal survey in the Sine-Saloum area have been published and appear more plausible.[15] The national sample project begun in 1969 in Liberia combines semi-annual rounds with independent information obtained from monthly visits by separate teams, a procedure which should permit cross-evaluation of the two sets of data;[16] no results of this survey are available at the time of writing. The Liberia project appears to be the most intensive of its kind yet started on a national scale in West Africa, similar in design to population growth estimate projects carried out elsewhere in the world. However, experience has shown that even such intensive projects yield results that are far from perfect in terms of completeness.[17] Moreover, while intensive procedures may reduce omissions and the degree of age misreporting, they cannot eliminate the latter entirely; it remains an intractable impediment to the generation of any fertility estimates more detailed than the overall birth rate.

SPECIALIZED LOCAL SURVEYS. In addition to a number of general demographic surveys of local areas, there have also been several investigations designed to examine particular fertility differentials or processes. Notable among these have been the series of pioneering studies in Ghana, mostly by Caldwell, and some surveys in Nigeria. The topics investigated have included socioeconomic fertility differentials; knowledge, attitudes, and practice with respect to contraception; perception of family obligations and its effects on fertility; the relationship between marital and fertility histories.

[14] Federal Office of Statistics, Nigeria, *Rural Demographic Sample Survey*, 1965–66, (Lagos, October 1968), p. 15.
[15] Pierre Cantrelle, *Etude démographique dans la région du Sine-Saloum (Sénégal): 1963–65*, Office de la Recherche Scientifique et Technique d'Outre-Mer (Paris, 1969).
[16] Department of Planning and Economic Affairs, *Liberian Population Growth Survey: Handbook, 1969* (Monrovia, 1970).
[17] A recent summary of results from some of these projects is given in W. Seltzer, "Some Results from Asian Population Growth Studies," *Population Studies*, XXIII, 17 (November 1969), 395–406.

AVAILABILITY OF FERTILITY DATA. The available large-scale information on fertility is very uneven in its coverage. Certain areas and population groups, notably nomadic peoples, are excluded altogether from several national demographic data series, because of the especially severe problems of sample design and the practical difficulties of surveying. Only Mauritania includes information on a sizable nomadic population in its national survey data, while elsewhere Niger is the only country to have published the results of an inquiry designed specifically for its nomadic population element.[18] Differences between countries also occur in the definition of the population to which the collected data refer: for francophone areas this is generally the *de jure* population, while for other areas it is often the *de facto* population.

Comparability of data is limited by the staggered timing of data-collection programs. For most areas, published national data are available for only one survey, with dates ranging from 1950, Guinea (Bissau); to 1964–1965, Mauritania. Even within a single country, the information has sometimes been gathered and published on a piecemeal basis. The component regions of Cameroon were surveyed separately, with data collection starting in 1960–1961 (North Cameroon) and continuing to 1965–1966 (the Bamiléké area); similarly, detailed data for Ivory Coast come from several regional surveys rather than a single uniform national inquiry. It is common for data collection in urban and rural areas to be carried out separately; data for major towns in Cameroon, the Central African Republic, the People's Republic of the Congo, Mauritania, Niger, and Upper Volta were collected separately from data for their respective rural areas.

Comparability is reduced further by differences in the type of information collected, and in the detail of the published tabulations. Only minimal information on age and sex distribution is available for Gambia, Liberia, and Nigeria on a national

basis; elsewhere, retrospective fertility data are also available, but the extent of detailed cross-tabulation varies considerably, in particular, breakdowns by region, rural-urban location, and ethnic group are not always published as fully as one might like.

Finally we should note that even the limited published data are extremely uneven in quality. Official reports not uncommonly include references to failure to effect the sample design fully or to gain full cooperation in all sampled areas.[19] Even where the desired data have been obtained, they suffer more or less seriously from misreporting.

The weakest sections of the data series are those regions for which there are no recent data and those for which there is no possibility of comparing two or more independent types of data, such as the evidence of age distributions compared with that of retrospective fertility reports. In this respect Nigeria is conspicuous in having only dated and extremely limited information. Unfortunately, the 1963 census yielded no direct information on retrospective fertility reports, and examination of the recorded age distributions[20] indicated that age misreporting (probably combined with age-selective inflation of the population) is so extreme as to render the data quite unusable for fertility estimation. It is regrettable that the largest country in the region, containing roughly 40 percent of the total population, should have no sound information about its fertility

---

[18] Niger; France, Ministère de la Coopération, INSEE, *Enquête démographique et economique en milieu nomade* (Paris, 1966).

[19] For example: "Very often in the North, 80 percent of the population of the village was dispersed in about ten little farming-hamlets (*Dankouch*), occasionally a long way apart from each other, and it was very difficult sometimes to persuade the village-chief to guide us towards these *Dankouch*. It is for the latter reason, moreover, that a census could not be taken in the subprefecture of Iriba." Chad Service de Statistique: France, Secrétariat d'Etat aux Affaires Etrangères, INSEE, *Enquête démographique au Tchad, 1964: Résultats définitifs*, 1 (Paris, 1966), 3. "Material difficulties caused the omission of the Abomey-Bohicon urban complex, and the canton of Tchi in the Sud-Ouest department." Dahomey; France, Ministère de la Coopération, INSEE, *Enquête démographique au Dahomey, 1961: Résultats définitifs* (Paris, 1964), p. 3.
[20] Federal Office of Statistics, *Population Census of Nigeria, 1963*, Vol. II (for each region) and Vol. III "Combined National Figures" (Lagos, 1968).

levels. A consideration of fertility levels in West Africa without up-to-date information on Nigeria remains incomplete.

In summary, the situation with regard to fertility data in West Africa presently is not very satisfactory, and prospects for more complete and accurate data for large areas in the near future are limited. Given the incomplete and defective nature of the information available, especially with regard to age misstatement, its interpretation must remain somewhat tentative, and uncritical acceptance of a single set of data may be very misleading.

## REGIONAL DIFFERENTIALS IN ESTIMATED FERTILITY LEVELS

Given the extreme forms of age misstatement common to the data, it is too much to hope that they can be used to estimate such fertility characteristics as age-specific fertility rates with any confidence. We have focused here on less ambitious measures of fertility, principally the birth rate, but also the total fertility rate.

The methods and regional estimates reproduced here are essentially the same as those prepared at Princeton in a previous series.[21] Inherent in the preparation and presentation of an extensive series of estimates is the danger of generating an unwarranted appearance of certainty in the figures; no matter how numerous and stringent the caveats inserted in a text, they are rarely entirely successful in preventing a series of estimates, once tabulated, from acquiring the aura of established facts. Wherever possible, we have included estimates derived from alternative data or from complementary estimation procedures. The reader interested in a particular area will find additional, and sometimes conflicting, estimates in the subsequent area studies.

METHODS OF ESTIMATION. Stable population estimates have been derived from the Coale-Demeny "West" model stable populations, selected as matching the reported populations in terms of an index of mortality (in most cases based on the proportion dead among children ever born reported for women age 20–24 years, but where such data are not available on a guess as to the general level of mortality) and the proportion under 15 years. Total fertility estimates were obtained from the same models, using the mean age of the reported current fertility schedule where this was available, or some alternative indirect estimate or a guess of the mean age in other cases.[22]

The use of the selected index of child mortality is based on the following considerations. Single-round surveys tend to produce reported current mortality data (deaths during the preceding 12 months) of notoriously poor quality; omissions and age errors seem to be rife. Early childhood mortality levels, by contrast, can be estimated with somewhat greater confidence from the proportion dead of children ever borne (tabulated by age of mother), provided one has some indication of the time distribution of the births involved and also of the age structure of early mortality. The essential idea is that the proportion dead at any point of time among children born to a group of women can be viewed as a function of the life table to which the children have been subject.

The estimation procedure developed by Brass permits derivation of adjustment factors to convert the reported proportion dead into the proportion dying before a specified age in that life table.[23] The adjustment factor is different for each group of women because of the different time distribution of births each group has experienced. For women in a particular age group, this time distribution is given simply by the age-specific fertility schedule that they have experienced. For given mortality conditions, women experiencing earlier fertility will have borne their

[21] Hilary J. Page and Ansley J. Coale, "Estimates of Fertility and Child Mortality in Africa South of the Sahara" (Paper prepared for Seminar on Population Growth and Economic Development, (Nairobi, December 1969).

[22] For example, estimates based on reported parity for women aged 20–24 and 25–29, as suggested in United Nations, *Manual IV*, p. 25.
[23] The method is described fully in Brass and Coale, "Methods of Analysis and Estimation."

children longer before the survey, on average, and consequently these children will have been exposed to mortality risks over a longer time period and a larger proportion of them will have died than would be the case for children of women with a later age pattern of fertility. The Brass procedure provides conversion factors by which the proportion dead reported for women aged 15–19, 20–24, 25–29, 30–34, etc., can be converted into the probability of a child having died before age 1, 2, 3, 5, etc. Determination of the time distribution of births is required to select an appropriate conversion factor; this can be approached via the same "standard" age structure of fertility that varies only in its starting point as is used in the Brass fertility procedures, with an index such as $P_1/P_2$ (ratio of the average parity reported for women age 15–19 to that for women age 20–24) being used to identify the starting point. We have already pointed out that this standard schedule may be a slight over simplification; it should also be noted that the ratio $P_1/P_2$ may be rather sensitive to misreporting.

Our estimates here are derived from a slight modification of the basic procedures for estimating the time distribution of births. The modification, which was developed by Sullivan,[24] is based on a regression analysis of the relationship between the required conversion factors and an index of the age structure of fertility (in this case the ratio of $P_2$ to $P_3$) for a number of empirical fertility schedules available by single years of age, over various levels and age patterns of early mortality. Specifically, the proportion surviving to age $x({}_x q_0)$ for West model life tables is estimated for various fertility schedules from

$$ {}_2q_0/D_2 = 1.30 - 0.54(P_2/P_3) $$

$$ {}_3q_0/D_3 = 1.17 - 0.40(P_2/P_3) $$

$$ {}_5q_0/D_4 = 1.13 - 0.33(P_2/P_3) $$

where $D_2$ is the proportion dead of children ever born reported for women age 20–24,

$D_3$ that for women 25–29, and so on. Of these three possible indices of early mortality, we have chosen to use the first (the proportion dying before age 2) on two grounds. First, because it is derived from reports by young women and so is probably less affected by possible differential omission of dead children (age group 15–19 might be preferable on this count, but is ruled out because it is too sensitive to age misreporting). Second, because responses by younger women reflect more recent mortality conditions than do those of older women: for ${}_2q_0$ they reflect the average conditions during roughly the four or five years preceding the survey.

Where there are no strong violations of the assumptions underlying the procedures (which could arise from mortality-related omission of children, correlation between child's and mother's survival, age misreporting, mortality change, or the use of an inappropriate model age structure of mortality), the basic procedure has been shown to yield excellent results.[25] With the defective data available to us, estimation is much more uncertain. A particular problem arises over the choice of an appropriate model life table; indeed, it is a moot point whether any of the available models are appropriate for tropical Africa in general. Some similarity of the age structure of early mortality to that incorporated in the Coale-Demeny "North" models has been suggested:[26] There are some indications that mortality between ages one and five is quite high relative to infant mortality. Multiround surveys conducted in Senegal suggest that the age pattern may be even more extreme than any of the Coale-Demeny models.[27] We have chosen to use the "West" family of the Coale-Demeny series here, although these do not incorporate a feature of particularly high child mortality

[24] J. M. Sullivan, "Estimates of Childhood Mortality Conditions from Childhood Survival Statistics" (Ph.D. dissertation, Princeton University, 1970).

[25] United Nations, *Manual IV*, p. 36.

[26] Frank Lorimer, William Brass, and Etienne van de Walle, "Demography," in R. A. Lystad, ed., *The African World: A Survey of Social Research* (New York: Praeger, 1965), p. 291.

[27] Cantrelle, *Etude démographique*; Pierre Cantrelle *et al.*, *Mortalité de l'enfant dans la région de Khombol Thiénaba (Sénégal) 1964–1968*, Cahiers de l'ORSTOM., Série Sciences Humaines, VI, 4 (Paris, 1969), 43–72.

relative to infant mortality, on the grounds that these are the most general models of the set (they relate to the experience of a number of populations including some non-European ones, whereas the other families are based on the experience of a few countries in particular parts of Europe which exhibit characteristics deviating from the "West" model). When it comes to using the age distribution to estimate the birth rate from model stable age structures, it can be argued that the more general "West" models might be preferred, since there is little by way of evidence on the age structure of mortality at older ages to suggest the use of one of the more particularized models. The point is admittedly debatable. Fortunately, the choice of an inappropriate model in estimating the birth rate from the reported age structure and an index of child survival has only a minor effect on the estimate, compared with other possible sources of error, at least within the range of the four Coale-Demeny families of life tables. The differences in the birth rate between these four families is only of the order of 2–3 per thousand population when a stable population is selected on the basis of the proportion under 15 years and an index of child mortality, for values of these indices similar to those found in West Africa.[28] An error in the level of mortality estimated has a slightly larger but still not very great influence.

The use of the overall proportion under 15 as the index of the age distribution is based on two considerations. First, where mortality has been declining, estimates of the birth rate will be increasingly biased as larger portions of the cumulated age-distribution are included in the index: the lower the upper age limit considered, the less the error. Second, there is the practical consideration of choosing an age group that is accurately reported. The youngest age groups (under five and under ten) can rarely be used because of the marked effect of age misstatement around these areas. We have used the proportion under five only in the case of Zaïre where it has been suggested that the circum-

stances surrounding the survey, especially the existence of a nearly universal registration system and of identity booklets, imply that age reporting of young children was comparatively reliable and the overall count of these children fairly complete.[29] Elsewhere the age group under 15 has been used, since this may be quite well reported when both sexes are combined. Reported age-sex distributions from tropical Africa exhibit a tendency for the ages of teenage boys to be understated, leading to inflation of the proportion under 15 for males, and for the age of teenage girls to be overstated, leading to deflation of this proportion for females. To some extent these tendencies cancel out.[30] The overall proportion under 15 years is used here then on the grounds that, in general, it is likely to be the youngest age group that is fairly reliably reported; the effect of declining mortality on the birth rate estimate derived from this rather than the very youngest age group is only of the order of a 2–3 percent underestimate if expectation of life at birth has risen as much as from 35 to 45 years in little more than a decade.[31] The index selected can be justified in these general terms, but closer examination of the age-sex compositions and firsthand knowledge of particular populations and data series might well suggest that his index does not yield the "best" estimate in every case. The only departure from this index attempted here (other than the use of the proportion under five years for Zaïre) occurs for those area subdivisions in which the age-sex distribution is patently distorted, for instance by selective migration. In these cases, a slight variation was made by considering the proportion under 15 in the female population only and adjusting this by applying as a multiplier the ratio of the proportion under 15 in the overall population to that proportion in the female population only, as reported for the whole

[28] United Nations, *Manual IV*, p. 45.

[29] Brass and Coale, "Methods of Analysis and Estimation," p. 126.

[30] Ansley J. Coale and Etienne van de Walle, "Notes on Areas for which Estimates Were Made, but Not Subject to Detailed Study," in Brass et al., *Demography of Tropical Africa*, p. 171.

[31] United Nations, *Manual IV*, Appendix III.

national population of the subdivision considered or for some neighboring population that was not markedly affected by such distortion.

For comparison, Brass method estimates of the birth rate obtained from retrospective fertility reports also are given. The adjustment factor used here is based on the mean of the $P_2/F_2$ and $P_3/F_3$ values, that is, the ratios of reported parity to cumulated current fertility for the age groups 20–24 and 25–29. The Brass methods have not been used to estimate total fertility, because of the tendency in many cases to artificially concentrate women into the reproductive ages through age misstatement.

REGIONAL DIFFERENTIALS IN FERTILITY ESTIMATES. The estimates are reproduced in Table 2.4.[32] Total fertility estimates based on model stable populations are mapped in Figure 2.1.

The general pattern is one of high to very high fertility throughout most of the western half of the region. The highest estimates are concentrated in the Ashanti and Brong-Ahafo regions of Ghana (Ashanti culture is traditionally held in Ghana to epitomize the ideals of high fertility), in Togo and Dahomey, in the western and southern segments of Nigeria, and in parts of Niger. The belt of high fertility estimates extends across to the Atlantic, including Upper Volta, Mali, parts of Guinea, Senegal, and Mauritania, but there is a suggestion that fertility levels along the western portion of the coast, from Liberia westward, may be more moderate. Moderate levels also are estimated for northern Ghana, and in parts of Niger and northern Nigeria. Middle Africa, by contrast, is marked in general by the presence of low to moderate fertility estimates, with a narrow band of very high fertility along the eastern border of Zaïre and with high or very high estimates found also in the southern portion of Zaïre to the south and in Chad to the north. In the

central area of lower fertility the lowest estimates are found in two arcs: One stretches from North Cameroon southward to Gabon, and the other covers some of the central Congo basin, the northeast part of Zaïre and parts of the Central African Republic. Zaïre and the Central African Republic are two areas for which low fertility has been attested by medical studies over several decades and have been a subject of some administrative concern.

The general impression conveyed by Figure 2.1 is bound to be misleading in some respects, because of the great variations in size and in homogeneity of population between the regions for which estimates can be prepared. Each estimate is merely an average for that area. Extremely high or low values can emerge only when the regional boundaries coincide with the limits of populations showing particularly high or low fertility. More moderate estimates may represent either a relatively homogeneous population with moderate fertility, or a heterogeneous population containing both high and low fertility elements. A more detailed breakdown into smaller areas would no doubt produce a more variegated pattern in many parts of the map. For example, in the North Bénoué section of North Cameroon, which has a total fertility estimate of 5.1, a breakdown of the data into two further categories yields much more extreme estimates: 6.2 for predominantly pagan areas and 3.5 for predominantly Moslem areas.

Plausibility of the broad pattern of relatively high or low fertility levels rests on three grounds. First, those areas for which the medical or anthropological literature is full of r ferences and indications of particularly high or low fertility are included among the regions with the most extreme estimates. Second, there is some consistency between neighboring countries in that somewhat similar levels are often estimated for the two sides of an international boundary where one might expect fertility levels to be similar because of roughly comparable physical and cultural conditions, despite the fact that the data-collection systems were independent

---

[32] Brief notes outlining which areas, if any, were excluded from the surveys on which the estimates are based are included in the appendix.

TABLE 2.4

Birth rate and total fertility rate estimates for major regions in West Africa

| Area | Date of Survey | Survey Population ('000s) | Sample Size ('000s) | Birth Rate (stable) | (Brass) | Total Fertility (stable) | ($\overline{m}$) |
|---|---|---|---|---|---|---|---|
| Cameroon | — | — | — | — | — | — | — |
| North | 1960–61 | 1,393 | 68 | 39 | 37 | 4.8 | 26.4 |
| Nord Bénoué | | 1,150 | 53 | 41 | 38 | 5.1 | 26.7 |
| Sud Bénoué | | 243 | 15 | 31 | 29 | 3.9 | 24.8 |
| Southeast | 1962–64 | 1,186 | 39 | 33 | 32 | 4.3 | 26.9 |
| Northwest rural[a,b] | | 564 | 18 | 37 | — | 4.8 | 26.9 |
| Southeast rural[a,b] | | 514 | 17 | 28 | — | 3.6 | 26.9 |
| West[c] | 1964–65 | 1,031 | 113 | 50 | 53 | 6.5 | 26.5 |
| Northern[a,c] | | 574 | 38 | 54 | 53 | 7.2 | 26.7 |
| Southern[a,c,d] | | 457 | 74 | 47 | 53 | 6.0 | 26.3 |
| Central African Republic | 1959–60 | 1,017 | 102 | 44 | 41 | 5.5 | 26.7 |
| Central | | 240 | 24 | 37 | 33 | 4.6 | 27.0 |
| River | | 134 | 13 | 30 | 33 | 3.8 | 26.2 |
| West | | 643 | 65 | 50 | 46 | 6.4 | 26.6 |
| Chad | 1964 | 2,524 | 133 | 52 | 44 | 6.9 | 27.7 |
| North | | 1,010 | 53 | 46 | 40 | 6.0 | 27.0 |
| South | | 1,514 | 80 | 56 | 48 | 7.7 | 28.0 |
| Peoples Republic of the Congo | 1960–61 | 582 | 110 | 44 | 42 | 5.9 | 28.3 |
| Zaire[e] | 1955–57 | 12,777 | 1,360 | 44 | 40 | 5.8 | 27.0 |
| Equateur Province[e] | | 1,756 | 195 | 38 | 33 | 4.9 | 27.3 |
| Equateur[e] | | 302 | 33 | 31 | 23 | 4.0 | 26.5 |
| Mongala[e] | | 519 | 63 | 42 | 41 | 5.6 | 27.8 |
| Tshuapa[e] | | 395 | 40 | 27 | 23 | 3.5 | 26.9 |
| Ubangi[e] | | 539 | 59 | 47 | 39 | 6.2 | 27.4 |
| Kasai Province[e] | | 2,121 | 252 | 46 | 40 | 5.9 | 26.9 |
| Kabinda[e] | | 480 | 60 | 47 | 38 | 6.2 | 26.6 |
| Kasai[e] | | 493 | 56 | 49 | 42 | 6.3 | 27.2 |
| Lulua[e] | | 654 | 77 | 48 | 44 | 6.1 | 26.9 |
| Sankuru[e] | | 494 | 59 | 41 | 35 | 5.3 | 26.8 |
| Katanga[e] | | 1,501 | 147 | 50 | 40 | 6.7 | 26.7 |
| Elisabethville[d,e] | | 140 | 20 | 63 | 52 | 9.2 | 26.8 |
| Haut-Lomami[e] | | 454 | 45 | 46 | 35 | 6.0 | 26.6 |
| Lualaba[e] | | 320 | 27 | 47 | 36 | 6.0 | 25.8 |
| Luapula-Moero[e] | | 192 | 19 | 58 | 50 | 8.3 | 27.6 |
| Tanganika[e] | | 397 | 37 | 49 | 41 | 6.6 | 26.9 |
| Kivu Province[e] | | 2,013 | 201 | 52 | 52 | 6.8 | 26.6 |
| Maniéma[e] | | 447 | 43 | 37 | 34 | 4.5 | 24.8 |
| Nord-Kivu[e] | | 735 | 71 | 55 | 55 | 7.5 | 27.0 |
| Sud-Kivu | | 831 | 87 | 60 | 59 | 8.1 | 27.1 |
| Léopoldville[e] | | 3,050 | 343 | 48 | 48 | 6.6 | 28.0 |
| Bas-Congo[e] | | 412 | 51 | 51 | 49 | 6.8 | 27.5 |
| Cataractes[e] | | 439 | 41 | 50 | 57 | 7.2 | 29.4 |
| Kwango[e] | | 466 | 53 | 53 | 54 | 7.5 | 29.0 |
| Kwilu[e] | | 1,143 | 116 | 46 | 46 | 5.3 | 27.8 |
| Lac Léopold II[e] | | 271 | 38 | 46 | 38 | 4.7 | 27.5 |
| Léopoldville[d,e] | | 318 | 44 | 47 | 48 | 6.3 | 26.8 |
| Orientale[e] | | 2,336 | 223 | 31 | 27 | 3.9 | 26.0 |
| Bas-Uélé[e] | | 468 | 46 | 21 | 20 | 2.8 | 25.1 |
| Haut-Uélé[e] | | 582 | 60 | 24 | 21 | 3.1 | 24.9 |
| Ituri[e] | | 651 | 53 | 41 | 33 | 5.7 | 29.2 |
| Stanleyville[e] | | 635 | 64 | 35 | 30 | 3.1 | 24.8 |
| Dahomey | 1961 | 2,080 | 122 | 54 | 50 | 7.2 | 27.8 |
| North rural[d] | | 595 | 25 | 53 | 49 | 7.3 | 28.1 |
| South rural | | 1,302 | 79 | 54 | 50 | 7.2 | 27.6 |
| Gabon | 1960–61 | 448 | 45 | 27 | 28 | 3.5 | 27.0 |
| Gambia[a,f] | 1963 | 315 | 315 | 40 | — | 5.3 | 28.0 |

TABLE 2.4 (*contd.*)

| Area | Date of Survey | Survey Population Size ('000s) | Sample Size ('000s) | Birth Rate (stable) | (Brass) | Total Fertility (stable) | ($\overline{m}$) |
|---|---|---|---|---|---|---|---|
| Ghana | 1960 | 6,727 | 336 | 47 | 54 | 6.6 | 29.4 |
| Accra Capital District[a,d] | | 492 | — | 45 | 52 | 6.6 | 30.6 |
| Ashanti[a] | | 1,109 | — | 51 | 55 | 7.3 | 28.7 |
| Brong-Ahafo[a,d] | | 588 | — | 53 | 53 | 7.5 | 28.5 |
| Eastern[a] | | 1,094 | — | 49 | 57 | 7.5 | 30.6 |
| Northern and Upper | | 1,289 | — | 40 | 57 | 5.5 | 29.0 |
| Volta[a] | | 777 | — | 46 | 49 | 6.1 | 29.6 |
| Western and Central[a] | | 1,378 | — | 47 | 57 | 6.6 | 29.3 |
| Guinea (Bissau)[g] | 1950 | 544 | 544 | 39 | — | 5.1 | 28.0 |
| Guinea | 1954–55 | 2,570 | 300 | 50 | 48 | 6.4 | 27.3 |
| Forest | | 760 | — | 46 | 45 | 5.9 | 27.8 |
| Fouta Djallon | | 970 | — | 53 | 50 | 6.8 | 27.0 |
| Maritime | | 500 | — | 48 | 44 | 6.2 | 26.9 |
| Upper | | 340 | — | 52 | 51 | 7.0 | 27.6 |
| Ivory Coast | | — | — | — | — | — | — |
| First agricultural sector[d] | 1957–58 | 325 | 26 | 50 | 52 | 6.8 | 27.8 |
| Liberia[a,f] | 1962 | 1,016 | 1,016 | 40 | — | 5.2 | 28.0 |
| Mali | 1960–61 | 3,485 | 104 | 51 | 50 | 6.7 | 27.8 |
| Mauritania | 1964–65 | 963 | 143 | 46 | 40 | 6.5 | 29.6 |
| Niger | 1960 | 2,611 | 71 | 50 | 51 | 6.7 | 28.3 |
| Stratum 1 | | 150 | 5 | 28 | 32 | 3.7 | 28.4 |
| Stratum 2 | | 529 | 14 | 48 | 52 | 6.1 | 27.1 |
| Stratum 3 | | 389 | 11 | 54 | 56 | 7.3 | 27.6 |
| Stratum 4 | | 408 | 11 | 49 | 49 | 7.0 | 29.1 |
| Stratum 5 | | 351 | 10 | 52 | 51 | 7.6 | 29.3 |
| Stratum 6 | | 785 | 21 | 51 | 52 | 7.0 | 28.5 |
| Nigeria[a,f] | 1952–53 | 31,156 | 31,156 | 54 | — | 7.0 | 27.0 |
| Eastern[a,f] | 1953 | 7,968 | 7,968 | 57 | — | 7.4 | 27.0 |
| Bamenda[a,f,c] | | 429 | 429 | 55 | — | 7.1 | 27.0 |
| Cameroons[a,d,f,c] | | 324 | 324 | 45 | — | 5.7 | 27.0 |
| Calabar[a,f] | | 1,540 | 1,540 | 61 | — | 8.1 | 27.0 |
| Ogoja[a,f] | | 1,082 | 1,082 | 54 | — | 7.0 | 27.0 |
| Onitsha[a,f] | | 1,768 | 1,768 | 55 | — | 7.1 | 27.0 |
| Owerri[a,f] | | 2,078 | 2,078 | 61 | — | 8.1 | 27.0 |
| Rivers[a,f] | | 747 | 747 | 56 | — | 7.2 | 27.0 |
| Northern[a,f] | 1952 | 16,836 | 16,836 | 51 | — | 6.5 | 27.0 |
| Adamawa[a,f] | | 1,181 | 1,181 | 55 | — | 7.1 | 27.0 |
| Bauchi[a,f] | | 1,424 | 1,424 | 50 | — | 6.4 | 27.0 |
| Benue[a,f] | | 1,468 | 1,468 | 49 | — | 6.2 | 27.0 |
| Bornu[a,f] | | 1,596 | 1,596 | 46 | — | 5.8 | 27.0 |
| Ilorin[a,f] | | 531 | 531 | 54 | — | 6.9 | 27.0 |
| Kabba[a,f] | | 664 | 664 | 51 | — | 6.5 | 27.0 |
| Kano[a,f] | | 3,396 | 3,396 | 50 | — | 6.4 | 27.0 |
| Katsina[a,f] | | 1,483 | 1,483 | 52 | — | 6.6 | 27.0 |
| Niger[a,f] | | 716 | 716 | 47 | — | 5.9 | 27.0 |
| Plateau[a,f] | | 891 | 891 | 50 | — | 6.3 | 27.0 |
| Sokoto[a,f] | | 2,680 | 2,680 | 55 | — | 7.1 | 27.0 |
| Zaria[a,f] | | 805 | 805 | 55 | — | 7.1 | 27.0 |
| Western[a,f] | 1952 | 6,352 | 6,352 | 60 | — | 7.9 | 27.0 |
| Abeokuta[a,f] | | 630 | 630 | 54 | — | 7.0 | 27.0 |
| Benin[a,f] | | 901 | 901 | 61 | — | 8.0 | 27.0 |
| Colony[a,d,f] | | 505 | 505 | 47 | — | 6.0 | 27.0 |
| Delta[a,f] | | 591 | 591 | 54 | — | 7.0 | 27.0 |
| Ibadan[a,f] | | 1,650 | 1,650 | 71 | — | 9.7 | 27.0 |
| Ijebu[a,f] | | 348 | 348 | 51 | — | 6.5 | 27.0 |
| Ondo[a,f] | | 945 | 945 | 60 | — | 7.9 | 27.0 |
| Oyo[a,f] | | 783 | 783 | 62 | — | 8.1 | 27.0 |

TABLE 2.4 *(contd.)*

| Area | Date of Survey | Survey Population ('000) | Sample Size ('000) | Birth Rate (stable) | (Brass) | Total Fertility (stable) | $(\bar{m})$ |
|------|------|------|------|------|------|------|------|
| Senegal | 1960–61 | 3,028 | 62 | 47 | — | 6.3 | 28.3 |
| Sierra Leone[a,f] | 1963 | 2,180 | 2,180 | 42 | — | 5.4 | 28.0 |
|   Eastern[a,d,f] | | 546 | 546 | 38 | — | 4.9 | 28.0 |
|   Northern[a,f] | | 898 | 898 | 51 | — | 6.7 | 28.0 |
|   Southern[a,f] | | 542 | 542 | 35 | — | 4.6 | 28.0 |
|   Western[a,d,f] | | 195 | 195 | 47 | — | 6.1 | 28.0 |
| Togo | 1961 | 1,544 | 120 | 57 | 54 | 8.0 | 28.7 |
|   Centre rural | | 329 | — | 54 | 52 | 7.5 | 28.0 |
|   Maritime rural | | 381 | — | 54 | 50 | 7.7 | 28.7 |
|   Plateau rural | | 390 | — | 55 | 54 | 7.8 | 28.6 |
|   Savane rural | | 217 | — | 65 | 68 | 9.4 | 29.2 |
| Upper Volta | 1960–61 | 4,293 | 90 | 50 | 48 | 6.5 | 27.9 |

SOURCES: See appendix to this chapter.

[a] The following mortality indices were adopted for stable population estimation where $_2q_0$ could not be estimated directly from child survivorship data.

| Area | Index | Value | Basis |
|------|------|------|------|
| Cameroon | | | |
|   subdivisions of Southeast | $_2q_0$ | 134 | Estimate for whole region |
|   subdivisions of West | $_2q_0$ | 184 | Estimate for whole region |
| Gambia | $e_0^\circ$ | 35.0 | Guess |
| Ghana regions | $_2q_0$ | 194 | Estimate for whole country |
| Liberia | $e_0^\circ$ | 35.0 | Guess |
| Nigeria | $e_0^\circ$ | 30.0 | Guess |
| Sierra Leone | $e_0^\circ$ | 30.0 | Guess |

[b] No data available on age-specific fertility: mean age of fertility, $\bar{m}$, estimated as that for whole of Southeast Cameroon.

[c] The provinces of Bamenda and Cameroons, formerly administered as part of the Nigerian Federation, became West Cameroon in the Federal Republic of Cameroon in 1961. Estimates derived for these two provinces from the 1952–1953 Nigerian census refer to the same areas as the estimates for the north and south portions of West Cameroon based on the sample survey of 1964–1965.

[d] Stable population estimates based on proportion under 15 years in female rather than in total population, since latter proportion appears particularly distorted (usually as a result of migration). Regional values of the proportion under 15 for females were adjusted by the ratio reported for the whole country:

$$\frac{\text{proportion under 15 in total population}}{\text{proportion under 15 in female population}}$$

Corresponding Brass-method estimates also are adjusted for particularly severe sex imbalance.

[e] Stable population estimates based on proportion under 5 years in preference to proportion under 15 years.

[f] No data available on age-specific fertility: mean age of fertility, $\bar{m}$, guessed.

[g] No data available on age-specific fertility: mean age of fertility, $\bar{m}$, estimated as $(23.95 + 2.25(P_3 P_2))$, where $P_3$ is reported average parity for women aged 25–29 years and $P_2$ that for women aged 20–24 years.

and sometimes rather different. This consistency exists also across the borders of the area considered here into Eastern Africa: The low fertility belt estimated for northern Zaïre and the Central African Republic extends across into the southwestern portion of Sudan, and the high fertility of eastern Zaïre is continued in Rwanda, Burundi, and the western portions of the East African states.[33] Third, the retrospective fertility data, though more limited in their areal coverage than the age-distribution data, present the same overall pattern of relative levels. The Brass method estimates of the birth rate are highly correlated with the stable population estimates: At the national level (13 countries) the correlation coefficient is 0.87, while for the 26 districts of Zaïre which provide the largest number and broadest range of estimates within a single data-collection system, the correlation coefficient is 0.91. Consideration of the detailed parity distributions by age reveals that the same broad pattern of relative levels exists for the proportions childless among adult women. In populations where marriage is virtually universal, the proportions childless for women

[33] Ansley J. Coale and F. Lorimer, "Summary of Estimates of Fertility and Mortality," in Brass et al., *Demography of Tropical Africa*, p. 166.

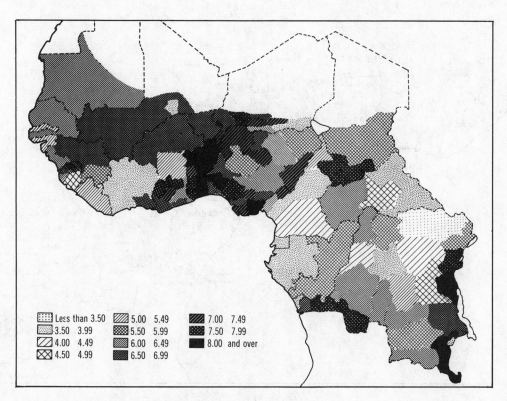

Less than 3.50
3.50   3.99
4.00   4.49
4.50   4.99
5.00   5.49
5.50   5.99
6.00   6.49
6.50   6.99
7.00   7.49
7.50   7.99
8.00   and over

FIGURE 2.1.   *Total Fertility Estimates for Major Regions of West Africa,*
*Based on Stable Population Models*

over, for instance, 30 years of age give a fair indication of the overall level of sterility. These proportions are exceptionally high in those areas where estimated fertility levels are lowest, an indication that a very high incidence of sterility may be a major factor in the generation of these low levels. The prevalence of venereal diseases in some of these communities is known to be high and may be the main cause of low overall fertility.[34]

Plausibility of the actual levels estimated is quite another question. The highest estimates, notably those for parts of Nigeria (for example, the birth rate of 71 estimated

for Ibadan province) are simply not credible. After detailed examination of the available age-composition data, van de Walle estimated very slightly lower levels,[35] but even these were only a little less incredible (a birth rate of 66 for Ibadan, for instance). The higher series may be more appropriate for some of the Nigerian provinces; at least, the estimates obtained from the West Cameroon survey of 1964–1965 are more nearly consistent with the higher estimates for the corresponding areas (Bamenda and Cameroon provinces) of the 1952–1953 census of Nigeria than with the lower ones. At the other extreme of estimation one might question the plausibility of those estimates which imply that the populations concerned are failing to replace

[34] A. Retal, quoted in J.-M. Cohen, "Fécondité: Facteurs," in INSEE, *Afrique Noire, Madagascar, Comores: Démographie Comparée* (Paris, 1967), pp. V10–V17; A. Romaniuk, *La Fécondité des Populations Congolaises* (Paris, 1967), chaps. 10, 11.

[35] Etienne van de Walle, "Fertility in Nigeria," in Brass et al., *Demography of Tropical Africa.*

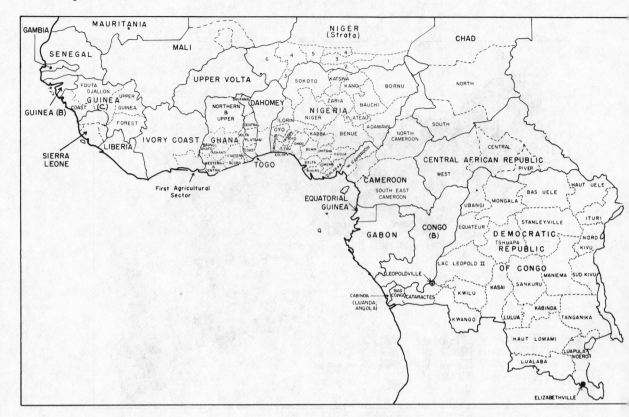

FIGURE 2.2. *Major Regions of West Africa for Which Fertility Estimates Are Given*

themselves or are only just achieving net replacement. These populations would have rapidly dwindled if such low fertility estimates had prevailed over any length of time, especially since mortality conditions were probably less favorable formerly. We have already considered parity sequences for some of these areas (Table 2.1); their suggestion of a possible fall in fertility levels is consistent with the estimated low net reproduction rate.

The birth rate estimates derived from retrospective fertility data are quite consistently a few points lower than those derived from the age distributions. The most obvious exception is Ghana, a case already mentioned as having a particularly suspect age-specific current fertility schedule. If we set aside the problem of age misstatement temporarily, we see that the Brass procedure is most likely to be biased downward because of the likelihood of some omissions in the reporting of parity by the younger women. Reintroduction of age misreporting may lead to an additional bias in either direction superimposed on this underlying downward bias. As a general rule, then, one might take the Brass-type estimates as representing roughly the lower limits of the range within which the actual birth rates can be expected to lie, although this rule of thumb may not hold good in particular cases. Whether the stable population estimates can be taken as representing a corresponding upper limit is more doubtful; detailed examination of the age-sex distribution for the area would be required to assess this in each individual case. We are not in a position to present a single estimate of fertility for each area, but only to indicate the probable range within which it lies. From essentially the same body of data and using similar techniques, a number of different estimates have been made at various times.

## REGIONAL DIFFERENTIALS IN NUPTIALITY AND MARITAL FERTILITY

In populations where fertility control is not widely practiced, marriage patterns, or, more specifically, patterns of regular cohabitation, are a major determinant of fertility levels. Marriage, and also parenthood, are universal ideals throughout the region. The reflections by Fortes on Tallensi attitudes toward celibacy are fairly typical: "[they regard marriage as] the normal state of life for every adult. They cannot conceive of anyone voluntarily refraining from marriage throughout life. There is something wrong . . . with men and women who never marry; and they are few."[36] Yet within the region there are deep differentials between cultures with respect to the precocity of marriage, the prevalence of different types of conjugal union, and the stability of unions. Each of these, together with customs relating to sexual abstinence within or before marriage, contribute to differentials in coital frequency. Cohabitation patterns assume even greater importance when it is allowed that they also influence the other major determinant of fertility levels, fecundity, through their effects on the spread and prevalence of venereal diseases and hence of sterility.

### MARRIAGE PATTERNS AND NUPTIALITY DATA.[37]

In most European and Asian societies the impact of nuptiality differentials on overall fertility patterns can fairly readily be assessed by decomposition of overall fertility levels into three main elements: nuptiality, marital fertility, and extramarital fertility levels and age patterns. The distinctions between currently married, ever married, and single are relatively clear cut in these societies: Regular cohabitation together with social and formal legal recognition of the union usually is initiated by a single civil, religious, or customary ritual (or by some combination of these performed within a very short space of time). In much of tropical Africa, by contrast, the traditional process of entering marriage can be stretched over a more or less extended time period. Rights and obligations between the couple and their respective kin may be developed in successive stages marked by different rituals,[38] with the process commonly being brought to its conclusion upon fulfillment of all bridewealth obligations on the part of the husband. Formal legal recognition of a union is often based on the payment of bridewealth, but completion of this does not necessarily coincide with either the point at which regular cohabitation commences or that at which the marriage is recognized in the community's kinship system. At one extreme a prospective union may not be fully accepted by the community until the birth of a child proves that the union is fertile, while at the other extreme, a widow may be formally "inherited" as wife by a close relative of her former husband without necessarily cohabiting. Current European and Asian notions founded on the concept of entry into marriage as a single unambiguous event are, therefore, not readily transferable to the traditional African systems where the marriage process is more complex and protracted.

The broad fourfold classification, single, currently married, widowed, divorced, has been adopted in most demographic surveys, with some subdivisions, but it is not always clear what criteria were used to sort the population into these categories. The United Nations recommends that "all persons habitually living together as man and wife even if they are not legally married" should be classified as currently married.[39] Thus the broad category "married" should include

---

[36] M. Fortes, *The Web of Kinship among the Tallensi* (London: Oxford University Press, 1949), p. 83.

[37] This section draws very heavily on the work of Etienne van de Walle, "Marriage in African Censuses and Inquiries," Brass et al., *Demography of Tropical Africa.*

[38] A. R. Radcliffe-Brown, "Introduction," In A. R. Radcliffe-Brown and D. Forde, eds., *African Systems of Kinship and Marriage* (London: Oxford University Press, 1950).

[39] United Nations, *Principles and Recommendations for National Population Censuses* (New York, 1958), p. 12.

persons living in consensual unions (defined as "socially recognized stable unions")[40] and those in incompletely formalized customary unions, besides those in fully regularized customary marriages. Where people classify themselves as currently married or not, the results may come close to this ideal. When additional categories are used, a proportion of unstable liaisons may be misreported as consensual unions; attempts to include a separate classification for unstable unions—"free unions"—have yielded negligible proportions reported in this category. Casual unions may develop into durable consensual unions. At what point does a casual union become a stable, socially recognized one? In Zaïre a distinction was made on the basis of the duration of the union to date. The lower limit for inclusion as a consensual union was set at six months; unions of lesser duration were omitted. Any such definition is arbitrary in nature, and is likely to exclude unions that are in fact stable although of very short duration to date.

Attempts to impose more rigorous definitions of marriage in order to distinguish between incompletely formalized and fully regularized customary unions have not been entirely successful. In Cameroon, where the distinction was based on payment of the bridewealth the results were acknowledged to be of doubtful meaning since the parties concerned often disagreed upon the status of the husband's payments.[41] In Zaïre the classification was based on the civil law which recognized only monogamous marriages for which bridewealth had been paid and fully formalized polygynous unions contracted before 1951 (when polygyny was outlawed). Polygynous marriages contracted after 1951 according to customary law were lumped together in a single residual category with customary marriages in-the-making and with consensual unions of some duration.

Further difficulties of classification occur in relation to dissolution of consensual or incompletely formalized customary marriage. Technically, a consensual union cannot be terminated by divorce, but it is not certain whether persons separated from consensual unions will report themselves as single or divorced. Similarly, there is doubt over the classification of persons separated from an incomplete customary marriage. Yet more difficulties arise in those cultures, such as the Gonja, where a marriage frequently ends in terminal separation rather than divorce.[42] The situation in which widows may be classified as married if they are technically inherited by one of their husband's kin, regardless of whether or not the two live together as man and wife, has already been mentioned. The classification adopted in Guinea for inherited widows introduced additional complexities, in that such a woman was classified as married or not according to whether or not she had borne a child in that union, a poor surrogate criterion for cohabitation.

It is evident that simple meaningful criteria of marital status are not easily specified, even for a homogeneous community; the definitional problems are compounded where marriages may be entered, observed, and dissolved in accordance with formal civil, Christian, or Moslem codes besides the local customary observances. With customary practices varying considerably from one community to the next it is almost impossible to find definitions that are meaningful, let alone comparable in meaning, across a number of communities. The many nuances that must be checked out to ensure that the classification criteria accommodate local variations in custom in some meaningful manner are well beyond the scope of large-scale demographic surveys. Yet the simple classifications usually adopted cannot cope with the complexities of the prevailing nuptiality customs; they tend to result in

[40] United Nations, *Multilingual Demographic Dictionary* (New York, 1958), p. 31.

[41] République du Cameroun, Service de la Statistique; France, Ministère de la Coopération, INSEE, *Enquête Démographique au Cameroun: Résultats Définitifs pour la Région Sud-Est, 1962-64* (Paris, 1966), pp. 32–33.

[42] E. N. Goody, "Conjugal Separation and Divorce among the Gonja of Northern Ghana," in M. Fortes, ed., *Marriage in Tribal Societies* (London: Cambridge University Press, 1962).

arbitrariness in definition and confusion in interpretation. Real similarities and dissimilarities may be obscured by the criteria adopted, so that comparative analysis of the existing large-scale nuptiality data can be approached only with a sizable measure of caution.

AGE AT MARRIAGE. There is little doubt that traditionally marriage has occurred at fairly early ages for women. A common ideal has been marriage soon after a girl becomes nubile; for males a slightly older age is more likely. Relating such broad generalizations to specific ages at marriage is extremely difficult. Anthropological investigations have rarely been of sufficient duration to pinpoint the actor's ages precisely. Such statements as "Ashanti girls marry between 16 and 18 years of age, youths between 20 and 25"[43] should be treated with some degree of scepticism, even when originating from researchers of high credentials, for they are only approximations. For larger demographic surveys in which the interviewers are not familiar with the respondents' personal histories and have not time to probe deeply in attempts to fix ages with any degree of precision (but rather, to the contrary, are likely to assign an age on the basis of reported marital and fertility status), generalizations regarding the age at marriage may bear only a sketchy correspondence to reality.

Direct questions as to the age at marriage have been asked in few large-scale surveys. Such data are not considered here since it is unrealistic to expect women who are not aware of their current ages to recall their age at the time of some past event, unless an exceptionally detailed personal history is constructed.

Age at first marriage can be computed indirectly from the reported proportions single, but the results usually are biased by the tendency for surveys to record marital status only for persons above a certain age (usually 14 or 15 years and over). Younger girls will be recorded as single regardless of their actual marital status; or more probably, their age will be inflated. Since the minimum age adopted varies from country to country comparability of the data is reduced. Hajnal's singulate mean age at marriage[44] can be computed, but has little meaning in the context of marital-status-related age misstatement in the first few age groups; it tends to indicate merely the age which is believed *a priori* to be the ideal or actual age at first marriage. Van de Walle has used an alternative strategy which requires only the overall proportion single in the whole population instead of the proportion in each age group, and hence is sensitive only to misstatement of marital status.[45] The method requires also an estimate of the age distribution, which can usually be approximated only through the adoption of a model stable population identified as being appropriate. Application of the procedure is, therefore, restricted to populations where the assumption of stability is tenable (which rules out its use for several regions and for study of rural-urban differentials) and to populations where a model age composition can be selected with some confidence. The method is sensitive to the choice of model and estimates obtained can vary considerably; its use is, accordingly, somewhat limited. Van de Walle has attempted to relate regional variations in the mean age at first marriage obtained from this procedure to the birth rate in a single country (Zaïre) where opposing biases from different survey procedures are less likely to reduce comparability than in international comparisons. The results were rather inconclusive. In fact, at the level of the smallest units considered (districts) the age at marriage was correlated positively with the crude birth rate estimates. Somewhat surprisingly, high fertility was associated with later rather than earlier marriage. The most plausible explanation, he suggested, was that high fertility

[43] M. Fortes, "Kinship and Marriage among the Ashanti," in Radcliffe Brown and Forde, *African Systems of Kinships and Marriage.*

[44] J. Hajnal, "Age at Marriage and Proportions Marrying," *Population Studies*, VI (1953), 129–31.
[45] Etienne van de Walle, "The Relation of Marriage to Fertility in African Demographic Inquiries," *Demography*, II (1964), 302–8.

tended to produce a later age at marriage, since it produces a steeper age distribution: Given the customary age difference between males and females at marriage, eligible men can find an adequate supply of brides at ages closer to their own age in a high fertility population than in a low fertility one.

By and large, the aggregrate data on age at marriage and its relationship to fertility levels is inconclusive, though at the individual level a strong relationship must exist. Delayed marriage in urban areas has been cited as one of the prime factors in rural-urban fertility differentials, a point we shall take up in more detail at a later time.

TYPE OF UNION AND MARITAL FERTILITY. Under the heading "type of union" may be considered marital category divisions cutting along two distinct dimensions: first, the form of union, fully legal customary unions being opposed in this sense to consensual unions; second, monogamous as opposed to polygynous unions. Whereas in the case of age at marriage there is usually only indirect evidence, direct information on type of union has been collected in several inquiries. We are no longer under the restraint of having to relate an overall measure of the type of union (such as the proportion in certain unions) to aggregate fertility levels, but can exploit fertility data gathered for individual women cross-tabulated by type of union at the time of the survey.

With respect to the first dimension, the available data suggest that the fertility of consensual unions is almost always lower than that of customary unions. The problems of discriminating between consensual customary unions for which full bridewealth has not yet been paid have already been mentioned; the data are not strictly comparable. The consistently lower fertility rates reported for consensual unions probably result from a number of causes. First, consensual unions tend to be less stable than customary unions so the women in consensual unions are more likely to have experienced infertile periods between unions and are more likely to have been exposed to venereal infections. Second,

subfecund women whose previous unions have been dissolved on account of their infertility may be less likely to find a spouse prepared to contract customary marriage and so they tend to be selectively recruited into consensual unions. Third, consensual unions as well as incompletely formalized customary marriages tend to be of shorter duration than fully regularized customary marriages, so average exposure to risk of pregnancy in them is less. Fourth, since these unions may develop eventually into stable customary marriages, a child conceived in a consensual union may be born after the marriage has been fully recognized according to customary law. There is, then, a fundamental lack of correspondence in the cross-tabulation of current fertility by marital status. These tabulations show conceptions that occurred, on average, some 15 months before the survey and births which occurred some 6 months before it; these events are tabulated by marital status of the mother at the time of survey. Any marital status which tends to be of comparatively short duration and is likely to lead to another status (e.g., from consensual marriage to customary marriage), thus has its apparent fertility artifically deflated at the expense of the other statuses. The differentials may be as much apparent as real.

Perhaps more meaningful are the fertility differentials between women in monogamous and polygynous marriages. Polygyny is often cited as a factor in lowering fertility. Possible mechanisms include lower coital frequency per woman, and increased risk of venereal infections. Since most polygynous males are in the older age groups and tend to take relatively young second and subsequent wives, there may also be a tendency for the fertility of young women in such unions to be reduced by the lower fertility of their husbands relative to the younger husbands of their monogamously married peers.[46] Table 2.5 gives the ratio of polygynous to monogamous fertility rates by age. The ratios are almost

[46] V. R. Dorjahn, "The Factor of Polygyny in African Demography," in W. R. Bascom and M. J. Herskovits, eds., *Continuity and Change in African Cultures*, (Chicago: University of Chicago Press, 1959).

TABLE 2.5

Ratio of polygynous to monogamous age-specific fertility rates

| Age Group | Central Niger Delta | Upper Volta | Guinea | Zaïre | |
|---|---|---|---|---|---|
| 15–19 | 0.87 | 0.97 | 0.95[a] | 0.77 | (0.93) |
| 20–24 | 1.01 | 0.95 | 0.93 | 0.86 | (0.91) |
| 25–29 | 0.93 | 0.90 | 0.96 | 0.81 | (0.85) |
| 30–34 | 0.85 | 0.87 | 1.03 | 0.74 | (0.83) |
| 35–39 | 0.82 | 0.71 | 0.91 | 0.71 | (0.75) |
| 40–44 | 0.80 | 0.68 | 0.95 | | |

SOURCES: See appendix to this chapter.
NOTE: Parentheses indicate figures based on fertility rates excluding childless women.
[a] Figure for age group 14–19.

all below unity and, except for some irregularities, decline fairly steadily with age. The decline with age is consistent with the first two factors stated above; it is also consistent with the notion that subfecund women may be progressively selected into polygynous unions as their husbands take additional wives in order to satisfy their desire for progeny. The additional data from Zaïre, which are restricted to women of proven fertility, yield ratios much closer to unity at the younger ages but decline rapidly with age. More detailed distributions by numbers of co-wives are available from four surveys (Table 2.6). The ratios here are much more irregular (especially the sequences for Gabon), which may or may not be a function of the small numbers of women involved. In general, the ratios decline with increasing numbers of co-wives as well as with age; the sequences from Upper Volta are quite remarkably regular in this respect.

MARITAL STABILITY AND FERTILITY. Marital instability reduces fertility levels through both the introduction of infertile periods between marital unions and the spread of venereal diseases. One of the classic investigations probing the detailed relationships between marriage customs and fertility levels was that conducted among the Bakweri in West Cameroon, an area noted for an exceptionally high sex ratio (from immigration of adult males), very low marital stability, and low fertility.[47] Age-specific parity levels by reported number of marriages contracted have been tabulated for a few surveys. While the number of marriages reported is undoubtedly understated in many cases, probably being grossly understated where survey interviews were particularly brief, the general picture is quite clear. The greater the deviations from the single marital experience, the lower the ratio. The ratios decline more or less regularly with increasing age. Once again, the selection of subfecund women into a particular category may be as much a cause as a consequence of the observed fertility differentials.

ABSTINENCE. The extent to which marital fertility may be reduced by abstinence in

[47] E. Ardener, *Divorce and Fertility: An African Study*, Nigerian Social and Economic Studies Number 3 (London: Oxford University Press, 1962).

TABLE 2.6

Ratio of polygynous to monogamous age-specific fertility rates by number of co-wives

| Age Group | Number of Co-Wives | | | | | | | | | |
|---|---|---|---|---|---|---|---|---|---|---|
| | Upper Volta | | | Gabon | | Guinea | | Congo | | |
| | 2 | 3 | 4+ | 2 | 3+ | 2 | 3+ | 2 | 3 | 4+ |
| 15–19 | 1.02 | 0.89 | 0.81 | 1.07 | 1.76 | 0.94[a] | 0.98[a] | 0.74 | 0.33 | 0.32 |
| 20–24 | 0.99 | 0.95 | 0.77 | 0.82 | 0.93 | 0.92 | 0.95 | 0.89 | 0.75 | 0.40 |
| 25–29 | 0.93 | 0.86 | 0.78 | 0.87 | 1.01 | 0.96 | 0.96 | | | |
| 30–34 | 0.95 | 0.79 | 0.67 | 1.03 | 0.56 | 1.04 | 0.98 | 1.07 | 0.86 | 0.67 |
| 35–39 | 0.71 | 0.76 | 0.66 | 0.97 | 1.02 | 0.91 | 0.92 | | | |
| 40–44 | 0.80 | 0.59 | 0.51 | 1.33 | 1.02 | 1.08 | 0.85 | 0.97[b] | 0.61[b] | 0.52[b] |

SOURCES: See appendix to this chapter.
[a] Figure for age group 14–19.
[b] Figure for age group 40–49.

various cultures is hard to assess until we have more detailed data on conjugal histories from several communities.

Two main forms of abstinence may be distinguished. First, enforced abstinence may be occasioned by separation of spouses for more or less lengthy periods of time. Thus the major source areas of migrant labor may have somewhat reduced fertility; this has been cited as one of the possible causes of relatively low fertility in the northern part of Ghana.[48] Second, there are a number of sexual taboos which are more or less strictly observed. The commonest, that following childbirth, often associated with the period of lactation, varies tremendously between cultures. Raulin, in a comparison of selected tribes, cites durations ranging from 40 days (the Maures of Mauritania, and Songhay of Niger) to 3–4 years (the Bété, Dida, Guéré, Malinké and Yacouba of Ivory Coast, Mossi of Upper Volta, and Gourmantché of Niger).[49] The data on such taboos are fragmentary, and the extent to which actual behavior corresponds to the ideal is uncertain. It might be argued that postpartum abstinence would reduce polygynous fertility less than monogamous fertility, since other wives are likely to experience more frequent intercourse than they otherwise would following the birth of a child to their co-wife. On the other hand, monogamous marriages may more often fall short of the ideal behavior.[50]

INTERRELATIONS OF MARITAL AND FERTILITY STATUSES. It is plain that, at the level of the individual, fertility is closely associated with age at marriage, type of marital union(s) experienced, and the number of these unions, fertility and marital histories being largely interdependent. At the community level, the evidence as to the relative importance of these interrelations cannot readily be assessed, partly because of the complexity of the interconnections, and partly because of the lack of detailed cross-tabulations or more data based on full conjugal histories for more communities.

## RURAL-URBAN DIFFERENTIALS, MODERNIZATION, AND FERTILITY TRENDS

In the absence of any valid time series of fertility estimates for most of the region, no direct inferences about general fertility trends can be drawn. One might speculate that periods of social disorganization and the development of labor migration may have affected patterns of cohabitation in some areas, or that the levels of fecundity have changed as a result of the spread of pathological sterility or the treatment of such conditions, but there is no sound evidence of such trends in most cases. In general there is little to suggest that overall fertility levels have changed markedly. The main case where roughly comparable large-scale data are available for quite widely separated dates is that of Ghana (age-specific parity data from samples of the 1948 and 1960 censuses); these show essentially no change in reported parity levels.[51] This text has already alluded to the only data appearing to reflect such change in the past—the anomalous parity and sterility sequences in parts of Middle Africa.

To detect possible current trends and to explore the mechanisms by which such changes operate, the only strategy commonly open is examination of fertility differentials between communities differentially affected by the processes of modernization. Rural-urban contrasts epitomize such distinctions, but one may also consider differentials by educational and other socioeconomic status categories, within both rural and urban areas.

RURAL-URBAN FERTILITY DIFFERENTIALS. The classic methods of estimating overall fertility are inapplicable in the case of rural-urban

[48] John C. Caldwell, "Population Change," in W. Birmingham, I. Neustadt, and E. M. Omaboe, eds., *A Study of Contemporary Ghana, II, Some Aspects of Social Structure* (London: George Allen and Unwin; Evanston: Northwestern University Press, 1967), p. 97.

[49] H. Raulin, "Commentaire Socio-Ethnologique," in INSEE, *Afrique Noire, Madagascar, Comores: Démographie Comparée* (Paris, 1967), p. VIII59.

[50] Dorjahn, "Polygyny in African Demography."

[51] S. K. Gaisie, "Estimated Mid-Twentieth Century Levels and Trends of Fertility in Ghana," *Proceedings of the International Population Conference, London, 1969,* I (Liège, 1971), p. 780.

contrasts: urban populations are neither closed to migration, nor, in most cases, do they possess a history of constant fertility and mortality; the Brass method of fertility estimation assumes constant fertility; the simpler child-women ratios are biased by age misstatement of young children (which may operate differentially between rural and urban areas, since the latter are more likely to have some system of vital registration and hence somewhat better reporting of the ages of young children), by the effects of children being separated from their mothers (children of rural residents attending schools in urban areas, or children of urban residents spending part of their childhood in the area of their ancestral home, for example), and by different mortality conditions between rural and urban areas affecting the survival probabilities of children born in the two environments. Bearing in mind these limitations, it still is possible to detect clear evidence of differentials between urban and rural fertility in some areas from consideration of reported child-woman ratios and retrospective fertility reports by age of woman.

Referring to the fertility reports for the major cities of countries of French expression, Cohen distinguishes three patterns:[52]

(1) Countries with higher urban than rural fertility: Congo, Gabon, and (to a lesser degree) Upper Volta
(2) Countries with roughly comparable urban and rural fertility: Chad and Senegal
(3) Countries with lower urban than rural fertility: Mali, Guinea, and Togo.

Zaïre shares some similarities with the first category,[53] and Ghana with the third category.[54] Cohen's suggested explanation rests on the idea that for early stages of urbanization in areas with generally low fertility caused by pathological sterility, the better

[52] J-M. Cohen, Fécondité: Facteurs," in INSEE, *Afrique Noire, Madagascar, Comores; Démographie Comparée* (Paris, 1967), p. V26.
[53] Romaniuk, *La Fécondité des Populations Congolaises*, chap. 5.
[54] John C. Caldwell, "Population Change," in Birmingham et al., *Contemporary Ghana*, pp. 98–102; Gaisie, *Dynamics of Population Growth*.

health facilities available in urban areas lead to a reduction in sterility; in areas with generally high fertility the processes of modernization that tend to erode high fertility norms predominate. Olusanya has taken the idea that the early stages of urbanization may lead to a rise rather than a fall in fertility a stage further. Even in the high fertility cultures of western Nigeria, urbanization may be associated with a relaxation of fertility restrictive practices such as postpartum sexual taboos.[55]

National values of child-woman ratios for urban and rural areas are fairly consistent with Cohen's patterns (Table 2.7), though

TABLE 2.7
Child-women ratios by area, urban and rural

| Area | National | Urban | Rural |
|---|---|---|---|
| Central African Republic | 0.557 | 0.516 | 0.569 |
| Chad | 0.643 | 0.655 | 0.642 |
| Congo | 0.596 | 0.699 | 0.582 |
| Dahomey | 0.837 | 0.871 | 0.833 |
| Gabon | 0.398 | 0.517 | 0.380 |
| Gambia | 0.552 | 0.687 | 0.541 |
| Ghana | 0.831 | 0.771 | 0.850 |
| Mali | 0.757 | 0.747 | 0.758 |
| Togo | 0.884 | 0.735 | 0.900 |

these data would suggest that urban fertility is not markedly below rural fertility in Mali.

RURAL-URBAN NUPTIALITY AND FERTILITY DIFFERENTIALS. Zaïre and Ghana will be taken here as two contrasted examples of rural-urban fertility differentials.

In Zaïre the overall age-specific fertility rates suggest that urban fertility is about 28 percent higher than rural fertility (Table 2.8).[56] Direct comparison of these rates does not consider the effects of differences in the proportions married. Allowance for nuptiality differentials must be made in order to indicate the relative importance of differentials in marital fertility as opposed to those in

[55] P. O. Olusanya, "Modernization and the Level of Fertility in Western Nigeria," *Proceedings of the International Population Conference*, pp. 812–25.
[56] Romaniuk, *Fécondité des Populations Congolaises*, pp. 173–76.

TABLE 2.8

Rural–Urban age-specific fertility differentials, Zaïre, 1955–1957, and Ghana, 1960

| | Zaïre | | | | | | | | | Ghana | | |
| | A | | | B | | | C | | | A | | |
| Age Group | Rural | Urban | U/R | Rural | Urban | U/R | Rural | Urban | U/R | Rural | Urban | U/R |
|---|---|---|---|---|---|---|---|---|---|---|---|---|
| 15–19 | 121 | 211 | 1.74 | 244 | 289 | 1.18 | 284 | 295 | 1.04 | 148 | 96 | 0.65 |
| 20–24 | 264 | 292 | 1.11 | 290 | 301 | 1.04 | 302 | 311 | 1.03 | 265 | 230 | 0.87 |
| 25–29 | 229 | 258 | 1.13 | 246 | 273 | 1.11 | 263 | 280 | 1.06 | 277 | 234 | 0.85 |
| 30–34 | 164 | 209 | 1.27 | 184 | 223 | 1.21 | 198 | 230 | 1.16 | 247 | 221 | 0.89 |
| 35–39 | 77 | 108 | 1.40 | 88 | 131 | 1.49 | 101 | 132 | 1.32 | 289 | 264 | 0.87 |
| 40–44 | | | | | | | | | | 106 | 94 | 0.89 |
| 45–49 | 16 | 20 | 1.25 | 22 | 31 | 1.41 | 26 | 26 | 1.00 | 46 | 45 | 0.98 |
| 50–54 | | | | | | | | | | | | |
| Total fertility | 4.77 | 6.12 | 1.28 | 5.92 | 7.06 | 1.19 | 6.50 | 7.16 | 1.10 | 6.39 | 5.43 | 0.85 |

SOURCES: Romaniuk, *La Fécondité des Populations Congolaises*, pp. 173–75; S. K. Gaisie, *Dynamics of Population Growth in Ghana*, Accra-Tema: Ghana Publishing Corporation, 1969.
*A* = rates based on all women.
*B* = rates based on customarily or consensually married women only.
*C* = rates based on women in monogamous customary marriages only.

nuptiality. Considering fertility rates based on married women only (including those in stable consensual unions), the differential is reduced to about 19 percent, the proportions married being higher in urban than in rural areas at all ages up to 35. When only those women living in fully recognized monogamous customary marriages are considered (hence those in consensual unions, incompletely formalized customary marriages, and polygynous unions are excluded) the differential is further reduced to 10 percent. About one-half of the differential between rural and urban fertility can thus be accounted for by different nuptiality patterns, leaving the other half of the excess of urban over rural fertility to be accounted for by such factors as improved health conditions and relaxation of sexual restrictions.

Although the urban-rural fertility differential appears to lie in the opposite direction in Ghana, this too is largely to be explained by nuptiality differences. The 1960 postenumeration survey data suggest that nuptiality differences are in the opposite direction from those found in Zaïre; the proportions married in the age group 15–24 in Accra Capital District were about half the proportions reported from the Northern Region, though the differential was minimal

at older ages.[57] More detailed investigations of conjugal histories suggest a rural-urban differential in age at marriage for women of about $1\frac{1}{2}$ to 2 years.[58] Age-specific marital fertility rates from the 1960 postenumeration survey are not yet available, but overall rates (included in Table 2.8) show urban total fertility rates some 15 percent below rural ones. The greatest differences are in the age group 15–19 years, where the ratio of urban to rural is only 0.65, while at other ages the ratios fall quite consistently between 0.85 and 0.90. These data are consistent with the limited information on marital status yet available from the survey, and are essentially similar to figures obtained in other surveys.[59] Age at marriage is probably the prime determinant in the rural-urban fertility differential, through its effects on the proportion of a woman's most fertile years spent in conjugal unions. Dissolution of marriage

[57] P. A. Tetteh, "Marriage, Family and Household," in Birmingham *et al.*, *Contemporary Ghana*, p. 202.
[58] John C. Caldwell, "Population: General Characteristics," in Birmingham et al., *Contemporary Ghana*, pp. 68–69.
[59] Caldwell, "Population Change," p. 102; D. I. Pool, "The Number and Type of Conjugal Unions as Correlates of Levels of Fertility and Attitudes to Family Limitation in Ghana" (Paper presented at Population Association of America meeting, Boston, 1968).

through widowhood or divorce is more likely to affect women further advanced in their childbearing span. With respect to possible rural-urban differentials in marital dissolution, it is probable that dissolution through widowhood is less frequent in urban areas because of the more favorable health conditions there, but it is not clear whether marital stability is greater or less in urban than in rural areas. Of two surveys of conjugal histories, carried out in 1963–1964 and 1965–1966 by Caldwell and Pool respectively, results from the first showed rural women in each age group reporting more conjugal unions than urban women, whereas the second suggested that rural women tended to report participation in a lower number of unions than urban women.[60] Overall, it has been estimated (from the former survey) that rural women spend on average 71 percent of their time between the ages of 15 and 44 living in conjugal unions, compared with only 63 percent for urban women.[61] The inference drawn from the nuptiality patterns is that delayed marriage is almost entirely responsible for the observed rural-urban fertility differentials in Ghana. Marital fertility levels are roughly comparable in both urban and rural environments, a situation not unlike that already outlined for Zaïre.

EDUCATIONAL AND FERTILITY DIFFERENTIALS. The postenumeration survey in Ghana shows clear evidence of an inverse relationship between educational attainment and fertility levels, the relationship being found in both rural and urban areas.[62] To a large extent this is due to the delay in marriage occasioned by prolonging education, but even among married women there is a slight inverse relationship between fertility and educational levels.[63]

CHANGES IN FACTORS INFLUENCING FAMILY SIZE. As one tries to penetrate deeper beneath the surface of rural-urban or educational

differentials in fertility to explore the underlying social and economic framework of existing differentials and possible future trends, one finds that the material available becomes increasingly confined to a comparatively small part of the region. Specifically, most of the detailed materials stem from the extraordinarily productive Population Council Survey Program in Ghana led by Caldwell between 1962 and 1964, though the supply of materials from subsequent projects in Ghana and elsewhere (notably Nigeria) is building up. A summary chapter is scarcely the place to retreat from the regional framework to focus on a vast quantity of detailed information relating to a relatively small portion of that region; discussion of the findings with respect to particular differentials can be found in relevant detailed chapters. However, the broad issue upon which most of the investigations have touched, the extent to which social and economic modernization will entail a reconsideration of the traditional high fertility ideals embedded in West African cultures, is a fundamental question throughout the region. Very broadly, the factors which might bring about a reconsideration of high fertility norms include the effects of declining mortality; the declining labor value of children with the spread of urbanization, with economic modernization in rural areas and the trend away from subsistence farming and with the spread of schooling; and changes in family structure, particularly in urban environments.

CONCLUSION. All three factors just outlined have been found to be associated with smaller family ideals to some extent, at least in Ghana,[64] and it appears quite likely that

[60] Caldwell, "Population: General Characteristics," p. 71; Pool, "Family Limitation in Ghana."
[61] Caldwell, "Population: General Characteristics," p. 73.
[62] Gaisie, *Dynamics of Population Growth.*
[63] Pool, "Family Limitation in Ghana," Table V.

[64] John C. Caldwell, "Fertility Attitudes in Three Economically Contrasting Rural Regions of Ghana," *Economic Development and Cultural Change,* XV, 2 (January 1967) 217–38; and *Population Growth and Family Change in Africa: The New Urban Elite in Ghana* Canberra: Australia National University Press, 1968). Both discuss the declining labor value/increasing costs of children including the costs of schooling. The latter also considers changes in family structure and obligations, as does "Extended Family Obligations and Education: A study of an Aspect of Demographic Transition among Ghanaian University Students," *Population Studies,* XIX, 2 (November 1965), 183–99.

social and economic change will have a similar impact on fertility elsewhere in the region. This chapter has scarcely been able to do more than touch briefly upon some few aspects of the patterns and trends of fertility in the region. For more detailed information about levels or trends of fertility in a particular area, about fertility control, or about population policy, the reader must turn to chapters devoted exclusively to that topic.

## Appendix: Major Statistical Sources

CAMEROON

Cameroun, Service de la Statistique; France, Ministère de la Coopération, INSEE, *Enquête Démographique au Cameroun, 1962–64: Résultats Définitifs pour la Région Nord* (Paris, 1968).

——, *Enquête Démographique au Cameroun, 1962–64: Résultats Définitifs pour la Région Sud-Est* (Paris, 1968).

Cameroun, Service de la Statistique; France, Société d'Etudes pour le Développement Economique et Social, *The Population of West Cameroon: Main Findings of the 1964 Demographic Sample Survey* (Paris, 1966).

North Cameroon survey population excludes nomadic M'bororos (15,000) and Tikar plain area (4,000).

Southeast Cameroon survey population excludes Yaoundé and Douala (280,000) and Bamiléké area (1,120,000).

CENTRAL AFRICAN REPUBLIC

République Centrafricaine, Service de la Statistique Générale; France, Ministère de la Coopération, INSEE, *Enquête Démographique en République Centrafricaine, 1959–60: Résultats Définitifs* (Paris, 1968).

Survey population excludes eastern portion of country (66,000), nomadic groups (40,000), and Bangui town (80,000).

CHAD

Tchad, Service de Statistique; France, Ministère de la Coopération, INSEE, *Enquête Démographique au Tchad, 1964: Résultats Définitifs*, two volumes, (Paris, 1966).

Survey population excludes northernmost part of country (Bourkou, Ennedi, and Tibesti and sparsely settled adjacent areas) and other nomad areas (630,000); it also excludes Lac prefecture and Fort-Lamy (100,000).

PEOPLES REPUBLIC OF THE CONGO

Congo, Service de Statistique; France, Ministère de la Coopération, INSEE, *Enquête Démographique, 1960–61* (Paris, 1965).

Survey population excludes Brazzaville (136,000) and Pointe-Noire (79,000).

ZAÏRE

Congo, Bureau de la Démographie, Tableau Général de la Démographie Congolaise, *Enquête Démographique par Sondage, 1955–57: Analyse Générale des Résultats Statistiques* (Léopoldville, 1961). Information by districts:

a) Congo Belge, 2e Direction Générale, 1e Direction, A.I.M.O., *Enquêtes Démographiques*, Vols. 1–5 (Cité Léopoldville, Territoire Suburbain, Bas-Congo, Cataractes, Tshuapa) and Vol. 7 (Maniéma).

b) Congo Belge, Affaires Economiques, Direction de la Statistique, *Bulletin Mensuel des Statistiques Générales du Congo Belge et du Ruanda-Urundi*, Série Spéciale, no 3, *Enquête Démographique, 1956–57*, Vols. b, e, f (Equateur Province excluding Tshuapa District, Katanga Province, Kasai Province).

c) République du Congo, Ministère du Plan et de la Coordination Economique, Service des Statistiques, *Résultats de l'Enquête Démographique*, Vols. 11, 12, and e (Lac Léopold II, Kwilu, Kwango, Nord- and Sud-Kivu, Katanga).

Survey population excludes part of Katanga (52,000).

DAHOMEY

Dahomey; France, Ministère de la Cooperation, INSEE, *Enquête Démographique au Dahomey, 1961: Résultats Définitifs* (Paris, 1964).

Survey population excludes Abomey-Bohicon and Tchi canton (1 percent of population).

GABON

Gabon, Service de Statistique; France, Ministère de la Coopération, INSEE, *Recensement et Enquête Démographique, 1960–61: Résultats Définitifs* (Paris, 1965).

GAMBIA

Gambia, *Report on the Census of Population taken on 17th–18th April, 1963*, by H. A. Oliver (Bathurst, 1965).

GHANA

Ghana, Census Office, *1960 Census of Ghana*, Vol. III (Accra, 1964). S. K. Gaisie, *Dynamics of Population Growth in Ghana*, (Accra-Tema: Ghana Publishing Corporation, 1969).

GUINEA (BISSAU)

Portugal, Provincia da Guiné, *Censo da População de 1950*, Vol. ii, *População não Civilizada*, (Lisbon, undated).

Data are for the "nonassimilated" African population only.

GUINEA

Guinée; France, Ministère de la France d'Outre-Mer, Service des Statistiques, *Etude Démographique par Sondage en Guinée, 1954–55: Résultats Définitifs* (Paris, undated).

IVORY COAST

Côte d'Ivoire, Service de la Statistique; France, Ministère de la France d'Outre-Mer, Service des Statistiques, *Etude Démographique du 1er Secteur Agricole de la Côte d'Ivoire, 1957–58: Résultats Provisoires* (Paris, 1958).

LIBERIA

Liberia, Office of National Planning, Bureau of Statistics, *1962 Census of Population* (Monrovia, 1965).

MALI

Mali, Service de la Statistique; France, Ministère de la Coopération, INSEE, *Enquête Démographique au Mali, 1960–61* (Paris, undated).

Survey population excludes nomads in northern part of country (210,000) and persons in the l'Office du Niger zone (30,000).

Mali, Mission Socio-économique 1956–1958; France, Ministère de la Coopération, INSEE, *Enquête Démographique dans le Delta Central Nigérien,* two volumes (Paris, undated).

MAURITANIA

Mauritanie; France, Société d'Etudes pour le Développement Economique et Social, *Enquête Démographique, 1964–65: Résultats Provisoires* (Paris, 1966). Survey population excludes nomad subdivisions of Tichitt and Boghé (20,000) and urban centers (70,000).

NIGER

Niger, Mission Démographique du Niger, 1960; France, Ministère de la Coopération, INSEE, *Etude Démographique du Niger; Résultats Définitifs* (Paris, 1963).

Survey population excludes Niamey city (30,000) and northern portion of country (240,000).

NIGERIA

Nigeria, Department of Statistics, *Population Census of the Eastern Region of Nigeria, 1953* (Lagos, undated).

——, *Population Census of the Northern Region of Nigeria, 1952* (Lagos, undated).

——, *Population Census of the Western Region of Nigeria, 1952* (Lagos, undated).

SENEGAL

United Nations, *Demographic Yearbook, 1969* (New York, 1970).

SIERRA LEONE

Sierra Leone, Central Statistical Office, *1963 Population Census of Sierra Leone,* Vol. I (Freetown, 1965).

TOGO

Togo, Service de la Statistique Générale, *Enquête Démographique, 1961: Résultats Définitifs,* Vol. II (Lomé, undated).

UPPER VOLTA

Haute-Volta, Service de Statistique; France, Ministère de la Coopération, INSEE, *La Situation Démographique en Haute-Volta: Résultats Partiels de l'Enquête Démographique, 1960–61* (Paris, 1962).

Survey population excludes Ouagadougou (60,000) and Bobo-Dioulasso (50,000).

# CHAPTER THREE

# Fertility Control

JOHN C. CALDWELL

WHAT may in time become mass family planning in tropical Africa will be based on earlier knowledge of, attitudes toward, and practice of fertility restriction much of which has not been specifically concerned with planning families. There are four important questions at the present time: (1) What have been the traditional antinatal practices and what influence have they had on fertility? (2) What change is at present under way in either antinatal practice or in knowledge and attitudes that may affect that practice? (3) If change is already occurring, what position has now been reached in the nontraditional areas of society and how significant is this for the whole society? (4) What implications have such changes for the future development of family planning and the level of fertility?

Some of the evidence must be derived from anthropological studies into a wider range of behavior and ideas, and many of these findings were summarized by Lorimer as early as 1954.[1] However, a knowledge of the importance of various practices among large populations and the directions of change has depended upon the so-called KAP studies[2] which date only from 1963. When these were first summarized in 1968,[3] those in West Africa which had released findings numbered only 12 encompassing interviews with fewer than 15,000 persons representing no more than about 20 million persons found in two countries.[4] Admittedly, these two countries were Ghana and Nigeria, which are not only among the three most populous of the region,[5]

[1] Frank Lorimer, *Culture and Human Fertility* (Paris: UNESCO, 1954).

[2] "KAP" means "knowledge of, attitudes to, and practice of family planning." These surveys normally also attempt to measure fertility. See John C. Caldwell *et al.*, *A Manual for Surveys of Fertility and Family Planning: Knowledge, Attitudes and Practice* (New York: The Population Council, 1970).

[3] John C. Caldwell, "The Control of Family Size in Tropical Africa," *Demography*, V, 2 (1968), 598–619.

[4] That is, the populations of the universes from which the samples were drawn and contiguous populations within the same countries of apparently the same type.

[5] West Africa is defined here as elsewhere in this volume to include all countries from Mauritania to Zaïre; it is the same as the United Nations' West Africa and Middle Africa with the omission of Burundi and Rwanda.

but appear to be the two destined to play the most significant role in terms of early governmental intervention aimed at reducing fertility and growth levels. The 1971 summary provided by this chapter covers 39 surveys totaling around 60,000 interviews representing about 75 million persons in eight countries. Perhaps more important are the following facts: They now allow more comparisons over time; francophone countries can now be contrasted with anglophone countries; and, while only one-fifth of persons interviewed up to 1968 lived in rural areas (where the vast majority of tropical Africans are found), two-thirds did so by 1971.

The mass and variety of this new material (much of it presented in this book for the first time) can hardly be overstated, subject only to the proviso that it is a close representation to the reality of West African life. There has been some debate on KAP surveys both in global and African terms, and the matter is so important for this chapter that it should be taken up at once.

## KAP SURVEYS AND THEIR DATA

In a recent review article, Hauser has charged that many KAP surveys together with other surveys, have failed to achieve sufficient reliability and validity and have lacked introspection about, or measures of, what they have achieved.[6] He added that they rarely measured the intensity of attitudes, and that the authors or others tended to misinterpret what the findings (for instance, the proportion passively agreeing that they would like to limit family size) meant in terms of likely behavior. The first two strictures can only be taken as a guide to better work and for a critical appraisal of the findings claimed by existing surveys; for a better understanding of the human condition, not least in the field of fertility and its control, there is little alternative to the survey. However, given that the surveys adequately present their data, they can

hardly be blamed for the further constructions built upon the evidence. Within West Africa, Pradervand[7] and Morgan[8] have made similar criticisms of KAP surveys in the region and Pool has made a more specific criticism.[9]

Morgan makes several very telling points. The first is his claim, made after years of working in this field in Nigeria, that probably all tropical Africans know that abstinence from sexual relations will prevent conception, that nearly all realize that withdrawal before the ejaculation of any spermatozoa (*coitus interruptus*) cannot lead to conception, and that the concept of abortion is known to nearly all, and, at least in Lagos, nearly everyone is aware that it is practiced. This leads him to cast severe doubt on the accuracy, and, by implication, the research methods of most West African KAP surveys. Thus, while his own survey of Lagos reported 98 percent of females and 89 percent of males knowing some method of birth control, that of Caldwell and Igun claimed only about three-quarters of the city's respondents of either sex having such knowledge.[10] In fact the proportion of respondents reporting family planning knowledge in rural areas declines from the 77 percent recorded by Dow in Sierra Leone in 1969–1970 to 4 percent recorded in Ghana by Pool in 1965–1966 and Gaisie in 1969–1970.

These contrasts are almost certainly neither as bad as they seem nor a measure of discrepancies in other KAP findings. The fundamental problem is the defining and measurement of knowledge of noncontraceptive forms of family planning such as withdrawal and abstinence. Thus the Morgan survey and the Caldwell and Igun one in

[6] P. M. Hauser, "Family Planning and Population Programs," *Demography*, IV, 4 (1967), 397–414.

[7] Pierre Pradervand, "Report to the Ford Foundation," mimeographed.

[8] Robert W. Morgan (in chapter 9 of this book).

[9] D. Ian Pool, "Ghana: A Survey on Fertility and Attitudes toward Family Limitation," *Studies in Family Planning*, XXV, (December 1967) 10–15; and "Ghana: The Attitudes of Urban Males towards Family Size and Family Limitation," *Studies in Family Planning*, LX, (December 1970), 12–17.

[10] John C. Caldwell and Adenola A. Igun, "The Spread of Anti-natal Knowledge and Practice in Nigeria," *Population Studies*, XXIV, 1 (March 1970) 23.

Lagos show much the same level of knowledge of modern contraceptives (around two-thirds of the respondents); but, for knowledge of traditional methods (withdrawal, abstinence, rhythm, local medicines, and so on), Morgan's figures are four times as high for males and almost eight times as high for females. Furthermore, in some surveys (for instance, both Gaisie's urban and rural surveys in Ghana), the level of knowledge reported for these methods becomes very low indeed.

To some extent, the low reporting may reflect imperfect research methods. There is no doubt that KAP survey interviewers often feel more embarrassment when asking about these antinatal methods than they do when asking other questions, and survey organizers sometimes reflect the same embarrassment when instructing interviewers. This is compounded by the fact that, especially in the case of withdrawal, there is often no common terminology between interviewers and interviewees, and if accuracy is to be attained, it is necessary to describe in some detail intimate behavior. However, it appears to this writer, after discussions with all KAP researchers in West Africa, that the major problems will remain even should research procedures approach perfection. They are problems of definition and even concept, and most researchers in Africa (and almost certainly elsewhere) have not thought them completely through. When we ask about knowledge of a method of contraception, do we not imply that we mean something that could conceivably be used by either the respondent or other members of the society? If there is no tradition of the use of withdrawal in marriage or if its use were abjured for cultural reasons or reasons of sexual satisfaction, is it in fact something which we may record as a known method? That these are no mere quibbles is shown by the fact that only 35 percent of any of the Lagos female respondents in Morgan's survey claimed knowledge of any one method among withdrawal, abstinence and rhythm.[11]

Morgan's second point is that most surveys probably underrecord knowledge of modern contraceptives too, because the respondents do not know the names, or at least the ones used by the interviewers, for these objects. He quotes (see Chapter 9) cases of persons recognizing contraceptives shown to them after failing to recognize the name or the description. The writer has expressed elsewhere[12] both his recognition of the force of this argument and his apprehension that respondents, faced by an object already described as a contraceptive, may dimly relate it to some earlier very vague knowledge and then claim more extensive knowledge. This seemed to be supported by the fact that Morgan's interviewers, displaying condoms, diaphragms, and orals but not foams or jellies, recorded 17 percent of both females and males as knowing diaphragms, which have usually been discreetly dispensed by doctors and clinics, but only 7 and 6 percent of females and males respectively having knowledge of foams and jellies which have long been available in pharmacies. However, this apprehension does not seem to be supported by a comparison of the Caldwell and Igun survey with the Morgan one, for the former recorded higher knowledge of about the order one might expect in view of the time between the two surveys. Perhaps one can conclude that the concept of condoms or oral contraceptives is so simple that we are ascertaining fairly "hard" facts here. However, a related matter is that of levels of knowledge. There is the problem of specificity: Ohadike reported from his 1964 survey of Lagos that 68 percent of respondents were aware that birth control was possible, while only 48 percent said they knew how, and only 32 percent could describe a method. Gaisie reported that in Accra in 1968–1969 more than seven times as many women had "heard" about various kinds of contraception than actually "knew" about them. This is then an area where the findings are significant only in terms of the exact wording of the

[11] Caldwell, "The Control of Family Size," p. 609.

[12] John C. Caldwell, "Anti-natal Practice in Tropical Africa," *Proceedings of the International Population Conference, London, 1969,* II, (Liège, 1971), p. 1124.

question and the probing and additional information supplied by the interviewer.

Morgan's third point, and one bearing some relation to the above discussion, concerns the practice of contraception. In the recent Lagos surveys Morgan reported much higher past contraceptive use than did Caldwell and Igun. Once again there was close correspondence between level of use of modern contraception (in fact the degree of accuracy in each survey appears to be such that we can obtain a measure of change over the intervening period). But the contrast in use of traditional methods (and hence of the totals of all methods) is huge: 71 percent and 51 percent respectively for Morgan's females and males compared with around 3 percent for each sex recorded by Caldwell and Igun. The latter figures are compatible with findings recorded in other West African surveys, but all may be low, especially in the area of the use of (presumably) largely ineffective folk medicines and talismans.

The major problem here is once again one of definition and concept with regard to contraceptive intent. The two surveys agree not only about the level of use of modern contraception but also apparently about that of withdrawal. The discrepancies are almost entirely explained by disagreement over the inclusion of postnatal abstinence in contraceptive methods. Such abstinence (as is discussed later in the chapter) is very widely observed in tropical Africa, and, if persisted with long enough, undoubtedly has a contraceptive effect which probably is realized by most Africans. But, in the vast majority of cases, the practice is followed primarily because it is felt that not doing so would be flying in the face of taboos which have a sanction somewhere between religion and cleanliness. Morgan's interviewers were told to count women who had observed the taboo as past contraceptors; the interviewers directed by Caldwell and Igun were specifically told not to do so unless the taboo would not have been observed but for its contraceptive effect, and this seems to have been, at least by implication, the intent of most other survey organizers. Perhaps the

truth, even in terms of intent, lies somewhere in between. Kumekpor, reporting in this book on investigations among his own people in Togo, certainly implies that some abstinence, whether it takes the form of prolonging the postnatal taboo beyond the point where the woman believes health or tradition to require it (which may still be less than the period observed by the society in the past) or visiting her relatives for longer than family sentiment may demand, has contraceptive intent. A full measure of this may necessitate separate interview questions on various parts of the period of abstinence or even a day-to-day registration of contraceptive intent. Dow (Chapter 21) claims that only 20 percent of women observing the postnatal taboo acknowledge that it has any contraceptive effect, and inevitably a very much smaller proportion would observe it only or mainly for this purpose.

Morgan's fourth point is the problem of language. He draws attention to dangers of the type faced by his research team when the "best number of children to have" was translated into a form much more akin to "proper number of children to have." Even "best" may carry an implication of social morality and tradition; we may have to concentrate on asking the newly married how many children they actually intend to have. The writer has elsewhere described the difficulties, which are greatest in the most traditional and hence fatalistic sections of society, encountered when asking questions about the future, and the hazards met in making the important distinctions between "hope" and "expect" or "anticipate."[13] These are not merely translation difficulties—although the problems of translation into a dozen or more languages for a country the size of Ghana should not be underestimated—but rather, difficulties of concept. Nor are they mainly the product of differences between European and African ways of looking at questions. The real difficulty is the assumption that people in fully or partly

[13] John C. Caldwell, *Population Growth and Family Change in Africa: The New Urban Elite in Ghana* (Canberra: Australian National University Press, 1968), p. 43.

traditional societies can understand the choices—or indeed realize that there are choices—of the kind open to, and often mandatory upon, the residents of the wealthier and more individualistic societies where such research began. While an awareness of these difficulties must underline every research decision and interpretation in West Africa, it is possible to disagree with Pradervand's pessimistic conclusion that the cultural gap may preclude any meaningful work. The writer has found that most of the decisions faced by the African elite are similar to those he himself has had to face, that a good deal of common ground now exists everywhere with people in urban, cash-cropping, and other areas of considerable economic and social change, and that in the remote subsistence village one sometimes is startled when hearing of family formation problems similar in kind, even if in a different guise, to those met in North America or Europe. The fundamental case for pursuing even the KAP attitudinal questions further in West Africa is that they seek to detect changes in fertility attitudes and practices that are bound up with a whole series of other changes which offer in much of life the possibility of alternative decisions. It is really to the extent that the respondents understand the attitudinal questions that there is a measurable possibility of their fertility patterns changing. The charge that there is little relation between expressed attitudes and likely behavior patterns can really only be tested by time. It may only be a kind of research culture shock; the solution may just be better research techniques, better questions, more communication with respondents about what is being attempted, and, as part of this, the playing of a more major research role by people born in the area.

Morgan's final point queries whether attitudinal data have a role at all. This is almost certainly a valid point in sociological and demographic studies of this type. The Caldwell and Igun study of change over time, socioeconomic condition, and distance from the coast in Nigeria confined itself entirely to the area of knowledge and prac-

tice, and future surveys may profitably concentrate on little more than practice (that is, behavior). But, in our pioneering attempts, over the last eight years, to understand the bases of family formation in West Africa the knowledge and attitudinal questions have yielded extremely instructive information particularly with regard to differentials and change within the societies.

It is true that West African KAP surveys (and all other systems for collecting data, including censuses) need more built-in checks and more subsequent checks.[14] It is equally true that measures of intensity are needed. These can be quite simple and yet point fairly accurately to where the truth lies. In a 1963 survey of the urban elite in Ghana, the addition of a rider saying that adequate contraception might involve the respondents in taking quite a lot of trouble, reduced the proportion who had already assented that they would like to practice contraception from 54 to 23 percent among females and from 65 to 29 percent among males.[15]

Pool has adopted a different position on the issue of obtaining data from all, or nearly all, respondents on many questions, especially those involving retrospective data and KAP-type questions.[16] He has claimed that large numbers of respondents genuinely "don't know" the answers in that they cannot "conceptualize" them and that they represent "a reservoir of uncommitted persons." He appears to imply that other researchers may have gone too far in probing and explaining and may have produced choice where no clear ideas really existed.

The problem is a difficult one and three observations should be made. The first is that, while some researchers might take issue with Pool on factual questions or the most straightforward attitudinal questions, there

[14] The largest-scale check in West Africa was probably the post-enumeration survey carried out on 5 percent of the enumerated population after the 1960 census of Ghana. However, it has taken 11 years to release the results, and such checks, to be effective, must produce findings fairly quickly.
[15] Caldwell, *Population Growth and Family Change*, pp. 138–40.
[16] Pool, in *Studies in Family Planning*.

is a considerable body of similar evidence for the most difficult or hypothetical questions. For instance, Pool recorded for females and males respectively "don't knows" of 39 and 24 percent in answer to the question about moral approval or disapproval of family planning in Accra;[17] for the same question, Ohadike had recorded three years earlier 36 percent for Lagos females, and Trevor four years later a higher proportion still in a northern Nigerian city (Trevor argued that she could have reduced this figure only by first undertaking an educational program).[18] Similarly, among rural females, Pool's 47 percent can be compared with Caldwell's 31 percent (in a household survey where "don't know" was recorded only if no one had an opinion) and the 60 percent found by Kumekpor in Togo.

However, some researchers recorded much lower figures for this question. Morgan in Lagos, Dow throughout Sierra Leone, Gaisie throughout Ghana, Reyna in Chad, and Lambo in the Western State of Nigeria scored persistently below 10 percent, and all claim that this was achieved by sufficient probing and explanation, or by graded multiple questions, or by anthropological techniques of inquiry without leading the respondents or putting new ideas into their heads. Certainly a series of questions can throw additional light on how a situation is viewed. In Ghana the writer probed ideal family size by asking four questions: (1) "If a friend were about to get married, and asked you the best number of children to have, what would you answer?" (2) "How many children do you hope your daughter will have?" (3) "How many more children do you want?" (4) "How many children does your husband/wife think is best?" By the third question the "don't knows" were down to 5 percent of females and 8 percent of males, and the uncertain and nonnumerical answers

to a further 3 and 5 percent respectively. In Gaisie's work in Ghana he attempted to estimate the extent of approval or disapproval of family planning along a seven-degree scale.[19] Social science has much to lose if it dispenses with interview probing, although there is undoubtedly much to be said in West Africa (and elsewhere) for recording responses before probing as well as afterward (and indeed even at intermediate stages).

The third observation is that Pool's findings do not provide very convincing support for the concept that those who "don't know" are those who have not conceptualized the issue. In his survey of Accra, males do not show the steep decline with increasing education that one might anticipate.[20] The suspicion remains that, in many surveys, this category can be eroded further without conceptualizing for the respondents and that it may contain a proportion who have obstinately not tried very hard to answer.

Perhaps the best evidence that nearly all the surveys are measuring something real and measuring it reasonably well is the consistent gradient in response recorded practically universally with movement through a continuum of respondents or environments. This will be observed throughout the rest of this chapter.

Something more should certainly be done to achieve consistency between the various surveys. Perhaps the most serious differences occur over the selection of female respondents. There is a divergence between those surveys which interview all females in a certain age range and those which interview only the "married" ones, a divergence which is particularly serious in the 15–24 age range in which many females, especially in urban or other transitional populations, are still unmarried. One of the problems of interviewing only the "married" is that of defining the condition adequately for all populations. There is greater room for agreeing to differ

[17] Pool, "Ghana: The Attitudes of Urban Males," p. 15.
[18] P. O. Ohadike, "Patterns and Variations in Fertility and Family Formulation: A Study of Urban Africans in Lagos, Nigeria" (Ph.D. thesis held by Department of Demography, Australian National University, Canberra, 1965); Jean Trevor (personal communication).

[19] S. K. Gaisie, *The National Demographic Sample Survey, 1968–69*, III (Legon, 1971), Table 16.
[20] Pool, "Ghana: The Attitudes of Urban Males," p. 13, Table 2, male data.

with regard to age as some researchers wish to investigate the behavior of women of currently reproductive age only, while others, of a more historical bent, wish to include older women as well so as to examine past behavior.

The following general conclusions are probably valid and will serve as a guide for the analysis in this chapter. (1) There are some difficulties in comparing the findings of various researchers because of differences in questions and interviewing methods, but the findings of the same team are very satisfactorily comparable. (2) Comparisons between the work of different teams on contraceptive practice are more likely to be satisfactory for modern than for traditional contraception. (3) Such comparisons may, with qualifications on some questions, be most satisfactory on questions of practice, knowledge, and attitudes in that order.

One should also add that much better data will almost certainly be gathered by continuous surveys. The reasons for this will become clearer after the next section.

## TRADITIONAL LEVELS OF FERTILITY AND FERTILITY RESTRICTION

If all West African fertility had originally been at much the same level, questions about declining fertility and the relative practice of antinatal methods could easily be answered by examining adequate analyses of the level of fertility. This is in fact not possible. The Princeton African project produced total fertility rates (i.e., figures probably close to average family size in West Africa) ranging from under 3.5 in Gabon to over 8.0 in the Ibadan area of West Africa[21] and no one believes that these differences are a result of recent change. Furthermore, the fertility estimates are still subject to a wide margin of error: Estimates for Ghana made at the Princeton Office of Population Research vary

by about one-sixth[22] and those for Western Nigeria are even more debatable.[23]

There is incontestable evidence of very great differences in fertility, often between one ethnic group and another, over short distances (see chapters on Ghana, Sierra Leone, and Cameroon). Some of the explanation may be in terms of nutrition and venereal disease and even innate fecundity. But most of the divergence, at least outside Middle Africa,[24] appears to result from differing social patterns governing sexual relations (age at marriage, length of postnatal taboo, and frequency of other taboos) and to a lesser extent various antinatal practices. Researchers have probably tended to underestimate the number of occasions when sexual relations are forbidden, such as during periods of mourning (see Chapters 34 and 27), and the extent of voluntary separation to avoid pregnancy (Chapter 34). Withdrawal also is known, as are traditional forms of abortion and methods of contraception ranging from use of herbs to beliefs in magic, but these are most likely to be used either in liaisons outside marriage or in attempts to prevent pregnancy during the period of lactation. Abortifacients are quite widely employed with increasing emphasis on such relatively new substances as washing blue or quinine.[25]

We cannot get, through retrospective one-round surveys, an adequate measure of why sexual relations occurred one day but not on another, or during one period and not subsequently, or why sexual relations at one

---

[21] William Brass et al., *The Demography of Tropical Africa* (Princeton, N.J., Princeton University Press, 1968), pp. 157–60.

[22] Cf. Hilary J. Page and Ansley J. Coale, "Fertility and Child Mortality South of the Sahara" in S. H. Ominde and C. N. Ejiogu, eds., *Population Growth and Economic Development in Africa* (London: Heinemann, 1972), p. 62., and Etienne van de Walle (chapter 30 in this book).
[23] See John C. Caldwell and Adenola A. Igun, "An Experiment with Census-type Age Enumeration in Nigeria," *Population Studies*, XXV, 2 (July 1971).
[24] See A. Romaniuk, "Infertility in Tropical Africa," in John C. Caldwell and Chukuku Okonjo, eds., *The Population of Tropical Africa* (London: Longmans, Ltd., and New York: Columbia University Press, 1968), pp. 214–24.
[25] P. O. Olusanya, "Nigeria: Cultural Barriers to Family Planning among the Yorubas," *Studies in Family Planning*, XXXVII (January 1969), 14; Lorimer, Culture and Human Fertility, passim; Caldwell, "Anti-natal Practice," pp. 1–2.

time were thought unlikely to result in conception. There is a great need to measure most of the major KAP indices on a day-to-day basis by means of a daily KAP interview with a very restricted questionnaire over a prolonged period.

## CHANGE AND THE EVIDENCE
## OF THE KAP SURVEYS

Major fertility change will be a product of other nontraditional changes: mortality decline, urbanization, the destruction of the old farming pattern, schooling, and the governmental provision of family planning services. Ultimately the main instrument is likely to be modern contraceptives.

When the writer made the first summary of tropical African KAP surveys in 1968,[26] the emphasis was on the level of KAP indicators. Most of this ground will not be traversed again here. For the first time now, we are in a position to begin estimating change. The reason is that we now possess the results of larger, and usually better, surveys, and that we now have more overlapping work.

Two national KAP sample surveys have now been undertaken: that of Gaisie in Ghana with almost 21,500 respondents and that of Dow in Sierra Leone with close to 6,000 respondents. In addition, in Nigeria, Caldwell and Igun have surveyed a south-north cross-section of Nigeria's society with 8,400 respondents, and Igun, Olusanya, and Acsadi have finished two rounds (with data from only the first yet available) of a continuing annual survey of a rural area with more than 5,000 respondents. These make a very impressive addition to the earlier work: Pool's 6,000 respondents in Ghana and Olusanya's surveys of almost 5,500 in Western Nigeria.

In the savanna, Pool and associates have interviewed nearly 3,000 persons in Niger and over 2,000 in Upper Volta, and Reyna has examined Chad; while on the francophone coast Kumekpor and associates have finished the first work in Togo and Ivory

[26] Caldwell, "The Control of Family Size," pp. 598–619.

Coast. Work on sections of society has expanded from Caldwell's earlier studies in Ghana to those of Okediji in Ibadan, Nigeria, Lambo in the same general area, Trevor in northern Nigeria, and Harrell-Bond in Freetown. Morgan has proceeded further with his Lagos study.

CHANGE OVER TIME. By far the most important measure is change over time; all others merely imply, perhaps sometimes wrongly, the probability of such change. Until the next round of data from Irrua is released by Igun, Olusanya, and Acsadi, we will have no comparison of populations drawn from the same universe by the same researchers using the same questionnaires and techniques. But, in Ghana, we can now compare the earlier work of Pool and Caldwell with the more recent findings of Gaisie; in Lagos we can compare Ohadike, Morgan, and Caldwell and Igun; and we have retrospective cohort data from Caldwell and Igun on Nigeria. All information which appears to be directly comparable in terms of population and form of question is summarized in Table 3.1.

The direction of change is clear and its magnitude is plausible. Every measure shows increases in both the knowledge and practice of family planning with the most rapid changes being in knowledge. This suggests that family planning knowledge is spreading to groups which are not as motivated or as able to practice it. There is some evidence that the use of modern contraception in Lagos by females (the important measure as a considerable proportion of the use by males may be outside marriage and with a relatively smaller total number of females) may be doubling about every five years. If this rate were to be maintained it would be the early 1980s before half of all married women in the city had used modern contraceptives. Even so, Morgan's figures indicate that the current usage is likely to run at only about half the level of all past usage. Thus, if this relationship were also to persist, about a quarter of married women would be employing modern contraceptives regularly by the early

TABLE 3.1

Comparisons of KAP information over time
(Pecentage of respondents in each category of information)

| | | | GHANA Investigator | | | | | NIGERIA Investigator | | |
| Information | Area | Sex | Caldwell, 1963 | Pool, 1965–66 | Gaisie, 1969–70 | Area | Sex | Ohadike, 1964 | Morgan, 1968 | Caldwell/Igun, 1969 |
|---|---|---|---|---|---|---|---|---|---|---|
| Ideal family size fewer than 4 children | Rural: all | F | | 2 | 4 | | | | | |
| | Northern & Upper regions | F | 2 | | 1 | | | | | |
| | Ashanti & Brong-Ahafo regions | F | 2 | | 4 | | | | | |
| | Eastern, Central, Western, & Volta regions | F | 3 | | 6 | | | | | |
| | Metropolitan (Accra) | F | | 6 | 11 | Metropolitan (Lagos) | F | 0 | 10 | |
| Knowledge of any family planning method | Rural: all | F | | 4 | 17 (4)a | | | | | |
| | Metropolitan (Accra) | F | | 11 | 29 (6) | Metropolitan (Lagos) | F | 52 | 98 | |
| Knowledge of any modern method of contraception b | | | | | | Metropolitan (Lagos) | F | 25–38c | 48 | 65 |
| | | | | | | Metropolitan (Lagos) | M | | 64 | 0 |
| Approves of family planning | Rural: all | F | | 22 | 21 | | | | | |
| | Northern & Upper regions | F | 2 | | 1 | | | | | |
| | Ashanti & Brong-Ahafo regions | F | 6 | | 24 | | | | | |
| | Eastern, Central, Western, & Volta regions | F | 24 | | 29 | | | | | |
| | Metropolitan (Accra) | F | | 37 | 63 | Metropolitan (Lagos) | F | 28 | 77 | |
| Interested in knowing about family planning | | | | | | Metropolitan (Lagos) | F | 43 | 77 | |
| Ever used family planning | Rural: all | F | | 3 | 4 | | | | | |
| | Metropolitan (Accra) | F | | 6 | 8 | Metropolitan (Lagos) | F | 8d | 21 | |
| Ever used modern contraception | | | | | | Metropolitan (Lagos) | F | less than 8 | 10 | 12 |
| | | | | | | Metropolitan (Lagos) | M | | 20 | 23 |

SOURCES: See Appendix to this chapter.
a Figures outside brackets are those who had detailed knowledge plus those who had heard of the methods; figures inside the brackets denote detailed knowledge only.
b That is, chemical or appliance methods or orals.
c Ohadike's data are available for separate methods; the lowest figures assume the maximum number of respondents overlapping in knowledge of methods while the maximum figures assume no overlap.
d 8 = ever used all forms of contraception totaled (thus possibly resulting in some double counting).

1980s and half by the early 1990s (a situation which might be altered radically by more massive government intervention than the present supply of family planning facilities in Lagos which is limited but nevertheless on a larger scale than anywhere else in West Africa). Certainly, from the mid-1960s on, family planning practice was growing more rapidly in Lagos than in Accra, partly because the earlier part of the period witnessed an attempt by the Ghana government to proscribe contraception parallel to the beginning of municipal family planning provision in Lagos.[27]

[27] This period has now passed in Ghana (see chapters 8 and 20 in this book).

The data from Ghana suggest movement toward further limiting of fertility in some rural areas, but a movement which has been perhaps solely a feature of the "transitional" rural areas where cash-cropping and the attendant spread of commerce, schooling, and other features of modernization have been important. Change in KAP indicators has been greatest precisely in those rural areas where economic change was greatest in the 1960s, in Ashanti and Brong-Ahafo where cocoa farming was spreading rapidly. It is doubtful if there has been any movement at all in the largely subsistence farming north of the country, almost certainly because there the economic gains from limiting family size are least and infant and child mortality is greatest. The relative lack of incentive to practice family planning in northern Ghana has already been recorded,[28] as has the relative lack of practice, even by those with the necessary knowledge, in the remoter parts of rural Nigeria.[29]

An acceleration during the 1960s in family planning knowledge, intent, and practice in all parts of Nigeria was substantiated by Caldwell and Igun.[30] They showed that, even among women who were over 40 years of age in 1969, and hence over 31 in 1960, and who had learned about family planning and were practicing it by 1969, half did not learn about family planning until the 1960s, and two-thirds neither knew about nor practiced modern contraception until then.

CHANGE WHICH IMPLIES CHANGE OVER TIME. In this section we have much more data and hence can confine the examination to that which is strictly comparable (usually the same investigation). Nearly all the comparisons are of a series of populations from the least to the most traditional and hence imply that we are examining change over time. This, however, is only an assumption, for, at least in theory, some of these differentials may indicate past occurrences while the present may be almost static. Such comparisons can never replace the repeated study of a single population over the years; the latter studies are as yet rare in West Africa and will be increasingly needed.

*Coast-inland or south-north differences.* Until the sixteenth century, outside influence on West Africa came almost exclusively from the north across the caravan routes. Subsequently, with the arrival of European ships on the coast, followed over the centuries by trading forts, ports, Christian missionaries, and associated Western schooling, and ultimately motor transport moving northward

from the ports on new roads, the flow of externally induced social and economic change has been in the opposite direction. For much of West Africa, and for the populations examined in detail in this chapter (that is, from Ivory Coast to Nigeria on the coast and the lands to their north), this is also a south-north movement.

In Table 3.2, cross-sections A, the B group, C, and D are each by the same researchers, although B(ii) and B(iii) were undertaken later than B(i).

It is clear that the inclination to restrict fertility, the ability to do so, and the record of having attempted to do it all decline dramatically with distance from the large West African ports through which ideas and ways of life have been imported as well as goods. This is especially striking if we follow Pool's researchers north from Ghana to Upper Volta and then northeast to Niger. It can also be noted if we proceed from the south-north cross-section of Nigeria and then leap northeast to Chad (where Reyna's questions do not allow direct comparability with Nigeria, but where the findings suggest levels of KAP indicators much below those recorded in northern Nigeria).

However, there are problems about such international comparisons. For instance, accepting the position that the Caldwell and Pool investigations are not directly comparable, it is still highly significant that in Caldwell's work the rural north of Ghana scores levels of about half its rural south, while for the one question which is on the same topic in both research programs (preference for small families) rural Upper Volta and Niger score only one twenty-fifth of the whole rural Ghana level of response in Pool's work. Thus the gradient from the coast steepens as it passes over Ghana's northern border. There appear to be two causes which interact. KAP indicators are lower in ex-French than in ex-British countries partly because of a difference in the past in the attitudes and laws of the metropolitan powers and partly because the African English-French language divide hinders ideas flowing from anglophone Africa

[28] John C. Caldwell, "Fertility Attitudes in Three Economically Contrasting Rural Regions of Ghana," *Economic Development and Cultural Change*, XV, 2 (January 1967), 217–38.
[29] Caldwell and Igun, "Spread of Anti-natal Knowledge and Practice in Nigeria," pp. 22–27.
[30] *Ibid.*

TABLE 3.2

Coastal-inland comparisons

(Percentage of respondents in each category of information)

| Investigator | Cross-section | Country | Year | Sex | Division by Urbanization | Coastal-Inland Division | Favor small families | Ideal Family Size Under 4 | Under 5 | Believe Family Planning a Good Thing |
|---|---|---|---|---|---|---|---|---|---|---|
| Caldwell | A | Ghana | 1963 | Household[a] | Rural | Coastal[b] | 42 (44)[c] | 3 | 21 | 17 |
| | | | | | | Inland[b] | 19 (19)[c] | 2 | 10 | 3 |

| Investigator | Cross-section | Country | Year | Sex | Division by Urbanization | | Favor small families | Has discussed family size with spouse |
|---|---|---|---|---|---|---|---|---|
| Pool | B (i) | Ghana | 1965–66 | F | Rural | | 25 (48)[c] | 13 |
| | (ii) | Upper Volta | 1969 | F | Rural | | 1 (2)[c] | n.a. |
| | (iii) | Niger | 1970 | F | Rural | | 1 (3)[c] | 1 |
| | B (i) | Ghana | 1965–66 | F | Capital[d] | | 49 (71)[c] | 25 |
| | (ii) | Upper Volta | 1969 | F | Capital[d] | | 16 (26)[c] | 10–22[e] |
| | (iii) | Niger | 1969 | F | Capital[d] | | 5 (11)[c] | 7 |

| Investigator | Cross-section | Country | Year | Sex | Division by Urbanization | Coastal-Inland Division | Knowledge of: condoms | orals | Ever Used: condoms | orals | Currently using: condoms | orals |
|---|---|---|---|---|---|---|---|---|---|---|---|---|
| Gaisie[f] | C | Ghana | 1969–70 | F | National[g] | Coastal[b] | 3.6 | 4.4 | 0.2 | 0.5 | 0.1 | 0.1 |
| | | | | | | Inland[b] | 0.7 | 0.5 | 0.004 | 0.004 | 0.00 | 0.00 |

| Investigator | Cross-section | Country | Year | Sex | Division by Urbanization | Coastal-Inland Division | Has discussed family planning with spouse | Knowledge of modern contraception | Knowledge of medical abortion | Ever used modern contraceptives[hf] |
|---|---|---|---|---|---|---|---|---|---|---|
| Caldwell & Igun | D | Nigeria | 1969 | F | Rural[f] | Coastal[i] | 3 | 7 | 5 | 0.4 |
| | | | | | | Inland[i] | 2 | 3 | 3 | 0.0 |
| | | | | F | Urban | Coastal[i] | 13 | 55 | 36 | 7 |
| | | | | | | Inland[i] | 4 | 11 | 12 | 1 |
| | | | | M | Rural[f] | Coastal[i] | 5 | 15 | 20 | 1.0 |
| | | | | | | Inland[i] | 1 | 7 | 5 | 0.4 |
| | | | | M | Urban[j] | Coastal[i] | 11 | 48 | 44 | 14 |
| | | | | | | Inland[i] | 1 | 34 | 20 | 1 |

[a] Answers by a kind of consensus derived from a household discussion.
[b] Coastal = Eastern, Central, Western, Volta, Ashanti, and Brong-Ahafo regions. Inland = Northern and Upper regions.
[c] Figures in brackets are the percentage of those respondents giving a definite reply.
[d] Ghana = Accra; Upper Volta = Ouagadougou; Niger = Niamey.
[e] Figure for main port of Ouagadougou = 22 percent and for Ouagadougou periphery = 10 percent.
[f] Because of small magnitude of responses decimal parts of percentages are shown.
[g] All regions except Accra Capital District.
[h] Chemicals or appliances or oral contraceptives.
[i] Coastal = Western State and Kwara State; Inland = Kano State.
[j] Note that in keeping with the definition in the previous footnote urban excludes Lagos State although it was surveyed and is included in other tables.

and from English-speaking peoples outside Africa (see below for an attempt to measure these phenomena). However, there is also a marked difference in economic development between coastal Ghana with its forest cash crops and minerals and drier, savanna Upper Volta and Niger, relatively inaccessible in terms of trade as well as behavioral innovation. The two latter countries are credited with per capita incomes of around one-fifth of that of the former.[31] Admittedly the gap in neither environment nor income is as great from northern Ghana to Upper Volta, but the former's position as part of the whole Ghanaian nation has meant a considerable

[31] Ghana was estimated at about U.S. $230 in 1966 (United Nations, *Statistical Yearbook, 1967* (New York, 1968). No sound estimates exist from Upper Volta or Niger, but amounts around $50 have been suggested.

flow of taxation moneys and commerce which makes the Ghana-Upper Volta border a real economic divide in spite of little difference in agricultural potential between the land on either side.

In both Ghana and Nigeria the ratio of KAP indicator levels in the southern part of the country to those in the north range from two-to-one or less up to ten-to-one or more, with the greatest differences being precisely in those measures most likely to imply a potential for fertility decline—familiarity with and use of modern contraceptives. That these are as much differences in culture and exposure to social change as in such economic conditions as whether the respondents were farmers or not is shown by the very large coastal-inland differential in Nigeria's urban population. The contrast here is greater than is the urban-rural differential in Ghana. It has a good deal to do with the Moslem traditions of northern Nigeria, but it is not a simple religious contrast, for Moslems make up nearly half the population in the Nigerian coastal areas investigated by Caldwell and Igun and form a substantial minority in northern Ghana (as well as some of the towns of southern Ghana). The difference appears to be explained by the strength of the traditional Islamic society which has endured in Nigeria's north and the extent to which it has held to a relatively low level many Western influences including modern (i.e., non-Koranic) schooling.

*Anglophone-francophone differences.* In West Africa, ex-British colonies are described as anglophone and ex-French and Belgian colonies as francophone. Admittedly, most of the populations of these countries speak either no English or French or have comparatively small vocabularies in the languages. But English and French are the languages of government and most education and are widely spoken in the towns and richer farming areas and universally by the new elite. Undoubtedly nearly everyone will speak the official languages within a few decades.

Until 1969 all data from surveys of antinatal knowledge and practice had derived from anglophone countries.[32] Since then, an effort has been made to secure cross-sectional information from Upper Volta, Niger, and Chad in the savanna and from Togo and Ivory Coast on the coast.[33] As yet comparatively little has been published (outside this book), but in the near future we should have comparative material on an important and largely representative block of contiguous countries, Ivory Coast, Ghana, Togo, Nigeria, Chad, Niger, and Upper Volta, containing almost 100 million people, forming over four-fifths of the population of West Africa as it is usually defined and almost two-thirds as it is defined in this book.

As yet, there is little comparative material. However, in the inland belt of land, we can compare one key question, with almost identical wording, in northern Ghana, Upper Volta, and Chad. This pertains to the disadvantages of the large family, and the results are shown in Table 3.3.

The question in Table 3.3 is perhaps the key one in distinguishing changing attitudes which must occur if fertility decline is ever to take place. By 1963, largely because Ghana's north was at last being invaded by schooling and to a lesser extent by cashcropping and other occupational alternatives to subsistence farming, but partly because new ideas were flowing from the south or being brought back by migrant workers, only a minority of rural residents could no longer see any disadvantages at all in the very large family (most of them, 80 percent of the whole sample, still thought large families were on balance the best thing to have). This was not the case in the francophone countries: In rural areas, and in Upper Volta towns outside the capital, and in Chad even in the capital, fewer than one-tenth felt the large family to have any disadvantages, and even in Upper Volta's capital, this proportion fell no lower than onefifth.

[32] A large survey in Senegal was recorded in Caldwell, "The Control of Family Size," as having taken place in 1967–1968, but the results are still not available.
[33] Data from the Kumekpor study in Ivory Coast were not available when this book went to press.

TABLE 3.3

Percentage distributions of responses on the disadvantages of large families

| Investigator | Country or Region | Year | Sex | Division by Urbanization | Disadvantages of the Large Family | | | |
|---|---|---|---|---|---|---|---|---|
| | | | | | Economic[a] | Social[b] | None or no response | Total |
| Caldwell | Northern Ghana[c] | 1963 | Household | Rural | 57 | 35 | 20 | 112 |
| Pool | Upper Volta | 1969 | Female | Capital (central) | 8 | 7 | 85 | 100 |
| | | | | Capital (periphery) | 6 | 16 | 78 | 100 |
| | | | | Other urban | 3 | 6 | 91 | 100 |
| | | | | Rural | 0 | 1 | 91 | 92 |
| Reyna | Chad | 1969–70 | Female | Capital | 2 | 2 | 96 | 100 |
| | | | | Rural | 3 | 3 | 94 | 100 |

[a] Includes economic difficulties of support, financial difficulties of schooling, and so on.
[b] Includes problems of child rearing, family crowdedness and noise, effect on parents' comfort and health, and so on.
[c] Northern and Upper regions.

The only comparative data we yet possess for coastal francophone areas is a part of the work of Kumekpor in rural southern Togo. There is little yet on family planning practice, and what there is suggests a lower level of modern contraceptives used than in southern Ghana and Nigeria, the result partly perhaps of the lesser availability of contraceptives. However, the attitudinal data resemble those of southern Ghana. In the Togo survey, 26 percent (46 percent of those giving a definite answer) believed family planning to be a good thing and almost two-thirds would like to have known more about it. The first finding compares with Caldwell's 1963 figure for the rural areas of the Eastern, Central, Western and Volta regions of Ghana of 24 (28) percent favoring family planning and of Pool's figure for the whole of rural Ghana of 8 (15) percent in 1965–1966. It is doubtful whether these figures are valid for all anglophone-francophone comparisons for two reasons: First, the Ewes of southern Togo have strong links with the Ewes in Ghana, and, for migrants, Accra is the nearest metropolis, so the penetration of the anglophone African way of life has been very great; second, the Ewes in both Ghana and Togo have probably adapted themselves to modernization more rapidly than most African peoples; Gaisie's findings for Ghana's Volta Region certainly imply this.

*Urban-rural differences.* Data on urban-rural differences are copious and the results unambiguous so Table 3.4 concentrates only on the more significant measures.

Although there is room for debate about relative levels between countries (see below), in all the larger surveys there is very considerable consistency within each survey.

Obviously the urban areas are, as in other matters, the places of innovation in both ideas and practices. The surveys demonstrate that the level of ideas in other urban areas is often similar to that found in the capitals, and that there is a marked contrast between the relatively high levels of these centers and those found in rural areas. However, there is also a marked differential between the capitals and the other urban areas, as well as between the latter and rural areas. The table implies that, as yet, nearly all the use of modern contraceptives is in the towns. The beginning of a desire for no more than four children is also there.

*Social class difference.* The only data by residential areas for whole societies is from the Caldwell and Igun study in Nigeria. In addition we have some information on the current use of modern contraceptives among Ghanaian elite females by occupation of husband and father. Table 3.5 also presents studies done by different investigators (and in one case at different times) in Accra and Sierra Leone, although the comparisons here are obviously much less satisfactory. Only

TABLE 3.4
Differentials in percentages of respondents answering certain questions in the same surveys by capital, other urban and rural divisions

| Investigator | Country (and region) | Year | Sex | Information | Capital | Division Other urban | Rural |
|---|---|---|---|---|---|---|---|
| Caldwell & Igun | Southern Nigeria[a] | 1969 | Female | Has discussed family size with spouse | 13 | 13 | 3 |
| | | | | Knowledge of modern contraception | 65 | 60 | 7 |
| | | | | Ever used modern contraception | 12 | 7 | 0 (0.4) |
| Caldwell & Igun | Southern Nigeria[a] | 1969 | Male | Has discussed family size with spouse | 11 | 11 | 5 |
| | | | | Knowledge of modern contraception | 70 | 48 | 15 |
| | | | | Ever used modern contraception | 23 | 14 | 1 |
| Caldwell & Igun | Northern Nigeria[b] | 1969 | Female | Has discussed family size with spouse | — | 4 | 2 |
| | | | | Knowledge of modern contraception | — | 11 | 3 |
| | | | | Ever used modern contraception | — | 1 | 0 |
| Caldwell & Igun | Northern Nigeria[b] | 1969 | Male | Has discussed family size with spouse | — | 1 | 1 |
| | | | | Knowledge of modern contraception | — | 34 | 7 |
| | | | | Ever used modern contraception | — | 1 | 0 (0.4) |
| Gaisie | Ghana | 1969–70 | Female | Ideal family size under 6 children[c] | 92 | 46 | 25 |
| | | | | Knowledge of: | | | |
| | | | | orals | 5 | 7 | 3 |
| | | | | IUDs | 8 | 5 | 2 |
| | | | | condoms | 7 | 8 | 3 |
| | | | | Ever used:[d] | | | |
| | | | | orals | 2.1 | 1.1 | 0.2 |
| | | | | IUDs | 0.5 | 0.2 | 0.01 |
| | | | | condoms | 0.7 | 0.3 | 0.01 |
| Pool | Ghana | 1965–6 | Female | Ideal family size under 5 children | 32 | — | 17 |
| | | | | Has discussed family size with spouse | 25 | — | 13 |
| | | | | Knowledge of any antinatal practice | 11 | — | 4 |
| | | | | Ever used any antinatal practice | 8 | — | 3 |
| Dow | Sierra Leone | 1969–70 | Female | Ideal family size under 5 children | 54 | 50 | 29 |
| | | | | Has discussed family size with spouse | 52 | 49 | 48 |
| | | | | Knowledge of: | | | |
| | | | | orals | 27 | 14 | 1 |
| | | | | IUDs | 31 | 15 | 1 |
| | | | | condoms | 36 | 33 | 8 |
| | | | | Ever used any antinatal practice | 18 | 12 | 4 |

TABLE 3.4 (*contd.*)

| Investigator | Country (and region) | Year | Sex | Information | Capital | Division Other urban | Rural |
|---|---|---|---|---|---|---|---|
| Pool | Upper Volta | 1969 | Female | Ideal family size under 5 children | 26e | 35 | 22 |
| | | | | Has discussed family size with spouse | 22e | 21 | n.a. |
| Pool | Niger | 1970 | Female | Has discussed family planning with spouse | 7 | — | 1 |
| Reyna | Chad | 1969–70 | Female | Ideal family size under 5 children | 7 | — | 8 |
| | | | | Believes family planning a good thing | 26 | — | 1 |
| | | | | Ever used any antinatal practice | 1 | — | 0 |

a Lagos, Western and Kwara states.
b Kano State.
c Under 6 children employed because data were not tabulated for under 5.
d Because of small numbers, decimal points of percentages are shown.
e Ouagadougou without the peripheral settlement.

Gaisie's comparisons include rural areas, but this may be no serious loss, for the developing social differentials in the Western sense are very much a phenomenon of the cities. As far as possible, Table 3.5 selects question data already used to measure other differentials.

Although the data are limited, their import is quite clear. There are substantial social differentials by residential area, and, within them, by the occupational class as specified both by the present marriage and by the respondents' childhood homes. It is equally clear that these differentials are much greater for family planning practice than they are for attitudes or knowledge. The richer respondents and those in occupationally higher jobs (and, related closely to these characteristics, those with better education) are much more likely to act upon the basis of knowledge, perhaps because their knowledge is more precise, or perhaps because they feel the pressure to limit family size much more strongly and are much more likely to persist with such action. It might also be noted that nearly all the family planning practice attributed to whole urban populations as yet occurs among the relatively small elite fractions of those populations.

*Differences by education.* In West Africa there is often a close correspondence between the extent of a man's education and, at least in urban areas, his social and occupational status and his income. This was particularly true in Nkrumah's Ghana where the government machine was far more important than Ghanaian business enterprises. Because of the copious information on the influence of education, the analysis in Table 3.6 is limited to antinatal practice.

Differentials in the practice of family planning by education or alternatively by literacy or level of knowledge (both perhaps strongly reflecting the fact of education and education levels attained) are strikingly consistent. However, the Sierra Leone study shows that the extent of education does not explain the whole urban-rural differential, and a Nigerian study confirms this.[34]

Ohadike's valuable contribution on the interaction of the education of husband and wife shows that the impact of education on influencing a woman to practice family planning is very much limited by whether her husband has had any education. This is not a severe limitation, as the sex imbalance in African education means that the great majority of educated wives have educated husbands.

[34] Caldwell and Igun, "Spread of Anti-natal Knowledge and Practice in Nigeria," especially p. 27, Table 4.

TABLE 3.5

Differentials in percentages of respondents answering certain questions in the same or comparable surveys by social class

| Investigator | Place | Year | Sex | Information | Social Class | |
|---|---|---|---|---|---|---|
| | | | | | Upper half[a] | Lower half[a] |
| Caldwell & Igun | Lagos | 1969 | F | Has discussed family size with spouse | 20 | 6 |
| | | | | Knowledge of modern contraception | 70 | 60 |
| | | | | Ever used modern contraception | 18 | 7 |
| Caldwell & Igun | Lagos | 1969 | M | Has discussed family size with spouse | 9 | 13 |
| | | | | Knowledge of modern contraception | 77 | 63 |
| | | | | Ever used modern contraception | 42 | 5 |
| Caldwell & Igun | Southern Nigeria other urban[b] | 1969 | F | Has discussed family size with spouse | 24 | 2 |
| | | | | Knowledge of modern contraception | 78 | 33 |
| | | | | Ever used modern contraception | 12 | 2 |
| Caldwell & Igun | Southern Nigeria other urban[b] | 1969 | M | Has discussed family size with spouse | 14 | 9 |
| | | | | Knowledge of modern contraception | 70 | 25 |
| | | | | Ever used modern contraception | 22 | 6 |
| | | | | | Husband white-collar worker[c] | Husband not white-collar worker[c] |
| Caldwell | Ghana urban elite | 1963 | F | Currently using modern contraception | 41 | 23 |
| Caldwell | Ghana urban elite | 1963 | M | Currently using modern contraception | 39 | 25 |
| | | | | | Upper quarter | All |
| Caldwell/Pool | Ghana urban | 1963 1965–6 | F | Ideal family size less than 5 children | 44 | 32 |
| | | | | Has discussed family size with spouse | 67 | 25 |
| | | | | Ever used any antinatal practice | 33 | 8 |
| Caldwell/Pool | Ghana urban | 1963 1965–6 | M | Ideal family size less than 5 children | 33 | 37 |
| | | | | Has discussed family size with spouse | 72 | 21 |
| | | | | | Small elite | All |
| Harrell-Bond/ Dow | Freetown | 1968–9 | M & F | Approval of family planning | 85 | 65 |
| | | | F | Ever used any antinatal practice | 84 | 18 |

[a] By dividing the towns into equal halves by quality of residential areas.
[b] Ibadan, Ile-Ife, Ilorin.
[c] That is, husband in the marriage; for a male respondent this means the respondent himself.

TABLE 3.6

Percentage of respondents claiming antinatal practice by various measures of education

| Investigator | Place | Year | Sex | Information | Highest Level of Education Reached | | | | |
|---|---|---|---|---|---|---|---|---|---|
| | | | | | No schooling | Elementary | Middle school[a] | Secondary | Tertiary[b] |
| Ohadike | Lagos | 1964 | F | Ever used any antinatal practice | 5 | 8 | — | 20 | 71 |
| | | | | Ever used modern contraception | 1 | 3 | — | 17 | 50 |
| Okediji | Ibadan | 1965–6 | F | Ever used any antinatal practice | 11 | 17 | 10 | 36 | 85 |
| | | | | Ever used modern contraception | 0 | 0 | 2 | 27 | 58 |
| Igun, Olusanya, & Acsadi | Irrua (rural Nigeria) | 1970 | F | Ever used any antinatal practice | 2 | 5 | — | 5 | —[c] |
| Caldwell & Igun | Lagos | 1969 | M & F | Ever used modern contraception | 10 | | | 22 | |
| Caldwell & Igun | Southern Nigeria (urban)[d] | 1969 | M & F | Ever used modern contraception | 2 | | | 14 | |
| Caldwell & Igun | Northern Nigeria (urban)[e] | 1969 | M & F | Ever used modern contraception | 0.7[f] | | | 1.3[f] | |
| Caldwell & Igun | Nigeria (rural)[g] | 1969 | M & F | Ever used modern contraception | 0.04[f] | | | 1.9[f] | |
| Dow | Freetown | 1969–70 | F | Ever used any antinatal practice | 12 | | | 29 | |
| Dow | Sierra Leone (other urban) | 1969–70 | F | Ever used any antinatal practice | 9 | | | | 20 |
| Dow | Sierra Leone (rural) | 1969–70 | F | Ever used any antinatal practice | 3 | | | | 16 |
| Caldwell | Ghana (urban elite) | 1963 | F | Ever used any antinatal practice | | 27 | | | 44 |
| | | | | Currently using contraception | | 20 | | | 36 |
| Caldwell | Ghana (urban elite) | 1963 | M | Ever used any antinatal practice | | 24 | | | 41 |
| | | | | Currently using modern contraception | | 20 | | | 36 |

| Investigator | Place | Year | Sex | Information | Joint Education of Husband and Wife | | | |
|---|---|---|---|---|---|---|---|---|
| | | | | | Neither with any education | Wife only with some education | Husband only with some education | Both with some education |
| Ohadike | Lagos | 1964 | F | Ever used modern contraception | 0 | 0 | 2 | 9 |

| Investigator | Place | Year | Sex | Information | Literacy | | Level of Information[h] | |
|---|---|---|---|---|---|---|---|---|
| | | | | | illiterate | literate | low | high |
| Dow | Freetown | 1969–70 | F | Ever used any antinatal practice | 11 | 24 | 10 | 31 |
| Dow | Sierra Leone (other urban) | 1969–70 | F | Ever used any antinatal practice | 8 | 20 | 8 | 23 |
| Dow | Sierra Leone (rural) | 1960–70 | F | Ever used any antinatal practice | 3 | 12 | 3 | 18 |

a In some ex-British colonies, a postprimary or postelementary school for improving educational standards for admission to secondary schools.
b All further education requiring at least some secondary schooling (or incorporating it).
c Numbers too low to be significant.
d Western and Kwara states.
e Kano.
f Decimal parts of percentages are given because of the very small numbers.
g Western, Kwara, and Kano states.
h Measured by a standardized series of questions on various subjects.

Clearly, the use of modern contraception is a measure of the disruption of the traditional agrarian society. Caldwell and Igun showed that, among rural women with no schooling, the use of modern contraception was almost zero (two persons in 2,000 had ever used it on any occasion and both had lived at some stage in a town), although such a generalization might well not hold in the circumstances of an extensive family planning program. In contrast, most urban women with any form of tertiary education had used contraceptives.

*Other factors.* Most other factors appear to play only a minor part. They are often merely reflections of the extent to which the traditional society has been broken.

Efforts to prevent conception among the Ghanaian elite were much more likely both in monogamous marriages and in first marriages.[35] There is, of course, an age and an associated education factor here, but the differentials are sufficiently wide to suggest that couples in monogamous, first marriages are everywhere the most likely contraceptors.

Religion has yielded few differentials that are not plausibly explained by nonreligious factors. Contraception seems to be more likely to be approved and practiced by Protestants, Catholics, and Moslems in that order, but the Protestant-Catholic differences tend to be small and even of no statistical significance, and the Christian-Moslem differential may disappear with standardization for education and urbanization at least in areas which are of mixed religious belief.[36]

There is one other factor, at least partly a measure of the extent to which the traditional society has been modified, which may be of fundamental importance: the level of infant and child mortality. One can show an indisputable correlation between areas of

likely lower than average mortality (towns, rich cash-cropping farmlands) or populations with likely lower mortality (the educated, the rich) and the level of contraceptive practice. Furthermore, interviews with high fertility populations invariably bring up the problem of the survival of sufficient children (see Chapter 10). The relationship between mortality and fertility levels has been much discussed with regard to the European fertility decline.[37] Nevertheless, there are differentials in the towns between the educated and uneducated wider than one might anticipate from mortality differentials alone. Among elite populations, where few children die, educational and occupational differentials in most KAP indicators are still very substantial.[38] Unless the very postulating that a family is large suggests that it has already overcome the mortality problem, it is significant that the West African KAP surveys, taken as a whole, record the insurance against the inroads of high mortality as the fourth most commonly advanced advantage of the large family, after labor productivity, security for the parents in old age and sickness, and prestige, and just ahead of pleasure in children's company. It may of course be that the aim is the first, second, and fifth of these; unrestricted fertility is a mechanism for ensuring getting there over the perils of infant and child mortality; prestige is the enshrinement of success in having attained such a difficult aim.

AN IMBALANCE WHICH MAY BE A MECHANISM FOR CHANGE OVER TIME: DIFFERENCES BY SEX. Throughout this chapter the term antinatal practice has been used more often than family planning. The reason is that a good deal of such practice in West Africa occurs outside marriage, at least partly because of late male marriage, partly because of postnatal taboos on sexual relations, and partly

[35] Caldwell, *Population Growth and Family Change*, p. 135 and elsewhere.

[36] *Ibid.*, pp. 31–33, 84, 179, 183–84; D. Ian Pool in Gavin Jones and Dorothy Nortman, "Roman Catholic Fertility and Family Planning: A Comparative Review of the Research Literature," *Studies in Family Planning*, XXXIV (October 1968), 9, 23; P. O. Ohadike, "A Demographic Note on Marriage, Family and Family Growth in Lagos, Nigeria," in Caldwell and Okonjo, eds., *Population of Tropical Africa*, pp. 390–91.

[37] Gosta Carlsson, "The Decline of Fertility: Innovation or Adjustment Process," *Population Studies*, XX, 2 (November 1966), 149–74. Kingsley Davis, "The Theory of Change and Response in Modern Demographic History," *Population Index*, XXIX, 4 (October 1963), 345–66.

[38] Caldwell, *Population Growth and Family Change*, passim.

because of the sex imbalance among young rural-urban migrants in the cities. This means that more males know of contraception, especially the use of modern contraceptives, and, as Table 3.7 shows, more have practiced it. Nevertheless, this male knowledge and experience may well allow family planning to be imported more rapidly into marriage, as it apparently did in nineteenth-century Europe. At the same time, it does have the effect of making many wives feel that contraception is something respectable married women do not practice; such a view has been recorded quite frequently by nearly every West African survey.

One has to be cautious with comparisons by sex. Experience in many parts of the world has shown that many females do not regard themselves as practicing contraception if their husbands are using a male method such as the condom, and that many males take a similar view when their wives are using diaphragms or oral contraceptives.

Male antinatal practice has been or is currently about double that of females except in two cases. The first is the Ghana urban elite where the levels of all practice are high within the family. The second is Morgan's findings for current use of all practices in Lagos; it is probable here that many more females observing the postnatal taboo on sexual relations agreed that they were practicing a form of family planning than did their husbands.

## FERTILITY CHANGE

The main purpose in analyzing change in the levels of most KAP indicators is to estimate the probability of fertility change or to

TABLE 3.7

Percentage of respondents claiming antinatal practice by sex

| Investigator | Place | Year | Males | Females | Ratio of male percentage to female percentage |
|---|---|---|---|---|---|
| *Ever used any antinatal practice* | | | | | |
| Morgan | Lagos | 1968 | 45 | 21 | 2.1 |
| Caldwell | Ghana urban elite | 1963 | 33 | 33 | 1.0 |
| *Ever used any antinatal practice successfully over a considerable period* | | | | | |
| Caldwell | Ghana urban elite | 1963 | 21 | 22 | 1.0 |
| *Currently using any antinatal practice* | | | | | |
| Morgan | Lagos | 1968 | 8 | 11 | 0.7 |
| *Ever used modern contraception* | | | | | |
| Morgan | Lagos | 1968 | 16 | 6 | 2.7 |
| Caldwell & Igun | Lagos | 1969 | 23 | 12 | 1.9 |
| Caldwell & Igun | Southern Nigeria Other urban | 1969 | 14 | 7 | 2.0 |
| Caldwell & Igun | Southern Nigeria (rural) | 1969 | 1 | 0.4 | —[a] |
| Caldwell & Igun | Northern Nigeria (urban) | 1969 | 1 | 1 | —[a] |
| Caldwell & Igun | Northern Nigeria (rural) | 1969 | 0.4 | 0.0 | —[a] |
| Caldwell | Ghana (urban elite) | 1963 | 27 | 28 | 1.0 |
| *Currently using modern contraceptives* | | | | | |
| Morgan | Lagos | 1968 | 2 | 1 | 2.0 |
| Caldwell | Ghana (urban elite) | 1963 | 27 | 27 | 1.0 |

[a] Ratios not calculated where no percentages exceed 1.

explain fertility change which has already occurred.

It is difficult to explain the fertility differences between most of West Africa's rural populations in terms of recent fertility shifts, but in some cases it may be the right explanation.[39] In some areas there may have been such movements arising from the recent spread of venereal disease rather than change in antinatal practice.[40]

There have been no attempts in West Africa to measure fertility change in terms of varying antinatal practice and few to measure differential fertility by differential antinatal practice. In Caldwell's 1963 study of the urban elite in Ghana an attempt was made to link successively all antinatal practice, the use of modern contraceptives, and claims of successful use of contraception over considerable periods to relatively lower fertility than that of the balance of the respondents.[41] No statistically significant differences could be established (admittedly the sample was small).

The most ambitious attempt has been made by Pool when analyzing his survey of Accra females. The results are summarized in Table 3.8.

The numbers are small and hence one cannot be very dogmatic about conclusions. In each of the important 20–24 and 25–34 age groups those who had ever practiced contraception approximate 50, and about half that number had ever used modern contraception. Nevertheless, in these two age groups there are clear signs of differentials: By 25–34 (admittedly a large age group in which the youngest might be more likely to be contraceptors) fertility falls short of that of those who had never practiced family planning by 12 percent for those who had ever practiced, 18 percent for those who were currently practicing, and 33 percent for those who had ever used modern contra-

TABLE 3.8

Fertility of Accra females, by antinatal practice, 1965–1966

| | Age Group | | | |
|---|---|---|---|---|
| Antinatal Practice | 15–19 | 20–24 | 25–34 | 35+ |
| Never used any practice | | | | |
| Percent of all females in age group | n.a. | n.a. | n.a. | n.a. |
| Average number of live births | 0.5 | 1.5 | 3.3 | 4.9 |
| Ever used any practice | | | | |
| Percent of all females in age group | 17 | 10 | 9 | 5 |
| Average number of live births | 0.1 | 0.7 | 2.9 | 4.9 |
| Currently using any practice | | | | |
| Percent of all females in age group | n.a. | n.a. | n.a. | n.a. |
| Average number of live births | 0.1 | 0.9 | 2.7 | 6.3 |
| Ever used modern contraception[a] | | | | |
| Percent of all females in age group | 10 | 5 | 4 | 2 |
| Average number of live births | 0.1 | 0.4 | 2.2 | 4.9 |
| All females[b] | | | | |
| Total number of respondents | 266 | 462 | 595 | 371 |
| Average number of live births | 0.4 | 1.4 | 3.1 | 4.6 |

SOURCE: D. I. Pool, "Ghana: Fertility Notes," mimeographed (May 1970,) Table XII.
NOTE: n.a. = not available.
a Excludes withdrawal, rhythm, abstention, herbs, etc.
b The categories above do not add to the total because of the exclusions of such groups as the sterile, those abstaining, etc.

ception. If there were any significant group consistently practicing modern contraception, one would expect their fertility to be much lower again, and their completed family size to be within the Western definition of the small family. These differentials were not found in 1965–1966 among the women over 35 years of age, but it might be noted that modern contraceptives were available to an even smaller extent during their younger years. Pool is probably also right in observing that many of them "have obviously adopted family planning because they are unhappy about their high fertility."[42]

Certain other fertility differentials may be

39 See Brass et al., *Demography of Tropical Africa*, for various references to apparent fertility declines in Cameroon, Central African Republic, Zaïre, Gabon, Niger, and Sudan.
40 Romaniuk, "Infertility in Tropical Africa."
41 Caldwell, *Population Growth and Family Change*, pp. 174–76.

42 D. Ian Pool, "Ghana: Fertility Notes," mimeographed (May 1970), p. 21.

partly explained by the differential incidence of antinatal practices. They will be briefly summarized.

In various parts of West Africa there is evidence of urban-rural fertility differentials, but they are not all in the same direction.[43] In Ghana, where by far the most detailed work has been done on the subject,[44] urban fertility is 10–20 percent below that in rural areas, and analyses enable us to determine some of the reasons. Certainly, contraception, and especially modern contraception, is practiced more frequently in the towns. Perhaps a more important explanation is later female marriage in the towns.[45] Pool has also produced data to show that mutual consent marriages (which in towns may describe very loose liaisons) are accompanied by lower fertility and are more frequent in Accra than in rural areas.[46] Morgan (see Chapter 9) and Olusanya[47] have argued that there is an opposing tendency, which at present has the upper hand in Nigeria. Urban fertility tends to rise above rural fertility because of the relaxation of a traditional practice with antinatal effect, namely the postnatal taboo on sexual relationships. Such changes in behavior patterns probably spring from the different attitudinal environment of the towns and the higher frequency of monogamous marriages which do not allow husbands to observe the taboo as easily as do polygynous marriages. Both changes may ultimately lead to greater contraceptive use followed by declining fertility.

There is evidence from Accra of substantial urban fertility differentials by social class with fertility around 14 percent lower in the richer quarter than in the poorer one.[48]

It is probable that all these differentials arise from relatively recent social change and especially from urbanization. The mechanisms for lowering fertility are (1) reduced time of exposure to risk of conception, (2) reduced risk of fertility during exposure, and (3) reduced likelihood of conception leading to birth. The first is at present almost certainly the most important being achieved, probably largely unintentionally, by delayed female marriage in the towns, and, perhaps to some extent, by greater instability of town marriage. However, a reduction in the average length of the postnatal taboo works in the opposite direction. The second is of increasing importance in the larger urban centers especially among the educated and richer people. The evidence appears to be that fertility decline is more likely to result from the spread of modern contraception than from an intensification of traditional methods; withdrawal may well be practiced more in the cities[49] but the evidence to date suggests that it is the users of modern contraceptives who are more efficient in preventing conception. The third is abortion; it is as yet illegal in all West African countries, but the evidence suggests that in such large centers as Lagos and Accra its incidence is rising markedly.

## OVERVIEW OF FAMILY PLANNING AS RECORDED BY KAP SURVEYS

No attempt will be made here to present the kind of detailed analysis undertaken above

[43] A. Romaniuk, "Fertility Trends in Africa," *Proceedings of International Population Conference, London, 1969*, I, pp. 739–50.

[44] Data have been collected in the 1960 census post-enumeration survey and by Caldwell, Pool, and Gaisie; see John C. Caldwell, "Population Change," in Walter Birmingham, I. Neustadt, and E. N. Onaboe, eds., *A Study of Contemporary Ghana*, II, *Some Aspects of Social Structure* (London: George Allen and Unwin; Evanston, Ill.: Northwestern University Press, 1967), pp. 98–103; John C. Caldwell, "Fertility Differentials as Evidence of Incipient Fertility Decline in a Developing Country: The Case of Ghana," *Population Studies*, XXI, 1 (July 1967), 5–7; S. K. Gaisie, *Dynamics of Population Growth in Ghana* (Accra-Tema: Ghana Publishing Corporation, 1969).

[45] Caldwell, "Fertility Differentials as Evidence of Incipient Fertility Decline," pp. 14–16; Caldwell, *Population Growth and Family Change*, pp. 172–74, 2, 11–12.

[46] Pool, "Ghana: Fertility Notes," pp. 1–3.

[47] P. O. Olusanya, "Modernization and the Level of Fertility in Western Nigeria," *Proceedings of the International Population Conference, London, 1969*, I, 812–25.

[48] Caldwell, "Fertility Differentials as Evidence of Incipient Fertility Decline," pp. 7–11; Caldwell, *Population Growth and Family Change*, pp. 190–211.

[49] Caldwell and Igun, "The Spread of Anti-natal Knowledge and Practice," 23–24, 34.

on change. The recorded levels of these indicators are available elsewhere[50] or in various chapters of this book. But some comments should be made on the broad canvas now available from almost 40 surveys. Certain general patterns are clearly visible even if some surveys probed less deeply for information than others.

Some parents in every society can see no advantage in the large family; the numbers are small in the rural savanna, but they increase in urban areas to two-fifths in Lagos and among fairly small urban elites may reach half. The most frequently described advantage of such a family is still the greater assurance the parents have of help in old age and sickness, a response which varies surprisingly little from farm to town or from poor to rich. However, some researchers report respondents observing that the assurance that children will eventually provide such support is declining with modernization. Ironically it is precisely the child who can most successfully enter and rise in the modern sector of the economy who can provide the greatest support. The value placed upon current household and farm help (in contrast to the discounted value in future emergencies) is second in importance but appears to be declining; presumably it was the main value in traditional, subsistence farming society.[51] The prestige of being the parent of a large family is still high, except among the urban elites where the most recent surveys show it (or its expression) falling right away. The only other two replies of any significance both appear to be changing, but probably in opposite directions, with socioeconomic change. The pleasure of children's company, the child as a consumption good, was probably little known, or at least little thought about, in the traditional society. It is still not recorded by surveys of savanna lands and stays at 6 percent or a lower proportion of all responses except in the most advanced cash-cropping areas (for example, in the older parts of Ghana's cocoa belt). But it rises as high as 25 percent in urban surveys and 36 percent in urban elite studies. However, an evaluation of the extent of change with modernization in the degree of favor for the large family as a guarantee against too great inroads by high infant and child mortality is much more difficult, largely apparently because responses vary according to the exact wording of the question and even more according to the extent of probing approved or encouraged by the survey organizers. Yet attitudinal change on this point, reflecting real change in vital levels, may be the key to the spread of contraceptive practice and fertility decline in West Africa. All that can be said is that, when the same researchers asked the questions, and where this response was given by substantial numbers of respondents (Olusanya in Nigeria and Caldwell in Ghana), mortality was a greater worry to rural respondents than to urban or urban elite respondents. But, where the level of all responses to this question was low (Dow in Sierra Leone and Pool in Upper Volta), the opposite was the case.

Nearly all surveys have asked about the disadvantages of the large family, and practically all (the exception being Pool's surveys of Upper Volta) have recorded the great majority of replies in terms of economic disadvantages. Where the same investigator has examined different societies (Caldwell and Gaisie in Ghana, Dow in Sierra Leone, Pool in Upper Volta), it is clear that the greatest economic disadvantages are in the city, followed in order by other urban, advanced cash farming and largely traditional subsistence farming. Where the economic problems were subdivided, they were dominated in urban areas, but not in rural areas, by the difficulties of keeping children at school: For instance, in Pool's survey of Ghana the proportions of female respondents complaining about school costs in contrast to other costs caused by children was 44 and 38 percent respectively in Accra compared with 8 and 36 percent in rural

[50] They are almost completely covered in the following four sources: Caldwell, "The Control of Family Size"; this book; Caldwell and Igun, "The Spread of Antinatal Knowledge and Practice"; S. K. Gaisie, Demographic Sample Survey, 1968–69, III.
[51] Caldwell, "Fertility Attitudes,"

areas. Two other responses are worth noting. The first is that the social problems of the large family—crowdedness, noise, fear of the children becoming delinquents—are not confined to advanced economies. In most surveys such problems were listed by between 10 and 40 percent of all respondents. Nor is it mainly an urban phenomenon: In national surveys of Ghana and Sierra Leone respectively, Gaisie and Dow recorded their highest levels of this response in rural areas. The second is the very low response level citing frequent births as a strain on the mother: above 10 percent in only one survey and, as might be anticipated, even lower among males than females.

Questions on preference for small as against large families are of debatable value in that the size criteria differ even in the same survey. It is, however, of undoubted significance that almost half of the respondents expressing an opinion favored small families in all surveys asking the question in Lagos, Ibadan, and Accra, and that, when the same researcher asked the question, the urban advocates of the small family outweighed the rural ones by very substantial margins in Ghana, Upper Volta, and Niger (Pool).

Where more exact criteria are employed in the questions on ideal family size, the percentage of respondents favoring fewer than four children has not yet risen above 6 percent in any large-scale rural survey,[52] but those favoring fewer than five children is frequently very much above this, reaching 29 percent in Sierra Leone. In towns, those favoring fewer than four children rarely exceed 10 percent, but those favoring fewer than five rise to almost 30 percent in many surveys and soar to over 30 percent in Lagos (Morgan) and Accra (Pool), to 54 percent in Freetown (Dow), and among elites to 40 percent in Caldwell's broad urban category in Ghana and Trevor's more restricted group in northern Nigeria and to 80 percent in Harrell-Bond's restricted Freetown group. The immediate demand for family planning services in West Africa appears to be greatest

[52] This excludes D. I. Pool's preliminary figures for Upper Volta.

in the area of providing assistance to prevent the conception of another child when a family already has four (presumably living) children. Such may soon be the desire of up to a third of the population of the larger towns, and up to a tenth of the population of rural areas (the latter may of course have little strong motivation; if they did, the rural demand for family planning would exceed the urban one in actual numbers, but it would be very diffused). Another measure of such demand is that of persons desiring no more children than they already possess. In national surveys, this reached 19 and 15 percent of the rural population of Ghana and Sierra Leone respectively (Gaisie and Dow), while in large-scale surveys of the more remote rural populations of Upper Volta, Niger, and Irrua (Nigeria) it was recorded as 11, 8, and 2 percent respectively. In contrast it was found to be around 30 percent in urban areas of Sierra Leone by Dow and of Ghana by Gaisie (the level Caldwell had recorded there six years earlier among the urban elite), but levels sank to about 10 percent in Pool's surveys in urban areas of Upper Volta and Niger.

As discussed above, the general question on the knowledge of any type of antinatal practice is not very satisfactory in most surveys. However, it is probably fair to say that Morgan has established that nearly all adults in Lagos have at least heard of a method, and that other investigators have shown that no more than a tenth of the rural population beyond the immediate coast and main cash-cropping areas knows any method which they believe would be usable in their circumstances to restrict their fertility if they wished to do so.

Apart from Dow's work in Sierra Leone and Gaisie's recent survey in Ghana, data on the knowledge of specific antinatal methods are all for urban populations where such levels of knowledge are high enough for satisfactory analysis. What these investigations show about modern contraception is that oral contraceptives, in spite of their relatively recent introduction, have already joined condoms as the most widely known methods. By 1970, probably one-third of the adults of reproductive age in the capitals of anglophone countries knew of each method. (Gaisie's preliminary results for Ghana do not fit into the pattern which appears to be emerging for this question and may well be too low.)

It is possible that some recorded knowledge and use of orals really refers to potions produced by traditional herbalists to be taken orally (Gaisie believes this to be so, and feels that he separated out this group successfully in his Ghana survey). Perhaps half this proportion know of IUDs or of jellies, foams, and diaphragms; the IUD figure is surprisingly high as no governmental IUD programs have yet been developed in the region. Outside the periphery of the towns or in the most advanced cash-cropping area (with inevitably a high overall level of urbanization) the level of knowledge of rural wives is not likely to exceed that found by Dow in Sierra Leone: 8 percent knowing of condoms, and 1 percent each knowing of orals and IUDs. Caldwell and Igun showed that male knowledge of all modern contraception in rural areas might be twice that of females, again because of the greater knowledge of condoms. It appears probable that in the cities more people know of induced abortion than know of any kind of modern contraception; a fact which might be of some importance to governmental family planning programs.

One hesitates to analyze the data on expressed views as to whether family planning is right or wrong, partly because those unfamiliar with it might cautiously answer that it was wrong (in Ghana, Caldwell, and Pool have shown that there is a high correlation between knowing about contraception or using it and approving of it)[53] and partly because any governmental or large-scale information program might easily shift the balance quite dramatically. However, it might be noted that every urban survey in coastal countries since 1968 has produced more "right" than "wrong" responses with

the exception of Gaisie's survey of Ghana where the failure of those approving to form a majority was solely the result of including many smaller urban areas more akin to large villages. Every elite survey at any date has produced very large majorities of approval (even among Catholic respondents). Rural surveys, almost without exception, and the only inland urban data yet available (Reyna from Chad) yield large "wrong" majorities, a clear indication of the urban-rural division in West Africa in matters of behavioral innovation.

A measure of such innovation, and probably a prelude to it in most cases, is the data on discussions between spouses on desired family size. In the larger urban areas of the coast such discussions seem to take place in between one-quarter and one-half of all marriages, but the level falls to one-fifth in Upper Volta and one-fourteenth in Chad. Dow in Sierra Leone and Pool in Ghana have shown that there is some urban-rural differential but it is not nearly as great as one might have expected: The greatest one, capital-rural, was only 8 percent in Sierra Leone (that is, the rural level was 8 percent below the capital). This is evidence that the lower inducement to restrict fertility in rural than urban areas may be a more important factor than lack of knowledge or means, or inadequate communication within the family.

All recent urban surveys show a majority of respondents wanting to know more about family planning (but there are no data from the inland countries) and rural surveys show about a quarter of respondents wanting to do so. Stated willingness to use family planning facilities if provided (only asked in a minority of surveys) runs surprisingly close to the levels quoted above, and far above the level of those replying that they wanted no more children.

When evaluating the impact of family planning, the best measure appears to be the use of modern contraception, for, although the pressures of modernization may well increase the use of traditional methods (especially withdrawal), the evidence suggests that this may be counterbalanced by the relaxation of some traditional prohibitions on

[53] Caldwell, "Fertility Attitudes," p. 232; Pool, "Ghana: Fertility Notes," p. 14.

sexual relations. All data are from Nigeria and Ghana, but fortunately in the former they are relatively plentiful and cover most sections of the population (Okediji, Morgan, Caldwell and Igun, and Lambo). In the female population as a whole, probably about 10–12 percent have used modern contraceptives in the largest cities of Nigeria (Lagos and Ibadan), perhaps half this level in other urban areas, and less than 1 percent in rural areas. In Ghana, the levels are lower, perhaps two-thirds. In Nigeria, male levels are about twice the female ones, the excess largely resulting from use outside marriage, probably with little effect on national fertility but possibly with considerable effect on the spread of information. Levels of past use in the elites (the so-called white-collar classes) are probably already well over 50 percent in Lagos, Ibadan, and Accra. The real problem is the discrepancy between these figures and the probable ones for near continuous use. There is only a small gap among the elites, but, among the population as a whole, current use is probably not over half of past use, thus perhaps yielding a figure for Nigeria of about 5 percent in the cities, $2\frac{1}{2}$ percent in other urban areas, and probably no more than $\frac{1}{4}$ percent in rural areas, perhaps a total of over a hundred thousand women within conjugal unions or less than 1 percent of the total. Three points should be noted. The "other urban" category is very heterogeneous; in large towns in the Lagos-Ibadan area use is probably close to the figure for those cities, while, in remoter and smaller towns, it is probably much closer to the rural figure. In spite of the huge rural population, including the great majority of Nigerians, no more than about one-fifth of the users of modern contraceptives are found there. These figures are for current use; that for near continuous, efficient use is undoubtedly considerably lower. If it were half the level for current use, and if such efficient practice increased interpregnancy intervals from three to six years (thus halving completed family size for this group), then such usage would lower the Nigerian birth rate by one-quarter of one point (per thousand).

The least measurable antinatal practice is induced abortion, partly because of its illegality (which, however, does not appear to be enforced with much vigor in many countries of the region). Morgan's survey in Lagos (see Chapter 9) recorded 1 woman in 50 as stating that she had experienced an abortion, but he attests that abortion is increasingly well known and increasingly regarded as a possible outcome of pregnancy in Lagos; he seems to suggest that the true level could be considerably higher. In the Caldwell and Igun survey one year later,[54] and with a question specifically restricted to medically induced abortion, $4\frac{1}{2}$ percent of Lagos females over 15 years of age agreed that they had experienced such an abortion (and $3\frac{1}{2}$ percent of males agreed that their partners had). Taking the female figure at its face value, and assuming that the abortions were all performed in Lagos, we reach an estimate of about 20,000 abortions. The survey also implies that about 8,000 of these would have been done in the second half of the 1960s and that by 1969 they might well have been running at a level of about 2,500 per year or about 4 percent of births in the city (perhaps depressing the birth rate by two points). Certainly a rise in the proportion of doctors undertaking abortion with little legal harassment, let alone legalization of abortion, could have a significant effect on the Lagos birth rate. It is quite likely that abortion is at present a more effective reducer of fertility in Lagos than is modern contraception. The medically induced abortion rate in Lagos is apparently about ten times that of the rest of the country; and the rest of the population, though perhaps 30 to 40 times as numerous, may not account for much more than thrice the number of abortions. To these figures for revealed abortions may be added an additional one-third in Lagos for nonmedical or "back yard" induced abortions and in the rest of the country a number considerably greater than the medically induced abortions. Such a level of abortion would depress the

[54] Caldwell and Igun, "The Spread of Anti-natal Knowledge and Practice," Table 1.

national birth rate by only a fraction of a point, but it is hard to regard such figures as anything but minimum ones.

## THE MECHANICS OF FAMILY PLANNING CHANGE

It is an assumption of most work on fertility control in developing countries that, while the extent of family planning practice may ultimately depend on economic and possibly social pressures to limit the number of dependents, the degree to which practice moves to its possible limits, and the speed with which it does so, is conditioned by the knowledge of suitable contraceptive practices and by the availability of suitable contraceptives. This is almost certainly the case in West Africa. It is true that nearly everyone may know of some possible antinatal practices, abstaining from sexual relations or withdrawal, but economic pressures, which are sufficient to make an African townsman use a condom or suggest that his wife have an IUD fitted, may not be great enough to encourage sustained and successful use of abstention or withdrawal. Hence, in these circumstances, a knowledge of contraception which is limited to the latter two methods may be insufficient knowledge to realize the potential existing for family planning practice. In West Africa (and elsewhere) one probably should plot family planning change not only in terms of the extent of (1) pressure to limit family size, (2) knowledge of how to do so in terms of acceptable methods, and (3) availability of certain contraceptives, but also (4) the legitimization of the practice of family planning, or of new methods of family planning, in the society. KAP surveys probe into at least the realized factors in the first by asking questions about the advantages and disadvantages of large families, about ideal family size, about whether another child is wanted and so on, and into the second by ascertaining familiarity with a range of contraceptive methods. Except where a major family planning program is under way, too little work has been done on the third; in West Africa practically nothing has been

done, although in Irrua (Nigeria) we may soon have data on the extent of practice as contraception became more available and as its availability became better known. Something is discovered about the fourth by questions on whether family planning is right or wrong. Often, however, such views are not held very firmly, and we need to learn much more about how they vary as the approval of government or local leaders or friends and neighbors for contraception becomes known.

In Nigeria, Caldwell and Igun examined the second and threw some light on the first.[55] From this study it was clear that, even without major governmental intervention in the family planning field (or any official intervention at all beyond Lagos), the knowledge and practice of most antinatal measures had increased much more rapidly than economic and social growth during the preceding decade. This was especially the case in three areas: the discussion of family planning between spouses, knowledge of modern contraception, and the use of modern contraceptives. Each of these probably increased more than fivefold during the 1960s[56] (and by a higher multiple still if absolute numbers, instead of the proportional incidence, are used, thus taking into account population growth); even among women over 40 by the end of the decade (and hence over 30 at its beginning) two-thirds of such knowledge or activities had occurred during this period. What is happening is undoubtedly more than a facet of general development. It is obviously part of a communications "explosion" in family planning in which what is happening in African countries is related to what is happening in other parts of the world: legitimization and availability of contraceptives.

The use of such dramatic terminology should not obscure two facts. First, initial

[55] *Ibid.*

[56] In the Caldwell and Igun survey, more than five times as many respondents had recorded each of these as beginning after 1960 as had done so before that date. However, some women who had begun before 1960 were excluded from the survey by 1969 because of their age.

levels of family planning were so low in West Africa that even by the 1970s they were still low in absolute figures and by world standards. Second, economic and social conditions play an intervening role in determining whether contraceptive knowledge is likely to be turned into contraceptive practice. This is clear from Table 3.9, although it should

also be noted that other factors, such as the availability of contraceptives, also play an intervening role.

The gap between contraceptive knowledge and usage is greatest for farmers, which may go far toward explaining the urban-rural differences; for the north, which is partly explained by Moslem attitudes but which in

TABLE 3.9.
Knowledge and practice of modern contraception in Nigeria, 1969, by subpopulations of respondents[a]

| First Subpopulations | Percentages: A. Knowing of modern contraceptives; B. Having ever used modern contraceptives | | Second Subpopulations | Percentages: A. Knowing of modern contraceptives; B. Having ever used modern contraceptives | | Ratios: Proportions for first subpopulations to proportions for second subpopulations[b] | | Greater likelihood of first subpopulation turning knowledge into practice than second subpopulation (B/A in preceding column) |
|---|---|---|---|---|---|---|---|---|
| Urban | A | 48 | Rural | A | 10 | A | 4.8 | |
| | B | 10 | | B | 1 | B | 15.6 | 3.3 |
| Urban rich (southern Nigeria) | A | 74 | Urban poor (southern Nigeria) | A | 37 | A | 2.0 | |
| | B | 20 | | B | 5 | B | 4.5 | 2.3 |
| Southern urban (southern Nigeria excluding Lagos) | A | 51 | Northern urban (Kano) | A | 22 | A | 2.3 | |
| | B | 11 | | B | 1 | B | 10.5 | 4.6 |
| Southern rural | A | 11 | Northern rural | A | 5 | A | 2.2 | |
| | B | 0.8 | | B | 0.2 | B | 3.5 | 1.6 |
| Having had some schooling | A | 60 | No schooling | A | 11 | A | 5.3 | |
| | B | 12 | | B | 1 | B | 13.5 | 2.5 |
| Nonfarmers | A | 40 | Farmers | A | 10 | A | 4.0 | |
| | B | 8 | | B | 0.5 | B | 16.2 | 4.1 |
| Ever lived in a large town (rural population only) | A | 19 | Never lived in a large town (rural population only) | A | 5 | A | 4.3 | |
| | B | 1 | | B | 0.1 | B | 8.8 | 2.1 |
| Ever employed for wages | A | 38 | Never employed for wages | A | 21 | A | 1.8 | |
| | B | 8 | | B | 2 | B | 2.5 | 1.4 |
| Christian | A | 42 | Moslem | A | 26 | A | 1.6 | |
| | B | 10 | | B | 2 | B | 4.6 | 2.9 |
| Married monogamously (currently married females only) | A | 38 | Married polygamously (currently married females only) | A | 21 | A | 1.8 | |
| | B | 8 | | B | 2 | B | 2.5 | 1.4 |

Source: Derived from John C. Caldwell and Adenola Igun "The Spread of Anti-natal Knowledge and Practice in Nigeria," *Population Studies*, XXIV, 1 (March 1970), p. 26, Table 3.
[a] All respondents, males and females, except where noted.
[b] Ratios before rounding of percentages.

turn partly explains emigrant Moslems in the south; and for the uneducated, which may explain much of the socioeconomic status gap in the towns. It is clear that there is lower motivation to use contraception to limit family size, even given equal knowledge, and possibly contraceptive availability—among farmers, savanna populations, and the urban poor. In at least the first two groups part of the explanation may be economic in that children are more likely to be producers and less likely to be under pressure to go to school; part may be demographic in that infant and child mortality rates are still relatively high. In the last case, at least one factor is that the urban poor inevitably feel smaller pressures to limit family size so as to allow the prolonged education of their children, in contrast to many of the better-off who feel real guilt if their children cannot aspire as adults to the standard of living they have enjoyed during their upbringing. It has been shown in urban Ghana, however, that there is an educational differential in the application of contraceptive knowledge even within the urban elite, evidence that the break with tradition fostered by education renders all kinds of innovational behavior easier.[57]

Investigating the mechanism of the accelerated spread of family planning knowledge in the 1960s, the Caldwell and Igun study showed that the major source of information was still friends (especially of the same sex) and relatives. The mass media are an increasingly important source of information on modern contraception and medical abortion, both as the direct source and more importantly as the originating source before one or more personal intermediaries. At least in Nigeria, news items and "answers to correspondents" are of much more significance than planted informative articles. Females derived more information than did males from medical and family planning workers, the latter being only of importance in 1969 in Lagos.[58]

[57] See Caldwell, *Population Growth and Family Change*, pp. 187–88.
[58] Caldwell and Igun, "The Spread of Anti-natal Knowledge and Practice," pp. 30–33.

## MODELS OF CHANGE AND IMPLICATIONS FOR THE FUTURE

The meaning of the survey results in the present and their implications for the future may not be clear because the surveys have not provided an equal coverage of all areas. The first step in an attempt to draw a picture of the present scene must be to distribute the population into groups exhibiting different levels of family planning knowledge and practice. In Table 3.10 this has been attempted in terms of a three-way division: geographic zones approximating to various distances inland and to progressively smaller changes in the indigenous society as a result of new ideas and ways of life permeating inland from the seaboard-coastal to the mid-inland (where this appears to be a distinct category differentiating the northern parts of coastal countries from the Black Volta to Lake Chad) and finally the inland areas; ecological zones according to the degree of urbanization—centers over 100,000 inhabitants (including capitals with smaller populations because even small centers experience rapid change when they become the seats of government), those with 20,000–100,000 and rural population (including persons living in centers with less than 20,000 inhabitants); linguistic zones (in terms of official language) which reflect both colonial heritages and access by language to cultural influences of the former metropolitian power and other countries speaking the same language—anglophone (ex-British areas plus Liberia) and francophone (ex-French and ex-Belgian areas) plus Guinea-Bissau. Table 3.10 suggests the likely 1970 subdivision of the estimated 140 million people in the region stretching from Mauritania to Zaïre.

When interpreting Table 3.10, it should be realized that all anglophone categories are dominated by Nigeria (five-sixths of the total) and the francophone coastal categories by Zaïre (three-sevenths).

The major feature of the distribution is that three categories each contain about one-quarter of the total population: anglophone coastal rural, francophone coastal rural and,

TABLE 3.10

Distribution of the population of West Africa[a], 1970

(a) *Population (in millions)*[b]

| | Anglophone | | | Francophone[c] | | |
|---|---|---|---|---|---|---|
| | Major urban[d] | Other urban[e] | Rural[f] | Major urban[d] | Other urban[e] | Rural[f] |
| Inland[g] | — | — | — | 0.6 | 0.1 | 18 |
| Mid-inland[h] | 1.1 | 2.5 | 32 | 0.0 | 0.0 | 2 |
| Coastal[i] | 7.0 | 2.4 | 36 | 4.0 | 1.6 | 34 |

(b) *Percentage Distribution of Total Population*[j]

| | Anglophone | | | Francophone[c] | | |
|---|---|---|---|---|---|---|
| | Major urban[d] | Other urban[e] | Rural[f] | Major urban[d] | Other urban[e] | Rural[f] |
| Inland[g] | — | — | — | 0.4 | 0.1 | 12 |
| Mid-inland[h] | 1 | 2 | 23 | 0.0 | 0.0 | 1 |
| Coastal[i] | 5 | 2 | 25 | 3 | 1 | 25 |

[a] Equivalent to the United Nations West Africa and Middle Africa excluding Rwanda, Burundi, and wholly insular countries.
[b] Decimal points shown for urban areas because of small numbers.
[c] Includes Guinea-Bissau where Portuguese is the official language.
[d] All capitals and all other urban centers with more than 100,000 inhabitants.
[e] All urban centers with 20,000–100,000 inhabitants except capitals.
[f] All rural population and population in centers with less than 20,000 inhabitants.
[g] Mauritania (because of climatic zone and cultural closeness to inland countries), Mali, Upper Volta, Niger, and Chad.
[h] Northern Ghana, northern Togo, northern Dahomey, northern Nigeria and northern Cameroon.
[i] Senegal, Gambia, Guinea, Sierra Leone, Guinea-Bissau, Liberia, Ivory Coast, southern Ghana, southern Togo, southern Dahomey, southern Nigeria, southern Cameroon (including the ex-British trusteeship), Equatorial Guinea, Gabon, Central African Republic, (included because of its close relationship to the Peoples Republic of the Congo and Zaïre and its climatic and vegetational separation from the inland and mid-inland zones of the West African lobe), Congo, and Zaïre.
[j] Under half of 1 percent shown to first decimal place.

anglophone mid-inland rural. Of the remaining quarter, a small majority is found in all urban areas and the remainder in inland rural areas. Thus the towns, where contraception is likely to spread fastest and where family planning programs would be most likely to succeed, and the inland savanna, where such changes will be slow and uncertain, together account for only one-quarter of the population. Ultimately, population will be significantly slowed down by what happens in the areas intermediate between these extremes (unless the fertility decline is delayed so long that it occurs only when most West Africans live in towns).

Several other important aspects of the population distribution can be read from the table. One West African in seven lives in a center with more than 20,000 inhabitants, of whom over two-thirds are found in anglophone areas and over half in anglophone coastal areas. One in eleven lives in a capital or other city. Just over two-thirds of the population are in coastal areas and just under two-thirds are in anglophone areas.

After eight years of KAP studies in West Africa, and with some results from almost 40 of them, it would be indefensible not to attempt to sketch an outline of the family planning pattern in West Africa. This, as one of the ultimate aims, has been a major justification of most of them. Such an attempt has been made in Table 3.11 and some of its implications have been spelled out in Table 3.12.

The anglophone half of the tables is probably fairly accurate. There is a mass of data from Nigeria, Ghana, and Sierra Leone, which contain over 98 percent of its population (although admittedly not all parts of Nigeria have been surveyed). Levels have varied somewhat, partly because the countries differ and partly because survey approaches vary, but the tables have attempted a meaningful compromise.

TABLE 3.11

Estimated levels of antinatal knowledge and practice among females of reproductive age in conjugal unions, West Africa, 1970
(Levels are percentages of all females of this type)

| | Anglophone | | | Francophone | | |
|---|---|---|---|---|---|---|
| | Major urban | Other urban | Rural | Major urban | Other urban | Rural |
| *Inland* | | | | | | |
| Have knowledge of modern contraception | | | | 2.5 | 1.75 | 0.5 |
| Have ever used any antinatal practice | | | | 1.0 | 0.5 | 0.0 |
| Have ever used modern contraception | | | | 0.15 | 0.075 | 0.0 |
| Currently using modern contraception | | | | 0.1 | 0.05 | 0.0 |
| Have ever had an induced abortion | | | | 0.2 | 0.2 | 0.1 |
| *Mid-inland* | | | | | | |
| Have knowledge of modern contraception | 10 | 7 | 2.5 | | | 1.25 |
| Have ever used any antinatal practice | 6 | 3 | 1.0 | | | 0.75 |
| Have ever used modern contraception | 1.5 | 0.75 | 0.1 | | | 0.0 |
| Currently using modern contraception | 0.6 | 0.3 | 0.05 | | | 0.0 |
| Have ever had an induced abortion | 0.5 | 0.4 | 0.1 | | | 0.1 |
| *Coastal* | | | | | | |
| Have knowledge of modern contraception | 60 | 40 | 15 | 30 | 20 | 7.5 |
| Have ever used any antinatal practice | 20 | 10 | 5 | 14 | 7 | 3.5 |
| Have ever used modern contraception | 10 | 4 | 1 | 5 | 2 | 0.5 |
| Currently using modern contraception | 5 | 2 | 0.5 | 2.5 | 1 | 0.25 |
| Have ever had an induced abortion | 3 | 1.5 | 0.5 | 2 | 1 | 0.3 |

The francophone half is based on wisps of information on relative levels of KAP indicators in comparable anglophone and francophone areas. KAP surveys have been carried out in Senegal, Ivory Coast, Togo, Upper Volta, Niger, and Chad (countries with 43 percent of the total francophone population) but only for the last four (28 percent of the total francophone population and seven-eighths of that from the inland zone) are any data available. More unhappily, hardly any of the data that are available shed

satisfactory light on the measures of family planning knowledge and practice used here. Thus, for francophone Africa, the tables are little more than a hypothetical design which may be substantiated or replaced by further research.

Practice of an antinatal method means in the tables one specifically employed to prevent conception, and not the following of taboos or traditions based largely on other sanctions. Modern contraception is restricted to chemical or appliance methods or oral pills

TABLE 3.12

Estimated distribution of antinatal knowledge and practice among females of reproductive age in conjugal unions, West Africa, 1970

(a) Total Regional Estimates

| | Number of Females | Percentage of Females |
|---|---|---|
| Have knowledge of modern contraception | 2,641,000 | 11.3 |
| Have ever used any antinatal practice | 964,000 | 4.1 |
| Have ever used modern contraception | 271,000 | 1.2 |
| Currently using modern contraception | 125,000 | 0.5 |
| Have ever had an induced abortion | 115,000 | 0.5 |
| *All eligible females* | 23,333,000 | — |

(b) Regional Distribution of Females Having Knowledge of Modern Contraception (in percent)

| | Anglophone | | | Francophone | | |
|---|---|---|---|---|---|---|
| | Major urban | Other urban | Rural | Major urban | Other urban | Rural |
| Inland | — | — | — | 0.1 | 0.0 | 0.6 |
| Mid-inland | 0.7 | 1.1 | 5.0 | — | — | 0.2 |
| Coastal | 26.5 | 6.1 | 34.0 | 7.6 | 2.0 | 16.1 |

(c) Regional Distribution of Females Ever Having Used Any Antinatal Practice (in percent)

| | Anglophone | | | Francophone | | |
|---|---|---|---|---|---|---|
| | Major urban | Other urban | Rural | Major urban | Other urban | Rural |
| Inland | — | — | — | 0.1 | 0.0 | 0.0 |
| Mid-inland | 1.1 | 1.3 | 5.5 | — | — | 0.2 |
| Coastal | 24.2 | 4.2 | 31.2 | 9.7 | 1.9 | 20.6 |

(d) Regional Distribution of Females Ever Having Used Modern Contraception (in percent)

| | Anglophone | | | Francophone | | |
|---|---|---|---|---|---|---|
| | Major urban | Other urban | Rural | Major urban | Other urban | Rural |
| Inland | — | — | — | 0.1 | 0.0 | 0.0 |
| Mid-inland | 1.0 | 1.2 | 2.0 | — | — | 0.0 |
| Coastal | 43.0 | 5.9 | 22.1 | 12.3 | 2.0 | 10.5 |

(e) Regional Distribution of Females Currently Using Modern Contraception (in percent)

| | Anglophone | | | Francophone | | |
|---|---|---|---|---|---|---|
| | Major urban | Other urban | Rural | Major urban | Other urban | Rural |
| Inland | — | — | — | 0.1 | 0.0 | 0.0 |
| Mid-inland | 0.9 | 1.0 | 2.1 | — | — | 0.0 |
| Coastal | 46.7 | 6.4 | 24.0 | 13.4 | 2.1 | 3.3 |

(f) Regional Distribution of Females Ever Having Had an Induced Abortion (in percent)

| | Anglophone | | | Francophone | | |
|---|---|---|---|---|---|---|
| | Major urban | Other urban | Rural | Major urban | Other urban | Rural |
| Inland | — | — | — | 0.2 | 0.0 | 2.6 |
| Mid-inland | 0.8 | 1.4 | 4.6 | — | — | 0.3 |
| Coastal | 30.3 | 5.2 | 26.0 | 11.6 | 2.3 | 14.7 |

and does not include withdrawal or rhythm. The most reliable figures are probably those on the current use of modern contraception. The most debatable are those on abortion; such questions were asked in fewer surveys and the replies are probably far from satisfactory. The level of abortion, especially without medical assistance, may be much higher than the table suggests.

The estimates are for women of reproductive age in conjugal unions and thus aim at measuring the level of knowledge and practice which may affect family formation. As with the surveys, they cover only the population of African origin. Survey data have been projected to give 1970 estimates.

Some of the figures in Table 3.11 are obviously based on assumed gradients from anglophone to francophone and from coastal to inland areas. All assumptions have some research basis. There is, for instance, a steeper coast-inland decline in knowledge and use of modern contraceptives than of "any antinatal practice" or of "all abortion" (but not of medical abortion). In Table 3.12 these proportions have been applied to the estimated 23⅓ million women in West Africa who, in 1970, were of reproductive age and in a conjugal union.

The estimates agree that family planning levels in West Africa are low by the standards of any other continent. In only one-ninth of marriages could modern contraception be practiced if the wife's knowledge had to be depended upon, although scattered survey data suggest it is possible that this fraction would rise to one-fifth if it were to depend on the husband's knowledge and perhaps to one-quarter if it were to depend on either spouse having sufficient knowledge. However, such practice has been tried in only 1 marriage in about 85 (there is necessarily no sex differential here although in addition a considerable number of husbands may have participated in extramarital sexual relations where contraception was employed) and is being tried at any given time in about 1 in 185.

Although all surveys give the impression (correctly) that antinatal practices are to a very considerable degree an urban phenomenon, it might be noted that over half the use of any antinatal practice and over half the knowledge of modern contraception has been in rural areas. The reason is that six-sevenths of the population lives in such areas. Even with this predominance, little more than one-third of the past modern contraceptive practice can be attributed to the rural population and not much more than one-quarter of continuing practice. However, such contrasts do highlight the problems of large-scale family planning programs: Contraceptive-use levels can often be raised quickly and cheaply in the major urban areas, but a rise in level of only one-tenth as much in rural areas can mean as many additional contraceptors.

The table underlines the significance of the coast: 92.3 percent of all knowledge of modern contraceptives is there, as well as 95.7 percent of all past use of contraceptives and 95.9 percent of all current use. The two-fifths of the region's population that lives further inland in the savanna lands of the great West African lobe has played little part in the advent of modern contraception and may not have a much greater part to play in the years immediately ahead.

It also underlines the significance of anglophone Africa, which with two-thirds of the total population, probably accounts for almost three-quarters of past practice and over four-fifths of current practice.

It is salutary to realize that almost half of all continuing modern contraceptive practice probably occurs in the major urban areas of anglophone coastal West Africa (Lagos, Ibadan, Abeokuta, Accra, Tema, Takoradi, Kumasi, Freetown, Monrovia, Bathurst, and so on) which contain only one-twentieth of the region's population.

Finally, where do the major gaps between potentiality and actuality lie? Of almost 2½ million women who know about at least one form of modern contraception but have never used any method, three-fifths are found in rural areas; of those women apparently having sufficient knowledge, only 15 percent of urban women and 7 percent of rural women have ever attempted to employ it at all. But, of the 150,000 who have used modern contraceptives but are not continuing to do so, only one-third are in rural areas, a similar fraction to that of all past users who are found there.

## THE FUTURE

Our knowledge of tropical African trends in both natural increase and contraceptive use is too poor to allow any real projections to be made, but we can sketch in a possible picture.

Accepting the United Nations' medium projection for 1980,[59] total regional population growth in the decade is likely to be around 40 million or almost 30 percent, taking the total figure from about 140 to 180 million. This will be far from even, largely because the more advanced areas tend to enjoy lower mortality and to attract more immigrants. Employing United Nations' and other more recent data (some from chapters in this book), a reasonable conclusion, in terms of the population divisions we have been using, would be that in anglophone countries coastal populations will grow by about 38 percent and mid-inland populations by 30 percent, while in francophone countries the increases will be about 29 percent in the coastal belt, 22 percent in the mid-inland one, and 13 percent in the inland one. Thus, if propensity to practice contraception increases with the surplus of births over deaths, then the areas of most change are likely to be the coastal belt and the anglophone mid-inland one (northern Ghana and northern Nigeria). For much the same reason, these are also the areas where the success of governmental family planning programs would be most important.

The same period will witness a continuation of rapid urbanization. If we accept the most recent United Nations' estimates for the increase of population in African centers with more than 20,000 inhabitants,[60] and assume that they hold for the West African region (as defined in this book), the number of people in such centers will climb by almost three-fifths during the decade—from 13.6 percent of the total population to 17.1 percent. In contrast, rural population will increase by less than one-quarter. Because of the marked urban-rural differential in contraceptive practice, this is an important shift in population balance. Nevertheless, it should be realized that, in absolute numbers, urban population will rise by only about $11\frac{1}{2}$ million during the 1970s (to almost 31 million) while rural population will increase by about 27 million (to almost 150 million).

Projecting these rates further forward (which may completely fail to take into account quite dramatic social, economic, and political changes), it is not until the last decade of the century that urban population increase in the region will be as numerically great as rural increase and not until a third of the way through the next century that the number of inhabitants of urban areas will exceed those of rural areas.

In the longer run, any substantial fertility decline in the region will probably be brought about by modern contraception and abortion. The spread of the latter is the more difficult to project, partly because the role of government is less predictable, and hence the detailed examination here will be confined to contraception. We have somewhat debatable evidence from Lagos and Ghana on trends in modern contraceptive use: on past and current use in the former and on past use only in the latter. In Lagos, the proportion of married females either using or having used modern contraception appears to have been doubling every five years; in Ghana (even in Accra) doubling seems to have taken nearer to ten years. In Table 3.13 the period for doubling in the region, without any further governmental intervention in the family planning field, is taken to be slightly under eight years, with a multiplication of the

[59] United Nations Economic Commission for Africa, *Demographic Handbook for Africa* (Addis Ababa, 1968), pp. 118–21. This is a revised version of United Nations, *World Population Prospects as Assessed in 1963* (New York, 1966).

[60] United Nations, *Growth of the World's Urban and Rural Population, 1920–2000* (New York, 1969), pp. 55–69.

TABLE 3.13

Projected 1970–1980 changes in past and current use of modern contraceptives among women of reproductive age in conjugal unions, West Africa

(a) Estimated 1980 Levels of Contraceptive Use (percent)

| | Anglophone | | Francophone | |
|---|---|---|---|---|
| | Urban | Rural | Urban | Rural |
| **Inland** | | | | |
| *Have ever used modern contraception:* | | | | |
| No more government intervention | | | 0.3 | 0.05 |
| Family planning programs | | | 0.6 | 0.1 |
| Crash programs | | | 1.0 | 0.15 |
| *Currently using modern contraception:* | | | | |
| No more government intervention | | | 0.2 | 0.03 |
| Family planning programs | | | 0.5 | 0.06 |
| Crash programs | | | 0.7 | 0.1 |
| **Mid-inland** | | | | |
| *Have ever used modern contraception:* | | | | |
| No more government intervention | 2.3 | 0.2 | | 0.1 |
| Family planning programs | 4.7 | 0.5 | | 0.2 |
| Crash programs | 7.0 | 0.7 | | 0.3 |
| *Currently using modern contraception:* | | | | |
| No more government intervention | 0.9 | 0.1 | | 0.0 |
| Family planning programs | 1.8 | 0.2 | | 0.1 |
| Crash programs | 2.8 | 0.3 | | 0.2 |
| **Coastal** | | | | |
| *Have ever used modern contraception:* | | | | |
| No more government intervention | 19.5 | 2.3 | 9.5 | 1.15 |
| Family planning programs | 39.0 | 4.7 | 19.0 | 2.3 |
| Crash programs | 59.5 | 7.0 | 29.0 | 3.5 |
| *Currently using modern contraception:* | | | | |
| No more government intervention | 10.0 | 1.15 | 4.8 | 0.6 |
| Family planning programs | 20.0 | 2.3 | 9.6 | 1.2 |
| Crash programs | 29.4 | 3.5 | 14.7 | 1.8 |

(b) Total Regional Levels

| | 1970 Number (thousands) | Per-cent | 1980 Number (thousands) | Per-cent | 1970–1980 Multiplication of numbers | change Increase in proportion (in percent) |
|---|---|---|---|---|---|---|
| *No government intervention* | | | | | | |
| Past use | 271 | 1.2 | 930 | 3.0 | 3.4 | +1.8 |
| Current use | 125 | 0.5 | 480 | 1.6 | 3.8 | +1.1 |
| *Family planning programs* | | | | | | |
| Past use | — | — | 1,860 | 6.1 | 6.9 | +4.9 |
| Current use | — | — | 960 | 3.1 | 7.7 | +2.6 |
| *Crash programs* | | | | | | |
| Past use | — | — | 2,790 | 9.1 | 10.3 | +7.9 |
| Current use | — | — | 1,440 | 4.7 | 11.5 | +4.2 |

(c) 1980 Percentage Distribution of Contraceptive Use in the Region[a]

| | Anglophone | | Francophone | |
|---|---|---|---|---|
| | Urban | Rural | Urban | Rural |
| Inland | — | — | 0.1 | 0.2 |
| Mid-inland | 2.4 | 1.5 | — | 0.04 |
| Coastal | 52 | 20 | 15 | 9 |

TABLE 3.13 *(contd.)*

(d) 1970–1980 Increase in the Numbers Currently Using Modern Contraception According to Government Policy (in thousands)

| | Anglophone | | Francophone | |
|---|---|---|---|---|
| *Inland* | Urban | Rural | Urban | Rural |
| No further govt. intervention | — | — | 0.2 | 1.0 |
| Govt. family planning programs | — | — | 0.7 | 2.0 |
| Crash programs | — | — | 1.1 | 3.3 |
| *Mid-Inland* | | | | |
| No further govt. intervention | 4.3 | 10.8 | — | 0.4 |
| Govt. family planning programs | 14.9 | 31.7 | — | 0.8 |
| Crash programs | 24.4 | 44.6 | — | 1.2 |
| *Coastal* | | | | |
| No further govt. intervention | 183 | 60 | 58 | 38 |
| Govt. family planning programs | 430 | 152 | 123 | 80 |
| Crash programs | 668 | 249 | 201 | 122 |

[a] The distribution presented here was calculated from past users of modern contraceptives without further governmental intervention, but the 1980 distributions of current users and distributions for both measures according to the scale of governmental intervention are almost identical. In this and the following distribution, decimal parts of thousands are shown for the inland and mid-inland zones because of the smaller numbers.

proportion of users of $2\frac{1}{3}$ times in a decade. The application of a constant fraction to all parts of the region might seem to be in conflict with the evidence on urban-rural and regional differentials in KAP indicators. This is not necessarily so: The initial lower proportions practicing modern contraception in rural areas and in inland ones means smaller increments there in the number of contraceptors even with constant rates of increase; and there is evidence elsewhere of precisely such a pattern of fertility decline (and, by implication, of the application of antinatal measures) from initially different levels.[61] A more difficult problem for the 1970s is estimating the impact of government family planning programs which will inevitably appear in many, if not most, of the countries during the decade (Ghana had moved this way in 1969 and Nigeria in 1970; see Chapter 8). Here, the rather simple assumption is made that the widespread occurrence of such programs could double the "natural" rate of contraception spread and that the widespread adoption of massive "crash" programs (of the Korean and Taiwan types) could multiply it by three. It may well be that the region as a whole may not see "crash" programs before the 1980s, although Ghana, Lagos, and one or two other areas could prove exceptions even to this prediction.

[61] Carlsson, "Decline of Fertility," pp. 149–74.

Even in the absence of further governmental intervention in the family planning field, it is likely that the number of women practicing family planning will multiply by about $3\frac{1}{2}$ times during the 1970s so that by the end of the decade almost a million wives will have used modern contraceptives at some time within marriage and almost half a million will be using them at any one time. Admittedly these figures represent only about 1 wife in 33 and 1 in 64 respectively. One can explain three-quarters of the increase in the number of contraceptors by the assumed rise in the proportion of women using contraception in either urban or rural areas, one-sixth by the increase in the number of women of this age because of past population growth, and one-sixteenth by the change in the urban-rural population balance. Leaving the effect of population growth aside and concentrating only on the rise in the proportion of all women practicing contraception, less than one-tenth of the increase is to be explained by intensified urbanization. The contribution to the increase in the rate of contraceptive use by wives remaining in a given residence zone to the rise in the proportion of all wives using contraception is, of course, higher again in the projections postulating increasing governmental involvement, accounting for all but 16 and 8 percent of the rise in the projected proportions in the widespread governmental programs and the crash programs projections respectively.

The projections do show the dimensions and the nature of possible family planning change. Applying the postulated increases in proportions of wives practicing contraception to the 1970 levels set out in Table 3.11 we observe that the 1980 levels for "ever used" and "currently using" modern contraception in the area with the highest levels (anglophone, coastal, major urban) are respectively $23\frac{1}{3}$ and $11\frac{2}{3}$ percent where there is no further government intervention, $46\frac{2}{3}$ and $23\frac{1}{3}$ percent with major government family planning programs, and 70 and 35 percent with crash programs. It is far from impossible that, with government assistance, the intermediate figures can be reached within a decade in the larger towns of southern Nigeria and Ghana (where the great majority of this population is to be found) and perhaps also in Sierra Leone, Gambia, and Liberia. The attainment of such levels would inevitably be possible only if higher levels still were achieved in cities such as Lagos and Accra, perhaps 35 percent of wives as current contraceptors in the case of the intermediate projection and 50 percent in the crash program projection. On the other end of the scale, the projections imply continuing very low levels of contraceptive use at the end of the decade in the poor inland savanna countries (Mauritania, Mali, Upper Volta, Niger, and Chad) where stubbornly high infant and child mortality rates (see Chapter 4) sustain high fertility attitudes. Even with widespread family planning programs in the region by 1980 (but incorporating the assumption that these countries are the ones likely to adopt them last), it is postulated that the proportion of wives currently practicing modern contraception in the inland zone will be no more than 1 in 200 in the towns and one in 1,667 in rural areas. Nor are much higher levels assumed to be likely in the francophone mid-inland zone. However, it is argued that the anglophone, mid-inland, urban areas (e.g., towns like Tamale and Bolgatanga in Ghana, and Kano, Zaria, Kaduna, Jos, and possibly Maiduguri in Nigeria) will display a considerably higher level of contraceptive use, with, by 1980, past use reaching 2.3, 4.7, and 7.0 percent respectively according to the three projections and current use 0.9, 1.8, and 2.8 percent. The justification for this is the pattern revealed for the 1960s by surveys in Ghana and Nigeria, and the fact that both areas belong to countries which have already decided upon governmental family planning programs or have forecast such decisions.

Two other points arise. First, are the projections probable in terms of what we know about demographic, social, and economic change in the various zones? Second, do the projections indicate the likelihood of sufficient fertility change to encourage governments to persist with the family planning programs necessary to achieve two of them?

The three types of change that most predicate the spread of family planning are probably a significant proportion of urban population, relatively low infant and child mortality levels, and relatively high educational levels in the community. Part (d) of Table 3.13 shows that about 95 percent of the increase in current contraceptors up until 1980 is projected for the coastal zone (95.3 for the no further intervention projection and 94.3 for the crash projection), around two-thirds for the urban areas of the coastal zone (67.8 and 66.0 percent for the two extreme projections) and over half (51.2 and 51.8 percent respectively) for the urban centers of the anglophone coast. Even the third of the increase outside the urban areas would come very largely from the smaller towns and, to a lesser degree, the villages of the advanced cash-cropping areas of the coast; to take perhaps an extreme example, much of the population of the old cocoa belt of Ghana enjoys health provision and feels the increasing pressure exerted by the large family of surviving children of much the same order as do the large towns.[62] There are data on the relative metropolitan and national death rates for four coastal zone countries, Senegal (also analyzed by Cantrelle in

[62] Caldwell, "Fertility Attitudes," pp. 217–38.

Chapter 4), Guinea, Dahomey, and Zaïre,[63] which show metropolitan rates varying between 39 and 71 percent of the national ones. Some of this striking difference must be explained by the urban age structure and perhaps by the choice of the right place to die, but there is no doubt that substantial mortality differentials also play a role. In Ghana, data are now available from the 1960 census postenumeration survey on child survival by residence; although the definition of urban population (the inhabitants of centers with population down to 5,000 instead of the 20,000 used in this chapter) tends to blur the differentials, it is noteworthy that in rural families the proportion of children who had died was almost a third higher than in urban areas.[64] It seems probable that in the major urban areas of the coast, child survival is already as high as it was in many Western countries when fertility rates had begun to fall steeply (the last decade of the nineteenth century), and, significantly, from a lower initial level; and in the "other urban" areas of substantial sections of the coast it is already as high as it was in the West when the first fertility falls became apparent.

The spread of education affects fertility control in two ways: First, parents may find large families more distressing because of the extra pressures of supporting school children, for education may cost money and may withdraw children from productive work; and second, educated parents may break with traditional high-fertility views. The impact of increased schooling has been felt widely in West Africa, partly because it has come so suddenly: In Nigeria, Zaïre, and Ghana, which are the key countries in terms of regional fertility change in that they contain two-thirds of the regional population and over three-quarters of that of the important coastal plus anglophone mid-inland zones, the UNESCO *adjusted school enrollment*

*ratio* approximately doubled in the first two between 1950 and 1965 and rose almost five times in the latter.[65] By 1965 most children in Zaïre and Ghana were experiencing some schooling and this was probably also true in coastal-zone Nigeria. By the latter date, the great majority of children in the urban areas of the coastal zone, taken as a whole, were probably obtaining at least some schooling. The full impact of education on adults has not yet been felt, although this apparent generational delay may not be as long as might first appear to be the case. Although the average age at childbearing of West African women is probably 27–28 years,[66] the age structure of the population means that almost half of all births, and at least half of all conceptions, are to women under 25. By 1965 a majority of Ghanaian girls, a third of girls in Zaïre, and a quarter of Nigerian girls (probably well over a third in the coastal zone) were receiving some schooling; these fractions will probably apply to the majority of women conceiving (or who would conceive but for contraception) in these countries by 1980. The education of women (and to some degree of either parent) probably also exerts an indirect influence on encouraging antinatal practice. The 1960 Ghana census postenumeration survey yielded data showing much higher levels of child survival where the mother had been to school. Even where the mother had only been to elementary school, the level of child survival above that of the uneducated mother was 27 percent in urban areas and 19 percent in rural ones.[67] Child

[63] United Nations Economic Commission for Africa, *Demographic Handbook*, pp. 81–82. This omits the Central African Republic which is included here in the coastal category only as a marginal case.
[64] Gaisie, *Dynamics of Population Growth.*

[65] These data are from Dorothy Nortman, "Population and Family Planning Programmes: A Factbook," *Reports on Population/Family Planning*, Population Council and the International Institute for the Study of Human Reproduction, Columbia University, 2 (July 1970), pp. 21–22. It is a rough indicator of the proportion attending school. See UNESCO *Statistical Yearbook, 1967* (Paris, 1968), p. 72.
[66] Page and Coale, "Estimates of Fertility and Child Mortality," pp. 57–60.
[67] Gaisie, *Dynamics of Population Growth;* John C. Caldwell, "The Demographic Implications of the Extension of Education in a Developing Country: Ghana," in *Symposium on Population and Socio-economic Development in Ghana, Ghana Population Studies,* 2 (Legon, 1969), pp. 98–99.

survival in families where the mother had enjoyed some elementary education was apparently already near the level of England and Wales just prior to World War I when birth rates there had already dropped below 25 per thousand. Education lessens the mothers' fatalistic acceptance of child ill health and renders mothers more capable of using modern facilities (even at such a level as being willing to argue with a nurse for immediate treatment for a sick child).

It is difficult to hazard even a guess at the effect on fertility levels of the projected increases in contraceptive use. For the whole region, the three projections suggest 1980 levels of current modern contraceptive use within marriage of 1.6, 3.1, and 4.6 percent respectively. If one were to assume that half as many marriages again will normally be using contraceptives, but are failing to do so at any given time because of pregnancy and its aftermath, temporary separation of spouses, and so on (thus inflating the figures by 50 percent), but were then to assume further that only half of all usual contraceptors represented couples consistently and successfully using contraceptives over long periods (thus halving the rates), the proportion of strongly motivated, successful users could be put at 1.2, 2.4, and 3.6 percent respectively for the three projections. If these couples (a woman and her conjugal partner, since neither formal marriage nor monogamy is necessarily implied by this usage) halve their fertility (and hence attain a completed family size of about three children), this would reduce regional fertility between 1970 and 1980 by about 0.6, 1.2, and 1.8 percent respectively, or by about 0.3, 0.6, and 0.9 crude birth rate points. However, the actual falls would probably be well above this. The declines in fertility occasioned by rises in modern contraceptive usage might well be paralleled by equal declines caused by a greater incidence of abortion and a greater, but less effective, use of modern contraception (that is, the remainder of the current users and the other past users) as well as traditional methods. Either the social change or the attitudinal changes resulting from govern-

mental family planning programs or the combination of both which led to the rising rate of contraceptive use would almost certainly affect all antinatal practice. Thus we might anticipate triple the change suggested above: reduction in fertility according to each of the three projections of 1.8, 3.6, and 5.4 percent or about 1, 2, and 3 birth rate points, which in 1980 would mean 180,000, 360,000, or 540,000 fewer births.

These changes would certainly not be spectacular, although they might be the necessary precursors of greater change to follow. They would, however, vary very much between different parts of the region and would be likely to be greatest precisely where governments would be most likely to introduce expensive programs. For instance, employing all the assumptions used above, fertility would decline in the francophone coastal urban areas by $12\frac{1}{2}$, 25, and $37\frac{1}{2}$ percent respectively by 1980, which would be sufficient to lower an initial birth rate of 50 per thousand to approximately 44, 38, and 31 respectively (birth rates might not actually be as low as this because rural-urban migration produces an abnormally large proportion of persons of reproductive age in the large towns). In anglophone coastal urban areas the projected falls would be 25, 50, and 75 percent respectively, yielding birth rates from an original 50 of 38, 25, and 13; this suggests that very substantial falls could be achieved in such centers as Lagos, Accra, and Freetown by providing comprehensive family planning facilities without the kind of high-pressure salesmanship of the crash program (in fact such a program might well achieve little more, certainly not birth rates of 13).

The projections, like many other projections, are unlikely to be exact, or even reasonably reliable, charts of the future. But they do show the parameters of the problems and the relationships they portray are probably reasonably accurate indicators upon which to base policy decisions. It is probably a fair conclusion then that family planning programs would achieve sufficiently obvious success by 1980 in coastal countries to ensure government continuation of programs and to guarantee a real return on investment. The most obvious successes would be in the towns. This would probably be welcomed, as per capita expenditure by West African governments is much greater on urban population (especially on increments to urban population) than on rural population. In inland countries, such programs might well be justifiable in terms of maternal and child health, and possibly even on economic grounds, but during the next decade it is unlikely that convincing statistical evidence could be adduced to show their impact on fertility levels.

If family planning programs are to appear, develop, and begin to curb high population growth rates within the 1970s, much depends on what happens within ten countries. First, there are the three populous ones, Nigeria, Zaïre, and Ghana, in all of which policies have already moved toward the adoption of programs. Perhaps the real doubt centers on Zaïre with its capital Kinshasa, a city which now has a million inhabitants. Second, there are the remaining anglophone countries, Sierra Leone, Gambia, and Liberia, all of which are likely to be influenced by family planning activities in other anglophone countries in Africa and beyond. Third, there are Senegal and Ivory Coast, the former likely to be concerned by the slow expansion of job opportunities, especially in its perhaps unduly large capital, Dakar (which was once the administrative center for a much larger area than Senegal), and the latter likely to be influenced by its rapid economic growth and probable steep declines in child mortality (see the projection of population in Chapter 32). Fourth, there are Dahomey and Togo, both of which have relatively low mortality and considerable employment problems in their more developed southern areas, and both of which are likely to be influenced by events in neighboring Nigeria and Ghana. If large-scale family planning programs do come into existence in some of these countries, then one of the first signs of their impact will probably be the coming into being, and subsequent widening, of urban-rural fertility differentials.

APPENDIX
West African KAP surveys which have released some findings

| Country | Area | Status | Sex | Age and Marital Status | Date | Investigator | Sample Size |
|---------|------|--------|-----|------------------------|------|--------------|-------------|
| *Anglophone* | | | | | | | |
| Nigeria | metropolitan | all | F | married | 1964 | Ohadike | 596 |
| | other city | all | F | married | 1965–6 | Okediji | 700 |
| | urban | all | F | married | 1966 | Olusanya | 2,248 |
| | urban | all | F | married | 1966 | Olusanya | 2,248 |
| | urban | all | F | married | 1966 | Olusanya | 2,248 |
| | metropolitan | all | F | married 15–49 | 1968 | Morgan | 732 |
| | metropolitan | all | M | married, 20+ | 1968 | Morgan | 834 |
| | rural (south) | all | F | married | 1967 | Olusanya | 682 |
| | national | all | F | all 15+ | 1969 | Caldwell & Igun | 4,200 |
| | national | all | M | all 15+ | 1969 | Caldwell & Igun | 4,200 |
| | urban (northern) | elite | F | all, about 27 married, wives | 1969–70 | Trevor | 167 |
| | urban (northern) | elite | M | about 27 | 1969–70 | Trevor | 96 |
| | rural (south) | all | M & F | married, 15–60 | 1970 | Lambo | 122 |
| | urban | transitional group | M & F | married, 15–60 | 1970 | Lambo | 95 |
| | urban | elite | M & F | married, 15–60 | 1970 | Lambo | 47 |
| | rural (south) | all | F | all | 1970 | Igun, Olusanya, & Acsadi | 5,287 |
| Ghana | metropolitan/ urban | elite | F | married, 18–44 | 1963 | Caldwell | 331 |
| | metropolitan/ urban | elite | M | married, wives 18–44 | 1963 | Caldwell | 296 |
| | rural | all | household | all | 1963 | Caldwell | 709 |
| | urban | all | F | all, 15–49 | 1965–6 | Pool | 2,700 |
| | metropolitan | all | M | all, 15+ | 1965–6 | Pool | 300 |
| | rural | all | F | all, 15–49 | 1965–6 | Pool | 3,000 |
| | national | all | F | married | 1969–70 | Gaisie | 21,484 |
| Sierra Leone | metropolitan | elite | M & F | all | 1968–9 | Harrell-Bond | 229 |
| | metropolitan | elite students | M & F | all | 1968–9 | Harrell-Bond | 130 |
| | metropolitan | all | F | married[a] 15–49 | 1969–70 | Dow | 1,676 |
| | urban | all | F | married[a] 15–49 | 1969–70 | Dow | 2,208 |
| | rural | all | F | married[a] 15–49 | 1969–70 | Dow | 2,068 |
| *Francophone* | | | | | | | |
| Togo | rural | all | F | all, 15+ | 1969 | Kumekpor | 293 |
| Upper Volta | metropolitan | all | F | all, 15–49 | 1969 | Pool | 1,028 |
| | metropolitan | all | M | all, 15+ | 1969 | Pool | 260 |
| | urban | all | F | all, 15–49 | 1969 | Pool | 365 |
| | rural | all | F | all, 15–49 | 1969 | Pool | 441 |
| Niger | metropolitan | all | F | all, 15–49 | 1970 | Pool | 2,053 |
| | rural | all | F | all, 15–49 | 1970 | Pool | 865 |
| Chad[b] | metropolitan | all | F | married, 14–50 | 1969–70 | Reyna | 301 |
| | rural | all | F | married, 14–50 | 1969–70 | Reyna | 155 |

[a] Includes by definition the unmarried who have given birth to a child.
[b] Preliminary results for 456 respondents in two areas. The total sample size in all areas was 1,600.

# CHAPTER FOUR

# *Mortality*

## *Levels, Patterns, and Trends*

PIERRE CANTRELLE

⊞

THERE is still a lack of precise West African mortality data in spite of the efforts which have been made in collection and analysis. However, the following general features are beginning to become clear: (1) a high level of mortality due largely to a very high mortality in childhood; and (2) large differences in the levels of mortality according to environment. Before specifying this level and indicating its variations, we should refer to some methodological aspects and the ecological context of African mortality.

## THE ENVIRONMENT

The common feature of the countries of West and Central Africa is that they are all in a tropical environment. The elements characterizing this environment have been analyzed by such geographers as Pierre Gourou,[1] who has shown that conditions are more difficult for man in the tropics, especially in Africa.

In Western Africa, climatic zones and hence geographical regions form horizontal strips from west to east, so that a north-south cross-section passes from the dryness of the Sahara to the saturating humidity of the dense forest with the exception of the more favorable climates of the western coastal strip and the plateaus, such as the Fouta Djallon and the Adamoua.

These climates create contrasts in the kinds of food production. In the savanna of the north, the basic foods are cereals, millets, and sorghum, which are better than rice in food value. Their yield, however, is generally low and exposed to the hazards of fluctuations in the annual rainfall, which is concentrated in only a few months of the year, from July to October. In the south, such tubers as yam and manioc are important and these are very poor in proteins.

Proteins in animal form generally are consumed in lesser amounts than the recognized requirements. In the north milk production is only seasonal because of the drought during most of the year. The cattle themselves rarely

[1] Pierre Gourou, *The Tropical World: Its Social and Economic Conditions and Its Future Status*, 2d ed. (London: Longmans, Green & Company, 1958).

are eaten, for they are regarded as capital. In the south, trypanosomiasis usually prevents cattle living there. Fishing in the two rivers, Senegal and Niger, along the Senegal coast or in the Dahomey lakes provides a considerable catch, but this only benefits the people living on the riverside or those, situated on the transport axes, who have sufficient means for buying the fish. Thus deficient and unbalanced diets are frequent but they vary from one region to another.

The tropics not only provide their inhabitants with deficient food but also encourage infectious diseases and their vectors. Besides infections commonly found in Europe, there are others such as malaria, trypanosomiasis, and yellow fever.

The physical environment makes a deep impression on man in the tropics and has made it difficult for him to rise above a precarious state of balance. It is probable that certain experiences, such as the slave trade, causing a loss of men and energy, have helped to destroy this balance and prevented man from progressively conquering his environment, in contrast to the experience of Europe over the last millenium.

Human types also vary greatly. There is a smaller difference between a Laplander and a Sicilian than between a Fulani (Peul) and a Yoruba in the Dahomey, or between a Tuareg and a Lobi in the Upper Volta. Ways of life depend not only on the physical environment, but also on the cultural and historical context. Inasmuch as the way of life influences health standards, we can expect differences of mortality levels and structures.

In addition we can postulate that health standards are linked to the medical and sanitary position (i.e., the direct means of fighting against disease). By world standards, there is a very low medical density in rural Africa. For example, in 1960 Upper Volta was divided into 22 medical districts, each under the responsibility of a single doctor. There was an average of one doctor per 200,000 inhabitants for the rural population; this proportion varied by a factor of four according to the district. Investigation has shown that the use of fixed medical facilities depends on the distance individuals live from them. For example, in the Sine-Saloum area of Senegal, where a population survey was carried out, it was noted that, for the two dispensaries in the zone (about one for 15,000 inhabitants), half or two-thirds of the consultants came uniquely from the village where the dispensary was situated; thus only a minority of the population benefited from the work of the dispensary.[2]

But, even with a low medical density, the effectiveness of medical action on the mortality level depends above all on the way it is carried out. Two systems operate, often apart: curative services from fixed facilities and preventive health services from mobile teams. The fixed medical facilities only deal with a small part of the population. Moreover, the training of their personnel is often insufficient, and their provision of medications is fairly small. Rural dispensaries, even if they relieve some illnesses, as the traditional healers do, cannot, as they are now constituted, solve the important problems of public health.

As for the mobile facilities, their work is limited to those infectious diseases which seemed the most urgent to combat: smallpox, trypanosomiasis, and yellow fever. Once the epidemics are stopped, the protection is maintained to avoid their reappearance. Other widespread infections, however, remain.

Despite the efforts made against malaria, the results so far have been disappointing. Although the gravity of measles in Africa has been known to doctors for a long time, the fight against them could only begin in 1962, after the perfection of a vaccine. As for diarrhea and other gastrointestinal complaints linked most frequently with the passing on of infections by flies, medical protection is almost nonexistent.

The situation is very different in the urban centers, where there is a concentration of medical equipment and personnel. Moreover,

[2] Pierre Cantrelle, "Mortalité: facteurs," Part 5 of Délégation générale à la Recherche Scientifique et Technique, *Démographie Comparée: Afrique Noire, Madagascar, et Comores* (Paris, 1965).

the struggle against the vectors, use of insecticides, removal of waste matter, and provision of drinking water, is systematic there. Finally, the income derived from wages, which are earned principally in the towns, allows the inhabitants to survive most crises when they appear.

## THE COLLECTION OF DATA

Different groupings of the methods of collecting data can be proposed according to the criteria considered (needs of the analysis, kind of intervention, and so on). The two main types of collection of mortality data are grouped according to whether the deaths are related individually or generally to the population concerned.

DEATHS RELATED INDIVIDUALLY TO THE POPULATION EXPOSED. The two main types of methods used are those calling solely upon the memory of persons interviewed concerning the deaths which had occurred, and those based on the comparison between two successive situations of the individual.

*Purely retrospective methods.* Information about deaths is extracted from two types of question: In the first the interviewer most often asks about the deaths which have occurred over the last 12 months before the survey (current mortality); that is, the deaths occurring during a defined period. The total issue of a woman subdivided into surviving and deceased children (total or retrospective mortality) is considered. Another possible question, which is complementary to the last one, asks for information, in contrast to that on the survival of descendants, on the survival of ancestors, almost always father and mother. This type of question was proposed by Louis Henry following his analyses of historical demography, but has rarely been used (it was first used in Chad, and more recently in East Africa).

*Comparison of two successive individual situations.* In this case, the interviewer does not ask if there has been a death in the family, a question which is not always well received, but deduces the death from the comparison of the situations recorded on two successive visits. A person is registered as resident, present or absent at a first inventory. When an interviewer goes to see him after a certain interval of time, this person is either still resident, emigrant, or dead.

Only the children born and deceased between two visits risk being left out, but this inconvenience can be limited by registering the pregnancies and, on the following visit, asking what became of them. The child is then either live-born or stillborn.

This technique is more or less applicable according to the population. Whatever the length of interval between two successive visits, it cannot provide a guarantee that all the births have been registered, but it does allow the computation of the infant mortality rate, at least for the births where the pregnancy has been registered. Subsequently the correction of the result, in terms of the probabilities of infant death according to the month of birth, can be made.

*Kinds of survey.* The comparison of two successive individual situations can only be made by multiround surveys. However, retrospective questions can be put in either single-round or multiround surveys.

Until the early 1960s most of the results had been obtained by the purely retrospective methods. This was true of all data for the francophone countries of tropical Africa, which were derived from representative population samples.[3] Multiround surveys have been employed more recently, in 1962 in Senegal,[4] and next in Cameroon.[5] Carried out first by small groups either on the occasion of health surveys or as experimental demographic surveys, they are beginning to be used on a national scale (Senegal). Indeed, demographers favor this method because of the accuracy it provides. Certain countries

---

[3] Y. Blayo, "Mortalité: niveau," Part 4 of *Démographie Comparée: Afrique Noire, Madagascar, et Comores.*
[4] Pierre Cantrelle, "Etude Démographique dans la Région du Sine-Saloum (Sénégal)," *Travaux et Documents de l'ORSTOM,* 1 (Paris, 1969).
[5] Andre M. Podlewski, "Un Essai d'Observation Permanente des Faits d'Etat Civil dans l'Amadaoua: Recherche Méthodologique," *Travaux et Documents de l'ORSTOM,* 5 (Paris, 1970).

(Cameroon and the Central African Republic Gabon, Chad, and the Peoples Republic of the Congo) are even considering the continuation of the survey in a population sample with partial replacement, in order to regularly construct annual indicators from it, at least for as long as other data are not available.

When this method is well applied, it yields far better results than those obtained by the previous surveys. Its advantages and drawbacks have been analyzed elsewhere.[6]

There is a further method, related to multiround surveys, and practicable in certain cases: the collation of parish registers with an associated survey. The trial carried out on a Senegal parish has provided the longest series of observations to date in Africa.[7]

Finally, one other method sometimes is used: the comparison of two independent data-collection systems, called the Chandrasekar-Deming method. It can consist of deaths declared voluntarily by the inhabitants as in a registry office, or registered through a systematic survey, either single or multiround. This comparison of two independent systems was used first in Senegal[8] and then in Liberia.

DEATHS RELATED GENERALLY TO THE POPULATION CONCERNED. Rates may be calculated from data collected by registration systems or from the comparison of two censuses. In the registration system, the deaths are declared by the families themselves. In rural areas the proportion of deaths registered is quite variable and, on the whole, very low, averaging about 5 percent. No swift progress with registration can be expected.

On the other hand, a complete coverage by registration may well exist in some urban centers. Even where this appears to be the case, a check should be made by an independent survey. A trial of this kind has been carried out in a Dakar suburb;[9] it showed that all deaths taken down in a sample survey (1968–1969) had been declared and registered in the registration offices.[10] Registration has the advantage that the procedure usually furnishes more precise information on the causes of death.

But, in the urban centers, when wishing to calculate death rates, it is often difficult to estimate the total number of the corresponding population, especially when no recent census is available.

The comparison of two censuses carried out at different periods makes it possible to draw up a life table for the whole population, possibly even according to ethnic group. However, prior to 1970 no country in West Africa had more than one modern census and these had been taken about 1960. But by 1971, certain countries possessed the results of two censuses conducted approximately ten years apart. These have been done by either complete enumeration, as in Ghana, Gabon, and Togo, or by sample censuses as in Senegal. Brass[11] has suggested the application of the Demeny and Shorter method[12] to this type of data.

However, it will be difficult to draw from these data conclusive results on mortality in childhood because of the interval between the censuses, and the lack of precision in determining ages.

## ESTIMATION OF THE MORTALITY LEVEL

The most numerous data have been obtained from single-round retrospective surveys. Adjustment of the results has been attempted by

[6] INED, INSEE, ORSTOM, "Les Enquêtes Démographiques à Passages Répétés. Application en Afrique d'Expression Française et Madagascar Méthodologie," (Paris, 1971).

[7] B. Lacombe, "Fakao (Sénégal) Dépouillement de Registres Paroissiaux et Enquête Démographique Rétrospective Méthodologie et Résultats," *Travaux et Documents de l'ORSTOM*, 7 (Paris, 1970).

[8] Cantrelle, "Etude Démographique dans la Région du Sine-Saloum."

[9] Pierre Cantrelle and J. Verdier, "Statistiques de Décès pour la Commune de Dakar, 1968" (à paraître).

[10] *Ibid.*

[11] William Brass, "Disciplining Demographic Data," *Proceedings of the International Population Conference, London 1969*, I (Liège, 1971), pp. 183–204.

[12] Paul Demeny and F. C. Shorter, *Estimating Turkish Mortality, Fertility and Age Structure: Application of Some New Techniques*, University of Istanbul, Faculty of Economics, Publication No. 218 (Istanbul, 1968).

TABLE 4.1
Crude death rate, infant mortality rates, probability of death at young ages

| Country | Year | Crude Death Rate (per thousand) | | Infant Mortality Rate (per thousand births) | | Probability of Death (per thousand) | | | |
| | | Uncorrected data | Corrected data | Uncorrected data | Corrected data | Under 2 years ($_2q_0$) | Between 1 and 2 years ($_2q_1$) | Between 1 and 4 years Estimated from current mortality | and 4 years Estimated from overall mortality |
|---|---|---|---|---|---|---|---|---|---|
| *Mauritania:* | | | | | | | | | |
| whole population | 1964–65 | 28 | — | — | — | 240 | — | — | — |
|   nomadic population | | — | — | 185 | — | 242 | — | — | — |
|   settled population | | — | — | 191 | — | 226 | — | — | — |
| *Senegal Valley:* | | | | | | | | | |
| whole population | 1957 | 24 | 28 | 173 | 224 | 283 | 76 | 169 | 199 |
| whole population | 1960–61 | 17 | — | 93 | — | — | — | — | — |
| *Mali:* | | | | | | | | | |
| whole population | 1957–58 | 41 | 38 | — | 354 | — | — | — | — |
| whole population | 1960–61 | 29 | — | 141 | — | 298 | — | 182 | 189 |
| *Portuguese Guinea:* | | | | | | | | | |
| Bissau | 1950 | — | 31 | — | 211 | 272 | 77 | — | — |
| *Guinea:* | | | | | | | | | |
| whole population | 1954–55 | 40 | 37 | 216 | 223 | 306 | 107 | 189 | 187 |
|   forest region | | 45 | 42 | — | 254 | 287 | 44 | — | — |
|   Fouta Djallon region | | 37 | 34 | — | 207 | 346 | 49 | — | — |
|   coastal region | | 38 | 31 | — | 227 | 299 | 93 | — | — |
|   Haute Guinea | | 39 | 42 | — | 203 | 277 | 93 | — | — |
| *Ivory Coast:* | | | | | | | | | |
| first sector | 1957–58 | 28 | 29 | — | 176 | 227 | 62 | — | — |
| *Ghana:* | 1960 | — | — | — | — | 194 | — | — | — |
| *Togo* | 1961 | 29 | — | 127 | — | 262 | — | 165 | 177 |
| *Dahomey:* | | | | | | | | | |
| whole population | 1961 | 26 | 33 | 111 | 206 | 267 | 77 | 166 | 203 |
|   north | | | 32 | — | 173 | 241 | 82 | — | — |
|   south | | — | 33 | — | 221 | 288 | 86 | — | — |
| *Upper Volta:* | | | | | | | | | |
| whole population | 1960–61 | 31 | 36 | 182 | 263 | 321 | 79 | 208 | 225 |
|   Mossi | | 33 | 38 | — | 292 | 350 | 82 | — | — |
| *Niger:* | | | | | | | | | |
| settled population | | 27 | | 200 | 212 | 262 | 63 | — | — |
| *Cameroon:* | | | | | | | | | |
|   North Bénoué | 1960–61 | 27 | 31 | 180 | 223 | 274 | 66 | 159 | 176 |
|   South Bénoué | 1960–61 | 17 | — | 100 | — | 174 | — | — | — |
|   Southeast | | 18 | — | 76 | — | 134 | — | — | — |
|   West | | 26 | — | 138 | — | 184 | — | 149 | 187 |
|   Bamiléké | | 25 | — | 159 | — | — | — | — | — |
| *Gabon* | 1960–61 | 30 | — | 229 | — | 206 | — | — | — |
| *Peoples Republic of the Congo* | 1960–61 | 24 | — | 180 | — | 225 | — | — | — |
| *Central African Republic* | 1959–60 | 26 | — | 190 | 192 | 263 | 88 | 103 | 185 |
| *Chad* | 1964 | 31 | — | 165 | — | 249 | — | 110 | 161 |

SOURCES: Uncorrected data and Between 1 and 4 years—Y. Blayo, "Mortality: niveau," Part 4 of *Démographie Comparée: Afrique Noire, Madagascar, et Comores* (Paris, 1965); Corrected data—William Brass et al., *The Demography of Tropical Africa* (Princeton, N.J.: Princeton University Press, 1968); Under 2 years—Hilary J. Page and Ansley J. Coale, "Estimates of Fertility and Child Mortality in Africa South of the Sahara," Seminar on Population Growth and Economic Development, Nairobi University College, 1969, mimeographed.

TABLE 4.2

Cameroons: probability of death according to data collected by retrospective and continuous observation

| Place | Age (in years) | Retrospective Observation 1965 | Continuous Observation 1966 | 1967 |
|---|---|---|---|---|
| Foulbé | 0 | 43 | 76 | 93 |
| | 1–4 | 44 | 52 | 64 |
| Dourou | 0 | 120 | 162 | 226 |
| | 1–4 | 129 | 109 | 124 |

SOURCE: A. M. Podlewski,"Un Essai d'Observation Permanente des Faits d'Etat Civil dans l'Adamoua: Recherche Méthodologique," *Travaux et Documents de l'ORSTOM*, 5 (Paris, 1970).

internal comparison (of various series of data gathered during the same survey).

Estimates are made mainly from data on current mortality on the one hand and the mortality of the women's children on the other. The estimation methods have been described by Brass in Chapters 3 and 7 of *The Demography of Tropical Africa*[13] and discussed in Part 4 of *Démographie Comparée*.[14] Some modifications have been made recently for the estimation of mortality of persons under two years of age.[15] Table 4.1 assembles various findings. We have shown for general mortality, infant mortality, and that of 1–4 year olds, the crude results as they are obtained from the question on deaths during the previous 12 months and the revised results. We have also included the probability of death under 2 years and that between 1 and 2 years, which has been calculated by deducting the infant mortality rate from the former.

It is possible to compare the results of various methods for collecting data. In Cameroon, the comparison has been made between the year before the observation, and the two years of continuous observation.[16] With retrospective data, the rate was higher—

a crude death rate of 26 per thousand as against 22 and 21.5 with continuous observation—but the mortality rate was lower for persons under 25 years of age (Table 4.2) and higher above this age than in continuous observation. In fact, we are comparing different years and cannot distinguish between errors in observation and annual variations.

In Senegal, in the Khombol survey zone, for the 1–4 age group, the following results were obtained:

Retrospective survey
over twelve months 1963–64 = 126 deaths
Continuous
observation         1965 = 184
                        1966 = 276
                        1967 = 237
Annual average   1965–67 = 233

The average for the three consecutive years is almost double that of the retrospective survey, thus suggesting at first sight an undercount of at least 46 percent in the latter. But the mortality for 1966 and 1967 was undoubtedly exceptional.[17] If we use 1965 alone for comparative purposes, the difference falls to 32 percent. In a neighboring zone, the Sine, the mortality in 1965 was the same as recorded in 1963 and 1964.[18] Therefore, this difference is very probably due to an underregistration in the restrospective survey.

With regard to mortality during the first year of life, which is always difficult to obtain accurately, a comparison has also been made between the retrospective survey and continuous observation, but this time for the same year of observation. The continuous observation was made by a registration of pregnancy. It has been shown that the months of birth, linked to the period of the survey, did not warrant in these cases an adjustment of the data. The result obtained in

[13] William Brass et al., *The Demography of Tropical Africa* (Princeton, N.J.: Princeton University Press, 1968).
[14] Blayo, "Mortalité: niveau."
[15] Hilary J. Page and Ansley J. Coale, "Estimates of Fertility and Child Mortality in Africa South of the Sahara," Seminar on Population Growth and Economic Development, Nairobi University College, 1969, mimeographed.
[16] Podlewski, "Un Essai d'Observation Permanente."

[17] Pierre Cantrelle, M. Diagne, N. Raybaud, and B. Vignac, "Mortalité de l'Enfant dans la Région de Khombol-Thiénaba (Sénégal), 1964–68," *Cahiers de l'ORSTOM*, Human Science Series, VI, 4 (Paris, 1969), pp. 43–72.
[18] Cantrelle, "Etude Démographique dans la Région du Sine-Saloum."

Senegal for Sine[19] and Thiénaba[20] is the following:

| Survey zone | Retrospective survey | Continuous observation | Difference |
|---|---|---|---|
| Sine 1965 | 165 | 238 | +37% |
| Thiénaba 1966–67 | 135 | 247 | +45% |

Other comparisons of all deaths have been made for the same year of observation on the whole of the deaths, in particular in the Sine-Saloum survey,[21] by a comparison of two independent registrations, one by the interviewer for each family on his annual visit, and the other, the village book, kept by a permanent resident of the village (see Table 4.3).

TABLE 4.3
Comparison of deaths recorded by two independent data collection systems in Senegal

| | Village Book Recordings | | | | | |
| | Sine | | | Saloum | | |
| | Yes | No | Total | Yes | No | Total |
|---|---|---|---|---|---|---|
| Recording by interviewer | | | | | | |
| Yes | 473 | 767 | 1240 | 85 | 354 | 444 |
| No | 38 | (62) | (100) | 11 | (46) | (57) |
| Total | 511 | (829) | (1340) | 96 | (405) | (501) |

SOURCE: Pierre Cantrelle, "Etude Démographique dans la Région du Sine-Saloum (Sénégal): Etat Civil et Observation Démographique," *Travaux et Documents de l'ORSTOM*, 1 (Paris, 1969). NOTE: The terms in brackets are calculated from the implications of the other data.

The computation by age has shown that for the Sine, more than half the omissions of deaths are of persons under one year of age with a disproportionate number under one month of age. The omissions, which are mostly unintentional, are not equally distributed over all the ages; usually they are of persons who did not yet have, or no longer had, any social importance (for example, old aunts with no children, and especially persons

[19] *Ibid.*
[20] Cantrelle et al., "Mortalité de l'Enfant."
[21] Cantrelle, "Etude Démographique dans la Région du Sine-Saloum."

of less than five years of age). The younger the child, the higher is the likelihood of omission, above all if he has not yet been baptized.

If we compare these results with the tables published by the United Nations[22] or those of Coale and Demeny,[23] we note significant differences. This is not surprising, for the published tables are based on populations where data were available, and these were essentially European populations.

Brass has proposed an "African standard" life table which takes into greater account the special structure of mortality in tropical Africa. From Brass's table,[24] we have deduced the probabilities of death by age, and have compared them with two tables computed in Senegal, one in a high-mortality zone, the Sine,[25] and the other in Fakao,[26] where living conditions are more favorable (see Table 4.4).

TABLE 4.4
Probabilities of death by year of age (per thousand)

| Age | African Table[a] | Fakao[b] | Sine[c] |
|---|---|---|---|
| 0 | 120 | 197 | 238 |
| 1 | 76 | 94 | 182 |
| 2 | 28 | 108 | 135 |
| 3 | 17 | 53 | 73 |
| 4 | 13 | 29 | 44 |
| 1–4 | 107 | 217 | 372 |

SOURCES: African Table—Brass *et al.*, *Demography of Tropical Africa*, p. 133; Fakao—B. Lacombe, "Fakao (Sénégal): Dépouillement de Régistres Paroissiaux et Enquête Démographique Rétrospective, Méthodologie et Résultats," *Travaux et Documents de l'ORSTOM*, 7 (Paris, 1970); Sine—Cantrelle, "Etude Démographique dans la Région du Sine-Saloum."

We can see that Brass's curve, which is for a lower mortality level, has a concave form as in European populations, whereas African curves are generally convex from zero to five years.

[22] ECOSOC, *Manuals on Methods of Estimating Population*; Manual III: *Methods for Population Projections by Sex and Age* (New York: United Nations, 1966).
[23] Ansley J. Coale and Paul Demeny, *Regional Model Life Tables and Stable Populations* (Princeton, N.J.: Princeton University Press, 1966).
[24] Brass et al., *Demography of Tropical Africa*.
[25] Cantrelle, "Etude Démographique dans la Région du Sine-Saloum."
[26] Lacombe, "Fakao."

When both complete registration of deaths and precise ages are available, we can see a dent in the population pyramid around the age of five years, due to a rapid fall in the survival rate under this age, a phenomenon which is unknown in nontropical populations.

Age is beginning to be known precisely in urban areas. In Dakar, at least two-thirds of those under 15 years old have a known date of birth. In rural areas, a low proportion of births is registered, and hence age is vague. One of the advantages of multiround surveys lasting several years is that they allow the researchers to determine the exact age at death during childhood. In fact, as Brass has often stressed, the adjustment of imprecise data provides a substitute which does not replace precise observation.

THE SPECIFIC ELEMENTS OF TROPICAL MORTALITY

Despite the lack of precision, we can say that the crude death rates in tropical Africa, which range from 15 to more than 40 per thousand, are among the highest in the world. This high general level of mortality is due most of all to the very high level of mortality in childhood. In order to characterize this, we have compared certain African data, most of which has been obtained by continuous observation, with data of the same quality from other nonindustrialized societies. Such data are rare, for generally the regions of high mortality are those where registration of the deaths is poor. The comparative materials used are from premodern France in Europe, Guatemala in Latin America, and China and India in Asia. In fact, they are very limited studies, of rural populations, using different kinds of sources, but they seem to offer the same guarantees of precision: data from either registers or multiround surveys.

Old parish registers have been collated above all in France. The data now published concern parishes in different regions of France, especially in the second half of the eighteenth century. We have restricted ourselves to the provinces of Brittany and Anjou, which provide a sample of 20,554 births from

1740 to 1829,[27] and the north of France.[28] The Guatemala study also uses registers, of a rural area of 10,000 inhabitants, mainly Amerindians.[29] The Chinese study is of a continuing observation over four years (1931–1935) of a rural population of 20,000 inhabitants in the delta of the Yangtze.[30] The Indian study was carried out on 11 villages in the Punjab, grouping 12,000 inhabitants divided into different castes.[31]

Table 4.5 shows that the probability of infant death for 1–4 year olds in West Africa commonly exceeds that in France of two centuries ago, and that recorded by the Yangtze and Punjab surveys. On the other hand, African mortality is not clearly higher in the first year of life.

But, if we consider mortality change by age, we note that mortality decreases much more slowly in Senegal (and in Guatemala) than in old France (see Tables 4.6 and 4.7).

Indeed, in old France, the mortality decreases fairly rapidly with age and the graphic curve is concave; whereas in Senegal or Guatemala, the mortality changes little from the first year to the second, giving a rather convex curve. This fact had already been revealed in the retrospective surveys (see Table 4.8). Its importance was partly hidden by the omissions, lack of precision in age determination, and an overestimation of

[27] Y. Blayo and L. Henry, "Données Démographiques sur la Bretagne et l'Anjou de 1740 à 1829," *Annals de Démographie Historique* (Sirey [Paris], 1967), pp. 91–171.
[28] R. Deniel and L. Henry, "La Population d'un Village du Nord de la France, Sainghin en Mélantois, de 1665 à 1851," *Population* (Paris, 1965), pp. 563–602.
[29] J. D. Early, "The Structure and Change of Mortality in a Maya Community (Guatemala)," *Milbank Memorial Fund Quarterly*, XLVIII, 2 (1970), 179–201.
[30] C. M. Chiao, W. S. Thompson, and D. T. Chen, *An Experiment in the Registration of Vital Statistics in China* (Oxford, Ohio: Scripps Foundation for Research in Population Problems, 1938).
[31] J. E. Gordon, S. Singh, and J. B. Wyon, "Causes of Death at Different Ages by Sex and by Season in the Rural Population of the Punjab (1957–9): A Field Study," *Indian Journal of Medical Research*, LIII (1965), 906–17; J. B. Wyon and J. E. Gordon, "A Long-Term Prospective-type Field Study of Population Dynamics in the Punjab (India)," in Clyde V. Kiser, ed., *Research in Family Planning* (Princeton, N.J.: Princeton University Press, 1962), pp. 17–32.

TABLE 4.5

Mortality: death rates and probabilities of dying (per thousand)

| | Probability Under 1 year | 1 to 4 years | Rate | Crude Death Rate of Whole Population |
|---|---|---|---|---|
| *Africa* | | | | |
| Senegal— | | | | |
| urban: Dakar, 1968 | 57[a] | | 16 | 10 |
| semiurban: Khombol, 1965–67 | 66[b] | 178 | 48 | — |
| rural: Fakao, 1943–63 | 193 | 217 | — | — |
| Saloum, 1963–65 | | 292 | 81 | 27 |
| Sine, 1963–65 | 233[b] | 372 | 109 | 34 |
| Thiénaba, 1965–67 | 247[b] | 433 | 141 | — |
| Gambia—1943–53 | 140 | 319 | — | — |
| Cameroon— | | | | |
| 1966–67 Foulbé | — | 72 | 16 | 16 |
| Dourou | — | 116 | 30 | 23 |
| 1954–67 Foulbé | — | 72 | — | — |
| agricultural laborers | — | 166 | — | — |
| *Other societies* | | | | |
| China— 1931–35 | 241 | — | 55 | 39 |
| Punjab— 1957–59 | 156 | — | 28 | — |
| Guatemala—1950–59 | 143 | — | 93 | 36 |
| 1960–68 | 113 | 164 | 44 | 23 |
| *France* | | | | |
| Brittany— 1740–1820 | 228 | 165 | — | |
| north: 1740–99 | 198 | 132 | | |
| 1800–49 | 240 | 111 | | |

SOURCES: Senegal urban—Pierre Cantrelle and J. Verdier, "Statistiques de décès pour la Commune de Dakar, 1968" (in preparation); Senegal semiurban—Pierre Cantrelle, M. Diagne, N. Rayboud, and B. Vignac, "Mortalité de l'Enfant dans la Région de Khombol-Thiénaba (Sénégal), 1964–68," *Cahiers de l'ORSTOM*, Human Science Series, VI, 4 (1969), pp. 43–72; Senegal rural, Fakao—Lacombe, "Fakao (Senegal)"; Senegal rural, Saloum, and Sine—Cantrelle, "Etude Démographique dans la Région du Sine-Saloum"; Senegal rural, Thiénaba—Cantrelle *et al.*, "Mortalité de l'Enfant"; Gambia—graphic estimation based on data published on a village, I. A. McGregor, "Patterns of Mortality in Young Children in Keneba Village (Gambia)," in Centre International de l'Enfance, *Conditions de Vie de l'Enfant en Milieu Rural en Afrique* (Paris, 1968), pp. 120–23; Cameroons, 1966–1967, Foulbé and Dourou—Podlewski, "Un Essai d'Observation Permanente des Faits d'Etat Civil dans l'Adamoua"; Cameroons, 1954–1967, Foulbé—J. Hurault, "Eleveurs et cultivateurs des hauts plateaux de Cameroun: La Population de Lamidat de Banyo," *Population* (1969), pp. 963–83; China—C. M. Chiao, W. S. Thompson, and D. T. Chen, *An Experiment in the Registration of Vital Statistics in China* (Oxford [Ohio]: Scripps Foundation, 1938); Punjab—(1) J. E. Gordon, S. Singh, and J. B. Wyon, "Causes of Death at Different Ages by Sex and by Season in the Rural Population of the Punjab (1957–59): A field study," *Indian Journal of Medical Research*, LIII (1965), 906–17; (2) J. B. Wyon and J. E. Gordon, "A Long-term Prospective-type Field Study of Population Dynamics in the Punjab (India)," in Clyde V. Kiser, ed., *Research in Family Planning* (Princeton, N.J.: Princeton University Press, 1962), pp. 17–32; Guatemala, 1950 and 1960—J. D. Early, "The Structure and Change of Mortality in a Maya Community (Guatemala)," *Milbank Memorial Fund Quarterly*, XLVIII, 2 (1970), 179–201; Brittany—Y. Blayo and L. Henry, "Données Démographiques sur la Bretagne et l'Anjou de 1740 à 1829," *Annales de Démographie Historique* (Paris, 1967), pp. 91–171; North France—Cantrelle and Verdier, "Statistiques de décès."

[a] Infant mortality rates.
[b] Computation based on what happened to pregnancies: Khombol, 1962–1967; Thiénaba, 1966–1967; Sine, 1965–1967.

TABLE 4.6

Probabilities of death per thousand persons—years

| | SENEGAL | | | | | FRANCE | |
|---|---|---|---|---|---|---|---|
| Age | Khombol[a] 1965–67 | Fakao 1943–63 | Saloum 1963–65 | Sine[a] 1963–65 | Thiénaba[a] 1965–67 | North 1740–99 | 1800–49 |
| 0 months | 300 | 984 | — | 638 | 1212 | | |
| 1–5 months | 37 | 128 | — | 218 | 48 | 198 | 240 |
| 6–11 months | 54 | 127 | — | 218 | 268 | | |
| 1 year | 93 | 94 | 125 | 182 | 222 | 68 | 55 |
| 2 years | 76 | 108 | 116 | 135 | 195 | 39 | 29 |
| 3 years | 10 | 53 | 62 | 73 | 69 | 17 | 18 |
| 4 years | 10 | 29 | 25 | 44 | 25 | 14 | 13 |

SOURCES: France—R. Deniel and L. Henry, "La Population d'un Village du Nord de la France, Sainghin en Mélantois, de 1665 à 1851," *Population* (1965), pp. 563–602; Khombol and Thiénaba—Cantrelle, *et al.*, "Mortalité de l'Enfant"; Fakao—Lacombe, "Fakao (Senegal)"; Saloum and Sine—Cantrelle, "Etude Démographique dans la Région du Sine-Saloum."

[a] See note b, Table 4.5.

TABLE 4.7

Mortality rates by age per thousand children

| Age (in years) | Senegal, 1963–65 | | Guatemala | |
| --- | --- | --- | --- | --- |
| | Sine | Saloum | 1950–59 | 1960–68 |
| 1 | 194 | 126 | 123 | 54 |
| 2 | 142 | 119 | 104 | 49 |
| 3 | 68 | 58 | 74 | 41 |
| 4 | 43 | 24 | 59 | 28 |
| 1–4 | 109 | 81 | 93 | 44 |

SOURCES: Senegal—Cantrelle, "Etude Démographique dans la Région du Sine-Saloum"; Guatemala—Early, "Structure and Change of Mortality."

TABLE 4.9

Punjab: probability of death per thousand persons—years

| Age (in months) | Cultivators | Leather Workers | Other Castes |
| --- | --- | --- | --- |
| 0 | 800 | 1252 | 1104 |
| 1–5 | 53 | 89 | 68 |
| 6–11 | 71 | 208 | 152 |
| 12–17 | 94 | 156 | 92 |
| 18–23 | 32 | 71 | 42 |
| 24–35 | 21 | 36 | 10 |

SOURCE: Wyon and J. Gordon, "Population Dynamics in the Punjab."

age, giving a rate lower than the real one, plus the fact that age overstatement occurs over a considerable age range and increases with age.

The phenomenon is more accentuated if we divide the years of age into fragments; in this case, the probabilities are converted to an annual basis to make them comparable (see Tables 4.6 and 4.9). The very high mortality during the first months drops rapidly, but then remains on a level, or even rises to reach a peak which is found at varying ages: (1) around the end of the first year in Senegal (Thiénaba, Sine), in Gambia (with a second peak around 3 years), and in the Punjab; (2) around 18 months at Khombol; (3) around 2 years at Fakao.

For the town of Dakar, the rates and probabilities could not be computed, but, judging by the figures, there is a similar

TABLE 4.8

Retrospective surveys: mortality rates by age per thousand children

| Age (in years) | Senegal Valley, 1956–1957 | | Guinea, 1954–1955 | |
| --- | --- | --- | --- | --- |
| | Rural | Urban | Rural | Urban |
| 1 | 61 | 67 | 68 | 57 |
| 2 | 68 | 81 | 76 | 75 |
| 3 | 43 | 24 | 54 | 49 |
| 4 | 30 | 25 | 33 | 24 |

SOURCE: Pierre Cantrelle, "Mortality: facteurs," Part 5 of *Démographie Comparée: Afrique Noire, Madagascar, et Comores* (Paris, 1965).

phenomenon[32] as can be seen by the number of deaths at each age: 0 month = 265; 1–5 months = 288; 6–11 months = 289; 12–17 months = 274, 18–23 months = 278; 2 years = 84; 3 years = 84; 4 years = 47.

Finally, with monthly probabilities,[33] we see the phenomenon more precisely; in Sine in Senegal, after the rapid drop of probabilities during the first months, we note a spectacular rise from the fifth to tenth months, the fall only starting again, but very slowly, toward one year. For the provinces of Brittany and Anjou, in old France, the mortality is higher during the first four to five months; from then on it quickly becomes lower, and the rise in the last quarter of the year is almost non-existent.

If we transfer the cumulated deaths to a graph, by the Bourgeois-Pichat method, with an abscissa of log-scale 3, we see a sharp break toward the sixth month in the different zones studied in Senegal.[34] When the graph is continued beyond 12 months, the curve bends again only around 3–4 years of age.

We can consider the rural parts of Senegal and old France, both with a subsistence economy, as having little medical protection. In point of fact, contemporary Africa benefits

[32] Cantrelle and Verdier, "Statistiques de Décès."
[33] Pierre Cantrelle and H. Leridon, "Infant and Child Mortality, Weaning and Fertility in a Rural Zone of Sénégal," *Population Studies*, XXV, 3 (November, 1971).
[34] Cantrelle, "Etude Démographique dans la Région du Sine-Saloum"; Cantrelle and Leridon, "Infant and Child Mortality"; Cantrelle *et al.*, "Mortalité de l'Enfant"; Lacombe, "Fakao."

by smallpox and yellow fever vaccinations, whereas in old France smallpox was an important cause of death.

This mortality curve is not peculiar to a subsistence economy since it is not found in old France, but does exist in the urban parts of Africa as well as the rural ones. It also is found in other tropical areas, Guatemala and Punjab, and so we could postulate that it is a tropical phenomenon. Observations in Cameroons,[35] although there is little detail for the childhood period, show, however, that there exist in the rural tropics areas which are privileged from the point of view of climate and food available, the one depending largely on the other.

Were the two basic components of morbidity in African childhood, infectious and deficiency diseases, less pronounced in old France? It is difficult to secure any proof, but we know that in tropical regions as well as universal infections such as measles and whooping cough, there are more specific infections, such as malaria. It is possible that the tropical climate favors the existence of certain germs, bringing an increased risk of infection at young ages. Moreover, the stock of protective antibodies present in the new-born baby decreases and becomes nonexistent by about the age of six months in the case of measles, for example. From this moment on, the child must face up to infectious attacks with his own means of defence, as MacGregor has stressed.[36] It is at this age that the protein contribution of the mother's milk has more and more difficulty in meeting the child's needs, for it is not being replaced by rich enough nourishment.

We have no proof either as to the meeting of protein needs of the child in old France. Perhaps the very young child did not eat eggs; but it is probable that dairy produce was more abundant and, above all, better spread

out over all the seasons. On the contrary, we know of the limited production of animal proteins, especially milk, in tropical Africa largely because of climatic conditions.

It is instructive to compare the mortality curve with the weight curve. We know that in tropical areas, and especially in Africa, the child puts on weight faster than the European child until about the age of six months; thereafter his weight increases much more slowly than that of his European counterpart, and it remains almost stable until about two to three years. But weight only expresses the effect of malnutrition and the attacks of many infections.

An analysis has been made of the relationship between weaning and mortality.[37] Among the data of the Sine-Saloum surveys, a group of children was chosen because they were weaned during the following pregnancy. The case is fairly frequent and the reason for weaning is then, from the point of view of the child, accidental enough for us to be able to take it as independent of his own state of health or development (see Table 4.10).

TABLE 4.10
Mortality after weaning: children weaned during the following pregnancy, Senegal (Sine), 1963–1965

| Age at Death (in months) | Annual Probabilities of Dying (per 1,000) by Age at Weaning (in months) | | | Annual Probabilities of Dying at Same Age as Weaning in Whole Population (per 1,000) |
|---|---|---|---|---|
| | 12–17 | 18–23 | 24–29 | |
| 12–17 | 483 | — | — | 194 |
| 18–23 | 172 | 256 | — | 168 |
| 24–35 | 159 | 120 | 230 | 139 |
| 36–41 | 123 | 82 | 103 | 95 |

SOURCE: Pierre Cantrelle and H. Leridon, "Infant and Child Mortality: Weaning and Fertility in a Rural Zone of Senegal," *Population Studies*, XXV, 3 (November 1971).

The risk is clearly the greatest with the earliest weaning. Whatever the age of weaning, there is some increase in the risk of death, but this is particularly so for the children weaned between 12 and 18 months,

[35] Podlewski, "Un Essai d'Observation Permanente." J. Hurault, "Eleveurs et Cultivateurs des hauts plateaux de Cameroun: La Population de Lamidat de Banyo," *Population* (Paris, 1969), pp. 963–83.
[36] I. A. McGregor, "Patterns of Mortality in Young Children in Keneba Village (Gambia)," in Centre International de l'Enfance, *Conditions de Vie de l'Enfant en Milieu Rural en Afrique* (Paris, 1968), pp. 120–23.

[37] Cantrelle and Leridon, "Infant and Child Mortality."

where mortality climbs to more than twice that of all children of this age (most of the rest will not yet be weaned and will have mothers who are not pregnant again). There is therefore a high excess mortality connected with weaning; but these cases are relatively few, and not frequent enough to weigh heavily in the balance of childhood mortality.

The average age for weaning noted in the Sine survey is 24.3 months; therefore it is not weaning which brings about higher mortality in tropical children. It is ultimately caused by malnutrition, which actually begins earlier than weaning in synergy with successive or simultaneous attacks of infections. Death being a cumulative process, it is therefore difficult to allocate the proper share of blame to each component.

### THE CAUSES OF DEATH

Similarly, the term "cause of death" is used for simplification. It is more a question of final condition. Medical administrators have introduced multiple-entry certificates distinguishing the main cause from the direct cause and the ancillary causes. For instance, a child suffering from malnutrition (ancillary cause), who catches measles (main cause), dies of a diarrheic dehydration (direct cause). Even if such multiple entries were practiced in Africa, which is not the case, special epidemiological studies would be necessary to tell which factor played the most important part in the death. Apart from accidents, the causes of death given have therefore only an indicative value, which is nonetheless far from negligible, for it gives us an idea of the importance of public health problems.

In urban areas, the causes of death are registered either directly by the hospitals or by the registering doctor or health officer after inquiry of the family. In rural areas, information has been obtained from certain population surveys where questions were put on this point: Senegal (Senegal Valley and Sine-Saloum), Upper Volta, Dahomey, Cameroon, and Lake Chad.[38] In some surveys the

[38] Cantrelle, "Natalité: facteurs."

questions were open and in others closed (that is, a list of suggested answers was supplied). It is obvious that this type of questionnaire should be used with great care. For greater convenience, we shall use the word "cause" to indicate the symptoms, diseases, or accidents declared by the families.

It is fairly easy to establish a relationship between the reply and certain causes, where it is a question of an accident, a confinement, or well-known specific illnesses, such as measles and smallpox. These two diseases are clearly distinguished, as the following examples from West African languages illustrate:

| Language | Measles | Smallpox |
|----------|---------|----------|
| Wolof | N'gnas | N'Diambal |
| Fulani | Douyodié, tiammé | Badé |
| Mossi | Bi | Gyéndiba |
| Dendi | Dobou-Dobou | Tadjidji |
| Bariba | Pouro-taou, Boussouka | Worou |
| Baoulé | Bli-Kissi | Ko-ouli |
| Fon | Azon-vovo | Sagbata |
| Yoruba | Eyi | Ilégbona |
| Hausa | Doussah, Bakwan dauro | Agana, ado |
| Tamachek | Loumi | Bedi |

On the other hand, the reply can only have an indicative value for such symptoms as coughing, diarrhea, bouts of fever, jaundice, and so on. Table 4.11 shows answers which direct us to diagnoses representing from 27–47 percent of deaths according to the survey. Precise circumstances (accident, confinement) and probable diagnoses (smallpox, measles, leprosy) total 9–29 percent of deaths.

Some of these causes will now be discussed in more detail.

*Accidents:* Generally speaking, the proportion is about 2 percent varying from 0.4 to 3.0 percent. Road accidents are more frequent in urban than rural areas, 35 against 2 per thousand in Dahomey, 11 against 1 per thousand in the Upper Volta. In contrast, accidents due to falling trees occur only in rural area. Deaths by drowning and animal

TABLE 4.11
Distribution of 1,000 deaths according to indicative value of replies

| | Valley | Senegal Niakhar | Paos-Koto | Upper Volta (rural) | Dahomey (total) |
|---|---|---|---|---|---|
| Indicative Value of Replies | 1957 | 1963–65 | 1963–65 | 1960–61 | 1961 |
| *Exact circumstances (probable diagnoses)* | | | | | |
| accident | 21 | 5 | 13 | 13 | 31 |
| pregnancy, confinement | 24 | 10 | 10 | 18 | 19 |
| smallpox | — | — | — | — | 33 |
| measles | 241 | 76 | 166 | 181 | 23 |
| leprosy | 5 | 2 | 2 | 2 | 2 |
| | 291 | 93 | 191 | 214 | 108 |
| *Indicative signs (possible diagnoses)* | | | | | |
| diarrhea | 97 | 103 | 71 | 176 | 55 |
| coughing | 76 | 58 | 46 | 98 | 74 |
| whooping cough | 16 | 7 | 8 | 25 | 4 |
| jaundice | 16 | 3 | 12 | 10 | 5 |
| stiffness of body | 58 | 8 | 6 | 51 | 34 |
| other fevers | 134 | 124 | 126 | 108 | 157 |
| | 397 | 303 | 269 | 468 | 329 |
| Other replies | 150 | 188 | 174 | 170 | 306 |
| *Not determined* | | | | | |
| old age | 18 | 89 | 45 | 19 | 54 |
| other | 144 | 327 | 321 | 129 | 203 |
| | 162 | 416 | 366 | 148 | 257 |
| Total | 1,000 | 1,000 | 1,000 | 1,000 | 1,000 |

SOURCE: Cantrelle, "Mortalité: facteurs."

attacks also are mentioned. The mortality rate from snake bite can be estimated for the year studied, at 11 per 100,000 inhabitants in Upper Volta, and 31 in Dahomey, almost half the deaths by accident in these countries; it is of about the same importance as the annual mortality rate due to road accidents, in the very motorized countries, where it is around 20 per 100,000 inhabitants.

*Maternal or obstetric mortality* includes all deaths due to complications in pregnancy as a result of confinement. The answers distinguish on the one hand, deaths which occurred during an illness related to a pregnancy or an abortion, and on the other hand, deaths related directly to a confinement or its consequences up to about a month after the confinement. The latter are three times more numerous than the former. The deaths directly related to a confinement expressed per thousand live births (that is, the maternal mortality rate) yield a rate of 10 in the Senegal Valley, 5.5 in the Sine, 4.1 in the Saloum, and 9.6 in Upper Volta. Comparative rates around 1955 were 4.5 in Ceylon, 3.5 in Chile, and 0.7 in Europe.

*Smallpox* was reported only in Dahomey, but with a relatively high frequency there; over the whole country the rate was 33 per thousand deaths, being higher in the south (57) than in the north (27). Rates were highest for children and adolescents as is shown by the following figures.

| Age | Number of deaths per thousand deaths attributable to smallpox |
|---|---|
| 0 years | 15 |
| 1–4 | 60 |
| 5–14 | 50 |
| 15–44 | 34 |
| 45–64 | 20 |
| 65+ | 9 |
| whole | 33 |

The relatively high frequency of deaths from smallpox revealed by the population survey is corroborated by the public health statistics, which are gathered during systematic attempts to track down each case. The rate in urban areas is lower, the rate for the same period as the statistics just quoted being 8 per thousand.

The population of central and southern Dahomey, in Yoruba and Goun country, are especially well acquainted with and fearful of smallpox. It is considered as the expression of a supernatural power "*Sagbatta*," to whom a particular cult is dedicated, and it is under this name that it is declared to the interviewers.

*Measles* seems to be a universal epidemic disease. Its gravity has long been known to doctors, but there were no exact cause-specific mortality rates. It has been easy to introduce questions on this illness into the population surveys, which have thus provided rich data on its morbidity, incidence, prevalence, case-fatality rate, and mortality.

The study of this illness was all the more interesting because a vaccine was perfected following the discovery of this virus by Enders. Senegal's demographic statistics have allowed an analysis of the effectiveness of the vaccination campaigns to be attempted.

In the Upper Volta and Senegal, the mortality rates computed for the periods observed are around 5 per thousand inhabitants (see Table 4.12).

In rural Dahomey the rate is 2.3 in the north as against 0.3 in the south. This is explained by the fact that during the month preceding the period observed, an important epidemic raged mainly in the southern part of the country.

Annual variations are indeed important. For the 1963–1965 period, the proportion of deaths by measles varied from 3–12 percent in the Sine, and 7–31 percent in the Saloum. At present, data are restricted to zones too limited and periods too short to allow extrapolation. However, for the whole of Senegal, we can make the reasonable hypothesis of a rate of mortality by measles of 2 per thousand inhabitants.

For the 1–4 years age group, the rate is about ten times higher than in nineteenth-century Europe. It is in this age group that mortality by measles is the highest in the African surveys. The deaths noted are spread out over the whole year, but most often with a marked upswing during the dry season.

*Diarrhea:* Under this term have been grouped all deaths for which diarrhea was declared as being the major symptom of the

TABLE 4.12
All mortality and mortality from measles for various ages

| Country | All Ages | | Under 1 Year[a] | | 1–4 Years | |
|---|---|---|---|---|---|---|
| | All causes[b] | Measles | All causes | Measles | All causes | Measles |
| *Senegal* | | | | | | |
| Senegal Valley, 1957 | 24 | 6 | 172 | 28 | 46 | 24 |
| Sine, 1963–65 | 34 | 3 | 170 | 4 | 109 | 15 |
| Saloum, 1963–65 | 27 | 5 | 129 | 9 | 81 | 21 |
| Khombol, 1965–67 | | | | | 48 | 15 |
| Thiénaba, 1965–67 | | | | | 138 | 31 |
| *Upper Volta* | | | | | | |
| rural, 1960 | 32 | 6 | 198 | 26 | 78 | 25 |
| *Dahomey*, 1967 | 26 | 1 | 110 | 2 | 44 | 4 |
| *England* | | | | | | |
| 1853–55 | | | 156 | 2 | | |
| 1896–1900 | | | 156 | 3 | 21 | 2 |

[a] These rates are related to the number of births and hence are infant mortality and cause-specific infant mortality rates, respectively
[b] Crude death rate.

disease, without concern for the etiology, which varies widely (typhoid fever, bacillary dysentery, amoebic dysentery). The proportion of all deaths is around 10 percent as is shown by the figures below.

|  |  | *Percent of deaths at all ages* | *Percent of deaths at 1–4 years* |
|---|---|---|---|
| Senegal, | Senegal Valley | 10 | 14 |
|  | Sine | 10 | 17 |
|  | Saloum | 7 | 12 |
|  | Khombol, Thiénaba | — | 35 |
| Upper Volta, rural |  | 18 | 23 |
| Dahomey, whole |  | 6 | 6 |

There are important variations according to age: The highest proportion of deaths is found in the 1–4 years group in all the surveys, except in Dahomey where the maximum is shared equally with the bordering age groups.

In Upper Volta where data are available by single years of age, the proportion of deaths is highest during the second year of life as is shown by the following figures.

| *Age* | *Percent of all deaths* |
|---|---|
| 0 months | 4 |
| 1–11 months | 13 |
| 1 year | 27 |
| 2 years | 24 |
| 3 years | 19 |
| 4 years | 18 |
| 5–9 years | 19 |

The causes of death are certainly more precise in the urban centers, where medical certification exists, all the more so as a large proportion of deaths takes place in hospitals (55 percent in Dakar in 1968).[39] The collation of this city's registers has been attempted, and the given causes of death have been coded according to the World Health Organization (WHO) international classification of 1965,

[39] Cantrelle and Verdier, "Statistiques de Décès."

and then grouped according to the list of 50 headings. The results appear to be of interest, strongly suggesting that it would be a good thing if these documents were collated more systematically. This would allow a comparison at least between the large urban centers of the different African countries. For instance, for the 1–4 years age group, nutritional deficiencies are described as the cause of death in 13 percent of cases; among infections, diarrhea is named in 19 percent of the cases, measles in 16 percent, and meningitis in 15 percent. In contrast, malaria, which is perhaps the most important cause of mortality in childhood in West African rural areas, seems from this evidence to have lost its virulence in the urban areas. However, this view is put forward cautiously as the year studied—1968—was an exceptionally dry one, causing an unusually low frequency of malaria.

## PERINATAL AND INFANT MORTALITY

Table 4.13 contains some perinatal and infant mortality data based on different sources used in Senegal: urban registers at Dakar, prenatal

TABLE 4.13
Perinatal and infant mortality: Senegal

|  | Large Center Dakar | Small Center Khombol | Rural Areas Sine | Fakao |
|---|---|---|---|---|
|  | 1964–65 | 1962–67 | 1965–67 | 1943–63 |
| Number of Births | 46,890 | 1,240 | 554 | 1,919 |
| Stillbirths | 39 | 27 | 40 | n.a. |
| Endogenous mortality | n.a. | 20.25 | 30.40 | 67 |
| Mortality rate[a] |  |  |  |  |
| first week | 19 | 17 | 33 | n.a. |
| first month | 34 | 32 | 53 | 84 |
| 2d–12th month | 50 | 34 | 180 | 106 |
| Infant mortality rate | 84 | 66 | 233 | 190 |

NOTES: n.a. = not available.
[a] Expressed per thousand births.

survey interviews at Khombol, the registration of pregnancies and their outcome in the Sine surveys, and parish registers at Fakao.

Satgé has shown that in Dakar, during 1964–1965, one-quarter of the babies who died in the neonatal period (under one month) were prematurely born; in addition, infection was responsible for a further one-fifth of the deaths (usually a belated infection, after the seventh day).

The mortality rate computed for umbilical tetanus was 1.4 per thousand live births. We have no comparable information for the rural zone.

## VARIATIONS IN CHILD MORTALITY WITHIN A SINGLE COUNTRY

In Senegal, for mortality rates from 1–4 years, the following levels have been noted:

| | | |
|---|---|---|
| Rural areas: | Thiénaba, 1965–67 | 141 |
| | Sine, 1963–65 | 109 |
| | Saloum, 1963–65 | 81 |
| | Fakao (coastal village), 1943–63 | 60 |
| Semirural areas: | Khombol (market village of 5,000 inhabitants), 1965–67 | 48 |
| Urban areas: | Dakar (town of 600,000 inhabitants), 1968 | 16 |

The highest rate is nine times the size of the lowest one. In European countries it apparently ranged from 30–50 at the end of the eighteenth century; in England it was 20 per thousand around 1900 and now is 1 per thousand.

## INDICATORS OF MORTALITY LEVELS

The Economic and Social Advisory Council of the United Nations had proposed a certain number of indicators of living standards, which were relatively easy to estimate quantitatively and which lent themselves to international comparison. Among these elements chosen to represent the standard of living, those concerning health and certain demographic measures hold an important place. The demographic indicators employed were expectation of life at birth, the infant mortality rate, age-specific mortality, and the annual number of deaths from infectious disease per 100,000 persons.

For the countries which do not have complete registration of deaths at least of a representative population sample, it is clear from the discussion above that it is illusory to compute expectation of life at birth. Similarly, in many countries, sufficient data are not available on deaths attributable to infectious diseases. The crude death rate, if it can be estimated, cannot lend itself to international comparison, because of differences in the age structures of populations.

With regard to age-specific death rates, we have seen that the system of repeated observations of a population sample provide, in a reasonable time, precise rates or probabilities of death in childhood. Moreover, we have seen that this latter measure is especially sensitive to the conditions of environment.

Data on infant mortality of the same quality are more expensive to obtain, for they alone necessitate more numerous survey visits to ensure a coverage of all births. Moreover, the elements involved in infant mortality, called endogenous and exogenous, have very different degrees of significance; whereas the latter is sensitive to environmental conditions, endogenous mortality is much more resistant, thus lowering the value of this indicator.

Finally, few of the indicators can be justified on the grounds of international comparability, for there are few of them which are available for all countries.

For tropical countries, the best demographic indicators at present would be the rates or probabilities of mortality during the second year of life; biologically, the grouping of mortality from six months to two or three years would be preferable, but, to facilitate international comparisons, the usual group of one to four years is more convenient. The probability of survival to five years would be valuable, but can only be computed if infant mortality is known with precision.

## BIOLOGICAL FACTORS

Irrespective of age, we know that mortality is generally a little higher for men than women, young and old alike. In the Dakar region neonatal mortality is 43 per thousand live births among the boys and 37 for the girls, and the infant mortality rate is 90 as against 76. Women's mortality only exceeds men's during the fertile life, 15–45 years. When medical conditions improve, this phenomenon disappears, as is illustrated by the series of mortality rates for the urban center of Dakar (see Table 4.14).

TABLE 4.14
Dakar: mortality rates by age (per thousand persons), 1968[a]

| Age | Both Sexes | Males | Females |
|-----|-----------|-------|---------|
| 0 | 71.8 | 75.0 | 68.2 |
| 1–4 | 16.8 | 17.0 | 16.5 |
| 5–9 | 2.3 | 2.5 | 2.1 |
| 10–15 | 1.2 | 1.7 | 0.8 |
| 15–19 | 2.2 | 2.3 | 2.1 |
| 20–24 | 2.9 | 4.1 | 2.0 |
| 25–29 | 4.2 | 4.7 | 3.7 |
| 30–34 | 4.5 | 4.6 | 4.4 |
| 35–39 | 6.0 | 6.3 | 5.7 |
| 40–44 | 6.6 | 7.8 | 5.0 |
| 45–49 | 8.8 | 10.1 | 6.7 |
| 50–54 | 12.1 | 12.6 | 11.3 |
| 55–59 | 14.7 | 15.5 | 13.6 |
| 60–64 | 23.2 | 26.5 | 19.1 |
| 65–69 | 38.7 | 53.2 | 24.4 |
| 70–74 | 55.0 | 53.7 | 56.7 |
| 75–79 | 74.9 | 78.5 | 70.7 |
| 80+ | 105.8 | 67.2 | 171.7 |
| All ages | 10.3[b] | 11.5 | 9.1 |

SOURCE: Cantrelle and Verdier, "Statistiques de décès."
[a] Total deaths in 1968 = 6,523.
[b] Crude death rate.

Neonatal mortality varies according to the age of the mother, being highest for mothers aged 15–19 years and over 35 years in Upper Volta and Dahomey.[40] This fact is confirmed by the figures for birth order in the Sine

[40] Cantrelle, "Mortalité: facteurs."

survey in Senegal. Two deviations are significant: for the first born clearly higher mortality up to two years, but especially concentrated in the first three months; for higher birth orders seven and over, excessive mortality up to one year, spread over the whole period.[41]

Infant mortality is much higher for twins than for other children: the probability of death during the first three months is four times as high, 294 per thousand in contrast to 73 for the whole population, and that of the second year is at least twice as high, 476 against 205 (Senegal, Sine).[42] Twins have, in fact, a lower average weight at birth than other children, an unfavorable situation in present-day living conditions in rural Africa, despite the attentions they are surrounded with in certain countries from their moment of birth.

## VARIATIONS ACCORDING TO ENVIRONMENT

We can schematize by distinguishing physical and human environments. Elements, such as climate together with its seasonal variations, should be classed in the physical environment; others, like the care normally given to sick children, belong to the human environment. But, availability of food, to take an example, is linked both with the physical environment (nature of the soil and rainfall) and the human environment (population density and the improvement of production by changed techniques). A factorial analysis would help us to distinguish better those environmental elements which are largely interdependent. But we do not yet possess sufficient data.

The different vital levels listed in Table 4.1 are often for different survey years; while levels often are very different from one year to another. Thus it is difficult to distinguish differences caused by variations from year to year from those arising from different environments. However, within the same survey

[41] Cantrelle and Leridon, "Infant and Child Mortality."
[42] *Ibid.*

we can see regional differences, as for example, in Guinea, where the crude death rate ranges from 31 in the maritime area to 42 in the forest region and Upper Guinea, or in Upper Volta, where mortality is highest in the Mossi country.

But the explanation of the differences cannot be found by relating them to a global context. We shall therefore confine ourselves here to some specific examples: the relationship between mortality levels and agricultural production, climate, urbanization, and public health services.

MORTALITY AND AGRICULTURAL PRODUCTION. The differences noted in rural Senegal are instructive (see Table 4.5). The coastal village of Fakao consumes a large part of its catch of fish, and thus is favored by available nourishment of high food value. The 1–4 years mortality rate, 60 per thousand, is significatively lower than those of the villages further inland.

But, even among the latter, we can distinguish meaningful differences between the Sine and the Saloum (see Table 4.15).

In Sine, the area available per person is smaller, the soil is less fertile, and the rainfall less heavy than in the Saloum, which is the cause of a much lower agricultural production per capita in the former than the latter. This

TABLE 4.15
Senegal: mortality and agricultural production, 1962–1965

|  | Sine | Saloum |
|---|---|---|
| 1–4 years mortality rate (per thousand) | 109 | 81 |
| Amount of rainfall (in inches) | less than 30 | over 30 |
| Density (inhabitants per square mile) | 200 | 100 |
| Cultivable area per person (in acres) | 2.5 | 6.2 |
| Cultivated area per person (in acres) | 2.2 | 3.7 |
| Annual peanut production per person (in pounds) | 617 | 1,904 |
| Annual millet and sorghum production per person (in pounds) | 736 | 1,263 |

level of production determines both food consumption (especially cereals, millet, and sorghum) and also income (especially the peanuts).

Now Sine's excess of births over deaths appears to be absorbed locally. If this tendency persists, the density, which is already over 200 persons per square mile, will rise still further. All the cultivable lands apparently are occupied and the fallow fields are disappearing. Production could increase only by the use of fertilizers or by technical changes, new techniques, and the improvement of seeds, but such gains would be quickly limited by the amount of rainfall. Irrigation would give rise to technical problems, which would be difficult to overcome; even more significant, the cost would be out of proportion to the results that could be expected.

It is probable that, faced with such a situation, the population, although strongly attached to the soil, will tend to emigrate toward areas such as the Saloum where conditions seem more favorable. Otherwise mortality, spurred by malnutrition, will start to rise again, at least given the means of production we can now foresee. The situation is still more critical in the neighboring region of Thiénaba. But the rate of 141 registered deaths corresponds to a period during which there was a very bad crop. The study of Gambia, in an environment fairly similar to that of Saloum, shows a similar mortality level.

Rural investigations in Cameroon have been made in a very different environment, the Adamoua Plateau, at least 1,000 meters in altitude, where heavy rainfall allows grazing all year round and provides different resources as well. The mortality rate approximates that of the urban parts of Senegal; but within this geographical environment, there are perceptible differences between the different ways of life. The rate for cultivators (Dourous and Serfs) is twice that of the Peul (or Foulbé) shepherds, who are milk producers. We might note the close agreement between the mortality probabilities computed for the Foulbé based on two different series of observations.

In nomadic circles in Niger, a difference was found in 1963 between two different ethnic groups, the Peuls and Tuareg; these results are less exact because they were obtained by a purely retrospective survey.[43]

| *Mortality rate* | *Peuls* | *Tuaregs* |
|------------------|---------|-----------|
| Under 1 year | 117 | 127 |
| 1–4 years | 49 | 67 |

Mortality variations linked with environment not only determine regional differences, but also are manifested by annual variations. The Khombol-Thiénaba survey sheds some light on this point (see Table 4.16). Nutritional and

TABLE 4.16
Annual mortality fluctuations, Thiénaba (Senegal) 1965–1969 1–4 years mortality rate (per thousand)

| Year | Rate | Observations |
|------|------|--------------|
| 1965 | 100 | Apparently an average year. |
| 1966 | 163 | Reduced availability of food because of the unusual pattern and deficient amount of rainfall, a situation which lasted until the following year's crop. |
| 1967 | 147 | Above average rainfall, causing a high incidence of malaria. |
| 1968 | 83 | Exceptional dryness and little malaria, but a very deficient crop. |
| 1969 | 210 | Reduced food because of the bad crop of the preceding year. |

infectious factors (malaria) doubtless act independently here, and in this particular case, the influence of nutrition, undernourishment, and malnutrition seems especially pronounced.

MORTALITY AND CLIMATE. Climate is one of the main components of the physical environment and its role in determining the regional differences is especially manifested in West Africa by the clear distinction of climatic zones from north to south. But, as we have already stressed, we do not yet have sufficient data to compare mortality in

[43] Cantrelle, "Mortalité: facteurs."

different climatic zones. We can, however, bring out the close relationships between climate and mortality level by noting (in addition to the annual variations already seen in Table 4.16) the seasonal mortality variations in a homogeneous population living in the same geographical area. We can, moreover, without comparing the levels, at least compare the seasonal variations of different regions. The Sine study zone in Senegal illustrates this (see Table 4.17).

TABLE 4.17
Monthly mortality fluctuations by age, Sine (Senegal) 1963–1965 (per mille distribution of deaths)

| Month | All Ages | 1–4 Years | 5–44 Years | 45 Years and Over |
|-------|----------|-----------|------------|-------------------|
| January | 61 | 51 | 62 | 86 |
| February | *77* | 58 | *110* | *133* |
| March | 63 | 52 | 104 | 91 |
| April | 60 | 59 | 83 | 74 |
| May | 58 | 45 | 86 | 79 |
| June | 48 | 41 | 66 | 65 |
| July | 54 | 50 | 53 | 60 |
| August | 91 | 106 | 59 | 66 |
| September | 140 | 151 | 92 | 87 |
| October | *174* | *209* | *127* | *105* |
| November | 99 | 105 | 88 | 73 |
| December | 82 | 73 | 70 | 81 |
| Totals | 1,000 | 1,000 | 1,000 | 1,000 |

SOURCE: Cantrelle, "Etude Démographique dans la Région du Sine-Saloum."
NOTE: Distinct maximums are in italics.

The distribution of all deaths by month of death shows a very sharp maximum in October and a slight climb in February. But this distribution is influenced above all by children's deaths, which are the most numerous. If we distinguish between the age groups, we see that in the 1–4 years group the range of variation is such that the maximum month exhibits five times the deaths of the minimum one, whereas after five years the ratio is only somewhat greater or smaller than double. Thus, the 1–4 years group is the most sensitive to environmental conditions. The reaction to environmental conditions varies in another way according to age; in the 1–4 years group, the maximum is very pronounced at the end of the wet season, in October; the distribution is reversed in the oldest group, where the dry season peak, February, is higher than the wet season one; it is in between for the middle age group.

In the survey zone, mortality tables have been drawn up for the first three years of age, according to the quarter of the year in which the birth occurred:[44] The children born in November, December, and January have, at three years, a survival rate of scarcely 50 percent; at the other extreme, those born in February, March, and April have a survival rate of 58 percent. Calculated in monthly cohorts, the differences are still more significant: 45 percent of survivals among those born in November, as against 59 percent among those born in February. It so happens that the distribution of births according to the month of year in this area does not influence this mortality pattern, since the maximum and minimum incidences of births are not widely separate and approximately correspond to the average probabilities of death.

Children born in November, December, and January reach the end of their first year (a delicate age when malnutrition and infection begin to rage) at the worst season of the year; it is at this period, in fact, that malaria is at its maximum, the new crops have scarcely come in to restock the food stores, and the combination of temperature and humidity is the least bearable.

Seasonal mortality variations differ according to climatic zone. In the coastal section of the so-called Sudanese zone (that is, Senegal and Guinea coasts) the mortality maximum occurs in the wet season. This characteristic appears to continue inland beyond the geographic limits of the coastal environment (as the Sine-Saloum example demonstrates). Conversely, in areas of inland climate (Sudanese and Sahelian), maximum mortality is more likely to be experienced in the dry season (data from Bamako, Upper Volta, and north Dahomey surveys support

this observation). In this part of West Africa there appear to be two bioclimatical regions. In addition, there are the Guinea equatorial climates, such as are found in Ivory Coast, and Dahomey, where maximum mortality occurs at the end of the dry season and the beginning of the wet one.[45]

MORTALITY AND URBANIZATION. All African data demonstrate lower mortality in urban than rural areas. The case of Senegal, described above, with its precise data can be cited. The crude death rate, around 30 per thousand in rural areas, drops to 10 per thousand in the capital, Dakar. For the 1–4 years group, the difference is still more pronounced—about 100 to 20 per thousand. The crude death rate in Dakar, 10 per thousand, is lower than that of European countries; this is largely a result of the population structure, for the 1–4 year death rate, for instance, remains almost 20 times higher than that found in Europe. There are numerous factors which explain these differences, but we cannot really measure their relative importance. African urban centers exhibit a concentration of wage earners who earn much higher incomes than are found in rural areas, and this assures them of a better and more regular diet than is enjoyed in rural areas. The concentration of medical facilities ensures better health conditions in the towns than the countryside; improved sanitation makes a considerable difference, as do the hospitals and clinics and the short distances to the nearest health facilities.

The possibility should not be ruled out that this differential between rural and urban mortality will continue to increase in the years ahead. In some rural areas mortality may well increase, whereas in the towns there appears to be every possibility of further decline. In Dakar, for example, infant mortality has dropped from 175 per thousand in 1942–1945 to 70 per thousand at the present time.

In Europe, during the industrial revolution, health conditions were generally worse in urban areas. In African towns health levels

[44] Cantrelle and Leridon, "Infant and Child Mortality."

[45] Cantrelle, "Mortalité: facteurs."

are rising faster than they did in Europe at that time. It is this drop in urban mortality, accompanied by almost unchanged fertility, that is responsible for the rising rate of natural increase. In a city like Dakar, the crude birth rate is about 40 per thousand which with a mortality of 10 per thousand, yields a rate of natural increase of around 3 per cent. The creation of new employment in Dakar does not seem to be keeping up with national population increase and was apparently averaging 5–6 percent yearly for the ten years from 1960 to 1970

It is possible that in the coming years, migratory increase, which until now has formed the main element of urban demographic growth, will gradually, with the continuing discouragement to potential immigrants of urban underemployment, become of smaller importance than urban natural increase.

MORTALITY AND MEDICAL SERVICES. It is very difficult to measure the role of medical services in the drop in urban mortality. The situation is perhaps clearer in rural parts, where we can assume that medical activities have had only a limited influence. Indeed, even in the absence of public health activities, mortality and morbidity variations from one year to another or from one region to another are considerable and arise from a fine ecological balance upon which life in these areas depends.

Proof can be adduced by comparing, in similar ecological conditions, the mortality of a population benefiting from medical provision with a population without it. This type of study has been partly carried into effect in the Khombol-Thiénaba survey zone in Senegal,[46] where a campaign of nutritional education has been carried out in one group of villages and vaccination against measles in another. The difference between the mortality in these two groups is not significant, but both enjoy significantly lower death rates than a control population which has been under observation by a population survey and which has not benefited from any health campaign. However, the margin of lower mortality in the first two populations over the control population is smaller than variations between populations caused by differing conditions of the physical environment. It might also be noted that the public health campaign affected only a few villages; it could not be extended to all rural areas of the country because of the cost and the limited budgetary provision.

At this economic and health level and with these conditions of mortality, an improvement in economic conditions would have an indirect effect on the drop in mortality (through a rise in the health level) more important than a direct public health program.

All health and other social and economic programs should include indicators to measure their effectiveness. The mortality level in childhood seems to be one of the better indicators. In addition measures of per capita production and real income should be attempted; trends in these indices would doubtless be of value in predicting mortality trends.

[46] Cantrelle et al., "Mortalité de l'Enfant."

THE MAJOR purpose of this chapter is to examine the relations between resources and population in West Africa. This is a difficult task because we do not have adequate information on either of these subjects. In the physical realm there is need for far more detailed data on soils, hydrology, land capability, and insects and diseases, not to mention mineral, forest, and fishery resources. In the demographic sphere we do not have truly satisfactory maps of population densities or distributions. The francophone countries have had only sample censuses and some of these cover only portions of the eight countries involved; and the 1962 and 1963 censuses for the most populous country, Nigeria, are considered to contain serious distortions, the 1963 census probably giving an overcount of 10 million people.

An additional difficulty arises in attempting to relate population to single factors such as climate, soils, and landforms since they are often closely interrelated and since a complex of interacting features, physical and cultural, usually is required to explain the existing population distributions. The element of scale is also of great importance: gross distributional features may be broadly related to one set of environmental factors while internal, detailed examination may reveal that other physical factors become more significant. This is particularly true for soil, landform, and hydrological conditions as contrasted with climate and vegetation. Finally, far too little attention has been paid to analyzing population distributions and the dearth of documentary sources is not likely to be corrected for some years.

Following these several caveats, the following section will very briefly present some basic data on the population of West Africa and the broad distributional patterns that may be discerned. Next, an attempt is made to correlate population with physical resources, which are seen to be inadequate to explain the existent distributions. This section is succeeded by a brief look at historical and socioeconomic factors which help to elucidate the population patterns. Explanations for the population characteristics of the four belts

# CHAPTER FIVE

# *Population & Resources*

WILLIAM A. HANCE

which are delineated below then are summarized. Finally, attention is given to the question: Are portions of West Africa subject to pressure of population on resources?

## BASIC DATA

The United Nations' figures for the populations of West African countries in mid-1967 are given in Table 5.1. The validity of many of the population estimates, as is developed more fully in other chapters, is open to serious question, particularly in the case of Nigeria. The total population of the area, 104 million, gave West Africa the highest crude density for any of the major regions of the continent delineated by the United Nations: 43.9 persons per square mile, as compared to 28.4 per square mile for the whole continent and its appurtenances.

These crude densities are rather meaningless, if not even dangerous, however, for they bear little relation to the densities actually experienced by the bulk of the inhabitants. Indeed, as Table 5.1 shows, eight countries have crude densities above the average, four have crude densities about twice the average, and one has a crude density about four times the average. Furthermore, large segments of

nearly empty desert country in Mauritania, Mali, and Niger distort the overall density figure; if one subtracts the areas of these three countries with densities under 10 per square mile, the average density for the rest of West Africa jumps from 43.9 to 84.3 per square mile.

Pursuing this line a little further to illustrate the misleading character of crude density figures and to present some concept of population concentration and dispersion on an abstract basis, it may be seen from Table 5.2, which gives density ranges calculated by subdivisions of various orders for the 15 countries, that about 85 percent of the population of West Africa lived at densities above the crude density on about a quarter of the total area; that about two-thirds of the population was concentrated on about a tenth of the area at densities over twice the average; and that a third of the total population was confined to less than one-fortieth of the whole area at densities above seven times the average.

Turning to more specific features of population distribution in West Africa, the two broadest-scale features to be noted are: (1) the large empty to very sparsely populated belt associated with the desert and sahel

TABLE 5.1
Estimated population of West African countries, mid-1967

| Country | Population (in thousands) | Area | | Density | |
|---|---|---|---|---|---|
| | | Sq. miles (in thousands) | Sq. kilometers (in thousands) | Per sq. mile | Per sq. kilometer |
| Mauritania | 1,100 | 398 | 1,031 | 2.8 | 1.1 |
| Senegal | 3,670 | 76 | 196 | 48.3 | 18.7 |
| Gambia | 343 | 4 | 11 | 85.8 | 31.2 |
| Mali | 4,697 | 479 | 1,240 | 9.8 | 3.8 |
| Upper Volta | 5,054 | 106 | 274 | 47.7 | 18.4 |
| Niger | 3,546 | 489 | 1,267 | 7.2 | 2.8 |
| Guinea (Bissau) | 528 | 14 | 36 | 37.7 | 14.7 |
| Sierra Leone | 2,439 | 28 | 72 | 87.1 | 33.9 |
| Guinea | 3,702 | 95 | 246 | 39.0 | 15.0 |
| Liberia | 1,110 | 43 | 111 | 25.8 | 10.0 |
| Ivory Coast | 4,010 | 124 | 322 | 32.3 | 12.5 |
| Ghana | 8,139 | 92 | 239 | 88.6 | 34.1 |
| Togo | 1,724 | 22 | 56 | 78.4 | 30.8 |
| Dahomey | 2,505 | 44 | 113 | 56.9 | 22.2 |
| Nigeria | 61,450 | 357 | 924 | 172.1 | 66.5 |
| Total | 104,017 | 2,371 | 6,138 | 43.9 | 16.9 |

Source: United Nations *Statistical Yearbook, 1968* (New York, 1969), pp. 78–79.

TABLE 5.2
Estimated population density ranges for West Africa, mid-1967

| Density (persons per sq, mile) | Percentage of Population | Percentage of Area | Cumulative Percentages | | Reverse Cumulative Percentages | |
|---|---|---|---|---|---|---|
| | | | Population | Area | Population | Area |
| Less than 10 | 3.3 | 52.5 | | | 100.1 | 99.9 |
| 10–20 | 3.1 | 9.8 | 6.4 | 62.3 | 96.8 | 47.4 |
| 20–30 | 2.9 | 5.5 | 9.3 | 67.8 | 93.7 | 37.6 |
| 30–40 | 4.4 | 5.8 | 13.7 | 73.6 | 90.8 | 32.1 |
| 40–50 | 4.8 | 4.8 | 18.5 | 78.4 | 86.4 | 26.3 |
| 50–60 | 3.3 | 2.6 | 21.8 | 81.1 | 81.6 | 21.5 |
| 60–70 | 5.7 | 3.8 | 27.5 | 84.8 | 78.3 | 18.9 |
| 70–80 | 1.7 | 1.0 | 29.2 | 85.9 | 72.6 | 15.1 |
| 80–90 | 2.7 | 1.5 | 31.9 | 87.3 | 70.9 | 14.1 |
| 90–100 | 4.1 | 1.9 | 36.1 | 89.2 | 68.2 | 12.6 |
| 100–200 | 19.8 | 6.4 | 55.9 | 95.7 | 64.1 | 10.7 |
| 200–300 | 11.0 | 1.9 | 66.9 | 97.6 | 44.3 | 4.3 |
| 300–400 | 4.2 | 0.6 | 71.1 | 98.2 | 33.3 | 2.4 |
| 400–500 | 6.7 | 0.7 | 77.7 | 98.8 | 29.1 | 1.8 |
| 500–600 | 2.4 | 0.2 | 80.1 | 99.0 | 22.4 | 1.1 |
| 600–700 | 2.8 | 0.2 | 82.8 | 99.2 | 20.0 | 0.9 |
| 700–800 | 2.5 | 0.1 | 85.3 | 99.3 | 17.2 | 0.7 |
| 800–900 | 0.2 | —[a] | 85.5 | | 14.7 | |
| 900–1,000 | 3.2 | 0.1 | 88.7 | 99.5 | 14.5 | 0.6 |
| Over 1,000 | 11.3 | 0.5 | 100.1 | 99.9 | | |

SOURCE: William A. Hance, *Population, Migration, and Urbanization in Africa* (New York: Columbia University Press, 1970) p. 60.
[a] Less than 0.05 percent.

regions along the north, and (2) the higher densities toward the southeast of the region. In fact, four countries, Ghana, Togo, Dahomey, and Nigeria, which account for 21.7 percent of the area of West Africa, have about 71.0 percent of its total population.

Another very important distributional feature is the rural-urban division; calculations show that for 1967, 16.6 percent of the population of West Africa resided in centers of 5,000 and more, 11.7 percent in towns above 20,000, and 8.8 percent in cities of 100,000 and over. Each of these figures is somewhat below the comparable levels for Africa as a whole, which were estimated at 19.8, 15.8, and 11.5 percent respectively for the same year. The urban percentage varies markedly from country to country, however; it is below 10 percent in the northern countries of Mauritania, Mali, Niger, and Upper Volta, and above 20 percent in Senegal, Ivory Coast, and Ghana. Western Nigeria is also highly urbanized, although many of its large traditional Yoruba towns still contain a high percentage of agriculturalists.

Numerous observers have professed to see parallel belts of population in West Africa, each of which often is said to show relationship to climate/vegetation zones. Three such belts normally are delineated, although it might be appropriate to add a fourth zone across the sparsely populated north. As used here the four belts serve only as a device for generalizing part of a very complex pattern and no effort is made to confine them rigidly to physical zones. Very briefly these belts are as follows:

(1) The northern desert/sahel belt, roughly north of the 15° N parallel, is empty or very sparsely populated except for bands along the Senegal and Niger rivers and lesser nodes associated with the Aïr and Adrar des Iforhas Massifs. (2) A northern belt contains a series of high-density nodes, including those in Senegal and Gambia, the Fouta Djallon Mountains of Guinea, around Bamako in Mali, the Mossi country of Upper Volta, around Korhogo in northern Ivory Coast and Navrongo in northern Ghana, the Kabrai country of northern Togo, the Atakora region

of northern Dahomey, and regions around the emirate cities of northern Nigeria, particularly Sokoto, Katsina, Kano, and Maiduguri. The areas of relative high density around Kaduna and on the Jos Plateau may also be assigned to this belt. (3) The so-called middle belt, occurs south of the northern high-density belt and is generally more sparsely populated than the belts to either side. Overall densities are higher in the east of the belt than in the west, particularly in Nigeria, and regions of higher density occur in Sierra Leone, upper Guinea (the inland southeast), around Bouaké in Ivory Coast, and in Tivland, Nigeria. The population pattern in Sierra Leone is atypical—Clarke notes, in addition to the high-density node centered on Freetown, two zones or belts of higher density, which he calls the two "lungs" of that country.[1] The first, north and northeast of the capital, contains the most intensive zone of swamp-rice farming, important fishery operations, iron-ore mining around Marampa, and market-gardening in the Bullom Peninsula. The second, in the south and southeast, has been influenced by diamond mining and cash-crop farming and displays a notable correlation with the series of towns along the railway upline from Bo. (4) A southern belt is sparsely populated to the west and densely populated to the east. It contains zones of particularly high density as follows: (a) Ashanti, Ghana; (b) a coastal belt running from southern Ghana through Togo, Dahomey and western Nigeria, and coalescing with (c) Yorubaland in the Western State and its extension into the Mid-West State in Nigeria; (d) Iboland in the East-Central State; and, (e) Ibibioland in the Southeastern State of Nigeria. West of Ghana there are lesser nodes in southeastern Ivory Coast in the hinterland of Abidjan, and around Monrovia, Liberia.

With this brief sketch of the major features of population distribution in West Africa in mind, it is now appropriate to turn to the correlations of population with physical factors. It will be apparent already, however,

that the population patterns are somewhat inchoate and only partially simplified by reference to the commonly accepted three- or four-belt concept.

## CORRELATIONS BETWEEN POPULATION AND PHYSICAL FACTORS

The existing population patterns of West Africa are the result of a complex of inter-acting factors whose relations are so involved as to defy accurate measurement of the relative importance of each. Vegetation, for example, largely is conditioned by climate; soils are related to geology, landforms, climate, and vegetation; diseases may be related to climate, hydrology, and other factors; and, of course, soils and vegetation may be affected greatly by differing land-use systems. Nevertheless, a single-factor analysis is of value in understanding the population distributions of the area.

CLIMATE. The temperature regimes in all of West Africa are tropical and would permit year-round production and winds are seldom a limiting factor; hence it is the third element of climate—precipitation—which is of prime importance. Indeed, rainfall is probably the single most important physical determinant in the population pattern of West Africa. This is most clearly apparent in the transition zone from the sudan to the sahel and desert zones. The highest densities in the north generally are found between the 12th and 14th N parallels where rainfall ranges from about 40 to 24 inches per annum. Below the 24 inch isohyet the rainfall regime is too unstable for rain-grown crops, even small variations making the growing of drought-tolerant millet a risky venture. Population densities fall immediately northward of the cultivation zone to about 8 per square mile in a narrow band and then vary rapidly to less than 3 per square mile finally reaching zero over vast desert stretches. Exceptions to this generalization are explained either by the existence of through-flowing streams (the Senegal and the Niger),

[1] J. I. Clarke, *Sierra Leone in Maps* (London: London University Press, 1966), pp. 41–42.

by higher-than-average rainfall due to the orographic influence, or by the presence of springs and easily reached aquifers.

A second major relationship between population and precipitation is seen in the high densities of the southern belt, which may be explained in part by the ability to produce two crops per year. This is not possible, except under irrigation, in the northern belts.

However, if precipitation were the all-controlling factor in population distribution, one would expect to see a downward gradation of population densities as one moved across the generally east-west trending isohyets. As was indicated in the brief description of population belts, this does not occur except from the south to the middle belt and from the northern high-density belt to the Sahara. Other factors must, therefore, be sought to explain both the relatively lower densities of the middle belt and the high-density nodes of the northern belt.

VEGETATION. The major vegetation belts of West Africa have, like precipitation belts, a general east-west alignment. In the desert and sahel areas the absence or sparseness of vegetation, climatically controlled, helps to explain the population patterns. In the sahel and sudan belts the open grassy or wooded steppes provided easy routes for human movement and this may, therefore, help to explain the greater number of high density nodes and their spacing along the full length of the northern belt as contrasted with the concentration of nodes toward the eastern half of the southern belt, where movement through the high forest was very much more difficult.

Focusing on the southern belt, it is apparent that the areas where the rain forest continues to dominate are sparsely populated. This is particularly true for the large sections of high forest in the west of Loffa County and the southeastern third of Liberia and in the southwest of Ivory Coast; lesser areas of high forest in Ghana and in parts of southern Nigeria are also sparsely populated.

The absence of dense forest in southeast Ghana and southern Togo and Dahomey, which have lower precipitation than the coastal zones to the east and west, is cited as an explanation for the high densities existing there. The coastal high-density belt of Ghana accounted in 1960 for 53.9 percent of the total population of that country, while 34 percent of Togo's 1968 population was concentrated in the four maritime circumscriptions which occupied only 12.5 percent of its area, and the southern 15 percent of Dahomey contains almost half of that country's population. Similarly, a break in continuity of the southern rain forest helps to explain the Yoruba concentration in southwestern Nigeria.

The savanna rain forest boundary also appears to have been a favored zone because fire could be used to cause the gradual retreat of the forest. Elsewhere, as in Ibibio-land, the high forest has essentially been replaced by oil palm forests and unusually high densities are found in what would be, under climax conditions, a zone of selva or rain forest. Again, therefore, one must look to factors other than vegetation to explain the population patterns in the rainy tropical zone, because within it there are both areas of remarkably high densities and areas which are practically empty.

The character of the local vegetation may also help to explain the settlement pattern in different parts of West Africa, particularly the dispersion of small groupings in existing rain forest regions, but also the concentration of peoples in hamlets and small villages in these regions, presumably because clearing could be better accomplished by men working together.

In the southern, middle, and northern belts, natural vegetation has sometimes been left standing in rings surrounding the settlements to provide barriers against neighboring tribes. The Annang and Ibibio in eastern Nigeria, for example, left successive rings of high forest around their villages for this purpose. Wooded zones also helped to protect hill refuge sites in the north, since they made incursion by mounted warriors difficult, while thorn bush sometimes served the same purpose between plains inhabitants.

Mangrove swamps, especially those in the Niger Delta, have tended to repulse occupation, though a number of environmental difficulties besides vegetation also account for the characteristically low densities in that region.

The resources of the natural flora of West Africa are relatively unimportant in attracting population. Exploitation of the tropical rain forests is best developed in Ivory Coast, Ghana, and Nigeria, but the total number of persons involved is not particularly high. Mention might be made of the towns of Samreboi in Ghana and Sapele in Nigeria, which owe their existence in part to the presence of lumber and plywood mills. A variety of fruits, nuts, gums, and other products are derived from natural trees but, again, none could be said to have had any notable effect on population distribution.

SOILS. The broad zonal-soil patterns of West Africa also display, though much less clearly than do climate and vegetation, an east-west alignment, but it is difficult to relate population distribution to these zones. The bulk of West Africa has relatively poor soils, with leached latosols extending well into dry regions where they might by analogy not be expected to occur. The worst soils are found on comparatively level sites where an impervious crust has developed with only a thin horizon or no soil at all. No other part of the world has a comparable formation of sterile duricrusts.

West Africa is also relatively disadvantaged with respect to the availability of rich, azonal soils such as alluvials and volcanics, and most of the alluvials that are present, such as those in the inner Niger Delta in Mali, do not compare with the fertile soils of the Nile or the alluvials of southeast Asia.

Considerable skill is sometimes evident in the selection of soils on a local scale but, as will be seen, this generalization is subject to important exceptions.

Of very great significance in setting some of the present population patterns was the ease of working specific soils with the primitive implements which were in use and which continue to be the main tools of the farmer. In many cases, ease of working took precedence over inherent fertility. Sandy soils in the wetter areas were, for example, much more readily cleared and worked than clay soils, and they were also more suitable for staples such as yams and for the oil palm. In the sudan belt, too, the ease of working soils has been an important attraction in such areas as the groundnut zone of Senegal or the drift-soil regions of northern Nigeria.

But there are examples of the use of heavy soils in densely populated areas such as in parts of the Ghanaian and Nigerian cocoa belts or in the Abakaliki region of eastern Nigeria, where huge mounds are laboriously formed to produce yams on the low-lying, heavy clay soils.

Relatively good soils are found along some of the river floodplains, in parts of Yorubaland, and in some of the highland regions such as the Atakora Mountains and parts of the volcanic sections of the plateau and mountain belt along the eastern border of Nigeria. Yet, for every densely populated area correlated with good soils, it is possible to find poor soil regions supporting heavy population concentrations. Examples are found in the Fouta Djallon, the Mossi country of Upper Volta (where better soil regions occur both to the east and to the west), and in Iboland where the highest densities are associated with the worst soils.

LANDFORMS. West Africa is predominantly a region of low or moderately high plains. Higher and more rugged areas are present but they often are isolated and cover a relatively small portion of the whole area. Thus most of the region could be said to have landforms permissively favorable to human occupation.

The landform pattern of West Africa is nowhere nearly as important in affecting population distributions as it is in East and Central Africa. Topography did not present important barriers to movement across the region; the orographic factor is much less significant than in the east; and the sedimentary or basement complex character of most of the uplands contrasts with the rich volcanic plateaus and mountains of parts of Ethiopia and East Africa.

The following are probably the two most important positive influences of landforms on population distribution in West Africa: (1) the upgrading of many of the higher lands through increased rainfall orographically induced and (2) the attraction of many of the higher lands as refuge areas for peoples who sought to escape domination by stronger groups. The first is certainly true for the windward sides of all the uplands away from the coasts, and the two great massifs in the desert intercept enough rain to support settlements in areas which would otherwise be waterless. Some of the highlands close to the coast, however, receive too much rainfall, as on the windward slopes of Mount Nimba in Liberia or the southern part of the Cameroon highlands. Examples of the second influence, refuge sites, include: the Bandiagara Plateau east of Mopti in Mali, where the Dogon occupy some of the cliffs and mesas at densities up to 400 per square mile; the Atakora Mountains in northwestern Dahomey, where a variety of ethnic groups were driven by the conquering Bariba and where the Somba, in particular, live at especially high densities; the Jos Plateau, whose topography presented difficulties to the Fulani horsemen and helped to save the local pagans from their domination; the Biu Plateau, where compounds of Burra pagans still are scattered all over the rugged landscape; and the Mandara Mountains.

In lower regions smaller landform features also frequently influenced the settlement of various groups. Some examples are: the rock outcrops and ridges in Yorubaland, where Abeokuta and other centers occupy fine defensive sites; the dissected uplands south of the Niger River in western Nigeria, where numerous hill settlements were formed as a response to Yoruba and Nupe raids in the nineteenth century; some of the most densely populated parts of Iboland, including the Nsukka Plateau; and, in a different situation,

the coastal flats west of Lagos which were used as refuge sites because protection was provided by the lagoon to the north.

The very high densities sometimes prevailing in these refuge areas, the landforms of which were in other respects often unfavorable for occupancy, led to some remarkably intensive land-use practices such as terracing and, in the case of the Dogon, transporting soil to form new fields.

The siting of some of the major coastal cities was influenced, sometimes rather precisely, by detailed features of the land and water scape. This is true for Nouadhibou (Port Etienne) in Mauritania, Dakar in Senegal, Bathurst in Gambia, Freetown in Sierra Leone, Abidjan in Ivory Coast, and to a lesser extent for many of the other ports.

HYDROLOGY. The availability of surface and easily reached underground water (in turn related to climate, geology, and landforms, and combinations of these) sometimes permits the support of considerably higher population densities than would otherwise occur.

The most striking examples related to surface water are seen in the bands of population along the Senegal River and along the Middle Niger, particularly between Lake Débo in the inner delta in Mali and Tillabéri in Niger. Both of these streams flow through regions with inadequate rainfall for tillage agriculture. South of Mopti in Mali and of Niamey in Niger, the attraction of the Niger is less marked.

These and lesser rivers in the north often flood extensive areas seasonally, providing, as the waters recede, lands which can be planted to catch crops, or ponds and lakes which can be used for irrigation of fields in the dry period. Partial control of the Niger by the Sansanding Dam and of the Senegal east of Saint-Louis by a long dike protecting 75,000 acres being developed mainly for rice production, has increased the supporting capacity of the zones, and future infrastructural installations may further increase this capacity.

The correlation between inundation and

population density is not always close, however. In some cases in the inner Niger Delta the annual flooding attracts only fishermen; elsewhere, as in the dead dune country where the Niger divides into numerous branches, conditions are eminently suitable for intensive occupancy, and densities are quite high from Lake Débo to Timbuktu. A narrow band along Lake Chad also has higher population densities, and polderization for rice and wheat should permit even more intensive occupancy.

Most of the other river valleys of West Africa are sparsely populated, including those of the lower Niger and its main eastern affluent, the Benue; exceptions are seen in the valleys of Gambia, Mono in southern Togo, and Dahomey. This pattern is in marked contrast with that of Europe, eastern North America, and south and southeast Asia where some of the highest densities are associated with river valleys. The explanation is primarily the higher incidence of diseases, onchocerciasis in the north and trypanosomiasis, malaria, and other diseases in the south. A secondary explanation is the lack of navigability and the difficulty of constructing roads along most of the rivers, which are rarely the route ways that they are in the other continental regions mentioned above. The major exceptions are the Niger, the Senegal, and the Gambia rivers, and the navigability of the two larger streams is interrupted by rapids, reduced to shorter stretches in the low-water period, and plagued by shifting sandbanks and difficult mouths. Neither has proved to be a backbone of transport in francophone West Africa, a role that was originally contemplated for them and which is enshrined in all of the coast to Niger railways, only one of which, the Dakar–Niger Railway, has thus far reached that river.

The importance of the inland waters of West Africa in fishery resources should be noted. This is briefly discussed in the next section.

The easy availability of groundwater helps to explain the relatively high densities in a number of areas in West Africa as, for example: the close-settled zone around Kano where the water table can readily be reached by crude and shallow wells; the quaternary Dallol-Bosso valley east of Niamey, where densities correspond to the depth of the underground aquifer which is about 33–48 feet below the surface at its shallowest levels; and numerous dry valleys of the sudan belt where wells can be readily dug and where water tables usually rise in the dry period. Many deeper wells and bore holes have been sunk with modern techniques, particularly in the years since World War II, to the advantage of both human and livestock populations, but in some regions the great depth of the water table makes such improvements too expensive to be justified.

Conversely, the lack of available surface or ground water helps to explain the relatively low densities of some rather large areas, not always confined to the dryer parts of the region. Sandy areas in particular are often plagued by water shortages and the depth of aquifers. The Ferlo district in northwest Senegal, for example, could support crops in the rainy season, but lack of potable water in the dry season accounts in considerable part for its sparse population. Other examples of areas which suffer from at least seasonal water shortages are the Oti Plateau of Togo, portions of the Volta basin, much of the middle belt of Nigeria, and large parts of the Bauchi and Biu plateaus and of Bornu.

The development of hydroelectric resources has had an impact on population in only a few areas. It has caused the displacement of some tens of thousands of people who inhabited the lands now occupied by the lakes created by the Akosombo Dam in Ghana (Lake Volta) and the Kainji Dam in Nigeria. Electricity from the former installation has helped to attract industry to Tema, particularly the aluminium smelter, which guaranteed purchases of large blocks of power, thus justifying the heavy investment required. The impact of the Kainji Dam is less apparent because output from its generating station is fed into a grid serving large areas of the north and west, and because only a small settlement is required to support operations at the station.

FAUNA. Disease-carrying insects play a very significant role in the distribution of population in West Africa. Most important is the tsetse fly, the bearer of both human and bovine trypanosomiasis, whose presence in rainy, tropical, and savanna regions has precluded keeping cattle in an enormous area, with the minor exceptions of the resistant, midget West African shorthorn and Ndama breeds. This has essentially confined the major cattle-keeping groups to the sudan and sahel areas and provides an important explanation for the comparative sparseness of population in the middle belt. The greater risk of human trypanosomiasis in the middle belt and in riverine areas and mangrove swamps in the southern belt also helps to explain both widespread and more local zones of low density.

The danger of contracting onchocerciasis is so great along the rivers and their tributary streams that these areas are virtually devoid of population. In Upper Volta the retreat from such areas is a continuing phenomenon despite the presence of good soils and better water supplies, in part because villages along the frontier become subject to attack by animals, including lions. Only a major clearing effort followed by reasonably dense settlement and land use may be expected to reverse this trend.

West Africa is much less famed for game animals than eastern and southern Africa, which helps to explain the lower receipts from tourism which has become a major source of revenue and provided many jobs in such countries as Uganda, Tanzania, and, above all, Kenya. Nonetheless, there are a number of game parks which are beginning to attract substantial numbers of tourists and other parks could be established and better stocked to stimulate this potentially important activity. Both existing and prospective parks are likely to be established in areas where competition between man and wild animals is minimal, that is, practically empty lands.

The fishery resources of West Africa are substantial, both in inland rivers, lakes, swamps, inundated lands, and lagoons and in the adjacent seas. Fishing is the prime activity of some tribes, a supplementary activity for others. Ironically, the drier countries in the north export fish in considerable tonnages to those in the south which front the sea. But sea fisheries have received greater attention in the past few decades with the provision of better nets, power boats, and improved harbor facilities. Tuna and sardine fishing are the most modern and commercialized branches and contribute in some measure to such centers as Nouadhibou, Dakar, Freetown, Monrovia, Abidjan, and Tema. Most fishing, however, is still characterized by primitive techniques and very low annual catches per man.

MINERALS. Mineral resources have not been particularly significant in West Africa in altering the pattern of population distributions, though in some places there are small nuclei based on the extraction and processing of minerals. Minerals are, however, of considerably greater importance in a number of countries in supporting rail and port activities and in providing foreign exchange. This is particularly true in Mauritania, Guinea, Sierra Leone, Liberia, Ghana, and Nigeria.

The largest numbers of people in mining are probably to be found in the labor-intensive extraction of alluvial diamonds and gold by individual pot-holers. At the height of the diamond rush in Sierra Leone an estimated 75,000 persons were engaged in pot-holing; as many as 20,000 may be engaged in mining for gold and diamonds in Ghana in addition to the 24,300 reported engaged in mining in 1967. The fact that mining of gold, diamonds, and manganese in Ghana occurs in a relatively small part of the country between Kumasi and Takoradi has meant that this activity has had a recognizable impact on population concentrations.

The booming crude oil production of Nigeria has attracted more people to the generally rather sparsely populated producing areas and to such centers as Port Harcourt and Bonny, while the availability of large quantities of low-cost gas, most of which is now being burnt off, could attract more industries to such centers as Afam, Ughelli, and Aba. Coal mining in that country, now in decline, was an important impetus for the rise of Enugu, and the tin-columbite mines of the Jos Plateau attracted substantial numbers of people to that area, not only for mining and smelting but for the various supporting services.

Other mining nodes in West Africa include: F'dérik and Akjoujt in Mauritania; Fria, Boké, and Conakry in Guinea; Marampa in Sierra Leone; the four iron mines in Liberia plus processing and shipping at Buchanan and Monrovia, and Arlit in Niger.

CONCLUSION. To conclude this section on the correlation of population with physical resources, it is apparent that not one nor all of the factors is adequate to provide a satisfactory explanation for the existing distributions. As Morgan and Pugh put it, "the distribution of tribes and other social groups in West Africa does not appear to correspond with physical distributions."[2]

There are too many contradictions, too many anomalies. There are rainy tropical areas with remarkably high densities and those which are virtually empty; there are highly populated zones on mediocre and poor soils bounded by sparsely peopled areas with better soils; and there is the major anomaly of the less densely populated middle belt which cannot be explained satisfactorily solely by reference to its physical limitations.

## THE CORRELATION OF POPULATION WITH NONPHYSICAL FACTORS

It follows that one must turn to historical, cultural, and economic factors to fill in at least some of the gaps and possibly help to explain some of the anomalies. Discussion of these factors must perforce be very brief. Of very great significance in the present distri-

butions are the migrations which have been going on from time immemorial to the present, many of which are still inadequately documented.

Differing patterns may also be related to the great variety of ethnic groups and societies inhabiting the area. Urvoy notes that different tribes following the same way of life and enjoying more or less identical resources are likely to have characteristic population patterns and densities varying from one to the other.[3] And Morgan and Pugh state that "no demographic account of West Africa can . . . be satisfactory if it fails to discuss the societies to which its statistical units belong, and which therefore directly affect the distributions studied."[4]

One of the most important explanations for the existence of well-marked population nodes was the formation of more or less powerful empires, kingdoms, and chiefdoms whose coherence gave political and economic strength to their regions, permitting the formation and protection of intensively settled zones, often increased by the addition of captured slaves. Some of these kingdoms have been destroyed and others have disintegrated, but many are still clearly visible on the population map of West Africa. Great empires seem to have found the most favorable environment in the sudan belt where the largest number of strong ethnic groupings still are found. This has been related by some observers to the civilizing character of grain production as well as to the ease of movement in the region. Present population nodes which owe their significance in part to ethnic strength include: the Fouta Djallon; the Mossi empire in Upper Volta; the Hausa-Fulani emirates of Sokoto, Katsina, and Kano; and the Kanuri of Bornu.

In the south, important nodes were and are associated with the Asante of Ghana, the Fon and Goun of Dohomey, and the Yoruba and Bini of the present Western and Mid-West states of Nigeria. The node occupied by the

[2] W. B. Morgan and J. C. Pugh, *West Africa* (London: Methuen and Co., 1969), p. xxi.

[3] See Y. Urvoy, *Petit Atlas Ethno-Démographique du Soudan entre Sénégal et Tchad*, Mémoires de l'Institut Français d'Afrique Noire, 5 (Paris, 1942).

[4] Morgan and Pugh, *West Africa*, p. 3.

Ibo, who did not have well-developed political systems, appears to be an exception to the rule, but it may be explained by the centralized economic structure and the cultural cohesiveness of that group.

Both the more powerful and the lesser ethnic groupings are frequently surrounded by a kind of no-man's-land or zone of relatively low density. Examples are seen in the areas surrounding the Balante of Guinea (Bissau), the Bousansi, Senoufo, and Lobi of Upper Volta, and the Ibo and Ibibio of Nigeria. Corridors of lower density separating two important groupings are seen in the lands between the Yoruba and the Bini, the Ibo and Ibibio, and the Nupe and the Gwari.

It is particularly notable that almost all the powerful tribal groupings are found either in the southern or the northern high-density belt, and the relative emptiness of the middle belt may certainly be explained in part either by contraction into the others, by slaving within it from both sides, or by the inability of the northerners to extend their empires too far into the tsetse-ridden zone.

Intertribal wars and slaving played a major role in influencing the population pattern in many areas, though the significance of slaving in explaining the middle belt should not be exaggerated in view of the likelihood that many more slaves were taken from regions which are now densely populated than from that belt. Examples of areas which are purported still to reflect the impact of slaving activities are: the Yoruba portion of middle Dahomey where weak Yoruba groups were attacked by Fon and other Yoruba clans from Nigeria; the upland region of the middle belt in Nigeria affected by Yoruba and Bini slaving from the south and Nupe incursions from the north; the line of march of slaves in the Bende-Bonny basin between the two high-density cores in eastern Nigeria; the middle and upper Cross River basin; and portions of Sokoto Province.

The colonial period in West Africa brought slaving and most intertribal fighting to an end. It tended, on the one hand, to stabilize patterns of ethnic distribution existing at the time of entry, and, on the other hand, to make some population movements possible, such as "downhill" or outward migration from refuge areas. Individual migration, as contrasted with group movements, became much more significant, bringing greater intermingling of peoples in some rural areas and in many cities. Some new cash-cropping areas received large numbers of migrants as did older production "islands" and many urban communities, particularly the port-capital cities along the coast. Yet inertia has remained strong in most areas, as is amply illustrated by the high density nodes of the Mossi or by those in eastern Nigeria.

One very important shift, which began before the partition of West Africa but was strengthened by it, was the reversal of trade direction for most of the northern belt. That zone had long maintained contacts across the Sahara and trade and handicraft production were far more advanced there than in the south. With the development of sea routes, the caravan trade declined, as did many of the former great caravan centers, and the northern cities found themselves much less favored than the coastal zone. Only the region inland from Saint-Louis and Dakar escaped in full this impact, while only a few centers such as Bamako and Kano found the handicap considerably reduced by the construction of rail lines from the coast.

The development of modern transport has had an important bearing, not only on the grand scale of interior versus coastal belts and productive "islands" versus largely subsistence areas, but also in the details of population distribution within each region, as there has been a strong tendency for people to move to roadside locations and to towns and cities served by rail lines. The coastal zones rapidly surpassed the north in the production of cash crops; mining and urban growth were also far more important in the south and, when modern, market-oriented industries were introduced, the coastal cities again were the major beneficiaries.

Postcolonial years have seen a general reinforcement of these patterns. There has been an accelerated movement to the cities, which now appear to be gaining population at a rate out of all proportion to their economic growth. This helps to explain a series of expulsions of foreign Africans from several countries, the largest of which occurred in Ghana in late 1969. Despite the powerful new economic and political forces of the past century, however, the gross pattern of population distribution today would not be very strikingly different from that of the past. Innate conservatism and attachment to tribal lands remains a powerful determinant of that distribution.

### THE POPULATION BELTS REASSESSED

Returning to the concept of population belts, it is possible to reorder much of the data covered in the discussion of correlations between population distribution and physical and other factors.[5]

THE SOUTHERN BELT. Explanations that help to explain the high-density portions of the southern belt and many of the lesser nodes west of Ghana include the following: the ability to produce crops on a year-round basis; the comparative ease of producing such subsistence crops as manioc, corn, yams, plantains, and palm oil; the ecological suitability of the belt for many important export crops; the particular attractiveness of the rain-forest/savanna border zone for ease of clearing; the presence of some relatively favorable soils; the occurrence of most of the mineral-producing areas of West Africa; the existence of a number of kingdoms whose political stability permitted the rise of more intensive and diversified economies; the longer and more intensive contacts with the outside world during the modern period when technological advances have been most dramatic and levels of trade far higher than when the sudan belt was trading by trans-Saharan caravan; the concentration of modern political, commercial, financial, manufacturing, and cultural activities at

[5] Adapted from William A. Hance, *Population, Migration, and Urbanization in Africa* (New York: Columbia University Press, 1970), pp. 78–86.

coastal points for all of the states fronting on the sea; and the greater impact of in-migration in this belt.

THE MIDDLE BELT. The population pattern of the middle belt is considerably more difficult to explain than that of any of the others. Factors which are significant include the following: presence of the tsetse fly precluding movement into the area by cattle herders and leading to a higher incidence of human trypanosomiasis; the widespread absence of permanent water supplies; the restricted suitability of the area for many valuable tree crops; the existence of powerful kingdoms on both margins and their general absence in this belt; the impact of slave raids and intertribal conflict on the area; the less developed transport pattern; and the meager production of cash crops in the belt. In toto, these do not provide a fully satisfactory explanation, however, because there are a number of exceptions and because the belt is ecologically suitable for a rather broad range of crops which presumably could have supported considerably higher densities.

THE NORTHERN BELT. Explanations for the series of high density nodes characterizing the northern belt include the following: ability to grow such subsistence crops as sorghum, millet, groundnuts, and beans and such cash crops as groundnuts and cotton; the presence of some through-flowing streams and of easily tapped underground water in several areas; the availability of some relatively good soils; the use of some relatively advanced agricultural techniques, including heavy application of animal and human waste permitting annual cropping without fallow in some areas; the relative ease of movement across the belt; the early development of commercial nodes; the buildup of artisan activity in the urban centers; the more recent provision of improved transport to specific centers; the atypical advantage of the westernmost nodes of closeness to the coast; the existence of powerful states permitting and sustaining the economic development required to support dense populations; and the concentration of some groups in refuge areas in several parts of the belt.

THE SAHEL AND DESERT BELT. The general sparseness or lack of population in the sahel and desert belt is obviously climatically controlled. The major exceptions are explained by the presence of through-flowing streams, availability of groundwater or higher than average precipitation due to the orographic influence. Minor exceptions are explained by the occurrence of minerals (e.g., iron ore at F'dérik and copper at Akjoujt in Mauritania, fissionable raw materials at Arlit in Niger), and by fishing activities along the Mauritanian coast.

It must be reiterated that much more study and research will have to be done in a wide variety of disciplines, from soil science and hydrology to archaeology and human ecology, before a satisfactory presentation of the patterns of population distribution and the correlations with a wide range of physical and socioeconomic factors can be made. The preceding discussions can lead to only tentative conclusions and, while the relative importance of individual factors is clear for some regions, the factors influencing most areas are so numerous and so complexly interwoven as to preclude any more than very subjective weightings.

## POPULATION PRESSURE ON RESOURCES

It is appropriate in a discussion of population and resources to ask such questions as the following: What is the man/resource ratio? Is there overpopulation or underpopulation in West Africa? And is there pressure of population on resources? These questions are a great deal more complex than they may at first appear. Trying to calculate resources in the man/resource ratio involves adding unlike things such as acres of alluvials, kilowatts of electricity, and tons of bauxite; it is a tricky, hazardous, and almost impossible task when so much needed data are lacking. Such a ratio would also imply that there was homogeneity throughout the region and that it would be possible somehow to equalize the

ratio if the population were distributed appropriately, both of which are grossly misleading suggestions. A few valid generalizations might be forthcoming from such an analysis broken down by regions, such as that the carrying capacity of the vast arid and semiarid zones is strictly limited, that the soils over the bulk of the area compare unfavorably with numerous world regions, or that only very few political units are known to have mineral resources which would rate them above average on a world scale, but that is about all. The exercise would be further complicated by the sometimes very great differences between the achievable and scientifically potential production levels, at least over the short run, and by very inadequate knowledge and understanding of just what the potentials are in various ecological regions.

The question regarding overpopulation and underpopulation runs into conceptual difficulties which make the use of these terms of questionable utility. They each imply that there is a definable optimum population which should presumably be the goal for planners. But it is rarely possible to calculate that optimum under any specific set of economic and technological conditions with any degree of acceptability; the optimum can be set at widely varying levels depending on the standard of living one is prepared to accept; it is next to impossible to engineer demographic dynamics in order to achieve and maintain a hypothetical optimum; and, finally, optimum levels may be expected to differ with the stage of development of a country and particularly in accordance with the strength of extractive pursuits.

Because of these considerations, this section is focused on the last of the three questions posed: Is there pressure of population on resources? The concern is with places where, under existent land use and technology and at the present stage of development, there is pressure on the land or in the urban centers. It does not follow that there will always be pressure on these areas. And relieving the pressure may be as much involved with such things as soil regeneration, intensification, rationalization, creation of new and diversified employment opportunities, and the removing of inhibiting cultural conditions as it is with population per se. In most cases, however, the pressure would probably be far easier to reduce with a lower population and certainly with a less rapidly growing population.

Indications that there may be excessive pressure in a given area include the following: (1) soil deterioration, degradation, or outright destruction; (2) the use of excessively steep slopes and other marginal lands; (3) declining crop yields; (4) changing crop emphases, especially to soil-tolerant crops such as manioc; (5) the reduction of the fallow period and the lengthening of the cropping period without measures to retain soil fertility; (6) the breakdown of the indigenous farming system; (7) food shortages, hunger, and malnutrition; (8) land fragmentation, disputes over land, landlessness; (9) rural indebtedness; (10) unemployment and underemployment in rural and/or urban areas; (11) certain types of out-migration.

Obviously, some of these indicators need not always be related to pressure. Malnutrition, for example, may be explained by improper dietary practices and may exist in regions with bountiful and varied harvests. Migration may be motivated by other considerations than pressure in the source area. But all of the areas in West Africa denoted as suffering from pressure on the land are characterized by one or more, usually more, of the indicators listed above.

Some very large parts of West Africa may be considered to have pervasive problems of pressure, while many smaller regions, often with dense populations, show unmistakable evidence of pressure on the land.

The vast stretches of desert and sahel country in Mauritania, Mali, and Niger are characterized by a disequilibrium between the available pastures and the pastoralists dependent upon them. The effects of overstocking are widespread, while the recent increases in population growth further threaten the land and its inhabitants.[6] Refuge areas in

these countries, such as the Bandiagara Plateau, must also be included among regions affected by pressure on the land, while most of the oasis communities live at appallingly low standards.

Parts of Senegal suffer from soil exhaustion, which has forced a shift of the groundnut producing zone. The region around and including Dakar experiences severe unemployment and underemployment which existing plans are totally inadequate to relieve. In Guinea, the high density Fouta Djallon Plateau shows numerous indications of overuse. The Mossi country in Upper Volta experiences considerable demographic pressure. Much of that country is characterized by poor and fragile soils which have been badly eroded and it cannot properly support its present population.[7] As much as 20 percent of the working population of Upper Volta is more or less forced to migrate to relieve pressure in the home areas.

Smaller regions in northern Ivory Coast, Ghana, Togo, and Dahomey may be delineated as pressure areas. The arable surface of the Korhogo Cercle in Ivory Coast is totally exploited and apparently deteriorating. Northern Ghana has a number of areas which have been depopulated by soil exhaustion followed by soil erosion. Elsewhere the densely populated areas are characterized by fragmented holdings, land shortage, widespread removal of topsoil, and precarious nutrition levels. At least half a million people in northern Ghana are affected by pressure on the land.[8]

Refuge areas in the north of Togo and in the Atakora Mountains of Dahomey show definite signs of overuse and consequent

[6] UNESCO, *Nomades et Nomadisme au Sahara* (Paris, 1963), p. 100.

[7] Frank Lorimer, "The Population of Africa," in Ronald Freedman, ed., *Population: The Vital Revolution* (New York, 1964), p. 211.

[8] See T. E. Hilton, "Population Growth and Distribution in the Upper Region of Ghana," in John C. Caldwell and Chukuka Okonjo, eds., *The Population of Tropical Africa* (London: Longman, Green & Company and New York: Columbia University Press, 1968); John M. Hunter, "Population Pressure in a Part of the West African Savanna: A Study of Nangodi, Northeast Ghana," *Annals of the Association of American Geographers*, LVII, 1 (March 1967), 101–14.

deterioration. The Samba, for example, experience chronic undernutrition; they live at densities four to seven times those of other north Dahomeyan groups and some have been obliged to move to lower lands or to migrate to southern Togo and Ghana.

Northern Nigeria contains several populous zones which have problems of pressure on the land. Prothero notes rapid depletion of soil fertility, land hunger, and out-migration as evidence of deteriorating man/land relationships in the present Northwest State.[9] In the densely settled zones around Katsina, Kano, and Zaria, the fertility of the land is reasonably well maintained near the cities by heavy application of human and animal manure, but elsewhere fertility is not being sustained and the condition of the soils is thought to be deteriorating, while erosion is serious over large areas.[10] Densities are remarkably high in portions of the sudan belt of Nigeria, much above the critical carrying capacities as estimated by Allan.[11]

Except for a number of refuge areas and Tivland, there are few parts of the middle belt which could be classed as pressure areas. Writing about southern Tivland, Vermeer notes "too many people on the land, diminishing soil fertility and crop yield, and a shift to rapidly maturing crops yielding well on degrading soils."[12] He considers that changes that have been introduced in the traditional system are evidence that it is under extreme stress related to the pressure of population.

Turning to the coastal lands and again moving from west to east, Sierra Leone, which has one of the highest crude densities of continental African countries, is faced by acute problems due to overuse of the land and a notable reduction in the fallow period which is resulting in widespread deterioration of the soil.[13] Parts of southern Ghana, Togo, and Dahomey are obviously afflicted, and some very high rural densities make amelioration of the problem quite difficult. The major cities in this belt and its continuation into Nigeria are also characterized by surplus populations in relation to employment opportunities.

In southern Nigeria there is evidence of deterioration around many of the large Yoruba towns, though this is less well documented than the more striking and more apparent situation in eastern Nigeria, which has been noted for many years. With respect to the former Eastern Region, Floyd notes "spectacular examples of soil erosion and 'badland' topography ... less pronounced though equally insidious sheet and gully erosion ... [and] soil deterioration and degradation ... well-nigh universal due largely to over-farming and primitive, destructive methods of cultivation."[14]

Iboland is probably the most seriously affected part of the east. In this region, shortened fallows have reduced soil fertility to the point where some lands have had to be abandoned, yields have deteriorated, and cassava (manioc) has more and more replaced the more respected yams, despite taboos against consumption of *garri* (grated, soaked, and dried cassava). There has also been extreme fragmentation of holdings, a breakdown in both family and communal land control, and frequent land disputes. Rural densities of well over 1,000 per square mile are found in a number of divisions and in at

[9] R. Mansell Prothero, *Migrants and Malaria* (London, 1965), p. 21.

[10] See A. T. Grove, "Population Densities and Agriculture in Northern Nigeria" in K. M. Barbour and R. Mansell Prothero, eds., *Essays on African Population* (London: Routledge and Kegan Paul, 1961), pp. 115–136; M. J. Mortimore and J. Wilson, *Land and People in the Kano Close-Settled Zone*, Ahmadu Bello University, Department of Geography, Zaria, Occasional Paper No. 1 (1965); Reuben K. Udo, *Geographical Regions of Nigeria* (London: Heinemann, 1970).

[11] See William Allan, *The African Husbandman* (Edinburgh: Oliver and Boyd, 1965).

[12] Donald E. Vermeer, "Population Pressure and Crop Rotational Changes among the Tiv of Nigeria" (paper presented to the Annual Meeting of the African Studies Association, Los Angeles, November 1968), mimeographed.

[13] See H. Reginald Jarrett, "Sierra Leone," *Focus*, VIII, 4 (December 1957).

[14] Barry N. Floyd, "Soil Erosion and Deterioration in Eastern Nigeria," *Journal of the Geographical Association of Nigeria*, III, 1 (June 1965), 33.

least four divisions of the coastal palm belt to the south.[15]

It may be very roughly, conservatively, estimated that about 35–40 million people in West Africa are now affected by more or less serious problems of population pressure. The amelioration of these problems will involve every aspect of planning in the countries involved, and the necessity to devote attention to them is made more urgent by the present rates of population increase which are estimated for the area.

## *Bibliography*

Allen, William. *The African Husbandman.* Edinburgh: Oliver and Boyd, 1965.

Barbour, Kenneth M., and R. Mansell Prothero, eds. *Essays on African Population.* London: Routledge and Kegan Paul, 1961.

Barlet, Paul. "La Haute-Volta (Essai de présentation géographique)," *Etudes Voltaiques,* no. 3 (1962), 5–77.

Birmingham, Walter, I. Neustadt, and E. N. Omaboe, eds. *A Study of Contemporary Ghana,* I, *The Economy of Ghana.* London: George Allen and Unwin, 1966; II, *Some Aspects of Social Structure.* London: George Allen and Unwin, 1967.

Buchanan, K. M., and J. C. Pugh. *Land and People in Nigeria.* London: University of London Press, 1955.

Caldwell, John C., and C. Okonjo, eds. *The Population of Tropical Africa.* New York: Columbia University Press, 1968.

Church, R. J. Harrison. *West Africa: A Study of the Environment and of Man's Use of It,* 6th ed. London: Longmans, Green and Co., 1968.

Clarke, J. I. *Sierra Leone in Maps.* London: London University Press, 1966.

de Wilde, John C., et al. *Experiences with Agricultural Development in Tropical Africa.* 2 vols. Baltimore: The Johns Hopkins Press, 1967.

Floyd, Barry. *Eastern Nigeria: A Geographical Review.* London: Macmillan, 1969.

——"Soil Erosion and Deterioration in Eastern Nigeria: A Geographical Appraisal," *The Nigerian Geographical Journal,* VIII, 1 (June 1965), 33–44.

Gleave, M. B., and H. P. White. "The West African Middle Belt: Environmental Fact or Geographer's Fiction?" *The Geographical Review,* LIX, 1 (January 1969), 123–39.

Grove, A. T. *Land Use and Soil Conservation in Parts of Onitsha and Owerri Provinces.* Zaria: Gaskiya Corporation, 1951.

——"Soil Erosion and Population Problems in Southeast Nigeria," *The Geographical Journal,* CXVII, 3 (September 1951), 291–306.

Hance, William A. *The Geography of Modern Africa.* New York: Columbia University Press, 1964.

——*Population, Migration and Urbanization in Africa.* New York: Columbia University Press, 1970.

Hunter, John M. "Population Pressure in a Part of the West African Savanna: A Study of Nangodi, Northeast Ghana," *Annals of the Association of American Geographers,* LVII, 1 (March 1967), 101–14.

Jarrett, H. Reginald. "Sierra Leone," *Focus,* VIII, 4 (December 1957).

Lacoste, Y. Problèmes de Développement Agricole dans la Région de Ouagadougou (Haute-Volta)," *Bulletin de l'Association de Géographes Français,* nos. 346–47 (July–August 1966), 4–18.

Lorimer, Frank. "The Population of Africa." In *Population: The Vital Revolution,* edited by Ronald Freedman. New York: Doubleday, 1964.

May, Jacques. *The Ecology of Malnutrition in Middle Africa.* Darien, Conn.: Hafner, 1965.

Morgan, W. B. "Farming Practice, Settlement Pattern and Population Density in South-Eastern Nigeria," *The Geographical Journal,* CXXI, 3 (September 1955).

——and J. C. Pugh. *West Africa.* London: Methuen and Co., 1969.

Mortimore, M. J., and J. Wilson. *Land and People in the Kano Close-settled Zone.* Ahmadu Bello University, Department of Geography, Zaria, Occasional Paper No. 1 (March 1965).

Prothero, R. Mansell. *Migrants and Malaria.* London: Longmans, Green and Co., 1965.

——"La Région de Korhogo en Côte d'Ivoire," *Industries et Travaux d'Outremer,* XV, 161 (April 1967), 299–300.

Steel, Robert W. "Some Problems of Population in British West Africa." In *Geographical Essays on British Tropical Lands,* edited by R. W. Steel and C. A. Fisher. London: George Philip and Son, 1956. Pp. 17–50.

Udo, Reuben K. *Geographical Regions of Nigeria.* London: Heinemann, 1970.

[15] See Barry N. Floyd,"Rural Land Use in Nsukka Division," in University of Nigeria, Department of Geography, "Nsukka Division: A Geographical Appraisal" (1965), mimeographed; Akin L. Mabogunje, "A Typology of Population Pressure on Resources in West Africa" (paper presented to the Symposium on the Geography of Population Pressure on Physical and Social Resources, Pennsylvania State University, September 17–23, 1967), mimeographed; Reuben K. Udo, "Patterns of Population Distribution and Settlement in Eastern Nigeria," *Journal of the Geographical Association of Nigeria,* VI, 2 (December 1963), 73–88.

——"Patterns of Population Distribution and Settlement in Eastern Nigeria," *The Nigerian Geographical Journal*, VI, 2 (December 1963), 73–88.

UNESCO. *Nomades et Nomadisme au Sahara*. Paris, 1963.

Urvoy, Y. *Petit Atlas Ethno-Démographique du Soudan entre Sénégal et Tchad*. Mémoires de l'Institut Français d'Afrique Noire, no. 5. Paris: Librairie Larose, 1942.

Vermeer, Donald E. "Population Pressure and Crop Rotational Changes among the Tiv of Nigeria." Paper presented at the Annual Meeting of the African Studies Association, New York, 1967.

Verrière, Louis. *La Population du Sénégal*. Dakar: Université de Dakar, 1965.

# CHAPTER SIX

## Population & Development

ETIENNE VAN DE WALLE

## INTRODUCTION

THERE are two ways of defining the field of demography. The first way is by its content: Demographic questions are those concerned with the components, determinants, and consequences of population growth. The second approach is more simplistic, but also more operational: Demographic topics are those investigated in a census or a demographic inquiry. There are usually economic questions in censuses, such as the questions on employment and professions. There are often also questions on education, tribal affiliation, religion, and so on. All these topics frequently are considered demographic by association.

In this chapter, we shall restrict ourselves to the first interpretation of demography, and deal specifically with the economic consequences of population growth and structure, as they result from the combined effects of fertility, mortality, and migration. We shall not be concerned with the inverse relation: the effect of economic variables on fertility, mortality, and migration. Despite pioneering efforts such as those of Caldwell in Ghana,[1] there is very little knowledge on fertility differentials by socioeconomic status. The very measurement of mortality encounters such problems that we cannot with certainty identify areas of low or of high death rates, let alone trace the source of the differences to precise social, economic or environmental causes. And even where reliable information exists on mortality levels, the information on economic characteristics is usually too scanty to permit discrimination between the factors at play. For example, Cantrelle and his colleagues have used exceptionally good data to compare infant mortality in two areas of Senegal. In one (Niakhar in the Sine), literacy is widespread and medical occupation is relatively dense, but population density appears excessive for the available resources, and the productivity of agriculture is low. The other area (Paos Koto in the Saloum) has been less marked by scholarly and medical progress, but its population is sparse

[1] John C. Caldwell, *Population Growth and Family Change in Africa: The New Urban Elite in Ghana* (Canberra: Australian National University Press, 1968).

and its crop yields are high.[2] Over three years of intensive and continuous demographic observation, the latter region consistently had lower mortality than the former, and it would be tempting to conclude that economic influences weighed more heavily than the quality of education and medical care in this instance. However, one would have to isolate these factors from the interplay of all the social and environmental variables about which we possess little, if any, information. Until more evidence has come forth, a comparison with other areas in the world provides a strong presumption that the present fast population growth rate in West Africa is the result of a fairly recent drop in mortality, and that the latter has been caused by economic and social development, mostly in the form of better public health and medical facilities. Finally, although economic motives are an important explanation of migration, the question will not be further treated here (since it is dealt with by A. L. Mabogunje, N. O. Addo, R. K. Udo, and others in this book).

In the absence of comprehensive vital registration in West Africa, censuses and demographic inquiries constitute the most important sources of knowledge of the demographic characteristics which are economically important: population size, age distribution, and the rate of growth itself. Although these sources provide the denominator of many economic equations (for example, income per capita, amount of land per person, etc.), they give no reliable or precise information on the more narrowly defined economic variables. Under African conditions, census takers have not yet solved satisfactorily the problems of definition and methodology that stand in the way of the collection of meaningful information on matters such as employment, manpower qualification (including education), land use, consumption, income, or migration patterns. It is sufficient here to give as examples some of the well-known

pitfalls of the subject of employment: (1) the difficulty of defining economically active and unemployed persons in the presence of widespread underemployment; (2) the incorrect classification of women in agriculture as housewives, and not as members of the labor force; (3) the treatment of petty trade in West African cities either as a traditional occupation (Ghana, 1960) or as part of the modern sector (Dahomey, 1961). A critical analysis of these data collected in past West African censuses seems overdue.[3] A new United Nations manual offers many guidelines for taking future surveys.[4]

In the present circumstances of West Africa, information on the subject of the economic consequences of population growth must come from a wide variety of sources, ranging from special inquiries into specialized subjects to employment statistics compiled from employers' declarations, from anthropological surveys describing how the subsistence economy reacts to the pressure of numbers, and from descriptions of overcropping by soil scientists; to the global views of national plans. The present writer is a demographer, and has only an imperfect knowledge of this diverse literature. He will attempt here both to provide a logical classification of research topics on population and economic development in West Africa and to indicate how a few recent studies fit into the classification.

The essential question to be answered is: What happens to the economy when the population starts to grow? And, since population in West Africa apparently has been growing at a relatively fast rate for some time, another question presents itself: What are economic characteristics of the present that can be attributed to past growth? The effects of population on the economy can be

[2] Pierre Cantrelle, M. Diagne, and B. Fall, "Mortalité de l'enfance dans la région du Sine-Saloum (Sénégal) 1963–65" in Centre International de l'Enfance, *Conditions de vie de l'enfant en milieu rural en Afrique* (Paris, 1968), pp. 136–39.

[3] A useful, but very brief discussion is available for the period 1955–1964 in Yuki Miura, "A Comparative Analysis of Operational Definitions of the Economically Active Population in African and Asian Statistics," United Nations, World Population Conference, 1965, IV (New York, 1967), pp. 372–79.

[4] United Nations, *Methods of Analyzing Census Data on Economic Activities of the Population*, ST/SOA/Series A/43 (New York, 1968).

classified under three headings: effects of population size, of the rate of growth, and of the age distribution. The threefold classification is borrowed from the classic study by Coale and Hoover.[5]

The need for a classification scheme of this order originates in the confusion of the concepts, and the absence of focus in much of the theory and research. Often, very general questions are asked, such as: Is West Africa (or a single country) overpopulated? The multitude of points of view gives rise to a series of conflicting answers, each of which may be true in a particular context. For instance, the idea that there is shortage of population until recently often was based on the difficulty of recruiting labor for mines or plantations. It must also be said that the attitude of official spokesmen on the subject range from alarmism to optimism, sometimes for reasons that have more to do with philosophy and the traditions of the ex-colonizing power, than with economic arguments. In French-speaking countries, there is still a widespread feeling that West Africa is underpopulated, although the notion rarely is defined, and is likely to rely mainly on an index as crude as overall density. In the preface to an otherwise balanced volume on the economy of Cameroon, André Philip states that "The country is underpopulated, despite its growth rate of 2.5 percent in the south and 1.5 percent in the north, which constitutes a factor of progress, but creates problems of adaption . . . ."[6] In English-speaking countries, however, there is now a diffuse feeling that "population growth is outstripping the rate of economic development."[7] The phrasing is often rather vague, as the above examples show.

[5] Ansley J. Coale and Edgar M. Hoover, *Population Growth and Economic Development in Low-Income Countries: A Case Study of India's Prospects* (Princeton, N.J.: Princeton University Press, 1958).
[6] Preface to Philippe Hugon, *Analyse du sous-développement en Afrique Noire, L'exemple de l'économie du Cameroun*, P.U.F. (Paris, 1968), p. v.
[7] Vice-Chancellor's "Opening Address" in N. O. Addo, G. Benneh, S. K. Gaisie and G. M. K. Kpedekpo, eds., *Symposium on Population and Socio-Economic Development in Ghana*, Ghana Population Studies, No. 2, Demographic Unit, University of Ghana (Legon [Accra] 1968), p. v.

## DENSITY AND POPULATION SIZE

The question asked in this section is essentially that to which Malthus and the classical economists were addressing themselves. With a finite amount of resources, including a fixed supply of land and capital, and at a certain level of technology, is a large population advantageous? Or does it keep production per worker, and income per head of population down? The classical view is expressed in the theory of the optimum population. Optimum theory states that population size in itself is of little importance; what matters is the combination of factors of production in the right proportions. For a given area of land and a fixed supply of capital, there is an optimum number of workers. If the labor force does not reach that number, there is not enough manpower to exploit the available resources, and additional workers would bring forth increasing returns per head, by virtue of division of labor and specialization. In this situation, one may talk of underpopulation. Conversely, above the optimum amount of manpower, average product goes down and there is underemployment—a stage of overpopulation has been reached. The argument is used primarily under conditions of stagnant technology. (With technical progress, the shape of the production function, and the optimum size of the population itself, would be modified.) The classical model is behind the often-stated opinion that West Africa is underpopulated, because it possesses plenty of unused land and unexploited mineral resources.

For example, Abdoulaye Wade supports "Adam Smith's optimism about the existence of a positive correlation between population and economic activity," and concludes that a large population will permit further division of labor resulting in higher productivity.[8] Wade also states that "quantitative demographic insufficiency has been recognized as one of the obstacles to the industrial development of Black Africa."[9] In discussing the

[8] Abdoulaye Wade, *Economie de l'Ouest Africain* (*Zone Franc*), Présence Africaine (Paris, 1964), p. 248.
[9] *Ibid.*, p. 249.

advantages of the division of labor, Adam Smith himself was restricting the relevance of his argument to industrial production. The effects of population size on industrial development will be discussed further at the end of this section.

There are possible advantages and disadvantages of population size in agriculture. In small-holder agriculture, where most of the population of West Africa makes its livelihood, there is little room for specialization and division of labor. Within the production unit, population increase is not likely to bring about economies of size. On the contrary, it will result typically in the addition of new production units, usually smaller than previous ones. A great deal of fragmentation of holdings has been going on in most densely populated areas of the region. The nations of West Africa have often attempted to intervene in order to reverse the dominance of small-holder agriculture and increase the size of production units. But large production units, plantations and resettlement schemes, do not typically accommodate large numbers of people. Even when they seek to relieve demographic pressure in neighboring areas resettlement schemes often fail to attract a large number of settlers.

An interesting aspect of the effect of population size on one of these schemes is discussed by de Wilde.[10] He gives as one of the reasons for the lack of success of the *Office du Niger* in Mali, its failure to attract a sufficient number of colonists and wage laborers. De Wilde contends that the absence of population pressure in Mali led to the under-utilization of the invested capital, to diseconomies of size, costly recruitment of settlers, compulsion to resort to expensive mechanization, and to insuperable labor bottlenecks. It would seem, however, that the failure to attract colonists must be explained by other factors than the assumed underpopulation of the area. After all, in 1961, when the total settled population of the *Office* reached its maximum with 38,000

persons, this represented much less than one year of natural increase in Mali (ignoring Upper Volta, from which settlers also were recruited). A more likely explanation of the shortage of manpower could be simply that life at the *Office du Niger* was not attractive enough to lure settlers. In this context, de Wilde's view of population pressure appears to be of a situation where things are so desperate for the peasant, that there is no alternative but to participate in a resettlement scheme!

As a matter of fact, plantations and resettlement schemes in West Africa, although they allow economies of size and division of labor, have not been conspicuously successful in recent times. The advantages of the large scale have not been sufficient to compensate for the comparative advantages of peasant agriculture in the production of both food and cash crops. And the capacity of small-holder land arrangements to absorb additional population has exceeded that of the large-scale operations. Eicher contends "that under West African ecological, political and social conditions, small-holders can produce almost any crop as efficiently as large-scale production units such as plantations or state farms." He notes that

for some crops such as cocoa, land with suitable qualities . . . is scattered and not amenable to farming in large units. Large-scale government production units are usually overcentralized, subject to manipulation by politicians and pay wages 20 to 30 percent higher than open market rates . . . .[11]

Resettlement schemes and plantations have large overhead costs, such as housing and welfare expenses for their employees, that the small farmer avoids. There are, it is true, functions of the agricultural unit that can only be performed satisfactorily and economically for a certain size. Among those belong agricultural research, seed selection, and international marketing operations. Fortunately, these tasks can be taken over by government agencies, even when production

---

[10] J. C. de Wilde, *Experience with Agricultural Development in Tropical Africa* (Baltimore: The Johns Hopkins Press, 1967), p. 288.

[11] Carl K. Eicher, *Research on Agricultural Development in Five English-Speaking Countries in West Africa* (New York: Agricultural Development Council, 1970), p. 15.

remains in the hands of the small holder. This has been done readily enough for cash crops in the past. Food crops as a rule have received little attention, perhaps because their marketing and consumption is as fragmented as is their production.

The effect of population size on small-holder agriculture must be considered under two headings: food crops and cash crops. Furthermore, the effects on the supply and on the demand for these crops must be considered separately. It should be emphasized in the beginning that the population problem in West Africa is not a food problem: Population is not, in the Malthusian sense, pressing on subsistence so that the supply of food cannot keep up with the demand created by the large population. The consensus of research shows that there has been no overall deficiency in the supply of food in recent times, despite the fast population increase. For instance, Boateng in Ghana notes that "agricultural production for local use, especially food farming, fishing and the raising of small livestock and poultry, has been largely neglected and left to fend for itself."[12] But with the help of official agencies providing selective breeding material and ensuring an adequate network of feeder roads, "there is no reason why, with only a few minor cultural improvements, Ghana should not be able to meet its own domestic food requirements and increase them substantially to cope with the needs of its rising population."[13] The same conclusion was reached in Nigeria by the Consortium for the Study of Nigerian Rural Development (CSNRD):

In general it is believed that [the subsistence food sector] has grown and will continue to grow at about the same rate as population unless present policies are changed either for better or for worse ... Nigeria does not run the risk of having population press on food supplies to the point of starvation and deprivation for the next two or three decades despite the [projected] enormous population figures.[14]

The West African countries import food, but imports are mostly high-grade products that cannot be grown locally, or luxury items for the restricted market of the cities. Moreover it appears to be often the lack of effective demand, rather than overpopulation, which restricts overall food production in the area. At prevailing prices, local producers often cannot compete; given a sufficient price incentive, the farmers would generally be eager to enter the market.

One spectacular example of growth of food production because of a larger effective demand occurred in Zaïre after independence.[15] The rapid population growth in Kinshasa after 1960 coincided with a disruption of the traditional sources of supply in Kasai. The prices of food products rose, and, as a result, the cultivated area close to the capital doubled in a very short period, and there was an enormous increase in the deliveries of food to the urban markets. We shall have the opportunity to come back to the indirect consequences of a fast expansion of this kind: The cultivated areas expand to keep up with the demand, at the cost of a sharp reduction of the usual fallow period, and the effects of overcropping on the land are severe. At this point, however, we are quoting the Zaïre example because it demonstrates how production can increase in reaction to an increase in prices. Similar reactions have occurred near other urban markets, as an adjustment to population increase. The mechanism at play here, however, has little to do with the classical model discussed earlier. The increase in production is not the result of the existence of a supply of

[12] E. A. Boateng, "Agricultural Practices and Population Growth: The Ghana Case" (Paper prepared for Seminar on Population Growth and Economic Development, Nairobi, 1969), 5.
[13] *Ibid.*, p. 13.

[14] Glenn L. Johnson, Orlin J. Scoville, George K. Dike, and Carl H. Eicher, *Strategies and Recommendations for Nigerian Rural Development, 1969/1985*, CSNRD 33 (July 1969), pp. 22–24.
[15] See E. Ndongala, "Mutations structurelles de l'économie traditionnelle dans le Bas-Congo sous l'impact de la colonisation et de la décolonisation," *Cahiers Economiques et Sociaux*, IRES, IV, 1 (Lovanium, 1966).

labor that is complementary to existing land and capital. Indeed, there is probably widespread underemployment of the labor force in West African agriculture. However, the expanding number of consumers creates its own demand, while the absence of a market for surplus production and the poor storage facilities available to the farmer would otherwise discourage any tendency he might have had to produce a surplus beyond the needs of himself and his family. In general, and within limits discussed later, such as the availability of cultivable land, food production tends to increase abreast with population.

The production of the various cash crops of West Africa appears to follow similar rules. It is also in the hands of a growing population of smallholders, and in several places there is now the prospect that population pressure will induce shortages of the relatively scarce land that is suited to the growing of such crops as palm oil or cocoa. The decreasing export of crops such as palm oil or peanuts, that can be consumed locally instead of finding their way to the world market, is yet another possible consequence of population growth. In fact the production of most cash crops has increased faster than has population in recent years, but one limiting factor to continued growth, perhaps the most important of all today, is the slow increase in world demand. Part of the problem is technological change, one aspect of which is the development of synthetic substitutes for primary products. But part of the problem also is the increasing number of producers, in West Africa and in developing countries elsewhere. At a time when the growth in the number of consumers in developed countries is slow, an increasing number of producers means a deterioration of the terms of trade between the two groups of countries. The FAO commodities projections for 1985 indicate a rate of growth of the demand for coffee in the world of 2.2 to 2.6 percent per year, slower than the expected population growth of West Africa; and there is little prospect for a rise in world prices. The outlook is similar for cocoa, and rather worse for cotton and palm oil. Growth in output for these products will mainly depend on the home market.[16] These facts do not mean that cash crops have no further role to play in increasing the productivity of subsistence agriculture. The CSNRD has argued in the instance of Nigeria that improved productivity and better pricing arrangements (including a revision of marketing boards' operations and a reduction of export taxes) could substantially increase the revenues derived by farmers from export crops.[17] In this economic context, we will now examine the possible effect of population growth on West Africa's terms of trade.

The first consideration is the effect of increasing population density on the production of food and cash crops (as opposed to the effect on their consumption). We have noted that production expands with population and demand does likewise, at least within certain limits. These limits are set by (1) the extent of man's ability to change agricultural techniques to keep up with increasing density, and (2) the carrying capacity of the land, with current techniques and land use systems. In many parts of West Africa, however, land is still plentiful. It has been argued that population growth would have beneficial effects in opening up new areas.[18] For the time being, however, we can assume that the occupation of new areas would require some capital investment to create roads and public services, to clear the land, and to settle the people. The present argument assumes that no new capital investment takes place, and that technology remains stagnant.

Now it may be said that these assumptions are unrealistic under conditions of population growth. E. Boserup has maintained that increases in density tend to force technical change.[19] Among other examples drawn from

[16] Food and Agricultural Organization of the United Nations, *Agricultural Commodities: Projections for 1975 and 1985*, I (Rome 1967), pp. 23–26.

[17] Johnson et al., *Nigerian Rural Development*, chaps. VI and VII.

[18] E. N. Omaboe, "The Population Pressure and the Development of New Areas," in United Nations, *World Population Conference, 1965*, III (New York, 1967), pp. 400 ff.

[19] E. Boserup, *The Conditions of Agricultural Growth* (London: G. Allen, 1965).

various areas of the world, she has invoked an often-quoted paper by Grove on densities and agriculture in northern Nigeria, in which the author documents the spread of mixed farming and of soil improvement practices around the larger towns and cities of Hausaland.[20] Better farming techniques are the result of high density, and of the existence of a ready urban market where agricultural products are bought at a good price that repays the efforts of intensification of cultivation. Grove himself points to the less promising outlook in the more remote districts, where the techniques of intensification are not applied and the land deteriorates under the pressure of population. Intensification, the substitution of labor and capital for the scarce factor—land—is usually possible. The paradox of unemployment in subsistence agriculture is that there is always plenty of work that needs to be done, from conservation to manuring, and that such work would substantially increase the productivity of the land and preserve its fertility in the long run. However, intensification will not easily come about spontaneously, because productivity does not increase proportionately to the labor invested. In any concrete situation, where there is an implicit choice between working more on the same piece of land, or cultivating more land, the peasant will choose extensive agriculture. Frequently, the economic calculus is rational in the short run. In the *Office du Niger*, the failure to intensify was blamed on the low density of settlement, which was leaving the choice open to the peasant to continue his practice of shifting cultivation on the rich land of the Niger Delta.[21] Even in cash cropping, technically sound agricultural practice may not make much sense economically if one balances the immediate prospects of saving some hard labor, against the more distant benefits to be obtained from conserving the farmer's capital. In Central Cameroon, for

instance, "the smallholder who treats his [cocoa] plantation correctly, who prunes, cares and protects against diseases, of course increases his production; but his hourly productivity does not rise!"[22] However the result of intensified cultivation is inexorable deterioration and erosion. But, even in the "badlands" of eastern Nigeria, where erosion and gullying have reached monumental proportions as a result of excessive use by man, the peasants have been most reluctant to invest their labor in conservation and have been wary of the effect of erosion control on land tenure arrangements.[23]

Thus, it would seem wrong to assume that higher population densities lead necessarily to more intensive forms of cultivation. In Senegal, there has been in recent times a marked shift to animal-drawn ploughing. SATEC, a rural development consortium, had recommended the introduction of agricultural implements, under the assumption that the time thus freed from other work would be spent to intensify land use. In fact, the ploughs are used to expand cultivated areas, and the owners of modern material have been able to appropriate areas previously under communal ownership, creating a landless class.[24] The paradox is that it has been a constant policy on the part of extension services since the 1930s to attempt to introduce animal traction and the plough.[25] Actually, the present process may be more the result than the cause of population pressure. It may well be that the extension of cultivation into new, less fertile areas, and the deterioration of land not left fallow long enough, compels peasants to cultivate larger areas to harvest comparable amounts. Since this situation did

[20] A. T. Grove, "Population Densities and Agriculture in Northern Nigeria," in K. M. Barbour and R. M. Prothero, eds., *Essays on African Population* (London: Routledge and Kegan Paul, 1961), pp. 115 ff.
[21] De Wilde, *Agricultural Development*.

[22] H. Marticou, *Les structures agricoles du Centre Cameroun, République Fédérale du Cameroun* (Paris, no date [data collected in 1959]), p. 42.
[23] Barry Floyd, "Soil Erosion and Deterioration in Eastern Nigeria," *The Nigerian Geographical Journal*, VIII, 1 (June 1965), 33 ff.
[24] J. Roch and G. Rocheteau, "Economie et population, le Cas du Sénégal" (Paper presented at the Colloque de Démographie Africaine organized by INED, INSEE, and ORSTOM, Paris, 6–9 October 1970), mimeographed, 5.
[25] See for instance H. Labouret, *Paysans d'Afrique Occidentale* (Paris, 1941), pp. 235 ff.

not exist before, its advent may explain the adoption of labor-saving devices used extensively. There are in West Africa many examples of areas where they have led to a shortening of the fallow period, and where manioc has replaced the more demanding crops cultivated in earlier times, and thus made up for the loss of fertility. For similar situations in Southern Africa, Allan has coined the term "critical density of population," meaning the density beyond which deterioration of the land is bound to set in.[26] Allan's concepts have been used in West Africa, for example by G. J. Afolabi Ojo.[27] Ojo points out that there are in southern Nigeria many physical and social factors of a changing nature that can affect the critical density. Although he judges that there is today "everywhere, a defined upward trend bringing the population densities closer and closer to the CDP [critical density of population] in areas where it has not actually been reached and surpassed,"[28] he feels that one cannot talk of overall population pressure in the area. There is a need for examining the characteristics of local areas and microregions in order to understand the determinants of critical density and the possibilities for an optimum use of the land that would reduce the pressure.

Even though the shortage of land is not a general problem in West Africa, overpopulation in the classical sense, namely that diminishing returns are setting in, exists in many areas. Hance has indicated that the following danger signals are suggestive of population pressure:

(1) Declining soil fertility, soil deterioration, degradation or outright destruction, often associated with a shortening fallow period, or with overstocking and overgrazing; (2) use of excessively steep slopes; (3) declining crop yields, a trend

toward more soil-tolerant crops such as manioc; (4) a breakdown of the indigenous farming system; (5) food shortages, hunger and malnutrition; (6) disputes over land, land fragmentation, excessively small holdings, landlessness among the rural population; (7) some types of out-migration; (8) unemployment and underemployment in rural and urban areas.[29]

Hance has attempted to map areas of population pressure in Africa. He points out that pressure may exist at high or low population densities depending on the carrying capacity of the land. Among others, he quotes the example of areas of northeast Ghana and the former Eastern Region of Nigeria where erosion and degradation are far advanced, and the Sokoto Province of northern Nigeria where there is widespread land hunger. Hilton has described some high density areas of northern Ghana. They seem to represent a climax, preceding the total exhaustion of the soil by overcropping and a lowering of the water table. In some areas close by, the cycle of occupation is coming to its close. The land has become too poor for cultivation, and the population is either dying out or migrating away.[30] In certain coastal regions of Sierra Leone, degradation of the soil has induced the migration of large numbers of farmers.[31] In the district around Porto Novo, Dahomey, the productivity of food crops in the once rich land of the palm forest is declining with the total disappearance of the bush fallow.[32] There are many other areas where the danger signals of population pressure are visible.

The existence of these zones of pressure does not necessarily contradict the frequent observation that there is still plenty of empty land in West Africa. It only indicates that the empty land is not available in the regions where the excess population needs it most.

[26] William Allan, *The African Husbandman* (Edinburgh: Oliver and Boyd, 1965), p. 89.

[27] G. J. Afolabi Ojo, "Some Cultural Factors in the Critical Density of Population in Tropical Africa," in John C. Caldwell and C. Okonjo, eds., *The Population of Tropical Africa* (London: Longmans, Green & Company, and New York: Columbia University Press, 1968), pp. 312 ff.

[28] *Ibid.*, p. 314.

[29] W. A. Hance, "The Race Between Population and Resources," *African Report* (January 1968), p. 8.

[30] T. E. Hilton, "Population Growth and Distribution in the Upper Region of Ghana," in Caldwell and Okonjo, *Population of Tropical Africa*, pp. 278 ff.

[31] R. G. Saylor, *The Economic System of Sierra Leone* (Durham, N.C.: Duke University Press, 1967), pp. 22–23.

[32] J. Serreau, *Le développement à la base au Dahomey et au Sénégal* (Paris, 1966), p. 23.

In several West African countries, there exist large "middle belts" with potential for denser human settlement.[33] The great diversity in the intensity of occupation can be explained in part by history, the scars left by slavery, and in part by tribal customs of land occup- ation and agricultural technology. Diseases also play a role: for example, river blindness in northern Ghana and sleeping sickness in the middle belt of Nigeria. There are islands of high density in the interior, frequently in mountainous areas that offered protection from enemy attacks. These areas have often developed uncommonly sophisticated systems of intensive agriculture, including terracing of slopes, mixed farming, and the use of manure. To this category belong the Jos Plateau of Nigeria, the Atakora Mountains of Dahomey, the Kabre country of Togo, the Bamiléké and Kirdi regions of Cameroon, all characterized by high density, population pressure, poverty, and seasonal or permanent out-migration toward the coastal regions. These are essentially insular situations, left over from the precolonial period. Their expansion to neighboring areas of low density has often been restricted by the land rights of other tribes; so the young men migrate to regions where there is a demand for their labor. Even in the middle belt, net emigration has been common, because, despite the availability of land, economic opportunities are not great.

It is likely that the large variation in the degree of occupation is also to a major extent the result of the unequal development of transportation systems.

Settlement and cultivation have both tended to be attracted to roads, to move away from areas without them, and to follow them into previously unoccupied areas .... In the development of export crop cultivation, the pattern of the trans- port system has clearly been as potent a factor as

soils and moisture supply in the distribution of planting and settlement.[34]

And, of course, a great deal of the population redistribution, that has led to the building up of new areas of population pressure on the land, has resulted from the existence of economic opportunities in a limited part of the country, because of the adequacy of the soil and climate for cash crops, or because of the proximity of markets. Morgan and Pugh note that "the development of commercial cultivation, in particular the cultivation of export crops, has been the most potent factor in the redistribution of population in West Africa."[35] In Senegal, groundnut production has opened up enormous areas that had been previously almost unoccupied.[36] In Ghana, cocoa has been grown in previously thinly peopled or even uninhabited forest, and has totally transformed the pattern of settlement. There was for a long time an abundance of land suitable for cash crops and the supply of labor was the only bottleneck preventing further expansion. Today, after many years of occupation, some of the old groundnut areas of Senegal and northern Nigeria are depleted, and the expansion of production depends on an ever widening search for new land. In southern Ghana, where a large inflow of people has taken place, there is now a shortage of land for food crops. The length of fallow has dropped, the yields have declined, and cassava (manioc) is in places replacing yams, cocoyams, plantains, and maize as the staple, because it is more tolerant of exhausted soils. Benneh estimates that the critical density has been reached on food crop land in many areas of the closed forest region of Ghana, and that it has become imperative to introduce im- proved methods of cultivation, such as the growing of leguminous plants and their use as green manure.[37] The cash crop not only

[33] See, for example, FAO, *Agricultural Development in Nigeria 1965–1980* (Rome, 1966), pp. 9 ff. This survey reaches the conclusion that because of population growth, "it seems inescapable ... that Nigeria is faced with a major task in the opening up, development and settlement of new areas" (p. 14).

[34] W. B. Morgan and J. C. Pugh, *West Africa* (London: Methuen, 1969), p. 441.
[35] *Ibid.*, p. 447.
[36] P. Pélissier, *Les paysans du Sénégal* (Saint-Yrieix, 1965), pp. 32 ff.
[37] G. Benneh, "Agricultural Land-Use and Population in the Closed Forest Region of Ghana," in *Symposium on Population and Socio-economic Development in Ghana*, Ghana Population Studies No. 2 (Legon, 1968), pp. 62 ff.

attracts a large population to the land but also occupies land that might be used to grow food, and it competes for the manpower that could be used to intensify the production of the food crop and to limit the exhaustion of the soil. We shall come back to the question of employment in the next section, when we discuss the problems inherent in fast population growth.

So far we have reviewed the effects of size and density both on the consumption and production sides of agriculture. One conclusion emerges: There are now many areas in West Africa that cannot easily accommodate the densities that have built up in recent times. Soil exhaustion sets a limit to the size of population in scattered areas, although not yet in West Africa as a region. We must now turn briefly to the effects of population size on the industrial sector of the economy. The expected advantage here is that of having a large market for manufactured products. There is little doubt that Nigeria's large population is a favorable factor in the drive for industrialization, while small nations, such as the Democratic Republic of the Congo or Gambia, have few prospects for the development of sizable, autonomous, industrial sectors. However, it must be remembered in this connection: (1) that a greater benefit can accrue from intraregional cooperation and a West African common market, than from population growth in individual countries; and (2) that, to the extent that population growth hampers the improvement of the standard of living and the purchasing power of the inhabitants, it also hampers the development of a sizable effective demand. There is more opportunity for industrialization in growing income per head than in growing numbers.

## POPULATION GROWTH

The preceding section discussed the consequences of a large population size and of high density. Now we proceed one step further, and ask: How does an economy cope with the growth of its population? The distinction between these two points is somewhat artificial, but it is intellectually clear. It has been accepted in general, even by those who consider that a country is underpopulated and would benefit from more people. For example, N'Diaye says that "Senegal offers a typical example of a country which is underpopulated and which is nevertheless experiencing great difficulties as a result of its population."[38] The view presented in this case is that the population of Senegal is under the optimum size, but that its growth exceeds the optimum rate of growth. From a static point of view, there are economies of scale, as overhead expenditures and public services are shared among more persons; from a dynamic point of view, additional investments are needed (and not necessarily forthcoming) to maintain, or improve, the ratio of existing capital stock to the growing population.

Most development plans aim at realizing a level of investment which expands faster than population growth, so that a substantial increase in income per head is possible. The projected investment is financed out of savings or, if the latter are insufficient, out of foreign capital invested in the country, loaned, or granted. As a rule, there has been considerable disparity between the recorded investment and that projected in development plans on the basis of their overall targets. "Planning without facts" cannot be expected to be very realistic. In the absence of detailed and accurate statistics, the most sophisticated instrument used by the economic planners to integrate population growth into their computations, has been a version of the so-called development equation:

$$g = s/c - r$$

where $g$ is the rate of increase of income per head; $s$, the percent saved of total income; $c$, the capital-output ratio; and $r$, the rate of population increase. (Thus, if the population of a country grows at 2 percent a year, and the capital-output ratio is equal to 3, 6 percent of the GNP should be saved and invested yearly simply to keep income per head

[38] A. L. N'Diaye, "The Difficulty of Rapid Population Growth in an Under-populated Country. An example: Senegal," in United Nations, *World Population Conference, 1965*, IV (New York, 1967), p. 85.

constant, and 9 percent is needed to make it grow by 1 percent a year.) The development equation, however, provides no practical guidelines in West Africa, because little is known about the actual value of most, if not all, of the terms in the equation. How much is saved and invested by the overwhelming majority living in subsistence agriculture? What is the capital-output ratio of investment ranging from the clearing of new lands to the erection of administrative buildings in the capital city, through to the supply of housing and educational equipment? And finally, the rate of population growth itself is in most countries conjectural.

Although the equation provides no real clue for planning, there is a basic truth behind the argument underlying it. Either the capital stock, or the efficiency in using it, must improve faster than the population increases, if development is to take place. As expressed in Ghana's policy paper on population,

Increases in agricultural or other production, in housing, in the provision of classrooms and hospital beds and jobs assure progress towards national goals only when this expansion exceeds the rate of population growth .... Even the most ambitious and successful program for the creation of new jobs will have no effect on the scale of unemployment if the number of prospective workers increases as fast as or faster than the numbers of available jobs ....[39]

Most development plans express a similar concern.[40] Although they register some polite recognition of the need to invest in traditional agriculture, to keep up with population growth on the land,[41] the plans concentrate on investment prospects in the industrial, urban part of the economy, and in capital intensive agriculture with irrigation and machinery. Two items have particularly drawn the attention of planners, and hence need elaboration here: the problems caused by the growth of the labor force, and the consequent need to expand the number of jobs; and the problems caused by the expansion of the educational system.

POPULATION GROWTH AND EMPLOYMENT. We must abandon the viewpoint of the "single target" development plan, and recognize that saving, and investment, for the purpose of creating more jobs, starts among the small production units which make up the employment sector in the economy of West Africa. One convenient point of departure is the model discussed in the previous section devoted to the implications of population size. For a certain amount of land and capital and with unchanging technology, the state of "overpopulation" is one of decreasing returns to increasing population density; this state is characterized by the fact that the marginal productivity of labor is below the average productivity. Some economists have argued that the marginal productivity in subsistence agriculture is normally equal to zero—i.e., that much of the abundant labor can be removed from agriculture and employed in the modern sector, without any detrimental effects on production. In recent years more nuances appear to have entered the discussion.[42] The decreasing returns model itself seems somewhat inadequate. As shown above, overpopulation is defined for practical purposes, not in terms of the marginal productivity of labor, but by reference to the

[39] Republic of Ghana, *Population Planning for National Progress and Prosperity*, Ghana Population Policy (Accra, March 1969), pp. 7–8.

[40] D. K. Ghansah, "Population Growth, Family Planning and Economic Development in Africa," Seminar on Population Growth and Economic Development, Nairobi, December 1969, mimeographed, especially pp. 8–13.

[41] "[R]apid population growth in the high density zones . . . in a way sterilized an important mass of investments for the sole purpose of preventing the degradation of the level of living . . . ," République du Dahomey, *Plan de développement economique et social, 1966–1970* (Cotonou, 1966), p. 25.

[42] See, for instance, C. Kao, K. Anschel, and C. K. Eicher, "Disguised Unemployment in Agriculture: A Survey," in C. Eicher and L. Witt, eds., *Agriculture in Economic Development* (New York: McGraw-Hill, 1964); or, more specifically: E. M. Godfrey, "Labor-Surplus Models and Labor-Deficit Economies: The West African Case," in *Economic Development and Cultural Change*, XVII, 3 (April 1969), 382 ff. The latter writer postulates that West Africa "appears to be suffering from a labour deficit in agriculture" (p. 382), a position which seems somewhat unrealistic as a general description, although it may fit certain regions at certain times.

damage caused to the land when a critical density has been exceeded. Of course, in the static model, where only the size of population changes, and where land, capital, and technology are kept constant, there is no place for modifications in productive techniques induced by high density. In the real conditions of West Africa, zero marginal productivity must be rare; either the population intensifies its land use (and, as Dumont comments, a modernizing agriculture need not worry about underemployment)[43] or it leaves the area of pressure in search of more favorable economic opportunities.

There is a great deal of underemployment, however, in the agricultural sector in West Africa. It is wrong to equate all underemployment with zero marginal productivity of labor or with overpopulation. An important form of underemployment exists because the seasonal pattern of cultivation often alternates periods of idleness with periods when labor shortage constitutes a bottleneck preventing the expansion of production. There is direct information on the subject, because several rural surveys in French-speaking West Africa have investigated the use of time in peasant societies for periods up to one year on a longitudinal basis.[44] These studies all show strong seasonal fluctuations in the level of activity, and serious underemployment during a large part of the year. Unfortunately the methodology of the surveys is not always comparable. Some surveys have attempted to keep track of the detailed schedule of daily tasks, including work in the home. Most studies have been content to count working days spent in the field, whatever the length of the day. This way of reckoning automatically leaves out household work which goes on even when there is a slack in the cultivation cycle. And it pays no heed to what capital maintenance—that is, repair or construction of buildings or of agricultural equipment—goes on when there is no demand for directly productive labor on the fields.

Thus the surveys of use of time may, or may not, include as "labor," some essential activities of the farm or the household as agricultural labor. Among these are the carrying of water and the preparation of food. The distinction between house and farm labor is ambiguous at best. One of the reasons for the adoption of manioc in a widening area of West Africa is the relatively light labor force required to cultivate it, and the fact that its harvest can be distributed over a long period, without creating a labor bottleneck. On the other hand, the preparation of cassava is usually very laborious. In other words, the shift to manioc means that the reduction in the amount of agricultural labor is largely compensated by the increase in house labor. If the latter is not counted, a misleading picture of the labor cost of manioc production may emerge. In the Senegal Valley, an adult man is reported to work on the average 153 days per year; an adult woman works only 57 days, but this excludes so-called domestic activities.[45] In the Adamoua region of Cameroon, however, men average 4 hours and 45 minutes daily (2 hours and 5 minutes agricultural, 2 hours and 40 minutes nonagricultural) and women, 6 hours and 10 minutes per day (1 hour and 45 minutes and 4 hours and 25 minutes respectively) including 2 hours and 15 minutes for cooking and 40 minutes for the water carrying chore. In the manioc area of Adamaoua, inhabited by the Baya tribe, the time spent on preparation of food is well above these averages.[46]

The point worth noting here, however, is that direct investigation has left no doubt that there is often considerable underemployment in agriculture, whether the estimates are expressed in average number of days per year or hours per day. A survey in Senegal estimated that underemployment amounted to 180 days per adult male per day.[47] In

---

[43] R. Dumont, *L'Afrique Noire est mal partie* (Paris, 1965), p. 213.

[44] See also chapter 14 in this book by Goddard, Mortimore, and Norman.

[45] J. L. Boutillier et al., *La Moyenne Vallée du Sénégal* (Paris, 1962), p. 110.

[46] République Fédérale du Cameroun, *Le niveau de vie des populations de l'Adamoua*, ORSTOM-INSEE (Paris, 1967), pp. 164 ff.

[47] Quoted by J. Serreau, *Le développement à la base*, pp. 36–37.

south Dahomey, where two yearly crops are possible, and where the calendar of agricultural labor has fewer seasonal peaks and troughs, the estimate is still high: 122 days per worker.[48] In a cotton-producing area of Oubangui, in the Central African Republic, where twice as much time is spent on the cash crop as on the food crop, there are also slack times and peaks of activity, and the average duration of the working day fluctuates between extremes of four and seven hours for the men. As is often the case, women work longer, even if only strictly agricultural tasks are considered and work in the household is omitted.[49]

Incidentally, these kinds of surveys are a useful complement to the results derived from censuses. They restore to the women their true importance in West African agriculture, while censuses often classify them simply as housewives. And they provide information over time, while the census must be content with the present status of employment, or with employment during a short base period. Underemployment may have many other causes, which are not directly seasonal: the health of the population, its customs, and the opportunities open to it within a reasonable distance. In the studies just discussed, and in others of their kind, there is a lack of empirical evidence linking underemployment and population pressure, although the relationship is plausible. It is postulated by the classical model (discussed earlier). Hance makes of underemployment one of the danger signals indicating that there is population pressure. And areas known to have passed the critical density often lose great numbers of their young men to migration. But seasonal underemployment exists in most of West Africa as a result of the climate, and it characterizes areas of abundant as well as of scarce land. As noted before, the cure of overpopulation may well lie in the intensification of agriculture, including the diversification of activities and their distri-

bution over the whole year. This in itself would relieve underemployment. The introduction of cash crops such as cocoa have played that role in the past, and created a considerable seasonal demand for labor, which coincided with a slack period in the hinterland. There are instances where the critical density on food-producing land is passed, and where there is nevertheless a shortage of labor to work on the cash crop.[50] Other forms of intensification consist in supplying more capital to agriculture, as a complement to the abundant labor. The result may be occasional, localized shortage of labor, as in the instance, already mentioned above, of the *Office du Niger*.

The reasoning behind the development equation finds its application at this point. The theory says that investment should increase at least at the same rate as the labor force so that the latter can be kept employed to the same or a greater extent. But precise measurement is impossible. Most investments in subsistence agriculture are done by peasants themselves, and take nonmonetary forms.

A very great deal of the capital in farms, in the form of perennial orchards, of cleared and developed land, of terraces and drains, has been built up simply by the labor of the cultivator, frequently by labor that could find no other employment because of the seasonal rhythm of farming.[51]

As to the capital-output ratio, it may well be going up with the increasing scarcity of good land. There are, however, investments in extension and research that have a very low capital-output ratio.

Economists and planners feel on firmer ground when they are dealing with the developed part of the economy. However, there are two reasons why they have to pay heed to the subsistence sector, even when

---

[48] *Ibid.*, pp. 37 and 334.
[49] République Centrafricaine, *L'emploi du temps du paysan dans une zone de l'Oubangui central 1959–1960* (Paris, 1961), pp. 21 ff.

[50] Benneh, "Agricultural Land-Use," p. 78. Godfrey ("Labor-Surplus Models," p. 382) appears to accept the idea of a general labor deficit in agriculture in West Africa on the basis of the large demand of the cocoa belt.
[51] A. M. Kamarck, "Notes on Under-Employment," in E. F. Jackson, ed., *Economic Development in Africa* (London: Blackwell, 1966), p. 78.

they are dealing with the modern sector. First, the modern sector receives a large inflow of migrants from the countryside, urbanization proceeds at a pace that greatly taxes the resources of the state, and unemployment increases dramatically in the cities. Second, population growth of such magnitude is expected in the near future in West Africa, and the capacity for absorbing labor in the modern sector is so small, that a large increase of employment in agriculture seems to be the only realistic prospect. Both of these reasons for employment and development in the modern sector of the economy being affected by employment in the subsistence sector have demographic implications.

To what extent are the rural-urban drift and unemployment in West Africa's cities a result of the growth of rural populations and of their underemployment? No doubt they contribute to the problem, but the question of urban unemployment is complex, and such unemployment has many different causes. Not very long ago wage labor was scarce in Africa. In 1956, Richard-Molard was commenting that the supply of manpower in almost all of French West Africa was insufficient.[52] About that time, there were only 28,000 salaried workers employed in manufacture in the whole of French West Africa.[53] In Nigeria, the modern sector accounts for only 5 percent of the total labor force.[54] The modern sector is usually so small that it can easily be overwhelmed by the drift of even a small portion of the underemployed from the countryside. One must explain, however, why the rural labor force now is attracted to the cities, and why it was

not a few years earlier. The primary cause seems to be the existence of substantial income differentials between the urban dwellers and the peasants. In spite of wide-scale unemployment, wages have been rising steadily in the modern sector.[55] These wages, and other opportunities in the city, may be sufficiently attractive to compensate for the risks of unemployment. At the same time, employment in the modern sector has failed to expand at the rate of population growth; in many countries, the total number of jobs has stagnated, or even decreased. In Ghana, it is estimated that the number of unemployed has tripled between 1960 and 1967; in November 1969, the Prime Minister estimated that 25 percent of the total labor force was unemployed. Addo blames this situation on the interaction of high population growth and inadequate economic expansion and contends that, as a result, "family planning is an economic necessity in contemporary Ghana."[56] In other West African countries, even though demographic causes of, and solutions to employment problems are not always as clearly referred to,[57] the growth of employment is not sufficient to absorb the growth of the labor force. Frank shows that a high rate of growth of the modern sector will normally not result in a large demand for additional labor, and that attempting to use labor-intensive techniques in that sector will have only a very limited effect.[58] Most of the large employers in West Africa (and the governments are the largest of them all) are labor intensive in their methods already; and the technical constraints of mining and industry are such that capital intensive

[52] J. Richard-Molard, *Afrique Occidentale Française* (Paris, 1956), p. 185. See also A. Byl, "The Evolution of the Labor Market in French-Speaking West Africa," *Weltwirtschaftliches Archiv.*, 97, 1 (1966). It should be noted that French West Africa in this context had a political sense, covering a different area than what is meant by West Africa in this book.

[53] The figure is given for 1954 in Morgan and Pugh, *West Africa*, p. 448.

[54] C. R. Frank, "Urban Unemployment and Economic Growth in Africa," *Oxford Economic Papers*, XX, 2 (July 1968), 252. Frank defines the modern sector by the scale of operation, including establishments employing ten workers or more.

[55] R. G. Hollister, "Manpower Problems and Policies in Africa," *International Labour Review*, 99, 5 (May 1969), 515 ff.

[56] N. O. Addo, "Urbanization, Population Growth and Employment Prospects in Ghana," Seminar on Population Growth and Economic Development, Nairobi, December 1969, mimeographed.

[57] See, however, E. R. A. Forde, "The Implications of Rapid Population Growth for Employment in Sierra Leone," Seminar on Population Growth and Economic Development. For a review of data on the growth of employment up to 1965, see Frank, "Urban Unemployment."

[58] Frank, "Urban Unemployment," 255 ff.

methods have a competitive advantage. Furthermore, eradicating unemployment may be impossible as long as there is an unlimited supply of labor in the rural areas waiting for an opportunity to join the urban labor force. With the unequal development of cities and countryside in West Africa, the concentration of investment in the urban sector will attract more migrants, and only a narrowing of the income differential would reduce the drift. The conclusion, that most of the quite large population growth expected in West Africa will have to be absorbed on the land, has far-reaching policy implications. It is a far cry from the "industrial fundamentalism" once professed by the Economic Commission for Africa.[59]

POPULATION GROWTH AND THE EXPANSION OF THE EDUCATION SYSTEM. Whereas the growth of capital stock in a country occurs either in subsistence agriculture where it is not easily measurable, or in the modern sector where it is not felt to affect directly the welfare and employment of a majority of the population, the growth of the educational system is easily measurable and concerns equally both the governments and the people of all countries of West Africa. To the individual and his family, even in remote villages, schooling appears the door to the improvement of one's condition and to success. To the state, education is an essential element of nation building and of the transformation of society necessary for economic development. Therefore it is not surprising that the impact of population growth on the size of the school-age population, and on the prospects of attaining the goal of universal primary education, is one of the most convincing arguments for a reduction of fertility and natural increase. The point is made cogently in the Ghana policy paper on population:

In the 1966–67 school year, only about 60 percent of the children of appropriate age were attending school. Had the Ghanaian population over the previous 20 years grown at half the rate at which it did grow, the facilities and personnel of 1966–67 would have been adequate for all the children of school age and the nation's goal of universal education could have become a reality.[60]

The growth of the population in the primary school years is expected in West Africa to be of the order of a two-thirds increase between 1965 and 1985, a period during which little reduction in fertility is anticipated.[61] The quality of programs must still be upgraded and the cost of education has escalated with the inflation of wages in recent years. However, the share of educational services in most national budgets has reached almost the maximum conceivable. Not only is the goal of universal primary education out of reach for this century, but the absolute number of illiterates is expected to increase even if enrollment continues to make slow progress.[62] Jones has considered the implications of alternative courses of fertility and population growth on education in Africa, with special attention to Ghana. He concludes that it would take decades to provide universal education, even under optimistic assumptions on the course of fertility.[63]

We shall return to education, as one of the most important costs of a young age distribution, in particular from the point of view of individual families. In this section, we have particularly stressed the investment need created by a fast expansion of the population. Our main theme has been that the need for improving the endowment of the existing population (by *economic* invest-

---

[59] The expression "industrial fundamentalism" is used by Eicher, *Research on Agricultural Development*, pp. 11 ff. The ECA position was given in *Economic Bulletin for Africa*, IV (January 1964), and in A. F. Ewing, *Industry in Africa* (London: Oxford, 1968).

[60] Republic of Ghana, *Population Planning for National Progress and Prosperity*, p. 11.

[61] The estimate is derived from Etienne van de Walle, "The Population of Tropical Africa in the 1980s," Symposium on Africa in the 1980s, mimeographed, Adlai Stevenson Institute (Chicago, 1969), p. 25.

[62] For the "disappointing" experience of Sierra Leone, see T. E. Dow, "Population Growth and Primary Education in Sierra Leone," Seminar on Population Growth and Economic Development, Nairobi, December 1969, mimeographed.

[63] G. W. Jones, "The Demographic Obstacle to the Attainment of Educational Goals in Tropical Africa," Seminar on Population Growth and Economic Development, in particular pp. 22 ff.

ments) competes with the demands of the additional population for an equal share in economic opportunities (thus forcing *demographic* investments which do not improve income per head).

## ECONOMIC IMPLICATIONS OF THE AGE DISTRIBUTION

The structure of investments (discussed in the previous section) will be influenced, at the macroeconomic level, by the age distribution of the population. In countries with a high birth rate, such as most West African nations, a large part of the population consists of children, usually more than 40 percent under 15 years of age. Expenditures on health and welfare, housing, and education, which are not productive directly and in the short run, will tend to receive more emphasis than in countries of low fertility where the average age is older. An index of age distribution, the so-called burden of dependency index,

$$BD = \frac{\text{Proportion of the population under 15 and over 60}}{\text{Proportion between 15 and 59 years}}$$

has often been used to express the relationship between the number of dependents and the number of active, productive members of the population. Whereas the burden of dependency in a typical West African nation is probably between 0.8 and 1.0 dependent per adult, in a typical Western country, with low fertility, it is closer to 0.7. Thus, with the young age distribution resulting from high fertility each adult has to provide for more dependents.

Although this macroeconomic argument tends to be appreciated by governments having to provide for the education of the young in the age distribution, it is often queried whether it has any value from the individual family's point of view. It is almost a cliché that children do not constitute a burden in a subsistence economy. The following quotation is fairly representative:

Economically and socially, the child . . . only represents a small expenditure, quickly reimbursed; it is even a good bargain: poorly fed and clothed, hardly or not at all educated, he engages very early in work productive of goods and services (agricultural or industrial labor, tinkering, begging, stealing and prostitution, etc.)[64]

The validity of this statement can be ascertained in two ways. The first approach consists of interviewing parents about what they feel is the economic contribution made by their child, and the costs involved in bringing up the child. This has been done in KAP surveys. The second approach would consist of an actual economic analysis of the costs and benefits of children in a family budget. The KAP surveys often include questions on the desirability of a large number of children. In his survey of urban residents in Ghana, Caldwell was able to assess that more than half of the female respondents and more than a quarter of the male ones believed that restricting family size would raise the family's standard of living.[65] It could be argued that this is only true under urban conditions, where "expenses do increase with family size, while income does not."[66] In a parallel study of rural areas, Caldwell found that over half of the respondents associated large families with lesser economic well-being.[67] The data also suggest that the economic value of children declines as one moves from the areas of traditional subsistence farming to those involved in the cash economy. The economic strains associated with schooling increase in the process. Finally, the economic value of the child differs greatly with its age. Of particular interest is the tabulation of answers to the question: "Do children earn their keep (that is, do they do enough work, or produce enough food or earn enough money to make up for the expense they cause)?" The proportions answering "no" (that children did not earn

[64] O. Afana, "L'Economie de l'Ouest-africain," *Economie et socialisme* 4 (Paris, 1966), p. 16.
[65] John C. Caldwell, *Population Growth and Family Change in Africa* (Canberra: Australian National University Press, 1968), p. 48.
[66] *Ibid.*, p. 53.
[67] John C. Caldwell, "Fertility Attitudes in Three Economically Contrasting Rural Regions of Ghana," *Economic Development and Cultural Change*, XV, 2, Part 1 (January 1967), 217 ff.

their keep) varied significantly according to economic region (subsistence farming in the north or cash cropping in the south), to the age of the child, and to whether or not he was attending school.[68] The results are shown below.

|  | *Percentage of Children Reported as Not Earning Their Keep* | |
| --- | --- | --- |
|  | *Not Attending School* | *Attending School* |
| (1)  Subsistence area | | |
| Age:    0–4 | 98 | — |
| 5–9 | 51 | 79 |
| 10–14 | 26 | 66 |
| (2)  Modernizing area | | |
| Age:    0–4 | 99 | — |
| 5–9 | 80 | 92 |
| 10–14 | 54 | 83 |

The proportions of respondents disagreeing with the opinion that children earn their keep, were thus very substantial in all instances.

The evidence from budgetary surveys and agricultural inquiries on the economic contribution of children is not conclusive, perhaps because this question has not drawn the attention of survey takers. Studies of use of time often do not consider the activities of children under 15 years old.[69] This in itself may be significant in indicating that work accomplished by children is not very important. However, there is plenty of evidence that children participate actively in field and house work.[70] They gain in efficiency between 6 and 15 years of age, but it is difficult to say at what age they produce more than they consume. In situations where there is considerable underemployment, child labor may

only make a contribution at the time of seasonal labor shortages. Research would be needed to establish microeconomic relationships such as those between the number of dependent children and the following: the size of the cultivated area, individual production and consumption of food, the ability to send one's children to school, and so on. Some of these relationships are suggested by other studies relating the size of the household to the cultivated area (the two are usually highly correlated)[71] or to food consumption (the coverage of dietary requirements usually is decreasing with increases in the size of the households).[72]

## CONCLUSION

This chapter set out to review some of the literature on the effect of population on the economy of West Africa. We discussed successively the effect of population size, of population growth, and of the age distribution. The population of West Africa will undergo an enormous increase in the coming years; the economic implications of this fact will become more and more visible as time goes by. There is the beginning of a body of valuable research on the subject, but much more is needed. The advantages to be expected from fertility reduction are still greatly misunderstood and underestimated, despite increasing interest in the last few years, and the breakthrough of the Ghanaian policy paper. A decrease in fertility would immediately reduce the burden of dependency. In the medium term, it would reduce the investment needs to keep up with employment and equipment of the labor force. In the long run, it would substantially reduce the dangers of overcropping that threaten many West African lands.

[68] *Ibid.*, summarized from Table 4, p. 227.
[69] For example, République Centrafricaine, *L'emploi du temps.*
[70] For example, the details in Boutillier et al., *La Moyenne Vallée*, pp. 106–11.

[71] See, for example: République du Sénégal, *Enquête agricole 1960–1961* (Paris, 1962), pp. 33–35.
[72] République Fédérale du Cameroun, *Le niveau de vie*, pp. 91–93.

WEST Africa has been a zone of considerable population movement from very early times. The myths of origin of most of the thousand or more ethnic groups in the area tell of their having migrated into the territory which they now occupy. From the Middle Ages onward, evidence of long-distance movements of people across the whole region starts to accumulate. The rise of various West African kingdoms and empires such as Ghana, Mali, Songhai, or Kanem often involved the dispatch of members of the conquering group to serve as administrators and soldiers in the conquered territory, as well as the forced migration of some of the conquered people as slaves to the metropolitan center of the new political state. More important, however, were the peaceful movements of people over long distances particularly for trade purposes but also for a variety of other reasons.

Prothero provides a typology of African mobility (see Figure 7.1) which very well summarizes the position. Basically, he distinguishes between the noneconomic and the economic types of movement. The former includes in particular religious pilgrimages, especially of Moslems, as well as the movements of political refugees. In West Africa, the movement of Moslem pilgrims has always been a very important phenomenon, involving each year tens of thousands of people. Until recently, it was a stage-by-stage affair in which the pilgrims gradually worked their way to Mecca, stopping to work for months or years at different places on the way. In consequence, it occasioned a considerable net loss of population from different parts of West Africa. It is estimated for instance, that such hopeful pilgrims from West Africa made up by 1956 nearly 75 percent of the 250,000 immigrants into the Republic of Sudan.[1] Today,

[1] See K. M. Barbour, "Population Shifts and Changes in Sudan Since 1898," *Middle Eastern Studies*, II, no. 2, (January 1966), 98–122; see also I. A. Hassoun, "Western Migration and Settlement in the Gezira," *Sudan Notes and Records*, no. 33 (1952); D. B. Mather, "Migration in the Sudan," in *Geographical Essays on British Tropical Lands*, R. W. Steel and C. A. Fisher, eds. (London: George Philip and Son, Ltd., 1956), pp. 113–44, and H. R. J. Davies, "The West African in the Economic Geography of Sudan," *Geography*, XLIX (1964), 222–35.

# CHAPTER SEVEN

# *Migration & Urbanization*

AKIN L. MABOGUNJE

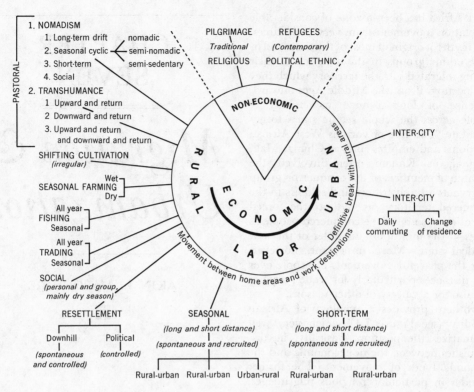

FIGURE 7.1. *A Typology of African Mobility (after Prothero)*

the provision of airline connections has considerably shortened the time required for the journey and obviated the need to work or stop over at intermediate points on the way.

In contrast, movements of refugees have become increasingly important in recent times. The consolidation after 1960 of the boundaries of the new African states as well as of their political stability has continued to generate internal strife and has given rise in a few cases to civil wars, notably in Nigeria and Chad. The result has been mass movements of people from one part of the country concerned to another as well as actual emigration. It is not possible to estimate the number involved, although it is obvious that this must be considerable. The internal strife that preceded the civil war in Nigeria, for instance, is said to have led to the movement of about 2 million people from one part of the country to another, while the civil war itself led to movement out of the country, especially of children, to Gabon and Ivory Coast.

Migration movements with economic orientations include pastoral nomadism, shifting cultivation, fishing, and trading. All of these have continued from the past right into the present. The Fulani continue to engage in migratory shifts of very indeterminate direction, length, and timing to ensure an adequate supply of water and pasture for their cattle.[2] In restricted areas of West Africa, farmers such as the Lobi in Ivory Coast and Ghana continue to move from one area to another in search of cultivable land.[3] The Sorkawa

[2] D. J. Stenning, "Transhumance, Migratory Drift, Migration: Patterns of Pastoral Fulani Nomadism," *Journal of the Royal Anthropological Institute*, LXXXVII, part 1 (January–June 1957), 57–74.
[3] Georges Savonnet, "La Colonisation du Pays Koulango (Haute Côte d'Ivoire) par les Lobi de Haute Volta," *Cahiers d'Outre Mer*, XV, no. 57 (January–March, 1962), 25–46. See also H. Labouret, *Tribus du rameau Lobi*, Institut d'Ethnologie (Paris, 1931), and W. Manshard, "Land Use Patterns and Agricultural Migration in Central Ghana (Western Gonja)," *Tijdschrift voor economische en sociale geografie*, LII, no. 9 (September 1961), 225–30.

fishermen on the Niger River migrate from the Gao area upstream as far as Timbuktu and downstream to Onitsha in search of new fishing grounds, while the Ewe fishermen of Ghana and Togo are found all along the coast from Sierra Leone to Zaïre.[4] Traders, especially those of Mandingo, Zerma, Hausa, or Yoruba origin, continue to be found in different parts of the region, their presence, especially in the urban areas, having become institutionalized in the administrative setup of the host area.[5]

## COLONIAL DEVELOPMENT AND LABOR MIGRATIONS

These traditional types of migration movements underwent tremendous modification under the impact of changes resulting from the establishment of the colonial regimes in West Africa. Three of these changes were of special significance in terms of the new direction they gave to the movements and the number and characteristics of the majority of migrants.

The first major change was in the field of transportation. The prelude to the European colonization of Africa was marked by the Berlin Conference of 1884 which, apart from reconciling the competing European countries to accepting each other's claims to "trading spheres of influence," introduced the concept of "effective occupation" as a test of the validity of these claims. A most important means of operationalizing this concept came to be the construction of railway systems within the area. From 1885 until about 1930, the present railway network in West Africa was established. It was, however, not much of a network since, except in the case of Nigeria and Ghana, there were few interconnections. Instead a series of isolated lines was established running from the coast inland. Nevertheless, the railway did occasion a revolution

in reducing traveling time and in knitting together areas which were formerly so far apart. After 1920, roads and motor vehicles came to play an important role in facilitating closer spatial integration. And since the end of World War II, airplanes have also become of increasing significance. All these various means of transport came to be used by an increasing number of people in migrating from one part of West Africa to another.

The second major change to affect the character of migration in West Africa was the increasing monetization of the economy. It was not that there were no monies in circulation long before the European penetration but that these tended to be restricted in their areas of circulation and to vary in their exchange rate from place to place. What the colonial regime did was to replace a multiplicity of currencies with no more than three (the pound, the franc, and the escudo). More important, the colonial regime gave monetary value to a wide variety of local resources such as land, trees, and animals and expressed their new importance in monetary terms. In other words, a major change in West Africa came with the introduction of the economy to a vast and largely expanding world market.

Both the improvement of transport and the monetization of the economy were predisposing elements for the third major change, the increasing specialization of production. Different parts of West Africa gradually discovered that the way to increase income rapidly was to concentrate on producing those crops for which they were best suited. In consequence, by the second quarter of this century, distinctive agricultural regions were starting to emerge in West Africa producing palm produce, cocoa, coffee, rubber, bananas, kolanuts, soya beans, benni-seed, groundnuts, and cotton. Most of these products were for export. However, the returns to the farmers from their production varied not only in relation to world demand for the individual crops but also in relation to the distance of the producing areas from the coast. In general, farmers in the areas close to the coast got a higher return for their effort compared with those further inland who had

---

[4] Jean Rouch, "The Sorkawa, migrant fishermen of the middle Niger," *Africa*, XX, no. 1 (January 1950), 5–55; and also Polly Hill, "Pan-African Fishermen," *West Africa*, no. 2430 (December 28, 1963), 1455; no. 2431 (January 4, 1964), 14–15.

[5] See A. L. Mabogunje, *Regional Mobility and Resource Development in West Africa* (Montreal: McGill University Press, 1972) p. 156.

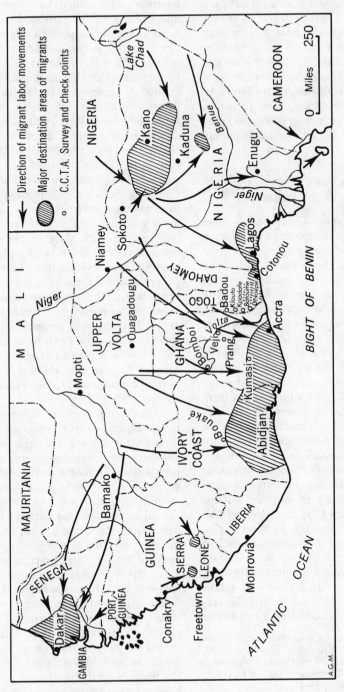

FIGURE 7.2. *Labor Migration in West Africa*

to receive prices for their crops which had been considerably discounted because of high transport costs. Moreover, the climatic regime favored the coastal areas with their longer agricultural season and two harvest seasons while the interior regions were always faced with the problem of how to tide over the relatively long dry season with the meager food supplies from their single yearly harvest.

In terms of migration, the most important consequence of these various changes in the social milieu was the emergence of a new pattern involving seasonal movements of population from the interior to the coastal areas of West Africa every year (see Figure 7.2). This seasonal movement of people across West Africa came to overwhelm the traditional movements in its volume, direction, and characteristics. To deal with the last two aspects first, the direction was almost invariably north to south as distinct from the crisscross pattern of traditional movements. The interior states of Mali, Upper Volta, and Niger became major source regions of migrants while coastal states, notably Senegal, Gambia, Ivory Coast, Ghana, and Nigeria became important destinations. In a large country such as Nigeria this north-south shift of population occurred within the country which also received migrants from other interior countries.

The dominant characteristic of this new migration was that it consisted largely of agricultural labor moving down to work on southern farms or plantations for a limited and clearly defined period each year. Or, to put it in the language of northern Nigeria, it was the migration of people (*mai cin rani*) who ate away the dry season elsewhere. When farming employment became inadequate, these people took up jobs as laborers in public works, mining, and forestry, or as carriers in the cities.

The volume of this colonial labor migration is difficult to assess. Most West African countries keep no records from which information on seasonal migration can be extracted. In consequence, we are reduced to extrapolating from the results of various surveys conducted at different times since the end of World War II, or to using census returns of Africans who are nonnative to a particular country. To summarize the evidence from these surveys, Jarrett's study in Gambia showed that the number of "stranger farmers" coming into the colony fluctuated sharply from year to year from a low of 2,585 in 1942 to a high of 19,979 in 1945.[6] Senegal also annually receives its *navetanes* who since 1946 are said to number between 40,000 and 45,000 a year.[7] A far more comprehensive survey of migrants conducted for Ghana and Ivory Coast from March 1958 to March 1959 revealed that some 400,000 to 500,000 persons moved into these two countries over the one-year period and that more than 80 percent of these stayed for less than one year.[8] Prothero, in a survey conducted from October 1952 to March 1953 in Nigeria, indicated that some 259,000 persons were involved in southward migration through Sokoto Province alone.[9] Of these, 73 percent originated in Sokoto Province, another 10 percent came from other parts of northern Nigeria, while the remaining 17 percent were from the neighboring territory of Niger. If Sokoto Province alone recorded over a quarter of a million such migrants, it is no exaggeration to suggest that probably a million people were involved in these movements within Nigeria. All in all, it can be assumed that the movement of seasonal agricultural labor from the northern to the

[6] H. R. Jarrett, "The Stranger Farmers of the Gambia," *Geographical Journal*, XXXIX, no. 4 (October 1949), 651.

[7] Virginia Thompson and Richard Adloff, *French West Africa* (London: G. Allen, 1958), p. 493.

[8] This survey was organized jointly by the Statistics or Research Division of the Governments of Ivory Coast, Ghana, Upper Volta, Niger, Togo, and Dahomey. Its results were presented as a series of Working Documents at a Symposium: "Study of Migrations in West Africa," especially CCTA/CSA., Joint Project No. 3, MIG. (61), (January 2, 1961). Similar information can be found in the monographic study by Jean Rouch, "Migrations en Ghana Enquête 1953–55," *Journal de la Société des Africanistes*, Tome 26, fasc. 122 (1956), 33–196.

[9] R. M. Prothero, "Migratory Labour from Northwestern Nigeria," *Africa*, XXVII, no. 3 (July, 1957), 251–61.

southern parts of West Africa is probably of the order of 2 million people.

## THE SOCIODEMOGRAPHIC CHARACTERISTICS OF COLONIAL LABOR MIGRANTS

No comprehensive study of the social and demographic characteristics of the labor migrants has been made. However, the survey already referred to which was conducted for migrants into Ghana and Ivory Coast in 1958–1959 provides much information which confirms to a large extent the general impression of the basic characteristics of labor migrants in West Africa. The survey was based on a 25 percent sample (104,587 individuals) of migrants passing through the major road and rail junction town of Bouake (Ivory Coast), the ferry-crossing towns of Yeji, Bamboi, and Otisu in Ghana and the Togo-Ghana frontier posts of Aflao, Batoume, Noepe, Kpadape Klouto, and Badon. It revealed a predominance of migrants from ethnic groups in the interior of West Africa. Some 60 percent of migrants belong to the Voltaic group, of whom the most important were the Mossi, the Dagari, the Lobi, the Gurunsi, and the Kotokoli. Another 13 percent belonged to the Mande group especially the

Bambara and the Malinke. The Niger group of Hausa, Zerma, and Songhai accounted for 10 percent while the remainder was made up of groups such as the Fulani and the Yoruba.

The variations in the age and sex distribution of the migrants are well brought out in Table 7.1. For most ethnic groups something like 30 percent of total male migrants were in the age group 25–29 while between 65 and 75 percent were between 20 and 34 years old. This, of course, corresponds to the well-known fact that it is the young men who go to seek work away from their home country. The situation for the women is also interesting. Apart from confirming the youthfulness of this category of migrants, it highlights the economic independence of the Yoruba women who formed a sizable proportion (nearly 25 percent) of the total of their ethnic group as compared with less than 2 percent in the case of most other groups. A similar situation is found among the Kotokoli and the Fon who are neighbors of the Yoruba.

Of the total migrants recorded, some 52 percent were single, a situation which can be regarded as normal given the relatively youthful age of the majority. Of married migrants, 85 percent were traveling alone. In other words, the great majority of labor migrants to the coastal areas were single,

TABLE 7.1

Demographic characteristics of major migrant groups into Ghana-Ivory coast, 1958–1959 survey

| Age | Mossi M | Mossi F | Bambara-Diola M | Bambara-Diola F | Zerma M | Zerma F | Hausa M | Hausa F | Yoruba M | Yoruba F |
|---|---|---|---|---|---|---|---|---|---|---|
| Under 14 | 102 | 3 | 10 | 3 | 13 | — | 20 | — | 13 | 1 |
| 15–19 | 1,420 | 11 | 73 | 11 | 239 | 3 | 167 | 14 | 100 | 36 |
| 20–24 | 4,499 | 13 | 731 | 29 | 631 | 2 | 685 | 28 | 205 | 87 |
| 25–29 | 7,959 | 30 | 1,753 | 40 | 926 | 10 | 1,025 | 41 | 471 | 122 |
| 30–34 | 3,023 | 17 | 578 | 35 | 520 | 6 | 517 | 32 | 304 | 82 |
| 35–39 | 1,812 | 14 | 676 | 41 | 458 | 8 | 432 | 25 | 197 | 36 |
| 40–44 | 544 | 4 | 99 | 11 | 213 | 1 | 181 | 11 | 102 | 35 |
| 45–49 | 357 | 2 | 104 | 4 | 121 | 1 | 112 | 8 | 51 | 11 |
| 50+ | 187 | 2 | 58 | 1 | 61 | 1 | 131 | 14 | 56 | 11 |
| Undeclared | 30 | 6 | 12 | — | 4 | — | 5 | 2 | 5 | 2 |
| Total | 19,933 | 102 | 4,094 | 175 | 3,186 | 32 | 3,275 | 175 | 1,504 | 423 |

Source: CCTA/CSA Working Document for Symposium on Migrations in West Africa, Niamey, MIG. (61) (January 2, 1961).

either actually or temporarily. The colonial labor migration would thus appear to be not an attempt at colonization and settlement but a short-term, often premarriage, adventure by young men who continue to maintain firm links with their country of origin. The Zerma, Kotokoli, and Yoruba were exceptions to this general pattern and showed a higher proportion of married males (about 60 percent) to single ones and of married men traveling with their wives. For these groups, it would appear that migration is less an individual venture than a family affair in which the man and the woman will each work at their own job for their general well-being.

The duration and frequency of migration is also of some interest. It would appear that the majority of migrants (nearly 80 percent) stayed for less than a year at a time. Distribution by ethnic groups reveals that the Zerma, Fulani, Hausa, and Yoruba made the shortest stays, some 50–60 percent of them staying less than six months. By contrast, the Mossi and Senoufo stayed much longer, often for up to a year or more. The explanation for this may be found in the different occupational interests of the various ethnic groups during their stay. The Voltaic groups were for the most part agricultural laborers and it is natural that they should stay longer than the Zerma, Fulani, Hausa, and Yoruba who were largely traders. This tendency is further confirmed by the number of journeys, which tended to be much higher for the latter group than for the former.

The occupational pattern of the migrants shows agricultural labor as the most common employment accounting for 46 percent and 52 percent of total migrants to Ivory Coast and Ghana respectively. It is followed by trading (20 percent) while unspecified occupations represented 15–25 percent of the total number of migrants. More interesting is the ethno-occupational specialization among the various ethnic groups. The Voltaic peoples, especially the Mossi and Senoufo, were mostly agricultural workers (65–70 percent). The Bambara-Diola were divided almost equally between agricultural work and trading. The Zerma and Hausas were mainly engaged in trade and transport or porterage (80 percent in all), while the Yoruba were mainly in trade and mining labor (60 percent).

This pattern of occupational specialization explains the different emphasis of the various ethnic groups on urban or rural residence at their destination. Table 7.2 shows the variation for the major ethnic groups. The trading groups, notably Zerma, Hausa, Fulani, and Yoruba showed a marked preference for urban destinations with between 65 and 85 percent of their number making for cities. The

TABLE 7.2
Urban/rural destinations of migrants into Ghana-Ivory coast, 1958–1959 survey

| Ethnic Group | Urban | | Rural | | Not Declared | | Total |
|---|---|---|---|---|---|---|---|
| | Number | Percent | Number | Percent | Number | Percent | |
| Mossi | 11,122 | 55.5 | 8,542 | 42.6 | 371 | 1.9 | 20,035 |
| Bambara | 1,874 | 43.9 | 2,195 | 51.4 | 200 | 4.7 | 4,269 |
| Zerma | 2,394 | 74.4 | 738 | 22.9 | 86 | 2.7 | 3,218 |
| Senoufo | 950 | 42.3 | 1,206 | 53.6 | 92 | 4.1 | 2,248 |
| Kotokoli | 718 | 29.6 | 1,705 | 70.2 | 7 | 0.2 | 2,430 |
| Hausa | 2,953 | 85.3 | 437 | 12.6 | 72 | 2.1 | 3,462 |
| Fulani | 2,040 | 68.3 | 860 | 28.8 | 86 | 2.9 | 2,986 |
| Yoruba | 1,484 | 77.1 | 425 | 22.1 | 17 | 0.8 | 1,926 |
| Fon | 286 | 42.3 | 390 | 57.6 | 1 | 0.1 | 677 |
| Total | 60,759 | 61.2 | 35,541 | 36.2 | 1,883 | 2.6 | 98,183 |

SOURCE: CCTA/CSA Working Document for Symposium on Migration in West Africa.

Mossi, Bambara, and Fon show no clear preference while the Senoufo and Kotokoli tended to be very strongly oriented to rural areas. Nevertheless, it is important to stress that even in the groups making for urban areas, only a few of their members are engaged in the upper sectors of employment as skilled workmen or clerks. Most of them remain primarily as unskilled laborers or tradespeople of the traditional type.

One important reason for this state of affairs is the relatively low level of education among most of the migrants. The survey revealed that between 75–80 percent of them were illiterate, some 10–15 percent had attended Koranic schools, and barely 2–5 percent had attended European-type schools. This education factor turns out to be a crucial element in any study of migration and urbanization in West Africa. It distinguishes the colonial from the more modern pattern of human movement in West Africa.

## MODERNIZATION AND THE RURAL-URBAN MIGRATION

The leaders of the nationalist movements in West Africa in the period soon after World War II saw their struggle as directed toward emancipation not only from colonial rule but also from the grip of ignorance, poverty, and disease. For many of them, it was almost a cardinal obligation that as soon as they could exercise power, they should vastly increase the educational opportunities available to their people. It is thus no wonder that one of the most remarkable changes that took place in West Africa with the end of the colonial era was the very rapid increase in enrollment in educational institutions. Table 7.3 shows the position for the 15-year period after 1950. A detailed examination of the table reveals tendencies in the training of young people which significantly affect both their attitudes to residence in rural as opposed to urban areas and their ability to function gainfully in either of these locations.

Three of these tendencies need to be highlighted. First, there is the very rapid rate of growth from an enrollment of 1.6 million in

TABLE 7.3
West Africa: Enrollment in educational institutions, 1950–1965

| Levels of Institutions | 1950 | 1955 | 1960 | 1965 |
|---|---|---|---|---|
| First Level | | | | |
| number ('000) | 1,528 | 2,684 | 4,555 | 5,549 |
| percent | (96.6) | (96.0) | (91.5) | (87.8) |
| Second Level | | | | |
| General | | | | |
| number ('000) | 39 | 70 | 361 | 646 |
| percent | (2.5) | (2.5) | (7.2) | (10.2) |
| Vocational | | | | |
| number ('000) | 5 | 13 | 19 | 60 |
| percent | (0.3) | (0.5) | (0.4) | (0.9) |
| Teacher training | | | | |
| number ('000) | 9 | 25 | 36 | 49 |
| percent | (0.5) | (0.9) | (0.7) | (0.8) |
| Third Level | | | | |
| number ('000) | 1 | 3 | 8 | 19 |
| percent | (0.1) | (0.1) | (0.2) | (0.3) |
| Total | | | | |
| number ('000) | 1,582 | 2,795 | 4,979 | 6,323 |
| percent | (100.0) | (100.0) | (100.0) | (100.0) |
| Rate of Growth | — | 11.21 | 11.23 | 10.49 |

SOURCE: UNESCO, *Statistical Yearbook* (1966).

1950 to 6.3 million in 1965. This gives a rate of growth of 11.0 percent per annum, compared with 2.5 percent per annum for total population and 4 percent per annum for the Gross Domestic Product.[10] Second, there is the sharp tapering off of enrollment in post-primary education. Although the relative importance of primary education has been declining over the period, it still accounts for nearly 88 percent of all enrollment in educational institutions compared with 61 percent in Canada, 59 percent in the United States, 51 percent in France, and 48 percent in Britain. In other words, a large proportion of primary school leavers are being thrown into the labor market at the rather tender age of 11–15 years. Third, at the secondary level, vocational training which could have equipped most school leavers with really salable skills within the modern industrial economy has received relatively scant attention. The ratio of enrollment in liberal education to each 100 of those in vocational education in

[10] United Nations, *Statistical Yearbook, 1968* (New York, 1969), p. 29.

1965 stood at approximately 1,100 in West Africa compared with 300 in France, 200 in Britain, and 75 in Germany.

This pattern of education means, in essence, training the youths mainly for clerical and similar white-collar occupations. It certainly discourages an acceptance of agricultural work and rural residence as an attractive way of life. The result has been a massive exodus of young school leavers from the rural areas into the cities. However, if the intense social change taking place all over West Africa, especially in the field of education, serves as the "push" factor encouraging many to leave the rural areas, the direction and destinations of their migrations have been determined to a large extent by the pattern of industrial development in most West African countries over the last 15 years. The major principle which has guided this development is that of import substitution, whereby instead of importing final consumer goods countries import the machinery, the skilled personnel, and very often the semi-processed raw materials needed to produce these goods locally. Because of the high import component of this form of industrialization, it is easy to appreciate why location at port cities was found most convenient and economic by many of the foreign industrialists. Besides, many of these port cities had served as the colonial capitals of the countries. They were also the seat of the head offices of most foreign commercial firms, some of which owned many of the new industrial plants, and most of which had already established efficient distribution systems for the goods now being produced. In the period of political independence, the preeminent position of these port-cum-commercial-cum-capital-cities was confirmed further by the indigenous governments which meant that numerous foreign embassies and legations were opened in these cities. All in all, then, the rate of employment creation in these coastal centers was hardly paralleled anywhere else in West Africa and hence they attracted a vast stream of youthful migrants, particularly the educated and those with very high hopes and aspirations.

Although less significant in terms of its overall impact, a second principle of industrialization in West Africa has been the semiprocessing of agricultural produce for export. This is especially important for distant interior areas which suffer considerable transfer cost disadvantages with their bulky, low-value agricultural produce. By semiprocessing such produce, the bulkiness is reduced, the value is raised, and the ability to bear transport cost is enhanced considerably. Semiprocessing has been applied in particular to groundnuts, cotton, hides, and skins from Northern Nigeria as well as to palm oil, rubber, cocoa, and timber from Southern Nigeria and Ghana. In some instances, such as in Kano and Kaduna in Northern Nigeria, the concentration of such industrial plants has attracted others more oriented toward production of final consumer goods. Outside of the coastal areas, therefore, a few industrial centers have emerged in the interior which also exert some pull on migrants leaving the rural areas for the cities.

## THE PATTERN OF WEST AFRICAN URBANIZATION

One of the most striking consequences of both the modernization and the industrialization processes in West Africa therefore has been not only the very rapid rate of urban development in the period after World War II, but also the increasing concentration of this population in a few large centers (see Figure 7.3). Assuming an urban center to be a compact settlement with a population of at least 5,000, it is found that in most countries while the total population has been increasing at a rate of between 2.5 and 3.5 percent per annum, the urban population has been growing at a rate of between 5 and 8 percent per annum over the period. Indeed, if we confine ourselves to urban centers with populations of 20,000 and above, the rate of growth is even more phenomenal, reaching in many countries well over 10 percent. Thus, by 1960, it was estimated that about 10.6 million people (or 12.4 percent of total population) lived in these larger centers in West Africa.

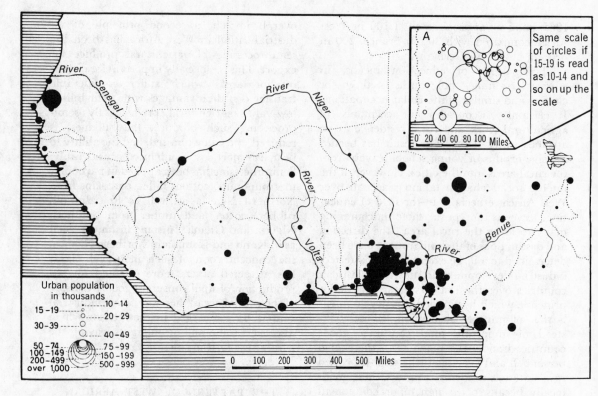

The inset contains the following text:
Same scale of circles if 15-19 is read as 10-14 and so on up the scale

0 20 40 60 80 100 Miles

River Senegal

River Niger

River

River Volta

River Benue

Urban population in thousands

15 – 19 ········ 10 – 14
                  20 – 29
30 – 39 ········
                  40 – 49
50 – 74       75 – 99
100 – 149     150 – 199
200 – 499     500 – 999
over 1,000

0   100   200   300   400   500   Miles

FIGURE 7.3.   *Pattern of Urban Development in West Africa*

This compares with a figure of 13 percent for the whole of Africa and about 5 percent for Eastern Africa.[11]

Table 7.4 gives the pattern of distribution of the urban population among different size classes of cities in selected West African countries. It reveals, first, the relatively lower level of urban development in the interior states of Mali, Niger, and Upper Volta, a fact not unrelated to the problems of economic growth in these countries. Second, the table emphasizes that except in the case of Togo and Ghana, settlements of less than 20,000 people account for less than 40 percent of the total urban population. Third, the very large urban settlements, those with population of 100,000 and above, accounted in nearly all countries for at least a third of total urban population. It is estimated that for all of West

[11] See United Nations, *Economic Bulletin for Africa*, VI, no. 2 (July 1966), 91.

Africa in 1960 some 6.5 million (or 7.6 percent of total population) were to be found in this category of settlements alone.

The question of the increasing concentration of the urban population highlights the recent tendency toward the emergence of primate cities in most West African countries. These are the cities which are so very large relative to the total urban population of the country. Table 7.5 shows the position in the 14 West African countries. It emphasizes that in nearly all cases, the primate city accounted for more than 30 percent of the urban population. In Senegal, Sierra Leone, and Liberia, these cities represented more than 50 percent of the urban population while in Gambia, the smallest West African country, the primate city is also the only city. Also, each of these cities is the capital of its country, and where the country is on the coast, the city is also the major port.

All over West Africa therefore, rural-urban

TABLE 7.4
Pattern of urban development in selected countries of West Africa

| Country | Year | Urban Population by Size Class as Percent of Total Population | | | | | | Urban Population by Size Class as Percent of Total Urban Population | | | | |
|---|---|---|---|---|---|---|---|---|---|---|---|---|
| | | Total | 5–9 | 10–19 | 20–49 | 50–99 | 100+ | 5–9 | 10–19 | 20–49 | 50–99 | 100+ |
| Dahomey | 1965 | 15.8 | 1.8 | 2.7 | 2.9 | 3.3 | 5.1 | 12.0 | 16.8 | 18.4 | 20.6 | 32.2 |
| Ghana | 1960 | 23.8 | 5.8 | 4.5 | 4.0 | — | 9.5 | 24.3 | 18.8 | 16.8 | — | 40.1 |
| Ivory Coast | 1967 | 22.0 | 2.3 | 2.7 | 4.3 | — | 12.7 | 10.5 | 12.2 | 19.5 | — | 57.8 |
| Mali | 1965 | 9.4 | 1.5 | 1.7 | 2.6 | — | 3.6 | 15.8 | 18.6 | 27.2 | — | 38.4 |
| Niger | 1968 | 5.4 | 1.2 | 0.6 | 1.7 | — | 1.9 | 21.3 | 11.2 | 31.5 | — | 36.0 |
| Senegal | 1960 | 24.0 | 1.9 | 0.6 | 3.5 | 6.1 | 12.0 | 7.9 | 2.1 | 14.5 | 25.3 | 50.2 |
| Sierra Leone | 1963 | 12.7 | 2.7 | 1.7 | 1.2 | — | 7.1 | 21.9 | 13.0 | 9.3 | — | 55.8 |
| Togo | 1966 | 19.5 | 1.3 | 9.3 | 1.2 | — | 7.7 | 6.7 | 47.7 | 6.1 | — | 39.5 |
| Upper Volta | 1966 | 6.5 | 1.9 | 0.5 | 0.5 | 1.4 | 2.2 | 29.8 | 8.1 | 6.8 | 21.1 | 34.2 |

SOURCE: W. A. Hance, *Population, Migration and Urbanization in Africa* (New York: Columbia University Press, 1970), p. 228.

migration shows a coastward tendency, similar in part to the preceding colonial labor migration movement. However, there are within most countries other centers which attract these migrants and therefore decrease the overall north-south effect. These are usually major trading centers found on railway lines or, more recently, at nodal points on the road-transport network. They used to be important as centers for the collection of export commodities or the distribution of imported manufactured goods. Today, with political independence and the desire to develop a spatial organization more relevant to the needs of the people, most of these cities have acquired new social and political functions such as being educational centers, locations for general or specialist hospitals, provincial headquarters, or state capitals. They have also attracted to themselves other functions in the commercial and industrial spheres and have in consequence shown a remarkable growth in their population. Examples of such centers include Thiès, Kayes, Kankan, Bouaké, Bobo-Dioulasso, Kumasi, and over a dozen noncoastal

TABLE 7.5
Primate cities of West Africa

| Country | City | Year | Population (in thousands) | Percent of Urban Population[a] | Percent of National Population |
|---|---|---|---|---|---|
| Dahomey | Cotonou | 1965 | 120 | 32.1 | 5.2 |
| Gambia | Bathurst | 1966 | 43 | 100.0 | 12.8 |
| Ghana | Greater Accra | 1966 | 600 | — | 8.9 |
| Guinea | Conakry | 1967 | 197 | — | 2.4 |
| Ivory Coast | Abidjan | 1967 | 400 | 45.4 | 10.8 |
| Liberia | Monrovia | 1962 | 81 | 64.8 | 8.0 |
| Mali | Bamako | 1965 | 165 | 38.4 | 3.6 |
| Mauritania | Nouakchott | 1966 | 22 | 35.5 | 2.1 |
| Niger | Niamey | 1968 | 71 | 36.0 | 1.9 |
| Nigeria | Greater Lagos | 1963 | 1,100 | — | — |
| Senegal | Greater Dakar | 1961 | 375 | 50.1 | 12.0 |
| Sierra Leone | Greater Freetown | 1963 | 163 | 55.8 | 7.1 |
| Togo | Lomé | 1966 | 129 | 39.4 | 7.7 |
| Upper Volta | Ouagadougou | 1966 | 110 | 34.2 | 2.2 |

SOURCE: Censuses and surveys; also UN *Demographic Yearbook* (1967).
[a] Urban population refers to places with at least 5,000 people.

Nigerian cities such as Ibadan, Abeokuta, Oshogbo, Benin, Onitsha, Aba, Enugu, Jos, Kaduna, Kano, and Maiduguri. Outside of these centers, modest growth continued in the relatively small towns which mainly perform central place functions for the rural masses. However, the extent to which their growth is the product of in-migration rather than of natural increase remains somewhat unclear.

In a number of older African cities which were large in the precolonial era but were not integrated into the colonial economy, the pattern of urbanization has been significantly different. Even where such centers report increases, this has been in the face of defective demographic structures. In other words, such places tend to suffer a net migration loss of young men and women and to show a preponderance of children, aged people, and women in their populations. This phenomenon has been associated with a strong feeling of social identification noticed among urban migrants who, even when they leave their home towns to look for employment elsewhere, not only maintain kinship ties with the place but often leave, within the polygamous structure, one or two of their wives, some of their children, and their aged parents behind.[12]

These various patterns have consequences for the character and quality of life in West African cities. The primate cities often reveal a most variegated pattern of housing types, neighborhood characteristics, land-use categories, and standards of environmental sanitation. There is also a basic distinction between such cities in the French-speaking and the English-speaking countries. In the former, the French seemed to have created cities, such as Dakar, Abidjan, and Conakry, of very strong European character. Although there are slum areas such as the Medina in Dakar, the main city is usually solidly built, well laid out and paved, and with the basic infrastructure of sewage, water supply, and telephone and electricity lines properly in place. In the English-speaking countries, modern town planning was only indifferently pursued.

[12] See A. L. Mabogunje, *Yoruba Towns* (Ibadan, 1962), p. 20.

Outside the European reservations, the general colonial policy was to provide the minimum facilities in these cities consistent with the needs of environmental sanitation and traffic flow.

## SOCIODEMOGRAPHIC CHARACTERISTICS OF WEST AFRICAN CITIES

Detailed description of the sociodemographic characteristics of these cities as well as of the changes that have taken place since the end of the colonial era is difficult to present because of the very unsatisfactory state of the data. Of the 15 West African countries, none of the 9 French-speaking ones have any census of population worth mentioning and the same is true of Portuguese Guinea. Liberia had its first census in 1962. Among the English-speaking countries, the 1963 census of Gambia was the only comprehensive one ever undertaken in that country, although some form of enumeration for various limited areas has been undertaken since 1881. Sierra Leone has had a long history of census taking, but again only the last one of 1963 covered the whole country. In Nigeria, the first full-scale census was in 1952. While a second census was undertaken in 1963, its results are of little value for analytical use because of the allegations of inflation which surround it. Only the censuses of Ghana provide us with some valuable data which can be assumed to typify in broad terms the conditions in most of the major West African cities.

The most significant aspect of the sociodemographic characteristics of West African cities as revealed by the Ghanaian examples is that essentially they are dominated by males. In 1948, for instance, while the sex ratio for Ghana as a whole was only 102 males for every 100 females, the figures were 110 for Accra, 112 for Kumasi and 129 for Sekondi-Takoradi. The sex inequality was even more pronounced for the critical adult age group of 14–45 year olds. While for Ghana as a whole, there were in fact fewer men than women in this group, the sex ratio being only 99, the ratio for Accra was 127, for Kumasi 131, and for Sekondi-Takoradi 153.

This pattern of sex composition emphasizes the well-known tendency in Africa to give education to boys rather than to girls and to be more permissive of the rural out-migration of boys than of girls. It also underscores the nature of the colonial nonindustrial economy which provided rather restricted employment opportunities for women. The pattern, however, is typical only of those cities which were closely integrated into the colonial economy. In Nigeria, for instance, the same pattern was noticed in 1952. While the sex ratio for the country as a whole was only 96, it was for Lagos 115, for Ibadan 107, for Kano 102, for Port Harcourt 170, for Enugu 164, for Jos 141, and for Kaduna 125. In those precolonial cities which were not so well integrated into the spatial economy, the position resulting from a net out-migration of males shows a sex ratio for Cape Coast in Ghana of 95. In Nigeria, such places included Sokoto 92, Katsina 96, Ife 87, and Ijebu-Ode 90.

By the 1960s, the changing socioeconomic situation as well as the vast improvement in transport, notably the construction of a denser network of roads, was further affecting the sociodemographic situation of the cities. In most of the growing centers, except the primate cities, there was a tendency toward a greater equalization of the sexes resulting from a higher volume of migration of women from rural areas to the cities, a higher proportion of women undergoing education and training, and increasing employment opportunities for women in the cities. Thus, while the total sex ratio for Accra rose from 110 in 1948 to 115 in 1960 (for those in the age group 14–45 it rose from 127 to 139 in the same period) it went down in Sekondi-Takoradi from 129 to 117 (for those between 16 and 45 years it fell from 153 to 135).

Apart from the changing sex distribution, the cities moved toward greater youthfulness in their populations reflecting, among other things, the massive rural-urban migration of young school leavers under 16 years. Table 7.6 shows the percentage of people under 16 years of age in the major Ghanaian cities in 1948 and 1960. The table reveals that

TABLE 7.6
Children as percentage of total population in Ghanaian cities, 1948–1960

|  | 1948 | | 1960 | |
|---|---|---|---|---|
|  | M | F | M | F |
| Ghana | 43.6 | 42.5 | 44.4 | 44.6 |
| Accra | 32.9 | 39.5 | 34.5 | 43.6 |
| Kumasi | 34.1 | 44.5 | 36.1 | 47.2 |
| Sekondi-Takoradi | 29.1 | 40.8 | 35.3 | 45.8 |
| Cape Coast | 37.1 | 38.6 | 39.6 | 43.1 |

SOURCE; Censuses of Ghana, 1948 and 1960.

whereas for the country as a whole this age class has increased only marginally in proportion to the total population, for the cities the increases have been more striking.

It is, of course, possible to argue that these increases are due to higher rates of natural increase in the cities than in the rural areas. And there is evidence, notably from Nigeria, to show that fertility levels far from being depressed in urban areas tend to rise.[13] However, the evidence from Ghana would tend to imply that fertility levels in the cities are as a whole lower (by about 10 percent) than in the rural areas.[14] Figures from four other West African countries (Table 7.7) also support the existence of such a differential. In all cases, fertility is between 5 and 20 percent lower in urban than in rural areas. Birth rates are also lower in the urban than in the rural areas but so are the death rates and the infant mortality rates. The result is that although fertility levels are lower, the rate of natural increase tends to be higher in urban than in rural areas. This notwithstanding, it

[13] See, for example, P. Olusanya, "Some Social Psychological Aspects of Fertility among Married Women in an African City: Comments," *Nigerian Journal of Economic and Social Studies*, X, no. 1 (March 1968), 117–23; and A. L. Mabogunje, "Urban Land Policy and Population Growth in Nigeria" (Paper presented at the Seminar on Population Growth and Economic Development, Nairobi, December 1969).

[14] See N. O. Addo, "Urbanization, Population Growth and Employment Prospects in Ghana" (Paper presented at Seminar on Population Growth and Economic Development, Nairobi, December 1969), p. 4; also John C. Caldwell, *Population Growth and Family Change in Africa* (Canberra: Australian National University Press, 1968), p. 38.

TABLE 7.7
Birth and death rates in urban and rural areas of selected West African countries

| Country | Year | Urban Rates of: | | | | Rural Rates of: | | | |
|---|---|---|---|---|---|---|---|---|---|
| | | Birth | Fertility | Death | Infant mortality | Birth | Fertility | Death | Infant mortality |
| Guinea | 1955 | 52 | 186 | 29 | 189 | 63 | 226 | 41 | 218 |
| Mali (Niger Valley) | 1957 | 52 | 185 | 31 | 246 | 54 | 205 | 47 | 320 |
| Senegal | 1960–61 | 44 | 175 | 10 | 36 | 43 | 184 | 19 | 109 |
| Dahomey | 1961 | 48 | — | 12 | — | 54 | — | 27 | — |

SOURCE: *Economic Bulletin for Africa*, V. (January 1965), 59.
NOTE: Fertility is calculated per 1,000 women aged 14–49 years.

would appear that a sizable proportion of the increases recorded in the youthful population has been due largely to in-migration to the cities.

Other demographic characteristics such as marital status and size of households in the cities are more difficult to discuss owing to lack of data. It would appear, however, that the urban areas tend to have a higher proportion of monogamously married couples than the rural ones. This purely intuitive notion has to be balanced against the growing body of evidence that monogamous marriages tend to result in higher female fertility than polygamous marriages. If urban fertility levels are lower than rural, it may be that no clear distinction exists between the two areas in terms of the type of marriage.

On the question of size of household, there is some evidence that this is smaller in urban than in rural areas. Caldwell, for instance, noted that in Ghana in 1963, the average urban household comprises 5.4 persons as compared with 7.7 in the rural households.[15] In Nigeria, however, the evidence is somewhat inconclusive. The rural demographic sample survey in 1965–1966 showed that the average size of rural households in the country was 5.6, varying from 4.9 in Western Nigeria to 6.0 in Northern Nigeria.[16] By contrast, urban consumer surveys conducted in various cities, notably Lagos, Ibadan, Oshogbo, Onitsha, Enugu, and Kaduna

between 1960 and 1967 revealed that while the average size of a household in the low-income class was smaller than in rural areas and varied between 3.4 in Kaduna and 5.2 in Ibadan and between 3.0 for clerks and 5.5 for artisans, that for the middle-income group was much higher varying between 4.7 in Kaduna and 7.4 in Lagos, the median being 6.6.[17]

The sociodemographic pattern of African cities also reveals some very striking contrasts with cities in the industrialized countries of the world. In the latter, although the sex balance in the cities tends to be in favor of females, this accompanies a lower rate of natural increase. In contrast, cities in West Africa while showing a tendency toward male dominance also exhibit rather high levels of natural increase. This situation has implications for the average size of household, and poses, with other features of West African urbanization, numerous problems in terms of the role of cities in the economic development of the region.

## PROBLEMS OF RAPID URBANIZATION

The rapid rate of urbanization has put various strains and stresses on the economies of West African countries. Perhaps the most important has been in the area of employment.

[15] John C. Caldwell, *African Rural-Urban Migration* (Canberra: Australian National University Press, 1969), p. 24.
[16] Nigeria, Federal Office of Statistics, *Rural Demographic Sample Survey, 1965–66* (Lagos, October 1968).

[17] Nigeria, Federal Office of Statistics, *Urban Consumer Surveys*, Lagos (1959–60), Ibadan (1966), Oshogbo (1966), Onitsha (1967), Enugu (1966), and Kaduna (1966). Low-income families are those with income from their main occupation not exceeding £350 per annum; middle-income families earn between £350 (U.S. $833) and £800 ($1,904) per annum from their main occupation.

Modern industrial development in the cities has served to raise the level of employment expectations far beyond its capacity to fulfill them. Because of the imported nature of industrial technology, there is considerable constraint on the choice of machines and equipment. More often than not, industrial plants tend to be capital rather than labor intensive. Increases in their number also have not been consistent, varying a great deal with the foreign capitalists' estimation of the degree of political stability in each country and their feeling of security of investment. Furthermore, internal plant expansion has been limited by the rather slow rate of growth in per capita income which in turn is dependent on the vagaries of the world market for export agricultural commodities.

The failure of industry to rapidly generate new employment opportunities in West African cities is emphasized further by the relatively slow rate of growth of the two other major sectors of the urban economy: administration and trade. Both of these sectors are characterized by the fact that they require simply the ability to read, write, and do a few manipulative sums. The educational systems in most countries of West Africa seem to have been designed to cater to this particular market. But as the output of the system increased and greater competition for jobs set in, both government and commerce became more selective in their recruitment policies and began increasingly to consider those in the lower levels of the educational ladder as hardly employable.

Moreover, most of these people were relatively young school leavers, usually less than 15 years old. Their tender age made them physically less attractive for industrial employment and in addition they have hardly any industrial skills. One of the more hopeful aspects of the situation is that after the initial frustration, an increasingly large number of these youthful unemployed are taking up apprenticeships in the numerous African-owned, small-scale production units in shoe repairing, carpentry, electrical fittings, machine and motor repairs, and tailoring. In this way, they are making up in part for their lack of skill. For instance, according to Callaway, in most years nearly 2 million such apprentices are to be found all over Nigeria.[18] Whether ultimately these apprentices are in a better position to secure permanent urban employment remains a moot question. However, it is clear that once possessed of a salable skill, these young men are in a much better position to make their livings either in the cities or back in the rural areas. And there is some evidence that this type of return urban-rural migration already is taking place.

The unemployment problem gives rise to a number of other subsidiary problems, the most important of which is the high dependency load of the average urban household. Not only does a household head have to bear the responsibility of his relatively large family but very often he also has to support two or three relatives still looking for jobs. Such dependency loads are inimical to capital formation and a rise in the average standard of living. Rather, they create a situation in which rural subsistence is gradually being transferred into the cities with more disastrous implications.

The high dependency load also creates housing problems. Most West African cities have numerous districts where overcrowding is acute and standards of environmental sanitation have deteriorated to critical levels. In Lagos, for instance, a 1950 census showed that densities per square mile had increased on the island from 50,039 in 1921 to 87,492 in 1950. In the two oldest wards, the respective densities in the latter year were 110,987 and 140,820 per square mile.[19] Only improved public health measures, notably in the field of vaccination, have kept virulent epidemics at bay. In the 1920s before this fortunate development, most of the important West African cities, such as Dakar, Accra, and Lagos, were ravaged by epidemics of one type or the other. Such outbreaks have had positive aspects in that they forced the

[18] A. Callaway, "Nigeria's indigenous education: the apprentice system," *ODU.*, I, no. 1 (July 1964), 63.
[19] Nigeria, Department of Statistics, *Population Census of Lagos, 1950* (Lagos, 1951), pp. 26 and 29.

administrators to be aware of the importance of town planning and urban renewal.

Other problems of West African urbanization such as traffic congestion, inadequate and inefficient infrastructural equipment, and poor land-use and zoning regulations need not concern us here. They all, however, emphasize the fact that the most serious problem of these cities is proper management. West Africa still needs to breed a class of urban administrators who take pride in the efficient performance of the city both as a place of work and a home for people, and who are able to plan the resources available to achieve these ends.

## CONCLUSION

In the preceding sections, migration has been shown as a population response to changing social and economic conditions. As these conditions have changed, so has the type of migrant and the object of movement. More than ever before, urban centers have emerged as the destination of the major strand in the crisscross flow of people over West Africa. And in this sense urbanization becomes also part of the response to social change.

Nevertheless, this response is not an isolated event but an intrinsic component of the significant structural transformation taking place today in West African society. Its ultimate result is a redistribution of the population in such a way as to make it easier to organize the people for social action to bring about still more social change. The increasing agglomeration of the population defines a new configuration of both purchasing and political power which will attract still more people, and hopefully more economic activities to these centers. But the process is not all positive and where the basic expectations of the people are not met, it could become a major factor of political instability and of dissipation of economic potentialities.

Concentration of people in urban centers has also been part of the modernization process taking place in most developing countries. It operates as a method of exposure, introducing people from rural and folk backgrounds to new styles of life, new behavior patterns, new habits, and new attitudes. The migrant to the city then undergoes a transformation of personality and a fundamental change in his values and expectations. He becomes in a sense "civilized," a fuller member of society, more sensitive to the effects of the actions or lack of action of those who lead and direct society.

It is for this reason that urbanization is seen as a focal process in the development of new nations to which leaders in these nations should pay greater attention. This is not simply in regard to such issues as the optimum size they desire for the cities or the physical layout or plan they would like them to have. Their concern should focus more seriously on considerations of the role cities should play in the modernization process, the strategy to make them play this role effectively, the need to see cities as a form of social organization for human enjoyment of "the good life," and the importance of maintaining them physically as a healthy environment without the debilitating problems of pollution. To achieve these objectives, leaders in these countries have the unusual advantage of having the experience and expertise of the more developed nations to draw upon. According to Lerner:

the hope is that this enriched sense of alternatives derived from more developed foreign countries will help Africans to select and refine a more workable image of their own development . . . . What Africa has gained, by being the last of the world's continents to undertake its own development, is a greater variety of "pictures" presented by developed societies elsewhere . . . . It would be a pity if Africa neglected this most important of all capabilities bestowed by modern systems of international and intercontinental communication in order to seek short-term gains by the blackmail-or-bribery routine.[20]

Against a perspective such as this, one can assert that the pattern of future development of most West African countries will depend very much on the manner in which their present leaders deal with these challenging phenomena of internal and international migration and the increasing urbanization of their populations.

[20] Daniel Lerner, "Comparative Analysis of Processes of Modernization," in H. Miner, ed., *The City in Modern Africa* (London: Pall Mall, 1967), p. 38.

THE MOST notable feature of governmental population policies in West Africa is their absence. Only the governments of Ghana and Nigeria among the countries of West Africa have adopted such policies; that is, they have officially stated intentions to influence the growth and/or movement of the country's population. In fact, though, every government in West Africa regularly undertakes actions that profoundly, if unintentionally, alter population growth and movement. On balance, these actions have greatly increased both the rate of population growth and the flow of people from rural to urban areas.

## THE PRESENT STATUS OF GOVERNMENTAL POPULATION POLICIES IN WEST AFRICA

In March 1969 the government of Ghana became the first government in West Africa to outline officially, publicly, and fully the elements of its population policy. Nigeria issued a briefer statement in November 1970 as part of its second National Development Plan. Concern with population problems in the other countries in West Africa is to be found only in private conversations with individual government leaders, occasional statements at international meetings by a government official (often representing a single ministry rather than the government as a whole, and speaking with an unknown degree of authority), or an occasional passage or two from a national development plan. Migration, particularly immigration, has received somewhat more attention, but primarily in the form of sporadic actions—hastily organized and only partially executed—to deal with specific problems of the moment, rather than in the form of a carefully developed longer-range policy.

## POLICIES ON POPULATION GROWTH

West African governments fall into three categories: those committed to or thinking about introducing large-scale family planning programs directed in part toward slowing population growth; those which have expressed little or no awareness of population growth; and those concerned that their populations should grow more rapidly. The second of these groups is by far the largest, comprising roughly three-quarters of the 20 or more governments of West Africa.

INTEREST IN SLOWING POPULATION GROWTH: GHANA AND NIGERIA. The West African government most concerned with slowing its rate of population growth is Ghana. The government's March 1969 policy statement, which has been deservedly accorded a chapter of its own in this book (Chapter 20), calls for the encouragement and undertaking of "programs to provide information, advice, and assistance for couples wishing to space or limit their reproduction," in recognition of "the crucial importance of a wide understanding of the deleterious effects of unlimited population growth . . . ."[1] The government has subsequently begun to implement this policy by initiating a national family planning program, announced by the Commissioner of Finance and Economic Affairs in February 1970.

Although official concern with population growth was originally expressed much earlier in Nigeria than in Ghana, it remains more tentative. Reference to the need for a population policy was contained in the June 1966 "Guideposts for the Second National Development Plan" prepared by the Ministry of Economic Development. Title VII, entitled "Population Growth," tentatively placed the rate of population growth at between 2.0 and 2.5 percent per year, called for a demographic sample survey to provide more accurate information, and declared that, despite a population growth rate seen as relatively modest, "there is a need to evolve a population policy (including spatial distribution) as an integral part of the national development effort."[2]

Since then, more and more government leaders have publicly expressed concern about population growth and the need for family planning. Those having issued public, written statements include four federal government commissioners (the Commissioners of Economic Development/Agriculture/Natural Resources, Health, Information/Labor, Education); two federal government permanent secretaries (Health, Economic Development); the military governors of 3 states, from a total of 12 (Lagos, Kano, and North-Central); and the Commissioners of Health and Social Welfare of five states (Lagos, Western, Mid-Western, Kwara, and Northeastern).[3] While all these statements express support for family planning, many of them cite only such benefits as maternal and child health, family welfare, and the basic human right to determine the number of children borne, without reference to a possible relation between family planning and overall fertility and population growth.

These statements have been reinforced by numerous and substantial state and local government "in kind" contributions to family planning, particularly to the work of the private Family Planning Council of Nigeria. Such support takes the form of allowing the council to operate family planning clinics in government facilities during hours when they are not otherwise in use, of allowing government health personnel to work in the Family Planning Council clinics outside their regular hours (an exception to the usual practice of prohibiting health personnel from accepting outside employment), the assignment of government personnel to participate in training courses for Family Planning Council personnel, and in some cases the deputation of government personnel to work full time for the council.

This interest culminated in the issuance of an official government population policy in November 1970, as part of the second National Development Plan (1970–1974). The statement occupies approximately one of the plan's 344 pages. It begins by stressing the

[1] Ghana, *Population Planning for National Progress and Prosperity: Ghana Population Policy* (Accra, March 1969), p. 20.
[2] Nigeria, Ministry of Economic Development, *Guideposts for Second National Development Plan* (Lagos: Ministry of Information, June 1966), p. 3.

[3] These statements are reproduced in the 1967, 1968, and 1969 Annual Reports of the Family Planning Council of Nigeria, which solicited them.

potentially controversial nature of a population policy in Nigeria: "The issue of population policy in contemporary Nigerian context must be handled with perception and discretion." It outlines briefly the country's demographic situation, notes the problems associated with rapid population growth, but also points to the Nigerian resource base and development potential as factors offsetting these problems. It concludes that

the magnitude of the country's population problem is unlikely to be such that calls for extensive emergency or panic action . . . . What seems appropriate in the present circumstances of Nigeria is for government to encourage the citizens to develop a balanced view of the opportunities for individual family planning on a voluntary basis, with a view to raising the quality of life in their offspring. Facilities are to be designed to protect mothers, on a long-range basis, from repeated and unwanted pregnancies, as well as to enable parents to space their children for better feeding, clothing and education.

The statement concludes by announcing that,

during the plan period, the government will pursue a qualitative population policy by integrating the various voluntary family planning schemes into the overall health and social welfare program of the country. Families would have access to information, facilities, and services that will allow them freedom to choose the number and spacing of their children. The work already done by the Family Planning Council of Nigeria has contributed much toward preparing some communities for family planning services. A government program would be able to move with greater assurance, certainty, and vigor in bringing family planning facilities within reach of many more willing communities, always with the emphasis on the voluntary nature of the family planning operations. The government will establish a National Population Council to implement this population policy and program, and to coordinate all external aid support for family planning activities throughout the country.[4]

Thus Nigeria has committed itself to the provision of family planning services through

existing health facilities. But Nigeria's policy clearly places much less emphasis on the need for reducing the rate of population growth than does that of Ghana.

UNCONCERNED AND UNAWARE OF POPULATION GROWTH: THE SILENT MAJORITY OF WEST AFRICAN GOVERNMENTS. Outside of Ghana and Nigeria, official concern about population growth is limited. In most countries a few advocates from the health fields are seeking to alert their governments to the need for family planning and to the importance of the related topic to population growth. Simultaneously, a limited number of policy makers, particularly those associated with economic planning, in most of these countries are becoming uncomfortable at their lack of knowledge about their country's population growth and are actively seeking further information. But that is about all.

The situation can best be understood by referring briefly to a number of representative "silent majority" countries.

*Dahomey's* economic planners displayed what was probably West Africa's first official concern with population growth in the 1961–1965 Economic Development Plan. This plan devoted several prominent pages to population, concluding that:

The Dahomean population is growing rapidly, at 2.65 percent per year . . . . It is doubling every twenty-six years. Half the population is massed in the south, in a coastal band representing 7 percent of the country's land area, which is heading toward a high density.

The Departments of the South-East and the North-West find themselves grappling with formidable problems of local overpopulation. Forty-six percent of the population is less than fifteen years of age, which renders more acute the problems of food, education, and employment.[5]

Although this analysis was not followed by any apparent action, individuals within the government have remained interested in the question of population growth. This led to a government request that the Population

[4] Federal Republic of Nigeria, *Second National development Plan 1970–74* (Lagos: Ministry of Information, 1970), pp. 77–78.

[5] Dahomey, *Plan de Développement Economique et Social du Dahomey*, Vol. I, Société Générale d'Etudes et de Planification (Paris, 1961), p. 175.

Council send a mission to study the country's population situation, which was done in June 1969. The final mission report was submitted in the summer of 1970, but the government's reaction is not yet known. In the meantime, the country has no population policy.

In *Gambia*, interest in the size and growth of the population was spurred by the 1965 publication of the final 1963 census results. By 1968, medical interest in family planning was increasing rapidly, resulting in the establishment of a private family planning association with the moral support of the government. Subsequent reports on the Gambian economy by the International Monetary Fund and an expert from the British Ministry of Overseas Development stressed the fertility element in the country's population growth.

The result of these various strands was a government request for a Population Council mission to study the available data and to recommend an appropriate government policy. This mission was undertaken in the summer of 1969. Its final recommendations were submitted in June 1970, but government reactions to them are not yet available.

In *Senegal*, several leading planners became concerned with the impact of rapid population growth and planned a special fertility survey for 1970–1971 for the express purpose of obtaining the information necessary to serve as a basis for a more reasoned decision in the field of population growth. The government has also given its informal but strong encouragement to the pioneering Senegalese founders of French-speaking West Africa's first family planning association.[6]

*Sierra Leone* is a strict neutralist on the question of family planning. As Thomas Dow reports,

while the Government maintains an official position of . . . neutrality with regard to family planning, it allows the Planned Parenthood Association to provide services in public as well as private facilities . . . . the effect of existing family planning activities is negligible. Whether this will continue to be the case will depend largely on the Government's policy. If it maintains

[6] Personal conversations in Dakar.

its present position of neutrality, this will effectively preclude any significant increase in family planning in Sierra Leone. Conversely, if it endorses and financially supports family planning, substantial progress might be possible in the near future. At the moment, there is no indication that such a change is in the offing.[7]

But, for Sierra Leone, such neutrality is a new development. In a 1965 survey of governmental population policy in Commonwealth Africa undertaken by John Caldwell, Sierra Leone was distinctly pronatalist, being the only country in West Africa to indicate it believed it would benefit from a much larger population and to express the hope that the birth rate might rise.[8]

In *Togo*, if a government spokesman has ever uttered an official word about population growth in that country, it has escaped all notice. On the related question of family planning, in fact, the Togolese Council of Ministers has explicitly decided to remain neutral.[9] But such silence should not be taken to mean that the government favors rapid population growth. For David and Jeane Stillman, who solicited the views of numerous government officials, report that

. . . those members of the government interviewed did not appear to believe that the country would benefit from a population much larger than at present, but were concerned rather with redistribution and improved living standards for those who already make up the populace. The government avoids the notion of seeking to fill up empty lands with a population boom . . . . Although the rate of population growth is not presently a matter of alarm, government planners do feel that rapid growth could hinder attempts to raise living standards. Those thinking in terms of

[7] Thomas Dow, "Sierra Leone," *Country Profile* (New York: Population Council and International Institute for the Study of Human Reproduction, September 1969), p. 4.

[8] John C. Caldwell, "Population Policy: A Survey of Commonwealth Africa," in John Caldwell and C. Okonjo, eds., *The Population of Tropical Africa* (London: Longmans, Green & Company; New York: Columbia University Press, 1968), pp. 369, 371.

[9] Personal conversation in Lomé.

the educational realm are particularly cognizant of this.[10]

INTEREST IN PROMOTING POPULATION GROWTH: CAMEROON, GABON, AND IVORY COAST. In three West African countries, such governmental concern as exists about population growth is directed toward its present inadequacy rather than toward its over-abundance.

Participants at the 1969 World Health Assembly in Boston report that the Cameroon government representative addressed himself to an alarming population decrease in Central Africa brought about by high mortality, especially infant mortality and expressed a special interest in the development of measures to combat sterility as a means of counteracting this. He suggested that an increase in population would help the countries achieve their development goals more quickly. More recently, Cameroon government representatives have referred to the government's intention not to contemplate any measures to limit population growth until a target population of 15 million is achieved (the present Cameroon population is around 6 million). To encourage population growth toward that goal, the government is said to be utilizing a variety of women's employment policies, including paid maternity leave, children's allowances, and nursing breaks during office hours to allow mothers to attend to their children. At the same time, however, the Cameroon government does not appear to oppose contraception prescribed by a physician, demonstrating once again the compatibility of an overall expansionist population policy and family planning for reasons of maternal and child health or women's liberties.

Gabon appears to have been concerned with raising its birth rate for some time. In 1963, the 1963–1965 Gabon Intermediate Development Plan predicted with satisfaction that the spread of general public health and maternal and child health would allow an increase in the country's population growth rate, then seen as insufficient.[11] The 1966–1971 Gabon plan forecast a shortage of manpower in the modern sector beginning in 1970.[12] And, according to an Economic Commission for Africa survey of the demographic content of African development plans, "Gabon's aim is to maintain its present birth rate . . . at 35 per 1,000."[13] The government has recently passed a law that prohibits the importation of contraceptives, institutes severe fines and prison penalties for people contravening the law, and calls for the appointment of special inspectors to enforce the law.[14]

Such measures should be viewed in the context of Gabon's unique geographical and economic situation. Gabon has by far the highest per capita income in West Africa, estimated at around $400 per year in 1966. Its birth rate of around 35 per thousand is the lowest in the region. Taken in conjunction with continuing high mortality, this birth rate produces the extraordinarily low population growth rate of around 1 percent per year, about half that of the next most slowly growing West African country, and more European than African. Gabon's average population density (about 6 per square mile) is also extremely low, even by African standards. The country is bountifully endowed with both forest and mineral resources requiring large amounts of labor for their exploitation.[15]

[10] David Stillman and Jeane Stillman, "Policies Affecting Population in Togo" (Paper read at the Seminar on Population Growth and Economic Development, Nairobi, December 1969, mimeographed), p. 8.

[11] C. de Buttet, "Bibliographie Sommaire sur les Politiques Démographiques en Afrique," Service de Documentation, Institut National d'Etudes Démographiques (Paris, 1970), introductory page.

[12] Anon., "When More Jobs Mean More Workless," *West Africa*, no. 2775 (August 15, 1970), 925.

[13] United Nations, Economic and Social Council, Economic Commission for Africa, "Demographic Content of African Development Plans" (E/CN.14/POP/5) (April 30, 1969), p. 12.

[14] Pierre Pradervand, "Obstacles to and Possibilities of Family Planning in Francophone Countries of West Africa and the Republic of Congo" (Paper presented to *Expert Group Meeting on the Family Planning and Population Policies in Africa*, Paris, 6th–8th April, 1970, Development Centre of the Organization for Economic Co-operation and Development), document no. CD/P/153, mimeographed, p. 17.

[15] Figures taken from "Gabon," *Afrique 1969 Jeune Afrique* (Paris, 1970), pp. 349–52.

The reports of recent visitors to Ivory Coast indicate the existence of a similar but publicly unexpressed governmental interest in promoting population growth for economic reasons.[16] But like Gabon, Ivory Coast is a unique country in West Africa. Ivory Coast's gross national product has been expanding steadily at a rate of 10 percent per year, making it the only country in West Africa (and one of the few in the world) able to finance a rapidly rising standard of living despite a population growth rate estimated at 2.3 percent. Whether government policy would remain the same should its economic growth rate fall to a level typical of West Africa as a whole is perhaps questionable.

## POLICIES ON MIGRATION

Migration has received somewhat more West African governmental attention than has population growth. This concern has focused primarily upon two specific issues: migration across international boundaries, particularly immigration; and rural-urban internal migration.

INTERNATIONAL MIGRATION. As John Caldwell reported in his survey of population policies of Commonwealth Africa,

in most countries, the oldest type of population policy has been that relating to the regulation of migration. Such regulation has had to be considered more in recent years, because many of what are now international borders were little more than internal boundaries in the extensive British and French empires. Furthermore, independent governments are much more likely to feel a prior responsibility for securing employment for their own nationals than is a colonial government.[17]

This certainly applies to the present immigration policy of Ghana, which again has the most clearly articulated position of any West African government. Leaving aside the lengthy history of the government's concern with immigration, several recent pronouncements and actions have indicated a keen desire to ensure that immigrants participate in economic activities that complement rather than compete with those of Ghanaians. The government's population policy paper said that "The government will adopt policies and establish programs to . . . reduce the scale and rate of immigration in the interests of national welfare." The reason for this stand, the paper continued, is that, "uncontrolled immigration of labor, especially of the unskilled type, reduces employment opportunities for citizens. It is intended that immigration will be used primarily as a means of obtaining needed skills and stimulating social and economic development."[18]

More recently and spectacularly, the Ghanaian government decreed on November 18, 1969, that all aliens who did not obtain within two weeks the residence permits required under preexisting Ghanaian law would be expelled from the country. The following are among the varying explanations for this sudden action which have been given: a desire to open up jobs to absorb the increasingly large numbers of unemployed in Ghanaian cities; concern over reportedly high crime rates among alien communities; the wish to make political capital by playing to a latent popular hostility to outsiders; a desire to curb the activities of specific, relatively small segments of the alien population (such as the Syrians and Lebanese, prominent in commerce) while leaving the great majority of aliens unaffected. Whatever the purpose, the result was a scramble to obtain residence permits, and a dramatic exodus of thousands toward their neighboring countries of origin (particularly Upper Volta, Togo, Dahomey, and Nigeria).[19] Although the quality of statistics is doubtless open to question, the government announced in late January 1970 that nearly 200,000 of Ghana's million or so

---

[17] Caldwell, "Population Policy," p. 370.
[16] Personal communications and conversations in Abidjan.

[18] Ghana, *Population Planning*, p. 23.
[19] Anon., "Strangers in Trouble," *West Africa*, no. 2739 (November 29, 1969); conversations in Accra.

alien residents had left.[20] The continuing efforts of the government to track down non-complying aliens through police action leaves no doubt about government determination to control immigration more closely in the future. And while government spokesmen present its actions as law enforcement rather than as anti-alien, the impression nonetheless persists among neighboring countries that the government of Ghana is pursuing at least a *de facto* anti-immigration policy.

Outside Ghana, governmental concern has taken the form of sporadic incidents rather than cohesive policies. Details of some of the more noteworthy cases, such as the expulsion of Dahomeans and Togolese from Ivory Coast in 1958 follow. As Akin Mabogunje has reported, Dahomey

was the most educationally advanced of the French colonial territories in West Africa. As such, it had supplied most of these territories as well as French Equatorial Africa and even the Belgian Congo with skilled manpower such as doctors, teachers, clerks and traders. As the movement toward independence gathered momentum, the presence of Dahomeans in all these positions began to attract unfavorable attention. In October 1958, on the alleged suspicion of a new influx of Dahomean and Togolese immigrants, there was a violent outbreak in Abidjan, capital of the Ivory Coast, in which one man was killed, fifty others injured and several houses were damaged. In consequence, more than a thousand Togolese and Dahomean men and women left the Ivory Coast to return to their homes.[21]

This was followed by the expulsion of Dahomeans from Niger in 1963–1964. Again, Mabogunje reports, ". . . in 1963, over a dispute with Dahomey, Niger suddenly ordered all Dahomeans living in the territory, esti-

mated at about 16,000, to leave the country before the end of the year. Later in 1964 it agreed to expel only Dahomean civil servants and not all Dahomeans as had been threatened . . . ."[22]

Some Ghanaians were expelled from Sierra Leone in 1968.

In December, 1968, the Sierra Leone Government ordered over a hundred Ghanaian fishermen to leave the country. A government statement pointed out that there were many thousands of Ghanaian fishermen in Sierra Leone and the problem had exercised the attention of previous governments. The statement argued that these Ghanaians exclude Sierra Leoneans from fishing and did not pay taxes; that they made beaches unsightly and unhygienic with their settlements and that in so doing they damaged tourist prospects. At present, they were also a security problem in the event of attempts to infiltrate Sierra Leone from the sea. The intention of the government was therefore to repatriate all anaian fishermen, although it recognized that many were now in other occupations. In response to this development, the Ghana Government appointed an ad hoc committee to prepare to tackle the problem of resettling more than 2,000 Ghanaian fishermen who face expulsion from Sierra Leone.[23]

*West Africa* cites the above and other cases in arguing that the November 1968 Gahanaian action has been relatively gentle:

Ghana is not expelling all aliens but only those without residence permits; permits will, no doubt, be readily issued to those in certain occupations such as mining. In other West African countries since the advent of independence aliens have not been treated so gently. The Fanti fishermen forcibly repatriated to Ghana and the Foulahs to Guinea from Sierra Leone, the Dahomeyans forced to return to their small country from several states of former French Africa, the Ewe who fled from Nkrumah's Ghana to Togo, the aliens from many countries expelled from the Ivory Coast, all those found themselves suddenly in the plight, but without the status, of refugees. Elsewhere in Africa the story has been the same . . . .[24]

[20] *Accra Daily Graphic* (January 23, 1970), 1. For a more thorough discussion of this action and its historical precedents, see N. O. Addo, "Immigration into Ghana: Some Social and Economic Implications of the Aliens Decree Order of 18 November 1969," presented to University of Ghana Department of Sociology staff seminar, mimeographed (January 20, 1970).
[21] Akin L. Mabogunje, *Regional Mobility and Resource Development in West Africa* (Montreal: McGill University Press, 1972).

[22] *Ibid.*
[23] *Ibid.*
[24] *Ibid.*

*West Africa* concludes from these examples and the Ghanaian case that:

The trend is clear. To a greater or lesser degree, it is the ambition of each of the governments of the entirely artificial but now rigidly entrenched units into which West Africa is divided, to reserve the right to live and work within its country for those who can pass a restrictive citizenship test. The object of turning this great and potentially rich area into a zone of free trade and free movement seems more remote than ever.[25]

Mabogunje agrees:

Pan-Africanism appears everywhere to be on the retreat. It is being replaced by economic chauvinism which sees the contribution of the migrants not as resulting from their special circumstances but from an usurpation of the "rights and privileges" of the members of the host community. Restriction rather than competition is now the battle-cry. Instead of positive programs of strengthening the competitive effectiveness of indigenes or nationals vis-à-vis the immigrants, most governments find the short-term political advantage of sacrificing the interests of the immigrants on the altar of national cohesion too tempting to resist.[26]

RURAL-URBAN MIGRATION.  Those West African governments that have noted and voiced an opinion about rural-urban migration are unanimously against it.

Again, Ghana has expressed its views most clearly. The March 1969 government policy statement says: "The government will adopt policies and establish programs to guide and regulate the flow of internal migration, influence spatial distribution in the interest of development progress . . . ."[27] The statement continues to explain that:

As indicated in the Two-Year Development Plan, the government intends to influence the flow of migration within the country so as to avoid excessive and uncontrolled concentration of population in urban areas . . . . it intends also to provide incentives for the siting of industries away from the major metropolitan areas . . . . the

government will also urge industries in both private and public sectors to decentralize some of their functions. The headquarters of all enterprises need not be in Accra, and business establishments will be urged, whenever possible, to locate their principal offices away from the Accra-Tema metropolitan area . . . . The government believes that development of ten towns with a population of 50,000 each, for example, will benefit the nation more than development confined largely to one city of 500,000 . . . . The government intends to intensify its efforts to supply rural areas with facilities such as safe pipe-borne water and improved means of refuse disposal. It is expected that the provision of these and other amenities will help make rural life more attractive and thus also slow down the rate of rural-urban migration.[28]

Programs to slow rural-urban population flows have proven equally popular in French-speaking West Africa where the rallying cry of *retour à la terre* (return to the land) remains eternally attractive to political leaders seeking solutions to their countries' urban ills. The Stillmans report, for example, that internal population distribution and rural-urban population movements constitute the government of Togo's principal population interest:

[Togolese] government policies in realms of demographic interest have been to emphasize rural development, rural-rural migration, slowing of the exodus to urban centers, improvement of agricultural methods and production, improvement of road systems, and increase of health and educational facilities.

Possible questions of population pressure have been averted by reference to the relatively empty but potentially fertile lands which still take up about half the country. Return to the land is a popular mystique in official viewpoints.[29]

The same "return to the land" theme is also to be found in Zaïre. An effort was made in 1967 to implement a "return to the land" policy through the establishment of a youth organization to develop agricultural communities. And 1968 was a year of emphasis on agriculture including the establishment of rural communities because of bad crops the

[25] *Ibid.*
[26] *Ibid.*
[27] Ghana, *Population Planning*, p. 22.

[28] *Ibid.*
[29] Stillman and Stillman, "Policies Affecting Population," p. 5.

preceding seasons and the resulting shortage of food in urban areas.

The results of these efforts were less than spectacular, suggesting that the warning about their potential effectiveness contained in the government's own 1966 Agricultural Preplan may have been correct. That plan predicted that 50 percent of the country's population would be living in urban and semiurban areas within 30 years; it expressed considerable concern about the ability of the country's agricultural areas to provide adequate food for so large an urban population. But the preplan dismissed a "return to the land" program as being incapable of providing a solution, arguing that "even should this return be realized, one cannot forsee that these men and women will become more than rural consumers,"[30] that is, they could not be expected to become effective producers without massive supporting investments of capital, nor would they be sufficiently content with rural life and its lack of amenities to work effectively.

Senegalese efforts to stem rural-urban migration have included attention to the capital requirements of resettlement. The Senegalese speak not of a "return to the land" but of the opening up of "new lands" through the organization of communities supported with adequate infrastructure and capital investment in sparsely settled areas of the country. This "regional program" was described as a principal long-term objective of the Second Development Plan (1965–1969) designed in part "to prepare over the long run a more satisfactory regional equilibrium [in terms of population distribution]" and "to face the demands of demographic growth by increasing production above the present level . . . ."[31]

Numerous other West African governments have developed their own variants of a "return to the land" or a "new lands" program. The Upper Volta Plan Outline of 1967–1970, for example, adopted its emphasis of rural development in part because of a wish to stem potential rural-urban migration.[32] The Niger 1965–1968 Four-Year Plan expressed its concern at the rapid rate of urbanization, noting the expense to the government of providing for city dwellers what rural people either go without or provide for themselves through collective actions.[33] Many similar examples could be quoted.

## GOVERNMENTAL POLICIES THAT AFFECT POPULATION IN WEST AFRICA

Although few West African governments have consciously sought to influence the growth and movement of their populations, each of them has unintentionally exerted such influence by adopting development policies with unintended population side effects. The most obvious and doubtless the most powerful of these policies are related to the extension of health services, which have lowered mortality without a significantly affecting fertility, thus accelerating population growth. There is good reason to believe that a wide range of other policies—the introduction of education and children's allowance programs, for example—also affect population growth through their impact on fertility; and that an even wider range of governmental projects and programs exert a cumulatively powerful impact on rural-urban migration.

Not enough is known about the quantitative significance of the population side effects of nonpopulation programs to allow anything approaching a precise measurement of their impact. But in view of the undoubted and overwhelming predominance of mortality-reducing health measures, the overall effect of governmental social programs certainly must

---

[30] Zaïre, Haut Commissariat au Plan et à la Réconstruction Nationale, *Etude d'Orientation pour la Relance Agricole* (Prepared by the Institute de Recherches Economiques et Sociales, Université Louvanium) Bureau d'Etude du Haut Commissariat au Plan et à la Réconstruction Nationale (Kinshasa, July 1966), p. 19.

[31] Sénégal, *Deuxième Plan Quadriennale de Développement Economique et Social*, 1965–1969 (Dakar, 1970), p. 54.

[32] Haute-Volta, Ministère du Plan, *Plan-Cadre de Développement*, 1967–1970, Vol. 1 (Ouagadougou, 1971), passim.

[33] Niger, *Plan Quadriennale*, 1965–1968, Vol. 1 (Niamey, 1969), p. 168.

be to increase population growth significantly. And since, as will presently be demonstrated, a wide range of government development policies can be shown to contain hidden benefits to urban residents, the net impact of such policies must surely be to increase rural-urban migration. Thus, when the government of Ghana speaks of trying to reduce population growth, and when the governments of Ghana and other West African countries refer to a need for slowing rural-urban migration, they are not speaking of action against natural, inevitable phenomena. Rather, they are acting to correct problems primarily of their own making.

Among nonpopulation policies that have thus unintentionally affected population are those dealing with health, education, family allowances, and rural-urban migration.

HEALTH. Every West African government is understandably and appropriately dedicated to improving the health of its citizens. This dedication is reflected not just in the speeches of health ministers but also in the amounts of money devoted to health. Table 8.1 gives the latest information available on the health expenditures of West African countries. None of those listed devotes less than 7 percent of its recurrent budget to health; the average is about 10 percent.

The per-capita health expenditure ranges between U.S. $0.68–$4.40, with the average per capita expenditure for the countries listed as a whole (after weighting for their different sizes) being about $1.25–$1.50. In addition, many of the countries listed provide sizable amounts of capital investment funds for health over and above the amounts listed in Table 8.1.

The absence of adequate mortality data prevents an accurate measurement of the impact of these health expenditures. But enough is known to state with confidence that they have indeed succeeded in reducing mortality and that they will continue to do so. The regionwide smallpox-measles program, for example, has just completed its "attack" phase, which involved giving over 100 million smallpox vaccinations. According to the World Health Organization, which assisted the program as part of its worldwide campaign against smallpox, West and Central Africa recorded only 10 percent as many

TABLE 8.1
Health expenditures of West African governments

| Country | Year | Amount Spent[a] (million U.S. dollars) | Percent of Total Government Expenditure[a] (approximate) | Amount per person (expressed in U.S. dollars) |
|---|---|---|---|---|
| Dahomey | 1965 | 3,946 | 12 | 1.75 |
| Ivory Coast | 1965 | 12,435 | 10 | 3.40 |
| Niger | 1965 | 2,256 | 9 | 0.68 |
| Senegal | 1965–66 | 12,232 | 9 | 3.65 |
| Upper Volta | 1965 | 3,335 | 10 | 0.70 |
| Mali | 1965 | 4,506 | 11 | 0.98 |
| Central African Republic | 1965 | 2,785 | 10 | 1.85 |
| Chad | 1965 | 3,327 | 10 | 1.00 |
| Peoples Republic of the Congo | 1965 | 3,077 | 8 | 3.60 |
| Gabon | 1965 | 2,777 | 9 | 4.40 |
| Cameroon | 1965–66 | 8,817 | 11 | 1.75 |
| Togo | 1965 | 1,850 | 9 | 1.15 |
| Nigeria | 1969 | 67,200 | 10 | 1.02 |
| Liberia | 1964 | 2,618 | 7 | 2.50 |

SOURCES: U.S. National Academy of Sciences, National Research Council, Division of Medical Sciences, *Public Health Problems in Fourteen French-speaking Countries in Africa and Madagascar*, V.II, *A Survey of Resources and Needs*. United Nations, World Health Organization, *Third Report on the World Health Situation, 1961–1964*, Official Records of the World Health Organization, No. 155, Geneva (April 1967).
a Recurring budget.

cases of smallpox in 1969 as in 1968.[34] Ghana estimates that life expectation at birth rose from about 28 years in 1921 to 48 in 1965, which means that life expectation has been rising at a rate of nearly one-half year per year over the past 20 years.[35] Similarly, Nigeria estimates that its mortality level has fallen by one-sixth from 29 per thousand to 24 per thousand in the ten years since independence; and projections of the Nigerian population made by the demographic unit of the University of Ife envisage a steadily continuing fall in the mortality level to 14 per thousand population in 1990. Such additional information as has since become available has thus only confirmed the general view prevailing at the 1966 Ibadan Population Conference, reported by John Caldwell: "despite the uncertainty about levels and trends, the conviction is widespread that death rates are falling, perhaps rapidly."[36]

But there has been no corresponding fall in birth rates. As the other contributions to this volume convincingly document, this is the basic cause of the unusually rapid and increasing population growth in West Africa. Thus, an unintended result of governmental policies and programs aimed at disease control has been, and will continue to be, a rapid increase in population growth.

EDUCATION. West African governments have shown even more interest in education than in health. In none of the countries listed in Table 8.1 for which information is available is the amount spent on education less than that spent on health. In most of them, educational expenditures run at two, three, or four times the level of health expenditures. As a result, ever-increasing proportions of school-age children actually attend school: the number of children in school increased by over one-third in the three years between 1960–1961 and 1963–1964 in the French-speaking

countries of West Africa;[37] primary enrollments tripled in Nigeria between 1952 and 1960, with secondary school enrollments tripling in the decade between 1956 and 1966;[38] and so on.

The demographic effects of these government expenditures on education and the resulting spectacular rises in school enrollments are far less clear than are the results of the comparable expenditures on health. But there is a basis for speculation (if no data adequate to prove the point) that the spread of education is beginning to exert a significant depressing effect on fertility.

Sub-Saharan African surveys have shown the importance of educational levels in bringing about a reduction in family-size ideals, particularly among urban elites. As John Caldwell reported in his summary article on these studies,

... the chief problem of the large family is clearly that it is an economic burden, a view that the majority of respondents expressed in all surveys which specifically asked them about the drawbacks of such families. Equally clear is the fact that educational costs climb steadily from subsistence to cash farming areas and from the latter to the towns culminating among the urban elite where these costs are the major factor which could lead to the limitation of family size. These costs include the expenses of schooling, school equipment, better clothing, the withdrawal of children from productive work, and the ability of educated children to exact more money from their parents.[39]

Such findings lead to the suggestion that, given West Africans' intense interest in education for their children, the availability of education at a moderate cost to parents is a potentially powerful factor in bringing about a reduction in fertility desires; but that education's downward influence on fertility becomes less strong as its price is either

[34] Lagos *Morning Post* (January 11, 1970), 12.
[35] *Ghana, Population Planning*, p. 6.
[36] John C. Caldwell, "Introduction," in *Population of Tropical Africa*, p. 11.

[37] J. Hallak and R. Poignant, *Les Aspects Financiers de l'Enseignement dans les Pays Africains d'Expression Francaise*, Monographies Africaines, no. 3; UNESCO, Institut International de Planification de l'Education (Paris, 1966), p. 18.
[38] Nigeria, Federal Ministry of Education, *Statistics of Education in Nigeria, 1968*, Series No. II, Vol. I (Lagos: Federal Ministry of Education Printing Division, 1966).
[39] John C. Caldwell, "The Control of Family Size in Tropical Africa," *Demography*, V, 2 (1968), p. 604.

increased or reduced from the "moderate" level. If education were not available at all or available only at exorbitant cost, parents would realize their inability to provide education regardless of how severely they limited their fertility and would continue their former reproductive patterns. Inexpensive or totally free education could likewise be expected to have no effect on family size ideals, since parents could be assured of education for all their children, regardless of their number.

Do the costs of schooling to parents in West Africa fall into the range described above as "moderate," where they represent a restraining influence upon the family's fertility desires? Not enough information exists about how much parents pay for education or how much education they want for their children to provide anything approaching a definite answer. But two things are clear: first, governments cover by far the greatest part of educational costs in West Africa; and second, despite this, parents must still pay substantial amounts relative to their incomes in order for their children to attend school.

In Ghana, for example, the government pays the entire estimated U.S. $20 annual cost of a child's primary school attendance, asking the child's parents to contribute only a $1.50 book fee; in secondary school, the government pays about $160 per year, requiring parents to contribute only about $11 per year for books and uniforms if the student does not board in the school.[40] In northern Nigeria, it has been the practice to levy no charge for children attending native authority primary schools except for the cost of uniforms, while the government contributes approximately $12 per year per child.[41] In French-speaking Africa, governments have contributed between $25 and $75 per child-year of primary education, while parents have been asked to pay very little directly. According to Hallak and Poignant's study of educational financing in French-speaking Africa:

In the aggregate, the [financial] role [of parents] is very modest: in so far as public education is free the expenses of families represent essentially the school fees in the private institutions of instruction. However, in certain cases, the initiative of individuals takes the form of "in kind" financing, varying greatly with the particular conditions of the region under consideration: thus voluntary construction, the housing of or gifts to the instructor or teacher, etc.[42]

While education would be clearly beyond the reach of parents were it not for these overwhelming government subsidies, education nonetheless remains a much more costly item for the individual family than the above figures suggest. They omit the cost of feeding and clothing children in a more expensive manner than would otherwise be necessary; in many cases, they omit the cost of books and other expenses, which can add up to a sizable sum; and they do not refer to the foregone labor of the children attending school, which may well be significant, at least in traditional rural areas. In Lagos, for example, education is "free" in that children attending municipal schools need pay no tuition or school fees. Nonetheless, each child enrolled in primary school costs his parents about U.S. $20 annually. Of this amount, $11–12 goes to buy prescribed books; the remainder pays for required school uniforms, school lunches, and contributions for parents' associations to be used for various school activities.[43] The Lagos working man earning perhaps $500 per year will clearly encounter difficulty in trying to keep more than a few children in school: To support five would require for these listed costs alone 20 percent of his limited income. The same appears to be true in rural Togo, where midwives questioned claimed it cost some $80 per year to maintain a child in primary school. Only $2 of this was in school fees, the rest going for books ($12–15), children's meals ($50) and uniforms ($20).[44]

[40] Information supplied by Ghana Ministry of Education.
[41] Information supplied by Nigerian Federal Ministry of Education.

[42] Hallak and Poignant, *Les Aspects Financiers*, p. 31.
[43] Interviews with Lagos parents, checked with Nigerian Federal Ministry of Education.
[44] Nurse-midwives interviewed in Klouto, Togo in January 1970 by Togo Health Ministry training team.

Even allowing for the possibility that this figure includes considerable cost that the parent would have to cover anyway (such as meals) and that a majority of midwives may have husbands who can be expected to help support their children's education, primary education would seem a major expense for these women, who earn not much over $200 per year.

Still another cost is brought about by the need for parents to provide an increasing number of years of education to ensure an acceptable standard of living for their children. Every major city of West Africa already has its share of unemployed school leavers unable to obtain the relatively prestigious jobs that could have been theirs only a few years ago. As education continues to spread, the need for more years of schooling on the part of the individual wishing to compete effectively on the job market will continue to increase. And a higher level of education means for parents the need to finance not only additional years of school, but more expensive ones. As noted above, the cost for schooling to Ghanaian parents rises from $3 annually at the primary level to $11 at the secondary level, plus as much as $125 boarding fee unless the student is able to obtain a government bursary. In Nigeria, the least expensive secondary schools are those run by the federal government, at a cost of over $150 annually for tuition, boarding, and books. The average is much higher.

In sum, the pattern of educational expansion in a country like Nigeria may well have been the primary cause of the growing, if still limited, interest in fertility regulation. The threefold expansion of primary education referred to earlier has brought education close enough for millions of Nigerian families to aspire to it for their children, at a price they could afford but high enough to require financial sacrifice and family limitation. Such educational expansion seems likely to continue to act as a stimulus to reduced fertility for some time to come. Education may become somewhat cheaper for parents as politicians continue to succumb to the almost irresistible temptation to lower or abolish school fees.

But as the above examples indicate, school fees represent only a minor portion of parents' total educational expenditures—and they are certainly minor compared to the additional expense of supporting children through more and more years of schooling, which will become increasingly necessary to achieve the good life as the primary certificate becomes the norm rather than a mark of distinction.

FAMILY ALLOWANCES. All of the more than 15 French-speaking countries of West Africa have a system of family allowance for government employees and salaried employees of private establishments. The government makes a cash payment to each family to cover the costs of pregnancy and delivery (often in addition to the medical costs, since deliveries are frequently handled in government health facilities at little or no charge); and, in addition, monthly payments are made to the family, based on the number of children, to help defray the costs of the children's upkeep.

The details of the program vary from country to country, but in most cases the amounts of money involved are rather substantial relative to families' income. In general, the programs provide monthly prenatal payments during the entire nine months of pregnancy, plus a lump-sum payment at the time of delivery. The combined value of these vary from around U.S. $25 (Chad, Mali) to $50 (Senegal) and $70 (Guinea), with the average being around $35–40. The subsequent monthly child support payments range from $1.25 per child per month (Chad) to about $4 per month per child (Guinea, Gabon), with most paying between $2 and $3 per month per child. These payments continue until the child reaches an age of 14–15 years (12 in Guinea, 17 in Gabon), with provision for its being extended to 18 or 21 years if the child remains in school, becomes an apprentice, or is an invalid.

In at least three of the countries (Cameroon, Gabon, Mali), there is no restriction on the number of births or children to which these payments apply. The more common pattern is for the lump-sum payments to be limited to the first three births, with prenatal allowances and the monthly child support payments being available for an unlimited number of children. Only one country (Guinea) places a limit on the number of children for whom monthly support will be given. When the employee concerned is male, there appears to be no limit on the number of wives whose children can be supported through the family allowance system.[45]

An illustration of the relative significance of these allowances can be provided from Dahomey. In Cotonou and Porto Novo, Dahomey, typists earn roughly U.S. $45 per month, while more highly skilled sales personnel or telephone operators earn about $60 per month.[46] Under the Dahomean system of family allowances, such personnel would receive prenatal payments totaling about $25 for each birth, plus a lump-sum payment of $20 at the time of the first birth, $10 for the second and third births, and nothing for subsequent births. They would then receive a monthly child support payment of approximately $2.50 per child.[47] A Dahomean clerk would thus receive around $45, or about a month's salary, in prenatal and birth benefits for his first child. His second and third children would bring $35 each; the following births $25 each. Were he to have six living children, he would receive about $15 in children's payments per month, an addition of between one-quarter and one-third of his base salary.

Beyond the programs just outlined, many French-speaking West African countries have another, higher schedule of benefits for upper-level government employees. In Dahomey, this provides payments of about $10 per month per child for a professional- or administrative-class government official (*fonctionnaire*).[48] Such people can normally expect

to receive a monthly salary after taxes of $150–200 at the beginning of their careers, which would rise to $250–300 per month after ten years or so of service.[49] A civil servant with six children would be drawing about $60 per month additional in family allowances, or around one-quarter of his take-home pay.

The significance attached to these payments by the higher civil servants is demonstrated by the strike which resulted in 1969 when the Dahomey government, faced with one of its periodic financial crises, tried to cut the $10 monthly "child support" payments for high-level government employees to the $2.50 per month enjoyed by the remainder of the Dahomean wage-earning population. The government eventually capitulated, retaining the $10 monthly payment level but limiting to six the number of children for whom payment would be made.

In no country, to be sure, do these systems of family allowances affect more than a rather small fraction of the population. Government employees and salaried workers in private institutions constitute only about 10–15 percent of the labor force in Dahomey and Togo. In some countries of West Africa, the proportion would be less than 5 percent; in few countries would it exceed 20 percent. But this is nonetheless an important group from the point of view of fertility reduction, for it includes the urban elite among whom a concern for fertility regulation can be expected to develop first and from which it can be expected to spread to other sections of the society. Any government policy or program that lessens the concern of this group for fertility reduction can be expected to slow the spread of fertility regulation throughout the society as a whole.

Before drawing any population policy conclusions from the existence of family allowances, however, it is necessary to ask whether they actually do significantly reduce the interest of the receiving couples in fertility regulation, thus contributing to the maintenance of high birth rates. No one knows that they do. But, if family allowances paid on the basis of number of children born have any

[45] Information in preceding section from U.S. Department of Health, Education and Welfare, Social Security Administration, Office of Research and Statistics, *Social Security Programs Throughout the World* (1967), passim.

[46] Dahomey, Office of Statistics.

[47] U.S. Department of Health, Education and Welfare, *Social Security Programs*, pp. 60–61.

[48] Interviews in Cotonou, Dahomey, February 1970.

[49] *Ibid.*

effect on fertility at all, it is clearly in the direction of raising rather than lowering it; and the hypothesis that family allowances of the magnitude paid in French-speaking West Africa are substantial enough to exert a significant profertility influence is at least plausible and worthy of further investigation.

GOVERNMENTAL POLICIES AND RURAL-URBAN MIGRATION. The foregoing examples have dealt primarily with population growth. But government policies unintentionally affect migration, as well. Almost all West African governments, for example, are promoting industrialization and modernization as fast as their resources will allow. But many industries do best if situated close together, where they can share such expensive infrastructure items as transportation facilities, electric power grids, and water supplies. There is thus a natural tendency for them to be located in urban areas, which in turn promotes a flow of people from the surrounding countryside in search of employment.

Thus, to some extent, any West African government promoting industrialization is by that policy alone contributing to its rural-urban exodus. In many cases, this tendency is compounded by the efforts of government to provide the required infrastructure in industrial estates, almost always situated near urban areas. Tema in Ghana and Ikeja in Nigeria are two obvious examples.

Further, government financial policies often tend to depress rural incomes relative to urban incomes. An example is the common practice of granting government marketing boards a monopoly on purchases of such export crops as cocoa, rubber, or groundnuts at a price well below the world market, diverting the resulting profits to the public treasury. Another is charging rural people at the same rate as urban dwellers for services not provided in rural areas (such as the "water rates" charged in western Nigeria). As Sir W. Arthur Lewis expressed the situation in his 1968 Aggrey-Fraser-Guggisberg lecture at the University of Ghana:

The fundamental reason for this [current drift to the towns] is the big gap which has now opened up between urban wages and the farmers' incomes . . . . An unskilled laborer in Lagos, in full employment, is paid twice as much as the average farmer earns. The fundamental explanation of heavy migration and unemployment is this big gap in incomes. Moreover, the gap is not confined to personal earnings, for there is an even bigger gap in public services. The governments levy taxes on the farmers and use the money to provide water supplies, medical services, secondary schools, electricity and transport not in the rural areas but in the town. In these circumstances any young man who stayed in the countryside instead of migrating to the towns ought to have his head examined.[50]

Another government policy which ironically serves to promote rural-urban migration, is the effort to provide education in rural areas. Professor Lewis, while not questioning the potential contribution of widespread primary education to productivity, notes the problems created by its rapid spread:

In Africa this swift transition [from limited to widespread primary education in rural areas] has raised the additional and more negative problem of the effect of frustrated expectations. For, in a country where only 10 percent of children finish primary school, and there are virtually no secondary schools, any boy who finishes primary school is assured of a clerical job in town at a high salary. The primary school is thus established in the minds of parents and children as a route to a white collar urban job. But, when 50 percent are finishing primary school, and in addition a new flow of secondary school boys are taking the clerical jobs and the jobs for elementary school teachers, the primary school graduate can no longer find this kind of work. However, it takes time for people to recognize that times have changed. For some years the primary school graduates continue to make a beeline for the towns, where they become unemployed. Depopulation of youth from the countryside, coupled with heavy unemployment in the towns, is now standard in most African countries which have been accelerating primary education. One starts off opening up schools in rural areas in the hope of having literate farmers, and finds instead the

[50] W. Arthur Lewis, "Some Aspects of Economic Development," *The Aggrey-Fraser-Guggisberg Memorial Lectures 1968* (Accra, 1969), pp. 29–30.

effect is that the brighter minds simply emigrate from the countryside into unemployment.[51]

INTENDED AND UNINTENDED CONSEQUENCES OF GOVERNMENT POLICIES. Many more examples of government policies unintentionally affecting population could be cited. But the foregoing suffice to prove the point that such unintentional influence is both frequent and quantitatively significant. To say that any given policy has an unforeseen effect on population, however, is not to say it should not be undertaken. As noted above, for example, the spread of health programs has greatly reduced mortality and thus has been a leading cause of population growth in West Africa. For those who believe that rapid population growth creates grave social and economic problems, this is most unfortunate. But to pay attention only to this problem created by health programs is to ignore completely the multitude of benefits that they also bring. Good health is obviously of inestimable humanitarian, social, and economic value, which is the reason why governments undertake such programs in the first place.

The point is thus not that government policies having undesirable population effects should not be undertaken. The point is rather that government policy makers should be aware of the entire range of effects of their policies and programs before deciding whether to undertake them or how to structure them. Education in rural areas, for example, might well still be worth undertaking even if it does lead to an exodus to the cities. But only if policy makers are conscious that the spread of rural education will have this as one of its effects can they intelligently decide whether to promote it. And only then can they shape their programs so as to minimize the effects found to be undesirable: by developing new educational curricula relevant to rural situations, for example; or by simultaneously undertaking employment programs to make full use of the school-leavers' talents; or, in the case of health services and population growth, by making family planning services available at the same time mortality reduction efforts are introduced.

[51] *Ibid.* pp. 27–28.

## CONCLUSION

As argued above, West African policy makers have by and large failed to indicate an awareness of the population changes described throughout this volume. This is far from surprising. For one thing, the data available to document the changes are far from plentiful, as the other chapters in this volume amply indicate. Nor, fortunately, has West Africa yet been subjected to the kind of population pressure on resources that leads to the periodic famines so well known in such countries as India and Pakistan. And the population changes occurring in West Africa, though profound, are not dramatic. As the Ghana population policy statement puts it, "the welfare of the nation is now endangered by a subtle, almost imperceptible demographic change." Such subtle changes can hardly be expected to attract the attention of the policy maker, who in any country must spend most of his waking hours simply responding to the flood of issues of the moment pressing themselves upon him. He is thus left with no time to identify or deal with subtle, imperceptible changes, regardless of how important such changes may be over the long run. Nor is it surprising that policy makers are not aware of the population implications of the development policies they are implementing: Nowhere in the world has much thought been given to the population implications of general development programs.

Limited as it may still be, concern for population in West Africa is growing. Seven years ago, few would have predicted that Ghana and Nigeria would by now have adopted population policies; or that Dahomey and Gambia would have been concerned enough about their population situation to request study missions; or that any of a number of other French-speaking West African countries would be according a high priority to a census. Thus, while the level of population awareness among West African governments is still lower than in any other part of the world, the trend is clearly toward greater awareness; and time is on the side of those who believe that questions of population are of enough significance to merit explicit consideration.

# PART
# TWO

## *Nigeria*

WHEN he visited Lagos a few years ago, a well-known demographer was heard to say, "My goodness! If it's bad luck for a woman to tell how many children she has, let alone how many children may have died, I don't see how you can do any demographic research here."

His point is well taken, and demographic research in Nigeria has its difficult aspects. People do not like to talk freely about the number of children they have had, and vital events are in general not registered, except in a few scattered areas of the country. If, however, one views demographic research as a joint exercise in social and medical science, rather than as an exercise in simple statistics alone, then the picture becomes brighter.

The following example is perhaps illustrative of the cooperation one can receive from respondents, provided the research situation is properly structured. During one of the important Moslem holidays in Nigeria, the writer had occasion to visit the northern parts of the country and one of the ancient walled towns along the fringes of the Sahara Desert, and he happened to see a colorful procession on horseback enter one of the town gates and proceed to the Emir's palace. At the center of the procession was a young boy, in magnificent green robes, and we were informed that this was a son of the Emir, along with his retinue, and that they had ridden out to welcome some official guests who were coming for the holiday. As the procession was entering the palace, the writer inadvertently asked one of the sentries at the gate how many sons the Emir had.

The question at first caused consternation among the guards. On the one hand, they knew it was dangerous to discuss this topic aloud and in public, because to do so might cause the fertility spirits who deal with matters of this kind to become interested in the topic themselves, and they might decide not to send any more sons to the Emir, which would be serious. On the other hand, they knew it would be most impolite not to answer the question of an interested stranger, particularly one who had done them the honor of coming all the way from Lagos.

# CHAPTER NINE

# Fertility Levels & Fertility Change

ROBERT W. MORGAN
Incorporating a report
by P. O. Ohadike

Finally, the guards solved the problem in the following manner. One of them beckoned to me to accompany him some distance along the outside of the palace walls. We turned a corner, out of sight of the people at the gate, and the guard, after looking cautiously to right and to left, bent forward and whispered, "Seventeen."[1]

As one attempts any kind of social research in Nigeria, one becomes impressed with the willingness of the people to assist.

[1] Evidence of this taboo on the discussion of fertility matters has been elicited largely from my own researches. Ojo writes, "The Yoruba have always been preoccupied with the problems of fertility of human beings as well as crops. *Every worship, no matter what the deity,* is incomplete without solicitations for children or for their long life." [G. F. Afolabi Ojo, *Yoruba Culture* (London: University of London Press, 1966), p. 185, italics mine.] Despite the obvious preoccupation of our respondents with human fertility, the apprehensions of young Nigerian women about their own ability to bear young, and the interest shown in family planning sub-fertility clinics in the country, one finds only scant mention of this subject in the classic works on Nigerian religions. Much greater attention is paid in the literature to fertility behavior with respect to crops: see for example J. Olumide Lucas, *The Religion of the Yorubas* (Lagos, 1948); S. F. Nadel, *Nupe Religion* (London: Routledge and Kegan Paul, 1954); Geoffrey Parrinder, *Religion in an African City* (London: Longmans, Green & Co., 1953).

With respect to vital events, these have been recorded in Lagos and a few other areas of the country, but in general they are not recorded. Even in Lagos, however, where registrations have been carried out for more than six decades, certain sociological factors distort to some extent the data received, tending to inflate the number of births registered and deflate the number of deaths. For example, children whose births are registered in Lagos are entitled to a free primary education in the Lagos schools, and hence some children born elsewhere in Nigeria are registered in Lagos under local addresses. Elderly people who have retired from gainful employment, and persons suffering from chronic illnesses, may return to their villages where they can be more easily housed and cared for, and tradition sometimes decrees that a person return to his village to die. This writer is aware of one instance in which a person died in an urban hospital, and the body was secretly returned to the person's village so that the death could be announced as having occurred there. In its 1968 Annual Report, the Lagos City Council Health Department gives a birth rate figure of 57.89 and a death rate figure of 6.89 for the city. These would appear to err respectively on the high side and the low side.

Provided one observes the customs of the place, allows time for rapport to be established, and shows a genuine concern for the problems of the people being studied, then one is likely to find a greater degree of cooperation in Nigeria than in many other places in the world. Demographic studies combining the social science approach with the techniques of random sampling have in fact been carried out successfully by a number of researchers in Nigeria.[2] In a few instances these studies have been further combined with medical research programs, with a resultant high degree of rapport being established with the respondents.[3]

Actually, a more serious defect with respect to demographic research here has been not so much the quality of the data as the fact that most studies have been confined to one area of the country. Nigerian population estimates based on the 1963 census varied between 55 and 65 million persons,[4] and within this population there are contained an estimated 250 different language groups,[5] ranging in size from a few hundred persons to 10–15 million. The largest tribal groups, according to the 1963 federal census, were the Hausas (11,652,745); the Yorubas (11,320,509); the Ibos (9,246,388); the

[2] In addition to Nigerian census materials and the ambitious Federal Office of Statistics undertaking, "Rural Demographic Sample Survey, 1965–1966," mimeographed (Lagos, October 1968), the principal sources for this chapter have been the researches of Patrick O. Ohadike, T. Daramola, R. D. Wright, and myself in the Lagos area, and of Francis Oluokun Okediji and P. O. Olusanya in Ibadan and adjacent Yoruba towns and villages. Part of the data of Ohadike and Olusanya, and a large part of my own data, have not been published, and a number of citations are hence made in this chapter to private memorandums and correspondence.

[3] As an outstanding example of the value of medically related demographic research in a developing country, see the publications of the Pakistan-SEATO Cholera Laboratory, Dacca, East Pakistan.

[4] For a discussion of Nigeria's overall population, see chapter 11 in this book. Preliminary figures for the 1973 census are close to 80 million although these are under review.

[5] James S. Coleman, *Nigeria: Background to Nationalism* (Berkeley, Calif.: University of California Press, 1958), pp. 15–16.

Fulanis (4,784,366); and nine other tribes numbering half a million or more persons each.[6] With only a few exceptions, demographic research in Nigeria has been focused on the large Yoruba tribe, occupying approximately the southwestern quarter of the country by area, and comprising the dominant population group in 3 of the 12 Nigerian states: Lagos, Western, and Kwara. This quarter of the country is far from typical either of Nigeria as a whole or of most other areas of tropical Africa.[7] It contains, for example, the two largest urban complexes not only in Nigeria but in all of tropical Africa. The first is the federal capital, Lagos, with at the end of 1963 according to the census a population for the metropolitan area, including Mushin and other immediately contiguous urban places, in excess of 950,000. The Department of Community Health has estimated the population for the end of 1968 at more than 1,200,000 and presently at more than 2 million.[8] The second center, Ibadan, the capital of Western State, lying 90 miles north of Lagos, had at the end of 1963 according to the census an urban population of 627,379 and an urban-rural population for the extensive political area called Ibadan Division of 1,258,625.[9]

The area also contains three of the six universities in Nigeria, the two largest hospitals (the teaching hospitals attached to the Faculties of Medicine in Ibadan and Lagos), and the largest concentration of teachers and doctors generally to be found anywhere in Nigeria.[10] The Yoruba economy is based on agriculture, and here too the area is better off than most other parts of tropical Africa, containing a variety of profitable cash crops including cocoa, palm oil, and rubber. The Yoruba farmer, and particularly the cocoa farmer, frequently is an extremely wealthy man.[11] Additionally, the three-state area serves as a communications and transportation thoroughfare between the northern states and the sea. Lagos contains one of the largest ports and busiest international airports in West Africa,[12] and the principal railroad and highway links between Lagos and the north pass through the other two state capitals, Ibadan and Ilorin. In terms of educational and medical facilities, agricultural productivity, communications and transportation links, opportunities for contacts with other societies, and nontraditional ideas, southwestern Nigeria thus appears to be uniquely endowed within the context of tropical Africa generally.

[6] Federal Office of Statistics, *Population Census of Nigeria, 1963* (Combined National Figures), III (Lagos, 1968).

[7] Tropical Africa is taken here to mean all of Africa south of the Sahara excluding the Republic of South Africa.

[8] Federal Office of Statistics, *Population Census of Nigeria, 1963*, Lagos, Vol. I, and Western Region, Vol. I. The Metropolitan Area was taken to include the urban areas of Mushin, Ajegunle, Ikeja, and Agege in addition to the former Federal Territory of Lagos. The end-1968 figure of 1.2 million was derived from my own research data; see R. W. Morgan and V. Kannisto, "A Population Dynamics Survey in Lagos, Nigeria," *Social Science and Medicine* VII (1973), 1–30.

[9] Federal Office of Statistics, *Population Census of Nigeria, 1963*, Western Region, Vol. II. While recent censuses for various African countries are not always available or accurate, one gathers that for the continent as a whole, cities larger than Lagos or Ibadan include Cairo, Alexandria, Algiers, Casablanca, Capetown and Johannesburg. While a full breakdown of the 1973 Census figures will not be available for some time, it seems likely that Lagos has grown to approximately twice the size of Ibadan in the past decade.

[10] R. W. Morgan, "Medical Students in Nigeria: A Case Study in Social Change" (doctoral dissertation, Boston University 1965). The ratio of doctors to population for the various sections of Nigeria in 1961 was estimated as follows: North, 1:109,000; East, 1:46,000; West, 1:27,000; Lagos, 1:2,050; overall, 1:44,000. See also Lord Hailey, *An African Survey, Revised 1956* (London: Oxford University Press, 1957), for an overview of the developmental pattern of educational and medical facilities elsewhere on the continent. Recent population shifts make it difficult to estimate the proportions in Nigeria today, although the proportion in Lagos has probably deteriorated to something like 1:5000 because the city's population has grown faster than the number of doctors.

[11] Most Nigerian agriculture is well endowed in the tropical African context, and within Nigeria the Yorubas are not exceptional in this respect. See Gerald Helleiner, *Peasant Agriculture, Government and Economic Growth in Nigeria* (Homewood, Ill.: Richard D. Irwin, Inc., 1967).

[12] From the sociological viewpoint under specific consideration here (i.e., ideas and persons flowing into and through port and airport), Lagos may far exceed the other competing West African coastal centers (i.e., Abidjan, Dakar, Accra-Tema).

Furthermore, within the southwestern Nigerian complex, it is apparent that the Lagos Metropolitan Area itself is unique. Mabogunje writes, "In many ways Lagos is the most spectacular of that class of Nigerian cities which owe their growth and development largely to European influence. When the era of industrial development began, the port location and political pre-eminence gave Lagos a peculiar advantage and transformed it into the major focus of the urbanization process in the whole country."[13]

By contrast, Ibadan is essentially a traditional Yoruba town grown very large. Again turning to Mabogunje, we read that Ibadan "represents the highest achievement of pre-European, pre-industrial urbanism in Nigeria," whereas Lagos is to be regarded as "the leviathan of our modern industry-oriented urbanism."[14] Besides Lagos and Ibadan, there are throughout Yorubaland a number of smaller towns of varying sizes, many of them, like Ibadan, representative of what Mabogunje calls "pre-industrial urbanism in Nigeria." Outside of Lagos, the demographic data particularly quoted in this chapter relate to Ibadan, surrounding villages, and two of the nearby towns, Ife and Oyo.

In addition to the Ibadan and Lagos areas, historians generally regard all of southern Nigeria as having been exposed for a longer time and to a greater extent to the impact of European trade, education, and medicine than the larger expanses of northern Nigeria. The latter, and particularly the extreme northern areas of Nigeria, have for centuries been under the control of strong, well-organized Moslem states. With the coming of Christian mission schools and hospitals, as well as the commercial traders, to the coastal areas of Nigeria, it is easy to understand not only why northern Nigeria was reached at a

later date but also how the advance of the educational and medical facilities sponsored by Christian missions into these areas was to a considerable extent rebuffed. Even today, the levels of educational and medical facilities in northern Nigeria are not equal to those of southern Nigeria, although for some years now northerners have been making a determined effort to catch up. These historical trends have been well documented by a number of Nigerian and foreign historians.[15]

In this chapter the fertility data will be examined within the framework of the following four-part sociocultural gradation: (1) Former Northern Nigeria, which now comprises the six northernmost Nigerian states. (2) Southern Nigeria, excluding the Ibadan and Lagos areas. (3) The Ibadan area is extended to include such nearby villages and the towns of Ife and Oyo, partly because, as stated previously, Yorubaland in general is thought to have been exposed to certain nontraditional influences to perhaps a greater extent than other areas of Nigeria, and partly because the Ibadan-Oyo-Ife area has been subjected to a greater amount of demographic research. (The two large geographical areas, identified broadly as northern and southern Nigeria, may themselves contain extreme internal variations in fertility pattern; unfortunately our present data are insufficient to explore the possibility of such variations further.) (4) The Lagos Metropolitan Area, defined here and in the research to be cited as the former Federal Territory of Lagos, an area of 27 square miles, plus immediately adjacent urban areas.[16]

Having made this four-part distinction, a word of caution must now be introduced.

---

[13] Akin L. Mabogunje, *Urbanization in Nigeria* (London: University of London Press, 1968), p. 238. The development of Nigeria's richest "crop" of all—oil—in the Midwest and Rivers states, is producing far-reaching changes in the power and wealth structure in the country, but these too appear to be focused in Lagos.
[14] *Ibid.*, p. 184.

[15] See for example Mabogunje, *Urbanization in Nigeria*, pp. 107 ff.; Kenneth Dike, *Trade and Politics in Niger Delta, 1830–1885* (Oxford, 1956); Coleman, *Nigeria*, especially Parts I and II. For a brief historical overview, see J. D. Fage, *An Introduction to the History of West Africa* (London; Cambridge University Press, 1962).
[16] Until 1967, when the 12 Nigerian states were created, the Federal Territory was a separate political entity and the adjacent urban areas of Lagos lay in western Nigeria. All of the Metropolitan Area now lies in Lagos State.

While there is evidence that the four areas just defined lie at different points along the scale of sociocultural progression, ranging from what is broadly called "traditionalism" to what is broadly called "modernism" or "industrialism," one must avoid the danger of magnifying these differences or of assuming that they are all-pervasive. The coexistence of the traditional and the modern is a fact of social life in almost every corner of Nigeria today. Even in the remotest villages, one finds the automobile and the radio, and not infrequently one hears the resident of some small settlement mention a relative who is studying at a university abroad, or describe a recent trip to Lagos or overseas. Geographically, the Nigerian population is mobile, and trade and travel between the farms and the urban areas is extensive. In terms of urbanization, Nigeria, as well as much of West Africa, has a history of city and town development going back many centuries.[17] While it has been documented that many of these urban centers are essentially traditional or African in character, and defy the classic theories or definitions of "urbanization,"[18] it has nevertheless also been documented that a form of secularization and specialization away from traditional rural patterns has occurred, and that the West African cities and towns now stand at some point midway between the traditional and the modern.[19] Conversely, Lagos itself is not nearly as secularized or as removed from tradition as some writers might have us believe. It is true that Lagos has one of the most heterogeneous urban populations in West Africa; nevertheless, the population remains predominantly Yoruba (70 percent according to the 1963 census,

rising to an estimated 84 percent during the recent crisis when many eastern Nigerians left the city).[20] Large areas of Lagos remain essentially traditional, and the traditional patterns of family life continue to be observed.[21]

In summary, then, one might say that, for the purposes of data analysis in this chapter, a four-part sociocultural gradation is postulated in relation to the four geographical areas of Nigeria defined above. Nevertheless, the reader is cautioned against exaggerating these differences and is advised of the extensive sociocultural similarities pervading all four areas.

## A PARADIGM FOR THE STUDY OF FERTILITY CHANGE

As an approach to studying fertility levels and fertility change in Nigeria, a paradigm is offered (see Figure 9.1). Some data are available for each of the facets of this paradigm, and an attempt will be made in this chapter to review the more important data pertaining to each facet. Again, it must be emphasized that, with only a few exceptions, available data pertain to only one of the many tribal groups in Nigeria, albeit one of the largest of such groups.

The assumption is made here that fertility levels can be measured directly in terms of Groups I and II variables, and that these in turn are affected directly or indirectly by Groups III and IV. The Group III factors are thought to relate particularly to individual families or couples, and the Group IV factors to broader patterns in the society. Group III (e) variables are thought to be influenced in particular by the special set of factors under Group V, and all of the above are assumed to be affected directly or indirectly by Group VI.

[17] For two historical works documenting the rise of West African cities, see Fage, *History of West Africa*, and E. W. Bovill, *The Golden Trade of the Moors* (London: Oxford University Press, 1968).

[18] Mabogunje, *Urbanization in Nigeria*, chap. 7 and especially p. 177; see also the early monograph by William R. Bascom, "Urbanization as a Traditional African Pattern," *Sociological Review*, VII (1959), 29–43.

[19] In addition to Mabogunje, see Hilda Kuper, ed., *Urbanization and Migration in West Africa* (Berkeley, Calif.: University of California Press, 1965), in which this question is explored in a number of chapters.

[20] Morgan and Kannisto, "Population Dynamics Survey."

[21] In particular see Peter Marris, *Family and Social Change in an African City: A Study of Rehousing in Lagos* (Evanston, Ill.: Northwestern University Press, 1962); Alison Izzett, "Family Life Among the Yoruba in Lagos, Nigeria," in Aidan Southall, ed., *Social Change in Modern Africa* (London: Oxford University Press, 1961), pp. 305–315.

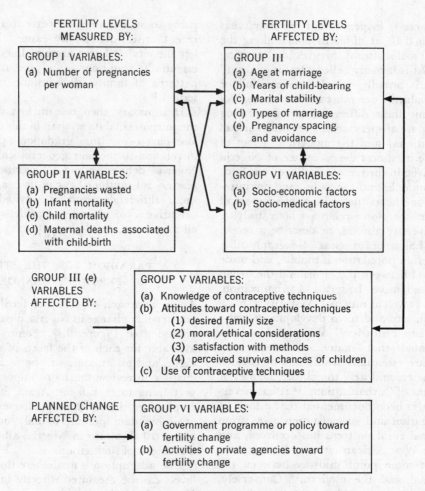

FERTILITY LEVELS
MEASURED BY:

GROUP I VARIABLES:
(a) Number of pregnancies
    per woman

GROUP II VARIABLES:
(a) Pregnancies wasted
(b) Infant mortality
(c) Child mortality
(d) Maternal deaths associated
    with child-birth

FERTILITY LEVELS
AFFECTED BY:

GROUP III
(a) Age at marriage
(b) Years of child-bearing
(c) Marital stability
(d) Types of marriage
(e) Pregnancy spacing
    and avoidance

GROUP VI VARIABLES:
(a) Socio-economic factors
(b) Socio-medical factors

GROUP III (e)
VARIABLES
AFFECTED BY:

GROUP V VARIABLES:
(a) Knowledge of contraceptive techniques
(b) Attitudes toward contraceptive techniques
    (1) desired family size
    (2) moral/ethical considerations
    (3) satisfaction with methods
    (4) perceived survival chances of children
(c) Use of contraceptive techniques

PLANNED CHANGE
AFFECTED BY:

GROUP VI VARIABLES:
(a) Government programme or policy toward
    fertility change
(b) Activities of private agencies toward
    fertility change

FIGURE 9.1. *A Paradigm for the Presentation of Data on Fertility Behavior through Time, in a Developing Country*

Many readers would doubtless prefer another organization of these boxes entirely, and the present one is offered merely for the purpose of simplifying and ordering the data presentation.

THEORETICAL BACKGROUND

Nigerian fertility data presented in this chapter will be assessed within the framework of the classical *demographic transition theory*, which postulates four stages in the population growth rate of a developing country: (1) a traditional period with a high birth rate and a high death rate in approximate balance,

and stable population growth; (2) a high growth period, affected by a lowered death rate and a continuing high birth rate; (3) a transitional period during which the birth rate also declines; and (4) the establishment of a new low birth rate and low death rate population balance.

It is further postulated that, in stage 3, the birth rate declines because of a combination of socioeconomic factors associated with the broad evolutionary forces variously called "modernization," "urbanization," "secularization," and "industrialization." Stolnitz writes: "All nations in the Modern Era which have moved from a traditional, agrarian-based economic system to a largely industrial urbanized base have also moved from a condition of high mortality and fertility to low mortality and fertility.''[22] These interacting forces, including the subtle process—referred to in this present chapter as "secularization"—whereby traditional values are challenged and eventually weakened or overthrown, have been defined and analyzed by numerous writers. In particular, the reader is referred to Crane Brinton's *The Shaping of the Modern Mind.*[23]

For the purpose of our discussion, it is assumed that Nigeria is in stage 2 of the demographic transition. All indications point to a stationary population continuing up to some period in the present century, after which the death rate began to fall, probably under the impact of mass immunization programs and the development of modern medical facilities, especially in the area of pediatric care. The censuses, such as they are, suggest a national population slowly growing past 20 million through the first four decades of the century, rising to some 30 million at mid-century and to something between 55 and 65 million in the 1960s.[24]

The questions to be asked in this chapter, then, involve what has happened to the fertility rate: whether it has continued at a high level, whether it has begun to fall under the impact of the broad evolutionary forces outlined above, or whether for various reasons it may even have risen a little.[25]

A secondary set of questions deals with forces opposing the traditional way of life which may be at work in Nigeria, and which might be causing fertility levels to rise or fall. It would seem to be an overstatement to say that either "urbanization" or "industrialization" was a prominent feature of the country at the present time. Mabogunje, as we have already noted,[26] has shown that the process of urbanization, though ancient, is nevertheless of a different quality from that found in modern industrial society. And while industry has a foothold in Nigeria, the majority of the population remains rural and agrarian based.[27]

What we do see in Nigeria is an infusion of ideas and artifacts that are the products of modern industrial society. The automobile, the motorbike, and the radio or rediffusion are everywhere; and everywhere, one finds people who want to fly in a plane, visit Lagos, or travel overseas. Education in the modern sense has become a primary value and a primary item in the country's annual budgets. Most important, the introduction and extension of the cash economy, even into the agrarian sectors, has afforded succeeding generations the opportunity, if they want it, of escaping in whole or in part from the controls of traditional society and traditional family life.

This latter set of processes, which certainly have affected and will affect fertility levels in the country, are for the purposes of this chapter lumped together under the broad, single heading of "modernization." Primarily, we mean by modernization any complex of forces serving to challenge, disrupt, weaken, or supplant traditional ideas, values, and behavior patterns.

Finally, it must be emphasized that we are not trying to look at either the traditional or the modern as "good," and their opposites as "bad." There is a tendency, in traditional and particularly rural societies, to view the

---

[22] George J. Stolnitz, "The Demographic Transition: From High to Low Birth Rates and Death Rates," in Ronald Freedman, ed., *Population: The Vital Revolution* (Chicago: Aldine, 1965), p. 30.
[23] Crane Brinton, *The Shaping of the Modern Mind* (New York, 1959).
[24] R. R. Kuczynski, *Demographic Survey of the British Colonial Empire,* Vol. I, West Africa (London: Oxford University Press, 1948), p. 597, and chapter 11 in this book.
[25] Short-run increases in fertility levels in various countries have generally been attributed to special factors outside the mainstreams of demographic transition theory. See for example Charles F. Westoff, "The Fertility of the American Population," in Freedman, *Population,* pp. 110–22; Judith Blake, "Income and Re-productive Motivation," *Population Studies,* XXI, 3 (November 1967), 185–206.

[26] See footnote 18.
[27] Federal Office of Statistics, *Rural Demographic Sample Survey, 1965–1966* (Lagos, 1968), p. 3, in which it is stated that 84.0 percent of Nigeria's population is officially classified as rural.

old ways as the good ways, and anything that challenges these as bad. And for those who champion modern causes, there is the tendency to hold the opposite view. No such moral questions are being raised in this chapter. We are simply trying to report what is happening in Nigeria today.

## GROUP I VARIABLES: PREGNANCIES PER WOMAN

While crude birth rates, crude death rates, and rates of natural increase are not specifically named under the set of Group I variables these data nevertheless are available for large segments of Nigeria and constitute our only immediate insight into the fertility characteristics of the population as a whole. The three studies considered here are as follows: (1) The Rural Demographic Sample Survey was carried out in a random sample of the rural population—representative of an estimated 84 percent of the total population of the country[28]—in two survey rounds conducted approximately 12 months apart in 1965 and 1966.[29] More than 200 units comprising some 1,500–3,000 persons each were surveyed.[30] (2) A demographic survey was conducted by Olusanya between March and May 1967, in 5 sample villages located within 60 miles of Ibadan in Western State.[31] A total of 682 ever-married women were interviewed, and pregnancy histories were taken. (3) The Lagos Population Dynamics Survey was carried out by the Department of Community Health of the University of Lagos College of Medicine in 30 sample blocks of some 400–500 persons each in the metropolitan area, in three sample rounds covering a 12-month period in 1967–1968.[32]

[28] Ibid.
[29] Although three rounds were carried out in whole or part, it will be seen that data analysis examined almost exclusively the first and third rounds. Ibid., especially pp. 5–8.
[30] Ibid., pp. 1 and 15.
[31] P. O. Olusanya, "Rural Attitudes to Family Size and Its Limitation in Western Nigeria," memorandum (typescript), Nigerian Institute of Social and Economic Research (no date).
[32] Morgan, and Kannisto "Population Dynamics Survey."

TABLE 9.1
Vital rates computed in three Nigerian surveys

| Area Surveyed | Crude Birth Rate (per 1,000) | Crude Death Rate (per 1,000) | Rate of Natural Increase (percent) |
|---|---|---|---|
| Nigeria, rural | 50.2 | 26.9 | 2.33 |
| Ibadan area villages | 46.3 | 15.0 | 3.13 |
| Lagos metropolitan area | 52.9 | 12.4 | 4.05 |

As Olusanya computed birth and death rates for his study population, a set of vital rates is available for each of these three sample areas, and final figures for each survey are given in Table 9.1.

In the first and third of these surveys, correction factors were employed to adjust for presumed errors in the data, primary among these being a probable underreporting of infant deaths. Because these two surveys were carried out in several stages, and because in the Lagos survey medical tests were available to check on actual pregnancies (such statistical and medical techniques not having been at the disposal of Olusanya during his one-round retrospective survey), the corrected data for surveys one and three are probably more accurate than the data for survey two.[33] To get a better comparative picture, therefore. let us examine that portion of the data from each survey prior to correction for missing infant deaths. We gain here, additionally, from the fact that, for the uncorrected data, the Rural Demographic Sample Survey reproduces figures separately for northern Nigeria and southern Nigeria.[34] The uncorrected figures are given in Table 9.2.

In each column, a progression now appears. It is the progression in the fertility column which most concerns us here. Furthermore, the four areas surveyed correspond rather

[33] Rural Demographic Sample Survey, pp. 16–18; Morgan, "Population Dynamics Survey," pp. 7–10 and Table XX. In the Lagos survey, Gravindex (pregnancy) tests were administered to a subsample of the female respondents and used as a check on infant deaths at a subsequent round of the survey, this correction factor then being applied to the entire sample.
[34] Rural Demographic Sample Survey, p. 13.

TABLE 9.2

Vital rates (uncorrected data), Nigerian surveys

| Area Surveyed | Crude Birth Rate (per 1,000) | Crude Death Rate (per 1,000) | Rate of Natural Increase (per-cent) |
|---|---|---|---|
| Nigeria, rural north | 45.0 | 25.6 | 1.94 |
| Nigeria, rural south | 45.9 | 20.4 | 2.55 |
| Ibadan area villages | 46.3 | 15.0 | 3.13 |
| Lagos metropolitan area | 49.4 | 8.9 | 4.05 |

closely with the four areas defined earlier as lying along a theoretical four-part gradation from the traditional to the modern. If our data and our suppositions are correct, then what we see here is evidence not only of a declining death rate and a rising rate of natural increase as one proceeds from the more traditional to the more modern sector, but also some increase in fertility itself. Olusanya has in fact argued this directly, based on data obtained in Ibadan and two smaller Yoruba towns,[35] and the author's Lagos data fit into this progression (see Tables 9.3 and 9.4), Oyo and Ife showing fewer live births per wife than Ibadan and

[35] P. O. Olusanya, "Modernization and the Level of Fertility in Western Nigeria," *Proceedings of the International Population Conference, London, 1969* (Liège, 1971), pp. 812–25.

Lagos, and the two former towns also showing lower age-specific fertility rates and lower fertility rates than Lagos.[36]

In Table 9.3, the Lagos data are taken from a survey by Ohadike,[37] carried out in 1964 among a random sample of 596 currently married females in the Lagos Federal Territory (Ohadike having done full pregnancy histories, which were not done in the 1967–1968 Population Dynamics Survey).

From Table 9.3, it is seen that average live births per mother increase as one shifts from Oyo to Ife to Ibadan to Lagos. Ife is considered midway between Oyo and Ibadan in the "modernization" scale. Olusanya mentions in his report that Ife is occupationally more diversified and somewhat more urbanized than Oyo. Educational levels are considerably higher in Ife (see Table 9.20). From the point of view of fertility variables, furthermore, another argument can be put

[36] Table 9: 4, Lagos rates, computed from Lagos Population Dynamics Survey data, 1967–1968.

[37] P. O. Ohadike, "A Demographic Note on Marriage, Family and Family Growth in Lagos, Nigeria," in John C. Caldwell and C. Okonjo, eds., *The Population of Tropical Africa* (London: Longmans, Green & Company, and New York: Columbia University Press, 1968), pp. 379–92; and "Patterns and Variations in Fertility and Family Formation: A Study of Urban Africans in Lagos, Nigeria" (Ph.D. thesis, Australian National University, Canberra, 1965), p. 260; also personal memorandum (January 1970), 29 pages.

TABLE 9.3

Live births per mother, Nigerian surveys

| Age | Oyo Number of women | Oyo Average number of live births | Ife Number of women | Ife Average number of live births | Ibadan Number of women | Ibadan Average number of live births | Lagos Number of women | Lagos Average number of live births |
|---|---|---|---|---|---|---|---|---|
| 15–19 | 82 | 0.65 | 87 | 0.71 | 17 | 1.00 | 33 | 1.0 |
| 20–24 | 460 | 1.21 | 517 | 1.24 | 36 | 1.89 | 112 | 1.8 |
| 25–29 | 658 | 2.03 | 662 | 2.38 | 62 | 2.19 | 129 | 2.9 |
| 30–34 | 462 | 2.96 | 427 | 3.42 | 68 | 3.49 | 115 | 4.2 |
| 35–39 | 234 | 3.53 | 250 | 3.96 | 42 | 3.88 | 75 | 5.1 |
| 40–44 | 126 | 4.11 | 134 | 4.60 | 23 | 4.19 | 52 | 6.2 |
| 45+ | 138 | 4.58 | 171 | 4.93 | 14 | 4.71 | 80 | 6.8 |
| Total | 2,160 | 2.44 | 2,248 | 2.75 | 262 | 3.05 | 596 | 4.0 |

SOURCES: Oyo, Ife, and Ibadan—P. O. Olusanya, "Modernization and the Level of Fertility in Western Nigeria" (1969); Lagos— P. O. Ohadike, 1964 survey of random sample of females, Lagos Federal Territory, see footnote 37.

TABLE 9.4
Age-specific fertility rates, in Nigerian surveys

| Age | Nigeria (rural) | Oyo | Ife | Lagos |
|---|---|---|---|---|
| 10–14 | 0.014 | — | — | — |
| 15–19 | 0.181 | 0.070 | 0.098 | 0.145 |
| 20–24 | 0.266 | 0.276 | 0.218 | 0.305 |
| 25–29 | 0.233 | 0.264 | 0.262 | 0.329 |
| 30–34 | 0.172 | 0.213 | 0.239 | 0.296 |
| 35–39 | 0.123 | 0.131 | 0.179 | 0.203 |
| 40–44 | 0.068 | 0.058 | 0.117 | 0.104 |
| 45+ | 0.063 | 0.042 | 0.055 | 0.079 |
| Total fertility ratio | 5.600 | 5.277 | 5.842 | 7.309 |

SOURCES: Nigeria—*Rural Demographic Sample Survey;* Oyo and Ife—P. O. Olusanya, "Modernization and the Level of Fertility in Western Nigeria" (1969) (Ibadan data not given); Lagos—R. W. Morgan, computed from Lagos Population Dynamics Survey data, 1968.

forward that Ife is more "modernized," since the town is on the main highway linking two of the more impressive pediatric care units in Nigeria, namely the one at University College Hospital, 55 miles to the west in Ibadan, and the one at Wesley Guild Hospital, only 20 miles east in Ilesha. Oyo, although 35 miles north of Ibadan and on the main highway to the north, is not so specifically linked to an area of intensive pediatric care.

The differences in fertility in Tables 9.2 and 9.3, showing higher levels for Ibadan and Lagos, might be explained in terms of a possible larger number of women in the younger age groups in those two cities, who had migrated from the villages looking for jobs. The 1963 census data for the Lagos Federal Territory did in fact show a large population "bulge" in the 20–30 age group for both males and females. This bulge was much reduced at the time of the Department of Community Health survey in 1967–1968. It is likely that, by then, with increasing political tensions in the country, many young migrants had returned to their villages and others among the males had been recruited into the Nigerian army. In any event, any such bias in the Lagos data appearing in

Tables 9.2 and 9.3 is offset by the age-specific data in Table 9.4. The apparently much higher fertility of Lagos women throughout the 20–39 age span is particularly striking, as is the very much higher total fertility rate for Lagos.

The two Lagos surveys reported so far were done approximately four years apart, and based on these surveys, one might be tempted to look for a fertility trend. In spite of Ohadike's total fertility estimate of 6.8, one would hesitate to suggest an upward fertility trend in Lagos over the four-year interval, as the methodology of the two surveys, and the corrections applied to the findings, undoubtedly differed.

The above analysis has been based on data collected in random samples of the total population of an area. A number of other surveys have been carried out in both Lagos and Ibadan in which to one extent or another special segments of the population have been studied. These surveys have, among other things, shed light on the question of whether fertility levels may be changing in specific segments of the population, for example in particular socioeconomic or religious groups. The studies of Daramola and Wright in Lagos [38] and of Okediji, as well as of Olusanya, in the Ibadan area[39] have been especially helpful in this connection. A review of these

[38] T. Daramola and R. D. Wright, "Attitudes Toward Family Planning in Lagos, Nigeria," mimeographed, Department of Community Health (Lagos, 1968). See also Daramola, Wright et al., "Attitudes in Nigeria Toward Family Planning," in Caldwell and Okonjo, *Population of Tropical Africa,* pp. 401–9.

[39] F. O. Okediji, "Some Social Psychological Aspects of Fertility among Married Women in an African City," *Nigerian Journal of Economic and Social Studies,* IX, 1 (March 1967), 67–79; "Attitudes Use and Knowledge of Family Planning Techniques among Married Women in the City of Ibadan," *West African Medical Journal,* XVII, 6 (December 1968), 211–218; "Differential Fertility in the City of Ibadan: Its Comparative Implications for Studying Population Change in Other African Countries," *Proceedings of Eighth International Congress of Anthropological and Ethnological Sciences* (Tokyo, 1969). Also see P. O. Olusanya, "The Educational Factor in Human Fertility: A Case Study of the Residents of a Suburban Area in Ibadan, Western Nigeria," *Nigerian Journal of Economic and Social Studies,* IX, 3 (November 1967), 351–74

surveys will be undertaken in the analysis of Group III and Group IV variables below.

Approaching the data from the random sample surveys with caution, one is tempted nevertheless to make the following generalizations with respect to fertility levels and fertility trends in Nigeria today: (1) Based on the data available, Nigeria has entered stage 2 of the demographic transition cycle and its population is increasing at an extremely rapid rate, possibly in the vicinity of 2.5 percent per annum. (2) The fertility rate is not declining; in other words there is no evidence that stage 3 of the demographic transition cycle has begun or is about to begin. (3) There are even indications that, with the onset of modernization forces, the fertility rate may, in the short run at least, be rising.

The possible reasons for such a rise in fertility will be discussed below, under the treatment of Group III and Group IV variables. Olusanya in particular has produced a most interesting treatment of this question, in which he argues that modernization factors not only among Group III variables but also among the specifically medical Group IV variables act directly to produce an increase in actual fertility per woman.[40]

## GROUP II VARIABLES: INFANT MORTALITY AND RELATED FACTORS

In assessing the effective fertility of a female population, it is necessary, in addition to considering actual pregnancies, to consider also the related factors of wasted pregnancies, infant and child deaths, and maternal deaths related to childbirth. Data on most of these variables are fragmentary throughout the developing world, and Nigeria is not an exception. The reader is also assumed to be familiar with the problems of definition associated with these variables, and the resultant difficulties which thus enter into the comparative analysis of those data which are available.

In the Lagos Population Dynamics Survey, this writer estimated pregnancy wastage at 10 percent. This was defined to include identified pregnancies which failed to result in a live birth. The figure is largely impressionistic and based on conversations with a number of obstetricians. Ohadike, in his 1964 survey, reported an average of 4.0 live births for all respondents at the time of the survey and an average of 4.3 total pregnancies.[41] This would mean a pregnancy wastage of about 7 percent. No data on rural pregnancy wastage are available, but one assumes that the rural figure is higher.

A presumed reduction in pregnancy wastage associated with improved medical services might be partially offset by an increased figure for abortions in the more urbanized areas. In 1962 and 1963, 1,500 and 1,000 abortions respectively were reported by the Federal Ministry of Health in Lagos hospitals.[42] In 1968, the reported figure was "over 2,000."[43] These figures obviously reflect only those cases brought to official attention, and the actual abortion rate in Lagos is doubtless much higher. In a recent survey of family planning attitudes in the Lagos Metropolitan Area, 69 percent of women interviewed stated that they knew what was meant by the term "abortion."[44] This is a much higher proportion than has been recorded elsewhere, especially among rural populations, in West Africa.[45] It would seem reasonable that in traditional African society abortions were seldom desired, since having many children was a mark of prestige for both the husband and the wife. It is likely that the pressures of

[40] Olusanya, "Modernization and the Level of Fertility in Western Nigeria."

[41] Ohadike, "A Demographic Note on Marriage," p. 386.

[42] O. Akinla and B. K. Adadevoh, "Abortion—A Medico-Social Problem," *Journal of the Nigeria Medical Association*, VI, 3 (July 1969), 16–22.

[43] G. A. Williams, *Annual Report of the Medical Officer of Health, Lagos, for the Year 1968*. Dr. Williams, who also is chairman of the Family Planning Council of Nigeria, has made a number of public statements in recent years citing the rise in the incidence of abortions in the Lagos Metropolitan Area.

[44] Robert W. Morgan, unpublished data, family planning KAP survey (1968).

[45] John C. Caldwell, "The Control of Family Size in Tropical Africa," *Demography*, V, 2 (1968), 598–619.

city life and the cash economy are causing more and more young women to turn to abortion as a means of preserving their status in their new urban way of life. The sad fact remains, however, that outside of random impressions, we have little to guide us with respect to dimensions or trends regarding pregnancy wastage in Nigeria, particularly in the vitally important area of abortions.

Some quantitative data are available on infant and child mortality. The Rural Demographic Sample Survey and the Lagos Population Dynamics Survey produced infant mortality figures for rural Nigeria and for Lagos. Additionally the Lagos figures were divided between those parts of the metropolitan area lying in the former Federal Territory (and hence having the benefits of pipe-borne water, sewage and refuse collection, paved roads, and more intensive medical facilities), and the peripheral areas of the city lying in the former Western Region and in general not enjoying these social and medical benefits. The respective infant mortality rates for these three areas are given in Table 9.5.

TABLE 9.5
Infant mortality rates per 1,000 live births, Nigerian surveys

| Area Surveyed | Infant Mortality Rate |
| --- | --- |
| Nigeria, rural | 178 |
| Lagos (former Western Region areas) | 143 |
| Lagos (former Federal Territory) | 79 |

A child mortality rate (children from birth up to five years) of 322 for males and 306 for females for rural Nigeria was reported in the Rural Demographic Sample Survey. (No combined figure for males and females was given.) Interestingly, the figure for males is slightly higher than that for females. No interpretative material is available, nor are there any trend figures.

Anyone familiar with the anthropological literature for almost any area of the develop-

ing world will appreciate the exceptionally high hazards of infant and child mortality and maternal deaths in childbirth. Quoting just briefly from the Bohannans' classic work on the Tiv, we read that delivery normally "takes place in a hut, the woman sitting in a . . . chair and the midwife . . . seated on a stool before her . . . . As soon as the woman is delivered, the midwife or another of the older women cuts the cord with a sharp bamboo splinter or cornstalk and binds the umbilical cord with raffia; she then bathes the child in hot water, scrubbing it with earth if no soap is available."[46] It is apparent that, among other things, the chances of tetanus are pronounced. The Bohannans also go on to record the hazards of difficult or obstructed labor, which usually is ascribed either to adultery or the intervention of an evil spirit, in which case the mother must either confess or appease the spirit in some way, a situation likely to aggravate both physically and mentally the already critical condition of the female.

Obviously, under these conditions, any introduction of modern medical facilities is likely to result in a sharp reduction in infant and maternal deaths, and may well be responsible, more than any other single factor, for the dramatic increases in effective fertility being observed in developing areas. Few quantitative data on these processes are available for Nigeria, but several interesting reviews of the efforts being made by present-day physicians to combat and reduce the hazards of infant and maternal deaths in some of the larger Nigerian hospitals have been published and are available.[47]

At this point, one would like to be in a position to offer summarized data from the surveys mentioned so far on average number of pregnancies, number of live births, number of child deaths, and number of surviving children, for each of the areas of Nigeria we

[46] Laura Bohannan and Paul Bohannan, *The Tiv of Central Nigeria*, International African Institute (London, reprinted 1962), p. 63.
[47] See for example, O. Akinla, "Social Obstetrics in Africa," *West African Medical Journal*, XVIII, 2 (April 1969), 47–49; I. Essien, "Grande Multiparity," *Dokita*, VII (April 1965), 11–13.

TABLE 9.6
Pregnancy outcome paradigm, rural Nigeria and metropolitan Lagos

| Area Surveyed | Estimated Number of Pregnancies | Estimated Pregnancy Wastage | Average Number of Live Births | Child Mortality (0–15 yrs.) | Average Child Deaths | Average Surviving Children |
|---|---|---|---|---|---|---|
| Nigeria, rural | 6.4 | 12% | 5.6 | 370 | 2.1 | 3.5 |
| Lagos Metropolitan Area | 7.9 | 7% | 7.3 | 220 | 1.6 | 5.7 |

SOURCES: Nigeria—live births and child mortality from Rural Demographic Sample Survey; pregnancy wastage and average pregnancies based on estimates alone; Lagos—live births from Lagos Population Dynamics Survey; child mortality and pregnancy wastage based on Ohadike's 1964 survey.

have been considering. Unhappily, the retrospective data on child mortality, on which most of these surveys rely, present such obvious discrepancies that one hesitates to do so. Instead, the following paradigm is offered (see Table 9.6) based on the Rural Demographic Sample Survey and the two Lagos surveys. For rural Nigeria, live births and child mortality (in this case taken to include children up to age 15) are given in the rural survey data, other figures being computed from these. A 12 percent pregnancy wastage figure has been assumed by this writer in the absence of any other data. For the Lagos area, we start with the figure of 7.3 live births derived from the 1967–1968 Population Dynamics Survey. Ohadike, in his 1964 study, estimated completed fertility at 6.8 and surviving children at 5.3, yielding a child mortality rate of approximately 220; for his total sample, he reported average pregnancies per woman of 4.3 and average live births of 4.0, giving a pregnancy wastage figure of 7 percent.[48] Because Ohadike's retrospective data may be subject to memory errors and may err on the low side, his rates have been used and the figures given in the paradigm have been scaled up slightly, based on the figure of 7.3 births. The results, as given in Table 9.6, suggest a range of 6.4 pregnancies and 3.5 surviving children in rural Nigeria and of 7.9 pregnancies and 5.7 surviving children in Lagos.

We turn now to an examination of Group III and Group IV variables, and possible explanations of this apparently higher fertility level in urban Nigeria. Unless otherwise

specified, the term "fertility" will hereafter be taken to mean number of pregnancies per woman; we will not be concerned during the remainder of this chapter with the mortality factors associated with pregnancy and childbirth which have been discussed under the Group II variables above.

GROUP III VARIABLES: MARRIAGE AND CONJUGAL UNION FACTORS

Most of the data to be presented in the sections which follow suggest that fertility levels in Nigeria should be decreasing as one moves from the traditional to the modern sector. We have seen already from reviews of broad surveys of vital events in the country that fertility levels in fact appear to be increasing, at least at the present time, as one moves from the traditional to the modern. Data on Group III and Group IV variables will be presented for each factor separately, and at the end of each section an attempt will be made to reconcile these apparently conflicting patterns. The set of Group III variables with which we are dealing here includes those factors which affect marriage and the individual childbearing couple. Among these factors are age at first marriage, types and duration of marriage, marital stability, and techniques employed to plan or space out pregnancies. The important set of factors dealing specifically with contraceptive practices and the data produced from the several family planning KAP surveys[49] conducted in Nigeria are dealt with in a separate section (pp. 213–225).

[48] Ohadike, "A Demographic Note on Marriage," p. 386.

[49] Surveys of knowledge, attitudes, and practice with respect to family planning.

TABLE 9.7
Age at first marriage, Nigerian surveys

| Areas Surveyed | Age (in years) | |
|---|---|---|
| | Males | Females |
| Katsina Province, northern Nigeria (median values) | — | 10–14 |
| Five villages, Ibadan area (mean values) | 27 | 20 |
| Ibadan, two suburban areas (mean values) | 25.8 | 19.4 |
| Lagos (mean values) | 28.1 | 19.8 |
| Surulere area, Lagos (mean values) | — | 15–19 |

SOURCES: Katsina Province and Surulere area—T. Daramola and R. D. Wright, "Survey of Attitudes in Nigeria toward Family Planning"; Ibadan villages—P. O. Olusanya, "Rural Attitudes to Family Size and Its Limitation in Western Nigeria," memorandum, Nigerian Institute of Social and Economic Research (no date); Ibadan suburban—P. O. Olusanya, "The Educational Factor in Human Fertility: A Case Study of the Residents of a Suburban Area in Ibadan, Western Nigeria," *Nigerian Journal of Economics and Social Studies*, IX, 3 (November 1967); Lagos—P. O. Ohadike, "A Demographic Note on Marriage, Family and Family Growth in Lagos, Nigeria," in John C. Caldwell and C. Okonjo, eds., *The Population of Tropical Africa* (London: Longmans, Green & Company, and New York: Columbia University Press, 1968).

Several surveys have produced data on age at first marriage for both men and women; these data are summarized in Table 9.7. Outside of the Yoruba areas, the only quantitative data we have derive from the Daramola and Wright survey conducted in 1965,[50] which included interviews carried out by a vacationing Lagos medical student among 73 mothers attending two pediatric clinics in Katsina Province in northern Nigeria. Data from two Ibadan area and two Lagos surveys are also included in Table 9.7. While we have very little to go on, the table does bring out strongly the fact that age at first marriage for women is considerably lower than for men in all groups. The table also suggests that, in the area of northern Nigeria surveyed, age at first marriage for

[50] Daramola and Wright, "Attitudes in Nigeria," p. 404.

women was less than 15 years, whereas, for each of the four other areas in southwestern Nigeria, age at first marriage for women was approximately 20 years.

These findings conform in a general way with the data on age-specific fertility, in different areas of Nigeria, given in Table 9.4, which suggest that, in rural Nigeria generally, childbearing begins at an earlier age than in the more modern and urban southwestern Yoruba sector. To highlight these differences, data from Table 9.4 for fertility in the younger

TABLE 9.8
Percentage of births occurring in younger age groups, Nigerian surveys

| Areas Surveyed | Menarche Up to 20 Years |
|---|---|
| Nigeria, rural | 17.4 |
| Oyo | 6.6 |
| Ife | 8.4 |
| Lagos | 9.9 |

SOURCE: Age-specific fertility rates, Table 9.4.

age groups have been analyzed separately in Table 9.8. It will be seen that, in rural Nigeria, 17.4 percent of births occur to women less than 20 years old, whereas, in the Yoruba towns and Lagos, a range of only 6.6–9.9 percent of births occur to women aged less than twenty. The anthropological literature also leads us to believe that marriage and childbearing in traditional society commence shortly after puberty when females become capable of bearing young. Contrary to a sometimes prevalent opinion, two Nigerian surveys suggest that the onset of menstruation among Nigerian girls parallels that among women in other parts of the world, with the mean age pinpointed at approximately 14 years. Akingba in a questionnaire survey of 2,200 girls at Nigerian schools and other institutions derived a mean age for the menarche of 13.95 years with a spread of 10–19 years.[51] Tanner, in an earlier survey cited by Ohadike, gave an average age for the

[51] J. B. Akingba, "Some Aspects of Menstruation in Nigerian Females," *Journal of the Nigeria Medical Association*, V, 4 (October 1968), 27–34.

menarche of 14 years with a range of 11–17 years.[52] It does appear from available data that, in traditional rural Nigeria, childbearing begins much closer to this menarchal age than in the more urbanized areas.

Turning to the other end of the fertility spectrum, an investigation of the data in Table 9.4 suggests no such pronounced differences between the rural and urban areas with respect to the cessation of child-bearing (see data analyzed separately in Table 9.9). One might suggest, therefore,

TABLE 9.9
Percentage of births occurring in older age groups, Nigerian surveys

| Areas | Ages 35+ | Ages 40+ |
|---|---|---|
| Nigeria, rural | 22.7 | 11.7 |
| Oyo | 21.9 | 10.0 |
| Ife | 30.1 | 14.8 |
| Lagos | 26.4 | 12.6 |

SOURCE: Age-specific fertility rates, Table 9.4.

that a longer childbearing period is to be found among females in the rural areas, ranging from 20–30 years with a possible median of 25 years. For the urban areas, on the other hand, a shorter childbearing period of 15–25 years seems more appropriate, with a possible median of 20 years. On the face of it, this should mean higher fertility levels in the rural areas.

With respect to types and duration of marriage, the rural data suggest much greater stability than do the urban data. Olusanya in his study of five villages near Ibadan writes, "Marriage here is very stable. About 95 percent of all extant marriages were first marriages and there were hardly any of the women who had been married more than twice before."[53] While data are lacking, this writer would hazard the guess that the same would be generally true in

rural Nigeria. In Ibadan and Lagos, on the other hand, we have data to suggest that marriages are much less stable. Okediji and Okediji have presented a study of divorce patterns in the city of Ibadan.[54] In this study, the authors perceive a weakening of the controls of the traditional patrilineal family group, and the rise of divorces initiated in the Customary Courts in Ibadan, particularly by women and frequently with the idea of obtaining a wealthier husband. This pattern is reported as not present to the same extent in traditional Yoruba society.

The complexity of traditional marriage, involving long rituals, family meetings, and the exchanging of gifts, and the equally complex forms of traditional divorce, an institution which apparently was possible in traditional society but presumably on rarer occasions, have been documented by numerous anthropologists. While quantitative data are lacking for most of Nigeria, we do have some measure of the extent to which the family influence on marriage and divorce proceedings has been reduced in Lagos and Ibadan.

According to our Lagos family planning survey carried out in 1968, marriage by native law constituted only 46.9 percent of all conjugal unions. Legal or court marriage, in which the couple sign a register at City Hall comprised 4.0 percent, while church marriage comprised 31.2 percent (this latter includes both Moslem and Christian rituals, and it might further be noted that church marriages also involve the signing of the court register). Mutual consent unions, an institution widely recognized in Lagos, in which a couple enter into a conjugal union which they and their associates define as "marriage" but which implies no involvement by family or governmental agencies, comprised 17.6 percent of all Lagos unions. Prostitution constituted 0.3 percent of the unions surveyed, and here it should perhaps be noted that a number of married women also engage in prostitution,

[52] J. M. Tanner et al., "Age at Menarche in Nigerian School Girls with a Note on Their Heights and Weights from Age 12 to 19," *Human Biology*, XXXIV, 3 (September 1962), 188.
[53] Olusanya, "Rural Attitudes to Family Size."

[54] O. O. Okediji and F. O. Okediji, "Marital Stability and Social Structure in an African City," *Nigerian Journal of Economic and Social Studies*, VIII, 1 (March 1966), 151–63.

TABLE 9.10
Types of conjugal union, Lagos females

| Type of Union | Number | Percent |
|---|---|---|
| Marriage by native law | 291 | 46.9 |
| Legal or court marriage | 25 | 4.0 |
| Church marriage | 194 | 31.2 |
| Mutual consent marriage | 109 | 17.6 |
| Prostitution | 2 | 0.3 |
| Totals | 621 | 100.0 |

SOURCE: R. W. Morgan, family planning attitude survey, 1968.

so that the figure for this kind of activity is undoubtedly higher (see Table 9.10).

Our data on the outcome of the most recent marriage of Lagos women showed that 82.1 percent were still married and living with their spouses; 12.7 percent were still married but living separately; 2.9 percent were divorced or separated; and 2.3 percent were widowed (see Table 9.11). This suggests a pattern of continuing stability for Lagos marriages, but the appearance is illusory. Obscured by Table 9.11 is the rate of divorces among married women. It may be that a significant number of our respondents at the time of our survey had recently left one spouse in favor of another, in which case these women would be recorded in Table 9.11 under one of the "still married" categories.

A better picture of the actual situation may be gathered from data on number of marriages per woman, and these are presented in Table 9.12, along with comparable data from two surveys in the Ibadan area. It will be seen that 26.1 percent of Lagos females

TABLE 9.11
Outcome of most recent marriage, Lagos females

| Marital Outcome | Number | Percent |
|---|---|---|
| Still married, live together | 505 | 82.1 |
| Still married, live apart | 78 | 12.7 |
| Divorced or separated | 18 | 2.9 |
| Widowed | 14 | 2.3 |
| Totals | 615 | 100.0 |

SOURCE: Morgan, family planning attitude survey, 1968.

have been married more than once, the comparable figures for two Ibadan suburban areas and for five villages near Ibadan being 11.0 percent and 5.0 percent respectively. These figures indicate a growth in marital instability as one moves from the villages to Ibadan to Lagos.

At this point, we must face the question as to whether marital instability in the urban areas contributes to higher or lower fertility per female. Ohadike's Lagos data argue very strongly for a higher rate of fertility with longer duration marriages and lower fertility rates with shorter duration marriages. This writer's own impression would be that marital instability does in fact contribute to lower fertility, partly because the fact of instability

TABLE 9.12
Number of marriages per woman, Three Nigerian surveys (percentage distributions)

| Area | Number of Marriages | | |
|---|---|---|---|
| | One | Two | Three + |
| Ibadan area villages | 95.0 | n.a. | n.a. |
| Ibadan, two suburban areas | 89.0 | 10.7 | 0.3 |
| Lagos | 73.9 | 23.2 | 2.9 |

SOURCES: Ibadan villages—Olusanya, "Rural Attitudes to Family Size and Its Limitation in Western Nigeria"; Ibadan suburban—Olusanya, "The Educational Factor in Human Fertility"; Lagos—Morgan, family planning attitude survey, 1968.

suggests some dissatisfaction with the marital partner, and partly because the hiatus in marital status produces, to that extent, a hiatus in conjugal activity. Ohadike has argued further that an earlier age at marriage and a longer marriage duration each contribute to increased fertility (shorter marriage duration producing lower fertility rates as well as lower fertility, see his data summarized in Table 9.13). Data from our ten family planning clinics in Lagos, which have served about 10,000 patients wishing to restrict their fertility, show that once-married women are overrepresented at the clinics vis-à-vis the population at large, whereas women married two or more times are underrepresented. This too might suggest higher fertility on the part

TABLE 9.13
Fertility by age at marriage and duration of marriage, Lagos females[a]

| Marital Characteristics | Present Age | | | | | | |
|---|---|---|---|---|---|---|---|
| | 15–34 | | 35+ | | | | Total |
| | Number of respondents | Mean births | Number of respondents | Mean births | Number of respondents | Mean births | Adjusted mean[b] |
| | 389 | 2.8 | 207 | 6.1 | 596 | 4.0 | — |
| *Age at marriage* | | | | | | | |
| 10–19 | 216 | 3.1 | 72 | 6.3 | 288 | 3.9 | 4.2 |
| 20+ | 173 | 2.5 | 135 | 6.0 | 308 | 4.0 | 3.7 |
| *Total years married*[c] | | | | | | | |
| 0–9 | 255 | 2.1 | 1 | 1.5 | 256 | 2.1 | 1.9 |
| 10–19 | 103 | 4.6 | 57 | 5.2 | 160 | 4.8 | 4.8 |
| 20+ | 1 | 5.5 | 97 | 6.8 | 98 | 6.8 | 5.9 |

SOURCE: Ohadike, "A Demographic Note on Marriage, Family and Family Growth in Lagos, Nigeria," p. 387. Adjusted mean computed on basis of equalized number of wives in each category.
[a] Currently married women.
[b] Excludes three women who refused to answer and another 79 who had been married more than once but for whom actual duration of marriage could not be assessed. The periods between marriages were not counted in the totals.
[c] Adjustment of sample to allow for houses with different numbers of potential respondents.

of once-married females and lower fertility as a result of marital instability. In summary, then, given our findings of later age at marriage and greater marital instability in Lagos and Ibadan, one would expect to find here still another set of arguments in favor of reduced fertility in the Nigerian urban areas.

Another factor to be considered in this section on Group III variables is whether fertility varies between polygynous and monogamous unions. All surveys point to an increase in the proportion of monogamous marriages as one moves from the traditional to the modern (some of these data are summarized in Table 9.14). It will be seen that, in the villages surveyed by Olusanya, 68 percent of marriages were recorded as polygynous, whereas in Ibadan and Lagos, the proportion was substantially lower. In two suburban areas of Ibadan studied by Olusanya, the percentage of polygynous marriages fell to 17.5. The data appear to show a higher proportion of polygynous marriages in Lagos than in Ibadan, but this may be an artifact of the sampling situation.[55] Several researchers also have reported a relationship between increased education and monogamous marriage, but a discussion of this factor is deferred until later in this section.

With increasing urbanization in Nigeria, monogamy may well be increasing; but there is nevertheless no clear indication that fertility is being affected significantly by this shift in marital mode. With respect to Lagos women, Ohadike writes, "There were some

[55] In recounting his difficulties in drawing his Ibadan sample, Okediji mentions "outright refusals, working away from home . . . , and frequent temporary migration to home-village" (see Okediji, "Differential Fertility.") He also notes the completion of only 700 schedules out of a projected sample of 1,005. It is entirely possible that polygynous wives are more traditional and hence more conservative in outlook than monogamous wives, and thus formed a greater proportion of the refusing respondents. The Lagos Population Dynamics Survey, because of greater resources including vehicular transportation, was able eventually to circumvent these difficulties and the final refusal was virtually nil.

It might also be noted that Ohadike in his Lagos sample reported 68.6 percent monogamous marriages and 31.4 percent polygynous marriages. Ohadike's data, however, show that only 37.2 percent of his total sample was Moslem, which may be too low a figure for the Lagos Federal Territory, where the 1963 federal census reported 46.8 percent of the female population as Moslem and the Lagos Population Dynamics Survey found 51.7 percent of females, aged 15–49, to be Moslem. With the exception of the religious and polygynous-monogamous marriage breakdown, Ohadike's sample appears to be exceptionally good vis-à-vis other available social data, and particularly in the critical area of educational breakdown.

TABLE 9.14

Percentage of polygynous and monogamous marriages, females, Nigerian surveys

| Area | Type of Marriage | |
| --- | --- | --- |
| | Polygynous | Monogamous |
| Ibadan area villages | 68.0 | 32.0 |
| Ibadan traditional area | 32.9 | 67.1 |
| Ibadan, two suburban areas | 17.5 | 82.5 |
| Lagos Metropolitan Area | 41.0 | 59.0 |

SOURCES: Ibadan villages—Olusanya, "Rural Attitudes to Family Size and Its Limitation in Western Nigeria"; Ibadan traditional—F. O. Okediji, "Differential Fertility in the City of Ibadan; Its Comparative Implications for Studying Population Change in other African Countries," *Proceedings of Eighth International Congress of Anthropological and Ethnological Sciences* (Tokyo, 1969); Ibadan suburban—Olusanya, "The Educational Factor in Human Fertility"; Lagos—Morgan, family planning attitude survey, 1968.

observed differences in fertility between women married to monogamists and those married to polygnists. The association, though statistically significant, was only slight and perhaps too much should not be made of it." He concludes his section on polygyny: "Considering the greater incidence of illiteracy among wives of polygynists, complemented by the less youthfulness of their age structure, there appears to be little justification for ascribing observed differences to the type of marriage." (See Table 9.15.)[56]

One interesting note in this connection is that an examination of attendances at the ten family planning clinics in the Lagos Metropolitan Area shows virtually no difference in the proportion of monogamously and polygynously married women, vis-à-vis the proportions of these females in the Lagos

[56] Ohadike, "A Demographic Note on Marriage," pp. 388–89.

population at large. This suggests some equality of fertility between the two types of marriage, with respect to the individual females involved. Of course, it is recognized that numerous other factors affect the attendance of monogamously and polygynously married women at these clinics, in addition to actual fertility.

Before trying to analyze further the effect of monogamy versus polygyny on fertility levels in Nigeria today, it would perhaps be appropriate to digress for a moment and make some comments about the nature of polygyny itself. First, it is not necessarily restricted to the Moslem religion. Ohadike records that in his Lagos sample, 17.3 percent of Roman Catholics and 23.3 percent of Protestants were polygynously married. Second, it should be emphasized that, in both urban and rural Nigeria, and in both modern and ancient times, polygyny has to a large extent been the prerogative of the rich. Just as in other parts of the world, in Nigeria wives cost money, and a poor man has difficulty supporting one wife, let alone two or three. Nadel, in his study of the Nupe, a strong Moslem state in northern Nigeria, carried out in 1934–1936, recorded a mean of 1.5–2 wives per man in two peasant village samples (see Table 9.16). Of Bida, the capital of Nupe, Nadel writes,

To quote a similar average for Bida would be meaningless; the great inequality of wealth and status is reflected in the widely varying range of polygamy. In the houses of the *talakazi*, the "poor ones," monogamy is the rule; in the "middle class" the conditions are much the same as in the peasant districts; but as regards the men of substance and rank, though it would be correct to say that they have rarely less than four wives, the

TABLE 9.15

Mean births by type of marriage, Lagos females

| Type of Marriage | Present Age of Wives | | | | | | |
| --- | --- | --- | --- | --- | --- | --- | --- |
| | 15–34 | | 35+ | | Total | | |
| | Number of wives | Mean births | Number of wives | Mean births | Number of wives | Mean births | Adjusted mean |
| Monogamous | 296 | 2.7 | 113 | 6.1 | 409 | 3.6 | 3.9 |
| Polygynous | 93 | 3.3 | 94 | 6.1 | 187 | 4.7 | 4.2 |

SOURCE: Ohadike, "A Demographic Note on Marriage, Family and Family Growth in Lagos, Nigeria."

TABLE 9.16
Number of wives per man, Nupe villages,
Northern Nigeria, 1934–1936

| Number of Wives | Sample 1 (2 Villages) | | Sample 2 (1 Village) | |
|---|---|---|---|---|
| | Number of men | Percent | Number of men | Percent |
| One | 68 | 34.5 | 44 | 56.5 |
| Two | 96 | 48.7 | 28 | 35.9 |
| Three | 20 | 10.2 | 3 | 3 8 |
| Four | 11 | 5.6 | 3 | 3.8 |
| Five | 1 | 0.5 | 0 | 0.0 |
| Six+ | 1 | 0.5 | 0 | 0.0 |
| Total | 197 | 100.0 | 78 | 100.0 |

SOURCE: S. F. Nadel, *A Black Byzantium* (London: Oxford University Press, 1942), p. 151. (Nadel's totals differed from the figures given, possibly through a typographical error, and corrected totals have been given here.)

upper limits of their polygamy are very fluid . . . . Popular notions attribute to certain royal princes and, above all, to the kings of Nupe, numbers of wives varying between 100 and 200.[57]

Nadel's comments about the relationship between wealth and polygyny, made in 1934–1936, would seem to apply with equal force to both rural and urban Nigeria today. The great majority of men who are polygynously married have two wives only, and those men with greater numbers of wives are rare (unfortunately, none of the researchers has produced specific data on this question for either Lagos or Ibadan).

As another note on polygynous marriage, it must be observed that while monogamy is becoming the more frequently observed official pattern in Nigerian urban areas, in actuality polygynous relationships continue to be practiced. A number of Lagos men of means (usually the more educated segment of the population) maintain one monogamous wife and one or more "girl friends" who are recognized by their associates and sometimes even by the wife herself as additional cohabiting partners of the man. In these cases, the man may be the recognized supporter of the girl friend and of the children

whom she may produce by him.[58] This raises the question as to whether these sets of relationships constitute "monogamous" or "polygynous" unions and further obscures the question of whether fertility levels really are higher under one set of relationships or the other.

Summarizing what we know about polygyny and fertility, then, it appears that (a) while officially recognized monogamous unions are becoming more prevalent in urban Nigeria, monogamous unions were nevertheless fairly prevalent in traditional society, and the extent to which they are actually increasing in the more modern sector is difficult to measure; and (b) while it does appear that fertility may be somewhat higher in polygynous unions, the measured differences are small.

Reviewing the Group III data so far, we find that an older age at first marriage, a shorter total childbearing period, increased marital instability, and possibly to some extent the increased incidence of monogamous marriages, all point to what should be decreased fertility levels in urban Nigeria. How, then, do we explain the measured fertility increase? The answer is to be found in what is undoubtedly the most significant single factor to be reported under this section, namely, the profound change one now observes in Nigerian urban areas in the childbearing interval.

Throughout the developing world, the classical anthropological literature has reported a widespread taboo on sexual relations between man and wife during the period when a new baby is being breast-fed, that is to say, for two to three years after the birth of a child. Various reasons are given for this taboo: for example, that the man's semen would spoil the mother's milk, that a new child in the womb would "overheat" the existing infant, and so on. In traditional polygynous society, the man normally finds satisfaction with one of his other wives during this period, or in casual relationships with

[57] S. F. Nadel, *A Black Byzantium* (London: Oxford University Press, 1942), p. 151.

[58] See Marris, *Family and Social Change,* and Izzett, "Family Life Among the Yoruba."

other women.[59] Given a lactation taboo of two to three years, plus an additional year for the wife to conceive and deliver, we get a childbearing interval in traditional society of three to four years. The traditional Yoruba weaning period has been recorded as three years.[60]

This pattern is definitely breaking down in the modernized and urbanized sectors of Nigeria today. Olusanya writes, "There is a tendency, as far as the educated wives are concerned, towards a break with traditionally held, though erroneous, beliefs, such as the belief that sexual intercourse with a nursing mother as well as the pregnancy that might result is injurious and sometimes lethal to the unweaned baby."[61] Other data suggest that this breakdown in the weaning period is not confined to the educated woman alone. Morley, in his studies in Ilesha in southwestern Nigeria, 20 miles east of Ife, reported a median weaning period of 23–25 months,[62] and our own Lagos data suggest a still shorter weaning period of 15–18 months.[63]

This makes it highly probable that, in the urban areas of Nigeria, men are resuming sexual relations with their wives much sooner after each childbirth than in the traditional areas, and this probably contributes more than any other single factor to the current rise in total fertility in the urban areas. If one goes back to our estimated median childbearing period of 25 years for rural females

[59] Marris, *Family and Social Change*, p. 48.
[60] Olusanya writes: "The most rigid form of the lactation taboo among the riverine peoples of Nigeria is found among the Yoruba .... A three-year period of suckling a baby is prescribed by custom without any provisos, while among the other groups the period is contingent upon various factors, e.g., the existence of other wives, the child's ability to walk and its sex. See P. A. Talbot, *The Peoples of Southern Nigeria* (London: Oxford University Press, 1926), II, pp. 378–83. From P. O. Olusanya, "Modernization and the Level of Fertility" (quote is from footnote 7 of Olusanya's paper).
[61] Olusanya, "The Educational Factor in Human Fertility," p. 372.
[62] D. C. Morley, J. Bicknell, and M. Woodland, "The Epidemiology of Childhood Undernutrition in a Nigerian Village," mimeograph report, Child Health Unit, Wesley Guild Hospital (Ilesha, no date).
[63] R. W. Morgan, unpublished data.

and of 20 years for urban females (reported above in this section on Group III variables), and if one further takes the figures for estimated total pregnancies of 6.4 for rural females and 7.9 for urban females (see paradigm, Table 9.6), then one can develop a pregnancy interval paradigm for Nigeria today which gives a figure of 4 years for rural areas and 2.5 years for the Lagos Metropolitan Area (see Table 9.17). These two paradigms,

TABLE 9.17
Pregnancy interval paradigm, based on Nigerian surveys

| Area Surveyed | Recorded Total Fertility Ratio | Estimated Number of Pregnancies | Estimated Average Years of Childbearing | Computed Average Interval between Pregnancies (in years) |
|---|---|---|---|---|
| Nigeria, rural | 5.6 | 6.4 | 25 | 4 |
| Lagos metropolitan area | 7.3 | 7.9 | 20 | 2.5 |

SOURCE: See Table 9.6, plus discussion on Group III variables. Pregnancies computed from total fertility rates, assuming 12 percent pregnancy wastage in rural Nigeria and 7 percent wastage in Lagos.

Tables 9.6 and 9.17, present a consistent summarizing picture of the demographic data presently available, and they also yield average childbearing intervals roughly consistent with our presently known data on the lactation taboo and the childbearing interval in the two segments of Nigeria depicted. One can argue, if one wishes, that the ideal intervals are probably less than 4 years or 2.5 years, and doubtless during the earlier years of marriage the actual intervals might be closer to 3 and 2 years respectively. Given accidents of life and a probable broadening of these intervals in the older age groups, however, the average for the total childbearing period of 4 years and 2.5 years, respectively, would seem to be quite reasonable.

This concludes our discussion of Group III variables, relating to factors affecting the individual childbearing couple, with the previously noted exception that data on contraceptive techniques and family planning attitudes will be presented in a separate section below.

## GROUP IV VARIABLES: SOCIO-ECONOMIC AND SOCIOMEDICAL FACTORS

One of the hottest disputes among population researchers in Nigeria today centers around whether improved socioeconomic status for a family produces decreased or increased fertility. Okediji, in a survey of females in three areas of Ibadan carried out in 1965–1966, has produced a number of publications showing that improved education, advanced occupational prestige, and higher income are all positively associated with decreased fertility.[64] His data are perhaps best sum-

[64] Okediji, "*Differential fertility.*"

marized in a table from his most recent publication (see Table 9.18).[65] Ohadike, in his 1964 survey of a random sample of Lagos females, examined these same variables, but found lowered fertility to be clearly associated only with the factor of improved education (see Table 9.19). Actually, what Ohadike found was that more education was associated with later age at marriage, and that these two factors together appeared to be associated with decreased fertility. Occupation, type of residence, and several other economic variables examined did not present any clear-cut relationship with fertility. As we have seen in the discussion of Group III variables above, Ohadike also found a positive relationship between longer marriage and higher rates of fertility. To

[65] F. O. Okediji, "Socio-economic Status and Differential Fertility in an African City," *Journal of Developing Areas*, III (April 1969), 339–354.

TABLE 9.18
Mean births per wife, by age and socioeconomic characteristics, three areas of Ibadan

| Socioeconomic Characteristics | Wives in Traditional Areas by Present Age | | | | Wives in Immigrant Areas by Present Age — Hausa | | | | Ibo | | | | Wives in Modern Areas by Present Age | | | |
|---|---|---|---|---|---|---|---|---|---|---|---|---|---|---|---|---|
| | 15–34 | | 35+ | | 15–34 | | 35+ | | 15–34 | | 35+ | | 15–34 | | 35+ | |
| | Number | Mean births | Number | Mean births | Number | Mean births | Number | Mean births | Number | Mean births | Number | Mean births | Number | Mean births | Number | Mean births |
| *Age at marriage* | | | | | | | | | | | | | | | | |
| 15–19 | 210 | 4.8 | 86 | 6.8 | 31 | 4.2 | 22 | 6.4 | 34 | 4.8 | 21 | 6.7 | 6 | 3.8 | 5 | 4.5 |
| 20 & above | 124 | 3.6 | 35 | 5.6 | 10 | 3.5 | 10 | 5.5 | 20 | 3.6 | 11 | 5.7 | 35 | 3.1 | 39 | 3.9 |
| *Education* | | | | | | | | | | | | | | | | |
| University/ professional | — | — | — | — | — | — | — | — | — | — | — | — | 23 | 2.6 | 21 | 4.0 |
| Secondary school | 14 | 4.8 | 8 | 5.7 | — | — | — | — | 13 | 4.6 | 4 | 7.0 | 11 | 3.7 | 11 | 4.1 |
| Primary/ modern | 55 | 5.2 | 18 | 6.1 | — | — | — | — | 21 | 4.7 | 12 | 6.6 | 7 | 4.1 | 9 | 4.3 |
| No schooling but literate | 38 | 5.3 | 21 | 6.5 | — | — | — | — | 11 | 4.8 | 9 | 7.0 | — | — | 3 | 4.6 |
| Arabic education | | | | | 11 | 4.5 | 8 | 6.2 | | | | | | | | |
| Nonliterate | 127 | 5.3 | 74 | 6.8 | 30 | 4.6 | 24 | 6.3 | 10 | 5.0 | 8 | 7.1 | — | — | — | — |
| *Occupation* | | | | | | | | | | | | | | | | |
| Professional/ white-collar | 8 | 4.7 | 9 | 5.7 | — | — | — | — | 11 | 5.0 | 5 | 6.5 | 21 | 2.5 | 21 | 3.7 |
| Skilled worker | 77 | 5.4 | 14 | 6.1 | — | — | — | — | 16 | 5.4 | 9 | 6.4 | 11 | 3.1 | 12 | 3.6 |
| Retail trader | 46 | 5.4 | 21 | 6.3 | — | — | — | — | 13 | 5.4 | 6 | 7.0 | 6 | 3.3 | 8 | 4.0 |
| Petty trader | 203 | 5.4 | 77 | 6.3 | 10 | 5.0 | 9 | 6.6 | 24 | 5.6 | 13 | 6.3 | 3 | 4.0 | 3 | 4.0 |
| Unemployed | — | — | — | — | 31 | 5.1 | 23 | 6.7 | — | — | — | — | — | — | — | — |
| *Income of family* | | | | | | | | | | | | | | | | |
| High (£500 & above) | 19 | 4.4 | 14 | 5.8 | — | — | — | — | 9 | 5.1 | 5 | 6.5 | 28 | 3.1 | 31 | 4.3 |
| Middle (£200–500) | 47 | 5.0 | 18 | 5.5 | 10 | 4.9 | 8 | 6.0 | 18 | 5.3 | 12 | 6.4 | 13 | 3.0 | 13 | 4.1 |
| Low (under £200) | 268 | 5.1 | 89 | 6.3 | 31 | 5.0 | 24 | 6.6 | 27 | 5.7 | 16 | 6.7 | — | — | — | — |
| Total | 334 | 4.6 | 121 | 6.2 | 41 | 4.3 | 32 | 6.1 | 54 | 4.6 | 33 | 6.2 | 41 | 3.3 | 44 | 4.3 |

SOURCE: F. O. Okediji, "Socio-economic Status and Differential Fertility in an African City," *Journal of Developing Areas*, 3 April 1969), pp. 339–354.

TABLE 9.19

Mean births per wife, by age and socioeconomic characteristics, Lagos Federal Territory

| Characteristics | Present Age of Wives | | | | | | |
| | 15–35 | | 35+ | | Total | | |
| | Number of wives | Mean births | Number of wives | Mean births | Number of wives | Mean births | Adjusted mean |
|---|---|---|---|---|---|---|---|
| Total wives | 389 | 2.8 | 207 | 6.1 | 596 | 4.0 | — |
| *Age at marriage* | | | | | | | |
| 10–19 | 216 | 3.1 | 72 | 6.3 | 288 | 3.9 | 4.2 |
| 20+ | 173 | 2.5 | 135 | 6.0 | 308 | 4.0 | 3.7 |
| *Wife's education* | | | | | | | |
| Secondary & over | 69 | 1.8 | 21 | 6.4 | 90 | 3.3 | 3.4 |
| Primary & others | 169 | 2.7 | 54 | 6.2 | 223 | 3.5 | 3.9 |
| None | 151 | 3.3 | 132 | 6.0 | 283 | 4.5 | 4.2 |
| *Husband's education* | | | | | | | |
| Secondary & over | 183 | 2.6 | 77 | 6.1 | 260 | 3.6 | 3.8 |
| Primary & others | 145 | 3.0 | 72 | 6.2 | 217 | 4.0 | 4.1 |
| None | 61 | 3.3 | 58 | 5.9 | 119 | 4.6 | 4.2 |
| *Wife's occupation* | | | | | | | |
| White collar | 55 | 2.1 | 18 | 6.5 | 73 | 3.2 | 3.6 |
| Traders | 97 | 3.4 | 85 | 6.1 | 182 | 4.7 | 4.3 |
| Craftswomen | 17 | 2.7 | 9 | 6.2 | 26 | 3.9 | 3.9 |
| Unskilled | 1 | — | 8 | 6.0 | 9 | 5.3 | 1.8 |
| None | 219 | 2.8 | 87 | 5.9 | 306 | 3.7 | 3.9 |
| *Husband's occupation* | | | | | | | |
| White collar | 202 | 2.6 | 74 | 6.0 | 276 | 3.5 | 3.8 |
| Artisans | 109 | 2.9 | 49 | 6.0 | 158 | 3.9 | 4.0 |
| Traders | 38 | 3.5 | 39 | 6.3 | 77 | 4.9 | 4.5 |
| Unskilled | 33 | 3.1 | 28 | 5.7 | 61 | 4.3 | 4.0 |
| None | 7 | 3.5 | 17 | 6.8 | 24 | 5.8 | 4.6 |
| *Residence* | | | | | | | |
| High | 51 | 2.9 | 29 | 5.8 | 80 | 3.9 | 3.9 |
| Middle | 104 | 2.6 | 54 | 6.7 | 158 | 4.0 | 4.0 |
| Lower | 234 | 2.9 | 24 | 5.9 | 358 | 4.0 | 3.9 |

SOURCE: Ohadike, "A Demographic Note on Marriage, Family and Family Growth in Lagos, Nigeria," p. 383.

quote his own summation of his findings: "Maternal age and marriage duration apart, the one single social trait associated clearly with fertility differences was education, obviously a factor that impedes early marriage."[66]

[66] Ohadike, "A Demographic Note on Marriage," p. 389.

In contrast to these two surveys, we have the several studies by Olusanya in Ibadan, Ife, and Oyo, and from these data Olusanya argues very strongly for a positive relationship between improved education and increased fertility. Part of Olusanya's Ibadan data are summarized in Table 9.20, and from these data Olusanya concludes: "The pattern is so consistent as to leave us with little

TABLE 9.20

Average size of families (to all women who have borne at least one child) by date of marriage and education, Ibadan suburbs

| Date of First Marriage | Education of Wife | | |
|---|---|---|---|
| | None | Primary & higher | All groups |
| Before 1946 | 4.7 | 5.6 | 5.2 |
| 1946–1955 | 3.9 | 4.3 | 4.1 |
| 1956–1965 | 2.1 | 2.3 | 2.2 |
| All dates | 3.3 | 3.4 | 3.3 |

SOURCE: Olusanya, "The Educational Factor in Human Fertility."

doubt that the educated among our survey population tend to be more prolific than their uneducated counterparts."[67] Of his Oyo and Ife data, Olusanya mentions "the tendency for fertility to be directly related to educational status," and he writes, "The differentials are, no doubt, small. Nevertheless, the consistency of the pattern for both towns is rather convincing." His data for Ife and Oyo are summarized in Table 9.21.[68]

In commenting on these three sets of investigations, one might point out first of all

[67] Olusanya, "The Educational Factor in Human Fertility," p. 368.
[68] Olusanya, "Modernization and the Level of Fertility."

TABLE 9.21

Average number of live births per wife at given duration of marriage, by date of first marriage, by education of wife

| | Number of Women | Duration of Marriage (years) | | | | | |
|---|---|---|---|---|---|---|---|
| | | 1 | 2 | 5 | 10 | 15 | 20 |
| Ife: Educated Wives | | | | | | | |
| Date of first marriage | | | | | | | |
| before 1946 | 15 | 0.40 | 0.60 | 1.27 | 2.80 | 4.07 | 4.93 |
| 1946–50 | 48 | 0.69 | 0.83 | 1.63 | 2.92 | 4.00 | — |
| 1951–55 | 93 | 0.73 | 0.92 | 1.87 | 3.42 | — | — |
| 1956–60 | 238 | 0.76 | 0.95 | 2.06 | — | — | — |
| 1961–65 | 379 | 0.79 | — | — | — | — | — |
| Ife: Uneducated Wives | | | | | | | |
| Date of first marriage | | | | | | | |
| before 1946 | 187 | 0.55 | 0.75 | 1.35 | 2.53 | 3.55 | 4.28 |
| 1946–50 | 199 | 0.64 | 0.84 | 1.59 | 2.89 | 3.92 | — |
| 1951–55 | 277 | 0.73 | 0.92 | 1.82 | 3.26 | — | — |
| 1956–60 | 439 | 0.70 | 0.94 | 1.93 | — | — | — |
| 1961–65 | 313 | 0.74 | — | — | — | — | — |
| Oyo: Educated Wives | | | | | | | |
| Date of first marriage | | | | | | | |
| before 1946 | 13 | 0.38 | 0.69 | 1.23 | 2.15 | 3.23 | 4.23 |
| 1946–50 | 26 | 0.54 | 0.92 | 1.88 | 3.08 | 4.19 | — |
| 1951–55 | 43 | 0.58 | 0.79 | 1.70 | 2.93 | — | — |
| 1956–60 | 116 | 0.56 | 0.86 | 1.73 | — | — | — |
| 1961–65 | 171 | 0.71 | — | — | — | — | — |
| Oyo: Uneducated Wives | | | | | | | |
| Date of first marriage | | | | | | | |
| before 1946 | 224 | 0.33 | 0.54 | 1.10 | 2.09 | 3.05 | 3.83 |
| 1946–50 | 192 | 0.39 | 0.61 | 1.24 | 2.31 | 3.25 | — |
| 1951–55 | 330 | 0.52 | 0.74 | 1.50 | 2.65 | — | — |
| 1956–60 | 633 | 0.56 | 0.80 | 1.62 | — | — | — |
| 1961–65 | 362 | 0.61 | — | — | — | — | — |

SOURCE: Olusanya, "Modernization and the Level of Fertility in Western Nigeria."

that Okediji's sample was drawn purposefully from three radically different areas of Ibadan: (1) the traditional central Yoruba area known as "Old Ibadan"; (2) a peripheral immigrant area occupied by Hausas from the north and Ibos from eastern Nigeria; and (3) a planned suburban community occupied by upper-class government officials and professionals. In such a case, the social variables of education, occupation, and income would tend to go together for each group, and any differentials in fertility which might be attributable to one of these social variables (i.e., education) might thus appear in the data analysis to be associated with all (which in general is what Okediji found). Ohadike, on the other hand, worked with a random sample of the entire population of Lagos. That education might thus be related to fertility, whereas occupation and income might not, is entirely consistent with what we know about contemporary Nigerian society. Improved social status and wealth are achieved by many Nigerians—wealthy traders, contractors, or cash-crop farmers—without the benefit of advanced education. What Ohadike and Okediji may have found then, is that education in Ibadan and Lagos is positively related to decreased fertility, while the latter, because of an artifact in his sampling method, also concluded, perhaps erroneously, that occupation and income were similarly related. Based on presently available data, one would hesitate to say that this latter was necessarily the case.

We now come to the difficult task of relating Olusanya's data to those of Ohadike and Okediji. It may be that Olusanya himself has given us the key. In the concluding paragraph of one of his monographs, he writes, "The apparent rise in fertility . . . may well be a temporary phenomenon and is probably a prelude to the emergence of an inverse association of socioeconomic status with reproduction leading eventually to an actual decline in overall fertility, in this society."[69] Quite possibly Ife and Oyo are somewhat less advanced on the urbanization scale than are Ibadan and Lagos, and the educated groups

in these two towns may be undergoing a period of increased fertility previously experienced by the educated groups in Lagos and Ibadan but now no longer in effect. Nor do Olusanya's Ibadan data necessarily refute this proposition. Olusanya's Ibadan sample consisted of two communities: (1) an atypical peripheral community predominantly Yoruba but with about two-fifths of its population comprising representatives of numerous other immigrant tribes, and (2) the same upper-class suburban community surveyed by Okediji. In his data analysis, Olusanya lumped these two samples together and it may be that his findings reflect a mixture biased by certain peculiarities of the large number of immigrant groups.

Perhaps the most important difference between Olusanya's approach and that of Ohadike and Okediji is that the former measured fertility by marriage duration and not age, thus making it difficult, or impossible, to corroborate Ohadike's finding that the mechanism for reducing fertility among educated females is later age at marriage. It is quite possible that such deferred marriage could reduce cumulated fertility, at least in the younger age groups, while, at the same time, giving rise to somewhat higher fertility rates by marriage duration.

One is tempted, therefore, to accept the findings of Ohadike and Okediji in this regard, and say that, at the present time in Ibadan and Lagos (but not necessarily in Oyo, Ife, or the other smaller Nigerian towns) education per se is having a negative effect on fertility. Summarizing Ohadike's findings, we find that Lagos wives with primary or modern school education and those with no schooling at all were 14.7 and 23.5 percent more fertile, respectively, than women with a secondary education and above, and that women with no education at all were 7.7 percent more fertile than women with a primary or modern school education.[70]

Numerous questions remain. What we have, presumably, is a good random sample survey of Lagos showing that education is

[69] *Ibid.*

[70] Ohadike, "A Demographic Note on Marriage," p. 390.

related to decreased fertility and two presumably equally good random sample surveys of Oyo and Ife showing at least by marriage duration, the opposite. Granted that Lagos is unique and not typical of other Nigerian towns, one then is forced to ask how accurate Olusanya's findings may be. Are they to be generalized to the other smaller Yoruba towns? Are they to be generalized to other urban areas elsewhere in Nigeria? Are they, as Olusanya suggests, short-run effects, or are they likely to last a long time? Obviously these are all subjects for further intensive research, and future demographic studies are to be recommended in this direction.

Unfortunately, we do not have a comparable random sample survey of Ibadan. Perhaps the mind of the methodologist boggles at the prospect of this huge, sprawling labyrinth of alleys, byways, tin roofs, and uncounted people. Olusanya, as previously noted, based his findings on a study of two atypical areas only. Okediji, after confronting the minotaur and drawing out a sample from the central maze of Ibadan, was then plagued by a high percentage of interview refusals, a factor he has never sufficiently analyzed for us in any of his publications. It would be good, now, if one of our researchers addressed himself anew to this problem of an Ibadan random sample, so that we would have data directly comparable with those of Oyo, Ife, and Lagos.

A further primary question is one raised by Olusanya himself: If education is positively related to increased fertility in the smaller Yoruba towns, and possibly in the other more distant urban areas of Nigeria as well, is this a short-run phenomenon only and what are its causes? Olusanya has produced a most interesting monograph on this subject, which is especially commended to the reader ("Modernisation and the Level of Fertility in Western Nigeria," see footnote 35). In this paper, Olusanya argues that our Group IV variables (improved socioeconomic and sociomedical conditions) operate not only on Group II variables alone, as is widely supposed (i.e., contribute to reduced mortality associated with childbirth), but also

act directly on Group I variables (i.e., produce an actual increase in fertility per woman). The reasons he gives may be summarized as follows:

(1) Improved school education and association with modern medicine act together to weaken the traditional lactation taboo, thus decreasing the interval between pregnancies and increasing the actual number of pregnancies per woman.

(2) Improved public health measures, such as malaria control and environmental sanitation, have been shown in a number of countries to produce not only a reduction in infant and maternal mortality but also an actual increase in fertility per woman; quoting Hertzler, he attributes this "to increased vitality, which [makes] for greater likelihood of conception and births."[71]

(3) The prevalence of certain diseases, as well as a generalized gross inadequacy of medical services, may produce infertility in some women,[72] and also a negative attitude toward childbirth; improved medical facilities as well as a rising standard of living may act together to reverse these tendencies.

(4) To quote Olusanya directly, "With the diffusion of middle-class culture to the lower class, both educated and uneducated mothers have increasingly resorted to bottle-feeding so that the belief in the relationships between sex, mother's milk, and the child's illness or death no longer holds"; this also

[71] J. O. Hertzler, *The Crisis in World Population* (Lincoln, Neb.: University of Nebraska Press, 1956), pp. 46–47.
[72] The relationship between extensive infertility in traditional Central African rural areas, and various diseases, including in particular venereal disease, has been examined in a provocative monograph by A. Romaniuk, "Infertility in Tropical Africa," in Caldwell and Okonjo, *Population of Tropical Africa*, pp. 214–24. Unfortunately we have little quantitative data on the prevalence of venereal disease in rural Nigeria. Some anthropologists have commented on the existence of prostitution as an important institution in traditional rural societies. See, for example, S. F. Nadel, *Nupe Religion*, in which he describes, sometimes with poetic fervor, the role of prostitutes among the Nupe of northern Nigeria. It is interesting to speculate on the possible relationship between increased fertility in the urban areas, and a reduction in venereal disease due to improved medical research. This, too, is a recommended subject for further research.

leads to a decline in the lactation taboo and shorter pregnancy intervals.

(5) Further evidence that this increase in fertility is related to the progressive "modernization" and "urbanization" processes at work in Nigeria today is derived from the observed "consistent increases in mean live births from the oldest down to the most recent marriage cohort examined" (see data in Table 9.21).

Olusanya might have added, as point (6) to all this, that improved socioeconomic and sociomedical status produce, initally at least, the awareness that a family can raise and support more children.

The reader might ask, at this point, to what extent education has gained a foothold in Nigeria. Data on the extent of education of males and females in the various surveys reported are given in Table 9.22. The majority of persons with "no schooling" undoubtedly belong to the older age groups, in each of the areas surveyed, and to an increasing extent the majority of Nigerian children are gaining access to at least a few years of free primary education. Most secondary education is fee paying, however, and few Nigerians attain this level even in Lagos.

Summarizing the high priority placed on education throughout Nigeria, Yesufu wrote in 1966:

The importance of education for Nigeria's development . . . has received special attention in

the last few years . . . . The result is that, today, education constitutes the greatest single "industry" in Nigeria (excluding agriculture) accounting for 113,297 of our 530,167 employed persons covered in the National Manpower Board Survey of 1963. This importance is reflected in the Development Plan 1962–1968, in which £69.8 million, or 10.3 percent of all expenditure under the Plan, is earmarked for education . . . . In Northern Nigeria, for example, the Plan makes provision for an annual primary school enrollment of 720,000 new pupils by 1968, as compared with the 1962 level of 259,934.[73]

Contrary to reports in the popular press, the Ibos of eastern Nigeria are not the only persons in Nigeria with high attendance rates at school, as the above figures demonstrate. This writer concluded, on the basis of investigations carried out in 1962–1963, that because of various artifacts of geography and politics, the Ibos, at that time, did not have as high a proportion of children enrolled in primary schools as did the Yorubas or several other tribal groups in southern Nigeria.[74] For Nigeria as a whole, it can be said that a school education in the modern sense is one of the highest social values, as well as one of the highest political priorities. "The Nigerian masses have a faith in education to improve their lot," wrote Pendleton Herring. "It is

[73] T. M. Yesufu, "The Politics and Economics of Nigeria's Population Census," in Caldwell and Okonjo, *Population of Tropical Africa*, p. 113.
[74] Morgan, "Medical Students in Nigeria," p. 33.

TABLE 9.22
Educational levels, Nigerian surveys

| Educational Level | Katsina Province (percentage distributions) M | F | Oyo M | F | Ife M | F | Ibadan M | F | Lagos M | F |
|---|---|---|---|---|---|---|---|---|---|---|
| No schooling | 55.3 | 80.0 | 71.0 | 92.0 | 46.0 | 63.0 | — | 70.7 | 23.1 | 58.0 |
| Primary only | 43.6 | 19.2 | 29.0 | 8.0 | 54.0 | 37.0 | — 29.3 | | 53.1 | 29.2 |
| Secondary + above | 1.1 | 0.0 | | | | | | | 23.8 | 12.8 |

SOURCES: Katsina Province—T. Daramola and R. D. Wright, "Attitudes Toward Family Planning in Lagos, Nigeria," Department of Community Health (Lagos, 1968); Oyo and Ife—Olusanya, "Modernization and the Level of Fertility in Western Nigeria"; Ibadan—Okediji, "Differential Fertility in Ibadan City," data for traditional or "Old Ibadan" area; Lagos—Morgan, Lagos Population Dynamics Survey.

said that every mother feels her child must have an elementary education."[75]

It has already been demonstrated by our researchers that this increase in education has had a profound effect on increased Nigerian fertility, because of its action in reducing the lactation taboo and the pregnancy interval. We also have evidence that, for the more educated groups in the larger cities of Lagos and Ibadan, a countertrend and some reduction in fertility is now being recorded. One is tempted to say, on the basis of present evidence, that, for the immediate future, the impact of education in Nigeria is going to be one of continued increased fertility; when, and if, a countertrend toward reduced fertility might be experienced in the population at large, as education becomes further diffused throughout the country, is a question for further research.

One additional social variable which should be examined in this section is religion. Ohadike, on the basis of his Lagos data, concluded that:

Moslem and traditional worshippers, with an average of 4.2 children ever born, appeared to be some 10.5 percent more fertile than Christians with an average of 3.8 . . . . Catholics were slightly lower than Protestants and far lower than Moslems. But whatever the differences, the degree of association between fertility and religious affiliation was not statistically significant, and the differences appeared to be smoothed out when averages were standardized by maternal age.[76]

Unfortunately, most of our data on religion relate to the southwestern Yoruba area, where significant differences have not been observed. What the pattern might be in the strongly Moslem areas of northern Nigeria, or the more predominantly Christian areas of eastern Nigeria, are also questions for further research.

## GROUP V VARIABLES: FAMILY PLANNING KNOWLEDGE, ATTITUDES, AND PRACTICE

Henry Ford is supposed to have said, "History is bunk," and sometimes this writer is inclined to feel the same way about the "attitude" portions, and perhaps even the "knowledge" portions, of some of the family planning KAP surveys done in the developing world.

In the realm of "knowledge," the dimensions of the problem may be suggested from the following. Certainly the traditional period of abstinence for several years following childbirth constitutes one form of pregnancy control or "family planning"; Olusanya, for example, refers to traditional abstinence as a form of "birth control" or "family planning"[77] and certainly the overwhelming majority of persons born and raised in tropical Africa must be familiar with this ancient and prevalent technique. One survey of Lagos females went so far as to assume that *all* respondents were familiar not only with traditional abstinence but also with abortion, and interviews were aimed rather at finding out how much they knew.[78] And yet, we find most KAP surveys done in tropical Africa reporting only about half the respondents as having "knowledge of a specific method" of pregnancy control.[79] In some studies, the figure falls to less than 10 percent. Apparently, the research situation in these cases was structured incorrectly, and the questions, to put it briefly, were being asked wrongly.

Or is it possible, in metropolitan Lagos where condoms are sold in chemist shops, that a large proportion of men (and women, too, for that matter) do not know what a condom is? If you ask the average man in Lagos, "What is a condom?" he will say he does not know. But if you show him a condom,

[75] Pendleton Herring, "The Future of Democracy in Nigeria," in R. O. Tillman and Taylor Cole, eds., *The Nigerian Political Scene* (Durham, N.C., 1962), p. 258.
[76] Ohadike, "A Demographic Note on Marriage," p. 390. A good deal of comparative data relating to religion pertains to the KAP material which is reviewed in a later section of this chapter.

[77] P. O. Olusanya, "Nigeria: Cultural Barriers to Family Planning Among the Yorubas," *Studies in Family Planning*, XXXVII (January 1969), 13–16.
[78] Daramola and Wright, "Attitudes Toward Family Planning in Lagos."
[79] Caldwell, "Control of Family Size in Tropical Africa," p. 607.

he will say, "Oh, that is a Durex" (using one of the local trade names) and proceed to tell you for what it is used. Research shows that about three-fifths of the men and about one-third of the women in Lagos Metropolitan Area fall into this category.[80] And yet we have KAP surveys carried out in Lagos reporting knowledge of the condom to be as low as 1 percent!

With respect to "attitude" questions, the problem is more subtle and more acute. To cite one minor example: During the pilot phase of our 1968 KAP survey in Lagos, we included a standard set of questions about "the *best* number of children to have?" The interview schedule was subsequently translated into Yoruba and put to work in the field. After some days, we reconvened in the office and asked the interviewers to translate the questions back into English. The above question came back, "What is the *proper* number of children to have?" Clearly, this is not what we wanted to find out, and after a period of trauma in the office, we managed to locate a Yoruba word with a meaning closer to "desirable" rather than "proper." This was one disaster we probably managed to avert, but how many others escaped our notice?

One researcher, Pradervand, whose work has been focused on the francophone areas of North Africa, has gone so far as to say that it is usually *not possible* to conduct Western-type "attitude surveys" in traditional societies, and therefore data so derived are of the most dubious value.[81] It would be an injustice to Pradervand to attempt to summarize his hundred-page document in a single paragraph, but one of his arguments is that, in traditional society, conversation is regarded as a cultural game which, when played in isolation from the actual event under discussion (i.e., when played in the interviewer-respondent setting which we recognize in the Western sense), does not require of the player the intellectual exercise involved in

relating his or her words to an actual situation; in fact, to do so may violate the rules of the game! Medical research carried out in conjunction with our Lagos Population Dynamics Survey has shown time and again that stated attitudes may have no relationship *at all* to actual medical behavior.[82]

With these words of caution before us, how are we to approach the KAP data for Nigeria? The answer would seem to be, with caution and a measure of scepticism. One could add that, in these vitally important areas, the personal impressions of key informants might also be taken into account. A second step would be to make as rigorous a distinction as possible between knowledge and attitudes relative to "traditional" contraceptive methods (i.e., abstinence, abortion, native medicine, some forms of surgery, and withdrawal) and "modern" methods (the diaphragm, condom, pill, IUD, foams and similar preparations, injections and implants, tubal ligations and vasectomies, and probably also the safe period or rhythm method). Most respondents would be expected to know about the former, but not about the latter.

A third step, which for better or worse has been adopted, has been to deal with the "knowledge" and "practice" portions of the data concurrently, and to discuss the "attitude" data separately. One tends to accept data on "practice" with a greater measure of assurance than that on "knowledge" and "attitude," partly because practice relates to actual events and can be partially tested against observed reality.

The use of traditional family planning methods among the Yoruba has been documented by Olusanya,[83] who mentions the following: (1) abstinence after a childbirth ("traditionally . . . the main method of birth control"); (2) abortifacients (four preparations are mentioned, which are administered by native doctors; these include three mixtures taken internally depending on the stage

[80] R. W. Morgan, family planning KAP survey, 1968.
[81] Pierre Pradervand, "Quelques Remarques Critiques sur la Methodologie des Enquêtes 'C.A.P.' dans le Tiers Monde," private memorandum, June 1969.
[82] For example, data on the relationship between attitudes toward smallpox and measles vaccination and actual vaccination behavior, where a wide divergence was found, are being analyzed for separate publication.
[83] Olusanya, "Nigeria: Cultural Barriers to Family Planning Among the Yorubas."

of the pregnancy, and a suppository);[84] (3) contraceptive devices or mixtures (three are mentioned, which are prepared and administered by native doctors; these include an iron ring worn on the woman's finger or a leather belt "stuffed with charms," either to be worn during intercourse, and a salt water mixture to be taken immediately after intercourse; (4) withdrawal (for which the Yorubas have a word, *adaye*).

Two Lagos surveys (Ohadike, 1964; Morgan, 1968) produced mention of either a surgical or more probably a traditional technique called "womb displacement" or "turning of the womb." Unfortunately the interviews did not bring out clearly whether this was regarded as a product of modern clinical medicine or not; probably it was so regarded, and perhaps the idea has arisen from reports of hysterectomies or tubal ligations done in Lagos hospitals. None of the researchers either rural or urban, appear to have asked about castration, although it is likely that a number of respondents would have been familiar with this ancient surgical procedure. Fortunately, in the most ambitious KAP survey in Nigeria (actually a knowledge and practice survey), carried out by Caldwell and Igun among 8,400 respondents in 22 urban and rural locations in the country in 1969, a distinction was made between traditional and modern methods.[85] Similar (though not identical) distributions were made in two of the Lagos KAP surveys, the 1965 Daramola and Wright study in a random sample of 642 mothers in Surulere, and this writer's 1968 survey of 1,565 males and females in the metropolitan random sample.

Caldwell and Igun sought to show, among other things, the relationship between contraceptive knowledge and practice, on the one hand, and geography and chronology in Nigeria. It was suspected that changes in contraceptive behavior would be related inversely to distance from the coast. A 500-mile strip of country was selected extending from Lagos on the southwestern coast to Kano in the far north, and including sections of Lagos, Western, Kwara, and Kano states. Ten urban and twelve rural gross sample areas were selected purposefully, on the basis of geographical and socioeconomic criteria (see Table 9.23), after which the gross areas were subdivided into smaller blocks and random selections made. All resident Nigerians over 15 years of age were interviewed in successive blocks until a quota of 200 males and 200 females was achieved in each of the 22 areas.

Some of the major results of the Caldwell and Igun survey are shown in Tables 9.24–9.27. Inspection of Table 9.24 shows that the authors have successfully demonstrated a relationship between knowledge and practice of contraception, on the one hand, and (a) nearness to the coast, (b) urban as opposed to rural residence, and (c) improved socioeconomic status. These relationships seem to apply to some extent to traditional as well as modern techniques.[86] The authors note that the data show "little change (perhaps only because of the small numbers involved) from predominantly cash-cropping areas to areas of mainly subsistence agriculture."

[84] The mixtures are described by Olusanya as follows: (a) for a pregnacy not more than one month old, potash and lime juice taken three times daily for three days; or (b) cactus juice and fresh eggs taken repeatedly; (c) for a pregnancy two months old or more, the first mixture described reinforced with blue dye and local gin.

The suppository is made from leaves, seeds, and juices of local trees to form a paste, which is formed into small balls and inserted into the vagina.

[85] John C. Caldwell and Adenola Igun, "The Spread of Anti-natal Knowledge and Practice in Nigeria," *Population Studies*, XXIV, I (March 1970), 213–34.

[86] Variations in the data pattern which may be observed in the "southern urban-richer" category might be explained in terms of the sociology of Nigerian cities. In Ibadan, Ife, and Ilorin, the "rich" areas tend to be more uniformly "rich" than the "rich" areas of Lagos. In the former three cities, as in most other growing Nigerian urban areas, elite families tend to live in defined and specially built high-income estates or reservations; in Lagos, on the other hand, with the exception of Ikoyi, Apapa, and a few other small areas, all parts of the city are much more heterogeneous, including the so-called high-income areas. This heterogeneity might well have depressed the figures in the "metropolitan-richer" category in Table 9.2 vis-à-vis the "southern urban-richer" figures.

TABLE 9.23

Twenty-two survey areas, Caldwell-Igun KAP study, 1969

| | | | Socioeconomic Divisions | | | |
| | | | Cash farming more important | | Cash farming less important | |
| Areas | Richer | Poorer | largest center over 1,000 | largest center under 1,000 | largest center over 1,000 | largest center under 1,000 |
|---|---|---|---|---|---|---|
| Metropolitan (Lagos) | 1 | 1 | — | — | — | — |
| Southern urban (Ibadan, Ife, Ilorin) | 3 | 3 | — | — | — | — |
| Northern urban (Kano) | 1 | 1 | — | — | — | — |
| Southern rural (Western, Kwara states) | — | — | 2 | 2 | 2 | 2[a] |
| Northern rural (Kano state) | — | — | 1 | 1[b] | 1 | 1 |

[a] One male survey omitted.
[b] One female survey omitted.

TABLE 9.24

Distribution of contraceptive knowledge and practice by major survey subdivisions, Caldwell-Igun (responses given as percentage of all respondents in subdivision)

| | | Responses (responses given as percentages of all respondents in subdivision) | | | | | | | | |
| Sex | Subdivision | Knows a method of traditional contraception[a] | Knows of traditional abortion[b] | Knows of modern (introduced) contraception[c] | Knows of medical abortion[d] | Has practiced traditional contraception | Has practiced abortion (or partner has) | Has practiced modern (introduced) contraception | Has practiced medical abortion (or partner has) | Number of respondents in subdivision |
|---|---|---|---|---|---|---|---|---|---|---|
| Male | Metropolitan—richer | 24 | 16 | 77 | 75 | 4 | 1 | 42 | 7 | 200 |
| | Southern urban—richer | 22 | 31 | 70 | 61 | 5 | 1 | 22 | 3 | 600 |
| | Metropolitan—poorer | 15 | 8 | 63 | 73 | 2 | 0 | 5 | 0 | 200 |
| | Southern urban—poorer | 14 | 6 | 25 | 27 | 2 | 1 | 6 | 1 | 600 |
| | Northern urban | 11 | 1 | 34 | 20 | 1 | 0 (0.3) | 1 | 1 | 400 |
| | Southern rural | 5 | 8 | 15 | 20 | 1 | 1 | 1 | 1 | 1,400 |
| | Northern rural | 1 | 1 | 7 | 5 | 0 | 0 | 0 (0.4) | 0 | 800 |
| | All male respondents | 10 | 9 | 30 | 29 | 2 | 1 | 7 | 1 | 4,200 |
| Female | Metropolitan—richer | 12 | 13 | 70 | 34 | 4 | 3 | 18 | 4 | 200 |
| | Southern urban—richer | 9 | 29 | 78 | 52 | 0 | 0 | 12 | 0 (0.2) | 600 |
| | Metropolitan—poorer | 12 | 5 | 60 | 25 | 1 | 0 | 7 | 5 | 200 |
| | Southern urban—poorer | 4 | 2 | 33 | 20 | 0 | 0 | 2 | 0 | 600 |
| | Northern urban | 4 | 13 | 11 | 12 | 0 (0.3) | 1 | 1 | 0 (0.3) | 400 |
| | Southern rural | 3 | 2 | 7 | 5 | 0 (0.4) | 0 (0.3) | 0 (0.4) | 0 (0.4) | 1,600 |
| | Northern rural | 2 | 3 | 3 | 3 | 0 (0.2) | 0 (0.2) | 0 | 0 | 600 |
| | All female respondents | 5 | 8 | 26 | 16 | 0 (0.4) | 0 (0.3) | 3 | 1 | 4,200 |

[a] Includes all "natural" methods (including *coitus interruptus* and rhythm methods).
[d] Includes mechanically induced abortion by persons without medical training.
[c] Appliance, chemical or oral methods.
[b] By medically trained persons.

From Table 9.24, they conclude:

The use of modern contraceptives in the towns (and most clearly amongst the better-off), is inversely related to the distance from Lagos, by far the most "modern" and cosmopolitan city of Nigeria, and not to population size. This is not merely a measure of the impact of Lagos, but of the diffusion of external influences and cultural change which have long flowed from the coast, and predominantly from Lagos, up country.[87]

Table 9.25 demonstrates the relationship between knowledge and practice of modern contraception, and educational levels as well as urban-rural residence. In analyzing these and other differential response patterns, the authors comment on the wide divergences between reported knowledge and practice as follows (italics theirs):

A comparison of the extent of contraceptive *practice* amongst those with the necessary *knowledge* is illuminating. The fraction recorded is less

[87] *Ibid.*, pp. 22–24.

TABLE 9.25
Respondents having knowledge of modern contraception and ever having practiced it, by urban-rural and educational divisions, Caldwell-Igun survey

| Residence | (Percentage of respondents in each subdivision) | | | |
|---|---|---|---|---|
| | Knowledge of Contraception | | Ever Practiced Contraception | |
| | Schooling | No schooling | Schooling | No schooling |
| Metropolitan Lagos | 71 | 47 | 22 | 10 |
| Southern urban (Ibadan, Ife, Ilorin) | 67 | 16 | 14 | 2 |
| Northern urban (Kano) | 31 | 12 | 1.3[a] | 0.7[a] |
| Rural (combined figures) | 40 | 7 | 1.9[a] | 0.04[a] |

[a] Figures not expressed to nearest whole percentage for levels under 2 percent.

than one-twentieth amongst both urban and rural populations in the North and amongst farmers everywhere. In the North this is partly a measure of the extent to which such actions are still alien to the *mores* of the savanna peoples, living in relatively unchanged societies, and partly of some Moslem resistance to what are regarded as non-Moslem influences. The figure for farmers reflects the fact that they feel little need to restrict family size . . . . Very different is the position of the urban upper classes, where children can only be assured of retaining their socioeconomic position if savings are concentrated on the education of a few; two-sevenths of those with the necessary knowledge in this group had practiced contraception.[88]

Table 9.26 presents cohort analyses, based on retrospective data gathered during the interviews, of first knowledge and practice of modern contraception by age and parity of the respondents. To the extent that the memories of respondents were accurate and the interviewers sufficiently patient, these data on a relatively small percentage of all respondents suggest a substantial increase in access to contraceptive knowledge over the past two decades, and, once knowledge is obtained, the extensive practice of contraception at low parities and even among the childless.

Table 9.27 gives reported sources of information on contraception, as well as the importance of friends and relatives of both sexes and also, perhaps surprisingly, of the mass media being borne out here.

In commenting on this very important survey, one is inclined to make the following perhaps too broad observations: (1) Qualitatively, the *direction* of the findings, suggesting higher levels of contraceptive knowledge and practice among the more urban and better educated, would seem to be valid and entirely consistent with data from other surveys, including the various attitude surveys to be reported upon below. (2) Quantitatively, the *rural data* are most revealing and, with the exception of Olusanya's study of five villages near Ibadan, to be discussed presently, constitute what must be our first such data

[88] *Ibid.*, pp. 26–27.

TABLE 9.26
First knowledge and practice of modern contraception, by age and parity, subdivided by age at survey, Caldwell-Igun data (in numbers of respondents)

(a) Age at First Knowledge and Practice

| Sex | Age at Event | First Knowledge[a] | | | | First Practice[a] | | | |
|---|---|---|---|---|---|---|---|---|---|
| | | 10–19 | 20–29 | 30–39 | 40+ | 10–19 | 20–29 | 30–39 | 40+ |
| Males | 10–19 | 173 | 204 | 33 | 6 | 30 | 18 | 3 | 0 |
| | 20–29 | | 370 | 179 | 15 | | 105 | 28 | 5 |
| | 30–39 | | | 108 | 76 | | | 19 | 20 |
| | 40+ | | | | 103 | | | | 19 |
| Females | 10–19 | 208 | 213 | 7 | 4 | 25 | 6 | 0 | 1 |
| | 20–29 | | 260 | 69 | 8 | | 50 | 33 | 6 |
| | 30–39 | | | 87 | 20 | | | 17 | 2 |
| | 40+ | | | | 58 | | | | 3 |

(b) Parity at First Knowledge and Practice

| Sex | Parity at Event | First Knowledge[a] | | | | First Practice[a] | | | |
|---|---|---|---|---|---|---|---|---|---|
| | | 10–19 | 20–29 | 30–39 | 40+ | 10–19 | 20–29 | 30–39 | 40+ |
| Males | 0 | 159 | 500 | 161 | 49 | 21 | 113 | 27 | 14 |
| | 1–2 | 1 | 78 | 84 | 25 | | 21 | 13 | 7 |
| | 3–4 | | 4 | 50 | 61 | | 1 | 7 | 8 |
| | 5–6 | | 1 | 16 | 42 | | | 2 | 7 |
| | 7+ | | 1 | 7 | 33 | | | | 5 |
| Fema es | 0 | 197 | 289 | 47 | 4 | 24 | 30 | 13 | 5 |
| | 1–2 | 23 | 158 | 40 | 14 | | 21 | 13 | 2 |
| | 3–4 | 15 | 48 | 55 | 22 | | 6 | 15 | 3 |
| | 5–6 | | 3 | 20 | 22 | | 1 | 7 | 2 |
| | 7+ | | | 2 | 14 | | | | 1 |

NOTES: A few respondents have been omitted in the parity table because of the difficulty of establishing the correct parity.
[a] Numbers in these column headings indicate respondents' ages at time of survey.

for Nigeria. The figures in Table 9.24, the authors point out, "may be compared with a figure of 4 percent reported as the proportion of females ever having practiced contraception in rural Ghana."[89] (3) The *urban data* with respect to modern contraceptives are gratifyingly consistent with earlier Nigerian surveys. Comparing the "metropolitan-poorer" figures in Table 9.24, for example, with Morgan's data for the former Lagos Federal Territory (see Table 9.29), one finds reported levels of knowledge to be 63 percent as opposed to 68.1 percent for males, 60 percent as opposed to 55.6 percent for females; and reported levels of use to be 5 percent as

[89] The reference cited is the work of D. I. Pool.

opposed to 22.8 percent for males,[90] 7 percent as opposed to 9.6 percent for females. Considering the different sampling methods used and the problems of methodology involved, these figures would seem to be remarkably

[90] The difference in the figures for males here may perhaps be traced to a slight difference in definitions. Caldwell and Igun defined the rhythm method as traditional; Morgan defined this method as modern. In the latter survey, 7.4 percent of males reported use of this method. More likely, however, Morgan's figure was higher because 17.8 percent of males reported use of the condom, and were shown a condom at the time of the survey (see Table 9.28). It might also be mentioned here that Morgan's random sample data are perhaps best compared with the Caldwell-Igun "metropolitan-poorer" data, since the "metropolitan-richer" segment of the Lagos population is so small.

TABLE 9.27

First source of information about fertility restriction, by urban-rural residence and sex, Caldwell-Igun data

(Percentage of respondents in each group)

| Information,[a] by Residence and Sex | Relatives M | Relatives F | Friends M | Friends F | Medical[b] | Paramedical[c] | Media[d] | Residual Responses | All Responses |
|---|---|---|---|---|---|---|---|---|---|
| **(1) Knowledge that fertility can be restricted:** | | | | | | | | | |
| Urban males (1,128) | 9 | 4 | 39 | 3 | 10 | 1 | 29 | 5 | 100 |
| females (975) | 3 | 8 | 1 | 44 | 12 | 6 | 20 | 6 | 100 |
| Rural males (429) | 8 | 1 | 54 | 2 | 2 | 3 | 23 | 7 | 100 |
| females (278) | 20 | 29 | 0 | 26 | 4 | 2 | 11 | 8 | 100 |
| **(2) Learning about traditional contraception:** | | | | | | | | | |
| Urban males (337) | 10 | 4 | 61 | 17 | 2 | 3 | 1 | 2 | 100 |
| females (138) | 6 | 21 | 10 | 57 | 3 | 3 | 0 | 0 | 100 |
| Rural males (80) | 10 | 3 | 71 | 2 | 2 | 5 | 7 | 0 | 100 |
| females (59) | 8 | 28 | 13 | 48 | 3 | 0 | 0 | 0 | 100 |
| **(3) Learning about traditional abortion:** | | | | | | | | | |
| Urban males (273) | 7 | 4 | 66 | 12 | 1 | 2 | 6 | 2 | 100 |
| females (273) | 3 | 13 | 4 | 73 | 2 | 3 | 1 | 1 | 100 |
| Rural males (124) | 7 | 1 | 73 | 1 | 1 | 8 | 9 | 0 | 100 |
| females (48) | 11 | 24 | 23 | 38 | 4 | 0 | 0 | 0 | 100 |
| **(4) Learning about modern contraception:** | | | | | | | | | |
| Urban males (982) | 4 | 4 | 37 | 7 | 8 | 8 | 27 | 5 | 100 |
| females (968) | 2 | 6 | 6 | 41 | 12 | 8 | 23 | 2 | 100 |
| Rural males (271) | 4 | 3 | 53 | 2 | 3 | 0 | 34 | 1 | 100 |
| females (130) | 6 | 8 | 20 | 23 | 6 | 6 | 30 | 1 | 100 |
| **(5) Learning about medical abortion:** | | | | | | | | | |
| Urban males (902) | 5 | 8 | 39 | 7 | 10 | 5 | 21 | 5 | 100 |
| females (597) | 3 | 7 | 6 | 51 | 8 | 8 | 15 | 2 | 100 |
| Rural males (315) | 10 | 4 | 35 | 7 | 3 | 2 | 37 | 2 | 100 |
| females (93) | 8 | 24 | 5 | 23 | 15 | 1 | 10 | 14 | 100 |

[a] Definitions as in Table 9.24. Numbers in brackets are those of all respondents having such information (i.e., the numbers shown as percentages in Table 9.24).
[b] Doctors, nurses, health and family planning workers, and pharmacists.
[c] Midwives and herbalists.
[d] Newspapers, magazines, radio, cinema, television, books.

consistent. The authors also note a similar compatibility with the findings of Okediji and Olusanya in Ibadan and Ife. (4) With respect to *traditional methods*, the Caldwell and Igun data appear at first glance to be entirely unsatisfactory. In line with the polemical argument presented at the beginning of this section, knowledge of traditional contraception should be high in most areas of West Africa, and might well verge on 100 percent. The much lower figures reported in Table 9.24 in this category, ranging from 1–24 percent, must therefore be questioned, and by extension one must also question the practice figures, which are in the very low range of 0–4 percent. Morgan reported much higher figures for Lagos in these categories (see Table 9.29). It may be that the Caldwell and Igun interviewers excluded abstinence after a childbirth from their list of traditional methods; if so, the residual figures would come more closely into line with Morgan's figures for native medicines, withdrawal, and abortion (see Table 9.28). Given this method-ological ambiguity in the Caldwell and Igun material, one hesitates to accept such interesting assertions by the authors as their finding, based on Table 9.24, that "by far the greatest knowledge of traditional methods is in the metropolis (Lagos) and southern towns, especially amongst the middle and upper classes." What they have probably found is that the use of *coitus interruptus* is greater or has increased among these groups, a finding also suggested in the Morgan data (see below). Regrettably the Caldwell and Igun data shed no light on trends in the use of traditional abstinence anywhere in Nigeria, a factor of critical importance to the main argument of this chapter. (5) The survey demonstrates the strengths and weaknesses of the stratified sample, at least with respect to the fertility surveys being reported upon here. If the demographic data reviewed earlier in this chapter are at all accurate, then present fertility in Nigeria is highest in the very urban areas where Caldwell and Igun report the highest incidence of contraceptive prac-tice. The explanation of this apparent paradox, of course, is found in the shortened pregnancy interval in the cities today, such that the slightly increased levels of contra-ceptive practice in these areas are insufficient to offset the substantially increased frequencies of pregnancies and births. The trouble with stratified sample surveys is that they tend to tell us what we want to hear; and while this type of research does bring different aspects of the overall picture into focus, an adequate synthesis of the whole normally can be achieved only through random sample sur-veys of the overall population.

In the Lagos Metropolitan Area, there are two surveys in which a distinction was made between traditional and modern contra-ceptive techniques: the 1965 Daramola and Wright survey of a random sample of 642 mothers in Surulere, and this writer's 1968 survey of males over 20 years of age and females aged 15–49 in a random sample of 1,565 respondents in the Metropolitan Area. Results are summarized in Table 9.28, and the astonishing similarity between the pro-portions of female respondents in the two surveys who have "heard of," as well as "have used," the various methods, both modern and traditional, will strike the reader at once. The proportions are almost identical in many of the categories.

Since most of Surulere is a recently developed residential community, partly for families resettled from Lagos Island slums into planned housing areas, and partly for middle- and upper-class business and pro-fessional persons in new, good quality housing units, the suburb is significantly different in character and, on the whole, of a higher socioeconomic status than almost any other section of the Lagos Metropolitan Area. The results of the two surveys done three years apart may thus indicate some increase in contraceptive awareness in the urban popu-lation as a whole during this period (i.e., the lower socioeconomic portions of the city may have moved in the three-year interval to the awareness level of the upper socioeconomic section in the earlier survey). This would conform with what we know of actual events. Beginning in late 1966 and continuing through 1967, a family planning educational program was initiated at several pediatric clinics and birth registration centers in the city, as one component of the Lagos Family Health Project, an activity of the Department of Community Health of the University of Lagos College of Medicine, which also carried out the 1967–1968 demographic and family planning surveys already cited. The number of family planning clinics in the Metro-politan Area also was increased from four to ten during this period, five new clinics being opened by the Family Planning Council of Nigeria, a voluntary agency, and a research and training clinic being opened by the

TABLE 9.28

Percentage of respondents having heard of, and having used, specific methods of contraception, two Lagos surveys

| | Surulere, Random Sample, 1965 | | Lagos Metropolitan Area Random Sample, 1968 | | | | | | | | |
|---|---|---|---|---|---|---|---|---|---|---|---|
| | Mothers (N = 642) | | Females aged 15–49 (N = 729) | | | Males aged 20+ (N = 836) | | | Total sample (N = 1565) | | |
| Modern Methods[a] | heard of | have used | heard of | have used | using now | heard of | have used | using now | heard of | have used | using now |
| Condom | 38 | 4 | 36.6 | 6.2 | 0.8 | 61.2 | 17.8 | 2.3 | 49.6 | 12.4 | 1.6 |
| Diaphragm | 16 | 2 | 16.9 | 1.1 | 0.4 | 17.6 | 1.0 | 0.1 | 17.3 | 1.0 | 0.3 |
| Oral pills | 37 | 3 | 35.2 | 3.3 | 0.3 | 37.6 | 5.9 | 1.0 | 36.4 | 4.7 | 0.6 |
| IUD | 6 | 1 | 14.7 | 1.5 | 0.8 | 5.1 | 0.7 | 0.1 | 9.6 | 1.1 | 0.4 |
| Jelly, cream (foam) | 6 | 0 | 6.6 | 0.7 | 0.1 | 5.5 | 0.7 | 0.0 | 6.0 | 0.7 | 0.1 |
| "Foam tablet" | 17 | 1 | —[b] | —[b] | —[b] | —[b] | —[b] | —[b] | —[b] | —[b] | —[b] |
| Rhythm method | 14 | 3 | 18.7 | 7.1 | 0.5 | 19.5 | 7.4 | 0.7 | 19.1 | 7.2 | 0.6 |
| Tubal ligation | 27 | 0 | —[c] | —[c] | —[c] | —[c] | —[c] | —[c] | —[c] | —[c] | —[c] |
| Douche | 6 | 0 | —[d] | —[d] | —[d] | —[d] | —[d] | —[d] | —[d] | —[d] | —[d] |
| Sponge | 4 | 0 | —[d] | —[d] | —[d] | —[d] | —[d] | —[d] | —[d] | —[d] | —[d] |
| Traditional methods | | | | | | | | | | | |
| Abstinence after childbirth | —[e] | —[e] | 84.5 | 59.2 | 23.4 | 74.8 | 46.4 | 16.7 | 79.2 | 52.2 | 19.7 |
| Abstinence generally | —[e] | —[e] | 44.7 | 18.2 | 6.3 | 28.7 | 11.1 | 3.2 | 36.2 | 14.6 | 4.7 |
| Native doctors' methods | —[d] | —[d] | 21.4 | 1.6 | 0.3 | 24.4 | 3.2 | 1.0 | 23.0 | 2.5 | 0.6 |
| Withdrawal | 18 | 1 | 19.5 | 7.7 | 0.8 | 28.7 | 9.4 | 1.1 | 24.4 | 8.6 | 1.0 |
| Abortion | —[e] | 1 | 68.9 | 1.9 | —[f] | 61.0 | 1.2 | —[f] | 64.8 | 1.5 | —[f] |
| "Surgery" | —[c] | —[c] | 46.8 | 0.1 | —[f] | 39.6 | 0.2 | —[f] | 42.9 | 0.2 | —[f] |

SOURCES: Daramola and Wright, "Attitudes Toward Family Planning in Lagos, Nigeria"; Morgan, family planning attitude survey, 1968, from previously unpublished data.
[a] In the Lagos survey, a condom, diaphragm, and plastic container of pills were shown to each respondent. This writer also favored showing an IUD but was vetoed by the doctors on the grounds that this would "frighten" respondents, who, they said, did not normally see an IUD at the clinics before insertion. See discussion in text.
[b] Lagos survey interviewers asked about "jelly, cream, salve, or foam for women"; Surulere interviewers asked about "foam tablets" separately, and a confusion which may have arisen in respondents' minds between foam tablets and oral pills may account for the higher Surulere percentage here. In Lagos, the word "tablet" generally is used to mean "pill."
[c] The only surgical procedure asked about in the Surulere survey was tubal ligation. The Lagos interviewers asked about "surgery or sterilization to prevent a man or woman from producing children." It was thought (obviously erroneously) by this writer in designing the survey, and the thought was passed on to the interviewers, that only traditional surgical methods such as "turning of the womb" would be familiar to Lagos respondents. The responses to the two surveys are therefore not comparable and are listed respectively under "modern" and "traditional" techniques. See discussion in text.
[d] Not asked.
[e] The Surulere interview schedule was framed in such a way as to assume that all respondents were familiar with abstinence and abortion and practiced the former. Hence the only question asked in this area was on practice of "induced abortion," to which 1.1 percent of respondents replied affirmatively.
[f] Not applicable.

Department of Community Health. Two subsequent programs of house-to-house motivational visits initiated by the Family Health Project and the Council were carried out too late to influence the results of the 1968 survey.

From Table 9.28, it will be seen that the only significant differences in levels of knowledge and use among female respondents are an increase of almost two-and-a-half times in reported knowledge of the IUD, an increase in knowledge and use of the rhythm method, and a considerable increase in the use of withdrawal.[91] While all these results could arise from artifacts of the surveying methods, it should nevertheless be pointed out that the results do conform with what we know about the expanded educational and clinic programs in the interval between the surveys.

[91] Since both males and females were interviewed in the 1968 Lagos KAP survey, questions to males about female contraceptive devices (i.e., the IUD) were framed so as to refer to the respondent's wife or cohabiting partner, and vice versa.

The IUD was the method most strongly recommended in these programs, so that more women would be expected to know about it; nevertheless many women including the family planning field workers themselves were reluctant to use the IUD (for reasons to be discussed in the "attitude" section) and hence actual use did not rise commensurate with knowledge. What did rise in the "use" categories were methods involving improved knowledge of the physiology of sexual reproduction itself (i.e., the rhythm method, withdrawal, and possibly also reliance on the condom); this is reasonable when one considers that basic sex education also was emphasized in the expanded family planning program in Lagos. The impressions of clinic workers, as well as responses to some questions in our 1968 KAP survey, suggest that well over half the Lagos public have had basic misconceptions about the process of reproduction, that only about 11 percent of males and 8 percent of females understand the fertile period during the menstrual cycle, and that males who initially are less prone to adopt family planning than women generally have a better knowledge of the physiology of sex than females. Basic misconceptions about sex found in Lagos included (1) that a woman can have intercourse during one menstrual period and become pregnant during the next one; (2) that pregnancy occurs because of prolonged contact with a man and not because of one specific coital act; (3) that a woman can become pregnant because of sperm taken through the mouth; and so on. If these misconceptions are prevalent in Lagos, they are doubtless more prevalent in the rural areas. It would seem reasonable that more extensive sex education in Nigeria would help those families who wanted to practice family planning to do so; and it may be that the principal initial result of the expanded family planning program in Lagos has been increased knowledge that pregnancies do not just happen, and that there are ways to prevent or space pregnancies even if one is presently unwilling to accept any of the new clinical methods such as the pill or the IUD.

A further breakdown of the 1968 Lagos KAP data has been made in Table 9.29, in which the proportions of persons familiar with any modern method, any traditional method, and any contraceptive method, are given. Table 9.29 also brings out the distinction between data on former Federal Territory residents and former residents of the immediately contiguous urban areas of western Nigeria, a distinction which is of the greatest

TABLE  9.29

Percentage of respondents using modern and traditional contraceptive methods, Lagos metropolitan area

| Area | Modern Methods | | | Traditional Methods | | | Any Methods | | |
|---|---|---|---|---|---|---|---|---|---|
|  | Heard of | Has used | Using now | Heard of | Has used | Using now | Heard of | Has used | Using now |
| Former Western Region Areas |  |  |  |  |  |  |  |  |  |
| Males (N = 362) | 58.8 | 15.5 | 0.6 | 85.4 | 54.7 | 26.5 | 90.1 | 58.8 | 26.7 |
| Females (N = 328) | 39.6 | 4.6 | 1.2 | 93.0 | 67.4 | 32.3 | 93.6 | 69.2 | 33.3 |
| Former Federal Territory Areas |  |  |  |  |  |  |  |  |  |
| Males (N = 474) | 68.1 | 22.8 | 1.9 | 80.0 | 48.9 | 14.1 | 88.8 | 54.9 | 15.8 |
| Females (N = 401) | 55.6 | 13.7 | 4.7 | 97.0 | 73.8 | 26.2 | 97.8 | 75.8 | 29.9 |
| Lagos Metropolitan Area |  |  |  |  |  |  |  |  |  |
| Males (N = 836) | 64.1 | 19.6 | 1.3 | 82.3 | 51.4 | 19.5 | 89.4 | 56.6 | 20.6 |
| Females (N = 729) | 48.4 | 9.6 | 3.2 | 95.2 | 70.9 | 28.9 | 95.9 | 72.8 | 31.4 |
| Total (N = 1,565) | 56.8 | 15.0 | 2.2 | 88.3 | 60.5 | 23.9 | 92.4 | 64.2 | 25.6 |

importance. The former Western Region, or peripheral, areas were developed largely during the 1950s and 1960s from small villages and open fields, and today (according to this writer's estimate) constitute almost 50 percent of the metropolitan population.[92] Obviously most of this population is migrant and of a different character from the longer-settled areas of Lagos Island, Ebute Metta, and Yaba in the former Federal Territory. The peripheral areas were governed from Ibadan, 90 miles away, and gained or suffered accordingly. They lack, for the most part, pipe-borne drinking water, sewage and refuse collection, paved roads, police and fire protection, and the extensive educational and medical facilities available to most residents in the Federal Territory.

Although by 1968 the entire urban area had come under the jurisdiction of the newly created Lagos State, these important social and environmental differences continued to exist at the time of the survey.

The data from Table 9.29, if correct, are far-reaching in their implications, and probably should form the basis for any immediately contemplated further research or activity programs in family planning in Nigeria, whether in the urban or the rural areas. (1) For *modern methods*, levels of knowledge are substantially higher in the longer urbanized area, and though the numbers involved are small, levels of use are also substantially higher (1.9 as opposed to 0.6 percent for males, 4.7 as opposed to 1.2 percent for females, employing the "using now" category). This is the part of the city in which the expanded family planning educational and clinical activity was focused during the period between the 1965 and 1968 surveys. These activities have since been extended to the peripheral areas. (2) For *traditional methods*, on the other hand, levels of knowledge are not especially different in the longer-urbanized area and knowledge is slightly higher among females and lower among males. This supports the contention made in the preamble to this chapter that traditional ideas continue to be observed in all sections of Nigeria, including Lagos, and that what we are seeing to varying degrees in different parts of the country is an infusion or "overlaying" of selected modern ideas. (3) *Reported use of modern methods by females* is three times that by males, reinforcing the impressions of clinic workers that 75 percent of women using modern methods do so without their husband's knowledge. This doubtless relates to male views that modern contraceptive techniques permit the wife to be unfaithful, and hence should be opposed. (4) With respect to the *use of traditional methods*, this is clearly much higher for both males and females in migrant or peripheral areas (26.5 percent as opposed to 14.1 percent for males; 32.3 as opposed to 26.2 percent for females). Among females, the difference may be accounted for partially (but not entirely) by a substitution of modern for traditional methods in the longer-urbanized area. A look at the "any methods" column will show (perhaps to the surprise of many readers) that use of pregnancy-control measures in the Lagos Metropolitan Area is substantially higher in the peripheral or more recently urbanized areas, and a look at the entire table will show that this is due to an overwhelming reliance on traditional rather than modern methods. All of this tends to bear out the contention of Olusanya,[93] also strongly supported in this chapter, that pregnancy control is practiced in Nigeria, but that the greatest obstacle to effective pregnancy planning is a continuing reliance on traditional methods, which include either (a) the abstinence period which is declining in the urbanized areas or (b) traditional medical methods which for the

[92] Morgan, "Population Dynamics Survey" (see footnote 8 of this chapter). The Lagos Metropolitan Area was defined to include the Federal Territory plus the adjacent urban areas of Mushin, Ajegunle, Ikeja, and Agege. The urban sections called Shomolu, Bariga, Itire, Shogunle, and Oshodi are politically part of Mushin. Likewise the Araromi-Ajegunle-Ajeromi complex, politically under the Ajeromi District Council, is referred to collectively in common parlance as Ajegunle. All of these areas came within the 1967–1968 survey sample; more distant places like Ikorodu were omitted.

[93] Olusanya, "Nigeria: Cultural Barriers to Family Planning Among the Yorubas."

most part are ineffective.[94] (5) For the Lagos Metropolitan Area as a whole, it will be seen that almost everyone knows about pregnancy control, that most people have practiced it, and that about one-quarter were doing so at the time of the 1968 survey. What the distinction between the Western Region and Federal Territory areas brings out is that with increasing urbanization one finds an apparent decline in reliance on traditional methods (i.e., the lower use in the Federal Territory); at the present time the observed increased use of modern methods does not compensate for this decline. This supports the basic contention made throughout this chapter that the modernization process in Nigeria is producing heightened fertility (in addition to decreased mortality) in the longer-urbanized areas.

In two other knowledge and practice surveys carried out in rural Nigeria, a distinction unfortunately does not appear to have been made between modern and traditinoal methods, so that the data are extremely hard to interpret. Olusanya, in his survey of five Ibadan area villages, asked the question, "Do some women sometimes try to stop having babies either by preventing pregnancy or causing abortion? The responses were "yes," 47.1 percent; "no," 9.9 percent; and "don't know," 43.1 percent. In commenting on these replies, Olusanya writes:

It seems . . . that a large proportion of the respondents know about these practices, though almost as many of them either did not want to give an opinion or were simply ignorant. It is interesting that only a small fraction were categorical in their opinion that women do not sometimes prevent births. Of course, this is not to say that the respondents had in mind modern methods of birth control. They might well be thinking of Yoruba traditional methods.[95]

In Irrua in Midwest State, a largely rural area, a sample of 5,287 women aged 15–45 were given KAP interviews by a research team from the University of Ife, again under the direction of Olusanya. According to preliminary results of this survey, 11.1 percent of respondents reported knowledge of a "method of family planning" and 2.9 percent reported that they had "ever practiced family planning." One suspects that the questions were asked with respect to specific methods of contraception apart from traditional abstinence, in which case one might say that the figures for both knowledge and use are several percentage points higher than the Caldwell-Igun figures for southern rural Nigeria generally (11.1 as opposed to 7 percent; 2.9 as opposed to 0.4 percent; see Table 9.27). A further analysis of this difference would be most interesting, but unfortunately is not available at this time.[96]

In Western State, at Wesley Guild Hospital in Ilesha (referred to previously), 20 miles east of Ife, an educational effort aimed at informing the public about the IUD has been in effect since 1957, and has been in an intensive phase since 1965. During the 1965–1968 period, a total of 400 Lippes Loops were inserted.[97] As the total population of the area

---

[94] This writer does not wish to assert that native medicine is not effective; he has been impressed with specific instances of apparent native medicine effectiveness, particularly in the realm of what might be classified as psychiatric or psychomatic disorders. Obstetricians in various countries have noted an apparent relationship between psychic states and infertility; and it may be that a young Nigerian girl holding an esteemed native practitioner in awe may put on one of his "contraceptive" rings and either (a) become psychologically infertile or, (b) if she does become pregnant, procure a secret abortion rather than risk proving the native practitioner wrong. It seems reasonable to assert that the average Western-trained physician, on reviewing the types of native contraception described in this chapter, would consider all but traditional abstinence as essentially ineffective.

[95] Olusanya, "Rural Attitudes to Family Size." Both Okediji and Olusanya have similarly not distinguished between traditional and modern methods in their Ibadan studies, see for example Okediji, "Attitudes, Knowledge, and Practice of Family Planning Techniques among Married Women in the City of Ibadan," p. 13 table and discussion, in which he specifically includes traditional abstinence as a "method" and reports 80–85 percent of women with a low level of education as "not knowing any method." This cannot be correct.

[96] Irrua data from John C. Caldwell, personal memorandum.

[97] V. J. Hartfield, "Experience with the Lippes Loop in a Provincial Hospital," *West African Medical Journal* (August 1969), pp. 125–35.

served is estimated at about 300,000, this would mean some 60,000–70,000 women in the childbearing age and an insertion rate of about 0.6 percent, about half the rate in metropolitan Lagos (Table 9.28, "having used" category, females, IUD) but, even so, an impressive achievement in this rural community 165 miles northeast of the federal capital. What this means is that 400 women decided, on the basis of an educational program conducted in conjunction with a pediatric clinic held in high regard locally, to practice a form of pregnancy control based on modern clinical methods. It would also appear that this decision was motivated, not by support for the lactation taboo (otherwise, why not the usual abstinence?), but rather by a direct desire to limit fertility (perhaps "to reduce the burden of having too many children").

ATTITUDINAL DATA, FAMILY PLANNING SURVEYS. Surveys on attitudes toward family planning have been carried out in Nigeria in the following places:

(1) *Lagos Metropolitan Area*, three surveys (Ohadike, 1964, in a random sample of 596 currently married females in the former Federal Territory;[98] Daramola and Wright, 1965, in a random sample of 642 mothers in Surulere, a suburban area largely built and developed in the past dozen years;[99] Morgan, 1968, in a random sample of 836 males aged 20 and over and 729 females aged 15–49, irrespective of marital status or parity, in the Metropolitan Area as a whole).[100]

(2) *Ibadan Metropolitan Area*, two surveys (Okediji, 1965–1966, in three sampling areas as follows—455 married women predominantly Yoruba in the indigenous or central city area, 160 Ibo and Hausa married women in an immigrant residential area peripheral to the central city, and 85 married women in a

planned suburb for upper-class families;[101] Olusanya, 1966, in two contiguous peripheral areas as follows—155 wives in a migrant but predominantly Yoruba area, and 108 wives in the same elite area surveyed by Okediji).[102]
(3) *Five villages within 60 miles of Ibadan*, one survey (Olusanya, 1967, a total of 682 ever-married women).[103]
(4) *Irrua area, Midwest State*, survey of 5,287 women aged 15–45 (directed by Olusanya; preliminary results available only).[104]

The 1965 Daramola and Wright survey included interviews among 73 mothers in Katsina Province in extreme northern Nigeria, but since about three-quarters of these respondents refused to answer attitudinal questions or made highly qualified answers, the attitude portions of the data were not scored.[105]

Some of the response patterns produced in the six Ibadan and Lagos area surveys were as follows:

(1) *Expressed ideal family size* was about six to seven children for most respondents, but varied significantly when controls for socio-economic characteristics were introduced. Some of the Ibadan data are summarized in Tables 9.30 and 9.31, and Ohadike reported essentially similar values for Lagos (average "ideal" and "expected" family size of 6.5 and 6.1 children respectively; average "expected" family sizes of 6.7 for wives without schooling, 6.2 for wives with primary or secondary schooling). The 1968 Lagos survey done four years after Ohadike's, produced an average "best number of children to have" of 5.5, or one child less than the earlier survey.

(2) *Expressed approval and disapproval attitudes* toward family planning or pregnancy spacing techniques inquiries found a majority of Lagos respondents approving and a majority of Ibadan respondents disapproving. While the method of asking such a question can greatly

---

[98] See footnote 37.
[99] See footnote 38. Data on 73 mothers interviewed in Katsina Province in the north were not scored, as noted in the text, because so many women refused to answer the attitude questions.
[100] See footnote 44.

[101] See footnotes 39 and 65.
[102] See footnote 39.
[103] See footnote 31.
[104] See footnote 94.
[105] For example, to the question about the ideal number of children to have, virtually every mother answered: "As many as God gives."

TABLE 9.30

Mean ideal number of children by socioeconomic characteristics, three sampling areas in Ibadan

| Age and Socioeconomic Characteristics of Wives | Traditional Areas | | Immigrant Areas Ibo | | Hausa | | Modern Areas | |
|---|---|---|---|---|---|---|---|---|
| | Percentage of wives | Mean idea children | Percentage of wives | Mean ideal children | Percentage of wives | Mean ideal children | Percentage of wives | Mean ideal children |
| *Age* | | | | | | | | |
| 15–24 | 45.05 | 6.1 | 37.8 | 6.2 | 54.7 | 5.8 | 15.29 | 3.5 |
| 25–34 | 30.99 | 6.3 | 28.9 | 6.2 | 19.1 | 5.8 | 52.94 | 4.2 |
| 35–44 | 21.45 | 6.4 | 27.5 | 7.2 | 16.5 | 6.2 | 24.71 | 4.1 |
| 45 + above | 2.42 | 6.4 | 5.8 | 8.0 | 9.7 | 6.0 | 7.06 | 4.2 |
| *Education* | | | | | | | | |
| University/ professional | — | — | — | — | — | — | 56.47 | 3.6 |
| Secondary school | 7.02 | 5.7 | 25.28 | 6.0 | — | — | 27.06 | 4.2 |
| Primary/modern | 22.20 | 6.5 | 39.08 | 6.7 | — | — | 18.82 | 4.2 |
| No schooling but literate | 13.19 | 6.8 | 16.10 | 7.4 | — | — | 2.35 | 4.0 |
| Arabic education | | | | | 27.4 | 6.3 | — | — |
| Nonliterate | 57.59 | 6.8 | 19.54 | 7.4 | 72.6 | 6.4 | — | — |
| *Occupation* | | | | | | | | |
| Professional/ white-collar | 9.96 | 5.2 | 13.79 | 6.3 | — | — | 56.47 | 3.9 |
| Skilled worker | 20.52 | 6.2 | 24.14 | 7.1 | — | — | 27.06 | 4.2 |
| Retail trader | 16.92 | 6.4 | 20.69 | 7.7 | — | — | 9.41 | 4.4 |
| Petty trader | 55.60 | 6.5 | 41.38 | 8.1 | 28.77 | 6.2 | 7.06 | 4.1 |
| Unemployed | — | — | — | — | 71.23 | 6.2 | — | — |
| *Income of family* | | | | | | | | |
| High (£500 and above) | 9.89 | 6.0 | 16.09 | 6.8 | — | — | 58.82 | 4.0 |
| Middle (£200–500) | 29.32 | 6.5 | 35.63 | 7.1 | 21.53 | 6.4 | 41.18 | 4.2 |
| Low (Under £200) | 61.79 | 6.4 | 48.28 | 8.2 | 78.47 | 6.4 | — | — |
| Total | (455) | 6.2 | (87) | 7.1 | (73) | 6.1 | (85) | 4.1 |

SOURCE: Okediji, "Socioeconomic Status and Differential Fertility in an African City."
NOTE: Percentages within categories do not always total 100 because of rounding separate figures.

TABLE 9.31

Mean ideal number of children, by age group, five Ibadan-area villages

| Age Group | Number of Women | "Up to God" | 1 | 2 | 3 | 4 | 5 | 6 | 7+ | Total | Mean |
|---|---|---|---|---|---|---|---|---|---|---|---|
| | | | Percentage of Women Giving as Ideal Numbers of Children | | | | | | | | |
| 15–29 | 238 | 27.7 | — | — | 0.4 | 17.6 | 7.6 | 31.1 | 15.5 | 100.0 | 6.3 |
| 30–39 | 231 | 31.2 | — | — | 1.3 | 13.9 | 8.7 | 27.6 | 17.3 | 100.0 | 6.4 |
| 40–49 | 117 | 37.6 | — | — | — | 12.8 | 8.5 | 18.8 | 22.2 | 100.0 | 6.7 |
| 50+ | 92 | 35.9 | — | — | 1.1 | 11.9 | 7.6 | 22.8 | 20.7 | 100.0 | 7.4 |
| Total | 678 | 31.7 | — | — | 0.7 | 14.7 | 8.1 | 26.7 | 18.0 | 100.0 | 6.6 |

SOURCE: Olusanya, "Rural Attitudes to Family Size and Its Limitation in Western Nigeria."

influence the result, the difference was so pronounced as to command attention. Again, there was a significant variation when controls for socioeconomic characteristics were introduced. It is also striking that the proportion of Lagos respondents approving rose with each succeeding survey during the 1964–1968 interval, the period when the extensive family planning educational program was initiated in the city and eight of the ten present family planning clinics were opened, (see Tables 9.32 and 9.33).

(3) *Ethical/moral considerations* were given as the primary reason for disapproval of family planning in the Ibadan area. In the five-village survey, to the question, "Do you think

TABLE 9.32
Percentage of respondents expressing various attitudes toward use of contraceptive techniques, Lagos and Ibadan surveys (by education) and Ibadan-area villages

|  | Approve | Dis-approve | Don't Know No Reply |
|---|---|---|---|
| *Lagos*(Ohadike,1964): |  |  |  |
| No education (N = 283) | 35.0 | — | — |
| Primary, modern Arabic schools (N = 223) | 57.0 | — | — |
| Secondary school (N = 76) | 72.0 | — | — |
| University, pro-fessional (N = 14) | 100.0 | — | — |
| *Ibadan* (Okediji, 1965–6, combined data given for three survey areas): |  |  |  |
| No education (N = 310) | 0.0 | 97.0 | 3.0 |
| Primary only (N = 121) | 9.5 | 90.5 | 0.0 |
| Modern school (N = 104) | 11.6 | 88.4 | 0.0 |
| Secondary school (N = 80) | 25.0 | 62.5 | 12.5 |
| Technical/pro-fessional (N = 65) | 86.0 | 7.6 | 6.4 |
| University (N = 20) | 85.0 | 5.0 | 10.0 |
| *Ibadan-Area villages* (Olusanya, 1967; N = 682) | 18.5 | 65.5 | 16.0 |

TABLE 9.33
Percentage of respondents expressing positive attitudes toward family planning, three Lagos surveys

|  | Males | Females | Total |
|---|---|---|---|
| *1964 survey:* |  |  |  |
| Approve doctors rendering birth control advice | — | 48.9 | — |
| Approve establishment of family planning clinics | — | 49.4 | — |
| *1965 survey:* |  |  |  |
| Approve use of family planning methods | — | 75.0[a] | — |
| *1968 survey:* |  |  |  |
| Approve use of family planning methods | 78.0 | 76.8 | 77.4 |
| Think "Nigerian government should have a program to give information to people who want to space the births of their children" | 86.7 | 81.7 | 84.3 |

[a] As previously noted, the 1965 survey was carried out in Surulere, an area of higher socioeconomic status than the Lagos Metropolitan Area generally.

(some women) should do this (i.e., prevent pregnancies or cause abortion)? a total of 447 women or 65.5 percent said "no"; among these 447 women, 224 or 50.2 percent gave as the reason, "It is a sin; we should not tamper with God's work." It is interesting that in most areas surveyed, approximately the same proportion of respondents gave the reply, "As many as God gives" or similar to the question about the "ideal" or "best" number of children to have, i.e., 31.7 percent in the five-village survey and 26.7 percent in the 1968 Lagos Metropolitan Area survey. To the direct question as to why some couples have difficulty in producing as many children as they would like, 30.7 percent of respondents in the 1968 Lagos survey attributed this to the will of God. In view of the extensive other attitudinal differences between the Lagos and Ibadan areas (for example, most Lagos respondents approved family planning), one wonders if ethical-moral considerations are not becoming secondary to other considerations (that is, economic and clinical ones, see data to be presented below).

An exception to the above statement would be the concern voiced by many males in both Lagos and Ibadan over the possibility that the use of modern contraceptives would permit their wives to become unfaithful. Coupled with this is the prevalent belief that infertile women are prostitutes. Unfortunately, quantitative assessments of the importance of these beliefs were not available from any of the reports; the impression is that these related beliefs, which produced highly emotional responses in a number of males, constitute one of the more serious obstacles to family planning in areas where modern techniques are known.

(4) *The "good" and "bad" things about having a lot of children* were explored in several surveys. Traditional beliefs about the value of a large family were expressed by a minority of respondents in surveys in both the Ibadan area (see Table 9.34) and in Lagos. A larger number of respondents gave answers related to economic or clinical factors as reasons both "good" and "bad" for having a lot of children. In the Lagos 1968 survey, only 41.0 percent of males and 37.7 percent of females gave answers related to family pride or prestige, in response to the open-ended question asked of all respondents, "What are the good things about having a lot of children?" Another 41.2 percent answered, "There is nothing good about having a lot of children." To the open-ended question, "What are the bad things about having a lot of children?" asked of all respondents, 73.8 percent of males and 70.5 percent of females replied, "too costly to support them" or "too costly to educate them." A total of 20.3 percent said, "There is nothing bad about having a lot of children." To the question, "How much education do you plan to provide for your children?" the median response for the Lagos Metropolitan Area was "university" for sons and "school certificate" for daughters! In answer to the question, "How do you plan to achieve this educational goal for your children?" 29.5 percent said, "God or chance will provide," 67.4 said "savings or investments," and 9.0 percent said the child would win a scholarship, with

TABLE 9.34

Responses to questions, "Do you think it is a good thing to have a lot of children? Why do you think so?" Five Ibadan-area villages

| Responses | Number | Percent |
|---|---|---|
| Yes | 416 | 61.4 |
| No | 262 | 38.6 |
| Total | 678 | 100.0 |
| **Reasons (Yes)** | | |
| Fear of child mortality + lack of of survivors | 172 | 41.4 |
| God gives children | 46 | 11.1 |
| Help to parents, especially in old age | 106 | 25.5 |
| Parental pride | 27 | 6.5 |
| The family increases | 20 | 4.8 |
| Other | 45 | 10.7 |
| **Reasons (No)** | | |
| Having a lot of children entails trouble | 14 | 5.4 |
| Children cost a lot to bring up nowadays | 108 | 41.2 |
| Having a small family enables each child to receive a sound education | 140 | 53.4 |

SOURCE: Olusanya, "Rural Attitudes to Family Size and Its Limitation in Western Nigeria."

other replies making up the remainder (some multiple-choice answers).[106]

(5) *The fear of child mortality* was given as a "good" reason for having a lot of children in both the Ibadan and Lagos areas (Table 9.34). In the 1968 Lagos survey, 17.3 percent of respondents replied that "many children mean some will survive to be adults," including 15.9 percent males and 19.0 percent females. To the direct question "Do you think a person is likely to have more surviving children now, or fewer ... than in our father's time or in our grandfather's time?" 66.7 percent of Lagos males and 60.7 percent of females replied, "more now" (about one-fifth of the females said they were undecided or did not know). The great majority of Lagos respondents attributed these increased child-survival chances to better medical facilities and health education.

[106] The full results of the 1968 KAP survey in Lagos are being prepared separately for publication.

Olusanya asked a somewhat similar question of respondents in his Ibadan suburbs sample ("Do you think that in future the population of Nigeria will be less than now, same as now, or more than now?") with 82.5 percent replying "more than now." By contrast, however, when those replying "more than now" were asked to give reasons for their answer, 89.9 percent gave reasons related to increased fertility per woman (rate of childbearing increasing; girls marrying earlier) whereas only 6.9 percent gave reasons related to decreased mortality and better medical services.[107] Unfortunately present data are insufficient to judge whether a basic difference in perceived child-survival chances exists between the two areas, or whether the results are an artifact of the interviewing method.[108]

(6) *The anticipated strong preference for male children* was expressed in all surveys, including the most recent (1968) Lagos survey in which a median preference of four boys and two girls—six children in all—was voiced by both males and females in the Metropolitan Area.[109]

(7) *Religion* as a factor in attitudes toward family planning was explored in the 1964 and 1965 Lagos surveys, with the rank order of both approval and use coinciding in the two reports (again it should be pointed out that the 1965 survey was done in an upper-middle-class area); see Table 9.35.

The preliminary Irrua data do not in general afford direct comparisons with the data from the other surveys. Irrua is a largely rural area, with comparatively little cash cropping and only medium-size villages, located in Midwest State about 200 miles east of Ibadan. The area does have a large

TABLE 9.35
Approval and use of family planning, by religion, two Lagos surveys (in percent)

|  | Protestants | Catholics | Moslems |
|---|---|---|---|
| *Lagos random sample, 1964* | | | |
| Support establishment of birth control clinics | 60 | 51 | 38 |
| Have used contraception | 14 | 11 | 4 |
| *Surulere random sample, 1965* | | | |
| Approve family planning methods | 79 | 77 | 65 |
| Have used a method | 19 | 9 | 6 |

timber mill and a 120-bed hospital privately operated. As previously noted, 11.1 percent of respondents reported knowledge of a method of family planning, and 2.9 percent reported having used a method. These figures are somewhat higher than the figures for southern rural Nigeria generally reported by Caldwell and Igun. In reply to the question, "Would you like to be able to stop having babies when you have enough, or to stop having them for a while (i.e., only become pregnant when you want to?)," 27.1 percent of respondents said "yes," again a figure that is high compared with other surveys. Olusanya's figure for the five Ibadan area villages was 18.5 percent; the Irrua figure is also considerably higher in comparison with the replies of the lower-educated respondents in Okediji's Ibadan survey (see Table 9.32). This is particularly interesting when one considers that some 71 percent of the Irrua respondents had no schooling and another 23 percent had primary schooling only. However, the doctor at the Irrua hospital had been recommending family planning and offering services. Again, one must await with interest a further analysis of these differences.

The Irrua figures for ideal family size appear to be consistent with those reported for other West African surveys; 95 percent of respondents wanted four or more children

[107] Olusanya, "The Educational Factor in Human Fertility," p. 360.
[108] In the 1968 Lagos survey, the question about increased perceived child survival chances was asked three different times in different wordings, with similar response patterns throughout.
[109] The one-quarter of respondents answering "as many as God gives" or similar were scored as above the median. The result was not greatly different if only numerical replies were scored, i.e., an average of 5.5 children preferred as opposed to a median of 6.

and 92.6 percent wanted five or more.[110] Mean or median figures in this category have not been reported.

This concludes our brief overview of the attitude data in southwestern Nigeria, except for the following impressionistic observation, based on conversations with Lagos clinic workers.

(8) *With respect to satisfaction with methods,* despite the strong approval of family planning expressed in Lagos, it is felt that there is a growing dissatisfaction with the four modern contraceptive methods considered most reliable—the diaphragm, condom, pill, and IUD most Lagos patients receive either the pill or the IUD). At Lagos University Teaching Hospital and the College of Medicine, where this writer is employed, a number of female staff members and their spouses who want to practice family planning have rejected all four of these techniques. It may be that, in the long run, some other satisfactory contraceptive method will prove to be more important in the development of a Nigerian family planning program than the presumed obstacles imposed by traditional beliefs.

It now falls to us to assess the impact of these attitudinal data, particularly with respect to (a) the apparent conflict between expressed attitudes in southwestern Nigeria, and the observed fertility increase reported upon in the earlier sections of this chapter, and (b) the negative comments about attitudinal surveys made by this writer above. Two observations, only, will be made.

(a) It must be clear that the attitudinal data, for the present time at least, do not reflect what is happening in Nigeria. They may be predictive of what is going to happen, but until evidence to this effect is produced,

the research worker must remain sceptical. One cannot help but note, for example, that expressed "ideal family size" reflects almost precisely the measured actual fertility level in the country today. And so it may be with much of the other data. Respondents may be answering to a very great extent in terms of what they see happening rather than what they would like to see happen, or in terms of what they consider is expected of them (that is, what they think is "proper" rather than "best").

(b) Fertility probably is declining in the upper socioeconomic groups. But these groups are small and the decline is small. Measured against this decline is the greater fertility increase among the very large numbers of lower-socioeconomic persons moving into the modern economic sector (among the urban proletariat, if you will). Until, and unless, this group responds to pressures driving fertility down rather than up, attitude surveys based on socioeconomic status are going to lead us astray.

To sound two optimistic notes, actual attendances at Lagos family planning clinics, though small, suggest the following: (1) The attitudinal surveys are correct in recording an eventual correlation between increased education and decreased fertility, the educational factor becoming operative with as little as a primary school education. Patients at Lagos family planning clinics at each educational level including "primary only" are overrepresented vis-à-vis the metropolitan population at large; women with no education are underrepresented at the clinics (see Table 9.36). (2) The attitudinal surveys may be incorrect in recording "ideal" family size and may in fact be recording some other mental set entirely. For women who do know about family planning and do come to the clinics, the "ideal" family size clearly is three (see Table 9.37), a figure also established in a number of other developing countries in which contraceptive programs have eventually become diffused.

Following completion of this chapter, information was received about a family planning KAP survey in progress in the

[110] Since this chapter was completed, the Nigerian government has published its *Second National Development Plan 1970–74* endorsing the establishment of family planning services on a voluntary basis in the country, and calling for the creation of a National Population Council to coordinate family planning activities and external aid programs for family planning. These developments, while not satisfying the advocates of a strong population control policy nevertheless represent a significant change of thinking in Nigeria over the previous five years.

TABLE 9.36
Educational levels, women aged 15–49, Lagos metropolitan sample and Lagos family planning clinic attendants

| Education | Lagos Survey | | Clinics | |
|---|---|---|---|---|
| | Number | Percent | Number | Percent |
| No schooling | 1,605 | 56.9 | 1,931 | 38.7 |
| Primary only | 803 | 28.5 | 1,876 | 37.6 |
| Secondary plus | 411 | 14.6 | 1,180 | 23.7 |
| Total | 2,819 | 100.0 | 4,987 | 100.0 |

SOURCES: Morgan, "Lagos Population Dynamics Survey," Family Planning Council of Nigeria, Lagos clinic records 1958–1968.

Ibadan area, under the direction of Drs. T. A. Lambo, psychiatrist, and C. G. M. Bakare, psychologist. The emphasis in this survey is on the emotional and psychological correlates of contraceptive behavior, and the study is being conducted in three sample populations: (1) Ilewo Village, a traditional rural area; (2) Abadina Village, described by the authors as "transitional" and accommodating junior and domestic staff working at the University of Ibadan; and (3) Bodija, the same upper-class residential suburb studied by several other authors reviewed in this chapter.

TABLE 9.37
Number of living children, women aged 15–49, Lagos KAP sample and Lagos family planning clinic attendants

| Number of Living Children | KAP Survey | | Clinics | |
|---|---|---|---|---|
| | Number | Percent | Number | Percent |
| 0 | 123 | 18.2 | 63 | 0.9 |
| 1 | 135 | 20.0 | 297 | 4.1 |
| 2 | 140 | 20.8 | 706 | 9.7 |
| 3 | 108 | 16.0 | 1,206 | 16.5 |
| 4 | 72 | 10.7 | 1,648 | 22.5 |
| 5 | 50 | 7.4 | 1,532 | 21.0 |
| 6 | 28 | 4.2 | 1,077 | 14.7 |
| 7 | 12 | 1.8 | 455 | 6.2 |
| 8 | 4 | 0.6 | 230 | 3.1 |
| 9+ | 2 | 0.3 | 97 | 1.3 |
| Total | 674 | 100.0 | 7,311 | 100.0 |

SOURCES: R. W. Morgan, Family Planning KAP Survey, Family Planning Council of Nigeria, Lagos clinic records, 1958–1968.

A few preliminary results available from this study suggest that the final report may be extremely valuable, and may give insights into the family planning situation in Nigeria which are not being obtained in the other surveys. It is hoped that the authors will interpret the data with exceptional care. Of special interest is the Abadina Village sample, which is not a typical "transitional" area but rather what amounts to a laboratory for the study of special features of social change. The village, on the border of the University of Ibadan compound, houses a population ranging in social status from junior staff clerks with some education and career prospects in the university administration, to illiterate domestic servants and their relatives who are unable to obtain housing in the vicinity of their employers' residences. The population thus offers the prospect of a group of individuals of lower economic and educational status who have nevertheless had exceptional exposure to Western customs and ideas.

Analysis of some of the Lambo-Bakare data suggests that, whereas Ilewo and Bodija run more or less according to form, Abadina contains a few surprises. Respondents in the three samples include married men and women aged 15 and over. The numbers interviewed include 122 in Ilewo, 95 in Abadina, and 47 in Bodija. The age and sex distribution is somewhat erratic in the three areas and perhaps arises from methodological problems such as nonresponse. The data in Table 9.38, "Reasons for Preferring a Large Family," seem to follow generally expected patterns, but the data in Table 9.39, "Reasons for Preferring a Small Family," contain some interesting variations. Concern over the cost of educating or raising a large family was less in Abadina than in either the traditional or modern area, whereas concern for the health of the mother or concern over the trouble and worry of a lot of children was higher in Abadina, the so-called middle or transitional area, than in Ilewo or Bodija. The numbers involved are small, and one would want to see these results further specified according to the social condition of the respondent; nevertheless, the data suggest possible lines of

TABLE 9.38
Reasons for preferring large family

| Reasons Given | Ilewo Village (N = 122) | | Abadina Village (N = 95) | | Bodija Estate (N = 47) | |
|---|---|---|---|---|---|---|
| | Number | Percent | Number | Percent | Number | Percent |
| To increase chances some children will survive, etc. | 52 | 36.6 | 8 | 16.7 | 10 | 14.9 |
| To be sure of having heirs, continuing family name, etc. | 9 | 6.3 | 9 | 18.8 | 21 | 31.3 |
| For support + happiness in one's old age, etc. | 40 | 28.2 | 12 | 25.0 | 7 | 10.4 |
| Family prestige, fame, wealth, etc. | 11 | 7.7 | 7 | 14.6 | 9 | 13.4 |
| Pleasure + enjoyment of having children, etc. | 7 | 4.9 | 5 | 10.4 | 4 | 6.0 |
| Because couple can afford it | 3 | 2.1 | 1 | 2.1 | 2 | 3.0 |
| Desire for male child | 0 | 0.0 | 1 | 2.1 | 1 | 1.5 |
| Will of God, religious or traditional belief | 5 | 3.5 | 1 | 2.1 | 2 | 3.0 |
| Ignorance, primitiveness, etc. | 0 | 0.0 | 0 | 0.0 | 3 | 4.5 |
| Not good to have many children. | 0 | 0.0 | 0 | 0.0 | 3 | 4.5 |
| Don't know | 15 | 10.6 | 4 | 8.3 | 5 | 7.5 |
| Total responses[a] | 142 | 100.0 | 48 | 100.0 | 67 | 100.0 |

[a] It appears that Ilewo and Bodija respondents were allowed multiple-choice answers; Abadina respondents, single-choice answers. Unfortunately, the authors were not available for clarification.

TABLE 9.39
Reasons for preferring small family

| Reasons Given | Ilewo Village (N = 122) | | Abadina Village (N = 95) | | Bodija Estate (N = 47) | |
|---|---|---|---|---|---|---|
| | Number | Percent | Number | Percent | Number | Percent |
| Cost of educating or raising children, etc. | 95 | 68.8 | 27 | 57.4 | 47 | 78.3 |
| Danger to health of mother, or combined economic and health reasons | 7 | 5.1 | 5 | 10.6 | 5 | 8.3 |
| Trouble and worry caused by many children, etc. | 6 | 4.3 | 8 | 17.0 | 7 | 11.7 |
| Woman doesn't want to be controlled by husband | 0 | 0.0 | 1 | 2.1 | 0 | 0.0 |
| Will of God | 1 | 0.7 | 0 | 0.0 | 0 | 0.0 |
| Ignorance | 1 | 0.7 | 0 | 0.0 | 0 | 0.0 |
| Prefers small family | 2 | 1.4 | 0 | 0.0 | 0 | 0.0 |
| No reason for having small family | 0 | 0.0 | 0 | 0.0 | 1 | 1.7 |
| Don't know | 26 | 18.8 | 6 | 12.8 | 0 | 0.0 |
| Total responses[a] | 138 | 100.0 | 47 | 100.0 | 60 | 100.0 |

[a] See Table 9.38.

TABLE 9.40
Use of contraception, Ibadan area survey

| Type of Use | Ilewo Village (N = 122) | | Abadina Village (N = 95) | | Bodija Estate (N = 47) | |
|---|---|---|---|---|---|---|
| | Number | Percent | Number | Percent | Number | Percent |
| Would use family planning clinic | 3 | 2.5 | 19 | 20.0 | 23 | 48.9 |
| Have ever used modern contraceptives | 1 | 0.8 | 25 | 26.3 | 27 | 57.4 |
| Currently using modern contraceptives | 0 | 0.0 | 15 | 15.8 | 27 | 57.4 |

interpretation. It may be that persons with essentially traditional backgrounds and career horizons, plus exceptional proximity to Western ideas, retain their interest in a large family, are less worried about the problems of cost of a large family (because, relatively, their career expectations are still reasonably low, but their financial opportunities are somewhat higher), are more worried about health (because they attend the university clinic), are more worried about trouble and bother (because of exposure to that Western value), and so on. All this is conjectural, and offered simply as one possible line of analysis when further results are available. The data on preferred family size support these propositions, to the extent that 59.0 percent of respondents in the traditional area and 32.0 percent in the modern area expressed a preference for five or more children, whereas in Abadina Village the higher figure of 76.8 percent was obtained.

Data in Table 9.40 on use of contraceptives run according to generally expected patterns, with use in the traditional area being virtually nil (in fact, actually nil for the "using now" category). Further results from this interesting project must now be awaited.

GROUP VI VARIABLES:
PLANNED CHANGE

Unlike Ghana and several other African countries, the Nigerian government does not have an official program affecting population size.[111] However, the Federal Ministry of Economic Development and the Federal

[111] As mentioned above, the 1970–74 National Development Plan supports family planning advice and service on a voluntary basis.

Ministry of Health have made declarations in support of a national population policy. Because the 12 Nigerian states have a large measure of political autonomy, the position of the states is also important and a number of state ministries have made similar declarations.

In the 1968 KAP survey in Lagos, 85 percent of respondents gave a "yes" answer to the question, "Do you think the Nigerian government should have a program to give information to people who want to space the births of their children, or who want to plan the time when the woman will become pregnant?" A total of 78 percent of the 1,565 male and female respondents interviewed approved the use of contraceptive methods, and of the 22 percent who disapproved, 28 percent said they "might approve" if advised to do so "by Nigerian government over radio or in the newspapers."

In the area of privately sponsored programs, the Family Planning Council of Nigeria, a voluntary agency supported by the International Planned Parenthood Federation, operates nine clinics in the Lagos area and in the past five years has opened numerous clinics in other parts of the country, including five in Ibadan. The first clinic was opened on Lagos Island in 1958 but the program began to grow during 1964–68 when additional clinics were opened in Lagos (see Table 9.41). The Council (1972 Annual Report) now has about 20,000 new acceptors per year in 46 places throughout Nigeria and total acceptors as of the end of 1972 were 67,629 or an estimated 0.5 percent of all women aged 15 to 49 in the country.

The Lagos Family Health Project, an activity of the Department of Community

TABLE 9.41

Patients registered for fertility control in each year, Lagos metropolitan area family planning clinics[a]

| Year | Lagos Island Clinics | Lagos Mainland Clinics | Suburban Lagos (former Western Region) Clinics | Total |
|---|---|---|---|---|
| 1968 | 1,388 | 1,938 | 97 | 3,423 |
| 1967 | 1,146 | 853 | 43 | 2,042 |
| 1966 | 771 | 356 | — | 1,127 |
| 1965 | 398 | 154 | — | 552 |
| 1964 + before | 91 | 9 | — | 100 |
| Total | 3,794 | 3,310 | 140 | 7,244 |

[a] Not including 121 patients for whom year of registration was not recorded, and 350–400 patients registered at the original Broad Street Clinic during 1958–1964, whose cards cannot be found.

Health of the University of Lagos College of Medicine, began a research, educational, and clinical program in 1966, supported by the Ford Foundation, the College of Medicine, and the International Planned Parenthood Federation. The research activities, including the Lagos Population Dynamics Survey and the 1968 KAP survey, have been reported upon extensively elsewhere in this chapter.

Some of the results of the field motivational exercises accompanying this research have been as follows:

(1) Free IUD insertions and free transport to clinics, tried briefly in several areas, have produced dramatic short-run increases in clinic attendances.
(2) A trial coupon referral system to clinics has produced response rates of 5–10 percent, varying with individual field workers, based on single visits to women in homes. This corresponds with the Taiwan experience.[112]
(3) Unlike the experience in a number of other countries, males proved as suitable as females in family planning motivational interviewing in Lagos; and in some respects males proved to be more effective and steadier workers.

[112] Mrs. Tessie Huang, Taiwan Population Studies Center, personal communication, 1969.

(4) The use of fieldworkers as intermediaries between clinic and patient has been widely adopted by the Family Planning Council and other programs in the country, and has proved to be the most important single factor affecting clinic attendances.

It is evident that none of the planned programs have had an impact on fertility up to this time. An intensive pilot family planning program based in one or more of the Nigerian states has been recommended by this writer in a memorandum distributed by the Family Planning Council.[113]

SUMMARY

(1) Several random sample demographic surveys indicate a correlation between modernization forces and heightened fertility in Nigeria, with total fertility ranging from a measured 5.6 in rural Nigeria to 7.3 in Metropolitan Lagos, for women who pass through the childbearing age.
(2) Whether or not this is a short-run phenomenon remains to be seen. It may presently be attributed to a weakening of the traditional belief in abstinence from sexual relations for up to three years following the birth of a child, or during the period when the infant is being breastfed. The weakening of this taboo may in turn be related to improved educational and medical facilities in the more modernized areas. Surveys suggest that the average pregnancy interval ranges from about 4 years in rural Nigeria to about 2.5 years in metropolitan Lagos.
(3) Virtually all other measurable factors associated with modernization, urbanization, and improved socioeconomic status suggest attitudes and practices conducive to reduced fertility.
(4) Opposition to family planning, where modern techniques are known, apparently is related not so much to traditional beliefs in a large family as to the following: (a) fear of

[113] R. W. Morgan, "Family Planning in Asia and the Middle East, with Implications for the Development of a Program in Nigeria," mimeographed, Family Planning Council of Nigeria (1970).

child loss, i.e., child mortality; (b) dissatisfaction with modern contraceptive methods; (c) belief by men that contraceptive techniques will permit the wife to become unfaithful (but strong concern was expressed in both urban and rural areas over the cost of raising and educating a large family).

(5) It would appear that nearly every couple practices some form of traditional family planning; but use of modern techniques is extremely low even in Lagos and probably verges on nil in most areas.

# CHAPTER TEN

# *Family Change in Sokoto*

## *A Traditional Moslem Fulani/Hausa City*

JEAN TREVOR[1]

▦

Sokoto is known locally as "Shehu's City" after Shehu dan Fodio because it owes its foundation, in 1809, to Shehu's Jihad or Holy War, when it became the headquarters of his Moslem Reform Movement. Then the plan was for Sokoto to be a pure Islamic state, and in a spirit of moral austerity, personal ambitions were to be subjected to the discipline essential to establishing a social system in accord with the Shehu's interpretation of the teaching of the Koran. Shehu himself came as a reformer but the elders today quote his teachings to support a rigid orthodoxy and the young are told that he expects them to conserve all the old traditions and social institutions which made Sokoto great.[2]

The Sokoto Islamic tradition includes extensive Koranic learning and interpretation, spiritual allegiance to the Arab world, the writing of Hausa in Arabic script, and until recently the opposition to secular, "Western" education. The social institutions justified by the traditional interpretations of the Koran presuppose total respect for, and obedience to, the religious leaders and the hierarchical order which is believed to be essential for the peaceful running of an Islamic state. Within the family this means total obedience is given to the male head of the compound. Women, being lower in the hierarchy, accept strict purdah, polygamy (which sometimes includes concubines as well as the four wives allowed in Islam), and very early arranged marriages, and their main way of gaining respect and status is by having as many children, preferably male, as possible. Among traditional families the seclusion of women has become much

[1] Jean Trevor, now at Exeter University, England, returned to Ahmadu Bello University seventeen years after she had taught in northern Nigeria to relocate and study her former pupils. The study is being reported as a Ph.D. thesis for Exeter and a report for the Population Council.

[2] For histories of Sokoto see Murray Last, *The Sokoto Caliphate* (London: Longmans, Green & Company, 1967); H. A. S. Johnston, *The Fulani Empire of Sokoto* (London, 1962). For an assessment of the Jihad and examples of the Shehu's writings see Thomas Hodgkin, *Nigerian Perspectives* (London: Oxford University Press, 1960), pp. 35–44 and 188–98.

more strict than that advocated by the original Islamic reformer, the Shehu, who said those who "Shut up their wives, their daughters, and their captives in the darkness of ignorance—in truth, they act out of egoism."[3]

Beginning in the 1960s a new revivalist movement, the Jama'atu Nasril Islam, has been re-examining the traditional social institutions to see if they are expressing the spirit of the Koran and the Sunna. Many of these reformers feel that their women should be given more freedom and education, and that forced early marriages bring unhappiness, instability, and ill health. The men feel too that they must be more positively responsible for their children's welfare and less fatalistic than their fathers. An important result of these discussions on men's moral responsibilities toward their families may be that women are made more conscious of their worth and less fatalistic; the women may also take a more active part in decision making. But it would be wrong to assume that this conscious reassessment is the only factor in the change in the style of family life. The discussion is taking place at a time when economic pressures and the redistribution of resources is forcing a breakdown of the huge extended families of old aristocrats.

The elders cannot now afford to support huge families at today's higher standards. At the beginning of this century the head of a rich aristocratic family was responsible for feeding all his relations, dependents, and servants; 150 persons was quite a usual number. Today there are very few men who could afford to do this, even if their sons would agree to be supported by their fathers.

In the past all decisions were made by the head of the family, and sons owed their father total obedience. Today the young men prefer the freedom of being masters in their own smaller homes even if they have to do without their father's financial help.

Sometimes the breakup of the huge old family is due to the son's work. An educated

son leaves home for work in the civil service. This son is unlikely to follow the pattern of his father, that is, to establish a great compound with four wives, concubines, and numerous dependents and servants. If he is away from Sokoto he will probably live in a government-owned bungalow too small to accommodate more than two wives.[4] Anyway, he can probably only afford two wives, since he has to pay for food now that he is away from the family farm. Also, in order to keep up appearances at work, he must be able to afford the new status symbols of a car, smart clothes, and a good education for his sons, so he cannot afford the traditional status symbol, a large harem. These men are living in a modern life style even though they were born in traditional elite families.

However, a surprising number of well-educated civil servants who remain in Sokoto do maintain big harems. The inquiry revealed that some of the most autocratic husbands, who kept their wives in strict purdah, themselves came from peasant families where women have more freedom. In traditional Sokoto, as in Bornu described by Cohen, "Authority is essentially hierarchical and is essential to a proper religiously sanctioned social existence."[5] It seems that those men of humble origin who have achieved status because of their Western education or skills have to show they know how to live a "proper religiously sanctioned social existence," which they do by following the life style of the traditional leaders. Only those men who have the security of an aristocratic origin, or move away from Sokoto, dare to be flexible in their attitude to women and allow them the freedom of a modern marriage. The newcomers to power in Sokoto have to show they know how to conform to the old accepted system. In spite of these exceptions, the future trend is toward more independence

---

[3] Uthman dan Fodio Nur al-abab, quoted by Thomas Hodgkin, *Nigerian Perspectives*, p. 194.

[4] For a discussion on architecture and the breakup of the extended family see Peter Marris, *Family and Social Change in an African City: A Study of Rehousing in Lagos* (London: Routledge & Kegan Paul, 1961).

[5] R. Cohen, "Power Authority and Personal Success in Islam and Bornu," in M. J. Swartz, U. W. Turner, and R. Tuden, eds., *Political Anthropology* (Chicago: Aldine, 1966), pp. 129–39.

for sons and their small family groups. This is significant because away from the parental home there is more self-determination for the young wives to bring up their children in a modern way.

## THE BREAKDOWN OF LARGE EXTENDED FAMILIES

In the last 20 years the huge extended families of the Sokoto aristocrats have been breaking down into smaller conjugal units both from choice and because of economic pressures. A traditional compound head or *maigida* liked to have as many people dependent upon him as possible. The number of people dependent on him was an idea of his *girma* or prestige. Although not every man managed to achieve this ideal, *every* man tried to establish as big a compound as was economically possible. The figures given in Table 10.1 are representative of the urban upper-middle class, who in Sokoto are the leaders of change.[6] The traditional aristocrats have even bigger households. In a traditional elite household there are concubines in addition to the four wives allowed in Islam. Within the hierarchy of the compound these concubines are disciplined by the wives and are treated as domestic servants. For example, in one compound each of the four wives has four concubines to help her with her domestic work, there being sixteen concubines in all. Each wife, in turn, prepares the evening meal for the entire compound. This she does with the help of "her" concubines. On the night the wife is responsible for the preparation of the food the husband sleeps in her hut. The concubines do not rate a "sleeping night," but their *maigida* calls for them at odd times when he wants them. The large proportion of women to men is made possible because

[6] For a consideration of the *rural* peasant Hausa-Fulani household and particularly the breakup of *gandu* (the group of relations working together on common land), see A. D. Goddard, "Are Hausa-Fulani Family Structures Breaking Up," *Samaru Agricultural Newsletter*, XI, 3 (Zaria, June 1969), pp. 34–48.

TABLE 10.1
## Change in household size

| Number of Persons in Household | Percent Distribution of Respondents at 7 Years of Age | Present Percent Distribution of respondents (about 20 years later) |
|---|---|---|
| Full distribution | | |
| 2 | 0 | 3 |
| 3 | 3 | 4 |
| 4 | 4 | 5 |
| 5 | 5 | 7 |
| 6–9 | 13 | 22 |
| 10–14 | 22 | 22 |
| 15–29 | 29 | 20 |
| 30–49 | 10 | 15 |
| 50–69 | 7 | 1 |
| 70–99 | 1 | 1 |
| 100 + | 6 | 0 |
| Summary distribution | | |
| Under 10 | 25 | 41 |
| 10–49 | 61 | 57 |
| Over 50 | 14 | 2 |

women marry much earlier than do men and so there are more women of marriageable age, and because concubines are brought from Niger.[7]

In a traditional household some of the first-born children are sent out of the compound to be looked after by their grandmothers or a respected relation or friend. Similarly, other children will be brought into the household. Boys over the age of seven are not allowed in the women's quarters. It is thus very difficult to secure accurate data on the number of children (see below). In addition to wives, concubines, and children, traditional households contain old dependents and servants. The servants may be the offspring of the family slaves, or clients who have attached themselves to the family. There is usually a responsible female servant, a *jakadiya*, who communicates between the separate male quarters at the front of the compound and the women's quarters at the back. There are often long-staying male visitors whose only claim on the *maigida* is that they are in need.

In Table 10.1 note that 20 years ago only 25 percent of the people lived in small

[7] See Vernon R. Dorjahn, "The Factor of Polygamy in African Demography," in William R. Bascom and M. J. Herskovits, eds., *Continuity and Change in African Cultures* (Chicago: University of Chicago Press,

households containing less than ten people, but now as many as 41 percent are living in these smaller households. Fewer people live in very big households today; only 2 percent are in households of over 50 people, while 20 years ago the figure was 14 percent. In Sokoto, as in the Arab countries described by Goode, "there is a secular trend, accelerated in the last decade, in which a young couple breaks away from an extended family and establishes their own home, but does not then develop another extended family made up of their own married sons and grandchildren."[8]

## THE DIFFICULTY OF OBTAINING ACCURATE DATA ON TRADITIONAL FAMILIES

Little is known about the family life of the traditional elite Moslem Fulani-Hausas because only women are allowed inside the women's purdah quarters and then only with the husband's permission.[9] This writer was very fortunate to have helpful friends in Sokoto, having taught there in 1953–1955 and having already made a study of the effect of Western education on Moslem women. The Sultan and officials[10] generously provided help, and ex-pupils and Hausa friends enthusiastically educated me until I understood and respected the peace, contentment, mutual support, and discipline of the harem. It was essential to spend long friendly days in the compounds, watching and taking part in everyday life. Interviewing alone would not have been enough, and only interviewing the male household head would have given totally inaccurate data.

Census-type questions were asked of the compound head by male student helpers.

The answers to these questions hardly ever gave the correct number of people in the compound as checked by observation and interviews with the women in the women's quarters. This was because the male heads of the compound did not like answering the questions, but, instead of objecting, they gave polite but inaccurate answers. For example, one man said when interviewed by a male student, that he only had 3 wives; but visits proved that he actually had 4 wives and 16 concubines. He explained that he wanted to appear to be "modern" and he said, "It is worse than a civil servant having his bank account looked into, for, if you know my family size, you know my resources and commitments and the political influence I have with the big families because I have married their daughters." He could have added that one would also know which adult sons were now eligible for tax and how many daughters he should have sent to school or had vaccinated. It is essential, therefore, for accuracy to go into the women's quarters and observe the family in addition to interviewing the compound head and a wife. It is also essential to have an assistant from the same community.[11]

The census-type questionnaire used was devised only after long observation in the compounds, but it was soon clear that there were snags. For example, if a man and a woman were asked about their mutual children, three different answers constantly were received. After early exasperation at the informants' "inconsistency," it was realized that the problem was one of terminology: "mother" in the questions meant "biological mother" to me, but not to the Hausa (the survey was necessarily conducted in the Hausa language). As Bohannon writes,

---

[8] W. Goode, *World Revolution and Family Patterns* (New York: The Free Press, 1963), p. 124.

[9] Mary Smith's *Baba of Kano* was invaluable to me, but Baba came from Bornu, and is, as she says on p. 143, "a Kado, Habe Barebare, not a Fulani," and she lived in villages so is different from urban Fulani Hausa women. Mary Smith, *Baba of Kano: A Woman of the Muslim Hausa* (London: Faber and Faber, 1954).

[10] I am particularly grateful to Alhaji Ahmed dan Baba, the Marafan Sokoto, for his patience, encouragement, and help at all times.

[11] See R. Mansell Prothero, "The Population Census of Northern Nigeria, 1952: Problems and Results," *Population Studies*, X, 2, 173, "The enumeration in 1952 aimed to include all, and the same importance was given to females as to males. This was not without its problems. There is the inclination among certain tribes to conceal the number of children, particularly the first-born. Among Moslem communities there is the impossibility of checking the number of married women who are in purdah "

"The most important fact about a kinship system is that it is a set of role tags which make it possible for a person to know what to expect from his kinsmen and what they expect from him. It is only secondarily true that in all societies some or all of these categories include persons who are related by bio-physical links."[12]

In Fulani-Hausa society, "mama" describes a woman of appropriate age or relationship who gives motherly attention to a child.[13] So one child has many "mamas"— that is, sociological mothers who may play the role of mother to him. But a first-born child in a traditional Fulani-Hausa household must not call his *own* biological mother "mama"; that is, he must not call upon her for motherly attention because there should be a shame-avoidance relationship between a first-born child and his or her biological mother. So, if one asks in a Fulani-Hausa family, "Who is the 'mama' of this child?" one gets information on who "mothers" the child—that is, the woman who plays the sociological role of mother to him—not information on the woman who gave birth to him.

First-born children are usually sent to their paternal grandmother or aunt after weaning,[14] or, in a large compound, they are looked after by a co-wife or *Kishiya* in order to avoid the intense emotional situation of the direct meeting of first-born child and mother which would upset the strict discipline of the compound. A woman may give motherly care to the later born of her own children, to children of co-wives and of wives who have left the compound, to children she has been given to hold—*riko*, and sometimes to children whose parents are poor, who have given them to her because she can give them a better life.

To give a woman a child to hold—*riko*— is a great compliment to her. In traditional

families a woman likes to mother as many children as possible, and this is regarded as her *dukiya* or happiness and good fortune, not as a burden or responsibility. But the number of children a woman mothers may have no relationship to the number to whom she has given birth. There is a different Hausa word for biological mother, *maihaifiya* (one who has given birth to), but the women thought it impolite and pedantic to make the distinction between *mama* and *maihaifiya*. What matters to the women is sociological motherhood; they explain that a woman who can say "I carried him" or *na goya shi* has at least as much influence on the child and as much claim to him as the woman who gave birth to him.

Of course, it was information on biological motherhood which mattered in the study of population trends. The only way to find out how many children a woman had given birth to was to ask her how many pregnancies she had had, and the result of each pregnancy. Even then this was not straightforward. A Fulani-Hausa woman should not mention her first and sometimes her second-born child, so that it was necessary to ask her or her co-wife or a friend after questioning, "Did this include the first and second born?" Since it probably did not, the first answers had to be corrected. It is also "shameful" and thought to harm the fetus if a woman speaks of a pregnancy that is less than four months old.

The figures in Table 10.2 show the number of children born to 100 educated and 100 uneducated women (i.e., "biological" children) compared with the number of children the women said they mothered (i.e., "sociological" children). From these figures it can be seen what a wide difference there is between the answers on biological and sociological motherhood and how easy it would be to get inaccurate data from census-type interviews alone.

The third category above, "economic children," is the answer given when the informant is thinking of the question, "How many children have you?" as "How many children am I responsible for feeding

[12] P Bohannan, *Social Anthropology* (New York: Holt, Rinehart and Winston 1963), p. 70.
[13] For Hausa kinship terms, see M. G. Smith, *The Economy of Hausa Communities of Zaria: A Report to the Colonial Social Science Research Council* (London, 1955), pp. 41–43.
[14] Smith, *Baba of Kano*, pp. 144–46.

TABLE 10.2

Comparison of biological, social, and economically dependent families, by education of "mother"

| Type of Family | Children per 100 Educated Women | Children per 100 Uneducated Women |
|---|---|---|
| Own biological children | 306 born alive *minus* 45 left home for adoption total = *261* children left in own biological mother's compound (but not all alive now) | 206 born alive *minus* 131 left home for adoption total = *75* left in own biological mother's compound (but not all alive now) |
| Sociological children | 62 foster children given to them *plus* 261 own children (as above) still with them (not all alive) total = *323* | 68 foster children given to them *plus* 75 own children (as above) still with them (not all alive) total = *143* |
| Economic children | How many children do you have a financial responsibility for? Total = *196* | How many children do you have a financial responsibility for? Total = *276* |

now?" This is the most usual way for a Hausa *man* to think of the question. Indeed many surveys have made the mistake of describing the household, defined as the people who use the same cooking pot, as though they were a biological group.[15] In all estimates of population growth, fertility, and infant mortality, it is essential to know that one is talking about the number of biological children given birth to by that household. But (as far as I know), figures so far published on population in this area have been about sociological or economic parentage, and not biological parentage; for example, Abell gives estimates of infant mortality but her data are based on households as socioeconomic rather than biological units.

[15] John C. Caldwell *et al.*, *A Manual for Surveys of Fertility and Family Planning: Knowledge, Attitudes, and Practice*, Population Council (New York, 1970); H. Abell, "Home Economics Aspects" in Food and Agriculture Organization of the United Nations, *Socio-economic Survey of Peasant Agriculture in Northern Nigeria*, FAO (1962). Dr. Murray Last has told me that in Magazawa villages among non-Moslem Hausas a mother looks after her children herself, so sociological and biological families are the same.

It is almost certain that the following data are about biological, not sociological or economic children, and so are relevant to research on population trends and may be of use to demographers whose statistics are often the basis of development programs. It is essential to understand the family structure of a people before starting to count them, so as not to construct tidy academic statistics which would have had little relevance either to the biological facts of reproduction or to patterns of responsibility for child rearing.

## THE MOVE TOWARDS SMALLER CONJUGAL FAMILIES

The modern small conjugal family is much easier than the traditional extended family for an outsider to understand. The former consists of a household with one man as the head living with one or two wives (but not concubines) and their children and perhaps some unmarried siblings of the parents. In families where there are more than two wives the status of the women is lowered and they do not take the active role in decision making which is part of the definition of a modern Hausa family. Modern families usually are headed by an educated man. But there are six modern families in my sample where the family's life style is determined by an educated woman with a high salary who has chosen to marry a man of lower status because he will allow her to go on with her career. This type can be classed as a modern marriage because it is certainly a departure from the traditional way of life, and because the woman has a higher status than traditional women. This type of family cannot be called a nuclear family; as Goode[16] explains, even though the family is living in a small household unit they have definitely not cut off ties with their extended kin, although they have more independence than if they were living in a common extended household. If there is a serious marital quarrel, wives go back to their parental home, and wait for their husbands to fetch them.[17] Modern wives, who are normally happy to be free from the traditional discipline of the elders, are still careful to keep very close contact with their parents, who give them security in time of trouble.

The young husband's break from the extended family is possible at an earlier age than it was for the previous generation because of his earlier economic independence. This independence is usually the result of Western schooling. Most heads of modern families are educated.

Although Western schooling generally has a direct effect on the subsequent life style of men, this is not so for women. In Sokoto the fact that a girl has Western schooling does not necessarily mean that she is likely to have a modern style of marriage, improve her status, be able to use her education in a career, or send her own children to school.

The plan of the study was to compare the families and attitudes of educated and uneducated women, partly to ascertain the influence of education, and partly, by so doing, to compare traditional and modern families. The working hypothesis used was that modern educated women have modern ideas and modern family lives, and uneducated women have traditional ideas and traditional families.[18] This was not at all true in Sokoto, because until recently the community was opposed to education for women. Sometimes an educated girl was considered a bad marriage risk because of her education; it was thought that she would be too self-determined to make a pliable wife, and that she would challenge the old hierarchical rules of domestic life and so threaten the groundwork of the Islamic state. So the sample of educated/uneducated women does not show the polarity between traditional family life and secular modern life. The sample does show some difference between the two sets of women, and the trend from traditional to modern, but it does not show the very strong contrast between the extremes of those living in traditional and modern life styles, which is a much wider division. Although this contrast is not as clear as was anticipated, the approach adopted in the survey was probably the right one, because it allowed for the comparison between women who had experienced Western schooling and those who had not. If the survey had compared modern and traditional women, it could not have been objective. It was, for example, impossible to construct a modern/traditional scale for Hausa women in an objective manner. Even the definition' 'educated" and "uneducated" is oversimplified and very specifically defined. The "educated" group of women had

[16] Goode, *World Revolution*, pp. 70 and 370–71.
[17] For a comparative situation in western Nigeria, see Tanya Baker and Mary Bird, "Urbanization and the Position of Women," *Sociological Review*, VII, 1 (1959).

[18] This hypothesis is employed in P. Lloyd, *The New Elites in Tropical Africa* (London: Oxford University Press, 1966), and in H. Miner, *The City in Modern Africa* (London: Pall Mall Press 1967). See Professor Lorimer's directive to K. A. Busia, "Some Aspects of Social Conditions Affecting Human Fertility in the Gold Coast," in F. Lorimer, ed., *Culture and Human Fertility* (Paris, 1954), p. 343, "To investigate the effect of certain 'modern' conditions such as education, urban residence, or changes in the standard of living on human fertility through their influence either on age at marriage or on family limitation within marriage or both."

Western-style secondary school education at Sokoto girls' boarding school. The "uneducated" group of women of the same age and social status did not have *this* education. But they may well have quite advanced Koranic education, including the ability to read, understand, and write Arabic and Hausa in Arabic script. Nearly all of them also have had an extensive home education in cooking and crafts which the "educated" girls would have missed when away at school.

The sample consisted of 100 women aged 24–30 and 40–44 years who have been to school, and 67 women who have not been to school, but who are matched with the other group for age and social status. In addition, 96 husbands[19] of these two groups of women were interviewed by male students. The control group of uneducated women was chosen by asking each educated woman for the name of her *kawwa* or bond friend. This was done because it seemed to be the only way to pick women of approximately the same age; Hausa women are usually vague about their ages, but the educated ones know theirs. It was also a way of choosing a control group whom the women themselves regarded as being of equal status in origin. But the disadvantage, of course, was that these uneducated women all had educated friends who would influence their opinions. Because of this, the difference in these two groups is less than one would expect to find in women at opposite ends of the traditional/modern scale. But the trend to greater differentiation is clear—a trend which will inevitably accelerate now that much more support is given to the education of women.

## MARRIAGE

A Sokoto woman's life style usually depends much more on the education and status of her father or husband than on her own education and personal attributes.

Educated women are more likely to be in a

[19] I regret not having been able to interview at least 100 in each group, but my grant came abruptly to an end.

compound with fewer wives than are the uneducated women, but there is no guarantee in Sokoto that a girl's education will lead her into a small modern conjugal household. However, some educated girls who were forced into marriages with powerful old chiefs with a large harem, later made their own arrangements to marry fellow school teachers. Some educated women (11 percent of the total) who wanted to work as teachers or nurses arranged to be divorced by their husbands and then married poor farmers or craftsmen who would let them work and could not afford a large harem. Not that

TABLE 10.3
Percentage distribution of respondents by education and number of current wives of husbands

| Number of wives | Educated | Uneducated |
| --- | --- | --- |
| 1 | 36 | 30 |
| 2 | 23 | 31 |
| 3 | 23 | 21 |
| 4 | 10 | 11 |
| 5 | 1 | 1 |
| 6 | 2 | 0 |
| 7 | 2 | 1 |
| 8 | 1 | 0 |
| 9 | 1 | 0 |
| 10 or more | 1 | 5 |
| Totals: percentage | 100 | 100 |
| number | 100 | 67 |

educated women all object to co-wives; some say they would welcome *one* other co-wife as a companion and a help with domestic tasks.[20] But the wives have noticed that, if a man has a superfluity of women, they lose their scarcity value and status.

The figures in Table 10.3 were obtained from interviews and were checked and corrected by observation and requestioning. The husband's information was, as emphasized before, usually unreliable if he was the head of a big compound, but it was usually accurate if he was head of a small compound. These results can be compared

[20] See Smith, *Baba of Kano*.

with figures for *rural* Sokoto families[21] where only 30 percent of husbands had more than one wife. The women in Table 10.3 are in contrast urban elite women, where husbands can afford more wives.

The women interviewed were not a random sample. They do not represent a cross section of all social groups. Most of the educated girls came from traditional elite families, but Table 10.4 shows that a large

TABLE 10.4

Occupations of respondents' husbands, by respondents' education (percentage distribution)

| Husband's Occupation | Educated | Uneducated |
|---|---|---|
| Traditional aristocrat | 16 | 11 |
| Traditional aristocrat with modern qualification & job | 10 | 6 |
| Civil servant, Western-type school teacher (not traditional elite) | 43 | 37 |
| Islamic learned man | 4 | 12 |
| A big trader | 3 | 1 |
| A small trader | 9 | 22 |
| Craftsman | 6 | 8 |
| Farmer | 9 | 3 |
| Servant | 2 | 0 |
| | 100 | 100 |

proportion of them have married modern elite men—that is, men whose status depends on education, not birth (civil servants and school teachers amount to 43 percent, and sons of traditional leaders who also have a modern job to another 10 percent, making 53 percent in all). The educated women's marriages to farmers and servants number 11 percent, and were almost invariably to obtain the freedom to work.

Educated women married later than uneducated women, but their marriages were more stable. When educated women were divorced it was usually to get away from a forced marriage in order to marry the man of their choice; often if they were teachers it was a colleague at school. Table 10.5 shows that

TABLE 10.5

Number of marriages of respondents, by education (percentage distribution)

| Number of Marriages | Educated | Uneducated |
|---|---|---|
| 1 | 61 | 5 |
| 2 | 31 | 17 |
| 3 | 6 | 23 |
| 4 | 2 | 39 |
| 5 | 0 | 10 |
| 6 | 0 | 5 |
| | 100 | 99[a] |

[a] Adds up to 99 because o frounding.

among the educated women, 61 percent had experienced only one marriage and 31 percent two marriages. This is a very low number of marriages for Hausa women—compare this with the uneducated group and with Smith, "On average most Hausa women will make three marriages between the age of 13 to the menopause, and probably another one thereafter."[22] The stability of the marriages of educated women would surprise the traditionalist men who oppose secular education for girls on the grounds that they would "not stay in marriage." In fact 61 percent of the educated were still in their first marriage compared with 5 percent of the uneducated, while only 2 percent of the former had been married four or more times compared with 54 percent of the latter.

Educated women are given more freedom than uneducated women. Among the uneducated women, 86 percent were kept in purdah by their husbands, compared with only 46 percent of the educated wives. The amount of freedom a woman is given has an influence on her status; if she is allowed out of purdah she is better known by other people and by discussing her views with others she is encouraged "to act and behave more individualistically than is customary under the traditional system."[23] These are the women who are questioning traditional beliefs about women's status, their roles as mothers, and the ideal size of their family.

[21] A. D. Goddard, *Samaru Agricultural Newsletter* (June 1969).

[22] Smith, *Economy of the Hausa Communities of Zaria*, p. 64.
[23] Kenneth Little, *West African Urbanization* (London: Cambridge University Press, 1965), p. 137.

TABLE 10.6
Extent to which husbands allow
respondent wives out of the home, by
education of respondents (percentage
distribution)

| Extent | Educated | Uneducated |
|---|---|---|
| Very strict, no outings | 2 | 3 |
| Purdah, limited evening outings only | 46 | 86 |
| Go out for work only | 40 | 9 |
| Not restricted | 12 | 2 |
| | 100 | 100 |

Table 10.6 shows the men's answers to the question, "Do you keep your wives in purdah, or do they go out to visit relations, to work, or to go shopping?" Their actual practice was checked by observation and further inquiries.

Accurate information on the total number of marriages men had made was not available because the men thought their virility was being questioned. For example, two men (a trader and a driver) had taken 35 and 37 wives each, as well as additional concubines. When the accuracy of these figures were checked, we were told that such figures were not out of the ordinary. (One of these men had never had a child, but he still thought his wives were to blame.) However,

modern young men pride themselves on the stability of their marriages. Even in traditional society, a man's first wife usually only makes one marriage.

Educated women marry later than uneducated women (see Table 10.7) because they must first finish their schooling. Traditional fathers think that girls should be married at or before the menarche, so that it is not possible for them to become pregnant before marriage. Such marriages are not supposed to be consummated until the brides are "ready", but in practice the husbands are not always patient. This practice leads to much misery and ill health because the girls conceive before they are fully grown and often either the mother or child is injured, sometimes incurably. Many women told me that, after a difficult miscarriage or delivery at 13 years of age, they had not been able to become pregnant again. The present generation of Moslem reformers is discussing this malpractice which they say is a misinterpretation of the Prophet Mohammed's instructions to care for the morals of one's womenfolk.

As educated women marry later, they almost always have their first pregnancy later. But although the uneducated women start married life earlier, ultimately they do not average as many pregnancies as educated women of

TABLE 10.7
Age at first marriage and first pregnancy, by education
(Percentage distribution)

| Age of Woman | Age at First Marriage | | Age at First Pregnancy | |
|---|---|---|---|---|
| | Educated | Uneducated | Educated | Uneducated |
| 13 years or less | 8 | 66 | 2 | 12 |
| 14 | 21 | 18 | 4 | 15 |
| 15 | 20 | 10 | 8 | 18 |
| 16 | 21 | 6 | 17 | 19 |
| 17 | 11 | 0 | 21 | 3 |
| 18 | 5 | 0 | 16 | 9 |
| 19 | 6 | 0 | 8 | 2 |
| 20 | 3 | 0 | 4 | 3 |
| 21 | 2 | 0 | 12 | 4 |
| 22 | 3 | 0 | 0 | 0 |
| Never pregnant | | | 8 | 15 |
| | 100 | 100 | 100 | 100 |

the same age. The main reasons for this seem to be the following:

(1) Uneducated women's marriages are less stable so they are "out" of married life for a larger proportion of the time subsequent to their first marriage.

(2) Some were injured by having their first pregnancy when they were too young, and are afterward subfertile or infertile.

(3) Uneducated women are more strict than educated women about keeping the taboo on sexual intercourse until their child is weaned around one year and seven months age. This leads to a natural spacing of children of one on average about every two-and-a-half years.

## CHILDREN

Among traditional elite families, men have more children than the women because each wife is often only one of many past or present wives. This is brought out clearly in Table 10.8. Thus the number of live children born per hundred educated women is 306, and per hundred uneducated women is 206 at the same age (i.e., around 30). The educated women have more children than the same aged uneducated women, even though they started later.

A surprisingly large number of the un-educated group of women—one-quarter—have had no live children born to them (they have adopted children whom they treat as their own). Of the total uneducated women, one-fifth said they had not been able to become pregnant. It is not known if this was because they were totally infertile or because they had been damaged by a too early pregnancy or miscarriage. It would not have been humane to press on with these questions because the women became very distressed since infertility is such a disaster to a Hausa. The women who had no children were all from big harems. It is suspected by gynecologists at Ahmadu Bello University that the risk of venereal disease to a woman, and consequent infertility, goes up according to the number of other women with whom her husband has intercourse. More husbands (15 per cent) of the uneducated women have no children than the husbands (5.2 percent) of the educated women.

It is worth noting that many more people asked about ways of increasing fertility than asked about family spacing or restriction. Many local medicines are used, ranging from talismans containing verses from the Koran, to herbal mixtures and sympathetic magic.

The live birth figures refer to women whose average age is 30 years. The 100 educated women have had 306 live births between them, of whom 67 children have died,

TABLE 10.8
Live births to respondents and their husbands, by education of respondents (percentage distribution)

| Live Births | Educated Women | | Uneducated Women | |
|---|---|---|---|---|
| | Respondents | Husbands | Respondents | Husbands |
| 0 | 9 | 5 | 26 | 16 |
| 1 | 19 | 9 | 18 | 13 |
| 2 | 16 | 14 | 18 | 10 |
| 3 | 15 | 14 | 12 | 21 |
| 4 | 20 | 15 | 10 | 8 |
| 5 | 11 | 13 | 13 | 8 |
| 6 | 5 | 2 | 3 | 8 |
| 7 | 3 | 9 | 0 | 3 |
| 8 | 0 | 3 | 0 | 0 |
| 9 or more | 2 | 16 | 0 | 13 |
| | 100 | 100 | 100 | 100 |

leaving 239, an average of 2.39 per woman. The uneducated women had given birth to 206 live children, of whom 56 have died, leaving 150, an average of 1.5 per woman. Of course these women will probably have more children, but they have already been married an average of 12 years and it is surprising that they have not had more. This hardly seems to be a "population explosion." When we separate modern from traditional women, a definite trend emerges. Women in modern conjugal homes have babies more frequently than do women in traditional homes. This is probably because they do not keep the lactation taboo as practiced in traditional homes.

In traditional Hausa homes, women maintain the ban on sexual intercourse before their child is weaned at one year and seven months. This taboo is most strictly kept among the non-Islamized Hausa, the Maguzawa, who roughly reckon the age of a child by counting his siblings and multiplying by three for the years in between their births.[24] Koranic scholars have told me that this taboo is an old Hausa custom and not a Moslem one. One devout Moslem said that, contrary to this old taboo a good Moslem should sleep with his wife as soon as she is ritually clean, to express his pleasure that she has given him a child; and anyway, he added, she is not likely to become pregnant so soon after she has given birth.

Whatever the origins, many Hausa families very strongly adhered to this taboo. The educated women rationalize and say it is a good custom, because a new pregnancy which comes too soon would "poison" the milk of an infant not yet ready for weaning so that he will not grow strong. Some of the uneducated women say that conceiving a child before one has weaned the last is "filthy, and shows lack of control over lust." Their opinions are summarized in Table 10.9. The disgrace of having another pregnancy too quickly is called *rurrutsa* in Sokoto, and *gwanne* in Zaria. It is thought that such children will not grow strong.

[24] Information from Dr. Murray Last who is at present studying the Maguzawa.

TABLE 10.9
Reasons given by respondents for maintaining the taboo on sexual relations during the lactation period (percentage distribution)

| Reasons | Educated | Uneducated |
|---|---|---|
| Mother's health suffers | 80 | 27 |
| Child's health suffers | 9 | 19 |
| Too expensive | 4 | 3 |
| Child will not be well looked after | 7 | 6 |
| It is dirty, taboo, or not right | 0 | 5 |
| If it happens, it is what Allah wills | 0 | 40 |
| | 100 | 100 |

## IDEAL FAMILY SIZE

In Table 10.9 the main difference between the educated and uneducated women is that the uneducated are much more fatalistic, while the educated women base their decisions on the belief that frequent pregnancies are bad for the health of mother and child. The biggest difference between women in the traditional extended families and women in the modern secular conjugal families is in their attitudes to the ideal family size, as can be seen in Table 10.10. Traditional women, whose status largely depends on their children, want as many as possible; they

TABLE 10.10
Ideal family size expressed by respondents, by education (percentage distribution)

| Ideal Number | Educated | Uneducated |
|---|---|---|
| 0 | 0 | 0 |
| 1 | 0 | 0 |
| 2 | 3 | 5 |
| 3 | 11 | 12 |
| 4 | 30 | 18 |
| 5 | 18 | 22 |
| 6 | 7 | 3 |
| 7 | 2 | 3 |
| 8 | 2 | 1 |
| As many as Allah brings | 22 | 36 |
| Too many already | 5 | 0 |
| | 100 | 100 |

feel that the number of children they have is determined by fate, and that the gift of children is a sign of Allah's approval. Modern women are less fatalistic; they feel that they as individuals must take responsibility for their own children, and not "just let things happen." These modern women are beginning to think more about the quality of life that they are able to provide for their children rather than the quantity of children they are able to produce. This trend is shown in the Table 10.10, although, as stressed before, the contrast is not as marked as it would be between traditional and modern women, because some of the educated women are living in a traditional way. Those fatalistic women saying they want "as many children as Allah brings" are all in traditional extended harem families.

The five educated women who said they had too many children already are all modern women. They did not like to state an ideal family size which was less than their actual family size because they would then be open to criticism. From the table, it can be seen that most educated women think that four children is an ideal family and most uneducated women prefer five. Most women said that they must have at least one son. A very modern educated woman, the sole wife, with four daughters, said, "I wish I could stop, but I must produce a son for my husband, so that his family goes on; if I don't he will probably take another wife." Most women wanted one daughter "to have one of my own kind to talk with and live through and enjoy admiring her when I have bought her new clothes, and arranging her marriage ceremony." But they thought too many daughters would be too expensive.

For comparison, Table 10.11 shows the ideal family size expressed by the respondents' husbands. Note the large proportion of men who want over ten children or as many as possible. Note also the lack of a clear difference between the two sets of husbands.

Modern men seem to cling to the traditional ideal of a large family, at least in theory, even when their wives are beginning

TABLE 10.11

Ideal family size expressed by respondents' husbands, by education of respondents (percentage distribution)

| Ideal Number | Husbands of Educated Women | Husbands of Uneducated Women |
|---|---|---|
| 0 | 0 | 0 |
| 1 | 0 | 0 |
| 2 | 2 | 8 |
| 3 | 3 | 5 |
| 4 | 14 | 8 |
| 5 | 28 | 11 |
| 6 | 12 | 16 |
| 7–9 | 0 | 0 |
| 10 + | 10 | 21 |
| As many as possible | 28 | 13 |
| Whatever number Allah gives me | 3 | 5 |
| Don't know | 0 | 13 |
| | 100 | 100 |

to think that they have all the responsibility with which they can cope. Men are still given respect if they have large families. Traditionalists quoted the old Hausa saying *Mutano, su ne aziki*, "one's people make one's fortune," saying it meant that one's future depended on having many children, and explaining that they needed many sons to look after them in their old age when they would have no other income. Some modern men said that they wanted many sons, whom they would educate in all the different professions, so that in their old age they would have vast political power and everyone would hear the family name.

In Hausa society a large family is a culturally acceptable aim. The men stressed that having a large number of children brings personal happiness and the respect of the community. Since these might be unthinking public statements, we asked the question in different ways to see if their thoughtful private views were the same. When asked "have you enough children now?" about a quarter of the men admitted they had (see Table 10.12).

The men did not admit that their children were a financial burden or a worry to them.

TABLE 10.12
Replies of respondents' husbands to question, "Have you enough children now?" (percentage distribution)

| Replies | Husbands of Educated Women | Husbands of Uneducated Women |
|---|---|---|
| Yes | 32 | 23 |
| No | 65 | 71 |
| What Allah decides | 0 | 5 |
| Don't know, and other | 3 | 1 |

They were then asked how they would spend a gift of money on their children to see how they viewed their responsibilities (see Table 10.13).

The men also were asked if they needed the children's help on the farm or with their craft, but they were reluctant to admit that their children were an economic asset to them when young, although they were an insurance for their old age. The women did say that their daughters were a help in their marketing activities and to purdah women they were an essential link with the outside world; but these elite women said that any profit from marketing was put aside for the daughter's dowry. There were different answers from the poorer respondents who needed the children's economic contri-

TABLE 10.13
Replies of respondents' husbands to question "What would you buy for your children if you were given a gift of money?" (percentage distribution)

| Replies | Husbands of Educated Women | Husbands of Uneducated Women |
|---|---|---|
| Food | 17 | 7 |
| Clothes | 21 | 31 |
| School fees | 43 | 31 |
| Toys | 8 | 7 |
| Their future | 10 | 21 |
| No response or residual | 1 | 3 |
| | 100 | 100 |

TABLE 10.14
Reasons for wanting a large family, by respondents' education (percentage distribution)

| Reasons | Educated Women | Uneducated Women |
|---|---|---|
| Perhaps some will die | 15 | 22 |
| Need help when I'm old | 9 | 33 |
| Children bring joy | 38 | 16 |
| Help at home | 3 | 2 |
| Don't want above four anyway | 34 | 15 |
| It is Allah's will not mine | 1 | 12 |
| | 100 | 100 |

bution to the family income, but the majority of the families studied were not poor.

When we talked to the men about the ideal family size, most started by vaguely quoting the culturally acceptable ideal that one should have a large family, in contrast to the women who had thought much more carefully about the number of children they personally wanted and about their reasons (see Tables 10.14 and 10.15).

There are striking differences between the two groups here. Educated women are more

TABLE 10.15
Reasons for wanting a small family,[a] by respondents' education (percentage distribution)

| Reasons | Educated Women | Uneducated Women |
|---|---|---|
| Women's health suffers with large number of pregnancies | 6 | 8 |
| Child's health suffers with large number of mother's pregnancies | 3 | 5 |
| Economic stress | 8 | 16 |
| Children well looked after | 45 | 15 |
| Don't want small family, personal decision | 38 | 10 |
| Don't know any reason for wanting small family, or children show the approval of Allah | 0 | 46 |
| | 100 | 100 |

positive; they want children because they bring joy, but the advantage of a small family is that children are well looked after. Uneducated women are pessimistic; they feel they ought to have a big family because some may die, and to insure their old age. They are also more fatalistic; they feel they should leave their fate to Allah. And 57 percent do not know of any reason at all for preferring a small family to a large one.

In order to find out why the women wanted more or less children than they already had, the women were asked about their attitude to *riko* or foster children. This is the easiest way to discuss attitudes to family size with them, because they have more choice about foster children. Many traditional women feel that giving birth should be left to fate. If one questions fate, then somehow one's own children, whom one loves even if there *are* too many of them, will be spirited away.

The traditional women feel that being given additional *riko* children is a compliment, and gives them enhanced status. Many of them use these girls (as well as their own) to help in housework or to sell cooked food in the market, so they are an asset in their trade and contacts with the outside world, though they do admit that the responsibility of giving these girls a dowry is expensive.

On the whole, educated women who live in a modern way, resist being given *riko* children because they say rearing children to today's standards is a heavy financial and psychological responsibility. If they are away from the family, farm food has to be bought; there is not much room in a small modern house; schooling is expensive and in their social position they could not, even if they wished, send the children trading in the market. A civil servant's wife said, as she was struggling to get her five children off to school in clean clothes and with a good breakfast, "In the past children were as cows are to the Fulani, the more the better; you turned them out to work on the farm, and they brought in their own food, and you felt proud when you counted them. But now we have to pay for everything from our fixed salary with no family nearby to help us out with domestic help or presents of food." Increasingly in families of this type the wife is the only adult woman, and she frequently has a job as well; thus it is a great worry to her to arrange for her own children to be cared for adequately, without taking on others. Also, like all good Sokoto Moslems, she realizes that character training, *tarbiya*, is primarily the mother's responsibility and must not be neglected.

In summary, traditional women want as many children as possible to give them status and interest, and to help with their work or craft. Modern women are much more aware of the responsibilities entailed in looking after children. Because there are fewer women in modern homes, babies come more quickly, and they have fewer people to help look after the children; then, too, they may have the additional responsibility of a job.

There is a marked difference between modern and traditional women's ideal family size. This difference is not so clearly shown up in the figures for educated and uneducated women in Table 10.16, but is nevertheless still visible. The educated women often qualify the statement that they have sufficient children by adding, "if Allah wills and they all survive."

The modern women seem to be moving away from the traditional ideal of wanting as many children as possible, but most

TABLE 10.16
Respondents' replies to question "Have you enough children now?" By education (percentage distribution)

| Replies | Educated Women | Uneducated Women |
|---|---|---|
| Yes | 62 | 20 |
| No | 26 | 65 |
| Whatever Allah brings | 6 | 14 |
| Don't know | 5 | 1 |
| No, want a boy | 1 | 0 |
| No, want a girl | 0 | 0 |
| | 100 | 100 |

modern men still say they want large families and do not like to admit that this may cause financial hardship. Modern women have more children, closer together than traditional women, but they are becoming concerned for their own and their children's health now that the traditional methods of spacing children are breaking down.

## FAMILY PLANNING

Does this mean that Hausa men and women would, if they had the knowledge, use modern birth control techniques to regulate the size of their families? The Grand Khadi, who is himself from Sokoto and is the head of Moslem Law, was asked if birth control was acceptable to Hausa Moslems. The Grand Khadi quoted the Koran and the Hadith to show that birth control is allowed in Islam and he made a public statement to this effect in 1968 in reply to the Papal encyclical. He said that in Islam a person's life must not be endangered and so, if a woman is likely to become ill if she is pregnant, we should do all we can to stop her if it is dangerous for her. When told that many Hausa men say it is their duty as Moslems to produce many children, the Grand Khadi replied that all the Prophet Mohammed had said was that we should get married, that marriage produces children, and children are a help in old age. He pointed out that there is another Hadith which says that "having a small family is a way of ensuring a higher standard of living for one's children."

So it does not appear that there is any public religious objection among modern Moslem thinkers to the use of modern birth control techniques for those whose health would suffer from continuous pregnancy. There is also the well-established traditional belief in the benefit of two-and-one-half year's spacing between children. But, among traditional people, it is considered wrong to challenge fate by taking decisions into one's own hands. Those traditional women who had heard about modern birth control methods were doubtful about their use just because they were more efficient than traditional methods and so cut out the element of fate. The women could not be asked directly if they knew about modern birth control methods since it had been agreed with the authorities that the subject would not be introduced, but questions about traditional methods of birth control were permitted (see Table 10.17).

TABLE 10.17

Knowledge of traditional contraception, by respondents' education (percent distribution)

| Responses | Educated Women | Uneducated Women |
| --- | --- | --- |
| Know and approve of use | 20 | 31 |
| Know | 22 | 18 |
| Know, but their use is not right | 0 | 7 |
| I wish I knew | 4 | 2 |
| Don't know | 51 | 42 |
| Keep away from husband | 3 | 0 |
| | 100 | 100 |

The traditional methods of birth control include abstaining from sexual intercourse, wearing a charm tied around the waist, drinking water which has been used to wash off a verse of the Koran written on a wooden board, and placing a charmed bowl under the bed to "catch" the baby. The method of *coitus interruptus* is well known but generally not thought of as a practical possibility which can be successfully managed. Those women who spoke about traditional methods of birth control did not think that they could ask their husbands to practice *coitus interruptus*, because it would be unfair to them or because their husbands might reject them in favor of other wives. The Grand Khadi in his public statement on birth control in 1968 stated that *azl* or *coitus interruptus* is a legitimate method of birth control. Abortion is considered a crime in Islam, but many women spoke about ways of obtaining abortions using charms, or local medicines such as the roots of henna which cause violent bowel movements.

TABLE 10.18
Knowledge and use of traditional methods
to promote fertility, by respondents'
education (percentage distribution)

| Responses | Educated Women | Uneducated Women |
|-----------|----------------|------------------|
| Know and use | 24 | 27 |
| Know | 26 | 17 |
| Wish I did | 4 | 10 |
| Don't know | 46 | 46 |
|  | 100 | 100 |

These traditional practices show that there is a concern for the spacing of children, but not necessarily a reduction of the total number of children. There is also great concern for knowledge of methods to increase fertility, as can be seen in Table 10.18. Women believe that a pregnancy can "go to sleep"—*kwanciyar ciki*—and they take local medicines to "wake it up." If this is not successful, they feel they must get rid of the "old sleeping pregnancy" before a new one can take its place. Many traditional women who would not go to a hospital for anything else, would like to have a dilation and curettage in the hope of being able to establish a new pregnancy.

This concern for spacing of children, and the desire for more knowledge about fertility, shows that there is a need for more knowledge about family planning in the broadest sense—that is, how to make responsible plans to have children at the best times. But it is probably not yet true to say that most people are interested in using modern birth control methods to cut down the total size of their families.

Traditionalists are afraid to challenge fate by taking personal initiative, and modern men still see large families as a means of gaining status, prestige, influence, and an insurance for one's old age. Modern women have thought more deeply about the problems because they are personally more affected. They want to space their pregnancies to safeguard their own and their children's health. They have more children more quickly than traditional women and are

finding the responsibility too great when they have no relatives to help and probably the burden of a job as well. It is this group, the modern women, who may ask for instruction on modern birth control techniques, *if* their ideal number of children survive. Those women who want to use modern birth control techniques primarily need a rest between children. They are at present reluctant to plan to have a small family because they are afraid that some of their children will die. No evidence has been collected so far that the children of educated women who are taken to the hospital when sick are less likely to die than those of uneducated women who are treated with local medicines. The Hausa greeting at the birth of a child is "May Allah let him live," and this is heartfelt in places where 50 percent or more of the children die before reaching adulthood.[25] Hausa people need children to look after them in their old age, and they dread the thought of dying without children. As one teacher said after her son had died of cerebro-spinal meningitis in spite of her care and that of the hospital, "We are afraid to say we want fewer children, and take fate into our own hands. Who knows when our healthy children will suddenly be struck dead? To die without children is to go from earth without leaving one's immortality." And a thoughtful modern man said, "Unfortunately we can never say we have enough children, because we do not know how many will survive. If we knew they would survive, our attitude to birth control would be different, but now we are always fearful." There is a Hausa saying, *Da ya fi dukiya*—a son is better than riches, because a son is seen as social insurance for one's old age, as well as a source of joy.

These people did not admit any economic reasons for restricting their total number of children. The men did not find it difficult to feed and clothe the children they had. The traditional men with large numbers of

[25] Estimated by J. Moore, Professor of Gynecology, Ahmadu Bello University, from figures at Zaria and Malamfashi hospitals, representative of city and rural areas.

wives, concubines, and children usually had family farms. Modern young men restricted the number of wives they had and consequently those men had fewer children than their fathers. They did not find feeding the children difficult but were beginning to worry about school fees. Of course this was an elite group and the story would be different for a poor group. But those poor people interviewed thought of their children as an economic *asset* in that they could help in crafts and farming and would look after their parents in their old age. Doctors at Sokoto and Zaria have said that there is little malnutrition among Hausa children because of lack of food, and where it does occur it is usually because of intestinal parasites or because of slow change over to protein food at weaning time. The Hausa people I spoke to do not feel they should restrict the number of children because of food shortages.

It seems that, until general infant mortality rates drop further, parents, even in small modern families, will not be interested in restricting the total size of their families. But modern women particularly may well be interested in the use of modern techniques for the healthy spacing of children. Modern women say that the well-established Hausa custom of abstaining from sexual intercourse until the baby is ready for weaning at one year, seven months is much easier to manage in a large harem than it is in a small modern family with only one or two wives, and, although the women would like to keep the taboo, they say their husbands will not agree. These modern women had discussed their problems with their husbands, but by no means all the husbands were sympathetic with their wives' difficulties in running the house and a job while being continually pregnant. As one husband said, "I haven't enough children yet; my father had 15 and I can bring another female relative from home to look after them"; but the wife said that she wanted peace when she came home from work, not more of his female relations cluttering up the house. Only three educated women (all living away from Sokoto) reported that their husbands had agreed that they should not have any more children for a while because they had so many responsibilities and had agreed to their being fitted with an IUD. They planned to have more children after a rest.

Probably most people would be interested in family planning information in the widest sense—that is, help with problems of infertility and healthy spacing of children if it were provided as an integral part of the maternal and child welfare services. There is a big demand for help with problems of infertility, a long-established belief in the importance of the healthy spacing of children, and a need for knowledge of modern spacing techniques in modern families where traditional taboos have broken down. It is unlikely that there will be a general demand for the restriction of total family size until infant mortality figures drop. Modern women have more children, closer together, than traditional women do, and if they see that these children survive, and they dare to take fate into their own hands, they may stop wanting to give birth to more children. But until a larger number of the children born survive the dreadful childhood illnesses of northern Nigeria there is not likely to be a general demand for restriction of family size.

It is impossible to be a responsible rational planning parent until one is more or less in control of the environment in which one's children grow up. In northern Nigeria, where about half the children die, Hausa people cannot feel certain that their children will survive. In such a situation it is understandable that they either overinsure by having more children than their ideal number, or because the situation is not in their control, they leave it to fate. Both from the viewpoint of responsible family planning, and on broader grounds of humanitarianism, the first priority is the general improvement of the maternal and child welfare services. Once parents see that their children have a greater chance of surviving they may well take the responsibility of restricting their numbers.

# CHAPTER ELEVEN

# Population Growth & Its Components

## The Nature and Direction of Population Change

P. O. OLUSANYA

⸬

THE 1963 census claimed for Nigeria a population of 56 million people. Since the area of the country is 356,669 square miles, this implied a density of 156 persons per square mile. This area is about three times that of the rest of anglophone West Africa, and it apparently contains almost 60 percent of the total population of West Africa and almost one-fifth of that of Africa as a whole. It is by far the most populous African country, although it covers only about 3 percent of the continent's total land area and only 15 percent of that of West Africa.

Because of Nigeria's latitudinal extent from about 4° to 14° North, its physical conditions, vegetation, ethnic groups, and economy are exceptionally varied. Rainfall ranges from about 120 inches in Calabar in the southeast to about 25 inches in the Chad basin in the northeast extremity. In the former there is an excess of rain all year, while in the latter there is adequate rain only during two or three months. In the delta area of the Niger the number of rainy days in each month is about 20 and rain falls throughout the year. Consequently, communications are difficult and settlements can only be reached through creeks. The roads, where they exist, are mainly poor, waterlogged, and unmotorable. These varied conditions constitute a severe handicap, not only in achieving the uniform development of the country, but also in securing uniformity of quality in population census data.

The geographical entity, now known as Nigeria, has not always been one country. The earliest reported European contact was by the Portuguese in 1472.[1] With the development of the overseas slave trade, the Portuguese were followed by other nations. After the abolition of the slave trade by the British in 1807, the penetration of the interior began. Lagos was taken in 1861 in order to suppress its illegal slave trade. In 1879 the United Africa Company (UAC) finally opened up the Niger River and undertook the government of the interior. While these designs were

[1] See Sir Alan Burns, *History of Nigeria* (London, 1948), for details.

still being accomplished, Oil Rivers Protectorate was proclaimed in 1885 over most coastal territories from Lagos to the Cameroons.

The process of colonizing the hinterland continued gradually, leading to the proclamation of the Protectorates of Southern and Northern Nigeria in 1900, the introduction of indirect rule to Northern Nigeria through the emirs in 1903, the merging of Lagos with Southern Nigeria in 1906, and, finally, the amalgamation of the Southern and Northern Protectorates in 1914 with Lugard as the first Governor of Nigeria.

Thus, Nigeria became a single country gradually and by stages, and this, as will be seen later, has had an important influence on its census coverage until very recent times. Moreover, the diversity of its cultures, the differences in the timing of European contacts, the varied physical environments, all of which have led to the development of different kinds of socioeconomic patterns and distribution of social amenities, are likely to have far-reaching demographic implications for the future of the country.

## PAST POPULATION RECORDS

As far as population counts are concerned, Nigeria is probably one of the poorest countries in the world. This situation has arisen from its history. Population counts in Nigeria began in 1866 when the enumeration was confined to the Lagos area. Another count followed two years later, and yet another three years later in 1871. From the third one, that of 1871, population censuses became decennial, though still confined to the Lagos area until 1911. Estimates had, of course, been made for parts of the country before this time, though they were no more than mere guesses.

In the 1911 population count, however, an attempt was made to cover a wider area in the southern provinces, but, even then, enumeration could be extended only to the main ports, while, for the rest, estimates for the southern provinces as a whole were made on the basis of the best available data in each district. It

was a very similar story in the northern provinces. A total population of 15.9 million was estimated for Nigeria as a whole.

An attempt was made in 1921 to widen the scope of enumeration. Consequently, the operation was divided into two parts, the township census and the provincial census. The former was said to be fairly accurate but the latter was an utter failure. A total estimate of 18.6 million persons, including the Trust Territory of the Cameroons, was given for Nigeria.

As for the 1931 "census," it was "a mere compilation of existing data,"[2] though it originally was planned to cover the whole country. The disturbances in parts of eastern Nigeria discouraged a countrywide population count so that the population of 19.9 million returned for Nigeria was obtained largely from existing records. In short, it is clear that the population estimates for specific years up to the World War II can give us at the best, only the vaguest idea of the number of Nigeria's inhabitants over the years.

The first census of population worthy of that name was taken in Nigeria in 1952–1953. Even today, the 1952–1953 census is regarded by many as the best source of demographic information on Nigeria. The more important shortcomings of the census, particularly in relation to completeness of enumeration, have been dealt with in detail elsewhere.[3] Unfortunately the figures are now out of date.

Although the timing of the population census of 1963 in terms of the increased overall level of literacy, the content of the questionnaire, and the preparations that preceded the

[2] "Report of the Census Officer," *Census of Nigeria, 1931*, Department of Statistics (Lagos).

[3] See P. O. Olusanya, "Adequacy of Existing Census and Vital Statistics for Demographic Research and Planning," *Nigerian Journal of Economic and Social Studies*, VIII, 1 (March 1966), pp. 143–46; C. Okonjo, "A Preliminary Medium Estimate of the 1962 Mid-Year Population of Nigeria," in John C. Caldwell and C. Okonjo, eds., *The Population of Tropical Africa* (London: Longmans, Green & Company, and New York: Columbia University Press, 1968), pp. 79–82; R. C. Duru, "Problems of Data Collection for Population Studies in Nigeria with Particular Reference to the 1952/53 Census and the Western Region," *ibid.*, pp. 71–77.

counts were all conducive to highly reliable results, the whole exercise was vitiated by political considerations which have led to heated arguments as to its validity and reliability. Much of the controversy has centered around the extent to which the published population figures reflect the actual numbers counted. The conclusion has invariably been that the figures were substantially inflated, considering the phenomenal increase indicated for the 1952–1963 intercensal period.[4]

Table 11.1 reveals several interesting facts about population censuses and estimates since

TABLE 11.1
Apparent population growth, 1921–1963

| Period | Population Increase (000's) | Percentage Increase | Average Annual Percentage Increase |
|---|---|---|---|
| *Intercensal periods* | | | |
| 1921–31 | 1,303 | 7 | 0.7 |
| 1932–52 | 10,489 | 53 | 2.1 |
| 1952–63 | 25,203 | 83 | 5.6 |
| *Certain combined periods* | | | |
| 1921–52 | 11,792 | 63 | 1.6 |
| 1921–63 | 36,995 | 199 | 2.7 |
| 1931–63 | 35,692 | 179 | 3.2 |

SOURCE: Computed from censuses of Nigeria.

1921. As would be expected from the account of the nature of these estimates, the 1921–1931 and the 1952–1963 intercensal periods show unusually low and unusually high average annual rates of growth respectively, which do not seem justified on the basis of the prevailing conditions in the two periods. In the case of the 1921–1931 intercensal period, the fault probably lies mainly with the 1931 population figure, which may well have been a gross underestimate, thus showing hardly any increase over the 1921 population. This has probably been responsible also for an apparent average annual rate of growth as high as 2.1 percent between 1931 and 1952, a

[4] For detailed discussions of the 1963 census see R. K. Udo, "Population and Politics in Nigeria," in Caldwell and Okonjo, *Population of Tropical Africa*, pp. 97–104; and T. M. Yesufu, "The politics and Economics of Nigeria's Population Census," *ibid.*, pp. 106–9.

period when the death rate presumably would have been still so high as to yield only a moderate rate of natural increase.

With regard to the 1952–1963 period, a number of studies[5] have suggested that the annual rate of growth of 5.6 percent indicated is much too high, and that the conditions under which the 1963 census was taken indicate that the numbers were probably inflated, though substantial underenumeration in 1952–1953 is not to be ruled out. Moreover, while the overall increase for the 1921–1952 intercensal period was only 63 percent or 1.6 percent per annum, the period 1921–1963 shows an overall increase of 199 percent or an annual rate of 2.7 percent. In fact, the two periods which include the 1963 census show average annual rates of increase, which, if accepted, would imply that the 1952 census undercounted the population by about 40 percent if the 1921–1963 rate is employed, and by about 30 percent if the 1931–1963 rate is used, which is highly improbable. True, censuses of Ghana show an annual rate of growth of 4.2 percent during the period 1948–1960,[6] but the well-known fact of mass immigration into that country (including large numbers from Nigeria) probably accounts for a large part of this high rate.

The crux of the matter, however, is that the 1921 and 1931 figures, being merely estimates, might also be partly responsible for the apparent high rates of growth. Comparisons of the various census figures, therefore, do not yield acceptable rates of growth. However, the 1963 census, in spite of its shortcomings,[7]

[5] See the section on "Estimates of Population Growth Rates and the Components."
[6] See John C. Caldwell, "Population: General Characteristics," in W. Birmingham, I. Neustadt, and E. N. Omaboe, eds., *A Study of Contemporary Ghana*, II, *Some Aspects of Social Structure* (London: George Allen & Unwin; Evanston, Ill.: Northwestern University Press, 1967), p. 23.
[7] From discussions with those who directed and those who participated in the census operation, it seems that the problem was largely that of multiple enumeration of the same individuals (probably confined to young adults) rather than of deliberate falsification of the census figures by the authorities concerned The nature of the census propaganda was probably responsible for this situation.

may be used, with reservations, in conjunction with data from other sources to give a rough idea of the characteristics of Nigeria's population.

## POPULATION CHARACTERISTICS

The 1963 census asked only five questions: age, sex, ethnic origin, religion, and occupation. The rural demographic sample survey, which was carried out two years later, obtained responses to questions on age, sex, and marital status in addition to those on fertility, mortality, and migration.[8] Unfortunately, one of the most important social characteristics, education, was not inquired into in either the census or the sample survey. The analysis of the population characteristics in this section will be based mainly on these two sources.

AGE AND SEX COMPOSITION.   A feature of the age structure, which is immediately visible on inspection, is that it is badly distorted—so much so that it is unnecessary to apply any of the rigorous tests of accuracy in order to demonstrate the inconsistencies. Examining the age structure from the youngest to the oldest, there is first a sharp fall in the proportions of persons aged 10–14 years (and 15–19 in the case of males), then a sharp rise in the next age group, a gradual fall to age groups 25–29 and 30–34 years and finally a precipitous drop at age group 35–39 years, followed by rapidly decreasing proportions down to the last age interval. In other words, there is an unusual concentration of the population in ages 20–34 years (15–34 in the case of females) and large deficits in the ages between 15 and 19 years inclusive, particularly in the case of females whose age structure is by far the most distorted.[9]

Four possible factors might have been responsible for the inconsistencies in the age structure:

(1) Advancement of age statement by males

TABLE 11.2
Percentage distribution of the 1963 census population by sex and age

| Age Group | Males | Females | Both Sexes |
|---|---|---|---|
| 0–4 | 16.8 | 17.6 | 17.1 |
| 5–9 | 15.5 | 14.8 | 15.2 |
| 10–14 | 11.6 | 9.7 | 10.7 |
| 15–19 | 8.9 | 10.0 | 9.4 |
| 20–24 | 11.2 | 13.7 | 12.4 |
| 25–29 | 9.3 | 10.7 | 10.0 |
| 30–34 | 7.5 | 8.0 | 7.8 |
| 35–39 | 4.8 | 4.1 | 4.5 |
| 40–44 | 4.7 | 4.0 | 4.3 |
| 45–49 | 2.4 | 1.8 | 2.1 |
| 50–54 | 2.4 | 1.9 | 2.2 |
| 55–59 | 1.0 | 0.7 | 0.8 |
| 60–64 | 1.6 | 1.2 | 1.4 |
| 65+ | 2.3 | 1.8 | 2.1 |
| Total | 100.0 | 100.0 | 100.0 |

aged 15–19 years and females aged 10–19 thus bringing about apparent large deficits in these ages

(2) Immigration of young adults between the ages of 20 and 34 years and emigration of males aged 15–19 and females aged 10–19 years

(3) Unusually high mortality in ages 10–19 years

(4) Overenumeration of persons in ages 20–34 years

While there is hardly any doubt that there are gross errors in age recording, the distortions shown here are such that they cannot be wholly explained by the ordinary type of digit preference which is certainly also prominent in the data.[10] The fact that the census figures were to be used in compiling the voters' list might have led to large numbers of persons, particularly between ages 15 and 20, deliberately giving their ages as between 20 and 25 years. On the other hand, it is very unlikely that mortality could be so age-selective as to affect in such a drastic way only persons

[8] Federal Office of Statistics, *Rural Demographic Sample Survey, 1965–1966* (Lagos, 1968).

[9] This pattern of distortion is shown to varying degrees in all the regions of the country.

[10] Apart from the deep "troughs" and the excessive concentration noted, differencing the population figures shows small drops to digit "0" and large drops to digit "5," i.e., heaping is pronounced at ages ending in "0" particularly at ages after 35.

between 10 and 20 years of age, so that this cannot explain the distortions. Mass immigration or emigration cannot do so either.[11] It is highly probable that substantial upward shifts in age by persons in the 10–19 age group to ages between 20 and 30, as well as over-enumeration of persons in the latter age range explain by and large the distortions observed in the age structure.[12] As a result of these distortions, particularly in the younger ages, any estimates of vital rates based on the unadjusted data will be grossly in error.

In Table 11.3 the data are arranged into larger age groupings. However, in spite of the broad age categories employed, the faults discussed above are still present. For example, the proportion aged 15–44 years seems

too large, particularly in the case of females, for the simple reason that persons aged below 15 years have been transferred en masse to higher ages and, in addition, some of those aged 45 years and above might have understated their ages. This is supported by the relatively small proportion of persons below age 15 and the rather small proportion of those aged 45 years and above.[13]

TABLE 11.3

Percentage distribution of the 1963 census population of Nigeria by broad age groups and sex

| Age Group | Males | Females | Both Sexes |
|---|---|---|---|
| Under 15 | 43.8 | 42.1 | 43.0 |
| 15–44 | 46.4 | 50.5 | 48.4 |
| 45–64 | 7.4 | 5.6 | 6.5 |
| 65 and over | 2.4 | 1.8 | 2.1 |
| Totals | 100.0 | 100.0 | 100.0 |

In spite of all these inconsistencies, there is no doubt that at least 40 percent of the population are under the age of 15 years and, as in nearly all African countries, the proportion of the population of working age (15–64 years) is below 60 percent. The large proportion of children, apart from the fact that it implies, other things being equal, a high level of current fertility, also indicates the likelihood of high fertility for many decades to come since the large number of children today are the potential parents of the future.

The large proportion of children also means, as it does in most developing countries,

[11] Patterns of age distribution similar to this have been noted in Angola, Mozambique, and Portuguese Guinea. In all these cases, as in the case of Nigeria, the female age structure is much more distorted than the male structure and the distortion has been attributed mainly to errors in age recording (see Don F. Heisel, "The Demography of the Portuguese Territories: Angola, Mozambique, and Portuguese Guinea," in William Brass et al., The Demography of Tropical Africa (Princeton, N.J.: Princeton University Press, 1968), pp. 444–46). The pattern is evident to a more limited extent in the 1960 population of Ghana and Caldwell attributes it to immigration as well as age misstatement and other factors (see Caldwell, "Population: General Characteristics," p. 32.) One strange fact about Nigeria, however, is that the Eastern and Mid-Western regions show the worst distortion. For example, Mid-Western females aged 20–24 years are about three times those 15–19 and about twice those 10–14. Eastern females aged 20–24 are over twice those aged 15–19. Yet in these two regions the level of literacy is probably double that of the North where the age structure, as in the West, is far less distorted.

[12] It might be noted that if half of the total number of persons returned by the census for ages 20–34 years is subtracted from the total population of 56 million, a total of 47 million is obtained, which is close to the various estimates of the November 1963 population of Nigeria (i.e., the 1963 census which was not released). However, the assumption that the 1963 census was a substantial overcount has been queried. First, there is the possibility that the "people concerned may have had stronger reasons for calling attention to flagrant overcounts in some areas than to inefficiency elsewhere." Second, in some places medical groups have found "as many people as one would expect if the 1963 census were correct." See John C. Caldwell, "The Population Outlook in Nigeria," Demographic Unit, University of Ife, mimeographed (Nigeria, 1969), p. 7.

[13] Cf. proportions of about 43 percent for the population aged 15–44, 9–10 percent for the population aged 45–64 years, and over 3 percent for persons aged over 65 years in Ghana in 1960. In the case of persons under 15, the omission of infants and young children certainly accounts partly for the depressed proportion as an examination of the distribution of the population aged 0–5 clearly shows. Those aged under one are in all regions only about three-quarters of those enumerated as age one and the population rises consistently to age three or four before a decline sets in.

TABLE 11.4
Males per 100 females,
Nigeria, 1963

| Age group | Ratio |
|-----------|-------|
| 0–4 | 97 |
| 5–9 | 107 |
| 10–14 | 121 |
| 15–19 | 91 |
| 20–24 | 84 |
| 25–29 | 88 |
| 30–34 | 95 |
| 35–39 | 118 |
| 40–44 | 119 |
| 45–49 | 141 |
| 50–54 | 128 |
| 55–59 | 149 |
| 60–64 | 132 |
| 65+ | 142 |
| Total | 102 |

a heavy load of child dependency[14] with the concomitant social and economic problems. This is especially true nowadays, when the country is preoccupied with the difficulties of economic development, and when education, particularly at the primary and secondary school levels, is very high on the list of priorities of each of the Nigerian states.

Table 11.4 shows the relative weights of the sexes in the population. It will be recalled that, in dealing with age, it was mentioned that the distortion of the age distribution is more pronounced in the case of the females (i.e., the population is more deficient where a deficiency occurs, and more excessive where large numbers are concentrated). As a result, the sex ratio is high in the age group 10–14 years and very low thereafter up to the age group 30–34 years. After this age group, the sex ratio becomes extremely high and remains so throughout all the older ages.

This pattern, of course, is not peculiar to Nigeria. It was shown in censuses by the

[14] A child dependency load (i.e., the ratio of the numbers aged 0–14 to those 15–64) of 78 percent (the proportion would be much higher if necessary adjustments are made to the population aged 0–14 years) with a total dependency ratio (i.e., the ratio of the numbers 0–14 and 65+ combined to those 15–64) of 82 percent for Nigeria may be compared with total dependency ratios of about 68, 52, and 51 percent respectively for the U.S.A., U.K., and Sweden.

Ugandan population in 1959 and by that of Ghana in 1960 and seems to stem from the same source, gross age misstatement. Of course, it is conceivable that maternal mortality, in a developing country with inadequate medical services, might have been responsible for a part of the very high sex ratios in the ages above 34, although the fact that in those parts of the world with adequate data, male mortality usually exceeds that of females means that we might have expected a reduction of the excessive sex ratios in the higher ages.

POPULATION DISTRIBUTION AND URBANIZATION. The 1963 census was based on the 4 political subdivisions of the country at that time (North, East, West, and Mid-West) plus the Federal Territory of Lagos. Since 1967, however, the country has been split into 12 smaller subdivisions. The boundaries of these 12 states are not sufficiently clearly defined at present to permit the discussion of population distribution by states.

Nigeria's population density, with 156 persons per square mile according to the 1963 census is exceeded in mainland Africa only by the two tiny territories of Rwanda and Burundi; it is three times that of the world and six times the figure for all Africa, but still only two-thirds that of Europe, which is admittedly in a late stage of industrialization and urbanization. There are, however, large differences between and within regions. The old Eastern Region is clearly the most densely populated part of the country averaging 420 persons per square mile, but with densities soaring to thousands of persons per square mile in several areas. The West (337) is a distant second, especially if Colony Province (particularly Ikeja) is excluded. Next comes Mid-West (170 persons), with the North (106 persons) trailing behind.

The density in northern divisions ranges between 10 persons in Borgu Division of Ilorin Province to 383 persons in Kano Division of Kano Province. In the East the range is from 103 persons in Ogoja Division to 23,692 persons in Port Harcourt Division or 1,632 persons in Orlu Division of Owerri Province

TABLE 11.5

Population growth in the city of Lagos, 1881–1963

| Year | Period | Population | Increase Number | Increase Percent |
|------|--------|-----------|--------|---------|
| 1881 | | 37,452 | | |
| | 1881–1911 | | 36,314 | 96.9 |
| 1911 | | 73,766 | | |
| | 1911–1931 | | 52,342 | 71.0 |
| 1931 | | 126,108 | | |
| | 1931–1950 | | 104,148 | 82.6 |
| 1950 | | 230,256 | | |
| | 1950–1963 | | 434,990 | 188.9 |
| 1963 | | 665,246 | | |

SOURCES: Nigeria, Department of Statistics, *Census of Lagos, 1950* (Lagos, 1951); Federal Office of Statistics *Population Census of Nigeria, 1963* (Lagos, 1968).

if urbanized Port Harcourt is excluded. In the West, density varies from 112 persons per square mile in Oyo Division to 1,246 persons in Ikeja Division, and in the Mid-West from 99 persons in Western Ijaw Division to 309 persons in Urhobo Division.

Lagos, being a center of heavy in-migration from all parts of Nigeria, has of course, no equal as far as population density is concerned. Its density, according to the 1963 census, was 24,639 persons per square mile. As a result of the influx of people, the city has grown greatly since its first population census in 1881. By far the most rapid growth was between 1950 and 1963, a period of only 13 years which coincided with the beginning of accelerated development and an increased tempo of internal migration in Nigeria. During this period, the population multiplied itself almost 3 times as Table 11.5 shows; it has multiplied itself about 17 times since 1881.

Of course, Lagos is not unique in this regard. Many Nigerian towns, particularly in the West, have grown at phenomenal rates as a result of mass movements into them from rural areas.[15]

Table 11.6 shows the high level of urbanization in Nigeria. It is well above that found in

[15] See Federal Office of Statistics, *Rural Demographic Sample Survey*, p. 30. According to this survey, about 600,000 more persons moved from the rural areas into towns than in the opposite direction during the survey period.

TABLE 11.6

Urban population, Nigeria, 1963[a]

| Area | Populations 20,000+ | 50,000+ | 100,000+ |
|------|---------|---------|----------|
| *Nigeria* | | | |
| Number of towns | 183 | 55 | 24 |
| Total town population | 10,691,664 | 7,074,231 | 4,908,299 |
| Percent of total Nigeria | 19.2 | 12.7 | 8.8 |
| *Northern Region* | | | |
| Number of towns | 70 | 16 | 5 |
| Total town population | 3,133,187 | 1,724,622 | 960,023 |
| Percent of total region | 10.5 | 5.8 | 3.2 |
| *Eastern Region* | | | |
| Number of towns | 29 | 5 | 4 |
| Total town population | 1,385,082 | 688,473 | 612,055 |
| Percent of total region | 11.2 | 5.6 | 4.9 |
| *Western Region* | | | |
| Number of towns | 77 | 30 | 13 |
| Total town population | 5,224,371 | 3,778,935 | 2,570,271 |
| Percent of total region | 50.9 | 36.8 | 25.0 |
| *Mid-West Region* | | | |
| Number of towns | 6 | 3 | 1 |
| Total town population | 283,778 | 216,955 | 100,694 |
| Percent of total region | 11.2 | 8.6 | 4.0 |
| *Lagos* | | | |
| Number of towns | 1 | 1 | 1 |
| Total population | 665,246 | 665,246 | 665,246 |

SOURCE: Computed from *Population Census of Nigeria, 1963*, III, pp. 58–65.
[a] The census defines as "urban" any settlement with 20,000 population or more.

most of tropical Africa and ranks next to Senegal (with 22.5 percent of its inhabitants living in towns of 20,000 or more inhabitants in 1960–1961)[16] in West Africa. The country is, nevertheless, predominantly rural.

[16] See United Nations Economic Commission for Africa, *Demographic Handbook for Africa* (Addis Ababa, 1968), p. 40. This report contains some inaccurate figures, particularly on Nigeria.

In terms of urbanization, western Nigeria is unique in Nigeria and indeed in the whole of Africa, with about 51 percent of its population living in towns with 20,000 or more inhabitants. Even French Somaliland, with 58 percent of its people in such centers has no single community with population as high as 100,000, while a quarter of the population of western Nigeria live in towns with 100,000 or more people.[17]

The urban dwellers of western Nigeria alone constitute about one-tenth of the total population of the country. Of the total urban population of the country, urban dwellers in western Nigeria make up over half. Nigerian urbanization may, therefore, be said to be largely Yoruba urbanization.

Many of these towns (including those with 10,000–20,000 people, which, if included in the urban population, would raise the urban proportion in western Nigeria to over 60 percent) are undergoing changes in social structure and are becoming economically diversified, though a large proportion of the inhabitants are farmers. The reason for this is to be found in their history of development.[18] Today, however, many of the towns have progressively moved to varying degrees from the original agricultural economic base depending on the size of their population.[19] They do conform to the generalization that the higher the degree of urbanization, the lower the proportions of the male population engaged in agriculture,[20] though difficulties arise when cross-cultural comparisons of the occupations of communities in the same size group are attempted.

OCCUPATIONAL COMPOSITION. The distribution of the population by occupational status is given in Table 11.7, which shows that

TABLE 11.7
Percentage distribution of the occupied population by major occupational groups, Nigeria, 1963

| Occupational Group | Males | Females | Both Sexes |
|---|---|---|---|
| Professional, technical, etc. | 2.8 | 1.5 | 2.4 |
| Administrative, executive, and managerial | 0.3 | 0.1 | 0.2 |
| Clerical | 1.5 | 0.5 | 1.3 |
| Sales | 8.2 | 38.9 | 15.6 |
| Farmers, fishermen, hunters, loggers, etc. | 67.7 | 22.5 | 56.8 |
| Miners, quarrymen, etc. | 0.1 | 0.1 | 0.1 |
| Transport and communication | 2.0 | 0.1 | 1.5 |
| Craftsmen, production process workers, and laborers | 12.3 | 11.8 | 12.2 |
| Service, sports, and recreation | 4.7 | 5.3 | 4.9 |
| Unspecified | 0.4 | 19.2 | 5.0 |
| Total | 100.0 | 100.0 | 100.0 |

SOURCE: Computed from *Population Census of Nigeria, 1963*.

Nigeria is predominantly an agricultural economy, with about 9 million, or two-thirds, of the working males engaged in agricultural and related occupations. Nevertheless, it seems that there has been a continuing shift from agriculture, probably as a result of the accelerated pace of urbanization noted above and the related fact that most migrants from rural areas come to the urban centers in search of nonagricultural occupations. In 1952–1953, for example, 78 percent of all occupied males were reported as being in agriculture,[21] while in 1963 the proportion

[17] *Ibid.*, p. 41. Even as far back as 1952, about 52 percent of the population were living in communities with 5,000 or more people, 43 percent in communities with 10,000 or more, and about 38 percent in communities with 20,000 or more.

[18] For a discussion of the pattern of development of Yoruba towns, see P. O. Olusanya, *Socio-economic Aspects of Rural-Urban Migration in Western Nigeria*, NISER (Ibadan, 1969), pp. 6–11.

[19] Mass migration from rural areas in western Nigeria is partly a movement away from agriculture. Rural in-migrants, found in very large numbers in both small and large Yoruba towns, are those who have come from widely scattered areas into environments where in the majority of cases they have no family land and consequently cannot engage in agriculture even if they wished to do so. The volume of in-migration, moreover, tends to vary directly with town size. See H. A. Oluwasanmi, *Agriculture and Nigerian Economic Development* (London: Oxford University Press, 1966), p 68.

[20] T. E. Smith and J. G. C. Blacker, *Population Characteristics of the Commonwealth Countries of Tropical Africa* (London: Oxford University Press, 1963), p. 21.
[21] *Population Census of Nigeria, 1952–53*.

was 67 percent. If this trend describes the actual situation, and if it continues (as it may, considering the current mass exodus of young adults from agriculture), the proportion in agriculture may well be below 50 percent by the end of the 1970s. This may lead to one of two results: either the proportion in non-agricultural activities or the rate of unemployment will increase considerably.

It would appear from the comparison of the regions in Table 11.8 that there is an inverse relationship between the degree of urbanization and the proportion employed in agriculture, if we exclude the Mid-West. The North, which is the least urbanized, has by far the highest proportion of males in agriculture (78 percent) followed by the East with almost 60 percent and then the West with 53 percent.

TABLE 11.8
Percentage of the occupied population in each region engaged in agriculture and related occupations, Nigeria, 1963

| Region | Males | Females | Both Sexes |
|---|---|---|---|
| Northern | 78.2 | 29.2 | 72.1 |
| Eastern | 58.9 | 43.5 | 54.4 |
| Western | 53.2 | 5.6 | 33.6 |
| Mid-West | 67.2 | 47.6 | 62.3 |
| Lagos | 3.0 | 0.4 | 2.3 |

SOURCE: Computed from *Population Census of Nigeria, 1963*.

Lagos, by virtue of its unique position as the capital of Nigeria, the seat of the federal government, and a very busy port, has, of course, a very insignificant proportion of its occupied male population in agriculture and such related activities as fishing in the surrounding lagoons, creeks, and sea.

The distribution also shows another interesting fact, and this is that, whereas, in the East, Mid-West and, to a lesser extent, the North, agriculture is a male as well as a female occupation, an insignificant 6 percent of females in the West and less than 1 percent in Lagos were recorded as being engaged in agriculture and related activities. In these two areas, the function of the women is not to cultivate the land or do the actual fishing but largely to market the produce. This is why

TABLE 11.9
Percentage distribution of the occupied population in each region engaged in sales, Nigeria, 1963

| Region | Males | Females | Both Sexes |
|---|---|---|---|
| Northern | 5.5 | 26.4 | 8.1 |
| Eastern | 13.5 | 15.3 | 14.0 |
| Western | 10.0 | 58.2 | 29.9 |
| Mid-West | 8.3 | 35.1 | 15.0 |
| Lagos | 11.5 | 70.9 | 26.0 |

SOURCE: Computed from *Population Census of Nigeria, 1963*.

much larger proportions of the females in both the West and Lagos were returned as sales workers (Table 11.9). The proportion for Lagos is considerably higher than for any other area because of the presence of many retail shops employing large numbers of sales girls.

ETHNIC AND RELIGIOUS COMPOSITION. Although Nigeria has numerous ethnic groups, only eight of them are of numerical importance (Table 11.10). These eight, the largest of which are the Hausas, the Yorubas, and the Ibos, constitute three-quarters of the total population with about 42 million persons.

Perhaps because it has very little to offer by way of economic opportunities, Nigeria does not attract large numbers of immigrants.

TABLE 11.10
Distribution by ethnic group, Nigeria, 1963

| Ethnic Group | Population (thousands) | Percentage Distribution |
|---|---|---|
| Hausa | 11,653 | 20.9 |
| Yoruba | 11,321 | 20.3 |
| Ibo | 9,246 | 16.6 |
| Fulani | 4,783 | 8.6 |
| Ibibio | 2,002 | 3.6 |
| Tiv | 1,394 | 2.5 |
| Ijaw | 1,061 | 1.9 |
| Edo | 939 | 1.7 |
| Others | 13,109 | 23.6 |
| Non-Nigerians | 152 | 0.3 |
| Unspecified | 10 | 0.0[a] |
| Total | 55,670 | 100.0 |

SOURCE: *Population Census of Nigeria, 1963*.
[a] Less than 0.05 percent.

TABLE 11.11

Percentage distribution of the population in each region by religion, Nigeria, 1963

| Religion | Northern | Eastern | Western | Mid-West | Lagos | Nigeria |
|---|---|---|---|---|---|---|
| Christians | 9.7 | 77.2 | 48.7 | 54.9 | 54.6 | 34.5 |
| Moslems | 71.7 | 0.3 | 43.4 | 4.2 | 44.3 | 47.2 |
| Others | 18.6 | 22.5 | 7.9 | 40.9 | 1.1 | 18.3 |
| Total | 100.0 | 100.0 | 100.0 | 100.0 | 100.0 | 100.0 |

SOURCE: *Population Census of Nigeria, 1963.*

Foreigners make up less than half of 1 percent of the total population.[22]

In all the regions except the North, Christianity appears to have more adherents than Islam. Thus religiously the country is split into two: the North which is overwhelmingly Moslem, and the South which is more Christian than Moslem, particularly in the East where there are hardly any Moslems. For Nigeria as a whole, however, the Moslems predominate with almost half of its population being adherents of Islam (see Table 11.11).

THE HOUSEHOLD. In most African surveys, the household is defined as a group of persons who "eat from the same pot" daily. This was the definition adopted in the Rural Demographic Sample Survey carried out by the Federal Office of Statistics. The data from this survey are mainly used in this section.

The survey shows that there is little variation in the size of households from one region to another (Table 11.12) except in the case of western Nigeria, which shows a rather low average size. What accounts for this is probably the fact that large extended families, comprising a couple, their married sons and their wives and children, and unmarried children (that is, the three-generation type of household), as single economic units are rarely found among the Yorubas.[23] In the case of Lagos, the average of 4.6

[22] Cf. Ghana where the foreign-born constituted about 8 percent of the total population in 1960. See John C. Caldwell, "Migration and Urbanization," in Birmingham, *et al., A Study of Contemporary Ghana,* p. 112.

[23] An average size of household of 4.9 persons was also obtained in rural survey in western Nigeria. See Olusanya, *Socio-economic Aspects of Rural-Urban Migration,* p. 58. The survey described will henceforth be referred to as S(1).

TABLE 11.12

Percentage distribution of households by size and by region, Nigeria

| Size of Household | Northern | Eastern | Western | Mid-West | Total | Lagos |
|---|---|---|---|---|---|---|
| 1 | 3.1 | 10.3 | 12.1 | 11.9 | 7.4 | 5.5 |
| 2 | 10.5 | 11.2 | 12.5 | 11.6 | 11.1 | 9.8 |
| 3 | 14.1 | 13.5 | 15.5 | 11.5 | 13.8 | 12.7 |
| 4 | 14.2 | 13.6 | 14.8 | 11.8 | 13.8 | 15.0 |
| 5 | 13.1 | 13.8 | 12.3 | 11.3 | 12.9 | 12.9 |
| 6 | 11.0 | 11.1 | 9.0 | 9.3 | 10.5 | 12.1 |
| 7 | 8.3 | 7.9 | 6.7 | 7.8 | 7.9 | 8.1 |
| 8 | 6.1 | 5.1 | 4.4 | 5.6 | 5.6 | 7.2 |
| 9 | 4.7 | 3.6 | 3.6 | 4.0 | 4.2 | 4.7 |
| 10+ | 14.9 | 9.9 | 9.1 | 15.2 | 12.8 | 12.0 |
| Total | 100.0 | 100.0 | 100.0 | 100.0 | 100.0 | 100.0 |
| Average | 6.0 | 5.2 | 4.9 | 5.7 | 5.6 | 4.6 |

SOURCES: All except Lagos—Federal Office of Statistics, *Rural Demographic Sample Survey, 1965–1966;* Lagos—R. W. Morgan, "A Population Dynamics Survey in Lagos, Nigeria: Preliminary Memorandum," mimeographed (1969), Table 23.

TABLE 11.13

Percentage distribution of households by structural types, rural Western Nigeria, 1967

| Household Types | Percent |
|---|---|
| Immediate family only[a] | 73.4 |
| Family and parents of husband and/or wife | 1.5 |
| Family, parents, other relatives, and nonrelatives | 0.8 |
| Head only | 8.2 |
| Family and other relatives | 4.6 |
| Other | 11.5 |
| Total | 100.0 |

SOURCE: S(1). See footnote 23.
[a] Immediate family here refers to a man, his wife or wives, and their children, i.e., a two-generation group.

persons probably is influenced by the preponderance of Yorubas in the population as well as by the lack of adequate accommodation for a large household.

It would be interesting to have data showing the distribution of households by structural type for Nigeria as well as the regions. This would have shed more light on the data in Table 11.12. Unfortunately, such data are not available from the Rural

Demographic Survey of 1965–1966. However, such a distribution is shown in Table 11.13 for rural western Nigeria.[24] The distribution shows that the rather low average size of households in the rural West is largely to be attributed to the predominance of the husband-wife-child type of household.

As in many developing, largely agrarian societies, marriage comes early in the life of the Nigerian, particularly the female. Table 11.14 shows that although there are hardly any males recorded as having ever-married below the age of 15 years, in the age group 15–19 years about one-tenth had been married at least once before the survey. Of the ever-married females, about one out of every ten were married before they had reached age 15 and a little over seven-tenths between ages 15 and 19 years. Approximately half and over nine-tenths respectively of men and women in the age group 20–24 had been married. Virtually no women were reported as never-married in the age group 25–29, while one-quarter of the men were still unmarried in the same age group.

[24] *Ibid.*, p. 58, data from S(1).

TABLE 11.14

Percentage distribution of the sample by marital status and age, rural Nigeria, 1965–1966

| Age Group | Males Married | Males Widowed | Males Divorced or separated | Females Married | Females Widowed | Females Divorced or separated |
|---|---|---|---|---|---|---|
| 10–14 | 0.2 | — | 0.0 | 8.4 | 0.0 | 0.1 |
| 15–19 | 10.3 | 0.1 | 0.5 | 70.0 | 0.4 | 1.6 |
| 20–24 | 44.9 | 0.6 | 2.2 | 90.5 | 1.0 | 2.4 |
| 25–29 | 72.0 | 0.9 | 2.9 | 94.4 | 1.9 | 2.1 |
| 30–34 | 85.8 | 1.3 | 3.7 | 92.1 | 4.3 | 2.7 |
| 35–39 | 91.2 | 1.1 | 2.7 | 86.8 | 9.0 | 3.3 |
| 40–44 | 91.4 | 2.0 | 3.4 | 78.1 | 16.6 | 4.4 |
| 45–49 | 92.4 | 2.3 | 3.1 | 65.1 | 27.8 | 6.0 |
| 50–54 | 92.0 | 2.7 | 3.4 | 50.3 | 42.3 | 6.4 |
| 55–59 | 91.5 | 3.8 | 2.6 | 40.2 | 52.5 | 6.1 |
| 60–64 | 90.6 | 4.3 | 3.1 | 29.4 | 64.9 | 4.7 |
| 65–69 | 88.3 | 6.4 | 3.3 | 21.9 | 69.0 | 7.3 |
| 70–74 | 86.6 | 7.8 | 3.2 | 13.4 | 78.3 | 6.7 |
| 75–79 | 87.3 | 7.0 | 3.5 | 12.0 | 81.1 | 5.0 |
| 80–84 | 85.0 | 8.6 | 4.3 | 11.0 | 83.1 | 4.6 |
| 85+ | 75.7 | 16.2 | 5.0 | 8.2 | 87.0 | 4.2 |
| Total | 59.7 | 1.5 | 2.3 | 69.9 | 11.3 | 2.8 |

SOURCE: Federal Office of Statistics, *Rural Demographic Sample Survey, 1965–1966.*

The rather early age of marriage among the women implies, other things being equal, early childbearing and rapid population growth since the interval between successive generations is short. Any tendency toward excessively high fertility implied by the low age of marriage might be offset by the significant proportions of widowed females which are as high as about one-twentieth in the 30–34 age group, one-tenth in the 35–39 age group, and almost one-fifth in the age group 40–44 years. However, for women whose age at marriage is around 15 years, a large proportion of their fertility will probably have been achieved by the age of 35, so the sharp increase in widowhood at higher ages is of

TABLE 11.15

Percentage ever married in each age group, by region, Nigeria 1965–1966

| Age Group | Northern M | F | Eastern M | F | Western M | F | Mid-West M | F |
|---|---|---|---|---|---|---|---|---|
| 10–14 | 0.4 | 16.7 | — | 1.5 | — | 0.1 | — | 0.9 |
| 15–19 | 18.1 | 90.7 | 1.5 | 35.9 | 1.2 | 26.3 | 1.6 | 41.7 |
| 20–24 | 64.7 | 98.2 | 16.8 | 84.1 | 17.4 | 89.0 | 15.2 | 88.0 |
| 25–29 | 87.5 | 99.4 | 54.9 | 95.9 | 63.0 | 98.4 | 46.6 | 95.7 |
| 30–34 | 94.5 | 99.5 | 81.5 | 98.2 | 85.9 | 99.0 | 79.7 | 97.8 |
| 35–39 | 97.5 | 99.6 | 90.1 | 98.3 | 93.2 | 99.0 | 87.6 | 97.7 |
| 40–44 | 98.2 | 99.8 | 94.0 | 98.2 | 95.3 | 98.7 | 91.9 | 97.8 |
| 45–49 | 99.0 | 99.7 | 96.7 | 97.5 | 96.4 | 99.9 | 95.2 | 97.5 |
| 50–54 | 98.9 | 99.1 | 95.8 | 98.6 | 98.6 | 99.6 | 97.1 | 97.3 |

SOURCE: Federal Office of Statistics, *Rural Demographic Sample Survey, 1965–1966.*

little demographic consequence even if it is assumed that widows recorded as above the age of 35 years at the time of the survey are unlikely to have subsequently remarried. This applies also to divorced or separated women.

Among the males, in contrast, there are very few widowers. This is attributable largely to the institution of polygyny. A man with two or more wives cannot be said to be widowed simply because one of the wives is dead.

However, not every region conforms to the picture of early marriage with a low incidence of early widowhood and divorce, as hitherto depicted for the country as a whole, as

TABLE 11.16

Percentage widowed in each age group, by region, Nigeria, 1965–1966

| Age Group | Northern M | F | Eastern M | F | Western M | F | Mid-West M | F |
|---|---|---|---|---|---|---|---|---|
| 10–14 | — | 0.1 | — | | — | | — | |
| 15–19 | 0.2 | 0.4 | — | 0.6 | — | 0.1 | 0.0 | 0.2 |
| 20–24 | 0.8 | 0.7 | 0.1 | 2.8 | 0.2 | 0.3 | 0.1 | 0.6 |
| 25–29 | 1.1 | 0.9 | 0.8 | 5.4 | 0.4 | 0.6 | 0.4 | 1.7 |
| 30–34 | 1.2 | 2.7 | 1.7 | 9.9 | 1.2 | 2.0 | 0.5 | 3.7 |
| 35–39 | 1.1 | 5.3 | 1.5 | 19.7 | 0.6 | 3.5 | 1.0 | 6.4 |
| 40–44 | 1.6 | 14.2 | 3.3 | 28.4 | 2.1 | 8.2 | 1.1 | 12.2 |
| 45–49 | 1.5 | 26.1 | 3.9 | 39.9 | 2.2 | 13.6 | 1.4 | 21.0 |
| 50–54 | 2.2 | 42.9 | 4.4 | 54.4 | 2.1 | 26.0 | 2.6 | 31.8 |

SOURCE: Federal Office of Statistics, *Rural Demographic Sample Survey, 1965–1966.*

Tables 11.15, 11.16, and 11.17 clearly show. The North is outstanding as the region of very early marriages, with almost one-fifth of its males in the age group 15–19 and almost two-thirds in the age group 20–24 married at least once. This contrasts with the situation in the other regions where there are no males recorded as ever married in the age group 10–14, only about 2 percent in the age group 15–19, and less than 20 percent in the age group 20–24 years.

The northern females present as sharp a contrast as their males to the females of the other regions. Virtually all northern females in the age group 15–19 and almost one-fifth in the age group 10–14 were reported as ever-married. In the other regions (except in the

TABLE 11.17

Percentage divorced or separated in each age group by region, Nigeria, 1965–66

| Age Group | Northern M | F | Eastern M | F | Western M | F | Mid-West M | F |
|---|---|---|---|---|---|---|---|---|
| 10–14 | 0.0 | 0.2 | — | 0.0 | — | | — | |
| 15–19 | 0.8 | 1.8 | 0.2 | 1.8 | 0.1 | 0.2 | — | 1.4 |
| 20–24 | 3.0 | 2.1 | 0.8 | 4.4 | 0.4 | 1.0 | 0.5 | 2.8 |
| 25–29 | 3.5 | 1.6 | 1.7 | 4.0 | 2.3 | 0.9 | 0.7 | 4.0 |
| 30–34 | 4.4 | 2.1 | 2.3 | 4.4 | 2.3 | 1.9 | 2.7 | 4.7 |
| 35–39 | 2.7 | 2.6 | 2.8 | 4.4 | 2.9 | 2.3 | 2.1 | 7.3 |
| 40–44 | 3.5 | 4.0 | 3.4 | 5.5 | 3.1 | 3.0 | 2.7 | 7.1 |
| 45–49 | 2.8 | 6.0 | 3.5 | 6.4 | 3.1 | 3.2 | 3.2 | 10.6 |
| 50–54 | 3.4 | 7.3 | 3.5 | 6.2 | 3.4 | 2.8 | 2.9 | 9.8 |

SOURCE: Federal Office of Statistics, *Rural Demographic Sample Survey, 1965–1966.*

East where an insignificant 1.5 percent were reported as ever married) the proportion ever married is almost nil in the age group 10–14 and ranges from one-quarter to two-fifths in the age group 15–19. The West shows by far the lowest proportion ever married in this age group. From about the age of 25, however, marriage is almost universal for all the regions.

Thus, in terms of comparative lateness in the timing of marriage, the regions may be ranked as follows: With regard to males, the Mid-West come first, the East second, the West third, and the North last. The comparative lateness in the Mid-West and the East is probably connected with the high bride price in these regions. In the case of the females, the order in the 15–19 age group is West, East, Mid-West, and North, although the West slips to third place in the 20–24 age group.

If marriage among males, as we have seen, comes later in the East and the Mid-West than in the West, and if this position is reversed among the females, it follows that there must be a greater disparity in the ages of spouses in both the East and the Mid-West and, consequently, that the incidence of widowhood among females will be likely to be higher than in the West. Table 11.16 clearly confirms this. It may be added that widowhood is far more pronounced in the East than in any other region, while its incidence seems to be least in the West.

As far as divorce and separation are concerned, there is not much difference between the situation of males in the various regions. There are, however, substantial differences between the regions in the case of the females, as Table 11.17 shows. Their incidence appears highest in the Mid-West, followed by the East and the North; the lowest figures are found in the West.

Considering these facts about marital conditions in the regions, it may be concluded that the North, with a very low age at marriage and a rather low incidence of widowhood and divorce (at least in the young ages), is likely to be the most fertile region. In the West, the relatively high female age at marriage is offset, to some extent at least, by

the low incidence of widowhood and divorce. The possible influence of the incidence of widowhood and divorce on fertility should, however, not be overemphasized in a society where polygyny is practiced and where women quickly remarry after widowhood or divorce. Therefore, if the unusually long period of lactation practiced by the Yorubas[25] is taken into account, it may be said that the West, in terms of Nigeria as a whole, probably displays relatively lower fertility than any other region. In the East and the Mid-West the relatively low female age at marriage is likely to result in somewhat higher fertility than in the West, but nevertheless probably lower than in the North, the relatively high incidence of widowhood and divorce notwithstanding.[26] It should be remembered, however, that there are other factors apart from marital status, such as health conditions in each region, which might influence the level of fertility.

## ESTIMATES OF POPULATION GROWTH RATES AND THE COMPONENTS

If the population census of 1963 has done anything, it has awakened the policy makers as well as the general public in Nigeria to the need for something to be done about this bumper harvest of human beings, the controversy surrounding the census notwithstanding. For some years now, lively debates have been going on in local newspapers and magazines as to the merits and demerits of family planning in a manner previously unheard of in this society. At present no positive action is being taken by the government in

[25] The longest and most rigid recorded in Nigeria. The period is usually about three years; but sometimes longer. See P. A. Talbot, *The Peoples of Southern Nigeria*, III (London: Oxford University Press, 1926), pp. 378–83.
[26] The relative levels of regional fertility surmised here differ from those estimated from 1952–1953 census data in Etienne van de Walle, "Fertility in Nigeria" in Brass *et al.*, *Demography of Tropical Africa*, pp. 515–27; also "An Approach to the Study of Fertility in Nigeria," *Population Studies*, XIV, 1 (July 1965), 5–16; but, as is shown below, they agree with estimates based on the 1963 census data if similar methods of analysis are employed.

the field of population control. It seems, however, that the decade of the seventies will be one of action in this direction. It is, therefore, necessary to have an idea, however vague, of the rate of growth of the country's population and its components.

Since the controversial 1963 census, with the unusually high growth rate implied for the preceding intercensal period, suggestions have not been lacking as to what rates of growth seem plausible under the circumstances obtaining up to the census date. Eke, for example, suggested a rate of growth of 2.7 percent.[27] Okonjo, after adjusting the 1952–1953 and 1963 census data, arrived at an estimate of 2.8 percent per annum.[28] A study of the internal consistency of the 1963 census data by Green and Milone led them to the suggestion of a 2.9 percent per annum growth rate.[29]

The estimates in this study are based on the age structure of the 1963 census population. For the purpose of the estimates a number of assumptions had to be made.

(1) The Nigerian population has the characteristics of a quasi-stable population.[30] The justification for quasi-stability is that net migration is virtually nil, and that, although mortality may have fallen somewhat within the past decade or so, fertility has probably remained very high and fairly constant.

(2) The growth rate almost certainly lies between 2.0 and 3.5 percent, taking into account the rates for other West African countries with similar socioeconomic conditions.

(3) Expectation of life at birth was probably not below 35 years and not above 45 years in 1963.

(4) The birth rate is not below 40 per thousand and not above 60 per thousand.

(5) The death rate in 1963 was not less than 15 per thousand and not higher than 30 per thousand.

These assumptions, particularly with regard to the rate of growth, were made in order to narrow the range of possible stable populations to which the 1963 population might conform. The estimates would have been more straightforward, if, in addition to the age structure of the population, the rate of increase or the expectation of life at birth were exactly known. These, unfortunately, are some of the parameters to be estimated. In the circumstance, the age structure of the population had to be heavily relied upon.

From our analysis of the age structure of the 1963 population, it is obvious that using the original data as the basis for the estimates of vital rates is out of the question. Consequently the age distribution was cumulated, plotted on a graph, and smoothed. The points dividing major age groups were then read off.[31] With the above assumptions and the smoothed age distribution, the estimating procedure is simply one of selecting the stable age distribution in Coale and Demeny "West" models[32] having the same proportion under a given age as the actual population. Interpolation between two distributions was often necessary. In addition, life tables, based on the Brass system,[33] were used to obtain estimates by reverse survival and by locating a stable population having the same ratio of children 0–14 to persons 15–44 years old.

FERTILITY. Table 11.18(a) and (b) shows that the birth rate for Nigeria as a whole probably lies between 52.7 and 54.1 per thousand or 53.4 per thousand[34] if the

[27] I. I. U. Eke, "Population of Nigeria: 1952–1965," *The Nigerian Journal of Economic and Social Studies*, VIII, 2 (1966), 289.

[28] C. Okonjo, "A Preliminary Medium Estimate of the 1962 Mid-year Population of Nigeria," p. 84.

[29] L. Green and V. Milone, *Physical Planning Research Programme Interim Report No. 1.*, N.I.S.E.R. (Ibadan, March 1969).

[30] See Ansley J. Coale, "Estimate of Various Demographic Measures through the Quasi-Stable Age Distribution," *Emerging Techniques in Population Research*, Proceedings of the Annual Conference of the Milankb Memorial Fund (1962), p. 178.

[31] The adjusted age distribution will be found in the appendix to this chapter.

[32] Ansley J. Coale and Paul Demeny, *Regional Model Life Tables and Stable Populations* (Princeton, N.J.: Princeton University Press, 1966).

[33] Population Investigation Committee, London School of Economics, "Tables Based on the Brass System of Model Life Tables," mimeographed.

[34] Compare the birth rate of 50.2 per thousand for Nigeria (Federal Office of Statistics, *Rural Demographic Sample Survey*).

TABLE 11.18

Estimates of birth and gross reproduction rates, Nigeria, 1963

(a) Employing Coale-Demeny "West" Stable Population Models and the Cumulated Age Distributions [C(x)]

| Index and Area | Birth Rate | | | Gross Reproduction Rate | | |
|---|---|---|---|---|---|---|
| | M | F | Median value | M | F | Median value |
| Nigeria | | | | | | |
| C(x) | | | | | | |
| 5 | 50.81 | 51.34 | 51.08 | 3.38 | 3.58 | 3.48 |
| 10 | 49.22 | 49.28 | 49.25 | 3.24 | 3.40 | 3.32 |
| 15 | 49.40 | 49.18 | 49.29 | 3.26 | 3.39 | 3.32 |
| 20 | 50.50 | 50.00 | 50.25 | 3.35 | 3.46 | 3.41 |
| 25 | 51.69 | 51.39 | 51.54 | 3.45 | 3.59 | 3.52 |
| 30 | 52.31 | 52.70 | 52.51 | 3.50 | 3.71 | 3.61 |
| *35* | *53.56* | *54.62* | *54.09* | *3.62* | *3.90* | *3.76* |
| 40 | 54.77 | 50.36 | 52.57 | 3.73 | 3.97 | 3.85 |
| 45 | 55.50 | 54.95 | 55.23 | 3.79 | 3.92 | 3.86 |
| C(35) | | | | | | |
| Northern region | 57.03 | 51.60 | 54.32 | 3.84 | 3.61 | 3.73 |
| Eastern region | 56.48 | 54.95 | 55.71 | 3.88 | 4.00 | 3.94 |
| Western region | 47.23 | 48.00 | 47.62 | 3.06 | 3.31 | 3.19 |
| Mid-West region | 50.89 | 50.13 | 50.51 | 3.32 | 3.46 | 3.39 |

(b) Employing Brass System Life Table Models by Reverse-Survival Method and Ratio of Persons 0–14 to Those Age 15–44

*Birth Rate Estimates (reverse-survival method)*

| Expectations of Life at Birth (years) Area | (35) | (37.5) | (40) | (42.5) | (45) | Median value[a] |
|---|---|---|---|---|---|---|
| Nigeria | — | 53.86 | 52.60 | 51.58 | — | 52.72 |
| Northern region | 54.52 | 53.14 | 51.88 | — | — | 53.20 |
| Eastern region | — | — | 50.95 | 49.97 | 49.04 | 49.99 |
| Western region | — | — | 45.57 | 44.79 | 43.95 | 44.76 |
| Mid-West region | 46.15 | 45.16 | 44.18 | — | — | 45.17 |

*Gross Reproduction Rate Estimates (0–14/15–44 ratio)*

| Area | M | F | M & F |
|---|---|---|---|
| Nigeria | 3.02 | 3.06 | 3.04 |
| Northern region | 3.20 | 3.28 | 3.24 |
| Eastern region | 3.21 | 3.25 | 3.23 |
| Western region | 3.02 | 3.04 | 3.03 |
| Mid-West region | 3.00 | 2.84 | 2.92 |

[a] Median value between lowest and the highest rate.

mid-point of the two values derived respectively from Brass and Coale-Demeny[35] is taken. These mid-points are shown in Table 11.21. The estimates suggest differences in the level of the birth rate from one region to another. Both the estimates from Coale-Demeny and Brass methods show the North as the most fertile of all the regions (Table 11.21), followed closely by the East, the Mid-West, and the West. The birth rates are respectively 53.8, 52.9, 47.8, and 46.2. It is not surprising that the birth rate is lower in the West and the Mid-West than in the North and the East, considering the marital patterns in the two former regions discussed above—in the West a comparatively late age at marriage for women coupled with extended lactation, and in the Mid-West a relatively early age at marriage for women coupled with a high incidence of divorce and separation (the highest of the regions).

The *gross reproduction rate* (GRR) for Nigeria is estimated as 3.4, that is, the mid-point of the range 3.04–3.76 derived from Brass and Coale-Demeny.[36] It should be mentioned, however, that although the sets of estimates derived by the Brass and Coale-Demeny methods show the same rank order (except in the positioning of the North and East which keep in the same order relative to each other), the set based on the Brass methods tend to give lower results. This probably stems partly from the fact that the models were derived from different sources. Which of the two sets is superior is difficult to determine, since the estimates are based on very inadequate data. It is possible that both are minimum estimates, but the true figure may not be far from the mid-points derived from the two sources.

MORTALITY. Estimates of the death rate and expectation of life at birth are given in Table 11.19(a) and (b). Although considerable progress has been made in the provision of medical facilities in Nigeria within the past two decades, the level of mortality is still moderately high. However, the estimated death rate of about 23 per thousand[37] is not unique in Africa where, except in a few countries, the death rate is generally above 20 per thousand.

The estimated rate for all Nigeria is lower than the 26.9 per thousand derived from the Federal Office of Statistics (F.O.S.) rural survey.[38] Two factors might account for this. One is that the urban centers, where most of the medical facilities are concentrated, were excluded from the survey. The inclusion of the urban centers would certainly have reduced the rate somewhat. Another is the rejection of some of the data from the survey on the grounds that they were poor. For example, the rather low birth rate of 45.4 per thousand obtained from the unadjusted data was attributed to errors of omission in a large number of survey units, and this led to the rejection, not only of recorded births, but also of deaths in 68 of the 250 units, even though it was admitted that deaths were far more accurately reported even in those units where recording of births was grossly incomplete.[39]

[35] The figure derived from Coale-Demeny (*Regional Model Life Tables*) is for $C(35)$.
[36] Compare the range 3.2–3.5 given by van de Walle, "Fertility in Nigeria," p. 515. Compare also the GRR of 2.7 obtained by the Federal Office of Statistics (*Rural Demographic Sample Survey*) from its rural survey. If adjustments could be made for possible underreporting of births and an amount added for the urban component, the resulting GRR would probably not be higher than 3.5.

[37] If the mid-point of the values is taken i.e., 23.66 and 22.23.
[38] The Federal Office of Statistics survey shows an unusual pattern of mortality in which the incidence is higher among females in most of the age groups. This is probably due to gross age misstatement. At the same time, the method of selecting the survey data for inclusion in the final result might have been responsible for the distortions (see footnote 39).
[39] One other factor which makes the crude death rate of 26.9 suspect is that the author of the report accepted all the units where the death rate from the original data lay between 20 and 50 per thousand while rejecting a large number of those units which yielded rates below 20 per thousand; the 50 per thousand rate did not strike him as unusual. It is, however, conceivable that in certain units the actual death rates might be unusually low either because of unusual mortality conditions or because the year of survey was an unusually good one for the areas constituting the units. Federal Office of Statistics, *Rural Demographic Sample Survey*, p. 14.

TABLE 11.19
Mortality estimates, Nigeria, 1963

(a) Employing Coale-Demeny "West" Stable Population Models and the Cumulated Age Distributions to Age [i.e., $C(35)$]

| Area | Crude Death Rates (per thousand population) | | | Expectation of Life at Birth (in years) | | |
|---|---|---|---|---|---|---|
| | M | F | Median value | M | F | Median value |
| Nigeria | 23.86 | 23.46 | 23.66 | 38.50 | 40.00 | 39.25 |
| Northern region | 27.93 | 23.80 | 25.87 | 36.10 | 38.75 | 37.43 |
| Eastern region | 24.18 | 19.75 | 21.97 | 40.41 | 43.75 | 42.08 |
| Western region | 24.83 | 22.50 | 23.67 | 38.51 | 41.25 | 39.88 |
| Mid-West region | 27.27 | 24.90 | 26.09 | 36.10 | 38.80 | 37.45 |

(b) Employing Brass System Life Table Models[a]

*Crude Death Rates (life table central death rates $[_5M_x]$)*

| Assumed expectations of life at birth (years) Area | (35) | (37.5) | (40) | (42.5) | (45) | Median value[b] |
|---|---|---|---|---|---|---|
| Nigeria | — | 24.72 | 22.29 | 19.94 | — | 22.33 |
| Northern region | 27.47 | 24.62 | 22.21 | — | — | 24.84 |
| Eastern region | — | — | 21.70 | 19.36 | 17.50 | 19.60 |
| Western region | — | — | 22.01 | 19.77 | 17.92 | 19.97 |
| Mid-West region | 27.99 | 24.84 | 22.08 | — | — | 25.04 |

*Expectation of Life at birth (0–14/15–44 ratio)*

| Area | M | F | M & F |
|---|---|---|---|
| Nigeria | 40.47 | 41.78 | 41.12 |
| Northern region | 35.00 | 39.40 | 37.20 |
| Eastern region | 40.11 | 44.38 | 42.24 |
| Western region | 38.00 | 43.88 | 40.94 |
| Mid-West region | 37.40 | 41.13 | 39.27 |

[a] The relevant tables can be found in the following: Population Investigation Committee, London School of Economics and Political Science, Demographic Training Program, "Tables Based on the Brass System of Model Life Tables and Stable Population Models," mimeographed (September 1967). They were constructed by Mr. N. H. Carrier of the LSE from Brass's logit system and his standard African life table. See W. Brass, "Uses of Census and Survey Data for the Estimation of Vital Rates" (Paper presented to the ECA Seminar on Vital Statistics, Addis Ababa, December 1964), paragraphs 30 ff.
[b] Median value between the lowest and the highest rate.

In fact, the death rate of 23.4 per thousand obtained from the original data is close to our estimate.

If the F.O.S. original death rate of 23.4 per thousand is accepted, then the expectation of life at birth for Nigeria should be higher than the 37 years obtained from the survey by some two years, which means a life expecta-

tion at birth of about 39 years for the rural sector and about 40 years for the whole of Nigeria, which is close to estimates we have derived (39.25 to 41.12 or 40.18 years).

As in the case of fertility, it appears there are differentials in mortality between the regions. The Mid-West appears to have the highest mortality with a death rate of 25.6 per thousand, followed by the North with 25.4 per thousand. The East and the West have lower death rates, the rate for the East at 20.7 being the lowest of all.

This pattern of differentials is, to some extent, supported by medical evidence. For example, the Northern Region annual report on medical services of 1952–1953 has this to say about the use of health facilities in the North:

Except in the riverain provinces where there is an increasing demand for the small village maternity homes which are so popular a feature of the medical services of the Eastern and Western Regions, the available maternity facilities continue to be utilized predominantly by women of Southern extraction, temporarily or permanently resident in the North.[40]

Then, in the report of 1953–1954, the following comments were made in connection with maternity and child welfare in the North:

When a northern woman did go to hospital for delivery, she was all too often *in extremis*, following prolonged and fruitless attempts by *ungozomai* and other incompetent persons, to effect delivery. It was often too late to save her or the infant. The maternity services lose face as a result of such "failures." One or two more enlightened northern leaders have set an example by having their wives delivered in a hospital, but these "pioneers" are still scorned by the majority of their contemporaries.[41]

Such an attitude has persisted to a considerable degree in the North, and this, coupled with many endemic and epidemic diseases such as meningococcal meningitis which until recent years frequently took a heavy toll of life in the North, makes the higher level of mortality in this region plausible. In the case of the Mid-West, an explanation is difficult to find. One possible explanation, however, is that the region,

[40] *Annual Report on the Department of Medical Services of the Northern Region of Nigeria 1952–53*, p. 18.
[41] *Annual Report of the Department of Medical Services of the Northern Region of Nigeria 1953–54*, p. 49.

apart from its gross inadequacy of medical facilities (except in a few large towns), includes part of the delta area where communications are so difficult because of the presence of numerous creeks that the medical facilities would be far more inadequate than in other parts of the region.

THE GROWTH RATE. In spite of the differences in the birth and death rates derived from the Coale-Demeny and Brass systems, there seems to be close agreement between the growth rates derived from the two sources (Table 11.20(a) and (b)). If the assumptions

TABLE 11.20
Rates of natural increase implied by the various estimates of birth and death rates

(a) Employing Coale-Demeny Stable Population Models

| Area | Growth Rates[a] (percent per annum) |
|---|---|
| Nigeria | 3.04 |
| Northern region | 2.85 |
| Eastern region | 3.37 |
| Western region | 2.40 |
| Mid-West region | 2.44 |

(b) Employing Brass System Life Table Models

| Area | Growth Rates[b] (percent per annum) |
|---|---|
| Nigeria | 3.04 |
| Northern region | 2.84 |
| Eastern region | 3.04 |
| Western region | 2.48 |
| Mid-West region | 2.01 |

a Differences between the median values in Tables 11.18(a) and 11.19(a).
1 Difference between the median values in Tables 11.18(b) and 11.19(b).

underlying the estimates are accepted, then it appears that Nigeria was growing by natural increase at a rate of about 3 percent per annum in 1963. This figure is very close to the various estimates and suggestions of the growth rate made for Nigeria since the census of 1963.[42] By 1970 the census was seven years past, so that it might not be far wrong to say that the rate of increase had risen a few points above the 3 percent mark.[43]

The estimates show differentials between the regions. The North and the East seem to be growing much faster than the West and the Mid-West, where rates of increase are only a little over 2 percent. The case of the East is noteworthy. Here, the rate of increase (3.2 percent) is above the overall rate for Nigeria, and this, as has been shown, has resulted from the fact that the region has the lowest death rate[44] and one of the highest birth rates

in the country.[45] In the near future at least, rather than falling, the rate of growth will tend to be higher since it is probable that the birth rate will remain at its high level for some time to come.[46]

[42] See footnotes 27, 28, and 29.

[43] A death rate of 28.4 per thousand has been estimated for 1952–1953 (See Olusanya, "Socio-economic Aspects of Rural-Urban Migration," p. 153). The 1963 rate of 23 per thousand thus represents a decline of about five points within a period of roughly ten years or half in a year. If it can be assumed that this trend has continued after 1963, then the 1970 death rate would be about 20 per thousand and with an unchanging birth rate, the rate of increase would be about 3.3 percent. This, of course, does not take into account the effect of the recent civil war in Nigeria and of the arrival of deportees from Ghana.

[44] See footnote 40. In the author's experience, persons from old Eastern Region who live in Lagos regardless of educational status, seem to make much more use of existing medical facilities (particularly maternity services) than even Yorubas among whom they live. In a study of patients at the Surulere Health Center in Lagos, for example, 41 percent of the sample were Ibo wives, 39 percent Yoruba wives, and 19 percent wives belonging to other southern ethnic groups (see T. Daramola, et al., "Survey of Attitudes in Nigeria towards Family Planning" in Caldwell and Okonjo, Population of Tropical Africa, p. 403.

[45] Very little demographic research has been done in the East, but a study of fertility in 1958 gave an average completed family size of 7.0 for Ogoja Province. At about the same time an average size of around 6 live births was obtained in a survey of 12 villages in the North and a crude birth rate of 56 per thousand (see B. M. Nicol, "Fertility and Food in Northern Nigeria," The West African Medical Journal, VIII, New Series (February 1959), 20–22). In contrast, a birth rate of 32.7 and a death rate of 19 per thousand were obtained in 1952 from a study of cocoa farmers in western Nigeria (see R. Galletti, et al., The Nigerian Cocoa Farmers (London: Oxford University Press, 1956), p. 203). Another set of vital rates was provided in 1964 in a rural health project at Igbo-Ora, a small, semi-rural town. This project yielded a birth rate of 32 per thousand and a death rate of 15 per thousand; see C. R. Barber et al., "Vital Statistics at Igbo-Ora" (Paper presented at the First African Population Conference, Ibadan, January 3–7, 1966). A rural demographic survey in western Nigeria in 1967 gave a birth rate of 46 (when adjusted for possible omissions), a death rate of 15 per thousand and a rate of increase of 3.1 percent. See Olusanya, "Socio-economic Aspects of Rural-Urban Migration."

[46] Even in Lagos, which is far more advanced economically and much more heterogeneous and literate than any other urban center in Nigeria, and where, consequently, it might be expected that the birth rate would only be moderately high, the birth rate in 1967–1968 was estimated at 52.9 per thousand and the death rate at 12.4 per thousand; see R. W. Morgan, "A Population Dynamics Survey in Lagos, Nigeria: Preliminary Memorandum," mimeographed (1969), Table 19.

TABLE 11.21
Summary of vital rates[a]

| Area | Birth Rate (per thousand) | Death Rate (per thousand) | Growth Rate (percent) | GRR | Expectation of Life at Birth (in years) |
|---|---|---|---|---|---|
| Nigeria | 53.40 ± 0.69 | 23.00 ± 0.67 | 3.04 | 3.40 ± 0.36 | 40.18 ± 0.93 |
| Northern region | 53.76 ± 0.56 | 25.35 ± 0.51 | 2.84 | 3.48 ± 0.24 | 37.31 ± 0.11 |
| Eastern region | 52.85 ± 2.86 | 20.70 ± 1.18 | 3.20 ± 0.16 | 3.58 ± 0.35 | 42.16 ± 0.08 |
| Western region | 46.19 ± 1.43 | 21.82 ± 1.85 | 2.44 ± 0.04 | 3.11 ± 0.08 | 40.41 ± 0.53 |
| Mid-West region | 47.84 ± 2.67 | 25.56 ± 0.52 | 2.22 ± 0.21 | 3.15 ± 0.23 | 38.36 ± 0.91 |

[a] The figures given here are the mid-points of values derived from Coale-Demeny and Brass systems. The ± values indicate respectively the difference between the mid-point and the higher and the lower figures.

## POPULATION GROWTH PROSPECT

The year 2,000 is less than 30 years ahead. The size and composition of Nigeria's population, as well as success in restraining its rapid population growth, will be crucial factors in its attempt at rapid socioeconomic development and its position in the international scale of modernization in the new century. It is, therefore, necessary to examine what, under different assumptions of the growth rate, the country's population will be at the end of the present century. The questions of the economic and social implications of the population growth and the possibility of widespread fertility control are taken up in detail in later chapters. It is enough to say here that antenatal practices on an appreciable scale do not yet exist in Nigeria and it seems unlikely that the proportion of families practicing modern contraception will become substantial within the next two decades unless radical measures are taken by the government, for Nigeria is a large and socially complex society. Fortunately or unfortunately, there are increasingly vigorous efforts to provide more and better medical facilities in the component states of Nigeria so that mortality will continue its downward trend.

The need for a radical approach to the population problem is obvious in the sample population projections shown in Table 11.22. The object of the exercise is not to trace the most plausible course of population but to demonstrate the relative sizes of population that would be generated by different possible rates of growth that seem to encompass the actual current rate of growth.[47] According to assumed growth rates of 2, 2.5, and 3 percent, Nigeria's population at the end of the present century will be approximately 114, 128, and 162 million respectively on the basis of the 1963 census population of 56 million, and 98, 109, and 138 million respectively on the basis of an estimated 1963 population of 48 million.

Whichever population is taken as the starting point, the fact remains that the development race will be one against the rate of human increase. Even with a 2 percent per annum growth, the population will double itself at the end of the century. But, with a 2.5 percent growth, there will be a reduction in the doubling time of about five years. However, with a 3 percent growth (the rate at which Nigeria's population already appears to be growing), the population will double itself about 15 years before the end of the century—that is, between 1984 and 1989. In fact, by the end of the first year of the next century, the 3 percent growth would have

[47] For detailed projections and their implications for Nigeria, see John C. Caldwell, "The Population Outlook in Nigeria," Demographic Unit, University of Ife, Nigeria, mimeographed, pp. 6–12.

TABLE 11.22
Projections of Nigeria's population based on assumed rates of growth (in millions)

| Year | Higher Series[a] | | | Lower Series[b] | | | Index: 1963 = 100 | | |
|------|------|------|----|------|------|----|------|------|----|
| | 2% | 2.5% | 3% | 2% | 2.5% | 3% | 2% | 2.5% | 3% |
| 1963 | 65 | 56 | 56 | 48 | 48 | 48 | 100 | 100 | 100 |
| 1969 | 63 | 65 | 67 | 54 | 55 | 57 | 113 | 116 | 120 |
| 1974 | 70 | 73 | 78 | 60 | 62 | 66 | 124 | 130 | 139 |
| 1979 | 77 | 82 | 90 | 66 | 69 | 77 | 137 | 146 | 161 |
| 1984 | 85 | 91 | 104 | 73 | 77 | 89 | 151 | 163 | 186 |
| 1989 | 94 | 102 | 121 | 80 | 87 | 103 | 167 | 183 | 216 |
| 1994 | 103 | 115 | 140 | 89 | 97 | 119 | 184 | 204 | 250 |
| 1999 | 114 | 128 | 162 | 98 | 109 | 138 | 203 | 229 | 290 |

a Accepting the 1963 census population of 56 million.
b Assuming a November 1963 population of 48 million. See P. O. Olusanya, *Socio-economic Aspects of Rural Urban Migration in Western Nigeria*, N.I.S.E.R. (Ibadan, 1969).

resulted in a population three times the 1963 figure. The probable continued fall in the death rate, coupled with the current high birth rate which does not show any indication of a spontaneous decline for many years to come, even suggests that the doubling might come sooner than 1984; any decline in the birth rate will probably be more than offset

by a decline in the death rate,[48] unless, as has been mentioned, a radical approach to the problem is adopted.

[48] The division of the country into small states each with its own central administration may well quicken the rate of decline in mortality. In the place of a single central administration of medical and health services in the North, for example, there will be 6 as a result of the creation of the 12 states.

Appendix: Unadjusted percentage age distribution of the population of Nigeria by region, 1963[a]

| Age Group | Nigeria[b] M | F | North M | F | East M | F | West M | F | Mid-West M | F |
|---|---|---|---|---|---|---|---|---|---|---|
| 0–4   | 16.8 | 17.6 | 17.9 | 18.3 | 17.9 | 19.0 | 12.7 | 13.8 | 16.0 | 16.5 |
| 5–9   | 15.5 | 14.8 | 16.1 | 14.7 | 16.8 | 16.4 | 12.6 | 12.9 | 15.9 | 15.7 |
| 10–14 | 11.6 | 9.7  | 12.0 | 9.7  | 11.6 | 9.8  | 11.0 | 9.9  | 10.3 | 8.6  |
| 15–19 | 8.9  | 10.0 | 9.1  | 12.7 | 7.7  | 6.0  | 9.9  | 8.2  | 7.7  | 5.3  |
| 20–24 | 11.2 | 13.7 | 10.3 | 13.6 | 11.0 | 13.3 | 13.3 | 14.2 | 12.4 | 14.5 |
| 25–29 | 9.3  | 10.7 | 8.5  | 9.4  | 9.2  | 11.6 | 11.4 | 13.4 | 9.1  | 11.6 |
| 30–34 | 7.5  | 8.0  | 7.7  | 7.9  | 6.5  | 7.6  | 8.2  | 9.0  | 6.4  | 7.6  |
| 35–39 | 4.8  | 4.1  | 4.3  | 3.2  | 5.2  | 5.2  | 5.4  | 5.2  | 5.5  | 5.6  |
| 40–44 | 4.7  | 4.0  | 4.7  | 3.9  | 4.4  | 4.0  | 5.0  | 4.5  | 4.5  | 4.4  |
| 45–49 | 2.4  | 1.8  | 1.9  | 1.2  | 3.0  | 2.3  | 2.9  | 2.4  | 3.5  | 3.0  |
| 50–54 | 2.4  | 1.9  | 2.6  | 2.0  | 2.1  | 1.6  | 2.4  | 2.1  | 2.4  | 2.1  |
| 55–59 | 1.0  | 0.7  | 0.9  | 0.5  | 1.1  | 0.8  | 1.1  | 0.9  | 1.4  | 1.2  |
| 60–64 | 1.6  | 1.2  | 1.6  | 1.2  | 1.4  | 1.1  | 1.6  | 1.4  | 1.8  | 1.5  |
| 65+   | 2.3  | 1.8  | 2.4  | 1.7  | 2.1  | 1.3  | 2.5  | 2.1  | 3.1  | 2.4  |
| Total | 100.0 | 100.0 | 100.0 | 100.0 | 100.0 | 100.0 | 100.0 | 100.0 | 100.0 | 100.0 |

a The percentages for Nigeria may be applied to either 56 million or 48 million to obtain the number of persons in each age group.
b Includes the population of Lagos and thus exceeds the sum of the four regional populations.

## INTRODUCTION: HISTORICAL TRENDS IN HEALTH PROBLEMS AND HEALTH PLANNING IN THE WESTERN STATE

The quality and duration of life are variables which have always been influenced by a very wide range of economic, social, and health factors. In modern times, the most important of these factors have been the levels of medical knowledge and services, the levels of real income, nutrition, quantity and quality of housing, sanitation, sewage, water supply, working conditions, and the public provision of the basic social services of which formal education is the most important. Most governments in the nations of the developing world have given serious attention to the provision of such public health and social welfare services, believing that measures to improve education and health can improve the quality of life of their peoples and their efficiency as productive agents, thereby accelerating the general socioeconomic development of these nations.

In Nigeria, as in other nations of the third world, the popular demand for more and better services, especially in the fields of formal education and health, has been insistent. Since at least 1946, the governments of the Federation have not only been anxious to satisfy some of these demands, but also have devoted a substantial proportion of their available resources to provide some of these services. The first positive attempt to plan for the health services of Nigeria was made in 1946 as an integral part of the ten-year (1946–1956) colonial development and welfare programs when about one-tenth of the projected capital expenditure was allocated to the provision of public health facilities. The health plan was as modest as the ten-year colonial development and welfare programs; and it was not properly coordinated with the provisions of other services in the overall plan, such as agriculture and rural development, education, and small-scale industries.

Constitutional advancement in Nigeria from the late 1950s ushered in political autonomy as the nationalist leaders assumed political responsibility. Greater attention came to be paid to the development of social

# CHAPTER TWELVE

# *Socioeconomic Status & Attitudes*

## *to Public Health Problems in the Western State: A Case Study of Ibadan*

FRANCIS OLU. OKEDIJI

services throughout the Federation. The government of the Western Region (now Western State) had blazed the trail in 1952 by publishing a policy paper on public health.[1] This public health policy included curative and preventive health services as well as free school medical services and a pilot insurance scheme. The Eastern and the Northern regions of Nigeria followed the example of the Western Region; and each of these governments, during the 1955–1962 Development Plan, allocated between 20 and 25 percent of their capital expenditures to the provision of educational and health facilities. On average, about one-third of this amount was invested in education. In the 1962–1968 National Development Plan, about 2.5 percent of the total projected capital expenditure of £676.8 million by all the governments of the Federation was devoted to the provision of public health services.[2] This percentage is rather small, however, compared with many other West African countries at the time.

A further discussion of the status of health services in relationship to other items in the 1962–1968 National Development Plan, with specific reference to the Western State, is necessary at this point.[3] The Western (including what subsequently became the Mid-West) Region presented the following statement on health in the 1962–1968 plan: "The government has already one hospital for each administrative division, and the number of dispensaries and maternity centers has more than doubled."[4] It also presented the following proposals: (1) an increase in the number of specialist hospitals, training of

nurses and midwives, and the provision of loans to private practitioners for hospital construction; (2) the expansion of preventive and rural health services, the rehabilitation of disabled leprosy patients, the control of certain common endemic and epidemic diseases, the establishment of better public health laboratory facilities, and the expansion of dental health services; (3) the development of government housing estates at Moba Village and in two or three other places in the region.

Although these stated health objectives were quite impressive, the resources allocated to public health and medical facilities were rather inadequate for the needs of the growing population of what is now the Western State. Of the funds allocated to health, higher priority was placed on the provision of curative health services than of preventive services. A large proportion of the illiterate masses in the Western State (in contrast to the small elite groups who live in the well-planned residential areas of Yoruba towns) is still vulnerable to the onslaught of infectious and other preventable diseases.

The population of the Western State in 1968 was estimated at almost 10.5 million.[5] Table 12.1 shows the population by division according to the controversial 1963 census on which the estimated population projection for 1968 was based. It would appear that the estimated figures were computed on an assumption of a 2 percent per annum rate of increase since 1963. The Western State government, while seemingly conforming to its stated health objectives in the 1962–1968 National Development Plan, has made the following expenditures on medical and health services: £2,206,082 or 8.8 percent of the total expenditures for the financial year 1962–1963;[6] £1,974,965 or 8.2 percent of the total expenditures for 1963–1964;[7] £1,733,298 or 8.2 percent of the total expenditures for

[1] Public Health Policy for the Western Region of Nigeria (Ibadan, July 1952).

[2] Federation of Nigeria National Development Plan, 1962–1968 (Apapa, Lagos, n.d.).

[3] For a critical assessment of the disjunction between stated health objectives in the 1962–1968 National Development Plan and the actual state of health in the Nigerian communities, see F. O. Okediji, "Socioeconomic Aspects of Public Health in Relation to 1962–68 Nigeria's National Development Plan" (Paper presented to the Seminar on Population Growth and Economic Development, Nairobi, Kenya, December 14–22, 1969).

[4] Federation of Nigeria National Development Plan, 1962–1968.

[5] Ministry of Health, Western State, Annual Statistical Bulletin (Ibadan), p. 6.

[6] Calculated from the Report of the Accountant General for the Year Ended March 31, 1963 (Ibadan, Western Nigeria Official Document No. 2 of 1966), p. 125.

[7] Calculated from the Report of the Accountant General for the Year Ended March 31, 1964 (Ibadan, Western Nigeria Official Document No. 2 of 1966), p. 125.

TABLE 12.1

Population in Western Nigeria, by division (Census 1963 and Estimation 1968)

| Divisions | Population Census 1963 | Estimated Population at the End of 1968 |
|---|---|---|
| Egba | 629,565 | 693,702 |
| Egbado | 345,321 | 380,653 |
| Ekiti: central | 351,283 | 387,020 |
| north | 216,158 | 239,154 |
| south | 344,120 | 379,129 |
| west | 529,363 | 583,217 |
| Okitipupa | 275,709 | 303,760 |
| Akure | 278,311 | 306,624 |
| Ondo | 258,063 | 284,316 |
| Akoko | 284,819 | 313,795 |
| Owo | 189,847 | 209,160 |
| Ibadan City | 627,379 | 691,205 |
| Ibadan less city | 514,298 | 566,619 |
| Ibarapa | 116,948 | 128,845 |
| Oshun: central | 590,589 | 650,672 |
| northeast | 551,817 | 607,955 |
| northwest | 455,574 | 501,921 |
| south | 608,518 | 670,424 |
| Ife | 376,718 | 414,739 |
| Ilesha: north | 177,428 | 195,486 |
| south | 304,292 | 335,248 |
| Oyo: north | 412,491 | 454,455 |
| south | 472,832 | 520,935 |
| Ijebu-Ode | 420,355 | 463,178 |
| Ijebu-Remo | 155,725 | 171,547 |
| Total region | 9,487,523 | 10,453,759 |

SOURCE: Ministry of Health, Western State, *Annual Statistical Bulletin* (Ibadan, 1968), p. 6.

1964–1965;[8] £2,057,423 or 8.5 percent of the total expenditure for 1965–1966;[9] £1,731,491 or 8.3 percent of the total expenditures for 1966–1967;[10] and £1,815,000 or 8.1 percent of the total expenditures for 1967–1968.[11]

When we examine the number and distribution of hospitals and health centers in the state in relation to the population served in the different divisions or districts as well as the number of patients per doctor, a reasonable judgment is that the funds expended on medical and health services are clearly inadequate. Table 12.2 shows the number and names of hospitals and health centers in the state as of 1968–1969 classified by divisions or districts and population served. Throughout the state, the ratio of hospital beds to population ranges from 1 bed per 4,000 to 1 bed per 10,000 people.[12] The ratios of different categories of medical staff to the population of the whole Western State are as follows: 1 doctor to 43,642 persons; 1 midwife to 6,047 persons; and 1 nurse to 8,656 persons.[13] Obviously, not only is the number of hospitals and health centers in the state small, but the available number of the different categories of medical staff is also small. Planning authorities seem to place a higher priority on the provision of curative health facilities than on the provision of preventive health facilities. Table 12.3, which shows the approved estimated expenditures of the Western State for medical and health services for the financial year 1968–1969, supports this observation. It is very doubtful whether this overemphasis on the provision of curative medical facilities as compared with the provision of preventive medical facilities is justified. First, it has been argued that it is a waste of taxpayers' money to build many expensive hospitals which are poorly equipped with human and material resources; and part of such funds should have been more rewardingly invested in providing preventive medical facilities. Second, recent health statistics obtained from government sources reveal that the commonest diseases in various communities are preventable ones such as malaria, anemia, dysentery, diarrhea, measles, gastrointestinal diseases, and respiratory infections.

Tables 12.4, 12.5, and 12.6 show the pattern of morbidity in the Western State according to hospital records. Before discussing the morbidity trends in these tables, we must point out an important omission which is common to them. The coverage of diseases did

[8] Calculated from the *Report of the Accountant General for the Year Ended March 31, 1965* (Ibadan, Western Nigeria Official Document No. 10 of 1966), p. 127.

[9] Calculated from the *Western Nigeria Estimates, 1967–1968*, (Ibadan) p. 13.

[10] Calculated from the *Report of the Accountant General for the Year Ended March 31, 1967* (Ibadan, Western State of Nigeria Official Document No. 1 of 1970), p. 13.

[11] Calculated from the *Approved Estimate of the Western State of Nigeria, 1969–1970* (Ibadan, 1971).

[12] Calculated from the Ministry of Health, *Annual Statistical Bulletin* (Ibadan, 1968), pp. 43–44.

[13] *Ibid.*, p. 47.

TABLE 12.2

Distribution of hospitals and health centers in the Western state classified by divisions or districts and population served from 1962–1969

| Divisions or Districts | Hospitals and Health Centers | | Population Served (based on 1963 census) |
|---|---|---|---|
| | Number | Name | |
| Akure & Ondo | 3 | State Hospital and Dental Care; Akure General Hospital; Ondo Rural Health Center, Araromi Obu | 536,374 |
| Egba | 4 | State Hospital and Dental Center, Abeokuta; Aro Mental Hospital; Abeokuta District Hospital Ottah; Sacred Heart Hospital, Abeokuta | 629,565 |
| Egbado | 5 | General Hospital, Ilaro; District Hospital, Ipokia; Rural Health Center, Ilaro; Rural Health Center, Imeko; Medical Field Unit, Ilaro | 345,321 |
| Ekiti | 12 | General Hospital, Iddo-Ekiti; District Hospital, Ijero; Rural Health Center, Aramoko; District Hospital, Iyin; District Hospital, Ijan Maria; Assumpta Hospital, Ado-Ekiti; Ile-Abiye Hospital, Ado-Ekiti; District Hospital, Ikole; District Hospital, Aiyede; District Hospital, Ikere; Otun District Hospital, Ijero; Ipoti District Hospital | 1,418,114 |
| Ibadan | 9 | State Hospital, Ibadan; Jericho Nursing Home, Ibadan; Chest Clinic, Ibadan; Orthopaedic Rehabilitation Center, Ibadan; St. Mary's Hospital, Eleta Ibadan; Catholic Hospital, Oke-Offa Ibadan; University College Teaching Hospital, Ibadan; District Hospital, Eruwa; Rural Health Center, Igboora | 1,258,625 |
| Ife | 2 | State Hospital, Ile Ife; Seventh Day Adventist, Ile-Ife | 515,194 |
| Ijebu-Ode | 4 | State Hospital and Dental Center, Ijebu-Ode; District Hospital, Odogbolu; District Hospital, Ijebu-Ife; General Hospital, Ibiade | 420,353 |
| Ijebu-Remo | 2 | General Hospital, Shagamu; Rural Health Center, Ishara | 155,725 |
| Ilesha | 4 | Rural Health Center, Imesi-Ile; General Hospital, Ilesha; Wesley Guild Hospital; Medical Field Unit, Ilesha | 481,720 |

TABLE 12.2 (contd.)

| Divisions or Districts | Hospitals and Health Centers Number | Name | Population Served (based on 1963 census) |
|---|---|---|---|
| Oshun | 8 | State Hospital, Oshogbo; District Hospital, Ede; Medical Field Unit, Oshogbo; Rural Health Center, Oyan; General Hospital, Iwo; Rural Health Center, Ikire; General Hospital, Ogbomosho; Baptist Hospital, Ogbomosho | 2,068,022 |
| Owo, Akoko, and Okitipupa | 2 | St. Louis Hospital, Owo; General Hospital, Ikare; General Hospital, Okitipupa | 497,478 |
| Oyo | 3 | General Hospital, Oyo; General Hospital, Igbetti; Baptist Hospital, Shaki | 885,323 |

SOURCE : Statistics Division, Ministry of Economic Planning and Social Development, Western State, *Statistical Abstract* (Ibadan, 1968), chap. VI; Ministry of Health, Western State, *Annual Statistical Bulletin*; and personal communications.

not include the following sources: maternity and health centers, dispensaries, privately owned hospitals, and chemists' and herbalists' establishments. Besides, there are hundreds of thousands of cases not reported to any of these health institutions because of cultural taboos or lack of access to any modern health institution.

Although these limitations are glaring, the tables show some interesting trends. Table 12.4 demonstrates clearly that in the period, 1963–1967, more than 60 percent of the notifiable diseases reported in the Western State hospitals each year (i.e., malaria, nervous system and sense organ diseases, dysentery, anemia, and respiratory diseases) are strongly connected with the unsanitary environment in which the masses of people of low socioeconomic status in the Western State, and generally in Nigeria, live.

Table 12.5 shows the number and percentage of cases of water-borne diseases treated in hospitals in the Western State for the same years 1963–1967. The number of reported cases seemed to fluctuate from year to year. The large rural population of the Western State suffers more from these water-borne diseases than the town population because the former lacks piped water and thus

depends on water supply from rivers, streams, and ponds.[14]

Table 12.6 shows similar morbidity trends as revealed by hospital records which were classified by provinces for 1967 alone. Ibadan Province appeared to have the largest number of reported cases of those diseases which are mostly preventable. The highest percentage

[14] A socioeconomic survey of rural communities in Egba and Egbado divisions done between 1968 and 1969 reported the following sources of water supply for a sample or rural and urban dwellers:

| Source of Water Supply | Percent of Inhabitants Having Villages | Towns |
|---|---|---|
| Own tap | 0.0 | 1.5 |
| Public tap | 0.0 | 73.5 |
| Well | 37.8 | 1.5 |
| Pond | 6.1 | 0.0 |
| River, stream | 56.1 | 23.5 |
| | 100.0 | 100.0 |

The surveys went further to indicate that the spread of intestinal diseases, dysentery and diarrhea was four times as high in the villages as in the town. The reason for this is that the villages lack piped water. See K. Borger Poulsen, "A Socio-economic Survey of Women in Rural Areas of the Western State of Nigeria," mimeographed (Ibadan, June 1969), pp. 88 and 94.

TABLE 12.3

Approved estimated expenditures of the Western state for medical and health services 1968–1969

| Type of Expenditure | Approved Estimated Expenditure (£000) | Percent of Total |
|---|---|---|
| Curative | 966,690 | 56.2 |
| Preventive | 315,430 | 18.3 |
| Other[2] | 437,650 | 25.5 |
| Total | 1,719,770 | 100.0 |

SOURCE: *Approved Estimates of the Western State of Nigeria, 1969–1970* (Ibadan, 1971).
[a] Other includes expenditure on Administrative and General Division, Finance and Establishment Division, and miscellaneous allowances.

of people (i.e., 65.5 percent) attacked by malaria was also reported for Ibadan.

Mortality statistics collated by the Western State Ministry of Health, which are subject to the same limitations inherent in the morbidity statistics, show that, of all the deaths recorded in the Western State hospitals in 1968, infective and parasitic diseases were the most important (35.4 percent), respiratory diseases came second (16.8 percent), diseases of the digestive system came third (9.6 percent), while the remaining 37.2 percent of diseases were unclassified.[15]

[15] Ministry of Health, *Annual Statistical Bulletin*, p. 42.

TABLE 12.4

Number and percentage of cases of notifiable diseases reported in the Western State hospitals, 1963–1967

| Types of Diseases | Number and Percentage of Persons Treated | | | | | | | | | |
|---|---|---|---|---|---|---|---|---|---|---|
| | 1963 | | 1964 | | 1965 | | 1966 | | 1967 | |
| | Number | Percent | Number | Percent | Number | Percent | Number | Percent | Number | Percent |
| Anthrax | 23 | 0.01 | 9 | 0.005 | 50 | 0.01 | 36 | 0.01 | 46 | 0.02 |
| Anemia | 12,937 | 5.6 | 11,285 | 6.7 | 11,020 | 3.9 | 14,510 | 4.7 | 19,453 | 9.4 |
| Asthma | 2,943 | 1.3 | 1,811 | 1.1 | 2,176 | 0.7 | 2,198 | 0.7 | 1,832 | 0.9 |
| Chicken pox | 1,341 | 0.6 | 297 | 0.1 | 454 | 0.1 | 1,189 | 0.3 | 483 | 0.2 |
| Cholera | 16 | 0.006 | 16 | 0.009 | 18 | 0.006 | 227 | 0.07 | 152 | 0.07 |
| Diphtheria | 300 | 0.01 | 113 | 0.06 | 210 | 0.07 | 40 | 0.01 | 27 | 0.01 |
| Dysentery | 26,432 | 11.3 | 15,998 | 9.5 | 20,916 | 7.5 | 27,390 | 8.9 | 25,439 | 12.3 |
| Epilepsy | 333 | 0.01 | 137 | 0.08 | 671 | 0.2 | 337 | 0.1 | 286 | 0.1 |
| Heart disease | 913 | 0.4 | 1,175 | 0.7 | 1,302 | 0.4 | 1,182 | 0.3 | 928 | 0.4 |
| Leprosy | 1,170 | 0.5 | 617 | 0.3 | 75 | 0.02 | 108 | 0.03 | 70 | 0.03 |
| Malaria | 97,274 | 41.8 | 56,452 | 33.6 | 138,810 | 49.7 | 148,365 | 48.1 | 104,581 | 50.5 |
| Measles | 8,651 | 3.7 | 5,821 | 3.4 | 7,046 | 2.5 | 13,125 | 4.2 | 11,900 | 5.7 |
| Neoplasm | 1,221 | 0.5 | 973 | 0.5 | 917 | 0.3 | 1,853 | 0.6 | 817 | 0.4 |
| Nervous system & sense organ diseases | 30,578 | 13.1 | 35,100 | 20.9 | 46,988 | 16.8 | 51,059 | 16.5 | 2,104 | 1.0 |
| Plague | 79 | 0.03 | 24 | 0.01 | 40 | 0.01 | 8 | 0.003 | 4 | 0.002 |
| Poliomyelitis | 38 | 0.02 | 121 | 0.07 | 124 | 0.04 | 107 | 0.03 | 90 | 0.04 |
| Pneumonia | 11,379 | 4.9 | 9,270 | 5.5 | 9,612 | 3.4 | 13,106 | 4.2 | 10,407 | 5.0 |
| Rabies | 141 | 0.06 | 197 | 0.1 | 1,033 | 0.4 | 900 | 0.3 | 109 | 0.05 |
| Relapsing fever | 436 | 0.2 | 43 | 0.02 | 208 | 0.07 | 301 | 0.09 | 44 | 0.02 |
| Rheumatic fever | 1,753 | 0.7 | 1,191 | 0.7 | 1,749 | 0.6 | 1,680 | 0.5 | 780 | 0.04 |
| Scabies | 14,064 | 6.0 | 7,612 | 4.5 | 7,850 | 2.8 | 9,146 | 2.9 | 5,815 | 2.8 |
| Smallpox | 103 | 0.04 | 467 | 0.2 | 630 | 0.2 | 380 | 0.1 | 165 | 0.08 |
| Syphilis | 3,475 | 1.5 | 2,937 | 1.7 | 3,312 | 1.2 | 3,945 | 1.2 | 252 | 0.1 |
| Tetanus | 846 | 0.3 | 834 | 0.5 | 953 | 0.3 | 927 | 0.3 | 1,046 | 0.5 |
| Trypanosomiasis | 141 | 0.06 | 15 | 0.0u8 | 69 | 0.02 | 325 | 0.1 | 4 | 0.002 |
| Tuberculosis | 8,123 | 3.5 | 7,600 | 4.5 | 7,355 | 2.6 | 7,178 | 2.3 | 4,356 | 2.1 |
| Typhoid fever | 174 | 0.07 | 229 | 0.1 | 187 | 0.7 | 285 | 0.09 | 275 | 0.1 |
| Typhus | 783 | 0.3 | 360 | 0.2 | 9,206 | 3.3 | 42 | 0.01 | 10,407 | 5.0 |
| Whooping cough | 4,612 | 1.9 | 3,977 | 2.3 | 4,351 | 1.6 | 5,026 | 1.6 | 4,130 | 2.0 |
| Yaws | 2,498 | 1.1 | 3,046 | 1.8 | 1,705 | 0.6 | 3,109 | 1.0 | 844 | 0.4 |
| Yellow fever | 130 | 0.05 | 154 | 0.09 | 278 | 0.1 | 98 | 0.03 | 155 | 0.07 |
| Total | 232,907 | 100.0 | 167,881 | 100.0 | 279,315 | 100.0 | 308,182 | 100.0 | 207,001 | 100.0 |

SOURCE: *Statistical Abstract*. We calculated the percentages which were not available in the original source.
NOTE: 1967 figures exclude those of the former Colony Province of Western Nigeria which is now part of Lagos State.

TABLE 12.5

Number and percentage of cases of water-borne diseases treated in hospitals in the Western State, 1963–1967

| Type of Disease | 1963 Number | 1963 Percent | 1964 Number | 1964 Percent | 1965 Number | 1965 Percent | 1966 Number | 1966 Percent | 1967 Number | 1967 Percent |
|---|---|---|---|---|---|---|---|---|---|---|
| Skin infections other than ulcers | 20,581 | 18.8 | 10,006 | 12.5 | 20,903 | 21.7 | 15,025 | 14.5 | 8,582 | 1 |
| Gastroenteritis and colitis | 26,311 | 24.0 | 27,438 | 34.1 | 27,828 | 28.9 | 35,286 | 34.3 | 24,251 | 3 |
| Dysentery | 34,372 | 31.3 | 22,293 | 27.8 | 24,095 | 25.1 | 30,581 | 29.7 | 25,439 | 3 |
| Typhoid, paratyphoid, and salmonella infections | 226 | 0.2 | 193 | 0.2 | 208 | 0.2 | 289 | 0.3 | 290 | |
| Helminthiasis | 25,794 | 23.5 | 17,637 | 22.0 | 20,310 | 21.0 | 18,819 | 18.2 | 17,053 | 22.0 |
| Infectious viral hepatitis | 2,338 | 2.2 | 2,680 | 3.4 | 2,986 | 3.1 | 3,089 | 3.0 | 1,273 | 1.7 |
| Total | 109,622 | 100.0 | 80,246 | 100.0 | 96,330 | 100.0 | 103,089 | 100.0 | 76,888 | 100.0 |

SOURCE: *Statistical Abstract* p. 106.
NOTE: Figures for 1967 exclude those of former Colony Province which is now part of Lagos State.

TABLE 12.6

Number and percentage of cases of notifiable diseases reported in the Western State hospitals by provinces, 1967

| | Provinces | | | | | | | | | | |
|---|---|---|---|---|---|---|---|---|---|---|---|
| Type of Diseases | Abeoukuta Number | Abeoukuta Percent | Ibadan Number | Ibadan Percent | Ijebu Number | Ijebu Percent | Ondo Number | Ondo Percent | Oyo Number | Oyo Percent | Total Number | Total Percent |
| Anthrax | 10 | 0.03 | 7 | 0.008 | — | — | 20 | 0.05 | 9 | 0.03 | 46 | 0.02 |
| Anemia | 5,572 | 15.4 | 5,036 | 6.0 | 2,073 | 8.7 | 3,125 | 8.2 | 3,625 | 14.0 | 19,431 | 9.4 |
| Asthma | 460 | 1.3 | 883 | 1.1 | 213 | 0.9 | 139 | 0.3 | 137 | 0.5 | 1,832 | 0.9 |
| Chicken pox | 71 | 0.2 | 249 | 0.3 | 48 | 0.2 | 86 | 0.2 | 29 | 0.1 | 483 | 0.2 |
| Cholera | — | — | 4 | 0.005 | 122 | 0.5 | 20 | 0.05 | 6 | 0.02 | 152 | 0.07 |
| Diptheria | 8 | 0.02 | 15 | 0.02 | 1 | 0.004 | — | — | 3 | 0.01 | 27 | 0.01 |
| Dysentery | 2,391 | 6.6 | 8,674 | 10.4 | 5,324 | 22.5 | 6,789 | 17.9 | 2,261 | 8.7 | 25,439 | 12.3 |
| Epilepsy | 108 | 0.3 | 66 | 0.08 | 12 | 0.05 | 25 | 0.07 | 75 | 0.3 | 286 | 0.1 |
| Heart disease | 51 | 0.1 | 202 | 0.2 | 385 | 1.6 | 46 | 0.1 | 244 | 0.9 | 928 | 0.4 |
| Leprosy | 11 | 0.03 | 12 | 0.01 | 26 | 0.1 | 15 | 0.03 | 6 | 0.02 | 70 | 0.03 |
| Malaria | 13,459 | 37.3 | 54,610 | 65.5 | 8,118 | 34.0 | 17,537 | 46.3 | 10,857 | 42.0 | 104,581 | 50.5 |
| Measles | 1,085 | 3.0 | 3,162 | 3.8 | 1,171 | 4.9 | 4,372 | 11.6 | 2,110 | 8.2 | 11,900 | 5.7 |
| Neoplasm | 50 | 0.1 | 58 | 0.07 | 342 | 1.4 | 68 | 0.2 | 299 | 1.2 | 817 | 0.4 |
| Nervous system and sense organ disease | 14 | 0.04 | 1,595 | 1.9 | 112 | 0.4 | 175 | 0.5 | 208 | 0.8 | 2,104 | 1.0 |
| Plague | — | — | — | — | 1 | 0.004 | 3 | 0.008 | — | — | 4 | 0.002 |
| Poliomyelitis | 1 | 0.003 | 21 | 0.03 | 43 | 0.12 | 4 | 0.01 | 21 | 0.08 | 90 | 0.04 |
| Pneumonia | 2,644 | 7.3 | 3,086 | 3.7 | 1,681 | 7.0 | 1,904 | 5.0 | 1,092 | 4.2 | 10,407 | 5.0 |
| Rabies | — | — | 32 | 0.04 | 16 | 0.06 | 36 | 0.09 | 25 | 1.0 | 109 | 0.05 |
| Relapsing fever | 1 | 0.003 | 26 | 0.03 | 3 | 0.01 | 12 | 0.03 | 1 | 0.004 | 43 | 0.02 |
| Rheumatic fever | — | — | 98 | 0.1 | 391 | 1.6 | 227 | 0.6 | 64 | 0.2 | 780 | 0.3 |
| Scabies | 320 | 0.9 | 1,182 | 1.4 | 643 | 2.7 | 1,675 | 4.4 | 1,995 | 7.7 | 5,815 | 2.8 |
| Smallpox | 16 | 0.04 | 46 | 0.06 | 84 | 0.3 | — | — | 19 | 0.07 | 165 | 0.08 |
| Syphilis | 2 | 0.006 | 9 | 0.01 | 51 | 0.2 | 174 | 0.5 | 16 | 0.06 | 252 | 0.1 |
| Tetanus | 219 | 0.6 | 330 | 0.4 | 176 | 0.7 | 104 | 0.3 | 217 | 0.8 | 1,046 | 0.5 |
| Trypanosomiasis | — | — | 4 | 0.004 | — | — | — | — | — | — | 4 | 0.002 |
| Tuberculosis | 495 | 1.4 | 2,376 | 2.9 | 415 | 1.7 | 439 | 1.2 | 613 | 2.4 | 4,338 | 2.0 |
| Typhoid fever | 9 | 0.02 | 148 | 0.2 | — | — | 24 | 0.06 | 94 | 0.4 | 275 | 0.1 |
| Typhus | 8,567 | 23.7 | 288 | 0.3 | 1,511 | 6.3 | 23 | 0.06 | 18 | 0.07 | 10,407 | 5.0 |
| Whooping cough | 347 | 1.0 | 886 | 1.1 | 744 | 3.1 | 461 | 1.2 | 1,692 | 6.5 | 4,130 | 2.0 |
| Yaws | 190 | 0.5 | 217 | 0.3 | 124 | 0.5 | 216 | 0.6 | 97 | 0.4 | 844 | 0.4 |
| Yellow Fever | 9 | 0.02 | 2 | 0.002 | 2 | 0.008 | 118 | 0.3 | 24 | 0.09 | 155 | 0.07 |
| Total | 36,110 | 100.0 | 83,324 | 100.0 | 23,832 | 100.0 | 37,837 | 100.0 | 25,857 | 100.0 | 206,960 | 100.0 |

SOURCE: *Statistical Abstract* p. 104. We calculated the percentages which were not available in the original source.

Despite the limitations in the morbidity and mortality statistics to which we have referred, they point to the primacy of diseases which are strongly connected with malnutrition, very poor housing conditions, unhygienic health habits and unsanitary environmental conditions.

Some important empirical questions can be raised at this point. Why should this condition of public ill health persist? Although we have demonstrated clearly that the financial resources allocated to health in the 1962–1968 Development Plan were inadequate and that the priority placed on curative medicine as compared with preventive medicine is unjustified, yet there are other sociological, cultural, and social-psychological factors which contribute to high morbidity and high mortality within the population of many communities in the Western State.

### THE SOCIOLOGICAL PROBLEM

The objectives of this investigation are as follows: (1) to review critically the important sociological theories which attempt to explain the development of cities and the residential patterns in these cities, with special reference to the existence of blighted areas (modifications of these theories will be suggested insofar as they can probably help us to understand the residential structure of Nigerian cities, with special reference to the city of Ibadan); (2) to provide reliable empirical evidence of public health conditions, with special reference to changes in morbidity and mortality levels, in selected residential communities in the city of Ibadan; (3) to determine the extent to which public health conditions, health habits, and morbidity and mortality levels differ according to the socioeconomic characteristics of families or the heads of households of the families selected for study; (4) to determine the extent to which differences in beliefs and knowledge of health problems, attitudes to and use of modern medical facilities, and care of children can be explained by the differentials in the socioeconomic characteristics of these families.

A CRITIQUE OF THEORIES OF THE ORIGIN OF BLIGHTED AREAS IN CITIES. Sociological literature is rich in theories explaining the development of cities in Western countries and of the residential patterns in these cities, with special reference to the existence of blighted areas and the socioeconomic characteristics and the public health status of the families living in these areas. The situation presented by cities or towns in the nations of the developing world has not given rise to the formulation of any systematic theory of the growth of such cities and of their residential structure. The available theories attempt only to explain the growth and the internal structures of cities in the highly industrialized nations. These theories will be critically discussed briefly insofar as they can possibly help us understand the residential structures of Nigerian cities, especially Ibadan. These theories have commonly emphasized that changes in urban land-use patterns and inadequate housing will bring about overcrowding, poor building maintenance, and public ill health.

One theory, which was derived from a study of cities in the United States by Burgess, postulated that slums develop within the core surrounding the central business district.[16] Earlier in the development of the city, this area was the home of the upper-income group. The expansion of industrial and commercial activities caused the higher-income group to move further out away from the center of the city. Thus, they were succeeded by lower-income groups who became the exclusive inhabitants of the area. Housing conditions deteriorated; the houses became overcrowded and the buildings were not properly maintained because the rather meager rental returns to the landlords were unprofitable.

This theory has been criticized principally on the grounds of its claim to universal generalization. Such criticisms have led to its

[16] E. W. Burgess, "The Growth of the City," in R. E. Park and E. W. Burgess, eds., *The City* (Chicago: University of Chicago Press, 1925); and L. Wirth, *Contemporary Social Problems* (Chicago: University of Chicago Press, 1939), p. 32.

modification, in another theory postulated by Hoyt, who conceptualized the growth and structure of the city as a pie, divided into wedge-shaped sections. Because industrial areas follow river valleys, waterways, and railways out of the center and workingmen's settlements cluster around them as well as factories located on some of the outskirts of the city, the high-quality houses do not fringe the entire city but only parts of it.[17] However, Sjoberg has claimed that the pattern of land distribution in which the slum is located in or near the central city represents a generalization applicable to industrial cities with their characteristic prominence of centralized commercial and industrial activities, but that this generalization does not apply to preindustrial cities.[18] In such cities which were commonly found in medieval Europe and are found even now in developing countries, the traditional elite groups resided close to the center of the city while the lower income groups resided in the slum areas which were located around the periphery of the city.[19] It is extremely doubtful whether Hoyt's sector view of city development can help very much in explaining the residential structure of the city of Ibadan which still manifests preindustrial characteristics. Industrialization is still at the formative stage and a modern transportation system is no more than planned.

There is also the multiple-nuclei theory postulated by Harris and Ullman who argue that the growth of many cities takes place around many nuclei and not around a single nucleus.[20] In other words, divergent forces shape the development of specialized activities

within a city; and these same forces also affect the divergent residential structure of the city. It would appear that this multiple-nuclei theory is of greater help in understanding the residential structures of Nigerian cities, such as Ibadan, than the two theories previously discussed.

THE RESIDENTIAL STRUCTURE OF THE CITY OF IBADAN. In the previous section, we discussed critically the concentric- and the sector-zone theories of the development of cities with special reference to the existence of blighted areas and the socioeconomic and public health status of families living in these areas within American cities. The common factor in both theories is the central business district which was conceptualized as the point from where socioeconomic, technological, and cultural influences are radially diffused to the city periphery. A conceptual modification of the theories is necessary in order to understand the residential pattern of the city of Ibadan. The residential structure of Ibadan can be conceptualized as traditional in nature in the core settlements, with a gradual transition into the more recently built and high-quality residential settlements around the periphery of the city.

The city of Ibadan was founded as a war camp around 1830,[21] and subsequently became a large Yoruba settlement. In the disturbed atmosphere in which refugees and other early settlers flocked into the oldest part of the city, such planning rules as "measure and divide" or "zoning" were entirely out of the question.[22] As the wars of the early nineteenth century subsided, the residential pattern of the oldest part of the city became more haphazard due to rural-urban migration and the desire of the indigenes to build houses on the already overcrowded lands which belonged to their respective lineages. Since its establishment, the city of Ibadan has

[17] Homer Hoyt, *The Structure and Growth of Residential Neighborhoods in American Cities* (Washington, D.C.: Federal Housing Administration, 1939), pp. 75–77; and Homer Hoyt, "The Structure of American Cities in the Post-War Era," *American Journal of Sociology*, XLVII (January 1943), 475–81.
[18] Gideon Sjoberg *The Preindustrial City: Past and Present* (New York: The Free Press, 1960), chap. 4; and N. P. Gist "The Ecology of Bangalore, India; An East–West Comparison," *Social Forces*, XXXV (May 1957), 356–65.
[19] *Ibid.*, p. 98.
[20] C. D. Harris and E. L. Ullman, "The Nature of Cities," *The Annals of the American Academy of Political and Social Sciences*, CCXLII (November 1945), 7–17.

[21] See S. O. Biobaku, *The Egba and Their Neighbors, 1842–72* (London: Oxford University Press, 1957), p. 14.
[22] See G. A. Onibokun, "Socio-cultural Constraints on Urban Renewal Policies in Emerging Nations: The Ibadan Case," *Nigerian Journal of Economic and Social Studies*, XI, 3 (November 1969), 344.

become a center of colonial administration and commerce, a regional capital and an educational center within Nigeria.[23] These forces of sociocultural change contribute significantly to the current heterogeneous population of the city which consists of: (1) the indigenous Yoruba people who are still deeply rooted in their traditional compounds, (2) the diverse immigrant groups from other parts of Nigeria who were and still are attracted to Ibadan in search of jobs; and (3) the highly placed educated elite groups who hold key positions in the bureaucratic, industrial, and educational institutions of the city.

The first or more traditional of these groups forms a dense population; the vast majority are descended from the earliest settlers. The most important unit of their traditional social structure is the lineage, which comprises descendants who can trace their ancestry from the same male ancestor. The families are organized in extended family groups whose members lodge in the same compound. Physically, a compound is a residential unit whose wall connects mud-built houses which are arranged around a series of rectangular courtyards. A typical compound contains several dwelling units occupied by many related families. Environmental sanitation is extremely precarious in these areas.[24] Most of the dwelling units are structually and qualitatively deficient; dwellings are chaotically and densely jumbled together; existing roads traversing the built-up area are extremely few and badly maintained and the basic urban amenities necessary for good health and happy existence are very scarcely and sporadically distributed.[25] Although the

core settlements are blighted, overcrowded, and deteriorated, they cannot be described as slum areas. This is another modification which must be made in the concentric-zone and sector-zone theories of the city of Ibadan. The core settlements of Ibadan are not slum areas because they are neither disorganized nor are they the breeding grounds of criminal and delinquent activities as are the slum areas of the highly industrialized European and American cities.[26] The inhabitants of the core settlements in the city of Ibadan are deeply rooted in these areas: They have developed well-organized and intimate relationships, and they generally are satisfied with their way of life.

Usually, the compounds in the traditional residential settlements range in size from fewer than 50 to more than 450 inhabitants.[27] The smallest compounds can be described as disintegrated units, since some of their members have migrated either to other parts of the city or elsewhere in the Western State. Polygyny is frequent in the traditional settlements; and between 35 percent and 60 percent of the married women are plural wives.[28] Each wife has a room of her own, although kitchen and toilet facilities are shared with other women who reside in the compound. The head of the family or household has his own room, and the authority structure converges on him. Life involves a wide range of social intercourse with a large number of persons who are mutually oriented to the traditions of the compound.

[23] See A. Mabogunje, *Yoruba Towns* (Ibadan, 1962); and P. C. Lloyd, A. Mabogunje, and B. Awe, eds., *The City of Ibadan: A Symposium on Its Structure and Development* (London: Cambridge University Press, 1967), chaps. 1 and 2.

[24] See F. O. Okediji, "Socio-economic Status and Differential Fertility in an African City," *Journal of the Developing Areas*, III, 3 (April 1969), 342; and F. O. Okediji and O. Aboyade, "Social and Economic Aspects of Environmental Sanitation in Nigeria: A Tentative Report," *Journal of the Nigerian Society of Health*, II (January 1967), 15–25.

[25] Onibokun, "Socio-Cultural Constraints," p. 345.

[26] F. O. Okediji and O. O. Okediji, "The Sociological Aspects of Prison Reorganization in Nigeria," in T. O. Elias, ed., *The Prison System in Nigeria* (Lagos, 1968), pp. 90–138.

[27] In a study of the compounds of Oje by Robert Levine and others, the range in size of Oje compounds is put between under 40 and more than 340 inhabitants. See Robert Levine, N. H. Klein, and C. R. Owen, "Father-Child Relationships and Changing Life-Styles in Ibadan, Nigeria," in H. Miner, ed., *The City in Modern Africa* (London: Pall Mall Press, 1967), p. 227.

[28] The percentage of polygyny in Oje, which is 58 percent, falls within our general estimated range of the incidence of polygyny in the traditional settlements of the city of Ibadan. See Levine et al., "Father-Child Relationships."

In contrast are the well-planned and high-quality residential settlements of the elite groups (group 3) which are located around the periphery of the city. The history of these settlements shows a kind of ecological succession of the indigenous elite who gradually replaced the Europeans. With the growing centralization of economic, educational, governmental, industrial, and religious functions during the early 1940s, many Europeans flocked to Ibadan as engineers, civil servants, merchants, and educators, to live in what was then known as the "European reservation." The Agodi Reservation to the north was the oldest and European administrators lived there. Later, the Commercial and Links reservations were established. The Western Nigeria Housing Corporation constructed a planned housing estate for high and low income groups around 1959. The universities of Ibadan and Ife also established separate planned residential areas for their senior, intermediate, and junior workers respectively. The Nigerianization policy, which started about 1952, meant that qualified Nigerians were recruited into top posts in the civil service. Automatically they were assigned houses in the so-called European reservations. Today, both Africans and non-Africans in high-status categories live in these planned areas. By virtue of a long period of education and exposure to overseas experience, the elite groups have deviated in some ways from the traditional culture which permeates the settlements in the core area.

In selecting groups for study, we decided to sample the two polar ends of the traditionalism-modernism continuum: that is, heads of households or families from the residential settlements in the core areas and from the high-quality residential settlements around the periphery of the city.

## METHODS OF STUDY

This inquiry is based on a special survey conducted between July and September 1969. The methodological orientation involved a comparative study of public health conditions, health habits, and morbidity and mortality levels in the two residential areas which we have already described.

*Definition of concepts.* Three important methodological concepts are relevant to the investigation: a one-person household, a multiperson household, and a head of household. A one-person household is defined as a person who lives alone in (the whole or part of) a separate housing unit or who, as a lodger, occupies a separate room or rooms in a part of a housing unit but does not join with any of the other occupants of the housing unit to form part of a "multiperson household." A multiperson household is a group of two or more persons who combine to occupy the whole or part of a house and to provide themselves with food or other essentials necessary for living. The group may be composed of related persons only or of unrelated persons or of a combination of both. A head of household is that person who is acknowledged as such by the members of the household.

The household sample survey was strictly limited to private households, and we were careful not to include institutional households comprising persons who live together in boarding houses, dormitories of schools and colleges, correctional and penal institutions, convents, hospitals, or military barracks.

The head of the household was chosen as the reliable source of information. But, when information about individual members of the households selected for study was needed, such members were directly interviewed with the cooperation of the heads of households.

*Sampling design.* The planning stage of this small-scale public health survey involved the construction, pretest, and finalizing of the questionnaire, and the selection of a sampling scheme which would allow a fair representation of the universe of study. The principal determinants of the size of the sample were the availability of time and other scarce resources and it was decided that a total sample of 350 heads of households would be adequate.

Through the Assistant Health Superintendent at the Ibadan City Council Health Office, we learned that the city is divided into four health districts, labeled A, B, C, and D.[29] District D was selected as being the most representative of the old residential settlements in the center of the city. It was then divided into blocks from which a systematic sample of one in five blocks was taken.[30] The interviewers were instructed to list the households in the selected blocks, and from this list we selected every tenth household for interview. The first 260 heads of households were selected for interview.

The elite residential settlements that we grouped together for sampling purposes are Agodi Reservation and Bodija Housing Estate. The same procedure as in the core settlements of Ibadan was followed in selecting the first 45 heads of households in each of the two settlements, thus giving us a total of 90. The total sample of heads of households selected was thus 350.

*The interview.* An interview schedule was constructed so that interviewers could obtain uniform data. The following classes of variables were included in the schedule: (1) general social background characteristics such as length of residence in the house and area, education, occupation, income, and expenses; (2) health matters such as water supply,

cooking facilities, refuse and excreta disposal, and nature of economic activities in the neighborhood; (3) morbidity and mortality, especially infant mortality; and (4) beliefs, knowledge, and attitudes to public health problems, use of modern medical facilities, and care of children.

Three undergraduate students in the Department of Sociology and three clinical students in the Medical College of the University of Ibadan were employed to conduct the survey and they were given a week of training. The students were supervised in conducting a preliminary pilot survey of 15 households in an area of central Ibadan to test the clarity of the items in the questionnaire. Individual and group discussions were held with the students after the pilot survey. Interviews were later conducted with the sampled 350 heads of households.

Out of the 350 respondents, 340 cooperated fully in the interview. The remaining ten interviews were not completed. Of these, seven were from the core residential settlements while three were from the residential area of the elite groups.

RELATIONSHIP BETWEEN SOCIOECONOMIC CHARACTERISTICS, ENVIRONMENTAL SANITATION, MORBIDITY, AND MORTALITY IN THE AREAS. *Socioeconomic characteristics of families in the core settlements.* The distribution of the heads of household in district D by length of residence in their houses at the time of interview was as follows: 16 percent reported that they had lived in their houses for under 10 years, 15 percent for 10–19 years, 38 percent for 20–29 years, while the remaining 31 percent had resided in their houses for 30 or more years. The responses to a similar question about length of residence in the area showed that 16 percent indicated that they had lived in the area for under 10 years, 15 percent for 10–19 years, while 37 percent and 32 percent reported that they had lived in the area for 20–29 years and 30 or more years respectively.

The distribution of heads of households by education was as follows: 12 percent had attended secondary school, 18 percent had attended primary school, and 70 percent had

[29] The important areas in each district are as follows: A comprises Ekotedo, Adamasingba, Sabo, Inalende, Ayete, Amunigun, Agbeni, Ogunpa, Adeoyo, Oke-Are, and Orita Mefa; B consists of Oke-Bola, Oke-Ado, Foko, Gege, Oja-Iba, Isale-Jebu, Molete, Ibuko; C comprises Bere Square, Oranyan, Kobi-Owun, Sleta, Agbongbon, Ile-tentun, Oke-Oluokun, Elekuro, and Ita-Ege; and D encompasses Isale-Afa, Labiran, Afara, Oje, Gbenla, Aremo, Agodi, Oke-Adu, Oke-Ofa Atipe, Oja'gbo, Aperin, Jegede, Oke-Ofa Babasale, Mato, and Lago.

[30] A block is defined as a rectangular or polygonal piece of land clearly bounded by identifiable streets. To this end, the interviewers were instructed to take a trip around the survey area to identify each street that was shown on the map, and to check other streets not named as this would facilitate the breakup of large blocks or enable a combination of two or more blocks. The inhabited part of the survey area then was divided into blocks from which every fifth block was selected.

received no formal education. Occupational[31] information showed that 10 percent were white-collar workers, 16 percent were skilled workers, 39 percent were unskilled workers, 8 percent were retail traders, and 27 percent were petty traders.

Three rough income levels were delineated: 10 percent of the respondents were in the higher income group (i.e., earned more than £500 per annum), 25 percent were in the middle income group (i.e., earned from £200–£500 per annum), while the remaining 65 percent were in the lower income group (i.e., earned below £200 per annum). It would appear that some 90 percent of the respondents earned well below £500 per annum, and, with the increasing cost of living in the city of Ibadan, this earning per family is rather low, especially when judged in relation to the dependency burden of each of the heads of the households. About 18 percent had up to five dependents, 40 percent claimed that they had between six and nine dependents, while 42 percent bore the economic and social burden of more than ten dependents. Thus about 82 percent of the heads of households had more than six dependents, and each family lived on a tight budget which was well below £500 per annum. In addition to paying income taxes, water and electricity rates, each head of household had to feed, clothe, and pay the school fees of his children. Financial demands from distant kinsmen added to the already heavy burden.

The important socioeconomic characteristics of families in the old residential settlements in the center of the city are that most of them had lived in this congested area for more than 20 years, had received no formal education, were unskilled workers and petty traders, earned below £200 per annum, had

heavy dependency burdens of well above six persons, and were deeply rooted in the slowly changing traditional way of life. It would appear that the socioeconomic status of these families in the core residential settlements and their density of settlement do much to explain the appalling health conditions in this core sector.

*Environmental sanitation in the core settlements in relationship to morbidity and mortality.* Demographically, this area is heavily populated, and the density of population may be as high as 250 persons per acre.[32] This area is filthy, unhealthy, and highly susceptible to epidemics. Most houses are built of mud and sticks, and cow dung is used to wipe the surface of the floors which are anything but smooth. A small number of houses are built of cement blocks and covered with corrugated iron sheets. A few beautiful modern buildings are scattered here and there in these areas. Most of the houses have no kitchens and cooking is done in the corridors. An observer can see beads of carbon on the walls of the corridors. Most of the clay pots used for cooking are unwashed, and often contain dirty water on the surface of which one can see dead flies and cockroaches. Cobwebs are common features of the corners of the dwelling units. In places where there are separate kitchens, these are usually unswept and full of obnoxious odors, aggravated by uncovered *salgas* (latrines) directly behind the kitchen. There are usually bits of dried excreta all over the *salgas*. In some houses the *salga* is used by all the members of the compound and responsibility for emptying it is not assumed by anybody. Standing water all over the place affords breeding grounds for flies and mosquitoes. Most of the gutters are uncemented and full of foul-smelling water. Some houses have no *salga*, and, as the inmates cannot afford to employ night-soil men, the members of the households go to the nearby bush or pit to excrete. Walking near the walls of any building, one is struck by the

---

[31] The occupational categories are broken down as follows: *professionals* include physicians, lawyers, accountants, university lecturers, graduate teachers and engineers; *white-collar workers* comprise clerks and kindred clerical and sales workers and technicians; *skilled workers* consist of carpenters, blacksmiths, goldsmiths, barbers, masons, plumbers, machinists, printers, etc.; *unskilled workers* include construction workers, farmers, laborers, janitors, night watchmen, etc.; *retail traders* and *petty traders*.

[32] This is a 1962 estimate and it could be higher by now. See A. Mabogunje, "The Growth of Residential Districts in Ibadan," *Geographical Review*, LII (1962), 66.

terrible odor of urine passed there by the inmates or passersby. Most of the houses do not have pail latrines.

Some houses have what is regarded as a bathroom, a small area fenced around with palm leaves. The floor is muddy, filthy, and full of stench, because it is used by inmates for disposing of feces. Flies and mosquitoes breed with the utmost facility. The kitchens in most of the houses are dirty. Feces of dogs and goats are regular features of the premises. Economic activities are carried on around most of the core residential settlements, and consequently the neighborhoods are always littered. Undoubtedly the habits of members of the sampled households contribute to the unsanitary environment of the core residential settlements. Information was therefore collected about the following: sources of water supply, purification of water, refuse disposal, and the frequency of refuse disposal.

The distribution of responses concerning the sources of water supply was as follows: 10 percent reported that they paid for exclusive use of pipe-borne water, 49 percent obtained water from public pipe-stands, 21 percent obtained water from wells, and 20 percent fetched water from rivers, streams, or ponds. Water supply, especially in the core residential settlements during the dry season, always is restricted. Consequently, during this time even the majority of the heads of households owning exclusive pipe-stands in their compounds, and those whose regular supply of water was from public pipe-stands, were forced to obtain water from rivers, streams, or wells. To ensure safe water, it must be boiled and filtered or some chemicals must be added to it. Three-quarters of the respondents reported that they did nothing to ensure the safety of water which they fetched from rivers, streams, or wells. The remaining one-quarter usually added a chemical called alum to purify the water consumed by the younger members of the household.

As regards refuse disposal, 15 percent reported that refuse is piled up in dustbins and then disposed of in public incinerators, 48 percent threw refuse into open pits, 13 percent piled refuse within the yard and later burned

it, while the remaining 24 percent carried refuse to nearby public incinerators. The frequency of the disposal of refuse is linked with the sanitary or unsanitary conditions of the environment. Nevertheless, 49 percent indicated that they had no fixed intervals for the disposal of refuse, 21 percent reported that they did so about twice a week, and 30 percent mentioned that the garbage was collected weekly.

The risk to life depends on such factors as age, sex, occupation, location of residence, health habits, environmental sanitation, and so forth. These factors taken in combination account for differentials between social groups. The reference period for morbidity and mortality in this survey was one year (July 1968–July 1969). A census count of the inhabitants of the sampled households in the core residential settlements during the period of interview was about 8,360. The age-group distribution of this population is presented in Table 12.7. In order to understand the

TABLE 12.7
Age-group distribution in the core residential settlements, 1968

|  | Age Group | Percent |
| --- | --- | --- |
| Dependent children | 0–14 | 48.5 |
| Active population | 15–54 | 45.7 |
| Dependent aged | 55+ | 4.8 |

incidence and pattern of morbidity among the inhabitants of the sampled households in the core residential settlements, the interviewers were instructed to collect data on the number of adults and children who had been taken ill during the previous year. From the responses, it appeared that the informants knew the symptoms rather than the causes.

About 55 percent, or slightly more than half, of the adult population were reported to have been ill during the year preceding the survey. The causes of the illness were classified by the interviewers and cross-checked by the principal investigator in collaboration with medical experts as follows: fever (mostly malaria), 42 percent; respiratory infections,

10 percent; gastrointestinal diseases, 10 percent; guineaworm, 11 percent; accidents, 21 percent; nervous system and sense-organ diseases, 4 percent.

The majority (65 percent) of the children in the sampled population of the core residential settlements were reported to have suffered from diseases. The following were the causes of the illness: malaria, 51.4 percent; respiratory infections, 11.4 percent; malnutrition, 21.4 percent; gastrointestinal diseases, 11.6 percent; smallpox and measles, 4·2 percent.[33]

The pattern of the diseases among the majority of the children was slightly different from that of the adults. For example, malnutrition, smallpox, and measles were confined mostly to the child population. However, the pattern and causes of illness for both children and adults are comparable to the statistics of the most common diseases reported in Western State hospitals as previously shown in Tables 12.4, 12.5, and 12.6.

Attention will now be focused on the mortality trend, with special reference to infant mortality. The infant mortality rate is of particular importance since it usually is considered as a direct indicator of health levels of living. It is approximately calculated by relating in the reference period infants' deaths to live births. The reference period for infant mortality in this survey is the same as that for morbidity, that is, from July 1968–July 1969. The number of live births for the reference period was 300, while the number of infant deaths reported was 19. Thus, the infant mortality rate for the reference period was 63.3 per thousand, which is about three times the level found in industrialized countries. However, Galletti, et al., in their survey of Nigerian cocoa farmers for the period from June 1951–May 1952 recorded

an infant mortality rate of 180 per thousand for the Ibadan and Ijebu areas.[34] Although there is evidence of a significant change in infant mortality when we compare our figure with Galletti's, yet a cautious interpretation of this change is necessary. Galletti's figure represented both the urban and rural areas in Ibadan and Ijebu provinces for the specified period. Our figure represented the infant mortality rate only in the traditional residential settlements of the city of Ibadan. Within a period of about 17 years, it is obvious that the Western State government has intensified its efforts in providing more medical and public health facilities in some sections of the state. Piped water is probably reaching more people, and health education and immunization campaigns are being intensified. Apparently, an increasing proportion of the illiterate masses are gradually becoming more aware of modern medical institutions, and are probably being motivated to use them. The apparent decline in infant mortality rate, on the basis of the comparison of our figure with Galletti's, is undoubtedly too optimistic. However, empirical evidence will be provided later to buttress the suggestion offered here of a very substantial decline in infant mortality rate. On the other hand, the statistics of notifiable diseases already presented in Tables 12.4, 12.5, and 12.6 indicate that ill health is still the lot of many Nigerians, although reference here is confined to the Western State communities. And, furthermore, the infant mortality rate of 63 per thousand which we have obtained from our present survey is still too high. Our findings are similar to those of Cunningham who recorded infant mortality rates of 53 per thousand and 73 per thousand for Imesi-Ile and Oke-Messi respectively for the period from September 1966–August 1967.[35] Both

[33] Although the percentage distribution of the classes of illness suffered by most children in Oje compounds (which are located in the core residential settlements of the city of Ibadan) was not provided by Robert Levine and others, yet the pattern of diseases which they discovered is comparable to what our study revealed. See Levine et al., "Father-Child Relationships," p. 236.

[34] B. Galletti, K. D. S. Baldwin, and I. O. Dina, *Nigerian Cocoa Farmers: An Economic Survey of Yoruba Cocoa Farming Families* (London: Oxford University Press, 1956), p. 36.

[35] Nicholas Cunningham, "An Evaluation of an Auxiliary-Based Child Health Service in Rural Nigeria" (Paper presented to the Annual Congress of the Nigerian Society of Health, University of Ibadan, March 1968), p. 4.

rural communities are very close to Ilesha which is about 70 miles from Ibadan. Our findings are also close to those of Ajani who obtained an infant mortality rate of 50 per thousand for Ebute-Metta and Yaba in Lagos for the period July 1968–July 1969.[36]

It has been indicated earlier that, as a pre-colonial city and a center of modern commercial, intellectual, and political activity, Ibadan encompasses within its city limits features of traditionalism and modernism which, usually on a smaller scale, are characteristic of Yoruba towns in general. We have analyzed the socioeconomic characteristics of the heads of households in a district within the traditional residential settlements, and have shown the extent to which the unsanitary environmental conditions (which also account in part for the high morbidity and high infant mortality levels in this area) are consequent on these characteristics. For purposes of comparison, we will discuss the socioeconomic characteristics of the elite families who reside in the high-quality residential settlements located on the periphery of the city. These socioeconomic characteristics will also be related to the quality of environmental sanitation in the area, and the effects of the latter on morbidity and mortality will be discussed.

*Socioeconomic characteristics of the elite families in the well-planned residential settlements.* A subsample of 85 heads of households was selected from residential areas. The distribution of responses on length of residence showed that 65 percent had lived in their houses for under 10 years, and the remaining 35 percent reported that they had lived in their houses from 10–19 years. The length of residence in the area was under 10 years for 68 percent and 10–19 years for 32 percent.

The educational qualifications of the heads of households were as follows: 81 percent had received university education, while 19 percent had only completed secondary school. Occupational information showed that 82

[36] H. A. Ajani, "Demographic Sample Survey of Ebute-Metta and Yaba" (Thesis presented for a Diploma in Statistics, Department of Economics, University of Ibadan, 1969), p. 27.

percent were either professionals or university lecturers, and 18 percent were businessmen. All the heads of households earned much above £500 per annum, which placed them in the highest income group. Their dependency burden was lower than that of the heads of households in the old residential settlements: 71 percent had up to 5 dependents, while the remaining 29 percent had 6–9 dependents. About two-thirds reported that they owned their houses, while one-third were tenants.

As these residential settlements are well planned, the highly placed elite groups are more attracted to live there. They can afford to do so, and (in some areas) are eligible to do so because of their jobs.

*Environmental sanitation in the high-quality residential areas in relationship to morbidity and mortality.* The dwelling units in the residential sectors are well planned, modern, well ventilated, well lighted, and spacious. It is customary to find well-trimmed lawns around the dwelling units, and some of the occupants cultivate beautiful gardens, thus adding freshness to the general appearance of the area. The sanitary facilities include pipe-borne water and sewage and are generally adequate; each dwelling unit has one or two garbage disposal pails (depending on the number of families living in the unit which may be a flat, or duplex, or a bungalow) which are regularly collected by the Ibadan City Council vans or the universities of Ibadan and Ife maintenance vans. Usually pigs, goats, or sheep are not raised in the area. Fowls are raised by some of the occupants, but facilities for raising them are modern and usually located in a section of the garden. Some occupants commonly keep dogs as well.

Inside, the dwellings are clean. There is usually a well-decorated room supplied with cushioned chairs, tables, and stools; and the sitting rooms as well as the sleeping rooms are properly lighted. Window curtains are generally made from high quality materials and an observer finds an assorted collection of high-status symbols such as radios, radiograms, pianos, television sets, African art, paintings, and shelves with assorted books. Each dwelling unit has at least two rooms, plus a toilet, and a kitchen with modern facilities such as a refrigerator, sink, cooking stove, and a pantry where food is arranged carefully. Each dwelling unit has servants' quarters attached to it, and these quarters are kept fairly clean. Each family has modern toilet facilities such as washing bowls, bathtubs equipped with showers, and shelves where shaving equipment and deodorants are arranged neatly. Except for the ugly sight of a few dustbins, standing water in some gutters and some roads which are not properly maintained, this area is generally clean and the quality of environmental sanitation is high.

The reference period for analyzing the morbidity and mortality levels was also one year (July 1968–July 1969). A census count of the inhabitants of the sampled households in the elite residential settlements was 838. The age-group distribution of this population is presented in Table 12.8.

TABLE 12.8
Age-group distribution in the high quality residential settlements

| Status | Age Group | Percent |
| --- | --- | --- |
| Dependent children | 0–14 | 46.4 |
| Active population | 15–54 | 50.0 |
| Dependent aged | 55+ | 3.6 |

In order to understand the incidence and pattern of morbidity among the inhabitants of the sampled households in the elite residential settlements, the interviewers were instructed to collect data on the number of adults and children who had been taken ill during the previous year.

Only 15 percent of the adult population were reported to have been ill during the year preceding the survey. The causes of illness were classified as follows: fever, 21.4 percent; ulcers, 32.4 percent; accidents, 15.4 percent; minor colds, 14.4 percent; infections of ears, eyes, and nose 11.4 percent; and miscellaneous, 5.0 percent.

Only 20 percent of the children in the sampled population of the elite residential settlements were reported to have been ill during the reference period. The causes of illness were classified as follows: malaria 27.5 percent; minor colds, 43.5 percent; chicken pox and measles, 2.1 percent; accidents, 16.4 percent; infections of ears, eyes, and nose, 5.5 percent; and miscellaneous, 5.0 percent.

The reference period for infant mortality was the same as that for morbidity, that is, from July 1968–July 1969. The number of live births for the reference period was 79, while the number of reported deaths was 2. Thus, the infant mortality rate was 25.1 per thousand which is moderately low. Such a low infant mortality rate among children of elite parents is not surprising, since this is an obvious result of superior housing, well-balanced diets, and adequate medical care.

*Comparison of the traditional and modern residential settlements.* The following empirical generalizations can be made about differences in socioeconomic status and environmental sanitation in both residential settlements: Families in the core residential settlements have a lower socioeconomic status than the elite families who live in the high-quality residential settlements located around the periphery of the city. Houses in the core sector are unplanned and older than those in the elite group residential settlements. Toilet and cooking facilities are appallingly inadequate and filthy in the core settlements, whereas these same facilities in the well-planned residential settlements are very adequate and fairly clean. There are hardly any motorable roads in the core residential areas, nor are there gutters. Many places are littered. The roads in the high-quality residential areas are tarred and gutters are provided on both sides. The refuse pails are collected regularly by the services of the Ibadan City Council. Obviously, the elite groups are a privileged class.

Not only are differences in socioeconomic characteristics related to differences in the quality of environmental sanitation, but the latter also has differential effects on morbidity and mortality levels. The adult population in the core traditional settlements is much less healthy than the adult population in the high-quality residential settlements. The same observation holds true for the health of children. Elite children are better fed, better housed, and have more access to superior medical treatment than the children of families in the core residential settlements. The infant mortality rate in the core settlements was twice as high as that in the high-quality residential settlements for the reference period from July 1968–July 1969. Not only are these observed differences explained by the variations in socioeconomic status, but also by differences in knowledge and attitudes to public health problems, use of medical facilities, and care of children.

KNOWLEDGE, ATTITUDES TO HEALTH PROBLEMS AND USE OF MODERN HEALTH FACILITIES. We cannot meaningfully discuss the scope of knowledge of health problems, attitudes to and use of modern medical facilities by the vast majority of the illiterate Nigerians without an adequate understanding of their traditional systems of medicine and care for the sick. Although we have discussed in the earlier sections of this study the linkages between unsanitary environmental conditions and high rates of morbidity and mortality especially among children, yet most illiterate Nigerians have developed some degree of self-reliance and have acquired through a long history a body of empirical knowledge to cope with these heavy rates of morbidity and mortality. These traditional systems of medicine and care for the sick which have been known and practiced over the years are, by contemporary standards, rather inadequate. Nevertheless, these beliefs and traditional medical practices have persisted in spite of the availability of modern medical care, which is now being gradually accepted by many illiterate Nigerians who have learned to welcome its successful curative and preventive services.

From the sociological point of view, there are ways of analyzing these traditional systems of medical care so that they can be understood not as a haphazard agglomeration of customs without tangible meaning, but as institution-alized patterns of social relationships and cultural patterns of behavior and thought. There appear to be three important analytically distinct, but mutually related, elements in these systems of traditional aid in sickness:[37] (1) the social structure and social organization of the people, from which arise the nature and degree of the mutual dependence of individuals in sickness and in health, in childhood and in age, and their respect for and dependence on those who are legitimized as highly skilled traditional healers; (2) the methods of treatment in sickness and the precautions taken to prevent and ward off accidents and illness; (3) the concepts of the natural and the supernatural world, which give people some basis for their beliefs about the onset of sickness, the likelihood of care, and the preservation of health.

Each of these elements in the system of traditional aid in sickness will be discussed briefly with particular reference to Yoruba society. It will be recalled that Ibadan is principally a Yoruba town. The Yoruba people over the years have developed a well-established medical-care system, which is based on ideas about the causes and treatment of diseases in terms of their environment, their way of life and their beliefs about human, environmental, and supernatural relationships. This medical care system is highly institutionalized in the rural areas and also among the illiterate families in the urban areas as well.

From the perspective of the social structure and social organization, when a person is taken ill (for example, in the core residential settlements of the city of Ibadan), he turns to people related to him who live in the same household or in contiguous households. The network of consultation extends to other known groups, within the kinship structure, who perform supportive functions. Some members of the kin group will certainly endeavor to observe the symptoms in order to determine the causes of the sickness. It is when they are unsuccessful that the accredited traditional healers are consulted. These traditional healers apparently rest their claims to competence in the art of healing on their pool of knowledge, their widely accepted popularity, integrity, and successes. There are four types of healers in the Yoruba system of medical care. The first category is women healers who use highly skillful techniques which include purgatives, poulticing, and traditional birth practices. There is the second category of those who set bones, give injections and vaccinations, and also perform some forms of traditional surgery. The herbalists, who constitute the third category, have a wide knowledge of the properties and use of herbs and the roots and bark of trees. The fourth category constitutes the Ifa diviners who cast lots of cowries or kola nuts and through certain combinations claim to be able to tell the causes of particular illnesses and suggest appropriate remedies.

In the Yoruba system of belief, health is defined as wealth. Illness is caused by natural and supernatural forces; and it is believed that diviners and herbalists have acquired a body of knowledge and techniques to treat different kinds of diseases which fall within human experience.

The institution of modern medical care of sickness has become a force disruptive, albeit functional, to the traditional system of medical care. Consequently, differential responses to its acceptance or rejection are linked with variations in socioeconomic status. The highly educated elite groups in our sample have more knowledge of the available modern medical facilities and are more disposed to use them. A few of them are at the same time aware of the potency of the traditional healers and diviners, and even resort to soliciting their services when the occasion demands. Most illiterate families in the rural areas and also in the urban areas still accept the traditional system of medical care, although there is a gradual acceptance of modern medical care especially when it successfully cures their ailments.

In order to understand the relationship between socioeconomic characteristics and attitudes to public health problems and use of modern medical facilities, the following themes were probed: relationship between health and environmental sanitation, care of

children, and use of modern medical facilities.

*Relationship between health and environmental sanitation.* We asked the respondents whether there was any connection between the health of the members of their families and the sanitary conditions in their neighborhoods. Table 12.9 shows clearly that there is a

TABLE 12.9
Perception of connection between health of family and environmental sanitation[a]

| Respondents | Connection | No Connection |
|---|---|---|
| Elite parents | 85 | 0 |
| Nonelite parents | 34 | 221 |
| | 119 | 221 |

[a] Differences between elite and nonelite significant at 0.001 level.

significant correlation between socioeconomic status and perception of connection between health and environmental sanitation. In other words, all the elite parents were aware that there is a connection between the health of the members of their families and the quality of sanitation of their neighborhoods. On the other hand, most of the nonelite parents in the old residential settlements said that there was no connection between the health of the members of their families and the sanitary conditions in their neighborhoods.

Within-group comparison of families in the old residential settlements shows an interesting trend. All the 34 nonelite parents who recognized some connection between the health of their families and their insanitary neighborhoods had completed either primary or secondary education. The most frequently reported connection was that unhygienic neighborhoods or environment can lead to outbreak of epidemics; the recognition of such a relationship apparently required the acquisition of formal education.

We probed further by asking attitudinal questions about the public health problems pertaining to their environment as follows: (1) "Are you satisfied with the standard of sanitation in your neighborhood?" (2) "If not, are you planning to move to another house located in the same area where you now live? or, are you planning to move to another house located in a less congested area?"

The pattern of responses by families in the core traditional settlements concerning satisfaction with the standard of sanitation in their neighborhoods was as follows: 32.5 percent were highly satisfied, 37.7 percent were fairly satisfied, 17.3 percent were highly dissatisfied, and 12.5 percent were fairly dissatisfied. The group who expressed dissatisfaction with their filthy neighborhoods were those who had received primary and secondary education; this was also the group who perceived some connection between their unsanitary neighborhoods and the ill health of members of their families. Surprisingly, when this same dissatisfied and moderately educated group were asked whether they planned to move to another house located in the same area where they were already living or to move to another house located in a less congested area, about three-quarters of them indicated that they did not plan to move at all. In this they were similar to the uneducated group who also expressed the desire not to move. The reason for their unwillingness to move is the traditional sentimental attachment which they have for the area. Besides, in a society where modern social welfare programs are within the reach of only a few (i.e., a small elite group), attachment to kinsmen becomes a functional alternative which guarantees access to traditional social welfare programs within the compounds.

Unlike most of the families who live in the core residential settlements, all the elite families were satisfied with the high quality of environmental sanitation in their neighborhoods, and also expressed the desire not to move.

*Patterns of child care.* As we have mentioned in the earlier sections of this chapter, the structure of the family in the traditional residential settlements tends to be patrilocal, polygynous, and deeply rooted in the extended family system. Division of labor is defined both by sex and age. Mothers in the traditional residential settlements are always engaged in their occupational activities

TABLE 12.10

Preference for where child is delivered[a]

| Respondents | Hospital or Maternity Center | Traditional Midwife |
|---|---|---|
| Elite parents | 85 | 0 |
| Nonelite parents | 44 | 211 |
| | 129 | 211 |

[a] Differences between elite and nonelite significant at 0.001 level

(especially trading) and household activities. Obviously, there is little time left for them to care for their children. Greater responsibility for child care and child rearing is often left to grandparents, sisters and brothers, or other relatives.

The structure of the family of elite groups tends to be neolocal, nuclear, and monogamous (although there were many examples of members of these groups who completely rebuilt the houses in their original home compounds or villages so that they could reside there when paying short visits to their kinsmen). Children of elite parents often are reared and cared for by servants, who usually are instructed to follow specific diet schedules for the children when both parents are away at work. As many elite parents, during periods of studies overseas, have been exposed to other cultures, it is to be expected that such exposure will have some effect on the way they rear and care for their children. Tables 12.10, 12.11, and 12.12 compare the patterns of child care and child rearing between elite and nonelite parents.

As indicated by Table 12.10, there is a high correlation between socioeconomic status and preference for where child is delivered. The highly privileged families preferred hospitals

TABLE 12.11

Father has bathed and fed the child[a]

| Respondents | Sometimes | Never |
|---|---|---|
| Elite parents | 72 | 13 |
| Nonelite parents | 14 | 241 |
| | 86 | 254 |

[a] Differences between elite and nonelite significant at 0.001 level.

TABLE 12.12
Father eats together with wife and children[a]

| Respondents | Sometimes | Never |
|---|---|---|
| Elite parents | 78 | 7 |
| Nonelite parents | 24 | 231 |
| | 102 | 238 |

[a] Differences between elite and nonelite significant at 0.001 level.

and exclusive maternity centers for the delivery of their children, while most of the parents who live in the core residential areas of the city preferred the services of the traditional midwives. Besides the fact that the latter have developed intimate relationships with the traditional midwives over the years, they also pointed out that they could not afford to pay the hospital expenses which would be incurred in delivering their children in modern institutions and furthermore that they had heard that most of the nurses in the hospitals were harsh and abusive.

Table 12.11 shows that the highly privileged fathers had participated in child care, such as feeding or bathing the child, thus lessening the burden on their wives. They frequently did so when both husband and wife were studying overseas. They both took turns when either of them was away for education or work in order to sustain the family. However, some of the elite parents mentioned that they had hardly bathed or fed their infants since they returned to Nigeria, because they could now afford to pay for the services of housemaids. Nonelite parents conform strictly to the traditional patterns; that is, the mothers or other women in the compounds are exclusively responsible for child care.

As Table 12.12 shows there are also socioeconomic differentials in eating habits. The highly privileged parents eat together with their wives and children, thus giving them the opportunity to make sure that their children consume a balanced diet. On the other hand, fathers in the core residential areas hardly ever eat together with their wives and children. The ideology of seniority in feeding and available food usually prevails.

Our findings concerning child care and child rearing practices in relationship to socioeconomic status compare with those of Uka and Levine.[38]

*Use of modern medical facilities.* The following questions were asked the respondents concerning their use of modern medical facilities: (1) "Are you aware of immunization campaigns in this city?" (2) "If you are not aware of such campaigns, would you like to be immunized together with the members of your family?" (3) "If you are aware of such campaigns, have you and members of your family ever received any immunization?" (4) "Whenever any member of your family is sick, do you take him either to a traditional healer or a hospital/health center?"

With regard to the awareness of immunization campaigns in the city, 22 percent and 78 percent of heads of households in the core residential settlements reported that they were aware and not aware respectively. Of the 78 percent heads of households who were not aware of immunization campaigns in the city, about half said that they would like members of their households to be immunized against infectious diseases. The remaining half were not in favor of immunization since they claimed that indigenous herbalists are more competent to treat most of these diseases such as smallpox, measles, and convulsions, and they preferred this treatment to what they called "European medicine." All the heads of households who reported that they were aware of immunization campaigns also affirmed that members of their households had received immunization at one time or the other. These heads of households had all either completed primary or secondary education. All the heads of families in the high-quality residential areas had heard of the immunization campaigns, and the members of their families always received immunization.

All the elite parents informed us that whenever any member of their family is sick

[38] See Ngwobia Uka, *Growing Up in Nigerian Culture: A Pioneer Study of Physical and Behavioral Growth and Development of Nigerian Children*, Occasional Publication No. 6, Institute of Education, University of Ibadan (Ibadan, 1966), chaps. 4, 5, and 9; and Levine et al., "Father-Child Relationships," pp. 238–41.

he or she is taken immediately to a hospital or a health center. Of the nonelite parents, one-quarter claimed that a sick member of their family usually is taken to a chemist, nearby dispensary, or hospital. The remaining three-quarters, who were mostly the illiterates within the nonelite sample, reported that their first choice would be to take such a sick person to any traditional healer. If the case got more serious, they said that he might be taken to the hospital although the doctor would be unable to see him for days; "So, why bother," one respondent remarked.

Important differences in knowledge and attitudes to health problems and the use of modern health facilities were evidently strongly related to differentials in socio-economic characteristics of the families in the two residential settlements. As one moves from the core residential settlements to the high quality residential areas of the elite families, there tends to be an increasing awareness of a strong relationship between a filthy environment and public ill health. Within-group comparison shows that, although the few fairly well-educated heads of families in the core sector of the city expressed dissatisfaction with the low quality of environmental sanitation in their neighborhoods, yet they preferred not to move even if they were given such an opportunity because of their traditional attachment to the area. In this respect, they were similar to the illiterate parents in the traditional residential settlements.

There are also socioeconomic differentials in patterns of child care and use of modern medical facilities. The highly privileged parents preferred their children to be delivered in hospitals; the husbands helped their wives in taking care of their children, especially during their sojourn overseas, when the situation demanded it; and ate together with their wives and children. The nonelite husbands neither ate together with their families nor helped their wives to take care of the children. Although some preferred traditional midwives to deliver their children, most of the small number of nonelite parents with some education were favorably disposed to the delivery of their infants either in hospitals or maternity centers when they could afford it and if the nurses could learn to be more patient.

## SUMMARY AND CONCLUSION

In the introductory section of this paper, we discussed briefly the historical trends in health problems and health planning in the Western State of Nigeria. Empirical evidence has been provided to show that: (1) The resources allocated to the provision of public health and medical facilities are inadequate for the needs of the growing population of the Western State. (2) Of the small percentage of funds allocated to health a greater priority is generally placed on the provision of curative rather than preventive health services. (3) A large percentage of the illiterate masses in the Western State is vulnerable to the onslaught of diseases which are strongly connected with malnutrition, deteriorated and blighted housing, and a filthy environment.

The city of Ibadan was selected for study in order to explore the sociological, cultural, and social-psychological factors which contribute to high morbidity and high mortality levels within the population of many communities in the Western State. A modification of the multiple-nuclei theory is suggested as of explanatory value in understanding the development of the city of Ibadan and its residential structure. Thus, the residential structure of the city of Ibadan is conceptualized as manifesting traditional characteristics in the core residential settlements with a gradual transition into the more recent and high-quality residential settlements on the periphery of the city.

It has been demonstrated that differences in health habits, environmental sanitation, morbidity, and mortality levels can be largely explained by differentials in socioeconomic status. The study further showed that differences in knowledge, attitudes to health problems, and use of modern medical facilities can also be explained by such differentials. Exposure to a reasonably long period of formal education seems to be the strongest force of change.

It would appear from the analysis of the characteristics of the two types of residential settlements that the trend of change is along a continuum from traditional to modern. Families in the core residential settlements of the city of Ibadan are treated as a base line for change, while the elite families who live in the high-quality residential settlements are viewed as furnishing models of change for those below. Unfortunately in a neocolonial society where a large percentage of the population is illiterate and access to scare resources is largely limited to the elite, the groups at the top of the stratification system tend to manipulate the opportunity structures to benefit mostly themselves. This is precisely the situation in health planning and implementation in Nigeria as a whole, and this

may well be the case with national development planning and implementation in general.

The privileges enjoyed by the elite groups have deep roots in the colonial heritage. With respect to medical facilities, it was the colonial expatriate elite who benefited most. The exclusive medical privileges extended gradually to the indigenous Nigerians who were absorbed into the colonial administration, the intellectual elite, and the army officers. The gap between the illiterate masses and the elite group as regards access to superior medical care continues to be vast and even to widen, as this study has clearly demonstrated.[39]

[39] For guidelines as regards a reorganization of health programs in Nigeria, see Okediji, "Socio-economic Aspects of Public Health."

# CHAPTER THIRTEEN

## Migration & Urbanization

### in Nigeria

REUBEN K. UDO

▦

HISTORICALLY, there have been three types of population movement in Nigeria and indeed in all tropical Africa. These are the pre-colonial movements of people which featured colonization-type movements and forced migrations in the form of slavery; colonial-period migrations which were prompted by radical changes in the social situation and the monetization of the economy; and finally the recent or postcolonial-period migrations which are increasingly becoming rural-urban in character.[1]

General insecurity, the subsistence character of the economy and the poor state of transportation at the time were largely responsible for the relatively small numbers or people involved in precolonial-period migrations which were essentially short-distance movements. The main purpose of these migrations was the search for farmland, hunting ground, and grazing lands. Movement was from one rural area to another except perhaps in Yorubaland where there were already large urban settlements of over 30,000 persons, although most of these town dwellers earned their living from agriculture. Colonial-period migrations consisted largely of rural-rural migrations but with a considerable rural-urban component in the 1950s. The relative number of rural-urban migrants continues to increase but it is erroneous to suggest that postcolonial internal migration in Nigeria is synonymous with rural-urban migration, in view of the fact that a considerable number of migrants who leave one rural area end up by settling, at least for a short time, in another rural area.[2]

## THE PATTERN OF INTERNAL MIGRATIONS IN NIGERIA

According to the figures of the 1952–1953 national census of Nigeria, the percentage of

[1] See, for example, J. Gugler, "On the Theory of Rural-Urban Migration—The Case of Sub-Saharan Africa," in J. A. Jackson, ed., *Migration* (New York: Cambridge University Press, 1969), pp. 134–55; and W. A. Hance, *Population, Migration and Urbanization in Africa* (New York: Columbia University Press, 1970), pp. 128–39.
[2] R. K. Udo, "Migrations in Nigeria," *Nigeria Magazine*, CIII (1970), 616–24.

migrant population was largest in the northern provinces of Adamawa, Bornu, Ilorin, Kabba, Niger, Plateau, and Zaria, and in the two most industrialized southern provinces of Colony and Rivers where Lagos and Port Harcourt are located respectively. In broad terms, the direction of flow of migrants was mainly south to north and the migrants consisted largely of southern Nigerians going to the developing northern cities of Maiduguri, Yola, Jos, and Zaria. A small proportion of these migrants settled to work in the tin fields of Plateau Province but by far the greater majority went to urban centers. This was before the 30 months civil war which ended in January 1970; but the indications are that there will be a resumption of this flow in the postwar period.

Simultaneously with this south to north flow of rural-urban migrants, there has been a substantial flow of rural-rural and rural-urban migrants from the northern states into the three western states of Lagos, Western, and Mid-Western Nigeria. Migrants who settle in rural areas of these states consist largely of Hausas and Igbiras who provide agricultural labor in the cocoa, rubber, and food farms of the three western states. The Hausa farm workers are essentially seasonal migrants from Sokoto and Katsina provinces.[3] They leave home around November to work in the cocoa belt, and return home in March, in time to hoe their farms for the next farming season. Igbiras, on the other hand, are permanent migrants who stay on for many years and whose main occupation consists of working for wages on food farms or setting up as independent food farmers on land rented from the local Yoruba and Bini people. Some of these northern migrants settle in Yoruba towns where they dominate the cattle and kola nut trade between western Nigeria and the northern states.

There is also a considerable east to west movement of people originating largely from the congested districts of the three Eastern states, but also from the Urhobo and Isoko divisions of the Mid-Western State. Most of these migrants are agricultural workers with little or no formal education; their source of income consists of working for wages on cocoa, rubber, and food farms or establishing themselves as independent tenant food farmers. Isoko and Urhobo migrants specialize in harvesting and processing fruits from wild oil palms growing on groves leased to them for periods varying from one to more than five years. East to west migrants who have primary six certificates or better educational qualifications invariably migrate to the major urban centers of Lagos, Ibadan, and Benin City.

Finally, there is a small west to east component in the southeastern part of the country, consisting mainly of movements from Ibo and Ibibio areas into the Cross River district which is a very sparsely settled area with less than 50 persons per square mile. With the exception of the literate migrants who go to the growing port town of Calabar, the majority of these west to east migrants settle in rural areas where they grow food crops or exploit palm fruits for sale.[4]

A few obvious relationships may be observed when the pattern of migrations is examined together with a map showing the distribution of population in the country. As a rule, the main source regions for migrants are the very densely populated areas with over 800 persons per square mile as well as some medium density areas with 400–800 persons per square mile. A close study of the environmental and economic situations in various source regions reveals that the significant push factor in these migrations is not merely the high numerical densities, but the pressure of population on available resources such as farmland, forest products, and fish. This explains why relatively sparsely settled areas such as the Niger Delta, the Bariba area of Kwara State and Okitipupa Division of the Western State, with under 200 persons per square mile, export population both to the cities and to the more densely settled rural parts of the cocoa belt.

[3] R. M. Prothero, *Migrant Labor from Sokoto Province, Northern Nigeria* (Kaduna, 1952).

[4] R. K. Udo, "The Migrant Tenant Farmer of Eastern Nigeria," *Africa*, XXXIV (1964), 326–39.

Receiving areas or destinations for these migrants usually consist of (1) growing urban centers, (2) areas of intensive cultivation of tree crops for export, or (3) sparsely settled rural districts with abundant farmland. Insofar as rural-rural migration is concerned, the process can be seen as one of redistributing the population with a view to achieving some sort of balance between the number of people and available resources. Improved technology and rising economic expectations resulting in a fuller exploitation of local resources have already started to modify the migratory process from certain districts. The introduction of rubber cultivation in Ishan Division[5] and eastern Urhobo Division,[6] and the introduction of cocoa into Irun district in Ekiti Division[7] have provided employment opportunities in these areas, resulting in a marked decrease in the number of poorly educated migrants from these areas.

The few cases of migrations from sparsely settled rural areas such as the Bariba district of Kwara State to more densely settled rural areas like the cocoa belt are analogous in some ways to the process of urban-urban migrations which feature a movement of people from low-order central places into higher-order central places which usually offer greater and more varied employment opportunities. In the particular case cited here, the more densely settled but faster-growing and better-developed cocoa belt also offers better employment opportunities; but unlike the city, which, because of the nature of its economy, can go on absorbing more and more migrants, a thriving rural district has a limit to the number of migrants that it can absorb.

## CHARACTERISTICS OF MIGRANTS

Of the three major ethnic groups in Nigeria—the Hausas (6 million), Yorubas

[5] A. A. Eigbefoh, "The Rubber Economy of Ishan Farmers" (B.A. dissertation, Department of Geography, University of Ibadan, 1970).
[6] E. K. Anoliefo, "Peasant Rubber Production in Western Urhobo District" (B.A. dissertation, Department of Geography, University of Ibadan, 1966).
[7] M. A. Ogunjemi, "Local Migration in Irun" (B.A. dissertation, Department of Geography, University of Ibadan, 1964).

(10 million), and the Ibos (7 million)—the Ibos are the most migratory according to the 1952–1953 census. At the time of this census, Ibo migrants were found in all the administrative divisions of the country; in most divisions the great majority of them had settled not in urban but in rural areas. The Yorubas, who as migrants are essentially traders, were found in all but 4 of the 93 divisions in the country, while the Hausas were also found in all the divisions, though in much smaller numbers than the Ibos. As permanent migrants, the Hausas in southern Nigeria are essentially traders, but as seasonal migrants, they provide agricultural labor both in the south and in parts of the northern states.

In a recent survey by the author, of rural-rural migration in the country in which 1,200 male migrants were interviewed at various destinations in the southern states, it was found that 95 percent of the migrants belonged to 10 of the more than 200 ethnic groups in Nigeria. The more numerous groups were Ibos (31 percent), Urhobo (18 percent), Ibibio (13 percent), Yoruba (11 percent), and Isoko (9 percent). The large number of Urhobo and Isoko migrants is surprising since these are among the smallest groups in the country, but one reason for this situation appears to be the fact that many interviews were carried out in areas which are not very far from Urhobo and Isoko districts.

The well-known fact that migration is selective in that young adults are more migratory applies to both rural-rural and rural-urban migrations in Nigeria. In the sample referred to in the last paragraph, 72 percent of the migrants were between the ages of 15 and 45 and this compares favorably with Ejiogu's findings that in the Greater Lagos area, about 71.9 percent of the migrant adult population were under 35 years of age.[8] The selective character of the age of the migrant population is obvious when we compare these

[8] C. N. Ejiogu, "African Rural-Urban Migrants in the Main Migrant Areas of the Lagos Federal Territory," in John C. Caldwell and C. Okonjo, eds., *The Population of Tropical Africa* (London: Longmans Green & Company, and New York: Columbia University Press, 1968), pp. 320–30 (reference on p. 323).

figures with those of the Nigerian census of 1963 which showed that for the country as a whole, the proportion of people between the ages of 15 and 45 was 53 percent.

A total of 920 migrants (about 77 percent) of the 1,200 rural-rural migrants were married and of these 72 percent were living with at least one wife. Of the adult migrants in the Lagos area study by Ejiogu on the other hand, about 50 percent were married and of these 89 percent had their wives living with them. These figures are revealing in view of the widely held belief that married men migrating to urban areas tend to leave their wives at home until they can get established in the town. Shortage of housing and the high cost of accommodation in urban areas are thought to be responsible for this. Although it is dangerous to generalize from a single localized study, it appears from Ejiogu's findings that high rent and shortage of accommodation in urban areas result in extreme congestion and slum conditions rather than in keeping male migrants apart from their wives. The fact that only about 31 percent of Lagos-born adult males, who would normally find it less difficult to obtain housing in the city, were married as compared with 50 percent of adult migrants[9] further suggests that the problem of housing is not such an important consideration when urban Nigerians in the low income group decide to marry.

The situation in rural destinations is not surprising since housing is not so much of a problem in rural areas where a mud hut can be put up within a short time and at very little cost. In addition, migrants to rural areas generally depend on family labor supplied by their wives; among Urhobo and Ibo migrants, most of whom are self-employed tenant farmers, the percentage of those living with their wives was 99 and 90 respectively.

The proportion of unmarried male migrants is, however, much higher in urban areas (50 percent in the Lagos area) as compared with the situation in rural areas where only 23 percent of the 1,200 migrants interviewed were bachelors. One possible

reason for this appears to be that migrants settling in rural areas tend to adjust more quickly in that they are readily employed either as farm hands or as independent tenant farmers shortly after arrival. In urban areas, on the other hand, young migrants including those who have completed high school often remain unemployed for many months, while those who are employed may prefer to remain bachelors because they consider their wages rather inadequate to support a family.

Postbasic education in Nigeria, by which is meant education above the primary school level, can be considered to be training for urban jobs since educated Nigerians rarely take to farming and since there are few other jobs available to them in rural areas. It is not surprising therefore that illiterate migrants generally settle in rural areas while migrants to urban areas usually consist of those with at least primary six certificates, the minimum qualification required for unskilled jobs both in industry and in the civil service. There are, however, many less qualified migrants who obtain jobs in urban areas as domestic servants, dock workers, or bar attendants; but in most cases such migrants must be able to write and speak English.

There are also some striking differences in the frequency of home visits between migrants settling in rural areas and those settling in urban areas. Generally, Nigerians who are working in areas outside their home villages or towns normally spend their annual vacation leave in their village of origin and not in holiday resorts. Those working for wages in the cities usually go home once in a year, whenever their employers find it convenient to release them, but self-employed migrants such as traders and migrant tenant farmers usually time their home visits to coincide with the Christmas season. Fortunately for the migrant farmers, the Christmas season falls during the slack season in the farming calendar; since the next farming year does not start till late in February, migrant farmers tend to spend longer perlods away from home than do urban migrants. It is also a striking feature of the survey data on the 1,200 migrant farmers that, although they are

[9] *Ibid.*, p. 325.

not entitled to paid vacation and leave travel allowances like wage-earners in the cities, they visit their home districts more frequently than the latter group of migrants. As many as 520 or 43 percent of the sample visited home at least twice a year, and, curiously, the distance factor was not important in the decision to visit home more than once a year. Improved and faster means of transport appear to offer part of the explanation for this, but the main reason for the greater frequency of home visits by migrant farmers than by city wage earners appears to be the independence of the self-employed farmer who is his own boss.

We conclude this section on the characteristics of migrants by noting the ethno-occupational specializations among self-employed migrants both in rural areas and in the cities. In rural areas, Ibo and Igbira migrants specialize in growing food crops while Illa Yorubas are noted for their special skill in tapping palm wine. Isoko and Urhobo migrants specialize in the harvesting and processing of semiwild palm fruits for sale while self-employed Hausa migrants in the Yoruba cocoa belt concentrate on the purchase and bulk handling of kola nuts for export to markets in northern Nigeria. In the cities, self-employed migrants engage primarily in trade, but there is also a considerable ethno-specialization in the goods sold by migrants. Thus, Abiriba migrants to Aba, Port Harcourt, and Onitsha specialize in selling cheap textiles like singlets, rough ready-made dresses, and second-hand clothes, while Nkwerre migrants trade primarily in high-quality textiles as well as in stockfish and imported tobacco. In the main urban centers of Lagos and Ibadan, Ibo women sell uncooked food unlike the local Yoruba women who deal in cooked food, textiles, and assorted manufactured goods.

## MIGRATION AND URBANIZATION

Colonial-period and present-day migrations in Nigeria are a product of the increasing modernization of the society and economy. In the first place, improved and faster means of transportation have made traveling easier, resulting in greater contacts between different peoples and different areas of the country. Among other things, this has in turn resulted in increasing specialization in agricultural production. The rising economic expectation of the people and the increasing monetization of the economy are related aspects of the modernization process and have played an important part in the increased flow of people from one part of the country to another.

Internal migration in Nigeria is therefore largely a product of recent economic development and so is the process of urbanization. In this section, the relationship between migration and urbanization in the country is examined. There has been a growing tendency to regard internal migration in Nigeria as synonymous with rural-urban migration. This has been the case, partly because the rapid growth of urban centers, particularly in those parts of the country where the urban way of life is a twentieth-century phenomenon, and partly because, in the present stage of the country's economic development, a large percentage of the increase in urban population consists of migrants (see Table 13.1). Various government functionaries have expressed concern about the drift to the towns and now and again the local press has come out with demands and requests that the government should do something to arrest the movement of people from rural areas to the cities.

TABLE 13.1
Sample of non-Yoruba peoples in the Lagos urban area

| Ethnic Group | Total | Migrant | Lagos Born |
|---|---|---|---|
| Ibo | 688 | 409 | 279 |
| Edo & Urhobo | 296 | 164 | 132 |
| Ibibio and Efik | 228 | 159 | 69 |
| Hausa | 40 | 36 | 4 |
| Other Nigerian | 43 | 32 | 11 |
| Non-Nigerian Africans | 58 | 41 | 17 |

SOURCE: C. N. Ejiogu, "African Rural-Urban Migrants in the Main Migrant Areas of the Lagos Federal Territory," in John C. Caldwell and C. Okonjo, eds., *The Population of Tropical Africa* (London: Longmans, Green & Company; New York: Columbia University Press, 1968), pp. 320–330.

It is true that since the end of World War II, an increasing number of people have been flocking into the cities. But, although the drift to the towns has received so much attention, the true position is still that a considerable proportion of these migrants settle in other rural areas. The reason why the movement into the cities has attracted so much attention appears to be associated with the fact that large-scale migration, such as that witnessed in Lagos immediately after the civil war, results in extreme shortage of housing and in congestion and creates excessive demands on available water supply and public transport.

A major reason why many migrants still go to settle in other rural areas is the relatively low level of education of the majority of these people. In the author's 1966 survey of rural-rural migration in Nigeria referred to above, a substantial majority (71 percent) of the 1,200 migrants interviewed were illiterate. It is fair to add that about 68 percent of these migrants were over 25 years of age and this means that they became of school age prior to 1946 when educational facilities were still very limited. In any case the nature of the jobs which these migrants do is not such that demands formal education in the Western sense. The main point, however, as already pointed out, is that illiterate and poorly educated migrants go to rural areas while the better-educated ones go to the cities. This is so because non-English-speaking migrants find it virtually impossible to get jobs in the cities since most businesses require their gatemen, messengers, cleaners, and even watchmen to be able to express themselves in English. The cosmopolitan character of the population of cities like Lagos and Port Harcourt has also made it necessary for domestic servants to be able to speak English since they may be obliged to serve those who speak different Nigerian languages and since domestic servants do much of the shopping for the family.

It is reasonable to expect that, with the present rate of expansion of primary education in the country, particularly in the southern states, more and more migrants will move into the cities. Today the secondary school is no longer a monopoly of the city but

is to be found in many rural areas of Nigeria. But on graduation, high school leavers in rural areas are obliged to migrate to the cities since the types of jobs they wish to do are rarely available outside the cities. The indications are of continued desertion of the countryside for the cities, a trend which is likely to be accelerated if the government carries out a policy of land reforms with a view to modernizing agricultural production.

The older generation of Nigerians and the Christian Church in the country tend to associate city life with what they consider to be the ways of the devil; and some of the outcry against the so-called depopulation of the countryside is engineered by these conservative groups of people. Yet the process of rural-urban migration is a sign of economic modernization. It is indeed difficult to reconcile the present all-out drive by government to modernize the economy through large-scale industrialization with the repeated statements by some government officials that steps be taken to arrest the drift of population into the cities. This naturally leads us to a consideration of the place of urbanization in economic development.

## URBANIZATION AND ECONOMIC DEVELOPMENT

In Nigeria, as in other African countries, the cities, or at least the main ones, are the chief centers of modernization. "They are the intellectual and social capitals, the seats of governments, the main foci of political activity of all sorts" and usually the economic capitals of their respective provincial states.[10] In the economic sphere, the cities are not only the main transport centers, but also the major financial nodes, the trans-shipment points, and the sites of market-oriented manufacturing industries. As Hance properly pointed out, one of the notable characteristics of many African cities (including those of Nigeria) is the rapid fading away of the signs of modernity as one leaves the urban centers. It is therefore not surprising that in Nigeria the

[10] Hance, *Population, Migration, and Urbanization*, p. 209.

city has come to be associated with what is modern and fashionable at least to the younger and more progressive generation. This is a basic cause of the increasing migration of educated rural people into the cities.

The experience of the developed nations of the world indicates that urbanization is a necessary process in economic modernization. Today, the most developed economies are those with predominantly urban population and one cannot but associate the process of urbanization in Nigeria with the increasing modernization of the economy through a structural transformation from a predominantly agricultural-based to an increasingly industrial-based economy. It is in the city, where great numbers of people are concentrated, that a market exists for the products of certain manufacturing industries. It is there that the basic infrastructure for manufacturing and labor exists, and even the basic social and cultural infrastructure; it is the city that sets the pace in education, invention, and fashion. Indeed, some writers hold the view that urbanization is the first phase in economic modernization and that, in the words of Adelman, *et al.*, "until a country reaches some critical minimum extent of urbanization, substantial extensions of literacy, mass communication, and the associated capacity for industrialization are impossible."[11]

It is, however, essential that the economic base of the city, as well as its basic services including transportation and housing, should expand fast enough to cater to the influx of rural population. The problem in Nigeria's cities today is that there are not enough jobs for the increasing migrant population many of whom roam the streets and sleep in petrol filling stations because of the shortage of housing. Many others are obliged to be parasites on relatives and fellow clansmen to such an extent that in the big cities it is common to find five people occupying a room

[11] Irma Adelman and C. Y. Morris, *Society, Politics and Economic Development* (Baltimore: Johns Hopkins Press, 1967), pp. 25–27; see also D. Lerner and L. W. Peusner, *The Passing of Traditional Society* (Chicago: The Free Press, 1966), pp. 57–68.

normally meant for one. The consequence of the overutilization of cooking and toilet facilities, coupled with poor drainage and irregular removal of garbage, is the growth of extensive slums. It is a situation such as this which gives rise to the futile, and perhaps dangerous, campaign to limit the migration of people into the cities.

One of the points usually made against the so-called depopulation of rural areas is that it results in the loss of able-bodied persons since rural-urban migration is essentially selective of age and sometimes of sex. In various parts of rural Nigeria it is common to hear complaints about labor shortage for hoeing yams and repairing houses, and often this is blamed on the loss of young people to the cities. There are some observers who even believe that the rapid change from yam to cassava cultivation in certain parts of southern Nigeria is prompted by the loss of young men to the cities, yam being traditionally a crop grown by men and cassava being the women's crop. A closer study of this particular question, however, reveals that deteriorating soil conditions and the market situation are responsible for the change. The amount of underemployment in most rural parts of the country makes it difficult to sustain the theory of labor shortage resulting from migration. Indeed, migration should result in a more effective utilization of rural resources if the reduced labor force in rural areas is fully utilized.

Rural-urban migration, by reducing the number of people depending on the land in the source regions, should lead to an increase in the amount of land available to cultivators; and consequently to the modernization of the agricultural sector which has to keep pace with industrial development and increasing urbanization. Unfortunately, in the more congested districts of the eastern states of Nigeria, rural-urban migration does not offer much hope for land consolidation owing to local ideas about the land. Usually the migrant leases out his land while he is away in a distant city or another rural area, since he hopes to return some day to his natal village. In a situation where landholding is very fragmented, there is little hope of the emergence of economic farm holdings for cultivation by those who have chosen not to migrate. In the northern states, where the land is held not by individuals but by the state government in trust for the people, such reforms are possible and necessary so as to create more opportunities for those migrants who cannot be absorbed in urban industries and services.

## THE PATTERN OF URBANIZATION IN NIGERIA

The largest concentrations of pre-European towns in Africa are found in the far north of Nigeria, where the ancient cities of Kano, Zaria, and Katsina are located, and in the more recently urbanized Yoruba west where Ibadan, the largest indigenous city in tropical Africa, is located. These pre-European cities were largely administrative, religious, and even educational centers, and, in the case of Hausa towns, trade and crafts formed the main basis of the economy. Yoruba towns, on the other hand, were largely agricultural and still are occupied by predominantly agricultural populations.

Along the coast, another series of traditional urban centers grew up; these were based on the trade in slaves and later in palm oil between the coastal people and European traders. They formed the city states of the Cross River estuary, the Niger Delta and the lagoon port towns of Yorubaland. Compared with the pre-European towns of the interior, the coastal port towns had a more cosmopolitan population and were usually smaller in size. With the exception of Calabar, Warri, and Lagos, these port towns, which depended solely on trade, have declined or ceased to exist following the loss of their middleman position in the country's export trade which has since been reorganized.[12]

The third group of urban centers consists of the new towns of the colonial period. These include the new port towns of Port Harcourt, Sapele, and Koko, and the mining towns of Jos and Enugu. In the already urbanized west and far north, existing towns served as administrative headquarters for the various administrative divisions and districts, but in the eastern states where the village form of settlement still predominated, the colonial government selected a few villages to serve as local administrative headquarters. Usually, a newly selected local headquarters was located as near as possible to the center of the unit of administration. The rapid transformation of these erstwhile villages into urban centers was remarkable. The establishment of a police station, prisons, district office, post office, magistrate's and customary courts, as well as primary schools and a church added new functions to these settlements[13] which started to attract more and more migrants. It was to cater to the increased nonfarm population that markets in such places as Onitsha, Awka, Umuahia, Ikot Ekpene, and Oron began to be held every day of the week instead of once every week as was the case in pre-British days. Today these new towns continue to attract migrants from the surrounding districts which serve as their tributary areas and the process is bound to continue as each town broadens its economic base.

The functional and morphological transformation of villages which were selected to serve as administrative headquarters has been quite astonishing. The development of new housing areas and the use of durable building materials combined to give these villages a new look. In Yorubaland and in the Nigerian Sudan, where some existing large traditional towns were selected as administrative headquarters, modifications of the townscape consisted of the establishment, outside the town walls, of new residential areas for Nigerian strangers and for the high-income group which at that time consisted primarily of expatriate administrative staff from Britain and traders from the Middle East and Europe. The administrative buildings and the

[12] See R. K. Udo and B. Ogundana, "Factors Influencing the Fortunes of Ports in the Niger Delta," *Scottish Geographical Magazine*, LXXXII (1966), 169–183; and R. K. Udo, "The Growth and Decline of Calabar," *Nigerian Geographical Journal*, X (1967), 91–106.

[13] See R. K. Udo, "Transformation of Rural Settlements in British Tropical Africa," *Nigerian Geographical Journal*, IX (1966), 129–44.

commercial center were located in this newly settled part of the town.[14]

Unlike the new mining towns and new administrative towns, the old traditional towns are still less functionally differentiated although the more favorably located ones such as Kano and Ibadan are now becoming industrialized. The population of the traditional towns is rather homogeneous while the new towns are more cosmopolitan. Marked differences also exist in the general layout, architecture, and cultural importance of these two groups of urban centers.

We now go on to consider the position of these towns in the continuing processes of migration and urbanization in the country. Today the most rapidly growing urban centers are the industrial port cities of Lagos and Port Harcourt whose increase in population is still largely due to migration. These are the two major industrial towns in the country and, in addition, Lagos is the country's political and commercial capital, thus offering a wide range of job opportunities for school leavers. Lagos, in particular, has witnessed an unprecedented surge of immigrants following the end of the civil war and the consequent destruction of the economy of the war-affected areas, many of whose inhabitants are now flocking to Lagos and other cities.

The old traditional towns are attracting or losing population according to the degree of modernization of the urban economic base. In general, those traditional towns like Ibadan and Kano, which have a number of manufacturing industries, have continued to attract migrants from various parts of the country; while towns like Ilesha, Badagry, and Katsina, whose economy is still based on agriculture and traditional craft industries, either are suffering a net loss in their population or are growing at a very slow rate. Understandably such conservative towns offer little or no prospects for the intending migrant, while at the same time they are

losing some of their more dynamic population to the bigger and fast-growing industrial centers of Lagos, Kano, Kaduna, and Port Harcourt. The increase in population, if any, is largely by natural increase unlike the position in the industrial cities where the increase in population is largely a result of immigration.

Educational institutions and commerce have contributed considerably to the growth of provincial towns which were selected as local administrative headquarters. The increasing number of secondary schools in these provincial towns has brought into them a number of primary school graduates from the surrounding countryside, but since these provincial towns cannot provide jobs for most of their secondary school graduates, they act as training and transit centers for rural youths who on graduation are obliged to migrate to look for jobs in the bigger cities. People who are familiar with the ancient Yoruba town of Ile-Ife, which is also the administrative headquarters of Ife Division, will agree that the opening in 1966 of the Ife campus of the University of Ife has brought about a considerable change in the urban economic base of the town. In a similar way, the opening of advanced teachers' colleges in the smaller provincial headquarters of Ondo, Abraka, Owerri, and Uyo has helped in the growth of these towns. It is not surprising therefore that many politicians struggle to have advanced government institutions located in their areas of origin and the removal of Queen's School from Ede to Ibadan was not well received by the traditional chiefs and people of Ede.

Finally, the creation of new states in Nigeria since independence has brought about the rapid growth in the population of the state capitals, some of which like Calabar, Sokoto, and Benin City, are pre-British cities. The sudden upgrading of 9 of the 12 state capitals from provincial headquarters with a few government establishments to major administrative centers with all the necessary civil service ministries and departments has meant new job opportunities for citizens of these states. Each state has virtually become a

[14] Details of the institution of township status by the colonial administration and of the modernization of the physical structure of Nigerian towns are given in A. L. Mabogunje, *Urbanization in Nigeria* (London: University of London Press, 1968), pp. 111–20.

planning unit and, as may be expected, the state capitals have been the first choice in the location of various market-oriented industries. The creation of more states has also brought a new lease of life to the smaller provincial towns in a period of progressive decentralization of government departments and armed forces barracks and training bases.

At the state level, therefore, the flow of rural-urban migrants is first toward the state capitals which are important and growing administrative, commercial, educational, and industrial centers and second toward the provincial administrative headquarters which also serve as educational and commercial centers for the immediate rural districts. At the national level, an increasing number of rural-urban migrants move north to south and east to west to the booming oil cities of Port Harcourt and Warri and to the country's largest industrial concentration in the Greater Lagos area.

It is pertinent to conclude by observing that the large influx of migrants into the rural areas of the three western states is partly connected with the high degree of urbanization in this part of the country. It is true that the migrants to what are now the rural parts of the Western, Mid-Western, and Lagos states were originally attracted by the vast employment opportunities in private cocoa farms, rubber farms, and the timber concessions of the Benin and Ondo forests. But since the late 1950s, an increasing number of these migrant laborers have established themselves as independent food farmers who produce food for both the nearby urban population and for some of the indigenous rural population who devote so much time to tree-crop production that they do not produce enough food for home consumption. Self-employed migrant food farmers are particularly numerous in the creeks and lagoons area of Lagos State where they specialize in producing garri and vegetables for the Lagos metropolitan market.[15] It is these migrant farmers who also supply the Lagos urban market with such forest products as firewood and a special leaf for wrapping cooked food for sale in the city.

[15] See H. I. Ajaegbu, "Recent Migrations and Settlement in the Coastal Areas of Southwestern Nigeria," *Nigerian Geographical Journal*, XI (1968), 61–78.

# CHAPTER FOURTEEN

# Metropolitan-ization

## The Growth of Lagos[1]

CHARLES N. EJIOGU

## INTRODUCTION

LIKE most developing countries, Nigeria has experienced rapid population increases in the past 25 years. Its annual rates of population growth have been estimated at 2.0 percent in the period 1931–1953.[2] These estimates are regarded, at best, as showing only trends because of the inaccuracies in the censuses.[3] The growth rate was estimated at 2.7 percent in the period 1953–1962[4] although Smith and Blacker had earlier estimated the 1952–1962 population growth rate at between 1.5 and 2.0 percent.[5] The rate for Nigeria compares with 2.5 percent per annum for Uganda during the period 1948–1959, and current estimates of 2.8 for Dahomey, 3.2 for part of Ivory Coast, 2.4 for Senegal, 3.4 for Rwanda and Burundi,[6] and 2.8 for Kenya between 1948 and 1962.[7]

The rates of urban population growth in Nigeria during these periods, as shown in Table 14.1, have been far above those of the rural population. By the 1931–1953 period, the average growth rate of the urban population was twice that of the rural population. During the 1953–1962 period, the urban population increased at more than twice the rate of the rural population. The comparable United Nations rates, bottom line in the table, are computed for urban areas as defined in the table. The U.N. team of experts on urbanization observed from a study of three groups of regions with different levels of urbanization that "where the level of urbanization was already high (i.e., over 25 percent by 1920), only moderate rates of growth in

---

[1] The study described here was undertaken before Nigeria's division into 12 states in 1967 and hence the old regional boundary names have been retained.

[2] Nigerian Government, *Population Census of Nigeria, 1952–1953*, pp. 6–7, 15.

[3] T. E. Smith and J. G. C. Blacker, *Population Characteristics of the Commonwealth Countries of Tropical Africa* (London: Oxford University Press, 1963), pp. 47–48.

[4] John C. Caldwell and C. Okonjo, *The Population of Tropical Africa* (London: Longmans, Green & Company, and New York: Columbia University Press, 1968), p. 93.

[5] Smith and Blacker, *Population Characteristics*, p. 48.

[6] *Ibid.*, pp. 48–49.

[7] Kenyan Government, *Kenya Population Census* (1962, 1966), p. 77.

TABLE 14.1

Average annual percentage rate of rural and urban population growth, 1931–1962

| Period | Total | Rural | Urban[a] |
|--------|-------|-------|----------|
| 1931–53 | 2.1 | 1.9 | 3.8 |
| 1953–62 | 2.7 | 2.3 | 7.3 |
| 1950–60 | 1.9 | 1.5 | 4.5 |

SOURCE: 1931–53—censuses 1932, p. 101, and 1952–1953, Table 9; 1953–62—population center, Ibadan, 1954; 1950–60—United Nations, *World Urbanization Trends, 1920–60* (New York, 1967), pp. 30–32.
[a] Places 20,000 and over.

TABLE 14.2

Urban population growth in Nigeria, 1931–1962

|  | 1931 | 1952–53 | 1962 |
|--|------|---------|------|
| Urban population (thousands) | 1,488 | 3,228 | 6,294 |
| Total population (thousands) | 19,131 | 30,418 | 45,332[a] |
| Percentage of population in urban areas | 7.8 | 10.6 | 13.8 |

[a] Estimate by the Population Center, University of Ibadan, based on a population growth rate of 2.7 percent per annum. To many demographers, this gives a more realistic estimate of the population of Nigeria in 1962 than the 56 million returned in the 1962 and 1963 censuses. See John C. Caldwell and C. Okonjo, eds., *The Population of Tropical Africa* (London: Longmans, Green & Company; New York: Columbia University Press, 1968), p. 93; Etienne van de Walle, "An Approach to the Study of Fertility in Nigeria," *Population Studies*, xix, no. 1 (July, 1965), p. 5.

both the urban and rural population occurred; but where the level of urbanization was low (i.e., below 25 percent in 1960) both the urban and the rural populations grew with great rapidity."[8] It could be assumed from the foregoing that the estimates for Nigeria present reasonable trends since the world regions considered by the U.N. team include countries with wide variations in level of urbanization.

Although towns in Nigeria with 20,000 inhabitants contained only 10.6 percent of the country's population in 1953, they had absorbed 15.3 percent of the intercensal population increase between 1931 and 1953 and were to absorb about 20 percent of the population increase during the period 1953–1962. The population living in urban areas more than doubled in the 22-year period between 1931 and 1953 and increased more than one-and-a-half times in the next decade. Urban centers, particularly the capital cities, ports, rail and road centers, in other parts of tropical Africa have also shown similar rapid growth during these periods.[9] During the period 1931–1962 the number of people living in urban areas, as shown in Table 14.2 multiplied more than fourfold. However the era of "rural exodus" in Nigeria is still in the remote future since more than 80 percent of the population live in rural areas.

[8] United Nations, *World Urbanization Trends, 1920–1960* (1967), pp. 30–32.
[9] Smith and Blacker, *Population Characteristics*, pp. 21–22; John C. Caldwell, *African Rural-Urban Migration* (Canberra: Australian National University Press, 1969), pp. 11–14.

The main factor in the rapid growth of the population of urban centers has been an acceleration in the migration of individuals and families from the rural areas as a response to economic and social pressures. Modern cities in developing countries are the centers of large-scale in-migration because they form the focuses of economic development. They are the new administrative, commercial, industrial, and transportation centers and also the location of most of the few processing and manufacturing plants established in every region. The principal products manufactured are: food, beverages, and tobacco; textiles and wearing apparel including footwear; timber, wood, and paper products; rubber; chemicals, oils, paints, and petroleum products; clay, glass, and cement products; metal products; machinery and transport equipment; miscellaneous products such as surgical, medical, and scientific products. As shown in the *Industrial Directory of Nigeria*, 70 percent of all manufacturing plants in the Western Region in 1964 were established in Ibadan and suburbs adjoining Lagos Federal Territory. In the Mid-Western Region, 93 percent of the industries cited were in Sapele, Benin, and Warri; 79 percent of those in the Northern Region were located in Kano, Kaduna, Jos, and Zaria. In the Eastern Region, 73 percent of all industries were found in Port Harcourt, Onitsha, Aba, Enugu, and Calabar. These towns are among the largest urban areas in the regions.

However, although economic needs play an important part in rural-urban migration, the conditions favorable for migration involve the interactions of the place of migrant origin and the place of destination as well as the background characteristics of those who migrate.

Of all cities in the country, however, Lagos had by far the largest number of industries. These account for more than 26 percent of all major manufacturing plants in the country. In fact, the Lagos Metropolitan Area is the site of 34 percent of the nation's manufacturing plants, thus forming the largest industrial concentration in Nigeria. The distribution of plants by number of employees indicates that the industries in these urban areas employ the largest number of workers. Thus, the number, size, and degree of industrial concentration in an area can serve as indices of its "pull" force on rural migrants and hence its population growth.

In this respect, the Lagos Metropolitan Area is very attractive to migrants. In addition to the high concentration of manufacturing and processing industries, Lagos is also the seat of the federal government and thus houses all the federal ministries, headquarters of public corporations, and banking, insurance, and mercantile houses. It is also the major port of Nigeria and the largest commercial and educational center in the country. These are activities in which large numbers of workers are employed. Hence Lagos attracts many migrants from all parts of the country and has the most cosmopolitan population in Nigeria. Other considerations which governed the choice are examined in some detail in other sections of this chapter.

## LAGOS

The Federal Territory of Lagos has undergone tremendous physical, demographic, and socio-economic transformation in the twentieth century due to a combination of political and economic circumstances which stem from its geographical situation and administrative importance. It has expanded from an island settlement of 1.55 square miles and about 40,000 people at the turn of the century to 37.22 square miles of built-up area with a population of 450,000 in 1962. Although its physical features are the least advantageous to its growth, they are closely associated with its urban development and hence with its population distribution.

Physically the territory consists of four islands and a mainland stretching only about six miles into Western Region, where the boundaries are lost amid the sprawling suburbs of Mushin, Shomolu on the north, and Ajegunle and Araromi on the south-west.[10] Thus any expansion of the city to the north and west is restricted by the close proximity of the then Western Region boundaries; expansion to the east and south is restricted by the sea. These features are obstacles in the way of planning a rapidly developing national capital.[11]

The islands within the legal boundary of the Federal Territory include the nucleus settlement of Lagos Island, the most densely populated of the four, Ikoyi and Victoria Island to the east, and Iddo Island which forms a stepping-stone to the mainland. Large areas of the islands as well as the mainland are covered by swamps and intersected by lagoons, creeks, and gulfs which require heavy expenditure on reclamation and drainage. Besides, communication between the islands and the mainland has only been effected by the construction of a number of bridges and causeways. Housing schemes in southeast and southwest Ikoyi and Victoria Island and the development of Ijora Industrial Estate were possible only after the reclamation of low-lying swamplands. Projects have been envisaged to reclaim the swampy areas in Yaba east, Suru-Lere south, and Apapa south on the mainland and the rest of Victoria Island. It was only by constant dredging and deepening that Lagos

[10] These suburbs are now in the new Lagos State.
[11] Charles Abrams *et al., A Report on Metropolitan Lagos,* Federal Ministry of Lagos Affairs, Annex 1 (1962), pp. 7–9.

harbor became safe for ships to enter and berth.

## HISTORY OF MIGRATION TO LAGOS

The physical obstacles to the urban development of Lagos were the main factors which attracted its earliest inhabitants. These were a Yoruba subgroup, the Awori, who migrated into Lagos from Isheri, 20 miles north of the Ogun River. The main motive for their movement was to escape the insecurity of life caused by civil war in their home area. They first settled at Ebute Metta where they built a town and engaged in traditional farming and fishing. The exact date of the first settlement in Lagos varies with historical sources but the earliest occupation could be estimated to date as far back as between the fifteenth and seventeenth centuries. However, there is consensus among Yoruba historians that during the Fulani and civil wars among the Yoruba in the seventeenth and eighteenth centuries, defense positions were essential conditions for all settlements. Hence farmers and fishermen from neighboring towns and villages sought refuge on the islands of Lagos which provided natural defense from enemies on the mainland.[12]

With continuous threat of war from Yorubaland, the first settlers were forced to move from Ebute Metta to Iddo Island and later to Lagos Island (or Eko), the larger of the two islands, in order to meet the defense and agricultural needs of the growing number of settlers. The Awori group were later joined by the Ijebu who first made Lagos Island the site of a temporary fishing village before settling permanently. The natural defense of the island attracted more refugees from other Yoruba towns and villages who were fleeing the raids by the Fulani of northern Nigeria. It also protected them from attacks by rival

towns and from the effects of the civil war which ravaged the Yoruba states in the eighteenth century.

The wars in the hinterland provided rich sources of merchandise for the slave trade which made Lagos an important center in the eighteenth century. Thus the population of Lagos increased through the captives brought to be sold into slavery and refugees who fled to the island for safety. During the heyday of the slave trade John Adams in 1789 estimated the population of Lagos at 5,000.[13]

The suppression of the slave trade and the conquest of Lagos by Britain in 1851 opened the way for a different migration stream into Lagos. Indeed the British occupation of Lagos marked the beginning of a new phase in the urban development of Lagos. When Lagos became a British colony in 1861 the population was estimated at 30,000 inhabitants. Repatriated slaves from America, Brazil, and Sierra Leone, most of whom were Yoruba by origin, formed the new wave of migrants. Captured slaves who escaped from the hinterland fled to Lagos from Dahomey, Abeokuta, Ibadan, and Ijebu provinces. The impression must not, however, be created that the town was at this time peopled only by ex-slaves, for legitimate trade in tropical products attracted both foreign and indigenous merchants and businessmen. In order to maintain the peaceful progress of commerce and trade, free movement, and security of life and property, the administration provided institutions of public order such as a constabulary, the police court, and prisons. By the last decade of the nineteenth century, missions, merchant houses, government offices, and other European-type buildings extended along the present Marina Road on the island. The missions built churches and schools to propagate Christianity and education, while trading firms built depots for the growing export of palm oil. The government established a hospital and provided other administrative departments many of which are still found on Lagos Island.

In 1891 the census of Lagos returned a

---

[12] Sources of the history of the earliest settlement in Lagos are mainly from P. A. Talbot, *The Peoples of Southern Nigeria*, I (1926), pp. 79–82; A. C. Burns, *History of Nigeria* (London: Allen and Unwin, 1948), pp. 33–40, and especially A. L. Mabogunje, "Lagos: A Study in Urban Geography" (unpublished, 1961), pp. 26–31.

[13] Burns, *History of Nigeria*, p. 36.

figure of 32,508, thus showing an estimated increase of only 2,508 in 30 years. If the 1861 population of 30,000 was not an overestimate or the 1891 one a gross underestimate, the growth rate was very slow indeed. It could suggest the effect of the prolonged warfare between the Yoruba states which hampered trade and movement of people from the interior. Or it could be a result of high mortality typical of the period. The cessation of civil war brought into prominence the importance of Lagos as the capital and port of the colony and within the next 20 years the population more than doubled, owing primarily to the freer movement of people to the capital. During the period, the railway from Lagos to Ibadan was opened in 1900, thus facilitating transportation from the immediate hinterland. The installation of electric light in most streets of Lagos by 1898 had its attractions in a country where the oil lamp was still the common form of illumination.

The increased migration to Lagos caused overcrowding on the island settlement which could not be extended naturally because of its physical nature. Increasing population concentration on the island worsened the overcrowded conditions in the African section and created the urgent need for suburban expansion. In fact, it was estimated that, with the construction of the MacGregor (drainage) Canal between the island and Ikoyi in 1904, and the reclamation of the swamps in Isaleganga, Okesuna, and Alakoro Island between 1905 and 1907, all available land space on the island had been utilized. Future population increase would have to look to the mainland and the suburbs for accommodation, as indeed has been the case since the early part of the second decade of the century.

As population began to spread to the mainland, the need for the construction of bridges between Lagos and Iddo islands (Carter Bridge), and Iddo Island and the mainland (Denton Bridge), became urgent. When, for the first time, the two new suburbs of Ebute Metta and Ikoyi were included in the census of Lagos Territory in 1901, their population was only 2,500 out of a total 42,000. The population figures in Table 14.3 exhibit the acute overcrowding on the island and the shift of population to the suburbs during the period 1901–1962. The average densities given in the table greatly underestimate the serious congestion in the residential areas of Lagos Island and some areas in the suburbs. Overcrowding caused a great deal of slum and unsanitary conditions leading to serious outbreaks of smallpox in 1903, 1919–1920, and 1933–1934, yellow fever in 1913, and the influenza epidemic in 1918 as well as an outbreak of plague in 1924.[14] The post-World War II urban "population explosion" caused further overcrowding on Lagos Island.[15] Conditions have not improved very much east of the slum-cleared area, since some of the displaced families, rather than accept resettlement on the mainland, moved into this area and worsened existing congestion and slum conditions.

The solution to the problem of slums and congestion was sought as early as 1931 and on a larger scale in 1956, by clearing the slum area and resettling the displaced families on the mainland. The move received a limited sympathetic response together with much resistance on each occasion. The objections originated from the economic dependence of the affected families on the commercial center and the large market close to their homes on Lagos Island. To be removed to places over six miles from the island would entail long and expensive journeys to their places of work. The move also was regarded as disruptive of their long established corporate family existence. Many had lived in family houses for which no rents were paid. To move to the housing estates on the mainland would not only separate them from their extended families but would also impose a heavy financial strain on their resources. Most of the island is an African city where the earliest settlers have lived and owned

[14] H. N. G. Thompson, *Population Census of Lagos, 1931, 1932*, pp. 129–30.
[15] Peter Marris, *Family and Social Change in an African City: A Study of Rehousing in Lagos* (London: Routledge and Kegan Paul, 1961), vii.

TABLE 14.3
Population of Lagos Federal Territory by main districts,[a] 1901–1962

| | Lagos Island | Ikoyi and Victoria | Mainland Suburbs | Total |
|---|---|---|---|---|
| *1901* | | | | |
| Area in square miles | 1.55 | n.a.[b] | n.a. | n.a. |
| Total population | 39,387 | n.a. | 2,460 | 41,847 |
| Population density | 25,411 | — | — | — |
| *1911* | | | | |
| Area in square miles | 1.55 | 8.00 | 8.45 | 18.00 |
| Total population | 58,580 | 2,628 | 12,558 | 73,766 |
| Population density | 37,793 | 328 | 1,486 | 4,098 |
| *1921* | | | | |
| Area in square miles | 1.55 | 8.62 | 10.00 | 20.17 |
| Total population | 80,867 | 2,326 | 16,497 | 99,690 |
| Population density | 52,172 | 270 | 1,650 | 4,942 |
| *1931* | | | | |
| Area in square miles | 1.55 | 8.62 | 15.42 | 25.59 |
| Total population | 93,250 | 5,419 | 27,439 | 216,108 |
| Population density | 60,161 | 626 | 1,779 | 4,928 |
| *1950* | | | | |
| Area in square miles | 1.55 | 8.71 | 16.96 | 27.22 |
| Total population | 135,612 | 15,058 | 79,586 | 230,256 |
| Population density | 87,492 | 1,729 | 4,693 | 8,459 |
| *1952* | | | | |
| Area in square miles | 1.55 | 8.71 | 16.96 | 27.22 |
| Total population | 151,900 | 17,500 | 98,000 | 267,400 |
| Population density | 98,000 | 2,009 | 5,778 | 9,824 |
| *1962* | | | | |
| Area in square miles | 1.55 | 8.71 | 16.96 | 27.22 |
| Total population | 173,850 | 38,800 | 236,850 | 449,500 |
| Population density | 119,354 | 4,455 | 13,965 | 16,514 |

SOURCES: Department of Statistics, *Population Census of Lagos, 1950* (Lagos, 1951), p. 26; Charles Abrams *et al.*, *A Report on Metropolitan Lagos*, Federal Ministry of Lagos Affairs, Annex 1 (1962), p. 5.
[a] Floating populations in 1911, 1921, and 1931 are distributed proportionately in the districts.
[b] n.a. = not available.

the land. Except for land expropriated by the state, most land on Lagos Island is family property and four-fifths of the properties in the city are subject to Yoruba law and custom.[16] In a fast-changing economy in which land is highly valued, the disposition of family land has become the subject of long drawn-out litigation. The registration of ownership of family land featured prominently in two committees set up by the Federation government in 1960 to examine the registration of title to land in the Federal Territory.

The traditional Yoruba patterns of settlement in large compounds of extended patrilineal families were established among the predominantly Yoruba inhabitants of the island. However, this form of family organization has been greatly modified by urban redevelopment and the changes it has caused in the social structure. The resistance to change amid unhealthy slum surroundings can be explained further in terms of the large

[16] R. S. Simpson, *A Report on the Registration of Title to Land in the Federal Territory of Lagos* (Lagos, 1957), pp. 44–49.

TABLE 14.4
Distribution of population by residential districts, Lagos Federal Territory, 1911–1962

| Census | Lagos Island | | Ikoyi & Victoria | | Mainland Suburbs | | Total | |
|--------|------------|---------|------------|---------|------------|---------|------------|---------|
| Year | Population | Percent | Population | Percent | Population | Percent | Population | Percent |
| 1911 | 58,580 | 79.4 | 2,628 | 3.6 | 12,558 | 17.0 | 73,766 | 100.0 |
| 1921 | 80,867 | 81.1 | 2,326 | 2.3 | 16,497 | 16.5 | 99,690 | 100.0 |
| 1931 | 93,250 | 73.9 | 5,419 | 4.3 | 27,439 | 21.8 | 126,108 | 100.0 |
| 1950 | 135,612 | 58.9 | 5,058 | 6.5 | 79,586 | 34.6 | 230,256 | 100.0 |
| 1952 | 151,900 | 56.8 | 17,500 | 6.5 | 98,000 | 36.6 | 267,400 | 100.0 |
| 1962 | 173,850 | 38.7 | 38,800 | 8.6 | 236,850 | 52.7 | 449,500 | 100.0 |

SOURCES: D.O.S., *Population Census of Lagos, 1950*, p. 26; Abrams *et al.*, *Report on Metropolitan Lagos*, p. 5.

number of Lagos-born families among the residents who have lived in the affected areas for many years. The response to rehabilitation in the new suburbs, as to other changes in manner of living, came more readily from migrants and the younger generation of native born, who wanted freedom from parental family control, than from the middle-aged and older indigenous community of traders and craftsmen, whose economic existence depended largely on the commercial center of the island.

The suburbs, on the other hand, are mainly residential, and contain nine-tenths of the area of the Federal Territory. The distribution of population after 1952 in favor of the mainland as presented in Table 14.4 was a direct consequence of increased congestion on the island, and the consequent slum clearance and rehabilitation programs coupled with increased migration into the mainland suburbs in recent years. As a result, by 1962, 61 percent of the population of Lagos Territory lived outside the island. Unlike the residential area on the island, the mainland suburbs, Ikoyi and Victoria Island give the impression of effective attempts at town planning in their structural layout. They also exhibit population structures distinct from those of the island.

## POLITICAL DEVELOPMENT AND MIGRATION

Every constitutional advance made by Lagos since the pacification of Yorubaland in 1897

enlarged the hinterland it served as a capital and thus increased the source area of migration flow. Its political status was raised when, in 1906, it was declared the capital of the colony and Protectorate of Southern Nigeria. Eight years later Lagos became the capital of the colony and Protectorate of Nigeria when the northern and southern provinces were amalgamated under the Lugard administration.[17]

Thus Lagos became the seat of colonial administration in Nigeria. However, a major political event which gave Lagos a national outlook and encouraged the migration of various Nigerian groups into the territory was the creation of the Nigerian Federation in 1954. Under this constitutional development Lagos ceased to be part of Western Region and became the seat of a government of representatives from each of the four regions of the federation. The government in turn sought to make the public service and its agencies representative of all the regions and their diverse ethnic groups.

With the attainment of independence in 1960, the existing ministries and other arms of the government were enlarged. Furthermore, it became federal government policy to recruit staffs for the ministries and corporations from all regions for obvious political reasons. This policy helped to resuscitate the hitherto declining numbers in the city belonging to ethnic groups from northern Nigeria, and further increased those of southern origin among the better educated.

[17] Burns, *History of Nigeria*, p. 201.

Henceforth, the population became more cosmopolitan and heterogeneous in character. At the same time the internal administration of the city became more complex as the number of functionaries expanded.

## ECONOMIC DEVELOPMENT AND MIGRATION

The position of Lagos as the chief port of Nigeria and the rich hinterland served by the port increased the economic activities of the territory after World War II. The improvement of the harbor and port facilities opened up overseas trade and communication. The extension of the railways to join the northern and eastern lines provided means of transporting export products—palm products, cocoa, groundnuts, and cotton—from the interior to Lagos, and imports from Lagos to the interior. It also facilitated the movement of people from the distant regions to the Federal Territory. The development of roads and telegraph communication after 1920 to important towns in the hinterland provided essential services for the growth of trade and commerce between Lagos and the rest of Nigeria.

Consequently, imports and exports through Lagos increased from values of £807,000 and £831,000 respectively in 1901[18] to £45 million and £51 million in 1950, and £159 million and £89 million in 1961. These figures represent an average of over 63 percent of the total trade of the country between 1950 and 1961. The growth of external trade was reflected in the increased shipping and tonnage of cargo handled in the harbor. The number of ships which entered Lagos harbor increased from 1,522 in 1957–1958 to 2,126 in 1960–1961, and to 2,174 in 1962–1963. This represented, on average, more than 52 percent of all ships using Nigerian ports in the same period. Until 1961 nearly 60 percent of the external trade of Nigeria passed through Lagos port. The drop in the proportion of cargo in 1961 was a result of the export of crude oil from Bonny near Port

[18] Talbot, *Peoples of Southern Nigeria*, p. 126.

Harcourt. This does not, however, indicate any decline in the volume of foreign trade handled at Lagos port in that year.

The increases in trade promoted wholesale and retail trade in Lagos, and offered opportunities to importers and exporters, dock workers, businessmen, traders, clerical and transport workers, as well as craftsmen and unskilled laborers, thereby encouraging a greater influx of job seekers to the Federal Territory. Its important position on the seaward and inland trade routes and its large urban population constitute additional economic advantages for the establishment of manufacturing and processing industries. The records of existing industries in 1960–1961 showed that 434 of the 1,062 industrial firms registered in Nigeria were located in the Lagos Metropolitan Area; the largest number, in proportion to area and population, in a single region of the country.

Although it is not easy to assess the internal commercial transactions in statistical terms, it is illuminating to note that in 1961 more than half of the total employment and cash earnings in the territory was accounted for by commercial enterprises of all kinds as shown in Table 14.5.

## POPULATION GROWTH

The period from 1900 to the time of the study was marked by rapid population increases especially in the suburban areas as seen in Table 14.6. The population trend is that of rapid growth in the period under review, being reflections of mortality and fertility (and their difference), and net migration trends in the area.

The physical characteristics of Lagos, its insular position, and its unplanned beginning disposed it to serious overcrowding early in its development. These conditions promoted poor sanitation, with associated periodic outbreaks of epidemics, ultimately increasing mortality especially of infants who tend to be the main victims of unhealthy surroundings. Indeed the conditions presented health hazards in the city early in the century when the official crude death rate was estimated at

TABLE 14.5

Total employment and cash earnings by type of employer, Lagos, 1961

| Employer | Number Employed | Percent of Total Employed | Cash Earnings (£ '000) | Percent of Total |
|---|---|---|---|---|
| *Government* | | | | |
| Federal | 19,623 | 23.4 | 5,871 | 28.4 |
| Local | 4,513 | 5.4 | 334 | 1.6 |
| Public corporations | 12,856 | 15.3 | 3,105 | 15.0 |
| *Commercial* | 46,052 | 54.8 | 11,107 | 53.7 |
| Voluntary agencies | 934 | 1.1 | 261 | 1.3 |
| Total | 83,978 | 100.0 | 20,678 | 100.0 |

41.4 per thousand population and infant mortality was 450 per thousand live births.[19]

However, health measures were initiated by Governor William MacGregor, who arrived with Ronald Ross from the School of Tropical Diseases in Liverpool, fresh from his epoch-making discovery of the cause of malaria. The Health Boards set up in 1900 and 1908 began projects for the improvement of sanitation, sewage disposal, and supply of pipe-borne water to the city population. Antimalarial precautions were started by the reclamation of swamps, construction of canals

and drainage, and the regular taking of quinine. Vaccination campaigns were organized to check the constant outbreaks of smallpox epidemics. Between 1900 and 1930 the sanitary staff of Lagos increased from 1 medical officer to 5 and from 2 sanitary inspectors to 55 and 110 health visitors.[20] Though these records might sound impressive, the ratio of doctors to population in 1931 was still rather low at 1 doctor to 25,000 persons.

However, the health and medical services provided in the Federal Territory subsequently expanded greatly and in 1962 there

[19] Thompson, *Population Census*, p. 129.

[20] *Ibid.*, pp. 129–30.

TABLE 14.6

Population growth of Lagos Territory, 1901–1962

| Census Year | Population of District | | | Average Annual Percentage Growth Rate since Previous Census | | |
|---|---|---|---|---|---|---|
| | Lagos island | Lagos suburbs | Total | Lagos island | Lagos suburbs | Total |
| 1901 | 39,387 | 2,460 | 41,847 | — | — | — |
| 1911 | 58,580 | 15,186 | 73,766 | 4.0 | 19.9 | 5.8 |
| 1921 | 80,867 | 18,825 | 99,690 | 3.3 | 2.2 | 3.0 |
| 1931 | 90,250 | 32,858 | 126,108 | 1.2 | 5.7 | 2.3 |
| 1950 | 135,612 | 94,644 | 230,256 | 2.0 | 5.7 | 3.2 |
| 1952[a] | 151,900 | 115,500 | 267,400 | 5.8 | 10.5 | 7.7 |
| 1962 | 173,850 | 275,650 | 449,500 | 1.4 | 9.1 | 5.3 |

Sources: D. O. S., *Population Census of Lagos, 1950*, p. 26; Abrams et al., *Report on Metropolitan Lagos*, p. 5.
a If the 1952 census figures are disregarded, the 1950–1962 average rates of increase are: Lagos Island: 2.1 suburbs: 9.3, total 5.7.

were 264 medical practitioners, 19 dentists, more than 300 other medical personnel, and 87 hospital establishments which included special and general hospitals, maternity homes and child welfare centers, outpatient dispensaries, clinics and consulting rooms, leprosarium and leprosy clinics.[21] These represent ratios of 1,600 persons per doctor and 194 persons per hospital bed. Improved sanitary conditions, health practices, and cheap medical aids have very much reduced the incidence of common diseases. In terms of the needs of the growing population, these facilities are still insufficient and Lagos hospitals often are overcrowded with outpatients, some of whom wait for long hours before receiving attention. The records of medical and indeed other social services in Lagos show a city in which increased urban facilities continue to chase an ever-inflating population. There is no doubt, however, that these facilities are the best in the country on a per capita basis and greater use is being made here of medical services than elsewhere or in Lagos' own past.

The practical results of these health measures and medical facilities are reflected in the reduction in mortality rates, especially in infant mortality, and in the increase of births over deaths within the period. The death rates declined from an average of 38 per thousand population during the period 1900–1904 to 21 in 1925–1929, 15 in 1950–1959, and 13 per thousand on average in 1960–1961. The falling trend in infant mortality is much more pronounced, from an annual average of 409 per thousand live births between 1900 and 1904 to 177 in 1925–1929, 114 in 1945–1949, through an average of 86 in the 1950–1954 period to 71 in 1960–1961, a decline of 17 percent in less than ten years. Maternal mortality rates have also declined markedly from 14 per thousand live births in 1949 to 6 in 1958 and 5 in 1959, a fall of almost 70 percent in a decade, thus being a factor in the apparent climb of crude birth rates from 36 per thousand population during the period 1940–1944 through 50 per

[21] Nigerian Government, *Health Statistics*, II, 9, (Lagos 1964).

thousand in 1950–1954 to 60 per thousand in the 1960–1961 period.

The vital rates given here are derived from the registration of births and deaths and population estimates of doubtful accuracy. Although the history of registration of vital events in Lagos dates back to 1863 when it was first introduced on a voluntary basis before being made compulsory in 1892,[22] the rates given above should be interpreted with some reservations. It is generally believed that before the introduction of universal free primary education in the Federal Territory of Lagos in 1956, underregistration was common. In a predominantly migrant population, in which wives often return to their home villages to have babies, the probability of vital events escaping registration is very high. On the other hand, after 1956, registration of births from outside the territory is known to exist "as parents use Lagos addresses of relatives to register their children so that they may qualify for the free primary education on attaining school age." Although all deaths in Lagos are supposed to be medically certified and no burial takes place without a valid burial and registration certificate, some deaths escape these procedures owing to the custom of migrants taking seriously ill relatives to their home towns or villages. There are also cases of those who die without attending the hospital and whose corpses are conveyed home for burial.

Defects and improvements in registration over time can cause the fluctuations observed in the vital rates. Better registration, and an increased tendency to come to the city for childbirth, have much to do with the rise in birth rate. Nevertheless the available data illustrate falling trends in mortality and rising fertility, and marked declines in maternal and infant mortality.

## MIGRATION

The major factor which accounts for the population growth of the territory, however,

[22] R. R. Kuczynski, *A Demographic Survey of the British Colonial Empire*, I, *West Africa* (London: Oxford University Press, 1948), pp. 542, 622–24.

is the large influx of people from all over the country. As the seat of the federal government, the chief port of the country, the largest commercial and industrial center in Nigeria, a railway terminus and an educational center, Lagos has experienced a continuous inflow of population from all regions as well as a few migrants from outside the country. The factors cited above have increased employment opportunities which have attracted all kinds of workers, school leavers, and other job seekers. Development in education by the federal government since 1956 has increased educational facilities in the city. The introduction of free primary education in the same year attracted many children of school age and families with children. Compared with the regions, the Federal Territory of Lagos has the largest number of educational institutions in proportion to population.[23]

The first indication of large in-migration is seen in the very high rates of population growth over the period shown in Table 14.6. The rates of population growth could also have been affected by variation in the levels of coverage in the population enumeration during the censuses. The results shown in the table should at best be regarded as showing trends, especially before 1950.

The increases in population were most rapid between 1901 and 1911, a period which marked the beginning of peace, legitimate trade, and urban development in Lagos. Migration from the interior following the end of internecine wars in the hinterland, the resettlement of repatriated slaves and refugees of intertribal wars, as well as the natural increase of the settled residents were the main factors for growth during this period. The growth in population was apparently retarded during the next decade, due to a combination of events, namely the 1914–1918 war, the influenza epidemic from 1918–1920, and the postwar slump in trade. The population increased by only 3.0 percent per annum during the period, less than half as

fast as during the previous decade. The effect was even more marked in the suburbs where many migrants settled, thus showing that the events of the period had profound effects on migration into the territory. The rate of population increase continued to decline on the island after 1921 due to more deaths from bubonic plague during the period 1924–1930 and the general world economic depression which caused a fall in prices of Nigerian exports and a general decline in port activity. These occurrences tended to slow down the stream of migration to Lagos and the trend is reflected in the lower average rates of population growth in the period 1921–1931, especially on the island, where most of the population lived at the time. However, during the same period, the annual growth rates of the suburbs more than doubled.

World War II was accompanied by an upward trend in migration, which by 1950 had raised the population size to almost double that of 1931. Many workers who were laid off in the regions during the war moved into Lagos where they believed greater employment opportunities existed. The influx of unemployed was so great after the war that the Department of Labor in 1945–1946 passed orders to prevent registration as unemployed workers of people from the provinces. This measure, however, failed to reduce the rate of migration into Lagos, in fact, the number of migrants increased by the addition of returned servicemen, whose reinstatement in employment was made compulsory by law throughout the country.

Although the growth of population in this period can be attributed to the increasing surplus of births over deaths, the proportion of the population of persons born in Lagos to the total population fell from 41 percent in 1931 to 37 percent in 1950, showing evidence of increasing in-migration. During the period 1931–1950 migration accounted for 69 percent of the population increase in the territory. Moreover, growth by natural increase rose because of the large-scale migration of young adults of reproductive age and as a result of improved health practices and

[23] See Nigerian Government *Report on Educational Development in Lagos* (1957); *Annual Abstracts of Statistics* (1963), pp. 159–64; and *Annual Digest of Educational Statistics* (Lagos, 1962), pp. 38, 49–50, 56.

medical facilities which helped to reduce mortality rates.

Throughout the period 1931–1950 the suburbs continued to attract large proportions of fresh migrants with the result that their population had almost tripled by 1950 while the island increased its population to just over one-and-a-half times that of 1931. In recent years the annual growth rate of the suburban population has risen from 5.7 percent in 1950 to 9.1 percent in 1962, while the island showed a relative decline in its annual average growth between 1952 and 1962 as seen in Table 14.6. At the 1952 census, 57 percent of the population of the Federal Territory lived on Lagos Island, and 43 percent on the mainland and Ikoyi and Victoria Island. By 1962 there was a complete reversal in the population distribution so that more than 60 percent were now living in the mainland and Ikoyi-Victoria suburbs.

These patterns of population growth and redistribution indicate the direction of recent migrant settlement and urban expansion. The decline in the growth rate of the island population is due to lack of space for further expansion and subsequent out-movement from the congestion. It was also a result of the recent slum clearance in central Lagos which removed nearly 20,000 residents to the mainland suburbs.

### AGE AND SEX STRUCTURE

The structure and composition of the population bear strong evidence of its large migrant segment. The age structure shows that adults under 40 years of age formed 53 percent of the population in 1931 and 51 percent in 1950. The proportion of persons under 15 years of age rose from 27 percent in 1931 to 32 percent in 1950 partly because of growth by natural increase during the period and partly as a result of in-migration of young persons aged 10–14 years. The effect of understatement of age cannot be disregarded in producing these results.

Between 1901 and 1961, the population of the city, as evidenced from the sex composition given in Table 14.7, remained predominantly masculine. But the trends in

TABLE 14.7

Sex Composition of Lagos population 1901–1961

| Year | Male | Female | Sex Ratio (males per 100 females) |
|---|---|---|---|
| 1901 | 21,176 | 20,671 | 102.4 |
| 1911 | 39,865 | 33,901 | 117.6 |
| 1921 | 57,337 | 42,353 | 135.4 |
| 1931 | 70,227 | 55,881 | 125.7 |
| 1950 | 124,858 | 105,398 | 118.5 |
| 1952 | 143,280 | 124,127 | 115.4 |
| 1961 | 200,100 | 185,200 | 108.0 |

SOURCES: D.O.S., *Population Census of Lagos, 1950*, p. 26, *1952*, p. 10; *Lagos Housing Enquiry, 1961*, p. 5.

the masculinity ratio clearly reveal the changes in the pattern of migration into Lagos over the period. In the early part of the century, when transportation was still rudimentary, migration was limited to the immediate Yoruba countryside; and the relative security of life in this commercial and administrative center vis-à-vis the areas of out-migration attracted whole families, hence the comparatively low sex ratio of 102.4 males per 100 females in 1901. At the early stage of its urban development, the sex composition of Lagos differed little from that of any other rural Yoruba city. As transport and communication improved and expanded in later years, and knowledge of opportunities in the city spread into other parts of the country which were now peaceful, there was a growing tendency for males to leave their homes to seek their fortunes in Lagos while the wives and children usually remained at home. Residence in the city was not permanent as married men moved back to the home town or village to see their families. This pattern reached its peak in the 1920s and 1930s when masculinity ratios were at the highest level of 135.4 and 125.7 males per 100 females in 1921 and 1931 respectively. The migrant population was most unstable during this period. By 1950 the downward trend in the sex ratio observed in the previous census continued as more migrants tended to bring their wives and more females migrated. The migrant population thus became more settled and included an increasing proportion of

TABLE 14.8

Percentage distribution[a] of ethnic groups in Lagos, 1931, 1950, 1964

| Ethnic Group | 1931 Lagos | 1950 | | | 1964 Lagos suburbs |
|---|---|---|---|---|---|
| | | Lagos territory | Lagos island | Lagos suburbs | |
| Yoruba | 77.2 | 70.9 | 79.9 | 57.9 | 58 |
| Ibo | 4.1 | 11.1 | 5.6 | 18.9 | 21 |
| Edo-Urhobo-Itsekiri | 3.3 | 5.0 | 4.1 | 6.4 | 9.0 |
| Hausa-Fulani | 2.8 | 1.7 | 1.1 | 2.6 | 2.0 |
| Ijaw-Kalabari | 1.1 | 1.5 | 1.0 | 2.2 | 2.0 |
| Efik-Ibibio | 0.6 | 1.4 | 1.1 | 2.0 | 5.0 |
| Other groups | 1.1 | 0.7 | 0.5 | 1.0 | 3.0 |
| Not stated | 3.0 | 1.9 | 2.4 | 1.2 | — |
| Percent | 93.2 | 94.4 | 95.8 | 92.3 | |
| Total Nigerians no. | 117,554 | 217,301 | 129,899 | 87,402 | |

SOURCE: D.O.S., *Population Census of Lagos, 1950*, pp. 44, 49.
[a] Non-Nigerian Africans formed only 5.6 percent of the total population in 1931 and 2.8 percent in 1950.

families and a decreasing proportion of single men. Consequently, increases by natural growth contributed further to lowering the masculinity ratio, with a marked fall from 118.5 to 108.0 males per 100 females between 1950 and 1961. In spite of the falling trend in the sex ratios of the general population of the territory, masculinity in the suburbs, where most of the migrants reside, remained high, at 130 males per 100 females in 1950 and 115.5 in 1961, compared with 111.1 and 99.1 respectively on the island.

## ETHNIC COMPOSITION

The diversity of the ethnic groups in the population, as shown in Table 14.8, is a further indication of the large number of migrants from all parts of the country. No other city in the Federation presents such a variety of Nigerian peoples as the Territory of Lagos. All important ethnic groups are represented with the Yoruba in the majority because of their social and physical proximity to the city.

The gradual but significant decrease in the proportion of this dominant group from 77 percent in 1931 to 71 percent in 1950 and the simultaneous increases in the proportion of non-Yoruba groups, particularly the Ibo, indicated the increased in-migration by the non-Yoruba groups as the urban area expands. The distribution of ethnic groups in the suburbs testifies to the expanded areas of migration to the city and its metropolitan character in recent years.

## CONCLUSION

The pattern of ethnic distribution within the city is a reflection of the phases of its urban expansion, and the growing diversity of its population suggests the widening migrant catchment area. It has been argued in a study by Mabogunje that the major influx of the Ibo from the Eastern Region began just before 1931, about the time the eastern railway was completed from Port Harcourt through the Ibo country to join the western line from Kano at Kaduna. This partly explains the significant growth in Ibo population in Lagos from 4 percent of the population of Lagos in 1931 to 11 percent in 1950, an increase of 397 percent during the period. Other non-Yoruba groups, except the Hausa, as shown in Table 14.8 exhibited comparable increases during the period. The new expanding suburbs provided the main residential area for them. The attractions of Lagos as a major port and main center of trade, industry, and learning, are sufficient to ensure continued inflow into these areas of people from distant parts of the country.

THE SIX northern states of Nigeria occupy an area of 281,782 square miles and contain a population which was 17,007,377 in 1952 and may now have reached or surpassed the inflated figure of 29,808,659 given by the census of 1963. However, the distribution of this population is conspicuously uneven, with rural densities rising above 600 per square mile in some areas, while extensive tracts are virtually uninhabited. Such figures are far above the average density for western tropical Africa and, by African standards, the northern states as a whole are relatively densely peopled with an average at the present time of the order of about 100 persons per square mile.

The most important areas of dense population (Figure 15.1) include the Kano close-settled zone with its extension to Katsina, the Sokoto region and the Rima valley, the Jos Plateau State, and the Ilorin-Offa areas in Kwara State. But there are numerous smaller concentrations often associated with important towns such as Okene in Kwara, or with mountainous areas such as the Gwoza Hills in North Eastern State. All these densely populated areas have arisen primarily in response to political factors which operated in precolonial times. Such was the premium set on security that only the centers of political power were able to attract migrants and sustain demographic growth, while the areas between remained largely unoccupied. The polarization between Moslem societies and those which resisted Islam, and the ensuing conflict, accentuated this tendency and led to high population densities in some regions where soil conditions were poor. Thus the distribution of population often fails to relate to the potential productivity of the land.

The rate of natural increase of the population also varies from place to place, but few data exist. It appears likely, however, that, whatever regional variations exist, they are of less importance to the present discussion than the growth which has taken place in the rate of natural increase since the beginning of the colonial era in 1903, and especially during the last 30 years. This upward trend affects all societies, though to

# CHAPTER FIFTEEN

# Some Social & Economic Implications

*of Population Growth in Rural Hausaland*

A. D. GODDARD,
M. J. MORTIMORE,
AND D. W. NORMAN

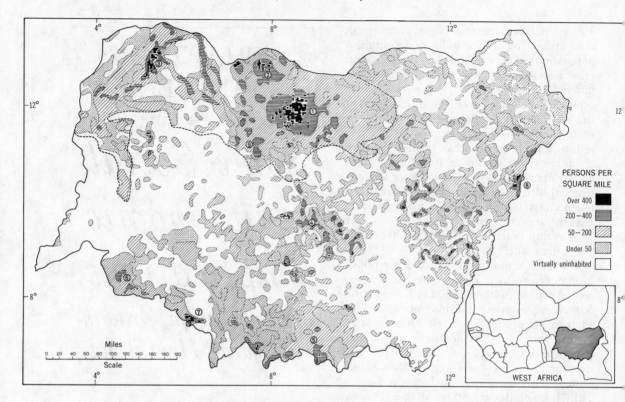

FIGURE 15.1.    *Population Density Map of Nigeria*

different degrees. A high rate of natural increase, in the context of a highly variable density of population, has serious implications for some rural communities and calls for substantial modifications to the farming system, for increased dependence on other activities, or for migration.

The greater part of the material available on the social and economic implications of demographic growth in northern Nigeria has been acquired from the study of rural societies in Hausaland. These studies have been undertaken principally in Katsina, Kano, Zaria, and Sokoto and the discussion which follows will draw on their conclusions. Hausaland, by which is meant those areas inhabited predominantly by people speaking Hausa as the first language, contains about one-third of the population of the northern states, and to this extent such an emphasis is justified.

For the present analysis, data should ideally

be organized in time series relating to particular areas. Such data would show the nature of chronological change in response to a growing population. They are, however, almost entirely lacking. Instead, a comparative spatial approach will be adopted. An attempt will be made to isolate, in areas of differing population density, those social and economic characteristics which can be interpreted, other things being equal, as responses to demographic growth. Although it is fully recognized that in rural Hausaland great diversity exists, the assumption is made (and believed to be justified) that divergences from the norm are not sufficient to invalidate the comparison in these case studies.

### LAND USE

The pattern of land use observed around rural settlements in Hausaland is the result of the interplay of three principal factors: the type or types of land available; distance of land from the village, hamlet, or compound; and population density.

The first of these factors is most commonly expressed in a fundamental distinction, made by all farmers, between *fadama* and upland. *Fadama* is low-lying land subject to seasonal flooding or waterlogging, along the banks of streams or in depressions. Upland varies in quality from place to place but is always elevated relative to *fadama*, if only by a matter of a few feet. *Fadama* can often be used either for irrigated cultivation during the dry season or, where the water table is high, for the cultivation of crops all the year round; cultivation of the upland on the other hand is confined to the wet season. The amount and distribution of *fadama* is determined by topography, and it rarely constitutes more than 10 percent of the cultivated area. It is favored for higher value, more labor-intensive crops such as sugarcane, onions, rice, vegetables, and tobacco, and the extent of its use is influenced by market accessibility. Upland, on the other hand, is used for growing the staples, millet and sorghum, which together with groundnuts, cotton, and cowpeas make up the main crops of Hausaland.

The role of distance from the place of residence has influenced the division of upland soil between annual cultivation with manuring to maintain fertility, and short-term cultivation with periods under bush fallow to restore fertility. Since in the long run annual cultivation requires greater inputs, the nearer zone is devoted to this, while fields at greater distances are bush fallowed. In between there may be a transitional zone of short or grass fallow where the fallow period never exceeds two years. The larger the size of the settlement, the larger the zone of annual cultivation tends to be. This system, combining the advantages of annual cultivation and bush fallowing, seems to be typical of those parts of Hausaland where population densities are relatively low.[1]

It is possible to see the ratio of manured land to fallow[2] as a function of population density since, if there is insufficient land to maintain the community by means of a long fallowing system, some land must be cultivated more frequently. On the other hand, all villages, and even small hamlets, have some manured land even in sparsely populated districts, and it has been claimed that Hausa farmers prefer annual cultivation to bush fallowing.[3]

The impact of a growing density of population on the pattern of land use becomes apparent when population rises to the point where there is no longer sufficient land to permit effective bush fallowing, and this zone disappears as neighboring villages enlarge their annually cultivated or short-fallowed land. It has been suggested that this may be expected to occur when the density reaches 150–220 persons per square mile.[4]

Over extensive areas of Hausaland this density has been reached and only residual islands of woodland remain, usually on land of marginal agricultural value. A second stage may be reached when grass fallowing disappears. This may have taken place in central parts of the Kano close-settled zone within the last 60 years, for early colonial reports speak of one-third of the land under fallow, whereas today the proportion is so small in any one year that it appears likely to be due to accidents, such as sickness, rather than to systematic fallowing.

After the disappearance of a reserve of uncultivated land further intensification must take the form of increased inputs of manure or fertilizers, labor, or other changes. If these fail to take place, serious deterioration of the land may ensue, especially in drier areas, and its capacity to support population may be

---

[1] R. M. Prothero, "Land Use at Soba, Zaria Province, Northern Nigeria," *Economic Geography*, XXXIII (1957), 72–86.

[2] Perhaps a more significant distinction is between short and long fallowed land, since even upland cultivated annually lies fallow for a few months each year.

[3] P. Hill, *Studies in Rural Capitalism in West Africa* (Cambridge: Cambridge University Press, 1970), pp. 146–59.

[4] A. T. Grove, "Population Densities and Agriculture in Northern Nigeria," in K. M. Barbour and R. M. Prothero, eds., *Essays on African Population* (London: Routledge and Kegan Paul, 1961), pp. 115–36.

permanently impaired. In Sokoto, for example, it has been suggested that there is a critical density of 200–250 persons per square mile beyond which intensification must take place if this is to be avoided.[5] This approaches closely the concept of the critical density of population formulated by Allan.[6] It also appears that a critical situation may develop in the event of the resources of manure falling below the level necessary for the maintenance of soil fertility of all the land under annual cultivation belonging to a community. The existence of such a situation presents obvious difficulties. Northern Sokoto may perhaps be considered an example, with persistently low and declining yields and low manure inputs. By contrast the Kano close-settled zone, despite its high densities, shows no sign of having reached a similar situation.

## LAND TENURE

Land tenure in Hausaland has a double ancestry: in traditional African concepts of communal ownership and in Islamic land law which recognizes individual tenure. The basis of the present system was communal, whereby it was recognized that members residing within the village community had the right to use as much of the communal land as they required, but in no sense could the land be alienated from the community. Little is known of legal conditions under the Hausa rulers, but after the Fulani conquered Hausaland during the nineteenth century they arrogated to themselves ownership of land. However, the customary rights of the individual farmer to occupy and use a portion of the land of his community survived. Rights to land were held by the family, while the village head maintained the traditional community control of land. Land was allocated by him to immigrants settling in the community and to resident families who required additional land. Land only reverted to the community in the event of migration, land left fallow beyond a recognized number

[5] R. M. Prothero, "Some Observations on Desiccation in Northwest Nigeria," *Erdkunde*, XVI (1962), 111–19.
[6] W. Allan, *The African Husbandman* (London: Oliver and Boyd, 1965).

of years, and the death of an heirless cultivator. Normally at death, land was transferred to the heirs of the cultivator. Where there was high population density, the impossibility of rotating land in agriculture has encouraged the trend toward individualization of land tenure, and this is expressed in a considerable degree of permanency in the pattern of land holdings. In the annually cultivated zone, fields often are edged with thatching grass, henna bushes, and other useful plants. Where little unused land remains, the traditional role of the village head has been reduced to witnessing inheritance and transfer, which no longer require his sanction.

A second important result of land shortage is the increasing frequency of alienation by sale, and temporary transfers of cultivation rights by loan. Table 15.1 illustrates this contrast in tenure patterns between two villages near Zaria where land is still relatively easily available, and three villages in central Sokoto where all the land suitable for agriculture is cultivated each year. Within the Sokoto villages sale prices vary largely in

TABLE 15.1
Land tenure types in areas of low and high population densities

|  | Two Zaria Villages [a] (1967) | Three Sokoto Villages (1968) |
|---|---|---|
| Approximate population density per square mile | 250 | 500 |
| Proportion of land acquired by: |  |  |
| Purchase | 3.7 | 22.1 |
| Loan | 5.7 | 10.4 |
| Other[b] | 90.6 | 67.5 |
| Total | 100.0 | 100.0 |

SOURCES: D. W. Norman, "An Economic Study of Three Villages in Zaria Province: 1. Land and Labor Relationships," *Samaru Miscellaneous Paper No. 19*, Institute for Agricultural Research, Ahmadu Bello University (Samaru, 1967); A. D. Goddard, J. C. Fine, and D. W. Norman, "A Socio-economic Study of Three Villages in the Sokoto Close-Settled Zone: 1. Land and People in a High Density Rural Setting," *Samaru Miscellaneous Paper No. 34*, Institute for Agricultural Research, Ahmadu Bello University (Samaru, 1971).
a Village C (in section on northern Zaria) was omitted from the comparison for two reasons: The village has a population density of 700 per square mile in an area of generally low densities; and the tenure pattern in the village has been influenced by the close proximity to Zaria town, and some of the land is owned either by the township or by Zaria landowners.
b Other forms of tenure include inheritance, gift from a relative, allocation by the village head, or land held in trust for absent relatives.

accordance with economic factors, particularly type of land (upland or *fadama*), size of field,[7] quality, and location. It is etiquette to offer land for sale first to close relatives, but there is no restriction on who may buy the land if the relatives refuse. The increase in loaned land has not usually led to a marked increase in rents, which still tend to be customary. It is suggested in the section, "Agriculture: Northern Zaria," that the increase in such temporary transfers of land may be due to social pressures operating against the practice of fallowing by large landowners in densely populated areas. However, the appearance of share cropping in the more densely populated parts of Sokoto[8] and Kano[9] may indicate the first stage of a move toward commercial rents.

The trend toward land becoming a transferable economic commodity is not new. As early as 1860 the Sultan of Sokoto unsuccessfully sought to prohibit the sale of land.[10] The same trend probably occurred earlier in Kano, where Lugard recognized its development as inevitable in 1903.[11] Sale within the community has since become generally accepted in the densely populated areas around Kano, Katsina, and Sokoto, but the practice of sale outside the village, or sale by emigrants leaving the community is still not universally recognized in these areas. However, where official sanction is lacking such transactions may be disguised as less permanent transfers.[12] In Kano it is reported

that land values have increased from little more than £1 an acre 20 years ago to £10–£20 an acre at present, giving many family holdings a value of £100–£200.[13]

The growth of a demand for land under the stimulus of high and increasing population densities, the formalization of landholdings, and the growth of commercial transactions in land have helped to bring land tenure closer to the English concept of freehold than is usual in Africa, particularly in Kano, Katsina, and Sokoto. Although the farmers' legal right to land is usufructuary, it is clear that in custom the farmer has effective security of tenure both for himself and his heirs, giving him the necessary incentive to make long-term improvements. On the other hand, the lack of a clear legal title means that land, the farmers' most important asset, cannot be used as equity for raising credit. Furthermore, on the death of a farmer, Islamic law provides for the division of the holding between the heirs,[14] or for its sale intact and the subdivision of the proceeds. Divisible inheritance encourages both the subdivision of holdings and fragmentation.

Counteracting the trend of subdivision and fragmentation through inheritance is a process of expanding and consolidating farms particularly by purchase in the densely populated areas. Thus a farmer with capital may both expand and consolidate his holding. Supporting statistical evidence for this trend has been derived from Sokoto.[15] Unfortunately in Sokoto there were no time series data from

[12] H. A. Luning, *An Agro-Economic Survey in Katsina Province* (Kaduna: Government Printer, 1961).

[7] Regression analysis between the price and the size of field for a sample of sales involving upland in the past five years in the Sokoto survey villages gave correlation coefficients ranging between 0.57 and 0.62, all significantly different from zero at 5 percent (see footnote 8). There were too few observations in Zaria to attempt such an analysis.

[8] A. D. Goddard, J. C. Fine, and D. W. Norman, "A Socio-economic Study of Three Villages in the Sokoto Close-Settled Zone: 1, Land and People in a High Density Rural Setting," *Samaru Miscellaneous Paper*, *No. 34*, Institute for Agricultural Research, Ahmadu Bello University (Samaru, 1971).

[9] C. W. Rowling, *Report on Land Tenure, Kano Province* (Kaduna: Government Printer, 1952).

[10] E. J. Amett, *Gazetteer of Sokoto Province* (London: Waterlow, 1920).

[11] Rowling, *Report on Land Tenure*.

[13] M. J. Mortimore and J. Wilson, *Land and People in the Kano Close-Settled Zone*, Occasional Paper No. 1, Department of Geography, Ahmadu Bello University (Zaria, 1965).

[14] Unless joint occupancy is agreed. However, it is noted elsewhere that such arrangements tend to be of short duration.

[15] Regression analysis gave rise to two conclusions. First, that there was no significant relationship between the size of present holding and the proportion of that holding received through inheritance or gift, or held in trust. This implies that the size of holding inherited by a farmer does not necessarily determine his scale of future operations. Second, that the extent of fragmentation does increase initially with an increase in size of holding, but that larger farmers are in a position to reduce the fragmentation of their farms. See Goddard, Fine and Norman, "A Socio-economic Study of Three Villages."

which to assess the relative speed at which these two counteracting forces have been operating. In certain parts of Kano, however, taxation was based on land holdings until 1956, and it is possible to compare the present pattern of tenure with the surveys of land holdings which were made for this purpose.

In one central village between 1932 (the date of the Revenue Survey) and 1964 the number of separately occupied plots in an area of 448 acres increased by 42 percent to 185. The number of landholders also increased from 95 to about 115. During the same period the cultivated area was increased by the clearance of 26 acres of bush, mostly marginal land situated in depressions and low in productivity. Of all the plots registered in 1932, 41 percent had been subdivided by 1964, while only 16 percent had been consolidated with adjacent holdings. Thus subdivision gained at the expense of consolidation. Fragmentation is also increasing. The average plot decreased in size by 22 percent between 1932 and 1964, whereas the average holding decreased by less than 11 percent.[16]

## DOMESTIC ORGANIZATION

It is generally recognized that the basic unit of production in the Hausa rural economy is domestic, but surprisingly little work has been done on the organization of this unit since it was described by Greenberg[17] for the pagan Hausa, and by Smith for Moslems.[18] More recent studies in Zaria,[19] Katsina,[20] and

[16] M. J. Mortimore, "Land and Population Pressure in the Kano Close-Settled Zone, Northern Nigeria," *The Advancement of Science*, XXIII (1967), 677–86.
[17] J. H. Greenberg, "The Influence of Islam on a Sudanese Religion," *Monographs of the American Ethnological Society*, X (1946), 1–17.
[18] M. G. Smith, "The Economy of Hausa Communities of Zaria," *Colonial Research Studies*, no. 16 (London: Colonial Office, 1955).
[19] B. J. Buntjer, "The Changing Structure of *Gandu*," in M. J. Mortimore, ed., *Zaria and Its Region*, Occasional Paper No. 4, Department of Geography, Ahmadu Bello University (Zaria, 1970).
[20] P. Hill, "The Myth of the Amorphous Peasantry: A Northern Nigeria Case Study," *Nigerian Journal of Economic and Social Studies*, X, 2 (1968), 239–60.

central Sokoto[21] provide indications that the static picture of the structure of family organization presented by the earlier writers is changing. Although large family groups appear traditionally to have been accorded high prestige throughout Hausaland, there is evidence to suggest that the incidence, size, and functions of the institution have declined under the impact of a monetary economy. This process has been accelerated in densely populated rural areas where the relative significance of farming in the domestic economy has diminished.

In rural areas the significant economic group is the "farming unit" defined as those men who work together on a farm under a common leadership, together with their dependents.[22] Two basic types of institutions may be recognized—simple and complex. Simple farming units are most numerous, and normally comprise a simple family and other unmarried dependents. Complex units (*gandu*, pl. *gandaye*) contain two or more male adults, usually married. There is a cyclical relationship between the two types, for a simple unit becomes a *gandu* when the eldest son marries if he continues working with his father. After the death of the father, married brothers may continue in *gandu* under the leadership of the eldest, but it is common for such units to dissolve once each brother has a family.

Although the number of case studies is very limited, some of the results from central Sokoto may be used to suggest the effects of increasing population densities compared with those from Zaria and Katsina, where land is not yet in short supply (Table 15.2). Even in the latter areas where the *gandu* is accorded high prestige, composite units comprise only about 30 percent of all farming units, containing 47–54 percent of all married men. The most common link is between a father and his married son or sons, and complex units involving brothers alone only

[21] A. D. Goddard, "Are Hausa-Fulani Family Structures Breaking Up?" *Samaru Agricultural Newsletter*, XI, 3 (Samaru, June 1969), 34–48.
[22] It should be emphasized that this production unit does not necessarily correspond to a consumption unit, for example, in the Sokoto area. *Ibid.*

TABLE 15.2

The incidence of *gandaye* in rural villages studied in Zaria, Katsina, and central Sokoto

| | Zaria (1967) | Katsina (1967) | Sokoto (1968) |
|---|---|---|---|
| *Gandaye* as a percentage of all farming units | 23.9 | 29.4 | 19.0 |
| Percentage of married men in *gandu* | 53.7 | 46.5 | 34.8 |

SOURCES: B. J. Buntjer, "The Changing Structure of *gandu*," in M. J. Mortimore, ed., *Zaria and Its Region*, Occasional Paper No. 4, Department of Geography, Ahmadu Bello University (Zaria, 1970); P. Hill, "The Myth of the Amorphous Peasantry: A Northern Nigerian Case Study," *Nigerian Journal of Economic and Social Studies*, X, 2 (1968), 239–60; A. D. Goddard, "Are Hausa-Fulani Family Structures Breaking Up?" *Samaru Agricultural Newsletter*, XI, 3 (Zaria, June 1969), 34–48.

account for about one-quarter of all *gandaye*. However, it is reported that both in Zaria and Sokoto there has been a decrease, compared with the past, in both the incidence and the size of *gandaye*, which had previously embraced a wider range of kin.[23]

This process has clearly progressed further in Sokoto than in Zaria or Katsina. Not only are there fewer *gandaye* in Sokoto (Table 15.2), but the functioning of many of the complex farming units differs markedly from institutions described in Zaria and Katsina. In the latter areas the *gandu* head, in return for the labor of subordinate men on the common farm, normally provides the seed and tools used by the unit, pays for expenses of the tax, marriage, and childbirth of its members, and provides dwelling places. He also supplies food and provides male members with personal plots of land over which they have complete control. However, it was found in Sokoto that only 15 percent of the *gandaye* conformed to this description. In 66 percent of cases, subordinate males were expected to provide their own tax money, either from the produce of their own fields or from off-farm occupations. In more than half of these cases the *gandu* head was regarded only as the leader of a cooperative farming group which

[23] Buntjer, "The Changing Structure of *Gandu*."

had no communal field, the title to all the land having already been distributed to the members. In such cases the *gandu* head has only powers of persuasion to enforce his decisions and subordinate members may split off at any time. The remaining one-fifth had one or more members either too old to work or infirm. In such cases, although authority may still be invested in them, the aged and infirm may be regarded as dependents in the sense that they receive their food and sometimes other needs from the active members of the *gandu*. Clearly these units perform a welfare function.

Therefore, not only is the incidence of complex units in central Sokoto smaller than is found in the studies conducted in the less densely populated parts of Hausaland, but where *gandaye* are found many of the powers of *gandu* heads have normally been delegated to subordinate members. It is an accepted practice in central Sokoto for a father to provide a married son with a field at the time of his marriage, or more commonly after the birth of the first child, and for the son at this time to separate from his father's farming unit.

The critical factor accounting for the greater disintegration of the complex farming unit in central Sokoto compared with Zaria and Katsina appears to be the large and increasing rural population and its attendant land shortage in that area. One of the common strategies of farming units short of land is to place greater reliance upon off-farm activities as a source of income (see the next three sections of this chapter). Such occupations as crafts, trading, and services have traditionally been organized outside the farming unit, with earnings accruing to the individual. Therefore, for the *gandu* head to meet both the food requirements and the social obligations of a large family it is necessary to derive a substantial income from the communal activities of *gandu* members on the common farm. The increase in the importance of off-farm activities, noted in areas with land shortages, weakens the central authority of the *gandu* by substituting earnings by individuals for communal earnings under his direction, and at the same time diminishes the benefits accruing to subordinate members of the *gandu*. Thus it is to be expected that the decrease in the relative importance of farming within the family budget which accompanies population increase is likely to be correlated with a weakening of the *gandu* structure.

## AGRICULTURE: NORTHERN ZARIA

The quantitative data presented in this section resulted from a survey, undertaken from April 1966–March 1967, of 106 farming families in three villages in northern Zaria.[24] In analyzing the results it was sometimes difficult to differentiate between those differences due to location and those due to population density because of the increase in density in the three villages (A, B, and C in Table 15.3) with ease of access to Zaria. However, this may not be an unusual problem since density around urban areas often tends to be related to accessibility.

As population density increases land becomes more limiting in relation to labor. Table 15.3 implies that the main influence of an increase in population density is a decrease in the average size and relative variation in the size of holding. It is possible to derive tentative explanations as to why this relationship exists. The increase in population logically accounts for the decrease in the size of holding. At the same time there is increasing pressure on those families with land under fallow to transfer temporarily the usufructuary rights to other families with land shortages. In other words the opportunity cost of leaving land fallow becomes too great. This may partly account for the decrease in the relative variation in size of holding as population density increases. Evidence in support of such an explanation is the decrease in the amount of fallow and an increase in land transfers by loan and sale. However, there could well be other explanations. For example, one could

argue that there may be social pressures exerted on those farmers who could normally have fallow land thereby forcing them to relinquish their rights temporarily to families suffering from land shortage. In such cases an alternative strategy would be for farmers to cultivate land which would otherwise be fallow, with the help of hired labor. However, it is probable that in areas accessible to urban centers, for example, in the modern sector, the returns for labor would be higher in off-farm employment, which would effectively limit the supply of labor available for farm work.

In terms of capital investment the only clear trend is an increase in the numbers of small livestock, such as goats, sheep, guinea fowl and chickens, with higher population densities. Under indigenous conditions such livestock are partly scavengers and are largely independent of the size of holding. Such livestock are often kept for substantial periods inside the compound and provide a source of manure for the annually cultivated fields. Because all farm work is undertaken with hand tools there is little difference in the value of investment in tools and equipment.

In northern Nigeria agricultural activity is highly seasonal in nature. In the survey area the main agricultural activity starts at the beginning of the rains in April with the planting of millet and sorghum followed by groundnuts; it rises to a peak in June and July when weeding is the main activity; and it tapers off after the end of the rains in October, with the harvest of sorghum, groundnuts, cowpeas, and cotton in November and December. These crops are confined largely to the upland fields. There also are limited amounts of *fadama* which primarily support sugarcane, a labor-intensive crop. However, the amount of land that can be handled during the peak labor demand period determines the level of agricultural activity during the rest of the year. With increases in population density, land availability rather than labor eventually becomes more limiting in determining the level of agricultural activity. Since a landless laboring class does not exist in the rural areas, the bulk of the labor is provided from family

[24] D. W. Norman, "An Economic Study of Three Villages in Zaria Province: 1. Land and Labor Relationships, 2. Input-Output Relationships, 3. Maps," *Samaru Miscellaneous Papers Nos. 19, 33, and 23,* Institute for Agricultural Research, Ahmadu Bello University (Samaru, 1967, 1971, 1967).

TABLE 15.3

Some comparisons between three northern Zaria villages April 1966–March 1967

| Variable Specification[a] | | Village A | Village B | Village C |
|---|---|---|---|---|
| Population per square mile[b] | | 81 | 396 | 709 |
| Land farmed per resident (acres) | | 1.9 | 1.3 | 0.6 |
| *Resource availability* | | | | |
| Land holding[c]: | Average size (acres) | 11.9 | 9.8 | 5.5 |
| | Coefficient of variation | 88.4 | 78.9 | 70.2 |
| | Percent of average holding: | | | |
| | upland | 91.6 | 87.8 | 87.3 |
| | *fadama* | 8.4 | 12.2 | 12.7 |
| Labor: | Average number of male adults per family[d] | 1.7 | 2.0 | 2.9 |
| Durable capital: | Average value of livestock (shillings) | 113.6 | 167.2 | 188.5 |
| | Average value of farm tools, grain stores & equipment (shillings) | 45.6 | 56.8 | 30.4 |
| *Resource utilization* | | | | |
| Land: | Percent fallow of average holding: | | | |
| | total | 21.2 | 26.8 | 2.6 |
| | upland | 19.2 | 28.9 | 2.8 |
| | *fadama* | 42.1 | 12.4 | 1.0 |
| | Intercropping index[e] | 2.4 | 2.5 | 2.7 |
| | Percent of acres devoted to crop mixtures | 76.3 | 70.7 | 83.9 |
| Labor: | Work on average farm | | | |
| | Total man hours[f] | 1,516.3 | 1,634.2 | 2,109.4 |
| | Percent contributed by: | | | |
| | family—male adults | 62.9 | 82.7 | 76.5 |
| | female adults | 0.1 | 0.3 | 0.7 |
| | grown children | 8.3 | 10.9 | 9.9 |
| | nonfamily | 28.7 | 6.1 | 12.9 |
| Inputs per cultivated acre: | | | | |
| | Fertilizer—organic (tons)[g] | 0.4 | 0.5 | 1.5 |
| | inorganic (shillings) | 0.1 | 0.1 | 0.1 |
| | Manhours upland[h] | 149.8 | 193.3 | 349.8 |
| | *fadama*[h] | 458.2 | 462.5 | 745.8 |
| *Income* | | | | |
| | Net income per acre (shillings) | 131.3 | 169.1 | 277.5 |
| | Disposable income per resident (shillings) | 290.6 | 227.5 | 214.9 |

[a] Where relevant these are expressed in terms of an average farm.
[b] The figures on population density were calculated from sources of secondary data and may not be accurate (see footnote 24). Nevertheless they do reflect the relative population densities between each village.
[c] A holding is defined as the sum of the acreages of all the fields over which the family had usufructuary rights during the survey year.
[d] A family is defined as "those people eating from one pot." In contrast to central Sokoto the units of consumption and work in northern Zaria are generally identical. The plot definition includes both simple and complex farming units defined above (see "Domestic Organization" section).
[e] The higher the value of the index the greater is the emphasis on intercropping or planting crops in mixtures. The index which can vary between one and six in value is defined elsewhere (see footnote 24).
[f] The work undertaken by family members was converted to man-hour terms as follows: one hour of work by a male adult (more than 14 years old) equals 1.0 man hour, by a female adult (more than 14 years old) equals 0.67 man hour, and by a child (7–1 years old) equals 0.5 man hour.
[g] Includes estimate of manure produced by corralled cattle.
[h] Fields that were partly upland and partly *fadama* were not included.

sources, primarily male adults. Islamic tradition discourages women from participating in heavy farm work. Nevertheless the significance of hired labor is greater in areas of low population density where labor is more limiting.[25]

In any area the relationship between land and labor is of importance in determining the intensity of farming. In the three villages the effects may be seen in the following: the amount of land left fallow; man-hour inputs and net farm income per acre; and the priority given to cultivating labor intensive *fadama* rather than upland (Table 15.3).[26] Explicit attempts are made to maintain the fertility of annually cultivated land through the application of household refuse, manure from small livestock, and through corralling of cattle often owned by nomadic Fulani. Table 15.3 shows that the application of manure is markedly greater in the village with the highest population density. Greater reliance will, however, have to be placed on the use of inorganic fertilizer in view of limitations in the supply of manure as population density and the area of permanent cultivation increase. As yet there is little evidence of the widespread use of inorganic fertilizer. Farmers are not convinced of the value of inorganic fertilizer and often do not have ready cash to buy it before the farming season begins: to them fertilizer is costly and not always readily available at the right place and at the right time. Factors such as these hamper the use of fertilizer at the present time.

Differences in population density appear to have little influence on the variety of crops grown. The basic strategy of farmers in the survey villages appears to be to grow enough food (primarily millet, sorghum, and cow-peas) for the family with cash crops (mainly groundnuts, sugarcane, and cotton) being essentially of secondary importance. The practice of growing these crops in mixtures, which under indigenous conditions is consistent with the goals of both profit maximization and security,[27] is also seemingly independent of population density. However, it should be noted that on the upland of larger family farms sole crops of sorghum and cotton are more common. Such sole crops and cotton-based mixtures require low labor inputs and give low returns per acre relative to most crop mixtures. Sorghum, cotton, and cotton-based mixtures are dropped in favor of crop mixtures giving a higher return per acre as land becomes more limited relative to labor. Nevertheless even on the bigger farms, a large percentage of the land is devoted to crop mixtures.

The bulk of the work on the family farm continues to be supplied by family members who are male adults, irrespective of population density. However, the extent to which a man works on the family farm is determined by a number of factors. The results (Table 15.4) imply that, other things being equal, a man will work less on the family farm if there is more than one man in the family, if fewer acres are cultivated, or if more hired labor is used. Consequently with increases in population density men have a progressively greater need to find alternative sources of income other than from the family farm. Indeed, the emphasis on off-farm activities is likely to change from the part-time dry-season commitment prevalent at the present time, to an increasing concentration on such activities throughout the year.

The quantity and type of off-farm activities are, among other things, influenced by location and population density (Table 15.4). In areas of high population density, implying nearness of urban areas, increased employment opportunities exist in the modern sector.

---

[25] The figure in Table 14.3 for Village B is low because of the efforts of the village head to extract tax from laborers originating from outside the village, who therefore found work elsewhere.

[26] A complication is introduced in the form of location. For example, the nearness of Village B to a main road has encouraged the cultivation of sugarcane which is expensive to transport. Indeed such cultivation is undertaken at the expense of off-farm activities. The cultivation of *fadama*, an all-year-round occupation, is being pursued at the expense of cultivating upland.

[27] D. W. Norman, "Intercropping" (Paper read at Seminar on Traditional African Agricultural Systems and Their Improvement, organized by the Ford Foundation, IITA, and IRAT at Ibadan, November 1970).

TABLE 15.4
Work per male adult in three northern Zaria villages, April 1966–March 1967

(a) Determinants of the Amount of Work Undertaken per Male Adult on the Family Farm[a]

| Variable | | Partial Regression Coefficient | Standard Error | t-Value |
|---|---|---|---|---|
| Dependent | Independent | | | |
| Number of days worked per male adult on the family farm | Constant | 181.51 | | |
| | Number of male adults in family | −23.70 | 5.13 | −4.61[b] |
| | Number of cultivated acres | 4.57 | 1.32 | 3.46[b] |
| | Number of man-hours nonfamily labor hired | −0.05 | 0.01 | −3.86[b] |
| | $R = 0.47$[b] | | | |
| | $Sy_x = 59.90$ | | | |

(b) Composition of Work per Male Adult

| | | Village A | Village B | Village C |
|---|---|---|---|---|
| Days: | Total | 262.7 | 198.2 | 211.1 |
| | On family farm | 140.1 | 158.7 | 124.6 |
| | At off-farm occupations | 122.6 | 39.5 | 86.5 |
| Percentage composition of off-farm work: | | | | |
| Traditional | manufacturing | 21.2 | 29.3 | 11.2 |
| | services | 40.1 | 27.2 | 20.9 |
| | trading | 35.0 | 24.7 | 3.4 |
| Modern[d] | services | 3.7 | 18.8 | 64.5 |

[a] Multiple regression analysis was used in order to investigate the determinants.
[b] Significantly different from zero at the 5 percent level. Sample size = 106.
[c] The traditional sector consists of those jobs that are fairly independent of modern development, e.g., barber, blacksmith, trader, etc. Average wage rate of such occupations equals 2.5 shillings per day.
[d] The modern sector consists of those jobs which have arisen directly or indirectly as a result of improved communications and the development of large cities, commercial firms, and government bodies, e.g., commission agents, drivers, messengers, night watchment, etc. Average wage rate of such occupations equals 4.1 shillings per day.

Work in the traditional sector is less dependent on proximity to urban areas. In Village C, with its close proximity to Zaria, men may prefer to obtain employment in the modern sector, which is generally more remunerative, than work in the traditional sector. In Village A the relative inaccessibility precludes employment opportunities in the modern sector. This, together with the presence of a market which meets twice weekly, has encouraged activities in the traditional sector. In Village B, employment opportunities in the modern sector are also very limited. However, the accessibility to a main road has encouraged farmers to concentrate on growing the more remunerative sugarcane than to participate in off-farm activities. Such activities in the traditional sector probably do not provide such certain sources of income.[28]

In terms of income Table 15.3 indicates that as population density increases net farm income has been maintained by increasing the inputs per acre which have produced a greater output per acre. Disposable income per resident, which takes into account income from both farm and off-farm activities, is, however, negatively correlated with population density. This implies that the economic position of farming families, at least under existing conditions, tends to worsen with increases in population density.

[28] An alternative explanation is given elsewhere (see footnote 24).

## AGRICULTURE: THE KANO CLOSE-SETTLED ZONE

The Kano close-settled zone is the largest concentration of dense population in the area under consideration, containing some 2.4 million inhabitants in 1962 at an average density of about 500 per square mile excluding the city and township of Kano. The distribution of population follows a regular pattern, diminishing toward the periphery. A comparison of four outlying villages with a group of villages in the center of the zone allows certain provisional conclusions to be drawn on the relationship between population density and certain aspects of the agricultural economy.[29] The central villages are 4–7 miles from Kano and have densities of 790 per square mile. The four outlying villages are situated 28–45 miles from Kano and have densities ranging in 1962 from about 289–518 per square mile. Against such variations, a reduction in the intensity of agriculture could be predicted together with a diminution in the intensity of relations with the central metropolis (Table 15.5).[30]

The demand for agricultural land at the center, where the available land is of the order of 1.1 acres per head of the rural population, has led to the appropriation of all but the worst land for cultivation, and annual cultivation is practiced on approximately 85 percent of the surface, including 4.2 percent of irrigated *fadama* which is double cropped every year. This proportion falls to 45 percent in the least densely populated of the outlying villages.[31]

[29] M. J. Mortimore, "Population Densities and Rural Economies in the Kano Close-Settled Zone, Nigeria," in W. Zelinsky, L. Kosinski, and R. M. Prothero, eds., *Geography and a Crowding World: Essays on Population Pressure upon Resources* (New York: Oxford University Press, 1970), pp. 380–88.

[30] It should be stressed that the average density of the outlying villages, although significantly lower than that of the center, is still very high by northern Nigeria standards. No attempt has yet been made to test these trends at lower densities and greater distances from Kano.

[31] In the other three, however, much higher densities exist and the percentages under cultivation, although not measured, are known to approach those of the center.

TABLE 15.5

Some comparisons between central and outlying villages in the Kano close-settled zone, 1964

| | Center | Outlying Villages |
|---|---|---|
| Average distance from Kano (miles) | 5 | 37 |
| Population density per square mile (district average)[a] | 609 | 439 |
| Percent of land under cultivation | 85 | 45[b] |
| Percent of land under bush or grazing | 7.5 | 53[b] |
| Percent of holdings partly or wholly purchased | 31 | 24[c] |
| Average size of holding (acres)[d] | 3.3–3.7 | 6.5 |
| Cultivated land per adult male (acres)[e] | 2.6 | 2.9 |
| Average number of adult males per holding | 1.42 | 2.24 |
| Percent of holdings applying less than one ton of manure per acre[f] | 36 | 76 |
| Percent of holdings applying more than one ton of manure per acre[f] | 64 | 24 |
| Percentage of families growing 5 or more sacks of groundnuts in 1962[g] | 32 | 9 |
| Percentage of families deriving some income from secondary occupations | 100 | 48 |

[a] Densities for the district as a whole are given because those for individual villages are only known for the center.
[b] One village only.
[c] The percentages for the four villages are 11, 21, 26, and 39.
[d] For the center a range must be given because of some uncertainty about the exact number of landholders. The value given for the outlying villages must be treated with great caution because of the small size of the sample.
[e] Adult males are taxpayers of 16 years or older, not necessarily married.
[f] These are estimates since there is no way of measuring manure inputs accurately.
[g] The term "family" is used here to mean farming unit as defined in the section on "Domestic organization."

It has been suggested (see section on "Land Tenure") that in the area closest to Kano the increasing frequency of sale of agricultural land is an indicator of its shortage. This conclusion is supported by Table 15.5. The average size of holding appear to be greater in the outlying villages, there is more cultivated land per adult male, and families are larger, i.e., the number of adult males per family holding is greater.[32] At the center, fragmentation and subdivision are increasing as the population grows. No comparable study has been made in the outlying villages.

There is evidence of a greater intensity of agricultural inputs at the center. Manure inputs, which reach an average of 1.5 tons per acre at the center, are noticeably smaller in the outlying villages. In these, an organized trade in this commodity, which is a conspicuous feature of relations between Kano city and its rural environs, is lacking.

Both the agricultural and the nonagricultural sectors are more commercialized at the center. Despite a smaller average size of holding and family, the production of groundnuts is greater.[33] Dry-season irrigated agriculture is more developed, although figures are not available to support this observation. Every family at the center derives some income from secondary sources, although these incomes vary from a few shillings to over £30 per annum, whereas only 48 percent do so in the outlying villages. Rural manufactures from the central villages, especially handwoven cotton cloth, and firewood from farm trees find an outlet in the city markets but this relationship disappears at greater distances from Kano.

Government policy toward agricultural land use in Kano State is a logical development from the situation described above. Its primary objective is to bring into perennial production a very extensive area within the close-settled zone, by means of irrigation from dams on the Kano River and its tributaries. A pilot scheme is already in operation and, if this succeeds, it may be possible, by extending the growing season throughout the year, to double production and develop commercial farming beyond the constraints previously imposed by the prior needs of subsistence. Such intensification appears to be the only

way to economic growth in the agricultural sector, since the reserves of usable uncultivated land are smaller than in any other of the northern states.

## MIGRATION: CENTRAL SOKOTO

Despite the lack of adequate and reliable statistics it is clear that the population densities in rural areas such as the Kano close-settled zone and central Sokoto continue to increase. Industrialization and urbanization are insufficient to absorb more than a small proportion of this additional labor force, the majority of which is employed in the rural economy. In these areas land shortages mean that a growing proportion of the population are living on farms too small to provide their food and cash requirements at present levels of production. Despite this apparently Malthusian situation, the small farmer has some other choices open to him other than the abandonment of his holding and a move to an area where land is more plentiful.

Off-farm activities traditionally play an important role in the economy of rural Hausaland. This partly, at least, adjusted to a climatic regime that effectively limits the farming season to between seven and ten months of the year, and to a marked peak labor demand in June or July, which determines the extent of the farming operation for the remainder of the season (see section on "Agriculture: Northern Zaria"). Most farmers therefore engage in one or more additional off-farm activities. For them, the farm is viewed as one part of an integral household economy, and farmers inheriting small farms inadequate for their needs normally find it easier to devote relatively more time to off-farm activities, rather than face the upheaval and uncertainty of starting life afresh elsewhere.

Accessibility to large and growing urban markets is advantageous to the practice of rural crafts.[34] Thus, for example, villages near

[32] Although the number of holdings which were measured in the outlying villages was very small (17 compared with over 100 in the central area), these results are suggestive.

[33] This conclusion is seemingly inconsistent with the results from Zaria. However, groundnuts have a greater comparative advantage in Kano where the range of available crops is more limited.

[34] Work in the modern sector only becomes a feasible alternative in areas very close to an urban center, for example, Village C (see "Agriculture: Northern Zaria").

Kano are able to sell in the city woven cloth and firewood cut from trees (see previous section). Elsewhere, however, access to local urban markets is more limited and the ability of such areas to absorb the products of rural craftsmen also is limited. Many farmers in the central Sokoto area find themselves in this position. The high population densities in this area are essentially of recent origin, resulting from the establishment of the Fulani Empire centered on Sokoto at the beginning of the nineteenth century.[35] The conquest of Sokoto and its integration into Nigeria at the beginning of the present century produced a dramatic change in fortune for the area. From being the capital of an extensive empire receiving tribute from vassal states in the form of both wealth and slaves, Sokoto became a relatively remote and inaccessible province bypassed by the railway to the south. Cash crop farming, particularly of groundnuts and cotton, never developed in this densely populated zone which was only marginally suited climatically and edaphically to the new crops.[36] Faced with limited local opportunities for off-farm activities, a large proportion of the men of working age have left their home villages during the long dry season to find work in more favorable localities. The development of this practice of seasonal movements is obscure. The Resident of Sokoto Province noted in 1936 that the customs and practices of seasonal migration "have existed since time immemorial."[37] However, from an analysis of government records in the colonial period, it has been argued that "the general lack of reference is indicative of the fact that seasonal migration, though not unknown, was at an incomparably smaller scale in the early decades of the century."[38] Such an argument is more consistent with the notion presented above of a

densely populated prosperous area having to adjust itself to drastically altered circumstances.

The only widespread and systematic census of labor migrations in the northern states of Nigeria was attempted for Sokoto Province in the dry season of 1952–1953. By this time it was estimated that between 25 and 33 percent of the male working population[39] of the whole province were involved, rising to more than 50 percent of those from the districts containing the highest population densities in central Sokoto. During this period, 60 percent of migrants were traveling to destinations outside the northern states, western Nigeria and Ghana together being the most popular destinations.[40]

A recent survey of migrant laborers conducted during the dry season of 1967–1968 in three villages located in the central Sokoto area illustrates some of the present characteristics of this movement. The villages were chosen to represent each of three locational types of economic importance in this area: One was 11 miles from Sokoto on a main road and therefore had reasonable access to the city market, a second was located on one of the major river valleys, and the third was relatively remote from either the city or the major valleys. Population densities in these villages ranged from 250 to more than 500 per square mile. In these villages only 56 percent of farmers regarded farming as their primary occupation, and 88 percent had two or more occupations.

Labor migration was found to be almost entirely practiced by men. The highest proportion of labor migrants is found in the most active age groups, with a definite peak between the ages of 20 and 29, falling markedly beyond the age of 40. Expressed as a proportion of men of working age a marked contrast was found between the villages in the number of labor migrants (Table 15.6). The incidence increased from 12 percent in the riverine village to 41 percent in the accessible

[35] M. Last, *The Sokoto Caliphate* (London: Longmans, 1968).
[36] Food and Agriculture Organization of the United Nations, *Soil and Water Resources Survey of the Sokoto Valley, Nigeria*, I-VI, FAO and UNDP (Rome, 1969).
[37] R. M. Prothero, *Migrant Labor from Sokoto Province Northern Nigeria*, 18 (Kaduna: Government Printer, 1959).
[38] *Ibid.*

[39] Between the ages of 15 and 49.
[40] Department of Statistics, "Report on a Labor Migration, Sokoto Province," mimeographed (Lagos, 1954).

TABLE 15.6
Characteristics of labor migration in three central Sokoto villages, April 1967–March 1968

| | Riverine Village | Accessible Village | Remote Village |
|---|---|---|---|
| Percentage of all away between the ages of 15 and 49 | 11.6 | 40.8 | 65.9 |
| Percentage of migrants aged between 20 and 39 | 72.2 | 61.3 | 61.7 |
| Average length of trip (months) | 2.3 | 3.2 | 4.1 |

village and 66 percent in the remote village. Such a distribution is consistent with a decrease in local employment opportunities in the dry season. *Fadama* comprises 40 percent of the average farm holding in the riverine village compared with less than 3 percent in the other villages, while the river provides good fishing grounds for five months of the dry season. Weaving for the Sokoto market is an important occupation in the accessible village, where the road station also provides opportunities for trading. On the other hand, in every respect the remote village is poorly endowed. The most common period spent away from the village was between the harvest of millet and the first planting rains. Only 11 percent were absent for more than six months, half of these not returning within a year.

In the Zaria area (see "Agriculture: Northern Zaria") increasing rural population density was accompanied by an increased reliance upon off-farm sources of income, but this also led to smaller disposable incomes per resident. This relationship is marked in central Sokoto where standards of living are low compared with other parts of rural Hausaland. Neither local off-farm activities nor labor migration are adequate substitutes for a substantial farm income in maintaining or raising living standards for the majority of

the rural population. Faced with this comparatively bleak economic situation, a section of the population emigrates. No adequate official statistics are available even for net migration movements, but some idea of their importance may be judged from the fact that in the three central Sokoto villages 19 percent of married sons had left their father's *gandu* and emigrated.[41] It is difficult to determine the relative importance of rural-rural and rural-urban migration in the absence of comparative studies, but the process of short distance movements of farmers from areas of relatively high to low population densities has been noted both in Sokoto[42] and Katsina,[43] and in the expanding agricultural area of Gombe the same process has been noted involving migration over longer distances.[44]

CONCLUSION

From the examples outlined above, it appears that farming families in rural Hausaland have three possible strategies available to them, when population rises beyond the point where income levels can be maintained or improved simply by increasing the cultivated area. In such densely populated districts, they may farm the land more intensively, they may seek income from off-farm sources, or they may migrate permanently elsewhere.

Intensification of agriculture has proceeded a long way, notably in Kano, making use of traditional methods. However, it appears doubtful whether such a gradual process of intensification can cope with the accelerating rates of natural increase which result from

[41] The distribution of this permanent movement conformed closely to the relative incidence of labor migrations, rising from 14 percent of married sons in the riverine village, to 19 percent in the accessible village and 24 percent in the remote village.
[42] Prothero, *Migrant Labor.*
[43] A. T. Grove, *Land and Population in Katsina Province* (Kaduna: Government Printer, 1957).
[44] M. Tiffen, "Changing Patterns of Farming in *Gombe* Emirate, North Eastern State, Nigeria," *Samaru Miscellaneous Paper No. 32*, Institute for Agricultural Research, Ahmadu Bello University (Samaru, 1971).

improved health services, and can provide an improvement in income levels commensurate with today's rising expectations. In the long run, if the agricultural sector is to continue to feed the burgeoning nonagricultural sector and to produce crops for export, governmental programs must concentrate on increasing the productivity of the land through the use of improved inputs, such as inorganic fertilizers, insecticides, and improved seeds. A special responsibility for bringing this about rests on the agricultural extension services.

Income may be augmented from off-farm sources in the vicinity or by means of seasonal migration to other areas. Opportunities in the vicinity may occur in the traditional or the modern sectors. Small-scale craft manufactures, services, and trade have always played a significant role in rural Hausaland, in association with a network of periodic markets and a relatively dense distribution of small urban centers. Kano provides an example of an area where such sources of income make a measurable contribution toward maintaining high population densities on the land. On the other hand, Village C in northern

Zaria provides an example of the importance which may be assumed by employment opportunities in the modern sector. The increase of rural educational facilities may provide greater opportunities. However, full-time employment in the modern sector is likely to remain confined to those living close to larger towns, or to institutions employing wage labor, and cannot yet be considered a solution to be adopted on a large scale.

If off-farm sources of income are not available on an adequate scale in the vicinity, they may be obtained by seasonal migration, either to towns or to commercial agricultural regions. This is the option which has been taken up widely in central Sokoto.

The third strategy, permanent emigration, is widespread in Hausaland. Its impact is greatest in central Sokoto, but quantitative information generally is lacking. It has contributed to the diffusion of Hausa farming populations over wide areas of northern Nigeria, but as a solution to the economic problems posed by population growth, it is only available while vacant land remains.

# PART THREE

## *Ghana*

# CHAPTER SIXTEEN

# *Fertility Trends & Differentials*

S. K. GAISIE

THE AVAILABLE demographic statistics indicate that Ghana's population is growing at a rate of about 3 percent per annum. Projections[1] prepared at the Demographic Unit, University of Ghana, show that, if the present levels of fertility remain unchanged, the rate of population growth will climb over 3.5 percent per annum during the years following 1970, and that the natural increase would reach 3.5 percent by 1980. With mortality declining and with that trend expected to continue, the future course of fertility will determine the pace of increase of Ghana's population in the coming years. A solution to the population problems probably lies more in a decline in fertility than in anything else. Consequently, an understanding of the demographic situation in Ghana requires an understanding of fertility levels, trends, and differentials and the factors responsible for them.

## FERTILITY LEVELS

Prior to March 1960 there was very little reliable fertility information. The paucity of such important information may be attributed to lack of a complete and efficient registration system for the provision of reliable data on births and deaths. In addition, the results of the censuses conducted by the colonial government were so defective and unreliable that very little use can be made of them. Thus, during the last 60 years the data on the age-sex structures of the population and the available vital statistics were so meager and defective that very little, if any, progress was made in the determination of fertility levels and trends in Ghana. In spite of the inaccuracy and incompleteness of the vital statistics, it has been possible to utilize the 1960 census and survey data to estimate both the present levels of fertility and past trends. The nature and quality of the available material have necessitated the use of various demographic techniques, some of which have been devised specifically for the derivation of

[1] S. K. Gaisie, *Dynamics of Population Growth in Ghana* (Accra-Tema: Ghana Publishing Corporation, 1969), Table 1, pp. 3, 19.

TABLE 16.1

Estimated and recorded crude birth rates for Ghana

| Year/Period | Estimated | Recorded |
|---|---|---|
| 1945–1949 | 52 | — |
| 1948 | 49 | — |
| 1950–1954 | 51 | — |
| 1955–1959 | 50 | — |
| 1959–1960 | 47–55 | 47 |
| 1963–1964 | 52–54 | — |
| 1968 | — | 47 |
| 1969 | — | 47 |

SOURCES: 1945–49—United Nations, *Demographic Yearbook, 1963* (New York, 1964); 1948—S. K. Gaisie, "Some Aspects of Fertility Studies in Ghana," in John C. Caldwell and C. Okonjo, eds., *The Population of Tropical Africa* (London: Longmans, Green & Company, and New York: Columbia University Press, 1968), p. 239; 1950–54 and 1955–59—United Nations, *Demographic Yearbook, 1963*; 1949–60—S. K. Gaisie, *Dynamics of Population Growth in Ghana* (Accra-Tema: Ghana Publishing Corporation, 1969), Table 1, pp. 3 and 19; 1963–64—John C. Caldwell, "Population Change," in W. Birmingham, I. Neustadt, and E. N. Omaboe, eds., *A Study of Contemporary Ghana*, II, *Some Aspects of Social Structure* (London: George Allen and Unwin, and Evanston: Northwestern University Press, 1967), p. 89; 1968 and 1969—From Demographic Sample Survey (1968–1969), Demographic Unit, University of Ghana, preliminary results (unpublished).

plausible estimates of fertility rates from limited data on vital events. Table 16.1 gives estimates on the approximate level of the crude birth rate during the period 1945–1969. Both the estimated and the recorded crude birth rates are over 40 per thousand, and, although all the estimates were not prepared by a uniform method, they all show that Ghana's fertility is high and that it has remained unchanged during the past quarter of a century.

In view of the limits set by the available material, the census data on children ever born by age of mother have been used to compute an index (i.e., completed family size) to gauge the fertility level in Ghana. The average number of children ever born to women by the end of the childbearing period is between six and seven (see Table 16.2).

In Table 16.3 Ghana's completed family size is compared with that of other countries. The fertility of Ghana is as high or higher than that of Latin American and Asian countries and is apparently higher than that of some other tropical African countries. It is certainly one of the highest in the world.

A more refined measure of the level of current fertility is provided by age-specific fertility rates and total fertility ratios. The current fertility data obtained from the 1960 postenumeration survey were adjusted for underreporting of births and the distorted shape of the age-specific fertility distribution also was corrected for misstatement of age and then graduated to give a more plausible and smoother shape. The total fertility ratio (6.3) yielded by the corrected age-specific fertility rates is definitely lower than the actual rate and it was therefore adjusted by Brass's method which raised the figure to 7.1.[2] Total fertility ratios ranging from between 6.5 and 7.6 have been estimated for the country (see Table 16.4).

The estimated gross reproduction rate (GRR), based on the age composition of a stable population model, for Ghana in 1960 was between 3.1 and 3.5. The application of different methods to the 1960 census age data yielded an estimated GRR of about 3.3 (estimates based on girls aged 0–4 years and

[2] *Ibid.*, Table 2, Appendix 1, p. 79.

TABLE 16.2

Children ever born per woman at specified ages

| | Ages of Women | | | | | | | |
|---|---|---|---|---|---|---|---|---|
| | 15–19 | 20–24 | 25–29 | 30–34 | 35–39 | 40–44 | 45–49 | 50+ |
| 1948 census | 0.59 | 1.59 | 2.60 | 3.70 | 4.68 | 5.36 | 6.14 | 6.56 |
| 1960 postenumeration survey | 0.46 | 1.72 | 3.06 | 4.24 | 5.08 | 5.70 | 5.85 | 6.16 |
| 1961 sample survey | 0.61 | 2.61 | 2.57 | 3.60 | 4.69 | 5.71 | 5.11 | 6.00 |
| Demographic sample survey, 1968 | 1.22 | 2.09 | 3.30 | 4.44 | 5.36 | 5.87 | 5.83 | 6.00 |

SOURCES: 1948—1948 Census Report, Table 31, p. 396; 1960 and 1961—Gaisie, *Dynamics of Population Growth in Ghana*, Table 7, p. 20; 1968—Demographic Sample Survey, 1968–1969, preliminary results.

TABLE 16.3
Mean numbers of children born to cohorts of completed childbearing by various countries

| Country | Year | Ages | Children per Woman |
|---|---|---|---|
| Ghana (census) | 1948 | 50+ | 6.6 |
| Ghana (sample) | 1961 | 50+ | 6.0 |
| Ghana P.E.S. | 1960 | 50+ | 6.2 |
| Ghana D.S.S. | 1968 | 50+ | 6.0 |
| Puerto Rico | 1946 | 45+ | 6.6 |
| Brazil | 1948 | 49–53 | 5.7 |
| | 1940 | 50+ | 6.2 |
| India | | | |
| (Travancore-Cochin) | 1951 | 50+ | 6.6 |
| (Banaras Tehsil) | 1956 | 45–49 | 6.6 |
| (Poona) | 1951 | 50+ | 6.4 |
| Guinea (Fouta Djallon) | 1955 | 50+ | 5.5 |
| West Cameroon (Bakweri) | 1958 | 50+ | 4.5 |
| Zanzibar | 1958 | 46+ | 2.9 |
| Pemba | 1958 | 46+ | 3.7 |
| Tanganyika | 1948 | 45+ | 4.4 |
| Buhaya sample | 1952 | 45+ | 3.7 |
| Uganda | 1948 | 45+ | 4.8 |
| Buganda sample | 1952 | 45+ | 3.0 |

SOURCES: Ghana census—*The Gold Coast Census of Population, 1948, Report and Tables*, Tables 30, 31, p. 396; Ghana sample—S. K. Gaisie, "An Analysis of Fertility Levels in Contemporary Ghana" (M.A. Thesis held by the University of London, 1964); Ghana P.E.S.—Gaisie, *Dynamics of Population Growth in Ghana* (P.E.S. = 1960 census postenumeration survey); Ghana D.S.S.—Demographic Sample Survey, 1968–1969, preliminary results; Puerto Rico—Lydia J. Roberts and Rosa Luisa Stefani, *Patterns of Living in Puerto Rican Families* (Rio Piedras: University of Puerto Rico, 1949), Table 30, p. 287; P. K. Hatt, *Backgrounds of Human Fertility in Puerto Rico* (Princeton: Princeton University Press, 1952), Table 282, p. 341; Brazil—Quoted in Hatt, *Backgrounds of Human Fertility*, p. 343; India—Travancore-Cochin and Poona in C. Chandrasekar, "Fertility Trends in India," *Proceedings of the World Population Conference, 1954*, (New York, 1956), pp. 787–833; S. R. Rele, "Some Aspects of Family and Fertility in India," *Population Studies*, XV, 3 (1962), 271; Guinea—R. Blanc, *Handbook of Demographic Research in Underdeveloped Countries* (New York: International Publications Service, n.d.), p. 90; West Cameroon—E. Ardener, *Divorce and Fertility: An African Study* (London: Oxford University Press, 1962), Table 39, p. 159; Zanzibar and Pemba—J. G. C. Blacker, "Population Growth and Differential Fertility in Zanzibar Protectorate," *Population Studies*, XV, 3 (1962), 261; Buhaya, Uganda, and Buganda—F. Lorimer, *Culture and Human Fertility* (Paris: UNESCO, 1964), p. 399.

TABLE 16.4
Estimated and recorded total fertility ratios for Ghana for recent dates

| Dates | Ratios |
|---|---|
| 1959–1960 | 6.5–7.3 |
| 1959–1960 | 7.2–7.6 |
| 1960–1961 | 6.5–7.3 |
| 1963–1964 | 6.2 |
| 1967–1968 | 6.5 |
| 1968–1969 | 6.7[a] |

SOURCES: 1959–60—Gaisie, *Dynamics of Population Growth in Ghana* p. 19; 1959–60 and 1963–64—Caldwell, "Population Change", p. 87; 1960–61—Gaisie, *Dynamics of Population Growth in Ghana*. Table 4, p. 14; 1967–68 and 1968–69—Demographic Sample Survey, 1963–1964 preliminary results.
[a] Based on the projected 1968 female age structure (i.e., proportions 15–19, 20–24, etc.) and registration data.

TABLE 16.5
Total fertility rates for Ghana and selected countries

| Country | Rates |
|---|---|
| Ghana (1968–1969) | 6.7 |
| (1967–1968) | 6.4 |
| (1959–1966) | 6.2–7.6 |
| Central African Republic (1959–1960) | 4.6 |
| Zaïre (1955–1957) | 4.1 |
| Dahomey (1961) | 6.9 |
| Gabon (1960–1961) | 4.1 |
| Guinea (1955) | 6.5 |
| Togoland (1961) | 6.7 |
| Argentina (1961) | 2.7 |
| Mexico (1960) | 5.9 |
| Ceylon (1962) | 4.7 |
| England and Wales (1964) | 2.9 |
| France (1963) | 2.8 |
| Australia (1964) | 3.0 |

SOURCES: Computed from United Nations, *Demographic Yearbook, 1965* for Ghana's figures see Table 15.4.

TABLE 16.6
Gross and net reproduction rates for recent dates (Ghana and some other countries)

| Country | GRR[a] | NRR[b] | Year |
|---|---|---|---|
| Ghana | 3.2–3.4 | 1.98–2.0 | 1959–1960 |
| | 3.0–3.3 | — | 1967–1968 |
| | 3.3+ | — | 1968–1969 |
| Cameroon Oriental | 2.3 | 1.8 | 1960 |
| Cameroon Occidental | 3.1 | 1.8 | 1964–1965 |
| Central African Republic | 2.5 | 1.5 | 1959–1960 |
| Chad | 2.4 | 1.4 | 1963–1964 |
| Mali | 3.8 | — | 1960–1961 |
| Togo | 3.5 | 2.1 | 1961 |
| Niger | 3.1 | 1.7 | 1959–1960 |
| Dahomey | 3.3 | 2.0 | 1961 |
| Ivory Coast | 3.2 | — | 1957–1958 |
| Upper Volta | 2.9 | 1.4 | 1960–1961 |
| Senegal | 2.6 | 2.1 | 1960–1961 |
| Madagascar | 2.4 | — | 1950–1954 |
| Zaïre | 2.4 | — | 1955–1957 |
| Gabon | 2.1 | 1.4 | 1960–1961 |
| United Kingdom | 1.5 | 1.4 | 1964 |
| Sweden | 1.1 | 1.0 | 1963 |
| U.S.A. | 1.62 | 1.56 | 1963 |
| Austria | 1.53 | 1.47 | 1964 |
| Bolivia | 2.9 | — | 1940–1945 |
| Brazil | 3.0 | — | 1940–1945 |
| Venezuela | 3.0 | — | 1963 |
| Pakistan | 3.4 | — | 1962 |
| India | 2.7 | — | 1951–1960 |

SOURCES: Ghana GRR, 1959–60—Gaisie, *Dynamics of Population Growth in Ghana*, p. 73; Ghana GRR, 1967–68—Demographic Sample Survey, 1960–1969, preliminary results; all other data are from United Nations, *Demographic Yearbook 1965*, Table 30, p. 605.
[a] GRR = gross reproduction rate.
[b] NRR = net reproduction rate.

TABLE 16.7

Urban-rural differentials as measured by total fertility ratios

| Region | Total Fertility Ratios Urban | Rural | Amount Urban Below Rural Fertility (percent) |
|---|---|---|---|
| Total country 1960 | 5.42 | 6.39 | 15 |
| 1968 | 5.86 | 7.64 | 13 |
| Accra Capital | | | |
| District | 5.46 | 6.30 | 13 |
| Western/Central | 5.46 | 6.61 | 17 |
| Eastern | 5.74 | 6.48 | 11 |
| Volta | 6.15 | 6.53 | 6 |
| Ashanti | 4.72 | 7.40 | 36 |
| Brong-Ahafo | 5.88 | 7.59 | 25 |
| Northern/Upper | 5.00 | 5.14 | 3 |

SOURCE: Gaisie, *Dynamics of Population Growth in Ghana*, p. 30.

5–9 years respectively). Friedlander's estimates for certain Ghanaian towns range from 3.4 to the rural towns (i.e., Tsito, Anomabo, Mpraeso, and Larteh) to 3.1 for Sekondi-Takoradi. The net reproduction rate (NRR) for Ghana has been estimated to be 2.0 per woman around 1960. Ghana's GRR and NRR are compared with those of other countries for recent dates (see Table 16.7). In general the picture is one of high and constant fertility.

It is undoubtedly clear from the rates presented above that Ghana's fertility has remained unchanged during the period under discussion and that there is no strong evidence of either rising or falling trends. What therefore will be the future course of fertility in Ghana? What are the factors which will determine changes in fertility, perhaps making it start a downward trend? Attempts have been made to provide partial answers to these questions by examining differential fertility by residence and educational and economic status. The following discussion tries to bring together some factual evidence in the hope of providing a basis for future research.

## FERTILITY DIFFERENTIALS

With data from the 1960 census and post-enumeration survey it has been possible to establish the existence of urban-rural differentials in fertility. Rural fertility is higher than urban fertility by between 10 and 15 percent[3] (see Tables 16.7 and 16.8). Studies based on child-woman ratios have also disclosed the same pattern of urban-rural differences.[4] Analysis of fertility differentials between the populations of the bigger towns and the areas immediately surrounding them and also between the bigger towns and the regions in which they are located shows that the fertility differentials between the towns and the rural areas near them are larger than those between the national urban and rural populations as defined in the 1960 census. Unfortunately the available data do not permit this type of analysis in terms of total fertility and completed family size. Nevertheless there is ample evidence of an urban-rural differential; but the real size of the differential is masked by a plethora of complex factors which are not adequately explained in the available statistics. The magnitude of the fertility differentials between the urban and rural populations is suggestive of the existence of certain factors which are responsible for the reduction of the level of fertility among the town and city communities.

[3] *Ibid.*, pp. 25 ff.
[4] *Ibid.*

TABLE 16.8

Urban-rural differentials as measured by completed fertility (i.e. average number of children born per woman aged 45 and over)

| Region | Completed Fertility Urban | Rural | Amount Urban Below Rural Fertility (percent) |
|---|---|---|---|
| Total country 1960 | 5.59 | 6.22 | 10 |
| 1968 | 5.45 | 6.04 | 10 |
| Accra Capital | | | |
| District | 5.38 | 6.69 | 20 |
| Western/Central | 5.80 | 6.51 | 11 |
| Eastern | 5.92 | 6.46 | 9 |
| Volta | 5.53 | 5.98 | 8 |
| Ashanti | 5.22 | 6.93 | 25 |
| Brong-Ahafo | 6.16 | 6.66 | 7 |
| Northern/Upper | 4.62 | 5.18 | 11 |

SOURCE: Gaisie, *Dynamics of Population Growth in Ghana*, p. 31.

Most of the urban-rural differential has been attributed to a relatively higher age at marriage in urban areas and the use of contraceptives to a much greater extent by women in the cities than by their rural counterparts. Extended formal education is one of the main factors responsible for the postponement of marriage among educated women.

While this factor may have very little, if any, effect on the marriage patterns of the uneducated urban women, economic security and the use of contraceptives may play an important role in the reduction of fertility in the urban areas. These factors are likely to operate more effectively among the educated and the well-to-do urbanites than among the uneducated and the poor town dwellers. Thus, fertility differentials are more likely to exist between the various socioeconomic classes in the cities and the big towns. And part of the observed urban-rural differential may be explained in terms of fertility differences between the socioeconomic strata in the towns. Caldwell's analysis of fertility differentials shows that about half of the rural-urban differential ". . . can be explained by a fertility difference between rural populations and even poor urban populations, and the other half by a socioeconomic fertility differential within the towns themselves."[5] The influence of socioeconomic status on fertility can be measured by one of a number of indices like occupation, income, and education, etc. Caldwell constructed a socioeconomic status index from occupational and educational data and applied it to subdivisions of Ghana's major towns.[6] His analysis revealed the existence of fertility differentials among the socioeconomic groups (i.e., quartiles) of the urban population. In a recent study Gaisie used the level of formal education achieved by the mothers as a measure of

[5] John C. Caldwell, "Fertility Differentials as Evidence of Incipient Fertility Decline in a Developing Country: The Case of Ghana," *Population Studies*, XXI, 1 (July 1967), 20.

[6] *Ibid.*; John C. Caldwell, *Population Growth and Family Change in Africa: The New Urban Elite in Ghana* (Canberra: Australian National University Press, 1968), pp. 189–213.

TABLE 16.9

Fertility by educational status of women

| Educational Status | Total Fertility Ratio | Completed Fertility |
|---|---|---|
| No education | 6.2 | 6.2 |
| Elementary | 6.4 | 5.5 |
| Secondary | 2.9 | 2.1 |
| University | 4.1 | 0.4 |

SOURCE: Gaisie, *Dynamics of Population Growth in Ghana*, p. 32.

socioeconomic status.[7] Tables 16.9 and 16.10 present the total fertility ratios and completed fertility by education of women. Most of the fertility differences between the illiterates and the women with elementary schooling and that between the secondary- and the university-educated women can probably be explained in terms of sampling errors. Out of 184,575 women in the sample, only 1,995 (i.e., 1 percent) and 85 (0.1 percent) had had secondary-commercial-technical and university education respectively. The average numbers of children ever born to women in the consecutive age groups[8] show clearly the negative relationship between fertility and educational status. The completed fertility (i.e., the number of children ever born per women aged 45 and over) is also inversely related to educational status; for the four groups in ascending order of status, the figures are 6.2, 5.5, 2.1, and 0.4. In both urban and rural areas fertility is related negatively to educational status. The non-educated women exhibit higher fertility than

[7] Gaisie, *Dynamics of Population Growth*, pp. 32 ff.

[8] *Ibid.*, Table 5A, Appendix III, pp. 92–93.

TABLE 16.10

Fertility by educational status and urban-rural residence

| Educational Status | Total Fertility Ratio | | Completed Fertility | |
|---|---|---|---|---|
| | Urban | Rural | Urban | Rural |
| No education | 5.5 | 6.4 | 5.7 | 6.2 |
| Elementary | 5.8 | 6.9 | 5.2 | 5.9 |
| Secondary | 2.8 | 3.4 | 2.5 | 1.0 |
| University | 4.5 | 2.5 | 0.5 | — |

SOURCE: Gaisie, *Dynamics of Population Growth in Ghana*, p. 33.

TABLE 16.11
Fertility by religion of women

| Religion | Total Fertility | Completed Fertility |
|---|---|---|
| Christian | 6.4 | 6.2 |
| Moslem | 5.8 | 5.3 |
| Traditional | 6.1 | 6.1 |
| No religion | 6.1 | 6.3 |

SOURCE: Gaisie, *Dynamics of Population Growth in Ghana*, p. 35.

women with elementary schooling and the latter's completed fertility exceeds that of the secondary-educated women by 51 and 85 percent in urban and rural areas respectively. It will be seen from Tables 16.9 and 16.10 that the university-educated mothers exhibit the lowest fertility.

FERTILITY AND RELIGION. With the exception of the Moslems, who exhibit the lowest fertility, there are no significant fertility differentials among the major religious groups (Tables 16.11 and 16.12). Within each religious group, rural fertility tends to be higher than urban, and there are relatively no significant differences among either urban or rural women with different religious affiliations. Although the real size of the fertility differences, if any, among the major religions might have been obscured by the fact that the data were not collected on the basis of the intensity of religious devotion, but instead according to "a person's own declaration or profession of religious faith,"[9]

[9] Census Office, *1960 Population Census of Ghana*, *Special Report "E," Tribes in Ghana* (Accra, 1964), pp. Lxxx ff.

TABLE 16.12
Fertility by religion of women and urban-rural residence

| Religion | Total Fertility Urban | Rural | Completed Fertility Urban | Rural |
|---|---|---|---|---|
| Christian | 5.4 | 6.8 | 5.6 | 6.6 |
| Moslem | 5.2 | 6.1 | 4.9 | 5.5 |
| Traditional | 5.7 | 6.2 | 5.8 | 6.1 |
| No religion | 5.2 | 6.4 | 5.5 | 6.5 |

SOURCE: Gaisie, *Dynamics of Population Growth in Ghana*, pp. 35, 36

TABLE 16.13
Fertility by major tribal groups

| Tribe | Total Fertility | Completed Fertility |
|---|---|---|
| Akan | 6.6 | 6.6 |
| Ga-Adangbe | 5.8 | 6.0 |
| Guan | 6.3 | 6.4 |
| Ewe | 6.6 | 5.6 |
| Central Togo tribes | 6.4 | 7.2 |
| Gurma | 5.6 | 6.8 |
| Mole-Dagbani | 5.3 | 5.1 |
| Grusi | 5.0 | 4.6 |
| Lobi | 6.2 | 5.4 |

SOURCE: Gaisie, *Dynamics of Population Growth in Ghana* p. 38.

it appears that religion, unlike urban-rural residence and socioeconomic or educational status, has little or no influence on fertility levels in Ghana.

TABLE 16.14
Fertility by tribes

| Tribe | Total Fertility | Completed Fertility |
|---|---|---|
| Akan | 6.6 | 6.6 |
| Asante and Ahafo | 7.3 | 6.9 |
| Fante | 6.5 | 6.4 |
| Nzema | 5.2 | 6.1 |
| Akyem | 5.9 | 6.6 |
| Akuapem | 5.2 | 6.3 |
| Kwahu | 7.3 | 6.6 |
| Wasa | 5.3 | 6.5 |
| Boron (including Banda) | 7.2 | 6.6 |
| Ga-Adangbe | 5.8 | 6.0 |
| Ga | 5.6 | 5.4 |
| Adangbe | 5.8 | 6.6 |
| Guan | 6.3 | 6.4 |
| Ewe | 6.6 | 5.9 |
| Gurma | 5.6 | 6.8 |
| Konkomba | 4.4 | 5.6 |
| Lobi | 6.2 | 5.4 |
| Grusi | 5.0 | 4.6 |
| Central Togo tribes | 6.4 | 7.2 |
| Mole-Dagbani | 5.3 | 5.1 |
| Dagomba | 4.8 | 5.2 |
| Mamprusi | 6.3 | 5.2 |
| Dagaba | 6.6 | 6.1 |
| Builsa | 5.1 | 4.3 |
| Frafra | 4.0 | 4.3 |
| Kusasi | 5.2 | 5.0 |
| Mossi | 5.9 | 4.7 |
| Yoruba | 6.1 | 5.5 |

SOURCE: Gaisie, *Dynamics of Population Growth in Ghana*, pp. 39, 40.

FERTILITY AND TRIBE.   In general the tribes may be grouped into three broad fertility categories:

(1) High fertility tribes—Asante and Ahafo, Akyem, Kwahu, Boron, Adangbe, Gurma, and Central Togo tribes

(2) Moderately high fertility—Fante (including the Agona), Nzema, Akuapem, Ga, Wasa, Guan, Ewe, Dagaba, Mamprusi, Lobi, and Yoruba

(3) Low fertility—Grusi, Builsa, Frafra, Kusasi, Mossi, Konkomba, and Dagomba

There are indications of the existence of fertility differentials between tribes and this may be attributed in part to education, degree of urbanization, physical mobility, and distorted sex ratios, and in part to malnutrition, diseases, and constitutional and aetiological sterility which tend to depress fecundity. Superstitions, leading to differential reporting of vital events, may also account for part of the differential. The Akan tribes show the highest fertility rates, followed by the remainder of the non-northern tribes with moderately high fertility. The lowest fertility is found among the northern tribes, except the Mamprusi, Gurma, and the Dagaba, who exhibit high fertility levels.

# CHAPTER SEVENTEEN

# Population Growth & Its Components

S. K. GAISIE

GHANA is situated on the coast of Guinea, bounded on the west by Ivory Coast, on the north by Upper Volta, and on the east by Togo. It extends from the coast to the north for a distance of about 420 miles between 4° 44′ north and 11° 10′ north; and for a distance of about 259 miles between longitudes 1° 12′ east and 3° 15′ west. The Greenwich Meridian passes through the country, the southernmost point of which is about $4\frac{1}{2}$° from the equator.

Its total area is about 92,000 square miles, which is approximately the size of the United Kingdom. Of this area, however, about one-third is covered by forests which stretch from the south to approximately latitude 30° 17′ north. The Accra plains in the south and the northern half of the country are covered by savanna vegetation. The southern forest areas contain most of the country's wealth and the northern area, with its extreme aridity, is the poorest region of the country. Thus geographic, economic, and climatic factors have been responsible, to a large extent, for the uneven distribution of the population; and the general demographic characteristics of the populations in the major regions have been influenced by these factors.

Prior to World War II comparatively little was known about the size and the structure of the population of Ghana. The available demographic statistics were of such dubious validity that no plausible population estimates could be based on them. The quality of the censuses conducted during the colonial era was so questionable that no definite conclusions about the past population trends can be arrived at without intensive examination of administrative documents and scholarly reports. However, post-World War II witnessed an improvement in data collection in Ghana. The year 1960 ushered in a considerable improvement in census taking in Ghana with regard to techniques, objectives, and scope. The departure of the colonial government left the Africans with the task of nation building and it was at this

TABLE 17.1
Population size, 1921–2000 (thousands)

| 1921 | 1931 | 1948 | 1960 | | 1970 | 1980 | 1990 | 2000 |
|------|------|------|------|-----|------|------|------|------|
| 2,296 | 3,164 | 4,118 | 6,727 | (a) | 9,521 | 13,624 | 19,771 | 28,878 |
| | | | | (b) | — | 13,435 | 18,205 | 24,398 |
| | | | | (c) | 9,748 | 14,279 | — | 31,916 |
| | | | | (d) | 9,648 | 13,233 | — | 22,341 |

SOURCES: (a) and (b)—S. K. Gaisie, *Dynamics of Population Growth in Ghana* (Accra-Tema: Ghana Publishing Corporation, 1969), Tables 42A and 42B, pp. 59, 60; (c) and (d)—John C. Caldwell, "Population Prospects and Policy," in W. Birmingham, I. Neustadt, and E. N. Omaboe, eds., *A Study of Contemporary Ghana*, II, *Some Aspects of Social Structure* (London: George Allen and Unwin; Evanston: Northwestern University Press, 1967), Table 4.4, p. 170. (a) and (c), and (b) and (d) are based on the assumptions of constant fertility and declining fertility respectively.

juncture that the African governments became aware of the need for adequate and reliable statistics as a tool for efficient administration and planning. They therefore devoted significant fractions of their meager national incomes to the collection of better demographic statistics. In this exercise Ghana did better than her colonial masters had done. Ghana spent 1 shilling 2 pence per head on her 1960 census as compared with a tenth of a penny per head in 1931.[1] It is therefore not surprising that comparatively high quality demographic data were collected in the 1960s.

The first census of the population of Ghana was taken in 1891 and it was followed by decennial censuses until World War II interrupted the sequence in 1941. However, the 1921 census was the first to cover the whole area now known as the Republic of Ghana. The 1960 census provided for the first time reasonably detailed and reliable data on the size and composition of Ghana's population, and most of the population estimates presented below are based on the the age and sex structure of the 1960 population. Ghana's population of just over 2 million in 1921 increased to 6.7 million in 1960; that is, it more than tripled in a short period of nearly 40 years. Although data for the early part of the century are not trustworthy, they are indicative of a rapid increase in Ghana's population. The projections presented in Tables 17.1 and 17.2 indicate

[1] See John C. Caldwell, "Introduction" to Part I in John C. Caldwell and C. Okonjo, eds., *The Population of Tropical Africa* (London: Longmans, Green and Company, and New York: Columbia University Press, 1968), p. 4.

that the 1960 population of Ghana would increase more than fourfold within a period of 40 years (1960–2,000) on the assumption of sustained fertility, and nearly fourfold on the assumption of declining fertility. The projections based on unchanged fertility produce an accelerated growth rate and a population reaching between 29 and 32 million by the year 2000, while in that year the population growing under declining fertility would reach 22–24 million. The indigenous population (i.e., that population which is not of foreign ancestry) would also increase by 1980 by 86 and 84 percent on the assumption of sustained and declining fertility respectively. Thus the indigenous population is also growing very rapidly and this may be attributed mainly to high fertility and declining mortality. Table 17.3 gives the percentages of population growth for the different periods considered in Table 17.1. The constant fertility projections show the greatest growth during 1960–2000. It is

TABLE 17.2
Projected population of Ghanaian origin, 1921–2000

| | 1970 | 1980 | 1990 | 2000 |
|-----|------|------|------|------|
| (a) | 7,918 | 10,952 | 15,462 | 22,256 |
| (b) | 7,918 | 10,826 | 14,366 | 19,031 |
| (c) | 9,329 | 13,267 | — | 28,918 |
| (d) | 9,235 | 12,287 | — | 20,084 |

SOURCES: (a) and (b)—Gaisie, *Dynamics of Population Growth in Ghana*, Tables 42A and 42B, pp. 59, 60; (c) and (d)—Caldwell, "Population Prospects," Table 4.4, p. 170. The populations projected in (c) and (d) are those of Ghanaian origin plus immigrants arriving before 1960 (i.e., the projections assume a cessation of immigration after 1960).

TABLE 17.3

Percentage population increases, 1921–2000

| 1921–31 | 1931–48 | 1948–60 | 1960–70 | 1970–80 | 1980–90 | 1990–2000 | 1980–2000 |
|---|---|---|---|---|---|---|---|
|  |  |  | (a) 42 | 43 | 45 | 47 |  |
| 38 | 30 | 63 | (b) 42 | 41 | 35 | 34 |  |
|  |  |  | (c) 45 | 46 |  |  | 124 |
|  |  |  | (d) 43 | 37 |  |  | 69 |

SOURCES: Based on the figures in Table 17.1.

considerably greater than the proportional increase forecast for other regions of the world. Table 17.4 presents the recorded rate of growth for the periods between 1921 and 1960. Although the data used in computing these rates are not trustworthy, the rates give a rough indication of the rapid acceleration of Ghana's population growth.

The estimated crude birth rate for 1959–1960 and the recorded crude birth rate for 1967–1968 were 50.0 and 47.5 per thousand population respectively.[2] The corresponding crude death rates for the same periods were 23.0 and 17.0 per thousand population. These fertility and mortality rates indicate that the rate of natural increase of the population of Ghana has risen from 2.7 percent per annum to about 3.1 percent during the 1960s. Estimates prepared by the author show an average annual rate of growth ranging between 2.8 and 3.0 percent for the whole period, 1948–1960. In comparison with rates of 1.8 percent for North America, 0.8 percent

for Europe, and 1.7 percent for USSR (1950–1960),[3] Ghana's rate of population growth may be regarded as one of the highest in the world. An annual rate of growth of between 2.7 and 3.0 percent would result in the doubling of the population in 25 years or less. The projected rates (see Table 17.5) indicate that eventually the rate of growth may climb over 4 percent per annum, although the recent exodus of "aliens" from Ghana may have a significant effect on the growth rate. Nevertheless, the rate of natural increase is now very close to 3.0 percent per annum and the country's population may still be growing at a high rate of natural increase. In fact, the results of the 1968–1969 Demographic Sample Survey show that the rate of natural increase has already passed 3 percent per annum. The projected rates in Table 17.5 show the population would be doubling itself every 30 years or 17 years on the assumptions of declining and sustained fertility respectively.

[2] S. K. Gaisie, *Dynamics of Population Growth in Ghana* (Accra-Tema: Ghana Publishing Corporation, 1969), and 1968–1969 Demographic Sample Survey (unpublished data) respectively.

TABLE 17.4

Recorded rates of growth, 1921–1960

| Period | Average Annual Rate (percent) |
|---|---|
| 1921–1931 | 3.2 |
| 1931–1948 | 1.6 |
| 1921–1960 | 2.8 |
| 1931–1960 | 2.7 |
| 1948–1960 | 4.2 |

SOURCES: Census reports.

### ETHNIC GROUPS

The great bulk of Ghana's population continues to be of indigenous African origin. There are, however, small minority groups of Asians, Europeans, Lebanese, and Syrians. The proportion of Africans among the Ghanaian population has never fallen below 99 percent. Africans made up 99.90 percent, 99.84 percent, 99.77 percent, and 99.85 percent of the country's population in 1921, 1948, 1960, and 1968 respectively.

[3] United Nations Economic Commission for Africa (ECA), *Economic Bulletin for Africa*, V (January 1965).

TABLE 17.5

Projected rates of growth, 1960–2000

## (a) Average annual decennial rates

| | Average Rate of Growth (percent) | | | |
| | Fertility assumed unchanged | | Fertility assumed to decline linearly by a total of 50% between 1975 and 2015 | |
| Period | without migration | with migration | without migration | with migration |
|---|---|---|---|---|
| 1960–1970 | 2.92 | 3.50 | 2.92 | 3.50 |
| 1970–1980 | 3.22 | 3.57 | 3.14 | 3.43 |
| 1980–1990 | 3.43 | 3.71 | 2.85 | 3.10 |
| 1990–2000 | 3.64 | 3.85 | 2.77 | 2.92 |

## (b) Rate of population growth for various periods

| Projections | Constant Fertility With immigration | Without immigration | Fertility Reducing by 1% per Annum With immigration | Without immigration | Fertility Reducing by 2% per Annum With immigration | Without immigration |
|---|---|---|---|---|---|---|
| Average annual rate of population growth (%) | | | | | | |
| 1960–5 | 3.8 | 3.3 | 3.8 | 3.3 | 3.8 | 3.3 |
| 1980–5 | 4.0 | 3.8 | 3.4 | 3.2 | 2.9 | 2.7 |
| 1985–2000 | 4.2 | 4.2 | 3.2 | 3.1 | 2.4 | 2.2 |

SOURCES: (a) Gaisie, *Dynamics of Population Growth in Ghana*, Tables 42A and 42B, pp. 59–60; (b) Caldwell, "Population Prospects," Table 4.15, p. 184.

Although the 1960 population census revealed that 12.3 percent of the total population of Ghana were foreigners, about 96 percent of the foreign-born immigrants hailed from the neighboring and nearby African countries of Togo, Upper Volta, and Nigeria. The nationals from these countries made up 34.0, 23.5, and 23.1 percent of the population of foreign origin respectively. There is no doubt that the number of foreigners has decreased considerably as a result of the recent enforcement of the immigration laws by the government, but at the time of writing nobody has any real idea of the number of foreigners who left the country after December 2, 1969. However, the 1971 census results show that the foreign component of the population has declined to about 6.6 percent. This must be attributed largely to the enforcement of the immigration laws. It must be noted that the non-African segment of the foreign population increased from 0.90 percent in 1921 to 1.6 and 2.3 percent in 1948 and 1960 respectively. The corresponding figure for 1968 was 1.5 percent. The number of non-Africans in Ghana increased considerably soon after Ghana obtained her political independence. The situation has been described by Caldwell as follows:

In actuality the numbers of the British in Ghana have not fallen. They rose between 1948 and 1960 from 4,211 to 7,420. But at the same time the non-British European population increased in size spectacularly. In the former year they numbered less than a thousand. In the ensuing twelve years they increased almost fivefold to 4,530.[4]

The Ghanaian population is also made up of a large number of ethnic groups, including the Akans, Ga-Adangbe, Guan, Ewe, Gurma, Lobi, Grusi, Central Togo tribes, and Mole-Dagbani (Table 17.6).

[4] John C. Caldwell, "Population: General Characteristics," in Walter Birmingham, I. Neustadt, and E. N. Omaboe, eds., *A Study of Contemporary Ghana*, II, *Some Aspects of Social Structure* (London: George Allen and Unwin; Evanston: Northwestern University Press, 1967), p. 24.

TABLE 17.6
Ethnic composition of Ghanaian population,
1960 and 1968

| Ethnic Group (percent of total population) | 1960 | 1968 |
|---|---|---|
| Akans | 44.1 | 43.3 |
| Ewe | 13.0 | 14.5 |
| Mole-Dagbani | 15.9 | 12.8 |
| Ga-Adangbe | 8.3 | 9.4 |
| Grusi | 2.2 | 4.8 |
| Guan | 3.7 | 2.2 |
| Gurma | 3.5 | 0.7 |
| Central Togo tribes | 0.8 | 0.4 |
| Non-African | 0.2 | 0.2 |

SOURCES: 1960—1960 census; 1968—S. K. Gaisie *et al.*, *The National Demographic Sample Survey*, vol. 2a, *General Characteristics of the Sample Population* (Legon, Accra: Demographic Unit, University of Ghana, 1970).

AGE AND SEX COMPOSITION

The 1960 census and the 1968–1969 sample survey data are presented in the form of pyramids shown in Figures 17.1 and 17.2. Although both sets of data might have been distorted to some extent by errors arising from age misstatement and errors in enumeration, and the survey may have been distorted by sampling fluctuations, they reveal clearly the main characteristics of Ghana's population. The most outstanding characteristic of Ghana's population is its extreme youth. The proportion of children under 15 years is more than 45 percent. The 1968 figures indicate that the Ghanaian population is becoming more and more youthful and the projected population also showed that the proportion of children in the population of Ghanaian origin would climb to 47.5 percent and 48.3 percent in 1970 and 1975 respectively.[5] In fact the figures in

[5] Gaisie, *Dynamics of Population Growth*, Appendix IV, Table VII, p. 106.

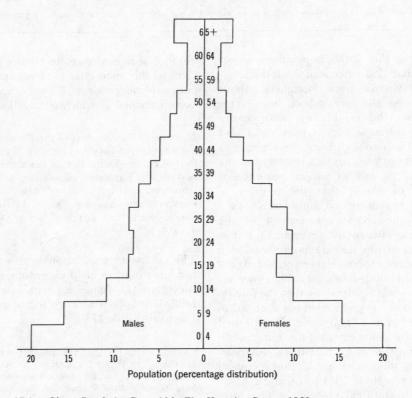

FIGURE 17.1. *Ghana Population Pyramid by Five-Year Age-Groups*, 1960

SOURCE: Population Census

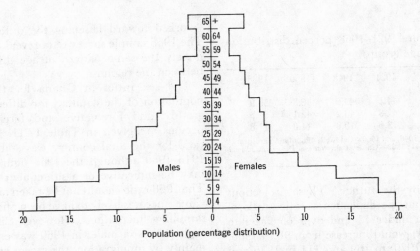

FIGURE 17.2. *Ghana Population Pyramid by Five-Year Age-Groups*, 1968

Table 17.9 show that the proportion of children under 16 years has never fallen below 43 percent since 1921, and, while the proportion between ages 15 and 64 years is decreasing gradually, the proportion of persons aged 65 years and over has remained nearly constant over the years (Tables 17.7 and 17.8). On the whole there have not been any major changes in the age structure, and, if fertility continues to remain constant in the coming years, about 50 percent of Ghanaian population will eventually be composed of children.

Indeed, the projected populations of Ghanaian origin indicate that the proportion of children under 15 years of age would increase from 45.6 percent in 1960 to 47.5 percent and 48.7 percent in 1970 and 1980 respectively. One of the serious problems arising from the age changes outlined above will be the provision of adequate schools for the rapid increase in the number of children who will be entering primary, middle, and secondary schools.

Another problem arising out of the unfavorable age distribution is the heavy dependency burden which tends to retard economic advancement. The imposition and intensification of a severe dependency burden in the coming years are revealed by the projections

TABLE 17.7
Age structure, 1960 and 1968 (percent distribution by five-year groups)

| Age | Both Sexes 1960 | Both Sexes 1968 | Males 1960 | Males 1968 | Females 1960 | Females 1968 |
|-----|------|------|------|------|------|------|
| 0–4 | 19.2 | 19.9 | 18.8 | 19.5 | 19.6 | 18.4 |
| 5–9 | 15.2 | 17.3 | 15.1 | 17.7 | 15.2 | 16.9 |
| 10–14 | 10.1 | 12.7 | 10.5 | 13.3 | 9.8 | 12.0 |
| 15–19 | 8.0 | 9.0 | 8.1 | 9.1 | 7.9 | 8.8 |
| 20–24 | 8.7 | 7.3 | 7.9 | 6.2 | 9.6 | 8.5 |
| 25–29 | 8.8 | 7.2 | 8.3 | 6.1 | 9.2 | 8.1 |
| 30–34 | 7.3 | 5.6 | 7.1 | 5.3 | 7.4 | 5.9 |
| 35–39 | 5.5 | 5.2 | 5.8 | 5.1 | 5.3 | 5.4 |
| 40–44 | 4.6 | 3.9 | 4.9 | 3.9 | 4.4 | 3.9 |
| 45–49 | 3.3 | 3.5 | 3.6 | 3.5 | 2.9 | 3.4 |
| 50–54 | 2.7 | 3.0 | 2.9 | 3.0 | 2.5 | 3.0 |
| 55–59 | 1.6 | 1.7 | 1.8 | 1.9 | 1.5 | 1.6 |
| 60–64 | 1.8 | 1.7 | 1.9 | 1.9 | 1.7 | 1.6 |
| 65+ | 3.2 | 3.0 | 3.3 | 3.4 | 3.0 | 2.5 |

SOURCES: 1960—1960 census; 1968—Gaisie et al., *National Demographic Sample Survey.*

TABLE 17.8
Age structure, 1960 and 1968 (percent distribution in broad age groups)

| Age Group | Both Sexes 1960 | Both Sexes 1968 | Males 1960 | Males 1968 | Females 1960 | Females 1968 |
|-----|------|------|------|------|------|------|
| Under 15 | 44.5 | 48.9 | 44.4 | 50.4 | 44.6 | 47.3 |
| 15–44 | 43.1 | 38.2 | 42.1 | 35.7 | 43.9 | 40.6 |
| 45–64 | 9.3 | 9.9 | 10.2 | 10.4 | 8.5 | 9.6 |
| 65+ | 3.2 | 3.0 | 3.3 | 3.4 | 3.0 | 2.5 |

SOURCES: Computed from Table 17.7.

TABLE 17.9

Age structure, 1921–1968 (percent distribution in broad age groups)

| Age Group | 1921 | 1948 | 1960 | 1968 |
|---|---|---|---|---|
| Under 16 | 44.1 | 43.0 | 46.3 | 50.9 |
| 16–45 | 42.3 | 43.2 | 42.1 | 37.3 |
| 46+ | 13.6 | 13.8 | 11.8 | 11.8 |

SOURCES: 1921, 1948, and 1960—Caldwell, "Population Prospects," Table 1.10, p. 41; 1968—Gaisie et al., *National Demographic Sample Survey.*

prepared by the author.[6] These projections indicate that the dependency ratio (ratio of population under 15 and over 65 years to that 15–64) would increase from 98 in 1968, to 105 in 1970, to 109 and 111 in 1975 and 1980 respectively. Under an assumption of declining fertility, however, the ratio would decrease from 109 in 1975, to 108 in 1980, and 98 in 1990. The view that the dependency burden in developing countries is lightened by putting children to work early and by allowing old people to continue to work as long as they are physically and mentally capable may be rebutted by the fact that in a nontraditional economy the contribution of children under 15 years of age and persons aged 60 years and over (the majority of whom have no skills of the type acquired by training) is too insignificant to lighten the load.

Table 17.10 presents age structures in the nine regions. Although some of the differences in the age compositions in the regions may be explained in terms of differential age reporting and the type of migration occurring in each region, the high fertility regions, i.e., Ashanti and Brong-Ahafo, inevitably have younger populations. In 1960 about 47 and 46 percent of the populations in Ashanti and Brong-Ahafo respectively were composed of children under 15 years of age. The corresponding proportions for the combined Northern and Upper regions, Eastern and the combined Western and Central regions were 43, 45.5, and 44.5 percent respectively. The differences in the age structure might have been greater if migration had not

[6] *Ibid.,* Table 44A, p. 66.

"worked toward lessening the differences." The 1968 sample survey data reveal approximately the same pattern of age differences between the regions.

The sex ratios in Ghana for the total population of the country, for different age groups, and for native and foreign-born persons are given in Table 17.11. The sex ratio for the total country was stable from 1948–1960 although the 1968 figure (94.0) may be indicative of a subsequent decline. The 1968 ratio should not be taken at its face value since it is likely to have been affected by sampling fluctuations. However, since the slight excess of males in 1960 was explained mainly by immigration, the recent exodus of "aliens" from Ghana may well have depressed the sex ratio, but probably not to the extent suggested by the 1968 figure. The sex ratios of the native-born population, as revealed by the 1960 census and 1968 sample survey were 97.7 and 91.5, respectively. The

TABLE 17.10

Percent distribution by age and region, 1960–1968

| Region | Year | Age Under 15 | 15–44 | 45–64 | 65+ |
|---|---|---|---|---|---|
| Accra Capital District | 1960 | 39.2 | 49.7 | 8.3 | 2.8 |
| | 1968 | 47.3 | 41.3 | 9.0 | 2.4 |
| Eastern | 1960 | 45.5 | 41.3 | 9.8 | 3.4 |
| | 1968 | 48.9 | 35.4 | 10.7 | 5.0 |
| Central | 1960 | — | — | — | — |
| | 1968 | 48.9 | 37.4 | 10.4 | 3.3 |
| Western | 1960[a] | 44.5 | 42.4 | 9.8 | 3.3 |
| | 1968 | 46.1 | 39.9 | 10.9 | 3.1 |
| Volta | 1960 | 45.6 | 40.0 | 10.1 | 4.3 |
| | 1968 | 49.7 | 35.7 | 11.2 | 3.4 |
| Ashanti | 1960 | 46.5 | 42.8 | 8.2 | 2.5 |
| | 1968 | 52.1 | 38.1 | 7.6 | 2.2 |
| Brong-Ahafo | 1960 | 46.1 | 43.5 | 7.9 | 2.5 |
| | 1968 | 51.3 | 35.9 | 9.5 | 3.3 |
| Northern | 1960[b] | 42.8 | 44.2 | 9.8 | 2.2 |
| | 1968 | 47.5 | 40.2 | 9.4 | 2.9 |
| Upper | 1960 | — | — | — | — |
| | 1968 | 45.1 | 42.5 | 10.6 | 2.0 |

SOURCES: 1960 census; Gaisie et al., *National Demographic Sample Survey.*
[a] Figures for western and central regions.
[b] Figures for northern and upper regions.

TABLE 17.11
Sex ratios, 1960 and 1968 (Males per 100 females)

| Age Group | 1960 | 1968 |
|---|---|---|
| 0 | 95.6 | 94.5 |
| 0–4 | 97.7 | 102.0 |
| 5–9 | 101.5 | 99.0 |
| 10–14 | 110.1 | 104.0 |
| 15–19 | 105.0 | 97.3 |
| 20–24 | 84.2 | 68.8 |
| 25–29 | 91.0 | 71.2 |
| 30–34 | 98.3 | 86.3 |
| 35–39 | 110.6 | 89.0 |
| 40–44 | 114.9 | 93.1 |
| 45–49 | 129.7 | 98.3 |
| 50–54 | 118.0 | 95.3 |
| 55–59 | 122.7 | 109.1 |
| 60–64 | 115.1 | 113.6 |
| 65+ | 114.0 | 123.8 |
| All ages | 102.2 | 94.3 |
| Native born | 97.7 | 91.5 |
| Foreign born | 170.6 | 115.0 |

SOURCES: 1960—Caldwell, "Population Prospects," p. 43; 1968—Gaisie et al., *National Demographic Sample Survey.*

excess of females over males probably may be explained in terms of higher male mortality. The sex ratios at birth in 1960 and 1968 appear to show an excess of female births over male births. This is the opposite of what is experienced in other parts of the world. In a number of specific populations the sex ratio at birth has varied from 113.2 in Greece to 101.1 in Cuba[7] (black population only). The average sex ratio at births

[7] P. S. Lawrence, *Quarterly Review of Biology* (March 1941), pp. 35–79.

TABLE 17.12
Sex ratios in broad age groups, 1948, 1960, and 1968 (Males per 100 females)

| Age Group | 1948 | 1960 | 1968 |
|---|---|---|---|
| Under 15 | 106.8[a] | 102.4 | 100.2 |
| 15–44 | 98.9[b] | 97.5 | 82.6 |
| 45–64 | 104.6[c] | 122.1 | 101.0 |
| 65+ | — | 112.6 | 124.6 |

SOURCES: 1948—Caldwell, "Population Prospects," Table 1.12, p. 44; 1960—computed from Table 17.10; 1968—computed from Table 17.10.
[a] Age group 1–15 years
[b] Age group 16–44
[c] Age group 45 and over.

throughout the world has been estimated to centre around 105 male births per 100 female births. Overstatement of boys' ages, heavy male infantile mortality, and underenumeration of infant boys may be cited as some of the explanations for the Ghanaian findings; but, since there is no evidence to show that only the ages of boys were overstated and that only boys were underenumerated, the imbalance between the sexes at birth may perhaps be attributed partly to comparatively heavy male infant mortality. On the other hand, a lack of a male excess of births may be a characteristic of African populations.

TABLE 17.13
Sex ratios by region, 1960

| Region | Ratio (males per 100 females) |
|---|---|
| Accra Capital District | 113.6 |
| Eastern | 101.9 |
| Western and Central | 101.6 |
| Volta | 95.2 |
| Ashanti | 104.9 |
| Brong-Ahafo | 111.2 |
| Northern and Upper | 97.2 |

SOURCE: 1960 census.

Table 17.12 shows quite clearly that, according to stated age, females outnumber males in the central age groups—i.e., 15–44—and that males assume supremacy beyond age 45. The latter phenomenon may be explained in terms of age misstatement (males overstating their ages and females perhaps understating theirs) and immigration. It must be noted that the picture portrayed in Table 17.12 has been found to be characteristic of other African populations.[8] Table 17.13 confirms that the immigrant regions exhibit the highest sex ratios.

POPULATION DISTRIBUTION

Ghanaian population density increased from 45 persons per square mile in 1948 to 73 in 1960 and the estimated density in 1970 is 94

[8] W. Joseph, Chapter 24 in this volume, Table 24.2.

TABLE 17.14

Population distribution by region, 1960 and 1968

| Region | Percent of the Population of Ghana | | | Percent of the Area of Ghana | Average Population Density (persons per square mile) | |
|---|---|---|---|---|---|---|
| | 1960 | 1968 | 1970 | | 1960 | 1970 |
| Accra Capital District | 7.3 | 8.3 | 10.0 | 1.1 | 494 | 853 |
| Eastern | 16.3 | 14.6 | 14.8 | 8.4 | 142 | 164 |
| Central | 11.2 | 10.8 | 10.4 | 4.1 | 197 | 134 |
| Western | 9.3 | 5.9 | 9.0 | 10.0 | 68 | 83 |
| Ashanti | 16.5 | 17.1 | 17.3 | 10.2 | 118 | 157 |
| Brong-Ahafo | 8.7 | 9.3 | 8.9 | 16.6 | 38 | 50 |
| Volta | 11.6 | 13.7 | 11.1 | 8.6 | 98 | 119 |
| Northern | 6.3 | 5.4 | 8.5 | 26.3 | 18 | 27 |
| Upper | 12.8 | 15.0 | 10.0 | 14.7 | 64 | 81 |
| Ghana | 100.0 | 100.0 | 100.0 | 100.0 | 73 | 93 |

SOURCES: 1960 census; Gaisie et al., *National Demographic Sample Survey*; 1970 census (provisional results).

persons per square mile. Table 17.14 shows that the greatest densities are in the Accra Capital District, followed by the Central, Eastern and Ashanti regions. The Brong-Ahafo and Northern regions exhibit the lowest population densities. Due to certain economic, historical, and cultural factors the population is unevenly distributed. As can be seen in Table 17.14, the Accra Capital District makes up only 1.1 percent of the territory but it contains about 8.0 percent of the total population of Ghana. On the other hand, the Northern Region occupies the largest land area in Ghana (26.3 percent of the total area) but only 6·9 percent of the country's inhabitants reside in this part of Ghana. The situation, however, changes from one of sparsity to one of comparatively dense concentrations as we move further north. Although the Upper Region accounts for only 14.7 percent of the area, its population is more than twice that of the Northern Region and the population density of the former is three-and-one-half times that of the latter. It must be noted that, although the Upper Region lacks the commerce and the industry that abounds in the south, it accommodates pockets of considerable human concentration who depend mainly on subsistence farming, particularly around the northwestern corner and the extreme north-

eastern part of the region. However, four regions in the south (Accra Capital District, Eastern, Central, and Ashanti) contain more than half of Ghana's population, 51.3 percent in 1960 and 50.8 percent in 1968, although they make up less than a quarter (23.8 percent) of the area. On the whole a greater number of Ghanaians reside in the southern half of the country where commerce, industry, and other economic activities are more developed than in the northern part. Thus the spatial distribution of Ghana's population reflects the way in which the individual economic activities are distributed within the society and this in turn determines the basis of the economic infrastructure.

In 1960, nearly half of the Ghanaian residents lived in localities with a population of less than 1,000 inhabitants and about 30 percent resided in villages with a population of between 1,000 and 5,000 persons. The urban population (i.e., those living in centers with more than 5,000 inhabitants) increased from 13 percent in 1948 to 23 percent in 1960 and to 30 percent in 1968. Although there have been few changes in the composition of urban-rural populations in the regions, Table 17.15 shows that, on the whole, the urban component of the Ghanaian population has increased considerably during the eight years following 1960.

TABLE 17.15

Urban and rural population by region, 1960 and 1968

| Region | Urban (localities with more than 5,000 inhabitants) | | Rural | |
|---|---|---|---|---|
| | 1960 | 1968 | 1960 | 1968 |
| Accra Capital District | 80 | 72 | 20 | 28 |
| Eastern | 20 | 20 | 80 | 80 |
| Central and Western[a] | 26 | 32 | 74 | 68 |
| Ashanti | 25 | 22 | 75 | 78 |
| Brong-Ahafo | 16 | 29 | 84 | 71 |
| Volta | 13 | 34 | 87 | 66 |
| Northern and Upper[a] | 8 | 23 | 92 | 77 |
| Ghana | 23 | 30 | 77 | 70 |

SOURCES: 1960 census; Gaisie et al., *National Demographic Sample Survey.*
a As in 1960.

## EDUCATIONAL STATUS

In 1948 only 4 percent of the Ghanaian population had received some kind of education. By 1960, however, the percentage had increased to 21 percent, and 27 percent of the population aged 6 years and over had attended or were attending school. The corresponding proportions in 1968 were 31 and 40 percent respectively; 50 percent of the males and 32 percent of the females aged 6 years and over had been to school at some time.

Between 1960 and 1968 the proportions of the urban and rural populations aged 6 years and over who had ever been to school increased from 43 to 55 percent and from 26 to 34 percent respectively. A little over a quarter of the females in the rural areas and less than a half of their urban counterparts had ever been to school at some time; and among the males nearly three-quarters of the urban dwellers and half of their rural brothers had received some kind of education. Although there is still a large number of Ghanaians who have never had any form of schooling, the proportions of children and adults who have ever been to school have continued rising since 1960. The proportion of boys in the age ranges 6–14 and 15–19 years who have received some form of education increased from 47 and 60 percent in 1960 to 66 and 73 percent in 1968 respectively; the female percentages also increased from 33 and 28 percent in 1960 to 57 and 48 percent in 1968 (Table 17.16). Despite the great increase in the proportion of Ghanaians going to school, the educational system has not expanded rapidly enough to provide at least elementary schooling for every boy and girl in the country. More than half of the females

TABLE 17.16

School attendance by sex and age, 1960 and 1968 (percent of each age-sex group)

| Age Groups | | Ever at School | | | | Never at School | | | |
|---|---|---|---|---|---|---|---|---|---|
| | | Males | | Females | | Males | | Females | |
| 1960 | 1968 | 1960 | 1968 | 1960 | 1968 | 1960 | 1968 | 1960 | 1968 |
| 6–14 | 6–14 | 46.8 | 65.5 | 39.9 | 56.9 | 53.2 | 34.5 | 60.1 | 43.1 |
| 15–19 | 15–19 | 60.3 | 73.3 | 36.6 | 47.7 | 39.7 | 26.7 | 63.4 | 52.3 |
| 20–24 | | 35.0 | | 22.0 | | 65.0 | | 70.0 | |
| | 20–29 | | 54.6 | | 24.1 | | 45.4 | | 75.9 |
| 25–34 | | 29.0 | | 8.0 | | 71.0 | | 92.0 | |
| | 30–39 | | 33.9 | | 10.4 | | 66.1 | | 89.6 |
| 35–44 | | 18.0 | | 5.0 | | 82.0 | | 95.0 | |
| | 40–49 | | 21.3 | | 6.1 | | 78.7 | | 93.9 |
| 45–54 | | 17.0 | | 5.0 | | 83.0 | | 95.0 | |
| | 50–59 | | 19.0 | | 4.9 | | 81.0 | | 95.1 |
| 55–64 | | 15.0 | | 4.0 | | 85.0 | | 96.0 | |
| | 60+ | | 15.7 | | 5.0 | | 84.3 | | 95.0 |
| 65+ | | 9.0 | | 3.0 | | 91.0 | | 97.0 | |

SOURCES: 1960 census; Gaisie et al., *National Demographic Sample Survey.*

aged 15–19 years had never attended school and over 40 percent of their younger sisters aged 6–14 years were illiterate in 1968 (Table 17.16). In the same year, about 40 percent of both the 6–14-year-olds and 15–19-year-olds had never attended school; 66 percent of the rural population and 45 percent of the urbanites had not received any formal education.

It must also be noted that education has not spread evenly among the different sections of the Ghanaian community. It will be seen from the figures presented in Tables 17.16, 17.17, and 17.18 that, in almost every age group, the proportion of males with some kind of schooling is higher than that of the females. In 1968, while almost half of the males had attended or were attending school, only one-third of the females had ever been to school. While in 1960, "well over twice as many males as females have ever been to school," the 1968 figures show that the ratio has decreased to nearly one-and-a-half times as many. That "this state of affairs is passing"[9] is borne out by the fact that, while in 1960 in the "younger years of primary school at the present time the males outnumbered the females by only one-and-a-half times,"[10] the proportion of females and males aged 6 years and over who had or were receiving primary schooling in 1968 was 62.4 and 48.9 percent respectively. Among the urban populations, more than three-fifths of both the 6–14-year-olds and 15–19-year-olds have ever been to school at some time, while only one-half of their rural counterparts have had the same opportunity (Table 17.17).

In 1968, 66 percent of the rural people and 45 percent of the urban dwellers had never attended school. It is interesting to note that in 1968 more urban girls aged 6–14 years (69 percent) were receiving some education than were rural boys in the same age range (60 percent) (Table 17.17). This partly reflects the concentration of educational facilities in the urban areas.

[9] Caldwell, "Population: General Characteristics," p. 52.
[10] *Ibid.*, pp. 53–55.

TABLE 17.17
School attendance by sex, age, and residence, (percent who had ever attended or were attending school)

| Age | Urban | | | Rural | | |
|---|---|---|---|---|---|---|
| | M & F | M | F | M & F | M | F |
| 6–14 | 73.5 | 78.5 | 68.9 | 55.8 | 60.1 | 51.2 |
| 15–19 | 70.7 | 82.8 | 60.1 | 55.3 | 69.1 | 41.6 |
| 20–29 | 53.7 | 71.6 | 40.8 | 28.2 | 45.9 | 16.1 |
| 30–39 | 36.2 | 52.9 | 21.6 | 14.9 | 25.6 | 5.5 |
| 40–49 | 29.5 | 44.1 | 16.4 | 7.8 | 13.4 | 2.3 |
| 50–59 | 26.5 | 42.2 | 12.8 | 7.0 | 11.8 | 2.0 |
| 60+ | 23.3 | 35.3 | 11.1 | 7.1 | 10.3 | 3.0 |

SOURCE: Gaisie et al., *National Demographic Sample Survey.*

An analysis of types of school attended and grades completed is one of the effective ways of examining in greater detail the educational status of the community. Table 17.18 presents the proportions attending different types of schools. It must be noted that, although the number of Ghanaians going to school has increased very rapidly over the years, only a small proportion of them actually go beyond middle school.[11] In 1960, for example, less than 8 percent of past school attenders had received either a secondary or university education, and by 1968 there had been little or no increase in the proportion receiving higher education. In absolute terms it appears that more and more Ghanaians are going to school, but only a small proportion of them go on to or complete secondary and university training (Table 17.18). In 1960, only 4.5 percent of those who had received some kind of education attended secondary school and only 1.8 percent had reached the fifth form. One percent had spent six years in the secondary school, 0.2 percent had spent four years in technical institutions, and about 1 percent had been in a university for three or more years. Of those currently experiencing full-time education in 1960, 0.2 percent, 0.4 percent, and 3 percent were in a university, technical institution, or secondary school respectively.

[11] A four-year, postprimary school, which can be wholly or partly omitted by students passing from primary to secondary schools.

TABLE 17.18

School attendance by type of school and grade (Percent of all enjoying full-time education in 1960; 1968 figures in parentheses)

| Type of School and Grade | Both Sexes | Males | Females |
|---|---|---|---|
| *Primary* | *69.4 (54.3)* | *66.5 (48.9)* | *75.3 (62.4)* |
| 1–3 years | 43.3 | 40.6 | 48.6 |
| 4–6 years | 26.1 | 25.9 | 26.7 |
| *Middle* | *24.9 (38.6)* | *26.7 (42.6)* | *21.2 (32.6)* |
| 1–2 years | 14.2 | 14.8 | 12.9 |
| 3–4 years | 10.7 | 11.9 | 8.3 |
| *Secondary* | *2.7 (6.5)*[a] | *3.3 (7.7)*[a] | *1.5 (4.7)*[a] |
| 1–3 years | 1.8 | 2.2 | 1.0 |
| 4–5 years | 0.8 | 0.9 | 0.4 |
| 6 years | 0.1 | 0.2 | 0.1 |
| *University* | *0.2 (0.5)* | *0.3 (0.6)* | *0.04 (0.2)* |
| (1–5 years) | | | |

SOURCES: 1960 census; Gaisie et al., *National Demographic Sample Survey.*
[a] For secondary teacher training, commercial, technical schools.

The problem of educating the young is becoming more acute as a result of the rapid increase in the number of children of school-going age. On the basis of the projected population of indigenous Ghanaians,[12] children aged five years would increase in number by 47 percent between 1960 and 1970 and by a further 35 percent within a period of ten years following 1970. The entire elementary school-age population would increase by 40 percent between 1960 and 1970 and would almost double itself by 1980. The percentage increases among the population of appropriate age for secondary education would be 31 percent between 1960 and 1970 and a total of 93 percent by 1980. The number of persons in the age group 19–24 years (i.e., school-age population of the higher educational institutions) would also rise by 30 percent within the same period. These percentages represent very large increases in the total number of children, adolescents, and adults for whom primary schooling and other forms of education should be provided.

There have been significant increases in the proportions of the regional populations aged 6 years and over who have ever been to school. These increases no doubt reflect improvements in educational facilities making

[12] Gaisie, *Dynamics of Population Growth*, p. 67.

it possible for more persons to go to school. The regions have maintained their positions on the educational scale as revealed by the 1960 census figures, and the more urbanized and the richer regions, possessing more educational facilities, still have a higher proportion of their peoples in schools (Table 17.19).

ECONOMIC ACTIVITY

In 1960, 89 and 57 percent of the males and females respectively aged 15 years and over

TABLE 17.19

School attendance by region, 1960 and 1968 (percent of population aged 6 years and over ever at school)

| Region | 1960 | 1968 |
|---|---|---|
| Accra Capital District | 47 | 63 |
| Eastern | 35 | 51 |
| Ashanti | 33 | 48 |
| Volta | 34 | 48 |
| Central | 28[a] | 42 |
| Western | | 40 |
| Brong-Ahafo | 20 | 36 |
| Northern | 6[a] | 21 |
| Upper | | 11 |

SOURCES: 1960 census; Gaisie et al., *National Demographic Sample Survey.*
[a] Central and Western regions combined and Northern and Upper regions combined.

were reported to be economically active; among this group, 94 percent of the males and 95 percent of the females were in employment. The corresponding figures for 1968 were 82 and 75 percent, and 95 and 98 percent respectively. However the proportions of the total male and female population who were employed were 46 and 30 percent in 1960 and 41 and 40 percent in 1968 respectively. The proportion of the employed among both the economically active males and females has remained relatively constant, but the proportion of the economically active males aged 15 years and over has declined by seven percentage points since 1960 and the proportion of their female counterparts increased from 57 to 75 percent. These changes also are reflected in the proportions of the total male and female populations who were employed during the periods under discussion. The proportion of employed males in the population fell from 46 to 41 percent between 1960 and 1968 while the female proportion increased from 30 to 40 percent during the same period. It must be noted, however, that these figures might have been affected by the seasonality of the tempo and the volume of economic activities in the country, expecially in the rural areas. For example, the 1968 data were collected at a time when harvesting of foodstuffs and cash crops was at its apogee and the comparatively large number of women who might have been working in the farms were probably reported as employed. On the other hand, the layoff of a large number of workers after the February 24, 1966, coup d'etat might have increased the proportion of male unemployed. In spite of

errors arising from sampling fluctuations which might have distorted the 1968 figures in one way or the other, the latter phenomenon may be explained in terms of gradually changing age structure which is made up of nearly 50 percent of children under 15 years of age. It may also be the case that, in a period of tight employment, fewer persons regard themselves as potentially economically active.

Table 17.20 presents the distribution of persons aged 15 years and over by economic activity. The pattern of economic activity also appears to have remained relatively constant since 1960, except that, while the proportion of students has increased over the years, the proportion of female homemakers has been slashed by more than 50 percent. The different times of the year during which the 1960 and 1968 data were collected may be one of the explanations of the wide difference between the proportions of female homemakers. The 1968 data were collected during the main cocoa season and it is probable that most of the female homemakers who were helping their husbands and relatives on the cocoa farms would have been listed as employed. During this period, too, the harvesting of millet (undertaken mainly by women) and onions was going on in the Northern and Upper regions and the Volta Region respectively. The rapid increase in the school population since 1960 explains the increase in the size of the student status component (see Table 17.16). Other important points to note about the economically active population are that 4.8 percent of the males and 4.1 percent of the females were aged over 65 years, and that 71 and 43 percent

TABLE 17.20

Economic activity of population aged 15 years and over by sex, 1960 and 1968 (in percent)

| | Employed | | Unemployed | | Homemakers | | Students | | Aged & Disabled | | Other | |
|---|---|---|---|---|---|---|---|---|---|---|---|---|
| | 1960 | 1968 | 1960 | 1968 | 1960 | 1968 | 1960 | 1968 | 1960 | 1968 | 1960 | 1968 |
| Males | 83.2 | 78.4 | 5.8 | 3.9 | 0.6 | 3.4 | 6.0 | 11.6 | 3.3 | 2.0 | 1.1 | 0.4 |
| Females | 53.6 | 73.5 | 3.0 | 1.6 | 36.7 | 16.7 | 1.8 | 4.9 | 4.8 | 2.6 | 0.3 | 0.3 |
| Both sexes | 68.6 | 75.8 | 4.4 | 2.7 | 18.4 | 10.4 | 3.9 | 8.1 | 4.0 | 2.3 | 0.7 | 0.3 |

SOURCES: 1960 census; S. K. Gaisie et al., *The National Demographic Sample Survey*, Vol. 2b—*Economic Statistics* (Accra, 1971).

TABLE 17.21
Population aged 65 years and over who are
economically active: selected countries
(in percent)

| Country | Year | M | F |
|---|---|---|---|
| Ghana | 1960 | 71.3 | 42.6 |
| Liberia | 1962 | 64.3 | 20.4 |
| Mozambique | 1950 | 76.9 | 1.4 |
| Venezuela | 1961 | 72.0 | 8.4 |
| Libya | 1964 | 50.9 | 1.6 |
| United Arab Republic | 1960 | 62.5 | 1.9 |
| Ceylon | 1953 | 67.8 | 23.3 |
| Japan | 1960 | 54.5 | 36.2 |
| United States | 1960 | 29.7 | 10.1 |
| Switzerland | 1960 | 41.9 | 11.0 |
| United Kingdom | 1961 | 24.7 | 5.4 |

SOURCE: International Labor Organisation, *1966 Year Book of Labor Statistics* (Geneva, 1966), Table 1.

respectively of males and females were employed. Table 17.21 shows that Ghana's figures in this regard are among the highest in the world. In developing countries, where the majority of the economically active population are employed in agriculture, the older people, especially the males, continue to work on the farms as long as they are physically and mentally capable of doing so. In comparison with other developing countries, the proportion of Ghanaian females aged 65 years and over who reported themselves as economically active is higher than that of any of the developing countries represented in Table 17.21. One plausible explanation of this situation is that Ghanaian females tend to occupy themselves with more than one job, and they therefore appear to be in employment most of the time. Farming, pottery, and petty trading are some of the commonest occupations of Ghanaian women.

Among the employed population, 56 and 76 percent of the males and females respec-

tively were either employers or self-employed. A little over one-tenth and less than one-fifth of the males were employed in the public and nonpublic sectors respectively. Apart from being employers or self-employed, a large number of the females were reported as family workers and only 1.4 and 2.3 percent were working in the public and nonpublic sectors of the economy as employees (see Table 17.22).

In 1960, about 6 percent of the economically active population aged 15 years and over were reported unemployed. The corresponding percentages for males and females in 1968 were 4.8 and 2.2 respectively. The problem of unemployment in Ghana is more acute in the urban areas than in the countryside. The 1960 census revealed that, although 23 percent of the population was classified as urban, 44 percent of the unemployed were roaming the streets of the towns. Caldwell observed that the ". . . incidence of unemployment is twice as high in the towns as in rural Ghana."[13] Furthermore, there is an inverse relationship between the size of town or locality and the incidence of unemployment. Thus proportion of males unemployed increases from 8 percent in towns with between 5,000 and 9,999 inhabitants to 17 percent in towns of more than 50,000 inhabitants (Table 17.23b).

The 1960 figures show quite clearly that both male and female unemployment is concentrated in the age range of 15–24 years (Table 17.23a). It must be noted that the proportion of urban population in this age range is higher than that of the rural population in the same age range. The proportion of this age climbs steadily as the size of the

[13] Caldwell, "Population: General Characteristics," p. 55.

TABLE 17.22
Employment status of the working population, 1960 (in percent)

| | Employers and Self-employed | Employees in Public Sector | Employees in Nonpublic Sector | Family Workers | Apprentices | Caretakers in Agriculture |
|---|---|---|---|---|---|---|
| Males | 55.6 | 11.3 | 17.8 | 9.8 | 2.5 | 3.0 |
| Females | 76.2 | 1.4 | 2.3 | 19.0 | 0.8 | 0.3 |
| Both sexes | 63.6 | 7.4 | 11.8 | 13.4 | 1.9 | 1.9 |

TABLE 17.23
Urban and rural unemployed and total population, 1960

(a) By Sex-Age Group (percent distributions)

| Age Group | Males Urban | Males Rural | Females Urban | Females Rural | Unemployed Over 15 Years of Age Urban | Unemployed Over 15 Years of Age Rural |
|---|---|---|---|---|---|---|
| 10–14 | 9.4 | 10.9 | 11.2 | 9.4 | — | — |
| 15–19 | 9.7 | 7.7 | 9.5 | 7.5 | 34 | 53 |
| 20–24 | 11.0 | 6.9 | 10.9 | 9.2 | 27 | 18 |
| 25–29 | 11.0 | 7.4 | 9.1 | 9.3 | 15 | 8 |
| 30–34 | 8.2 | 6.8 | 7.1 | 7.5 | 9 | 5 |
| All ages | 100.0 | 100.0 | 100.0 | 100.0 | 100.0 | 100.0 |

(b) By Urban-Rural Division and Size Group of Towns (percent, all persons or sex in location)

| Age Group | Urban M | Urban F | Rural M | Rural F | Size of Towns 5,006–9,999 total | Size of Towns 10,000–19,999 total | Size of Towns 20,000–49,999 total | Size of Towns 50,000+ total |
|---|---|---|---|---|---|---|---|---|
| 10–24 | 9.4 | 11.2 | 10.9 | 9.4 | 10.5 | 10.4 | 10.5 | 9.9 |
| 15–24 | 20.6 | 20.4 | 14.6 | 16.7 | 18.0 | 19.8 | 20.8 | 23.0 |
| 25–44 | 29.8 | 24.8 | 24.9 | 26.8 | 25.1 | 27.9 | 27.4 | 28.8 |

Proportion of Total Unemployed Resident in

| | | | | | 5,006–9,999 | 10,000–19,999 | 20,000–49,999 | 50,000+ |
|---|---|---|---|---|---|---|---|---|
| Males | | | | | 7.8 | 9.0 | 7.5 | 16.7 |
| Females | | | | | 8.9 | 8.5 | 9.7 | 19.9 |

SOURCES: (a) Caldwell, "Population Prospects," Table 1.21, p. 56. N. O. Addo, *Demographic Aspects of Urban Development in Ghana in the Twentieth Century*, Monograph 3 (forthcoming) Chapter 2, Table 12.

locality of residence increases (Table 17.23b). Thus the high incidence of unemployment is largely due to the constant influx of young adults from the countryside into the towns. The rural unemployment in the age groups 15–19 and 20–24 is the "cause of such migration."[14]

The labor force projections prepared by the author[15] indicate that, unless the number of jobs available is increased annually by 3 percent or more, the unemployment problem will become more acute in the future. The projections show that the indigenous labor force is likely to increase at the rate of 2.8 percent per annum between 1965 and 1970 and at 3.7 percent in the period following 1970; and that these rates would

[14] *Ibid.*
[15] Gaisie, *Dynamics of Population Growth*, p. 66.

increase the number of workers to 8.7 million in 1995 and 18.6 million in 2015.

In 1960, 52 percent of the country's labor force was employed in agriculture, forestry, hunting, and fishing. Of these, 58 percent were farmers engaged in "field crops and foodstuffs production including vegetables and flowers and mixed farming"; 35 percent worked on oil palm, tea, coffee, and rubber plantations and in cocoa and tobacco growing, and only 3.6 and 0.7 percent were employed in fishing and forestry respectively. Thus more than half of the country's agricultural labor force are subsistence farmers and subsistence farming is the main occupation of the employed persons in agriculture in the Northern, Upper, Volta, Western and Central Regions. On the other hand, although 80 percent and 62 percent of the labor force

TABLE 17.24

Persons employed in industries by sex, 1960
(numbers of employees in thousands)

| Industry | Males | | Females | | Both Sexes | |
|---|---|---|---|---|---|---|
| | Number | Percent | Number | Percent | Number | Percent |
| Agriculture, forestry, hunting, and fishing | 1,003 | 64 | 576 | 58 | 1,579 | 62 |
| Mining | 46 | 3 | 2 | 0 | 48 | 2 |
| Manufacturing | 136 | 9 | 99 | 10 | 235 | 9 |
| Commerce | 96 | 6 | 276 | 28 | 372 | 15 |
| Construction | 87 | 5 | 3 | 0 | 90 | 3 |
| Electricity, water, and sanitary services | 14 | 1 | 0 | 0 | 14 | 1 |
| Transport | 67 | 4 | 1 | 0 | 68 | 3 |
| Services | 124 | 8 | 31 | 3 | 155 | 6 |
| All industries | 1,573 | 100 | 988 | 100 | 2,561 | 100 |

SOURCE: Caldwell, "Population Prospects," Table 1.22, p. 58.

were employed in agriculture and its related pursuits in Brong-Ahafo and Ashanti respectively, only 41 and 37 percent were subsistence farmers. These are the main cocoa and coffee-growing areas of Ghana (Tables 17.24 and 17.25).

## MARITAL STATUS

In 1960, 65 percent of the males and 91 percent of the females aged 15 years and over had ever been married. The corresponding proportions in 1968 were 62 and 87 percent.

TABLE 17.25

Employment in agriculture by region, 1960

| Region | Labor Force Employed in: (percent) | | |
|---|---|---|---|
| | (1) Agriculture, forestry, hunting, & fishing | (2) Field crops & foodstuffs | Percent (2) of (1) |
| Accra Capital District | 13 | 6 | 48 |
| Eastern | 59 | 28 | 47 |
| Western and Central | 58 | 29 | 50 |
| Ashanti | 62 | 23 | 37 |
| Brong-Ahafo | 80 | 33 | 41 |
| Volta | 62 | 40 | 64 |
| Northern and Upper | 86 | 84 | 98 |
| Ghana | 62 | 36 | 58 |

SOURCE: Caldwell, "Population Prospects," Table 1.23, p. 59.

These figures show that most Ghanaians, especially the females, do marry. An analysis of marital status by age reveals some interesting features. While five-sixths of males, 15–24, were classified as bachelors, only one-quarter of the females were reported as spinsters. The proportions never married continued to dwindle along the age ladder to such an extent that only 0.4 percent of the females aged 50 years and over had never married although nearly 3 percent of the males in the same age group claimed to be bachelors. The proportions currently married increased with age and the highest points were reached in the age groups 45–49 for males and 35–44 for females (Table 17.26). The corresponding age groups in 1968 were 40–49 and 30–39. It appears, therefore, that, on average, men marry girls who are between 5 and 10 years younger than themselves. The percentages of the married males and females fall to 81 percent and 41 percent in the age group 50 years and over (Table 17.26). On the other hand, the proportions widowed and divorced increase with age without declining at any point on the age ladder. The increases are steeper after age 44, especially among the females whose remarriage problem at this age is much more acute than that of the males. Thus, while about 44 percent of the females aged 50 years and over are widowed, only

TABLE 17.26

Percent distribution of the population aged 15 years and over by age and marital status, 1960

| | Males | | | |
|---|---|---|---|---|
| Age Group | Never married | Married | Divorced | Widowed |
| *Total 15 years and over* | *34.4* | *58.6* | *5.1* | *1.9* |
| 15–24 | 84.1 | 14.8 | 1.0 | 0.1 |
| 25–34 | 28.0 | 66.8 | 4.6 | 0.6 |
| 35–44 | 8.4 | 83.0 | 7.0 | 1.6 |
| 45–49 | 4.2 | 85.0 | 8.0 | 2.8 |
| 50+ | 2.8 | 81.0 | 9.6 | 6.6 |
| | Females | | | |
| *Total 15 years and over* | *9.0* | *74.7* | *7.2* | *9.1* |
| 15–24 | 25.8 | 70.2 | 3.6 | 0.4 |
| 25–34 | 1.9 | 91.0 | 5.5 | 1.6 |
| 35–44 | 0.6 | 85.5 | 8.0 | 5.0 |
| 45–49 | 0.5 | 72.3 | 12.0 | 15.2 |
| 50+ | 0.4 | 41.0 | 15.2 | 43.5 |

SOURCE: D. J. Owusu, "Marriage Patterns and Their Effects on Fertility in Ghana" (Paper presented at the International Union of the Scientific Study of Population Conference, London, September 1969), Table 1.

6.6 percent of the males have this marital status. The proportions widowed, therefore, appear to be dependent upon the rate of remarriage, mortality differentials among the sexes, and the extent to which polygamy is practiced. The proportion divorced is higher among females than among males. In 1968, 5 and 9 percent of the males and females respectively were divorced at the time of the sample inquiry (Table 17.27). The 1960 postenumeration survey data recorded 5 and 7 percent respectively. It must be noted, however, that it is the comparatively high rate of remarriages among men that accounts for the low percentage of divorced males. Furthermore, a polygynist is not included in this figure if he divorces one of his wives.

It is interesting to note that the marriage pattern revealed by the 1960 census is, to a great extent, repeated in the 1968 figures (Table 17.27). But a feature revealed by the 1968 figures is that out of 122 children aged between 12 and 14 years who were classified as married, 107 or 88 percent hail from the Upper Region where very young betrothals are said to be common.

TABLE 17.27

Percent distribution of the population aged 12 years and over by age and marital status, 1968

| | Males | | | | |
|---|---|---|---|---|---|
| Age Group | Never married | Married | Divorced, separated | Widowed | Not reported |
| *Total 12 years & over* | *46.1* | *48.4* | *3.8* | *1.2* | *0.5* |
| 12–14 | 99.7 | 0.3 | — | — | — |
| 15–19 | 99.0 | 2.0 | — | — | — |
| 20–29 | 57.4 | 40.0 | 2.0 | 0.1 | 0.5 |
| 30–39 | 14.7 | 78.6 | 5.3 | 0.8 | 0.6 |
| 40–49 | 6.9 | 85.0 | 6.4 | 1.1 | 0.6 |
| 50–59 | 4.3 | 83.6 | 8.2 | 3.0 | 0.9 |
| 60+ | 9.8 | 73.0 | 9.7 | 6.4 | 1.1 |
| | Females | | | | |
| *Total 12 years & over* | *21.5* | *62.4* | *8.0* | *8.0* | *0.1* |
| 12–14 | 96.7 | 3.2 | 0.1 | — | — |
| 15–19 | 58.5 | 37.5 | 3.8 | 0.2 | — |
| 20–29 | 9.0 | 83.1 | 7.1 | 0.7 | 0.1 |
| 30–39 | 1.0 | 86.9 | 8.8 | 3.2 | 0.1 |
| 40–49 | 0.6 | 78.2 | 11.2 | 9.8 | 0.2 |
| 50–59 | 0.7 | 57.7 | 15.5 | 25.8 | 0.3 |
| 60+ | 2.2 | 26.8 | 15.6 | 54.6 | 0.8 |

SOURCE: Gaisie et al., *National Demographic Sample Survey*, Vol. 2a.

TABLE 17.28
Proportion ever married

| 1960 | | | 1968 | | |
|---|---|---|---|---|---|
| Age Group | M | F | Age Group | M | F |
| 35–44 | 91.6 | 99.4 | 30–39 | 85.3 | 99.0 |
| 45–49 | 95.8 | 99.5 | 40–49 | 93.1 | 99.4 |
| 50+ | 97.2 | 99.6 | 50+ | 92.7 | 98.5 |

SOURCES: Computed from Owusu, "Marriage Patterns," Table 1; Gaisie et al., *National Demographic Sample Survey*, Vol. 2a.

Three important points to note about the marriage patterns described above are: (1) females marry at younger ages than males and on the average, the former tend to be between 5 and 10 years younger than their husbands; (2) males remarry more rapidly than females, especially after age 45 years; (3) most Ghanaians get married at some stage in their lives (Table 17.28). The urban-rural differentials in marriage patterns also show certain marital characteristics. The proportions of both spinsters and bachelors are lower in the rural areas than in the towns and cities. On the other hand, the proportions currently married in each age group are higher in the countryside than in the urban centers. While almost 0.5 percent of rural females aged 12–14 years are married, none of the urban girls in the same age group are married. The level of divorce is almost as high among rural females as among their urban counterparts. Yet the urban male marriages appear to be more stable than the rural ones (Tables 17.29 and 17.30). It is clear from Tables 17.29 and 17.30 that both rural males and females marry at younger ages than their urban brothers and sisters. And although age at marriage may be determined by certain socioeconomic, cultural, and legal elements within a particular society, urban-rural residence has become an important variable determining female marriage patterns by age.

AGE AT MARRIAGE. One much documented conclusion in sociodemographic studies is that age at marriage, especially for females, is low in Ghana. As Fortes recorded, "a Tallensi woman is married as soon as she is nubile and very few fertile women reach the age of 20 without having had at least one pregnancy."[16] "Ashanti girls marry between 16 and 18 years of age, youths between 20 and 25." Busia observed that "on the average the age of first marriage for girls in the rural towns seemed to be about 18, but just over 21 for girls in the urban towns."[17] It has also been reported that 74 and 63 percent of the girls in Salt Town and Yeji respectively were first married before they were 19 years old.[18] A survey conducted by Friedlander and Smith[19] in 1961 revealed that 61 percent of the women in four rural towns in Ghana married between the ages of 16 and 18 and about 81 percent married before the age of 20. The corresponding figures for Sekondi-Takoradi were 54 and 70 percent respectively. Even 65 percent of the women interviewed in Caldwell's sample survey of the urban elite were under 23 years of age when first married.[20] According to the postenumeration survey, 91 percent of all females aged 15 and over were either married, divorced, or widowed. It was also noted that about 84 percent of 15–24-year-old females had been married at least once. A singulate mean age at marriage for females (based on the postenumeration survey data) has been estimated to be 17.7 years.[21] The singulate mean age at marriage for females is about 5 percent in the urban areas (18.7 years) than in the rural ones.

FORM OF MARRIAGE. The principal form of marriage in Ghana is the customary marriage,

[16] M. Fortes, "Kinship and Marriage Among the Ashanti," in A. R. Radcliffe Brown and D. Forde, eds., *African Systems of Kinship and Marriage* (London: Oxford University Press, 1950), p. 278.

[17] K. A. Busia, "Some Aspects of Social Conditions Affecting Human Fertility in the Gold Coast," in F. Lorimer, ed., *Culture and Human Fertility* (Paris, 1954).

[18] P. A. Tetteh, "Marriage, Family and Household," in Birmingham et al., *A Study of Contemporary Ghana*, p. 202.

[19] S. K. Gaisie, "An Analysis of Fertility Levels in Contemporary Ghana," (M.A. Thesis held by the University of London, 1964).

[20] John C. Caldwell, "Fertility Differentials as Evidence of Incipient Fertility Decline in a Developing Country: The Case of Ghana," *Population Studies*, XXI, 1 (July 1967), 14, Table 9.

[21] Unpublished figures, supplied courtesy of F. Aryee Demographic Unit, University of Ghana.

TABLE 17.29

Percent distribution of the population aged 15 years and over by sex, age, marital status, urban/rural

| Age Group | Urban | | | | Rural | | | |
|---|---|---|---|---|---|---|---|---|
| | Never married | Married | Divorced | Widowed | Never married | Married | Divorced | Widowed |
| | | | | *Males* | | | | |
| *Total 15 years & over* | *41.9* | *52.9* | *4.0* | *1.2* | *31.6* | *60.7* | *5.6* | *2.1* |
| 15–24 | 86.8 | 12.5 | 0.6 | 0.1 | 82.8 | 15.9 | 1.2 | 0.1 |
| 25–34 | 31.6 | 64.6 | 3.5 | 0.3 | 26.4 | 67.8 | 5.1 | 0.7 |
| 35–44 | 8.1 | 84.4 | 6.6 | 0.9 | 8.6 | 82.5 | 7.1 | 1.8 |
| 45–49 | 5.0 | 85.4 | 7.5 | 2.1 | 2.7 | 85.8 | 9.4 | 2.1 |
| 50+ | 4.0 | 79.6 | 9.6 | 6.8 | 2.5 | 81.3 | 9.6 | 6.6 |
| | | | | *Females* | | | | |
| *Total 15 years & over* | *13.3* | *70.7* | *7.8* | *8.2* | *7.7* | *75.9* | *7.0* | *9.4* |
| 15–24 | 32.8 | 63.6 | 3.3 | 0.3 | 23.1 | 72.6 | 3.8 | 0.5 |
| 25–34 | 2.9 | 89.0 | 6.9 | 1.2 | 1.6 | 91.6 | 5.0 | 1.8 |
| 35–44 | 0.9 | 83.4 | 10.5 | 5.2 | 0.6 | 86.0 | 7.3 | 6.1 |
| 45–49 | 1.1 | 68.1 | 15.4 | 15.4 | 0.5 | 73.4 | 11.0 | 15.1 |
| 50+ | 0.7 | 36.7 | 16.4 | 46.2 | 0.3 | 42.1 | 14.8 | 42.8 |

SOURCE: Owusu, "Marriage Patterns," Table 2.

TABLE 17.30

Percent distribution of the population aged 12 years and over by age, sex, marital status, and urban-rural differentials, 1968

| Age Group | Urban | | | | | Rural | | | | |
|---|---|---|---|---|---|---|---|---|---|---|
| | Never married | Married | Divorced or separated | Widowed | Not reported | Never married | Married | Divorced or separated | Widowed | Not reported |
| | | | | | *Males* | | | | | |
| *Total 12 years & over* | *49.9* | *46.2* | *2.9* | *0.7* | *0.3* | *44.6* | *49.3* | *4.2* | *1.4* | *0.5* |
| 12–14 | 99.9 | — | — | — | 0.1 | 99.6 | 0.4 | — | — | — |
| 15–19 | 99.1 | 0.7 | 0.1 | — | 0.1 | 97.4 | 2.5 | — | — | 0.1 |
| 20–29 | 62.7 | 35.4 | 1.4 | — | 0.5 | 54.7 | 42.5 | 2.3 | 0.2 | 0.3 |
| 30–39 | 12.5 | 82.6 | 4.5 | 0.2 | 0.2 | 15.7 | 76.9 | 5.7 | 1.1 | 0.6 |
| 40–49 | 5.6 | 88.4 | 5.1 | 0.6 | 0.3 | 7.3 | 83.8 | 6.8 | 1.3 | 0.8 |
| 50+ | 8.0 | 79.4 | 7.7 | 4.1 | 0.8 | 7.0 | 77.6 | 9.3 | 5.0 | 1.1 |
| | | | | | *Females* | | | | | |
| *Total 12 years & over* | *26.9* | *58.0* | *8.4* | *6.5* | *0.2* | *19.1* | *64.3* | *7.8* | *8.7* | *0.1* |
| 12–14 | 99.5 | 0.5 | — | — | — | 95.1 | 4.7 | 0.1 | — | 0.1 |
| 15–19 | 66.4 | 30.6 | 3.0 | — | — | 54.6 | 41.0 | 4.1 | 0.3 | — |
| 20–29 | 13.7 | 78.0 | 7.6 | 0.6 | 0.1 | 6.7 | 85.6 | 6.8 | 0.8 | 0.1 |
| 30–39 | 11.5 | 84.3 | 10.9 | 3.1 | 0.2 | 0.8 | 88.0 | 7.8 | 3.3 | 0.1 |
| 40–49 | 1.2 | 75.5 | 14.3 | 8.8 | 0.2 | 0.4 | 79.2 | 10.0 | 10.2 | 0.2 |
| 50+ | 1.8 | 44.8 | 16.0 | 36.9 | 0.5 | 1.3 | 42.2 | 15.4 | 40.6 | 0.5 |

SOURCE: Gaisie et al., *National Demographic Sample Survey*, Vol. 2a.

which is contracted in accordance with the provisions of the customary law. The customary marriage is celebrated by the giving of marriage payments and by the performance of a series of ceremonies, each of which is regarded as a necessary step toward the establishment of a legal union. Such a union is endowed with certain "legal sanctions" which are recognized by the members of the community. The elaborateness of the ceremonies and the kinds of payments made vary from one part of the country to another. For example, among the Akans, payment of *tiri nsa* which consists of drink and money validates the marriage. The *tiri nsa* varies according to the "social-economic" status of the girl. On the other hand, it is the ceremony of the powdering of the bride—*togbagba*—which validates marriage among the Anlo Ewes, not the marriage payments as such.[22]

Another form of marriage, which one comes across in Ghana, especially among the educated Ghanaians, is the marriage contracted under the "Marriage Ordinance" (*Cap. 127* of the *Laws of Ghana*). Unlike the customary marriage, it is monogamous and can only be dissolved in a court of law. This form of marriage is regarded as a prestige symbol and the educated women prefer it to other forms of marriage because "it gives them and their children security with regard to inheritance of the husband's personal property."[23] Two-thirds of the husband's personal property goes to the wife and the children if he dies intestate. The wife, however, gets only one-third of the property if the man is not survived by a child.

Islamic marriage is similar to the Christian church marriage in many respects. In both cases, the local minister of religion records the marriage and he is supposed to be consulted in case of divorce. The Islamic marriage is celebrated in accordance with the provisions of the *Marriage of the Mohammedans* (*Cap. 129*

of the *Laws of Ghana*) and one of the provisions is that the men can marry as many as four wives and no more. It must be noted that in Ghana a marriage can take more than one of the forms described above and in most of these cases the customary marriage forms an integral part of the other types of marriage (Table 17.31).

TABLE 17.31
Percent distribution of married males by form of marriage, total country, urban-rural, 1960

| Form of Marriage | Total Country | Urban | Rural |
|---|---|---|---|
| Customary | 86.1 | 80.3 | 88.0 |
| Ordinance (with customary and church as well) | 2.9 | 5.9 | 1.9 |
| Customary and church | 1.5 | 1.5 | 1.5 |
| Moslem with or without customary | 5.4 | 9.3 | 4.2 |
| Mutual consent | 4.0 | 2.9 | 4.4 |
| Other (by ordinance only, Hindu, etc.) | 0.1 | 0.1 | 0.0 |

SOURCE: Owusu, "Marriage Patterns," Table 3.

There is another type of union which usually is referred to as "mutual consent." It has no legal status. It is a *de facto* union which is characterized by the continuous cohabitation of the partners.

The 1960 postenumeration survey data show that, at the time of the inquiry, 86 percent of the ever-contracted marriages of the males were customary marriages (Table 17.31). The regional proportions ranged from 78 percent in Brong-Ahafo to 92 percent in the Northern and Upper Regions. In 1968, 80 percent of the currently married women were married under the customary law. About 96 percent of the women in the Upper Region and 68 percent of their Ashanti counterparts had been so married (Table 17.32). The figures in Table 17.31 and 17.32 show that the proportion of customary marriages in the rural areas is higher than in the urban centers. In 1960, the marriages contracted under the marriage ordinance accounted for only 2.9 percent (including both those with

[22] G. K. Nukunya, *Kinship and Marriage among the Anlo Ewe* (New York: Humanities Press, 1970).
[23] K. A. Busia, *Report on the Social Survey of Sekondi-Takoradi* (Westport, Conn.: Negro Universities Press, 1950 ed. reprint, n.d.).

TABLE 17.32
Percent distribution of married females by form of marriage total country, urban/rural, 1968

| Form of Marriage | Total Country | Urban | Rural |
|---|---|---|---|
| Customary only | 81.7 | 76.3 | 84.0 |
| Ordinance only | 0.3 | 0.8 | 0.1 |
| Ordinance, church, Moslem | 5.8 | 12.8 | 3.0 |
| Mutual consent | 11.0 | 9.0 | 11.8 |
| Other (Hindu or Buddhist custom, etc.) | 0.1 | 0.1 | — |
| Not reported | 1.1 | 1.0 | 1.1 |

SOURCE: Gaisie et al., *National Demographic Sample Survey*, Vol. 2a.

and without church blessing) of the ever-contracted marriages; the Accra Capital District had the highest proportion of such marriages (7.9 percent). A greater proportion of the urban dwellers than rural people have this type of marriage (Tables 17.31 and 17.32). In spite of the fact that the number of legal marriages is increasing, they still form only a comparatively small proportion of the total marriages contracted in the country. Among the currently married females, only 0.3 percent of their marriages were registered and only a very small number of the marriages classified under "church" fall into the category of ordinance marriages (Table 17.32).

Islamic marriages are also more common in the towns than in the countryside; the Ashanti and Brong-Ahafo regions top the list with about 8 and 10 percent respectively of the marriages contracted by males. These figures indicate that Islamic marriage is more important in the south than in the northern part of the country. The 1968 figures, however, show that about 42 percent of the currently married females in the Northern Region had marriages classified under "church" and about 90 percent of these were Moslem marriages. It is interesting to note that about 96 percent of the Upper Region marriages were classified as customary, and

2.4 percent were reported as church marriages. Thus Islamic marriages are more commonly found in the Northern Region than in the Upper Region where more than four-fifths of the female extant marriages were contracted under customary law.

The Christian church marriages accounted for only 1.5 percent of all the ever-contracted male marriages in 1960. While about 4 percent of the male ever-contracted marriages were classified as mutual consent in 1960, 12 percent of the currently married women were living in such a union in 1968. A large number of such unions were reported in Ashanti, Brong-Ahafo, Volta, and Eastern regions. A distribution of mutual consent unions by age indicates that the union represents a transitional stage in conjugal status.

TABLE 17.33
Percent distribution of married males by number of wives, total country, urban/rural, 1960

| No. of Wives | Total Country | Urban | Rural |
|---|---|---|---|
| 1 | 73.8 | 78.6 | 72.2 |
| 2 | 20.0 | 16.8 | 21.0 |
| 3 | 4.6 | 3.4 | 5.0 |
| 4 | 1.1 | 0.8 | 1.3 |
| 5 or more | 0.5 | 0.4 | 0.5 |

SOURCE: Owusu," Marriage Patterns," Table 4.

According to the figures provided by the postenumeration sample survey, about 26 percent of married men were polygynists, and among these polygynists, 76 percent had two wives and 5.8 percent had four wives or more. Table 17.33 also shows that polygyny is practiced more extensively in the rural areas than in the towns and the cities and that Volta and Northern regions exhibit the highest incidence of polygyny, followed by Ashanti and Brong-Ahafo Regions. The proportion of polygynous marriages ranges from 20 percent in Accra Capital District to 33 percent in the Northern Region.

# CHAPTER EIGHTEEN

# Immigration & Sociodemo-graphic Change

N. O. ADDO

ACCORDING to the 1960 census of Ghana, about 837,000 persons representing 12 percent of the total population, were of foreign origin. A considerable number of the immigrants[1] were found to have arrived only 18 months prior to the census. Immigration into Ghana nevertheless started long before 1960, and, indeed, immigrants had been associated with the development of the country since the early days of modernization. Although there are no statistics available to trace the growth of immigration in the past, historical evidence shows that the movement of foreigners into the country occurred rather slowly at first but became systematic in time. The movement did not occur smoothly throughout, but fluctuated during certain periods. It was not until after political independence that the country really received large numbers of immigrants; they arrived mainly from the neighboring African countries primarily to find work and improve their conditions of life. This chapter will concentrate on African immigrants in Ghana; this group formed 98 percent of the total immigrant population as of 1960.

The study will examine the relative impact of these immigrants on the social, economic, and demographic structure of the country around the mid-twentieth century. Our main source of data is the 1960 population census; we shall analyze the data on these immigrants with the aim of evaluating their relative position in the socioeconomic structure of the country. The analysis is based on the assumption that, by studying the characteristics of a group of the population and comparing them with other groups, one can demarcate with reasonable accuracy the areas of greatest development among these groups.

[1] The 1960 Ghana Population Census defines the country of origin of a person as the country where that person's father was born, if he was born outside Ghana. If the father was born in Ghana, then the country of origin was determined by the father's father's country of birth; where this was unknown, it was the mother's mother's country of birth which decided it. Anyone whose country of origin was outside Ghana was classified by the census as an "immigrant."

TABLE 18.1

Distribution of African Foreign origin population in Ghana by country of origin, 1960

| Country of Origin | Total Population | Males | Females |
|---|---|---|---|
| Togo | 34.5 | 31.2 | 39.3 |
| Upper Volta | 24.0 | 27.0 | 19.7 |
| Nigeria | 23.0 | 22.3 | 25.6 |
| Ivory Coast | 6.7 | 6.4 | 7.0 |
| Dahomey | 3.9 | 3.7 | 4.1 |
| Niger | 3.0 | 4.1 | 1.4 |
| Mali | 2.4 | 3.1 | 1.3 |
| Liberia | 1.0 | 1.0 | 0.1 |
| Other | 0.9 | 1.0 | 0.7 |
| *Totals:* | | | |
| percent | 100.0 | 100.0 | 100.0 |

N = 811,703　N = 482,402　N = 329,301

SOURCE: 1960 Ghana Population Census, III, Table 12.

## SOURCE OF ORIGIN OF THE IMMIGRANT POPULATION

The major sources of immigration in 1960 were Togo, Upper Volta, and Nigeria; together these formed about four-fifths of the total immigrant population in the country according to these data. The majority of the remaining immigrants originated from other West African countries, while less than 1 percent came from East, South, and North Africa combined (Table 18.1). Over one-third of the "immigrants" had been born in Ghana.

The immigrant population from each country is itself composed of different ethnic groups, such as Ibos and Yorubas of Nigeria; Dagabas and Grusi of Upper Volta; Lobis and others of Ivory Coast; Ewes, Atakpames, and Kotokolis of Togo; and other groups like the Hausas who came from various countries. These ethnic groups exhibit varied characteristics in respect of their educational level, occupational structure, residence patterns, age structure, sex ratios, and the level of integration achieved in the communities where they reside. This chapter is not intended to examine the ethnic differences among immigrants but rather the differences which exist between the group as a whole and the indigenous Ghanaian population.

## FOREIGN IMMIGRATION AND ITS EFFECTS ON THE SPATIAL DISTRIBUTION OF POPULATION

International migration into Ghana has made a considerable impact on the density of population throughout the various regions of the country. The addition of foreign immigrants has increased the density of population of the whole country from 64 to 73 persons per square mile, a rise of 14 percent (Table 18.2). The largest gains have been in the Eastern and Volta regions where foreign immigration has increased the density by nearly one-sixth while Northern Ghana received the smallest increase, one-tenth.

TABLE 18.2

Population density of various regions (persons per square mile)

| Region | (1) Without Foreign-Origin Population[a] | (2) With Foreign-Population | Percent Gain $\frac{(2) - (1)}{(1)}$ |
|---|---|---|---|
| All regions | 64 | 73 | 14.1 |
| Accra capital district | 387 | 494 | 12.8 |
| Western | 96 | 106 | 10.4 |
| Eastern | 123 | 142 | 15.4 |
| Volta | 85 | 98 | 15.3 |
| Ashanti | 103 | 118 | 14.6 |
| Brong-Ahafo | 34 | 38 | 11.8 |
| Northern | 31 | 34 | 9.7 |

[a] Persons of Ghanaian descent only.

TABLE 18.3

Regional distribution of foreign-origin population by place of birth and sex ratios

| Region | All Foreign-Origin | | Foreign-Origin Born in Ghana | | Foreign-Origin Born outside Ghana | |
|---|---|---|---|---|---|---|
| | Percent | Sex ratios | Percent | Sex ratios | Percent | Sex ratios |
| Accra capital district | 12.9 | 162 | 11.6 | 107 | 13.6 | 298 |
| Western | 14.7 | 163 | 13.3 | 108 | 15.4 | 202 |
| Eastern | 18.0 | 146 | 19.2 | 108 | 17.4 | 177 |
| Volta | 12.6 | 120 | 11.9 | 108 | 12.9 | 126 |
| Ashanti | 17.3 | 172 | 16.1 | 108 | 18.0 | 220 |
| Brong-Ahafo | 9.1 | 191 | 7.2 | 112 | 10.1 | 238 |
| Northern | 15.4 | 106 | 20.7 | 104 | 12.6 | 108 |
| All regions | 100.0 | 147 | 100.0 | 107 | 100.0 | 175 |

SOURCE: 1960 Ghana Population Census, III, Tables 1 and 2.

Nearly one-fifth of all immigrants in Ghana lived in the Eastern Region at the time of the census. The two major economic factors which influenced these immigrants to settle in relatively large numbers in this region were the cocoa industry and diamond mining. Although, in proportionate terms, this region still has large numbers of immigrants, nevertheless the attractive power of the region has consistently declined in recent years due to the very limited opportunities which now exist for expanding cultivable cocoa land. At the same time economic expansion has occurred at a relatively more rapid pace in some of the other regions, such as the Accra Capital District, Ashanti, and Brong-Ahafo, and this has resulted in a large inflow of immigrants into these regions (Table 18.3).

Indeed, if the total number of immigrants is expressed as a fraction of the population of each region, then the Accra Capital District (ACD) has the highest fraction and thus could be said to be the major attractive region to these immigrants. The proportion of foreign-origin population in each of the regions was as follows: ACD, 20.0 percent; Western 8.6 percent; Eastern 13.6 percent; Volta, 13.3 percent; Ashanti 12.7 percent; and Northern 9.9 percent.

Evidence from the 1960 post-enumeration survey (PES) data on length of residence among the immigrants showed that those resident in Northern Ghana had, on the average, been there longer than those in any other region. For example, the distribution of the foreign-origin population over 15 years of age by those who had been in residence for more than 12 years prior to the 1960 PES is shown in Table 18.4. Whereas only 17 percent of the immigrants in rural Brong-Ahafo had lived there for 12 years or more, 38 percent and 60 percent of those living in the Western and Northern regions respectively had been in residence there for this length of time.

TABLE 18.4

Proportion of foreign-origin population over 15 years of age with more than 12 years residence, by region of residence

| Type of Residence | Region of Residence | | | | | | |
|---|---|---|---|---|---|---|---|
| | Accra cap. dist. | Western | Eastern | Volta | Ashanti | Brong-Ahafo | Northern |
| All | 36.4 | 43.1 | 34.1 | 33.2 | 23.2 | 18.0 | 56.1 |
| Rural | 28.6 | 37.9 | 32.5 | 28.3 | 21.8 | 16.7 | 59.5 |

SOURCE: 1960 Postenumeration survey data (unpublished).

The development of the cocoa industry in Brong-Ahafo has taken place only over the last two decades; for this reason the immigrants who came to work on the cocoa farms have not been in residence for very long. Indeed, a considerable number of the immigrants in this particular region arrived from other regions of Ghana, especially the Northern, Ashanti, and Eastern regions.

Another important spatial characteristic of the immigrants is that they have been highly mobile in the country; at the time of the 1960 PES, approximately one-quarter of all the foreign-origin population aged 15 and over had lived somewhere in Ghana outside the region where they were enumerated. The most mobile groups were those living in the Accra Capital District and Brong-Ahafo: About 88 and 53 percent respectively of all the immigrants in these regions aged 15 and over had lived elsewhere in Ghana before arriving in their present region of residence. The majority of the foreign-origin population (66.4 percent) lived in rural areas at the time of the census. There were considerable differences among the regions; for example, 83 percent of the immigrants residing in the Accra Capital District lived in towns, compared with 13 percent in the Volta region. There is some evidence to show that immigrants, particularly the females, the young, the educated, and also those born in Ghana, show greater preference for living in towns than in rural areas. In general those towns with the highest level of urbanization have absorbed the largest proportion of immigrants. The relationship between urbanization and the capacity of the towns to absorb these immigrants could be measured by ranked correlation coefficients; the results obtained are slightly positive ($+0.29$), meaning that immigrants have a slight tendency to favor living in urban areas compared with rural areas where the ranked correlation co-efficient is $+0.11$ (Table 18.5).

Apart from the economic motivation, there are other factors which influence the spatial characteristics of the immigrant population; these are geographic proximity and tribal or ethnic affiliation. The Togolese are concentrated mainly in the Volta Region, which lies along the border with Togo, and the Eastern Region and Accra Capital District, which also are not far from Togo. Upper Voltaics constitute the largest group of immigrants in the Northern Region, Brong-Ahafo, and Ashanti; these three regions are not far from Upper Volta. Nigerians are mainly concentrated in the Western and Eastern regions; these persons are attracted into this region partly because of the diamond and gold mines which exist here. A census office report on patterns of internal migration in Ghana indicated that geographical proximity and tribal affiliation are major factors which influence settlement patterns in the country. For example, a large number of Ewes settled in Accra and the Eastern Region,

TABLE 18.5

Relationship between urbanization and urban/rural residential patterns among foreign-origin population

| | Region of Residence | | | | | | | |
| | Accra cap. dist. | Western | Eastern | Volta | Ashanti | Brong-Ahafo | Northern | Rs[a] |
|---|---|---|---|---|---|---|---|---|
| Percent of total population of region in urban areas | 80.1 | 27.3 | 19.9 | 13.3 | 24.7 | 15.8 | 8.1 | — |
| Percent of foreign-origin population among urban population of region | 22.5 | 12.9 | 19.0 | 13.3 | 20.4 | 12.7 | 17.9 | +0.29 |
| Percent of foreign-origin population among rural population of region | 18.3 | 7.4 | 12.3 | 13.4 | 10.4 | 12.8 | 9.2 | +0.11 |

[a] Ranked correlation coefficient.

which are not far from the Volta Region, their home area; similarly the Dagaba and Grusi settled mainly in the Northern Region, near their home area further east. This association between geographical proximity, tribal affiliation, and settlement patterns is very strong among immigrant groups, particularly among those from Togo, Upper Volta, and Ivory Coast. In the latter case, the historical evidence is that the Lobi tribes of Ivory Coast crossed the border into Northern Ghana some time during the second decade of this century as a means of escape from the high taxation to which they were being subjected by the French authorities.[2] The case of the Togolese in the Volta Region is also interesting, and exemplifies a group who have not let an international boundary interfere with their cultural and family ties. The Ewes are the predominant tribe on both sides of the border, and because of the character of the social organization, families have to farm lands on both sides. Major factors influencing migration were found to be the extent of knowledge about the possibilities of obtaining better opportunities elsewhere, the distance which the immigrant is likely to travel in order to reach his proposed destination, the availability of transport to reach this place, as well as the possibility of finding a relative or someone from his own country in the new area. Since a large amount of the migration takes place on a seasonal basis, it is possible that some of those who planned to stay longer preferred to stay close enough to their home countries to facilitate easy communication with relatives at home.

## IMMIGRATION AND DEMOGRAPHIC CHANGE

Foreign immigration had contributed about 12 percent of the total population of Ghana in 1960. Over one-third (35 percent) of these immigrants had been born in the country of residence; proportionately considerably more females were born in Ghana (40 percent) than

[2] Jack Goody, *Social Organization of the Lo Willi* (London: H.M. Stationery Office, 1956), p. 16.

males (31 percent) thus showing that there were fewer adult female migrants. The age composition of the immigrants showed a preponderance of persons within the economically active age group, 15–64; the proportion in this age group was 20 percent higher than in the indigenous population. Similarly, whereas 35 percent of the immigrants were below the age of 15 years, nearly 46 percent of the indigenous population fell within this age group. The age structure varies considerably among the various ethnic groups; for example, among the Central Togo tribes, 45 percent were below 15 years compared with 30 percent among the Hausas. Nearly half of the immigrant population aged below 5 years and over four-fifths (84 percent) of all children below 5 years were born in Ghana.

Although the age pattern of the immigrant population was found to contain a relatively high proportion in the economically active ages, nevertheless, since the numerical impact of the group was relatively small, these characteristics had not produced any very appreciable change in the country's age structure as a whole. Thus, whereas among the indigenous population, 54.1 percent fell into the economically active age group, for the country as a whole (i.e., including immigrants) the proportion within the same group was only 2 percent higher (55.5 percent). The indigenous population on average was about three years younger than the immigrants; the average age of the immigrants born abroad was, however, almost eight years higher than the average age for the Ghanaian population as a whole and about ten years above the average for indigenous Ghanaians. The average age of immigrants born in Ghana was about seven years (Table 18.6). Thus, by implication, the immigrant population had only recently begun to contribute to child dependency in the country.

## SEX RATIOS

The presence of immigrants in the country has influenced the general sex ratio of the population; the ratio of males to females among the indigenous population was 97 per

TABLE 18.6

Comparison of the age structure of Ghana-origin population with foreign-origin population, both sexes (percent)

| Age Group | All Ghana | Ghana-Origin | All Foreign Origin | African Foreign-Origin | |
|---|---|---|---|---|---|
| | | | | Born outside Ghana | Born in Ghana |
| 0–4 | 19.2 | 19.7 | 16.4 | 4.3 | 40.0 |
| 5–9 | 15.2 | 15.6 | 11.5 | 5.3 | 23.0 |
| 10–14 | 10.1 | 10.5 | 7.2 | 5.1 | 11.0 |
| 15–19 | 8.0 | 8.1 | 7.4 | 7.9 | 6.5 |
| 20–24 | 8.7 | 8.6 | 10.1 | 12.5 | 5.8 |
| 25–29 | 8.8 | 8.2 | 11.9 | 15.6 | 5.0 |
| 30–34 | 7.3 | 6.9 | 9.9 | 13.4 | 3.4 |
| 35–39 | 5.5 | 5.3 | 7.7 | 10.6 | 2.3 |
| 40–44 | 4.6 | 4.5 | 5.7 | 7.9 | 1.5 |
| 45–49 | 3.3 | 3.2 | 3.8 | 5.3 | 0.8 |
| 50–54 | 2.7 | 2.6 | 2.8 | 4.0 | 0.6 |
| 55–59 | 1.6 | 1.6 | 1.5 | 2.1 | 0.2 |
| 60–64 | 1.8 | 1.8 | 1.6 | 2.3 | 0.2 |
| 65+ | 3.2 | 3.3 | 2.6 | 3.7 | 0.3 |
| | | | | | |
| Total | 100.0 | 100.0 | 100.0 | 100.0 | 100.0 |
| Median age | 18.1 | 17.0 | 20.5 | 26.7 | 7.2 |
| Average age | 22.0 | 21.4 | 23.9 | 30.6 | 7.8 |

100 as compared with 146 among the immigrant population and 102 for the total population (i.e., Ghanaians and immigrants). Among the immigrants, there were more males than females at all ages, but the sex ratios were highest in the older age groups, 45 years and over; and, in general the younger the age group the lower the proportional difference between males to females. The higher ratios of males to females in the older age groups of the immigrant population are reflected in the general sex ratio for the country, where there were 102 males per 100 females compared with 107 males per 100 females among the indigenous population. The male to female ratio for the immigrant population born abroad is significantly higher than for the group born in Ghana; this is most noticeable within the labor force population group aged 15 years and over. Even among the Ghana-born immigrants the male-female ratio is above parity, particularly in the population 45 years and over; thus the age structure of the immigrant population is quite different from that of the indigenous popula-

tion in many respects. The explanation for the immigrants born in Ghana is probably that the females return, or are sent back home earlier, while the boys continue to stay in the country. It is also possible that some foreign-born immigrants, a group in which males predominate, claimed local birth at the census.

Assuming that endogamy is practiced among the two population groups and that there are no cross marriages between the indigenous population and the immigrants, then a rough measure of fertility levels among the groups could be indicated by the child-woman ratio. This index appears to show that the fertility of the immigrant was slightly below that of the indigenous population (Table 18.7). But this is by no means a true measure of the situation; the index assumes that all the immigrant children aged from 0–4 years are resident in the country with their mothers. This is not true since it is known that some immigrants send their young children back to their home countries for local training.

TABLE 18.7

Sex ratios by age and fertility ratios, foreign-origin and Ghana-origin populations

| Age Group | All Ghana | All Foreign-origin | Sex Ratios | | Ghana-origin |
|---|---|---|---|---|---|
| | | | Foreign-origin born in Ghana | Foreign-origin born outside Ghana | |
| 0–4 | 98 | 102 | 102 | 101 | 98 |
| 5–14 | 106 | 108 | 112 | 101 | 105 |
| 15–44 | 98 | 158 | 104 | 173 | 90 |
| 45+ | 120 | 305 | 172 | 322 | 107 |
| All ages | 102 | 146 | 107 | 175 | 97 |
| Fertility ratios (i.e., children 0–4/women 15–49) | 83 | 78 | — | — | 84 |

## MARITAL STATUS OF THE POPULATION AGED 15 YEARS AND OVER

Since marriage patterns influence the fertility of a population, a study of nuptiality among the different population groups may give us a rough indication of the extent of these differences in the demographic structure (Table 18.8). Proportionately a greater number of the female immigrants were married than were all females in the country. This situation also is confirmed in Table 18.9 where the proportion of homemakers among the female immigrant population over 15 years was found to be significantly higher than the proportion among the indigenous female population. It would appear that few unmarried female foreigners migrate into the country; those arriving accompany their husbands or join them after the husbands have been in the country for a while.

## ECONOMIC CHARACTERISTICS OF THE IMMIGRANT LABOR FORCE OVER 15 YEARS OF AGE

There were important differences between the types of activity of immigrants and those of the indigenous population; the male immigrant labor force was proportionately more in employment, less unemployed, and also contained fewer in the category of students compared with the indigenous population at the time of the census. The labor force participation rates for the two

TABLE 18.8

Percent distribution of population over 15 years of age by marital status

| Population Group | Marital Status | | | | | | | |
|---|---|---|---|---|---|---|---|---|
| | Females | | | | Males | | | |
| | never married | married | divorced | widowed | never married | married | divorced | widowed |
| All Ghana | 9.0 | 74.7 | 7.1 | 9.2 | 34.4 | 58.6 | 5.1 | 1.9 |
| Foreign-origin population | 3.6 | 87.8 | 5.5 | 2.0 | 33.6 | 58.9 | 5.5 | 2.0 |
| Akan (Ghanaian tribe) | 10.1 | 69.9 | 11.6 | 8.4 | 34.5 | 58.1 | 5.9 | 1.5 |
| Ewe (Ghanaian tribe) | 12.8 | 75.0 | 3.8 | 8.4 | 37.8 | 50.5 | 3.8 | 1.9 |
| Central Togo (Togolese tribe) | 18.7 | 66.2 | 6.2 | 8.9 | 39.9 | 54.2 | 5.1 | 0.8 |
| Yoruba (Nigerian tribe) | 5.5 | 91.7 | 0.8 | 2.4 | 34.5 | 61.3 | 3.1 | 1.1 |
| Ibo (Nigerian tribe) | 4.8 | 92.7 | 1.4 | 2.1 | 41.5 | 55.1 | 2.0 | 1.4 |
| Hausa (various countries of origin) | 3.5 | 83.1 | 5.0 | 8.4 | 34.3 | 55.7 | 7.5 | 2.5 |

groups were as follows:

|                       | Males | Females |
|-----------------------|-------|---------|
| Immigrants            | 87.1  | 40.4    |
| Indigenous population | 82.3  | 55.3    |
| All Ghana             | 83.3  | 53.6    |

The female immigrants were proportionately less employed than the indigenous population; a majority of the former were recorded as "homemakers"—53 percent, compared with 35 percent for the latter. The female immigrant labor force in the urban areas was proportionately more employed than those in the rural areas. This phenomenon is, however, reversed among the male group where those in the rural areas were proportionately more employed than those in the towns. The employment pattern observed among the female immigrant labor force runs directly opposite to that found among the indigenous females, for, among the latter, the women living in the rural areas are proportionately more employed than those living in towns.

Proportionately the most employed group in the country were the male immigrants born abroad and living in the rural areas; the

Ghana-born descendants of immigrants, particularly those living in towns, were found least in employment but this is because they were the youngest population and a considerable proportion of them were still students at the time of the census. A large number of those who had left school were unemployed as were the indigenous school leavers. It might reasonably be expected that as the Ghana-born descendants of the immigrant population gradually become integrated into the society, their job aspirations would approximate those sought by the indigenous population.

The proportion of immigrants aged 15 years and over still at school was below 2 percent; while among the indigenous population about 5 percent were still attending school at this age and above. Over nine-tenths of all the students in both groups were aged between 15 and 25 years. The student proportion of both groups was significantly higher in the towns than in the rural areas, particularly among the female immigrants (Table 18.9). The evidence suggests that the immigrants' influence has been in only

TABLE 18.9

Percent distribution of types of activity of foreign-origin and Ghana-origin populations (aged 15 years or over) by urban-rural and sex divisions

| Types of Activity | Males | | | | | | Both Sexes | | | |
| | All foreign-origin | | Foreign-origin born outside Ghana | | Foreign-origin born in Ghana | | Ghana-origin | | All foreign-origin | |
| | urban | rural | urban | rural | urban | rural | urban | rural | urban | rural |
|-------------------|-------|-------|-------|-------|-------|-------|-------|-------|-------|-------|
| Employed | 83.6 | 89.0 | 85.1 | 90.0 | 70.3 | 81.7 | 64.9 | 69.4 | 70.9 | 70.0 |
| Unemployed | 9.7 | 5.6 | 9.1 | 5.2 | 13.1 | 8.7 | 8.0 | 3.1 | 7.5 | 4.3 |
| Homemakers | 0.2 | 0.6 | 0.3 | 0.6 | 0.5 | 1.2 | 15.3 | 19.2 | 16.3 | 21.3 |
| Students/vocational trainees | 2.9 | 1.8 | 1.4 | 1.2 | 12.5 | 6.6 | 7.6 | 3.8 | 2.3 | 1.2 |
| Disabled/others | 3.6 | 3.0 | 3.5 | 3.0 | 3.6 | 2.8 | 4.1 | 4.5 | 3.0 | 3.2 |
| | Females | | | | | | | | | |
| Employed | 46.7 | 37.4 | 47.4 | 38.1 | 44.4 | 34.1 | — | — | — | — |
| Unemployed | 4.5 | 2.1 | 4.0 | 1.7 | 5.9 | 4.0 | — | — | — | — |
| Homemakers | 45.2 | 56.7 | 45.1 | 56.2 | 45.1 | 58.8 | — | — | — | — |
| Students/vocational trainees | 1.1 | 0.3 | 0.6 | 0.2 | 2.6 | 0.9 | — | — | — | — |
| Disabled/others | 2.5 | 3.5 | 2.9 | 3.8 | 2.0 | 2.2 | — | — | — | — |

SOURCE: 1960 Ghana Population Census, IV, Tables 1 and 15 and Advance Report of Vols. III and IV

particular sectors of the social and economic structure; in general, the group made very little inroad into the social organization of the country.

## OCCUPATIONAL CHARACTERISTICS OF THE LABOR FORCE OVER 15 YEARS OF AGE

The proportion of agricultural workers was smaller among the immigrants than among the indigenous population; whereas two-thirds of the male population of the latter group were agricultural workers only half of the former group were similarly employed (Table 18.10). Among the labor force, both the Ghanaians and immigrants were concentrated in two main categories, namely (1) farmers, fishermen, and loggers and (2) laborers. Of the male immigrant and the indigenous labor force, 84 percent and 73 percent respectively were in these two categories. The majority of the immigrant agricultural workers were in paid employment either as laborers or caretakers on farms and in timber occupations, but few worked as fishermen. In contrast, the indigenous farmers were mainly self-employed or employers.

TABLE 18.10
Relationship between urbanization and the agricultural activity of the foreign-origin labor force

| Country of Origin | Proportion of Foreign-Origin in Urban Area | Proportion of Foreign-Origin in Agriculture |
|---|---|---|
| Ivory Coast | 11.7 | 80.9 |
| Dahomey | 23.7 | 48.0 |
| Togo | 24.0 | 61.9 |
| Upper Volta | 24.0 | 65.6 |
| Niger | 47.6 | 26.3 |
| Nigeria | 54.5 | 12.5 |
| Mali | 58.7 | 21.5 |
| Liberia | 75.2 | 9.8 |

The female immigrant labor force was mainly employed in the sales occupations; 56 percent of the group were in this class, significantly higher than the indigenous female population among whom 26 percent were similarly employed. The proportion of both the immigrant and Ghanaian labor force in the top occupations, namely professional, administrative, managerial, and clerical, was quite insignificant, although the latter was more than double the former (Table 18.11).

TABLE 18.11
Percent distribution of major occupations of foreign-origin and Ghana-origin populations over 15 years of age by sex and urban/rural division

| Occupation | Sex | All Foreign-Origin | | | Ghana-Origin | | |
|---|---|---|---|---|---|---|---|
| | | All | Urban | Rural | All | Urban | Rural |
| Professional, technical | M | 1.5 | 2.5 | 1.0 | 3.4 | 4.6 | 1.8 |
| | F | 0.4 | 0.7 | 0.2 | 1.3 | | |
| Administrative, executive, managerial | M | 0.2 | 0.5 | 0.2 | 0.9 | 1.2 | 0.2 |
| | F | — | — | — | — | | |
| Clerical | M | 0.8 | 1.9 | 0.3 | 3.0 | 6.4 | 0.6 |
| | F | 0.3 | 0.4 | — | 0.3 | | |
| Sales | M | 11.7 | 19.8 | 7.7 | 2.6 | 27.1 | 8.3 |
| | F | 56.0 | 79.4 | 42.5 | 25.9 | | |
| Farmers, fishermen, etc. | M | 49.1 | 9.6 | 68.3 | 65.9 | 21.2 | 75.6 |
| | F | 28.6 | 2.0 | 43.9 | 60.6 | | |
| Miners, quarrymen | M | 5.5 | 4.4 | 6.1 | 1.3 | 1.4 | 0.1 |
| | F | 0.9 | 0.7 | 1.1 | 0.1 | | |
| Transport | M | 2.1 | 4.4 | 0.9 | 3.5 | 5.6 | 1.1 |
| | F | — | — | — | 0.1 | | |
| Craftsmen | M | 23.5 | 43.7 | 13.6 | 17.6 | 27.8 | 11.0 |
| | F | 10.0 | 9.3 | 10.4 | 10.3 | | |
| Service | M | 5.6 | 13.2 | 1.9 | 1.8 | 4.7 | 0.8 |
| | F | 3.9 | 7.5 | 1.9 | 1.4 | | |

Very few miners were found among the labor force population; in proportionate terms, the immigrants were found working four time more frequently in this field than the indigenous population. Indeed, the absolute number of indigenous persons working in this sector in 1960 was about the same as that of the immigrants. It is common knowledge that relatively large numbers of persons of Nigerian origin were working in the diamond business either as diggers or dealers. Approximately half the immigrant labor force in this field were of Nigerian birth; and about one-third of all persons working in this field were of Nigerian origin.

A considerable proportion of the immigrants were also working as craftsmen, particularly in the towns. These were employed as tailors, seamstresses, vulcanizers, carpenters and plasterers, skilled and unskilled workers in construction occupations, fitters, oilers and greasers, watch repairers, longshoremen, and freight handlers. The occupational characteristics varied considerably among the immigrants from the different countries (Table 18.12). In general, the higher the level of urbanization of the region, the higher also the proportion of the immigrant labor force working in nonagricultural activities. In each of the regions it was observed that the immigrants often made the maximum use of the economic opportunities available in the area; they entered into those spheres which promised them the highest returns for their level of skill and education.

Once the immigrants arrived in the

TABLE 18.12

Percent distribution of foreign-origin employed population over 15 years of age by country of origin and main occupation

| Country of Origin | Major Occupation | Sex | |
|---|---|---|---|
| | | M | F |
| Ivory Coast | Farmers, loggers, fishermen | 80.9 | 54.7 |
| | Craftsmen | 9.6 | — |
| | Sales workers | — | 24.5 |
| Liberia | Craftsmen | 62.2 | 24.0 |
| | Service, transport | 19.7 | — |
| | Farmers, loggers, fishermen | 9.8 | 20.1 |
| | Sales workers | — | 43.4 |
| Mali | Farmers, loggers, fishermen | 21.5 | 14.9 |
| | Craftsmen | 17.8 | 12.4 |
| | Sales workers | 19.7 | 66.2 |
| Upper Volta | Farmers, loggers, fishermen | 65.6 | 41.2 |
| | Craftsmen | 17.8 | — |
| | Sales workers | — | 43.4 |
| Togo | Farmers, loggers, fishermen | 61.9 | 46.0 |
| | Craftsmen | 24.9 | 12.4 |
| | Sales workers | — | 38.2 |
| Dahomey | Farmers, loggers, fishermen | 48.0 | 32.9 |
| | Craftsmen | 25.4 | 13.8 |
| | Sales workers | — | 50.4 |
| Nigeria | Farmers, loggers, fishermen | 12.5 | — |
| | Craftsmen | 27.1 | — |
| | Miners, quarrymen | 10.9 | — |
| | Sales workers | 33.3 | 84.4 |
| Niger | Farmers, loggers, fishermen | 26.3 | 16.1 |
| | Craftsmen | 26.5 | — |
| | Miners, quarrymen | 16.7 | — |
| | Sales workers | 19.9 | 69.8 |

SOURCE: 1960 PES (unpublished data).

TABLE 18.13

Region of enumeration by region of previous residence, foreign-origin population aged 15 years and over (percent distribution)

| Region of Enumeration | Region of Previous Residence | | | | | | | |
|---|---|---|---|---|---|---|---|---|
| | Accra cap. dist. | Western | Eastern | Volta | Ashanti | Brong-Ahafo | Northern | Total |
| Accra capital district | 11.6 | 22.5 | 25.2 | 11.2 | 24.6 | 1.1 | 3.8 | 100.0 |
| Western | 9.6 | 62.5 | 8.5 | 1.7 | 15.6 | 0.3 | 1.8 | 100.0 |
| Eastern | 7.0 | 10.2 | 63.2 | 4.1 | 12.4 | 0.9 | 2.2 | 100.0 |
| Volta | 9.1 | 4.0 | 10.6 | 68.3 | 3.6 | 0.7 | 3.7 | 100.0 |
| Ashanti | 3.8 | 7.7 | 21.3 | 3.6 | 51.5 | 8.9 | 3.2 | 100.0 |
| Brong-Ahafo | 2.2 | 4.0 | 9.2 | 6.2 | 28.2 | 47.2 | 3.0 | 100.0 |
| Northern | 5.2 | 3.3 | 1.0 | 8.9 | 9.0 | 1.3 | 71.3 | 100.0 |

SOURCE: 1960 PES (unpublished data).

country, they did not remain in the region where they originally settled, but kept on moving from one area to another in search of better opportunities. The movement is both intraregional and interregional (see Table 18.13). In the Accra Capital District and Brong-Ahafo in particular, the vast majority of the resident immigrant workers had moved in from other regions of the country where they previously resided. One may assume that some occupational mobility takes place when these workers move from one region to another, but there are no firm data on this phenomenon. On the other hand, it is reasonable to assume that an immigrant who previously worked as a laborer on a farm in, for example, Brong-Ahafo, is most likely to change to another occupation when he moves into the Accra Capital District. In general, the degree of occupational mobility will be determined by the skill and education of the individual; since most of the immigrants who enter the country are unskilled and illiterate, the occupational mobility which often results from moving across one region to another is a horizontal one. Thus laborers in agricultural areas may move into cities as watchmen, longshoremen, bottle sellers, or construction laborers. In their new capacity some of these immigrants may increase their income considerably, especially if they take up trading in the towns.

Occupational mobility occurred on a much greater scale among the local-born children of the immigrants. There were proportion-

ately more sales, transport, clerical, and professional workers and also slightly more farmers and craftsmen among the male local-born immigrants than among the foreign-born immigrants. In contrast the proportion of the male local-born immigrant workers in the mining and service occupations was significantly lower than the proportion of those born abroad.

These phenomena suggest that, apart from farming, the locally born immigrants had taken to more skilled and higher-grade types of jobs than had their parents who were born abroad (Table 18.14). This may be taken as

TABLE 18.14

Percent distribution of selected occupations of foreign-origin employed persons over 15 years of age by birthplace and sex

| | Foreign-Origin Population | | | |
|---|---|---|---|---|
| | Born Outside Ghana | | Born in Ghana | |
| Occupation | M | F | M | F |
| Professional, Administrative | 1.8 | 0.3 | 2.5 | 0.6 |
| Clerical | 0.7 | 0.1 | 1.5 | 0.2 |
| Sales | 12.0 | 54.7 | 8.9 | 61.8 |
| Farmers | 48.7 | 30.4 | 51.7 | 20.6 |
| Miners | 5.9 | 1.1 | 2.0 | 0.3 |
| Transport | 1.6 | 0.1 | 5.8 | 0.1 |
| Craftsmen | 23.3 | 9.4 | 24.5 | 12.3 |
| Service | 6.0 | 3.9 | 3.0 | 4.2 |
| Total | 100.0 | 100.0 | 100.0 | 100.0 |

TABLE 18.15

Percent distribution of male agriculturists running their own farms or working as laborers on farms

|  | Foreign-Origin Over 15 Years of Age | |
|---|---|---|
| Occupational Group | Born outside Ghana | Born in Ghana |
| Farmers and farm managers | 58.9 | 76.2 |
| Farm workers and agricultural laborers | 37.4 | 21.9 |

SOURCE: 1960 Ghana Population Census, IV, Table 19.

evidence of vertical mobility among some of the locally born immigrants. In the case of farming, even though a greater proportion of the locally born immigrants were in this field than were those born abroad, nevertheless it was observed that a basic structural change had occurred among the former group. There were proportionately more farm managers and fewer agricultural laborers among the locally born immigrants than among the foreign-born immigrants. Probably there is a growing tendency among the locally born immigrant farmers to run their own independent farms (Table 18.15). If this is the case, then it is a sign of the higher status which has occurred in the economic relationship between this group of workers and their Ghanaian landowners.

On the whole, the immigrant workers had little inroad into the skilled sector of the country's economy. But, as their occupations reveal, they were contributing quite significantly in some sectors of the economy, particularly as agricultural and mining laborers and as workers in the service sector. These characteristics also are confirmed by the distribution of the immigrant labor force among the various industries (Table 18.16). Contrary to popular belief in Ghana, there were proportionately fewer immigrants in the agricultural industries than there were indigenous Ghanaians. But the immigrant agricultural laborers were very important in cocoa growing. Nearly one-quarter of the total immigrant male labor force population aged 15 years or over was in the cocoa-growing sector; and about half (50.8 percent) of the male immigrant agricultural labor force was employed in the cocoa-growing sector alone.

## EMPLOYMENT STATUS OF THE LABOR FORCE AGED 15 YEARS OR OVER

Quite a substantial proportion (45.0 percent) of the male immigrant labor force were working for either wages or salary; only one-quarter (25.1 percent) of the indigenous labor force population were in similar status. The latter were often either employers or self-employed. The majority of the foreigners

TABLE 18.16

Percent distribution of industrial activities of employed foreign-origin and Ghana-origin populations aged 15 years or more, by sex

| Population Group | Sex | Type of Industry | | | | | | |
|---|---|---|---|---|---|---|---|---|
|  |  | Agriculture | Mining & quarrying | Manufacturing | Construction | Services & electricity | Commerce | Transport |
| All Ghana | M | 63.9 | 2.9 | 8.6 | 5.5 | 8.7 | 6.1 | 4.3 |
|  | F | 58.5 | 0.3 | 10.0 | 0.3 | 3.2 | 27.6 | 0.1 |
| All African foreign-origin | M | 49.3 | 6.7 | 8.3 | 6.7 | 10.6 | 14.4 | 4.0 |
|  | F | 28.9 | 1.1 | 9.2 | 0.3 | 4.8 | 55.6 | 0.1 |
| African foreign-origin born outside Ghana | M | 49.0 | 7.2 | 7.7 | 6.9 | 9.7 | 14.8 | 3.6 |
|  | F | 30.8 | 1.2 | 8.7 | 0.3 | 4.7 | 54.2 | 0.1 |
| African foreign-origin born in Ghana | M | 52.1 | 2.8 | 13.0 | 4.9 | 8.0 | 11.1 | 7.2 |
|  | F | 20.9 | 0.4 | 11.8 | 0.3 | 5.2 | 61.3 | 0.1 |
| Ghana-origin | M | 67.7 | 2.0 | 8.7 | 5.2 | 10.4 | 4.2 | 4.3 |
|  | F | 60.9 | 0.2 | 10.0 | 0.3 | 3.0 | 25.5 | 0.1 |

TABLE 18.17

Percent distribution of employment status of foreign-origin and Ghana-origin populations by sex (employed persons aged 15 years)

| Population Group | Sex | All | Employer/ self-employed | Public sector | Nonpublic sector | Family worker | Caretaker | Apprentice |
|---|---|---|---|---|---|---|---|---|
| | | | | | Employment Status | | | |
| Ghana-origin | M | 100.0 | 59.2 | 11.4 | 13.7 | 11.0 | 2.0 | 2.7 |
| | F | 100.0 | 76.6 | 1.4 | 2.0 | 19.0 | 0.2 | 0.8 |
| All foreign-origin | M | 100.0 | 40.9 | 10.3 | 34.7 | 4.7 | 7.4 | 1.9 |
| | F | 100.0 | 72.2 | 0.5 | 5.0 | 20.1 | 1.5 | 0.7 |
| Foreign-origin born in Ghana | M | 100.0 | 42.6 | 11.1 | 23.4 | 14.6 | 4.4 | 3.9 |
| | F | 100.0 | 77.2 | 0.9 | 3.7 | 16.6 | 0.6 | 1.0 |
| Foreign-origin born outside Ghana | M | 100.0 | 39.9 | 10.6 | 36.8 | 3.5 | 7.6 | 1.6 |
| | F | 100.0 | 70.0 | 1.2 | 5.9 | 20.6 | 1.7 | 0.6 |

were employed in the nonpublic sector of the economy; the proportion of the group in the public sector was almost the same as the indigenous population. Proportionately there were significantly more of the male immigrant labor force in the caretaker category (7.4 percent) compared with the indigenous labor force (2.0 percent). There is again evidence that some degree of social mobility has occurred among the local-born immigrant labor force population. For example, the proportion of the group born in Ghana working in the public sector was slightly higher than those born abroad; conversely a smaller proportion of the former worked in the nonpublic sector where manual work was mainly concentrated (Table 18.17). Indeed, the proportion of the locally born immigrant labor force in the public sector was almost the same as that of the indigenous population; this further suggests that the locally born immigrants were becoming gradually integrated into the society and adopting some of the values of the local population. The "employer/self-employed" and apprentice groups had both increased among the locally born group compared with those born abroad.

## EDUCATIONAL CHARACTERISTICS OF THE POPULATION AGED 6 YEARS AND OVER

The general level of literacy among the entire population is still relatively low when compared with that of the developed nations. There has, however, been rapid development in education during recent years. Thus 43.7 percent of those aged between 6 and 15 years were at school in 1960, although only 16.4 percent of those aged 15 years and over had ever been to school. The least educated group were the immigrants born abroad and resident in the rural areas; the most educated were the indigenous population resident in the towns. In the male population, the level of education among the indigenous group was significantly higher than that among the immigrant group. The proportion of the indigenous female population with some education was twice as high as that of the immigrant female group. The locally born immigrants were better educated; in the younger generation the proportion attending school was almost the same as that of the indigenous population. The intergenerational differences in the level of literacy were significant for each of the population groups in the country. Recently female education has advanced much faster than male education (Tables 18.18 and 18.19).

The literacy level of the population as a whole was significantly higher in the urban areas than in the rural areas. About 30 percent of the male and 15 percent of the female immigrants aged six years and over and resident in the urban areas were literate (i.e., past and present school attendants); only 14 percent of the males and 5 percent of the females resident in the rural areas were

TABLE 18.18
Percent distribution of population by education

| Population Group | Aged 6+ Years | | | Aged 6–14 Years | | | Aged 15+ Years | | |
|---|---|---|---|---|---|---|---|---|---|
| Males | Never | Past | Present | Never | Past | Present | Never | Past | Present |
| Ghana-origin | 60.1 | 19.3 | 20.6 | 45.2 | 3.8 | 51.0 | 67.1 | 25.7 | 7.2 |
| All foreign-origin | 80.9 | 11.2 | 7.9 | 61.4 | 2.4 | 36.2 | 84.8 | 13.0 | 2.2 |
| Foreign-origin born in Ghana | 64.3 | 11.0 | 24.7 | 58.6 | 1.7 | 39.7 | 70.2 | 20.8 | 9.0 |
| Foreign-origin born outside Ghana | 85.3 | 11.3 | 3.4 | 67.4 | 3.5 | 29.1 | 86.8 | 11.9 | 1.3 |
| Females | | | | | | | | | |
| Ghana-origin | 82.1 | 7.8 | 10.1 | 66.4 | 3.7 | 30.9 | 88.9 | 9.2 | 1.9 |
| All foreign-origin | 91.8 | 3.2 | 5.0 | 79.2 | 1.8 | 19.0 | 95.7 | 3.7 | 0.6 |
| Foreign-origin born in Ghana | 84.2 | 3.9 | 11.9 | 76.6 | 1.5 | 21.9 | 91.8 | 6.3 | 1.9 |
| Foreign-origin born outside Ghana | 95.0 | 3.0 | 2.0 | 85.0 | 2.2 | 12.8 | 96.6 | 3.1 | 0.3 |

literate. Indeed, whereas 28 and 30 percent respectively of the male and female immigrant population aged six years and over resided in the urban areas, 52 and 60 percent of the literates among these two groups were resident in such areas in 1960. Thus, like the indigenous population, the educated among the immigrants tend to live in the towns, where they may secure employment in the modern sector. The spatial distribution of the educated population was, however, closely related to the availability and distribution of education facilities within particular areas in the country. Since educational facilities were largely provided by the towns, a large proportion of those attending school was found in

these areas. It is generally found that where the school/population ratio was high the proportion of literacy among the population was also high and vice versa.

The vast majority of those with some education had reached the elementary level; in this respect there was no significant difference between the immigrant group and the indigenous population. As Table 18.20 shows, 95 and 98 percent respectively of the male and female immigrants aged six years and over who received education in the past, compared with 91 and 95 percent of the indigenous population of the same age bracket, had

TABLE 18.19
Proportion of total population aged 6–14 years in relation to proportion of group educated

| | Ghana-Origin | | Foreign-Origin | |
|---|---|---|---|---|
| Index | M | F | M | F |
| Proportion of total population aged 6–14 | 23.7 | 21.6 | 14.0 | 18.8 |
| Proportion of total educated persons in 6–14 age group | 42.2 | 54.2 | 34.5 | 62.9 |

TABLE 18.20
Past school attendants of population aged 6 years and over by type of school (percentage distribution)

| | Type of Education | | | |
|---|---|---|---|---|
| | Males | | Females | |
| Population Group | elementary | higher | elementary | higher |
| Ghana-origin | 91.0 | 9.0 | 95.0 | 5.0 |
| Foreign-origin born in Ghana | 95.0 | 5.0 | 98.0 | 2.0 |
| Foreign-origin born outside Ghana | 95.0 | 5.0 | 95.0 | 5.0 |

NOTE: Elementary = primary and middle school; Higher = secondary and commercial schools, teacher training, and university.

reached the elementary school (i.e., primary and middle). Indeed, among the entire immigrant population with any form of higher education in the country, only 5 percent were of African origin; the remaining 95 percent were of European, American, Asian, and other non-African origin.

There were considerable differences among the immigrants themselves according to country of origin. Nigerians, for example, showed much higher literacy rates than those from Niger or Upper Volta. These differences among the foreign groups usually reflected the general level of education in their original home countries. Thus, most probably the level of sophistication and education, cultural and social conditions in the home country, and perhaps the level of social interaction with the indigenous population are factors which influence the rate of absorption and integration among any of the particular foreign-origin groups resident in the country.

## SUMMARY AND CONCLUSION

Foreign immigration has greatly influenced the pattern of population distribution between the various regions of the country, and has also to some extent influenced the structure of the country's population. The overall density of population per square mile without foreign immigrants was, in 1960, found to be 14 percent below that which was obtained when foreign immigrants were included. The foreign-origin population already in residence was found to be highly mobile; they continued to move from one region to another, and from rural areas to towns in search of new opportunities for improving their standards of living. A considerable proportion of the group, particularly the locally born immigrants and the females, showed a much greater preference for living in towns than in rural areas. Nevertheless, at the time of the census, the majority of the immigrants still lived in the rural areas, and they were mainly employed in agriculture and mining.

In terms of demographic characteristics, the immigrant groups showed different features from the indigenous group. The former contained proportionately more persons in the economically active age group; there were fewer children; the average age of the group was higher than the rest of the population. The locally born immigrants were the youngest group; the average age for the group was about 8 years compared with average ages of 30.6 years and 21.4 years respectively for the immigrants born abroad and the indigenous population. The sex ratios among the immigrant group were significantly higher than those of the indigenous group. In general, the greater the distance of migration, the higher the sex ratio among the immigrant group. The present information on differential fertility between the indigenous population and the immigrants is crude and unreliable; nevertheless the general situation suggests that there are no significant differences in the levels of fertility between the two groups. Similarly, the nuptiality patterns of the male immigrant group are almost the same as those of the country as a whole. Among females, however, the proportion of immigrants married was considerably higher than the national figures. A large proportion of the female immigrants arrived in the country with their husbands, and the majority of them remained full-time housewives. The indigenous female labor force population showed a higher proportion in employment.

Both the immigrant and indigenous labor force populations were largely unskilled and illiterate. Among the two groups the proportion of the labor force in the top occupations was small. Proportionately more of the indigenous male labor force population was in agricultural occupations. However, the immigrants were more often found in the mining sector than the indigenous population. Whereas a majority of the immigrants worked for wages on the farms, in the mines, and more generally in the nonpublic sector of the economy, the indigenous population were often self-employed or employers. In both groups the female employed population were found mainly in trade, although a substantial proportion also worked in agriculture.

Considerable social mobility occurred among the locally born immigrants; thus, they were proportionately found less in unskilled jobs and proportionately more in the top occupations than those born abroad. Even among those working in agriculture, it was observed that those born in Ghana often served as farm managers and were very much more in control of their own affairs than the group born abroad, the majority of whom remained as farm laborers. The locally born immigrant group also was better educated; indeed the degree of absorption of the group in the community was such that the level of education, particularly among the younger generation, was almost the same as that of the indigenous population. Immigrants residing in the rural areas had also been migrating into the towns in search of opportunities for employment in the modern sector of the economy. It is anticipated that, as urbanization increases throughout the regions, proportionately more of the immigrant population will seek residence in the towns.

In conclusion, it may be remarked that immigration as a whole has produced some effects on the socioeconomic structure of the country. The changes, however, are still minor and not deep rooted, so that the overall social structure of society seems to have been affected surprisingly little by the phenomenon.

INTERNAL migration in Ghana has become an integral part of the demographic complexion of the country's social structure. Since almost three-quarters of a century ago, Ghana has been going through a period of rapid change in the course of which many of her institutions and social structures have become modernized. These conditions of social change also gave rise to an increased mobility of the population. The continuous movement of people from one place to another in turn produced conditions which altered the ways of living among persons in different communities and produced changes in their social and economic institutions and in their attitudes, values, outlook, and behavior. The majority of migrants had consisted mainly of young adults who moved elsewhere in search of work and new ways of life. Labor mobility therefore has changed the entire nature of life among the population living in the towns as well as those in the villages.

Much has been written on the subject of internal migration and urbanization in Ghana, and the reader is referred to these sources to obtain adequate understanding of the global aspect of the process.[1] The present chapter is a specialized study in the sense that the information presented describes some of the dynamic and differential aspects of internal migration and urbanization which were not available in the earlier migration studies. The work is confined to the southeastern section of the country for two main reasons: first, the survey which provided information for this chapter covered the southeastern area only; and second, the two administrative regions which comprise the study area, namely the Eastern Region and

# CHAPTER NINETEEN

# *Internal Migration Differentials*

## *and Their Effects on Sociodemographic Change*

N. O. ADDO

---

[1] For example, (a) N. O. Addo, "Demographic Aspects of Urban Development in Ghana in the Twentieth Century" (Paper Read at First African Population Conference, Ibadan, January 3–7, 1966); (b) John C. Caldwell, "Migration and Urbanization," in Walter Birmingham, I. Neustadt, and E. N. Omaboe, eds., *A Study of Contemporary Ghana*, II, *Some Aspects of Social Structure* (London: George Allen and Unwin, and Evanston: Northwestern University Press, 1967); (c) John C. Caldwell, *African Rural-Urban Migration: The Movement to Ghana's Towns* (Canberra: Australian National University Press, and New York: Humanities Press, 1969).

383

Accra Capital District, are not homogeneous in any sense and exhibit varying demographic and socioeconomic characteristics. The geographic, economic, and social conditions, as well as patterns of population distribution and growth, are different in the two regions. A comparative study of the two areas will be useful, for it will provide the opportunity to examine some of the differential aspects of internal migration and urbanization[2] in the country. Internal migration has not produced the same effects on all the communities and population groups in the country; a number of complex socioeconomic and cultural variables influence the situation from one place to another. A study of migration and urbanization in these two regions is likely to give some idea of the various factors that influence demographic changes in the country as a whole.

THE STUDY AREA. Geographically, the Accra Capital District (ACD) is strung along a distance of about 60 miles on the coast of eastern Ghana, and stretches northward for about 16 miles to reach the boundary of the Eastern Region (ER). See Figure 19.1. With the exception of a few low ridges, the country immediately surrounding the Accra Capital District forms an undulating area ranging between sea level and 2,000 feet in height and rising gradually to about 500 feet at the foot of the Akwapim ridges. Spatially the district covers only 0.9 percent of the total land surface area of Ghana and contained only 7 percent of the total population in 1960; nevertheless almost a quarter of the country's urban population was located there (Table 19.1). Only one-eighth of the total employed population in the district was doing agricultural work, raising cereals and vegetables partly for subsistence and partly for retailing in the local markets. There were also a few fishermen. In contrast with the rest of the country, where agriculture has been the basis of economic progress, the Accra Capital District has drawn much of her resources for development from the other regions and also

[2] For the purpose of this study, an urban area is defined as any locality with a population of 5,000 or over.

from outside the country. Her population growth is attributed much more to net migration than to natural increase. Again the infrastructure has been built mainly with the efforts of migrants; similarly much of the developmental funds for the improvement of the region have been drawn from government funds obtained primarily from tax collected on cocoa, a rural product. This region, therefore, is in a fortunate position and occupies a higher level on the scale of development than the other regions.

The Eastern Region lies immediately to the northwest of the Accra Capital District, covering an area of 7,698 square miles and with a density of population of 142 persons per square mile in 1960 (see Figure 19.1). Sixteen and fourteen percent of the total population and total urban population of the country respectively were concentrated in this region at the 1960 census (see Table 19.1). The economy of this region, unlike the ACD, is based primarily on agriculture; the region produces a considerable proportion (about 18 percent in 1965–1967) of the country's major export crop, cocoa, and also quite a substantial amount of the local foodstuffs. This region was the first area into which large-scale migration occurred, and into which migrants flocked from both within and outside the country to work on the cocoa farms and the mines which became established there toward the end of the nineteenth century. The region has undergone considerable demographic change since the early days when these economic developments began. In the last two decades many acres of the cocoa farms in the area have been destroyed by the swollen shoot virus disease; and over a longer period the major part of the forest land has been utilized for cocoa and other crops so that there is little land left for further cultivation. These developments have resulted in the last few decades in emigration of some of the population into the new forest regions of Brong-Ahafo and Ashanti to open new farming lands. Again recent developments in education and urbanization have created a situation whereby increasing numbers of the younger generation have

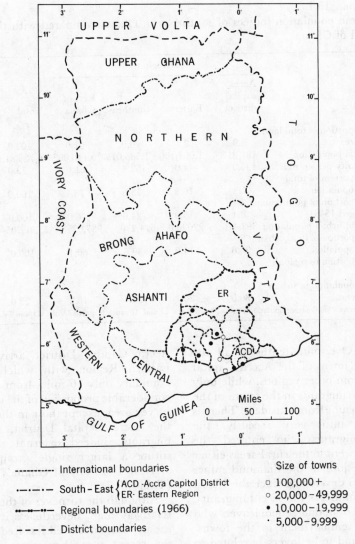

FIGURE 19.1. *Map of Ghana Showing Positions of the Regions and the South-East*

moved into the towns. These various movements have created some demographic changes in the Eastern Region which are quite different from those found in the Accra Capital District.

The aim of this chapter is to examine some of the social and demographic conditions of these two areas and to consider some of the reasons why these developments have occurred. We shall in particular study migration streams and the structure and characteristics of the migrant and nonmigrant population.

MIGRATION STREAMS AND THEIR COMPONENT PARTS. All the major groups of the country's population are represented in the towns of the southeast. All the towns, however, contain a core population which is indigenous to the area; almost half the population recorded in the survey area belonged to the indigenous

TABLE 19.1

Some population indices of southeastern Ghana compared with the rest of Ghana

| Index | Accra capital district | Eastern | Southeast | Rest of Ghana | Total |
|---|---|---|---|---|---|
| | **Region** | | | | |
| Proportion of total land area | 0.9 | 8.1 | 9.0 | 91.0 | 100.0 |
| Total population | 491,817 | 1,094,196 | 1,586,013 | 5,140,802 | 6,726,815 |
| Density per sq. mile | 494.0 | 142.0 | 182.4 | 61.6 | 73.0 |
| Proportion of total population | 7.3 | 16.3 | 23.6 | 76.4 | 100.0 |
| Proportion of population aged 15–64 | 8.1 | 15.9 | 24.0 | 76.0 | 100.0 |
| Total urban population | 393,410 | 220,860 | 614,270 | 937,035 | 1,551,305 |
| Proportion of total urban population | 25.6 | 14.0 | 39.6 | 60.4 | 100.0 |
| Proportion of region's population in urban areas | 80.0 | 20.1 | 38.7 | 18.2 | 23.0 |

SOURCE: 1960 Ghana Population Census, Vols. I and II and Advance Report of Vols. III and IV.

ethnic groups. Over nine-tenths of all the migrants in the towns of the Accra Capital District came from other regions, while only 42 percent of the migrants in the towns of the Eastern Region came from outside it. There is evidence that, until very recently, the majority of migrants who entered the Eastern Region went to the rural areas either to farm or take jobs in the diamond mines which have been developing since the 1920s. An increasing number of the recent migrants, however, consist of middle school leavers who are looking for employment in the towns. Migration is found to be inversely related to distance;[3] the majority of migrants in the towns as well as in the rural areas came from nearby areas. For example, nearly two-fifths of all the internal migrants in the towns of the Accra Capital District arrived from the Eastern Region with which it shares a boundary only 16 miles from the capital. A considerable proportion of the migrants in the survey area, except those in the rural part of the Accra Capital District, were external migrants; indeed external migrants constitute a larger single group than those arriving from any of Ghana's other regions (Table 19.2).

Although the turnover of the population is relatively high, nevertheless it appears that the population moved less frequently during the recent past than compared with the period soon after independence in 1957. A number of persons who moved may have done so temporarily, to visit relatives or conduct

[3] The relationship between distance and migration was measured by computing correlation coefficient between the X factor (that is the distance from the region of birth—origin of journey—to the region of destination—the area of enumeration) and the Y factor (that is, the percentage of the total migrants in the sample area who came from a particular region). N was taken to represent the number of regions in the country as at 1960, i.e., 7. The correlation coefficients computed for each of the sample areas are as follows:

| Sex Group | Urban | |
|---|---|---|
| | Accra Cap. Dist. | Eastern |
| Males | −0.6964 | −0.3588 |
| Females | −0.7256 | −0.5525 |
| | Rural | |
| Males | −0.4925 | −0.1542 |
| Females | −0.5415 | −0.6457 |

TABLE 19.2
Proportion of migrants from outside the region of enumeration, by region of birth

| | Sample Area of Enumeration | | | | | | | |
| | Males | | | | Females | | | |
| | Accra cap. dist. | | Eastern | | Accra cap. dist. | | Eastern | |
| Region or Country of Birth | urban | rural | urban | rural | urban | rural | urban | rural |
|---|---|---|---|---|---|---|---|---|
| Accra capital district | — | — | 9.8 | 13.4 | — | — | 16.8 | 17.5 |
| Western and central | 17.7 | 4.7 | 19.6 | 12.5 | 20.0 | 5.4 | 21.9 | 17.1 |
| Eastern | 26.7 | 64.9 | — | — | 30.7 | 70.9 | — | — |
| Volta | 13.1 | 14.6 | 13.6 | 15.5 | 14.8 | 11.3 | 14.2 | 16.0 |
| Ashanti | 6.6 | 5.8 | 18.4 | 8.9 | 7.1 | 3.8 | 18.0 | 13.2 |
| Brong-Ahafo | 0.8 | 0.6 | 3.4 | 1.8 | 0.8 | 1.1 | 3.0 | 3.9 |
| Northern and Upper | 4.3 | 0.6 | 7.5 | 11.0 | 3.2 | 0.5 | 6.4 | 7.2 |
| Outside Ghana | 29.2 | 8.8 | 25.0 | 35.7 | 22.5 | 7.0 | 18.8 | 24.6 |
| Not stated | 1.6 | — | 2.7 | 0.2 | 0.9 | — | 0.9 | 0.5 |
| *Totals:* percent | 100.0 | 100.0 | 100.0 | 100.0 | 100.0 | 100.0 | 100.0 | 100.0 |
| | N = 2,756 | N = 171 | N = 704 | N = 673 | N = 2,396 | N = 186 | N = 643 | N = 544 |

some business elsewhere and then return after a few weeks. About one-fifth and one-eighth respectively of the migrants who stated that they were born in the urban areas of the Accra Capital District and the Eastern Region stated that they previously lived in other regions before for varying periods. Similarly 5 percent and 17 percent, who were born in the rural areas of the Eastern Region and the Accra Capital District respectively, stated that they had lived in other regions at some time in the past. On the whole, the trend shows that the movement of population from all parts of the country into the towns of the Accra Capital District has continued since the last census thus making the area more and more cosmopolitan. In contrast, the majority of the migrants in the towns of the Eastern Region arrived from the nearby rural areas.

## URBAN AND RURAL STREAMS

Apart from the broad regional migration patterns, there are other characteristics of the migration process which relate to the nature of the flows and their effect on the population

TABLE 19.3
Classification of migration types

| Migration Type | Frequency of Move | Determinants |
|---|---|---|
| Type A | One movement since birth | Place of birth in Ghana and same as place of previous residence |
| Type B | two or more moves since birth | Place of birth in Ghana but different from place of previous residence |
| Type C | At least two moves involving return migration | Moved sometime in the past but has returned to birthplace in Ghana |
| Type D | One movement direct from external source, i.e., without any intermediate station. | Born outside Ghana with previous residence outside Ghana |

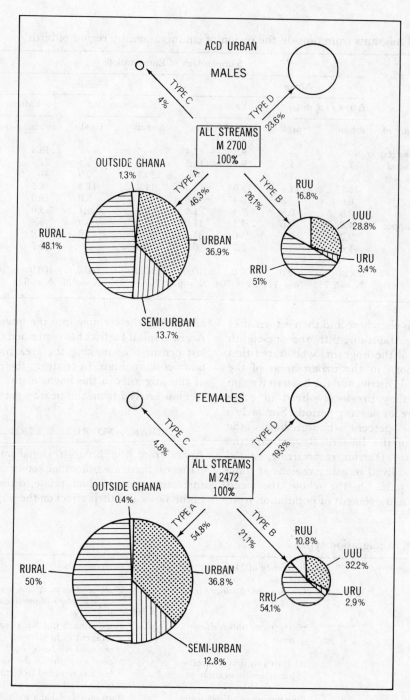

FIGURE 19.2.   *Migration Streams and Their Component Parts, South-East Ghana (ACD), 1966*

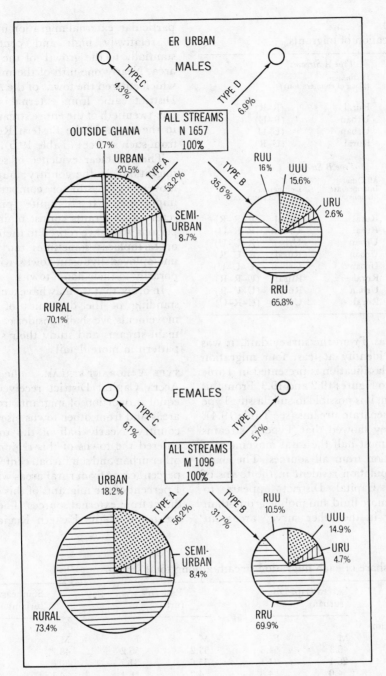

FIGURE 19.3.    *Migration Streams and Their Component Parts, South-East Ghana (ER), 1966*

TABLE 19.4
Subclassification of migrants

*Type A Streams*

| Origin (place of birth) | Destination (place of enumeration) | |
|---|---|---|
| (1) Rural | Rural | (R–R) |
| (2) Rural | Urban | (R–U) |
| (3) Urban | Urban | (U–U) |
| (4) Urban | Rural | (U–R) |

*Type B Streams*

| Origin (place of birth) | All Other Intermediate Stations | Destination (place of enumeration) | |
|---|---|---|---|
| (1) Rural | Rural | Rural | (R–R–R) |
| (2) Rural | Rural | Urban | (R–R–U) |
| (3) Rural | Urban | Urban | (R–U–U) |
| (4) Rural | Urban | Rural | (R–U–R) |
| (5) Urban | Urban | Urban | (U–U–U) |
| (6) Urban | Rural | Rural | (U–R–R) |
| (7) Urban | Urban | Rural | (U–U–R) |
| (8) Urban | Rural | Urban | (U–R–U) |

of these areas. From the survey data, it was possible to identify at least four migration types; the classification is presented in Table 19.3. See also Figures 19.2 and 19.3. From this classification, it is possible to subclassify Type A into four separate streams (see Table 19.4).

The survey showed that Type A streams represent almost half the total movement of the population from all sources. The male migrant population resident in the towns of the Accra Capital District appears to represent a more fluid and mobile group than those living in the other survey areas; in

particular, external migration into this region is relatively high and contributes substantially to the growth of the towns in the area. Nearly one-fifth of the migrant stream which entered the towns of the Accra Capital District came from external sources; only one-twentieth of the entire stream of migrants in the towns of the Eastern Region arrived from such sources (Table 19.5).

There is clear evidence of some "return-migration" in the country; but this type of movement is still of comparatively little importance. It is quite probable that returning migrants consist mainly of elderly persons who have retired to their home towns or birthplace; sometimes too some of the unemployed living in towns withdraw temporarily to their home towns.

In order that we may have a clearer understanding of the dynamics of the various movements, we shall consider each of the two main streams and study their structure and pattern in more detail.

TYPE A MIGRANT STREAM.  The towns in the Accra Capital District received an almost equal proportion of migrants from the rural areas and from other towns elsewhere in the country. Nearly half of the migrants who entered the towns of this region came from other urban and semiurban centers; almost 49 percent came from rural areas while less than 1 percent of the migrants of this stream came direct from external sources. The situation in the towns of the Eastern Region is in this

TABLE 19.5
Percentage share of each migration stream among total stream

| Migration Stream | Accra Cap. Dist. (urban) | | Eastern (urban) | | Southeast[a] (urban) | |
|---|---|---|---|---|---|---|
| | M | F | M | F | M | F |
| Type A | 46.3 | 54.8 | 53.2 | 56.2 | 48.7 | 55.5 |
| Type B | 26.1 | 21.1 | 35.6 | 31.7 | 30.0 | 25.6 |
| Type C | 4.0 | 4.8 | 4.3 | 6.1 | 4.1 | 5.5 |
| Type D | 23.6 | 19.3 | 6.9 | 5.7 | 17.2 | 13.4 |
| All types | 100.0 | 100.0 | 100.0 | 100.0 | 100.0 | 100.0 |
| | N = 2,700 | N = 2,472 | N = 1,657 | N = 1,898 | N = 4,357 | N = 4,370 |

[a] Southeast = Accra Capital District plus Eastern region.

TABLE 19.6
Percentage distribution of migrants of type A stream, by origin

| Type A | Urban | | | | Rural | | | |
| | Accra cap. dist. | | Eastern | | Accra cap. dist. | | Eastern | |
| Stream Origin | M | F | M | F | M | F | M | F |
|---|---|---|---|---|---|---|---|---|
| Urban | 36.9 | 36.8 | 20.5 | 18.2 | 42.4 | 35.7 | 21.9 | 19.1 |
| Semiurban[a] | 13.7 | 12.8 | 8.7 | 8.4 | 5.5 | 10.1 | 11.5 | 12.1 |
| Rural | 48.1 | 50.0 | 70.1 | 73.4 | 52.1 | 54.2 | 66.5 | 68.7 |
| Outside Ghana | 1.3 | 0.4 | 0.7 | — | — | — | 0.1 | 0.1 |
| Total | 100.0 | 100.0 | 100.0 | 100.0 | 100.0 | 100.0 | 100.0 | 100.0 |
| | N = 1,352 | N = 1,441 | N = 878 | N = 1,088 | N = 144 | N = 179 | N = 980 | N = 1,296 |

[a] Localities with population 5,000–9,999.

respect quite different from the Accra Capital District, for over seven-tenths of the migrants in residence in the former arrived from rural areas, largely from the adjacent villages (Table 19.6).

The character of the migration into the Accra Capital District is quite different from that into the Eastern Region mainly because the capital city is located in this region and it is into this city that large-scale migration has been directed in recent years. In the country as a whole it is within the largest towns that the greatest expansion of population has been occurring, and the migrants who contributed to this situation arrived from all parts of the country, particularly from the rural areas and the small towns.[4] Cities such as Accra, Tema, Kumasi, and Sekondi-Takoradi have all developed through this process. One would have thought that, if such demographic trends continued, the rural areas and small towns would eventually become depopulated; but the evidence suggests that no such development has occurred in the country, for the migration patterns assume different forms. The evidence is that a substantial proportion of the flow has been directed from the towns into the rural areas. The data suggest that about one-fifth and two-fifths respectively of the migrants in Type A stream who were resident in the rural areas of the Eastern Region and the Accra Capital District, were

[4] Addo, "Demographic Aspects of Urban Development."

found to have arrived from towns. It is reasonable to consider that the movement of the population into the rural areas of the Eastern Region and that into the Accra Capital District cannot assume the same measure of significance. Although both may be said to be motivated by economic reasons, it is clear that the conditions within these two areas are quite different. A large number of migrants in the rural part of the Accra Capital District in fact reside in nearby villages; from here they commute into the city daily to carry out their various activities. The majority of the migrants who moved into rural Eastern Region were engaged in farming and related activities.

TYPE B MIGRANT STREAM. The Type B stream consists of migrants who have resided in at least three places, three of which have been recorded, namely, place of birth, place of previous residence, and place of present residence. The record of this stream does not, therefore, cover all the movements which a person experienced in the past; the missing links are those towns, villages, and regions where the person may have stayed in the interval between where he was born and where he resided previously before he entered his present abode. We could conveniently ignore these intermediate stops in the migration history of these individuals in our analysis since the majority of the migrants in the survey area had only lately left their birthplace to stay in other areas. Most of them in fact are middle school leavers who have just passed out of school and have moved into the towns or other places to look for employment or seek higher education.

This stream's data also confirm that the major source of migration into the towns is from the rural areas; however, the complexity of the migration phenomena can only be realized if one recalls that the urban population itself has also been found to be highly mobile. Some of those born in the towns were found to have moved into other towns elsewhere, while others had gone into rural settlements; for example, about one-third of all the migrants enumerated in the survey area as having been born in towns were found to have moved into the rural areas. In spite of this observation, the chances that a person born in a town will eventually migrate to another town are much greater than that this person will move into a rural settlement. The same remarks could be made in respect of those migrants born in the rural areas, for, among this group too, the vast majority eventually migrated into other rural areas with only a few moving to towns. A close study of the data shows however that almost half of the migrants born in rural Ashanti lived in towns in that region at some time previous to leaving for the southeast. The majority of these had lived in Kumasi, and it is most probable that some of them were persons who were actually born in the city while others had come from places in rural Ashanti itself or from Brong-Ahafo or northern Ghana. Thus a large amount of migration into the towns as well as that into the rural areas of the southeast occurred in stages (Table 19.7).

The above account clearly shows that the migration patterns in the southeast assume various shapes and that the migration process throughout the region, and most probably also in other regions, assumes rather more complex forms than some earlier studies appeared to have shown. Nevertheless it remains true that the major stream of migration in the country is from one rural area to another; a second stream which has

TABLE 19.7

Direction of movement among town-born migrants of type B stream

| Type B Stream | Southeast | |
| | Male | Female |
| --- | --- | --- |
| Urban-urban-urban | 60.4 | 61.9 |
| Urban-urban-rural | 24.9 | 25.2 |
| Urban-rural-urban | 7.8 | 8.3 |
| Urban-rural-rural | 6.8 | 4.6 |
| Total | 100.0 | 100.0 |
| | N = 1,164 | N = 1,246 |

recently been developing rapidly is the rural-urban one. Rural settlements in Ghana can thus be seen as playing an important, dual role in the population distribution process. In the first place they supplied the bulk of the migrants into the towns. But perhaps even more important is the fact that the densest rural areas sent away some of their excess population to other rural areas, thus relieving themselves of the impending threat of overcrowding while simultaneously making available their excess labor force to sparse areas to augment the labor requirements for developing new resources in those areas. This process may then be looked upon as ultimately producing some beneficial results in that both the sending and the receiving areas gain; the process tends to create a balance by distributing the labor force more fairly over the regions. One cannot, however, make the same remarks about migration into the large towns from the rural areas because all the evidence on this phenomenon points to the increasing pressure of the population on the existing resources and services in these settlements.

LENGTH OF RESIDENCE OF THE MIGRANT POPULATION. The length of time migrants have stayed in a community could be taken as a fair measure of the nature of flow in the past and of the stability of migrant settlement in these areas. This index, however, ignores the effects of mortality and return migration, since it measures the length of time a migrant has stayed in his present abode. It is most

TABLE 19.8
Percent distribution of migrants age 15 or over by length of residence at place of enumeration

| Length of Residence (in years) | Accra Cap. Dist. (urban) | | Eastern (urban) | | Eastern (rural) | |
|---|---|---|---|---|---|---|
| | M | F | M | F | M | F |
| Less than 1 | 12.0 | 15.3 | 27.7 | 20.2 | 15.7 | 23.9 |
| 1 but less than 2 | 11.4 | 10.5 | 13.7 | 11.0 | 9.3 | 13.1 |
| 2 but less than 3 | 10.8 | 10.5 | 11.4 | 9.4 | 6.7 | 11.6 |
| 3 but less than 4 | 8.8 | 8.4 | 8.7 | 7.5 | 6.7 | 8.9 |
| 4 but less than 5 | 8.0 | 6.8 | 5.5 | 5.7 | 5.5 | 6.0 |
| 5 but less than 6 | 7.3 | 7.0 | 4.3 | 3.2 | 4.8 | 4.3 |
| 6 & over | 41.7 | 41.5 | 28.7 | 43.0 | 51.7 | 32.2 |
| Totals | 100.0 | 100.0 | 100.0 | 100.0 | 100.0 | 100.0 |
| | N = 2,178 | N = 1,757 | N = 1,070 | N = 1,178 | N = 1,932 | N = 1,882 |

likely that there is an inverse relationship between the age of a migrant and the likely duration of his migration; the older migrants are more likely to die earlier and also to return home earlier than the young adults. However, this study considers length of residence of the migrant population aged 15 years and above, and assumes that the shape of the curve relating to duration of residence is not affected by mortality or return migration.

The migrants in the survey area have been in residence for varying lengths of time; a substantial movement occurred over the past six years with three-fifths or more of the total migrants having come into residence during this period. It appears that the migration flow into the towns of the Accra Capital District occurred in a more continuous and systematic manner over the past six years than was the case in the towns of the Eastern Region (Table 19.8). In other words, it seems that migration either occurred at a more rapid rate into the towns of the Eastern Region in the 12 months prior to the survey as compared with the towns of the Accra Capital District, or that migration to Eastern Region towns always contains a larger proportion of short-term migrants.

There is another inverse relationship also between age and length of residence; the younger the age of the migrant the shorter on average the period the migrant had been in residence and vice versa.

## MIGRATION AND SOCIODEMOGRAPHIC CHANGE IN THE SOUTHEAST

MIGRATION AND ITS EFFECTS ON THE AGE STRUCTURE OF THE TOWNS AND VILLAGES. Migration has significantly influenced the age and sex structure of the urban as well as rural population; this influence could be discovered by first comparing the age structure of the migrant and nonmigrant population and in turn comparing each of these groups with the total population of the area as a whole. The nonmigrant population in particular contains an unusually large proportion of children below 15 years; over 60 percent of the non-migrants in the towns were found in this age group compared with 30 percent of the migrant population. Of the nonmigrant and migrant population residing in the rural areas 58 and 28 percent respectively were also found in this age group. Because the young adults migrate in large numbers, the population left behind is often composed mainly of children and the aged. The married men also often leave their wives and children behind, while the young single adults, of course, travel alone. The process produces different results in the receiving and the sending areas; in general a heavily emigrating community in Ghana is most likely to show a population which is unusually young, feminine, and highly dependent. Conversely, a community which is affected by large-scale in-migration is likely to be more masculine, and contains a low proportion of children; consequently such a community has a high proportion of persons within the labor force. A table of significance tests comparing two major age groups of the migrants with the nonmigrants (i.e., 0–14 and 15–64) shows quite clearly that the differences are highly significant (i.e., at the 1 percent level). The computed median ages for the towns of the Accra Capital District show that the male and female nonmigrants are younger than the migrants by nearly 14 and 11 years respectively; the corresponding differences in age between male and female nonmigrants and the migrants in the towns of the Eastern Region are 13 and 8 years respectively (Table 19.9).

The migrants living in the towns of the Accra Capital District were slightly younger than those residing in the towns of the Eastern Region; and in general female migrants were younger than males irrespective of place of birth or place of residence. Type A migrants were the youngest group and Type D (those who came direct from outside Ghana) the oldest, with Type B falling in between (Table 19.10).

The average age of the intermediate group of migrants living in the rural areas, both males and females, was higher than those living in the towns, the differences between the former area and the latter being about four years for males and between four and seven years for females. See Figure 19.4 for a graphic delineation of the age and sex structure of the population.

SEX RATIOS. A study of the sex ratios for the urban areas shows that the ratio of males to

TABLE 19.9

Age structure of migrants, nonmigrants, and total population (in percentage)

| Sample Area of Enumeration | Age Group | | | | Total | N | Average Age | Median Age |
| --- | --- | --- | --- | --- | --- | --- | --- | --- |
| | 0–14 | 15–44 | 45–64 | 65+ | | | | |
| Accra capital district urban | | | | | *Males* | | | |
| Migrants | 21.9 | 66.7 | 10.3 | 1.1 | 100.0 | 2,720 | 24.7 | 26.3 |
| Nonmigrants | 61.8 | 30.9 | 4.7 | 2.5 | 100.0 | 2,519 | 16.1 | 12.5 |
| Total | 41.0 | 49.6 | 7.6 | 1.8 | 100.0 | 5,239 | 21.6 | 19.4 |
| Eastern urban | | | | | | | | |
| Migrants | 33.2 | 51.9 | 11.3 | 3.6 | 100.0 | 1,675 | 25.4 | 22.5 |
| Nonmigrants | 73.0 | 22.9 | 3.3 | 0.7 | 100.0 | 1,128 | 12.9 | 9.1 |
| Total | 49.5 | 40.5 | 7.9 | 2.1 | 100.0 | 2,803 | 24.5 | 15.2 |
| Southeast rural | | | | | | | | |
| Migrants | 27.1 | 48.7 | 18.3 | 5.9 | 100.0 | 2,385 | 28.9 | 29.8 |
| Nonmigrants | 61.2 | 28.1 | 7.8 | 2.9 | 100.0 | 2,528 | 17.3 | 12.6 |
| Total | 44.7 | 38.1 | 12.9 | 4.3 | 100.0 | 4,913 | 23.4 | 17.0 |
| Accra capital district urban | | | | | *Females* | | | |
| Migrants | 29.1 | 65.0 | 4.7 | 1.2 | 100.0 | 2,472 | 20.4 | 22.5 |
| Nonmigrants | 57.9 | 31.3 | 7.2 | 3.7 | 100.0 | 2,834 | 18.4 | 11.7 |
| Total | 44.4 | 47.0 | 6.0 | 2.5 | 100.0 | 5,306 | 19.5 | 22.0 |
| Eastern urban | | | | | | | | |
| Migrants | 36.4 | 52.1 | 9.5 | 2.1 | 100.0 | 1,913 | 23.6 | 21.3 |
| Nonmigrants | 67.6 | 26.7 | 4.2 | 1.5 | 100.0 | 1,424 | 14.7 | 14.0 |
| Total | 49.7 | 41.4 | 7.0 | 1.9 | 100.0 | 3,337 | 19.8 | 15.2 |
| Southeast rural | | | | | | | | |
| Migrants | 29.5 | 49.6 | 16.3 | 4.6 | 100.0 | 2,298 | 27.2 | 20.5 |
| Nonmigrants | 55.0 | 33.0 | 8.3 | 3.7 | 100.0 | 2,651 | 19.3 | 11.3 |
| Total | 43.1 | 40.8 | 12.0 | 4.1 | 100.0 | 4,949 | 23.4 | 15.7 |

TABLE 19.10
Mean and median ages of migrants, by type of stream

| | | Migration Stream | | | | | |
| | | Males | | | Females | | |
| Sample Area of Enumeration | Index | Type A | Type B | Type D | Type A | Type B | Type D |
|---|---|---|---|---|---|---|---|
| Accra capital district (urban) | mean age | 23.1 | 27.5 | 32.6 | 18.6 | 23.8 | 27.0 |
| | median age | 23.1 | 27.2 | 32.4 | 20.3 | 23.5 | 26.8 |
| Eastern (urban) | mean age | 23.2 | 27.4 | 28.8 | 22.2 | 24.8 | 27.3 |
| | median age | 18.7 | 26.6 | 27.1 | 19.2 | 22.5 | 25.1 |

females declined in 1966 as compared with the 1960 census, i.e., 114.5 in 1960 and 98.7 in 1966 in the urban areas of the Accra Capital District and 99.9 and 84.0 respectively for Eastern Region urban areas. The sex ratios nevertheless were higher among migrants than among nonmigrants both in the urban and rural areas. It is most probable that increases which occurred in the female population in the towns were due to genuine increases recorded in the proportion of females among the migrants who arrived in the towns in the past few years. Education and improved transport systems have helped to increase the mobility rate among young females. On the other hand, it is strongly suspected that female mortality, particularly maternal mortality, declined relatively faster than male mortality, and this may have contributed to the disproportionate increase which occurred in the female population of the towns. Indeed there is some evidence which suggests that women and children visited hospitals more regularly than the male adults. For example, figures collected from the largest hospital in the country, Korle Bu in Accra, suggest that the number of children and women who attended the hospital increased six times between 1958 and 1966 compared with four times among adult males during the same period.[5] It is perfectly reasonable to assume that, if mortality declined among these groups, the rate of decline would have been higher among the

[5] N. O. Addo, "Dynamics of Urban Growth in Southeastern Ghana" (Ph.D. thesis, London, 1969), p. 93.

females and children than among the adult males for the simple reason that the former may well have obtained greater health attention than the latter.

SOCIAL AND ECONOMIC CHARACTERISTICS OF THE POPULATION. *Economic activity of the population aged 15 and over.* Types of economic activity are quite different among the migrants and the nonmigrants. For instance, the population of students among the former group is significantly higher than among the latter group irrespective of age and sex. Similarly, the male migrants exhibited a higher rate of employment than the nonmigrants (the differences between the two groups are both significant at the 1 percent level in the towns). Female migrants, however, exhibit a lower rate of employment than the nonmigrants; this relationship is still valid irrespective of the origin or the educational level of the group. The differences between these two groups are smaller and less significant. Wives normally accompany their husbands into the towns, and initially these women remain as full-time housewives. There are fewer full-time housewives in the rural areas than in the towns; by tradition married women in the rural areas conveniently combine their housework with farming or other forms of economic activity. Quite often, married women who join their husbands (say on civil service transfer into the villages), and also teachers' wives in these areas, take up full- or part-time farming to supplement the household provisions (Table 19.11).

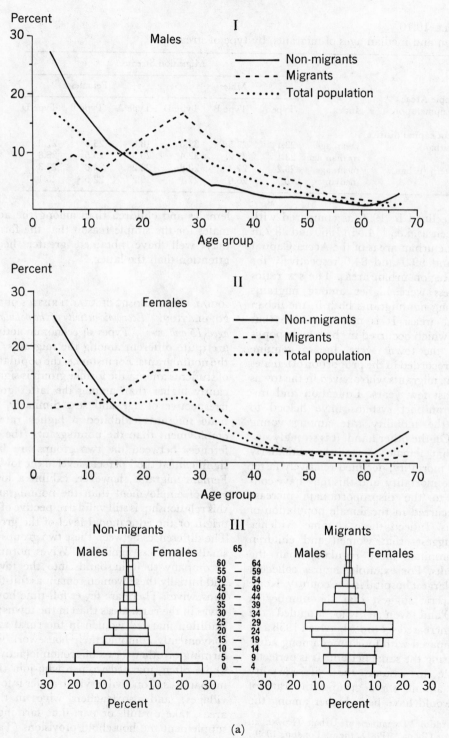

FIGURE 19.4. *Age and Sex Structure of Migrants, Non-Migrants, and Total Population*

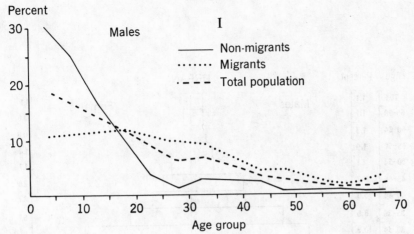

ER URBAN

I

Males

Non-migrants
Migrants
Total population

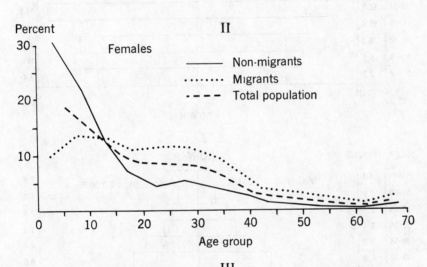

II

Females

Non-migrants
Migrants
Total population

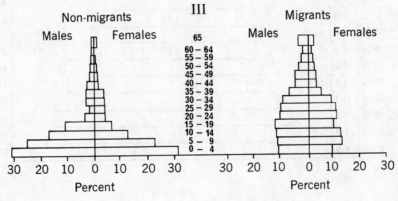

III

Non-migrants

Males    Females

Migrants

Males    Females

65
60 – 64
55 – 59
50 – 54
45 – 49
40 – 44
35 – 39
30 – 34
25 – 29
20 – 24
15 – 19
10 – 14
5 – 9
0 – 4

(b)

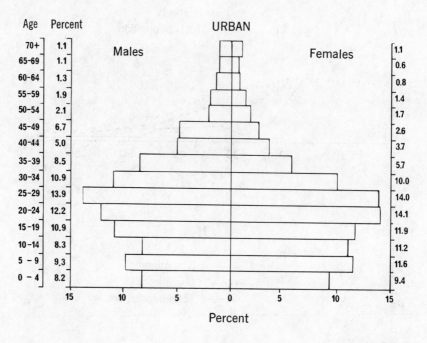

| Age | Percent | URBAN | | Percent |
|---|---|---|---|---|
| 70+ | 1.1 | Males Females | | 1.1 |
| 65-69 | 1.1 | | | 0.6 |
| 60-64 | 1.3 | | | 0.8 |
| 55-59 | 1.9 | | | 1.4 |
| 50-54 | 2.1 | | | 1.7 |
| 45-49 | 6.7 | | | 2.6 |
| 40-44 | 5.0 | | | 3.7 |
| 35-39 | 8.5 | | | 5.7 |
| 30-34 | 10.9 | | | 10.0 |
| 25-29 | 13.9 | | | 14.0 |
| 20-24 | 12.2 | | | 14.1 |
| 15-19 | 10.9 | | | 11.9 |
| 10-14 | 8.3 | | | 11.2 |
| 5-9 | 9.3 | | | 11.6 |
| 0-4 | 8.2 | | | 9.4 |

Percent

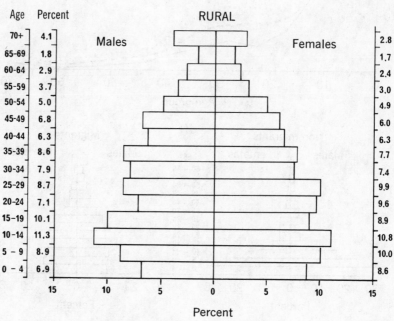

| Age | Percent | RURAL | | Percent |
|---|---|---|---|---|
| 70+ | 4.1 | Males Females | | 2.8 |
| 65-69 | 1.8 | | | 1.7 |
| 60-64 | 2.9 | | | 2.4 |
| 55-59 | 3.7 | | | 3.0 |
| 50-54 | 5.0 | | | 4.9 |
| 45-49 | 6.8 | | | 6.0 |
| 40-44 | 6.3 | | | 6.3 |
| 35-39 | 8.6 | | | 7.7 |
| 30-34 | 7.9 | | | 7.4 |
| 25-29 | 8.7 | | | 9.9 |
| 20-24 | 7.1 | | | 9.6 |
| 15-19 | 10.1 | | | 8.9 |
| 10-14 | 11.3 | | | 10.8 |
| 5-9 | 8.9 | | | 10.0 |
| 0-4 | 6.9 | | | 8.6 |

Percent

(c)

TABLE 19.11
Percent distribution of population age 15 and over by type of economic activity

| | Accra Cap. Dist. | | | | Eastern | | | |
| | Males | | Females | | Males | | Females | |
| Types of Activity | M | NM | M | NM | M | NM | M | NM |
|---|---|---|---|---|---|---|---|---|
| **URBAN** | | | | | | | | |
| Student | 7.0 | 19.8 | 3.7 | 8.1 | 11.9 | 32.2 | 6.5 | 11.1 |
| Working | 85.3 | 66.7 | 54.3 | 60.5 | 83.0 | 60.0 | 64.5 | 69.9 |
| Unemployed | 4.7 | 7.4 | 5.0 | 7.2 | 2.5 | 4.7 | 4.5 | 6.3 |
| Housewife | — | — | 32.7 | 15.9 | — | — | 20.3 | 9.7 |
| Pensioner/old age/disabled | 2.2 | 2.5 | 0.8 | 4.9 | 1.6 | 1.1 | 0.5 | 2.0 |
| Not stated | 0.8 | 3.6 | 4.7 | 3.4 | 1.0 | 2.0 | 3.7 | 2.0 |
| Totals | 100.0 | 100.0 | 100.0 | 100.0 | 100.0 | 100.0 | 100.0 | 100.0 |
| | N — 2,222 | N = 938 | N = 1,802 | N = 1,214 | N = 1,083 | N = 298 | N = 1,214 | N = 452 |
| **RURAL** | | | | | | | | |
| Student | 19.0 | 13.1 | 4.4 | 7.9 | 7.9 | 25.7 | 6.1 | 12.2 |
| Working | 76.8 | 75.0 | 60.5 | 70.2 | 89.3 | 67.1 | 72.0 | 72.3 |
| Unemployed | 2.8 | 7.0 | 4.4 | 8.0 | 1.7 | 5.7 | 3.0 | 5.8 |
| Housewife | — | — | 30.0 | 8.2 | — | — | 16.3 | 6.5 |
| Pensioner/old age/disabled | 1.4 | 4.9 | 0.7 | 5.7 | 1.1 | 1.5 | 2.6 | 3.2 |
| Not stated | — | — | — | — | — | — | — | — |
| Totals | 100.0 | 100.0 | 100.0 | 100.0 | 100.0 | 100.0 | 100.0 | 100.0 |
| | N = 142 | N = 76 | N = 182 | N = 114 | N = 1,394 | N = 858 | N = 1,458 | N = 1,096 |

NOTE: M = migrants; NM = nonmigrants.

Employment levels are generally higher in the rural areas than in the towns; and migrants are proportionately more employed than nonmigrants in each of the two areas. The differences in labor participation rates in the rural areas and the towns need to be qualified; it is well-known that underemployment is a widespread phenomenon in the rural areas and this situation reduces productivity among the rural population. In the towns on the other hand, one is usually either fully employed or completely unemployed.

A considerable number of people in the 15–20 years age group was found to be still attending school; those who were not at school and therefore theoretically available for work showed the highest unemployment rate for any age group. Female activity rates at this age interval were also found to be somewhat reduced due to the high incidence of marriage among the group. A number of newly married women, for various reasons, often remain full-time housewives for a while before they set out to find gainful employment. Factors such as early pregnancy, prolonged honeymoon, keeping domestic arrangements in order, and insufficient capital, may prevent married women from starting any serious trade in the early years of their residence in towns. In general the longer a married woman stays with her husband at one particular place the more likely it is that she may enter into some form of gainful employment.

The proportion of the labor force in employment rises sharply after the age of 20. The increase in male activity rates reaches a maximum plateau level around the ages between 30 and 54 years; thereafter the rates fall consistently till they nearly reach zero at the very old ages. In Ghana as a whole the reduction in activity rates among males, particularly those older than 65 years, is largely the result of the high incidence of disability among this age group; retirement is hardly known in the rural areas and healthy men usually remain active until very late in life. Female activity stretches over a longer period than male activity; the peak period of employment for males is between 40 and 44 years compared with females among whom activity rates are at the highest between 50 and 60 years. It is most likely that widowhood increases the tendency for women to find employment even at relatively late periods of their lifetime.[6]

Further examination of the data shows that the level of employment is lowest among migrants who arrived within the previous 12 months. For example, 57.3 percent of the males aged 15 and over who had been in residence for less than one year in the Accra Capital District urban area were found to be working compared with 75.7 and 78 percent of those who had been in residence for between one and six years and over six years respectively. The corresponding figures for the towns of the Eastern Region are 61.5, 66.9, and 69.1 percent respectively for those in residence of less than one year, between one and six years, and over six years. A similar phenomenon is observed in the rural areas. The conclusion from these observed patterns is that the longer the period of residence and the more stable the migrant the greater the chances that such a migrant will find employment. The observed patterns of activity rates among the population are explicable; usually migrants coming directly into the towns from

their rural homes arrive without any adequate skills to qualify them to obtain employment quickly. Again, since employment avenues are relatively scarce, these newly arrived members of the labor force often find it difficult even to make the necessary contacts, and can remain in the towns for varying lengths of time without any employment.

Analyzing only the population with some schooling, it is found that employment levels are higher among the more educated labor force than among the less educated for all population groups irrespective of migration status, origin, sex, or age. However, if those with no schooling are also included and contrasted with those with schooling, it is found that education as such has not increased the level of activity among the labor force as a whole to any significant degree. On the contrary, employment levels in general are higher among the noneducated than those with education. The difference is explained by the large proportion of middle and elementary school leavers within the educated labor force; and those with the lowest education register the highest rate of unemployment in the towns as well as in the rural areas. One cannot but conclude that large-scale elementary schooling throughout the country has produced great numbers of unemployed young men and women. Unemployment among elementary school leavers is indeed very widespread in the towns as well as the rural areas. Middle school leavers are highly oriented toward reporting themselves as unemployed but seeking work in the clerical sector, and this is the very area in the economy that is already saturated. The middle school graduates show a strong aversion to manual work, and will rarely accept positions as drivers' mates, apprentice craftsmen, and the like, occupations which hold out the prospect of raising them to semiprofessional and technical status in the economy.

The situation in the rural areas is rather surprising and probably more harmful in terms of its social consequences; here many of these boys and girls will neither submit to assisting their parents in petty domestic duties

---

[6] N. O. Addo, "Demographic Aspects of Manpower and Employment in Ghana," *The Economic Bulletin of Ghana*, XI, 3 (1967). The age-specific labor participation rates for females are as follow:

| Age group | 15–19 | 20–24 | 25–29 | 30–34 |
|---|---|---|---|---|
| Percent | 42.5 | 49.5 | 50.0 | 56.1 |
| Age group | 35–39 | 40–44 | 45–49 | 50–54 |
| Percent | 58.7 | 64.4 | 65.6 | 68.3 |
| Age group | 55–59 | 60–64 | 65+ | |
| Percent | 68.8 | 61.8 | 42.0 | |

nor take to any form of farming. They would rather be idle, waiting to be served by their illiterate mothers and hoping for a chance to go into a town. Our survey found, for example, that in the rural areas of the Eastern Region, 15 percent of nonmigrants with elementary education were unemployed; only 1.7 percent of the illiterates were similarly unemployed. Compared with the towns, the level of unemployment is low in the rural areas; but even in these areas about 2.8 percent of those with elementary education were still without employment compared with 1.1 percent of the illiterates.

Another related aspect of migration and employment, this time revealed by the 1960 census, is that there is a tendency for migrants born in towns to be proportionately less employed than those born in the villages (Table 19.12).

TABLE 19.12
Percentage of migrants, over 15 years of age, employed

| Status | Males | Females |
|---|---|---|
| Born in another town, currently in town residence | 78.9 | 59.3 |
| Born in another town, currently in village residence | 86.3 | 65.9 |
| Born in another village, currently in town residence | 81.4 | 59.9 |
| Born in another village, currently in village residence | 89.9 | 62.9 |
| Born in this locality (nonmigrant) in town residence | 75.0 | 68.9 |
| Born in this locality (nonmigrant) in village residence | 87.1 | 72.5 |

SOURCE: 1960 Census Postenumeration survey.

The association of urbanization, education, and employment is quite strong. The town-born person, because of circumstances which tend to make him better educated, more sophisticated, more rational in his choice between jobs and more knowledgeable about the differences in styles of living between clerical workers and manual or technical apprentice workers, is likely to be more selective in choosing between jobs than his rural counterpart who may not have such qualities. There is also another factor: Parents, particularly mothers, in the villages invariably encourage their young children, whom they cannot send to higher schools, to go into the towns to find white-collar jobs. Even rich farmers and great landowners are most unlikely to encourage their educated children to follow in their footsteps. This creates a psychological situation which leads many young middle school graduates in the rural areas to migrate to the towns.[7]

THE EDUCATIONAL BACKGROUND OF THE POPULATION OVER SIX YEARS OF AGE. The educational background of the population is influenced by a number of variables, including place of birth (urban/rural), place of residence (urban/rural), age, sex, and length of present residence. In urban areas the level of education among the male migrants is slightly lower than among the nonmigrants; however, this picture is distorted because it is heavily weighted by the inclusion of foreign immigrants from the neighboring African countries, over 95 percent of whom are illiterates. The true situation is that the local-born migrants show slightly higher levels of education, in terms of both quantity and quality, than the nonmigrants in urban as well as rural areas. The towns are of immense attraction to persons who have been to school.[8]

The proportion of migrants with higher levels of education who moved into the towns of the Accra Capital District is much greater than those who moved into the towns of the Eastern Region. Since the majority of the migrants in the towns of the latter region came from the nearby villages, most of even the more educated among them could not have gone beyond the middle school, which is the main type of education found in these areas.

Because of the expansion of the educational system in recent years, the education of the

[7] See also John C. Caldwell, "Determinants of Rural-Urban Migration in Ghana," *Population Studies*, XII, 3 (November 1968).

[8] See *ibid.* and also Caldwell, *African Rural-Urban Migration*, especially pp. 60–76.

young is considerably more extensive than that of the older generation. All groups among the younger generation, aged 6–14 years, migrants and nonmigrants, rural or town-born, have recently enjoyed substantial opportunities for entering elementary school. In particular, the younger females have achieved a tremendous advance in education, especially in the rural areas, and now there is a narrowing difference between their educational level and that of males. The greatest difference is in higher education, where the men still hold a significant lead over the women (Table 19.13).

On the whole, the town-born migrants proportionately reached much higher levels of education than the rural-born. One can however anticipate that some of these differences in education among the various groups and communities in the country will be greatly reduced or will even disappear as the educational system, particularly the higher forms, evenly penetrates the rural areas and all the regions (Table 19.14).

EDUCATION BY LENGTH OF RESIDENCE.   Recent developments in education in the rural areas have resulted in higher levels of education among recent migrants to the towns. Mobility has become particularly great among those with higher education. There has been an increase in the flow of those with educational qualifications into the rural areas, consisting mainly of trained teachers and other personnel in the civil service. However, it should be noted that education beyond elementary and middle school can now be obtained in some of the villages and small towns. It has become almost a fashion in recent years for local communities in rural areas and in some of the small towns, even those with easy access to urban services and adequate communications with the main towns, to establish higher educational institutions such as commercial and secondary schools for the children of the vicinity, by using communal labor and their own resources. Further, the government, in response to the needs of the country for more qualified teachers, recently opened a number of new training colleges, some of which are located in villages and small towns. A few of the small towns in the Eastern Region which provide some form of higher education are Anum, Old Tafo, Dodowa, Amanase, and Akropong. The population which enters these institutions is diverse and originates from all parts of the country.

TABLE 19.13

Percent distribution of population over 6 years of age, by type of education

| Sample Area | Type of Education | | | | | | | | | |
| | None | | Elementary | | Higher | | Not Stated | | Numbers | |
| | M | NM | M | NM | M | NM | M | NM | M | NM |
| Urban | | | | | *Males* | | | | | |
|   Accra capital district | 32.1 | 23.3 | 51.5 | 62.9 | 14.8 | 12.9 | 1.6 | 0.9 | 2,690 | 1,748 |
| Eastern | 29.7 | 25.2 | 62.6 | 70.6 | 7.0 | 3.9 | 0.7 | 0.3 | 1,574 | 727 |
| Rural | | | | | | | | | | |
|   Accra capital district | 34.9 | 43.2 | 55.2 | 56.1 | 9.9 | 0.7 | — | — | 212 | 139 |
| Eastern | 25.5 | 26.5 | 69.6 | 72.1 | 4.9 | 1.4 | — | — | 1,304 | 1,693 |
| Urban | | | | | *Females* | | | | | |
|   Accra capital district | 60.5 | 45.9 | 33.4 | 47.5 | 5.0 | 5.3 | 1.1 | 1.3 | 2,342 | 2,033 |
| Eastern | 54.6 | 41.2 | 41.4 | 56.9 | 2.9 | 0.9 | 1.1 | 1.0 | 1,679 | 908 |
| Rural | | | | | | | | | | |
|   Accra capital district | 58.9 | 60.2 | 39.1 | 39.7 | 2.0 | 0.1 | — | — | 248 | 156 |
| Eastern | 60.8 | 47.9 | 38.6 | 51.5 | 0.4 | 0.6 | — | — | 1,823 | 1,851 |

NOTE: M = migrants; NM = nonmigrants. Elementary education includes middle school; higher education covers any secondary schooling at all.

TABLE 19.14
Type of education of population over 6 years of age, by whether born in urban area, rural area, or outside Ghana

| Type of Education | Accra cap. dist. (urban) | | | Eastern (urban) | | | Eastern (rural) | | |
|---|---|---|---|---|---|---|---|---|---|
| | town | village | outside Ghana | town | village | outside Ghana | town | village | outside Ghana |
| | *Males* | | | | | | | | |
| None | 19.0 | 26.9 | 55.5 | 20.7 | 30.7 | 67.3 | 30.7 | 45.2 | 84.0 |
| Elementary | 60.2 | 57.7 | 34.2 | 67.9 | 61.3 | 29.8 | 64.0 | 52.6 | 15.7 |
| Higher | 19.2 | 13.6 | 9.3 | 10.8 | 7.1 | 2.9 | 5.3 | 2.2 | 0.4 |
| Not stated | 1.6 | 1.9 | 1.0 | 0.6 | 0.9 | — | — | — | — |
| Totals | 100.0 | 100.0 | 100.0 | 100.0 | 100.0 | 100.0 | 100.0 | 100.0 | 100.0 |
| | N = 872 | N = 938 | N = 773 | N = 352 | N = 858 | N = 171 | N = 496 | N = 989 | N = 246 |
| | *Females* | | | | | | | | |
| None | 49.3 | 62.5 | 76.4 | 40.7 | 56.4 | 94.0 | 44.2 | 65.4 | 96.2 |
| Elementary | 44.0 | 32.9 | 17.0 | 52.9 | 39.0 | 3.5 | 54.4 | 34.3 | 3.8 |
| Higher | 5.5 | 3.3 | 5.5 | 5.6 | 1.9 | 2.5 | 1.4 | 0.3 | — |
| Not stated | 0.8 | 1.3 | 1.1 | 0.8 | 0.7 | — | — | — | — |
| Totals | 100.0 | 100.0 | 100.0 | 100.0 | 100.0 | 100.0 | 100.0 | 100.0 | 100.0 |

OCCUPATIONAL CHARACTERISTICS OF THE POPULATION. The first impression one gets from comparing migrants with nonmigrants in the Eastern Region is that proportionately the former occupy higher occupational positions than the latter. Occupational mobility may have advanced faster in the towns of the Eastern Region than in the Accra Capital District, where the differences are relatively small between migrants and nonmigrants.

It is in agriculture and fishing that non-migrants predominate, largely because this invariably was the local traditional economic activity. Nearly three-fifths of the male non-migrants living in the towns of the Eastern Region were in agricultural occupations compared with only one-eighth in the towns of the Accra Capital District. Whereas the modern sector of the economy is relatively well developed in the Accra Capital District and is indeed the major source of work of the labor force, in contrast the population of the towns of the Eastern Region retain strong agricultural characteristics. The service industries, including police, fire, domestic, and conservancy services, are still largely operated by internal migrants from Northern Ghana and immigrants from neighboring African countries. The women who found employment in the towns of the Eastern Region essentially showed no differences in their occupations from those living in the rural areas. About three-quarters of the female nonmigrant labor force living in the towns, and almost the same proportion in rural areas of this region, were found to be occupied in agriculture while only one-sixth were in trading (Table 19.15).

The educational background of the various occupational groups are those to be expected in a society like Ghana which began the development process slowly but has recently been changing quite rapidly. Indeed, a substantial proportion of the labor force occupies professional and clerical positions with only elementary educational qualifications. There are many cases in the civil service, banks, and private Ghanaian and foreign business enterprises in which the top and intermediate positions still are filled by persons with middle school education. There are also many untrained pupil teachers in the

TABLE 19.15

Percent distribution of population over 15 years of age, by type of occupation

| Type of Occupation | Sex | Accra Cap. Dist. (urban) | | Eastern (urban) | | Eastern (rural) | |
|---|---|---|---|---|---|---|---|
| | | M | NM | M | NM | M | NM |
| Professional | M | 10.1 | 8.8 | 9.1 | 4.6 | 9.1 | 3.5 |
| | F | 4.1 | 4.8 | 4.1 | 1.3 | 2.8 | 1.2 |
| Clerical | M | 16.6 | 16.4 | 8.1 | 5.3 | 3.8 | 4.8 |
| | F | 7.2 | 7.7 | 1.5 | 1.0 | 0.2 | 0.2 |
| Sales | M | 13.7 | 16.1 | 14.2 | 5.4 | 6.5 | 1.2 |
| | F | 66.3 | 70.0 | 50.8 | 17.8 | 27.4 | 15.4 |
| Farmers/fishermen | M | 3.0 | 11.2 | 20.0 | 58.8 | 60.2 | 75.7 |
| | F | 1.5 | 1.6 | 25.9 | 71.3 | 59.0 | 75.7 |
| Miners, etc. | M | — | 0.6 | 0.2 | — | 5.8 | 0.7 |
| | F | 0.2 | 0.2 | — | — | 0.2 | 0.3 |
| Transport, etc. | M | 9.0 | 10.3 | 6.8 | 5.3 | 1.9 | 2.9 |
| | F | 0.9 | 0.5 | 0.7 | — | 0.2 | 0.5 |
| Craftsmen | M | 38.4 | 34.7 | 36.8 | 20.0 | 12.2 | 11.1 |
| | F | 13.6 | 11.5 | 14.4 | 7.4 | 10.3 | 6.7 |
| Service | M | 9.2 | 1.3 | 3.3 | — | 6.5 | — |
| | F | 6.2 | 4.1 | 1.9 | 0.3 | 0.9 | — |
| Not classified | M | — | 0.6 | 1.5 | 0.6 | — | — |
| | F | — | — | 0.7 | 0.9 | — | — |
| *Totals* | | | | | | | |
| Percentages | M | 100.0 | 100.0 | 100.0 | 100.0 | 100.0 | 100.0 |
| | F | 100.0 | 100.0 | 100.0 | 100.0 | 100.0 | 100.0 |
| | M | N = 1,956 | N = 638 | N = 909 | N = 187 | N = 1,241 | N = 577 |
| | F | N = 177 | N = 747 | N = 793 | N = 324 | N = 1,050 | N = 797 |

NOTE: M = migrants; NM = nonmigrants.

villages and small towns; this group constituted over three-fifths of the total teachers in the country in 1967–1968.[9] Pupil teachers, like those with full training, often describe themselves as professionals and appear as such in the statistics of occupations, which strictly speaking should not be the case. The occupations of the elementary school leavers are quite varied; however, they are found proportionately less in agricultural occupations than the illiterates (the differences being significant at the 1 percent level.) Those with secondary and commercial education are employed mainly in the clerical sector, while university graduates and those with other forms of higher education are in the professions and higher clerical occupations.

A substantial proportion of the labor force in the towns are craftsmen, mainly carpenters, builders, painters, weavers and spinners, tailors, goldsmiths, mechanics, etc. Females are often seamstresses; this activity is in increasingly becoming a popular vocation for young girls who obtain the qualification mainly through apprenticeship, but recently also through organized full-time vocational training in institutions. Petty trading still remains the most important activity for females in the towns; this work usually is taken up by illiterate women and young girls who dropped out of school quite early or servants working for their mistresses. It is more likely that a girl with a completed elementary education, choosing to work in the trading field, would seek employment in a large, organized, trade store as an employee salesgirl rather than enter into petty trading. For one thing, such a girl is motivated to maintain her standard of living at a level similar to her counterpart who for one reason or another may have gained employment in the civil service, a bank, or an office. Since the

[9] Ghana Government, *Two-Year Development Plan—Mid-1968 to Mid-1970* (Accra, July 1968), p. 83.

conditions of service are similar in many respects in these sectors for persons with such qualifications, no serious differences arise if such a girl moves into a store as a salesgirl. Petty trading on the other hand is not as respectable a vocation as clerical or sales work; the former is a much more tedious activity although sometimes it requires considerable entrepreneurial skill for its successful organization. This kind of occupation in the rural areas is considered to occupy a higher status position than farming. Young girls with elementary education may gladly take up this job rather than go into farming.

*Occupation by length of residence.* The trends shown in occupations reflect the changes occurring in the quality and skill of labor and also the opportunities that have developed in the recent past in employment in the two regions. In general the male professional, technical, and managerial class grew more than proportionately among the recent migrants both in the towns and rural areas as compared with those who had been residents for longer periods there. Although many of the professionals in the rural areas are school teachers, nevertheless recent developments in fields such as agricultural extension, surveying, and paramedical and rural health activities led to an increase in the demand for such skills there. The 1960 postenumeration survey showed that 30 percent of the professionals in the rural areas who had been in residence for less than two years were in the "draftsmen, engineering, technician" occupations compared with 11 percent of those migrants who had been in residence for two years or more. On the whole, the proportion of clerical workers appears to have declined among recent migrants; this indeed is further evidence that the emphasis in the economy now is on skilled technical and professional workers who could help directly, and in other ways, in the building up and improving of the infrastructure.

The proportion of female sales workers has also fallen in the towns since the 1960 census, but in rural areas the situation is the reverse and a considerable increase was recorded among this group. Trading has gradually expanded in the rural areas and is the second major activity for females following agriculture. Trade, in fact, has developed at the expense of agriculture; hence in these areas both the younger males and females are increasingly moving away from farming into the nonagricultural sector. Clearly this rapid decline of rural agricultural labor is an important economic trend; its implications must be thoroughly investigated as a basis for better agricultural and overall economic planning. Among those factors that have been mentioned as affecting adequate agricultural production are traditional methods of farming, inadequate feeder roads and bad transportation systems, poor storage facilities, the withdrawal of children into the classroom, the growing proportions of children in the population, and increased rural-urban migration. Our own statistics show that the proportion of the migrants to rural areas who enter agriculture has declined among the most recent migrants compared with those who came earlier in the 1950s and early 1960s (Table 19.16).

To repeat our earlier findings, migrants who were born in the rural areas were disproportionately more unskilled or semiskilled, and were found more in agricultural occupations, than those born in towns. The towns of the Accra Capital District attracted more skilled and professional workers than the towns of the Eastern Region. It is important to note, however, that the same "pull factors" in the town milieu attracted not only the skilled but also the unskilled workers; this is the social and economic dilemma of the urban process in Ghana. Thus the urban areas are seen by both the skilled and unskilled as the center within which they might maximize their efforts and achieve higher levels of living.

Occupational change between the generations is also another important measure of occupational mobility. One main economic effect of large-scale elementary education is that it has reduced labor participation rates among the population aged 15–20 years. In addition, a considerable proportion of those who were found working in this age group

TABLE 19.16

Type of occupation of migrants over 15 years of age, by length of residence, (percent distribution)

| Type of Occupation | Sex | Accra cap. dist. (urban) | | | Length of Residence Eastern (urban) | | | Eastern (rural) | | |
|---|---|---|---|---|---|---|---|---|---|---|
| | | Under 1 yr. | 1–6 yrs. | 6+ yrs. | Under 1 yr. | 1–6 yrs. | 6+ yrs. | Under 1 yr. | 1–6 yrs. | 6+ yrs. |
| Professional, technical, adminis- tration | M | 18.6 | 10.9 | 9.0 | 9.2 | 11.3 | 5.6 | 21.8 | 18.0 | 3.7 |
| | F | 7.8 | 6.1 | 2.2 | 4.6 | 4.6 | 2.1 | 7.8 | 7.6 | 1.0 |
| Clerical | M | 12.8 | 19.6 | 12.9 | 7.8 | 7.9 | 8.8 | 3.2 | 4.7 | 3.1 |
| | F | 4.3 | 8.6 | 5.5 | 3.1 | 1.8 | 0.3 | 1.0 | 0.6 | — |
| Sales | M | 8.1 | 11.1 | 17.2 | 11.1 | 12.1 | 18.3 | 3.2 | 5.6 | 7.0 |
| | F | 60.9 | 58.6 | 74.6 | 38.5 | 48.1 | 55.4 | 32.4 | 29.2 | 27.9 |
| Farming, fishing | M | 5.2 | 4.9 | 0.5 | 15.0 | 15.5 | 26.8 | 29.8 | 41.6 | 71.2 |
| | F | 7.8 | 2.4 | 0.5 | 23.8 | 27.7 | 28.6 | 39.2 | 45.1 | 61.9 |
| Mining, etc. | M | — | — | 0.1 | 0.6 | 0.4 | — | 9.7 | 11.2 | 2.6 |
| | F | 0.2 | 0.2 | 0.3 | — | — | — | 2.0 | 0.9 | — |
| Transport | M | 7.6 | 8.8 | 8.7 | 6.5 | 6.8 | 7.1 | 4.0 | 1.9 | 1.9 |
| | F | — | 0.6 | 1.2 | 1.5 | 0.7 | 0.3 | 1.0 | 0.3 | 0.1 |
| Craftsmen | M | 35.5 | 35.7 | 42.6 | 43.1 | 40.8 | 30.1 | 26.6 | 15.9 | 10.1 |
| | F | 9.6 | 15.1 | 11.9 | 19.2 | 13.9 | 12.7 | 12.7 | 14.0 | 8.7 |
| Service | M | 11.6 | 9.0 | 9.0 | 5.9 | 4.5 | 2.1 | 1.6 | 1.1 | 0.4 |
| | F | 8.7 | 8.4 | 3.8 | 7.7 | 2.5 | 0.6 | 3.9 | 2.2 | 0.4 |
| Not classified | M | 0.6 | — | — | 0.6 | 0.7 | 1.2 | — | — | — |
| | F | 0.7 | — | — | 1.5 | 0.7 | — | — | — | — |
| Total per- centages | M | 100.0 | 100.0 | 100.0 | 100.0 | 100.0 | 100.0 | 100.0 | 100.0 | 100.0 |
| | F | 100.0 | 100.0 | 100.0 | 100.0 | 100.0 | 100.0 | 100.0 | 100.0 | 100.0 |
| | M | N = 172 | N = 1,082 | N = 421 | N = 153 | N = 556 | N = 339 | N = 124 | N = 466 | N = 774 |
| | F | N = 115 | N = 510 | N = 421 | N = 130 | N = 563 | N = 377 | N = 102 | N = 315 | N = 734 |

were training as craftsmen. Thus the potential workers who in the past would have taken up agriculture or trade had now taken up different forms of training which generally held greater promise for them, in terms of raising their status into the semiprofessional and technical groups. Domestic service also increased among the younger female workers in the towns. Until very recently, this activity was virtually monopolized by girls from very poor homes, particularly the illiterates who originated from such tribes as the Ewes of the Volta Region, and Frafras and other tribes of the Northern Region. This sector has also expanded quite recently and has absorbed elementary school girls as well.

SUMMARY AND CONCLUSION

The above study revealed some of the dynamics of the internal migration process and its effect on the social, economic, and demographic structure of urban and rural areas in one of the most rapidly developing parts in Ghana. From this study, one cannot help but conclude that internal migration has made a deep and irreversible impact on the social and demographic structure of the region under review. This impact nevertheless occurred in different degrees within the towns and rural areas, and in the Eastern Region and the Accra Capital District.

Since migrants are not representative of the total population, their characteristics often tend to be different from nonmigrants. This study has shown, for example, that migrants are found proportionately more in the top occupations, are more likely to be employed, and more often have higher education than the nonmigrants. In demographic terms, migration has raised the proportion of the economically active population in the towns and thus has probably reduced the level of child dependency in these areas. The migrant population contains proportionately fewer children and more young adults than is found among nonmigrants. Part of the explanation is that some of the migrants leave their young children and families behind in their home towns and villages. Hence migration per se has probably not altered the overall pattern and level of child dependency in the country as a whole. There is no clear evidence yet that migrants are less fertile than the nonmigrants or that mortality rates are higher for one group than the other. It has been suggested however that one of the causes of relatively low fertility in Northern Ghana compared with other regions is the fact that large numbers of husbands separate from their wives and families and migrate seasonally or for longer periods to the southern regions to work.

This study has also led to some other observations: First, it is quite clear that the processes of change are themselves complex. The migration process consists of a network in which the movement of the population has assumed varying shapes and has occurred in various directions all of which in turn have affected the structure of the urban as well as rural areas. The movements have occurred, though to unequal extents, between the towns and rural areas on the one hand, and between the Accra Capital District and Eastern Region on the other. Second, both literates and illiterates, men and women, adults and children, of different ethnic backgrounds have been involved in these movements. Two basic causes have always been responsible for the movement of people from rural areas into the towns: the desire to obtain employment in the modern economic sector and the desire to obtain higher education. The towns so far have been fairly successful in giving education to those who want it; but they have not yet been successful in satisfying all those who come solely for employment. Although the movement of migrants into the rural areas is primarily for the purpose of farming, nevertheless a growing number of recent migrants are working on government and other projects designed to improve the infrastructure of these areas.

The characteristics of the migrant population show considerable variations even among the various subgroups. Thus, for example, unemployment among migrants living in towns was found to be higher among the most recent migrants (that is, those who arrived in the 12 months prior to the survey) than among those who came before them. Similarly the town-born migrants were proportionately more educated and occupied higher positions in employment than the rural-born migrants. In general, the social and economic characteristics of the migrants show a strong association with place of residence, place of birth, and the length of time in which the migrants have been in residence.

# CHAPTER TWENTY

# *Population Policy & Its Implementation*

S. K. GAISIE, N. O. ADDO,
AND S. B. JONES

One of the most significant features of Ghana's population is its rate of growth. At the beginning of 1921 the country had a population of just over 2 million, and by the first quarter of 1960 the population had increased to 6.7 million; that is, it more than tripled in the short period of 40 years. Although data for the early part of the century are not completely reliable, the recorded figures indicate that Ghana's population had been growing at an average annual rate of 2.8 percent for the 40-year period. According to the available census data, the rate of growth increased to over 4 percent per annum in the period between 1948 and 1960. Nevertheless, estimates prepared by the Demographic Unit of the University of Ghana indicate that the plausible rate of natural increase during this period lay between 2.7 and 3.0 percent per annum,[1] and that Ghana's population was tending to double in only 20 years.

In 1960 the crude death rate was 23 per thousand, the infant mortality rate about 160 per thousand, and the expectation of life at birth around 40 years.[2] Although these vital rates, based on retrospective data collected in 1960, indicate the existence of comparatively high death rates in Ghana, the mortality rate has undoubtedly been declining as a result of the widespread application of preventive and curative medicine. Thus the 1968 crude death rate was estimated to be 15 per thousand population,[3] apparently falling about one point every year. The rate of natural increase probably lay between 3.0 and 3.5 percent per annum in the 1967–1969 period.[4] There is no doubt therefore that the population has been increasing at an accelerating rate, until in 1970 nearly half a million persons are being added to the population every year. In 1960, 171,386 children aged 6 years (70 percent of

[1] S. K. Gaisie, *Dynamics of Population Growth in Ghana* (Accra-Tema: Ghana Publishing Corporation, 1969), p. 55.

[2] *Ibid.*, pp. 73 ff.

[3] 1968–1969 Demographic Sample Survey, Demographic Unit, University of Ghana, Preliminary results (unpublished).

[4] *Ibid.*

children at that age) were not in school, and 701,207 (or 58 percent) of children aged 6–12 years had never received any formal education. The 1960s witnessed a rapid increase in the school-age population and although "enrollment in primary and middle schools increased from around 825,000 in 1961–1962 to about 1.4 million in 1967–1968, and secondary enrollment from under 20,000 to around 44,000, large numbers of children still remain out of school."[5] It must also be borne in mind that the expenditure on education increased from NC30 million[6] to more than NC80 million during the period of seven years—i.e., 1961–1962 to 1967–1968. In 1960 about 163,643 (9 percent) of people whose labor could have contributed to the rapid development of the economy were out of jobs; and a large proportion of the employed were engaged in occupations of relatively low productivity. At the same time, the supply of insufficient high-level manpower is indicative of the urgent need for intensive training and expansion of higher education to provide the needs for the various sectors within the expanding economy. This expansion would involve the expenditure of huge sums of money.

That Ghana's population growth should be regulated in accordance with the growth of material resources is an obvious truth. Yet, although interest had been shown in family planning in various tropical African countries during the 1950s, it was not until the beginning of the 1960s that some concern was unofficially expressed about Ghana's high rate of population growth. In late 1961, the results of the 1960 census showed that the population had increased by two-thirds since the 1948 census and that the average annual rate of growth appeared to be 4.2 percent. The Bureau of Census pointed out that some of the increase was due to immigration and that the 1948 census was probably defective. It must also be noted that there was probably some overcount in the 1960 census and that

this might have exaggerated the rate of growth. Nevertheless, the bureau misled the planners by assuring them that the rate of growth was only 2.6 percent per annum. Although the former President of Ghana, Kwame Nkrumah, was dreaming of a Ghana with a population of 20 million within the shortest possible time, the planners of the economy who masterminded and prepared his Seven-Year Development Plan warned in 1963 that the high rate of population growth would slow down economic development.[7]

Before 1963, however, the Christian Council of Ghana had already begun showing interest in family planning for married couples. The council established medical advice centers in Accra, Kumasi, and Ho in 1961, 1964, and 1965 respectively.[8] One of the aims of these clinics is to make "available contraceptive advice for those who wish to limit or space their pregnancies." In addition to this the clinics "help to eliminate physiological obstacles in achieving happy marriage and, since sterility causes divorce by native customary practice, one purpose is to assist those suffering from this disability through investigation, treatment and education." Although the council's main aim in establishing these clinics is to help married couples to solve some of the problems arising from infertility which tends to cause divorce or, at least, to create unhappy marriages, it provides family planning services to those who request them. Among the contraceptives supplied at the clinics are diaphragms, IUDs, oral pills, and a variety of foam tablets.

It was not until the second half of the 1960s that public concern about the population problem really emerged. In 1965, the then President of the Republic of Ghana, Kwame Nkrumah, established an interdepartmental advisory committee headed by the government Chief Statistician, E. N. Omaboe, to consider a population policy for Ghana. The first and only meeting of this committee was

---

[5] Republic of Ghana, *Population Planning for National Progress and Prosperity* (Accra-Tema: Ghana Publishing Corporation, March 1969), p. 11.

[6] NC1 (or one New Cedi) = U.S. $1.

[7] Republic of Ghana, *Seven Year Development Plan, 1963–1964 to 1969–1970* (Accra: Government Printing Department, 1964) pp. 6 ff.

[8] N. O. Addo, "Family Planning Services in Ghana," 1965 (unpublished article).

attended by representatives from various departments and institutions; among them were medical practitioners, ministers of religion, demographers, senior civil servants, and politicians. The Central Bureau of Statistics submitted to this meeting a memorandum containing certain proposals for the committee to consider as the basis for formulating a population policy for Ghana. The meeting, which took only one hour to "complete" its work, was dominated by the politicians who were sent there to hammer out the official policy on population growth. That Nkrumah's government was advocating an expansionist population policy was confirmed by the government Chief Statistician who remarked at the meeting that the President himself had previously disclosed such a policy to him informally.

It is not surprising, therefore, that most of the recommendations submitted to the advisory committee by the bureau reflected the official policy the government intended to pursue in the future. Thus the committee recommended among other things that "it was one conclusion made by the advisory committee that for various reasons Ghana is capable of supporting a much larger population than it has at present and such a population increase is desirable." The bureau, of course, was one of the expert organizations which helped to draw up the 1963–1964 to 1969–1970 development plan; it was therefore quite familiar with the massive problems which high birth rates might create for the country's economic development. The Ghanaian planners rightly stated that the demographic facts, as revealed by the 1960 census, "must condition all economic policy in Ghana for years to come" and that the "demographic situation which lays this heavy burden of savings on the population is not likely to show any significant changes in the short-run." And yet the bureau thought that it was not necessary to take any positive steps to reduce the current birth rate, for "it may cause an unnecessary alarm which may make it impossible for Ghana to get the necessary increase in its population which it so badly needs now."

While the bureau played politics by trying to please the government of the day, it at the same time placed the advisory committee in a very embarrassing and difficult position as far as making a critical and objective examination of what the bureau had proposed as the basis of government official policy. But even despite this political pressure, the advisory committee expressed its concern about "the high birth rate and its concomitant high natural increase." It therefore advised that "any direct mass campaign to increase the population may ultimately lead to an unwanted population explosion in the future." The committee suggested that "where certain people willingly expressed the desire to stop reproduction, doctors should be allowed to give the relevant advice." The committee also advised that the government should explore ways and means to help those who want to stop reproduction for economic and health reasons. The use of existing health services or mobile family clinics was recommended.

These recommendations were not implemented; instead they were filed away. Prior to this meeting, the government had placed a ban on the importation and sale of contraceptives and had discussed the "possibility of penal sanctions against contraception." Although legislative action was not taken, it is a historical fact that Nkrumah's government was a pronatalist one and a strong advocate of an expansionist policy.

Nevertheless, a change of political administration in February 1966 ushered in a new attitude toward the population problem. On Human Rights Day, 1967, Ghana became the first sub-Saharan African nation to sign the *World Leaders' Declaration on Population* and to join the 30 nations affirming the following convictions:

. . . that the population problem must be recognized as a principal element in long-range national planning if governments are to achieve their economic goals and fulfill the aspirations of their people; . . . that the great majority of parents desire to have the knowledge and the means to plan their families; that the opportunity to decide the number and spacing of children is a basic human right . . . .

That the objective of family planning is the enrichment of human life, not its restriction; that family planning, by assuring greater opportunity to each person, frees man to attain his individual dignity and reach his full potential.

The Ghana Planned Parenthood Association was founded in March 1967 and it was incorporated in June of the same year. The aims of the association among other things are to:

(1) Assist national efforts aimed at improving the quality of the population
(2) Promote the physical and mental health of mothers through better spacing of births
(3) Encourage proper spacing of children, and ensure that families have children when they are ready and want them
(4) Promote the better health and nutrition of children

The association has expanded rapidly, has employed full-time field workers, and now has branches in Accra, Kumasi, Sekondi-Takoradi, and Cape Coast. The clinics established in these towns offer family planning advice and also supply contraceptives. The association also disseminates knowledge about family planning through lectures, debates, symposiums, and film shows. The association is affiliated with the International Planned Parenthood Federation and has continued to receive almost all of its financial support from the agency.

The two-year *National Development Plan*, published in 1968, contained a brief reference to the government's intention to establish family planning services. Thus the Ghana Manpower Board, which was created in January 1968 with the Commissioner for Economic Affairs as its chairman, was charged with the responsibility of reviewing "...the policy of the government on population and migration and advice on measures to be taken to ensure the fullest utilization of the human resources of the country." A special subcommittee of the board was set up to prepare a national population policy for the country. This time there were no political pressures and the subcommittee approached the issue with dili-gence and objectivity, paying more attention to demographic facts and their socio-economic implications than to the dictates of politicians. It took the subcommittee almost six months to complete its work and the prepared national population policy was submitted to the National Liberation Council for approval. The National Liberation Council approved it and it was published in March 1969, as an official policy paper, "Population Planning for National Progress and Prosperity."[9] The following are the major policy recommendations:

1. A national population policy and program are to be developed as organic parts of social and economic planning and development activity. Details of programs are to be formulated through the collaborative participation of national and regional entities, both public and private, and representatives of relevant professions and disciplines.
2. The vigorous pursuit of further means to reduce the still high rates of morbidity and mortality will be an important aspect of population policy and programs.
3. Specific and quantitative population goals will be established on the basis of reliable demographic data and the determination of demographic trends. To this end steps will be taken to strengthen the statistical, research, and analytical facilities and capabilities of the government and of public and private educational and scientific organizations.
4. Recognizing the crucial importance of a wide understanding of the deleterious effects of unlimited population growth and of the means by which couples can safely and effectively control their fertility, the government will encourage and itself undertake programs to provide information, advice, and assistance for couples wishing to space or limit their reproduction. These programs will be educational and persuasive, and not coercive.
5. Ways will be sought to encourage and promote wider productive and gainful employment for women; to increase the proportion of girls entering and completing school; to develop a wider range of nondomestic roles for women; and

[9] Most of this paper was republished, with a preface by E. N. Omaboe, Commissioner for Economic Affairs at the time, as "Ghana: Official Policy Statement," *Studies in Family Planning*, XLIV (August 1969).

to examine the structure of government prerequisites and benefits and if necessary change them in such a way as to minimize their pronatalist influences and maximize their antinatalist effects.

6. The government will adopt policies and establish programs to guide and regulate the flow of internal migration, influence spatial distribution in the interest of development progress, and reduce the scale and rate of immigration in the interests of national welfare.

7. Provision will be made to establish and maintain regular contact with the development and experience of population programs throughout the world through intensified relationships with international public and private organizations concerned with population problems.

It is clear that the population policy pledges the government to provide those who wish to restrict their family size with the means for doing so.

Following the adoption of the policy, steps were taken to develop an appropriate machinery for the family planning program

and to prepare for its implementation on a national scale. In January 1970 the government approved the machinery for the National Family Planning Program and authorized the requisite funds (NC93,000 for the first six months) to commence the program.

## STRUCTURE OF THE MACHINERY OF THE NATIONAL FAMILY PLANNING PROGRAM

The structure and location of Ghana's National Family Planning Program is unique. The structure consists of a National Family Planning Council, with a secretariat, which is an integral part of the Ministry of Finance and Economic Planning, and an executive committee, which provides the link between the council and the secretariat (see Figure 20.1). This machinery is related directly to a number of government agencies including the Ministries of Health, Information, Youth and

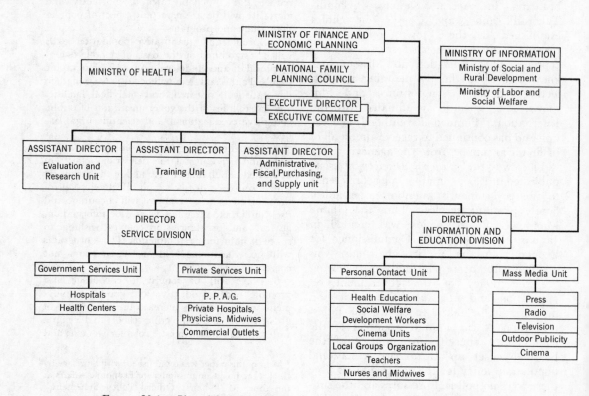

FIGURE 20.1. *Plan of Organization, Ghana National Family Planning Program,* 1969

Rural Development, and Labor and Social Welfare as well as several private agencies whose programs are related to the work of the national program. The Ministry of Finance and Economic Planning is charged with overall responsibility for the program.

The National Family Planning Council is made up of representatives of all public and private agencies whose activities are related to family planning. It thus represents a cross section of Ghanaian society. Its main role will be to give visibility and status to the National Family Planning Program. The council will thus play an active role in the mobilization of public opinion in support of that effort. Although the council may initiate policy, its role is mainly advisory.

As already indicated, the secretariat and its director are located in the Ministry of Finance and Economic Planning. The day-to-day administration of the program devolves on the director and his staff. The executive director is assisted by the executive committee composed of representatives of the participating governmental agencies (e.g., Ministries of Health, Information, etc.). The executive committee will monitor the development and progress of the program and will advise and assist the executive director in implementing approved policies and procedures. The executive committee approves annual budgets and requests for financial and technical assistance. The executive director also is assisted by three assistant directors in charge of the research and evaluation, training, and administration respectively.

There are two major line divisions of the secretariat: the services division, whose director is a physician, and the information and education division. The directors of both are administratively responsible to the executive director of the program.

SERVICE DIVISION. The services division is responsible for stimulating, coordinating, funding, and helping to design and operate service programs. The services division consists of two units: a government services unit which is responsible for services within government hospitals and health centers, and a private services unit which is responsible for contraceptive services supplied by other agencies, including the Planned Parenthood Association of Ghana, nongovernment hospitals and clinics, private physicians, and midwives. The private services unit will also be responsible for developing a contraceptive distribution program in the commercial sector.

The information and education division is responsible for stimulating, coordinating, funding, and helping to design and operate programs intended to provide couples with the knowledge and advice they need on regulating their fertility, and for acquainting people with the values of responsible parenthood. It is also responsible for informing the public about the importance of family planning for economic development and about the goals and achievements of the National Family Planning Program.

The machinery for the program was developed after careful consideration of the structure of national programs in other countries and represents an attempt to avoid many of the limitations apparent in these programs. A unique feature of Ghana's program is the location of the central secretariat in the Ministry of Finance and Economic Planning. This location was selected for several reasons. First, the family planning effort was viewed as an integral part of the country's development effort and therefore it was considered necessary to locate the secretariat in the ministry responsible for the formulation and implementation of the National Development Plan. Second, it was recognized that a successful national family planning program would require the active involvement and participation of personnel from a number of public agencies as well as the utilization of private sector resources. This could best be accomplished if the program were located in a ministry whose primary responsibility was the coordination of the responsibilities and activities of other ministries.

THE INFORMATION AND EDUCATION DIVISION. While the health aspects of family planning were clearly recognized and acknowledged, it was also realized that unless couples knew about family planning they could not avail themselves of the service. The information and educational aspects of the program were thus seen to be of critical importance. The Ministries of Information, Labor and Social Welfare, and Youth and Rural Development have a major responsibility for this component of the program. The Ministry of Health has primary responsibility for the provision of family planning services although it is also hoped to use commercial distribution channels, the Planned Parenthood Association, and private medical personnel in an attempt to extend services to parts of the population for whom government health services are not yet readily available. Family planning will be an integral part of maternal and child health services where they exist and a major effort will be made to recruit high-risk women for whom another pregnancy represents a threat to the mother or infant. It is felt that this strategy will contribute to a reduction in maternal and infant mortality while at the same time reducing the number of births that would otherwise have occurred.

The program is based on the following set of operating principles:

(1) The principal objective of the National Family Planning Program will be to reduce the rate of population growth in Ghana.

(2) The National Family Planning Program, in serving the national interest, will pursue its principal objective in such a way as to ensure the enrichment of family life and the promotion of individual dignity.

(3) Every effort will be made to ensure that barriers to public access, acceptance, and continued contraceptive use are kept to a minimum. This means attention to the convenience, comfort, privacy, and dignity of those served by the program. Fees shall be low and charged only when essential to serve program interests. Limitations shall be few, examination minimal and directly related to safety, waiting times will be short, additional supplies convenient to obtain, information adequate and accurate, while attention to

side effects will be prompt, and reassurance and encouragement readily given.

(4) Individual acceptance of family planning methods will be voluntary. Recruitment efforts will be informative and persuasive but not coercive.

(5) The fullest possible use will be made of existing institutions, facilities, and personnel.

(6) Private sector resources which can contribute toward the success of the program will be identified and used as far as possible.

(7) Specific targets and objectives, both long and short range, will be established early in the program.

(8) The establishment of services will be phased over a period of time with initial effort—emphasizing existing facilities—directed at that group of potential acceptors who are likely to be most receptive and easiest to reach.

(9) A choice of safe effective contraceptives will be made available.

(10) As contraception is reversible and birth spacing desirable, women will be eligible for service regardless of age or the number of children they have.

(11) Emphasis will be placed on assuring continuation of contraceptive practice as well as on obtaining initial acceptance.

(12) Incentive schemes to improve staff effectiveness and increase acceptance and continued contraceptive use will be tested and, where practicable, implemented.

(13) Administrative practices and policies, including basic reporting and record forms, will be uniform throughout all components of the program.

(14) An intensive and sustained educational campaign, emphasizing both mass media and person-to-person communication, to keep the general public well informed of the importance of the program will be developed to parallel if not precede the establishment of contraceptive services.

GOALS and OBJECTIVES. Preliminary planning targets have been based on an estimate of the effort needed to keep the present rate of population growth from increasing in the light of a rapidly falling death rate. These targets are based on the following assumptions:

(a) That the crude death rate could decline by as much as one point per year and that for each fall of one point in the death rate a comparable fall in the birth rate must occur to maintain a constant rate of growth
(b) That one-third of family planning acceptors and the same proportion of continuing users from previous years will discontinue contraception in a given year
(c) That it might be roughly estimated that one birth would be prevented for every four users of effective methods during a year

It is probable that the death rate may not decline as rapidly as suggested. In that event, a program of the magnitude envisaged would not only keep the rate of population growth from increasing but would also initiate a modest decline in the annual rate of increase. It also is recognized that the preliminary planning targets are only an approximate estimate of the effort required and are to be further refined on the basis of program experience and from additional demographic data as these become available.

The planning targets in Table 20.1 have been calculated on the basis of these assumptions. If the acceptor targets are achieved and the assumption regarding discontinuation is correct, there would be about 200,000 continuing users at the end of the fifth year. This represents approximately 10 percent of the expected female population in the childbearing ages.

ORGANIZATION AND RESPONSIBILITIES. The program will make full use of existing institutions, facilities, and personnel in the private as well as the public sector. The Ministry of Health will have major responsibility for the provision of contraceptive services, patient education, and training of technical personnel involved in the service program. The Ministry of Information will have responsibility for mass information and the education components of the program. Personnel from the Ministries of Youth and Rural Development and Labor and Social Welfare will also be involved with education and recruitment. It is planned that the Ministry of Education and the Ministry of Agriculture will also participate in the information and education program. The National Family Planning Program secretariat will assume overall responsibility for coordinating the various components of the program. The Planned Parenthood Association of Ghana, which provides contraceptive services, will be supported in their efforts both in respect of contraceptive services and in publicity work. The support and active involvement of a number of additional agencies, institutions, and professional associations will also be enlisted and encouraged.

PROGRAM PLAN. The initial phase of the service program will concentrate on establishing family planning services in the largest government hospitals. These hospitals are well distributed geographically and can can serve as training centers for medical and paramedical personnel. The initial training effort has begun with the preparation of job descriptions and task-oriented training materials for the several categories of personnel who will be involved. It is expected that

TABLE 20.1
Targets for family planning acceptors, Ghana, 1970–1975

| Fiscal Year | Users at Start of Year | Acceptors During Year | Total Users during Year | Users Discontinuing during Year | Users at End of Year | Estimated Births Prevented |
|---|---|---|---|---|---|---|
| 1970–71 | — | 54,000 | 54,000 | 18,000 | 36,000 | 9,000 |
| 1971–72 | 36,000 | 78,000 | 114,000 | 38,000 | 76,000 | 19,000 |
| 1972–73 | 76,000 | 96,000 | 174,000 | 58,000 | 116,000 | 39,000 |
| 1973–74 | 116,000 | 118,000 | 234,000 | 78,000 | 156,000 | 39,000 |
| 1974–75 | 156,000 | 144,000 | 300,000 | 100,000 | 200,000 | 50,000 |

specially trained nurse-midwives will play a major role in the provision of family planning services.

An intensive and sustained educational campaign, embracing all available media, is being developed along with the establishment of contraceptive services.

## IMMIGRATION POLICIES IN GHANA AND THEIR IMPLEMENTATION

Until very recently, Ghana could be adequately described as "a country of immigration."[10] At the time of the 1960 census, there were 827,000 persons of foreign origin in Ghana, which represented about 12.3 percent of the total population. Twelve years before this census the immigrant population stood at 176,000 or 4.3 percent of the total population; thus, in absolute terms, the immigrant population in Ghana multiplied nearly five times during the intercensal period between 1948 and 1960. The absolute number of immigrants prior to the 1948 census is not known; what is known historically is that systematic immigration into the country did not begin until the last quarter of the nineteenth century. This was the period when the country had just begun to modernize her economy; the development of the cocoa industry and the introduction of modern methods into mining initially triggered off this systematic relatively large-scale immigration from the neighboring countries into Ghana. On the whole, the movement of foreign workers into Ghana had been spontaneous; it was the economic attraction offered by the country and the possibility of improving their level of living above that achieved within their own country which motivated these foreign workers to come in relatively large numbers. This economic motivation has prevailed till today. Fluctuations in numbers entering occurred from one time to another, but on the whole the move-

ment can be associated with social, economic, and political developments in the country.[11]

THE LAISSEZ-FAIRE PHASE OF FOREIGN IMMIGRATION: THE COLONIAL PERIOD. Colonial Gold Coast did not possess separate laws of its own regulating the movement of immigrants either into or within the country. The country was ruled by British laws, and thus had the same immigration laws as the British Empire. For example, those who entered from West African countries, such as Nigeria, Sierra Leone, and Gambia, or from Asian countries, such as India, came under the same regulations as those who came from Britain, Australia, or Canada. Those who came from the nearby French territories, such as Togo, Ivory Coast, Upper Volta, or Niger, theoretically came under different regulations; it is known however that these regulations were not strictly enforced. British administrative policies in the colonial era did not cover matters concerning population growth. One could suggest two possible reasons why the colonial power was so inactive in this area. First, the country's population had been growing very slowly in the years before the fifties because the high birth rate was nearly matched by a high death rate. There was, therefore, no imminent threat of population explosion.

The second reason is largely economic. Like all colonial areas, the country did not receive any systematic assistance from the British toward the improvement of its economy. But there were two important economic factors which influenced population growth, particularly the immigration of foreign workers into the country. The two main economic activities which attracted foreign immigrants were modern mining and cocoa growing; these sectors produced export goods which in a direct way profited the colonial government. For a number of reasons, the local indigenous population

[10] See newspaper reports of the press conference held in Accra, December 17, 1962, by B. Gil on the occasion of the publication of the first three volumes of the 1960 Ghana Population Census.

[11] See N. O. Addo, "Immigration into Ghana: Some Social and Economic Implications of the Aliens Compliance Order of 18th November, 1969," Ghana Journal of Sociology, VI, 1 (February 1970).

generally felt disinclined to take up employment in these export-producing sectors. Wage employment, both in the mines and on the cocoa farms, involved mainly manual labor, and the indigenous population felt unwilling to join in this type of work.[12] Immigrant labor was therefore indispensable to the success of these activities. The flow of immigrants into these fields naturally benefited the export market, and, as such, immigration may have been looked upon either directly or indirectly by the colonial administrators as beneficial to the British economy. The foreign mining companies welcomed the immigrants who formed the bulk of the labor in their enterprises; similarly, the indigenous cocoa farm owners made extensive demands for immigrant labor to cultivate, harvest, and attend to the existing farms. The expansion of mining and cocoa farming throughout the forest regions created ever more demand for immigrant labor, with the result that the volume of immigration increased with time. There is, however, no evidence that the British authorities ever offered direct help or incentives to prospective immigrants to come and work in these export sectors.

Colonial laws regulating foreign immigration into the country were not effectively enforced. Thus, immigration was virtually left to run its natural course. Some of the immigrants probably arrived with the idea of settling permanently; many of those who came in with this intention may have eventually lost identification with their home countries. Many more, nevertheless, continued their contacts with relatives at home and often sent back part of their earnings to these relatives. Nigerians and Togolese were among the immigrant groups tending to settle permanently in the country; but in most cases even these immigrants married persons from their own country of origin. The immigrant groups in time expanded their interests, and became petty traders, cocoa brokers, building construction workers, car

repairmen, carpenters and plasterers, tailors, and so on. Nigerians in particular joined in the illicit diamond mining rush which began in the eastern part of the country during the latter fifties. The preindependence era could therefore be described as a laissez-faire period of immigration; immigrants entered and left "freely" with virtually no official or unofficial regulation binding their movements or their activities.

Such migration was made up mostly of Africans from the neighboring West African countries, notably Togo, Nigeria, Ivory Coast, Mali, Niger, Upper Volta, Dahomey, and Liberia. One most important characteristic of immigration in the preindependence days, which has remained till today, is that the majority arrived as seasonal migrants; they came only in certain seasons of the year to work as laborers, clearing the newly grown bush in the cocoa farms and harvesting the cocoa for the owners, after which they returned to their villages at the beginning of the rainy season. There was also a minority which formed a second category: those who stayed on, almost permanently, to act as caretakers on the farms, or who took up employment in other fields. Some of the workers on the mines also belonged to the seasonal category; this type of immigration is known to create serious problems for the mines since it leads to a very high labor turnover within these establishments and has always been a source of worry to the mining authorities.

A much smaller number of Europeans and Asians, notably Lebanese, Indians, and Syrians, also entered the country in the preindependence period. They lived mainly in the towns. In one sense one can hardly describe the Europeans as immigrants, for the majority were British and they came primarily to rule. A few others were businessmen and owned large private commercial enterprises, such as The United Africa Company (UAC), The Union Trading Company (UTC), and Busi and Stephenson, etc. All the banks were owned by European companies, such as Barclays Bank D.C.O. and the Bank of West Africa (BWA). European employees normally came to the country on transfer to

---

[12] Addo, "Immigration into Ghana"; E. Ampene, "Obuasi and Its Miners," *Ghana Journal of Sociology*, II (October 1967).

work in these establishments or in the colonial administrative service for a few years after which they left on transfer again to other countries.

Some Asian groups arrived soon after World War I; these people in particular entered into the trading field, and gradually established themselves in the commercial life of the country. The social and economic circumstances in the colonial period provided further incentives for the development of commerce among these groups of foreign workers. Since the local people did not possess the necessary capital and entrepreneurial skills, they were therefore unable to organize any large-scale trade of their own. Again, the indigenous small traders had little or no contact with importers abroad, and for this reason they relied heavily on the European and Asian importers for goods for retailing. The Asians had the advantages of possessing large-scale capital, entrepreneurial and commercial skill, and external contacts for importing goods into the country. These advantages meant that they could organize themselves better and more systematically in the commercial field and create near monopolies. The Asian traders could be said to have performed an essential service for the country at this time of its history; since the local population had no resources to trade on a large scale these Asian traders through their activities were able to fill this vacuum and thus activate the commercial life of the country.

Asian monopolistic influence in many fields of trade continued after independence to such an extent that by the mid-sixties some local pressure groups among the indigenous people had begun to express anxieties about the impending threat of these Asians to the economy. The question of continued alien domination of the retail trade was one of the important factors which influenced the government to bring the 1969 Aliens Compliance Order into force.

THE LAISSEZ-FAIRE PHASE OF FOREIGN IMMIGRATION: THE POSTINDEPENDENCE PERIOD UNTIL FEBRUARY 24, 1966. In theory, the laissez-faire period of foreign immigration under the colonial administration came to an end with the achievement of political independence in March 1957. However, the new constitution of that date did not make any reference to citizenship; a new definition of who was a citizen of Ghana did not come into being until May 11, 1957, when the Ghana Nationality and Citizenship Act was passed by Parliament. Under this act, a person who was born in Ghana before that date and who was a citizen of the United Kingdom and Colonies or a British-protected person became a citizen of Ghana, unless none of his parents or grandparents had been born in Ghana and he did not have British nationality.[13] Thus, in many cases persons born in the Gold Coast Colony, Ashanti, the Northern Territories, or British Togoland before 1957 became citizens of Ghana, if at least one of their parents or grandparents had been born in Ghana.

The new legislation on citizenship in 1957 did not seriously affect the rate at which immigration continued into the country. Indeed the general evidence is that immigration was at a faster rate immediately after independence than before. The ruling, indigenous Convention People's Party (CPP) government, largely for political but also probably for other ideological and economic reasons, followed a course of action which in effect "welcomed" all persons of other African descent irrespective of their social or political background, skill or education, into the life of the country. The years soon after political independence until around 1961–1963 could be described as "the period of accelerated immigration" into the country. As before, it did not matter whether the arriving foreigner sought to invest in the country, or was sick and wanted to come and receive free treatment in the country's hospitals, or was a political agitator who wanted to use Ghana as a base for his political activities, or was a criminal in

[13] G. K. A. Ofosu-Amaah, "The Position of Aliens in Ghana: A Review" (Unpublished lecture delivered on March 12, 1970, at the Auditorium, School of Administration, University of Ghana, Legon), p. 2.

his home town and wanted to take refuge elsewhere. All types of persons from foreign countries entered Ghana, since the country's doors were open to them; and once they had come in no apparent regulations restricted their movements and activities. Some political refugees are known to have entered the country within this period to be supported fully on government funds.

Thus, the period for four to five years after independence could also in a sense be described as a laissez-faire period of immigration. It differed, however, from the preindependence movement in that it was supported by an indigenous government with a pan-African outlook. This political policy was successful probably because rapid economic expansion was taking place in the country around this time, a situation even more meaningful to immigrants than the purely political policy of welcome. Political independence increased the tempo of economic and social development in the country, and, even without a deliberate political policy, it is likely that an increasing number of immigrants would have entered the country to exploit the opportunity of the economic boom.

FIRST ATTEMPTS TO ESTABLISH IMMIGRATION LAWS. The first real effort by the country to establish firm immigration laws was contained in the provisions of the Aliens Act 1963 (Act 160). This act sought to rationalize the existing laws on immigration by bringing them together under the same systems as other laws of the country. This act of the Parliament of the Republic of Ghana was meant to consolidate, with modifications, enactments relating to the immigration, residence, employment, and deportation of aliens. Among other things, the act declared that every alien should possess the necessary legal documents, such as a passport, work permit, etc., which legally permitted him to take up residence in the country. Section 2 was amended in 1965 under a government order entitled Aliens (Amendment) Act 1965 **(Act 265)**. The Amendment Act of 1965 states specifically that "a person other than a citizen of Ghana shall not enter Ghana except

by one of the recognized or normal places of entry into Ghana." The names of these entry points were given in the act.

The extent to which these immigration regulations were acted upon by the relevant authorities is not known; but it seems quite clear that the new immigration laws were not strictly enforced, with the result that immigrants still continued to enter the country illegally through unauthorized routes, especially along the land borders where proper security still was lacking. Indirect evidence seems to suggest, however, that immigration into the country may have slowed down after 1961–1962. The postindependence boom in economic activity and employment continued uninterrupted for a few years only; from 1961–1962 the country began to show signs of economic deterioration. Factors, such as the fall in world cocoa prices, a fall in the terms of trade, government overexpenditure, general economic mismanagement, and inflation, contributed to the slump which occurred in the economy from this period. The government, in an attempt to arrest the situation, placed restrictions on foreign exchange. These regulations put serious obstacles in the way of foreign immigrants continuing to send their usual cash remittances to relatives in their home countries. The evidence seems to suggest that as a result, a number of immigrants actually left for their home countries; this situation probably affected labor supply particularly on the cocoa farms and the mines. One may assume that the majority of those who left were seasonal migrants; those who had established themselves in the social and economic life, particularly in the towns, may not have been similarly affected and probably remained in the country.

Another factor which slowed down the rate of immigration during this period was the price of cocoa in the neighboring countries; cocoa prices were much higher in Togo and Ivory Coast than in Ghana. It is possible that the wages received by cocoa laborers in these countries were therefore higher and more attractive than in Ghana; thus the potential laborers, who would previously have migrated into Ghana, may have stayed on to work on farms in their own countries. Also some of the nearest countries became independent during the early sixties and soon thereafter began to expand their own economies; it is possible that some of the potential immigrants may have been drawn into new activities in their own countries.

TOWARD A POSITIVE IMMIGRATION POLICY FOR GHANA. The first organized attempt by the country to establish an immigration policy was made in 1965 when the government appointed the Advisory Committee on Population (described more fully in the earlier section, "Structure of the Machinery of the National Family Planning Program," in this chapter) to consider ways and means of formulating a population policy for Ghana. The committee met under the chairmanship of the government statistician in July 1965. The meeting was attended by representatives from various organizations and included participants generally qualified in their own fields, such as medical officers, ministers of religion, civil servants, demographers, and statisticians, as well as politicians. Among those matters discussed was a possible immigration policy for Ghana. The full recommendations on immigration which were submitted to the government by the committee read as follows:

On immigration, the meeting noted with some concern the high rate of immigration, especially of unskilled persons from the neighboring countries, into Ghana as revealed by the 1960 census. The representatives of the African Affairs Secretariat and the Ministry of Interior informed the meeting of the desirability of allowing the immigrants to come in since they come to Ghana to take up certain unskilled jobs in which Ghanaians are not generally interested. It was however generally agreed that some of the immigrants came in to swell up unemployment figures in the country since all of them do not usually get jobs. The meeting decided that in consonance with Ghana's policy of friendship with all countries, and, especially, in the interest of African unity *it would be undesirable for the government to take any direct steps* to stop immigration of Africans into the country. *It was, therefore, decided that the government*

*should enforce regulations already in force on immigration.* For example, the regulation that immigrants intending to stay in the country should have valid travel documents should be strictly enforced. *The meeting also decided that in order not to allow immigrants to create unemployment problems in the country the Labor Department should be advised to set up Labor Advice Centers at the customs posts along the borders.* Employers, especially the municipal and local authorities, should indicate to these Labor Centers their requirements in such jobs as conservancy and domestic services. This it is hoped will make it possible for the government to know how many immigrants have been found jobs and how many remain to be found jobs.

It is quite obvious that, had these recommendations been fully acted upon by the government, they would have produced far-reaching consequences on immigration and would have resulted in the mass return of immigrants to their home countries, since almost certainly the great majority of them would not have qualified for residence in the country under the Aliens Act (1963) and Aliens (Amendment) Act of 1965. The government, nevertheless, would not act upon these recommendations; whether this was due to a rejection of the recommendations submitted by the Advisory Committee or whether the proposals, either as they stood or modified, may have been acted upon at some future date can now never be determined. What is known is that these recommendations had still not been implemented by the time of the February 24, 1966, coup through which a new military government came to power. Thus foreign immigration into the country continued at a laissez-faire pace, regulated only by the economic and social conditions within Ghana and the interests or circumstances of the immigrants themselves.

POST-1966 FEBRUARY COUP ATTEMPTS TO CONTROL FOREIGN IMMIGRATION. The search for new ways to control foreign immigration into the country and also to regulate the activities of immigrants in residence continued under the new military regime. A number of decrees were passed by this regime during its lifetime on various aspects of immigration, and these referred particularly to those areas of the economy where they were not allowed to operate. For example, an order contained in the Aliens Act 1963 (Amendment) Decree, 1968, prohibited aliens from entering into or remaining in any of the diamond areas of the country. This measure was brought into effect in an attempt to control illegal diamond dealings in which a large number of immigrants, particularly Nigerians, are known to have participated. Other decrees were passed which prohibited aliens from operating in the following economic pursuits:

(1) Retail trade with annual sale volume of NC500,000 or less
(2) Wholesale trade with annual sales of NC1 million or less
(3) Taxi services, sales of taxis, hire-purchase
(4) Small-scale enterprises employing 30 persons or less which in the opinion of the Ghanaian Enterprises Committee require simple production or operational techniques or which have a capital of less than NC100,000, being an extractive, processing, manufacturing, or transport undertaking[14]
(5) Representation in Ghana of overseas manufacturers

The ultimate objective of these measures by the government was to encourage Ghanaian businessmen to operate in these sectors with minimum competition from foreign enterprises.

Another economic measure which had some indirect effect on immigration was the devaluation of the country's currency in July 1967. This action by the military government added to the existing difficulties in foreign exchange transactions faced by business enterprises and individuals in the country. Foreign exchange became more expensive, and created serious limitations on the ability of immigrant and expatriate workers to repatriate some of their earnings to their home country. It is believed that some expatriate workers left the country as a result

of the devaluation measures; it also is suspected that some prospective foreign investors may have been discouraged from coming to invest in the country. The effect of the devaluation was such that the British government was even compelled to institute a salary supplementation scheme for its citizens working in various enterprises in the country, particularly in schools and educational institutions, an action which actually deterred some of the British expatriate workers from leaving the country.

Another measure which also was instituted by the military government to regulate the inflow of foreign workers was the immigrant quota review. This review sought to restrict the importation of expatriate workers into business concerns to those with scarce skills which could not be obtained from local sources. The measure was designed to encourage foreign entrepreneurs to train and make use of local talents to assist in the running of their businesses.

SECOND ATTEMPT TO FORMULATE A POPULATION POLICY FOR GHANA. In May 1968, the Commissioner for Economic Affairs in the military government appointed a special subcommittee of the Manpower Board to consider a national population policy for Ghana (described more fully earlier in this chapter). Among some of the broad principles discussed by the committee at its various meetings were the conditions for the admittance of immigrants into the country, regulations regarding employment, work permits, property rights of immigrants, etc. This committee produced a most comprehensive report for the government regarding what it considered should form the basis of a future population policy for the country. The relevant part of the policy affecting immigration is contained in the final document on population policy, and reads as follows:

The government will take steps to evaluate and, as necessary, to control immigration and to ensure that the permitted immigration is in the best interests of the country. A principal cause for concern has been the size of immigrants' remittances to their countries of origin. The effects

[14] *National Liberation Council Decree (NLCD) 323.* The Ghanaian Enterprises Committee was established to ensure the efficient implementation of the decree.

of this outflow of capital will be studied and remedial action taken as necessary. A further cause of concern relates to the slow rate of assimilation among many immigrant groups. This problem will also be studied in detail and remedial measures introduced . . . . There is no evidence that the rate of immigration into Ghana is slowing down. Uncontrolled immigration of labor, especially of the unskilled type, reduces employment opportunities for citizens. It is intended that immigration will be used primarily as a means of obtaining needed skills and stimulating social and economic development. The government has introduced measures to ensure that would-be immigrants have work permits before entering Ghana so that services that can adequately be performed by Ghanaians may be reserved exclusively for Ghanaians. Additional measures under consideration include procedures for strictly enforcing the work permit scheme recently introduced, a new system of alien registration and periodic reporting, and measures for restricting and regulating the sale or lease of land to aliens. To implement these measures, the office of the Principal Immigration Officer will be strengthened and the Migration Section of the Central Bureau of Statistics will also be strengthened to permit it to develop and analyze relevant statistical information on immigrants. The government will continue to support research on immigration, and especially that relating to the contribution of immigrants to social and economic development and costs of absorbing them into the Ghanaian population.[15]

This recommendation by the subcommittee on population policy was fully accepted by the government, and in March 1969, this became the official immigration policy of the country. The machinery to implement it was subsequently established within the government department responsible for economic planning. It was in the course of implementing these policies that a new civilian government was elected into office in August 1969.

SECOND REPUBLIC ATTEMPTS TO CONTROL IMMIGRATION: THE FINAL AXE. The new civilian government took over the question of immigration policy and, in due course, came out with the most far-reaching order ever

[15] Republic of Ghana, *Population Planning for National Progress and Prosperity*.

issued on the subject. On November 18, 1969, this government published an Aliens Compliance Order in the *Government Gazette*; the provisions of this order briefly stated that all aliens resident in Ghana who did not possess the necessary immigration papers as required by the Aliens Act (160) 1963 and the Aliens (Amendment) Act 1965, should obtain them within a period of two weeks from the date of publication of the order; failure to do so would necessitate their departure from the country. The reasons for this sudden order by the new civilian government are not quite clear; the order probably was influenced by a number of social and economic as well as political factors.

In the first place, the country had been plunged into serious economic difficulties since the military regime took over power in February 1966; unemployment had been growing consistently month after month, and the government had been looking for the best solutions to counteract these developments in the economy. The impression had been growing throughout the country, from both official and unofficial sources, that the presence of large numbers of immigrants had been reducing employment opportunities for the citizens. Again a number of new local business associations and groups sprang up in various places soon after the military government came to power, and these were vigorously campaigning to advance the cause of business among Ghanaians. These groups are known to have exerted a certain amount of pressure on the military government and subsequently on the new civilian government to give Ghanaian businessmen prior consideration in respect of activity or contracts in certain fields which hitherto had been dominated by alien businessmen. Indeed it was partly the pressure from these local groups which influenced the military government to pass the Ghanaian Enterprises Decree, to which reference has already been made.

Politically also, the new civilian government had pledged to solve the unemployment problem and to raise the living conditions of the citizens of the country. These factors meant that the government was committed to explore all the means whereby it might create more opportunities within the economy for Ghanaians. Again the impression had been given in various quarters that aliens constituted a relatively high proportion of the hard core, incorrigible criminals in the country, particularly smugglers, burglars, habitual law breakers, contraband goods dealers, and persons indulging in large-scale systematic bribery and corruption. Many citizens had thus questioned whether it was indeed desirable to maintain such groups of aliens within the country since their behavior was felt to be not conducive to social stability.[16] These opinions about aliens had been gaining root among various communities throughout the country, particularly in official circles, and it is known that the courts were increasingly deporting alien criminals to their home countries. All these factors may have influenced the decision of the new civilian government to enforce the existing laws on immigration.

The Aliens Compliance Order is unique in the history of immigration laws in Africa, and the consequences of the order on the social and economic life of the country are yet to be fully known. Since the order came into force, a large number of immigrants have left the country for their home lands. The exact number of those who left is not known. It is quite obvious however that the mass return of foreign workers will have some repercussions, particularly on the economic life of the country.[17]

IMPLEMENTATION OF THE 1969 ALIENS COMPLIANCE ORDER. The responsibility for enforcing the Compliance Order rests primarily with the police and immigration officers. The enforcement of the law by the relevant authorities began soon after the dateline of

the order expired on December 2, 1969.[18] An important modification was made to the order some few weeks after it came into force. An exemption order granted all aliens working in agriculture (especially cocoa farming) and in the mines an indefinite period to remain in the country subject to the condition that their Ghanaian employers obtained the necessary legal documents on their behalf. This exemption order seems to have saved the country from immediately losing large numbers of farm and mine laborers who traditionally have been chiefly responsible for these two important export sectors. Apparently some of the immigrant farm laborers left the country before the new exemption order was announced.

FUTURE IMMIGRATION PROSPECTS. It is anticipated that the admission of immigrants into the country will become very restrictive. Government policy now lays emphasis on the positive role immigration should play in the future development of the country. Specifically, the policy notes that immigration should serve as a means of obtaining needed skills and stimulating social and economic development. In this respect, it is anticipated that the country will in future limit admission largely to the scarce and highly skilled personnel required to assist significantly in economic development. Nevertheless, the immigrant farm laborers/caretakers and mine workers will continue to be in demand for a considerable time to come. How soon local labor will take over most of the farm and mine work from the foreign workers cannot be predicted. It is well known that quite a large number of the local population is disinclined toward working in these particular sectors. This situation is not likely to change significantly overnight; until—and if—it does, the country will continue to need African immigrants for employment in these areas. It is difficult to forecast exactly long-term immigration into

[16] For example, a statement which was issued by the government soon after the Compliance Order came into force stating that about 90 percent of the hard-core incorrigible criminals in the prisons were aliens. This statement has been subsequently criticized in the country as an exaggeration.

[17] Addo, "Immigration into Ghana."

[18] At the time of writing this chapter, numerous press reports indicated that a number of aliens have been arrested in various parts of the country for contravening the Aliens Compliance Order (see for example, *Daily Graphic*, May 2 and 4, 1970).

the country; the situation will be greatly influenced by social, economic, and political circumstances prevailing in both the sending and receiving countries. What is fairly certain is that, if the present immigration policy remained in force, the future contribution of immigration to population growth would become negligible. Thus, instead of the view which was previously held, that immigration would accelerate the rate of population growth, the anticipation is that the phenomenon will become less and less significant in its contribution to Ghana's population growth.

# PART FOUR

## *Sierra Leone*

BACKGROUND. Prior to independence in 1961, the present territory of Sierra Leone was divided into a coastal Crown Colony, occupying 256 square miles, and a provincial Protectorate, occupying 27,699 square miles. The former was established in 1808; the latter, in 1896. Demographic analysis in Sierra Leone is conditioned and limited by this pattern of historical development.

During the nineteenth century, population counts were limited to the colony area. No enumeration or estimation of the provincial population was attempted. Accordingly, no national population totals or growth rate estimates are available for this period.

With the establishment of a Protectorate in 1896, the provincial population was estimated in 1901, 1911, 1921, 1931, and 1948. These Protectorate estimates may be combined with census results in the Crown Colony area to produce total population figures and inter-censal growth rates for Sierra Leone as shown in Table 21.1.

In interpreting these figures, it is useful to distinguish between the population data provided by the Crown Colony and the Protectorate. In the case of the colony, although census coverage may have been reasonably complete, the population was not large enough to appreciably affect national totals or national growth rates. National patterns were essentially a reflection of Protectorate population estimates. The accuracy of these estimates is therefore of some importance.

ESTIMATES OF PROTECTORATE POPULATION: 1901, 1911, 1921. District commissioners provided population estimates in 1901, 1911, and 1921 apparently based on personal observations carried out in a small number of arbitrarily selected villages. Such totals must

# CHAPTER TWENTY ONE

# *Demographic Trends & Implications*

THOMAS E. DOW JR.
AND EUGENE BENJAMIN[1]

[1] Benjamin and Dow have jointly written the section on Population Growth; Benjamin contributed the section on Government and University Activities in the field of demography; all other sections are by Dow. A supplementary paper on population growth in Sierra Leone prepared by Eugene Benjamin is on file at the Central Statistics Office, Freetown.

TABLE 21.1

Population totals and growth rates for Sierra Leone, 1901–1948

| Year | Colony | Protectorate | Total | Average Annual Rate of Increase (percent) |
|------|--------|-------------|-------|------------------------------------------|
| 1901 | 74,351 | 949,927 | 1,024,278 | — |
| 1911 | 75,395 | 1,324,577 | 1,399,972 | 3.2 |
| 1921 | 85,044 | 1,455,510 | 1,540,554 | 1.0 |
| 1931 | 96,422 | 1,672,058 | 1,768,480 | 1.4 |
| 1948 | 124,657 | 1,733,618 | 1,858,275 | 0.3 |

SOURCE: *Census of the Colony and Protectorate of Sierra Leone, 1948* (Freetown: Government Printer, 1949).

be considered little more than "reasoned guesses."[2]

In 1931 it was hoped that a genuine census could be carried out in the Protectorate, but this plan had to be abandoned in favor of an estimate based partly on enumeration. "Greater efforts, however, were made to secure adequate data on which to base the estimates."[3] District commissioners were asked to carry out complete enumerations in as many villages as possible. These villages were then to be used as key villages. "The population of the remainder of each chiefdom could then be calculated, the numbers of persons per house being ascertained from these [key village] counts and the house tax lists . . . ."[4]

In practice, only a small number of villages were actually enumerated and these were selected without regard for sampling principles. Table 21.2 indicates the number of key villages enumerated in each district.

In 1948, officials were asked "to make an exact count of the population in certain representative types of towns and villages and from the figures obtained to establish the

ratio of taxpaying males to the total population of the sample villages." The total population of each chiefdom would then be obtained "by multiplying the total number of taxpaying males by the ratio obtained from the sample data."[5]

Once again, no established statistical principles were followed in either the selection of the "sample" communities or in the decision to eliminate certain towns in which the taxpayer population ratio was considered too low. As the Central Statistics Office points out, "the reliability of estimates derived from this kind of sampling is . . . questionable."[6]

In view of the above, it seems clear that neither the size nor the growth rate of the national population can be established reliably from the demographic data available for the period 1901–1948. If anything, the erratic growth pattern observed in Table 21.1 would seem to confirm the improbable character of some or all of these estimates.

1963 CENSUS. The census of April 1963 was the first national count ever attempted in Sierra Leone. Following well-established enumeration procedures,[7] it indicated a

TABLE 21.2

Number and location of provincial villages enumerated in the 1931 census

| District | Number of Villages |
|----------|-------------------|
| Port Loko | 41 |
| Kambia | 34 |
| Karene | 58 |
| Bombali | 12 |
| Koinadugu | —[a] |
| Moyamba | —[a] |
| Bonthe | 36 |
| Pujehun | 13 |
| Bo | 32 |
| Kenema | 31 |
| Kailahun | 144 |
| Kono | 24 |
| Total | 425 |

SOURCE: *Report of Census for the Year 1931* (Freetown: Government Printer).
[a] No record of number of villages visited.

[2] John I. Clark, "Population Distribution in Sierra Leone," in John C. Caldwell and C. Okonjo, eds., *The Population of Tropical Africa* (London: Longmans, Green and Company; New York: Columbia University Press, 1968), p. 270.

[3] R. R. Kuczynski, *A Demographic Survey of the British Colonial Empire* I, *West* Africa (London: Oxford University Press, 1948), p. 35.

[4] *Report of Census for the Year 1931* (Freetown: Government Printer), p. 79.

[5] Central Statistics Office, *1963 Population Census of Sierra Leone*, 1 (Freetown, 1965), p. i.

[6] *Ibid.*

[7] *Ibid.*, pp. i–xii.

population of 2,180,355. The relative accuracy of this figure was confirmed in a postenumeration survey which indicated a "net undercount of about three-and-one-half percent subject to a sampling error of . . . one and one-half percent."[8] Noting the tendency toward underenumeration rather than overenumeration in an initial census, the enumerated population as of April 1 may be increased by 5 percent and adjusted to midyear 1963 to obtain a final total of 2,297,964.

When this adjusted figure is compared with the 1948 estimate, it indicates an annual intercensal growth rate of about 1.4 percent. The usefulness of this figure, however, is somewhat reduced by the manner in which the 1948 estimate was reached. Consequently, less direct techniques also are employed to estimate the approximate growth rate in 1963.

STABLE ESTIMATES OF POPULATION GROWTH. Estimates of population growth may be obtained by using the 1963 census female age distribution to locate appropriate stable populations in the "West" family of the Coale and Demeny tables[9] having (a) the same proportion of the population under the age of 10 years, and (b) the same proportion of the population under the age of 35 years, with, in each case, an expectation of life at birth of 30 years. With both sets of models a growth rate of 1.5 percent is obtained.

Of course, if a higher $e_0$ is assumed—e.g., $e_0 = 35$, 37.5, or 40 years—a more rapid growth rate would be observed. Given this degree of uncertainty, the lowest or most conservative expectation of life value is probably to be preferred. Accordingly, 1.5 percent is accepted as the approximate growth rate for the year 1963. Assuming no major changes in fertility or mortality in the 1960s, this figure also is used as the probable annual growth rate for the postcensus period producing a total population of 2,550,376 by 1970.

[8] *Ibid.*, pp. x–xi.
[9] Ansley J. Coale and Paul Demeny, *Regional Model Life Tables and Stable Populations* (Princeton, N.J.: Princeton University Press, 1966).

POPULATION GROWTH: 1970–1990. Population growth over the next generation was estimated in the following way. Initially, the 1963 census female age distribution was used to locate a stable population ("West" female) with the same proportion under the age of 10 years, $e_0 = 30$ years. Next, the total population was increased by 1.5 percent per year from 1963 to 1970 and apportioned according to the selected model age distribution. For the period 1970–1990, it was assumed that the expectation of life at birth would increase from 30 to 40 years, fertility remaining unchanged. Expectation of life values were estimated for the years 1970–1975, 1975–1980, 1980–1985 and 1985–1990. In conjunction with the birth-woman ratio obtained from the original model age distribution, the basis was established for a standard population projection by five-year survival rates and a general fertility rate. The results are summarized in Table 21.3. However, it might be noted that recent data on survivorship (see sections on "Family Planning" and "Mortality" in this chapter) suggest that the expectation of life at birth may already be approaching 40 years. Consequently, the projections are probably conservative estimates of possible population growth over the 20-year period.

Obviously, both the timing and specific totals of this projection are merely gross approximations of possible trends; yet the pattern of moderate-to-rapid population growth implied by the assumptions of constant fertility and declining mortality seems plausible. As the following treatment of

TABLE 21.3
Projected population totals and growth rates for Sierra Leone, 1963–1990

| Year | Population | Average Annual Rate of Increase (percent) |
|------|------------|-------------------------------------------|
| 1963 | 2,297,964 | — |
| 1970 | 2,550,376 | 1.5 |
| 1975 | 2,812,358 | 1.9 |
| 1980 | 3,130,816 | 2.1 |
| 1985 | 3,515,732 | 2.3 |
| 1990 | 3,987,800 | 2.5 |

fertility, family planning, and mortality make clear, a substantial increase in the population growth rate in the years ahead is to be expected.

## FERTILITY

Levels of fertility in Sierra Leone cannot be derived directly from vital registration or census material. Registration is reasonably complete only in the capital, while the country's only census failed to include any questions on fertility. Consequently, fertility estimates in this section are based on indirect analytical techniques and recent survey findings. The analytical material is considered first.

FERTILITY ESTIMATES DERIVED FROM THE 1963 CENSUS AGE DISTRIBUTION: CHILD-ADULT RATIOS.[10] Initially, the 1963 female age distribution is examined in the hope of establishing reasonable estimates of fertility in Sierra Leone. Ratios of those under 5 years, under 10 years, and under 15 years to those 15 years of age and over are computed for the observed female population and compared with corresponding ratios in an appropriate

[10] See Thomas E. Dow, Jr., "Fertility in Sierra Leone," *Sierra Leone Geographical Journal*, XIII (1969), pp. 3–12.

TABLE 21.4
Female child-adult ratios for a female expectation of life at birth of 30 years and for selected levels of the gross reproduction rate with a mean age of childbearing of 27 years—"north" model stable populations

| Gross Reproduction Rate | Various Child-Adult Ratios (numerator = children's age; denominator = adult's age) | | |
|---|---|---|---|
| | Under 5 Over 15 | Under 10 Over 15 | Under 15 Over 15 |
| 2.0 | 0.160 | 0.290 | 0.416 |
| 2.5 | 0.218 | 0.387 | 0.544 |
| 3.0 | 0.276 | 0.483 | 0.670 |
| 3.5 | 0.336 | 0.581 | 0.795 |
| 4.0 | 0.396 | 0.677 | 0.916 |
| 4.5 | 0.456 | 0.771 | 1.035 |

TABLE 21.5
Gross reproduction rates estimated from female age structure for the provinces and districts of Sierra Leone, 1963

| Area | Female Child-Adult Ratios Employed | | |
|---|---|---|---|
| | Under 5 Over 15 | Under 10 Over 15 | Under 15 Over 15 |
| Sierra Leone | 2.9 | 2.9 | 2.5 |
| Southern Province | 2.6 | 2.5 | 2.2 |
| Eastern Province | 2.8 | 2.7 | 2.3 |
| Northern Province | 3.3 | 3.3 | 2.9 |
| Western Area | 2.8 | 3.0 | 2.8 |
| Mean | 2.9 | 2.9 | 2.5 |
| Bo District | 2.5 | 2.4 | 2.1 |
| Bonthe District | 2.6 | 2.4 | 2.1 |
| Moyamba District | 2.6 | 2.5 | 2.2 |
| Pujehun District | 2.7 | 2.5 | 2.1 |
| Sherbro Urban District | 2.6 | 2.8 | 2.9 |
| Kailahun District | 2.8 | 2.7 | 2.3 |
| Kenema District | 2.6 | 2.4 | 2.1 |
| Kono District | 3.1 | 3.0 | 2.6 |
| Bombali District | 3.3 | 3.3 | 2.9 |
| Kambia District | 3.2 | 3.2 | 2.9 |
| Koinadugu District | 3.4 | 3.5 | 3.0 |
| Port Loko District | 3.1 | 3.1 | 2.7 |
| Tonkolili District | 3.3 | 3.3 | 2.9 |
| Mean | 2.9 | 2.9 | 2.5 |

series of stable populations. Table 21.4 indicates the relevant ratios for a series of stable populations at different levels of the gross reproduction rate.

Using Table 21.4 child-adult ratios in the observed population were located in the stable models and, by interpolation, gross reproduction rates were derived for the national, provincial, and district levels in Sierra Leone as shown in Table 21.5.

The under 5 years, under 10 years, and under 15 years ratios yielded gross reproduction rates of 2.9, 2.9, and 2.5 respectively. This disparity suggests serious underenumeration in the age class 10–14 years, which is reflected in the ratio for the under 15 years group. Accordingly, a gross reproduction rate based on this ratio is almost certain to be too low. The remaining ratios, with a common mean gross reproduction rate of 2.9, are to be preferred.

A REEXAMINATION OF THE GROSS REPRODUC-
TION RATES. By comparing observed child-
adult ratios with similar ratios in appropriate
stable populations, gross reproduction rates
were derived for the various provinces and
districts of Sierra Leone. The results gave
reasonable evidence of differential fertility.
But beyond this, the accuracy of these rates—
that is, their correspondence to the actual
gross reproduction rates in the real population—remains problematic.

If we accept the mortality level and mean
age of childbearing used in this analysis, all
that is left as a possible source of serious bias is
the observed age structure. Systematic errors
in this age structure, producing net excesses or
deficiencies in either the numerator or the
denominator of the child-adult ratio, would
obviously inflate or deflate the final fertility
estimate.

An indication of the specific biases in the
female age distribution may be obtained by
referring (under the continuing assumption of
a mean life expectation at birth of 30 years) to
stable populations that correspond to the
female age distribution in having either (A)
the same proportion of the population under
age 35, or (B) the same proportion of the
population under age 10. When this is done
(Table 21.6), it is clear that the dominant
feature in both comparisons is a net transfer
of females above the age of 15 with a net
deficiency below that age, this deficiency

being most pronounced in the 10–14 age
group.

In the previous analysis this distortion was
not adjusted in the computation of child-
adult ratios, but was compensated for to some
extent by the final selection of the under 10
years rather than the under 15 years ratio for
the estimation of gross reproduction rates. In
the former case, the final ratio was deflated
primarily by an excess of females over the age
of 15; while in the latter case, this excess was
combined with an equally serious deficiency
of children under 15 years to produce an
extremely low gross reproduction rate. Left
with these figures, one can only choose the
lesser of two evils by selecting the higher, and
apparently more accurate ratio.

Fortunately, data based on interviews with
5,952 women 15–49 years of age are now
available from a survey directed by the author
in 1969–1970. The survey findings supplement and extend these impressions. This
material is examined below.

SURVEY METHODOLOGY. *Sample and universe.*
The sample is made up of females, 15–49
years of age, either currently married or single
with children; it excludes single women
without children, and ever-married women
not currently married. Considering the
observed and estimated distribution of these
different marital statuses in Sierra Leone, it
can be said that the sample is representative

TABLE 21.6
Comparison of the recorded female age structure (1963) with certain model stable populations
("North" female stable populations having mean expectation of life at birth of 30 years)

| | Same Proportion Under Age 35 | | | | Same Proportion Under Age 10 | | | |
|---|---|---|---|---|---|---|---|---|
| Age in Years | Recorded | Model | Difference | Cumulative difference | Recorded | Model | Difference | Cumulative difference |
| Under 5 | 173 | 172 | +1 | +1 | 296 | 296 | 0 | 0 |
| 5–9 | 123 | 131 | −8 | −7 | | | | |
| 10–14 | 60 | 114 | −54 | −61 | 60 | 112 | −52 | −52 |
| 15–19 | 101 | 100 | +1 | −60 | 101 | 99 | +2 | −50 |
| 20–24 | 105 | 88 | +17 | −43 | 105 | 88 | +17 | −33 |
| 25–29 | 104 | 77 | +27 | −16 | 104 | 77 | +27 | −6 |
| 30–34 | 82 | 66 | +16 | 0 | 82 | 67 | +15 | +9 |
| Over 35 | 252 | 252 | 0 | 0 | 252 | 261 | −9 | 0 |
| All ages | 1,000 | 1,000 | 0 | 0 | 1,000 | 1,000 | 0 | 0 |

of approximately 92 percent of the total urban female population aged 15–49, and approximately 96 percent of the total rural female population aged 15–49.

*Sample design.* Survey work was carried out in three stages: the first stage examined Freetown,[11] Sierra Leone's only metropolitan area; the second, its other urban places; and the third, its rural population.

*Freetown.* An existing sampling frame was used in Freetown. It was developed in 1966–1968 to obtain social and economic information from a representative sample of households in the capital. Specifically, one-third of the city's 111 enumeration areas were selected as primary sampling units and a complete listing of all dwelling places in these areas was made. One-third of all dwellings listed were then selected in a random fashion for inclusion in the survey. Sampling in Freetown for the present study was based on this second stage listing.

*Other urban places.* Sampling frames similar in design to that described for Freetown were also available for 22 towns in Sierra Leone. Using an urban threshold of 1,000 population, these towns were divided into four size ranges: 1,000–3,999; 4,000–8,999; 9,000–13,999; and 14,000 and over. Three locations were then randomly selected for each size range, and sampling fractions adjusted to ensure an "equal" number of interviews in each location. Overall, approximately 500 interviews were to be obtained in each size range.

*Villages.* The 1963 census classified all rural places into four size ranges: under 100; 100–200; 200–500; and 500–1,000. To obtain approximately 500 interviews in each size range, all eligible women in approximately 100, 33, 14, and 7 villages, respectively, were to be interviewed. Villages in each size class were selected at random from a national

[11] The decision to treat Freetown as a separate stratum was based primarily on two considerations: first, its total size relative to other urban places (in the 1963 census Freetown had a population of 127,917 while Bo, the country's second largest "city," had a population of 26,613); second, its unusual history which resulted in the development of a distinct Creole group (descended from liberated slaves) 90 percent of whom live in the capital and its suburbs.

listing of all rural locations, the only qualification being that the number of villages to be selected from each province would be determined by the province's share of the total rural female population.

Table 21.7 summarizes the number of interviews completed in each of the three stages.

TABLE 21.7
Sample size and distribution

| Location | Number |
|---|---|
| Freetown (metropolitan) | *1,676* |
| Towns (urban) | *2,208* |
| Size range 1 (1,000–3,999) | 517 |
| Size range 2 (4,000–8999) | 735 |
| Size range 3 (9,000–13,999) | 575 |
| Size range 4 (14,000+) | 381 |
| Villages (rural) | *2,068* |
| Size range 1 (under 100) | 749 |
| Size range 2 (100–200) | 548 |
| Size range 3 (200–500) | 421 |
| Size range 4 (500–1,000) | 350 |
| Total | *5,952* |

*Stratification.* Community size was used as the basis for stratification in both the urban and rural samples. Within both samples, differences in behavior and attitudes were anticipated in the movement from small to large towns and small to large villages. In general, however, internal variations from size range to size range were either not significant or random in nature. This was in sharp contrast to the marked differences *between* rather than *within* the urban and rural communities. Reflecting this, the following findings are presented in terms of metropolitan-urban-rural comparisons, with the four urban and four rural size ranges combined to provide total urban and total rural results.

*Weighting.* To facilitate metropolitan-urban-rural comparisons and national estimates, a series of weights was developed so that the number of respondents in each stratum would be inflated, as shown in Table 21.8, to approximate the estimated number of females, 15–49, less single women without children and ever-married women

TABLE 21.8

Weight and sample size for each stratum

| Stratum | Weight | Sample Size | Weight × Sample Size |
|---|---|---|---|
| Freetown | 17 | 1676 | 28,492 |
| Town (urban) size range[a] | | | |
| 1 | 106 | 517 | 54,802 |
| 2 | 30 | 735 | 22,050 |
| 3 | 26 | 575 | 14,950 |
| 4 | 17 | 381 | 6,477 |
| Village (rural) size range[a] | | | |
| 1 | 176 | 749 | 131,824 |
| 2 | 206 | 548 | 112,888 |
| 3 | 305 | 421 | 128,405 |
| 4 | 155 | 350 | 54,250 |
| Total weighted sample | | | 554,138 |
| Total Sierra Leone female population aged 15–49 | | | 582,713 |

[a] See Table 21.7.

not currently married. In practice, the weights for the four town and four village ranges, respectively, are combined to produce total urban and total rural results. National estimates are obtained by combining these two strata with Freetown.

*Parity by age.* Although various qualifications must be considered in interpreting Table 21.9,[12] two basic impressions are clear: first, that rural women have significantly higher parity than urban and metropolitan

[12] Specifically, that only currently married and single women with children are included in the sample; that parity for the age group 15–19 is exceptionally high due, in part, to the omission of single women without children from the sample; and that the exceptional high parity of older rural women may be attributed, in part, to the tendency of interviewers, in cases where age was not definite, to exclude menopausal women.

women;[13] and second, that the national level of fertility, reflecting the rural character of the total population, is quite high.

DIFFERENTIAL FERTILITY. *Regional variations.* Although rural fertility is not greatly affected by village size, it does vary substantially by region. As Table 21.10 indicates, women in the Northern Province tend to have, desire, and idealize significantly larger numbers of children than do women in the Southern and Eastern provinces. This finding confirms the broad regional variations observed in the

[13] The only significant difference in parity levels between city and town women beyond the age of 30 occurred in the age group 40–45. Conversely, rural parity averages for women over 30 were significantly higher than those in Freetown and towns in the following age groups: 35–40, 40–45, and 45–50.

TABLE 21.9

Mean parity by age, Freetown, towns, villages, and Sierra Leone[a]

| | Age | | | | | | | |
|---|---|---|---|---|---|---|---|---|
| Location | 15–19 | 20–24 | 25–29 | 30–34 | 35–39 | 40–44 | 45–49 | Number |
| Freetown | 1.0 | 2.0 | 3.2 | 4.5 | 5.1 | 5.8 | 5.3 | 1,676 |
| Towns | 0.9 | 1.7 | 3.0 | 4.5 | 4.8 | 5.2 | 5.1 | 2,208 |
| Villages | 0.8 | 2.0 | 3.7 | 4.8 | 6.6 | 8.3 | 8.8 | 2,068 |
| Sierra Leone | 0.8 | 2.0 | 3.5 | 4.7 | 6.1 | 7.4 | 7.5 | |
| | N = 697 | N = 1,367 | N = 1,293 | N = 1,040 | N = 767 | N = 460 | N = 328 | N = 5,952 |

[a] All of the data in this report are weighted to account for different sampling fractions.

TABLE 21.10

Actual, expected, and ideal fertility values for rural women aged
15–49, by province

| Province | Mean Number of Live Births | Mean Number of Additional Children Desired | Mean Ideal Number of Children |
|---|---|---|---|
| Northern Province | 4.1(N = 1,259) | 6.1(N = 1,258)[a] | 6.8(N = 1,253)[b] |
| Southern Province | 3.6(N = 468) | 2.9(N = 468) | 5.7(N = 468) |
| Eastern Province | 2.7(N = 341) | 3.2(N = 341) | 5.7(N = 341) |
| Totals | N = 2,068 | N = 2,067 | N = 2,062 |

[a] One woman did not respond.
[b] Six women did not respond.

earlier analysis of gross reproduction rates
(see Table 21.5).

*Literacy.* With the possible exception of
older rural women, literacy had little effect on
parity in Freetown, towns, or villages. Within
the literate and illiterate groups, rural
women aged 30–39 and 40–49 had substantially higher fertility than their urban and
metropolitan counterparts (see Table 21.11).

*Information.* In the present survey a simple
ten-item information test was used in addition
to the more conventional measures. Individual
scores were grouped into "high" and "low"
categories for purposes of analysis. As
Table 21.12 indicates, substantial variations
in parity by level of information are evident

only at the village level. Similarly, within the
high and low information groups, the only
apparent contrast is between the fertility
levels of older metropolitan-urban women, on
the one hand, and rural women, on the other.

*Education.* At the village level, women
with some education had substantially less
children than women with no education. The
same relationship existed to a limited extent
in Freetown, where it held only for women
aged 40–49; it was not found at the town
level (see Table 21.13).

SUMMARY. Two main points emerge from
this analysis: first, that educated, literate and
well-informed rural women, in at least

TABLE 21.11

Mean parity by age and literacy for women aged 15–49, Freetown, towns, villages, and Sierra
Leone

| | Ages and Numbers of Respondents | | | | | | | | |
|---|---|---|---|---|---|---|---|---|---|
| | 15–19 | No. | 20–29 | No. | 30–39 | No. | 40–49 | No. | Total Number |
| *Freetown* | | | | | | | | | |
| Literate | 1.1 | 95 | 2.5 | 404 | 4.7 | 231 | 5.5 | 181 | 911 |
| Illiterate | 0.9 | 64 | 2.7 | 318 | 4.9 | 262 | 5.7 | 121 | 765 |
| *Towns* | | | | | | | | | |
| Literate | 0.8 | 67 | 2.3 | 323 | 4.5 | 177 | 5.4 | 82 | 649 |
| Illiterate | 0.9 | 153 | 2.5 | 619 | 4.6 | 576 | 5.1 | 211 | 1,559 |
| *Villages* | | | | | | | | | |
| Literate | 0.8 | 18 | 2.4 | 89 | 5.6 | 29 | 7.4 | 4 | 140 |
| Illiterate | 0.8 | 300 | 2.8 | 907 | 5.5 | 532 | 8.4 | 189 | 1,928 |
| *Sierra Leone* | | | | | | | | | |
| Literate | 1.1 | 180 | 2.4 | 816 | 4.9 | 437 | 5.7 | 267 | 1,700 |
| Illiterate | 0.8 | 517 | 2.7 | 1,844 | 5.3 | 1,370 | 7.6 | 521 | 4,252 |
| *Total number* | | | | | | | | | 5,952 |

TABLE 21.12

Mean parity by age and level of information for women aged 15–49, Freetown, towns, villages, and Sierra Leone

| | 15–19 | No. | 20–29 | No. | 30–39 | No. | 40–49 | No. | Total Number |
|---|---|---|---|---|---|---|---|---|---|
| | | | Ages and Numbers of Respondents | | | | | | |
| *Freetown* | | | | | | | | | |
| High information score | 1.2 | 61 | 2.4 | 264 | 4.8 | 162 | 5.5 | 140 | 627 |
| Low information score | 0.9 | 98 | 2.7 | 458 | 4.8 | 331 | 5.6 | 162 | 1,049 |
| *Towns* | | | | | | | | | |
| High information score | 0.7 | 40 | 2.4 | 245 | 4.1 | 213 | 5.3 | 98 | 596 |
| Low information score | 0.9 | 180 | 2.4 | 697 | 4.8 | 540 | 5.1 | 195 | 1,612 |
| *Villages* | | | | | | | | | |
| High information score | 1.0 | 9 | 2.1 | 50 | 40 | 10 | 7.5 | 2 | 71 |
| Low information score | 0.8 | 309 | 2.8 | 946 | 5.5 | 551 | 8.4 | 191 | 1,997 |
| *Sierra Leone* | | | | | | | | | |
| High information score | 0.9 | 110 | 2.3 | 559 | 4.2 | 385 | 5.5 | 240 | 1,294 |
| Low information score | 0.8 | 587 | 2.7 | 2,101 | 5.4 | 1,422 | 7.7 | 548 | 4,658 |
| *Total number* | | | | | | | | | 5,952 |

certain age groups, tend to have lower parity than their uneducated, illiterate, and un-informed neighbors; and second, that village women within each universe (e.g., literate-illiterate) tend to have substantially higher fertility than their urban and metropolitan counterparts. As there were very few educated, literate, or well-informed rural women, however, these findings are not conclusive.

Thus, one recognizes that rural residence seems to be associated with high fertility regardless of educational circumstances, without losing sight of the fact that parity differences apparently exist between rural women of different educational backgrounds.

*Religion.* Considering the largest religious group first (78.7 percent of the total weighted sample were Moslem), we find that Moslem women living in Freetown and towns tend to have lower parity than Moslem women living in villages (see Table 21.14). This implies the relative primacy of residence over

TABLE 21.13

Mean parity by age and education for women aged 15–49, Freetown, towns, villages, and Sierra Leone

| | 15–19 | No. | 20–29 | No. | 30–39 | No. | 40–49 | No. | Total Number |
|---|---|---|---|---|---|---|---|---|---|
| | | | Ages and Numbers of Respondents | | | | | | |
| *Freetown* | | | | | | | | | |
| One or more years of education | 1.2 | 72 | 2.4 | 299 | 4.8 | 158 | 5.2 | 141 | 670 |
| No education | 0.9 | 87 | 2.7 | 423 | 4.8 | 335 | 5.9 | 161 | 1,006 |
| *Towns* | | | | | | | | | |
| One or more years of education | 0.7 | 54 | 2.2 | 275 | 4.4 | 140 | 5.3 | 70 | 539 |
| No education | 0.9 | 166 | 2.5 | 667 | 4.6 | 613 | 5.1 | 223 | 1,669 |
| *Villages* | | | | | | | | | |
| One or more years of education | 1.0 | 14 | 2.1 | 69 | 4.9 | 17 | 7.5 | 2 | 102 |
| No education | 0.8 | 304 | 2.8 | 927 | 5.5 | 544 | 8.4 | 191 | 1,966 |
| *Sierra Leone* | | | | | | | | | |
| One or more years of education | 0.9 | 140 | 2.2 | 643 | 4.6 | 315 | 5.4 | 213 | 1,311 |
| No education | 0.8 | 557 | 2.8 | 2,017 | 5.3 | 1,492 | 7.6 | 575 | 4,641 |
| *Total number* | | | | | | | | | 5,952 |

TABLE 21.14

Mean parity by age and religion for women aged 15–49, Freetown, towns, villages, and Sierra Leone

| | 15–19 | No. | 20–29 | No. | 30–39 | No. | 40–49 | No. | Total Number |
|---|---|---|---|---|---|---|---|---|---|
| | | | | Ages and Numbers of Respondents | | | | | |
| *Freetown* | | | | | | | | | |
| Protestant | 1.1 | 35 | 2.7 | 191 | 4.8 | 149 | 5.3 | 132 | 507 |
| Catholic | 1.2 | 12 | 2.2 | 53 | 4.9 | 31 | 5.5 | 17 | 113 |
| Moslem | 1.0 | 112 | 2.6 | 473 | 4.8 | 311 | 5.8 | 152 | 1,048 |
| *Towns* | | | | | | | | | |
| Protestant | 1.0 | 26 | 2.6 | 130 | 4.3 | 96 | 5.7 | 47 | 299 |
| Catholic | 1.3 | 17 | 2.0 | 86 | 4.6 | 53 | 5.7 | 18 | 174 |
| Moslem | 0.8 | 176 | 2.4 | 719 | 4.6 | 589 | 5.0 | 225 | 1,709 |
| *Villages* | | | | | | | | | |
| Protestant | 0.8 | 30 | 2.4 | 103 | 5.2 | 43 | 7.0 | 17 | 193 |
| Catholic | 1.4 | 16 | 1.9 | 42 | 4.9 | 20 | 10.0 | 1 | 79 |
| Moslem | 0.8 | 240 | 2.8 | 770 | 5.5 | 451 | 8.5 | 165 | 1,626 |
| *Sierra Leone* | | | | | | | | | |
| Protestant | 0.9 | 91 | 2.5 | 424 | 4.9 | 288 | 6.2 | 196 | 999 |
| Catholic | 1.4 | 45 | 2.0 | 181 | 4.8 | 104 | 6.2 | 36 | 366 |
| Moslem | 0.8 | 528 | 2.7 | 1,962 | 5.3 | 1,351 | 7.5 | 542 | 4,383 |
| *Total number* | | | | | | | | | 5,748[a] |

[a] 204 women (8 in Freetown, 26 in towns, 170 in villages) did not fall into the three main religious categories.

religion in the conditioning of fertility levels and, with continued rural-urban migration, suggests the possibility of long-term reductions in parity.

Parity differences between Catholics and Protestants in Freetown, towns, and villages, on the other hand, were quite limited. (Apparent urban-rural differences in the older age groups are based on small numbers and are therefore inconclusive).

*Marital status.* Substantial numbers of single women with children were present only in Freetown and towns and, in both cases, their fertility tended to be lower than that of currently married women in the same locations. With the exception of rural women aged 40–49, there were no major parity differences between monogamous and polygamous relationships (see Table 21.15).

Of more importance would be the tendency of older rural women, whether polygamously or monogamously married, to have substantially higher fertility than their metropolitan and urban counterparts. Apparently, in the context of fertility, where one lives is more important than how one is married.

*Tribe.* The Mende and Temne are Sierra Leone's largest ethnic groups. According to the 1963 census, each contains approximately 25 percent of the total population. As Table 21.16 indicates, when one controls for location, parity differences between Mende and Temne are most apparent with regard to older rural women.

So isolated, the observed differences in parity might be attributed to tribal membership; while the narrowing of these differences, in town and city comparisons, would suggest the waning of tribal influence under urban-metropolitan conditions.

*Geographic mobility.* Table 21.17 examines the relationship between place of birth, present residence, and average parity. In practice, the effect of mobility on parity was most pronounced for rural women aged 40–49, in that those now living in a village other than that of their birth had substantially fewer children than those who had never moved.

This pattern is reversed at the urban level, in that older women born and bred in towns had substantially lower fertility than

TABLE 21.15
Mean parity by age and marital status for women aged 15–49, Freetown, towns, villages, and Sierra Leone

| | Ages and Numbers of Respondents | | | | | | | | |
|---|---|---|---|---|---|---|---|---|---|
| | 15–19 | No. | 20–29 | No. | 30–39 | No. | 40–49 | No. | Total Number |
| *Freetown* | | | | | | | | | |
| Never married | 1.2 | 51 | 2.2 | 157 | 4.8 | 43 | 4.6 | 34 | 285 |
| Polygamously married | 0.9 | 39 | 2.7 | 173 | 5.0 | 136 | 5.6 | 73 | 421 |
| Monogamously married | 1.0 | 69 | 2.7 | 392 | 4.7 | 314 | 5.7 | 195 | 970 |
| *Towns* | | | | | | | | | |
| Never married | 0.7 | 48 | 2.1 | 235 | 4.2 | 102 | 4.4 | 13 | 398 |
| Polygamously married | 0.9 | 93 | 2.5 | 387 | 4.6 | 398 | 5.1 | 172 | 1,050 |
| Monogamously married | 1.0 | 79 | 2.4 | 320 | 4.7 | 253 | 5.4 | 108 | 760 |
| *Villages* | | | | | | | | | |
| Never married | 1.1 | 15 | 1.6 | 20 | 1.0 | 1 | — | — | 36 |
| Polygamously married | 0.8 | 208 | 2.8 | 733 | 5.5 | 421 | 8.3 | 142 | 1,504 |
| Monogamously married | 0.7 | 95 | 2.7 | 243 | 5.4 | 139 | 8.8 | 51 | 528 |
| *Sierra Leone* | | | | | | | | | |
| Never married | 1.0 | 114 | 2.0 | 412 | 4.1 | 146 | 4.5 | 47 | 719 |
| Polygamously married | 0.8 | 340 | 2.8 | 1,293 | 5.3 | 955 | 7.5 | 387 | 2.975 |
| Monogamously married | 0.8 | 243 | 2.7 | 955 | 5.2 | 706 | 7.3 | 354 | 2,258 |
| *Total number* | | | | | | | | | 5,952 |

TABLE 21.16
Mean parity by age and tribe for women aged 15–49, Freetown, towns, villages, and Sierra Leone

| | Ages and Numbers of Respondents | | | | | | | | |
|---|---|---|---|---|---|---|---|---|---|
| | 15–19 | No. | 20–29 | No. | 30–39 | No. | 40–49 | No. | Total Number |
| *Freetown* | | | | | | | | | |
| Mende | 1.4 | 18 | 2.5 | 98 | 5.3 | 51 | 5.2 | 22 | 189 |
| Temne | 1.0 | 53 | 2.6 | 226 | 4.6 | 143 | 5.8 | 53 | 475 |
| Creole | 1.0 | 19 | 2.3 | 100 | 4.2 | 83 | 4.8 | 90 | 292 |
| *Towns* | | | | | | | | | |
| Mende | 0.6 | 64 | 2.2 | 251 | 4.1 | 284 | 4.9 | 134 | 733 |
| Temne | 0.7 | 62 | 2.4 | 294 | 5.1 | 201 | 5.2 | 62 | 619 |
| *Villages* | | | | | | | | | |
| Mende | 1.0 | 79 | 2.5 | 248 | 4.5 | 183 | 7.2 | 61 | 571 |
| Temne | 0.8 | 141 | 2.8 | 391 | 5.9 | 235 | 9.2 | 90 | 857 |
| *Sierra Leone* | | | | | | | | | |
| Mende | 0.9 | 161 | 2.5 | 597 | 4.4 | 518 | 6.4 | 217 | 1,493 |
| Temne | 0.7 | 256 | 2.8 | 911 | 5.7 | 579 | 8.4 | 205 | 1,951 |
| *Total number* | | | | | | | | | 3,736[a] |

a 2,216 women were excluded for the following reasons: 2,142 women (720 in Freetown, 782 in towns, 640 in villages) were not members of the three main tribes but were distributed among a large number of smaller tribal groupings; when broken down by age, there were too few Creole women in towns (N = 74) to permit analysis.

TABLE 21.17

Mean parity by age and current place of residence for women aged 15–49, Freetown, towns, villages, and Sierra Leone

| | 15–19 | No. | 20–29 | No. | 30–39 | No. | 40–49 | No. | Total Number |
|---|---|---|---|---|---|---|---|---|---|
| *Freetown* | | | | | | | | | |
| Same as birthplace | 1.1 | 73 | 2.5 | 271 | 4.8 | 146 | 5.4 | 123 | 613 |
| Different from birthplace | 0.9 | 86 | 2.7 | 450 | 4.8 | 347 | 5.7 | 179 | 1,062 |
| *Towns* | | | | | | | | | |
| Same as birthplace | 0.8 | 70 | 2.4 | 325 | 4.8 | 237 | 4.4 | 88 | 720 |
| Different from birthplace | 0.9 | 150 | 2.4 | 617 | 4.5 | 516 | 5.4 | 205 | 1,488 |
| *Villages* | | | | | | | | | |
| Same as birthplace | 0.8 | 119 | 2.7 | 394 | 5.4 | 229 | 9.3 | 73 | 815 |
| Different from birthplace | 0.8 | 192 | 2.8 | 573 | 5.5 | 321 | 7.9 | 117 | 1,203 |
| *Sierra Leone* | | | | | | | | | |
| Same as birthplace | 0.8 | 262 | 2.7 | 990 | 5.2 | 612 | 8.0 | 284 | 2,148 |
| Different from birthplace | 0.9 | 428 | 2.7 | 1,640 | 5.3 | 1,184 | 7.0 | 501 | 3,753 |
| *Total number* | | | | | | | | | 5,901[a] |

[a] 51 women (1 in Freetown, 50 in villages) could not answer the question concerning residence.

rural-urban migrants. A similar but less pronounced tendency was apparent with regard to Freetown.

In sum, rural women will have higher fertility than their city and town counterparts whether or not they have been geographically mobile; but where such rural mobility is present, it tends to be associated, at least for older women, with lower parity. Increasing mobility of the rural population, then, even on an intrachiefdom basis, may be expected to have some long-range effect on the overall level of completed fertility.

*Final note.* While the previous analysis seems to confirm the primacy of urban-rural differentials in fertility, it also suggests that intervening variables (e.g., literacy, tribe, and mobility) may have a significant effect on fertility within either or both communities. In Sierra Leone, however, these intraurban and intrarural differentials, pertaining as they often do to extremely small groups in the total population, will have little influence on national demographic trends.

## ATTITUDES TOWARD FAMILY SIZE AND FAMILY PLANNING

In addition to questions on parity, women in the Sierra Leone sample survey were asked about their attitudes toward family size and family planning. The findings are examined below.

CHARACTERISTICS OF THE SAMPLE. Table 21.18 suggests some of the social and economic characteristics of women in the capital, towns, and villages of Sierra Leone. One can note the diversity evident in city-town-village comparisons, as well as the dominant influence of the rural experience in the final weighted national totals.

PARITY AND SURVIVORSHIP. It may be assumed that the relationship between live births and surviving children plays a part in conditioning attitudes toward family size and family planning. In the case of Sierra Leone, most women lose substantial proportions of their children, but these losses are progressively greater as one moves from city to town to village (see Table 21.19).

Nevertheless, when these figures are measured against average ideal family size preferences of 5.1, 5.2, and 6.4 in Freetown, towns, and villages respectively, it is clear that older women at all levels will tend to have fewer surviving children than they would prefer. Under these circumstances, prospects for family planning are not very bright.

TABLE 21.18

Selected social and economic characteristics, Freetown, towns, villages, and Sierra Leone

| Characteristic | Freetown | Towns | Villages | Sierra Leone |
|---|---|---|---|---|
| Mean age of women (years) | 30.2 | 29.6 | 27.7 | 28.2 |
| Mean age at first marriage (years) | 18.4 | 16.5 | 15.2 | 15.7 |
| Percentage currently married | 83.0 | 81.8 | 98.2 | 94.5 |
| Percentage desiring additional children | 67.8 | 70.5 | 85.2 | 81.7 |
| Percentage with high information score | 37.4 | 25.7 | 3.6 | 9.2 |
| Percentage literate | 54.4 | 27.2 | 6.8 | 12.9 |
| Mean number of school years completed | 3.5 | 2.1 | 0.4 | 0.9 |
| Percentage employed in agriculture | 0.2 | 1.4 | 68.4 | 53.0 |
| Mean length of breast feeding of youngest child (months) | 15.9 | 16.5 | 19.3 | 18.6 |
| Percentage of women who had ever consulted with a Juju man or sorcerer on matters of health or personal conduct | 39.4 | 63.8 | 83.5 | 77.8 |
| | N = 1,676 | N = 2,208 | N = 2,068 | N = 5,952 |

IDEAL FAMILY SIZE BY SELECTED VARIABLES.

In the following sections, ideal family size preferences are cross tabulated by literacy, level of information, education, religion, marital status, tribe, and mobility. Major findings are summarized in Table 21.20.

*Literacy, information, and education.* Considering the first three variables in Table 21.20, it is evident that family size preferences in Freetown, towns, and villages vary substantially with literacy, information, and education. Moreover, within each group, metropolitan-urban expectations are sub-

stantially lower than those found in rural areas.

*Religion.* The major contrast was between Moslem and Christian women in Freetown and towns, with the former preferring substantially more children than the latter. This relationship was not apparent among rural women, although their fertility in general was substantially higher than that of their coreligionists in Freetown and towns. (The somewhat anomalous rural Catholic finding may reflect the small number of cases in this cell.)

TABLE 21.19

Mean number of live births and mean number of surviving children by age, Freetown, towns, villages, and Sierra Leone

| | Freetown | | | Towns | | | Villages | | | Sierra Leone | | |
|---|---|---|---|---|---|---|---|---|---|---|---|---|
| | (1) Live Births | (2) Surviving Children | (3) Proportion Surviving[a] | (1) Live Births | (2) Surviving Children | (3) Proportion Surviving[a] | (1) Live Births | (2) Surviving Children | (3) Proportion Surviving[a] | (1) Live Births | (2) Surviving Children | (3) Proportion Surviving[a] |
| 19 | 1.0 | 0.9 | 0.9 | 0.9 | 0.8 | 0.9 | 0.8 | 0.6 | 0.7 | 0.8 | 0.6 | 0.8 |
| 24 | 2.0 | 1.7 | 0.8 | 1.7 | 1.4 | 0.8 | 2.0 | 1.5 | 0.7 | 2.0 | 1.5 | 0.8 |
| 29 | 3.2 | 2.6 | 0.8 | 3.0 | 2.3 | 0.8 | 3.7 | 2.6 | 0.7 | 3.5 | 2.6 | 0.7 |
| 34 | 4.5 | 3.3 | 0.7 | 4.5 | 3.3 | 0.7 | 4.8 | 3.3 | 0.7 | 4.7 | 3.3 | 0.7 |
| 39 | 5.1 | 3.8 | 0.7 | 4.8 | 3.4 | 0.7 | 6.6 | 3.9 | 0.6 | 6.1 | 3.8 | 0.6 |
| 44 | 5.8 | 4.1 | 0.7 | 5.2 | 3.5 | 0.7 | 8.3 | 3.9 | 0.5 | 7.4 | 3.8 | 0.5 |
| 49 | 5.3 | 3.7 | 0.7 | 5.1 | 3.8 | 0.7 | 8.8 | 3.8 | 0.4 | 7.5 | 3.8 | 0.5 |
| | N = 1,676 | | | N = 2,208 | | | N = 2,068 | | | N = 5,952 | | |

E: Column (3) is calculated by dividing column (2) by column (1).

TABLE 21.20

Mean ideal number of children by selected variables for women aged 15–49, Freetown, towns, villages, and Sierra Leone

| Variable | Freetown | | Towns | | Villages | | Sierra Leone | |
|---|---|---|---|---|---|---|---|---|
| | Mean | No. | Mean | No. | Mean | No. | Mean | No. |
| *Literacy* | | | | | | | | |
| Literate | 4.5 | 908 | 4.6 | 648 | 5.9 | 140 | 5.1 | 1,696 |
| Illiterate | 5.8 | 759 | 5.5 | 1,556 | 6.4 | 1,922 | 6.3 | 4,237 |
| | | | | | | | | 5,933[a] |
| *Information score* | | | | | | | | |
| High information score | 4.2 | 627 | 4.8 | 596 | 5.7 | 71 | 5.0 | 1,294 |
| Low information score | 5.6 | 1,040 | 5.4 | 1,608 | 6.4 | 1,991 | 6.2 | 4,639 |
| | | | | | | | | 5,933[a] |
| *Education* | | | | | | | | |
| One or more years of education | 4.2 | 669 | 4.4 | 539 | 5.8 | 102 | 4.8 | 1,310 |
| No education | 5.7 | 998 | 5.5 | 1,665 | 6.4 | 1,960 | 6.3 | 4.623 |
| | | | | | | | | 5,933[a] |
| *Religion* | | | | | | | | |
| Protestant | 4.4 | 506 | 4.7 | 299 | 6.2 | 193 | 5.6 | 998 . |
| Catholic | 4.6 | 113 | 4.8 | 174 | 5.5 | 79 | 5.2 | 366 |
| Moslem | 5.5 | 1,040 | 5.3 | 1,705 | 6.3 | 1,621 | 6.1 | 4,366[a,b] |
| | | | | | | | | 5,730 |
| *Marital status* | | | | | | | | |
| Never married | 4.2 | 285 | 4.3 | 398 | 5.7 | 36 | 4.6 | 719 |
| Polygamously married | 5.5 | 417 | 5.5 | 1,047 | 6.5 | 1,499 | 6.3 | 2,963 |
| Monogamously married | 5.2 | 965 | 5.4 | 759 | 6.1 | 527 | 5.9 | 2,251 |
| | | | | | | | | 5,933[a] |
| *Tribe* | | | | | | | | |
| Mende | 4.8 | 188 | 5.1 | 733 | 5.7 | 571 | 5.5 | 1 492 |
| Temne | 5.4 | 472 | 5.2 | 618 | 7.1 | 851 | 6.8 | 1,941 |
| Creole | 3.9 | 291 | 4.2 | 74 | — | — | 4.0 | 365 |
| | | | | | | | | 3,798[a,c] |
| *Present residence* | | | | | | | | |
| Same as birthplace | 4.6 | 610 | 4.9 | 720 | 6.3 | 811 | 6.0 | 2,141 |
| Different from birthplace | 5.4 | 1,056 | 5.4 | 1,484 | 6.4 | 1,202 | 6.2 | 3,742 |
| | | | | | | | | 5.883[a,d] |

[a] Of the women, 19 (9 in Freetown, 4 in towns, and 6 in villages) did not express an opinion on ideal number of children.
[b] Of those that did express an opinion, 203 (8 in Freetown, 26 in towns, and 169 in villages) did not fall into the three main religions.
[c] Of those that did express an opinion, 2,135 (716 in Freetown, 779 in towns, and 640 in villages) were not members of the three main tribes but were distributed among a large number of smaller tribal groupings.
[d] Of those that did express an opinion, 50 (1 in Freetown and 49 in villages) could not respond to the question concerning residence.

*Marital status.* Polygamous wives in Freetown, towns, and villages tend to idealize slightly more children than their monogamously married counterparts. Single women with children in Freetown and towns, on the other hand, tend to want substantially smaller families than do either category of currently married women. Finally, within each marital category, there is a sharp contrast between village and metropolitan-urban expectations.

*Tribe.* Table 21.20 shows the Mende-Temne differential in ideal family size to be most pronounced at the rural level. It also indicates that in her expectations the rural Temne woman is further removed from her tribal sisters in city and town than is the rural Mende woman.

Lastly, the expectations of both Mende and Temne women in Freetown and towns are significantly higher than those of Creole women in the same communities. (Possible explanations for this difference are suggested later in this chapter.)

*Geographic mobility.* The effect of geographic mobility on ideal family size expectations is apparent in Freetown and towns. In both cases, women born in the urban environment wanted smaller completed families than did those born elsewhere. At the rural level, there was no significant difference between the expectations of women living in the village of their birth and those living in a different rural location.

SUMMARY. The above findings suggest that within the metropolitan, urban, and rural communities ideal family size preferences vary with different social and cultural factors. These variations imply the possibility of a gradual reduction in parity expectations over time. Change would be limited, however, by the fact that location, particularly rural residence, continues to have a dominant effect on such expectations regardless of intervening social or cultural variables.

Thus, for example, literate rural women are closer in their ideal family size expectations to their illiterate rural neighbors than they are to other literate women living in urban areas. That is to say, they are more in the rural universe than they are in the literate universe.

For city and town women, the pattern is somewhat different. In her ideal family size expectation, for example, the educated urban woman is about as far removed from her uneducated neighbor as she is from her educated country cousin. Or to put it in the opposite context, the ideal family size expectation of the illiterate, uninformed, and uneducated city or town resident will be quite similar to the corresponding expectation of the literate, well-informed, and educated rural woman. This demonstrates a good deal about the relative distance between the urban and rural worlds.

DESIRE FOR ADDITIONAL CHILDREN BY NUMBER OF LIVING CHILDREN. Fertility aspirations vary not only with social and cultural conditions, but with number of living children. This relationship is presented in Table 21.21.

In analyzing this table, one should note how closely the patterns in Freetown and towns resemble one another. In both cases, if we take as crucial marks the parity levels at which a majority of the respondents do or do not want additional births, we find that approximately 70 percent of the women with three living children in Freetown and towns desired additional births, while only 40.9 and 46.1 percent respectively with four living children wanted more.

TABLE 21.21

Percent desiring more children by number of living children, Freetown, towns, villages, and Sierra Leone

| Number of living children | Freetown | | Towns | | Villages | | Sierra Leone | |
|---|---|---|---|---|---|---|---|---|
| | Percent | Number | Percent | Number | Percent | Number | Percent | Number |
| Number of children born alive | 96.2 | 130 | 99.7 | 174 | 98.7 | 293 | 98.8 | 597 |
| Number of living children | 95.6 | 40 | 91.6 | 46 | 93.5 | 174 | 93.4 | 260 |
| 1 | 93.3 | 373 | 95.4 | 508 | 93.8 | 360 | 94.1 | 1,241 |
| 2 | 82.2 | 331 | 73.4 | 527 | 88.8 | 377 | 85.0 | 1,235 |
| 3 | 70.4 | 267 | 71.9 | 355 | 84.4 | 289 | 81.1 | 911 |
| 4 | 40.9 | 225 | 46.1 | 256 | 77.2 | 221 | 69.2 | 702 |
| 5 | 29.4 | 136 | 24.9 | 164 | 68.5 | 169 | 60.0 | 469 |
| 6 | 21.8 | 101 | 22.6 | 97 | 64.3 | 113 | 56.1 | 311 |
| 7 | 23.1 | 39 | 14.0 | 48 | 55.7 | 48 | 48.5 | 135 |
| 8 | 9.1 | 22 | 13.2 | 18 | 37.1 | 16 | 29.8 | 56 |
| 9 or more | 0.0 | 12 | 0.0 | 15 | 19.1 | 8 | 12.7 | 35 |
| All women | 67.8 | 1,676 | 70.5 | 2,208 | 85.2 | 2,068 | 81.7 | 5,952 |

This experience is in sharp contrast to the rural pattern in which 77.2 and 68.5 percent of the women with three and four living children respectively, desired additional births. Indeed, even with six living children, approximately two-thirds of the women wanted to increase further their family size.

From another point of view, by cumulating the proportions at all ages who do not want another child, we find that 32.2, 29.5, and 14.8 percent of the women in Freetown, towns, and villages respectively, are so involved. Thus, there is some potential for family planning in all sectors, but the "demand" is greater in Freetown and towns than villages.

FAMILY PLANNING: KNOWLEDGE, ATTITUDES, AND PRACTICE

KNOWLEDGE. Respondents were asked if they had ever heard of anything either a man

TABLE 21.22
Percent with specific knowledge of a family planning method, Freetown, towns, villages, and Sierra Leone

| Location | Percent | Number |
|----------|---------|--------|
| Freetown | 74.3 | 1,676 |
| Towns | 82.4 | 2,208 |
| Villages | 77.1 | 2,068 |
| Sierra Leone | 77.9 | 5,952 |

or woman could do to keep the woman from having children. Affirmative responses were accepted only if the woman had specific information on one or more methods. The results are summarized in Table 21.22.

In interpreting these results, it is necessary to specify the content of information held at each level. When this is done (see Table 21.23) it is clear that rural "knowledge" is limited essentially to traditional techniques,

TABLE 21.23
Percentages[a] knowing specific contraceptive methods, by women with some knowledge of family planning, Freetown, towns, villages, and Sierra Leone

| Method | Total Sierra Leone | Villages | Towns | Freetown |
|--------|--------------------|----------|-------|----------|
| Traditional abortion[b] | 84.8 | 89.2 | 75.3 | 54.1 |
| Native medicine[c] | 79.6 | 87.2 | 58.6 | 41.4 |
| Abstention | 60.4 | 68.3 | 36.1 | 30.4 |
| Cord talisman[d] | 25.3 | 26.2 | 27.6 | 3.7 |
| Breast feeding | 14.6 | 18.9 | 0.8 | 0.5 |
| Sheath | 14.4 | 8.4 | 33.0 | 36.5 |
| Medical abortion | 11.3 | 6.7 | 21.6 | 45.1 |
| Sterilization | 5.2 | 2.1 | 16.6 | 10.2 |
| Coil | 4.8 | 0.7 | 14.7 | 31.0 |
| Pill | 4.7 | 1.0 | 13.6 | 27.2 |
| Spells | 3.3 | 4.2 | 0.4 | 0.4 |
| Coitus interruptus | 2.2 | 2.1 | 0.8 | 9.7 |
| Vaginal spermicides | 1.1 | 0.1 | 3.7 | 7.1 |
| Rhythm | 0.3 | 0.4 | 0.0 | 0.6 |
| Diaphragm | 0.1 | 0.0 | 0.1 | 1.2 |
|  | N = 4,605 | N = 1,245 | N = 1,765 | N = 1,595 |

[a] Percentages do not add to total since some respondents were aware of more than one method.
[b] All nonprofessional techniques applied by the woman or unskilled others for the sole purpose of producing an abortion.
[c] All native mixtures or potions which are drunk to prevent conception and/or to induce abortion. (These two aims are not mutually exclusive.)
[d] A talisman worn around the woman's waist which may function either as a symbolic reinforcement of the prohibition against coitus during lactation, or as a "magical" property able to prevent conception in its own right.

while metropolitan and urban information is more modern in character.

In part this distinction may suggest selective underreporting in both groups in that, for example, many city and town women who could be expected to know of the existence of various traditional techniques may fail to perceive or acknowledge them in the context of a specific question on family planning. That is, they may feel that such "methods" do not safely or effectively "keep a woman from having children" and, accordingly, would fail to include them in their responses. Similarly, rural women "universally" engage in lengthy breast feeding, but only one in every five recognizes or acknowledges this technique in the context of deliberately "keeping a woman from having children." At the other extreme, there is almost complete recognition of "native medicine" and "traditional abortion." The possible effect of such perception on attitudes toward family planning is considered next.

ATTITUDES. As Table 21.24 indicates, the proportion approving family planning falls from two out of every three in Freetown and towns, to one out of every ten in villages. While such a distinction was expected, the actual level of rural disapproval was not fully anticipated; it requires further comment.

Actually the failure of most rural women to support family planning is not surprising in a situation where relevant knowledge is generally limited to "methods" that are ineffective, dangerous, and/or socially disapproved in stable unions.

Thus when asked what was the best reason not to practice family planning, 72.1 percent of the rural women indicated that family

TABLE 21.24
Percent approving of family planning, Freetown, towns, villages, and Sierra Leone

| Location | Percent | Number |
|---|---|---|
| Freetown | 64.9 | 1,676 |
| Towns | 64.7 | 2,208 |
| Villages | 10.0 | 2,068 |
| Sierra Leone | 22.6 | 5,952 |

planning was a violation of God's will, while 20.9 percent felt that it would produce personal injury or death. The former response apparently reflects the existing social taboo against the principle of prevention in stable marriages, while the latter response clearly suggests a rational concern over the reliability of "available" methods.

*Approval of family planning by selected variables.* Table 21.25 suggests the relationship between approval of family planning and various social and cultural factors. In general, approval of family planning varied positively with literacy, information, and education in Freetown, towns, and villages. It also varied with marital status, as single women with children at all levels tended to approve of family planning to a greater extent than their currently married peers.

Tribally, Creoles in Freetown and towns tended to support family planning to a far greater extent than either Mendes or Temnes. Given their historical, social, and economic background (as descended from freed slaves from different parts of Africa with continuous residence in the capital and full participation in the social, educational, and economic development of the area), one can understand this high level of support as a consistent part of the general Creole position on family size and family planning.

With reference to the major indigenous tribes, one finds that the Mende in city and town tend to favor family planning more than the Temne. At the rural level, this relationship is reversed.

With reference to geographic mobility, it appears that women born and bred in the capital are more likely than rural-urban migrants to support family planning. At the other extreme, rural women who were still living in the village of their birth were somewhat less likely than their more mobile rural counterparts to support family planning.

*Summary.* There is already extensive approval of family planning in Freetown and towns and, as the above findings suggest, some reason to believe that further gains will be made in these areas. At the other extreme, there is presently little support for family

TABLE 21.25

Approval of family planning by selected variables for women aged 15–49, Freetown, towns, villages, and Sierra Leone

| Variable | Freetown Percent | Freetown Number | Towns Percent | Towns Number | Villages Percent | Villages Number | Sierra Leone Percent | Sierra Leone Number |
|---|---|---|---|---|---|---|---|---|
| *Literacy* | | | | | | | | |
| Literate | 76.2 | 911 | 75.4 | 649 | 20.4 | 140 | 53.0 | 1,700 |
| Illiterate | 51.4 | 765 | 60.7 | 1,559 | 9.3 | 1,928 | 18.0 | 4,252 |
| | | | | | | | | 5,952 |
| *Information score* | | | | | | | | |
| High information score | 81.5 | 627 | 82.5 | 596 | 21.8 | 71 | 64.1 | 1 294 |
| Low information score | 54.9 | 1,049 | 58.6 | 1,612 | 9.6 | 1,997 | 18.3 | 4,658 |
| | | | | | | | | 5,952 |
| *Education* | | | | | | | | |
| 1 or more years of education | 79.8 | 670 | 78.9 | 539 | 24.4 | 102 | 58.6 | 1,311 |
| 0 years of education | 54.9 | 1,006 | 60.1 | 1,669 | 9.3 | 1,966 | 18.4 | 4,641 |
| | | | | | | | | 5,952 |
| *Religion* | | | | | | | | |
| Protestant | 76.3 | 507 | 74.3 | 299 | 14.6 | 193 | 35.8 | 999 |
| Catholic | 78.8 | 113 | 64.8 | 174 | 6.5 | 79 | 27.2 | 366 |
| Moslem | 57.8 | 1,048 | 63.2 | 1,709 | 9.1 | 1,626 | 21.0 | 4,383 |
| | | | | | | | | 5,748[a] |
| *Marital status* | | | | | | | | |
| Never married | 74.7 | 285 | 72.0 | 398 | 24.8 | 36 | 60.4 | 719 |
| Polygamously married | 56.5 | 421 | 63.7 | 1,050 | 10.1 | 1,504 | 18.1 | 2,975 |
| Monogamously married | 65.6 | 970 | 62.2 | 760 | 8.7 | 528 | 25.8 | 2,258 |
| | | | | | | | | 5,952 |
| *Tribe* | | | | | | | | |
| Mende | 68.8 | 189 | 75.2 | 733 | 2.9 | 571 | 18.7 | 1,493 |
| Temne | 60.8 | 475 | 64.8 | 619 | 14.4 | 857 | 23.7 | 1,951 |
| Creole | 83.6 | 292 | 89.6 | 74 | — | — | 86.0 | 366 |
| | | | | | | | | 3,810[b] |
| *Present residence* | | | | | | | | |
| Same as birthplace | 75.4 | 613 | 63.3 | 720 | 6.9 | 815 | 19.3 | 2,148 |
| Different from birthplace | 58.8 | 1,062 | 65.5 | 1,488 | 11.4 | 1,203 | 24.5 | 3,753 |
| | | | | | | | | 5,901[c] |

[a] 204 women (8 in Freetown, 26 in towns, 170 in villages) did not fall into the three main religions.
[b] 2,142 women (720 in Freetown, 782 in towns, 640 in villages) were not members of the three main tribes but were distributed among a large number of smaller tribal groupings.
[c] 51 women (1 in Freetown and 50 in villages) would not respond to the question concerning residence.

planning at the village level, and no convincing reason to anticipate a rapid improvement in the near future. Accordingly, while we might reasonably expect further gains in education, for example, to promote increased approval, the actual payoff will probably be very limited, in that only two out of every ten literate or educated rural women at present support family planning.

Still, there are indications that some rural disapproval at all social and cultural levels is based on a fear of available techniques. With the provision of safe and reliable alternatives to present procedures it is possible that some rural women, particularly those presently anxious to avoid another pregnancy, might adopt a more favorable attitude toward family planning.

PRACTICE. Tables 21.26 and 21.27 indicate the proportions ever practicing family planning and the methods used. In general, both

TABLE 21.26
Respondents who had ever practiced family planning, Freetown, towns, villages, and Sierra Leone

| Location | Percent | Number |
|----------|---------|--------|
| Freetown | 18.3 | 1,676 |
| Towns | 11.6 | 2,208 |
| Villages | 3.7 | 2,068 |
| Sierra Leone | 5.9 | 5,952 |

the level of practice and the use of safe and effective techniques increase as one moves from village to town to city.

These figures probably represent a conservative estimation of the amount of use, in that some women might have been reluctant to mention the practice of family planning, particularly the use of socially disapproved techniques, while other women might have failed to mention certain procedures which they did not think of as being primarily contraceptive in nature, e.g., prolonged breast feeding.

With these qualifications, one may conclude that total contraceptive use in Freetown and towns, particularly as this increasingly involves safe and effective modern techniques, may be responsible for some small decline in urban fertility. At the rural level, where knowledge and practice are limited largely to traditional methods and small numbers, one could hardly assume this much.

Still, as Table 21.28 suggests, family planning practice within metropolitan, urban, and rural communities already varies with certain educational variables. Consequently, the level of use is likely to increase with further improvements in literacy, information, and education. This form of change, however, will be more rapid in city and town than village, and will not result in a massive or rapid adoption of contraception.

INTEREST IN LEARNING MORE ABOUT FAMILY PLANNING. As Table 21.29 indicates, a majority of women in Freetown, towns, and villages wanted to learn more about family planning. Moreover, this interest was not limited to specific social and cultural contexts within communities, as Table 20.30 shows. At the rural level in particular, women with different backgrounds tended to show a similar interest in acquiring additional contraceptive knowledge.

SUMMARY AND CONCLUSION. The present survey revealed significant behavioral and attitudinal differences between villages, on

TABLE 21.27
Specific methods of family planning ever used by respondents, Freetown, towns, villages, and Sierra Leone (in percentage)

| Method | Freetown | Towns | Villages | Sierra Leone |
|--------|----------|-------|----------|--------------|
| IUD (Coil) | 20.5 | 8.3 | 7.8 | 10.0 |
| Pill | 21.2 | 13.4 | 6.0 | 11.0 |
| Diaphragm | — | 0.3 | — | 0.1 |
| Condom | 5.9 | 4.2 | 1.1 | 3.0 |
| Vaginal spermicide | 2.9 | 2.0 | 1.0 | 1.6 |
| *Coitus interruptus* | 0.7 | — | — | 0.1 |
| Abstention | 9.1 | 1.8 | — | 2.1 |
| Sterilization | 1.0 | 0.2 | — | 0.2 |
| Medical abortion | 9.4 | 4.8 | 1.3 | 3.8 |
| Traditional methods including native medicine and abortion | 29.0 | 62.6 | 80.9 | 66.2 |
| Prolonged breast feeding | 0.3 | 2.4 | 1.9 | 1.8 |
| | 100.0 | 100.0 | 100.0 | 100.0 |
| | N = 307 | N = 309 | N = 79 | N = 695 |

TABLE 21.28
Ever practiced family planning by selected variables for women aged 15–49, Freetown, towns, villages, and Sierra Leone

| Variable | Freetown | | Towns | | Villages | | Sierra Leone | |
|---|---|---|---|---|---|---|---|---|
| | Percent | Number | Percent | Number | Percent | Number | Percent | Number |
| *Literacy* | | | | | | | | |
| Literate | 24.4 | 911 | 20.1 | 649 | 11.7 | 140 | 17.6 | 1,700 |
| Illiterate | 11.1 | 765 | 8.4 | 1,559 | 3.1 | 1,928 | 4.1 | 4,252 |
| | | | | | | | | 5,952 |
| *Level of information* | | | | | | | | |
| High information score | 31.4 | 627 | 22.7 | 596 | 17.7 | 71 | 23.0 | 1,294 |
| Low information score | 10.5 | 1,049 | 7.7 | 1,612 | 3.2 | 1,997 | 4.1 | 4,658 |
| | | | | | | | | 5,952 |
| *Education* | | | | | | | | |
| One or more years of education | 28.4 | 670 | 20.2 | 539 | 16.0 | 102 | 20.3 | 1,311 |
| No education | 11.6 | 1,006 | 8.7 | 1,669 | 3.1 | 1,966 | 4.2 | 4,641 |
| | | | | | | | | 5,952 |

the one hand, and Freetown and towns, on the other. Specifically, village women on the average had more children, lost more children, expected more children, and idealized more children than did city and town women. At the same time, rural women were less likely to use or approve of family planning, and more likely to acknowledge traditional methods, than were either metropolitan or urban women.

Within each community, attitudes and behavior tended to vary with different social and cultural factors. Specifically, women who had been to school, were Christian, single, or members of the Creole tribe tended to be less pronatal in attitudes and behavior than women who were uneducated, Moslem, currently married, or members of the Temne

TABLE 21.29
Interest in learning more about family planning, Freetown, towns, villages, and Sierra Leone

| Location | Percent | Number |
|---|---|---|
| Freetown | 68.2 | 1,676 |
| Towns | 77.1 | 2,208 |
| Villages | 57.8 | 2,068 |
| Sierra Leone | 61.8 | 5,952 |

tribe. Finally, women born in Freetown and other towns tended to be less pronatal than their neighbors who were born elsewhere; conversely, rural women who were living in the village of their birth tended to be more pronatal than those living in a different rural location.

While these variations are encouraging, they must be viewed against the following background: Most women 15–49 years of age in Sierra Leone live in rural areas, are currently married, belong to the Temne or Mende tribes, consider themselves Moslem, and are living in the village of their birth. Moreover, those few rural women who are educated or literate, for example, tend to be closer in their positions to their illiterate rural neighbors than they are to their literate metropolitan and urban counterparts.

Basically, the path to a less pronatal position leads from village to town to city and tends, at all levels, to favor women with certain social and cultural backgrounds. Under these circumstances, prospects for the further diffusion and acceptance of family planning would be quite good in the capital and reasonably good in other urban places. At the rural level, the situation is less encouraging. Still, if present levels of infant and child mortality could be reduced, and the

TABLE 21.30

Interest in learning more about family planning by selected variables, Freetown, towns, villages, and Sierra Leone

| | Interested in Knowing More | | | | | | | |
| | *Freetown* | | *Towns* | | *Villages* | | *Sierra Leone* | |
| Variable | Percent | Number | Percent | Number | Percent | Number | Percent | Number |
|---|---|---|---|---|---|---|---|---|
| *Literacy* | | | | | | | | |
| Literate | 75.8 | 911 | 87.5 | 649 | 63.0 | 140 | 74.9 | 1,770 |
| Illiterate | 59.1 | 765 | 73.2 | 1,559 | 57.4 | 1,928 | 59.8 | 4,252 |
| | | | | | | | | 5,952 |
| *Information score* | | | | | | | | |
| High information score | 82.3 | 627 | 96.8 | 596 | 49.6 | 71 | 79.6 | 1,294 |
| Low information score | 59.8 | 1,049 | 70.2 | 1,612 | 58.1 | 1,997 | 60.0 | 4,658 |
| | | | | | | | | 5,952 |
| *Education* | | | | | | | | |
| One or more years of education | 82.4 | 670 | 91.4 | 539 | 56.9 | 102 | 76.7 | 1,311 |
| No education | 58.7 | 1,006 | 72.4 | 1,669 | 57.9 | 1,966 | 60.1 | 4,641 |
| | | | | | | | | 5,952 |
| *Religion* | | | | | | | | |
| Protestant | 78.3 | 507 | 88.1 | 299 | 56.6 | 193 | 66.2 | 999 |
| Catholic | 82.3 | 113 | 84.7 | 174 | 46.8 | 79 | 59.3 | 366 |
| Moslem | 61.9 | 1,048 | 74.7 | 1,709 | 58.7 | 1,626 | 61.8 | 4,383 |
| | | | | | | | | 5 748[a] |
| *Marital status* | | | | | | | | |
| Never married | 78.6 | 285 | 89.7 | 398 | 42.5 | 36 | 75.9 | 719 |
| Polygamously married | 61.5 | 421 | 74.3 | 1,050 | 59.9 | 1,504 | 61.8 | 2,975 |
| Monogamously married | 68.0 | 970 | 74.1 | 760 | 52.8 | 528 | 58.8 | 2,258 |
| | | | | | | | | 5,952 |
| *Tribe* | | | | | | | | |
| Mende | 77.8 | 189 | 93.4 | 733 | 46.6 | 571 | 56.6 | 1,493 |
| Temne | 63.4 | 475 | 73.5 | 619 | 51.0 | 857 | 54.8 | 1,951 |
| Creole | 81.2 | 292 | 96.2 | 74 | — | — | 80.2 | 366 |
| | | | | | | | | 3,810[b] |
| *Present place of residence* | | | | | | | | |
| Same as birthplace | 77.8 | 613 | 74.0 | 720 | 58.6 | 815 | 62.0 | 2,148 |
| Different from birthplace | 62.7 | 1,062 | 78.7 | 1,488 | 57.2 | 1,203 | 61.7 | 3,753 |
| | | | | | | | | 5,901[c] |

[a] 204 women (8 in Freetown, 26 in towns, 170 in villages) did not fall into the three main religions.
[b] 2,142 women (720 in Freetown, 782 in towns, 640 in villages) were not members of the three main tribes but were distributed among a large number of smaller tribal groupings.
[c] 51 women (1 in Freetown and 50 in villages) could not respond to the question concerning residence.

expressed interest in learning more about family planning met, it is possible that a vigorous program of family planning might have some chance of modest success in rural as well as urban areas.

## MORTALITY

FREETOWN AND THE WESTERN RURAL AREA. In Freetown and the Western Rural Area (WRA), registration data on births and deaths can be used to compute infant mortality rates. Average infant mortality rates for the years 1966–1968 for Freetown and the WRA were 126 and 166 respectively. If these figures are even approximately correct,[14] they suggest a marked increase in the level of infant mortality as one moves out of the metropolis. If this trend were to

[14] Figures for Freetown are more reliable than those for the WRA. In the latter case, some underregistration of both births and deaths seems likely.

continue with increasing distance from the capital and the coast, and with progressive deterioration in medical services, it is not unlikely that the provincial level of infant mortality might be as high as 200. Such external evidence as there is, tends to support this assumption.

NUTRITIONAL AND MEDICAL CONDITIONS. The nutritional state of infants is often a decisive factor in determining their resistance to a wide range of infectious diseases. In Sierra Leone, there is evidence of serious and extensive infant malnutrition.[15] Although children are usually breast fed for 18–24 months, there is little supplementation with solids. Moreover, that food which is added, primarily cassava, rice, and palm oil, contains very little high-grade protein. The resulting malnutrition reduces the child's resistance to infection and increases the chance of infant mortality should infection take place. This cycle may be observed in a recent analysis of approximately 1,000 juvenile deaths occurring between 1955–1964.[16] The principal causes of death are listed below.

| Principal Cause of Death | Percentage of All Deaths |
|---|---|
| Pneumonia | 24 |
| Diarrhea | 17 |
| Malaria | 15 |
| Malnutrition | 11 |
| Tetanus | 10 |
| Anemia | 9 |
| Measles | 8 |
| Native medicine intoxication | 5 |
| Other | 1 |
| Total | 100 |

It is significant that malnutrition was the principal cause of death in 11 percent of the cases and was reported to be a contributing factor in a much larger number of cases. In practice, iron anemia and protein deficiency

increase the child's vulnerability and he is likely to succumb rapidly to his first attack of pneumonia, diarrhea, malaria, measles, or other childhood diseases.[17] Conversely, these same diseases may convert a subnutritional state into a severe and perhaps fatal form of malnutrition.[18] Under these conditions, one would anticipate a high level of infant mortality.

MEDICAL SERVICES. If medical services were adequate, the effects of infection and malnutrition might less often be fatal. In fact, such services were not generally available in Sierra Leone during the 1960s. In 1964, there was approximately 1 doctor for every 15,000 people and 1 hospital bed for every 1,200 people. Of course, these services were not distributed evenly throughout the country. The hospital bed-population ratio, for example, was as low as 1:290 in the Western Area, which had only 9 percent of the total population; it was as high as 1:2,087 in the Northern Province, which had 43 percent of the total population.[19] In short, modern medical services were simply not available to most people living outside the Western Area and, in the absence of such services, it is difficult to see how an extremely high level of infant and child mortality could have been avoided.

PARITY and SURVIVORSHIP. Using information on live births and surviving children it is possible to obtain at least some crude estimates of mortality in Sierra Leone. Table 21.31 suggests specific findings.

Obviously, as a basis for national mortality estimates this material is severely limited in at least two ways: first, it represents only the experience of currently married women and single women with living children; and

[15] J. R. Rose, "Kwashiorkor in the Southeast Province of Sierra Leone," *Sierra Leone Studies*, VII (1956), p. 130.
[16] J. L. Wilkinson, "Children in Hospitals in Sierra Leone: A Survey of 10,000 Admissions," *Transactions of the Royal Society of Tropical Medicine and Hygiene*, LXIII, 2 (1969), pp. 263–269.

[17] Henry Wilde, "Health Problems and Conditions in Sierra Leone" (Report prepared for the United States Department of State, August 1968), p. 8.
[18] J. L. Wilkinson, Ecology and Prevention of Child Malnutrition in a Rural Community," *West African Medical Journal*, XIII (February 1964), p. 10.
[19] See John I. Clarke, ed., *Sierra Leone in Maps* (London: University of London Press, 1966), pp. 66–67.

TABLE 21.31

Estimation of mortality from reported numbers of children ever born and children surviving for currently married women and single women with children, Sierra Leone, 1968–1969

| Interval (i) | Age of Women | Average Number of Children Ever Born $(P_i)$ | Average Number of Children Surviving $(S_i)$ | $1 - S_i/P_i$ | Multipliers for Column (5) from $P_1/P_2$ and $\bar{m}$ | Age x | Proportion Dead by Age x $(x^q{}_0)$ | Expectation of Life |
|---|---|---|---|---|---|---|---|---|
| 1 | 15–19 | 0.822 | 0.626 | $1 - 0.762 = 0.238$ | 0.840 | 1 | 0.200 | 36.9 |
| 2 | 20–24 | 1.951 | 1.464 | $1 - 0.750 = 0.250$ | 0.930 | 2 | 0.232 | 39.5 |
| 3 | 25–29 | 3.493 | 2.578 | $1 - 0.738 = 0.262$ | 0.940 | 3 | 0.246 | 40.4 |
| 4 | 30–34 | 4.717 | 3.279 | $1 - 0.695 = 0.305$ | 1.046 | 5 | 0.319 | 35.9 |
| 5 | 35–39 | 6.100 | 3.784 | $1 - 0.620 = 0.380$ | 1.054 | 10 | 0.401 | 31.4 |
| 6 | 40–44 | 7.380 | 3.806 | $1 - 0.516 = 0.484$ | 1.037 | 15 | 0.502 | 25.7 |
| 7 | 45–49 | 7.478 | 3.812 | $1 - 0.510 = 0.490$ | 1.039 | 20 | 0.509 | 27.3 |

NOTE: For a statement of the methods employed, see William Brass and Ansley J. Coale, "Methods of Analysis and Estimation," in William Brass et al., *The Demography of Tropical Africa* (Princeton, N.J.: Princeton University Press, 1968), pp. 104–114.

second, it derives expectation of life values from child mortality experience only.

The former problem tends to inflate the parity of women 15–19, particularly in urban areas, and is only partially compensated for by the use of weighted national results; while the latter problem, namely the use of childhood survival rates to estimate the expectation of life at birth, assumes a certain relationship which is problematic about death at different ages.

With these qualifications, one may select the mortality levels and expectation of life values for ages two and three (that is, for women 20–24 and 25–29) as the most reasonable estimates that can be obtained from this limited data.

PROSPECTS. Efforts are presently under way to reduce infant malnutrition and generally improve the quality of child and maternal care. Under-five clinics, to be established in each district, will play a major part in this program. Four such clinics are already open. Parallel efforts also are being made to control infectious diseases, with the prospective eradication of smallpox and measles as the first major accomplishment in this area. These factors should tend to reduce the level of mortality, especially among the very young. But it is difficult to predict how rapid this decline will be.

Certainly, the immediate provision of adequate medical facilities throughout the country is not economically feasible. Still, increased expenditures in this area are anticipated and these funds will be used to strengthen and expand public health programs and specific medical facilities. In the latter case, it is difficult to say whether such static medical units, even with improved staff and equipment, will reach a majority of the rural population.[20] With a better road and transport system,[21] a larger proportion of the population should be able to visit such health centers.

On balance, serious problems persist in the areas of malnutrition and infectious disease—malaria, for example, is still hyperendemic and is apparently "one of the main direct or contributory causes of death in Sierra Leone,"[22]— but there are indications of present or prospective improvement in these fields. In particular, the problem of malnutrition, for infants, children, and pregnant women, is largely one of customary feeding procedures rather than direct scarcity and could therefore

[20] The use of mobile child welfare teams in a 200 square mile area in the Eastern Province was apparently quite successful in reducing infant mortality. That the same results might have been achieved by the use of static units is considered unlikely by the investigators. See J. L. Wilkinson H. Smith and O. I. Smith, "The Organization and Economics of a Mobile Child Welfare Team in Sierra Leone," *Journal of Tropical Medicine and Hygiene*, LXX (January 1967), pp. 14–18.
[21] In the 1969–1970 fiscal year 33 percent of the development budget will be spent to improve roads and transport.
[22] Wilde, "Health Problems and Conditions," pp. 8–9.

be remedied within the existing framework of available foodstuffs.[23] With such improvements in diet, the individual would be better able to resist infectious disease. At the same time, the continuing success of mass inoculation programs will tend to reduce the incidence of such diseases throughout the country.

Under these circumstances, and in conjunction with gradual improvements in the general standard of living,[24] one can reasonably expect a substantial decline in mortality over the next 10 or 20 years. In the absence of a parallel reduction in fertility, this will mean a significant increase in the rate of population growth. Such an increase will complicate Sierra Leone's already difficult problems of social and economic development.

## THE ECONOMIC AND SOCIAL IMPLICATIONS OF POPULATION GROWTH

GENERAL TRENDS. Since independence in 1961, Sierra Leone has made great efforts to improve social and economic conditions. These activities, frequently involving costly long-term development projects with little immediate economic return, had the following results. The public debt was increased two-and-one-half times between December

[23] *Ibid.*, pp. 8–10.
[24] Government of Sierra Leone, *Budget Speech* (Freetown: Government Printer, 1969), especially pp. 11–12.

1961 and December 1966; while the country's external reserves were reduced by almost half between 1960 and 1968. Unfortunately, the government was spending at a high rate during a period of low overall economic performance. As the figures in Table 21.32 suggest, the economy was growing, but the pace was very slow.

THE CIVILIAN LABOR FORCE. Of the 1,522,335 persons ten years of age and older in 1963, 937,737 or 61.6 percent were economically active—that is, either working or available for work. The ratio of males to females in this group was slightly less than 2:1—604,173 males and 333,564 females.

Analysis of those 584,598 persons over ten years of age who were not economically active—144,024 males and 440,574 females—suggests that only a small proportion of either sex was disabled, inmates, soldiers, students, or retired. Taking each sex separately, the majority of women were engaged solely in housekeeping, while the majority of men were neither working nor looking for work for unspecified reasons.

Clearly, most of these people, particularly the males, should have been part of the civilian labor force. That they were not, is an indication of the low level of economic activity and growth in Sierra Leone.

THE STRUCTURE OF EMPLOYMENT. Occupational patterns are described in Table 21.33.

TABLE 21.32
Economic growth, Sierra Leone, 1964–1967

| Economic Indicators | Year | | | | Percent Change | | |
|---|---|---|---|---|---|---|---|
| | 1964 | 1965 | 1966 | 1967 | 1964–65 | 1965–66 | 1966–67 |
| National income (millions of Leones)[a] | 182.2 | 203.9 | 214.2 | 223.5 | +11.9 | +5.1 | +4.3 |
| Total population (thousands) | 2,332 | 2,367 | 2,403 | 2,439 | +1.5 | +1.5 | +1.5 |
| Per capita national income (Leones)[a] | 78.1 | 86.1 | 89.1 | 91.6 | +10.4 | +3.4 | +2.8 |
| Gross national product (millions of Leones)[a] | 195.7 | 219.7 | 231.8 | 243.2 | +12.3 | +5.5 | +4.9 |

SOURCE: *National Accounts of Sierra Leone 1963–64 to 1966–67* (Freetown: Central Statistical Office, 1969).
[a] 1 Leone = U.S. $1.20.

TABLE 21.33

Percentage distribution of working population by occupation for males and females, Sierra Leone, 1963

| Occupational Group | Both Sexes | | Males | | Females | |
|---|---|---|---|---|---|---|
| | Number | Percent | Number | Percent | Number | Percent |
| Professional, technical | 11,066 | 1.2 | 8,121 | 1.4 | 2,945 | 0.9 |
| Administrative, managerial | 2,384 | 0.3 | 2,172 | 0.4 | 212 | 0.1 |
| Clerical | 6,953 | 0.8 | 5,842 | 1.0 | 1,111 | 0.3 |
| Sales | 47,243 | 5.2 | 25,210 | 4.4 | 22,033 | 6.6 |
| Farmers, fishermen | 700,174 | 77.1 | 403,123 | 69.9 | 297,051 | 89.7 |
| Miners | 42,891 | 4.7 | 42,612 | 7.4 | 279 | 0.1 |
| Transport and communications | 13,319 | 1.5 | 13,051 | 2.3 | 268 | 0.1 |
| Craftsmen, laborers | 69,971 | 7.7 | 63,563 | 11.0 | 6,408 | 1.9 |
| Service | 14,146 | 1.6 | 13,231 | 2.3 | 915 | 0.3 |
| *Total* | 908,147 | 100.0 | 576,925 | 100.0 | 331,222 | 100.0 |

SOURCE: Central Statistics Office, *1963 Population Census of Sierra Leone*, Vol. 3, *Economic Characteristics* (Freetown, 1965), p. 25.

The dominance of agricultural work (77 percent) in relation to all other activities (23 percent) is to be noted. With such a large proportion of the labor force, the agricultural sector will necessarily have a large impact on the nation's economy. As the 1969–1970 budget notes, "without healthy progress in agriculture, we can neither solve our immediate problems of alleviating unemployment in our urban centers, nor can we hope to generate the funds which we need to finance the country's infrastructure . . . and industrial projects."[25] Accordingly, economic development in Sierra Leone must be evaluated in the context of present and prospective agricultural productivity.

AGRICULTURE. Although agriculture's share of the working population approaches 80 percent, it contributes only about one-third to the gross domestic product. As the Bank of Sierra Leone points out, this is a conspicuously low proportion when compared with an average of 50–70 percent for all African nations.[26] Reflecting this imbalance, the proportion made up by subsistence agriculture of total agricultural output may be as high as 65 percent.

Noting this low level of agricultural productivity, the government hopes to "create the social organization needed to transform the traditionally subsistence farming sector into a modern industry where . . . farmers will contribute their full potential to [the] gross domestic product . . . ."[27] But, as everyone recognizes, the changes needed to bring about this transformation are very great.

At the moment, the low productivity of the agricultural sector may be attributed largely to the fact that the labor force is poorly educated, ill-trained, and inadequately equipped with capital. Under these conditions a rapid increase in the agricultural population would not necessarily increase individual productivity. On the contrary, an increasing rate of population growth would make it more difficult to improve the quality or training of the agricultural labor force, and provide the additional capital needed for its productive employment.

EMPLOYMENT. Sierra Leone at present faces serious problems of agricultural under employment and urban-industrial unemployment. Each condition reflects the failure of its respective sector to develop at an acceptable rate, relative to the needs of a growing

[25] *Ibid.*, p. 2.
[26] Bank of Sierra Leone, *Economic Review*, II, 3 (December 1967), p. 3.

[27] Government of Sierra Leone, *Budget Speech*, 1969, p. 4.

population.[28] As a result, rural-urban migration shifts, but does not solve, the problem of effective employment. As the government recognizes, "the employment potential of the industrial sector alone is relatively small [and] the employment opportunities created [in this area] are not likely to be considerable in the forseeable future."[29]

Thus, "despite the overall growth in employment, job opportunities have not kept pace with the supply of labor in the urban and industrialized areas; consequently, unemployment has been rising steadily and unfilled vacancies diminishing rapidly. This situation is reflected in the growing number of active job seekers who are unable to secure gainful employment. The statistics show that the number of registered unemployed rose by 100 percent, between December 1961 and December 1966."[30] Recognizing that registered unemployment represents only a small fraction of total unemployment, it is likely that the problem actually involves as much as 10 percent of the civilian labor force.

Since the present rate of economic development is not sufficient to eliminate unemployment, still less underemployment, it is clear that a rapid increase in the number of people seeking employment would only further aggravate the problem. Sierra Leone's present rate of population growth, therefore, is more than adequate to ensure a sufficient labor supply for the foreseeable future.[31]

SOCIAL WELFARE EXPENDITURES. In the post-independence period, the improvement of social and medical services has had a high priority. As a result, the proportion of total current expenditure used for such purposes increased from about 25 percent in 1963 to about 30 percent in 1966. In interpreting this

trend, the Bank of Sierra Leone concluded that "the growth in social expenditures accounts in large measure for an overall rate of growth in government expenditures much higher than that of GNP."[32]

The government expects to increase its development expenditure from Leones 10 million in 1968–1969 to Leones 11.8 million in 1969–1970. One-fifth of the development budget in 1969–1970 will be spent to improve social services, e.g., hospitals, schools, and water supplies.[33] Under these circumstances, a more rapid rate of population growth would simply increase the total demand for such improved services, with the result that a larger proportion of national income would have to be employed for this purpose and hence diverted away from more economically productive use. This pattern can be observed in the area of education.

EDUCATION.[34] Between 1963 and 1970, progress toward universal primary education in Sierra Leone was very slow. As Table 21.34 indicates, actual increases in enrollment were substantially offset by the growth of the school-age population.

PROJECTIONS OF PRIMARY SCHOOL-AGE POPULATION AND PRIMARY SCHOOL ENROLLMENT: 1970–1990. In this analysis, estimates of the normal primary school-age population are derived from the component projection described earlier in the section on "Population Growth," while anticipated enrollment figures are computed on the basis of an assumed 5 percent annual increase.[35] Both

[28] *Ibid.*, pp. 2–3.

[29] *Ibid.*, p. 3.

[30] Bank of Sierra Leone, *Economic Trends: September–October* (1967), p. 2.

[31] For a recent analysis of this situation, see Enid Forde, "The Implications of Rapid Population Growth for Employment in Sierra Leone" (Paper presented at the Seminar on Population Growth and Economic Development, University College, Nairobi, December 14–22, 1969).

[32] Bank of Sierra Leone, *Economic Review*, p. 11.

[33] Government of Sierra Leone, *Budget Speech*, 1969, pp. 11–12.

[34] See Thomas E. Dow, Jr., "Population Growth and Primary Education in Sierra Leone: 1960–1990" (Paper presented at the Seminar on Population Growth and Economic Development, University College, Nairobi, December 14–22, 1969).

[35] In a revised set of estimates for the period 1968–1971, the Ministry of Education assumed a 5 percent annual increase in primary school enrollment. This figure is used as the best available estimate for the entire period. In practice, it would mean that the number of children to be added to the school system each year would increase from approximately 8,000 in 1971–1972 to approximately 18,000 in 1989–1990.

TABLE 21.34
Primary school education, 1960–1970

| Year | Total Enrollment | Annual Increase | Percentage Annual Increase | Estimated Population, 5–13 Years of Age[a] | Percentage of Population, 5–13 in Primary Schools |
|------|-----------------|-----------------|---------------------------|-------------------------------------------|--------------------------------------------------|
| 1960–61 | 79,132 | — | — | — | — |
| 1961–62 | 91,132 | 12,000 | 15.2 | — | — |
| 1962–63 | 99,129 | 7,997 | 8.8 | — | — |
| 1963–64 | 113,631 | 14,502 | 14.6 | 518,141 | 21.9 |
| 1964–65 | 118,788 | 5,157 | 4.5 | 525,913 | 22.6 |
| 1965–66 | 121,482 | 2,694 | 2.3 | 533,801 | 22.8 |
| 1966–67 | 124,808 | 3,326 | 2.7 | 541,808 | 23.0 |
| 1967–68 | 131,545 | 6,737 | 5.4 | 549,935 | 23.9 |
| 1968–69 | 137,658[b] | 6,113 | 4.6 | 558,185 | 24.7 |
| 1969–70 | 144,541[b] | 6,883 | 5.0 | 566,558 | 25.5 |

[a] The primary school-age population in 1963 is arrived at by increasing the total population by 5 percent and apportioning this total according to an appropriate stable age distribution. (A model stable population, "West" female, was selected with the same proportion under age 10, $e_0 = 30$ years.) In each subsequent year (1964–1970), the total population is raised by 1.5 percent and similarly apportioned. The final school-age population in each year is obtained by combining the age groups 5–9 and 10–14, less one-fifth the latter total.
[b] Revised estimate (1968–69)—original goal was 153,253; revised estimate (1969–70)—original goal was 174,961.

sets of projections are brought together in Tables 20.35.

Under the assumptions stated, the percentage of the school-age population in primary schools will increase from about 25 percent in 1970 to about 40 percent in 1990. When compared with the original Sierra Leone Development Program in Education, which called for 70 percent enrollment by 1980 and 100 percent enrollment by 1990, the results must be considered disappointing. This is especially evident if one recognizes that the number of children outside the school system will actually increase by 165,202 or approximately 40 percent over the 20-year period.

Overall, the achievement of universal primary education in Sierra Leone is not to be expected in this century, and its attainment in the next will depend largely, but not exclusively, on how rapidly the school-age population increases. It now seems probable that this increase will be substantial, with progress toward complete enrollment retarded accordingly.

SUMMARY. Sierra Leone, like most developing nations, has an inadequate stock of capital per head, a poorly educated and poorly trained work force, and a low per capita income. Living at or near a subsistence level, most households tend to generate income or produce primarily for their own consumption. Consequently, the level of saving, investment, and economic growth is quite low, and is likely to remain that way if economic development is forced to compete with rapid population growth. At the very least, such expansive growth would greatly prolong the process of modernization.

TABLE 21.35
Projections of primary school-age population and school enrollment, 1970–1990

| Year | Population, 5–13 | Primary School Enrollment | Percent of Population 5–13, in Primary School | Number of Children 5–13, Outside School System |
|------|-----------------|---------------------------|----------------------------------------------|-----------------------------------------------|
| 1970 | 566,558 | 144,541 | 25.5 | 422,017 |
| 1975 | 621,398 | 184,475 | 29.7 | 436,923 |
| 1980 | 727,202 | 235,443 | 32.4 | 491,759 |
| 1985 | 851,454 | 300,492 | 35.3 | 550,962 |
| 1990 | 970,732 | 383,513 | 39.5 | 587,219 |

## GOVERNMENT AND UNIVERSITY ACTIVITIES IN THE FIELD OF DEMOGRAPHY

GOVERNMENT OF SIERRA LEONE. African governments today are becoming increasingly aware of the importance of demographic information for the efficient discharge of their functions. Effective administration, the formulation and implementation of plans for economic and social development, and successful requests for foreign aid all require to varying degrees the availability of certain basic statistical data. Demographic data are undoubtedly at the core of all such matters.

In Sierra Leone, the government's interest in demographic matters stems from two main considerations: namely, routine administrative needs, and economic and social development. There is no clearly defined policy or philosophy on demographic issues which the government can be said to follow. There is for instance no definite commitment by the government on family planning, although it is aware that a movement exists and government officials participate in it in a private capacity. However, the government requires basic demographic information, such as the size of the population and its geographical distribution and composition, size of the labor force, etc. The 1963 census provided for the first time some useful demographic information that has served a wide range of administrative purposes. It has also furnished the basis for surveys[36] thereby augmenting and enriching the country's stock of economic and social data. These surveys have no doubt provided valuable information which the government needs for its development projects. However, it is clearly recognized that there are important gaps which exist in the country's stock of demographic information and there are plans to put this right.

The most important kind of information which is lacking is the rate of population growth. Obviously the key issue in most developing countries today is the rate of growth of the population and its relationship to the rate of increase of food production and the rate of economic development. Consequently, no developing country can afford to be without this vital information.

The Sierra Leone government took another population census in 1973. Conducted on the same lines as the 1963 census, it should provide the means for arriving at some workable estimate of population growth. On the same issue proposals have been worked out for a phased extension of the country's civil registration system, in an effort to establish a sound basis for the calculation of annual rates of population growth. Because of the length of time that would elapse before the registration system would be working satisfactorily enough to yield the required information, it was decided to include in the proposals a plan for a sample survey. The survey is designed to serve two purposes: First, it would meet the urgent need of the country for information on fertility, mortality, and population growth; and second, it would constitute a check on the registration system. It is hoped that the project will be started by the mid-1970s with the financial and technical assistance of a foreign country. If the project materializes, Sierra Leone should be able to extend civil registration to cover the entire country before the end of the next decade.

UNIVERSITY OF SIERRA LEONE. The Geography Department at Fourah Bay College offers two courses in population. As a result of undergraduate experience in these courses, two M.A. candidates in geography have decided to prepare dissertations in the area of demography. Their graduate work was supported by the Population Council.

At the staff level, an Advisor in Demography from the Population Council was attached to Fourah Bay for two years. With his departure at the end of the 1969–1970 session, a demographic unit was established at the university.

[36] See the Central Statistics Office, *Agricultural Statistical Survey*, 1965–1966; *Household Multipurpose Survey*, 1966–1969; and *Survey of Business and Industry*, 1966–1967, Freetown.

THE POLITICAL paroxysms in the savanna region of West Africa during the fourteenth to fifteenth centuries caused waves of outmigration from this belt to the forested south. In the forested belt, each group occupied a locality to the exclusion of others.[1] Such a discrete spatial ordering was a reflection of the latent state of conflict between contiguous groups. In this type of environment, intergroup intercourse was minimal, and any form of interregional or long distance trade was impossible. Within the areas occupied by each group, physical geographical factors were so potent that they largely dictated the pattern of settlement, agriculture, and general behavior.

The creation of states in West Africa after the Berlin Conference of 1885, the introduction of a monetary exchange system, and the inception of interregional trade, have in the last century caused a complete spatial reallocation of population. The following are some of the consequences of this change in the socioeconomic landscape of the country:

1. Changes in demographic attributes
   (a) Variations in population densities
   (b) The redistribution of ethnic groups
   (c) The spread of Christianity and Islam.
2. Social and economic changes
   (a) Regional variations in age structure and dependency
   (b) Variations in educational, occupational, and industrial structure
   (c) Structural changes in the household, marriage and the general nature of the family

## CHANGES IN DEMOGRAPHIC ATTRIBUTES

POPULATION DISTRIBUTION AND DENSITY. As early as 1871, attempts were made to record decennial estimates of Sierra Leone's population. Such estimates were usually based on actual enumeration in the Crown Colony

[1] John I. Clarke, "Population Distribution in Sierra Leone," in John C. Caldwell and C. Okonjo, eds., *The Population of Tropical Africa* (London: Longmans, Green and Company, and New York: Columbia University Press, 1968), p. 14.

# CHAPTER TWENTY-TWO

# *The Nature & Movement of the Population*

MILTON F. HARVEY

TABLE 22.1

Population of Sierra Leone, 1921, 1931, and 1963

| Year | Crown Colony | Protectorate | Total |
|------|-------------|-------------|-------|
| 1921 | 85,163 | 1,455,510 | 1,540,673 |
| 1931 | 96,573 | 1,672,058 | 1,768,631 |
| 1963 | 195,023 | 1,985,332 | 2,180,355 |

(now called the Western Area) whereas in the Protectorate (now called the provinces) they were from tax rolls of adult males.[2] In spite of the gross inaccuracies that are bound to occur from such a method, the estimates do give us some idea of population growth in the country (Table 22.1).

The increases in population have been accompanied by marked internal population redistribution. For example, in 1931, the most densely populated districts with over 100 people per square mile were Kailahun and the Western Area. In 1963, there were six districts (Port Loko, Kambia, Bo, Kailahun, and the Western Area) with densities above the 100 per square mile threshold. Although the diamond mining district of Kono does not fall into the above group, it is worth noting that the population density there increased from 35 to 77 per square mile.

The changes in population densities between 1931 and 1963 are essentially the results of internal migration in response to the development of mining industries, the increasing employment opportunities in large towns, and the inception of the mechanical rice cultivation schemes of the Port Loko and Kambia districts.[3] The resultant pattern of population densities is largely related to the economic health of the locality. Operationally, this can be defined as the percentage of the active labor force employed in commerce

[2] R. R. Kuczynski, *A Demographic Survey of the British Colonial Empire*, I, *West Africa* (London: Oxford University Press, 1948).

[3] For a detailed discussion of these processes, see M. E. Harvey, "A Geographical Study of the Pattern, Processes and Consequences of Urban Growth in Sierra Leone in the Twentieth Century" (Ph.D. dissertation of Durham University, England, 1966).

($X_1$), and the number of cooperatives ($X_2$). For the 147 chiefdoms plus the Western Area, the above data were collected and a stepwise regression technique was used to test the hypothesized functional relationship between population density ($Y$) and the two independent variables:

$$Y = f(X_1, X_2)$$

The correlation matrix (Table 22.2) clearly shows that there is an evident relationship between the dependent and independent variables. The lack of any significant correlation between the independent variables is indicative of the absence of multi-collinearity (i.e., the individual influence of the independent variables on the dependent variable can be easily estimated.)[4]

The result of the regression (Table 22.3) showed that the two factors together explain 79.9 percent of the variations in population density; with $X_1$ accounting for 79.8 percent, a value which is significant at the 99 percent level.

The result of this analysis really isolates the main component of economic development in the country. In a developing economy without large-scale industrialization, trade in either cheap consumer goods or the production of raw materials for industrial countries are the main occupations. The former is largely urban based; the latter is essentially rural. Although a few light industries have developed in the post-independence period, their influence on the internal redistribution of population is still weak. Rather than generating a pool of labor,

[4] L. J. King, *Statistical Analysis in Geography* (Englewood Cliffs N.J.: Prentice-Hall, 1969), p. 163; J. Johnston, *Econometric Methods* (New York: McGraw-Hill, 1963).

TABLE 22.2

Correlation matrix

|  | Simple | Correlation | Coefficients |
|------|--------|-------------|--------------|
|  | $Y$ | $X_1$ | $X_2$ |
| $Y$ | 1.000 | | |
| $X_1$ | 0.893 | 1.000 | |
| $X_2$ | 0.782 | 0.198 | 1.000 |

TABLE 22.3
Summary for the regression model

| Step | Variable | $R$ | Standard Error | $R^2$ | Increase | Regression Coefficient | Standard Error | Variables Not Included | |
|------|----------|-----|----------------|-------|----------|------------------------|----------------|------------------------|--|
| | | | | | | | | Variable | Partial |
| 1 | $X_1$ | 0.893[a] | 87.09 | 0.789 | 0.798 | 27.918[b] | 2.249 | $X_2$ | 0.230 |
| 2 | $X_2$ | 0.889[b] | 85.86 | 0.799 | 0.001 | $b_1 = 27.617$[b] | 2.227 | | |
| | | | | | | $b_2 = 2.174$ | | | |

[a] Significant at the 99 percent level.
[b] Significant at the 95 percent level.

these industries are supplied from the existing labor market created by commerce and trade.

THE REDISTRIBUTION OF ETHNIC GROUPS. As previously stated, the various tribes in Sierra Leone formerly occupied discrete locations. Each group was separated from its neighbors by physical barriers like forest, large rivers, swamps, and mountain ranges. Neighboring groups cooperated only to fight against a common enemy. During the last half century, the situation has changed remarkably and the ethnic structure of every locality has become more heterogeneous. The main agents of these changes were essentially related to the colonial period. They include the slave trade, the growth of trade in general, missionary activity and the spread of educational and medical facilities, the proclamation of the Protectorate (1896), the construction of the railway (1905–1916), mining, road construction, and employment opportunities in town. All these factors could be regarded as components of modernization.[5]

The net effect of intense ethnic interaction during this century is evident from the large number of groups found in any of the chiefdoms (Table 22.4). It is interesting to note that the least number of ethnic groups found in any chiefdom is 8, whereas the mean number for all the chiefdoms is 13. A mode of 17 and a median of 13 reflect the large-scale population shifts of the colonial period.

[5] B. J. Riddell, "Structure, Diffusion and Response: The Spatial Dynamics of Modernization in Sierra Leone" (Ph.D. dissertation of The Pennsylvania State University, 1969).

So far the discussion of the distribution of the groups may give an impression that all tribes have the same propensity to migrate. Table 22.5 clearly shows that this is not the case. The propensity to migrate seems to be related to two main factors: the direction of flow of the original migrants and the size of the group. Of these, the former is the more important. As potential areas of trade and employment are mainly south of the core areas of the northern tribes, these groups had more urge to migrate either southward to centers like Bo, the bauxite mining center of Mokanji, and the diamond mining belt along the middle Sewa River valley, or westward to Freetown, or eastward to the diamond mining district of Kono. As a result of this,

TABLE 22.4
Ethnic composition of chiefdoms

| Number of Ethnic Groups (max. 18) | Number of Chiefdoms |
|-----------------------------------|---------------------|
| 18 | 8 |
| 17 | 22 |
| 16 | 17 |
| 15 | 20 |
| 14 | 21 |
| 13 | 17 |
| 12 | 21 |
| 11 | 10 |
| 10 | 8 |
| 9 | 3 |
| 8 | 1 |

SOURCE: 1963 census.

TABLE 22.5
Distribution of ethnic groups by chiefdoms

| Group | Population | Rank Size | Point of Entry into Country | Chiefdom Spread (out of 148) |
|---|---|---|---|---|
| Mende | 672,831 | 1 | Southeast | 148 |
| Temne | 648,931 | 2 | North | 148 |
| Susu | 67,288 | 7 | North | 148 |
| Fula | 66,724 | 8 | North | 148 |
| Mandingo | 51,024 | 10 | North | 147 |
| Limba | 183,496 | 3 | North | 144 |
| Kono | 104,573 | 4 | Southeast | 142 |
| Loko | 64,459 | 9 | North | 139 |
| Kissi | 48,954 | 11 | Southeast | 138 |
| Sherbro | 74,674 | 6 | Indegene | 132 |
| Kuranko | 80,732 | 5 | North | 127 |
| Creole | 41,783 | 12 | West | 124 |
| Yalunka | 15,005 | 13 | North | 87 |
| Krim | 8,733 | 14 | Southeast | 86 |
| Gallinas | 2,200 | 18 | Southeast | 84 |
| Vai | 5,786 | 15 | Southeast | 78 |
| Gola | 4,854 | 16 | Southeast | 54 |
| Kru | 4,793 | 17 | Southeast | 52 |

SOURCE: 1963 census and C. Fyfe, *A History of Sierra Leone* (London: Oxford University Press, 1962).

the most culturally heterogeneous chiefdoms are also the most developed.

THE SPREAD OF CHRISTIANITY AND ISLAM. The present social, cultural, and political structure of Sierra Leone gives evidence of its long contact with savanna West Africa and Western Europe. One of the major results of these interactions has been the superimposition of Islam and Christianity on the then existing pagan religions.

The history of Islam in Sierra Leone really dates back to the 1725 *jihad* (holy war) of the Futa Jallon. One direct consequence of this was the adoption of Islam by the Susu who subsequently migrated into Sierra Leone. Subsequently tribes conquered by them were forcibly converted to Islam. The religion also spread because of trade contacts between Islamic and pagan groups.

Quite independent of the Susu influence on the propagation of Islam in the country was the migration of the Islamized Fula, Mandingo and Kuranko into northern Sierra Leone. Through war and trade, Islam slowly diffused among the Loko, Limba, Temne, and in more recent times, among the southern tribes. In general, the popularity of Islam throughout the country is partly due to the similarity between its doctrines and traditional cultural codes.

Christianity and the influence of Christian missions in Sierra Leone date back to the coming of the settlers in 1792. These people established the Baptist, Methodist, and Huntingdonian churches in present-day Freetown. In the nineteenth and twentieth centuries many other religious groups, like the American Evangelical and United Brethren sects, have established churches, mission hospitals, and schools in different parts of the country. Until recently, education in the provinces was largely provided by missions. As a result of this, Christian influence spread throughout the country. Unlike Islam, the religion has been most successful among the educated urban people. In rural areas, however, Christianity has achieved very little.

The spread of Islam and Christianity followed very evident trends, the former from north to south, the latter from coastal west to east. Although the diffusion of these religions was nonrandom, the willingness of individual communities to construct either a mosque or a church was largely a fortuitous process.

## SOCIAL AND ECONOMIC CHANGES

REGIONAL VARIATIONS IN AGE STRUCTURE AND DEPENDENCY. Of the estimated 2,180,354 people in Sierra Leone in 1963, 50.4 percent or 1,099,232 were females. This female excess was not uniform throughout the country (Table 22.6). In the Western Area, the diamond mining belt, the rice cultivating areas of Kaffu Bullom and Loko Masama chiefdoms, and the two Dembelia chiefdoms of the Koinadugu District, there were marked male excesses. As may quickly be noticed, these areas are among the main zones of in-migration. Male excesses, therefore, reflect their greater propensity to migrate.

Within the country, there are marked regional contrasts in age structure. The main areas of employment show a marked excess of young adults whereas the subsistence agricultural areas of the southern sandy belt, the southeastern Gola Forest, the Tingi Hills, and the livestock region of the north, have a preponderance of both children and older people. This means that the dependency ratio is higher in the latter areas than in the former. To alleviate the strains on the active labor

TABLE 22.6
Sex ratios by districts, 1963

| Locality | Females per 1,000 Males |
|---|---|
| Sierra Leone | 1,017 |
| (Western Area) | 897 |
| Freetown | 902 |
| Rural areas | 888 |
| (Eastern Province) | 922 |
| Kono | 847 |
| Kenema | 851 |
| Kailahun | 1,145 |
| (Northern Province) | 1,099 |
| Bombali | 1,173 |
| Kambia | 1,083 |
| Koinadugu | 1,075 |
| Port Loko | 1,050 |
| Tonkolili | 1,120 |
| (Southern Province) | 1,021 |
| Bo | 963 |
| Bonthe | 1,056 |
| Moyamba | 1,124 |

SOURCE: 1963 census.

force in the areas of high dependency ratios, children are drafted very early into the productive sector. Some of the implications of contrasts in demographic attributes will be discussed elsewhere.

OCCUPATIONAL CONTRASTS. In 1963, there were 908,147 people over the age of ten who were actively employed (see Chapter 21, Table 21.34). Of that total, by far the highest percentage (77.3) was in agriculture, forestry, fishing, and hunting either as subsistence or plantation farmers, or as forest rangers, forest guards, or fishermen. This high percentage is generally characteristic of developing countries where the majority of the population still are tied directly to the soil and agricultural work is divided between the sexes. In addition, the implements used—the hoe, machete, and axe—are essentially primitive, and their use presupposes both a large farming group and many hours of hard work. In developed countries, where agriculture and fishing have been highly mechanized, and shifting agriculture abolished, a very small number of people are required to produce food for the many. Compare the 77 percent in Sierra Leone to the low percentages for Britain (4 percent), the United States (7 percent), Australia (15 percent), and New Zealand (20 percent).

Within the country, the eight occupational groups are not evenly distributed (Table 22.7). More people are engaged in agriculture, forestry, hunting, and fishing in the Northern Province than in any other area. In contrast, it contains the smallest proportion of people working in commerce. For commerce, the Western Area is the predominant region, followed by the Eastern Province. The former area has many large towns and includes Freetown, the national capital and the main commercial center. The importance of commerce in the Eastern Province clearly reflects the influence of diamond mining which has caused the easy circulation of money.

The importance of Freetown as the main center for transport and storage is responsible for the fact that the Western Area has more than 60 percent of all those engaged in this

TABLE 22.7
Percent distribution of occupational groups by province, 1963

| Occupational Group | Southern Province | Eastern Province | Northern Province | Western Province |
|---|---|---|---|---|
| Agriculture, etc. | 83.0 | 71.6 | 89.6 | 13.9 |
| Mining & quarrying | 4.1 | 12.5 | 1.0 | 0.3 |
| Manufacturing | 4.5 | 5.5 | 2.5 | 11.2 |
| Construction | 1.0 | 1.2 | 1.3 | 10.1 |
| Electricity, etc. | 0.1 | 0.1 | 0.1 | 2.0 |
| Commerce | 4.1 | 5.8 | 3.5 | 26.6 |
| Transport, etc. | 1.1 | 1.1 | 0.6 | 14.4 |
| Services | 2.1 | 2.2 | 1.4 | 21.5 |
| Totals | 100.0 | 100.0 | 100.0 | 100.0 |

occupational group. The Western Area is outstanding in services (the army, and administrators, teachers and doctors, clerks and messengers), transport (with a port and a well-developed public transport system), construction and electricity, gas, and water. For these five occupational groups, the Western Area employed 38.5 percent of the national totals. In manufacturing, the Eastern Province was numerically the most important and the Western Area the least important. Realizing that manufacturing includes the preparation of miscellaneous food products— *foofoo, agidi*, etc.—domestic handicrafts, the dyeing of native and imported clothes, and modern automated industries, one will understand why the three provinces are more important. Actually, if figures were available for modern industries only, the Western Area would have predominated. Diamond mining in the Eastern Province and sections of the Southern Province employs more people than iron ore mining (hence the explanation for the number employed in mining by province).

The regional employment pattern may change with the development of the new bauxite and rutile mines in the Southern Province, the creation of plantations in the Northern and Southern provinces, and increasing industrialization.

## POPULATION MOVEMENTS

The inclusion of West Africa, or perhaps more appropriately the forested region, within the sphere of international trade and a monetary system of exchange has affected the demographic structure of this region by triggering both international and internal migrations. Although the basic motives for both types of population mobility may be identical, the two groups of movers often differ considerably in their social and economic backgrounds and in their outlook to resource appraisal. Consequently, the two will be treated separately.

INTERNATIONAL MIGRATION. The 1963 national census showed that there were 59,482 foreigners in Sierra Leone. Table 22.8 reveals the main source areas and the sections of the country most popular to each group.

The table effectively shows the preponderance of citizens of Britain, Lebanon, Ghana, Nigeria, Gambia, Guinea, and Liberia. The last two countries share common boundaries with Sierra Leone, and consequently fluidity of movement across the common borders is very great. This is particularly true among tribes that stretch on both sides of the frontier. For these groups, professing citizenship of one or other of the countries depends on where, when, and how they are asked about the matter. Migration into Sierra Leone from Guinea and Liberia is largely the result of spatial contiguity and the complex ramifications of kinship ties across the borders.

In Africa, one of the advantages of the colonial period was the introduction of

TABLE 22.8
Nationality of non-Sierra Leonean population, 1963

| Country | Total | Male | Female | Locational Preference in Sierra Leone |
|---------|-------|------|--------|---------------------------------------|
| Gambia | 2,523 | 1,721 | 802 | 2—1—4—3 |
| Ghana | 3,419 | 2,059 | 1,360 | 4—3—1—2 |
| Guinea | 30,671 | 20,037 | 10,634 | 3—2—1—4 |
| Liberia | 8,286 | 4,043 | 4,243 | 4—2—1—3 |
| Nigeria | 5,573 | 3,807 | 1,766 | 4—2—1—3 |
| France | 162 | 107 | 55 | 4—2—1—3 |
| Germany | 65 | 42 | 23 | 4—2—1—3 |
| India | 278 | 219 | 59 | 4—1—2—3 |
| Lebanon | 3,102 | 1,789 | 1,313 | 2—4—1—3 |
| Switzerland | 79 | 59 | 20 | 4—1—2—3 |
| Syria | 199 | 111 | 88 | 1—3—2—4 |
| United Kingdom | 2,360 | 1,390 | 970 | 4—2—3—1 |
| U.S.A. | 429 | 225 | 204 | 4—3—1—2 |
| Other African countries | 1,401 | 665 | 270 | 2—4—1—3 |
| Others | 935 | 960 | 441 | 4—3—2—1 |
| *Totals* | 52,609 | 33,568 | 19,041 | 4—2—1—3 |

NOTE: 1 = Southern Province, 2 = Eastern Province, 3 = Northern Province, 4 = Western Area.

*linguae francae* that transcended the geographical territory of particular tribes. In West Africa, for example, nationals of the former British colonies can communicate either through English or English patois. Furthermore, immigration rules for members of the Commonwealth were very lenient. These two factors help explain the large numbers of Gambians, Ghanaians, and Nigerians, in contrast to the few citizens from most former French West African countries in Sierra Leone.

The migrants from other African countries to Sierra Leone are generally illiterate or semieducated, and are interested primarily in diamond mining and petty trading. Minor interests include fishing (especially the Ghanaians) and cattle herding in the northern savanna.

In attempting to explain non-African migration to the country, distance is quite unimportant. It is hypothesized that such flows are related to both the extent of trade links with Sierra Leone and the intensity of information flow between the country of origin and Sierra Leone. Operationally, we measure trade as the value of hard manufactured goods (machinery and transport equipment, mineral fuels, and chemicals) exported to Sierra Leone $(X_1)$. Here the underlying assumption is that most of the migrants from outside Africa come to Sierra Leone to either operate machinery or supervise the operation of foreign commercial organizations. The intensity of information flow $(X_2)$, we measure as the number of people, from a particular country, who were resident in Sierra Leone in 1931. The resultant model states that the number of immigrants $(Y)$ to Sierra Leone from any non-African country is a function of $X_1$ and $X_2$; that is, $Y = f(X_1, X_2)$.

To test this model, the relevant data for 1966 for the 18 countries with more than 10 nationals in Sierra Leone in that year were collected and analyzed by stepwise regression technique. The correlation matrix in Table

TABLE 22.9
Simple correlation matrix

| | Simple | Correlation | Matrix |
|---|--------|-------------|--------|
| | $Y$ | $X_1$ | $X_2$ |
| $Y$ | 1.000 | | |
| $X_1$ | 0.928 | 1.000 | |
| $X_2$ | 0.521 | 0.293 | 1.000 |

TABLE 22.10
Analysis of the stepwise regression model

| Step | Variable | $R$ | Standard Error | $R^2$ | Increase | Regression Coefficient | Standard Error | Variables Not Included Variable | Partial |
|------|----------|-----|----------------|-------|----------|------------------------|----------------|-----------|---------|
| 1 | $X_1$ | 0.928[a] | 188.78 | 0.862 | 0.862 | 1.6148[a] | 0.157 | $X_2$ | 0.241 |
| 2 | $X_2$ | 0.964[a] | 138.99 | 0.921 | 0.059 | $b_1 = 1.476^a$ | 0.121 | | |
| | | | | | | $b_2 = 0.00005$ | 0.00001 | | |

[a] Significant at the 99 percent level.

22.9 shows that there is a relationship between the dependent and the independent variables. In fact the result of the stepwise regression showed that the two variables explain 92.9 percent of non-African migration to Sierra Leone (Table 22.10). The contributions of the two variables were significant at the 99 percent level.

One similarity between internal and international migration is the age and sex differential. Analysis of the age structure of arrivals and departures of foreigners from Sierra Leone (Table 22.11) shows that the majority are males between the ages of 30 and 49. The similarity of the age distribution of the arriving and departing groups is partly an indication of the transient nature of many of the migrants from non-African countries. As one group leaves, another set with similar demographic traits arrives to replace it.

The occupational structure of these immigrants shows that they are largely professional, technical, and related workers; administrative, executive, and managerial workers; and sales workers. There is also a remarkable similarity between the occupational composition of "arrivals" and "departures." This is a further justification of our early assertion that as a group leaves, a comparable one arrives to replace it.

This rather short analysis of international migration to Sierra Leone throws light on the nature of economic development in the country. It shows that in spite of political independence, the economic structure of the country is still essentially colonial. Evidence of this fact is the absence of a local pool of skilled workers capable of effectively replacing the foreign experts. The transient nature of immigration does not allow the country to

TABLE 22.11
Age and sex distribution of non-Sierra Leoneans (non-African): Arrivals and departures, November 1966

| Age Group | Arrivals Total | Male | Female | Departures Total | Male | Female |
|-----------|-------|------|--------|-------|------|--------|
| 0–14 | 48 | 26 | 22 | 35 | 77 | 18 |
| 15–19 | 48 | 25 | 23 | 29 | 13 | 16 |
| 20–29 | 276 | 196 | 80 | 232 | 164 | 68 |
| 30–39 | 420 | 350 | 70 | 327 | 275 | 52 |
| 40–49 | 274 | 223 | 51 | 218 | 117 | 41 |
| 50–59 | 110 | 90 | 20 | 94 | 80 | 14 |
| 60+ | 40 | 28 | 12 | 20 | 14 | 6 |
| *Total* | 1,216 | 938 | 278 | 955 | 740 | 215 |

SOURCE: Data from Immigration Department, Ministry of External Affairs, Government of Sierra Leone.

have a group of experienced men capable of creating the economic atmosphere conducive to development. This situation will continue until many more Sierra Leoneans are qualified for executive and managerial posts. Much more important is the fact that a transformation of the occupational structure necessitates the development of more local enterprises and industries. To meet these challenges, the whole educational reorientation from a philosophico-literary bias to a technico-scientific inclination is inevitable. As Sierra Leone develops, she needs to optimize the utilization of both her natural and human resources.

INTERNAL MIGRATION. Internal population shifts in Sierra Leone fall into three time periods which reflect human responses and adaptability to contemporary social and economic situations. Transition from one phase to the next was marked by an increase in economic activity and more pronounced interregional mobility. Operationally, these three stages could be identified as the *traditional*, the *transitional*, and the *colonial*.

The inception of the traditional phase could be related to the disintegration of the states of the savanna partly because of constant interstate friction, and partly as a result of direct military intervention from north of the Sahara. The defeat of the Songhai Empire by a Moroccan detachment at the battle of Tondibi in 1591 may be regarded as the inception of the traditional phase. Characterizing this period was the absence of any appreciable interregional trade and interethnic cooperation. Indeed such a situation does not generate economic development nor does it create a hierarchical central place system which forms a framework for various types of intergroup and interpersonal frictions. Subsistence agriculture, hunting, and fishing are the characteristic occupations of such a society. Thus, besides certain social and cultural constraints on the individual's movement, there were no marked regional economic disparities serving to initiate the economic push-pull forces so important in both internal and international

migration. Concluding, we note that in this era intragroup mobility was the only evident type of population shift.

During the transitory period, vigorous missionary activity as well as exploration of the interior by people like Laing and Alldridge during the eighteenth and early nineteenth centuries slowly reduced ethnic suspicion; intertribal warfare was replaced by cooperation in trade. During the early period of this transitory phase, numerous trade routes developed to connect the interior to the coast. Along these caravan routes, villages at advantageous geographic sites slowly emerged as important collecting centers.[6] Interregional trade, based on the barter of hides, dyes, gum, and gold from the interior and imported rum, beads, gunpowder, and mirrors, flourished in this phase. Naturally, temporary sojourns outside one's own locality as a member of a trading caravan group were in some cases replaced by permanent residences. Freetown, the capital, was particularly attractive to migrants.[7] Other nodes of attraction included the coastal settlements of Bonthe, Port Loko, Kambia, and Rotifunk. Common characteristics of all these places was the presence of European commercial firms, many African trading establishments, churches, and mission schools. In summary, it may be noted that in this exploratory or transitory phase, local intragroup movement was replaced by intergroup mobility. Migration distances were longer and certain centers emerged as attractive destination nodes. The general trend of migration was from the interior to the coast.

The proclamation of the Protectorate over the hinterland in 1896 marks the beginning of the colonial phase. During the first four decades of this era, many innovations, such as

[6] M. E. Harvey, "Implications of Migration to Freetown: A Study of the Relationship between Migrants, Housing and Occupation," *Civilizations*, XXVIII, 2 (1968).

[7] M. Banton, *West African City: A Study of Tribal Life in Freetown* (London: Oxford University Press, 1957); M. E. Harvey, "Important Social, Political and Economic Schisms Between Town and Country in Sierra Leone" (Paper submitted at the INCIDI Conference at Aix-en-Provence, 1968).

the introduction of a local monetary system, education, medical facilities, mining, and road and rail construction, completely changed the scale of social and economic values. These components of modernization were not evenly distributed over the country, nor were they spontaneously established.[8] Consequently, marked regional schisms as regards employment opportunities, educational and social facilities, and the general rate of social change ensued. Recently, these regional disparities have become accentuated because the more developed areas have created some basic consumer industries and certain amenities like pipe-borne water supply, electricity, cinemas, and night clubs.

Over the resultant economic and social landscape, interregional migration has tended to be differential in terms of age, sex, ethnic group, and level of education. The basic reasons for such migration is the individual's ambition to maximize his welfare, social status, and money income. Invariably, therefore, there are many characteristics of the migrant himself, his place of origin and destination, and the nature of the intervening opportunities which could be included in an empirical study designed to explain interregional migration flows. From this multitude of factors, we assert that some quantifiable indices of economic motivation, of age differential between any two observation

units, and of the size of the units themselves will aggregatively explain the patterns of internal migration in the country. Table 22.12 summarizes the operational definitions of the variables. In that table, $i$ and $j$ represent the origin and destination nodes respectively.

For the 12 districts and the Western Area, data were collected on these variables. The 156 equations were used in a stepwise regression model involving

$$Y = f(X_1, X_2, X_3, X_4, X_5).$$

Table 22.13 of simple correlations shows that all our hypothesized relationships between the dependent and independent variables were valid. Correlations among the independent variables are low, an indication that the influence of multicollinearity on our regression results is very weak.[9]

The five factors were able to explain up to 72.15 percent of interregional migration flows. Relevant extracts from the stepwise regression results are shown in Table 22.14. The contributions of each of the individual independent variables were significant at the 95 percent level or more.

From the results of the analysis, the following conclusions could be made about the pattern of interregional migration in Sierra Leone: (1) Migration to a locality is conditioned by prior information about jobs, social conditions, housing, and general cost of

[8] Riddell, "Structure, Diffusion and Response."

[9] Johnston, *Econometric Methods*, pp. 201–7.

TABLE 22.12

Variables involved in the stepwise regression model of interregional migration in Sierra Leone

| Variable | Operation Definition | Hypothesized Relationship to $Y$ |
|---|---|---|
| $Y$ Population flow | Gross population flow $i$ to $j$ | |
| $X_1$ Employment opportunity | Number of salary workers $(j/i)$ | Positive |
| $X_2$ Information flow | Percent of dominant ethnic group of $i$ and $j$ | Positive |
| $X_3$ Cohort factor | Percent of active population (15–45 years) $(j/i)$ | Positive |
| $X_4$ Size of unit | Population density $(j - i)$ | Positive |
| $X_5$ Distance | Distance between $i$ & $j$ | Negative |

TABLE 22.13
Correlation matrix of the variables

|  | $Y$ | $X_1$ | $X_2$ | $X_3$ | $X_4$ | $X_5$ |
|---|---|---|---|---|---|---|
| $Y$ | 1.000 | | | | | |
| $X_1$ | 0.422 | 1.000 | | | | |
| $X_2$ | 0.731 | 0.199 | 1.000 | | | |
| $X_3$ | 0.507 | 0.477 | 0.243 | 1.000 | | |
| $X_4$ | 0.301 | 0.004 | 0.285 | 0.174 | 1.000 | |
| $X_5$ | −0.465 | −0.066 | −0.454 | −0.025 | −0.027 | 1.000 |

living at that place. As information flow was made a function of the ethnic structure of both the origin and destination nodes, the importance of this variable in the model shows that in spite of very evident ethnic admixture, intraethnic migration is still more important than interethnic mobility. (2) Migration is most prevalent among the young active population. This implies that the demographically active and virile people leave the rural areas for either the mines or the larger towns. Consequently, agriculture has been disrupted to such an extent that Sierra Leone now imports over 40,000 tons of rice per annum, although the *Agricultural Survey* of the country showed that 86.3 percent of all farmers produced rice.[10] (3) The importance of economic gains in migration motivation, stressed by researchers like Sjaastad[11] is confirmed by this study. When it is realized, however, that there are only a

[10] Central Statistics Office, *Agricultural Survey of Sierra Leone* (Freetown, 1967).
[11] L. A. Sjaastad, "The Relationship Between Migration and Income in the United States," The Regional Science Association, *Papers and Proceedings*, VI (1960), pp. 37–64.

few centers of employment in the country, we must concede that continued migration will cause serious social and economic problems. Some of the implications of migration in the country have been discussed by Harvey,[12] who advocated a regional development policy because such a strategy would reduce the dominance of the capital and the other growth poles of the country. (4) The rather weak effect of distance on migration in the country is indicative of the situation discussed in point (3) above. As there are few areas of employment with evident locational biases, a prospective job finder is not deterred by distance. It is, however, suggested that the influence of distance, so important in other migration studies,[13] will be more evident when local or interchiefdom migration is analyzed.

LOCAL MIGRATION.    Analysis of interchiefdom migration is based on the determination of the chiefdom to which another chiefdom sent most migrants. This technique we call First Preference Analysis (FPA). When FPA was performed on the figures for 1963 of migration from each of the 148 administrative units to the other 147, the influence of distance was

[12] Harvey, "Implications of Migration to Freetown"; M. E. Harvey, "Levels of Economic Development and Patterns of International Migration in Sierra Leone" (Papers submitted to the Seminar on Population and Economic Development, University College, Nairobi, December 1969).
[13] G. Olsson, "Distance and Human Interaction: A Migration Study," *Geografiska Annaler*, XLVII (1965), pp. 4–43; G. Kulldorf, *Migration Probabilities*, Lund Studies in Geography, Series B, Human Geography, 14 (Lund, 1955).

TABLE 22.14
Extracts from the results of the stepwise regression model

| Step | Variable | $R$ | Standard Error | Increase in $R^2$ |
|---|---|---|---|---|
| 1 | $X_2$ | 0.731 | 0.459 | 0.535 |
| 2 | $X_3$ | 0.806 | 0.400 | 0.110 |
| 3 | $X_5$ | 0.829 | 0.379 | 0.043 |
| 4 | $X_1$ | 0.841 | 0.368 | 0.019 |
| 5 | $X_4$ | 0.849 | 0.360 | 0.014 |

TABLE 22.15
Number of administrative units crossed by migrants

| District | Total Number of Chiefdoms | Number of Administative Units[a] | | | | | |
|---|---|---|---|---|---|---|---|
| | | 1 | 2 | 3 | 4 | 5 | > 5 |
| Bo | 15 | 8 | 4 | 2 | 0 | 0 | 1 |
| Bonthe | 12 | 10 | 2 | 0 | 0 | 0 | 0 |
| Moyamba | 14 | 8 | 2 | 2 | 2 | 0 | 0 |
| Pujehun | 11 | 9 | 0 | 0 | 0 | 1 | 1 |
| Kailahun | 14 | 9 | 1 | 2 | 0 | 0 | 2 |
| Kenema | 16 | 11 | 2 | 2 | 1 | 0 | 0 |
| Kono | 14 | 9 | 1 | 4 | 0 | 0 | 0 |
| Bombali | 13 | 6 | 0 | 2 | 2 | 3 | 0 |
| Kambia | 7 | 3 | 1 | 1 | 1 | 0 | 1 |
| Koinadugu | 11 | 6 | 3 | 1 | 0 | 0 | 1 |
| Port Loko | 9 | 8 | 0 | 1 | 0 | 0 | 0 |
| Tonkolili | 11 | 7 | 1 | 2 | 1 | 0 | 0 |
| Western Area | 1 | 0 | 0 | 0 | 0 | 0 | 1 |
| *Total* | *148* | *94* | *18* | *19* | *7* | *4* | *6* |
| *Percent* | 100.0 | 63.5 | 12.2 | 12.8 | 4.7 | 2.7 | 4.1 |

SOURCE: 1963 census.
[a] This means the minimum number of units other than the one of origin necessarily entered; thus moving to a contiguous unit counts as "1."

found to be very marked (Table 22.15). This table shows that in the majority of cases the place of first preference was a contiguous chiefdom. The 4.1 percent whose first preference is over five chiefdoms away consists of movement to units with one or more large urban centers.

For all movement from the provinces, the Western Area with Freetown the capital was the destination and for movement from the Western Area, Kakua which contains Bo, the second largest town, was the first preference. The predominance of the Western Area as the first preference node, followed by Kakua, Nongowa, and Jaiama Nimi Koro, points to the existence of a hierarchical ordering of preference nodes. From the FPA, only nine classes were delimited. In ascending order, these are:

(a) Nonnodal chiefdoms which were never selected as first preference by any other chiefdom. The 89 administrative units in this category are distributed all over the country. Generally, they are found in either poor physical areas, or very close to a chiefdom with a large urban center.
(b) Nodes for one other chiefdom. The selection of these 32 chiefdoms as first preference nodes is largely conditioned by distance.
(c) Nodes for two chiefdoms. These 14 chiefdoms could be associated with small central places that act as local centers of employment.
(d) Nodes for three chiefdoms. These 8 chiefdoms are most commonly found in the diamond mining area where the recent rapid growth of towns is the result of the heavy migration to this belt.
(e) The remaining five cases consist of single chiefdoms which have emerged as the centers of regional migration, and are the nodes for four or more chiefdoms.

From the above discussion and further study of the geography of Sierra Leone, we can come to the following conclusion about the pattern of local migration. First, except around large urban centers, migration is essentially stepwise. Confirmation of this is the fact that the country could be easily divided into migration regions. Interregional mobility is largely between the most important nodes associated with each region; otherwise the regions act as closed migration systems. Second, between rural and semi-urbanized chiefdoms, migration is largely a function of distance, but, for urbanized administrative units, flow is conditioned by the relative attraction of the places. Here a gravity-type model is operative. Finally, economically more advanced chiefdoms are important destination nodes whereas the more backward areas are zones of depopulation. The resultant internal redistribution of population has caused the development of towns and the creation of an urban hierarchy within which development and education are structured.

## URBANIZATION

As previously stated, the human landscape was completely altered by the introduction of certain innovations by the British, particularly by the pattern which initially consisted of a walled nucleated settlement with dependent agricultural hamlets within a five-mile radius. Although urbanization is a continuous process, we can isolate three phases in the development of towns in Sierra Leone. Phase I ended about 1910, phase II extended from 1911 to about 1930, and phase III stretches from 1930 to the present time.

GROWTH OF TOWNS. In the pre-1910 period, the main forces which changed the simple traditional settlement structure were the slave trade and trade in timber and oil palm. Related to these factors were the establishment of caravan routes to tap the resources of the peripheral areas, and the gradual termination of hostilities between contiguous tribes. The spread of mission schools and churches and of both indigenous and foreign trading firms gave larger villages some central place functions.

Another factor, the influence of which was to increase considerably during the 1911–1930 period, was the construction of the railway. Between 1896 and 1908, about 222 miles of rail were laid traversing the main oil palm belt joining Freetown to the eastern horn of the country. The completion of each phase stimulated trade in that area and resulted in the emergence of new centers of exchange.

For example, the opening of the Freetown-Songo line "brought a new life to the eastern villages, raising land values and enabling the people to send produce to Freetown."[14] Similarly, the Freetown-Bo line caused the emergence of Moyamba, Mano, Bo, and Rotifunk as collecting centers for produce. The railway not only generated a linear urban pattern which is directly related to it, but also stimulated the growth of intermediate collecting centers in the produce areas. Such centers were linked to a railway town by either bullock tracks or well-established trade routes.

At the beginning of the 1911–1930 phase, two developments occurred which eventually played important roles in the resultant urban structure. The first was the actual delimitation in 1911–1912 of the boundaries between Sierra Leone and her neighbors; the second was the gradual spread of Syrian traders into the interior after 1912. These two factors had different effects on urbanization trends. The former caused a truncation of the natural trading catchment of Freetown as well as the trading spheres of many frontier towns.[15] For example, by diverting the trade of the Niger headwaters to Guinea, the French seriously impaired the transit trade of places like Siemamaia, Falaka, and Kukuna. These centers eventually decreased in size and importance.

The movement of Syrian traders into the interior enhanced the commercial status of many centers, especially those along the railway. Closely associated with the diffusion of Syrian traders was the spread of European commercial establishments. Where European, Syrian, and African shops appeared in a town, a three-cornered competition ensued, and "those with large capital . . . squeeze out the small."[16] Eventually, the towns with commercial firms enlarged their trade area, and emerged as the most important centers.

[14] C. Fyfe, *A History of Sierra Leone* (London: Oxford University Press, 1962), p. 596.
[15] P. K. Mitchell, "Trade Routes of the Early Sierra Leone Protectorate," *Sierra Leone Studies*, New Series, No. 16 (1962), p. 596.
[16] Fyfe, *History of Sierra Leone*, p. 613.

The 1930 pattern is different from that of 1910 in many ways. The number of centers with more than 1,000 inhabitants increased during the period from 39 to 117, and the influence of the railway on the distribution of towns was more evident in 1930. River towns at the heads of navigation showed an absolute decline. Generally, however, the 1930 structure is a further development of the 1910 system—an infilling of the 1910 urban matrix. After 1930, the introduction of new potent forces of urbanization caused a complete remodelling of the size structure and distribution of towns in the country.

During the 1930–1969 era, the most important single stimulus to urban development was undoubtedly mining—of gold, chrome, iron ore, and diamonds. Ancillary factors included commercial rice cultivation, coastal fishing, and growth of a national road network.

Although gold mining in the Sula Mountains-Kangari Hills (east of Magburaka) commenced in 1927, it was in the post-1930 period that it attracted massive immigration into the area. Such movement resulted in the growth of many ephemeral centers. Makali, Bumbuna (an important trading center in the pre-European era), Boamahun, Gobwebu, Magbolonto, Mongeri, Mabonto, and even Magburaka all grew as a consequence of gold mining. But the gold became exhausted in the mid-1940s. Consequently there was a widespread decay of towns; only those centers like Magburaka, which had easy accessibility to roads and rail, continued to grow.

Contemporaneously with the decline of gold mining and its resultant ghost towns, was the increase in the mining of iron ore and chrome ore at Marampa near Lunsar and at Hangha, respectively. Iron ore induced the growth of Lunsar and the iron ore port of Pepel which is linked to Lunsar by rail, whereas chrome caused the rapid growth of Hangha which was already on the rail.

The highly centralized nature of iron and chrome mining considerably reduced their potency to change radically the preexisting urban situation. However, diamond mining, which is dispersed over a large area, has greatly altered the pattern since 1950 and even more so after the granting of alluvial diamond licenses to indigenes in 1956. This resulted in massive migration to the diamondiferous areas of the middle Moa and Sewa rivers. As a result, an area of traditional subsistence farming, infected by goiter and sleeping sickness, became one of the most prosperous and densely peopled sections of the country. Movement on such a scale caused alterations in the existing settlement pattern. First, many existing villages grew very fast and became commercial centers for the surrounding areas (Yormandu, Sedu, Koidu). Second, there was the growth of many new centers such as Bondayilahun, Mano Junction, and Tongo Field. And third, many large towns, outside the effective limit of diamond mining, either declined or stagnated (Kainkordu, Kayima, Jojoima). It was only in the core area of cocoa and coffee production, centered on Pendumbu, Segbwema, and Kailahun, that towns withstood the pull of the diamond mines. In essence, diamond mining caused the thinning out of the urban pattern in contiguous nondiamondiferous areas, but developed a new urban system in the valley of the Sewa River.

Besides mining, commercial rice cultivation, around the estuary of the Scarcies River, and commercial coastal fishing have caused the proliferation of small centers. The former is responsible for the dense urban cluster west of Mange, whereas the latter has made Katta, Plantain, Konakridee, and other towns along the Lungi shore into populous centers of commerce and trade.

The gradual spread of roads to join all sections of the country, as well as the increasing specialization of transport vehicles to replace the all-purpose "mammy-wagon," has caused what might be termed a transport revolution. Many remote areas are now easily accessible, and journey by road can be made in relative comfort. In addition, transport by road in Sierra Leone is more flexible and faster than by rail. The result of all this has been the concentration of trade away from the railway to the roads. This has caused a decline in the growth rate of many railway towns, but a marked increase in the population of nodal centers like Makeni, Port Loko, Kambia, Magburaka, and Kabala. One interesting fact to be observed is the persistence of towns at heads of navigation. Being served by roads, many of these have continued as collecting and marketing centers but with a new axis of trade. Produce is transported by the creeks in dugouts to these places from which they are sent by lorry either to larger interior trading centers or direct to Freetown. Of all the towns of this type, only Port Loko has continued a substantial trade by sea with Freetown, and here proximity to the capital has been an important factor. Freetown, including the nearby centers, continued to grow very rapidly during the 1930–1963 period.

The resultant urban pattern, revealed by the 1963 national census, exhibits many components. There is the new urban system of the Sewa River caused by diamond mining; the persistence of old linear developments along the railway and at heads of navigation; the extremely clustered structure around Freetown and the Scarcies River estuary; the new urban pattern of the road system; and the isolated mining towns of Lunsar and Pepel. Indeed, by 1963, there had developed in Sierra Leone an urban network consisting of both small and large towns. This pattern is quite unlike that of either 1910 or 1930.

CHANGES IN URBAN STRUCTURE AND RATES OF URBANIZATION. These processes of urbanization caused the concentration of people into larger nucleated settlements. It is clear from Table 22.16 that irrespective of the selected urban threshold, there has been an increase in the number of town dwellers. Between 1910 and 1930, the pattern of concentration of population seems to have largely maintained the 1910 position, but by 1963 the increase in size of centers with population between 2,000 and 5,000 was appreciable. From this, it could be inferred that the 1910–1930 pattern of migration was focused on all towns, whereas in the 1930–

TABLE 22.16
Percentage of total population in urban centers above various thresholds in 1910, 1930, and 1963

| Population Threshold | 1910 | 1930 | 1963 |
|---|---|---|---|
| 1,000 | 6.6 | 13.7 | 25.4 |
| 2,000 | 3.8 | 6.4 | 19.2 |
| 4,000 | 2.8 | 4.1 | 14.8 |
| 5,000 | 2.4 | 3.8 | 13.1 |
| Freetown | 2.4 | 3.1 | 5.9 |

1963 period, it was increasingly concentrated on the large towns with more employment possibilities.

By any Western standards, the level of urbanization is very low, still reflecting the basic colonial structure of the economy. In such a situation, the capital emerges as the only center of secondary production and the major link between the interior and the Western technological society. Such a city becomes the focal point of migration, experiences mercurial growth, and maintains a stranglehold on the whole national economy. This is more serious when this city is also the only important port in the country.

Increase in the number of urban residents caused both the growth of large centers and an increase in their number. The number of towns with a population above 1,000 grew from 39 in 1910 to 117 in 1930, and was 168 at the time of the 1963 national census (Table 22.17). As expected, there is an inverse relationship between size-class and the number of centers in that class. In spite of this evident preponderance of smaller centers, their relative dominance is decreasing. For example, in 1930, 83.8 percent of the towns had population between 1,000 and 1,999, but in 1963, their share had dropped to 63.7 percent. One direct cause of this is the increase in the number of larger centers in the 3,000–14,999 range; evidence of the development of a central place pattern characterized by the nesting of smaller lower-order centers in the trade sphere of the larger ones. All this

TABLE 22.17

Distribution of urban centers by size-class in 1910, 1930, and 1963

| Size-Class | 1910 | | 1930 | | 1963 | |
|---|---|---|---|---|---|---|
| | Number | Percent | Number | Percent | Number | Percent |
| 1,000–1,999 | 32 | 82.0 | 98 | 83.8 | 107 | 63.7 |
| 2,000–3,999 | 5 | 12.8 | 15 | 12.8 | 35 | 20.8 |
| 4,000–5,999 | 1 | 2.6 | 3 | 2.6 | 13 | 7.7 |
| 6,000–8,999 | — | — | — | — | 6 | 3.6 |
| 9,000–14,999 | — | — | — | — | 5 | 3.0 |
| 15,000–29,999 | — | — | — | — | 1 | 0.6 |
| Above 29,999 | 1 | 2.6 | 1 | 0.8 | 1 | 0.6 |
| | 39 | 100.0 | 117 | 100.0 | 168 | 100.0 |

has been possible because of large-scale road construction and diamond mining.

The relative decrease in the number of smaller towns is directly reflected in their decreasing share of the total urban population (Table 22.18), from 42.8 percent in 1910 to 24.6 percent in 1963. The trend, however, was more marked in the 1930–1963 period when their population increased by only 6,771 or 2.2 percent of the total urban population increase. Towns in the 2,000–3,999 size-class maintained a rather constant proportion: 17.4 and 17.8 percent of the urban population during the two periods respectively. Urban growth between 1930 and 1963 was largely focused on the larger towns, including the capital. During this period, towns in the 6,000–29,000 group received 41.9 percent of the urban population increase, and Freetown alone enjoyed the largest share of 23.2 percent. Looking at it from another angle, we see that of a total increase of 312,653 in the number of urban dwellers between 1930 and 1963, about 65.1 percent were concentrated in the 13 largest towns. The recent accelerated growth of inter-mediate-size towns such as these in Sierra Leone has also been reported by King in a developed Westernized country like New Zealand.[17]

Using grouped data for the analysis of urban population change completely obscures the behavior of individual towns. To compensate for this, population change for the 168 centers in 1963 was analyzed by comparing their populations in 1930 and 1963 respectively. On double logarithmic graph paper, the population of each center in 1963 was plotted against its population in 1930. Since it has logarithmic scale on both axes,

[17] L. J. King, "Urbanization in an Agriculturally Dependent Society; Some Implications in New Zealand," *Tijdschrift voor Economische en Geografie*, LVI (1965), 12–21.

TABLE 22.18

Population of urban centers by size-class in 1910, 1930, and 1963

| Size-Class | 1910 | | 1930 | | 1963 | |
|---|---|---|---|---|---|---|
| | Population | Percent | Population | Percent | Population | Percent |
| 1 000–1,999 | 34,488 | 42.8 | 129,865 | 53.7 | 136,636 | 24.6 |
| 2 000–3,999 | 14,121 | 15.3 | 40,067 | 16.5 | 95,631 | 17.2 |
| 4 000–5,999 | 4,616 | 5.0 | 16,639 | 6.9 | 63,156 | 11.4 |
| 6 000–8,999 | — | — | — | — | 39,893 | 7.2 |
| 9,000–14,999 | — | — | — | — | 64,737 | 11.7 |
| 15,000–29,999 | — | — | — | — | 26,613 | 4.8 |
| Above 29,999 | 34,090 | 36.9 | 55.359 | 22.9 | 127,917 | 23.1 |
| | 87,315 | 100.0 | 241,930 | 100.0 | 554,583 | 100.0 |

along "straight lines drawn upward to the right at an angle of 45°,"[18] all points have the same percentage population change. From a study of this graph, the following conclusions can be drawn:

(1) The centers which decreased in size are mainly small towns just above the threshold figure of 1,000. At the same time, the growth of many new small-sized towns shows that the decay of such towns in formerly prosperous areas often is compensated by a new development in regions of more recent economic prosperity.

(2) The extreme mutability of the urban system is evidenced from the fact that, of the 117 towns in 1930, only 69 maintained their urban status by 1963; and, of that number, 27 had decreased in size. The 1963 urban pattern therefore is made up of 69 old-established towns and 99 new towns. Perhaps by 1973, the date for the next national census, the internal reorganization of urban centers may have changed considerably, because new mining activities (bauxite and rutile) are now transforming the landscape, the ethnic structure, and the settlement pattern of the southwest.

(3) Centers which have experienced rapid growth are mainly those in which the predominant occupation is either mining, commercial rice cultivation, or commercial fishing. But the absence of large towns in the latter two categories shows that agriculture and fishing are not very potent generators of urbanization. At the same time, mining has evidently caused the phenomenal growth of towns like Lunsar, Koindu, Yengema, Fomaia, Pepel, and Peyima. Such rapid growth is bound to considerably influence the shape of the rank-size graph of the whole country.

As a result of the analysis of the urban dissimilarities in 1910, 1930, and 1963, it can be postulated that strong contrasts exist between their different town-size hierarchies. To test this, both the shapes of the actual rank-size graphs, as well as the extent to which each graph deviates from the generalized empirical rule relating city-rank to population, are examined and measured.

The rank-size graphs of the country in 1910, 1930, and 1963 show some common features. They are generally concave, and deviate considerably from the theoretical pattern. They also show "knick points," (i.e., points of abrupt change) which are especially striking on those for 1930 and 1963. In spite of these similarities, there are very marked contrasts between them. First, convexity decreases from 1910 to 1963, directly reflecting the decreasing primacy of Freetown. The city's index of primacy decreased from 13.5 in 1910 to 8.1 in 1930 and was as low as 4.8 in 1963. Second, the knick on the 1930 graph is between 2,000 and 3,000 along the population axis, whereas in 1963, it is between 7,000 and 14,000. Here an analogy seems to exist between the movement of the knick on the rank-size graphs and the retreat of knick points on rivers. To carry the analogy further, just as the final disappearance of the knick point upstream tends to result in a "graded" profile, so the development of larger provincial towns and the eventual decrease in Freetown's primacy may finally cause the knick point on the graph to disappear and a lognormal curve to result.

One persisting characteristic of all these rank-size graphs is the primacy of the capital. Such an urban structure, Berry[19] observed, is often true of fairly small territories where a few factors mold the urban system. It is also characteristic of countries with a dual economy, a low per capita income, an export-orientated economy, and a colonial past.[20] All these characteristics are found in Sierra Leone. It is hoped that with the diversification of the economic base by the development of industries outside the Greater Freetown area, as well as with the creation of an improved road network and the continuous

[18] B. L. J. Berry, *Geography of Market Centers and Retail Distribution* (Englewood Cliffs, N.J.: Prentice-Hall, 1967), p. 26.

[19] B. L. J. Berry, "Cities as Systems within Systems of Cities," *Regional Science Association, Papers and Proceedings*, XIII (1964), p. 149.

[20] A. S. Lansky, "Some Generalizations Concerning Primate Cities," *Annals of American Geographers*, LV (1965), 506–13.

growth of many large provincial towns like Bo, Makeni, Koidu, and Lunsar, the primacy of the city will continue to decrease.

The urban network of Sierra Leone is quite unstable and will remain so as long as the main agents dictating the spatial distribution of towns are still ephemeral. The country's urban mesh will only be stable if these temporary deforming factors are either neutralized by more permanent factors like commercial mechanized agriculture, expanded retail trade, and substantial secondary industries, or completely replaced by these more rooted and less evanescent agents.[21]

[21] M. E. Harvey, "The Changing Urban Network of Sierra Leone," *Proceedings of the 21st International Geographical Congress* (New Delhi, 1969).

CONSEQUENCES OF URBANIZATION. The uneven distribution of educational and social amenities in Sierra Leone has generated both urban-urban and rural-urban migration. Such large-scale population shifts have caused the rapid growth of many centers. With this continuous influx of migrants from different cultural and economic backgrounds, the towns of Sierra Leone, like those of other developing countries, have many problems—congestion, increasing separation of the individual from place of work, uncontrolled urban sprawl, unemployment, and problems of readjustment to an individualistic society.[22]

[22] Harvey, "A Geographical Study," chap. 15.

# CHAPTER TWENTY-THREE

# Some Influential Attitudes about Family Limitation

## and the Use of Contraceptives among the Professional Group in Sierra Leone

BARBARA HARRELL-BOND

THIS chapter surveys some of the ways in which traditional attitudes and values persist and influence the practice of birth control among the professional group in Sierra Leone.[1] The discussion rests upon data gathered in an anthropological study of marriage among this group. The statistical material was obtained from questionnaires administered to a sample of university students and from personal interviews with a sample of the adult professional group. Anthropologists have long been aware of the importance of what Davis and Blake called the "intermediate variables" which affect fertility control,[2] or, as Freedman put it, "The means of fertility control which stand between social organization and the social norms on one hand and fertility on the other."[3] Few studies have devoted themselves to an examination of these factors.

Stycos has accused demographers of ignoring psychological, social and cultural facts which influence human behavior and he noted that "even now . . . we know more about what people expect, want, and do with

---

[1] Although this study falls under the general rubric of "elite" studies in Africa, I prefer to avoid this term because of its imprecise nature. Since my aim was to provide some quantified data, I chose to narrow my definition of "elite" to include only those persons who held a university degree or equivalent professional qualifications and their spouses. Although there are many persons in what would be described as the "elite" group who do not hold such qualifications, all those persons who do hold a university degree in Sierra Leone are, almost by this criterion alone, members of the "elite."

"Traditional" in this paper is used in the sense that Hoselitz used it (B. F. Hoselitz, "Tradition and Economic Growth," in R. Braibanti and J. J. Spengler, eds., *Tradition, Values and Socioeconomic Development* (Durham, N.C.: Duke University Press, 1961), meaning that the attribute has a history and that it has characterized that society for a considerable time. In the case of Sierra Leone, it also refers to a pattern of social relations and the organization of family life which can be observed in villages today. Professional people, when discussing this pattern of life, refer to it either as the "traditional" or the "native" way of life.
[2] K. Davis and J. Blake, "Social Structure and Fertility: An Analytical Framework," *Economic Development and Cultural Change*, IV, 3 (April 1956).
[3] R. Freedman, "The Sociology of Human Fertility: A Trend Report and Bibliography," *Current Sociology*, X-XI, 2 (1961–1962).

respect to planting wheat or purchasing TV sets than with respect to having babies."[4] Part of the explanation for this lack of data, as Stycos pointed out, is that demographers are usually drawn from disciplines which are highly suspicious of "soft" data collected in the area of attitudes and opinions. DeMott has, however, suggested that this is only part of the problem.[5] He has accused sex researchers of being a "fearful lot" and noted that the reactions to the "sex-lab" approach reveal that the "long struggle waged by scientific and literary minds on behalf of the cause of intellectual inclusiveness, . . . a struggle which began in the 19th century, . . . [is still] unfinished." Studies of attitudes and behavior relating to sexuality are still relatively rare. Moreover, those that do appear tend to be limited to investigations of the "pathological."

Anthropologists' particular theoretical concerns have rarely led them to conduct studies of "sexology." Moreover, some of the anthropological data that have been collected around this topic have been misused or construed to support popular myths about the supposed promiscuity (or "naturalness," depending on the viewpoint of the commentator) of the "primitives." Now that these so-called primitives have moved into the contemporary world of town life, investigators have tended to approach their subjects with the same reticence they might feel when investigating sexual attitudes and behavior in their own culture. Even such research as the Masters-Johnson study has been accused of including elements of "evasiveness and self-censorship."[6] Their report included "testimonials" of participants who had been "cured" of certain sexual inhibitions as a result of their participation in the experiments. We can agree with DeMott when he says that to include such statements in a research re-

port looks all too much like defensive answers to those who would "vilify sex research as sin." For example, Bott's now almost classic study of marriage among a group of couples in London practically ignored the topic of sexual relations.[7] She discussed the reticence she encountered in her initial interview with couples, "Although few couples ever mentioned it directly, *it was obvious* that most of them were thinking about whether they would be called upon to discuss their intimate affairs, especially sexual relations . . . ."[8] The couples were assured this would not be required unless they were willing, and never with her but only with a psychologist. Bott reported on these subsequent interviews and stated that the psychologist took written notes on the conversations, "*except* when the couples were discussing physical sexuality or some topic that *seemed particularly embarrassing* . . . ."[9] Stycos has commented on another and somewhat related problem of investigations of sexual behavior and particularly contraceptive practices. This is the tendency to ignore the importance of the attitudes of men when they are perhaps deserving of "more attention,"

Given the fact of male dominance and the fact that fertility declines have historically been accomplished by means of male contraceptive techniques in many countries, males cannot be ignored. Moreover, because of their generally higher literacy, prestige, sophistication, and range of social relationships, they would not only be

[4] J. Mayone Stycos, "Problems of Fertility Control in Underdeveloped Area," in Garrett Hardin, ed., *Population Evolution And Birth Control* (London: W. H. Freeman and Company, 1969).

[5] Benjamin DeMott, "Literature, Science and the Sex-lab War," *New Society*, VIII (January 1970).

[6] *Ibid.*

[7] E. Bott, *Family and Social Network* (London: Tavistock 1957). These remarks are not meant to imply that the topic is not sensitive and difficult to research but only to emphasize some of the problems which have contributed to its neglect. In my own field work I encountered problems from an unexpected source. Members of the expatriate or European community were acquainted with members of the Sierra Leonean professional group. Sometimes these Europeans were curious about my research. I always described it as a study of family life and family organization. Frequently the response was, "Oh, you're doing a Kinsey report." On several occasions individuals would joke about this in the presence of Sierra Leoneans. One European asked my research assistant, who was an African, if I was finding out how many times Africans copulate each week.

[8] *Ibid.*, p. 18, emphasis added.

[9] *Ibid.*, p. 25, emphasis added.

accessible to more new ideas but more effective disseminators of these ideas.[10]

Although the design for this field study included roughly an equal number of men and women from the "elite group" when the investigation began of how information about the use of contraceptives was disseminated, the importance of considering the attitudes of men was emphasized. The research was an examination of marriage and family organization among the professional group in Sierra Leone.

One assumption underlying studies of "elite" groups in developing countries is that the patterns revealed are indicative of the direction of change taken by the society as a whole. It is based upon a kind of "commonsense" observation of how symbols of status "percolate" downward through a population. For example, in traditional society a high value was placed on having a large number of children. An examination of the attitudes and practices of the professional group as regards family limitation and practices of birth control might provide an indication of the presence of a new trend throughout society. But most likely the intersocietal relationships are so complicated that change is not so lineal.

Professional couples in Sierra Leone are still very much a part of the traditional extended family. It is important to see their behavior in relation to the large group of relatives who can claim traditional kinship obligations. Many of these relatives are illiterate villagers. Often they have together made a significant contribution toward the education of their professional relative. They now expect that in turn he will help them. They ask him to educate their children, assist them in achieving political favors, and help them to get jobs; and they expect him to provide hospitality when they come to the city. Professional people do not so much set a pattern of behavior for others to follow to acquire prestige in terms of urban values, but rather, because of their accomplishments and their position vis-à-vis their relatives, they

provide access to the resources for achievement in the urban setting for the other members of their family. That a professional couple carefully limit the number of children they produce may not even be very obvious since their households almost always include one or more of their relatives' children. In short, the household of professional couples does not provide a "model" of a small nuclear family. Rather, for them, family limitation appears to be an economic necessity because of the high cost of maintaining the standard of living expected of the professional group (this includes large cars, houses, Western-style clothing, and imported foods along with the costs of school fees for their children) and the enormous financial burden of extended family obligations.

Anthropologists have often noted the association of prestige with the production of large numbers of children in kin-based societies. Douglas has discussed this question and its relationship to fertility control, "A small primitive population which is homogeneously committed to the same pattern of values and to which the ladders of social status offer a series of worthwhile goals which had not required large families for their attainment is likely to apply restrictive demographic policies."[11] But, she continues, "When social change occurs so rapidly that the prestige structure is no longer consistent, we should expect population explosions to occur." She remarks on the apathy and resistance often encountered by the "well-educated and the well-to-do" in their efforts to influence the "teeming poorer classes" to practice birth control. She admonishes those who would succeed to examine their prestige structure and ask, "Have the ladders of high prestige enough rungs to reach into the most populous sections of the community?" She concludes her discussion with a recommendation which does not advance beyond suggesting that population control is simply a matter of manipulating the symbols of prestige, "If given the *right incentives* some kind of population control would be likely to

[10] Stycos, "Problems of Fertility Control."

[11] M. Douglas, "Population Control in Primitive Groups," *British Journal of Sociology* (September 1966).

develop among the poor as it apparently has amongst those who seek to administer the demographic policy."[12]

The traditional family system in Sierra Leone does associate high prestige with the person who could acquire a large number of wives, children, and dependents. Professional people are now fully aware that they cannot afford to support large numbers of children and also enjoy the symbols of prestige in the town, but in a society where large numbers of children are associated with prestige a whole potpourri of attitudes, beliefs, and practices has also grown up to support and maintain the "structure" of that association. When change occurs in such societies it may become patently clear to everyone that family limitation is highly desirable and that large families are an encumbrance to those climbing the "rungs of the ladders of high prestige." At the same time it may be less clear how certain beliefs, attitudes, and practices, often having intense emotional content, stand in the way of widespread adoption of methods of birth control.

Before discussing some of these beliefs, attitudes, and practices, it is necessary to distinguish between two groups of people in Sierra Leone, the Creoles and the provincials who make up the professional group, and to describe some of their characteristics. The British established Freetown on the peninsula in 1787 as a colony for the resettlement of slaves who had been freed and returned from the United States, Canada, and Great Britain. These people, who came to be called Creoles, had originated from many parts of the west coast of Africa. Cut off as they were from their own traditions, they were highly susceptible to the "benefits" of Western education and religion through the efforts of philanthropists, missionaries, and the British government. Although today they number less than 2 percent of the population of the whole country, they still represent the majority of the professional group.

The indigenous population of Sierra Leone is made up of about 16 tribal groups. Since the turn of the century these provincial people

have made rapid educational advances and already a significant proportion of the professional group is of tribal or provincial origin, but the vast majority continue to live in small villages and towns. Their education has come largely through the auspices of missionary-supported schools and their attitudes toward marriage have also been greatly influenced by religious ideas.

The majority of the professional group is Christian. All the members of this group claim to practice monogamous marriage. The majority of both students and adults disagreed with the statement, "I would prefer a system which allows a man more than one wife." Although marriages by customary law (exchange of bridewealth) and by Moslem law are legal in Sierra Leone, most of these people say that they would not feel "married" without a church wedding ceremony under the "general law" of Sierra Leone.[13]

All but 13 percent of the sample of men have lived either in Great Britain, Europe, or the United States and over half of their wives have also lived abroad. Both Creoles and provincials see the Western pattern of marriage and family life as superior to the traditional polygamous system.[14]

The professional group views itself as Westernized in both attitude and style of life. They approve the Western pattern of husband and wife cooperating in caring for the children and sharing the household tasks.[15] Although most have other relatives living with them, they express the belief that the ideal arrangement of the household would include only a

---

[12] Ibid., emphasis added.

[13] "General law" as practiced in Sierra Leone is based upon British law.

[14] "Western," although an imprecise term in sociological literature, has a definite meaning to Sierra Leoneans. It includes the way of life as they have observed it in their years of study abroad as well as from their observations of Westerners living in Sierra Leone. It also includes the information gathered from reading, films, and the teachings of missionaries. Their main criticisms of Western family life are the way in which old people are neglected and the formality of family relationships.

[15] In practice married couples maintain a more traditional pattern of segregation of roles in terms of division of domestic duties.

TABLE 23.1
Ideal number of children

| Number of Children | University Students (percent) | Professional Group (percent) |
|---|---|---|
| 1–3 | 21 | 31 |
| 4 | 62 | 49 |
| 5+ | 15 | 13 |
| Other ("no response" & one in each group stated "as many as possible") | 2 | 7 |
| *Totals* | 100 | 100 |
| | N = 229 | N = 139 |

man, his wife, and their children. Even though present conditions do not allow them personally to organize their households in this manner, 66 percent thought that in the future this would be the normative household composition in Sierra Leone. In interviews with the professional sample, 85 percent agreed with the statement, "My way of life as far as marriage and family life are concerned is based more upon Western ideas than upon traditional African ideas."

In contrast to the traditional value of having as many children as possible, they also favor "small" families, implying an awareness of the necessity of family limitation. Table 23.1 shows the responses of university students and the professional group to the question about the ideal number of children.[16] Clearly, they idealize having no more than four children.

[16] We cannot assume that if professional couples limit their families to four children or less this will significantly affect population growth. Both the university students and the professional sample were asked about the size of their family of orientation. Sixty-seven percent of the university students and 64 percent of the professional group had four or fewer brothers and sisters by the same mother and father. However, among the professional group 83 percent had three or fewer brothers and sisters still alive and 23 percent were now only children. On the other hand, this does not account for half brothers and sisters. Among the university students, 65 percent had at least one sibling on their father's side and 26 percent had at least one on their mother's side. Similarly, among the professional sample, 58 percent had at least one brother or sister on their father's side and 19 percent had at least one on their mother's side.

Whether or not they are succeeding in limiting the number of children to four is difficult to ascertain.

There are several problems involved in collecting accurate information on the numbers of children born to members of the professional group. Although education usually delays marriage, it is not unusual for men to have fathered several children before contracting a "formal" marriage. As one informant put it:

Sometimes before a man gets married, you have left school. You have got an ambition to become a doctor, lawyer, or anything. You are still struggling either to get a scholarship or to raise enough funds for you to go overseas to study but you are already full grown. You have gone to college and finished but you decide to work and save money. During that period you don't want to commit yourself by marrying, but still you have got girl friends. (Perhaps) one of them is impregnated and you get issue from her. You accept the children as your own children although the woman is not your wife. So by the time you get married, after your profession(al training) you will have four or five children outside. This is what happens in the majority of cases. Before you decide to choose a wife you will already have four or five children.

Married men also establish relationships with women outside the marriage. As one man said:

I think polygamy just continues here in Freetown (because) we men who have married one wife according to Christian or civil marriages, we have got girl friends here and there. A married man in Freetown will have four or five houses where he has got sweethearts. He is responsible for them, pays their rent and so forth, but he is still married.

Sometimes these "outside" wives, as they are called, have children. These children are a particular source of tension within the marriage and people are reluctant to report them. It was not possible to ask people *how many* outside children they had. The professional sample was asked to indicate if either they or their spouse were responsible for children born outside this marriage, and 24 percent indicated they were.

Respondents were asked about the age, sex, and the residences of each of their children.[17] (The hope was that perhaps this would provide more accurate information about the number of children professional couples had.) Seven percent of the children reported were living in another household. The following case study illustrates the problems of making an accurate count:

This informant had had two children by two different women before leaving Sierra Leone to study in Britain. One of these unions was regularized by the exchange of bridewealth. One child was being cared for by his [the respondent's] parents and the other was with its mother. While he was in Britain, this man lived with an Irish girl. They had two children. Upon his return to Sierra Leone, he "married" and he and his wife had four children. During my field work this man had another child with a girl friend. His wife had also had a child before this marriage and it was being cared for by her father. Nevertheless, in the interview, this couple only reported the four children living in the household.

Appreciating the extent of the inaccuracy involved, it is sufficient to state that the mean number of children reported by the professional group (which included 20 percent "never married" men and women) was 2.1. Only 10 percent of the sample reported having more than four children. It would appear that people tend to report a number of children within the range of the family size they consider as "ideal." Moreover, it is equally difficult to predict the size of the completed families of these professional couples since most of them are still of childbearing age (62 percent of the men and 66 percent of the women are under 40 years of age). Moreover, 65 percent of the sample of married couples said they wished to have more children and 15 percent of the wives were pregnant (or were "not sure" if they were pregnant) at the time of the interview. The persons in the professional sample were asked "open-ended"

[17] Under the law in Sierra Leone, mothers of illegitimate children have the first right to the custody of their children. It is, however, a general assumption that children belong to their fathers and sometimes married men will take their illegitimate children to their parents or another relative to be reared.

TABLE 23.2
Attitudes toward having a large family

(a) *"WHAT WOULD YOU SAY WAS THE BEST THING ABOUT HAVING A 'LARGE' FAMILY?"* (in percent)

| Response | Males | Females |
|---|---|---|
| Nothing good | 52 | 56 |
| Mutual financial assistance | 11 | 4 |
| Companionship | 11 | 37 |
| Security in old age | 4 | 1 |
| A better chance some will survive and make good | 6 | 1 |
| Better preparation for life to grow up in a large household | 1 | 1 |
| Perpetuate Creole group | 1 | 0 |
| Status | 8 | 0 |
| Preserve the family name | 5 | 0 |
| No response | 1 | 0 |
| *Totals* | 100 | 100 |
| | N = 82 | N = 59 |

(b) *"WHAT WOULD YOU SAY WAS THE WORST THING ABOUT HAVING A LARGE FAMILY?"*

| | Males | Females |
|---|---|---|
| Financial costs (specifically mentioned educational costs) | 19 | 20 |
| Finances | 50 | 58 |
| Too much responsibility | 4 | 1 |
| Individual child not well cared for | 10 | 12 |
| Burden on the mother's health | 4 | 3 |
| Loss of privacy | 4 | 1 |
| Nothing bad | 1 | 1 |
| Other | 6 | 3 |
| No response | 2 | 1 |
| *Totals* | Percent 100 | 100 |
| | N = 81 | N = 59 |

questions about their attitudes toward "large" families. Table 23.2 shows their responses to these questions. These answers reveal changing attitudes toward having many children and show that the financial requirements of large numbers of children are the chief reason for family limitation. It has already been noted that professional people are called on to support and educate large numbers of relatives' children. People often expressed the view that they would prefer to invest in the education of a few more of the children of these relatives than to have more than three or four children of their own. The more relatives who receive an education and move into the wage-earning economy, the more persons there will be to share the burden of extended family obligations.

The concern with the need for family limitation is reflected in the development of the professional groups of the Planned Parenthood Association of Sierra Leone. In 1969 they presented a play which was entitled *I de inɔ du* which is a Krio phrase meaning, "There is some, but not enough for anyone else." This phrase usually is employed when relatives make requests which cannot be honored. The play was very successful and performances were repeated by popular demand. It emphasized the constant problem of insufficient money to pay school fees and buy food and clothing for large numbers of children. This Krio song was part of the drama and became very popular in Freetown:

Who is there now that doesn't know the world has become difficult for us?
Who is there now that doesn't know the world has turned upside down?
Who is there now who doesn't know money is finished in town?
Money is finished
It is there, but it is insufficient.
Some people are better off than their mates.
Like our little children in their different homes.
Some have few children, others have many.
It is there, but it is insufficient.[18]

<hr>

18
U de nao wey nɔno se wɔl dɔɛ trɔɛ paɔ wi
U de nao wey nɔno se wɔl dɔn tɔn oba
U de nao wey nɔno se kɔpɔ dɔn
Kɔpɔ dɔn na tɔɛ
I de inɔ du
sɔm man you kin bɛtɛ pas in kɔmpin smɔl
Lɛkɛ dɛn wi lik piking dɛn na dɛn difrɛn om
I de inɔ du

TABLE 23.3
Methods of contraception ever used

| Method | Percent |
| --- | --- |
| Durex | 32 |
| Foam tablet | 2 |
| Jelly | 2 |
| Diaphragm | 5 |
| Rhythm method | 3 |
| *Coitus interruptus* | 7 |
| The pill | 17 |
| Surgery (either male or female) | 2 |
| Abstinence | 4 |
| IUD | 12 |
| Douche | 0 |
| Nothing | 12 |
| *Totals* | 100 |
| | N = 184[a] |

[a] N > than sample because some respondents indicated using more than one method.

Since the professional group as a whole approves of small families, the problem of methods of family limitation must be considered. The majority of the professional sample (85 percent) indicated that they "approved of the use of contraceptives. They were asked to state what methods of contraception they had used at any time in their lives. These responses are shown in Table 23.3.

We see that only 16 percent indicated they had never used any method of contraception. Nevertheless, when these people were asked about what methods they were presently using, quite a different picture emerged. These responses are shown in Table 23.4. Forty-seven percent were not using any method of contraception although they did not indicate that they wished to have more children.[19] It

<hr>

[19] Although 18 percent of these said they were planning to do so in the future, we cannot rely very much on these responses. The interview included a list of contraceptives and then an opportunity for the respondent to indicate, if he was not using any method, why not. The choices offered included: not using any method because wife is pregnant, because more children are desired, because of religious convictions, not using any now but plan to in the future, or not using any and do not plan to in the future. Respondents would be less likely to admit that they did not plan to use contraceptives because of their firm commitments to family limitation and the obvious question which this "inconsistency" would raise.

TABLE 23.4

Methods of contraception presently used

| Method | Percent |
|---|---|
| Durex | 9 |
| Foam tablet | 0 |
| Jelly | 0 |
| Diaphragm | 1 |
| Rhythm method | 2 |
| *Coitus interruptus* | 0 |
| The pill | 9 |
| Surgery (either male or female) | 2 |
| Abstinence | 2 |
| IUD | 10 |
| Douche | 1 |
| Not using any because wife is pregnant or more children are desired | 14 |
| Not using any now, but plan to in the future | 14 |
| Nothing; Not using any and never plan to do so | 36[a] |
| *Totals* | 100 |
| | N = 140 |

[a] Included two persons who were not using contraceptives because of religious convictions.

was also clear from discussion with married men that they were often reporting the method of contraception they were using in their extramarital relationships and that many of these were using no birth control methods in their marriages other than abstinence. So we see that the continued involvement of the professional person with the members of his extended family and the financial obligations this imposes, together with the high cost of educating his own children, motivates him to limit his family. Certain beliefs and attitudes which are part of his traditional background, however, complicate ready acceptance of the practice of contraceptive techniques.

To begin with there are practically no traditional methods of contraception in Sierra Leone. Some native medicine men do supply special cords which women tie around their waists to prevent conception. Sometimes women from the towns arrange to purchase them. The Temnes have a practice called "turning the womb" (*Ka lafthi an puthu*).

Certain manipulations are performed by old women who had acquired this skill and afterward the woman is incapable of conceiving. These practices earn much disapproval. Today older women will react to questions about family limitation with such comments as, "God, who separates the mouth at birth, will put food in it" (*gɔd we plit yu mɔt go put it di*) or, "God is not going to give you a load that you are unable to bear" (*gɔd nɔde gi yu lod we yu nɔgo ebul tot*). Women who complain about having too many children are admonished "You just have to be patient and put up with it" (*na fɔ biya*).

Abortion is also practically unknown in traditional society. Today abortion is thought to be quite common among educated single girls and some married women. As one informant put it:

Abortion is very rare in villages. Most villagers are afraid of committing artificial abortion. This abortion is actually committed with girls going to school. They are unmarried and they don't want to have issue . . . . Abortion is very common in the larger towns and it is mainly among school girls and young girls who have left school and are working. They are not engaged and so it is socially wrong for them to have issue when they have not yet married. It would spoil their chances of getting married. But the married woman (in the village) the happiest thing that can happen to her is to get children. A woman can get twenty. They are able to send them to school by and large or they can send them to work on their farms so there is no fear.

When the persons in the professional sample were asked if they thought abortion was common in Sierra Leone today, 55 percent responded that they thought it was very common and specified it occurred among the educated only, 21 percent said they "didn't know," and 22 percent said that it was not common. Among the professional sample 30 percent also agreed that they saw no objection to married couples using abortion as one means of limiting the number of children born to them. Of those who disagreed, very few had "religious" reasons for their objections; they were mainly concerned with the effects of abortion on the future fertility of the woman. (If abortions were made legal, many undoubtedly would cease to have objections if they were assured that such operations would be conducted under adequate medical conditions.)[20]

It is impossible to get an idea of how widespread the practice of abortion is a method of family limitation. Among the professional sample of the women who were reported as having had miscarriages, 20 percent admitted that they were induced.[21]

It is also difficult to determine how effective the methods are which these women claim they use. There are a variety of things which are thought to act as abortifacients: blueing mixed with gin, quinine, and some native leaves and herbs. Doctors report that women also resort to inserting an instrument to induce bleeding. In spite of the considerable number who do not object to abortion and those who admit to having had an abortion, the following excerpt from a college newspaper illustrates the concern over this problem.

*Abortionists in Our Midst.* The rate of abortion in the campus is increasing every term. I am not trying to be biased against anyone but to say the truth regardless of who gets hurt.

Right now in campus, three girls are suffering abortion. What pains me most is that these people have once suffered abortion. They have not got any steady boyfriends only the usual froys. Some abortion leads to sterilization and one cannot tell which one will lead to that. Many people have suffered abortion more (sic) once since they came

to college, and if the percentages of abortionists to non-abortionists (that is, people who have had abortions) is calculated, one would be surprises (sic). Does this mean that our girls are more sexually inclined? I can only advise them to control their sexual feelings.

Statistics shows that girls who go steady suffer abortion more frequently than other girls.[22]

The failure to use contraceptives is a serious problem among university students. Traditionally a girl married shortly after joining the secret society (see p. 482). Today education delays marriage, but young people view themselves as qualified to assume adult sexual behavior once they have been initiated into the secret society. Unlike the majority of the population, university young people have access to contraceptive devices through the college medical doctor. Part of the reason they fail to use contraceptives is due to lack of information and a sense of embarrassment about asking for them. Many fear that any contraceptive device could lead to sterility. Students told me of cases where they believed the condom had come off during intercourse and had gone up inside the uterus causing infection and sterility. Oral contraceptives are avoided because of the same fears. Students often related stories about friends and acquaintances, who were "the kind of girls who used those things" or had "dissolved" pregnancies, and who, when they married, were consequently unable to conceive.

There are more subtle complications to the ready acceptance of contraceptives. Women who use them are thought to be more susceptible to the temptation of promiscuity. In a traditional society women are viewed as being fundamentally promiscuous. One of the perpetual problems facing the polygamous husband in the village is controlling the sexual behavior of his wives. "Women damage" cases (women accused of committing adultery) are the most frequent problem brought before the local courts. Traditional

---

[20] Although abortions are illegal in Sierra Leone, no doctor has ever been charged with committing this offence. It is relatively easy to arrange for an abortion and one nursing home is known to cater mainly to abortion cases.

[21] Since people were being asked to admit to having committed an offense, we can assume that these figures do not exaggerate the numbers. Since these figures were reported by both husbands and wives they may under-represent the picture since husbands would be less likely to admit or even know that their wives had induced an abortion. They also do not show how many abortions a woman may have induced. In my intensive interviews I found that it was quite common for women at least to attempt to do this. One woman admitted inducing one abortion and then, after telling me how she accomplished this, said, "I always say I won't try anymore to dissolve a pregnancy after three months."

[22] Fourah Bay College mimeograph news sheet, 1968. "Froy" is a term for a casual girl or boyfriend and refers to the kinds of persons who just go from one person to another with no permanent attachments.

society has the institution of the women's secret society (*Bundu* or *Sande*). Part of the initiation of girls into adult roles includes the practice of female circumcision or the cliteridectomy. The whole question of the "dynamic" behind this practice is very complicated but one of the rationalizations which is given is that it reduces a woman's sexual desire and makes easier the husband's problem of management of a household which includes a large number of women. This practice continues among the professional women from the provinces, although only 21 percent of the professional (provincial) wives agreed they would want their children initiated into the society. This is in contrast to 42 percent of the men who stated they would prefer that their children join the society.[23]

It is not possible to say whether or not the continued practice of female circumcision is related to men's fears of their wives' potential promiscuity (42 percent of the provincial women in the sample had been initiated into the secret society), but certainly a very high premium is placed upon the good character of the girl who marries a professional man. For a professional, infidelity on the part of his wife is intolerable. As one informant put it, a husband's infidelity does not threaten the marriage, only the peace in the home. If a wife is unfaithful, the only result can be divorce. Fear of pregnancy is thought to be a deterrent to extramarital relations:

The way I see contraceptives affecting married life is that say the wife had a friend she could go on having relations with him when her husband was away without fear of being pregnant. If the husband returned and was told about it or got to know about it in some other way, he could get a divorce. But except the husband is told, he wouldn't know about his wife's sex relations. That's the way birth control aids affect one's married life.

Since women are thought to be potentially promiscuous, not many men would find it

[23] Sixty-nine percent of the provincial university students agreed with this statement. To illustrate how acceptable the practice continues to be, in 1961 the first Prime Minister, who was a medical doctor, was concerned about infections and offered and was allowed to do the operations himself.

easy to admit that their wives used contraceptives. Of the male university students 72 percent (in contrast to 45 percent of the females) stated that they agreed with the statement "Women who use contraceptives are more likely to be unfaithful to their husbands."

Another of the subtle considerations in the matter of the use of contraceptives is the great concern about being childless. The high rate of infant mortality in the village is a constant reminder that it is important to have as many babies as possible. Old people, and especially the women, are totally dependent upon their adult children for support in their old age. It was often mentioned that, although a person might have four or five children, perhaps only one would be alive to care for him in his old age. Childlessness is regarded as one of the worst tragedies which can befall a person. People who do not have children are considered abnormal. Sterile persons are even accused of being witches; among the Mende such persons are called *Ndelei* which means they have evil spirits. A *Ndelei* is a reptile whose spirit sucks the blood of children. Mothers are afraid to allow an old man or woman who is sterile near their children and would never allow them to be responsible for their care.

Another related belief among all of the tribes in Sierra Leone, including the Creole group, is the belief in the witchbird or *kaka*. When the very distinctive call of this bird is heard, everyone knows that the bird belongs to someone who is about to kill a child. When this bird appears, all the people around the entire village amass to drive the bird away, to identify the guilty person, and to force him or her to leave the area immediately. Almost invariably the person who is identified as the owner of the witchbird is a sterile man or woman. The following excerpts from two local papers illustrate the reactions this bird elicits:

*Witchbird at Police Station.* A large crowd of about 300 people stormed the Eastern Police Station yesterday, as word went round that the police had detained a "witchbird"—locally known as korkor.

Accompanying the bird to the police station

was a middle-aged woman from Blyden Lane at Gingerhall in Freetown's east end, who is helping the police in their investigations.

Residents around the area, particularly suckling mothers, had complained that they were terrified by the frequent cries of the bird which started shortly after the woman in question moved to the area recently.

A number of children are also reported to have died in the area recently at the rate of one almost every day.

Also being questioned yesterday was a jujuman from Kenema; alleged to have found the bird and named the woman as the owner.

The woman had to be rescued from an angry mob of women as they fell on her.

An army officer had to intervene to save the woman from molestation. Police later released the woman but the bird was left in a bucket of water at the police station.

The jujuman was also released.[24]

*Fire Force Alerted as "Witch Tree" Burnt Down.* A bid by unknown persons to destroy a "witch tree" in the west end of Freetown, nearly caused a major disaster at the last week.

The Freetown Fire Brigade had to be called out and the fire was brought under control.

It happened that for several days some residents of Bolling Street, King Tom, were molested by "cries" of a bird locally known as "koko" and believed to be a "witchbird."

On Wednesday evening some people in the neighborhood decided to burn the tree and get rid of the bird.

Efforts to drive it away on previous nights failed. Stones and sticks were hurled at the tree but the bird did not move. Dried grass and leaves were piled at the foot of the tree and set ablaze.

The fire was immediately greeted by a violent wind and sparks of fire went flying in all directions and threatened wooden houses in the area.

The threatening blaze and the wind were also interpreted by the people in the neighborhood as a sign of the anger as the "witch" bird flew off.

The Fire Force was immediately alerted and there was a sigh of relief as the fire was brought under control and a serious disaster averted.

There was also a sigh of relief that the "witch" bird has been silenced and residents in the area can now sleep in peace.[25]

One of the most serious abusive terms which can be applied to a person is to call him impotent (impotency being equated

with sterility).[26] It is a common belief that it is better to have three at the altar than two, or, in other words, a woman's fertility should be well established before marriage.[27] Young men are warned, "Don't marry a girl who is sterile" (*Med siɔ yu nɔ put man kak no yu os*).[28] It is also common to remind young couples that one child is not really a child (*Wan pikin nɔ to pikin*). You must certainly have more than one child. If you have only one and it dies, you will be left with an empty house.

In this light, a wife's adultery is considered a very serious offence, but if it proves that a couples' childlessness was the result of her husband's sterility, the husband is forced to overlook her behavior. The attitude is summed up in the Krio phrase, "The sterile man cannot frighten the pregnant woman" (*Okobo man nɔ de skia bɔl wuman*). In short, her adultery has proven that he is guilty of the sin of sterility of which she has been accused.

For example, two Sierra Leonean men were discussing how vitally important it is for everyone to have children and the lengths to which people will go to get them. They cited an example of one couple who had been childless for a long time:

This couple went to England and while they were abroad they reported back to their relatives that the wife was pregnant and that they would remain in England until she delivered. They have now returned with a small baby that is "whiter than you with straight hair and both of the parents are as black as the two of us sitting here." These parents were so desperate to get a child they would do anything.[29]

[26] Krio: *Okobo*; Temne: *ay hɔrɛ*, or *aɔ̆ bɔrk*; Mende: *Barrkeh.*
[27] In response to the statement, "It is preferable for a girl to be pregnant by her boyfriend before they are married so that they know that they are able to have children," 42 percent of the male and 27 percent of the female students "agreed."
[28] Literally this means, "Don't put a male hen in your house." The most serious abusive phrases a man can level at his wife or any woman are, "I have a male hen in my house" (*Kak na me os*) or, "You are a male hen" (*Yu na kak*).
[29] The implication of this story was that the husband had arranged for his wife to have an affair with some Englishman. One bachelor told me that he had "helped several such sterile couples" by getting the wives pregnant. In one case at least, the husband knew who had fathered his wife's child.

[24] *Unity*, Monday, May 12, 1969.
[25] *Daily Mail*, April 16, 1968.

With such concern with fertility, it is little wonder that young married couples do not wish to delay having a child. In response to the statement, "It is preferable for married couples to wait for two years before having their first child," 80 percent of the university student sample disagreed.[30] Marriage without children is unthinkable. Among the university students, 68 percent agreed that a couple may love each other sincerely, but, if their marriage is not blessed with children, it is bound to be unhappy. Those who disagreed pointed out that it is possible to adopt a relative's child or for the husband to have children outside. In no case was it thought possible to maintain a marriage without children. It is common for young married couples to have one or two relatives' children living with them for the beginning of their marriage. All couples who had no children of their own were raising some relatives' children.[31]

Although considerable tension exists between married couples over the husband's extramarital relationships, they are still considered to be a legitimate recourse for the childless couple. Both students and professionals ranked extramarital relationships as the chief source of conflict within marriages. Table 23.5 shows the responses of both groups toward the legitimacy of this practice for childless couples.

Other attitudes aggravate the tendency for men to have extramarital relationships. The traditional method of spacing children is based upon the postpartum sex taboo. Women are forbidden to have sexual intercourse during the time they are breast feeding their babies.

If a child becomes ill, the mother often is accused of having broken this taboo. Both samples were asked to respond to the statement, "Intercourse during the time a mother is breast feeding her child is harmful to the child." Of the university students 63 percent agreed that it is harmful, compared with 28 percent of the professional group. However, those who disagreed emphasized that scientific medical knowledge had disproven any direct connection, but that they personally would never have intercourse with a nursing mother. They described such a practice as "revolting" or "disgusting." Even those husbands who were able to overcome these feelings said that their wives would never agree.[32]

Traditionally, the child was breast fed for as long as two or three years; now mothers are weaning their babies much sooner. The longest time recorded was a professional wife's six-month nursing period. Usually the time is much shorter. Nevertheless, the observance of the postpartum sex taboo still is used as a justification for men to have extramarital sexual relations. As one man put it, "It is the time when men slip up. That is the only time I ever slipped up during that period."

In addition to the overriding importance of having children, particularly if the marriage is childless, and the inconvenience of long periods of sexual abstinence which surround birth, other traditional attitudes strengthen the tendency of men to establish extramarital relationships. The prestige associated with large numbers of children in traditional society continues to act as a motive for a man to father as many children as possible. It has already been mentioned how difficult it is to establish how many children have resulted from these relationships. Traditional society does not acknowledge the importance of a

[30] In the traditional family a wife who does not produce children may be divorced, sent back to her family, and the husband may demand repayment of the bride-wealth. One student who indicated that he agreed with this statement was questioned about his attitude. His answer illustrates the problems involved in collecting data through questionnaires, and also underlines the overriding importance of fertility. He said, "Yes, I agree. I'll give her two years and then if she isn't pregnant, I'll decide what to do with her" (i.e., whether or not to send her back to her family).

[31] One prominent professional couple had had no children and had raised two of the wife's nieces as their own. In the interview the wife claimed these two girls as her own daughters.

[32] Among the university sample there were significant differences between the responses of the males and females. Of the males, 56 percent agreed it was harmful to the child as compared with 74 percent of the female students. There were no significant differences between the responses of the men and women in the professional sample although 8 percent more provincials than Creoles agreed.

TABLE 23.5
"If a marriage does not produce children a wife should be understanding and permit her husband to have children outside" (in percent)

| RESPONSE | University Students | | Professional Group | |
|---|---|---|---|---|
| | M | F | M | F |
| Agree | 64 | 56 | 54 | 43 |
| Disagree | 31 | 41 | 36 | 43 |
| Other (including those who could not answer and those who felt it was justified but wouldn't consider wife's opinion) | 5 | 3 | 10 | 14 |
| *Totals* | 100 | 100 | 100 | 100 |
| | N=142 | N=97 | N=85 | N=72 |

husband's fidelity. There is no provision in customary law procedures for a wife to divorce her husband on the grounds of adultery. Today, under general law, adultery is the most common reason for a woman to initiate divorce proceedings.[33]

This might appear as evidence of a wider acceptance of the value of fidelity in marriage which is integral to the teachings of Christianity, at least as far as the wives are concerned. Such an interpretation, however, does not account for the widespread acceptance by both men and women of the inevitability of husbands' extramarital affairs nor for the extent to which men, who are partners in seemingly stable monogamous marriages, indulge in them.[34] Women who complain to their families about their husbands' affairs are always reminded, "What can you do, men are by nature polygamous" (*Au fɔ du, na so man tan*).

These illicit sexual relations of the husbands threaten the family unit in at least two vital ways. First, they pose an economic threat in terms of the claims upon the husband's resources for the day-to-day maintenance of the home and in terms of the inheritance rights of these children. Second, these relationships threaten the prestige role or superior status of the "legally" married woman.[35] It is, however, the financial threat, particularly regarding inheritance rights, that causes the most trouble over these outside relationships.

In 1965 there was an attempt by a small group of concerned lawyers in the Attorney General's office to pass legislation which would eliminate the concept of illegitimacy. Although most Sierra Leoneans would deny that the "outside" or illegitimate child suffered any handicaps because of the importance of children in African society,

[33] Usually these petitions are based upon other grounds than adultery because lawyers find it is not only difficult to prove adultery but it is also almost impossible to get anyone to act as witness in support of an adultery charge against a man. This is in considerable contrast to the ease with which husbands are able to get a divorce from their wives on the same grounds.

[34] Respondents in both samples were asked to react to the statement, "It is unfair for a wife to expect her husband to have sexual relations only with her." Such a question could not be expected to elicit a measure of actual behavior. Often men would laughingly respond, "It is not unfair, but it is unrealistic." Despite the inadequacy of the question and the tendency for respondents to answer in terms of their ideals, 41 percent of the male students and 28 percent of the adult professional males agreed. Only 18 percent of the female students and 15 percent of the professional wives agreed. When these responses were subdivided into Creoles and Provincials, the persistence of the traditional attitudes was even more pronounced. In the case of the professional wives, 17 percent of the Creole wives agreed compared with 31 percent of the provincial wives.

[35] The intricacies of the "game" which husbands play in order to continue these illicit relationships when the wife is fully aware of them and still maintain a stable marriage are discussed elsewhere (Harrell-Bond, 1968).

the judiciary was confronted with the obvious legal discrimination which these children face.[36] British law and the influence of missionaries were blamed for imposing the idea of illegitimacy on African society.[37] The new law would have sought to do away with all legal discrimination especially as it related to inheritance rights.

The attempt to pass this law raised such a furor that it was dropped. Not surprisingly, the "elite" wives were the most vocal in their opposition.[38] Because the bill had gained so much publicity, almost without exception, the persons in the professional sample thought it had been passed. Prior to this attempt, the maintenance law affecting illegitimate children was revised and there was a substantial increase in the numbers of women claiming maintenance under its provision.[39] As a result, the conflicts of married couples over their husbands' outside relationships have dramatically increased because men can no longer avoid these additional financial responsibilities. The issue over inheritance is a live one and opinion is divided. When asked if they thought a man's inheritance should be divided equally among all his children, both legitimate and illegitimate, 57 percent of the male and 49 percent of the female students agreed. The responses of the men and women in the professional sample who were faced with the problem reveal less agreement: 70 percent of the men agreed compared with

50 percent of the women. Women express a great deal of ambivalence over this aspect of the problem. They argue that they have worked and invested years of their lives helping their husbands build up the family estate. Why, they ask, should another woman and her children benefit when they have contributed nothing and have only been a constant drain on the family resources throughout the husband's life? They admit it is unfair for any child to suffer because of the conditions of its birth, but, at the same time, they are not willing to allow their children to be deprived of their rightful inheritance.

The acceptance of the ideal of family limitation within the marriage, which is complicated by the belief that women who use contraceptives may become promiscuous; continued observance, at least by some, of the postpartum sex taboo; and the conflicts which occur over the threat of outside relationships, all doubtless increase the tendency for men to seek refuge in extramarital affairs. However, it is necessary to examine these liaisons in the light of their effect on a man's relationships with his male friends.

As we have seen, a man's position and prestige in traditional society was measured largely in terms of the number of wives, children, and other dependents he could acquire. The prestige associated with procreative powers continues to act as a strong motive for men to beget as many children as possible. When a wife discovers her husband has had an illegitimate child, it is the occasion for intense conflict. Often she moves out of the household. All of the conciliatory resources of the extended family are required to persuade her to return. At the same time the husband is involved in such *palavars*, he is also being congratulated by his friends. They sympathize with him over the trouble his wife is causing, and another birth simply evokes their sincere approbation.

The desire to beget children is only one aspect of the attitudes of men which lead them to indulge in extramarital affairs. In the polygamous traditional household wives take turns sleeping with the husband. It is the

[36] These children have no legal relationship to their parents or other relatives; they can never be legitimized, etc. Most important they cannot inherit from their father's estate.

[37] Illegitimacy is a concept inherent to traditional family organization but it only becomes an important issue in such matters as inheritance or succession to chieftaincy.

[38] The women were also joined in the effort to stop passage of this bill by church organizations and the bar association. This latter group opposed it primarily because they saw an opportunity to make the proposed legislation into a political issue. The bill was supported by the political party dominated by provincials and the Creoles accused these provincials of trying to legitimize their "native" or primitive way of life and thereby striking at the heart of Creole Christian society.

[39] *Bastardy Laws Amendment Act, 1872* (35 & 36 Vict. c65) and *Bastardy Laws (Increase of Payments) Ordinance, 1961. Laws of Sierra Leone.*

responsibility of the husband to get these women pregnant. The importance of being successful is emphasized in the following comments:

Sterility worries them [the husbands] to death. In the native homes, especially when you are married in a polygamous family, the main reason why your parents sent you to be married to the chief is to get issue. Because the only benefit they can get from you, from that marriage, is issue.

Failure to impregnate one's wives is the occasion for public humiliation. Under customary law, impotency is one of the few grounds on which a woman may divorce her husband. Easmon described a chief who had not impregnated any of his wives and showed the extreme public humiliation he had to endure as a result.[40] At one ceremonial occasion a performer sang the following song:

> Chief Briwa beds with many a girl—
> But what does he all through the night?
> Keeps he the bedlight burning bright,
> Or snores his wives into a fright?
> His name is known through all the land,
> His word is good as gold band.
> But Briwa, Chief, your Chiefdom wants
> For other things than roads and grants.
> It would not have your sires forgot,
> Their fame and power decline and rot.
> So pray, O Chief: Let down your pants,
> Bring forth, O Chief, a boy or girl!
> All else is good but this most worth:
> *Bring forth, Briwa, bring forth.*

The stress on the husband's sexual performance as measured by resulting pregnancies is so great that it is a matter of intense anxiety among men. Complaints about impotency are a very frequent reason for men to seek medical advice.[41] These fears are not limited only to men involved in traditional family life. Professional men have similar concerns. Many consult medical doctors to receive injections of *testosterone* (male hormone) which they believe will increase their sex drive. Men fear situations which will expose their sexual limitations. Wives use this knowledge of their husbands' ego involvement in their ability to perform sexually to punish them for their extramarital affairs. When a husband comes in late and the wife is aware that he has been out with a girl friend, she may demand to be satisfied sexually. The husband is loath to refuse since the wife has full right to report his refusal to his family. Men joke about this problem and the way they try to stay out as late as possible in the hope that their wives will have gone to sleep and will not wake when they come in.

The social pressures on a man to participate in extramarital liaisons are intense. Groups of married men have informal clubs, the only activity of which is to organize parties to which they may bring their girl friends. Relationships with girl friends are the chief topic of conversation when men get together for drinks. Married men who attempt to be faithful to their wives do so over almost impossible odds.[42]

Men who are known not to have extramarital affairs are derided by their male friends. Even other women express scorn and derision. One man told me that never a day passes but someone, a man or woman, makes some sarcastic remark about his probable impotence. He said that it was fortunate that he had already had four children with his wife to prove his manhood. Such men are sometimes tricked into compromising situations

---

[40] R. S. Easmon, *The Burnt-Out Marriage* (London: Nelson, 1967), p. 117.

[41] Doctors discussed this problem. One epidemiologist who ran a clinic during his research, said it was the one most frequent complaint men brought to him. He referred to these common fears about impotency as a "type anxiety" in the society. During the short time I spent in a remote village almost all of the men came to me privately at one time or another asking me if I had an injection for them because they were suffering from impotency.

[42] One such husband thought he would make his position very clear. He had just returned from studying abroad with his new wife, who happened to be an American. He was invited to one of these parties and he took his wife. She was embarrassed because she found all her husband's friends there with their girl friends and she was the only wife. The other men were furious because of the possibility that she would expose them to their spouses. This couple noted that after this their friends never invited them to *any* social gatherings and for more than a year they were practically socially isolated.

with the full cooperation of the unmarried girl involved.

Men compare notes regarding one another's girl friends. They cooperate with each other in securing places where they can take these girls and protect each other from exposure to their wives. Although they claim to be absolutely loyal to one another in the sense that they would never try to compete with a friend for a girl another was courting, in practice a great deal of this kind of competition for particular girls takes place between them. However, there is beginning to be a greater emphasis on the sexual relationship itself rather than simply on the production of children since the financial resources of the husband are taxed by the addition of children.[43] A great deal of conversation goes on about the lovemaking abilities of both partners rather than about fertility. Men compare notes with each other on the relative attractiveness of the girls they admire and make guesses about their skill in making love. They argue about whether or not certain tribal girls are more passionate than Creole girls. These preoccupations are in some contrast to the traditional values as one informant discussed them:

As far as the native man in the village is concerned he is not particular about sexual education. All he requires is to satisfy himself. It is only by education, you have been to school, you read about sex and that women also had the same desire as you do and that there are certain areas of a woman that excite her, give her maximum feeling and so forth. But the man in the bush doesn't know that. They do not even know whether the existence of the clitoris gives a woman extra sensitivity. It is only by process of education . . . . And in fact in native's home, the people in the village, they don't have to caress a woman, to play with her, to excite her. All he does is go to the room straightaway and go to bed with her. When a woman expresses desire, a man feels that she is immoral.

[43] The amount of prestige gained from adding to the number of children a man has fathered is mitigated by the tension these children create in the home. The fact that the father's financial responsibility can now be effectively enforced has increased the tendency for men to deny paternity. In traditional society no man would think of denying that a child was his own.

Nowadays with the advent of education, young boys read about it in love stories, and they see film stars. This generation of school children, boys and girls, they are taking rapidly to Western ways of making love, caressing and so forth. Whereas to the average native man all that is unnecessary. It is not part of what he wants. He is more direct in his lovemaking. He only wants to have his sexual satisfaction.

As a result of the diminished value of having children and the greater emphasis upon the sexual relationship itself, men are beginning to use contraceptives in these outside relationships sometimes long before they would consider using them with their wives. Some of these married men have been known to assist girl friends in arranging for abortions and to pay for them. They also are known to encourage their girl friends to use oral contraceptives.

In conclusion, this chapter has not attempted to provide statistical data which would serve as a basis for comparison with the family size of "elite" groups in other developing countries. Rather, it has stressed that such measures or statements about the ideal family size, at least in Sierra Leone, may be misleading if they are taken as statements about future population growth. We have seen that the economic burdens associated with traditional kinship obligations are a strong incentive for professional people to limit the number of children they produce. These professionals have radically changed their attitudes from a traditional ideal family size, "as many as possible," to "four or less." But judging from the size of their families of orientation, if these professionals succeed in rearing four children to adulthood, these planned families will represent an actual population increase. In addition, other traditional attitudes continue to lead to the exposure of many more women than just wives to the possibility of conception. In spite of the meager returns on investments in family planning programs and research, these efforts continue to be heavily funded in many parts of the world dominating the approach to the problem of population control. Despite the avowed aim to limit births, we have seen how in Sierra Leone certain traditional attitudes and practices complicate the ready acceptance of methods of birth control. We have traced the manner in which it appears that the emphasis formerly placed upon procreation has gradually been modified to an emphasis upon sexual performance and upon the sexual relationship itself. Perhaps these data provide an important pointer for serious consideration.

Elite and nonelite Sierra Leoneans see films and read modern magazines.[44] They emphasize the importance of romantic love over the traditional family choice as the basis for the selection of a mate. Girls are incredibly fashion conscious and although the miniskirt faced a very considerable storm of protest, articles on the woman's page of the local newspaper supported the style with discussions on how women should dress to make themselves attractive to men.[45] A small boutique specializes in expensive lingerie and the customers include men buying these items for girl friends. Most certainly the revolution in sexual attitudes is not confined to the Western world. In the process of changing attitudes some of the former negative reactions toward the use of contraceptives, at least in relationships outside marriage, have been reduced and birth control methods are gradually becoming more acceptable. Birth rates are perhaps less likely to fall as a result of an emphasis upon family planning programs than as a result of these dynamic changes in sexual attitudes. This insight, if further documented, should provide a corrective to the present direction of expenditure in research and applied programs. Since traditional attitudes stand in such diametric opposition to the changes we have traced, examination of this basic area of human behavior promises to shed light on the theoretical problems of social change as well.

[44] *Playboy*, for example, is a popular magazine in many households. One provincial woman told me that her husband taught her about the female orgasm and used pornographic pictures he had purchased in Europe as a teaching aid. One Sierra Leonean girl now working as a "bunny girl" in London was interviewed in the local press and her achievement of securing such an attractive job was praised.

[45] One such article was captioned, "Is there such a thing as world beauty?" and noted that, "It is a woman's beauty that determines most of her future successes. It is the one thing that brings almost everything under her spell as though touched by a magic wand. A woman's beauty attracts a string of men to bow to her charms and ask her hand in marriage. In many cases, beauty makes women rich. Look at film stars and winners of beauty contests." (*Daily Mail*, January 6, 1968). Another such article asked, "How do men like to see women dress?" and the advice included, "Men love long hair" and "Men are particular about foot wear . . . . They say we look sexy [in] lacy stockings. Never on fat legs, they say," and "Men love perfume. They like to associate particular scents with particular women. But don't overdo it, they warn. A tantalizing whiff does it much more effectively than an overpowering dose does." (*Daily Mail*, March 9, 1968).

# PART
# FIVE

## *Other*
## *English-*
## *Speaking*
## *Countries*

EVEN BY African standards Gambia is a small country. By 1970 it probably consisted of just over one-third of a million inhabitants living on only 4,000 square miles of land forming a 15–30-mile-wide strip along the Gambia River in the westernmost part of the continent.

## DEMOGRAPHY

However, for the student of demography or of social and economic change, it does have its interest. Macroscopic population data are comparatively few, thus leading somewhat surprisingly not to diversity but to near consensus in various published estimates of its fertility levels. In contrast, the small-scale study of village demography has been of some importance for the whole of tropical Africa, because of the location of the British Medical Research Council Laboratories in the country. Interest also arises from a density of population greater than the world average and three times that of Africa, and from an agricultural economy that has been transforming significant sectors of itself fairly rapidly to production for the market.

The dominant climatic controls are heat and moisture which have important demographic effects in that they allow mosquitoborne and other diseases to flourish. The rainfall, and the incidence of sickness also, is markedly seasonal, four-fifths or more often falling from August to October, months during which the weakness of warriors, in the past, led to a cessation of tribal warfare and which now are responsible for most annual sick leave taken by public servants and other employees. Thus health and agriculture are determined by the nature of the country: rural, low lying with many swamps strung along a single river, monsoonal, absurdly long in proportion to its width with all transport up country starting at Banjul (Bathurst) on the sea and proceeding up the river or roads along the banks on either side. For most Gambians, life still centers around

---

# CHAPTER TWENTY-FOUR

# *Gambia*

JOHN C. CALDWELL
AND BARBARA THOMPSON[1]

---

[1] This chapter has been written as two separate sections: "Demography" by John C. Caldwell, and "Some Demographic Factors Illustrated in a Gambian Village" by Barbara Thompson.

the village and farming; but cash production is becoming important and per capita incomes are high by tropical African standards and have risen sharply during the 1960s.

THE POPULATION AND THE CENSUSES. At least part of the population of Gambia has been enumerated in censuses held every ten years since 1881, except for 1941 and the delay of the planned 1961 count to 1963 so as not to clash with preparations for pre-independence elections. Attempts to cover the whole country were made in 1901, 1911, 1921, 1931, and 1963, of which all but the first (which was certainly incomplete and estimated rather than counted a considerable proportion of the total population)[2] are summarized in Table 24.1.

TABLE 24.1

Enumerated census populations and apparent intercensal growth, 1911–1963

| Census Year | Enumerated Population | Apparent Percentage Growth since Previous Census Average | |
|---|---|---|---|
| | | Total | Annual |
| 1911 | 196,101 | — | — |
| 1921 | 210,530 | 7.4 | 0.7 |
| 1931 | 199,520 | −5.2 | −0.5 |
| 1963 | 315,486 | 58.1 | 1.4 |

SOURCE: H. A. Oliver, *Report on the Census of Population of the Gambia taken on 17th/18th April, 1963* (Bathurst: Government Printer, 1965), pp. 22–23.

Taking the record at face value, we could draw the conclusion that prior to 1931 (or perhaps some subsequent turning point), population growth was slow, or even uncertain, with increase or decrease determined almost at random by the occurrence and timing of epidemics. This would mean that mortality was very high, with birth and death rates probably both between 40 and 50 per

[2] R. R. Kuczynski, *Demographic Survey of the British Colonial Empire*, I, *West Africa* (London: Oxford University Press, 1948), p. 331. "The 1911 count was certainly incomplete, though more complete than that of 1901 . . . there is no evidence that this [1921] count was incomplete." On p. 332, "I suspect that the population had been overstated in 1921." (This chapter was written prior to the 1973 census, but see note at end of chapter.)

thousand, life expectation at birth little more than 20 years, infant mortality around 300 per thousand, and half of all live births having been succeeded by deaths by about 5 years of age.[3] Such a situation is far from inconceivable, and approximates to some extent that which has been described for the Mossi of Upper Volta and in Mopti in Mali as late as the period around 1960.[4] It would presumably represent little advance in health conditions over those which had traditionally prevailed. The fact that African censuses tend successively to become more complete, partly because of greater experience (although the rapid turnover in British officials and the lack of a continuing census or demographic statistical system mean that this point should not be overstated) but largely because of the extension of administration and commerce into traditional rural areas, is additional evidence that the real population growth rate was probably as low as the censuses indicated.

The grounds for feeling some doubt about this interpretation are that the evidence for this earlier, almost static growth rate depends heavily on the enumeration of 1931, a very atypical year. Because of the world economic depression, colonial administrations everywhere were economizing and the efficiency of Gambian census taking might well have suffered. Perhaps more significant is the fact that, while it is apparently true that the depression did not reduce population growth rates in the developing world taken as a whole (in contrast to the position in developed

[3] Assuming from the evidence presented below that the birth rate is (and was) over 40 per thousand and that over a sufficient period the death rate equaled it, and then choosing a matching stable population and life table (Mortality Levels 2 or 3) in the "North" family of tables in Ansley J. Coale and Paul Demeny, *Regional Model Life Tables and Stable Population* (Princeton, N.J.: Princeton University Press, 1966).

[4] William Brass et al., *The Demography of Tropical Africa* (Princeton, N.J.: Princeton University Press, 1968), pp. 157–58. The approximation is better in the comparison with infant mortality rates than with crude death rates, which probably are falling among the Mossi and in Mopti, although it may also be that the vital statistics surveys were carried out in years when major epidemics did not occur.

countries where fertility declines slashed rates of natural increase), growth rates did fall in some colonies which produced export crops with assistance from immigrant labor. Gambia has had an important groundnut cash-cropping industry all this century, and the industry itself, and the other economic growth it has fostered, have certainly attracted immigrants from the more purely subsistence-farming areas of Senegal across the border. It is particularly easy to move the short distances into Gambia, and it would have been equally easy to return in 1930 as the demand for groundnuts and their overseas market price crashed.[5] Thus there may well have been a positive rate of natural increase in the 1911–1931 period, although net immigration may have meant that it was considerably below the calculated annual growth rate for 1911–1921 of 0.7 percent. But, if it were no higher than 0.5 percent, this would still mean a crude death rate 5 points per thousand below the birth rate, with an expectation of life at birth possibly already higher than 25 years and rising. This would be more compatible with the common-sense view that British administration and some rural cash income must have had some effect on the reduction of mortality.

The first census that contains sufficient data for an attempt to resolve some of these questions is that of 1963, the only national count held in the last 40 years. Its value was unfortunately much diminished for our purposes by the 32-year gap that separated it from its predecessor, thus rendering it almost impossible to relate the average intercensal rate of population growth to that estimated for the period around 1963. Nevertheless, this is our major source of data and its form and accuracy must remain for us a great cause of concern.

The census was undertaken with a good deal of enthusiasm but, largely because of the size of the country, it could not be compared with the more professionalized full censuses of that period in Ghana or East Africa. Nor could its collection of retrospective fertility and mortality data compare with those being gathered in the ex-French territories. No one statistically trained was associated in Gambia with the undertaking. Nor could Gambia afford an expensive census. The fact that the whole operation was carried out for only £14,000 (U.S. $39,000) was a creditable financial achievement, but it meant that the cost per head of population was under 11 pence (compared with 1 shilling and 2 pence in Ghana's 1960 census) and must inevitably have led to some reductions in efficiency below that potentially possible. The enumeration, like most African censuses, took place over several weeks, a feature which almost certainly increases the chances of omission or duplication.

It is difficult to evaluate the accuracy of the actual head count. The numbers recorded closely agreed with the population estimates made by district commissioners, but this may merely show a similar tendency to omit certain groups, such as very young children or internal or external migrants. More reassurance was provided by two separate counts in small areas; Thompson (in this chapter) records that three census counts and two of her own in a village showed an extreme variation of only 5 percent, most of which could probably be explained by population movement (thus, however, emphasizing the danger of protracted enumeration). One might conclude that the total population figure for the country is probably not far out.

The position is inevitably very different when considering individual characteristics of the population or possibly the enumeration of some subgroups. Thompson's findings on birthplace and tribe that only one-twentieth of outsiders to the village were recorded as such is certainly sufficient to shake one's faith in the recording of the numbers of external and internal migrants and in many other data as well. Officials associated with the census argue that this finding is not a good measure of the extent of inaccuracy as there

[5] Kuczynski, *Demographic Survey*, p. 334, quotes the reports of the *Agriculture Department* to suggest that between 1921 and 1931 the number of "strange farmers" in the country declined by over 12,000 or more than the intercensal decline in total population.

are specific problems with tribal names and a self-consciousness about admitting an origin outside the place of residence.

The most important consideration when estimating the potential in the society for population growth is the nature of the age data and whether all apparent distortion can be explained by misstatement alone, or whether the selective omission of persons of some ages is probable. Accurate age data cannot be secured in Gambia, nor elsewhere in West Africa, because many people have never known their true ages and because the traditional culture has not encouraged them to remember age as a matter of importance. The 1963 census took the unusual step of publicizing beforehand that the census would require age statement and that thought should be given to the matter.[6] Whether this improved age statement or merely made respondents sound more convinced might be a matter for conjecture. Enumerators also employed an historical calendar for helping respondents to refresh their memories and to calculate their ages. This device must be used with time and care, and even then it might result in an over-statement of age and an under-reporting of the very young,[7] both phenomena which do in fact appear to have occurred in Gambia (but perhaps largely for other reasons). Thompson reports that it is possible to collect male age in terms of "age set" or *kafo* group membership, but is not clear whether these were actually used in the census (although presumably references were made to contemporaries in such sets when using the calendars to try to establish approximate age) and they appear to be somewhat imprecise (although doubtless much more valuable than nothing) in that they may span an age range of about three years.

Figure 24.1 shows that the recorded age pattern in Gambia departs considerably from that of a stable population model, even though it can be assumed that fertility has been sufficiently constant to ensure a real configuration approximating to stability. Most of the departures doubtless arise from age misstatement and closely follow patterns in misstatement which are common in tropical Africa.

Even so, the recorded number of persons 0–4 years of age is smaller than might have been anticipated. They exceed the number of 5–9-year-olds by less than 1 percent; indeed among the population of the furthest hinterland (the two-fifths who live in MacCarthy Island and Upper River) there are 10 percent fewer persons enumerated as 0–4 than as 5–9. In contrast, the selected stable population model has the former exceeding the latter by 28 percent and any other model gives a generally similar picture. In most tropical African censuses those enumerated under 5 years are fewer than would be expected, because of age misstatement and the failure to enumerate some of the very young, but in most the 0–4 group is nevertheless appreciably larger than the 5–9 one. It is difficult to avoid the conclusion that some Gambians of under 5 years were omitted by the 1963 census and these omissions were particularly bad in, or perhaps were largely confined to, the districts furthest up the river. Very young children are often sleeping out of sight when the enumerator calls; their parents may hesitate to call them to an official's notice if they were born so recently that a name has not yet been decided upon; careful enumeration using an historical calendar for consultation with respondents may convince households that no meeting with babies is envisaged (this seems to be supported by recent work in Nigeria).[8]

The pattern of age enumeration also shows other patterns commonly found across the continent, namely the recording of fewer females, 10–14, than in any 5-year age group between 20 and 35, possibly because of the

[6] H. A. Oliver, *Report on the Census of Population of the Gambia taken on 17th/18th April, 1963*, Sessional Paper No. 13 of 1965 (Bathurst, 1965), p. 7.

[7] For the historical calendar employed, see *ibid.*, p. 39. The problems encountered when using calendars are discussed in John C. Caldwell and Adenola Igun, "An Experiment with Census-type Age Enumeration in Nigeria," *Population Studies*, XXV, 2 (July 1971).

[8] *Ibid.*

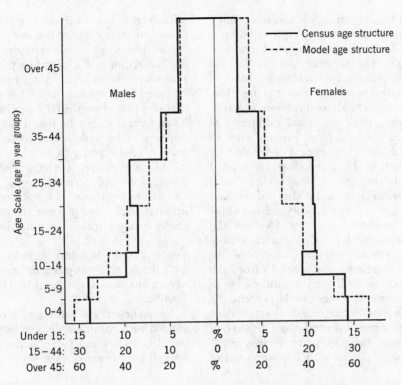

Figure 24.1. *Census and Model Age Pyramids, Gambia, 1963*

*Note:* Percentaged populations are for the sexes separately (the closeness of the totals for the two sexes at the census and the assumption of near parity in the sex ratio at birth in the model means that the pyramids do not appear appreciably different from pyramids percentaging the total population.

SOURCES: (i) Census: H. A. Oliver, *Report on the Census of the Population of the Gambia taken on 17th/18th April,* 1963, Sessional Paper No. 13 of 1965, Bathurst, 1965, p. 41.

　　　(ii) Model: Ansley J. Coale and Paul Demeny, *Regional Model Life Tables and Stationary Populations,* Princeton, 1966. Females "North", Mortality Level 7, BR-46, Males "North", Mortality Level 8, BR-46.

assumption that married 10–14-year-olds are really older than 15 years; and an implausibly great number of 15–34-year-olds, arising from the phenomenon just mentioned as well as the understatement of the ages of some women over 35 (possibly because they are still demonstrably fertile). Less common is the recording of half the anticipated females over 45 years, explained in the census report in terms of very high mortality in these years,[9] but possibly caused by age misstatement and omission as well.

[9] A model constructed from Brass's African Standard life table (see Brass et al., *Demography of Tropical Africa,* p. 133) would come closer to the recorded female population over 45 years of age than the one constructed from the Coale and Demeny "North" life tables employed in Figure 24.1.

The above paragraph has concentrated on the reported age structure of the female population, as there is a strong case for using this structure when estimating vital rates, because it is less affected by immigration. A larger proportion of the males than of the females were immigrants, 12.9 percent compared with 9.7 percent. But, more importantly, half the extra 6,000 males who made up this margin were believed by the Gambian administrators to be "strange farmers" arriving seasonally without dependents[10] and thus distorting the age structure to a greater degree from one formed solely by natural increase than would

[10] Oliver, *Report on the Census,* 1963, p. 35.

the typical female immigrants who are more likely to be accompanied by their children.

Some of Thompson's findings in the second part of this chapter bear directly on the problems of female age statement. Most of her information was provided by the older men of the household, as doubtless was that of the census. With the usual difference of age between spouses, most women over 45 years would have their ages stated either by very old men or by more distantly related males. With her more painstaking social anthropological approach, she did in fact establish that a considerably higher proportion of women were over 45 than the census had claimed for the area, and succeeded in raising the proportion of all population enumerated as over 45 from the census 15 percent to 19 percent and under 15 from the census 40 percent to 42 percent.

It is quite possible that female age statement is so much more distorted than is that of males because their ages are so frequently given by males, because their lower level of schooling is apt to make them less certain about their age, and because attempts to relate their age to their reproduction distort the pattern of statement at certain ages, and that therefore the male age structure should be taken into account as well in spite of our inability to remove the effects of immigration. Therefore, it might be noted that there also appears to be a deficit of males in the recorded 10–14 group, a small surplus in the 25–34 age range, perhaps reflecting the immigration of farmers, and, in striking contrast to the recorded female age structure, approximately the proportion over 45 years that we might anticipate from the model.

THE PATTERN OF VITAL EVENTS. As Table 24.2 shows, there appears to be considerable agreement about the level of vital rates in Gambia.

Nevertheless, the estimated levels must be viewed with considerable suspicion. They are in all cases a small subsection of a series of estimates for many countries and regions, and

TABLE 24.2

Estimated vital rates in Gambia, 1963

| Source | Crude Birth Rate (per 1,000) | Gross Reproduction Rate | Total Fertility Rate | Crude Death Rate (per 1,000) | Expectation of Life at Birth (years) | Rate of Natural Increase (percent) |
|---|---|---|---|---|---|---|
| (a) 1963 Census Report (uncorrected)[a] | 36 | | | 21 | | 1.5 |
| (a) 1963 Census Report (corrected)[a] | 39 | | | 22 | | 1.7 |
| (b) Princeton Project (DTA) | 40 | | 5.2 | [28][b] | [35][c] | [1.2][b] |
| (c) Princeton estimates (Nairobi Conf.) | 40 | | 5.3 | [29][b] | [35][c] | [1.1][b] |
| (d) United Nations estimates (PTA) | 39 | 2.5 | | 21 | 43 | 1.8 |

SOURCES: (a) H. A. Oliver, *Report on the Census of Population of the Gambia taken on 17th/18th April, 1963* (Bathurst: Government Printer, 1965); (b) William Brass et al., eds., *The Demography of Tropical Africa* (Princeton, N.J.: Princeton University Press, 1968); (c) Hilary J. Page and Ansley J. Coale, "Estimates of Fertility and Child Mortality in Africa South of the Sahara" (Paper presented at the *Seminar on Population Growth and Economic Development*, Nairobi, 1969); (d) R. K. Som, "Some Demographic Indicators for Africa," in John C. Caldwell and C. Okonjo, eds., *The Population of Tropical Africa* (London and New York, 1968), pp. 187–98. Estimates not essentially different are also given in R. K. Som, "Population Prospects in Africa" (*Seminar on Population Growth and Economic Development*, Nairobi, 1969).
[a] The only corrections made to the report were arithmetical ones of addition of births and deaths, and readjustment of the population (i) to include only those areas where vital statistics had been collected, (ii) to estimate a mid-year population for the period for which vital events were collected.
[b] Other estimates in keeping with the expectation of life at birth assumed and the model stable population tables employed.
[c] Assumption (based on the calculated expectation of life from the 1957 Senegal Valley survey and an assumption of declining mortality).

inevitably little time could be spent on the relatively scanty Gambian data. It is probable that the estimated levels seemed reasonable enough because the 1963 census produced estimates of birth and death rates which appeared to be compatible with certain aspects of the age structure (e.g., the proportion under 15 years of age) and with the rate of current population growth which could be deduced from the intercensal growth rate. Nevertheless, all this evidence is highly suspect.

It is noteworthy that the latest Princeton estimates from more detailed survey data in surrounding Senegal put birth rates in that country at 49 per thousand or nine points higher than their estimate for Gambia.[11] There may be cultural differences, developed both before and after colonization, between the two populations, but one would hardly expect fertility levels to differ to this extent.

Other available evidence from Gambia is perhaps more disconcerting. From an admittedly very small sample, Thompson found that the women of over 50 years of age who had married had experienced an average 6.4 live births, yielding a completed fertility rate of about 6.1–6.2 for all females of this age. Furthermore, in this part of Africa she might have anticipated such fertility levels because of the following observations she made on the area studied: female marriage is nearly universal and is almost continuous after menarche except for very short periods to be observed after the end of one marriage and before the necessary remarriage; sterile marriages are usually broken up and replaced by other unions, sterility being "a tragedy for the individual"; "children, both boys and girls, are wanted and the very idea of an unwanted pregnancy is quite incomprehensible"; the abortion rate is apparently low; antinatal practices are little known and even the lactation taboo on sexual relations is broken in at least half of all cases; there is hardly any venereal disease.

The evidence for the capital, Banjul, is of considerable interest. Here one might anticipate a birth rate lower than or equal to the national one, especially as the proportion of the population made up by women of childbearing age is markedly lower than the national one.[12] But the only birth registration system in the country yielded a crude birth rate for resident population of 47 per thousand in the year of the census and this level has remained approximately constant since. It is possible, of course, that the authorities have not succeeded in distinguishing all nonresidents coming into Banjul to give birth (these are held to be comparatively few), but on the other hand it is also quite possible that registration is not quite complete. The census, inevitably asking questions only of women being enumerated in the town, provided strong confirmatory evidence, by calculating a birth rate which, with adjustment to base it upon a mid-year population, was 49 per thousand for Banjul and 46 per thousand for the larger Banjul-Kombo St. Mary urban area.[13]

But the strongest reasons for suspecting the census birth rates are the figures themselves. The method for estimating the time period when securing retrospective fertility and mortality data may well have been better than in most work of this type in Africa; an exact period was established back to the apparently clearly remembered general election (the only one) 11 months earlier in the previous May and the figures were inflated

---

[11] Hilary J. Page and Ansley J. Coale, "Estimates of Fertility and Child Mortality in Africa South of the Sahara" (Paper presented at the Seminar on *Population Growth and Economic Development*, Nairobi, 1969), p. 18.

[12] If it follows the pattern from two other anglophone African countries, Ghana and Kenya, urban fertility would be lower than rural fertility. However, if francophone countries and perhaps Nigeria, are also considered, cases of apparently higher urban than rural fertility can also be shown. See A. Romaniuk, "Fertility Trends in Africa," *Proceedings of the International Population Conference, London, 1969*, I (Liège, 1971), pp. 739–50. It might be anticipated that crude birth rates would be relatively high in towns that attracted an abnormal number of young adult women, but females of reproductive age, 15–44, make up only 22.2 percent of the population of Bathurst-Kombo St. Mary compared with 25.6 percent in the country as a whole (part of the difference may be a statistical artifact, namely the reporting in rural areas of some women over 45 years of age as being under that age).

[13] Oliver, *Report on the Census, 1963*, p. 47.

proportionally to yield an estimate for a whole year. There is no strong likelihood that seasonality of births would make April—May so atypical that the annual estimate would be biased (but the mortality estimate may well be too high because of the seasonally low number of deaths during these months). The collection of birth and death data had none of the painstaking concentration on this theme and multiple questions found in the more purely demographic inquiries. Thus it is likely that in most areas some births have been omitted, often probably by omitting all births to particular respondents. Thompson feels that pregnant women may often have deliberately refrained from telling of babies who had recently been born and then died, for fear of endangering the coming child.

That some births and deaths were missed in the Gambia census is strongly suggested by the variations in the birth and death rates[14] from one district to another, the former ranging from 11.9–62.4 and the latter from 8.2–32.7. It is true that in some African countries there are substantial internal variations in the birth rate (e.g., in Zaïre where district birth rates varied in 1955–1957 from 20 to 60 partly at least as a result of a differential incidence of venereal disease[15] which is believed to be a much more serious problem in Zaïre than in Gambia). While some variation undoubtedly occurs in Gambia, this is almost certainly not the major reason that some of the districts have returned very low birth rates, for, were the phenomenon real, it would be reflected in the age structures of the district populations. But (confining our attention to areas which embrace several districts and hence are less likely to be affected by chance variations in numbers) the birth rate of the Kuntaur Area (the most extreme case) was 27.5 but was accompanied by an age structure almost identical to that of Gambia as a whole and

one incompatible according to any model with such a low birth rate. The fact that the age structure does not vary greatly from district to district, while the recorded birth rate does, means that there is little relation between the recorded birth rate and the recorded residual population from the previous five years' births; thus, while the *population 0–4* made up 73 and 61 percent respectively of *five times the recorded number of births* of Banjul and Gambia respectively, this proportion sank to 45 percent in Foni Brefet District which claimed a birth rate of 62 and rose to the extraordinary figure of 209 percent for Nianija District to which a birth rate of 12 had been attributed.[16]

If it is accepted that most districts did not quite record all births and deaths, while some districts fell well short and a few were quite aberrant, it appears likely that the true birth and death rates in 1963 were well into the 40s and 20s respectively. Unfortunately the Brass techniques for estimating fertility[17] cannot be used on the data, for births were not cross-tabulated by age of mother.

Further evidence of child mortality levels are available for Gambia. The director of Medical Research Council Laboratories (Dr. I. A. McGregor) has followed the fortunes of all persons born in the village of Keneba in the five-year period, 1949–1953 and reported that 13.4 percent died before one year of age and 43 percent before seven years.[18] The latter figure (incompatible with the former

[14] *Ibid.* The rates quoted are as printed in the report and have not been adjusted.

[15] A. Romaniuk, "Infertility in Tropical Africa," in John C. Caldwell and Chukuka Okonjo, eds., *The Population of Tropical Africa* (London: Longmans, Green and Company, and New York: Columbia University Press, 1968), pp. 214–24.

[16] According to the model chosen for comparison (in Figure 24.1 and in the population projections in Table 24.5) this ratio should be about 73 percent. The figure of 61 percent recorded by the whole Gambia, would, even assuming a lower birth rate, imply an expectation of life at birth in the low 20s and a low or negative rate of population growth. It should be noted that this ratio cannot be equated with the survivors from the previous five years' births, for five times the current annual number of births is greater in a growing population than the sum of five years' births to date. It should also be noted that the ratio is affected not only by the recorded number of births but also by the under-enumeration of 0–4-year-olds.

[17] Brass et al., *Demography of Tropical Africa*, pp. 89–104.

[18] Ian A. McGregor, W. Z. Billewicz, and A. M. Thomson, "Growth and Mortality in Children in an African Village," *British Medical Journal*, II (December 1961), 1661–66.

according to life tables based on experience outside Africa)[19] corresponds to a Coale and Demeny "North" life table with an expectation of life at birth of about $28\frac{1}{2}$ years. Because of the relatively high mortality in infancy and early childhood in contrast to later childhood, most of these deaths would have occurred a decade or more before the census, and would have represented the mortality level of this earlier period. If mortality declined at a rate which has been suggested by the United Nations and others for contemporary Africa, the study area might have exhibited an expectation of life at birth of about 34 years by the 1963 census year and perhaps 37 years by 1970.

These mortality levels, compatible with the Princeton estimates in Table 24.4 but not with those of the United Nations or the Gambia Census Report, are high, but it seems likely that they do not exaggerate Gambian national levels. The Keneba mortality figure for seven years of age has been chosen in preference to the infant mortality rate for selecting an appropriate model life table partly because so much mortality has occurred by this age that there must be less possible variation in choosing an approximate expectation of life at birth, and partly because it is believed that the major differences between the African child mortality pattern and that represented in published life tables from experience elsewhere occur largely below the age of seven but not under one year (i.e., toddler mortality is relatively high compared with infant mortality).

Thompson's work has shown that it is possible to miss deaths in Keneba even in a cohort under strict observation, so it is possible that mortality could have been a

little higher still. Furthermore, it can be shown that the researchers did something to improve the health of the area and of members of the group under observation.[20] But, when using the Keneba findings to estimate 1963 national mortality, the above considerations may be offset by the fact that a small proportion of Gambians, namely those living in Banjul-Kombo St. Mary and two or three other lesser towns, enjoyed better health facilities than Keneba, and by a possible faster improvement in mortality rates than the one postulated here (discussed below). Apart from these worries, it might be noted that Keneba is a village 100 miles inland from Banjul, larger but perhaps more isolated than the average, with probably similar mortality levels among its inhabitants, at least in 1949, to those experienced by the great majority of Gambians.

Two further observations should be made about Keneba mortality. First, the 1949–1953 cohort studied contained only 187 persons, thus leaving room for a good deal of random variation in mortality (as was necessarily also the case when studying a single village as far as the onslaught during five years of epidemics on one village but not another was concerned). Second, some subsequent mortality figures have been published for Keneba[21] and for the village of

---

[19] No tropical African data are incorporated in any of the four families of life tables in Coale and Demeny, *Regional Model Life Tables*, nor in the earlier United Nations, *Methods for Population Projections by Sex and Age*, Population Studies No. 25 (New York, 1956). Brass model life tables can also be constructed (see Brass et al., *Demography of Tropical Africa*, pp. 132–35) based on an "African Standard" life table, which it might be noted also suggests relatively higher survival to seven years, given the proportion surviving to one year, than was recorded at Keneba.

[20] McGregor et al., "Growth and Mortality in Children," pp. 1662–64, notes campaigns from 1950 against trypanosomiasis, malaria, bancroftian filariasis, and hookworm. They comment, "Some of the children in the present study must have received treatment for disease from which they might otherwise have died. Unfortunately it is not possible from the records to identify these children or to assess the nature and frequency of treatment given. However the availability of treatment depended on the presence or absence of a doctor at Keneba. and on this basis it may be assumed that seriously ill children could have been effectively treated during only about 30 percent of the 10-year period of study."

[21] A. M. Thomson, W. Z. Billewicz, Barbara Thompson, R. Illsley, A. K. Rahman, and I. A. McGregor, "A Study of Growth and Health of Young Children in Tropical Africa," *Transactions of the Royal Society of Tropical Medicine and Hygiene*, LXII, 3 (1968), 330–40. See also B. Thompson, "Marriage, Childbirth and Early Childhood in a Gambian Village: A Socio-Medical Study" (Ph.D. thesis, University of Aberdeen, 1965).

Sukuta,[22] near Banjul. In a 1962–1963 study of Keneba (referred to by Thompson in the second part of this chapter), 99 children were born during the two years; 24 of them died during the period. If these births were evenly distributed during the two years, the number of deaths recorded (now believed by Thompson to have been an undercount) as occurring to them was greater than would have been anticipated by applying the mortality experience of the 1949–1953 cohort[23] and even higher than that predicted by a model life table conforming with the survivorship of that cohort to seven years of age. As the Sukuta study was not based on all births, and was not a random sample of births in the center, the data are not suited to the kind of analysis applied here. However, given these qualifications, they provided confirmation (as was the main purpose of the inquiry) of the high level of disease among young children, especially the role in raising mortality levels of malaria, and associated anemia, malnutrition, and diarrhea, and of the likelihood of children being left behind with others during the daytime while their mothers were farming.

The only other major source of Gambian mortality data is that from the Gambian registration system. Death rates in West African capitals are often far below the national figures because of the concentration of doctors and health facilities in the large towns. Banjul should be no exception to this; although the Banjul-Kombo St. Mary area contains only about one-eighth of the country's population, five-sixths of practicing doctors in either private or government employ and the only large hospital are found there. The 1963 registered death rate for residents of 16 per thousand (slowly, but fluctuatingly, declining since) is entirely compatible with a national death rate at the time of 30 per thousand. What is less explicable is an adjusted death rate from the retrospective census figures on deaths of 26 per thousand for Banjul and 23 for the whole Banjul-Kombo St. Mary area. Perhaps the explanation is that dying people came to town for treatment. Perhaps also the fact that deaths cannot be attributable to a single respondent, as births can to a mother, meant that there was some overlapping in reporting; if this were widespread it would mean that the census mortality rates were nonsense, but overlapping (as well as omission) may be less likely in the villages than in the town. These difficulties mean that our mortality estimates must rest largely on the Keneba findings, a very unsatisfactory position but nevertheless better than that in many African countries, plus a likelihood that the death rate must be considerably higher than that calculated by the census from recorded deaths with obvious substantial omissions in a large number of centers.

An unproven assumption employed here is that of an improvement in mortality, to the extent that one year is added to the expectation of life at birth for every two years of time elapsed. This is the approximate rate apparently experienced by many developing countries outside Africa before World War II[24] and indeed is slower than the experience of many of these countries since.[25] It is a result of improving medical technology, the availability of this technology to larger proportions of the population, and an increasing willingness and ability of the populations to make use of available services. All those things seem to be happening in Gambia. Table 24.3 shows that during the 1960s expenditures on medicines and medical equipment by the Gambian government quadrupled, an increase which remains very substantial indeed even when offset by a rise

[22] P. D. Marsden, "The Sukuta Project: A Longitudinal Study of Health in Gambian Children from Birth to 18 Months of Age," *Transactions of the Royal Society of Tropical Medicine and Hygiene*, LVIII, 6 (1964), 455–89.

[23] That is, the experience set out for three- and then six-month intervals in McGregor et al., "Growth and Mortality in Children," p. 1665.

[24] It is incorporated in the projection methods recommended in United Nations, *Methods for Population Projections*.

[25] United Nations, *Population Bulletin of the United Nations, No. 6, 1962 with special reference to the situation and recent trends of mortality in the world* (New York, 1963), pp. 48–51.

TABLE 24.3

Expenditure by the Ministry of Health on "Drugs and equipment," 1960–1970

| Year | Budget Estimate (Gambian £)[a] | Actual Expenditure (Gambian £)[a] |
|---|---|---|
| 1960 | — | 7,806 |
| 1961 | — | 16,635 |
| 1962 | — | 24,820 |
| 1963 | 27,608 | 25,358 |
| 1964 | 26,200 | 22,937 |
| First half of 1965[b] | 27,200[c] | n.a. |
| 1965–6 | 26,530 | 22,937 |
| 1966–7 | 27,000 | 30,474 |
| 1967–8 | 27,000 | 28,605 |
| 1968–9 | 30,000 | n.a. |
| 1969–70 | 31,600 | — |

NOTE: In 1969–1970 all government expenditure on health and associated staff and facilities was estimated to be G£276,860 or 8–9 percent of the budget.
[a] Until November 1967, G£1 = U.S. $2.8; after that date G£1 = U.S. $2.4.
[b] Change in the financial year.
[c] Actual half-year budget estimate of £13,600 expressed here as annual rate.

in population of possibly one-fifth and by some inflation. At the same time roads have penetrated further and the number of lorries has increased, a greater proportion of production has been destined for commerce (by the mid-1960s the value of exports doubled in a three-year period)[26] and the number of families with children in schools was rising rapidly (enrolled pupils increased by 35 percent in three years in the mid-1960s).[27] Hospital admissions actually fell between 1963 and 1966[28] but this may have been a sign of improving health.

There is certainly scope for some gains against mortality which could be reasonably easily secured. "Toddler mortality" (i.e., that in the 1–3-year age group) is relatively high in both Gambia and much of West Africa compared with that of infants or most adult ages. The high death rate among these young children has been attributed among other

things to the poor sharing of the family food upon which the children are dependent after weaning, and to the years taken to build up resistance against malaria and other diseases after the effects of resistance passed on from the mother have disappeared. In Gambia, Thompson (in the second part of this chapter) reports that toddlers are also insufficiently cared for while their mothers (with the youngest babies on their backs) are farming. At least the first and last problems, being social rather than medical in nature, should be susceptible to attack.

The testimony of intercensal population growth should provide independent evidence of the likely level of natural increase. Unfortunately that testimony is confused by apparent evidence of growth and subsequent decline in the 1911–1931 period, by the possibility that the 1931 census produced an undercount, and by the 32-year period elapsing between the last two censuses. Nevertheless, this last period with its apparent average annual growth rate of 1.4 percent must remain our chief evidence.

Almost certainly the population did not grow at a constant rate, but started the period at a lower rate of increase which rose as death rates declined with the increasing penetration of health services. If we adopt the United Nations assumption[29] (very similar to the assumptions in the subsequent population projections) that the crude death rate is currently falling at about one point every two-and-one-half years, and add the extra assumptions that the prewar decline was about half as fast and that the rate of immigrational increase has been constant (the war period produced fluctuations which cannot be estimated), the following picture is obtained. The annual population growth rate may have been about 1.0 percent in 1931 (provided that any depression efflux was past by that time), 1.2 percent in 1941, and 1.9 percent by 1963. The same assumptions would suggest a rate of population growth of about 2.2 percent by late 1970.

[26] Gambia, *Statistical Summary, 1966–7*, Sessional Paper No. 9 of 1967 (Bathurst, 1968), p. 10.

[27] *Ibid.*, pp. 16–17.

[28] *Ibid.*, p. 18. They fell again between 1966 and 1967. See mimeographed "Statistical Summary—Gambia 1966–67 Medical Figures—Jan.–June, July–December 1967 and year 1967."

[29] United Nations Economic Commission for Africa, "Recent Demographic Levels and Trends in Africa," *Economic Bulletin for Africa*, V (January 1965), 78.

These rates will be higher than those of natural increase, because Gambia has a net intake of migrants and by 1963 over one-ninth of the population was recorded as being of foreign birth. Immigrants (mostly from Senegal) have contributed to population growth both by their arrival and their subsequent reproduction (the latter cannot be calculated from the 1963 census separately from that of the whole community). If the 1931 proportion of foreign-born were only a third of that in 1963, if their arrival had occurred in equal increments during the entire period, and if their fertility (as related to their total numbers and not merely the female immigrants) were as high as the native-born population, then they could have been responsible for an average annual growth rate of over 0.4 percent for the period. Apparently most of these qualifications do not hold: it is believed that the 1963 census was held shortly after a burst of (perhaps short-term) seasonal immigration, and immigrant fertility is apparently low both because of the predominance of males and because many of the farmers immigrate leaving children, or subsequently fathering them, outside Gambia. Thus, it would probably be unwise to estimate the past or future immigrational contribution to population growth at more than 0.2 percent per annum, and this figure will be employed in all calculations in this chapter.

It may well be that at the time of the 1963 census natural increase stood at about 1.7 percent and annual total population growth at about 1.9 percent, the former figure, probably fortuitously, close to that which could be deduced by correcting the census or that which has been estimated by the United Nations. Nevertheless, one should not overlook the fragility of the series of assumptions upon which our estimates here are based.

So far the evidence available from the age structures recorded by the censuses has been little used, although these are the bases for much of the estimation of vital rates in Africa now that sets of model life tables are available and have been employed for the Princeton estimates given in Table 24.2. The use of these tables in Gambia, and elsewhere in West Africa, depends on the fact that fertility levels, if not mortality levels, have probably been fairly constant and that no great exactness is needed in determining mortality levels as these define the age structure to a much smaller extent than does fertility. Nevertheless, it is instructive to observe in Table 23.4 that the quite modest (in terms of any certainty about Gambia) variations in mortality assumptions there do change the crude birth rate estimates by up to four points (only three points according to population under 15 years of age) and those of the rate of natural increase by seven points or a quarter (only four points at 15 years of age). If we contrast two more extreme mortality assumptions, namely that the national level is still that found during the 1950s in Keneba and that the United Nations estimate is correct, then we can vary the birth rate estimate by nine points (seven at 15 years of age). If one goes further and varies the family of life tables (for there is no certainty about the relative levels of mortality at different ages in Gambia) or accepts the probability that mortality has been changing for decades, then estimates can diverge further still. Admittedly one should not be guided by age structure alone but should choose at least one other demographic parameter; however, these parameters are in fact such measures as the Keneba mortality statistics or the census death rates which have yielded the different estimates given above.

A much greater problem encountered when attempting to apply stable population models in tropical Africa is the absence of reliable age data. The Princeton group has attempted to minimize difficulties by using not the often highly irregular individual age groups but the cumulated proportion of the population under a certain age. The real problem then centers on choosing an appropriate proportion. The youngest five-year age group, those 0–4 years of age, might seem to be the right choice as being the product of the most recent births, but underenumeration and misenumeration of the ages in this group render it almost unusable in Gambia and much else of West

Africa. The Princeton group has tended to choose the 0–14 fraction, which has the advantage of being a large proportion of the total population (around two-fifths). The disadvantage here, and it is a substantial dis-advantage in Gambia and probably else-where, is that two of the three five-year age groups included are peculiarly defective. The age misstatement among 0–4-year-olds is of no concern as they will still be reported in the 0–14 group, but the omission of some of them, which probably occurred in Gambia, is serious. Among the older ones, there is almost certainly a greater loss of 10–14-year-olds, especially among females and particularly those marrying or reaching the menarche early (apparently much the same group), upward than there is of 15–19-year-olds downward.

Various remedies can be attempted. If, when examining female age structure, one could cumulate population only to 10 years of age and make an estimate of those 0–4-year-olds not enumerated at all (thus assuming no net movement over the tenth birthday, which does not seem certain), or cumulate to 25, for research in Nigeria does not seem to indicate much net movement over this birthday,[30] the position might be improved. Cumulation beyond 25 years means that the proportion can be affected by difficulties, which do occur, in obtaining the age data of the older population who are less likely to be educated or to have come into contact early with the Western concept of age. One can examine the male age structure or that of both sexes together (as in the Princeton estimates presented to the Nairobi Con-ference). The case for including the males is that their age statement is likely to be better, as beyond a certain age they more often speak for themselves (Thompson's data was provided most often by the older men), they have on average higher educational levels,[31]

and estimates are apparently not confused so much by enumerators endeavoring to relate their age to their marital condition or number of children; the case against, in Gambia and some other West African countries, is that their age structure is much more affected by migration.

In Table 24.4 the "North" Coale and Demeny models are used in keeping with the observation in *The Demography of Tropical Africa*[32] that there are indications that the mortality pattern incorporated in them may fit more closely to African infant and child mortality (this is true in the case of the patterns observed in Keneba although the resemblance is still not very close). Thus the stable populations employed in Table 24.4 are the same as those used in the Princeton estimates (Nairobi Conference) of Table 24.2. However, the Princeton Project (DTA) used the "West" tables for Gambia, but the difference in fertility estimates is small; for instance, at mortality level 7 the "North" and "West" (latter shown in brackets) estimates of the Gambian crude birth rate according to population cumulated to 5, 10, 15, 25, 35, and 40 years respectively is 39 (39), 43 (44), 41 (41), 46 (44), 57 (56), and 60 (59). Mortality level 7 (used in the first Princeton estimate—as the expectation of life figure employed in the second one is the joint one, level 8 was probably used for the more recent Princeton estimate) is treated as the central mortality estimate here in keeping with the argument employed earlier in the chapter based on the survival of the Keneba children to seven years of age; but it should be noted that, if a model were chosen according to their survival to two[33] (the key rate for selecting models in the recent Princeton estimate), level 9 would be appropriate for the early 1950s and probably

[30] Caldwell and Igun, "An Experiment with Census-type Age Enumeration."

[31] Indices demonstrating worse female than male age statement for certain specific ages and better statement by school attendance for the 1960 Ghana census are given in John C. Caldwell, "Population: General

Characteristics," in Walter Birmingham, I. Neustadt and E. N. Omaboe, eds., *A Study of Contemporary Ghana*, II, *Some Aspects of Social Structure* (London: George Allen and Unwin and Evanston: Northwestern University Press, 1967), p. 31.

[32] Brass et al., p. 113.

[33] Calculations from McGregor et al., "Growth and Mortality in Children," p. 1665, yield $_2q_0 = 0.235$.

TABLE 24.4

Estimates of vital rates obtained by comparing the 1963 Gambia census age structure with stable population models (Coale and Demeny "North" Table)[a]

(a)    Proportion of Population Enumerated in Census under Certain Age

Percent of Population            Corresponding Rates (per 1000 except for GRR)

| (Mortality levels)[c] | Gross reproduction rate[b] | | | Crude birth rate | | | Crude death rate | | | Natural increase | | |
|---|---|---|---|---|---|---|---|---|---|---|---|---|
| | (6) | (7) | (8) | (6) | (7) | (8) | (6) | (7) | (8) | (6) | (7) | (8) |
| *Females* | | | | | | | | | | | | |
| 5 years = 14.4 | 2.6 | 2.6 | 2.5 | 40 | 39 | 38 | 31 | 28 | 25 | 9 | 11 | 13 |
| 10 years = 28.5 | 3.0 | 2.9 | 2.8 | 45 | 43 | 42 | 31 | 28 | 26 | 14 | 15 | 16 |
| 15 years = 37.8 | 2.8 | 2.7 | 2.6 | 42 | 41 | 39 | 31 | 28 | 26 | 11 | 13 | 13 |
| 25 years = 59.2 | 3.1 | 3.1 | 3.0 | 47 | 46 | 44 | 31 | 28 | 26 | 16 | 18 | 18 |
| 35 years = 80.4 | 4.2 | 4.1 | 4.0 | 59 | 57 | 56 | 33 | 30 | 27 | 26 | 27 | 29 |
| 45 years = 90.0 | 4.6 | 4.4 | 4.3 | 63 | 60 | 59 | 34 | 30 | 27 | 29 | 30 | 32 |
| *Males* | | | | | | | | | | | | |
| 5 years = 13.8 | 2.6 | 2.5 | 2.5 | 39 | 39 | 38 | 34 | 31 | 28 | 5 | 8 | 10 |
| 10 years = 27.8 | 3.0 | 2.9 | 2.8 | 45 | 44 | 42 | 34 | 31 | 29 | 11 | 13 | 13 |
| 15 years = 37.4 | 2.8 | 2.7 | 2.6 | 43 | 42 | 42 | 34 | 31 | 29 | 9 | 10 | 13 |
| 25 years = 54.2 | 2.7 | 2.6 | 2.5 | 40 | 39 | 38 | 34 | 31 | 28 | 6 | 8 | 10 |
| 35 years = 72.5 | 3.1 | 2.9 | 2.8 | 45 | 44 | 43 | 34 | 31 | 29 | 11 | 13 | 14 |
| 45 years = 84.1 | 3.1 | 3.0 | 2.9 | 47 | 46 | 44 | 34 | 31 | 29 | 13 | 15 | 15 |

(b)   Certain Special Measures

Percent of Population            Corresponding Rates (per 1000 except GRR)

| (Mortality levels)[c] | (6) | (7) | (8) | (6) | (7) | (8) | (6) | (7) | (8) | (6) | (7) | (8) |
|---|---|---|---|---|---|---|---|---|---|---|---|---|
| *Females* | | | | | | | | | | | | |
| 5–9 = 14.1 | 3.7 | 3.6 | 3.5 | 54 | 52 | 49 | 32 | 29 | 26 | 22 | 23 | 23 |
| If under 10 = 30.0 | 3.2 | 3.1 | 3.1 | 48 | 46 | 45 | 31 | 28 | 26 | 17 | 18 | 19 |
| If under 10 = 31.0 | 3.4 | 3.3 | 3.2 | 50 | 48 | 47 | 32 | 29 | 26 | 18 | 19 | 21 |
| *Males* | | | | | | | | | | | | |
| 5–9 = 14.0 | 3.7 | 3.6 | 3.4 | 55 | 52 | 50 | 36 | 32 | 29 | 19 | 20 | 21 |
| If under 10 = 30.0 | 3.3 | 3.2 | 3.1 | 49 | 48 | 46 | 35 | 32 | 29 | 14 | 16 | 17 |
| If under 10 = 31.0 | 3.5 | 3.4 | 3.3 | 52 | 50 | 49 | 35 | 31 | 29 | 17 | 19 | 20 |
| *Keneba females*[d] | | | | | | | | | | | | |
| *Census | | | | | | | | | | | | |
| Under 15 = 40 | 3.1 | 3.0 | 2.9 | 46 | 44 | 43 | 31 | 28 | 26 | 15 | 16 | 17 |
| Under 45 = 85 | 3.3 | 3.2 | 3.1 | 48 | 47 | 46 | 31 | 29 | 26 | 17 | 18 | 20 |
| **Thompson | | | | | | | | | | | | |
| Under 15 = 42 | 3.3 | 3.2 | 3.1 | 49 | 47 | 46 | 31 | 29 | 26 | 18 | 18 | 20 |
| Under 45 = 81 | 2.7 | 2.6 | 2.5 | 40 | 39 | 38 | 31 | 28 | 26 | 9 | 11 | 12 |

[a] From Ansley J. Coale and Paul Demeny, *Regional Model Life Tables and Stable Population* (Princeton, N.J.: Princeton University Press, 1966).
[b] Assuming average age at childbearing to be 29 years.
[c] Female, male, and joint (assuming sex ratio at birth near parity) expectations of life at birth are respectively for mortality level 6—32.5, 29.6, and 31.1 years, for level 7—35.0, 32.0, and 33.5 years, and for level 8—37.5, 34.5, and 36.0 years.
[d] See Thompson in the second part of this chapter.

level 11 for the census date.[34] A further problem is that age distributions in Gambia, as well as some other West African countries, suggest little sex differential in overall mortality (except perhaps in old age) while the model life tables assume a higher female expectation of life. It is probable (and we will do this later when projecting population) that the best way of aggregating female and male data in Table 24.4 is to employ a mortality level for males one level above that applied to the data for females. In Table 24.4 gross reproduction rates have been calculated on the assumption of a mean age at childbearing of 29 years (based, in the absence of Gambian figures,[35] on a survey figure of $28\frac{1}{2}$ for the middle Senegal Valley in 1957, although the 1961 figure for the whole of Senegal yields an age about one year lower) in contrast to figures of 28 and 27 years used in later and earlier Princeton estimates respectively. It might be noted that, for the mortality levels considered here, the estimate of the gross reproduction rate drops by about one point for every two years fall in the average age of childbearing for our lower fertility estimates (i.e., birth rates in the low 40s) and by one point for every year for our higher fertility estimates (i.e., birth rates in the high 40s). Although the attempt to estimate a fertility level by choosing a model based on a certain mortality level does not necessarily indicate agreement that mortality can be so easily identified to within a few death rate points, the implications of these choices for the levels of death and natural increase rates have also been shown in the table.

Three points stand out clearly in Table 24.4. The first is that, even employing the same stable population family of models, the Gambian age structure can give rise to a wide range of fertility estimates. The second is that the use of cumulated age to 15 years (or to 5 years) yields some of the lowest estimates. The third is that the most substantial change caused by considering males in addition to females is to lower the fertility estimates derived by cumulating age to 25 or beyond (the joint estimates for the oldest two age groups are, with crude birth rates of 50 and 53,[36] still high, a phenomenon contrary to what might be anticipated to be the result of declining mortality).[37]

Some of the special measures are of interest. If we regard the 5–9 age group as being less affected by underenumeration or age shifts than its predecessor or successor, we obtain rather high fertility estimates; if we take the population under 10 and assume (perhaps conservatively) that the omission of very young children, as well as the recording of some 9-year-olds as 10, has reduced its apparent proportion of the whole population by first about 2 percent and then about 3 percent, we obtain joint birth rates around 47 and 49 respectively. If we employ Thompson's correction in Keneba for the proportion of females under 15, we obtain an estimate around 47 (but a lower figure if we use her correction for older women).

Obviously the 1963 census provided insufficient data to resolve all these problems, although the weight of evidence is probably on the side of the Princeton fertility estimates being somewhat low. In the speculation about prospects for population growth later in this chapter we shall use birth and death rate estimates for 1963 of 46 and 28 respectively. These are compatible with mortality model 7 for females and 8 for males and are fairly central to the estimated rates in Table 24.4. They have certain advantages. They are close to those suggested by the analysis of survey data from Senegal which surrounds Gambia. They allow for an omission by the 1963 census of 15 percent of the births and

---

[34] That is, joint expectations of life around $38\frac{1}{2}$ and $43\frac{1}{2}$ years respectively, or levels approximating to the United Nations estimates in Table 25.2. These estimates are not used here because they assume that about half the life table deaths in the interval from one to five years of age occur between one and two while in Keneba the proportion was only just over one-third.

[35] The average age of the 106 women who delivered live or stillborn children during Thompson's two years in Keneba was 28.03 years.

[36] Employing mortality level 7 and assuming equal numbers of each sex.

[37] United Nations (Ansley J. Coale and Paul Demeny), *Manual IV, Methods of Estimating Basic Demographic Measures from Incomplete Data* (New York, 1967), p. 26.

TABLE 24.5

Possible population trends in Gambia, 1963–2000 (all rates per 1,000)*

(a) Assuming That the Mortality Decline is Independent of the Fertility Decline

| Measure | | 1963 | 1970 | 1975 | 1980 | 1985 | 1990 | 1995 | 2000 |
|---|---|---|---|---|---|---|---|---|---|
| Expectation of life at birth (in years)[a] | | 34 | 37½ | 40 | 42½ | 45 | 47½ | 50 | 52½ |
| Birth rate[b] | (1a) | 46 | 46 | 45 | 45 | 44 | 44 | 44 | 44 |
| | (2a) | 46 | 46 | 43 | 40 | 38 | 36 | 34 | 31 |
| | (3a) | 46 | 46 | 43 | 40 | 37 | 34 | 30 | 25 |
| Death rate | (1a) | 28 | 26 | 24 | 22 | 20 | 18 | 16 | 15 |
| | (2a) | 28 | 26 | 23 | 21 | 19 | 17 | 15 | 14 |
| | (3a) | 28 | 26 | 23 | 21 | 19 | 16 | 15 | 13 |
| Rate of natural increase | (1a) | 18 | 20 | 21 | 23 | 24 | 26 | 28 | 29 |
| | (2a) | 18 | 20 | 20 | 19 | 19 | 19 | 19 | 17 |
| | (3a) | 18 | 20 | 20 | 19 | 18 | 18 | 15 | 12 |
| Immigration rate | | 2 | 2 | 2 | 2 | 2 | 2 | 2 | 2 |
| Population growth rate | (1a) | 20 | 22 | 23 | 25 | 26 | 28 | 30 | 31 |
| | (2a) | 20 | 22 | 22 | 21 | 21 | 21 | 21 | 19 |
| | (3a) | 20 | 22 | 22 | 21 | 20 | 20 | 17 | 14 |
| Population (in thousands)[c] | (1a) | 315 | 365 | 408 | 463 | 529 | 610 | 708 | 828 |
| | (2a) | 315 | 363 | 405 | 452 | 503 | 558 | 618 | 681 |
| | (3a) | 315 | 363 | 405 | 452 | 501 | 550 | 597 | 639 |
| Population indices (1963 = 100) | (1a) | 100 | 116 | 130 | 147 | 168 | 194 | 225 | 263 |
| | (2a) | 100 | 115 | 129 | 143 | 160 | 177 | 196 | 216 |
| | (3a) | 100 | 115 | 129 | 143 | 159 | 175 | 190 | 203 |
| Population density (persons per square mile)[d] | (1a) | 79 | 91 | 102 | 116 | 132 | 153 | 177 | 207 |
| | (2a) | 79 | 91 | 101 | 113 | 126 | 140 | 155 | 170 |
| | (3a) | 79 | 91 | 101 | 113 | 125 | 138 | 149 | 160 |

21 percent of the deaths which seem reasonably cautious figures in view of the collection methods and the very small numbers collected in some of the districts; the differential in omissions is in line with the statement by the census controller that, "It was found generally that births were easily remembered, whereas deaths are quickly forgotten, not an unusual case with unsophisticated agricultural communities having day to day economies."[38] The level of births and deaths approximates

[38] Oliver, *Report on the Census, 1963*, p. 8.

that suggested from the scraps of evidence considered earlier, as does the rate of natural increase to that suggested by the discussion of intercensal growth. A completed family size of a little over six children is more in line with anthropologists' expectations than one of not much over five.

POPULATION PROSPECTS. The paucity of Gambian data does not warrant the construction of more than outline population projections. That shown in part (a) of Table 24.5 assumes that a rise in expectation of life

TABLE 24.5 (*contd.*)

(b) Supplementary Projection, 1980–2000, Assuming That Reduced Family Size Leads to More Rapid Mortality Decline so That Increase in Expectation of Life at Birth after 1980 in Projections (2) and (3) are $1\frac{1}{2}$ and 2 Times Increase in Projections (1)

| Measure | | 1980 | 1985 | 1990 | 1995 | 2000 |
|---|---|---|---|---|---|---|
| Expectation of life at birth (in years)[a] | (1b) | $42\frac{1}{2}$ | 45 | $47\frac{1}{2}$ | 50 | $52\frac{1}{2}$ |
| | (2b) | $42\frac{1}{2}$ | $46\frac{1}{4}$ | 50 | $53\frac{3}{4}$ | $57\frac{1}{2}$ |
| | (3b) | $42\frac{1}{2}$ | $47\frac{1}{2}$ | $52\frac{1}{2}$ | $57\frac{1}{2}$ | $62\frac{1}{2}$ |
| Birth rate[b] | (1b) | 45 | 44 | 44 | 44 | 44 |
| | (2b) | 41 | 38 | 36 | 34 | 31 |
| | (3b) | 41 | 37 | 34 | 29 | 25 |
| Death rate | (1b) | 22 | 20 | 18 | 16 | 14 |
| | (2b) | 21 | 18 | 15 | 13 | 11 |
| | (3b) | 21 | 18 | 15 | 13 | 11 |
| Population growth rate | (1b) | 25 | 26 | 28 | 30 | 31 |
| | (2b) | 22 | 22 | 23 | 23 | 20 |
| | (3b) | 22 | 21 | 21 | 18 | 16 |
| Population (in thousands)[c] | (1b) | 463 | 529 | 610 | 708 | 828 |
| | (2b) | 452 | 505 | 565 | 631 | 704 |
| | (3b) | 452 | 523 | 557 | 609 | 659 |
| Population indices (1963 = 100) | (1b) | 147 | 168 | 194 | 225 | 263 |
| | (2b) | 143 | 160 | 179 | 200 | 223 |
| | (3b) | 143 | 166 | 177 | 193 | 209 |
| Population density (persons per square mile)[d] | (1b) | 116 | 132 | 153 | 177 | 207 |
| | (2b) | 113 | 126 | 141 | 158 | 176 |
| | (3b) | 113 | 131 | 139 | 152 | 165 |

NOTE: All dates are mid-year ones except for 1963 (census date = April 17–18); thus 1963–1970 = 7.2 years, while all other periods = 5 years.
[a] Assuming the Coale and Demeny "North" mortality levels of 7 for females and 8 for males in 1963 and a rise of one level for each subsequent listed date. The matching female and male tables are so similar that the rates have been read off the female table only.
[b] See text for assumptions.
[c] Growth rates for each period are assumed to be the average of the rates at each end.
[d] Based on a land area of 3,995 square miles.
* For possible correction of this table see "Note on the 1973 census" at the end of this chapter.

at birth of one year for every two years of time can be maintained for the rest of this century. The projection of fertility is more difficult because organized family planning has already begun on a limited scale in Banjul and there is a considerable possibility that a government program will be established. Thus three fertility trends have been suggested, the two incorporating declining fertility assuming that any decline will have some tendency to accelerate with time. (*1a*) *The constant fertility projection* assumes that the family planning work will make no real impact and that women will tend on average to have the same number of live births at the end of the century as they do now (perhaps on average 6.4). (*2a*) *The sustained moderate fertility decline projection* assumes the kind of gentle decline during 1970–1975 which would reduce the birth rate by two points during this time, and a slightly steeper decline after 1975 which would yield a fall of three points during 1975–1980 and which would reduce fertility levels (as measured by age-specific birth rates) to the same extent during each subsequent quinquennium. In comparison with the initial 1963–1970 fertility level, this would mean a decline during the first five years of just under 1 percent per annum and thereafter of 1.3 percent per annum, with a total fall in fertility by the year 2000 of 37 percent yielding a total fertility ratio by then of approximately four live births per woman. (*3a*) *The moderate followed by steeper fertility decline projection* assumes that family planning programs around the world will be more efficient and more accepted by 1980 and hence points to a steepening in fertility decline by a third after 1980 and a further third of the pre-1980 rate beyond 1985 so that during the last 15 years of the century fertility would be falling at over 2 percent of the 1963–1970 level per annum, resulting by the year 2000 in a total fall of 52 percent and a total fertility ratio averaging just over three live births per woman.

There is insufficient detailed population data to be able to construct such projections without employing assumptions from elsewhere. The 1963 census population age structure has been redistributed according to a stable population model (Coale and Demeny, "North") with the same birth and death rates as those estimated above and the same fraction of the population under 35 years of age. Senegalese age-specific birth rates were employed and were adjusted to match the estimated 1963 birth rate and the model age structure. All calculated fertility declines were proportional reductions of these rates, and hence, because of changing age structures, sometimes appear at variance with changes in the crude birth rates. A sex ratio at birth of 103 males per hundred females was used. We have inevitably assumed that the 1963 census was a reasonably accurate count of the population, and have also estimated growth caused by net immigration as continuing at 0.2 percent per annum.

The implications of part (a) of Table 24.5 are clear enough (and would not be very different even if birth and death rates were both a few points below what we have assumed here). With unchanged fertility, the annual rate of population growth is likely to rise above 3 percent after 1995, or, if immigration is held to zero, after the year 2000. Such growth rates would be achieved even with an expectation of life at birth which would not rise above 50 years until nearly the end of the century, a level reached by many developed countries early this century and now passed by many Asian and Latin American populations. Population would more than double in the 30 years after 1970 and by 2000 its density would approximate that of contemporary East Asia.

It is quite conceivable that a fertility decline, almost certainly with government assistance if it is to be on any significant scale, could appreciably reduce birth rates by the late 1970s and potential population size by the late 1980s (and that of some subdivisions, such as children of school age by the early 1980s) below the level of the constant fertility projection. The projections bring out important points about the effect of changing age structure consequent upon changing fertility. For a long time initially high fertility populations experience little but economic advantage as their birth rates decline; their productive adult age groups continue to grow in size while the proportion of the population consisting of children needing support and education falls. Thus the so-called labor-force age group, 15–64 years of age, would in projections (1a), (2a), and (3a) grow between 1963 and 2000 by 136, 122, and 121 percent respectively, exhibiting relatively small differences. But the school-age population would increase by 178, 99 and 75 percent respectively, yielding great contrasts in terms of potential support and schooling costs. By the year 2000 the proportion of the population in the labor-force age range would be 52, 60, and 63 percent respectively according to the three projections, again yielding great contrasts in terms of economic efficiency.

Eventually fertility decline produces another demographic effect: At the same real level of mortality (as measured by age-specific death rates, life table functions, etc.), low-fertility countries exhibit higher crude death rates than do moderate-fertility ones. As fertility declines, this eventually becomes quite an important brake upon population growth. However, until 2000 and beyond this phenomenon is not witnessed, partly because insufficient time has elapsed for the numbers of aged to swell and partly because of the declining proportion of very young children at high mortality risk—indeed, so marked is the latter effect that by the year 2000 the lowest death rate is recorded by projection (3a) followed by (2a). It is quite possible that this differential will be even more marked, in that a decline in population growth will make it possible to raise living and health standards, and, perhaps more important, that children are better looked after in small families than they are in large ones.[39] These are undeniably community gains. But are they to some degree self-defeating in that they will tend to raise population growth rates? It has even been argued that fertility fall might be completely offset by the reduction in infant and child mortality it causes. The further use of the models for the supplementary projections in part (b) of Table 24.5 shows that this argument should not be overstated. Even the most extreme improvement in health, that envisaged for projection (3b) (with improvement in mortality after 1980 double that previously projected), does not reduce the gap which would otherwise have opened up at the end of the century between projections (1a) and (3a) by more than one-eighth in the rate of natural increase and one-ninth in population numbers.

One other interrelation of the variables has not been explored, because it is probably

[39] There is some evidence of this for Ghana (see John C. Caldwell, "The Erosion of the Family: A Study of the Fate of the Family in Ghana," *Population Studies*, XX, 1 (July 1966), 10–14).

not likely to have much effect in the period discussed, although the validity of this judgment may be debatable. That is the possibility of "Malthusian" pressures developing to the extent that the projected health gains in part (a) of Table 24.5 will ultimately not be attainable if fertility remains constant because of pressure on resources. Such an eventuality would of course be a major social loss, perhaps even a catastrophe, even though a slower growth rate were thereby attained.

Some of the demographic indices in Table 24.5 should be put into perspective. The birth rates attributed to the declining fertility projections (2) and (3) in the year 2000 are still higher than those now found in any developed country. The rates of population growth in 2000 in these two projections are higher than that of any industrializing country in Europe during the so-called population boom there during the late nineteenth century. The size of the quinquennial population increments does not begin to decline in the two projections until after 2000 and 1990 respectively, and at the point of decline the five yearly additions are greater than the seven-year one between the 1963 census and 1970. Even projection (3), with its very rapid fertility decline, envisages population more than doubling between 1963 and 2000.

The real paradox of the Gambian situation may be that the high rate of population growth and the increasing population density hamper the attempt to raise living standards, while, at the same time, the small size of the total population also tends to frustrate economic development. The latter problem is, however, an outcome of the country's very small area; the solution lies in joining with larger units either by political fusion or by the creation of trade pacts and common markets.

THE CHANGING SOCIETY. The demographer is necessarily interested in many aspects of a society in the sense that social changes can be the cause or result of demographic changes. The positions of declining birth rates in some of the projections in Table 24.5

indicates an anticipation that very great changes in attitudes and practices in some aspects of family life could take place; conversely, declining mortality, more a product of economic advancement and technological innovation than of sociological factors, must eventually profoundly change family and community behavior patterns. The relevant Gambian data are limited, so only a few key matters will be touched on here.

Social change in Africa, as elsewhere, has often proceeded furthest in the towns, where adjustments have to be made to conditions very different from the traditional farming village, and where new patterns of living are most easily imported from outside or adopted from foreign residents. The local population also tends to be atypical of the country as a whole, especially in such characteristics as educational levels and, of course, in occupation.

There are obvious limits to urbanization in Gambia, in that the population of the whole country is smaller than that of Accra and only a fraction of that of a real city like Lagos. These limits may impose economic difficulties in the development of manufacturing industries and may retard other aspects of modernization, such as the creation of a local university. By mid-1970, Gambia's only real urban area, the Banjul-Kombo St. Mary area, probably contained about 50,000 inhabitants or almost one-seventh of the population of the country (a much larger fraction than Accra or Lagos are of their own countries but comparable to Dakar's position in Senegal). Because of problems in developing industry, it is possible that this urban population will not grow much faster than the present town-planning estimate of 4 percent per annum, thus reaching 110,000 inhabitants in 1990 and 160,000 at the end of the century. Assuming that the falling fertility projections imply faster modernization and hence do not influence absolute urban population growth rates, this means that the population living within the chief urban area will climb from 14 percent of that of the whole country in 1970 to 18–20 percent in 2000. However, the

spread of rural schooling or the growth of rural unemployment could swell the rural-urban migration to a greater extent than just envisaged regardless of the occupational opportunities in Banjul. It should be emphasized that the Banjul-Kombo St. Mary area is not a single, nucleated, densely settled center (at the 1963 census this description would have applied only to Banjul making up about two-thirds of the total). Nor does it offer the variety of experience that a larger center would present to an immigrant from rural areas. However, it does contain a very high proportion of the elite of the new nation, and there is no doubt that Gambian behavior patterns are developing which are very different from the traditional ones. If fertility does fall, it is among this group that the phenomenon should first be detected.

The data from the *Statistical Summaries* and the 1963 Census Report (which contains nothing on occupation or education) allow the following observations on the contrast between Banjul-Kombo St. Mary and the rest of the country. As was noted earlier from the registration statistics, there is as yet no real evidence that fertility is lower in the town, but mortality is probably markedly lower. Certainly, as will be seen below, schooling is almost universal, while in the rest of the country it probably still impinges on only a minority of children. The town is cosmopolitan: In 1963 one-quarter of the population of Banjul-Kombo St. Mary was of foreign origin compared with one-eighth in the country as a whole; at the same date, one-fifth of the Gambian-born population of Banjul and nearly one-half of Kombo St. Mary[40] were immigrants from other parts of the country compared with a fraction of one-seventh for all the districts of the country. Nevertheless, Banjul is not yet by any means the destination for all the mobile or occupationally surplus population of the

[40] In each of these two centers, now really a single urban group, some of this movement may have merely originated in the other, but the published data do not allow these movements to be separated.

country. Between 1911 and 1931 its population grew by 91 percent compared with 37 percent for the whole country, while between 1931 and 1963 the respective percentages were 89 and 58 percent. But probably Banjul's faster growth can be explained largely in terms of a higher rate of natural increase, because of lower mortality, and a greater attraction for foreign immigrants. The 1963 census reported, in terms of moves since birth, almost as much movement out of Banjul as into it.[41] The relatively small importance of immigration has meant certain social gains; the male surplus over females in 1963 was only 10 percent in Banjul-Kombo St. Mary compared with 4 percent in the whole country (in 1960 in Ghana it was 14 percent in Accra and 17 percent in Sekondi-Takoradi compared with 2 percent in the whole country).

Migratory movements continue to be of demographic and social importance because of the small size of the country. In 1963 one-ninth of the population was enumerated as being foreign born—one-eighth of all males and one-tenth of all females. Of these, 51 percent came from surrounding Senegal (35 percent from that to the north of Gambia and 26 percent from that to the south), 15 percent from Guinea, 13 percent from Guinea (Bissau), 5 percent from Mali, and 2 percent from Sierra Leone.[42] Thus Gambia attracted Africans almost exclusively from the far west of the continent, almost all from distances of less than 500 miles and probably the majority from less than 100 miles. Of the 768 non-Africans enumerated in 1963 (i.e., 2.2 percent of all foreign immigrants and 0.2 percent of the total population), over half were British and only one-ninth were Asian.

A major source of change, and even more of potential change, in West Africa over the last decade or two has been the spread of formal education. The development of Gambia's education system during the 1950s was apparently slower than in some other parts of English-speaking Africa and coastal

Africa, so that by the 1963 census not much more than a quarter of the males and about a tenth of the females 5–14 years of age were currently attending school (compared with half of males and almost a third of females, 6–14, in Ghana, admittedly a leader in West Africa, as early as 1960).[43] But subsequent change was rapid, and attendance at both primary and secondary schools rose by about 10 percent per year over the next few years, so that by 1966–1967 it was possible that half of all young males and a quarter of all young females were receiving some years of schooling. The educational coverage was, of course, uneven; not only were almost two-and-one-half times as many boys as girls in school, but (in contrast to Ghana's history of the previous decade) the ratio was not improving. There was also a marked urban-rural differential; by 1966–1967 the numbers of males and females in all schools in Banjul-Kombo St. Mary made up 122 and 76 percent respectively of the size of the 5–14-year-old group in that area enumerated in the 1963 census (now 8–17, diminished by some deaths and doubtless supplemented to a greater degree by net immigration), suggesting that nearly all the town children now get some schooling and that there is a marked movement into Banjul and Kombo St. Mary for education. This is in fact so, especially in secondary education, for in 1966–1967 this area accounted for more than four-fifths of all secondary school places in the country contrasted with only two-fifths of primary school places. Finally, it might be noted that a continuation of the expansion of schooling at the rate experienced in the mid-1960s (economically rather a favorable

41 Oliver, *Report on the Census, 1963*, p. 36.
42 *Ibid.*, p. 122.

43 The Gambian educational data are from the *Statistical Summary, 1966–7*, pp. 16–17 and the population data from the *Report on the Census, 1963*, p. 41; the Ghanaian data are from *1960 Population Census of Ghana*, III, *Demographic Characteristics* (Accra, 1964), p. 11. To take certain other selected tropical African countries, Gambia's educational rate for males was similar to Liberia, worse than Ivory Coast, Senegal, Kenya, Uganda, and Tanzania and much better than Mali and Upper Volta; the ratio of females to males at school was very similar to all of them. See United Nations, *Compendium of Social Statistics: 1967* (New York, 1968), Tables 34 and 35.

period) would get all children into primary schools, with perhaps a quarter going on to some secondary schooling, by 1990 according to the constant fertility projection (1a) and by 1980 according to the declining fertility projections (2a) and (3a).

Significant economic changes are also under way. Among the limited range of statistics available for the years after the census,[44] one can note without any special selection for high rates of increase, such average annual rates of increase as the following (with no increase during the period in the retail price index): value of exports, 15 percent; number of letters posted 13 percent; number of motor vehicles licensed, 40 percent. This may have been a particularly favorable period for agricultural exports and hence for national and individual incomes, but it should be noted that important fundamental changes are continuing to occur in rural areas, which form the major sector of the economy. Cash agricultural production, dominated since the 1890s by groundnuts which still form well over 90 percent of all exports by value (local processing before export has been increasing), is forming a larger proportion of all agriculture. It has been conspicuously successful, in terms of West African comparisons, during the 1960s in adapting itself, with government assistance, to better plant varieties, the use of greater quantities of fertilizer, and the use of local cattle as draught animals for ploughing. The river valley is also proving to be one of the limited areas in West Africa suited to the new varieties of rice which depend on plentiful water (usually from irrigation), labor, and fertilizer. Innovation may be easier for local communities to agree on in cash-export-food production than in the subsistence production of local foodstuffs, partly because everything concerned with such production is relatively innovational, but perhaps partly too because (as Thompson points out) the men (who undoubtedly make most decisions) are

concerned with cash production while subsistence farming is largely a female monopoly.

One demographic measure, which is of very considerable significance for the future of rural Gambia, is that of density of settlement. By 1963 its population density, at 79 persons per square mile, was one-third higher than the world average, twice that of all West Africa, and three times that of the whole African continent. It was the same as the density of Ghana, and twice that of Kenya, the two countries in tropical Africa that have since established national family planning programs. Gambia's overall density was only one-third that of Europe, but such comparisons ignore the fact that much of Europe's population is concentrated in industrial cities; Europe's density of population economically dependent on agriculture is now well below that of Gambia. It is true that these densities reflect the riverine nature of much of the country, and that some recent agricultural innovations, particularly the growing of the new heavy-yielding varieties of rice, are labor intensive. Nevertheless it is unlikely that rural living standards can continue to rise indefinitely as annual growth rates increase from 2 percent to 3 percent. Satisfactory rises in living standards would seem to be more consonant with lower growth rates and with the moving of a substantial part of the population increment of the decades ahead out of agriculture. The first depends on whether a fertility decline can be induced, as is discussed below, and the second on whether nonagricultural employment can expand sufficiently rapidly. There are very real problems in a country of Gambia's size in creating an urban complex which can provide that employment. As economies have developed in many areas, the surplus rural population, no longer needed by modernizing more highly capitalized agriculture, has migrated to the industrial cities from which have come much of the goods and scientific research which have raised rural productivity. Migration streams flowed not only within European countries but east-west and south-north across the continent to the manufacturing cities of northwestern Europe, and

[44] These are all from the *Statistical Summary, 1966–7*, pp. 12 and 24.

beyond to North America. The main impetus which is raising rural productivity and rates of natural increase in Gambia comes from outside the country, and it is unlikely that Banjul will be able to import an urban, manufacturing technology on any significant scale, although (to examine some cities in larger countries) Lagos seems to have made a successful start, Accra-Tema may also make a breakthrough, and so perhaps may Dakar. Moreover, it is increasingly doubtful whether any significant number of Gambians will be able to migrate to London or Manchester, and eventually even movement to Dakar may be hindered. Thus rapid population growth may pose greater problems for countries the size of Gambia than it does for ones like Ghana or Senegal which may develop their own industrial metropolises.

FAMILY PLANNING AND POPULATION POLICIES. Doctors and hospital authorities in Banjul reported an increasing number of requests during the late 1960s for help with contraception or abortion. Nearly all the demand in the country for such services comes from the Banjul-Kombo St. Mary area and necessarily almost entirely from nonfarming populations with a heavy concentration among the new administrative elite. The family planning clinic reported that a woman was unlikely to seek its assistance unless she had at least some schooling.

Partly as a result of this rising internal demand, partly because local doctors were coming into contact with ideas about family planning at international and African medical conferences, partly because international technical personnel were increasingly regarding rapid population growth as a matter for either their individual or public concern, and partly because of visits by representatives of such organizations as the Pathfinder Fund and the International Planned Parenthood Federation (IPPF), a Gambian Family Planning Association was founded in 1968 and subsequent affiliation with the IPPF was secured. With assistance from these outside bodies, a family planning clinic was opened in Banjul in 1969. In addition at

least one doctor provides a considerable family planning service through his private practice. It is believed that some abortions also are performed.

An increase in government interest in population matters paralleled these developments. Population growth had been a matter for some administrative concern from the time of the 1963 census and from the publication of the Census Report in 1965. In 1968 and 1969 reports on the Gambian economy by the International Monetary Fund and by an expert provided by the British Ministry of Overseas Development emphasized the population component in prospective economic growth and included estimates of population change. On the request of the Ministry of Health, the Population Council sent a mission to the country in 1969 and submitted a report in 1970 recommending a government family planning program.

THE FUTURE.   Analogy with mortality trends elsewhere, the increasing expenditure by the Gambian government on health services, and the pace of educational and economic change in the country suggest that mortality will continue to decline, probably as fast as is postulated in Table 24.5. Educational change is probably important, as a striking differential has been shown for Ghana in child survival according to the educational levels reached by their mothers.[45] Nevertheless, the length of the country and the almost complete concentration of doctors and superior hospital facilities at one end of it in Banjul means that there will be considerable difficulty in markedly raising health levels in upcountry villages. Offsetting this is the improvement of the highway inland from Banjul the extensive system of rural health centers and dispensaries, and the large numbers of nurses, midwives, sanitary personnel, and medical auxiliaries now being trained in the new Gambian School of Nursing and Midwifery and the new Public Health School. With regard to the health staff, much will depend not on the

[45] S. K. Gaisie, *Dynamics of Population Growth in Ghana*, (Accra-Tema: Ghana Publishing Corporation, 1969), pp. 50–51.

numbers being trained but on how many will ultimately remain in Gambia, for nurses, at least, may still be able to migrate to Britain. Similarly there are sufficient Gambians already trained or now being trained outside Gambia in medicine to triple the existing supply of doctors, but it is doubtful if many of them will return.

The major question is whether fertility is likely to fall among any sections of the society. Such a fall would only be likely to occur if antinatal measures such as contraception or partial or total sexual abstinence or abortion, whether legal or illegal, became increasingly more common. This in turn depends partly on whether pressure to reduce family size becomes greater and partly on whether access to contraceptives and contraceptive knowledge spreads.

The evidence that we have on the desire to restrict family size in Africa suggests that urbanization and the spread of education are by far the most important determinants,[46] with the spread of cash farming possibly playing some role.[47] It would in fact be surprising if birth rates did not fall in Banjul-Kombo St. Mary in the next few years, but it might be noted that any decline confined to this area would mean only a seventh as much decline in national figures now, and perhaps one-fifth as much in 1990, and one-quarter as much in the year 2000 (i.e., a fall in the urban birth rate from 46 to 26 in 1990 would mean that the national rate would be 42 if the rate outside the capital

remained unchanged). Perhaps more fertility decline will derive from the rapid expansion of schooling in the 1960s and from the possibility that nearly all the children will be in schools some time in the 1980s. Ultimately this will mean educated married couples with a greater propensity to restrict family size, but even earlier it will mean the extra financial burdens of keeping children at school, forgoing some of their productive labor, and meeting the extra demands for expenditure that educated children seem to make. The pressure to keep children at school is particularly strong among the non-farming population which assumes that its children's earning power will be related to their training. Obviously, then, the educational aspect of fertility fall is to a large extent a component of the urban aspect. It is also possible that the tendency toward growth in real family size with falling infant and child mortality will also influence parents to try to restrict fertility.

World publicity during the 1960s, and the accompanying legitimation of private and press discussion of family planning has certainly spread knowledge about contraception in Africa, especially in the towns and among the educated. However, fertility is more likely to fall in the 1970s and 1980s in Gambia if such sources are supplemented by more exact information, and by the supply of free or cheap contraceptives, from a government family planning program or perhaps from a large voluntary association program supported by the government. In a country where nearly all rural medical help comes from the government, rural fertility is unlikely to fall without similar efforts in the family planning field. Analogy with what has been happening in Asia suggests that programs of this type will probably appear throughout tropical Africa during the 1970s, and that the real question is whether they appear in most areas during the earlier part of the decade or later.

## SOME DEMOGRAPHIC FACTORS ILLUSTRATED IN A GAMBIAN VILLAGE

The village of Keneba is situated in the middle of a peninsula, about 100 miles inland

[46] Various findings have been summarized by Caldwell in (i) "The Control of Family Size in Tropical Africa," *Demography*, V, 2 (1968), 598–619, and (ii) "Anti-natal Practice in Tropical Africa," *Proceedings of the International Population Conference*, (London, 1969), II, 1223–39, while the educational aspect has been treated at some length in (iii) *Population Growth and Family Change in Africa: The New Urban Elite in Ghana* (Canberra: Australian National University Press, 1968), esp. pp. 104–10.

[47] The evidence presented in John C. Caldwell, "Fertility Attitudes in Three Economically Contrasting Rural Regions of Ghana," *Economic Development and Cultural Change*, XV, 2 (January 1967), 217–38 seems to bear this out, as to a somewhat lesser degree do the data in John C. Caldwell and Adenola Igun, "The Spread of Anti-natal Knowledge and Practice in Nigeria," *Population Studies* XXIV, 1 (March 1970), 21–34.

from Banjul with a crescent of mosquito-breeding swamps to the south. In 1949, Keneba was chosen as a field station for entomological and medical research by the Medical Research Council (MRC) Laboratories.[48] Since then a villager literate in Arabic has kept a record of births and deaths and the people have been weighed, measured, and medically examined annually. These data showed[49] that the pattern of growth and mortality of children was similar to that in other developing countries, and by Western standards lightweight babies were the rule. Good growth occurred in the first few months of infancy; subsequently there was a faltering; and nearly half the children died before five years of age.

A research project focused on the growth and health of young children was therefore undertaken during two years of continuous residence (1962 and 1963) in the village to identify the factors involved and to study seasonal variations in the pattern. The research was based on daily observation, questioning, and regular measuring.[50] The work done in Keneba and in three adjacent villages, together with reports of other writers[51] indicate that in many respects the findings in Keneba are fairly typical not only of Gambia but also of other large parts of West Africa. Demographic processes too may be similar in much of the region. Partly because of its isolation, however, the

pattern of life in Keneba remained very traditional although it was being increasingly exposed to external pressures and the youths were beginning to question the accepted order. Unrest was accelerated in 1963 as a consequence of the opening of an all-weather road from Banjul which passed about 12 miles from the village.

THE VILLAGE ECONOMY AND ENVIRONMENT. Keneba is a Moslem village with pagan undertones. It has no market, transport, or school and there is no pipe-borne water or sanitation. The people are peasants practicing slash-and-burn, hand-hoe cultivation. Children are an economic asset with the minimum period of dependence; they enter the labor force at about 4–6 years, the boys as shepherds and the girls as "nursemaids." The sharp division of labor between males and females persists as they grow older and progress through various stages of training until they have acquired adult skills. During the rainy season (May–November) all able-bodied adults must farm; the men grow groundnuts, the only cash crop, and some millet for food, while the women cultivate rice at swamps up to eight miles distant. A few men have an additional source of income, usually from a dry-season occupation (e.g., weaving or tailoring), but such activities are restricted by other demands (e.g., building, thatching, and fence making).

The village is not entirely self-supporting as each year food has to be bought on credit to tide the people over until the new crops are harvested. Food is scarce during the rainy season when farming is at its peak and the people lose weight. This applies even to pregnant women, and babies born during the rainy season apparently tend to be lightweight.[52] Children of more than a few months old are left behind in the village during the daytime while the mothers work at the

[48] I. A. McGregor and D. A. Smith, "Health, Nutrition and Parasitological Survey in a Rural Village (Keneba) in West Kiang, Gambia," *Transactions of the Royal Society of Tropical Medicine and Hygiene*, XLVI (July 1952), 403–27.

[49] McGregor et al., "Growth and Mortality in Children."

[50] Thomson et al., "Study of Growth and Health of Young Children."

[51] For example: M. H. Haswell, *The Changing Pattern of Economic Activity in a Gambian Village* (London, 1964); D. P. Gamble, *Economic Conditions in Two Mandinka Villages* (London: Colonial Office Research Department, 1955); F. Lorimer, *Culture and Human Fertility* (Paris: UNESCO, 1954); D. Morley, J. Bricknell, and M. Woodland, "Factors Influencing the Growth and Nutritional Status of Infants and Young Children in a Nigerian Village," *Transactions of the Royal Society of Tropical Medicine and Hygiene*, LXII, 2 (March 1968), 164–99; and Marsden, "The Sukuta Project."

[52] A. M. Thomson, W. Z. Billewicz, B. Thompson et al., "Body Weight Change during Pregnancy and Lactation in Rural African (Gambian) Women," *Journal of Obstetrics and Gynaecology of the British Commonwealth*, LXXIII (October 1966), 724–33; B. Thompson, "The First Fourteen Days of Some West African Babies," *Lancet*, II (July 1966), 40–45.

swamps and child care is unsatisfactory.[53] Illness, notably malaria and other insect-borne diseases, but excluding measles and certain common infectious diseases, is more prevalent and severe in the rainy season.

POPULATION. There were 768 persons (382 males and 386 females) living in Keneba (excluding the MRC compound) when the national census was taken in April 1963. The census was carefully prepared and rehearsed. Enumerators visited in December 1962, numbered all huts and took a preliminary count; there was also a rehearsal just prior to the census. In October 1962 and 1963, this writer also took a census. These five counts of the population in Keneba ranged between 795 and 758 persons, differences being easily accounted for by migration, temporary absence (a feature of the dry season), births, and deaths.

In October 1963 the population of Keneba was 763, the loss of 31 persons in the year being almost entirely due to migration: 68 persons left Keneba, but only 38 came there, while 25 deaths were offset by 24 births. The migrants out were mainly families of ex-slave origin who moved to settle in villages springing up along the new trunk road to Bathurst. A review of the national census data in the light of two years' findings leads to the following conclusions:

(1) As a count of males and females, the national census was excellent.

(2) Ages were reasonably comparable having regard to the different methods of assessment. In the national census 40 percent of the population was recorded as under 15 years of age and 15 percent as aged over 45 years compared with my estimates of 42 and 19 percent respectively. In the national census, ages were estimated by senior men (grey hair and position in family rather than chronological age indicate seniority) in the family

and ages of older persons, particularly women, appear to be underestimated. Birth dates were known from the project's records for those born in Keneba or adjacent villages since 1950. For the remainder the physiological assessment of age by a medical officer (Dr. I. A. McGregor), made in the course of routine annual medical surveys were used and adjusted to agree with seniority within families. In addition approximate ages were checked with *kafo* group (age set) membership, which gives a reliable age for men and women born in Keneba. Since marriage is patrilocal, ages were more difficult to assess for wives who had come to live in the village. From dates of birth available for the most recently formed *kafo* groups it was established that members' ages spanned about three years, but there was some overlap between groups.

(3) The national census data and my information on place of birth and ethnic origin are very different. The former recorded only 8 persons as having been born outside Keneba, whereas I listed over 160 persons. In the national census all except two persons were given as Mandinka whereas I found that about one-third were of Jola ancestry. There were some glaring discrepancies in the census. For example, a Tilibonko born in Mali and a Jola born in Guinea were returned as Mandinka born in Keneba.

Questions on ethnic origin are difficult, however, because of the association with slavery. In the Keneba area, the pagan, matrilineal Jolas seem to have been converted to Islam and to have realigned themselves to accommodate to patriliny and to patrilocal marriage. Nevertheless, some customary restrictions on intermarriage persist and, without inherited wealth and access to the best agricultural lands, Jolas tend to be perpetuated as a lower social class if they remain in the village. I saw the original census records nearly a year later, as I was leaving Gambia and it was too late to investigate the reasons for differences, to find out exactly how questions were posed, to discover if there were any fears of discrimination, and so forth.

[53] B. Thompson and A. K. Rahman, "Infant Feeding and Child Care in a West African Village," *Journal of Tropical Pediatrics*, XII (September 1967), 124–38.

It is not known how far the experience in Keneba is typical of rural Gambia. It may be that Jolas now consider that they have become Mandinka and that the people consider their place of birth as the village where they inherit land. Differences in definitions could account for the discrepancies in the findings on ethnic origin and birth place. It is apparent that the census taken in Keneba gave a reliable count of males and females and provided a reasonable record of ages.

MARRIAGE AND FERTILITY HISTORIES. *Records used.* Histories of marriage and reproduction can never be accepted as accurate in conditions such as exist in rural Africa. Many factors militate against completeness as other researchers (for example, Ardener) have reported.[53] Information obtained may depend on whether men or women are interviewed, their knowledge of the interviewer, the circumstances and timing of the inquiries, and so forth.

In rural Gambia, women are blamed if marriages are childless while multiple wives are a sign of wealth and power, so that men were more likely to report infertile marriages which had already ended in divorce. The people have a strong belief in magic, spirits, sorcery, and witchcraft, and, possibly for these reasons, pregnant women sometimes give very inaccurate obstetric histories, omitting mention of abortions, stillbirths, or deaths for fear of harming the fetus. For example, antenatally a women presented herself as a primigravida but postnatally disclosed that she had no surviving children out of three previous pregnancies which had occurred elsewhere. In the belief that she was protecting him from harm, one mother would not acknowledge verbally her son, her thirteenth and only surviving child.

The situation in Keneba was particularly favorable for demographic inquiries. The people were used to a wide range of MRC activities; there was no hostility and cooperation was excellent. Added to this was

the knowledge of individuals and customs accumulated during daily work in the village over two years.

It was possible therefore to obtain a detailed family, marriage, and pregnancy history for each adult, to cross-reference those of siblings and spouses, and to check discrepancies. Births registered since 1950 provided valuable evidence of accuracy. In the early years, however, the registrar had usually only recorded births of children likely to be available for annual medical examination and therefore there was no previous record of most stillbirths and of about one-fifth of neonatal deaths. A further check on births was provided by a knowledge of customary naming practices; certain names were given to the first-born son, twins, a child following a twin pregnancy, and so forth. Care had to be taken in cross-referencing histories, however, as the mother and father sometimes referred to a child who had died in infancy by different names.

The proportion of abortions, stillbirths, and live births recorded among all pregnancies experienced by the women was similar to that which was found in Keneba in the two years of the study, namely 6:7:99. This abortion rate is very low and suggests that some early abortions may have been missed.

Of women past childbearing age, the oldest, who had usually outlived their husbands, tended to report fewer marriages and births than the younger women. For example, women in their fifties reported on average 6.3 live births compared with 6.0 live births for women aged 60 years and over. It is impossible to say whether aging may account for faulty memory or whether, being less exposed to the risks of childbearing and thus to maternal morbidity, the least fertile may live longer.

*The marriage pattern.* Marriage is clearly defined and the procedure is uniform. Both men and women marry in order of seniority within the family and all first marriages are arranged following circumcision and betrothal.

A girl is betrothed and "bride price" agreed upon any time after initiation in

54 E. Ardener, *Divorce and Fertility: An African Study* (London: Oxford University Press, 1962).

childhood. The operation is a minor form of clitoridectomy and does not usually complicate childbirth. As soon as she has passed the menarche, a woman starts visiting her husband's hut at night in rotation with any co-wives, two nights about. A wife does not transfer to live with her husband's family until the "bride price" has been paid and the defined obligations on both families fulfilled. Thus initially opportunities for coitus may be restricted if the couple live in different villages, as the husband must go to his wife's village and this may be impracticable during the rainy season when the pressure of farming is great. Coitus is taboo during menstruation and allegedly during lactation.

From the menarche on, a woman must be married continuously in order to go to Paradise, which the people believe can only be achieved at the instigation of the husband at her death. A specified time (about four months) must elapse, however, following divorce or widowhood in order to avoid any possible paternity disputes. All children belong to their father's family so that if the woman is pregnant, remarriage takes place whenever the pregnancy ends. Elderly women, if widowed or divorced, choose a "nominal" husband.

Table 24.6 shows that women usually are betrothed before age 15 and married before they are aged 20 years. Two older women remained unmarried. They were incapable of pounding grain and performing normal domestic and farming duties and were considered "as children"—one was "simple" and the other had been left badly crippled and mentally disturbed following a severe pyrexial illness in adolescence. At any time there are likely to be a few women in the transitional stage between marriages. Thus there was one divorced woman in Keneba in October 1962 and two older women who had recently been widowed.

As Moslems the men are permitted up to four wives at any time. However, the majority of married men (58 percent) had only one wife. Monogamy is considered only a temporary state and most men expect to achieve polygyny although it is only the oldest and wealthiest men who ever have the maximum of four wives. Only three men in Keneba had four wives; one of these had been married five times and had fathered the highest number of children (38), although only half had survived. No man had more than two wives of childbearing age. Most second and later wives (63 percent) had been married previously and had already "transferred as a bride," a ceremony which each woman goes through once in her lifetime. There are always plenty of offers made for a widow or divorced woman of childbearing age as the formalities are minimal and relatively cheap, in marked contrast to the elaborate and costly procedure of "transferring a bride."

Men who marry a virgin will expect to be

TABLE 24.6
Marital state of Keneba women by age, October 1962

| | Number of Women | | | | | | | |
| | 10–14 | 15–19 | 20–29 | 30–39 | 40–49 | 50–59 | 60+ | All Ages |
|---|---|---|---|---|---|---|---|---|
| *Never married* | | | | | | | | |
| Not betrothed | 20 | — | — | — | 1 | — | — | 21 |
| Betrothed | 30 | 8 | 1 | — | — | — | — | 39 |
| *Married* | 1 | 24 | 56 | 49 | 48 | 25 | 4 | 207 |
| *Divorced* | — | — | — | 1 | — | — | — | 1 |
| *Nominal state* | | | | | | | | |
| Unmarried | — | — | — | — | — | — | 2 | 2 |
| Married | — | — | — | — | — | 2 | 24 | 26 |
| *Total* | 51 | 32 | 57 | 50 | 49 | 27 | 30 | 296 |

responsible for her "transfer" although occasionally death or divorce may intervene, in which case a later husband will have to accept this commitment. "Transfer" takes place in the dry season after the husband has paid the "bride price" and reimbursed her father for the cost of her circumcision, any cosmetic operation such as lip tattooing, and certain other expenses of her upbringing. At night, following a day of preparation and ritual, most villagers attend the main ceremony, after which the bride goes in a procession to her husband's hut. The bride shares her husband's hut for a week during which time various customs are followed. The bride is feasted daily and for this one week in her life she is relieved of all domestic duties. A previously "transferred wife" is able to go and live with her new husband as soon as the waiting period has expired and the "bride price" can be paid later by installments.[55]

There are fairly equal numbers of men and women, but polygyny is feasible because, whereas women marry at the menarche, men do not marry until the late twenties and thirties. No man was betrothed before age 20 years, by which age woman were already married, but it was not until the age of 40 years that all men in Keneba were married.

It is obvious, therefore, that husbands must be considerably older than their wives. About 17 percent of husbands were senior by 20–45 years, and this of course has an important bearing on differential mortality experience. Twice as many women's as men's marriages had been ended by death, 30 and 16 percent respectively; of course, some men, when they die, leave more than one widow.

There are strong pressures and economic incentives to maintain the stability of marriage, but divorce is recognized as a regrettable necessity in certain circumstances. For example, a man is expected to divorce a woman who continually provokes him or who does not produce children "within a reasonable time." No pregnancy had occurred in 65 percent of women's marriages which ended in divorce, compared with 19 percent of those ended by death. A husband merely has to state his intention before witnesses and the couple are divorced. The wife, on the other hand, has to prove grounds for divorce such as cruelty, which means permanent bodily harm in this society where wife beating is accepted as a normal concomitant of marriage. Occasionally, a wife divorced her aged husband for impotence. Leprosy was a recognized ground for divorce but all lepers (about 40 were registered) married.

The village is divided into four exogamous *Kabilos*, which are founding families or clans. Choice of a husband is particularly restricted for a divorced woman, however, as she may not marry within her husband's *Kabilo*. In the past the people were able to marry in the village without committing incest (i.e., marrying within certain restricted degrees of kinship), although a few sons of freeborn origin were married to women from the area where they studied as Koranic scholars. Since the abolition of slavery, however, all sons are required to farm at home and now it would be only under exceptional circumstances that a boy would be sent away "for learning." As time has gone on the villagers have so intermarried that all are related to each other in some way, and the men of Keneba have had to look elsewhere for wives. Thus intermarriage between Keneba and three adjacent villages is increasing.

*Fertility.* The 216 ever-pregnant women in Keneba in October 1962 reported that they had delivered 1,056 live singleton births of whom 53 percent were still alive; this includes a relatively large number of babies born early in 1962 (see below). These women had also borne 11 sets of twins but only 2 of the 22 children had survived and only a further 2 had lived for more than one year.

A logical feature of the Keneba marriage pattern is that, with increasing number of marriages, a man is likely to augment the number of his children. On the other hand, as a woman must endure a period of celibacy between marriages and infertility may result

[55] B. Thompson, "Marriage, Childbirth and Early Childhood in a Gambian Village: A Socio-medical Study" (Ph.D. thesis, University of Aberdeen, 1965).

in divorce, each break in a woman's marital history is likely to be reflected in her reduced fertility. This can be illustrated by the men and women aged 50 and over. The men had had from two to eight wives and the number of their live-born children increased from an average of 6.3 for those married twice to 15.4 for those who had had six or more wives. In contrast women married only once had had an average of 6.9 children but this fell to 5.7 children when the women had been married at least four times before the menopause.

Children, both boys and girls, are wanted and the very idea of an unwanted pregnancy is quite incomprehensible to the people of Keneba. Sterility is uncommon but is a tragedy for the individual. Two of the four women over 40 years who had never conceived were co-wives of one of the three men aged 50 and over who were childless and were therefore thought to be bewitched by demons. Venereal disease is seen only occasionally: in the two years, two younger men reported with gonorrhea on return from visits elsewhere. Illegitimacy, which might be difficult to identify in any case, is apparently uncommon as the lives of the women are so ordered and circumscribed. A few persons in the area were known to be illegitimate, however, although none was in Keneba. In this traditional society, illegitimate children are in an anomalous position as they belong to the mother's family and have limited rights of inheritance.

The prohibition on marriage during pregnancy, the prescribed waiting period before remarriage, and the taboo on coitus during lactation provide safeguards in the interests of village harmony and of suckling infants. Apart from these restrictions, customary behavior exposes a woman to the risk of pregnancy throughout her childbearing years. The number of her pregnancies, therefore, depends on the span of her fertile years and the interval between pregnancies. All the evidence indicates that menarche is late in Keneba women and there is some suggestion that, in general, the menopause may be several years earlier than in Western society. Such features cannot be proved,

however, until exact ages are known. In a small village, over a period of two years, these events can only be dated for a very few women. The average age at menarche appeared to be 14–16 years. This would accord with a check made possible by a brief visit to Keneba in 1969, when it was found that 11 women whose dates of births were known, had now had their first baby at ages ranging from 14 years, 10 months, to 18 years, 9 months.

The implication of the taboo on coitus during lactation is that the interval between births depends on the length of survival of the previous child. Thus the average interval between births increased steadily from 14.8 months following a stillbirth to 15.9 months if the first baby of two died within one month, to 35.1 months if the first-born child survived at least two years. (These data were based on precise dates of 293 adjacent single births, intervals coincident with remarriage being excluded.)

The villagers reported that a child needed to be breast fed for at least two years. In fact this applied to only one-third of children who were fully weaned in the course of the study.[56] All the children however, were breast fed for at least 18 months. Walking and eating a diet of adult pattern were prerequisites for the cessation of breast feeding.

If the taboo on coitus during lactation had been strictly kept, then at least 9 months should have elapsed from full weaning to the birth of the next child. Evidence shows however that this was not always so (see Figure 24.2) and in fact the taboo was obviously broken in about half the cases where lactation was prolonged. When a lactating woman was known to be pregnant she was ridiculed and scorned. The number of couples who broke the taboo is not known, however, as pregnancy was the only proof and conception may not have occurred in some cases. The possibility of conception is, of course, affected by the duration of postpartum amenorrhea and the range was great (5–20 months) in the few women for whom reliable information

---

[56] Thompson and Rahman, "Infant Feeding."

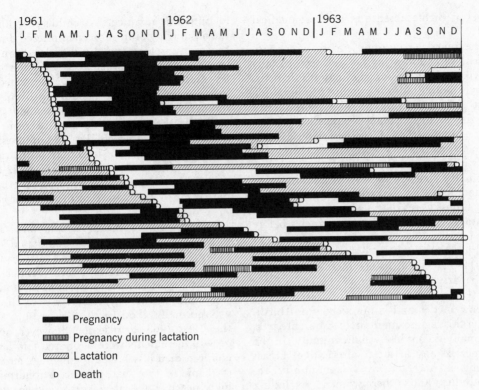

1961
J F M A M J J A S O N D | 1962
J F M A M J J A S O N D | 1963
J F M A M J J A S O N D

■ Pregnancy

▥ Pregnancy during lactation

▨ Lactation

ᴅ Death

FIGURE 24.2. *Pregnancy and Lactation Histories of All Keneba Women Having One or More Still Births or Child Deaths during Lactation, 1961–1963 Listed in Chronological Order by First Death*

was available, and one woman did not menstruate between births (23 months). The indications were that the taboo was kept as long as the baby was largely dependent on breast milk, that is for about 8–9 months.

CHILD MORTALITY. Although fertility is high in Keneba, this is offset by high mortality. In fact, parents need to have as many children as possible in order to ensure that some will survive. It has been reported that 43 percent of children died in Keneba before age seven years[57] but this is an underestimate as some early deaths were not registered, as already described.

The children are particularly vulnerable to death at two periods. First, during delivery and the following weeks and second, between the ages of 6 and 24 months.

[57] McGregor et al., "Growth and Mortality in Children."

*Birth and early experience.* There are no maternity services, and certain rituals are potentially harmful. Old women relying on empirical knowledge and evoking magical aids officiate at delivery, in the most unhygienic conditions. If severe difficulties arise both mother and baby die. Thus four maternal and fetal deaths were known to have occurred in the area in the two years. Babies are usually lightweight, however, a safeguard against disproportion particularly when the pelvis is not fully developed as in young women, or when the uterus is fibrotic as in elderly, high parity women. Stillbirth rates are high, 7 stillbirths occurring in 106 births during the two years. Three of the seven first-week deaths were due to a convulsive illness, probably tetanus neonatorum; another baby who was very premature and too weak to feed, and an iniencephalic, died. Specific diagnoses could not usually be made, however, in the absence of resident medical staff.

The marriage customs expose women to the risk of childbearing before they are fully grown, and pelvic damage may result if the baby is too big; also the young primigravida is at risk to eclampsia. The reproductive histories of these young women were poor. For example, the 11 women whose birth dates at first delivery were known, produced two stillbirths and four babies who had died within the first few weeks; in addition, one woman had had a previous abortion. The indications were that young women often had to have three or four pregnancies before they became efficient reproducers.[58]

Although babies are lightweight (average 6 lbs. 2 ozs. for 98 babies in the two years) particularly during the rainy season (average only 4 lbs. 12 ozs. for 10 first babies), breast feeding on demand is practiced from birth. Under this regime infants make rapid progress and many do not lose weight initially. In the absence of any artificial alternative, breast feeding is accepted as a community responsibility and other women (excluding certain kin) will feed a baby until the mother establishes lactation, and at other times in case of need. This latter is particularly important for children of the oldest women who may be inefficient lactators.

*Age 6–24 months.* Half the children who died in Keneba in the two years were aged 6–24 months. The cause of death is known for only a few children who died in the hospital when an autopsy was performed; these were highly selected children and pneumonia usually was implicated. Some deaths followed a series of illnesses usually including diarrhea, respiratory infection, sepsis, and malaria and were associated with weight loss, while other deaths were sudden. Most children died in the rainy season, but those likely to succumb could not usually be

identified in advance.[59] A child's reaction to the onslaught of infection encountered during the rainy season partly depended on its immunological competence. For the first few months of its life the child is protected by the passive immunity acquired from the mother, but thereafter it takes about two years for the child to develop its own immunity. Thus the child's immunity state when it encounters the infections of the rainy season is of vital importance to survival. This state depends on the child's age, and therefore date of birth, in relation to the rainy season.

SOME GENERAL FEATURES OF MORBIDITY AND MORTALITY. The seasons dominated the pattern of illness and death and full weaning was not an important factor.[60] The characteristic pattern was for children to lose weight during the rainy season but "catch-up" was normally good in the dry season.[61] In the 1962–1963 dry season however some growth increments were depressed and a few children died of whooping cough. A measles epidemic in 1961 had produced abnormally high death rates at a season when good growth and survival is expected.[62]

The severity of morbidity and mortality may have been slightly reduced by the activities of the research team in the two years 1962 and 1963. The pattern of illness and death was unaltered however as shown by comparison with other villages. All Keneba children were treated with antibiotics and antimalarials at some time, and a few children were admitted to the hospital. The lives of a few Keneba children may have been prolonged and occasionally saved. It is

[58] B. Thompson and D. Baird, "Some Impressions of child-bearing in tropical areas" and "Some Impressions of child-bearing in tropical areas: II Preeclampsia and Low Birth Weight," *Journal of Obstetrics and Gynaecology of the British Commonwealth,* LXXIV (June and August 1967), 329–38, 499–509.

[59] I. A. McGregor, A. K. Rahman, A. M. Thomson, W. Z. Billewicz, and B. Thompson, "The Health of Young Children in a West African (Gambian) Village," *Transactions of the Royal Society of Tropical Medicine and Hygiene,* LXIV, 1 (1970), 48–77.
[60] Thompson and Rahman, "Infant Feeding."
[61] I. A. McGregor, A. K. Rahman, B. Thompson, W. Z. Billewicz, and A. M. Thomson, "The Growth of Young Children in a Gambian Village," *Transactions of the Royal Society of Tropical Medicine and Hygiene,* LXII, 3 (June 1968), 341–52.
[62] I. A. McGregor, "Measles and Child Mortality in the Gambia," *West African Medical Journal,* XIII (1964), 251–57.

significant however that 77 percent of deaths occurred in the second half of the year, i.e., the main part of the rains and the early dry season.

There were marked socioeconomic differences in Keneba but these were submerged under the dominant factors in a child's life of climate, unhygienic conditions, agricultural demands on the women, malaria and other infections, seasonal food shortage, Islamic teaching, and traditional customs. Also the advantages of certain concomitants of prosperity were counteracted by disadvantages. For example, signs of wealth were tin-roofed huts and the ownership of cattle. Tin roofs carried a high tax however and therefore co-wives (and their children) often were crowded together in one building rather than being provided with a hut each; this increased dangers of infection. Also young children in the wealthiest families had easier access to supplementary milk from the animals but this was often highly contaminated.

THE PATTERN OF DEATHS AND BIRTHS. Figure 24.2 illustrates the pregnancy and lactation histories of all the women in Keneba who had had a stillbirth or had lost a breast-fed child during the three years 1961–1963 inclusive. The exact length of gestation was seldom known, as the women are very secretive about menstruation and fearful to disclose when they become pregnant. The people believe that pregnancy lasts 10 months. Although babies were lightweight, very few "arrived before their moon" or showed obvious signs of premature delivery. The chart shows that pregnancy usually followed soon after a death so that the women were almost continually either pregnant or lactating. Co-wives were often lactating at the same time and there was no suggestion that men tried to arrange it so that they always had a wife available for coitus. The taboo on coitus was never given as a reason for multiple wives.

The women are listed in order of the first death. Normally most deaths occur in the rainy season but the measles epidemic in

spring 1961 in which over one-fifth of children aged under five years died, upset the pattern. The lethal nature of measles in West Africa has been reported by others.[63] Then in the following dry season some deaths occurred during an epidemic of whooping cough. The resulting pattern in the two years of study may be summarized as follows:

(1) In 1962, many babies were born early in the year to replace children lost in the measles epidemic. It was a healthy year since few children were at the most vulnerable age during the rainy season and there were few deaths.

(2) In 1963, there were relatively few births, but some were replacing the children who had died of whooping cough. Many children were at a critical age during the rains, there was a great deal of illness, and more deaths.

The births and deaths in the two years are given in Table 24.7. It is obvious that

TABLE 24.7

Number of births and deaths of children aged under five years in 1962 and 1963

|  | 1962 | 1963 |
|---|---|---|
| *Births* | | |
| Live births | 68 | 31 |
| Stillbirths | 2 | 5 |
| *Deaths* | | |
| First week | 3 | 4 |
| 8 days–5 years | 7 | 19 |

erroneous conclusions could be drawn from using figures for a single year. For example, the birth rate in 1962 was about 87 per thousand population compared with 41 in 1963; also the perinatal mortality rate was 73 and 290 per thousand births in the two years respectively.

SUMMARY. This brief account of marriage, fertility, and child mortality in an isolated

[63] For example, D. C. Morley and K. M. MacWilliam, "Measles in a Nigerian Community," *West African Medical Journal*, X (1961), 246–253; and R. G. Hendrickse, D. Montefione, P. M. Shermann, and H. M. Van der Wall, "Studies in Measles Vaccination in Nigerian Children," *British Medical Journal*, I (February 22, 1964), 470–74.

Gambian village has demonstrated some of the problems encountered not only in the collection of accurate demographic data but also in the interpretation of findings.

It was relatively easy to demonstrate, in such a traditional, Moslem village, how the customary marriage behavior was translated into a fertility pattern and to show some of the implications for obstetrics and pediatrics.

A measles epidemic in the year prior to the study had a profound effect on the fertility and mortality in the two years. The findings highlighted the erroneous conclusions that could be drawn from basing fertility and mortality rates on the records of a single year, or from extrapolating to a whole population the findings of a particular village or area. The annual number of births and deaths in any Gambian village and probably over wide areas of rural West Africa may depend on the pathway and timing of an epidemic, especially measles.

### Note on the 1973 census

Since this chapter was written the preliminary results of the 1973 census have been released. These claimed a population of 494 thousand or 27 percent more than the figure of 388–90 thousand which can be obtained by interpolating in Table 24.5 This new figure is incompatible with that of the 1963 census implying an average annual rate of population growth for the intercensal decade of 4.6 percent. If net immigration had been zero and if the crude death rate for the period were taken to be 26 per thousand as implied by Table 24.5, then a crude birth rate of 72 per thousand is posited. This is beyond the bounds of demographic or biological possibility, as would also be a birth rate of 70 per thousand estimated by adhering to the assumption in Table 24.5 of a net immigration rate of 0.2 percent per annum. Reducing the death rate to the improbably low level of 20 per thousand does little to improve the situation.

Three explanations are obvious and it would seem probable that each is true: (1)

the 1963 census deficiencies included the omission of population in at least some areas and the real 1963 population was higher than that recorded; (2) the strong publicity in 1973 that urged everyone to be counted to secure facilities for their areas of residence resulted in an overcount; (3) the West African drought and possible other factors resulted in an unusually large number of "strange farmers" being in the country at the time of the census (this was in fact noted by the census organization).

It would seem to be unwise to multiply all projected population figures in Table 24.5 by 1.27, thus yielding estimates for the end of the century of 812,000 to 1,052,000. A reasonable guess might be that the vital rates estimated in the table are approximately correct and that projected population numbers can be obtained by using an inflation factor of either one-sixth or one-fifth. This would yield a range of projected populations for the end of the century of either 746–966 thousands or 767–994 thousands and population densities of either 187–242 or 192–248 persons per square mile. It would yield a 1973 figure (excluding the "extra" strange farmers) of 455 or 468 thousands according to Projection (1) and 453 or 466 thousands according to Projections (2) and (3). According to these ranges, the half million mark will be passed either in 1976 or early 1977.

The 1973 census of Gambia contained questions that allowed direct estimates to be made of both child and adult mortality. An attempt has now been made to estimate mortality from these data and the estimates suggest expectations of life at birth no higher than our projections show for the 1963 census (personal communications from J. G. C. Blacker). It is possible that mortality is improving much more slowly than we had anticipated when constructing the projections. Therefore, the adjustments suggested above should be regarded as providing an upper bound for Gambia's population. The real levels might be somewhat lower than this.

## A SHORT HISTORY OF CENSUSES AND SURVEYS IN LIBERIA

There is no record of any complete count of the Liberian population until 1962. However, note should be taken of the enumeration in November 1956 of the capital, Monrovia, which revealed a population of 41,391 people, and two years later of Greenville, the administrative seat of the county of Sinoe, which yielded a count of 3,628 persons. The main objectives of these limited enumerations were primarily to train local staff and acquaint them with problems of field work in preparation for a national census.

The census of April 1962 can be considered as a landmark in the development of statistics in Liberia. Besides providing information for the first time on the size, distribution, and composition of the Liberian population, it allowed the training of a number of students in the field of population censuses and statistics. It provided, most of all, a population dimension for planning purposes.

## EVALUATION OF THE 1962 CENSUS

Census statistics are always affected by errors, although the errors may be large or small. The importance of the errors, given their magnitude, depends on the uses to which the data are put. Some applications are valid even if the statistics are subject to large errors; other uses require more accurate data.

Many procedures for appraising the accuracy of population data have been worked out and described in various United Nations publications. An important one is the *postenumeration survey* which is a second enumeration of all, or a sample, of the localities or households within them, covered during the census proper within a period after the main operation which usually does not exceed two or three weeks. The results of postenumeration surveys in Africa are frequently disastrous. There are quite a number of reasons for this, apart from the techniques used and the planning of the operation itself. Africans traditionally are not in the habit of giving

# CHAPTER TWENTY-FIVE

# *Liberia*

WESNER JOSEPH

out information that they consider personal. Telling a stranger about their names and birth dates is like surrendering part of themselves. Besides, there is also some fear that the counting of people has to do with taxation or other government actions. As a result, most people do not hesitate to change their names, age, or whatever information they have to provide to the interviewer. It is clear that the basic elements for matching purposes are vitiated, and the chances of postenumeration surveys being successful and acceptable are small.

The assessment of the value of the census data of 1962 will therefore be limited to the study of the age and sex distributions of the population. Tests of the accuracy of age statistics are necessary, not only because such data are of major importance for population estimates and demographic analyses, but also because errors in these statistics are often indicative of deficiencies in the head count of the population. Sex, unlike age, is seldom reported incorrectly in census enumerations. However, statistics classified by sex may be in error because the enumeration or the recording of facts is more nearly complete for one sex than for the other. Analyses of statistics by sex, like the tests of age statistics, are useful in evaluating the reliability of head counts and the completeness and quality of other demographic characteristics. Tests carried out on the population arranged by single years of age have shown that usually a large number of individuals reported their ages around the terminal digits 0 and 5 and surprisingly in almost the same magnitude around the digit 8. The extent of preference for these digits is higher among females. There is no apparent heaping at digits 2 and 9, and there appears to be a marked deficiency in the population at ages with terminal digits 1, 3, 4, 6, and 7.

AGE RATIOS. Interpreting the male and female age ratios in Table 25.1 there appears at a first glance to be evidence of age misstatement in age group 5–9. A ratio of 64.4 for females and 80.5 for males of 10–14 years of age is hardly comparable to the ratios

109.3 and 110.0 observed in the preceding age group. The apparent excess in the age category 5–9 cannot alone account for the deficit observed in age group 10–14. We are forced to conclude that there was a large omission of children 10–14 which is much more pronounced for females. Such omissions have caused an upward bias in the 5–9 age ratio computed on the base of the under estimated adjacent age group 10–14. Thus the age group 5–9 appears to be in excess only by the fact of omission in age groups 10–14 and/or misstatement of children in the 5–9 age brackets. Actually the true size of the population 5–9 may well be underestimated.

Beyond this point (10–14 age group), the males show a pattern where any apparent excess in one age group is matched by an almost equal deficit in the following age group except for age groups 40–44 and 45–49. The situation is very different for the females, among whom inaccuracy in age reporting was much greater. This distortion also affects the sex ratios.

SEX RATIOS. The sex ratio (number of males per hundred females) at young ages is 97.5 for Liberia (see Table 25.2). This low ratio at young ages is followed by an increasing apparent excess of males aged 5–14. At ages 15–39 there is a deficit of males which is transformed to an excess at age 40, reaches a peak at age 59, and decreases slowly at older ages to a low of 113.9.

This contrasts with what has been observed in other countries, mostly Euro-American type, where the sex ratio is high at birth, balances around ages 15–19, and decreases slowly at older ages influenced by the higher mortality among males. This pattern, though common among most non-African countries for which accurate data are available, has not been found in the Liberian population.

The sex ratios of population of the United States of America and of several West African countries for which population data are available are presented in Table 25.2 and Figure 25.1. The contrast observed between African states and the United States is striking. No less surprising is the great similarity shown among the African states as

TABLE 25.1

Computation of age-accuracy index by the United Nations secretariat method, census of Liberia, 1962

| Age Groups | Reported Number | | Analysis of Sex Ratios | | Analysis of Age Ratios[a] | | | |
| | | | | | Males | | Females | |
| | Males | Females | Ratios | Successive difference | ratios | deviation from 100 | ratios | deviation from 100 |
|---|---|---|---|---|---|---|---|---|
| 0–4 | 81,625 | 83,757 | 97.5 | — | — | — | — | — |
| 5–9 | 68,809 | 64,953 | 105.9 | +8.4 | 110.0 | +10.0 | 109.3 | +9.3 |
| 10–14 | 43,483 | 35,112 | 123.8 | 17.9 | 80.5 | −19.5 | 64.4 | −35.6 |
| 15–19 | 39,248 | 44,049 | 89.1 | −34.7 | 100.3 | +0.3 | 104.0 | +4.0 |
| 20–24 | 34,757 | 49,601 | 70.1 | −19.0 | 87.5 | −12.5 | 100.1 | +0.1 |
| 25–29 | 40,220 | 55,072 | 73.0 | +2.9 | 112.5 | +12.5 | 116.1 | +16.1 |
| 30–34 | 36,750 | 45,241 | 81.2 | +8.2 | 98.4 | −1.6 | 100.5 | +0.5 |
| 35–39 | 34,459 | 34,979 | 98.5 | +17.3 | 101.2 | +1.2 | 96.5 | +3.5 |
| 40–44 | 31,367 | 27,244 | 115.1 | +16.6 | 106.1 | +6.1 | 99.9 | −0.1 |
| 45–49 | 24,715 | 19,547 | 126.4 | +11.3 | 96.7 | −3.3 | 93.5 | −6.5 |
| 50–54 | 19,746 | 14,547 | 135.7 | +9.3 | 103.9 | +3.9 | 100.2 | +0.2 |
| 55–59 | 13,296 | 9,481 | 140.2 | +4.5 | 80.9 | −19.1 | 74.9 | −25.1 |
| 60–64 | 13,130 | 10,751 | 122.1 | −18.1 | 118.8 | +18.8 | 128.1 | +28.1 |
| 65–69 | 8,808 | 7,298 | 120.7 | −1.4 | 97.4 | −2.6 | 96.6 | −3.4 |
| 70–74 | 4,963 | 4,358 | 113.9 | — | — | — | — | — |

*Total* (irrespective of sign) 169.6    111.4    132.5
Mean (total divided by 13) 13.04    8.57    10.19
*Index* (3 times the mean difference of sex ratios plus the mean deviations of the male and female age ratios) 57.88

Age ratios = persons in each age group as percentage of arithmetic mean of two adjacent age groups; i.e., the percentage the enumerated age group is of the "True size of the age group", where the true size of the age group is the mean or average of its two adjacent age groups.

TABLE 25.2

Sex ratios of African States and U.S.A. (males per 100 females)

| Age Group | U.S.A. (1966) | Liberia (1962) | Senegal (1961) | Sierra Leone (1963) | Niger (1962) | Togo (1961) | Ghana (1960) | Kenya (1962) | Uganda (1959) |
|---|---|---|---|---|---|---|---|---|---|
| All ages | 97.0 | 98.2 | 97.1 | 98.4 | 98.1 | 90.1 | 102.2 | 98.1 | 101.0 |
| 0–4 | 103.4 | 97.5 | 98.0 | 99.0 | 96.5 | 97.4 | 98.2 | 96.2 | 101.0 |
| 5–9 | 103.4 | 106.2 | 106.2 | 108.0 | 108.0 | 103.0 | 102.5 | 101.2 | 104.0 |
| 10–14 | 103.3 | 123.8 | 118.0 | 114.5 | 140.0 | 118.5 | 110.6 | 120.0 | 102.0 |
| 15–19 | 100.7 | 98.1 | 80.0 | 74.3 | 107.1 | 97.5 | 103.8 | 105.0 | 96.0 |
| 20–24 | 95.4 | 70.1 | 74.0 | 66.0 | 69.3 | 58.0 | 83.2 | 70.2 | 88.2 |
| 25–29 | 96.3 | 73.0 | 74.2 | 82.0 | 70.0 | 66.2 | 90.9 | 75.0 | 92.0 |
| 30–34 | 95.8 | 81.2 | 93.5 | 90.4 | 92.4 | 68.4 | 98.6 | 81.0 | 96.0 |
| 35–39 | 95.0 | 98.5 | 95.0 | 113.3 | 102.2 | 83.3 | 111.0 | 93.1 | 100.0 |
| 40–44 | 95.8 | 115.1 | 106.5 | 122.0 | 96.0 | 95.2 | 114.0 | 98.0 | 106.0 |
| 45–49 | 97.0 | 126.4 | 117.1 | 140.1 | 114.0 | 95.0 | 128.4 | 117.0 | 114.4 |
| 50–54 | 97.2 | 135.7 | 122.0 | 131.1 | 99.0 | 81.0 | 118.4 | 114.0 | 122.1 |
| 55–59 | 95.9 | 140.2 | 138.5 | 137.2 | 107.0 | 82.4 | 123.0 | 131.0 | 116.0 |
| 60–64 | 91.3 | 122.1 | 121.4 | 117.0 | 108.4 | 89.0 | 116.3 | — | 117.3 |
| 65–69 | 88.1 | 120.7 | 125.0 | — | 109.3 | 85.0 | 113.3 | — | 121.0 |
| 70–74 | 85.6 | 113.9 | — | — | 85.3 | 110.2 | 111.5 | — | 129.4 |
| 75+ | — | — | — | — | 108.2 | — | 113.0 | — | 122.2 |

SOURCES: Liberia—population census; Senegal—sample survey; Sierra Leone—population census: Niger—sample survey, provisional; Togo—sample survey; Ghana—population census; Kenya—population census; Uganda—population census.

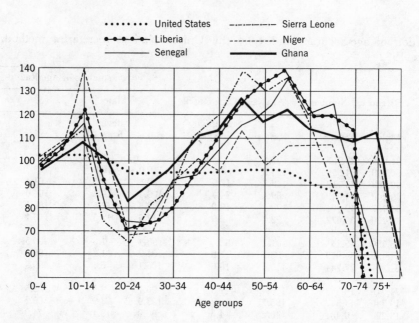

FIGURE 25.1.  *Sex Ration Curves for the United States and Selected African Countries*

they move close together in a pattern quite different from the one observed for the United States, which is a typical example of the Western pattern.

We can summarize the pattern of the African states as follows: low sex ratio at early ages, apparent predominance of males at ages 5–14 and apparent large deficit of males in the central age groups 15–39, with predominance of males at ages 40 and over. This is what Lorimer had to say about African data in a paper presented at the International Population Conference of Ottawa (Canada) in 1963:

The misreporting of ages in African surveys affects the reports of children, as well as those on adults, though there is generally no apparent underenumeration of children in Africa. There are large apparent deficits in the reported number of persons in age classes in the vicinity of puberty. One usually finds an apparent excess of females in the central childbearing classes.[1]

[1] Frank Lorimer, "Possibilities and Problems in the Estimation of Vital Rates in Africa," in International Union for the Scientific Study of Population, *International Population* Conference, 1963 (Liège, 1964), pp. 180–81 and 185.

The analysis of our data shows no marked deviation from Lorimer's findings. Even so, the great consistency in the pattern of the population of African states is striking. Census and survey errors cannot alone explain such consistencies in errors in such different areas which have in each case applied a different method of enumeration at a different period of time. More research is needed on African population age and sex structure. Cultural and other factors may have contributed to the shaping of this pattern which is so very similar and consistent among African states.

GEOGRAPHIC DISTRIBUTION. At the time of the 1962 census, the population and the country were divided into 12 administrative areas, as shown in the first part of Table 25.3. The Physical Planning Division (Department of Planning and Economic Affairs) has estimated the redistribution of this population within the boundaries of new administrative divisions following an act of legislature of 1964 that divides the country into nine major areas. This redistribution of the population is shown in the second part of Table 25.3.

Liberia as a whole is thinly populated with the major concentration of 101 persons per square mile in Montserrado County. The national average is 26 inhabitants per square mile. The population is not evenly distributed, as miles and miles of empty land lie in between small population clusters. Liberia is one of the few countries of the world which does not have to cope with demographic pressure and high rates of population increase. Rather, the population problems of Liberia are of a different nature: those of determining the optimum number of people necessary to develop fully the vast resources of Liberia, the implementation of measures to reach that population target, the improvement of the quality of the population by extending health measures, and the stepping up of the education campaign in order to provide the skilled manpower needed for an optimum development process.

ETHNIC DISTRIBUTION. Table 25.4 shows the tribal affiliation of the population by sex. Kpelle is the most important group, followed by the Bassas, Gios, Krus, Greboes, and Manos. Figure 25.2 shows geographically the areas where the major concentration of these various groups are found.

TABLE 25.3

Distribution of the population of Liberia according to old and new administrative divisions, 1962

| Counties, Provinces, & Territories | Old Administrative Divisions[a] | | New Administrative Divisions | | | |
|---|---|---|---|---|---|---|
| | Population | Percent | Population[a] | Percent | Area (sq. mi.)[b] | Density |
| All areas | 1,016,443 | 100.0 | 1,016,443 | 100.0 | 38,250 | 26.6 |
| Central Province | 325,230 | 32.0 | — | — | — | — |
| Gong County | — | — | 131,528 | 12.9 | 3,650 | 36.0 |
| Nimba County | — | — | 160,743 | 15.8 | 4,650 | 34.6 |
| Eastern Province | 63,712 | 6.3 | — | | | |
| Grand Gedeh County | — | — | 59,275 | 5.8 | 6,575 | 9.1 |
| Western Province | 170,942 | 16.8 | — | — | — | — |
| Lofa County | — | — | 123,165 | 12.1 | 7,475 | 16.5 |
| Montserrado County | 166.797 | 16.4 | — | — | — | — |
| Marshall Territory | 14,442 | 1.4 | — | — | — | — |
| Montserrado County | — | — | 258,821 | 25.5 | 2,550 | 101.5 |
| Grand Bassa County | 99,566 | 9.8 | — | — | | — |
| River Cess Territory | 28,756 | 2.8 | — | — | | — |
| Grand Bassa County | — | — | 131,840 | 13.0 | 5,075 | 26.0 |
| Sasstown Territory | 9,540 | 0.9 | — | — | — | — |
| Sinoe County | 44,639 | 4.4 | — | — | — | — |
| Sinoe County | — | — | 56,095 | 5.5 | 34,50 | 12.9 |
| Maryland County | 39,349 | 3.9 | — | — | — | — |
| Kru Coast Territory | 21,280 | 2.1 | — | — | — | — |
| Maryland County | — | — | 62,786 | 6.2 | 1,675 | 37.5 |
| Cape Mount County | 32,190 | 3.2 | 32,190 | 3.2 | 2,250 | 14.3 |

SOURCE: 1962 Census Report.
[a] 1962 population; the individual county's figures are estimates based on the county boundaries as determined by the Boundary Commission.
[b] The calculation of these figures is based on the planimetric map of Liberia (scale: 1,500,000) and the areas are estimated to within 25 sq. miles (Dept. of Public Works).

TABLE 25.4

Tribal affiliation of the Liberian population by sex, 1962 census

| Tribes | Total | Male | Female |
|---|---|---|---|
| All tribes | 1,016,443 | 503,588 | 512,855 |
| Bassa | 165,856 | 81,744 | 84,112 |
| Belle | 5,465 | 2,575 | 2,890 |
| Dey | 5,396 | 2,619 | 2,777 |
| Gbandi | 28,599 | 13,245 | 15,354 |
| Gio | 83,208 | 40,797 | 42,411 |
| Gola | 47,295 | 23,267 | 24,028 |
| Grebo | 77,007 | 36,617 | 40,390 |
| Kpelle | 211,081 | 105,916 | 105,165 |
| Kissi (Gissi) | 34,914 | 17,985 | 16,929 |
| Krahn | 52,552 | 24,956 | 27,596 |
| Kru | 80,813 | 39,026 | 41,787 |
| Lorma (Buzzi) | 53,891 | 26,253 | 27,638 |
| Mandingo | 29,750 | 15,742 | 14,008 |
| Mano | 72,122 | 35,647 | 36,475 |
| Mende | 4,974 | 3,107 | 1,867 |
| Via | 28,898 | 14,000 | 14,898 |
| Other tribes | 34,622 | 20,092 | 14,530 |

AGE STRUCTURE. The 1962 census recorded a population of 1,016,443 of whom 503,588 were males and 512,855 females. Liberia has a young population. Table 25.5 shows that children under 15 years of age constitute 37.3 percent of the total population while people in the age bracket 45 and over account for only 16.2 percent. A mere 4 percent of the total population is older than 65. The median age of the population is as low as 22.

EDUCATIONAL CHARACTERISTICS. The educational characteristics of the population are shown in Table 25.6. Out of 851,061 persons in the age group 5 and over in 1962, only 89,343 persons had ever completed a school grade while 761,718 had either left without completing any grade in school or had not been to school. Out of 212,357 children in the age range 5–14, only 44,607 were attending school full time at the time of census taking, and there were 165,742 children who were not attending. The size of this age group in the population could be taken as a yardstick to measure the facilities required to accommodate and educate all the children.

ECONOMIC ACTIVITY. Population in the age group of 10 and over is shown by activity in Table 25.7. The proportion of the economically active population in the census sense is determined partly by the age structure and partly by the extent of women's employment. Counting the economically active on an internationally comparable basis is difficult because it is not easy to know just how to classify farmers' wives. What the census shows has therefore always to be taken with caution.

The proportion of economically active women depends partly upon the ratio of women to men in the adult population and partly on the extent of women's work within the household. The extent of women's employment outside the household depends primarily on the stage of economic development which has been reached. As development continues, women will be emancipated from household drudgery. Therefore, in manpower planning, woman-power should not be relegated to a secondary position. Suitable occupations for women should be identified.

The proportion of children in school rises with economic development, and so does the average number of years of schooling. The age of retirement from active work tends to fall. Both factors will affect the future participation rates of the labor force.

In Liberia, almost two-thirds of the economically active population comes mainly from the age group 14–44, which constitutes some 46.5 percent of the total population. The census showed that the proportion formed by the economically active of the total population was 40.5 percent in 1962, which is slightly lower than that of the advanced countries. A noteworthy point is that 25.6 percent of the economically inactive population was classified as "others," most of them being teen-agers. Guidance and training is needed to convert them into economically active population.

INDUSTRIAL AND OCCUPATIONAL DISTRIBUTION. The geographic distribution of industries in Liberia in 1962 is shown in Table 25.8.

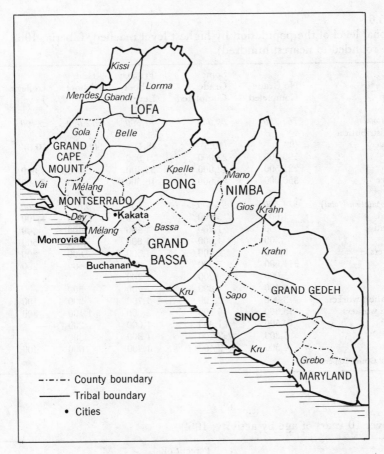

FIGURE 25.2.   *Tribes of Liberia*

TABLE 25.5
Age group structure of the population, 1962

| Age | Population | | | Males | | | Females | |
|---|---|---|---|---|---|---|---|---|
| | Number | Percent | | Number | Percent | | Number | Percent |
| *All ages* | 1,016,443 | 100 | | 505,588 | 100 | | 512,855 | 100 |
| *Important age groups* | | | | | | | | |
| 0–4 | 165,382 | 16.5 | | 81,625 | 16.2 | | 83,757 | 16.3 |
| 5–14 | 212,357 | 20.8 | | 112,292 | 22.3 | | 100,065 | 19.6 |
| 15–24 | 167,655 | 16.5 | | 74,005 | 14.7 | | 93,650 | 18.3 |
| 25–44 | 305,332 | 30.0 | | 142,796 | 28.4 | | 163,535 | 31.6 |
| 45–64 | 125,213 | 12.2 | | 70,887 | 14.0 | | 55,336 | 10.6 |
| 65+ | 40,504 | 4.0 | | 21,983 | 4.4 | | 18,511 | 3.6 |
| *Other age groupings* | | | | | | | | |
| 5+ | 851,061 | 83.5 | | 421,963 | 83.8 | | 429,098 | 83.7 |
| 10+ | 717,299 | 70.4 | | 353,154 | 70.1 | | 364,145 | 71.0 |
| 5–9 | 133,762 | 13.1 | | 68,808 | 13.7 | | 64,953 | 12.7 |
| 0–14 | 377,739 | 37.3 | | 193,917 | 38.5 | | 183,822 | 35.9 |
| 15–44 | 472,987 | 46.5 | | 216,801 | 43.1 | | 256,186 | 49.9 |
| 15–64 | 598,200 | 58.7 | | 287,688 | 57.1 | | 311,522 | 60.5 |

SOURCE: 1962 Census Report.

TABLE 25.6

Educational level of the population by highest level reached, Liberia, 1962
(number rounded to nearest hundred)

| Age Group | No Grade Completed | Some Grade Completed | Primary School Level | High School Level | College Level | Total |
|---|---|---|---|---|---|---|
| *5 and over* (*total*) | *761,700* | *89,300* | *71,800* | *12,000* | *5,400* | *851,000* |
| (percent distribution | | | | | | |
| 5 and over) | (89.5) | (10.5) | (8.4) | (1.4) | (0.6) | (100.0) |
| 5–14 | 190,200 | 22,000 | 21,900 | 80 | — | 212,300 |
| 1–29 | 221,500 | 42,000 | 33,300 | 6,800 | 1,800 | 263,000 |
| 30 and over | 350,000 | 25,600 | 16,500 | 5,400 | 3,600 | 375,700 |
| | | | | | | |
| *Working Population* (*total*) | *374,500* | *37,300* | *25,000* | *8,000* | *4,200* | *411,800* |
| Professional | 1,600 | 5,900 | 2,200 | 2,100 | 1,700 | 7,600 |
| Administrative | 900 | 1,200 | 400 | 400 | 500 | 2,100 |
| Clerical | 500 | 4,000 | 1,800 | 1,700 | 500 | 4,500 |
| Sales workers | 8,700 | 2,400 | 1,500 | 600 | 300 | 11,100 |
| Farmers | 311,600 | 7,300 | 6,700 | 400 | 200 | 319,000 |
| Fishermen | 5,000 | 200 | 200 | — | — | 5,200 |
| Miners | 6,100 | 800 | 700 | 500 | — | 7,000 |
| Transportation workers | 3,900 | 2,200 | 1,700 | 300 | 100 | 6,100 |
| Production workers | 15,300 | 6,500 | 5,000 | 1,100 | 300 | 21,000 |
| Other crafts | 10,500 | 1,900 | 1,600 | 200 | — | 12,400 |
| Services | 5,800 | 2,200 | 1,800 | 300 | — | 8,000 |
| Others | 4,500 | 2,400 | 1,300 | 600 | 400 | 6,900 |

SOURCE: 1962 Census Report.

TABLE 25.7

Population over 10 years of age by activity, 1962

| | Number | Percent of Total Population | Percent of Population over 10 Years of Age | Males Number | Males Percent | Females Number | Females Percent |
|---|---|---|---|---|---|---|---|
| *Activity* (*total*) | *717,299* | *70.4* | *100* | *353,154* | *100* | *364,145* | *100* |
| Economically active | 411,794 | 40.5 | 57.4 | 263,560 | 74.6 | 148,234 | 40.7 |
| Economically inactive | 305,505 | 29.9 | 42.6 | 89,594 | 25.4 | 215,911 | 59.3 |
| Student | 46,826 | — | 6.5 | 34,717 | 9.8 | 12,109 | 3.3 |
| Housekeeping | 144,780 | — | 20.2 | — | — | 144,780 | 39.8 |
| Inmate of institution | 1,343 | — | 0.2 | 933 | 0.3 | 140 | 0.1 |
| Retired | 33,358 | — | 4.7 | 12,560 | 3.6 | 20,798 | 6.7 |
| Others | 79,198 | — | 11.0 | 41,384 | 11.7 | 37,814 | 10.4 |

SOURCE: 1962 Census Report.

TABLE 25.8

# Geographic distribution of employed persons by industry in Liberia, 1962[a]

| | Whole Country | County | | | | | Province | | | Territory | | | |
| --- | --- | --- | --- | --- | --- | --- | --- | --- | --- | --- | --- | --- | --- |
| | | Grand Bassa | Cape Mount | Mary-land | Mont-serrado | Sinoe | Central | Eastern | Western | Kru Coast | Marshall | River Cess | Sasstown |
| *All Industry* | 411,794 | 41,450 | 13,443 | 14,442 | 59,695 | 17,209 | 142,514 | 32,611 | 62,726 | 10,449 | 5,178 | 9,803 | 2,275 |
| *Agriculture and Forestry* | 327,853 | 35,821 | 9,984 | 11,270 | 30,572 | 14,586 | 122,968 | 30,309 | 51,802 | 9,509 | 2,893 | 8,775 | 1,549 |
| Agriculture & livestock | 325,462 | 34,495 | 9,859 | 11,159 | 29,256 | 14,408 | 122,585 | 30,187 | 51,192 | 9,505 | 2,654 | 8,691 | 1,538 |
| Forestry & logging | 2,391 | 345 | 125 | 111 | 180 | 178 | 383 | 122 | 610 | 4 | 239 | 83 | 11 |
| *Hunting and Fishing* | 5,264 | 987 | 211 | 346 | 1,136 | 755 | 386 | 105 | 160 | 32 | 141 | 266 | 335 |
| Hunting, trapping & game | 1,313 | 104 | 107 | 26 | 39 | 306 | 323 | 98 | 109 | 23 | 6 | 124 | 47 |
| Fishing | 3,951 | 883 | 104 | 320 | 1,097 | 449 | 63 | 7 | 51 | 409 | 135 | 142 | 288 |
| *Mining and Quarrying* | 14,441 | 755 | 1,655 | 15 | 757 | 172 | 6,090 | 299 | 4,644 | 1 | 6 | 7 | 26 |
| Iron ore | 7,660 | 749 | 785 | 1 | 606 | 2 | 2,831 | 9 | 2,660 | 1 | 2 | | |
| Gold | 626 | 1 | 49 | 6 | 68 | 145 | 11 | 286 | 35 | — | — | 3 | 34 |
| Diamond | 6,127 | 5 | 821 | 4 | 33 | 16 | 3,245 | 4 | 1,949 | — | 4 | 4 | 2 |
| Others | 26 | — | — | 4 | 10 | 9 | 3 | — | — | — | — | — | — |
| *Manufacturing* | 8,472 | 504 | 439 | 342 | 3,035 | 258 | 1,038 | 174 | 1,572 | 21 | 194 | 123 | 28 |
| Food | 123 | 14 | 7 | 6 | 53 | 1 | 28 | 3 | 27 | | 2 | 3 | 1 |
| Beverage | 255 | 20 | 2 | 3 | 139 | 3 | 34 | 16 | 25 | 4 | 4 | 4 | — |
| Footwear & apparel | 3,292 | 193 | 216 | 140 | 964 | 118 | 774 | 58 | 713 | 13 | 47 | 47 | 8 |
| Wooden | 121 | 4 | 10 | 14 | 46 | 2 | 10 | 1 | 18 | — | 6 | 11 | — |
| Furniture & fixtures | 1,718 | 141 | 135 | 68 | 603 | 36 | 289 | 46 | 266 | 2 | 91 | 36 | 5 |
| Printing | 105 | 2 | — | 2 | 51 | 3 | 40 | — | 3 | — | 4 | — | — |
| Metals | 1,193 | 59 | 45 | 45 | 280 | 47 | 291 | 18 | 355 | 1 | 26 | 17 | 9 |
| Transport & heavy equipment (repair) | 1,263 | 65 | 16 | 53 | 787 | 35 | 179 | 60 | 73 | 1 | 11 | 3 | — |
| | 1, | | | | | | | | | | | | |
| Nonmetal mineral | 236 | 5 | 3 | 9 | 100 | 5 | 87 | 9 | 15 | — | — | — | 3 |
| Miscellaneous | 186 | 1 | 5 | 2 | 12 | 8 | 71 | 3 | 77 | — | 3 | 2 | 2 |
| *Construction* | 12,032 | 1,984 | 239 | 279 | 4,715 | 187 | 3,269 | 464 | 571 | 2 | 258 | 43 | 5 |
| Airfield & harbor | 110 | 99 | 1 | — | 6 | 2 | 1 | 1 | — | — | — | — | — |
| Electrical | 37 | 3 | 2 | — | 23 | 2 | 2 | — | 4 | — | — | — | — |
| Highway & road | 6,232 | 1,353 | 128 | 29 | 1,278 | 35 | 2,779 | 340 | 142 | — | 147 | 1 | — |
| Housing | 5,637 | 529 | 105 | 248 | 3,408 | 141 | 484 | 123 | 423 | 2 | 110 | 42 | 5 |
| Water & others | 16 | — | 3 | 2 | | 7 | 3 | — | 1 | — | — | — | — |
| Electricity, water, & sanitary | 375 | 20 | 9 | 30 | 276 | 5 | 18 | — | 10 | — | 5 | 2 | — |
| *Commerce* | 11,540 | 614 | 334 | 404 | 4,134 | 159 | 3,452 | 369 | 1,702 | 15 | 187 | 141 | 21 |
| Wholesale | 243 | 5 | — | 10 | 195 | — | 20 | — | — | — | 6 | — | — |
| Retail | 10,733 | 601 | 325 | 356 | 3,487 | 159 | 3,422 | 369 | 1,680 | 15 | 181 | 109 | 21 |
| Wholesale & retail | 404 | 5 | 9 | 33 | 302 | — | 10 | — | 13 | — | — | 32 | — |
| Banks & others | 160 | 3 | — | 5 | 150 | — | — | — | 2 | — | — | — | — |
| *Transport, Storage, & Communication* | 3,777 | 218 | 40 | 157 | 2,105 | 45 | 573 | 26 | 286 | 1 | 213 | 113 | 2 |
| Transport | 3,437 | 207 | 38 | 140 | 1,936 | 38 | 563 | 24 | 279 | — | 108 | 104 | 1 |
| Storage | 69 | — | — | 5 | 25 | 5 | 4 | 2 | — | — | 8 | — | — |
| Communication | 291 | 11 | 2 | 12 | 144 | 2 | 6 | — | 7 | 455 | 79 | 9 | 1 |
| *Services* | 24,938 | 1,369 | 488 | 1,530 | 12,382 | 978 | 3,284 | 809 | 1,807 | 455 | 1,217 | 304 | 291 |
| Government | 11,612 | 390 | 200 | 375 | 6,508 | 328 | 1,398 | 401 | 626 | 137 | 930 | 124 | 193 |
| Community (education) | 3,198 | 161 | 133 | 259 | 890 | 277 | 666 | 170 | 460 | 97 | 47 | 73 | 43 |
| Medical & health | 1,746 | 110 | 55 | 178 | 640 | 79 | 327 | 42 | 258 | 5 | — | 28 | 9 |
| Religion | 926 | 174 | 13 | 39 | 146 | 101 | 159 | 80 | 106 | 23 | — | 47 | 23 |
| Legal | 89 | 4 | 2 | 5 | 66 | 2 | 6 | — | 1 | 1 | — | — | — |
| Other community | 86 | 9 | 2 | 7 | 47 | 5 | 2 | 9 | 1 | — | — | 2 | — |
| Business | 3,773 | 363 | 13 | 437 | 2,344 | 27 | 154 | 62 | 102 | — | 156 | 14 | 1 |
| Recreation | 112 | 2 | 3 | 5 | 50 | 5 | 29 | 2 | 9 | — | 5 | 2 | — |
| Restaurant, cafe, bar & hotel | 889 | 24 | 22 | 36 | 592 | 18 | 99 | 14 | 30 | 10 | 79 | 6 | — |
| Laundry, cleaning & drying | 866 | 46 | 15 | 40 | 498 | 31 | 149 | 15 | 34 | — | — | 25 | 1 |
| Barber, beauty, & photo | 148 | 83 | 2 | — | 55 | 1 | 36 | — | 3 | — | — | — | — |
| Personal N.E.C. | 1,493 | 3 | 28 | 149 | 546 | 104 | 159 | 12 | 177 | 182 | — | 29 | 20 |
| N.E.S. | 3,102 | 159 | 44 | 69 | 1,716 | 64 | 671 | 56 | 172 | 13 | 64 | 29 | 18 |

SOURCE: 1962 Census Report.
[a] Table not additive.

TABLE 25.9

Employment by county and major industrial group public and private sector
(1968 Establishment Survey of the Government Sector and 252 Selected Establishments)

| County | All Sectors | | Private Sector | | | | | | | | Government Sector | | |
|---|---|---|---|---|---|---|---|---|---|---|---|---|---|
| | Employment | Percent | Total | Manufacture | Commerce | Transportation | Service | Agricultural | Mining | Construction | Total | Electricity & water | Government agencies |
| All counties | 74,572 | 100 | 54,672 | 6,157 | 10,272 | 1,505 | 5,777 | 20,523 | 8,834 | 1,604 | 19,900 | 709 | 19,194 |
| Percent | 100 | — | 73 | 8 | 14 | 2 | 7 | 27 | 12 | 3 | 27 | 1 | 26 |
| Montserrado | 47,873 | 64 | 34,409 | 5,079 | 6,467 | 1,229 | 3,409 | 13,967 | 2,869 | 1,362 | 13,464 | 530 | 12,934 |
| Remainder (Mont. Co.) | (19,919) | (27) | (10,700) | (1,088) | (390) | (—) | (917) | (13,905) | (2,294) | (183) | (1,142) | (11) | (1,131) |
| Monrovia | (23,954) | (37) | (15,632) | (3,991) | (6,077) | (1,229) | (2,492) | (62) | (602) | (1,179) | (12,322) | (519) | (11,803) |
| Maryland | 5,539 | 7 | 3,961 | — | 206 | — | 1,385 | 2,317 | 53 | — | 1,578 | 18 | 1,560 |
| Grand Bassa | 5,223 | 7 | 4,389 | 1,018 | 1,131 | 158 | 133 | 1,741 | 48 | 160 | 834 | 124 | 710 |
| Nimba | 4,860 | 7 | 4,042 | 60 | 522 | — | 377 | 776 | 2,307 | — | 818 | — | 818 |
| Bong | 4,312 | 5 | 2,743 | — | 523 | — | 212 | 99 | 1,909 | — | 569 | 11 | 558 |
| Sinoe | 2,378 | 3 | 1,381 | — | 164 | 118 | — | 1,099 | — | — | 997 | 13 | 984 |
| Cape Mount | 2,283 | 3 | 1,882 | — | 261 | — | — | — | 1,621 | — | 401 | 10 | 391 |
| Lofa | 1,862 | 3 | 1,011 | — | 834 | — | 177 | — | — | — | 851 | — | 851 |
| Grand Gedeh | 1,242 | 1 | 854 | — | 164 | — | 84 | 524 | — | 82 | 388 | — | 388 |

a Mainly Public Utilities Authority Staff and 11 persons from the private sector.

Although there have been changes in the distribution of manufacturing, construction, utilities, and transportation in recent years, census data still serve useful purposes in the discussion of industrial distribution in the country.

Due to the rapid expansion of mining and industrial production in many parts of the country, a serious shortage of professional and skilled workers exists, and a high proportion of these jobs are occupied by foreigners. Vocational education is still in the initial stage of development and few workers receive formal vocational training at trade schools or through vocational courses in high schools. The shortage of skilled manpower will continue for some years to come, particularly at the professional and managerial level.

The bulk of the labor force is unskilled and highly mobile. Although subsistence farming is still by far the most common occupation, many enter wage labor for various periods of time.

A first approximation to the immediate need for trained personnel is provided in the table by the number of aliens working in the country. A detailed breakdown of the occupations followed by the aliens would provide a useful indicator of the shortage of specific trained manpower. This information could be utilized to determine policy for the training of Liberians in the immediate future. In addition, a further stock of trained people would, of course, be needed to fill the current vacancies caused by retirement or death of existing Liberians working in these occupations, and to provide for needs arising out of future development plans.

## THE 1968 ESTABLISHMENT SURVEY

In 1968 the Bureau of Statistics (Department of Planning and Economic Affairs) conducted a nationwide survey of business establishments employing 31 or more employees. Questionnaires were returned by 252 establishments and were subsequently tabulated.

Table 25.9 shows employment in government and the 252 establishments engaged in the private sector by county and major economic activities. Nearly 37 percent of all employees work in Monrovia and 64 percent in Montserrado County as a whole. Maryland County, Grand Bassa, and Nimba follow with 7 percent each, and Bong with 5 percent of the labor force. Employment opportunities of this type are low in Sinoe, Cape Mount, and Lofa which each account for 3 percent. Grand Gedeh has only 1 percent of this work force.

The private sector is attracting more and more people. Now 73 percent of all employees work in the private sector. This percentage will increase further as people depend less and less on the government for a living and the occupational pattern approximates more closely that found in most developing countries.

In the private sector, agriculture is still the largest employer of labor in spite of its limited coverage in the survey. Next is commerce, followed by mining, which account for 14 and 12 percent respectively of the private sector. Construction has markedly decreased due to the fact that most construction projects started in the last decade have been completed.

OCCUPATIONAL STRUCTURE OF WORK FORCE. The occupational structure of the work force is given in Table 25.10.

## FERTILITY AND MORTALITY

It is difficult, in the absence of a vital registration system and two or more censuses, to determine, with any degree of certainty, what the fertility and mortality levels are in Liberia. An attempt has been made to arrive at some indication of these two important parameters in a paper by the writer.[2]

The national rates derived from this exercise are summarized as follows: crude birth rate, 44 per thousand; crude death rate, 28 per thousand; infant mortality rate, 188 per thousand; life expectation at birth, 38.6 years for females and 36.1 years for males.

## POPULATION MOVEMENT

Table 25.11 gives a picture of the foreign-born population by citizenship and place of birth.

Incomplete data from the Bureau of Immigration and Naturalization of Liberia indicates that the annual volume of new migrants is very small. It is a fact that earlier waves of migrants from the United States and the West Indies have long since settled down and established families. This statement is substantiated by the great similarity that has been observed in the sex-age distribution of the populations of citizen and alien. At the

[2] W. Joseph, "Estimates of the Birth Rate and Expectation of Life in Liberia on the Basis of Quasi-stability" (unpublished).

TABLE 25.10

Distribution of major occupation groups by sector: Monetary sector, 1968 (Establishment Survey)

| Major Occupation Groups | Grand Total | Total | Liberians | Private Sector | | Public Sector |
| | | | | Expatriates | | |
| | | | | Non-Africans | Other Africans | |
| All occupations | 74,572 | 54,787 | 48,831 | 3,921 | 2,035 | 19,785 |
| Professional, technical, and related | 9,062 | 3,622 | 2,646 | 757 | 219 | 5,440 |
| Administrative, executive, and managers | 7,016 | 3,269 | 1,665 | 1,114 | 490 | 3,747 |
| Clerical | 5,516 | 3,008 | 2,686 | 194 | 128 | 2,508 |
| Sales | 3,898 | 3,880 | 2,929 | 709 | 242 | 18 |
| Farmers, fishermen, hunters, and loggers | 15,482 | 15,362 | 15,068 | 30 | 264 | 120 |
| Miners and quarrymen | 1,490 | 1,481 | 1,388 | 88 | 5 | 9 |
| Transportation and communications | 3,537 | 1,528 | 1,263 | 142 | 123 | 2,009 |
| Craftsmen, production and process, and laborers | 22,117 | 19,003 | 17,712 | 810 | 481 | 3,114 |
| Service, sport, and recreation | 6,223 | 3,547 | 3,387 | 70 | 80 | 2,676 |
| Not classified by occupation | 231 | 87 | 77 | 7 | 3 | 144 |

**TABLE** 25.11

Citizenship of the population by age and sex, 1962

| Country of Birth | Total Population | | | Citizens | | | Aliens[a] | | |
|---|---|---|---|---|---|---|---|---|---|
| | Both Sexes | Males | Females | Both Sexes | Males | Females | Both Sexes | Males | Females |
| Total | 31,633 | 19,591 | 12,042 | 10,268 | 5,545 | 4,723 | 21,365 | 14,046 | 7,319 |
| Dahomey | 10 | 10 | — | 5 | 5 | — | 5 | 5 | — |
| Ghana | 6,896 | 4,095 | 2,801 | 1,359 | 778 | 581 | 5,537 | 3,317 | 2,220 |
| Guinea | 8,579 | 4,899 | 3,680 | 4,469 | 2,296 | 2,173 | 4,110 | 2,603 | 1,507 |
| Ivory Coast | 1,131 | 537 | 594 | 754 | 315 | 439 | 377 | 222 | 155 |
| Mali | 565 | 335 | 230 | 142 | 86 | 56 | 423 | 249 | 174 |
| Nigeria | 543 | 404 | 139 | 266 | 179 | 87 | 277 | 225 | 52 |
| Zaïre | 12 | 7 | 5 | 2 | 1 | 1 | 10 | 6 | 4 |
| Senegal | 156 | 94 | 62 | 36 | 26 | 10 | 120 | 68 | 52 |
| Sierra Leone | 4,685 | 2,934 | 1,751 | 2,601 | 1,496 | 1,105 | 2,084 | 1,438 | 646 |
| Togo | 155 | 119 | 36 | 56 | 41 | 15 | 99 | 78 | 21 |
| Other African countries | 278 | 198 | 80 | 86 | 63 | 23 | 192 | 135 | 57 |
| Australia | 9 | 4 | 5 | — | — | — | 9 | 4 | 5 |
| Canada | 112 | 63 | 50 | — | — | — | 112 | 62 | 50 |
| U.S.A. | 1,876 | 1,049 | 827 | 231 | 106 | 125 | 1,645 | 943 | 702 |
| Latin America | 400 | 255 | 145 | 132 | 79 | 53 | 268 | 176 | 92 |
| Haiti | 62 | 33 | 29 | 13 | 9 | 4 | 49 | 24 | 25 |
| Israel | 83 | 49 | 34 | — | — | — | 83 | 49 | 34 |
| India | 154 | 113 | 41 | — | — | — | 154 | 113 | 41 |
| Lebanon | 2,077 | 1,603 | 474 | — | — | — | 2,077 | 1,603 | 474 |
| Other Asian countries | 231 | 141 | 90 | — | — | — | 231 | 141 | 90 |
| Belgium | 24 | 13 | 11 | — | — | — | 24 | 13 | 11 |
| Denmark | 47 | 30 | 17 | — | — | — | 47 | 30 | 17 |
| France | 210 | 153 | 57 | — | — | — | 210 | 153 | 57 |
| Federal Republic of Germany | 275 | 189 | 86 | — | — | — | 275 | 189 | 86 |
| Italy | 699 | 652 | 47 | — | — | — | 699 | 652 | 47 |
| Netherlands | 481 | 317 | 164 | — | — | — | 481 | 317 | 164 |
| Norway | 28 | 20 | 8 | — | — | — | 28 | 20 | 8 |
| Spain | 470 | 384 | 86 | — | — | — | 470 | 384 | 86 |
| Sweden | 383 | 228 | 155 | — | — | — | 383 | 228 | 155 |
| Switzerland | 125 | 94 | 31 | — | — | — | 125 | 94 | 31 |
| United Kingdom | 293 | 184 | 109 | — | — | — | 293 | 184 | 109 |
| Other European countries | 198 | 126 | 72 | — | — | — | 198 | 126 | 72 |
| Country not reported | 386 | 260 | 126 | 116 | 65 | 51 | 270 | 195 | 75 |

SOURCE: 1962 Census Report.
[a] Total number of aliens born in Liberia: 4,506; males, 2,280; females, 2,226.

time of the census, 18 percent of the native population were enumerated outside their county, province, or territory of birth. The remaining 82 percent were found in their county of birth. This does not mean that people from that group have never migrated. They may have migrated many times before the census and then returned to their birth place where they were enumerated. From the census data it is not possible to measure all the moves that one person might have made and the time period in which they have taken place. Figures presented in Tables 24.12 and 25.13 express only the net result of all movements that took place up to the time of the census.

Column 5 of Table 25.12 shows that Montserrado County, Marshall Territory, and Maryland County are the only administrative areas out of 12 with immigration exceeding emigration. This is explained by the fact that Monrovia, the seat of the central

TABLE 25.12

Net migration by major administrative area

| County, Province, Territory | Population Enumerated in Area (1) | Persons Born in Area and Enumerated There (2) | Total Population Born in the Area (3) | Persons Born in Area and Enumerated in Other Areas (4) | Net Migration (5) |
|---|---|---|---|---|---|
| County | | | | | |
| Grand Bassa | 96,575 | 86,478 | 116,410 | 29,932 | −19,835 |
| Grand Cape Mount | 30,447 | 26,373 | 34,442 | 8,069 | −3,995 |
| Maryland | 38,520 | 24,970 | 31,419 | 6,449 | +7,101 |
| Montserrado | 150,648 | 54,396 | 64,275 | 9,879 | +86,373 |
| Sinoe | 44,127 | 41,387 | 51,764 | 10,377 | −7,637 |
| Province | | | | | |
| Central | 315,734 | 294,275 | 337,715 | 43,440 | −21,981 |
| Eastern | 63,075 | 60,837 | 76,045 | 15,208 | −12,970 |
| Western | 165,137 | 151,599 | 183,943 | 32,344 | −18,806 |
| Territory | | | | | |
| Kru Coast | 20,995 | 20,504 | 25,032 | 4,528 | −4,037 |
| Marshall | 13,826 | 6,737 | 8,804 | 2,067 | +5,022 |
| River Cess | 28,437 | 27,087 | 34,749 | 7,662 | −6,312 |
| Sasstown | 9,296 | 8,497 | 12,219 | 3,722 | −2,923 |
| All areas: persons | 976,817[a] | 803,140 | 976,817 | — | — |
| percentages | 100.00 | 82.22 | — | 17.78 | — |

SOURCE: 1962 Census Report.
NOTE: (2) + (4) = (3); (5) = (1) − (3).
[a] This total does not add up to the 984,810 natives residing in Liberia as the place of birth was not reported for 7,993 people who are excluded from this table.

government, and the Firestone Plantations, the oldest concession area in Liberia, are both within Montserrado County. Almost two-thirds of the people living in the county come from another county, province, or territory. Next to Montserrado County as an attraction for in-migrants are Marshall Territory and Maryland County. Firestone also has plantations in these two areas.

Western Central and Eastern provinces, which constitute the hinterland, are areas of net out-migration. The situation in Grand Bassa is bound to be reversed, or may already have done so, because of the new mining activities going on in that area and the large Port of Buchanan (Bassa) that serves as an outlet to the Nimba iron ore.

Many changes have taken place in the

TABLE 25.13

Net movement of migrants from place of birth to place of residence, 1962

| From Place of Birth in | To Place of Residence in | | | | | | | | | | | |
|---|---|---|---|---|---|---|---|---|---|---|---|---|
| | Grand Bassa | Grand Cape Mount | Maryland | Montserrado | Sinoe | Central | Eastern | Western | Kru Coast | Marshall | River Cess | Sasstown |
| County | | | | | | | | | | | | |
| Grand Bassa | | 333 | 242 | 18,787 | 147 | 5,144 | 198 | 1,688 | 23 | 2,858 | 483 | 29 |
| Grand Cape Mount | 211 | | 36 | 4,136 | 14 | 1,187 | 48 | 2,252 | — | 161 | 12 | 12 |
| Maryland | 189 | 91 | | 3,801 | 165 | 659 | 789 | 436 | 163 | 73 | 33 | 50 |
| Montserrado | 1,289 | 486 | 258 | | 218 | 4,270 | 81 | 2,289 | 43 | 789 | 122 | 34 |
| Sinoe | 442 | 148 | 845 | 6,935 | | 578 | 215 | 649 | 55 | 104 | 315 | 91 |
| Province | | | | | | | | | | | | |
| Central | 4,896 | 939 | 248 | 30,948 | 100 | | 267 | 4,539 | 35 | 975 | 207 | 286 |
| Eastern | 79 | 205 | 7,930 | 2,330 | 1,066 | 2,034 | | 1,037 | 102 | 130 | 105 | 190 |
| Western | 504 | 1,742 | 64 | 21,785 | 59 | 6,388 | 161 | | 6 | 1,551 | 32 | 52 |
| Territory | | | | | | | | | | | | |
| Kru Coast | 21 | 19 | 2,571 | 1,151 | 84 | 76 | 355 | 140 | | 48 | 11 | 52 |
| Marshall | 406 | 16 | 6 | 1,221 | 7 | 255 | 3 | 135 | 2 | | 15 | 1 |
| River Cess | 2,031 | 57 | 320 | 3,602 | 156 | 782 | 53 | 283 | 6 | 370 | | 2 |
| Sasstown | 29 | 38 | 1,030 | 1,556 | 724 | 86 | 68 | 90 | 56 | 30 | 15 | |

SOURCE: 1962 Census Report.

distribution of the population since the census of 1962 because of the large mining companies and other industries which have established themselves in Liberia in the last ten years. Soon the 1969 demographic survey will bring to light the latest facts.

## THE LIBERIAN POPULATION
## GROWTH SURVEY

In April 1969, a demographic survey was initiated in Liberia which is known as The Liberian Population Growth Survey. This survey is intended to meet the urgent need for information on the dynamics aspects of the population of Liberia.

Two of the major factors thought to influence fertility and mortality schedules in Liberia are living in a traditional "rural" or village area and residing in an "urban" type of community. Using this basic dichotomy for sampling purposes, demographic estimates have been restricted to Liberia, Liberia rural, and Liberia urban.

A two-stage sampling design was used. In the first stage, 50 clans were selected with probability proportionate to the number of localities in each. In the second stage, two villages or village groups were randomly selected in each clan. In all, 100 localities or villages were selected in the rural area and 100 blocks in the urban area. The sample size is approximately 58,000 persons or about 5 percent of the population estimated for 1969. Each sampling unit is being covered thoroughly once each month or 12 times a year. A dual system of enumeration is used in this survey, with each system independent of the other. The theory of this approach is based largely on the work of Chandrasekar and Deming.[3] The first enumeration is carried out by a registrar who makes monthly visits to each household in his assigned area and records the occurrence of all births, deaths, and migrations. The second enumeration is carried out independently by a staff member, called a supervisor, once every six months. The two reports are matched and all mismatches are checked in the field. This survey, which is intended to be a continuous one, will yield up-to-date information on fertility, mortality, and movements of the population. The first bulletin of the Liberian Population Growth Survey was released in November 1970.

[3] C. Chandrasekar and W. E. Deming, "On a Method of Estimating Birth and Death Rate and Extent of Registration," *Journal of the American Statistical Association*, XLIV (1949).

PART
SIX

*French-Speaking Countries*

THERE is an immense diversity in Cameroon, which covers over 180,000 square miles from 2°–13° north latitude, its southern base completely buried in the equatorial forest and its northern apex disappearing into the Lake Chad papyruses. The thick, damp forest zone of the south gives way to the grassy, scrubby savanna of the center, the high plateau of the Adamoua, the open forests of the Sudanese zone, and finally the Sahel's thorny steppes, not to mention the mountain formations of the west.

The 5,800,000 inhabitants of this territory (1970 estimate) are similarly divided into many ethnic groups, of which the two extreme forms are probably the pygmies of the far south and the Choa Arabs of the far north, and, in between, Bantu, semi-Bantu, Sudanese, and palaeonegritic and hamito-semitic populations. The religions practiced add still more to these differences, since, although the South has a very large Christian majority, the North remains half-traditional and half-Moslem, in spite of some islets of expanding Christianity.

Thus, imparting an idea of the demographic evolution of such varied human entities in a few pages will force us into wide regional generalizations. These unfortunately cannot take into account the ethnic factor, which remains nonetheless essential in demography when dealing with an endogamous region.

## SOURCES

For many reasons, which need not be set out here, the administrative censuses cannot provide the necessary basic data for this subject. This is the reason that since 1960, various sample surveys have been carried out for the whole of the Cameroon territory. It is the results of these surveys, carried out jointly by the Department of General Statistics of Cameroon and the Cooperation Department of INSEE[1] on one hand and SEDES[2] on the

[1] Institut National de la Statistique et des Etudes Economiques.
[2] Société d'Etudes pour la Développement Economique et Social.

# CHAPTER TWENTY-SIX

# *Cameroon*

ANDRÉ PODLEWSKI

other, which we shall use to establish the general outline of Cameroon demography.

Perhaps we should also mention the research work carried out by ORSTOM[3] in this field, which has made clear the basic role of ethnic cultural patterns and has also tried to perfect new methods of demographic investigations by repeated visits.

As well as the demographic studies used in this chapter, geographers and sociologists of ORSTOM have published the results of small-area studies. All these works illustrate the complexity of human phenomena in Cameroon.

## POPULATION INCREASE, PAST AND PRESENT

SAMPLE SURVEYS. There have been four sample surveys. Each is described below:

(1) A survey covering the whole of the federal inspection of Northern Cameroon was carried out in 1960–1961, and sampled about 1,400,000 persons. Two large main zones were distinguished, North Bénoué and South Bénoué, which we shall retain in this survey.
(2) One covering the South and East was carried out in 1962 and sampled about 1,200,000 persons (but excluded the town of Douala). Six large zones of rural population (excluding the urban centers) were distinguished, and regrouped into two unities, East and Mid-South.
(3) One covered the Bamiléké country and its neighborhood, in 1965–1966, and sampled about 1,100,000 persons. Two main zones were distinguished: the Bamiléké country on one hand, and the neighboring area on the other, each zone yielding results concerning the rural areas, the market villages, and the towns.
(4) One covering Western Cameroon was carried out in 1964–1965 and sampled about a million people. Three main zones were distinguished: North, Middle, and South. Very detailed results were published.

As it is impossible here to present findings

[3] Office de la Recherche Scientifique et Technique Outre-Mer.

on over 20 subdivisions of Cameroon, we shall distinguish only the six large zones which are shown on the map in Figure 26.1. The main characteristics of these are delineated in Table 26.1.

The sample surveys, on which the work here is based, have been carried out by the traditional procedure of collecting retrospective information by means of interviews (i.e., the data concerning fertility and mortality come from events which occurred in the 12 months preceding the survey). In addition to the fact that we have to depend upon the memory of the people being surveyed, problems arise also from the difficulty of specifying to people who often know nothing of the use of the calendar, the 12-month period being examined. These considerations and others have sometimes led those responsible for the surveys to alter the results obtained.

Despite these reservations, inherent to the region surveyed and the methodology in use at the time of the survey, the results obtained seem, on the whole, reasonable, at least for the large areas employed here. Finally, it should be noted that these surveys have been carried out at various dates between 1960 and 1965 according to the area. We shall thus be comparing results for information gathered in different years.

PAST POPULATION GROWTH. For the whole of Eastern Cameroon (i.e., excluding zone 6) administrative censuses have been carried out since 1925. Such censuses are merely the addition of the population numbers recorded by the administrative records in all parts of the country. The series of population totals obtained by these censuses, nevertheless, does not allow us to determine the natural increase of the population. The main reasons are that often the increases recorded are very irregular, and the totals at any date only correspond to more complete lists by adding population which has escaped censusing until that time. Thus, these old data can in no way be used to judge the natural increase or rate of growth of the population. However, for the record, Table 26.2 presents the total numbers

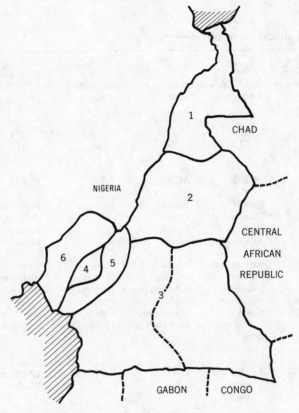

FIGURE 26.1. *Six Subdivisions of the Cameroons*

registered since 1944 by the administrative censuses.

The various sample surveys carried out between 1960 and 1965 give, for mid-1962, a total of about 4 million people for Eastern Cameroon. Comparing this with the figure for 1956, the implied increase would thus be 830,000 people, which corresponds to an average annual increase of about 4 percent. This is obviously an improbably high rate of increase, due very largely to the improvement in censusing methods. Natural increase, as we shall see, is at a much lower level.

There is other, and more exact evidence which allows us to affirm that the administrative censuses often underestimated population numbers. In the North, a comparison of the figures for villages in the survey sample with those of the most recent administrative census showed that the latter underestimated population by 16–22 percent in zone 1, and from 4–10 percent in zone 2. More recently, a complete list for two rural districts of the Adamoua plateau (zone 2) has also revealed an underestimate of 9 percent in the administrative totals. The errors appear to be smaller elsewhere, especially in the South, and range from an undercount of 3.6 percent to an overcount of a similar magnitude. Reasons for these underestimates have been given elsewhere.[4]

[4] From the interesting data obtained on the nomad populations (Foulbé, Mbororo, Akos, nomad stock breeders) in the Western Cameroon survey (zone 6), Service de la Statistique du Cameroun and INSEE, *La Population du Cameroun Occidental*, II (1969), pp. 208–10, supplemented by fuller data which the writer has gathered from a sample of a thousand Mbororo of the Mbabo Tchabbal (Adamoua) and which fit in well with the official survey proportion of less than 15 years old, Adamoua = 48 percent, Western Cameroon = 52 percent; total fertility ratios, Adamoua—5.1, Western Cameroon-5.1.

TABLE 26.1
Characteristics of six subdivisions of Cameroon

| | (1) | (2) | (3) | (4) | (5) | (6) |
|---|---|---|---|---|---|---|
| | | | | | Area around | |
| | North Bénoué | South Bénoué | Southeast | Bamiléké | Bamiléké | West Cameroon |
| *Survey date* | *1960* | *1961* | *1962* | *1965* | *1965* | *1964* |
| *Population* | | | | | | |
| *(thousands)* | | | | | | |
| rural | 1,112 | 228 | 1,078 | 578 | 344 | 932 |
| urban | 38 | 15 | 107 | 80 | 116 | 97 |
| *Area* | | | | | | |
| (sq. miles) | 14,900 | 48,300 | 84,900 | 2,400 | 10,600 | 16,200 |
| *Main ethnic groups* | Foulbé | Foulbé | Boulou, Eton | Bamiléké | Bamoun | Bantous |
| | Matakam | Dourou | Essel | | (Mbam) | Balundu-Mbo |
| | Massa | Baya | Ewondo | | Bamiléké | Ibos |
| | Toupouri | Mboum | Bassa | | Tikar | |
| *Economy* | millet | pastoralism | cocoa | maize | yams | palm-oil |
| | peanuts | millet | coffee | plantain | plantain | cocoa |
| | cotton | peanuts | cabbage-palms | bananas | bananas | bananas |
| | pastoralism | maize | timber-forests | coffee | coffee | coffee |
| | fishing | cassava | aluminium | pigs | pigs | tea |
| | rice | (manioc) | food cultivation | timber-forests | timber-forests | rubber |
| | | fruit | | | | |
| *Main religions* | Traditional | Traditional | Christian | Christian | Christian | Christian |
| | Moslem | Moslem | | | Moslem | Traditional |
| | | Christian | | | | |
| *Main towns* | Garoua | Ngaoundéré | Yaoundé | Dchang | Foumban | Victoria-Buéa |
| | Maroua | | (excluding | Bafoussam | Nkongsamba | Bamenda |
| | | | Douala) | Bafang | Loum | |
| | | | | Mbouda | Mbanga | |

It is still possible to speculate as to whether a single survey round can yield adequate population estimates. This is doubtful for the following reason. During a multiround survey carried out over two years on 15,000 people,

TABLE 26.2
Population of eastern Cameroon according to the administrative censuses[a]

| Date | Population |
|---|---|
| 1944 | 2,816,000 |
| 1946 | 2,820,000 |
| 1947 | 2,898,000 |
| 1950 | 3,073,000 |
| 1952 | 3,107,000 |
| 1956 | 3,170,000 |

[a] Zones 1–5 in Table 26.1.

it was discovered in the year following the drawing up of the initial list that an additional 4 percent of population, for one reason or another, had not been counted at the time of the first round. These additional people were found gradually during the two subsequent six-monthly rounds. As the same thing has been observed in Senegal, where a multiround survey has also been made, it can be assumed that a single round does not allow us to enumerate the whole of the population in tropical Africa.

ESTIMATING CURRENT GROWTH RATES AND TOTAL POPULATION FOR 1970. Remembering these reservations, Table 26.3 can be consulted for estimates of the Cameroonian population and its increase, based on the

TABLE 26.3
Estimates of population growth rates and size

|  | Date | Estimated Population (thousands) | Annual rate of Increase (percent) | Cameroons, 1960–1970 Population |
|---|---|---|---|---|
| Surveyed |  |  |  |  |
| (1) North Bénoué | 1960 | 1,150 | 1.2 | 1,300 |
| (2) South Bénoué | 1961 | 243 | 1.7 | 282 |
| (3) Southeast | 1962 | 1,180 | 1.6 | 1,340 |
| (4) Bamiléké | 1965 | 659 | 2.4 | 742 |
| (5) Area around Bamiléké | 1965 | 461 | 1.9 | 506 |
| (6) West Cameroon | 1964 | 1,029 | 2.3 | 1,146 |
| Not surveyed | Douala |  |  | 250 |
| Yaoundé + certain other rural and urban zones |  |  |  | 270 |
| Estimated total 1970 population |  |  |  | 5,836 |

sample surveys which cover almost the whole country.

DIFFERENTIAL GROWTH. Zones. Table 26.3 showed that the estimated growth differs significantly from zone to zone. Population growth in the northern zones (1 and 2) as a whole has recently been slower than that in the southern and western zones (3–6). The North, thus defined, has an increase of about 1.3 percent per year, while the South and West have one of about 2.0 percent. This difference of growth has been brought about by the double effect of slightly lower fertility and slightly higher mortality in the northern regions.

Ethnic groups. Growth in terms of entire zones is a very general measure, in the sense that it does not apply to the various ethnic groups in each zone considered separately. In fact, in the North, we can see two types of population which evolved in very different ways.

(1) The Foulbé, and populations which have adopted the Foulbé way of life (the Mandara, Kotoko), tend to exhibit stationary population growth.
(2) The populations retaining the traditional pattern, especially on the plain, are now tending to grow at a rate near to, or above, 2 percent per year.

Thus the average given above for the North is in fact only an abstract approximation which

does not really represent any of the large ethnic groups.

In the South, the Bamiléké zone does correspond to a homogeneous group with a rate of growth estimated at 2.3 percent per year, but in the other southern zones the ethnic differences are pronounced. Thus, for Western Cameroon, out of the three divisions—north, central, and south—the first (the Bantoides of the central plateau) are increasing most rapidly (2.9 percent).

In the Southeast there are also clear-cut differences between certain ethnic groups. Thus the Bassa are growing by over 2.3 percent per year, while other groups (Mvété, Yébékolo, etc.) exhibit the low level of 0.5 percent.

Religions. Another way of considering growth is to examine it in terms of the religion practiced. It appears that the Moslem populations tend to exhibit lower rates of growth than either the traditional or Christian populations. Traditionals and Christians both show rates of growth in the region of 2 percent per year, but the reasons differ: very high fertility and mortality for the traditionals, and lower fertility and mortality for the Christians. Table 26.4 summarizes the findings, giving very general estimates.

Rural and urban residences. Once more we must distinguish the North from the other regions. The urban centers of the North (Maroua, Garoua, Ngaoundéré) seem to show natural rates of growth far below those

TABLE 26.4

Religious differentials in demographic measures (all rates per thousand)

| | Fertility | Mortality | Natural Increase |
|---|---|---|---|
| Moslems | Low (20–25) | Low (20) | Low (0–5) |
| Traditionals | Very high (55) | High (35) | High (20) |
| Christians | High (45) | Medium (25) | High (20) |

observed in the neighboring rural populations. The opposite trend is to be found in the other zones, where the natural rates of growth are noticeably higher in the towns than in the neighboring rural areas. This difference is caused by very low fertility in the towns of the North, and very low mortality in the towns of the other zones.

POPULATION PROJECTIONS UNTIL 1980. In Table 26.5 the projections made by those responsible for the surveys are summarized, and those for each of the zones are presented separately.

TABLE 26.5

Population projections, 1970–1980, by zone (in thousands)

| Zone | 1970 | 1975 | 1980 |
|---|---|---|---|
| (1) North Bénoué | 1,300 | 1,380 | 1,460 |
| (2) South Bénoué | 282 | 308 | 335 |
| (3) Southeast | 1,340 | 1,450 | 1,570 |
| (4) Bamiléké | 742 | 835 | 940 |
| (5) Area around Bamiléké | 506 | 556 | 611 |
| (6) West Cameroon | 1,146 | 1,284 | 1,439 |
| Cameroon | 5,316 | 5,813 | 6,355 |

## THE STATE OF THE POPULATION

DISTRIBUTION, DENSITY, AND ETHNIC AND RELIGIOUS DIVISIONS. The distribution of population over the Cameroon territory is very unequal, since almost half the population is in zones 4, 5, and 6, as well as in the town of Douala situated far south of these zones. Together these areas cover only 17 percent of Cameroon.

Figure 26.2 shows that the other concentration of population is to be found in the North

(zone 1) and the West (zone 6). The highest population density is to be found in the Bamiléké country (zone 4) with 275 persons per square mile.

Densities of over 260 persons per square mile are also to be found in the barren mountains of the Matakam country and among the Mora "pagans" (zone 1).

In terms of the whole country, the North Bénoué region (zone 1) comes after the Bamiléké country, with an average density of 78 (85 in great Diamaré and only 18 in the far north, home of the pastoral Choa Arabs). Western Cameroon (zone 6) has a density of around 65 persons per square mile but we should distinguish the north (91), the center (28), and the south (62), which exhibit very varying densities. The area around the Bamiléké country (zone 5) has only 41 persons per square mile, despite the immigration of many Bamiléké. But this is only an average, the two extremes being the Mungo state (north of Douala) with 163, and the Tikar and Bamoun country with 23.

The large Southeast zone (zone 3) exhibits a density of only 16. A contrast exists between the high densities of the land around the capital (over 100) and the low densities east and north of this zone (less than 13).

Finally, Central Cameroon (zone 2) has an average of only 5 persons per square mile. However, locally there are more important population concentrations (i.e., the districts of the Dourou Plateau and Mbang-Foulbé).

Thus, there is a Central and Eastern zone of very low population density, while population concentrations are to be found in the North, the West, and around the capital (Yaoundé). It is not possible here to analyze the ethnic densities in detail. We have already stated that the Bamiléké (zone 4) and especially the Matakam or Mafa (in the north) showed unbelievably high densities considering the natural resources of the area.

Attention might be drawn to parts of the North with very high densities among certain traditional ethnic groups in the Mora Mountains (one rural district has up to 525 inhabitants per square mile), the neighboring Mofou district (260), and certain other

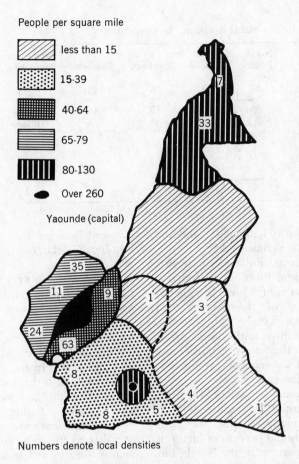

People per square mile

less than 15

15-39

40-64

65-79

80-130

Over 260

Yaounde (capital)

Numbers denote local densities

FIGURE 26.2. *Population Density by Zone*

districts—Massa, Toupouri, Moundang, and Guidar (130–260).

The lowest densities are found among the Foulbé of the Adamoua Plateau (who, with a million zebus, follow a pastoral way of life). It appears impossible to distinguish any relationship between religion and density. The Moslem regions can have a very high density (Diamaré) or a low one (Logone Chari, Adamoua), and the same can be said of the Christianized or traditional regions.

AGE STRUCTURE. Judging by the distribution of the percentage of under-15-year-olds by whole areas, urban populations are younger than rural ones for the country as a whole, but not in the North (zones 1 and 2). Rural-

urban results are very near to one another for zones 6 and 4. The proportion of the adult population, 15–59 years of age, is much the same for the urban (53.5 percent) and rural (54.0 percent) populations. In all zones the towns contain many fewer old people (60 years of age and over) than do the rural areas. Table 26.6 shows the urban-rural division in the very young and the oldest age groups.

Generally speaking, the proportion of young people (less than 15 years) is highest in the following places: the West among the Bamiléké (48 percent) and the populations of the north of Western Cameroon (49 percent); the North among the traditional plain and mountain populations (41 percent), including the Moundang (47 percent), Matakam (45

TABLE 26.6
Age structure by urban-rural division (in percentages)

| Age Group | Urban/Rural | North Bénoué | South Bénoué | Southeast | Bamiléké | Area around Bamiléké | West Cameroon | Total |
|---|---|---|---|---|---|---|---|---|
| 0–14 years | rural | 37 | 34 | 36 | 48 | 43 | 47 | 41 |
| | urban | 29 | | 43 | 48 | 49 villages | market-villages 47 towns 45 | 44 |
| 60 + | rural | 6 | 6.5 | 7 | 4 | 4 | | 5 |
| | urban | 5 | | 3 | 3 | 2 | 2 | 3 |

percent), and Mofou (43 percent); and the Southeast among the Bassa (44 percent), Yambassa (47 percent), Bafia (49 percent), Baya (43 percent), and Eton (43 percent).

The proportions are much lower among the Moslem population of the North; i.e., Foulbé (27 percent), Kotoko (31 percent), Mandara (32 percent), and Choa Arabs (33 percent). But in the South certain ethnic groups also exhibit a very low proportion; i.e., Yébékolo (24 percent).

However, note should be taken of the difficulties and differential difficulties met in estimating ages in many regions. (Registration now covers about 90 percent of births in the South, and 20 percent in the North, but this only includes the last few years.) When there is doubt, ages are estimated with the aid of local historical calendars and sometimes according to the fertility of the women.

Despite inevitable mistakes, it is striking that the average age of childbearing women in almost every region is recorded as between 26 and 28 years. However, it is also striking that all the age pyramids show a hollow in the female 10–19 years of age group, which no doubt corresponds to an underenumeration of young girls in this age range probably because of the overstatement of their age when they are already promised for marriage, or when they have reached puberty.

There is a continuing need for more exact estimates of age, despite the difficulties. However, by forming large age groups, we can reduce the risk of error, especially if the divisions between the groups are not round numbers (10, 20, etc.).

SCHOOL ENROLLMENT. The rate of enrollment (i.e., the proportion of those of school age actually at school) is low in the North (about 30 percent), average in Western Cameroon (55 percent), high in the South and the Bamiléké region (80 and 88 percent), and higher still in the urban centers (almost 90 percent, with the exception of the North).

Certain ethnic groups in the North (zones 1 and 2) have a higher enrollment rate (the Moundang, Dourou, and Mboum are all over 40 percent). The Foulbé of the Adamoua seem little inclined to accept either state or missionary schooling (10 percent), but prefer the Koranic teaching of the marabouts (20 percent).

Everywhere school enrollment is greater for boys than girls. Table 26.7 estimates the rate of illiteracy as a proportion of the total population for those zones with the necessary data.

In addition to the state schools, religious missions play an important role in the effort to achieve more complete schooling, and they work as much in the North as elsewhere.

DISTRIBUTION BY OCCUPATION. The use of different definitions makes a precise comparison between regions according to activities difficult, if not impossible. In general, we can say that, in all regions, agricultural and pastoral activities occupy 80–85 percent

TABLE 26.7
Percentage of total population illiterate

| Zone | Urban/Rural | Percent |
|---|---|---|
| (1) and (2) North and South Bénoué | rural | 96 |
| | urban | 81 |
| (3) Southeast | total rural & urban | 70.5 |
| | urban only | 55 |
| (6) West Cameroon | population of 15 yrs and over | 85 |

of the population aged 15 years or more, the secondary and tertiary sectors comprising only 5–10 percent of the total, and the inactive making up the remainder 5–15 percent.

In urban areas (for the whole of the country the rate of urbanization is close to 14 percent) the primary sector, the secondary, and tertiary together, and the economically inactive, each make up about one-third of the labor force.

MARRIAGE PATTERNS. The houses or dwellings are called "lodgings", "concessions", or *sarés* (North), in different surveys. These dwellings house one or more families. It is interesting to note that in certain regions there can be shown to be a relationship between the average number of inhabitants per *saré* and the level of fertility (for instance, in zone 1). As a general rule, it seems that the average number of residents per concession or *saré* is higher among the more traditional populations. Cultural evolution, by means of Christianity or Islam, seems, on the contrary, to individualize families.

When studying the marriage pattern, it is important to consider first what we call *ethnic endogamy*. In fact, in all the zones surveyed, almost all the unions had been made within the ethnic group; thus, in North Bénoué (zone 1), Southeast (zone 3), and Western Cameroon (zone 6) about 90 percent of the married men chose women of their own ethnic group (except the Douala, Maka, and

Kozimé groups in zone 3). In the South Bénoué region (zone 2), the proportion was 85 percent.

Thus it is possible to study ethnic fertility and to judge whether valid differences have been recorded, and to compare the findings with the fertility of "mixed" or interethnic group marriages, which, because of the direction of social change, will become ever more numerous in the decades to come. Indeed, it does seem that ethnic endogamy is tending to decline in the towns, where contacts with "modern" ways of life are many. But, at the present time, even in the urban centers ethnic endogamy is around 75 percent. We shall return to this point when discussing differential fertilities.

The difficulty of determining age to a year makes statistics of age at first marriage uncertain. For women, usual age at first marriage would be 16–17 years in Western Cameroon (zone 6), 15–16 in the Southeast, and 14–15 in the North (where the Moslems tend to marry earlier than those of the traditional religions). Marriage tends to take place later in urban centers, which apparently is an effect of schooling.

For men, the age at first marriage shows great variation. It seems to depend essentially on the amount of bridewealth asked. The higher it is (in the urban centers of the South), the later men marry. On the contrary, the more it is largely symbolic or traditional, the earlier men marry (i.e., the traditional mountain-population of North Cameroon). Everywhere, 70–75 percent of the men are monogamous, and this proportion rises to 81 percent in the Southeast (zone 3). Thus polygamy only concerns 20–30 percent of married men, varying according to the zone.

According to ethnic group, 100 married men will have an average number of wives varying between 112 in the Ewondo-Yaoundé region, and 160 in some traditional ethnic groups in the North (zone 1) and ethnic groups in the north of Western Cameroon (zone 6).

Everywhere, polygamy increases with age, and even more rapidly with wealth. The

TABLE 26.8

Average number of marriages experienced
by ever married women

| Zone | Number of Marriages |
|---|---|
| (1) North Bénoué | 2.1 |
| (2) South Bénoué | 1.7 |
| (3) Southeast | 1.4 |
| (6) Western Cameroon | 1.2 |

most polygynous populations are those which
have kept their traditional characters, followed by the Moslems, and finally the
Christians. There is less polygyny in urban
than rural areas, a fact perhaps largely
explained by religion since these centers have
large majorities of Christians and Moslems.

We might be surprised that Moslems are
less polygynous than those of traditional
religions. This is perhaps due to the fact that
Moslems tend to have successive wives rather
than simultaneous ones.

The number of remarriages for women
varies greatly with region as can be noted in
Table 26.8. The decrease is very noticeable
from north to south. This index shows
clearly that one of the main effects of Islam in
tropical Africa is the multiplication of remarriages among women. Table 26.9 confirms this. Among the Foulbé or North
Bénoué, who are mostly Moslems, an index of
2.7 has been recorded.

Thus, it seems that the more the population
is Christianized, the more solid are the bonds
of marriage (except for the coastal groups of
the South and Western Cameroon). Islam is
also one of the reasons for the low number of

TABLE 26.9

Northern Cameroon: average number of
marriages per ever-married woman, by
religion

| Religion | Number of Marriages |
|---|---|
| Moslem | 2.4 |
| Traditional | 1.8 |
| Christian | 1.4 |
| All religions | 2.0 |

marriage registrations in the North, where the
woman is afraid of "cementing the marriage
too much" by an official declaration. Thus,
we can generalize that in the South and West
at least two-thirds of the married women have
been married only once, whereas in the
North this proportion drops to half. Everywhere, women without children remarry
more often than women with children, and, in
urban centers, remarriages of wives are everywhere less frequent than in rural areas.

All the surveys also seem to indicate that
the marriage bonds are more fragile among
the young generations than among the older
ones, a fact which will probably have future
repercussions on fertility.

Finally, it might be noted that a multiround survey carried out in zone 2 showed
that in only 19 percent of the marriages
recorded in the course of a year, were the
wives marrying for the first time and into a
monogamous marriage. Table 26.10 presents
the distribution of the 181 marriages observed
during the year in the predominantly Moslem
area. It should be noted that the proportion of
first wives marrying for the first time must
have been all the higher as the fertility of the
ethnic group considered was the highest.

## FERTILITY

The sample surveys referred to here have
estimated the fertility by means of two
different procedures:

(1) By retrospective interviews, gathering
information on the births which occurred in
the 12 months before the survey
(2) By retrospective interviews, seeking information about all children ever born alive
to the women in the sample.

The first procedure essentially measures
current fertility. The second obtains total or
past fertility.

Here we shall examine only the data from
the 12 months preceding the survey and
concentrate on present-day fertility. The
total fertility approach places too great a
reliance on respondents' memories and on the
cooperation of those involved, and often

Table 26.10

Order of the wife in marriage, according to
the number of her marriages

| Wife's Order among Wives in Marriage She Is Entering (including herself) | Number of Wives by Number of Marriages (including present one) | | | |
|---|---|---|---|---|
| | 1 marriage | 2 marriages | 3 or more marriages | Totals |
| 1 | 35 | 24 | 14 | 73 |
| 2 | 31 | 37 | 12 | 80 |
| 3 | 1 | 6 | 8 | 15 |
| 4 | 3 | 2 | 4 | 9 |
| 5 | 2 | 1 | 1 | 4 |
| *Total* | 72 | 70 | 39 | 181 |

yields results very different from the other approach, thus forcing research workers into making many adjustments.

For the whole of Cameroon, the crude birth rate is apparently about 43 per thousand. This relatively high rate strongly affects the age structure of the country, 41 percent of the population being under 15 years of age.

The apparent sterility rate (women of reproductive age without children at the time of the survey) is 22.5 percent. The average age of childbearing is between 27 and 28 years.

Such is the general picture of Cameroon fertility which, however, varies greatly by the region. The regional total fertility ratio ranges from a minimum of 4.0 percent to a maximum of 6.3 percent. Fertility varies greatly also by religion (e.g., 3 for the northern Moslems to over 7 among those of traditional religion in the mountains).

All the denser zones reveal a crude birth rate of more than 40 per thousand (zones 1, 4, 5, and 6). Indeed, the Bamiléké country (zone 4) and Western Cameroon (zone 6) yield rates of 50 and 49 per thousand respectively.

But zones 2 and 3 (the most sparsely settled), which cover three-quarters of Cameroon exhibit rates of about 36 per thousand. Figure 26.3 maps the regional differences in total fertility ratios.

However, analysis by zone does not show the basic differences existing between one ethnic group and another. The leading researchers now seem unanimous in asserting that the ethnic factor is decisive where fertility is concerned. This is all the clearer in view of the demonstration that ethnic endogamy is the general rule everywhere. Looking at the fertility in this way we can detect huge differences within the same region.

In zone 1 (North Bénoué), the Foulbé, Bornouans, Mandara, and Kotoko present total fertility ratios of under 4. All these groups are Moslem. On the other hand, adherents of the traditional religions in the mountains, the Matakam, Mofou, Ouldémé, Podokwo, Guiziga, Daba, etc., exhibit total fertility ratios of over 6.

It seems that the transition from high fertility (total fertility ratios over 6) to medium fertility (4–5) occurs by a reduction of the birth rates during the first 15 years of reproductive age (the fertility maximum in the 20–24 years group tends to disappear). In the same way, the traditional ethnic groups on conversion to Islam experienced a drop in the age at first marriage of females, and, at the same time, a drop in fertility.

In zone 2 (South Bénoué) similar ethnic differences appear. The Laka of the Adamoua, former servants of the Foulbé, exhibit extremely low fertility of less than 1.7 (and only 17 percent of the population are under 15 years of age). Likewise, the Kolbila, a tiny isolated group of less than 1,000 people, remaining traditional in religion, record 2.1, and 21 percent of the population are under 15

TABLE 26.11
Measures of fertility by zone, age, and population subdivisions

| Zone | Population Type | Crude Birth Rate | Age-Specific Birth Rates (per 1,000) | | | | | | | Total Fertility Ratios | Percentage of Females 14–49 with No Live Births |
| | | | 14–19 | 20–24 | 25–29 | 30–34 | 35–39 | 40–44 | 45–49 | | |
|---|---|---|---|---|---|---|---|---|---|---|---|
| (1) North Bénoué | All religions | 42 | 161 | 287 | 198 | 152 | 104 | 53 | 10 | 4.7 | 24 |
| | Moslem | 29 | 122 | 150 | 131 | 95 | 60 | 24 | 6 | 3.1 | 33 |
| | non-Moslem | 49 | 188 | 285 | 232 | 182 | 129 | 72 | 14 | 5.7 | 19 |
| (2) South Bénoué | All religions | 36 | 196 | 213 | 148 | 105 | 78 | 13 | 8 | 4.0 | 30 |
| | Moslem | 25 | 145 | 133 | 148 | 72 | 91 | 18 | 10 | 3.2 | 37 |
| | Traditional | 42 | 220 | 220 | 153 | 120 | 67 | | 8 | 4.2 | 29 |
| (3) Southeast | All population | 36 | 140 | 228 | 196 | 166 | 98 | 57 | 12 | 4.6 | 33 |
| | Urban population | 45 | 138 | 279 | 190 | 190 | 116 | 80 | 16 | 5.2 | 30 |
| (4) Bamiléké | All population | 49 | 228 | 307 | 298 | 239 | 131 | 43 | 4 | 6.3 | 14 |
| | Urban population | 52 | 203 | 325 | 282 | 232 | 163 | 69 | — | 6.4 | 22 |
| (5) Area around Bamiléké | All population | 41 | 172 | 264 | 225 | 197 | 114 | 31 | 9 | 5.1 | 22 |
| | Urban population | 43 | 146 | 291 | 224 | 214 | 117 | 36 | 1 | 5.1 | 24 |
| (6) Western Cameroon | All population | 50 | 198 | 304 | 261 | 200 | 105 | 33 | 21 | 5.6 | 15 |
| | Urban population | 49 | 208 | 294 | 249 | 191 | 111 | 30 | 6 | 5.4 | 22 |

years old. The Bayas, on the contrary, exhibit total fertility ratios of 4.7, and more than 40 percent of the population is under 15 years of age. In zone 3 (Southeast), there is also a wide ethnic range; the two extremes appear to be the Bassa with a total fertility ratio of 6 (and about 44 percent of the population less than 15 years old), and the Yébékolo with about 3 (and 24 percent less than 15 years old). Zone 4 is almost entirely Bamiléké country, and the results in zone 5 lump together the various ethnic groups making no distinction between them except to point out that Bamoun fertility is near that of the Bamilékés. Finally, in Western Cameroon (zone 6), the two extremes are shown by the Bantoides of the forest, with a total fertility ratio of 6.6, and the coastal groups, whose fertility is around 3.

Table 26.11 summarizes the main findings on fertility and sterility by zone. It should be noted that in all the zones (except for the Moslem groups of zone 2) the maximum fertility rates are to be found in the 20–24 age group.

The differences in fertility between urban and rural areas are scarcely significant, except for zone 1, North Bénoué (not shown in Table 26.11), where there is significantly lower fertility in the urban centers with a total fertility ratio of 2.9 in contrast to 4.9 in the zone as a whole, and with a sterility rate

in the former of 40 percent compared with 21 percent in the latter.

This absence of a significant difference in the other zones is rather surprising, but it probably is explained by the fact that urban-rural fertility differentials develop only slowly. Since the urban centers of the South developed under European influence have only acquired a real numerical importance in the last generation, the results of urbanization have consequently not yet been deeply felt. This is confirmed when we consider the position in the northern towns—Maroua in particular—which are older essentially African market towns. Here the effect on fertility of population concentration has been working for a long time, and consequently has had an appreciable effect.

Then, too, the towns are inhabited by younger populations, a fact which we must also take into account for a better appreciation of the *apparent* sterility rates, which are generally higher in the urban centers than the rural zones (for the whole of Cameroon, this rate is 22 percent in rural areas and 28 percent in the towns).

Though polygyny does not seem to influence fertility, there does exist a significant association between fertility and the number of marriages a female has experienced. This relationship can be seen clearly within the various ethnic groups.

Per square mile

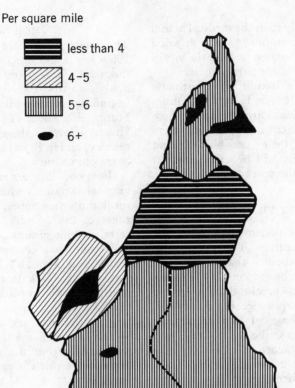

FIGURE 26.3.   *Total Fertility Ratios by Major Zone*

In certain regions (notably Western Cameroon) it has been shown that married women have distinctly higher fertility than those who are single, living in free union, separated, divorced, or widowed. In this same region, it was found in the towns that women married to executives or technicians had higher than average fertility.

It is impossible to determine secular fertility trends, and it is not certain that fertility has fallen. Studies made by comparing completed fertility with current fertility, a very debatable procedure, would suggest rising fertility.

We can, however, try to bring out the main conditions which could lead to either an increase or a decrease in fertility. Factors which could raise Cameroonian fertility include: (1) a reduction in the length of breast-feeding time, and a resulting decrease

in the period of culturally enforced sexual abstinence; (2) the development of health services to reduce maternal mortality, especially of young mothers following child-birth, thus leading to the possibility of their having other children; (3) the increasing success in combating the spread of sterilizing venereal diseases (usually more widespread in towns); (4) the rising standard of living, and the possibility of tranquillity resulting perhaps from a political and economic stability, which could tend to increase fertility, at least initially; (5) the development especially in the urban centers of supplementary feeding for children at the breast might also allow earlier conception.

Factors which might lower Cameroonian fertility include: (1) increased and quicker remarriage of women; (2) in certain urban centers, the spread of sterilizing venereal diseases more rapidly than the medical action seeking to stamp them out; (3) the growing schooling of young women beyond the age of puberty (especially in the urban centers).

At the present, it is difficult to estimate which of these two trends is predominating. Population projections carried out by those responsible for different surveys do not seem to favor any of these possibilities, and consider that fertility will be maintained at its present level in the years to come.

## CONTRACEPTIVE METHODS

There is very little documentation on the subject of contraceptives. The point most commonly written about is that the practice of abortion seems to be growing in the urban centers, although few precise data are given. In rural areas this practice is exceptional, largely because those of the traditional religion, as well as the Christians and Moslems, are frightened of breaking the "divine law" in this domain.

Traditional practices, attempting to combat sterility among both men and women, by what are claimed to be suitable medicines, are much more common than attempts to reduce fertility. This writer's only contact with the use of abortives was by a woman who had already given birth to eight boys and was afraid of having a ninth one, which would have provoked the hostility of her neighborhood at such an "excess of power." However, in a small ethnic group situated in the South Bénoué area, it was said that abortive methods were formerly used, but later given up once and for all because of the bad effects they could have on the social life of the group (this group has now scarcely more than a thousand persons).

Given the great risks of infant and toddler mortality which still exist in many regions, it is difficult to believe that such practices would traditionally have been widespread enough to have influenced fertility levels. Finally, it might be recalled that most of the rural population of tropical Africa honor the mother, and that a large family remains the crowning glory of the woman who has borne it.

## MORTALITY

The crude death rate of Cameroon in the 1960s has been estimated to be about 24 per thousand. This rate corresponds approximately to that recorded in England at the beginning of the nineteenth century, in France in about 1830, in Poland and Hungary toward the end of the nineteenth century, and in Brazil at the beginning of the twentieth century.

However, this general rate masks great internal variations which are found between rural and urban zones, between the different zones of the country, and finally between certain ethnic groups.

For all urban centers combined the crude rate is only about 14.5, whereas it is 26 in rural areas. This large differential results partly from the medical and social services that are much more plentiful in urban centers and accepted by the urban people (which is not always the case in rural areas), and partly from the age structure of the population which is younger in urban than rural areas.

In terms of mortality, the zones of the country fall into three groups. The first is the Southeast (zone 3) and South Bénoué (zone 2), where the crude rate is in the region of 20 (in zone 3: 17.8 in the western half and 21.7 in the east). The Southeast owes this moderate rate to its medical and social services whereas South Bénoué owes it above all to its climate, moderated by the attitude of the Adamoua Plateau, and to its varied food resources. Second are those of the West (zones 4, 5, and 6), where the crude rates are between 25 and 29. Finally, there is North Bénoué (zone 1), where the corrected rate is 31 (the uncorrected rate being 27). Within this region, we can distinguish the populations of the mountains, where the rate is at its highest level (40) and those of the plain (where the rate is 28).

Important differences have also been found between different ethnic groups, sometimes even those inhabiting neighboring lands. Thus the Moslem ethnic groups of North Cameroon (zone 1) and especially the Foulbé show much lower rates (of the order of 20) than those of certain neighboring traditional populations (more than 40 for the Matakam, Kapsiki, etc.).

In zone 2, which is healthier, the Foulbé have a rate of only 18 (verified by subsequent multiround surveys). The rate of the neighboring populations, mostly Moslems (Mboum, Dourou of the plateau) is also low, at about 22.

In zone 3, the ethnic groups in and near the capital (Eton, Ewondo, Bané) exhibit much lower rates (16) than those of the ethnic groups further east (Baya, Kaka, Maka, Kozimé), where the crude rates vary from 21–23. In the dense and prolific Bamiléké country (zone 4) we find a rate of 26, whereas the surrounding land has one of 28.

Finally, in Western Cameroon (zone 6), the overall rate of 27.5 covers very large regional differences (39 in the center and 27 in the south), which apparently result from different access to hospitals (19 percent of the deaths in the south are in hospitals, against only 7 percent in the north).

Thus, local variations are marked, and seem to be influenced by three main factors: malnutrition (especially in the mountains of zone 1); a favorable climate (especially Adamoua in zone 2); the presence and use of hospital services (especially in the south of Western Cameroon and the region around the capital).

In five zones out of six, higher male than female mortality has been recorded (the exception being zone 5 where the levels are similar). The sex differential varies, reaching its maximum in the Bamiléké country (zone 4) with rates of 30 for men and 23 for women. It is not impossible that the after-effects of the disturbances which arose in this region shortly before the survey, are the cause of this high excess mortality among the men. Before presenting mortality data which are more precise than the crude rate, it might be emphasized that in the population projections carried out on the basis of the sample surveys, in most of the zones the hypothesis of falling of mortality was employed for years to come. This hypothesis seems completely valid, all the more so as

certain rates (infant and toddler mortality) can presumably only decrease in view of their present high level contrasted with the development of medical and social services and the spread of concepts and knowledge of elementary rules of hygiene.

Summarizing the findings on infant mortality, we might note that: (1) it is generally less than 100 per thousand live births in the urban centers; (2) it is near to 100 in the Southeast region (zone 3) and the South Bénoué region (zone 2); (3) it is between 150 and 200 in the other rural areas. The most unfavorable regions are central Western Cameroon and the mountains of Northern Cameroon (zone 1).

It should be noted that infant mortality rates obtained by retrospective interviews generally are underestimated for various reasons (a tendency not to declare children who died before receiving a name in traditional regions, for example), and those responsible for the surveys have often had to correct the results obtained in this field. Only sustained observations with repeated rounds every three or six months can hope to include most of the deaths of this age. Only the sustained observations carried out over the past years in Cameroon and Senegal seem to have been sufficiently thorough to demonstrate Bourgeois-Pichat's relationship which makes it possible to distinguish between endogenous and exogenous causes of infant mortality (this necessitates a weekly classification of deaths during the first month of life, and a monthly one until the end of the first year of life).

From 1–4 years after birth, the total volume of mortality is generally equal to the one observed during the first 12 months. One example is the area surrounding Bamiléké (zone 5) which recorded 2,624 deaths under 1 year of age and 2,550 deaths at 1–4 years. Similar proportions are to be found in the Southeast (zone 3), Western Cameroon (zone 6), and South Bénoué (zone 2). Thus, in the zones where infant mortality is high, we find annual rates for 1–4-year-olds in the region of 40 per thousand. For children of up to 5 years of age, male mortality is higher than female mortality. The high rates of infant and toddler mortality are caused in the various parts of the country by malnutrition, absence of sufficient care taken of the young children, or more unfavorable local climatic conditions.

Minimum age-specific death rates are found in different parts of the country anywhere between 5 and 24 years of age (usually between 10 and 15) and thereafter rise gradually at first. From the various survivorship tables constructed we shall examine only the general figure of the median length of life (i.e., the age at which the generation is reduced by half, and which, at the Cameroonian level of mortality, is probably in most cases somewhat higher than the more widely used index, the expectation of life at birth). For Cameroon as a whole, this median length of life is about 41 years.

By zone the median lengths of life are: (a) under 30 years in the North (zone 1, 28 years), but this estimation is an average between two very different results, the Moslem areas reaching 42 years and the mountain people of traditional religion only reaching 14; (b) 38 years in Western Cameroon (32 for men and 42 for women); (c) over 40 years in the Bamiléké country and its surrounding area (rural zones 4 and 5, 45 years) and in the eastern part of the Southeast zone (40 years); (d) around 50 years in the western part of the Southeast (zone 3) (52 years for the whole area and 55 in the urban centers), and in the Bénoué (zone 2). In these regions the expectation of life at birth ($e_0$) and at 5 years ($e_5$) are given in Table 26.12. Thus the large differences in mortality which can exist between the different regions during the first five years of life are much reduced after 5 years of age.

The high figure of 52 years at 5 years of age, revealed by the Adamoua high plateau, is explained by the comparative healthiness of the plateau climate and the varied agricultural and pastoral resources of these high lands. Another multiround survey made recently in this region yields results similar to these; over a two-year period a mortality level has been observed with an expectation

TABLE 26.12

Expectations of life at birth and at five years, by zone

| Zone | Expectation of Life at Birth (in years) | Expectation of Life at 5 Years (in years) |
|---|---|---|
| (1) North Bénoué | 33 | 46 |
| (2) South Bénoué | 43 | 52 |
| (3) Southeast | 43 | 49 |
| (4) Bamiléké | 39 | 49 |
| (5) Area around Bamiléké | 40 | 47 |
| (6) Western Cameroon | 34 | 43 |

of life at 43 years at birth. (The same as the other survey and 50 years rather than 52, at 5 years of age.)

Finally, we should add that the expectation of life at birth of an inhabitant of Cameroon is about 37 years in rural areas and 50 years in urban centers. It is certain that hospital facilities and medical and social services are the reason for this difference. In rural areas even where hospital facilities exist it seems that the coverage is still insufficient despite recent efforts to improve the position.

We believe that rural social and paramedical aid would be more effective if practiced in the villages themselves (by means of frequent visits), rather than by treating everyone in stationary facilities in a prefecture or subprefecture. A determined effort does seem to have been made recently in the field of social and paramedical aid, as much by the state as by the missions. It is to be hoped that this will continue, will expand, and will be applied particularly to attempt to curtail the frightening infant and toddler mortality recorded in the mountainous regions of the North, which are more backward than other areas. Social and paramedical aid, destined above all to give preventive care, often is found to be much less expensive than medical efforts destined to provide curative care.

## MIGRATION

EXTERNAL MIGRATION. Looking at an ethnic map of Cameroon, we realize that at least 25 ethnic groups lie astride one of the country's boundaries. For zone 1 (North Bénoué) alone, taken as an example, the following ethnic groups spread into Chad or Nigeria: Choa Arabs, Kotoko, Mousgoum, Massa, Mousseye, Toupouri, Moundang, Margui-Kapsiki, Goudé, Ndjen, Foulbé, Bata, and Fali. Thus, it is obvious that population movements from one country to another are not generally recorded, and cannot be, for those coming or going hardly ever use the rare motorized tracks where customs points are established, but usually take the bush trails which are faster and more used by foot travelers, without any control taking place.

It is therefore illusory to try and reckon movements which are very numerous and elusive. Two examples follow: (1) To be able to wed, a young Massa man should give his future parents-in-law bridewealth consisting, among other things, of eight to ten head of cattle (zebus). Often, to save up a nest egg, the young man becomes for two or three years a fisherman among the Kotoko of Chad. None of them make an official declaration of departure. (2) At the eastern and western ends of the Adamoua Plateau are fairly numerous Mbororo populations who are mostly nomadic and follow their herds. If the tax on cattle becomes heavier, it is sufficient to make the herders, with their families and animals, cross the border and settle down on the side where the fiscal impositions are lightest.

RURAL-RURAL MIGRATION. In a single-round survey the easiest and best way of measuring the general volume of rural migration is to distinguish, among the resident population examined, the persons not born in the locality of their present residence. This is the procedure mainly used in the different sample surveys examined here.

Before giving the broad regional results, it might be noted that female mobility is every-where more important than male mobility for the following reason. The ethnic groups are made up of different clans, each of them generally claiming to be descended from a common male ancestor, regarded as the founder of the clan. In order to avoid con-

TABLE 26.13
Percentage of population currently living in place of birth, by zone and sex

| Zone | Males | Females | Both Sexes |
|---|---|---|---|
| (1) North Bénoué | 67.7 | 43.0 | 54.4 |
| (2) South Bénoué | 55.4 | 40.9 | 48.0 |
| (3) Southeast | 85.0 | 43.0 | 63.0 |
| (4) Bamiléké | 74.1 | 44.6 | 57.9 |
| (5) Area around Bamiléké | 60.9 | 52.1 | 56.4 |
| (6) Western Cameroon | 81.0 | 77.5 | 79.0 (in the south = 48) |

sanguineous marriages, almost all the clans practice clan exogamy (except most Foulbé and the Mbororo), in the sense that a man marries a woman of a clan other than his own. As the members of a same clan are usually united in the same villages, and as the wife usually goes to live in the husband's clan, a great volume of female migration is recorded.

By zone and by sex, Table 26.13 presents the proportion of population currently living in the village of their birth. The population is clearly more mobile in zone 2 (South Bénoué). The Adamoua is a land of stock raising where Foulbé and Mbororo graze their herds, and it is normal to note that among pastoralists change of place of residence is more important than among farmers of other types. Moreover, most of the population of this zone is Moslem, and such populations are more mobile than others.

Migration is next most important in zone 1 (North Bénoué) where Moslems are also an important part of the population and where certain ethnic groups follow economic activities which lead them to move frequently (i.e., the stock raising of the Choa Arabs). Moreover, this zone is densely inhabited, especially in the mountains, which are saturated with people massed together so that more and more mountain families are coming down on to the plain (i.e., among the Matakam and Mofou).

Then follow zones 4 and 5, the Bamiléké country and its surroundings. It is to be noticed that zone 5 shows a higher percentage of migrants among the men than zone 4. It seems that they are essentially Bamiléké migrants who have left their native soil (the most densely populated part of Cameroon) because they could not find land to cultivate there.

Zone 3 (Southeast) has one of the least mobile rural populations equaling the position in zone 6 (Western Cameroon) where 79 percent of the population in rural areas were born in the place of present residence. However, this immobility of the rural population is to be seen essentially in the north and center of the zone, since the south, home of the coastal groups, has only 48 percent of people born in their place of residence.

RURAL-URBAN MIGRATION.    The data in Table 26.14 are given in the same way as in Table

TABLE 26.14
Percentage of population currently living in place of birth, by zone and sex

| Zone | Males | Females | Both Sexes |
|---|---|---|---|
| (1) North Bénoué | 41.0 | 30.0 | 35.2 |
| (2) South Bénoué | 41.0 | 30.0 | 35.2 |
| (3) Southeast | 37.3 | 32.3 | 35.0 |
| (4) Bamiléké | 31.4 | 29.5 | 30.4 |
| (5) Area around Bamiléké | 49.7 | 49.2 | 49.4 |
| (6) Western Cameroon | — | — | 31.2 |

26.13 (i.e., considering the percentage of people born in the town of present-day residence). In all the regions except one (zone 5) only about one-third of the urban population was born in the town of present residence. Even in zone 5, the explanation is the existence there of the "capital" of the Bamoun country, Foumban, a traditional town where population immobility is very important (83.7 percent of the present-day residents were born at Foumban); this raises the average results for the zone, even though the other towns show a mobility similar to the towns of other zones.

All the data agree in showing that the rural exodus toward the towns is continuing at a sustained pace. The general rate of present day urbanization is on the order of 14 percent for the whole of Cameroon, and the rate of growth of the main towns (Yaoundé, Douala, Victoria) is on the order of 8 percent per year. Garoua, the capital of Northern Cameroon, with only 17 percent of the adult population born in the town, exhibits a very high rate of growth. Attempts are being made to reduce the rate of urban growth because of insufficient town employment, but there is little evidence of success.

It is probable that Douala (the commercial capital) has about 250,000 inhabitants. Yaoundé (the administrative and political capital), according to estimates made in 1964–1965, should have about 150,000 inhabitants in 1970.

Seasonal and other forms of temporary migration are important in all the regions. They generally take place wholly within the country.

ECONOMIC AND SOCIAL IMPLICATIONS OF
POPULATION GROWTH

When St. Vincent de Paul wanted to place an abandoned child with a family for adoption, he chose for preference a family already numerous and poor. Yet, in the middle of the seventeenth century in France, fertility must have been about equal to that of present-day Cameroon (about 5 children per woman in the Beauvais), whereas overall and infant mortality was probably higher (crude death rate, 30 per thousand, and infant mortality at least 200 per thousand). St. Vincent was certainly not unaware of the economic implications of an increase of numbers, but at the family level he did not think it was of great importance. The position may well be the same in the Cameroonian families of the twentieth century. But, passing from the family level to the regional or national level, it is obvious that the economic and social implications of sustained population growth become very considerable. These remarks lead us to observe that we should not,

from the beginning, concern ourselves much
with population pressure in regions of low
density. Rapid population increase only
becomes really disturbing in very populous
areas where family structures are changing.
As this circumstance occurs above all in the
towns, we shall leave to later the distinction
between rural and urban ways of life.

With an annual rate of natural increase of
about 1.9 percent, Cameroon is now increasing by about 100,000 persons per year,
80,000 of whom are added to the rural
population while another 20,000 are added to
the urban population. It is generally calculated that, with growth of this order, about
8 percent of the national income should be
invested for capital formation so that the new
arrivals will not relatively reduce the existing
facilities.

IMPLICATIONS IN RURAL WORLD AREAS. The
density of the rural population is less than 25
inhabitants per square mile for the whole of
the territory, and very large surface areas
remain available for farming.

However, zones of overpopulation appear
if we leave abstract averages to examine the
actual position. Overpopulation can come
either from an excess of inhabitants in relation
to the arable land surface or from soil
exhaustion. Thus the Bamiléké are spilling
out from their land in all directions under the
impact of ever greater numbers, and, likewise,
the Matakam of Northern Cameroon are
moving into the plains of the Mandara
country. This type of migration, caused solely
by the continuous pressure of demographic
increase, generally occurs almost imper-
ceptibly and smoothly. But, whereas, among
the Bamiléké, there is a high level of schooling,
and the migration consequently tends to turn
toward the towns, large villages, or modern
plantations in neighboring regions, among
the Matakam, with a very much lower level
of schooling, it will remain an essentially rural
movement.

Crop yields, decreasing to the point of
becoming insufficient, can, under the pressure
of an increase in population, provoke
similar movements. Certain Mofou mountains, which have become wasteland, force the
male population initially either to come
down to the plain, or to look for seasonal or
permanent engagement among the Moslems
of low lands. In certain other places (e.g., the
Guidar country), the growing of cotton on
poor, deteriorating soils leads inevitably after
10 or 12 years to lower yields, which in turn
lead to a noticeable rural exodus.

All these rural migrations, caused by the
imbalance between cultivable land and
population, seem to have in common the
desire not to go too far away from their
native soil, especially when the religion of
their ancestors has been retained, in order to
be able to come back and honor the dead (or
the pottery representing them) when tradition
demands it.

Thus, on the outskirts of overcrowded or
agriculturally worn-out microregions, it is
advisable to discern favorable in-migration
zones and, if possible, to improve them. Long
distance transfers of population, which have
been attempted with the best of intentions
(before 1960), seem to have failed for the
reasons discussed above, and it does not seem
that enforced movements of population have
much chance of success. Nonetheless, the
huge, cultivable, and practically deserted
territories, which are going to be crossed by
the construction of a railway linking Yaoundé
and Ngaoundéré, could be gradually colon-
ized by populations from high density and
highly educated areas.

Population increases in regions of low
density have therefore only local implications
for rural society. The two main instruments
giving rise to this pressure are the school and
the dispensary (and other paramedical and
social welfare facilities).

If the rural world is in general only indirectly concerned in the population growth
of the country, it is nevertheless affected in
quite another way. For it is the rural world
which remains the provider of food for the
population, and any increase in the nonproductive population in the agricultural
sense of the term, demands higher productivity of the remaining rural population.
That this may not be easy is suggested by the

fact that 99 percent of the Northern Cameroon lands are still cultivated by the hoe.
This increase in the agriculturally nonproductive population also means greater
demands for storage, preservation, marketing,
and the distribution of produce.

So that the rural population can meet the
effort demanded, it is necessary that it should
be encouraged by the realization of real
profits. If the opposite happens, it may be
discouraged and even abandon certain areas
of cultivation. Peanut growing combined with
the cultivation of millet for food has in the
past allowed the peasant of the North to pay
his taxes. If, under the pressure of wholesalers, the purchasing price tends to drop so
low that it no longer allows the peasant to pay
his tax (which on the contrary tends to rise),
there is obviously a strong possibility that the
extra effort will not be forthcoming.

IMPLICATIONS IN URBAN AREAS. As recorded
earlier, the larger towns of Cameroon have a
rate of growth (natural increase plus immigrants) of about 8 percent per year. It is
irrefutable that this increase does not correspond to employment possibilities and this
is a most important problem.

The major economic implication of current
urban growth is the need to create new
employment positions. If this is not possible,
new migrants should be discouraged or the
towns will soon contain, for every man with
work, several others who hope to have employment some day but in the meantime are
all living on the first man's wages.

The position of Yaoundé in 1964 was not so
alarming, since, at that date, the proportion
of economically inactive among the male
population of 15 years and over was only 29
percent. But, with a growth rate of about 8
percent the problem has inevitably grown
worse since then. By subtracting the rate of
natural increase from the rate of growth of
the capital, we obtain a measure of immigration showing that men 15–50 years of
age alone are arriving at over 1,600 per
annum, which corresponds to the minimum
number of positions which should be created
annually. Although it is not our purpose here

to specify purely economic needs such as the
amount and control of the necessary investments and their sources, we should
mention that the creation or support of
average-sized and small businesses (or
branches) throughout the rural prefectures
and subprefectures would help to slow down
the excessive growth of the larger towns,
while at the same time keeping the persons
thus employed in a semirural context.

In the current Cameroon position, the
following measures might help cope with the
forecast population growth: (1) modernization of agricultural techniques in subsistence
farming; (2) adjustment of tax and wholesale
prices so as not to turn the rural populations
away from certain desirable types of commercial farming (e.g., growing peanuts);
(3) strengthening of the means of communication and transport; (4) development of
preventive health measures; (5) creation of
small and medium-size businesses in urban
centers of average size; (6) encouragement of
the rural population to remain where it is and
thus avoid its exodus to the cities; (7)
addition to the government and private
primary school courses of practical agricultural work which might induce some
young people with the certificate of primary
studies to remain in farming.

However, it is difficult to generalize about
economic development for a country as varied
in social, economic, and human aspects as
Cameroon. This diversity means that the rate
of population growth has different implications from region to region, and that it would
be appropriate to study each region separately. An increase of 2 percent per year for
the mountain people of traditional religion of
Northern Cameroon, who have a low level of
schooling, cannot have the same economic
and social implications as a similar increase
among Christian or Moslem populations, or
populations with a high standard of schooling.

INTEREST IN POPULATION PROBLEMS

Cameroon has, until now, mainly been the
object of regional demographic studies by
sampling procedures. It appears that the

administrative and financial demands that a national census would make are considered too heavy at the present time.

The tendency is rather to maintain the administrative censuses which are carried out periodically and locally by the Territorial Administration service. These censuses aim at obtaining, in the same operation, basic demographic data (especially on the condition and structure of the population) and taxation and financial information. This double purpose is obviously detrimental to the accuracy of the information supplied.

For the collection of vital data, distinct areas exist: (1) the southern part of the country, where the great majority of births are registered, though deaths and marriages fare less well; and (2) the northern part of the country (zones 1 and 2), where the proportion of registrations is not more than 20 percent for births, and lower still for deaths and marriages. It might be noted that, in Cameroon, death registration is free; marriage certificates require a fiscal stamp; birth registration is free up to a fortnight after the birth, after which a fiscal stamp is required.

The Cameroonian authorities, conscious of the deficiencies in censusing and registration, seem willing to do their utmost to remedy this in different ways. At present only sample surveys can give a complete demographic picture of the main regions of the country.

The results of these surveys, some of which are very complete and detailed, have apparently not yet been made the object of a study in depth. It is only when this has been carried out that the government will, with a full knowledge of the facts, be able to choose among the possible demographic options those which seem to conform the most to the harmonious development of the country, and thus to define its own particular population policy.

The Statistics Department of Cameroon, helped by the Cooperation Department of INSEE and the SEDES (for the survey on zones 4 and 5 and the one on the standard of living in Yaoundé), has participated in all the surveys mentioned above. Moreover, it is training in Yaoundé, in a School of Instruction, staff for survey, coding, and tabulation work. Demographic research in Cameroon was pioneered mainly by ORSTOM (one research worker). This work was directed originally at the demography of areas which though especially populous were little known till then (i.e., Northern Cameroon), and has shown the basic role of ethnic groups where fertility and matrimonial patterns are concerned. More recently (1965–1968), an attempt at continuous recording of vital events in rural areas has shown that it is possible, at less expense thanks to multiround surveys, to obtain very complete demographic information and, to improve the quality of vital records kept by village registers.

Thus, after ten years spent usefully building up copious and good-quality basic documentation, the time now seems to have come for Cameroon to draw some conclusions from these observations and to proceed to construct and apply economic and social population policy. To be coherent and effective, this action should not only take into account the studies made, but also be guided by persons with a good theoretical and practical knowledge of one or several regions of this very varied country.

### Appendix

(A) ETHNIC DISTRIBUTION

*Zone 1 (North Bénoué):*
37 ethnic groups. Main ethnic group because of its civilization and total number: Foulbé (about 200,000). Important groups numerically or economically: Matakam or Mafa (about 120,000), Toupouri, Massa, Kotoko, Choa Arabs, Moudang, Guidar, Guiziga, Kapsiki, Fali.

*Zone 2 (South Bénoué):*
About 20 ethnic groups. Main one: Foulbé (about 100,000). Important ones: Bata, Dourou, Doayo, Mboum (former lords of the Adamoua), Baya, Mbororo. Minute ones: Voko (1,200), Kolbila (1,000), and some isolated groups.

*Zone 3 (Southeast):*
80 percent of the population of this zone is divided into 12 ethnic groups, the largest of which are: Boulou (167,000), Eton-Essel (164,000), Bassa (105,000), and Ewondo (101,000).

*Zone 4 (Bamiléké):*
Mainly Bamiléké.

*Zone 5 (area surrounding Bamiléké):*
Main ethnic groups: Bamoun, Tikar, Bakoundou, Mbam, Mbos, Bassa, and Bamiléké.

*Zone 6 (Western Cameroon):*
A dozen large ethnic distinctions are seen in the works relating to this region, but in all there are about 60 ethnic groups.

For the whole of Cameroon the two most important ethnic groups numerically, and probably economically, and the Bamiléké and the Foulbé.

(B) RELIGIOUS DISTRIBUTION
Three large groups are to be found:

*Christians:*
mainly in the South and the West. Zone 3 = 94

percent, zone 6 = 69 percent, no proportions for zones 4 and 5, which are nonetheless very strongly Christianized except for the Bamoun country.

*Traditionals:*
mainly in the north and center (Adamoua). Zone 1 = 59 percent, zone 2 = 30 percent.

*Moslems:*
also mainly in the north and center. Zone 1 = 40 percent, zone 2 = 60 percent, and also the Bamoun country (zone 4) which is mainly Islamized.

We can forecast in the long run a diminution of the number of "traditionalists" who will gradually be integrated to one of Cameroon's monotheistic religions, Christianity or Islam.

This chapter reports on a phenomenon in Chad of considerable significance for Africa: that of differential regional socioeconomic change and population growth. Chadian socioeconomic development has followed the ability of introduced technologies to exploit different environments. Two population trends have been isolated: one is a nation-wide, slow, natural growth; the other, a regionally varying growth rate, is dependent on in- or out-migration. Internal migration is at present the major demographic variable. These migrants are either (1) making attempts to avoid environments where the exploitative techniques have been less than successful, and thus where little development has occurred; or (2) trying to reach environments where exploitation has been successful, and where development has been comparatively rapid.

The chapter must necessarily have a stimulative rather than an authoritative function, for social scientific and demographic research in Chad is too tentative yet to permit definitive statements.

## ENVIRONMENT

The Chadian environment exhibits a major contrast. On one hand, the north encompasses some of the most inhospitable stretches of the Sahara, while a relatively benign wooded savanna stretches through southern Chad.

Chad is a basin limited by (1) the volcanic mountains of Tibesti to the north (culminating in Emi Coussi at an altitude over 10,000 feet; (2) the sandstone massif of Ennedi in the northeast; (3) the high plateau which runs from Guera to Darfour passing through the massif of Ouaddai in the east; (4) the plateaus of Oubangui in the south; and (5) (5) the mountains of Adamawa and Mandara

[1] The authors, both of whom are attached to the *Institut National Tchadien pour les Sciences Humaines* (INTSH) wish to acknowledge the expert aid they have received from J. Chapelle, Joint Director of INTSH, in matters pertaining to this and other demographic research efforts in Chad. They wish further to assign responsibility for the various sections of the article. Bouquet is responsible for the parts on environment and economy, and the remaining parts are Reyna's.

# CHAPTER TWENTY-SEVEN

# *Chad*

S. P. REYNA
AND CHRISTIAN BOUQUET[1]

in the southwest. Within these borders, Chad is a sedimentary basin, the lowest point of which is in the Djourab depression (just over 500 feet above sea level) south of Largeau. The immense Paleotchaddian Sea once covered most of this basin. During the Neolithic period, though already contracting, this sea covered 125,000 square miles, while all that now remains, known as Lake Chad, stretches over an area of only 10,000 square miles.

Three major bioclimatic zones can be distinguished within the Chadian basin. In the south there is a *tropical zone* which receives 30–50 inches of rain during six months (May–October). This region includes the Salamat swamps in the east and the two basins of the Chari and Logone rivers in the west. Vegetation is of the "Sudano-Guinean" type. The *Sahel zone* is located in the central regions of the country in the northern parts of Baguirmi, the Kanem, Batha, Guera, and Ouaddai. It receives 10–30 inches of rain from July to September, and is marked by a "Sahelo-Soudanlienne" type of vegetation. The *Saharan zone*, where it rarely rains, extends north from the 15th parallel. With the exception of the northern massifs of Tibesti and Ennedi, it is an area of denuded, plateau dunes.

The drainage systems of Chad are for all intents and purposes limited to the Chari and Logone river basins. The Chari River (750 miles in length) is formed from the union of several streams from the Central African Republic (the Gribingui, Bamingui, and Bangoran). It is further fed by the Bahr Aouk and Salamat rivers just before spreading out to form an immense swamp near Niellim. At N'Djamena (Fort Lamy) the Chari receives the waters of the Logone River (600 miles in length), flowing from the southwest, and originally formed by the junction of the M'Béré and Pende rivers. It is through a large delta that the Chari and Logone, flowing together, enter Lake Chad.

The action of the climates (with temperatures ranging from a moderate 70°–80° fahrenheit grade during the wet season from June to October; to a chilling 40°–65° from November to February; to the intense heat of 95°–105° during the March to May hot season), rainfall, and factors of erosion have resulted in several soil types which can be regionally distinguished. The southern part of Chad, between the Logone and Chari rivers, has lateritic soils in areas beyond flooding and hydomorphic soils in the flood plains. Both soil types favor the cultivation of millet and cotton. Between Pala and Sarh (Fort Archambault), laterite soils are found. These are less useful agriculturally. The elevated parts of the massifs in Ouaddai and Guera are not agriculturally exploitable, but the slopes and interior plateaus have lateritic soils. The soils north of the 15th parallel are of the steppe and semidesert types. Agriculture in this region is hardly possible.

Environmentally, two Chads exist. First, there is a zone bounded in the north by N'Djamena and in the south by the Central African Republic, extending from the west bank of the Chari to the Cameroon border. In terms of present administrative divisions, this zone includes the prefectures of Mayo-Kebbi, Tandjilé, Logone Oriental, Logone Occidental, most of Moyen-Chari, and the small southwestern portion of Chari-Baguirmi. This Chad is largely in the tropical zone. It has the major rivers and receives most of the rain that falls on the better soils. Its area is approximately 60,000 square miles. The second zone includes all of Chad east and north of the Chari; and consists of the prefectures of the BET (Borkou, Ennedi, and Tibesti), Kanem, the Lake, Batha, Biltine, Ouaddai, Salamat, Guera, Chari-Baguirmi east of the Chari, and Moyen-Chari east of Kyabé. In this zone are all the Sahel and Saharan portions of the country, as well as the difficult Salamat swamps. Its area is the remaining 450,000 square miles of Chad. It lacks important rivers, receives less rain than the other zone, and has poorer soils.

Seen in terms of human exploitation, Chad west of the Chari offers a far easier environment to exploit than east of the river. It is in this sense of human environmental potential that we distinguish two Chads: Chad the benign, and Chad the austere.

## HISTORY

Chad's history was almost unrecorded until colonial times. The archaeological record suggests that by 1000 A.D. settled village life among the Sao population had occurred around Lake Chad. Between 1000 and 1600 A.D. as Islam was spreading into Chad, there arose several statelike polities in the Sahel region. With the establishment of these polities, the full variety of socioeconomic systems that was to characterize Chad until the coming of the French was complete.

We can classify the pre-French social-economic organization into three types, arranged as to the methods of environmental exploitation. In the south were found swiddening acephalous peoples. Such populations exploited through shifting subsistence cultivation an environment favorable to agriculture, but often unfavorable because of trypanosomiasis to pastoralism. Their major food was millet supplemented to some extent by proteins from fish, or, in the southwest, some cattle meat. Their social organization consisted of patrilineage groupings, frequently within villages. Often the village can be identified as the resource-possessing unit (i.e., land-holding unit). The component extended families within lineages typically were re-source-exploiting units. It was the extended family that provided the labor and produced the crops. Such populations were acephalous in that few if any institutionalized inter-village political links occurred, with those ties that did exist between villages being primarily the result of kinship or religious organization. Nearly all the southern Chadian ethnic groups of today are of this type with the Sara in the majority. The sole exception is the Moudang who have a kingship.

In the north were found pastoral acephal-ous peoples. The pastoralists exploited the Saharan environment through herding. Their subsistence was largely dependent on camel or cattle products, to some extent supplemented by harvesting dates and by participation in trade as caravan guides (or raiders). The major groupings in the social organization were patrilineages and clans. Permanent villages rarely, if ever, were established, with the main residence unit being a "camp" consisting of as small a unit as an extended family or a small lineage segment. The resource-possessing and exploiting unit was the camp, which was the herd-holding unit and was responsible for producing what goods the herd could provide. While chiefdom existed among the pastoralists, it was largely along kinship lines and lacked institutional-ized spheres of administrative authority. The chief was largely *primus inter pares*. Thus, links between camps usually were kin based. Today, the Toubou populations of the desert are still of this type.

In the central regions of Chad were *multi-environment-exploiting statelike* peoples. The socioeconomic organization of these people was more complicated than that of the two previous types. It was marked by an organiza-tion which exploited the environment more thoroughly through (1) the use of both the previous types of exploitative technologies in the same socioeconomic system; and (2) the creation of a political system. Both pastoralists (largely cattle herders in contrast to camel herders in the north) and agriculturalists produced their distinctive goods using dif-ferent components of the same environment. Among these people were found not only the characteristic social groupings of the swid-dening and pastoral acephalous peoples described earlier, but a political system, with an administrative center and political officers responsible for coordinating intervillage and camp activities. It should be appreciated that the political system was also an environment-exploiting device. Through its army, the political system would raid environments outside of the territory over which it held sovereignty, returning with what resources it could plunder. In Chad, the major environ-ment raided was that of the swiddening acephalous peoples and the major plundered resource was people. The major statelike polities which have occurred in Chad were Kanem, Kotoko, the Bulalas, Baguirmi, and Ouaddai. Each polity has included a number of ethnic and economic groups ranging from pure pastoralists to semisedentary pastoralists, agriculturalists with some cattle, and pure agriculturalists.

By 1900 each of these three socioeconomic organizations already had a long history in Chad; but they were soon to be disturbed. At the turn of the century, a Sudanese ex-slave raider, Rabah, conquered much of southern Chad, Baguirmi, and Bornu. His defeat by Commandant Lamy in the Battle of Kousseri in 1900 opened the door to French colonization in Chad. French occupation moved from west of the Chari, eastward and toward the north. Abéché, capital of Ouaddai, was taken in 1909; Faya Largeau in 1913; Bardai in 1915; and finally, in the extreme north, Zouar was considered secured in 1917. Hence, by 1917 Chad ceased to be a military problem, becoming instead an even more recalcitrant economic problem. Colonial wars and administrations were costly. It became a matter of considerable interest as to how Chad could be exploited instead to becoming the economic liability it threatened to be. The military reports of the period of conquest speak of a "Chadian Mesopotamia between the Chari and Logone" in which modern techniques of cotton and rice cultivation could be introduced. Reports on the eastern, central, and northern regions noted with exasperation only the numbers of cattle and the difficulty of governing the cattle herders. Gradually, colonial administrators fell into the habit of distinguishing between two regions in their newly acquired colony: *Tchad utile* and *Tchad inutile*. It was in the former region, our benign Chad, that attempts were made to exploit the environment through the introduction of new techniques. In the latter Chad, only the tricolor flew.

## ECONOMIC DEVELOPMENT

Traditionally, the Chadian economy has been overwhelmingly dependent upon extensive agriculture, herding, and fishing, although there has also been a history of considerable commerce. Prior to the coming of the French, there were two main axes of trade: (1) south to north from Chad to Libya, and (2) west to east from northern Nigeria through Chad to the Sudan. Nineteenth-century trade was largely centered around the capitals of Baguirmi and Ouaddai. During the nineteenth century, the most important trade goods originating in Chad were probably slaves. The Djeilaha in Ouaddai, and the Bornuans and Hausa in Baguirmi once handled an extensive commerce. French colonization greatly curtailed traditional trade, and was especially restrictive of long-distance movement. The effects of the decline of this traditional trade in the regions strongly dependent upon it merit study. One report on the possibilities of development in Ouaddai states that the decline of the traditional trade led to a marked local recession.

Parallel to the traditional economy, modern sectors are developing as a result of diverse innovations in agriculture, herding, and fishing; slow industrialization of the principal urban centers; and the development of an infrastructure of communications. The following section will concentrate upon recent advances and the nature and importance of the traditional economy in six areas: agriculture, herding, fishing, mineral resources, industrialization, and communications.

AGRICULTURE. The Chadian diet is based upon millet porridge. Thus central to the traditional economy are millet and sorghum of which there are three major varieties in Chad: (1) rainy-season sorghums (*gros mils blancs* and *rouges*) grown to the west of the Chari, south of the 12th parallel, where they represent about 85 percent of the production of millets and sorghums (yielding 550–625 lbs. per acre); (2) Indian millet (*bérberé*) planted in the floodable zones of Chari-Baguirmi, Batha, and Guera (although yields can equal those of the rainy season sorghums, *bérberé* represents only 5 percent of the millet grown in the country); and (3) African millet (*pennisetum*) needing only 6–24 inches of rain and hence cultivable north of the 12th parallel (yielding about 550 lbs per acre). It is difficult to estimate total national millet yields, largely because so much of the crop is consumed by the subsistence cultivators and the total acreage planted with millet is not accurately known. Nevertheless, the annual report for agriculture in 1967–1968 showed that the $2\frac{1}{2}$ million acres planted with millet had produced 647,000 tons of millet, giving Chad an average millet yield of 570 lbs. per acre.

Other crops traditionally grown are groundnuts (between the 14th parallel and the latitude of Bousse), yielding 1 ton per $2\frac{1}{2}$ acres in good years, and wheat from around Lake Chad, which is mostly eaten locally although about 600 tons a year is thought to enter the traditional caravan trade going north across the desert. Of secondary agricultural importance are 20,000 tons of potatoes, 40,000 tons of beans, 5,000 tons of sesame, and smaller quantities of tubers (sweet potatoes and yams), as well as tare, okra, red pepper, and sorrel (grown in small quantities, usually around houses). Fruit is not traditionally grown in Chad with the exception of dates (25,000 tons yearly) in the Sahara. Manioc (cassava) has recently been introduced in the south as a hunger crop and is becoming increasingly popular. Production is currently estimated at 50,000 tons per year.

The introduction of modern farming began with the enforced production of cotton. In the 1920s, colonial administrators believed that cotton might well be the answer to their financial problems. In 1927 cotton production was begun in the southwestern prefectures where indigenous cotton already grew in small quantities. Agreements were signed between the administration and Cotonfran (*Compagnie Cotonnière Equatoriale Française*) giving the latter exclusive rights to develop cotton production. Every taxable individual was held responsible, under legal compulsion, for the production of a *corde* of cotton (about an acre). Each was supposed to place his *corde* at the head of his rotation cycle, a practice which was found to lead to a more rapid exhaustion of the soil. Considerable extra labor was demanded, as each person was supposed to prepare his *corde* perfectly and to weed it three times before harvest. It was by no means uncommon for farmers

who in some way defaulted on their crop to be in legal trouble with the administration. If the methods of the introduction of cotton were barbaric it does not negate the fact that southern Chad is a favorable environment for the production of cotton, providing that the proper June to mid-July planting dates are met. But this is frequently impossible, since these days are the same as those for the planting activities necessary for the production of food crops. As a result of constant improvements in seed (Allen variety and ultimately HG 9 and BJA 592) production in 1968–1969 attained 148,000 tons on 750,000 acres.

The exportation of cotton fiber represents 80 percent of Chad's export income. The principal buyers of her cotton are France, Yugoslavia, the United Kingdom, and the Benelux countries. Cotonfran continues to hold a monopoly of cotton production.

The production of rice, which was first grown commercially in Chad to feed Free French troops during World War II, has recently been expanded. Rice cultivation has traditionally been practiced in the flooded plains in the south, with "Marara" and "Garara" varieties being grown. Two companies, Sema (operating near Bongo) and Semalk (operating near Lai-Kelo) are the major concerns responsible for introducing new productive techniques, new seed strains, and commercialization of rice in Chad. In 1967–1968 on the 70,000 acres planted, 32,305 tons were produced, giving a yield of between 4 and 16 cwt. per acre. There are three rice mills in Chad which buy paddy from the farmer for 30 francs CFA per kilogram (about U.S. 5 cents per pound).

The northwestern banks of Lake Chad constitute a privileged region in an otherwise Saharan environment. Traditionally, farmers in this region have blocked off the arms of the lake with sand from the main body of water. Water left in the blocked arms dries, leaving an exceptionally fertile soil. Lands reclaimed in this manner are called "polders." Since 1950, administrators have realized the potential value of polder lands and have made considerable efforts to drain lands and to introduce modern agricultural techniques. By 1969, 55,000 acres of land had been isolated from the lake, of which 17,000 acres had been thoroughly drained and 8,000 acres were being effectively cultivated. However, the climate, the accessibility of the phreatic nappe to irrigation, and the exceptional fertility of the soils permit three harvests per year (wheat in November–March, maize in April–July and again in August–October) with a yield of 8 cwt per acre for wheat, 10 cwt per acre for traditional corn, and as much as 25 cwt per acre for hybrid corns. Commercialization of agriculture around the lake has not been without its problems. Sodelac, though given a monopoly for the commercialization of wheat in the polders, could only send 200 tons to the flour mills in N'Djamena in 1969, and 6,000 tons had been harvested. Still, the lake remains a region of great agricultural promise. Potatoes have been grown in the polders with excellent yields. Cotton has been experimentally grown with yields of 16 cwt per acre. Sugarcane has been tried with great success. The cold season is ideal for vegetable growth. The agricultural techniques of the populations remain, however, largely unadapted to exploiting the new crops. In addition to technical problems of production, suitable markets must be found before farming at the lake becomes commercially profitable.

In a further attempt to diversify Chadian agriculture, sugarcane and tobacco have been introduced. Sugar plantations have been started south of Sarh and a 180,000-ton harvest of cane from 5,500 acres is predicted for 1969–1970. The tobacco plantation near Koumra has yet to prove successful.

HERDING. Herding is the second largest traditional industry in Chad, but is largely restricted to the region east of the Chari and north of the 14th parallel by the presence of the tsetse fly in the moist southern areas. There were an estimated $4\frac{1}{2}$ million head of cattle in Chad in 1967, with the Arab-Zebu strain representing about 80 percent of the total. These cattle weigh 550–1,000 lbs and give around half a gallon of milk a day. Two other major strains found in Chad are Bororo-Zebu, belonging largely to the Fulani (which can attain 900 lbs) and Kouri, located around Lake Chad, which can surpass 1,100 lbs giving over one-and-a-half gallons of milk a day.

The herdsmen practice seasonal transhumance moving their herds, usually averaging only about a hundred head, south during the dry season and north with the rains in search of pasture and water. The cattle are exploited largely for their milk products. Meat usually is consumed only when animals die. Cattle are rarely sold except in cases of dire necessity. Milk products are either consumed or bartered for millet from agriculturalists. The nature of the milk-millet exchange is an important sector of the Chadian traditional economy, but it has not yet been studied.

Serious efforts have been started to modernize Chadian cattle raising. Major responsibility for development efforts in this sector lie with the *Services de l'Elevage*. Sickness among Chadian cattle is a pressing problem. The *Institut d'Elevage et de Médecine Vétérinaire des Pays Tropicaux* was created at Farcha in N'Djamena to conduct research relevant to Chadian cattle diseases. The *Institut* today produces cattle vaccines, of which large quantities are exported to neighboring countries. The *Travaux d'Hydraulique Pastorage* has put in over 500 wells in the Sahelian zone, while the *Service d'Agrostologre de Farcha* has studied the possibilities of improving pastures. Finally, a breeding center has been created at Sarh with the aim of producing breeds more adapted to Chadian conditions.

A refrigerated slaughterhouse was opened at Farcha in 1958, making possible, for the first time, large-scale commercialization of cattle in Chad. This plant rapidly attained maximum production as its capacity was restricted to only 7,000 tons of meat yearly. In 1968, 10,000 cattle were slaughtered at Farcha. A similar, but smaller, slaughtering plant was installed at Sarh. Frozen meat is largely exported by air and in 1968, 5,000 tons were exported, mostly to Brazzaville. It should be noted that the overwhelming majority of Chad's cattle raisers have not begun to change their techniques of herd management to more modern methods. Furthermore, the government's attempts to foster modernization are often associated by the pastoralists with efforts to improve tax collection.

In 1967, Chad was estimated to possess 4,150,000 head of goats and sheep. As opposed to cattle, these animals are raised to be eaten. Other livestock in the country are donkeys (300,000) used as beasts of burden, camels (350,000) used for transportation and for their milk in the north, and horses (150,000) used for transportation and regarded as a sign of prestige.

FISHING. Fishing is participated in by approximately 6,000 individuals full time, 24,000 seasonally, and 140,000 occasionally. Annual production is estimated at about 110,000 tons of fresh fish yearly. The height of fishing activity occurs during the beginning of the dry season between November and February, for then fish are found in the drying flooded zones and are easily caught by communal hunts in the shallow waters. When the waters are the lowest, from March to July, seasonal fishermen compete with specialists to catch the salanga (alestis), for then these fish are found plentifully along the beds of the small tributaries of the Chari and Logone. They are dried and sold in the markets of the interior. Finally, during the height of the flood (July–November), specialists, using nets and lines, go after the larger species, which they smoke and sell at local markets.

Further development of the fishing industry has consisted of the formation of fishing cooperatives in Sarh and N'Djamena. Nylon fishing nets and improved techniques of preservation were introduced. The success of the cooperatives has been less than might have been hoped, because they appear to be incompatible with the traditional organization of fishing.

It is almost impossible to measure fish production by species or by local production, but the Fishing Service estimated that, in 1967, 60,000 tons of fresh fish were produced in Bas-Logone, Bas-Chari and the delta of the lake. The lake, the region usually most bountifully endowed with fish, produced that year only 25,000 tons of fresh fish. Mayo-Kebbi produced 10,000 tons; the Moyen-Chari and Salamat area, 20,000 tons; Lake Fittri, 3,000 tons; and Lake Iro, 2,000 tons. At average market prices this production represents a value of 5 billion francs CFA (or over U.S. $20 million). It is, thus, a significant potential revenue in the Chadian economy encouraging attempts to modernize fishing techniques.

MINERAL RESOURCES. At present the only exploitable mineral resource in Chad is natron (sodium carbonate) which is used (like salt) for livestock. Natron has been extracted since ancient times by traditional means in the wadis of southwestern Kanem. Traditionally, natron is traded over vast distances, traveling as far as Togo, and frequently is exchanged for Kola. The total value of the controlled trade in natron for Chad has been estimated to be around 90 million francs CFA (or over U.S. $360,000).

TOWARD INDUSTRIALIZATION. The obstacles to Chadian industrialization are numerous: (1) scarcity of exploitable natural resources; (2) nonexistence of sources of energy, at least as presently understood; (3) high cost of equipment (since all must be imported); (4) nonexistence of a skilled labor pool; (5) nonexistence of a managerial labor pool; (6) small interior market; and (7) extremely rudimentary communications infrastructure. Yet, some industrialization has occurred.

Since 1926 Cotonfran has been responsible for constructing cotton gins. To date 22 have been built employing 2,580 workers. In 1967, a textile factory was built at Fort Archambault, with an annual capacity of 10 million yards of cloth. This plant employs 410 persons.

Although Chadian rice is largely eaten by the subsistence farmers themselves, three modern milling plants have been installed at Bongor, Lai, and Kelo employing respectively 62, 72, and 12 persons. In 1964, they produced 3,279 tons of rice.

In 1964, even before the prospects of polder wheat were envisioned, the *Grand Moulins du Tchad* had begun flour milling in Fort Lamy. The *Grand Moulins*, employing 22, has a capacity of 10,000 tons of flour yearly. This capacity is still far from being reached as the polders have only been able to send 200 tons of wheat annually to N'Djamena. PAM (*Programme Alimentaire Mondiale*) furnishes 3,000–4,000 tons of wheat yearly, permitting the *Grand Moulins* a 1965 output of flour of 2,571 tons.

Experiments with the production of groundnuts in Bokoro and Ouaddai have permitted the creation of an oil mill (Olafric) at N'Djamena, capable of annually furnishing 175,000 gallons of oil. But at present the plant operates for only seven to eight months each year. The plant employs 18 persons and in 1965 produced only 100,000 gallons. A small private plant at Kelo is in decline, while a large one was opened in August of 1969 in Abéché.

The abattoirs in N'Djamena and Sarh employ 93 and 30 persons respectively. These installations treat meat and skins. Milk products are not exploited although a small factory in N'Djamena makes yogurts, but they utilize imported powdered milk.

This exhausts the list of industralization of local products.

Other plants have been installed in Chad which utilize imported products. The most important of these is a brewery at Moundou that furnishes 330,000 gallons of beer annually and employs 130. In N'Djamena there is an establishment producing carbonated drinks which has 43 salaried personnel. Using raw sugar imported from the Congo, Sosutchad, employing 160, produces 6,000 tons of processed sugar a year. Palm oil is imported from the Central African Republic to supply a small soap factory in Sarh. The building industry is difficult to report on, since its main labor source comes from seasonal workers. The metal-workers' industry employs 350 people, the woodworking industry 300, and the electrical industry 50. All these enterprises are restricted almost entirely to N'Djamena.

At Moundou, Cycle-Tchad, employing 20, assembles bicycles and has an annual capacity of 10,000. Safripa (*Société africaine de parfumerie*) makes colognes and pomade at N'Djamena with 35 employees.

Thus, Chad has an industrial labor force of less than 4,500 people, of whom 2,288 are employed in the cotton mills in the south, 1,167 in N'Djamena, 455 at Sarh, and 223 at Moundou.[2]

COMMUNICATIONS. There are, in a country twice the size of France, 22,000 miles of routes designated as *pistes*, of which, perhaps, only 3,000 miles are all-weather routes. There are approximately 125 miles of paved road and no railways at all. During the rainy season and its aftermath, most movement is effected on foot or in dugout canoes.

SUMMARY. This economic survey shows three things. First, since Chad's most valuable natural resources are farmland, cattle herds, and fish, the key to the development of the country lies in the modernization of agriculture and fishing. Second, efforts to improve the economy have taken the line of least resistance, avoiding the barren region of the Chari. East of the river, apart from the polders at the lake, experiments in groundnut production in Bokoro and Ouaddai, and the oil-processing plant in Abéché, almost no economic development has occurred. Austere Chad still is confined to subsistence agriculture and wide-scale herding. In benign Chad cotton and rice have been introduced to complement traditional agriculture, organized fishing has begun, and industrialization has been initiated in Bongor, Moundou, Sarh, and N'Djamena. Third, it can be seen that economic development of Chad has only just begun. Over 90

[2] Ministère du Plan, *Recensement des Entreprises au 1 Janvier, 1968* Fort Lamy [N'Djamena], 1968).

percent of the labor force is engaged in agricultural pursuits and one study found that only one-tenth of the crops grown in Chad ever reach the market. The technology of this subsistence economy is still rudimentary. In 1961 an agricultural survey in the south (the most developed region of the country) found that the average farming unit had at its disposal no more than 3.5 hoes, 2 axes, 9 sickles, and 6 machetes.

## SOCIAL CHANGE

It is difficult to discuss adequately and briefly the nature of social change in Chad because of the inadequacy of the data available. Existing studies do suggest that there are marked regional differences in social development. Rapid social change was introduced by the colonial administration; since independence in 1965 it has been actively promoted by the Chadian government. During this period the two main determinants of social change have been cultural and politico-economic shifts.

Cultural change has been brought about by the introduction of European education and religious institutions. The present education system in Chad has been transported in its entirety from France. Its aim is to produce scholars who will attend universities abroad. At present, only some 23 percent of school-age children (those 6–14) receive schooling in Chad. West of the Chari the proportion reaches 31 percent, while east of the river it is only $5\frac{1}{2}$ percent. Education has long been more widespread west of the Chari, for with the French administrators came the missionaries, who restricted their Christianizing efforts to the south. In 1964, 48 percent of the population west of the Chari claimed to be Christian, with 32 percent professing Catholicism; only 4 percent said they were Moslem. Christians are rare east of the Chari, where 96 percent of the population professes to be Moslem. Christian and Western education creates a class which understands Western phenomena, especially technology, and which frequently wishes to adopt Western mores. Such a cadre exists in benign

Chad, but it is absent from the region east of the Chari.

We speak of a group of politico-economic initiated changes because most economic events which have affected social organization have originated from policy decisions in the colonial or Chadian governments. The first of these politico-economic change initiators was the *pax gaullois*. The French attempted to stop conflicts between ethnic groups. They were especially successful in ending the raids of the Baguirmi and Ouaddai against their southern neighbors. A major effect of more tranquil conditions was, and today still is, increased internal migration. An example of these migrations is provided by the border regions between the Baguirmi and their acephalous neighbors. Freed from the need to stay in compact villages or lineages, Sara and Massa have drifted north in search of lands along the Chari. Increased internal migration can be seen as only one result of the fact that the *pax gaullois* rendered obsolete the defensive aspects of traditional social organization. If squabbles with neighbors or need for more land made life miserable for a Sara, he now did not have to remain within his original village for reasons of protection, but had the option of moving on. The exact course of this internal migration, the times of its occurrence, and its intensity are matters for further study, as is the timing and distribution of the enforced peace. If frequently recurrent incidents between bands of pastoralists within Guera, Biltine, Batha, and the BET are any indication, the *pax gaullois* was a more ephemeral peace in austere Chad.

A second initiator of social change was direct central administration and, more recently, the Chadian state. Direct administration had different effects depending on the various types of socioeconomic system it was imposed upon and the success with which it was instituted. The exact chronicling of these matters is an important topic for further research. As has been suggested in an earlier section of the chapter, the administrative presence was more lightly felt in the central, northern, and eastern portions of Chad. It would, then, not be a surprise if future researchers found traditional authority structures operating more effectively independent of the central Chadian government in these areas than those in the south.

Thus, two important effects of direct rule on social organization should be stressed. (1) The French and (now) Chadian administration provides an alternative that, in terms of force, greatly supersedes traditional political authority. This means that the sanctions normally utilized by traditional authorities for maintaining traditional social behavior were greatly weakened. Thus, if the government wishes to put an end to certain traditional practices (facial scarification or initiation ceremonies for example), there is little the traditional authorities can do in opposition. (2) The formation of new social groupings has occurred in one of two ways: (a) In the early days of colonization, especially in the south, people were transferred to facilitate the implementation of government tax and cotton production policies (such moves resulted in multiethnic towns in which old ties of family and lineage tended to be disturbed). (b) Market-oriented economic activities tended to occur around the important administrative centers which resulted in the beginning of urban growth.

Chadian urbanization is in its earliest stages, having begun only during World War II. In 1964, there were only seven towns with populations near or over 10,000 (N'Djamena, 98,000; Sarh, 33,001; Moundou, 29,388; Abéché, 24,269; Bongor, 11,691; Doba, 10,272; Koumra, 9,802). By 1970 N'Djamena was still the only town in Chad with a population over 100,000 and Abéché the only center east of the Chari with more than 10,000 inhabitants. If urbanization is in its infancy, the point to be grasped is that it nevertheless does exist west of the Chari, offering alternative social units to the traditional Chadian social structures.

Throughout Chad, the socioeconomic systems we have described as existing before the French, are still, to a large extent, operative. However, it is possible to distinguish a region where more people look with favor on the adoption of Western forms, where the military reasons for remaining socially encapsulated have completely evaporated, where the traditional sanctions for maintaining conformity to traditional social forms have been heavily vitiated, and where a new social unit has begun to develop. This region is benign Chad. In austere Chad, these conditions have yet to come.

It is now possible to summarize Chadian socioeconomic development since French arrival. The French found two Chads. In the environmentally better-endowed region they began introducing new agricultural techniques, the beginnings of industrial technology, and market-based techniques of distribution. If we can assert that prior to the French the sole exploitative technique was extensive agriculture, it is apparent that the innovations promise (and in some cases already permit) more complete and efficient exploitation of environmental resources west of the Chari. The Chadian government since independence has continued and attempted to strengthen the use of these novel exploitative techniques which can be said to have spawned a new social form, the towns of the south, that facilitates the operation of the new economy.

East of the Chari, the French found an environment which they could rule, but for which they could find no use. They encountered a parched land unable to support any form of plantation agriculture, completely lacking in mineral resources, whose vast distances and lack of water made ordinary communication necessitate feats of daring. Finally, they had absolutely no control over the cattle, the one resource in the area. The economic technology of early twentieth-century colonialism simply was not capable of profitably exploiting this austere land. It is probable that since the coming of the French this area has been exploited even less efficiently, because of destruction or curtailment caused by state-associated economic activities, such as commerce and raiding. In a sense, the French occupation decapitated the economy, forcing peoples east of the Chari to rely almost exclusively on extensive herding or agriculture in a region disfavoring such efforts. As might be expected, no new social forms have arisen in this region to complement the occurrence of miniscule economic development. The Chadian government has intensified development efforts east of the Chari, but one wonders if this intensification has been sufficient.

## POPULATION GROWTH

Predictably, people strive to achieve perceived benefits. The final section of the chapter surveys the available demographic information on population growth. Two types of growth are distinguishable. The first, natural increase, which is nationwide and accelerating, reflects the still high, and apparently unchanging, natality. The second is a type where natural growth has been supplemented by immigration or reduced by emigration, and is restricted to the areas where the novel exploitative technologies have had the most and the least success respectively.

AVAILABLE DEMOGRAPHIC INFORMATION. Little demographic information for Chad exists. That available stems from four sources: (1) colonial political or economic reports; (2) administrative censuses; (3) ethnographic monographs; and (4) a very few professional demographic studies.

From the very beginning of colonization, administrators were responsible for including demographic information (usually of the census type) in their reports. Such information, deposited in archives throughout the country and in France, is potentially useful for studying the evolution of Chad's population since the turn of the century. It should be employed, however, with caution since it is often inaccurate, being collected by untrained personnel for purposes (usually tax collection) which prompted informant misstatement.

There are three major administrative censuses which have used trained personnel (those of 1954, 1960–1961, and 1968). Even these should be employed with care as they were frequently identified with government

purposes and almost certainly suffer from a deliberate lack of informant accuracy. For example, the 1968 census, conducted primarily to establish the number of taxable females, discovered one small village which remarkably had 3 adult women and 29 adult men.

The demographic information included in ethnographic accounts has been collected by professional social scientists with nonprofessional interests in population matters. It is usually not collected by sampling techniques and is, hence, meant to be accurate only for very restricted populations. It is, however, reliable in terms of the accuracy of answers.[3]

With one exception the professional studies are concerned with the collection of basic data using sampling techniques in selected regions of Chad. Important among these are a useful 1962 study by INSEE (*Institut National de la Statistique et des Etudes Economiques*) of N'Djamena[4] and a 1961 BDPA study (*Bureau pour le Développement de la Production Agricole*) of the lake region, that should be consulted by anyone concerned with the difficulty of working under Sahel and Saharan conditions.[5] There is a single sample survey which included the greater part of the country. This is another INSEE study, *Enquête Démographique du Tchad, 1964*, that is a model of modern sampling research designed to collect basic socioeconomic data, as well as the population's age-sex structure, fertility, mortality, migration, density, size, and

[3] The following are some useful ethnographic sources: (a) on the Massa: Igor de Garine, *Les Massa du Cameroun* (Paris: Presses univ. de France, 1964); (b) on the Goula: C. Pairault, *Boum le Grand! Village d'Iro* (Paris: Institut d'Ethnologie, 1966); (c) on the Sara: A. Adler, "Les Day de Bouna," INTSH Series A, 1 (Fort Lamy [N'Djamena], 1966); (d) on the Kotoko: A. M. D. Lebeuf, "Essai d'études démographiques chez les Kotoko," Séances Institut franç. d'Anthropologie, Fasc. 3 (January 1949, December 1949); (e) on the Teda: J. Chapelle, *Nomades noirs du Sahara* (Paris: Plon, 1967).
[4] INSEE, *Recensement démographique de Ft. Lamy, Mars–Juil., 1962, Résultats provisoires* (Paris: INSEE, 1962).
[5] M. Jacob and J. P. Delagarde, *Enquête démographique par sondage dans la République du Tchad: Rapport provisoire* (Paris: BDPA, 1963); *Enquête démographique par sondage: Zone des cuvettes lacustres et ouaddis du lac Tchad; Rapport définitif* (Paris: BDPA, 1964).

TABLE 27.1
Summary of Chadian demographic information[a]

| | Sex Ratio[b] | Males 0–14 | Males 15–59 | Males 60+ | Females 0–14 | Females 15–59 | Females 60+ | Total males | Total females | Total 0–14 | Total 15–59 | Total 60+ | Completed Fertility[c] |
|---|---|---|---|---|---|---|---|---|---|---|---|---|---|
| *Benign Chad* | 93 | 25.4 | 21.4 | 1.3 | 22.8 | 27.9 | 1.1 | 48.2 | 51.8 | 47.8 | 49.8 | 2.4 | 4.86 |
| Moyen Chari | 93 | 26.0 | 20.9 | 1.2 | 23.4 | 27.5 | 1.0 | 48.1 | 51.9 | 49.4 | 48.4 | 2.2 | 4.58 |
| Logone Oriental | 94 | 27.1 | 19.7 | 1.5 | 24.3 | 26.4 | 1.0 | 48.3 | 51.7 | 51.4 | 46.1 | 2.5 | 5.14 |
| Logone Occidental | 95 | 25.0 | 22.0 | 1.6 | 22.4 | 27.9 | 1.1 | 48.6 | 51.4 | 47.7 | 49.9 | 2.7 | 5.05 |
| Mayo-Kebbi | 91 | 23.1 | 23.8 | 1.2 | 19.8 | 30.9 | 1.2 | 48.1 | 51.9 | 42.7 | 54.7 | 2.4 | 4.61 |
| Tandjilé | 93 | 26.0 | 20.6 | 1.1 | 24.1 | 27.1 | 1.1 | 47.7 | 52.3 | 50.1 | 47.7 | 2.2 | 5.66 |
| *Austere Chad* | 87 | 22.2 | 21.7 | 2.5 | 21.1 | 27.8 | 2.6 | 46.3 | 54.0 | 43.4 | 51.1 | 5.1 | 4.14 |
| Ouaddai | 73 | 19.9 | 19.5 | 2.7 | 22.6 | 31.5 | 3.8 | 42.1 | 59.7 | 42.5 | 51.0 | 6.5 | 4.01 |
| Salamat | 88 | 22.9 | 21.1 | 2.7 | 21.2 | 29.6 | 2.5 | 46.7 | 53.4 | 44.1 | 50.7 | 5.2 | 4.81 |
| Batha | 81 | 23.0 | 19.5 | 2.2 | 23.5 | 29.2 | 2.6 | 44.7 | 55.3 | 46.5 | 48.7 | 4.8 | 4.71 |
| Guera | 92 | 24.8 | 21.3 | 1.9 | 21.1 | 29.2 | 1.7 | 48.0 | 52.0 | 45.9 | 50.5 | 3.6 | 4.47 |
| Chari-Baguirmi | 101 | 20.6 | 26.9 | 2.9 | 17.3 | 29.7 | 2.6 | 50.4 | 49.6 | 37.9 | 56.6 | 5.5 | 3.68 |
| *Urban* | 96 | 22.7 | 25.1 | 1.2 | 21.1 | 28.5 | 1.4 | 49.1 | 50.9 | 41.9 | 56.4 | 2.7 | 3.98 |
| *Chad* | 90 | 23.8 | 21.6 | 1.9 | 22.0 | 27.9 | 1.9 | 47.3 | 52.9 | 45.6 | 50.8 | 3.6 | 4.48 |

(column spanner: Population by Sex and Age (percent))

growth information.[6] Unless otherwise noted, all demographic data cited comes from the 1964 INSEE report. The prefectures of the lake, Kanem, the BET, and the northern parts of Batha, Ouaddai, and Biltine were not included in the 1964 study; this means that adequate information for these extreme northern areas is lacking.

AGE-SEX GROUPINGS. A summary of Chad age-sex information can be found in Table 26A.1, columns A–L. For the whole country, there appeared to be an average of 90 males for every hundred females. In the austere region the figure dropped to 87 per hundred, but west of the Chari it was 93 per hundred. The Chadian deficit has been attributed to higher male mortality. The greater deficit of men east of the Chari, the INSEE study suggests, is due to male migration out of the region. The urban figures are higher than the Chad average and show that there are 96 males for every hundred females; this would seem to reflect higher male migration to the towns.

With regard to age groupings, the INSEE study warns of possible errors in informants' statements. They believe that the age-group 0–14 years for the entire domain of their study was overestimated for males and underestimated for females. Chad has a young, typical of high fertility population,

with 45.6 percent of its people under 15 years; 50.8 percent between 15 and 59; and only 3.6 percent over 60 years of age. There is a slightly older population east of the Chari than west of the river with the former region showing 43 percent between ages 0–14; 51 percent between 15–59; and 5 percent over 60 years. West of the river, the figures show 48 percent between ages 0–14; 50 percent between 15–59; and only 2 percent over 60. The INSEE study suggests that the lower percentage of young east of the river is due to a lower fertility and the higher percentage of aged is due to a healthier climate than in moist southern areas.

FERTILITY. Chad exibits high fertility compared with developed countries, but only moderately high fertility compared with other African countries. Chad's fertility figures are presented in columns M–P of Table 27.1. An average of 4.5 live births are claimed by women over 50. The figure is higher west of the Chari (4.9) than east of the river (4.0). The other fertility measures also bear out the higher fertility of benign Chad.

Chad had a moderately high sterility rate, with 21 percent of its women over age 15 without live births (see Table 27.1, column P). The sterility figures for the two environmental zones are quite similar, though they are higher in the urban centers. The very high sterility in the prefecture of Chari-Baguirmi, the highest in Chad, should be noted. The high sterility in urban areas,

[6] INSEE, *Enquête démographique du Tchad, 1964: Résultats définitifs*, I & II (Fort Lamy [N'Djamena]: Service de Statistique, 1966).

TABLE 27.1 (*contd.*)

| General Fertility Rate[d] | Crude Birth Rate (per 1,000) | Sterility[e] | Infant Mortality Rate[f] | Crude Death Rate (per 1,000) | Population[g] | Density[h] | Rate of Natural Increase (percent) | Migration[i] M | F | M & F |
|---|---|---|---|---|---|---|---|---|---|---|
| 184 | 49 | 21 | 173 | 35 | 1,600,000 | 30.3 | 1.4 | 4.6 | 2.5 | 3.5 |
| 179 | 45 | 20 | 132 | 32 | 374,000 | 21.5 | 1.3 | 5.9 | 3.5 | 4.6 |
| 168 | 44 | 25 | 144 | 32 | 236,000 | 21.8 | 1.9 | 5.8 | 3.3 | 4.5 |
| 180 | 43 | 18 | 93 | 28 | 190,000 | 56.7 | 1.2 | 5.4 | 3.7 | 4.5 |
| 182 | 52 | 23 | 235 | 39 | 228,000 | 32.6 | 1.3 | 3.3 | 1.4 | 2.3 |
| 220 | 55 | 15 | 181 | 43 | 486,000 | 42.0 | 1.2 | 3.4 | 1.4 | 2.4 |
| 138 | 38 | 21 | 135 | 25 | 1,600,000 | 3.9 | 1.3 | 8.4 | 3.1 | 5.6 |
| 145 | 42 | 18 | 188 | 35 | 310,000 | 10.9 | 0.7 | 11.7 | 3.5 | 6.9 |
| 145 | 40 | 19 | 134 | 26 | 84,000 | 3.4 | 1.4 | 6.1 | 2.5 | 4.2 |
| 132 | 35 | 20 | 114 | 23 | 296,000 | 9.1 | 1.2 | 15.6 | 5.4 | 9.9 |
| 126 | 35 | 20 | 51 | 20 | 159,000 | 7.0 | 1.5 | 5.8 | 1.8 | 3.7 |
| 130 | 35 | 26 | 144 | 22 | 402,000 | 13.0 | 1.3 | 5.4 | 2.9 | 4.2 |
| 165 | 44 | 27 | 134 | 29 | 173,210 | — | — | 5.0 | 3.1 | 4.0 |
| 165 | 45 | 21 | 160 | 31 | 3,254,000 | 6.7 | 1.4 | 6.1 | 2.7 | 4.3 |

SOURCE: INSEE, *Enquête Démographique du Tchad, 1964: Resultats definitifs*, I & II (Fort Lamy [N'Djamena], 1966).
a This table does not contain all the prefectures in Chad. The B.E.T., Kanem, Biltine, and the Lake are excluded for lack of reliable data.
b Number of males per hundred females.
c Average number of births ever to females of completed fertility (i.e. 50+ years of age).
d Annual births per thousand females, 15–49.
e Percent of females over 15 years of age without live births.
f Deaths of those less than 1 year of age per thousand live births.
g All areas included.
h Persons per square mile.
i Percent absent from place of residence.

especially N'Djamena, may well be due to a high incidence of venereal disease, and possibly to some delay in female age at marriage.

The INSEE study found Chadian fertility to be negatively correlated and sterility to be positively correlated with the number of marriages contracted. They further reported fertility to be negatively associated with polygamy, and positively associated with kin marriage. It should be easy to account for the regional fertility differentials in terms of these social variables, but the evidence is in fact inconclusive.

Table 27.2 shows conjugal mobility to differ little between the two regions.

TABLE 27.2
Conjugal mobility

| Number of Marriages Contracted | Percent of Females over 15 Austere Chad | Benign Chad |
|---|---|---|
| 0 | 4.3 | 3.6 |
| 1 | 68.7 | 69.8 |
| 2 | 18.7 | 20.1 |
| 3 | 5.1 | 2.6 |
| 4 & over | 2.5 | 1.4 |
| Not stated | 0.7 | 2.5 |
| | 100.0 | 100.0 |

In each region nearly 70 percent of the women over 15 have contracted only one marriage. In the austere Chad, 26 percent of the women have contracted more than two marriages, as opposed to only 24 percent of the women west of the Chari. Although west of the Chari 2.5 percent of the informants did not respond to the question as opposed to only 0.7 percent in the other region, nevertheless, the possibility remains of slightly higher conjugal mobility in austere, and perhaps more traditional, Chad.

A surprising finding, in view of the association of lower fertility with polygamy, is that polygamy is commoner west of the Chari (i.e., in the areas with higher fertility). The polygamy rate, defined as the number of currently married females per hundred currently married males, is 140 west of the Chari and only 114 northeast of it. Thus polygamy appears to be more frequent in the more Westernized area.

A similar problem occurs with kin marriage. East of the Chari, where there is lower fertility, there is considerably higher kin marriage even though it has been shown to be associated with higher individual fertility levels. The INSEE study found 85 percent of the marriages occurring west of the Chari to be not between kin, while the figure fell to only 64 percent east of the river. It seems highly unlikely that differentials in fertility arising from polygamy and kin marriage can account for differences in fertility in the two regions. It is possible that differential conjugal mobility could be a contributing factor, but one could also argue that this too should work in the opposite direction tending to bring more husbands than wives as migrants from austere to benign Chad.

MORTALITY.    Mortality in Chad is still high. The calculated crude death rate of 31 per thousand in 1964 was exceeded by reported rates from only three African countries (Table 27.1, columns Q–R). Mortality, measured in terms of both the crude death rate and infant mortality, is considerably higher west of the Chari. Benign Chad is reported to have an infant mortality rate of 173, and a crude death rate of 35 compared with figures of 135 and 25 respectively for the other region.

These figures are surprising when one considers that the highest mortality is apparently found in the area with the most health services; but it must be borne in mind that the arid climate in the north and east greatly inhibits insect and parasite borne disease. The 1964 INSEE study claimed a high incidence of alcoholism contributing to the higher mortality in the south, although no figures were provided justifying this assertion. Until such figures are forthcoming the assertion that heavy beer drinking is a contributive factor to the high death rate might be regarded as a peculiar form of Gallic ethnocentrism.

At this point it should be clear that a "demographic transition" had not really begun in Chad by 1964. Birth and death rates were very high. The former indeed may well have been as high as it had ever been, although the latter had probably declined somewhat, from even higher levels, as a result of social and economic change.

POPULATION SIZE.    Since the 1964 INSEE study, there has been the 1968 administrative census. We prefer, however, to rely on the 1964 figures, as the 1968 census unaccountably found a smaller population in seven of the nine prefectures for which information is available.

In 1964 INSEE stated that Chad had a population of 3,254,000 (Table 27.1, column S), 730,000 inhabitants out of the total population being estimated from sources other than their own. The populations east and west of the Chari were approximately equal, each being around 1,600,000. Note, however, that the region west of the river is only $11\frac{1}{2}$ percent of the total area of Chad.

DENSITY.    Chad has one of the world's smaller populations. In terms of area, however, it is not one of the smaller countries, encompassing almost half a million square miles, approximately twice the size of France. Hence Chad had a population density in 1964 of less than 7 persons per square mile (Table 27.1, column T). The density for the region west of the Chari was over 30, while that east of the river was less than 4 per square mile. Here is one of the most striking differences between the two Chads: the austere region has a population density less than one-seventh that of the benign region.

NATURAL GROWTH RATE.    The significance of these differentials in density can only be evaluated after considering the natural growth rate. The INSEE report stresses that, given the uncertain nature of some of their data, the natural increase estimates should be taken only as rough approximations of population growth trends.

Their figures indicate that Chad probably has, by African standards, a slowly growing population, with an average annual rate of increase of only 1.4 percent, meaning that the population would take about 50 years to double itself (Table 27.1, column U). Further, the rates for the austere and benign Chads are not very different, with the former annually increasing at 1.3 percent and the latter at 1.4 percent. These regionally similar, slow growth rates are encouraging to a country that can little afford a galloping population. To us, however, at first glance, they appear puzzling in that if the two Chads can so clearly be distinguished environmentally, economically, socially, and demographically, why are they growing at about the same rate?

The answer to this question must stand as one of the major conclusions of this chapter. None of the demographic figures we have cited for either region would surprise an ethnologist. The high proportion of young in the populations, the high fertility and mortality rates, the low population sizes and densities are all well within the ranges of demographic data that anthropologists expect to find in underdeveloped countries of the African interior. As indicated earlier, the process of socioeconomic change in Chad has only just begun; the relatively low natural growth rate is merely another index of just how incipient is Chadian development.

The similar growth rates contrasted with marked density differentials between the two Chads underline a further point: It is extremely probable that the different pre-French socioeconomic systems had, and where still extant, still have, differential carrying capacities. It is extremely likely that extensive agriculture in the well-watered regions supported and supports a larger population in the same area than pastoralism, or pastoralism mixed with agriculture, in the Saharan or Sahelian regions. If this is the case, major demographic research problems in Chad become first the establishment of the carrying capacities for different types of exploitative techniques, and second the discovery of the sociodemographic mechanisms by which population density is regulated.

MIGRATION.    It has been indicated that socioeconomic development has occurred differently in the two Chads, and this should have produced some effects on population growth. To isolate these effects, we shall refine our focus, and concentrate our attention on two areas, each in one of the two Chads, where the extremes of development or nondevelopment have occurred.

The nondeveloped area is the prefecture of Ouaddai, which has experienced economic decapitation since the turn of the century. The developing area is N'Djamena, which, since 1900, has become the administrative, commercial, and industrial center of Chad. A comparison of the population growth of these two areas is shown in Table 27.3.

TABLE 27.3
Comparison of population growth in Ouaddai and N'Djamena

| Date | N'Djamena | Ouaddai |
| --- | --- | --- |
| 1945 | 17,800 | 271,000 |
| 1954 | 32,783 | 304,000 |
| 1957 | 45,700 | 306,000 |
| 1960 | 80,200 | 303,000 |
| 1964 | 100,000 | 310,000 |

The population figures for these two areas have been taken from administrative sources and the 1962 INSEE study of N'Djamena. No one who knows Chad would be surprised that between 1945 and 1964 Ouaddai has stagnated and N'Djamena almost exploded in terms of population growth. If we examine only the natural growth rates we will not explain the differential population trends. Ouaddai does indeed have a low natural growth rate, but that of N'Djamena is only 1.5 percent, hardly high enough to explain N'Djamena's rise. It is to migration we must look to explain the differentials in population trends between Ouaddai and N'Djamena.

In terms of the migration which has occurred in some other African countries, Chad has a fairly stable population. Four-fifths of the respondents in the 1964 INSEE study were residing in the villages in which they were born. If one examines columns V–X in Table 27.1 it becomes clear that migration is a considerably stronger phenomenon east of the Chari, where fully 5.6 percent of the population was absent from their prefecture of residence at the time of the study, in contrast to only 3.5 percent absent west of the Chari. The difference becomes even more marked when we look at males alone for then 8.4 percent of the eastern males were absent as opposed to only 4.6 percent of the southern males.

Differences also exist in the ages at which males migrate. The majority of the absent southern males are gone between the ages of 10 and 19, while the eastern men are absent between the more mature ages of 20 and 50. The youthfulness of the southern male migration is probably due to the fact that many of the migrants are students. It should be noted that migrants from east of the Chari are away during prime child-producing years. This possibly could affect fertility east of the Chari.

Important differences exist between the two regions as to where the migrants go. West of the Chari, 47 percent of those absent had not passed subprefectorial limits, and only 9 percent had left the country. East of the river fully 21 percent of the absent had left Chad. The INSEE study did not attempt to measure the size of migration out of Chad, but estimates from administrative sources range between 250,000 and 500,000. The bulk of these are said to go to the Sudan, and to come from east of the Chari.

We do not know accurately where the eastern population migrates to within Chad, but at least some of the people must go to urban centers judging by the population composition figures for N'Djamena. In 1962, about 52 percent of that city's population was composed of ethnic groups from north and east of the Chari, with Ouaddains composing 3.8 percent of the city's total population. The point is that migration of southerners consists for the most part of people moving about within the south, especially young scholars; while east of the Chari more people completely leave the region, migrating to other countries or to N'Djamena.

To return to the contrasts between Ouaddai and N'Djamena: We can account for population stagnation in Ouaddai in terms of comparatively low fertility and the second highest rate of net emigration in Chad (fully 12 percent of the men were absent during the 1964 INSEE study). On the other hand, the annual rate of increase due to net immigration in N'Djamena in 1962 was found to be 5 percent. Migration in Chad, then, may be compared to a pump drawing people out of austere areas, like Ouaddai, and into more benign ones, like N'Djamena.

There has been no study which adequately sought to understand migrants' reasons for leaving one area and going to another. When such studies are conducted, it is almost certain that they will show that Chadians regard the urban areas west of the Chari as places of economic advantage, and the rural places east of the river as places of stagnation. Or, as one Baguirmi informant patiently explained it to accommodate the author's halting command of the Baguirmi language, *Koro lolo, pu!* *N'Djamena, pet!* ("Bush here, nothing! N'Djamena, all!")

## CONCLUSION

We have isolated and contrasted two regions in Chad: an environmentally harsh one east and north of the Chari River, and an environmentally more benevolent one west and south of the river. Prior to the arrival of the French, three socioeconomic systems, each with distinctive exploitative technologies, operated within these regions. We suspect that each of the pre-French socioeconomic systems would have exhibited distinctive population-carrying capacities, and have argued that the carrying capacity east of the Chari would have been lower than that west of the river. In all of the socioeconomic systems we would have expected only slowly growing populations.

With the arrival of the French at the turn of the century, new exploitative technologies were introduced into Chad. These events were associated with strains on the old social forms and the introduction of new urban structures. It has been seen that the spread of new technologies and social forms has been slow, recent, small, and limited to the regions west of the Chari.

The population trends have been distinguished. The first is a moderate natural growth rate, resulting from the difference between high birth and death rates characteristic of the populations of the developing countries of the interior of West Africa. The second is a migration-nourished growth rate. It has been contended that in Chad this latter rate comes in two distinct varieties. In N'Djamena, where the novel technologies have been successful, in-migration has occurred leading to rapid population increase while in Ouaddai, where technological innovation has not yet occurred, out-migration has developed, leading to population stagnation. In-migration and out-migration represent one measure of the success or failure of exploitative technologies in Chad.

### Bibliography of Works Not Previously Cited

BIBLIOGRAPHIC

INTSH. *Bibliographie du Tchad*. INTSH, Series A, 4. Fort Lamy [N'Djamena], 1968.

ENVIRONMENT: There is no good single reference to the Chadian environment. However, excellent environmental research has been carried out almost exclusively under the auspices of ORSTOM. Accordingly, the reader is referred to:

ORSTOM. "Liste chronologique des études effectués par l'ORSTOM en République du Tchad." Fort Lamy [N'Djamena]: Centre ORSTOM de Fort Lamy, 1968.

HISTORY

Boissen, J. *L'Histoire du Tchad et de Ft. Archambault*. Paris: Ed. du Scorpion, 1966.

Lebeuf, A. M. D. *Les populations du Tchad*. Paris: Presses univ. de France, 1959.

Lebeuf, J. P. *Archéologie tchadienne*. Paris: Hermann, 1962.

——and A. Masson-Detourbet, *La civilisation du Tchad*. Paris: Payot, 1950.

Le Cornec, J. *Histoire politique du Tchad de 1900 à 1962*. Paris: Librairie générale de droit et de jurisprudence, R. Pichon and P. Durand-Auzias, 1963.

ECONOMY

BCEOM. *Plan routier du Tchad*. Paris: Bureau Central d'Etudes pour les Equipements d'Outre-Mer, 1963.

Diguimbaye, G., and R. Langue. *L'Essor du Tchad*. Paris: Presses univ. de France, 1969.

Le Rouvreur, A. *Sahariens et Sahéliens du Tchad*. Paris: Berger-Levrault, 1962.

Ministère de l'Agriculture. *Etude de la Moyenne Vallée du Chari, rive gauche*. Fort Lamy [N'Djamena], 1968.

Ministère du Plan et de la Cooperation. *Enquête agricole au Tchad, 1960–1961*. Paris: INSEE, 1961.

——*Quinquennial de développement économique et social, 1966–1970*. Fort Lamy [N'Djamena], 1969.

Poumaillou, P. *Etude du développement régional du Ouaddai*. Paris: Ministère de la Cooperation, 1965.

SEDES. *Perspectives d'industrialisation du Tchad*. Paris: Société d'études pour le développement Economique et Social, 1962.

USDA. *Range management and livestock industry, Chad Basin*. Washington: U.S. Dept. of Agriculture, 1968.

SOCIAL CHANGE

Brunschwig, H. *Mythes et Réalités de l'impérialisme colonial francais, 1871–1914*. Paris: Armand Colin, 1960.

Buisson, M. "Projet d'intensification de l'action de modernisation rurale dans le centre-est Tchadien." Paris: BDPA, 1964.

Lebeuf, J. P. *Fort Lamy, Rapport d'une enquête préliminaire dans les milieux urbains de la fédération*. Paris: Ed. de l'Union Français, 1954.

Le Brun and P. C. Le Fevre. "Fertilité de sols et éléments sociologie rurale en Afrique au Sud du Sahara." Brussels: CEDESA, 1964.

Marway, P. *Etude socio-économique de la ville d'Abéché*. Paris: SEDES, 1963–1965.

DEMOGRAPHY

Alverson, H. S. "Time series analysis of migratory stabilization, with special reference to sub-Saharan Africa." *African Studies*, 26, 3 (1967).

Anonymous. "Evolution démographique dans les Républiques gabonaise, du Congo, de centrafricaine, et du Tchad." *Chronologie de la Communauté*, 2 (October 1959).

Bemmoiras, J. D. "La situation démographique du Tchad. Résultats provisoires de l'enquête démographique 1964." Paris: SEDES, 1964.

Crocquevieille, J. "Essai d'étude démographique des Kaba du district de Kyabe." Memoire CHEAM, 2416 (1955).

Dainville, J. "Habitations et types de peuplement sur la rive occidentale du lac Tchad." *R. Géogr. Humaine et éthnol.*, 1 (April–June 1948).

Gourou, P. "Une géographie de sous-peuplement." *Homme*, VII, 2 (April–June 1967).

Gros. *Enquête sur les migrations des travailleurs tchadiens au Soudan*. Paris: Ministère des Affaires Etrangères, 1959.

Herbot, P. "Coup d'oeil sur l'AEF. Le peuplement." *Afr. Franc.*, V (1934).

Masson-Detourbet, A. and M. P. Vincent. "Essai d'étude démographique des Kotoko." *Population*, III (July–September 1951).

Mathais, Lt. "La population de l'Afrique Equatoriale Française, Cercle de Batha." *Rens.-col. Afr. franc.* (1928).

Nodinot, J.-F. "Une vieille société dirigeante baguirmienne au contact d'une poussée démographique non-baguirmienne." Paris: Memoir ENFOM, 1957.

# CHAPTER TWENTY-EIGHT

# *Pronatalism & Child Labor*

## Chadian Attitudes to Birth Control and Family Size[1]

S. P. REYNA

▦

"A WOMAN WITHOUT CHILDREN IS LIKE A TREE WITHOUT LEAVES"—Chadian proverb.

This chapter represents a preliminary report on certain findings of the Chadian KAP project. Attitudes toward family size and birth control methods, and knowledge of birth control techniques suggest a pronatalism among the population surveyed.

The household contribution ratio is introduced to measure subsistence yields of different labor tasks assigned in preindustrial populations. The ratio is applied to one ethnic group, the Barma. It shows that households with fewer children and more adults are in a more secure position vis-à-vis subsistence than households with many children and fewer adults. These results are utilized to suggest that pronatalist sentiments be examined in terms of the labor requirements of pre-industrial populations.

### DESCRIPTION OF THE CHADIAN KAP PROJECT

The Chad KAP project surveyed the family planning knowledge, attitudes, and practices, as well as fertility levels within the Republic of Chad. Slightly over 1,600 currently married women, aged 14–50, were interviewed in the capital, N'Djamena, and in selected rural areas of the prefecture of Chari-Baguirmi. Systematic sampling techniques were employed in the urban area. The sample was selected so that the full variety of ethnic groups present in N'Djamena were represented. Two ethnic groups (the Barma and the Arab), with subsistent economies typical of those found in the dry savanna, were interviewed in the rural area. In the countryside a woman with the proper qualifications was interviewed in each household with such women. Sampling was not employed because the project invested extra time in the rural area, gathering economic data relevant to fertility levels, and it was possible to examine each household.

[1] A preliminary report on research supported by a grant from the Population Council.

TABLE 28.1
Consideration of number of children wanted

|  | Urban Area | | Rural Area | | All Population | |
|---|---|---|---|---|---|---|
|  | Number | Percent | Number | Percent | Number | Percent |
| Ever considered | 107 | 36 | 24 | 15 | 131 | 29 |
| Never considered | 178 | 59 | 111 | 72 | 289 | 63 |
| No response | 16 | 5 | 20 | 13 | 36 | 8 |
| Total | 301 | 100 | 155 | 100 | 456 | 100 |

Field operations began in N'Djamena at the beginning of July 1970 and ended toward the latter part of September. The data is still being processed. The conclusions in this chapter are derived from 301 interviews conducted in three *quartiers* (neighborhoods) in N'Djamena and 155 interviews conducted in five largely Barma villages to the south of N'Djamena. Two of the three *quartiers*, Repos and Hille Leclerc, are predominantly Moslem. The third, Ragouta Djemal, has a large southern population and a substantial representation of various Sara ethnic groups. The Barma were interviewed in the villages of Guera, Bougoumene, Meskin, Mailao, and Dourbali.

## ATTITUDES TOWARD FAMILY SIZE

In the questionnaire the women were asked if they had ever previously thought about the number of children they wanted. It was a surprise to discover that 29 percent of the women indicated they had previously given some consideration to their desired family size (Table 28.1). If we consider that thinking about the number of children one wants is thinking about the sort of family desired, then it is clear that there may be some sort of family planning among about 30 percent of the women interviewed. The question remains as to the substance of this planning.

With regard to the number of children desired, only a small proportion (7 percent) of the women interviewed wanted four or fewer children; while almost two-thirds wanted five or more (Table 28.2). The large percentage of the "Do not know" or "No response" answers (28 percent) is a measure of the number of people too baffled or astonished at being asked such questions to respond. A slightly higher percentage of people in the rural area preferred smaller numbers of children than in the urban area.

Of the women interviewed, 7 percent stated that they wanted no more children than they had at present, and only 12 percent of the women had friends who had all the children they wanted (Tables 28.3 and 28.4). In the urban area 72 percent of the women wanted more children and 6 percent wanted no more, while in the rural area only about half those

TABLE 28.2
Desired number of children

|  | Urban Area | | Rural Area | | All Population | |
|---|---|---|---|---|---|---|
|  | Number | Percent | Number | Percent | Number | Percent |
| Less than five | 19 | 7 | 13 | 8 | 32 | 7 |
| Five or more | 204 | 68 | 92 | 59 | 296 | 65 |
| Don't know/no response | 78 | 25 | 50 | 33 | 128 | 28 |
| Total | 301 | 100 | 155 | 100 | 456 | 100 |

TABLE 28.3
Desire for more children

| | Urban Area | | Rural Area | | All Population | |
|---|---|---|---|---|---|---|
| | Number | Percent | Number | Percent | Number | Percent |
| Want more | 215 | 72 | 81 | 52 | 296 | 65 |
| Want no more | 19 | 6 | 13 | 8 | 32 | 7 |
| Don't know/no response | 67 | 22 | 61 | 40 | 128 | 28 |
| Total | 301 | 100 | 155 | 100 | 456 | 100 |

interviewed wanted more children, while 8 percent wanted no more. In the urban area about one-fifth of the women gave no response or said that they did not know, while the percentage approximately doubled in the rural area. With regard to friends wanting or not wanting children, the responses are somewhat different. In the urban area the percentage "wanting more" remains about the same (74 percent compared with 72 percent); but the "want no more" and the "Don't know" and "No response" proportions are changed. The percentage of "women with friends wanting no more" is double their own responses (moving from 6 to 14 percent), while the percent of "Don't know" and "No response" declines by almost half (from 21 to 12 percent). In the rural areas there was a large increase from personal answers to answers about friends in the number of women wanting more children (up from 52 to 86 percent); the percentage of women not wanting children remains about the same (8 percent); while the percentage of women

with friends answering "Don't know" or "No response" sharply drops (from 40 to 6 percent). What is at stake in the discussion of these discrepancies is whether more people in rural areas actually want no more children than said so. Possibly the low "want more" figure for the rural population respondents in Table 28.3 is the result of the high "Don't know" or "No response" figure in the same table, and would resemble the "want more" figure in Table 28.4 if its "Don't know" or "No response" cells were greatly reduced. What is clear is that most women and their friends want more children than they have at present; but a small, consistent number do not want any more children.

There were only 32 women who wanted four or fewer children. Their reasons for not wanting large families are recorded in Table 28.5. About 29 percent of this group did not know or gave no response as to why they wanted smaller families. Two women from N'Djamena did not want large families for religious reasons. These women did not feel

TABLE 28.4
Desire of respondent's friends for more children

| | Urban Area | | Rural Area | | All Population | |
|---|---|---|---|---|---|---|
| | Number | Percent | Number | Percent | Number | Percent |
| Want more | 224 | 74 | 134 | 86 | 358 | 78 |
| Want no more | 42 | 14 | 12 | 8 | 54 | 12 |
| Don't know/no response | 35 | 12 | 9 | 6 | 44 | 10 |
| Total | 301 | 100 | 155 | 100 | 456 | 100 |

TABLE 28.5
Reasons for preferring a small family[a]

| | Urban Area | | | Rural Area | | | All Population | | |
|---|---|---|---|---|---|---|---|---|---|
| | Number | Percent All respondents | Respondents wanting less than 5 children | Number | Percent All respondents | Respondents wanting less than 5 children | Number | Percent All respondents | Respondents wanting less than 5 children |
| Economic strain | 6 | 2 | 32 | 5 | 3 | 38 | 11 | 2 | 34 |
| Health of mother or children | 4 | 1 | 21 | 4 | 3 | 31 | 8 | 2 | 25 |
| Religion or belief system | 4 | 1 | 21 | 0 | 0 | 0 | 4 | 1 | 13 |
| Don't know/no response | 5 | 2 | 26 | 4 | 3 | 31 | 9 | 2 | 28 |
| Not applicable— respondents do not want less than 5 children | 282 | 94 | — | 142 | 91 | — | 424 | 93 | — |
| Total | 301 | 100 | 100 | 155 | 100 | 100 | 456 | 100 | 100 |

[a] Fewer than five children.

that a supernatural force disapproved of large families, but that for some unaccountable reason an exception had been made in their cases and they were doomed to bear only a few children. Two other N'Djamena women had personal belief systems which insisted that large families were not a "good thing." One-quarter of the women, four from N'Djamena and four from the rural area wanted small families for medical reasons. These women believed many children to be unhealthy for themselves (often referred to as "making them dirty") or their children. Older women especially felt giving birth to be dangerous to them. The largest group of women (34 percent) who gave a reason for not wanting large families felt that having many children would be an economic drag. Their attitude could succinctly be summed up as *La vie est chère.* If the responses of these 32 women are representative, there would appear to be some awareness that large numbers of children can be economically and medically disadvantageous.

The number of women wanting more than five children was 296, with their reasons falling into seven categories (Table 28.6). About 16 percent of the women either did not know why they wanted many children or gave no response. Nearly 14 percent of these women gave religious reasons for wanting many children, believing that a supernatural force either wished for or made inevitable large numbers of children. Barma respondents often expostulated: *Allah day,* which literally means "God come" but which implied "God sends." Almost the same percentage of rural women as urban women gave religious reasons for wanting large families. Most women felt that many children were good because they in some way supported the family. A higher percentage of rural women felt this to be the case, with the figures being 52 percent in the rural area in contrast to only 37 percent in N'Djamena. The women believed that children either supported the family by helping now or in the future in a wide variety of activities, or that they replaced

TABLE 28.6
Reasons for preferring a large family[a]

| | Urban Area | | | Rural Area | | | All Population | | |
|---|---|---|---|---|---|---|---|---|---|
| | Number | Percent All respondents | Respondents wanting 5 or more children | Number | Percent All respondents | Respondents wanting 5 or more children | Number | Percent All respondents | Respondents wanting 5 or more children |
| Family support | 76 | 25 | 37 | 48 | 31 | 52 | 124 | 27 | 42 |
| Will participate in benefits of modern-ization | 17 | 6 | 8 | 2 | 1 | 2 | 19 | 4 | 6 |
| Good of country | 8 | 3 | 4 | 1 | 1 | 1 | 9 | 2 | 3 |
| Religion or belief system | 65 | 21 | 32 | 31 | 20 | 34 | 96 | 21 | 33 |
| Don't know/no response | 38 | 13 | 19 | 10 | 7 | 11 | 48 | 11 | 16 |
| Not applicable— respondents do not want 5 or more children | 97 | 32 | — | 62 | 40 | — | 160 | 35 | — |
| Total | 301 | 100 | 100 | 154 | 100 | 100 | 456 | 100 | 100 |

[a] Five or more children.

its dead members. Almost 19 percent of the women had belief systems that held the giving of birth to many children to be a general moral duty, or a personally good thing. The rural and urban percentages in this category are quite similar. A small percentage of the women (6 percent), largely urban (8 percent in contrast to 2 percent in rural areas), thought having many children was good because the children would be able to participate in the opportunities that are occurring as a result of modernization. The most frequently perceived such opportunity was that children could become *fonctionnaires* (government officials). It was also felt that children would be able to "earn money" in other ways and to go to school. Finally, 3 percent of the women thought it was good to have many children for patriotic reasons, believing that the more children there were, the bigger Chad would be.

Large numbers of children appear to be wanted by most women to continue to provide labor for the family.

## ATTITUDES TOWARD AND KNOWLEDGE OF FAMILY PLANNING

Only 3 women out of the 456 in the sample analyzed here stated that they had ever utilized any type of birth control device (Table 28.7). The figures were also low for those who stated that they intended to use some form of birth control in the future (Table 28.8). When the question was made less personal and our respondents were asked if they had friends who used or intended to use such birth control methods in the future, the percentage went up: 10 percent said their friends used or intended to use some form of birth control; only 40 percent definitely did not intend to use birth control; and a huge

TABLE 28.7
Ever used any family planning method

| | Urban Area | | Rural Area | | All Population | |
|---|---|---|---|---|---|---|
| | Number | Percent | Number | Percent | Number | Percent |
| Ever used | 2 | 1 | 1 | 1 | 3 | 1 |
| Never used | 299 | 99 | 150 | 97 | 449 | 98 |
| Don't know/no response | 0 | 0 | 4 | 2 | 4 | 1 |
| Total | 301 | 100 | 155 | 100 | 456 | 100 |

50 percent did not know or made no response to the question (Table 28.9). The urban percentages are higher than rural ones in this category (12 percent of the urban women have friends who use or intend to use birth control, while only 5 percent of the rural women have such friends).

Tables 28.7 and 28.9 suggest a low incidence of the use of family planning. Untabulated urban data provide some ideas as to the nature of technique employed. In Repos nine people reported knowledge of birth control techniques. Six of these simply stated that they had heard from friends or relatives that births could be controlled. They were not, however, quite sure how it was done. One said you should go to a *marabout*. Another specified that you should take a folk medicine. The final person said something incoherent. In Hille Leclerc 13 persons responded. Seven said they had friends or relatives who insisted that births could be controlled. One said you should go to a doctor (in Chad the distinction between a doctor and a nurse is not always clear); and three said you should go to a *marabout*. One said you should take nivaquine, which is an antimalarial, and apparently also the generic for "medicine" among much of the population around N'Djamena. One person said you should take the contraceptive pill. In Ragouta Djemal, 12 women responded. Two said you could go to a doctor. Four said that they had heard from friends or relatives that you could control births. Two said you might go to *marabouts*. Three mentioned taking folk medicines. One reported reading about birth control techniques in magazines.

Of the 34 urban women reporting knowledge of different birth control methods, only 6 responded with knowledge that would appear to be "modern." Three of these reported that they would go to a doctor. It is by no means certain that the women going to the doctor had any idea of what the doctor might do to control births. Similar data for the rural area are not yet available.

Attitudes toward the utilization of birth

TABLE 28.8
Intend using family planning in the future

| | Urban Area | | Rural Area | | All Population | |
|---|---|---|---|---|---|---|
| | Number | Percent | Number | Percent | Number | Percent |
| Intend to do so | 11 | 4 | 1 | 1 | 12 | 3 |
| Do not intend to do so | 273 | 90 | 150 | 97 | 423 | 93 |
| Don't know/no response | 17 | 6 | 4 | 2 | 21 | 4 |
| Total | 301 | 100 | 155 | 100 | 456 | 100 |

TABLE 28.9

Knowledge of friends using or intending to use family planning

|  | Urban Area | | Rural Area | | All Population | |
|---|---|---|---|---|---|---|
|  | Number | Percent | Number | Percent | Number | Percent |
| Knows of such a friend | 37 | 12 | 8 | 5 | 45 | 10 |
| Does not know of such a friend | 104 | 35 | 77 | 50 | 181 | 40 |
| No response | 160 | 53 | 70 | 45 | 230 | 50 |
| Total | 301 | 100 | 155 | 100 | 456 | 100 |

control methods were not very favorable. Only 3 percent of the women interviewed intended to use birth control methods in the future (Table 28.8). The differential between urban and rural responses is marked. Only 0.6 percent of the rural women intended to use birth control as opposed to 3.6 percent of the urban women. Fully 71 percent of the women interviewed were not in agreement with the use of birth control techniques (Table 28.10). Again, the rural women were more adamant in their opposition, with 90 percent being against birth control as opposed to 62 percent in N'Djamena. Over three-quarters of the women interviewed believed it to be against their religion to employ birth control techniques (Table 28.11).

## PRONATALISM AND THE BARMA

The data indicate that Chadians value having many children; that a large percentage of the women see children as providing help and replacement for the family now and in the future; and that birth control is apparently neither widely known, nor approved of, nor practiced. The women surveyed exhibit what could be termed a "preindustrial, pronatalist" ideology. It is "pronatalist" because such an ideology is a collection of cultural rules which positively value things perceived to increase the child yield, and negatively value things perceived to decrease this yield. It is "preindustrial" because such an ideology has been associated with populations lacking complex industrial technologies. What is striking about the views of the women surveyed is their predictability. Chad lacks any substantial modern economic sector; hence Chadian women express strong natalist sentiments.

It is clear that pronatalist ideologies are associated with preindustrial populations. It is not yet quite so clear why this is so. Conventional wisdom observes the demographic parameters of preindustrial society, notes the high mortality (especially infant

TABLE 28.10

Approval of family planning

|  | Urban Area | | Rural Area | | All Population | |
|---|---|---|---|---|---|---|
|  | Number | Percent | Number | Percent | Number | Percent |
| Approve | 79 | 26 | 1 | 1 | 80 | 18 |
| Disapprove | 185 | 62 | 139 | 90 | 324 | 71 |
| Don't know/no response | 37 | 12 | 15 | 9 | 52 | 11 |
| Total | 301 | 100 | 155 | 100 | 456 | 100 |

TABLE 28.11
Belief that respondents' religion is against use of family planning

|  | Urban Area | | Rural Area | | All Population | |
|---|---|---|---|---|---|---|
|  | Number | Percent | Number | Percent | Number | Percent |
| Religion against | 227 | 75 | 132 | 85 | 359 | 79 |
| Religion not against | 55 | 18 | 7 | 5 | 62 | 14 |
| Don't know/no response | 19 | 7 | 16 | 10 | 35 | 7 |
| Total | 301 | 100 | 155 | 100 | 456 | 100 |

mortality), and argues that, for such populations to flourish, they need a high fertility. Pronatalism is the set of rules by which a population ensures its high fertility.

A problem with this position is that it tends to treat preindustrial populations as monolithically similar. In fact, preindustrial economies probably exhibit more quantitative differences between themselves than do industrial economies. One way in which preindustrial economies differ that has implications for pronatalism, is in the manner they organize labor. Preindustrial populations assign different labor tasks to different categories of persons who differentially contribute to the subsistence needs of the population. An ideology which values a group that makes no subsistence contribution must be carefully examined to ascertain just what that ideology values, for, while subsistence requirements are similar in all human populations, in preindustrial populations the means of filling these requirements are limited. The labor of children in certain populations contributes to subsistence, while in others it does not. In these latter populations pronatalism must be carefully scrutinized.

A case in point are the Barma whom we have already seen to exhibit a vigorous pronatalism. A striking characteristic of the Barma economy is that both male and female children are an apparent economic drawback, because, until nearly puberty, their labor was largely limited to play. Barma economic activity occupies three major sectors: fishing, swidden farming, and trading. Prior to the

arrival of the French there was a fourth sector, raiding.

Fishing is the work of adult males. It is principally conducted from dugout canoes. Nets, weirs, and spears are used to catch fish. Manual dexterity is required to handle a canoe and a net or spear at the same time; this type of dexterity is lacking in a small child. Fishing is a favored form of sport for boys between ages of 7 and 12, but boys fish with poles for fun and their catch is not infrequently left on the riverbank. Boys do not learn to use nets or to build weirs until puberty. Neither young nor adult women fish.

Barma agriculture is largely the production of millets, sorghums, okra, and peanuts. The labor tasks associated with the production of grains are restricted to adult males. Each adult woman has a field of okra and frequently a field of peanuts. It is not until after puberty that boys begin to actively enter the agricultural labor force. Girls begin slightly earlier.

Trading of two types is an important part of Barma economy. Postpubertal males exchange purchased goods—most frequently sugar, tea, or cloth. Young girls or boys do not sell at the market.

Barma children do not lead a life of utter leisure. Young girls will tend younger siblings, help their mothers prepare food and goods for market, gather wood, and sell kola nuts. Boys help their mothers carry things and frighten animals out of maturing fields. However, prepubertal Barma males and females do not contribute labor to subsistence tasks.

The implications of such a labor situation can be made more explicit if we introduce a ratio which measures the contribution of all household members to the household's subsistence. The ratio will be in terms of calories, a convenient measure of the energy required for subsistence. We shall define a household contribution ratio (*HCR*) as the sum of the average total number of calories consumed daily by each household member to the sum of the average daily total of calories produced by each household member. Thus:

$$HCR = \frac{(Ci)}{(Pi)}$$

where   $Ci$ = the total number of calories consumed daily for each $i$; where $i$ is each household member

$Pi$ = the total number of calories produced daily for each $i$

The larger $Ci$ is to $Pi$, the less secure a household is with regard to subsistence.

We shall apply the *HCR* to two hypothetical Barma families: one consisting of a man, his wife, and four children under 12 (family A); the other consisting of a man, his wife, his two children under 12, his full brother, and his brother's wife (family B). Table 28.12 presents the consumption and production figures for each family.

The figures are ideal ones in that they are not computed using Barma data, but are within the parameters for populations employing similar techniques inhabiting similar environments. The figures are only for the production of grains, fish, okra, and milk. Existing data suggest that a man daily provides about 5,200 grain calories when production is averaged for the year. The figure assumes that the stores after harvest have about 600 kilograms (about 1,350 lbs.)

TABLE 28.12
Calculation of "household contribution ratios"

| Family A | | | Family B | | |
|---|---|---|---|---|---|
| Household members | Average daily calorie production | Average daily calorie consumption | Household members | Average daily calorie production | Average daily calorie consumption |
| Husband | 5,200 (grain) 1,240 (fish) | 2,500 | Husband | 5,200 (grain) 1,240 (fish) | 2,500 |
| Wife | 60 (okra) 270 (milk) | 1,900 | Wife | 60 (okra) 270 (milk) | 1,900 |
| Child 1 | — | 1,500 | Child 1 | — | 1,500 |
| Child 2 | — | 1,500 | Child 2 | — | 1,500 |
| Child 3 | — | 1,500 | Brother | 5,200 (grain) | 2,500 |
| Child 4 | — | 1,500 | Brother's wife | 60 (okra) 270 (milk) | 1,900 |
| Total | 6,770 | 10,400 | Total | 12,300 | 11,800 |

of grain, with a kilogram providing about 3,150 calories. The daily average contribution from fishing is put at 1,240 calories estimating that the daily edible portion of his catch is 500 grams (just off 1 lb.) with 60 grams providing about 155 calories. A woman's contribution is estimated at 60 calories per day from okra and 270 calories a day from milk, assuming that a woman's edible harvest of okra is about 62 kilograms (about 135 lbs.) and that 100 grams of okra give about 29 calories in about half a cup. The consumption figures are commensurate with a WHO study partially conducted in the Barma region of Chad.[2]

With the values set as they are the HCR for household A is 0.65 while for household B it is 1.03. The family with four children produces on average only 6,770 calories per day, while it consumes 10,400. Such a family is in a perilous situation with regard to subsistence. Its members may attempt to increase the amount of labor they expend, while at the same time decreasing the amount they consume; they thereby put themselves in a less advantageous position with regard to a wide variety of diseases. The household with the two married brothers, one of whom does no fishing, still manages to produce 12,300 calories while it consumes only 11,800 calories. Such a family is making ends meet and in addition is producing a small surplus. It is free to decrease production and to take the time saved and invest it in other ways: in increased leisure or in trade, or alternatively to continue food production for the market or to vary the diet.

The Barma division of labor makes children what Alland has termed a "disjunctive" phenomenon.[3] On the one hand, children make subsistence more difficult; on the other, children are a necessity if subsistence is to continue into the next generation. Disjunctive situations, Alland has observed,

[2] WHO, "Report on a Mission by Dr. Paret, Nutritional consultant to WHO, to Chad, November 1964 to January 1965" (unpublished).
[3] Alexander Alland, Jr., *Adaption in Cultural Evolution: An Approach to Medical Anthropology* (New York: Columbia University Press, 1970).

resemble those successfully analyzable in terms of game theory.

The object of the game for the Barma is the development of strategies which maximize per capita caloric production over time. Ratios, such as the HRC, could help to predict optimal strategies. Such strategies, considering the Barma division of labor, would state the "best" household composition measured in terms of a ratio of adult males and females to children. An optimal household composition would provide the highest present caloric production, with the fewest number of children required to replace the present generation of adults.

Children are a necessary requirement of Barma society that inevitably have certain undesirable economic consequences. Seen in this light, it is reasonable to reinterpret Barma pronatalism as an ideology favoring children, but not too many children. Conceivably sentiments like a Barma woman's desire for ten children resemble the barroom brawler's challenge to "take on anyone, one at a time." In both cases after four or five the game gets to be a bit wearing.

It would seem valuable to ascertain whether the Barma example is atypical; that is, to note to what degree children's labor is utilized in subsistence activities elsewhere. Further, in populations like the Barma, detailed examinations of pronatalism might be carried out to identify whether the population really does want as many children as possible.

## CONCLUSION

This chapter has discussed the preliminary findings of the Chadian KAP project. It duly notes the predictable occurrence of pronatalist ideologies. It has examined the labor-requirements of one preindustrial population, the Barma, and concludes that their children are a disjunctive element and that their pronatalism should not logically call for *all* the children possible, but *enough* children. Finally, the chapter suggests that examination of the relation between the labor requirements of preindustrial populations and their natalist sentiments is in order.

# CHAPTER TWENTY-NINE

## *Zaïre*[1]

JOSEPH BOUTE

⊞

For many years before the proclamation of independence, it had been the custom in Zaïre[1] to assess the total population annually by adding the numbers in the permanent card index held by the district administrations. This card index was kept up to date by the declarations made by the residents to the local registrars. The extent of population growth could, in theory, be known at any time. All that was necessary was to decide to count the cards and to compare the result with that of the previous count.

A general summary of the population used to appear in each annual report of the Minister of Colonies in the Belgian Legislative Chamber. To compile this summary, the territorial administration checked the population count on the ground; the permanent card index was verified by an operation called a census during which the census takers passed through the various villages or urban districts and verified that a card existed for each declared person and that each departure and each death had been treated according to the instructions.[2]

This practice of an annual census was maintained more or less rigorously during the 1960s. The reforms effected by the country since November 24, 1965, have subsequently led to improvements in this particular field as well. Plans to resume the verification of the cards were considered on many occasions, and were finally implemented in the first half of 1970. The first official figures were published at the end of July of the same year.[3]

Apart from the administrative censuses, an extensive demographic sample survey was carried out from July 1955 to early 1958. The figures, published in a series of reports,[4] were submitted to a thorough analysis. The

---

[1] Formerly the Democratic Republic of the Congo, often referred to as Congo (Kinshasa). All references to the country throughout this book have been changed to the present name, Zaïre, except those in the titles of publications.
[2] See appendix to this chapter, RUFAST; J. Magolte, "Les Circonscriptions Indigénes—Commentaire du décret du 5 déc. 1933," *Dison Verviers* (1934).
[3] See Appendix, *1970 Administrative Census* (July 31).
[4] See Appendix, *1955–1957 Demographic Survey*.

results appeared in various publications.[5] The repetition of the inquiry in an improved form, planned for 1960, could not be achieved.

It was only in 1967 that a sample survey of one-tenth of the population was carried out in Zaïre, and then only for the capital. It constitutes the first serious inquiry of recent times in the most important city of Central Africa.[6] A similar work was undertaken for the town of Bukavu in October–November 1970 as part of the research associated with the economic renewal program of the north-eastern region, the one most affected by the successive rebellions. The President of the Republic has designated this region as the country's third pole of development.[7]

## ESTIMATING THE POPULATION OF ZAÏRE BEFORE 1970

Analyses, based mainly on stable population techniques of the 1955–1957 survey data, have increased our knowledge of the population prior to political independence.

The figures from this inquiry, uncorrected or adjusted in conformity with the results of the analyses mentioned above, are the ones which served as a starting point for the

different estimates made between the years 1955 and 1970 of population trends in Zaïre.[8]

Table 29.1 lists one set giving the totals obtained by the revised United Nations Population Division projections in accordance with different assumptions as to the rate of natural increase.[9] These projections take as their starting population an estimate by age and sex for 1965, based on the 1955–1957 demographic situation and assuming no significant changes during the subsequent decade. The different variants are in accord with relatively simple hypotheses. The low, medium, and high variants all assume a progressive fertility rise from a gross reproduction rate of 2.8 in 1965 to 3.0 for the 1980–1985 period. The mortality assumption varies, with mortality declining more steeply as we move from the low variant through the medium variant to the high variant. The fourth or constant fertility variant maintains a gross reproduction rate of 2.9 throughout the whole projection period while adopting the medium mortality assumption.

Thus these projections differ only long after 1955. It was natural to try to determine the demographic effects of the events which the country went through in the years following the 1955 survey. But the projections appear to assume that the political disorders and the rebellions had occurred over the whole of the country, whereas vast regions were never seriously troubled and have only suffered from a general slowing down of economic and medical activities. It has been very difficult to ascertain the demographic reaction to the state of the country during these ten years. Thus, because of a total lack of data, the components of demographic growth were considered as constant until 1965, even though nothing was preventing the population of much of Zaïre from experiencing accelerated growth.

[5] A. Romaniuk, "Evolution et Perspectives Démographiques de la Population au Congo," *Zaïre*, Louvain, XII, 6 (1959); A. Romaniuk, "L'Aspect Démographique de la Stérilité des Femmes Congolaises," Kinshasa, IRES-Lovanium (1961); A. Romaniuk, "Fécondité et Stérilité des Femmes Congolaises," *International Population Conference*, II (New York, 1961), pp. 109–16; A. Romaniuk, "Infertility in Tropical Africa," in John C. Caldwell and C. Okonjo, eds., *The Population of Tropical Africa* (London and New York, Columbia University Press, 1968), pp. 214–24; A. Romaniuk, *La Fécondité des Populations Congolaises*, La Haye, Mouton, and Kinshasa, IRES-Lovanium (Paris, 1967), p. 346; A. Romaniuk, "Estimation of the Birth Rate of the Congo through Nonconventional Techniques," *Demography*, IV, 2 (1967); A. Romaniuk, "The Demography of the Democratic Republic of the Congo," in William Brass et al., eds., *The Demography of Tropical Africa* (Princeton, N.J.: Princeton University Press, 1968), pp. 239–339.
[6] See Appendix, *1967 Socio-Demographic Survey (Kinshasa)*.
[7] See speech platform of the head of state, December 5 1970 in *Le progrès* newspaper, December 7–8 1970.

[8] M. Fabri and J. Mayer, "La Population Future du Congo," *Centre d'Etudes des Problèmes Sociaux et Professionels de la Technique* (Brussels, 1959).
[9] Information from M. Macura and the United Nations Population Division to the Institut National de la Statistique in Kinshasa.

TABLE 29.1

Summary of the United Nations population division projections of the population of Zaïre (in thousands)

| Year | Low Variant | | | Medium Variant | | | Constant Variant | | | High Variant | | |
|---|---|---|---|---|---|---|---|---|---|---|---|---|
| | M | F | M & F | M | F | M & F | M | F | M & F | M | F | M & F |
| 1965 | 7,566 | 8,061 | 15,627 | 7,566 | 8,061 | 15,627 | 7,566 | 8,061 | 15,627 | 7,566 | 8,061 | 15,627 |
| 1970 | 8,440 | 8,940 | 17,380 | 8,463 | 8,961 | 17,423 | 8,515 | 9,013 | 17,529 | 8,484 | 8,981 | 17,646 |
| 1975 | 9,512 | 10,019 | 19,531 | 9,606 | 10,107 | 19,712 | 9,653 | 10,154 | 19,808 | 9,694 | 10,190 | 19,884 |
| 1980 | 10,747 | 11,262 | 22,009 | 10,969 | 11,470 | 22,439 | 11,015 | 11,516 | 22,531 | 11,179 | 11,667 | 22,846 |
| 1985 | 12,250 | 12,771 | 25,021 | 12,675 | 13,171 | 25,847 | 12,651 | 13,148 | 25,799 | 13,077 | 13,549 | 26,626 |

The fertility rise shown in 1967 to have occurred in Kinshasa[10] and the results of the 1970 administrative census throw doubt on the hypothesis of constancy. They lead us to conclude, until proof to the contrary can be adduced, that the rate of natural increase was rising in the years prior to 1965 because of increasing fertility and diminishing overall mortality, in spite of unusual peaks of mortality in various places at certain times.

The results of the 1955–1957 demographic survey have already been the subject of numerous analyses and comments. At the time of writing, only a single, preliminary set of 1970 administrative census results has been published.

THE 1970 POPULATION OF ZAÏRE

The method used for the 1970 census was the administrative enumeration: Each head of the family had to go to the local census office to furnish the information required about himself and his dependents, and the enumeration recorded this information on an individual index card replacing the usually very defective older card. Each district had at least one census office. The operation started in February and ended around May 31. The totals were established on site by manual count. They were tabulated in accordance with models supplied with the instructions.[11] The only published set of

figures separates nationals and foreigners, and subdivides each by sex and by age into children and adults for each territory and town.

This administrative census is the first one since independence to have been effectively organized and publicized. Members of the *Mouvement Populaire de la Révolution* (the national party) encouraged the population to cooperate.[12] This operation, primarily carried out to draw up electoral lists,[13] had been preceded by preliminary efforts in 1968 and 1969.

Table 29.2 compares the 1970 results with those of the administrative censuses prior to 1960. The high quality of the 1956 figures had been recognized.[14] The administrative structure of Zaïre in 1970 comprises 8 provinces and an urban district having the rank of a province (Kinshasa); these are subdivided into 24 districts and 10 urban areas, and again into 134 territories. Each territory comprises one or several local districts.[15]

According to these figures, Zaïre has undergone an acceleration in its rate of growth. As we cannot determine the annual growth from current data an average annual growth

[10] *1967 Socio-Demographic Survey*, see "Rapport Général." p. 67.
[11] *1970 Administrative Census*, see April 30, 1968, p. 8; September 6, 1968, article 12 and Appendix.

[12] See *Bilan*, 1965–1970, Bureau de la Présidence de la République (Kinshasa, 1971), popular edition, p. 90.
[13] Banque Nationale du Zaïre, *Rapport Annuel, 1969–1970* (Kinshasa), p. 81.
[14] See Romaniuk, "The Demography of the Democratic Republic," p. 248.
[15] Following the Ordinance on territorial organization No. 67/221 of May 3, 1967, modified by the Ordinances No. 68/018 of January 12, 1968 and No. 68/180 of April 11, 1968; No. 69/275 of November 21, 1969 and No. 70/095 of March 15, 1970.

TABLE 29.2
Nationals (N),[a] foreigners (F), and total population (T), by province

| Province | | 1956 No. | 1956 Percent | 1959 No. | 1959 Percent | 1970 No. | 1970 Percent |
|---|---|---|---|---|---|---|---|
| Kinshasa | N | 348,763 | 94.7 | 380,781 | 94.4 | 1,099,009[b] | 84.0 |
| | F | 19,679 | 5.3 | 22,529 | 5.6 | 209,352[b] | 16.0 |
| | T | 368,442 | 100.0 | 403,310 | 100.0 | 1,308,361[b] | 100.0 |
| Bas- | N | 894,184[c] | 99.1 | 971,780 | 99.2 | 1,294,898[b] | 85.2 |
| Zaïre | F | 8,183 | 0.9 | 7,488 | 0.8 | 224,141[b] | 14.8 |
| | T | 902,367 | 100.0 | 979,268 | 100.0 | 1,519,039[b] | 100.0 |
| Bandundu | N | 1,781,155[c] | 99.1 | 1,948,579 | 99.7 | 2,592,426 | 99.7 |
| | F | 5,779 | 0.9 | 5,712 | 0.3 | 8.130 | 0.3 |
| | T | 1,786,934 | 100.0 | 1,954,291 | 100.0 | 2,600,556 | 100.0 |
| Equateur | N | 1,723,449 | 99.6 | 1,836,538 | 99.6 | 2,427,667 | 99.8 |
| | F | 6,224 | 0.4 | 6,985 | 0.4 | 4,145 | 0.2 |
| | T | 1,729,673 | 100.0 | 1,843,523 | 100.0 | 2,431,812 | 100.0 |
| Haut- | N | 2,347,745 | 99.3 | 2,506,398 | 99.2 | 3,320,347 | 98.9 |
| Zaïre | F | 16,459 | 0.7 | 18,994 | 0.8 | 36,072 | 1.1 |
| | T | 2,364,204 | 100.0 | 2,525,392 | 100.0 | 3,346,419 | 100.0 |
| Kivu | N | 2,112,477 | 99.4 | 2,329,262 | 99.4 | 3,014,618 | 89.7 |
| | F | 13,756 | 0.6 | 15,116 | 0.6 | 347,265 | 10.3 |
| | T | 2,126,233 | 100.0 | 2,344,378 | 100.0 | 3,361,883 | 100.0 |
| Shaba | N | 1,561,344 | 97.8 | 1,709,659 | 98.0 | 2,654,520 | 96.4 |
| | F | 34,936 | 2.2 | 34,074 | 2.0 | 99,194 | 3.6 |
| | T | 1,596,280 | 100.0 | 1,743,733 | 100.0 | 2,753,714 | 100.0 |
| Kasai | N | 882,415 | 99.7 | 940,089 | 99.7 | 1,870,853 | 99.9 |
| Oriental | F | 2,897 | 0.3 | 3,285 | 0.3 | 1,378 | 0.1 |
| | T | 885,312 | 100.0 | 943,374 | 100.0 | 1,872,231 | 100.0 |
| Kasai | N | 1,192,042 | 99.5 | 1,241,335 | 99.6 | 2,431,496 | 99.9 |
| Occidental | F | 5,463 | 0.5 | 5,566 | 0.4 | 2,365 | 0.1 |
| | T | 1,197,505 | 100.0 | 1,246,901 | 100.0 | 2,433,861 | 100.0 |
| Zaïre | N | 12,843,574 | 99.1 | 13,864,421 | 99.1 | 20,705,834 | 95.7 |
| | F | 113,376 | 0.9 | 119,749 | 0.9 | 932,042 | 4.3 |
| | T | 12,956,950 | 100.0 | 13,984,170 | 100.0 | 21,637,876 | 100.0 |

SOURCES: 1956 and 1959 AIMO Services, Léopoldville; 1970 Administrative Census (July 31). (See appendix to this chapter.)
[a] In 1956 and 1959, including Africans of bordering countries; in 1970 excluding Africans of bordering countries.
[b] In 1970, the commune of Maluku has remained in the province of the Kongo Central instead of Kinshasa for a better comparability.
[c] In 1956 and 1959, Kimvula Territory (estimation) is counted in Kongo Central and has been removed from Bandundu.

rate for the 1956–1959 period and another one for that of 1959–1970 has been calculated. In 1959, the number of inhabitants in Zaïre was 7.9 percent greater than in 1956, implying an average annual growth of 2.6 percent: in 1970, the results indicate a population 55 percent greater than in 1959, implying an average annual growth rate of 4.2 percent.

This chronological comparison is not rigorous, however, as we find when we seek to determine the significance of migration and natural increase in this growth. Direct information on natural increase was totally lacking for the 1959–1970 period; it is necessary to obtain it as a residue, after having determined the extent of migration. But the problem of estimating migration is tied to the definition given to nationals and foreigners.

### NATIONAL AND FOREIGN POPULATION

Special care was taken in 1970 to define what was meant by the term "foreigner." Prior to independence, the administrative census classified as "autochthon population" Africans of bordering countries and as "non-autochthon population" other Africans and foreigners from other continents.[16] For 1970, precise instructions were given. It had become necessary to register resident foreigners (i.e., those in possession of a residence visa),[17] refugees, immigrants (e.g., people from Rwanda living in Kivu). The instructions pointed out that numerous immigrants prior to 1960 own Zaïrien identity cards and that it was nevertheless necessary to obtain useful information on their nationalities and their

[16] See "La Situation Economique du Congo Belge et du Ruanda-Urundi en 1950–1959," *Situation Economique*, Belgian Ministry of Colonies, Department of Economic Studies (Brussels, 1959), p. 24.
[17] Persons on temporary or transit visas were omitted. See *1970 Administrative Census*, April 30, 1968, p. 2.

dates of immigration.[18] The foreigner is thus defined negatively as one who does not have Zaïrien nationality.[19] Nationality can be acquired by various means and enumerators had to endeavor to find how it was acquired by each person.[20] The precise definition of foreigner adopted in 1970, being more exact than the definitions used in the past, introduces difficulties in comparing this recent count of population with those prior to 1960 in which it will now be necessary to distinguish the "foreign population" from the "national population."

The influence of external migrations is especially conspicuous when it takes the form of a surplus of immigrants having taken refuge in certain fairly delimited regions. The regions where foreigners are the most numerous coincide with those where refugees of neighboring countries reside (Table 29.3). The volume by sex and per age of these refugees is not well known. The United

[18] *Ibid.*
[19] *1970 Administrative Census*, March 8, 1969, repeating article 1 of the *Ordonnance-loi* No. 67/302 of February 20, 1967, p. 4.
[20] *1970 Administrative Census*, March 8, 1969, repeating articles 2–10 of the *décret-loi* of September 18, 1965 embodying the legal provisions for claiming Zaïrien nationality.

TABLE 29.3

Towns and territories of Zaïre with more than 2 percent of foreigners, 1970

| Territory | Foreigners (percent) | Territory | Foreigners (percent) | Territory | Foreigners (percent) |
|---|---|---|---|---|---|
| City of Kinshasa | 15.8 | Fizi Territory | 5.1 | Town of Lubumbashi | 9.5 |
| | | Kalehe Territory | 12.5 | Town of Likasi | 6.4 |
| Town of Matadi | 20.4 | South-Kivu District | 3.4 | Kipushi Territory | 20.6 |
| Boma Territory | 14.5 | Goma Territory | 26.7 | Kambove Territory | 6.8 |
| Seke Banza Territory | 9.8 | Masisi Territory | 70.6 | Kasenga Territory | .2.3 |
| Bas Congo District | 5.0 | Rutshurur Territory | 24.4 | Sakania Territory | 21.7 |
| Songololo Territory | 58.9 | Walikale | 2.4 | Ht. Katanga District | 7.8 |
| Kimvula Territory | 2.6 | North-Kivu District | 20.0 | Kolwezi Territory | 6.6 |
| Thysville Territory | 24.3 | Pangi Territory | 3.0 | Dilolo Territory | 6.3 |
| Madimba Territory | 3.0 | Punia Territory | 3.7 | Lubudi Territory | 2.5 |
| Cataracts District | 20.1 | Province of Kivu | 10.3 | Lualaba District | 4.5 |
| Province of Kongo Central | 14.9 | | | Province of Katanga | 3.6 |
| | | Kahemba Territory | 2.2 | | |
| | | Kasongo Lunda Territory | 2.6 | Poko Territory | 3.8 |
| Faradje Territory | 6.1 | | | Aru Territory | 3.4 |
| Gungu Territory | 7.3 | | | | |
| Haut Uélé District | 2.5 | Town of Bukavu | 5.4 | | |

SOURCE: 1970 Administrative Census (July 31, 1970). (See appendix to this chapter.)

Nations High Commissioner for Refugees works in Zaïre by relying on the following estimates: about 50,000 Sudanese in the Ueles; about 24,000 people from Rwanda in the Kivu; about 15,000 Lumpa in the Katanga tongue; and approximately 350,000 people from Angola in the region stretching from Kinshasa to the Atlantic Ocean. This would constitute a total of approximately 440,000 persons.[21] This figure represents 2 percent of the total 1970 population or about half of all foreigners in Zaïre.

For the town of Matadi in particular, the foreign population, in part cosmopolitan because it is in a harbor district, comprises predominantly people from Angola who, by stages or in a single move, have settled themselves in the capital of the province. In Kinshasa also, the people from Angola form an important part of the foreign population; there were nearly 135,000 in 1967,[22] a number equal to more than 60 percent of the foreigners counted in 1970 in the capital city.

Since the definition of the foreigner has broadened, that of the national has become more restricted.[23] The total number of Zaïrien nationals living outside the country is not easily determined, with the exception of officials and students. The rebellions have led to temporary emigrations but no one is able to estimate the numbers of those who still live outside the frontiers. A clemency measure was proclaimed subsequent to the census, in the inauguration speech of the head of state delivered on the occasion of his taking the presidential oath on December 5, 1970. This measure has caused the return of many thousands of Zaïriens, who have been compelled to register before resuming a normal life.[24] The number of repatriates had reached almost 10,000 by mid-February 1971.[25] The number of those still living abroad could hardly exceed 20,000.

Even exact figures for the foreigners living in the country and the Zaïrien citizens living outside it would still establish only in a residual manner the share of international migrations in the total growth. It would be necessary to calculate separately the growth of nationals and the growth of foreigners, which the change of definition from one period to another forbids us from doing with exactness. What we know enables us to state positively that international migration remained a factor of minor importance in national population growth, even if this is not the case in certain specific areas.

## NATURAL INCREASE

There is at present insufficient data to estimate the national mortality or fertility levels. The results obtained for the city of Kinshasa in 1967 show for the capital a higher birth rate than in 1955, but a mortality rate of approximately the same level as 12 years earlier.[26] But these are data for a large city. The analysis of the data drawn from the 1955–1957 demographic survey suggested a national crude death rate of 26 per thousand. If this mortality had remained constant a crude birth rate of nearly 67 per thousand would have to be postulated to explain the population growth to 1970. In extreme contrast, if mortality had fallen to reach a national level of 10 per thousand by 1970, which would certainly represent amazing progress during the 15 years, the necessary crude birth rate would still be around 52 per thousand, a level already high compared with the 45 per thousand birth rate estimated for the country in 1955–1957.[27]

We can at least argue with some assurance that, for the country as a whole, the balance

[21] Information transmitted verbally by the Office of the HCR in Kinshasa.
[22] *1967 Socio-Demographic Survey*, "Rapport General," p. 40.
[23] *1970 Administrative Census*, March 8, 1969.
[24] See *Ordonnance-loi* No. 70/083 of November 30, 1970, providing amnesty for Zaïriens who had participated in activities held to jeopardize the safety of the state between July 1, 1960 and November 30, 1970. See *Le Progrès* newspaper of December 10, 1970 and of January 13, 18, 20, and 26, 1971.

[25] See declaration of President Mobutu to reporters in Dakar, *L'Etoile* newspaper, February 17, 1971, p. 2.
[26] *1967 Socio-Demographic Survey*, "Rapport General," pp. 63–68.
[27] See Romaniuk, "The Demography of the Democratic Republic," p. 339.

of births over deaths has considerably increased even if it is not possible to state precisely the level of either parameter. And we can agree with the National Bank that the rate of natural growth suggested by the 1970 administrative census "would be at the limit of physiological possibility."[28]

## REGIONAL GROWTH

The demography of Zaïre offers a very varied range of situations. The rate of natural increase in the years 1955–1957 showed great disparities between provinces and between districts, ranging from a minimum annual growth rate of −6.4 per thousand in Bas Uélé to a maximum rate of 46.0 per thousand in Lubumbashi.[29] Confining our attention to the provinces, three of them were growing rather slowly by African standards: Orientale, 0.86 percent per thousand; Kasai Oriental, 1.34; and Equateur, 1.57. Four other provinces kept close to the national average of 2.0 percent: Kasai Occidental, 2.08; Bandundu, 2.20; Kongo Central, 2.30; Kivu, 2.37. In contrast, natural increase in the Katanga was far higher with a rate of 3.01 percent.

In 1970, the 4.2 percent growth rate included natural increase as well as migration. No population declines were found any longer but the ranking of provinces according to growth rates had changed (see Table 29.6).

The Equateur Province increases at a moderate rate (2.66 percent). This province has been almost entirely free from disturbances. The Tshuapa District seems to have regained a new vitality.

The three provinces immediately above it in population growth were the center of the most important disorders since the independence: Bandundu, with the Kwilu rebellion (2.70 percent); Orientale (2.73 percent) and Kivu (3.47 percent), with the 1964–1965

rebellions and the incursion of mercenaries in 1967. The Kwilu District (in particular Bandundu) shows for the 1959–1970 period an average annual growth rate representing only 87 percent of the 1955–1957 natural growth rate. The Gungu Territory is the one which seems to have suffered the most serious demographic aftereffects while the population of the Idiofa Territory shows an annual growth close to its 1955–1957 annual growth.[30]

The Katanga secession took place at the beginning of the ten years of independence. It was important from the political point of view, but occasioned fewer deaths than the rebellions. The Katanga shows, for the 1959–1970 period, an annual total growth rate of 4.41 percent.

From the figures of the 1970 administrative census, the two Kasai provinces have enjoyed the most rapid growth in Zaïre since 1959. It must be remembered that already during the year which preceded political independence, this region had been shaken by tribal frictions which had caused large population movements as well as sporadic massacres. This situation had jeopardized the efficiency of the 1959 administrative census in these regions. It seems probable that at that period the Kasai population had been underestimated. This would explain at least partially the extremely rapid average rate of growth claimed for this region. The shifting of the population during the period is appreciated when we compare the natural increase estimated for each district in 1955–1957 with the total change between 1956 and 1959. In Kasai Occidental, natural increase is higher than population growth, evidencing a migratory loss; on the other hand, in Kasai Oriental, population growth exceeds natural increase, as a result of the return of the Baluba to their native region. But, after 1959, the rate of growth of the two regions is similar. It is in the Kasai provinces that the recent demographic figures are hardest to interpret.

[28] Banque Nationale du Zaïre, *Rapport Annuel 1969–1970*, p. 81.

[29] See Romaniuk, "The Demography of the Democratic Republic," p. 339; and *1955–1957 Demographic Survey*, general table, p. 185.

[30] Leon de Saint Moulin, "Les Statistiques Démographiques en R.D.C.," *Congo-Afrique (Kinshasa)*, X, 47 (August–September 1970), p. 6.

## REGIONAL DISTRIBUTION

For many years, the country has been divided administratively into six large provinces of unequal demographic importance, for contrasting densities mean that populations are not proportional to provincials areas. There has been very little relative change in this regard since 1939 (see Table 29.4).

TABLE 29.4
Percent of the total population at various dates and the total area in each province

| Province | 1939 | 1949 | 1959 | 1970 | Area |
|---|---|---|---|---|---|
| Leopoldville (Kinshasa)[a] | 20.4 | 22.0 | 23.9 | 25.1 | 15.4 |
| Kivu | 12.8 | 14.2 | 16.8 | 15.5 | 11.1 |
| Katanga | 10.1 | 11.6 | 12.5 | 12.7 | 21.2 |
| Equateur | 15.3 | 14.4 | 13.2 | 11.2 | 17.1 |
| Orientale | 22.8 | 20.7 | 18.1 | 15.5 | 21.5 |
| Kasai[b] | 18.7 | 17.2 | 15.7 | 19.9 | 13.8 |
| Total | 100.0 | 100.0 | 100.0 | 100.0 | 100.0 |

SOURCES: 1939–1959: Services of AIMO (Kinshasa); 1970: Administrative Census, Ministry of the Interior. (See appendix to this chapter.)
[a] Regroups the present Kongo Central and Bandundu provinces, as well as the city of Kinshasa.
[b] Regroups the present Kasai Oriental and Kasai Occidental provinces.

A comparison up to 1959 of the provincial share of population over time shows that three of these six regions are absorbing a higher and higher proportion of the total Zaïrien population whereas the proportion in the other three is declining. The most recent figures reveal a change in the trend of the relative importance of the Kivu and of the Kasai.

By 1970 population density of the whole country was 9 persons per square mile for the *de facto* population. This overall density is low by African and world standards, although not by those of Central Africa. None of the factors of explanation, such as the climatic zones, the inequality of the relief, the distribution of the forests, the distribution of traditional cultures, and the intensity of the contact with the industrialized world, explains in a really satisfying way this general characteristic.[31]

If we disregard small-area variations, extensive zones of similar population density appear. The densest area of occupation stretches along the great lakes (beside the eastern mountains) from Uvira to Aru, with a thinning out toward Beni-Butembo. A belt of high density stretches latitudinally from the Atlantic to north Katanga with peaks first in the Bas Congo and Cataracts districts, and then in the Kwilu, Lulua, and Kabinda districts (the 5th and 6th south parallels). Other dense areas in the northern part of the country are found mainly around Gemena, Bumba, and Isiro (3d and 4th north parallels). These aspects of the territorial distribution have scarcely changed since 1956.[32]

It has been noted[33] that the density zones in Zaïre correspond neither with the areas of greatest economical potential, nor with the network of natural and man-made means of communication. The Katanga, a geological miracle in its richness, displays the lowest population density. If we except part of the Kasai provinces, the railroads, built to join the Congo River with the important centers of economic activity, cross regions with few people. The main tributary of the Congo River, the Kasai, does not touch the populated zone of the Kwilu but runs parallel to it at a distance. Finally, the immense Lualaba-Congo River only crosses really dense population zones between Kinshasa and the ocean, the only stretch where navigation is impossible.

## INTERNAL MIGRATION

The 1970 census has as yet released no data which can be used to assess internal migration.

[31] See Pierre Gourou, "La Densité de la Population Rurale au Congo Belge," *Académie Royale des Sciences Coloniales, Classe des Sciences Naturelles et Médicales, Mémoires,* no. 8, new series, 2d edition (Brussels, 1955), p. 168, map.
[32] See Romaniuk, "The Demography of the Democratic Republic," pp. 253–57.
[33] Fernand Bezy, "Problèmes Structurels de l'Économie Congolaise," *Nauwelaerts* (Paris-Louvain, 1957), pp. 30–34.

One of the first ways of measuring internal migrations will be to compare the *de jure* and the *de facto* populations. Some of the most important data to be released are those distinguishing the enumerated into permanent or temporary residents. The population categories therefore used for this analysis are the following:

(1) Population enumerated in a usual residence without a temporary residence elsewhere

(2) Population enumerated in a usual residence with a temporary residence elsewhere

(3) Population enumerated in a temporary residence with a certificate of registration of more than three years

(4) Population enumerated in a temporary residence where they have stayed less than three years

(5) Visitors and transients

The census instructions are that the first three categories are to be classified as being enumerated in their places of usual permanent residence, while the last two are to be classified as being in temporary residence.[34]

Since the census wished to include *de facto* population,[35] this latter category can only be included in the totals at the place of the temporary residence, even if the locality of usual residence is sent a duplicate of the census card of this population[36] before proceeding with the manual count. Insofar as this principle has been applied, there has been no double count and the explanation for the explosive growth in certain regions must be sought elsewhere.

No one denies that the rebellions and the other disorders which marked the first years of independence were the cause of major population migrations within the provinces.[37] However, there has been no insurrection since 1967, and even that one was caused by

a few hundred soldiers under the instigation of foreign mercenaries. Therefore, many temporary refugees in the Orientale Province, Kivu, and Kwilu had already returned home at the time of the 1970 census. Not all have done so, since beside the ones who were granted amnesty and who came back from abroad relying on the word of the head of state (*supra:* note 24), we also noted, coming out of the jungle, nationals from north Katanga or from Kwilu who had never left the country, but still submitted themselves to census enumeration.[38] While the events have exercised a particular influence on the population movements in the interior of the country, they have contributed also, together with the usual economic factors, to the migration of rural inhabitants to urban centers.

## URBANIZATION

In the course of the decades which preceded independence, it was customary to classify the population in two categories: the ones who remained in their traditional environments were described as "traditional" (*coutumière*); the ones who emerged from such a life to dwell in newly created localities were described as "nontraditional" (*extra-coutumière*).

The 1955–1957 demographic survey divided the population into three groups according to residence in an urban area, a rural area, or a mixed urban/rural area, this last being characterized by a population below 2,000 engaged predominantly in nonagricultural activities.[39] This threefold division fits in quite well with older divisions if we regroup the mixed and the urban populations into a single class.

The low density of the rural population could have been regarded as constituting a safety valve for the rapid population growth if the growth had not simultaneously produced

---

[34] *1970 Administrative Census*, February 4, 1969, p. 3.

[35] *Ibid.*, April 30, 1968, p. 2.

[36] *Ibid.*, September 8, 1968, article 8; March 8, 1969, p. 6, c and d.

[37] Benoît Verhaegen, "Rébellions au Congo," Kinshasa, IRES and INEP, undated, I, p. 568; II (Maniema), p. 830.

[38] Examples in *Le Progrès* newspaper of January 13, 1971, and of February 1, 1971.

[39] *1955–1957 Demographic Survey*, general table, p. 19. Only exception: the labor camps of agricultural workers employed in European plantations appear in the mixed population.

TABLE 29.5

Percent of "nontraditional" population in each province

| Province | 1939 | 1949 | 1959 |
|---|---|---|---|
| Kinshasa | 8.0 | 19.4 | 26.9 |
| Equateur | 9.0 | 15.0 | 20.5 |
| Orientale | 14.2 | 21.5 | 23.1 |
| Kivu | 8.4 | 18.9 | 17.0 |
| Katanga | 14.3 | 27.5 | 33.3 |
| Kasai | 3.5 | 9.3 | 13.3 |
| Whole country | 9.4 | 18.3 | 22.3 |

SOURCE: Services of AIMO, Kinshasa.

an accelerated rural exodus. This phenomenon is clearly shown by the rise in nontraditional proportions in the six former provinces of Zaïre between 1939 and 1959.

The census data for 1970 on area of residence are as yet available only for the 11 main cities. In 1959 these centers had 1,118,284 inhabitants, or 8 percent of the country's population and 36 percent of the nontraditional population. By 1970, these same cities housed 3,241,777 persons or 15 percent of the Zaïrien population. If the proportion that city residents form of all nontraditional population was the same in 1970 as in 1959, this would mean that approximately 9 million persons or 46 percent of the population are living today outside their customary villages. But there is no definite evidence permitting us to assert that the population of all the nontraditional centers has increased as rapidly as that of the major cities; in fact it seems likely that the intermediate centers have lost in favor of a growing concentration.

It might be expected that the ratio of nontraditional population to total population would be highest in the low-density regions. This expectation is not justified in Kongo Central where the high rural densities have not prevented the growth of important agglomerations such as Matadi, Thysville, Boma, and Tshela, but the ratio of the nontraditional to the total population is very high in the sparsely populated regions. However, it would not have attained these levels if there had not been an almost total

coincidence between the sparsely populated regions and both the main centers of economic development and the network of the means of transportation.[40]

The formation of population agglomerations and the urban concentrations which dominate them has been occurring to some degree since the beginning of colonization. By 1950 the centers were exerting an increasingly powerful attraction on the rural population. This was a spontaneous development for the city represented not only occasions for paid work and hence money for purchases, but at the same time a favorable occasion to spend the money. Furthermore, the city provided freely or very cheaply a series of public services and establishments important to modern life: schools, public health services, medical care, spare-time activities, etc. Finally, the urban centers had become a symbol of getting on in the world and of individual freedom.

Toward the end of the colonial period, irresistible social pressure overcame the administrative and police barriers meant to protect the cities and their peripheries against the influx of rural populations. After independence, the fall in industrial activities and in the number of jobs offered by the European population was offset by the incredible inflation in the public service in terms both of the number of civil servants and the amount of their salaries. This new income was redistributed to a large clientele of relatives and others coming from the villages to escape the poverty or to benefit from the windfall. This general situation has continued, with variations from time to time according to the economic situation.[41]

The growth of the cities (see Table 29.6) differs enormously from one city to the other, not only in terms of average rates but also in propensity to fluctuate. Bukavu and Kisangani

[40] Bezy, "Problèmes Structurels," p. 33.
[41] C. Hoyoux and J. Houyoux, "Les Conditions de Vie dans Soixante Familles à Kinshasa" *Cahiers Economiques et Sociaux*, IRES, VIII, 1 (Lovanium, March 1970), 99–132, see the heading "Cadeaux" (gifts) in the structure of the expenditures of each socioprofessional category.

TABLE 29.6

Population, density, and growth 1959–1970, by district

| District or Town | Population | | | | Area (sq. miles) | Density (per sq. mile) | | Average Annual Natural Increase 55–57 (percent) | Total Increase 59–70 (percent) | Doubling Time (years) |
|---|---|---|---|---|---|---|---|---|---|---|
| | 1959 Number | 1959 Percent | 1970 Number | 1970 Percent | | 1959 | 1970 | | | |
| Kinshasa | 403,310 | 2.9 | 1,308,361a | 6.1 | 778a | 518.0 | 1,680.0 | 4.2 | 118.5 | 5.8 |
| Town of Matadi | 60,361 | 0.4 | 110,436 | 0.5 | 42 | 1,421.1 | 2,600.4 | — | 58.7 | 11.8 |
| Bas-Congo District | 358,891 | 2.6 | 522,053 | 2.4 | 5,525 | 65.0 | 94.5 | 2.2 | 36.1 | 19.2 |
| Cataracts District | 560,016 | 4.0 | 886,550a | 4.1 | 18,320a | 30.6 | 48.4 | 2.4 | 45.7 | 15.2 |
| *Bas-Zaïre Province* | 979,268 | 7.0 | 1,519,039a | 7.0 | 23,888a | 40.9 | 63.4 | 2.3 | 43.1 | 16.1 |
| Town of Bandundu | 11,500 | 0.1 | 74,467 | 0.3 | 86 | 134.2 | 868.7 | — | 193.1 | 3.6 |
| Town of Kikwit | 16,126 | 0.1 | 111,960 | 0.5 | 77b | 208.8 | 1,449.9 | — | 200.9 | 3.4 |
| Inongo District | 305,488 | 2.2 | 429,465 | 2.0 | 49,129 | 6.2 | 8.8 | 2.5 | 33.3 | 20.8 |
| Kwilu District | 1,175,805 | 8.4 | 1,370,454 | 6.3 | 30,123b | 39.1 | 45.6 | 2.1 | 18.8 | 37.0 |
| Kwango District | 445,372 | 3.2 | 614,210 | 2.8 | 34,739 | 13.0 | 17.6 | 2.2 | 29.3 | 23.7 |
| *Bandundu Province* | 1,954,291 | 14.0 | 2,600,556 | 12.0 | 114,154 | 17.1 | 22.8 | 2.2 | 27.0 | 25.6 |
| Town of Mbandaka | 51,397 | 0.4 | 107,910 | 0.5 | 178 | 289.3 | 607.6 | — | 73.6 | 9.4 |
| Equateur District | 277,521 | 2.0 | 340,823 | 1.6 | 39,939 | 7.0 | 8.5 | 1.5 | 19.5 | 35.6 |
| Tshuapa District | 405,360 | 2.9 | 466,286 | 2.2 | 51,335 | 7.8 | 9.1 | 0.4 | 13.4 | 51.9 |
| Mongala District | 541,759 | 3.9 | 739,813 | 3.4 | 39,192 | 13.7 | 18.9 | 2.3 | 29.9 | 23.2 |
| Ubangi District | 567,156 | 4.1 | 776,980 | 3.6 | 25,068 | 22.5 | 31.1 | 2.0 | 30.1 | 23.1 |
| *Equateur Province* | 1,843,523 | 13.2 | 2,431,812 | 11.2 | 155,712 | 11.9 | 15.5 | 1.6 | 26.6 | 26.1 |
| Town of Kisangani | 126,930 | 0.9 | 229,596 | 1.1 | 737 | 172.2 | 311.3 | — | 57.6 | 12.0 |
| Haut-Congo District | 566,936 | 4.1 | 714,545 | 3.3 | 76,315 | 7.5 | 9.3 | 1.4 | 22.1 | 31.3 |
| Bas-Uélé District | 496,446 | 3.6 | 588,768 | 2.7 | 57,271 | 8.5 | 9.8 | 0.6 | 16.3 | 42.6 |
| Haut-Uélé District | 624,383 | 4.5 | 795,619 | 3.7 | 34,627 | 18.1 | 23.1 | 0.06 | 23.2 | 29.9 |
| Ituri District | 710,697 | 5.1 | 1,027,891 | 4.8 | 25,351 | 28.0 | 40.7 | — | 35.5 | 19.5 |
| *Haut-Zaïre Province* | 2,525,392 | 18.1 | 3,356,419 | 15.5 | 194,301 | 13.0 | 17.4 | 0.9 | 27.3 | 25.4 |
| Town of Bukavu | 60,850 | 0.4 | 134,861 | 0.6 | 23 | 2,626.8 | 5,821.5 | — | 78.1 | 8.9 |
| Nord-Kivu District | 935,678 | 6.7 | 1,473,380 | 6.8 | 22,997 | 40.7 | 64.0 | 3.1 | 43.9 | 15.8 |
| Sud-Kivu District | 876,221 | 6.3 | 1,130,676 | 5.2 | 25,015 | 35.0 | 45.3 | 2.2 | 24.4 | 28.4 |
| Maniema District | 471,629 | 3.4 | 622,966 | 2.9 | 51,062 | 9.3 | 12.2 | 1.1 | 26.7 | 26.0 |
| *Kivu Province* | 2,344,378 | 16.8 | 3,361,883 | 15.5 | 99,097 | 23.6 | 33.9 | 2.4 | 34.7 | 20.0 |
| Town of Lubumbashi | 184,126 | 1.3 | 318,000 | 1.5 | 288 | 638.2 | 1,102.6 | 4.6c | 53.0 | 13.1 |
| Town of Likasa | 80,212 | 0.6 | 146,394 | 0.7 | 91 | 884.0 | 1,613.6 | 4.4c | 58.5 | 11.8 |
| Tanganika District | 469,697 | 3.4 | 696,363 | 3.2 | 52,134 | 9.1 | 13.5 | 3.0 | 37.9 | 18.3 |
| Haut Lomami District | 375,345 | 2.7 | 602,368 | 2.8 | 41,778 | 9.1 | 14.5 | 2.2 | 45.8 | 15.1 |
| Haut Katanga District | 278,696 | 2.0 | 394,316 | 1.8 | 50,750 | 5.4 | 7.8 | 3.5 | 33.4 | 20.8 |
| Lualaba District | 355,657 | 2.5 | 596,273 | 2.8 | 46,837 | 7.5 | 12.7 | 2.9 | 50.1 | 13.8 |
| *Shaba Province* | 1,743,733 | 12.5 | 2,753,714 | 12.7 | 191,878 | 9.1 | 14.2 | 3.0 | 44.1 | 15.7 |
| Town of Mbuji Mayi | 39,038 | 0.3 | 256,154 | 1.2 | 25 | 1,579.9 | 10,366.2 | — | 193.9 | 3.6 |
| Kabinda District | 490,150 | 3.5 | 1,118,725 | 5.2 | 24,641 | 19.9 | 45.3 | 1.2 | 81.1 | 8.5 |
| Sankuru District | 414,186 | 3.0 | 497,352 | 2.3 | 40,282 | 10.4 | 12.4 | 1.4 | 17.5 | 39.7 |
| *Kasai Oriental Province* | 943,374 | 6.8 | 1,872,231 | 8.7 | 64,948 | 14.5 | 28.7 | 1.3 | 66.9 | 10.3 |
| Town of Luluabourg | 121,113 | 0.9 | 428,960 | 2.0 | 146 | 829.8 | 2,939.1 | — | 127.0 | 5.5 |
| Kasai District | 505,945 | 3.6 | 833,468 | 3.9 | 36,923 | 13.7 | 22.5 | 2.4 | 48.3 | 14.3 |
| Lulua District | 619,843 | 4.4 | 1,171,433 | 5.4 | 23,536 | 26.4 | 49.7 | 1.7 | 62.0 | 11.2 |
| *Kasai Occidental Province* | 1,246,901 | 8.9 | 2,433,861 | 11.3 | 60,605 | 20.5 | 40.1 | 2.1 | 65.2 | 10.6 |
| *Zaïre* | 13,984,170 | 100.0 | 21,637,876 | 100.0 | 905,361 | 15.5 | 23.8 | 1.9 | 42.1 | 16.5 |

Sources: Statistics relative to the year 1959 (annual report)—indigenous and nonindigenous combined. 1970 administrative census (July 31) (See appendix to this chapter.) Areas: "Repertoire des Superficies des Provinces, Districts, Territoires et Villes de la République Démocratique du Congo," (Kinshasa, March 1, 1970). Romaniuk, "The Demography of the Democratic Republic of the Congo," in Brass et al., *The Demography of Tropical Africa* (Princeton, N.J.: Princeton University Press, 1968), p. 339.
a The territory of the "*commune*" of Maluku (3,069 square miles) has been joined to the Cataracts District.
b Nonofficial estimation of the area of the town territory—detached from that of the Kwilu District.
c 1955–1957 demographic survey, general table, p. 53.

fluctuated considerably before resuming, after 1967, a new and continuous spurt which brought them to their present size.[42] Kikwit received a large increment to its population by serving as a refuge for the people from the southeastern part of the Kwilu who were running away from the rebels. Mbuji-Mayi has grown richer with the Baluba being driven back from the Kasai and Katanga regions. The growth of Luluabourg is more

[42] The date of arrival of the residents, obtained during current surveys, will tell us more about present change.

difficult to explain. However, the neighboring territories also show very rapid growth.[43]

There is as yet little information on the relative contributions of rural-urban migration and urban natural increase to urban population growth. However, births in maternity hospitals and burials in cemeteries are regularly calculated,[44] although their

[43] de Saint Moulin, "Les Statistiques Démographiques," p. 11.
[44] "Bulletin Trimestriel des Statistiques Générales de la République Démocratique du Congo," *Institut National de la Statistique* (*ONRD*).

value for the calculation of the natural increase must still be evaluated. Vital registration data are too incomplete for use.

There are better data from Kinshasa thanks to the 1967 sociodemographic survey. The analysis of natural increase favors a crude birth rate of approximately 56 per thousand and a crude death rate of approximately 11 per thousand, yielding a rate of natural increase around 4.5 percent.[45] Nearly 47 percent of the Kinshasa people were born there, and, among these, only 4 percent are more than 25 years old. The remainder of the Kinshasa growth can be explained by migration (at a rate of 6.5 percent per year). In the last few years, migration from the nearest district (Cataracts District) has slackened while the flow from the more remote regions (Kwango-Kwilu and the remainder of the country) is growing stronger.[46]

## SEX DISTRIBUTION

The sex ratios of 94 males per hundred females recorded by the 1955–1957 demographic survey for the whole of the country did not seem abnormal in view of the low sex ratio at birth and the differential in mortality by sex. The 1970 administrative census claimed a national sex ratio slightly closer to parity.

Regional differences are considerable. Bandundu remains the province where the male ratio is the lowest. One should not blame the rebellion, for the Kwango District, which has not been troubled, exhibits the lowest sex ratio (88). Inside the Kwilu District, the territories of Gungu (90) and of Idiofa (94), the main center of the rebellion, exceed the territories of Bagata (85) and of Masi-Manimba (87) where the rebellion did not penetrate. The rural exodus from the province, particularly toward Kinshasa, constitutes a more plausible explanation of this situation.[47] This last factor is supposed to

have been important in Kongo Central as well, mainly in the Cataracts District (89).

This could be confirmed by the difference between the sex ratios for adults and children. The increase in the sex ratio of those over 18 years in relation to the one of the younger population means either that differential mortality increases rapidly with advance in age, or that male numbers are reduced by emigration, or perhaps that some adolescents were classified as adults. In Zaïre, provincial sex ratios for all ages are lowest where the difference between the ratios of children and adults is the most pronounced. Now, the Bandundu and the Kongo Central provinces, and in this last one the Cataracts District in particular, show a larger disparity between the male ratio of the age groups than anywhere else in Zaïre; thus it seems that these differences should be attributed to the adult male exodus.

The sex ratio has moved toward parity in the towns under the combined effect of the rising birth rate and the immigration of family groups. The example of the capital is extremely revealing: "Kinshasa is no longer a city with a strong proportion of adult immigrants."[48] In 1967, for all ages, there were found to be 110 men for 100 women, whereas there were 135 in 1955.[49]

## AGE STRUCTURE

In all African countries, where ages are known with precision only for part of the population, certain characteristic distortions creep into the age distribution.[50] It is particularly noticeable that many girls are considered as adult women because they have borne children, thus appearing to reduce the number under 18 years.

In 1970, the ratio of children to adults in all provinces was lower for the females than for males (Table 29.7). In 1959, the apparent difference was greater still. The passing of

[45] *1967 Socio-Demographic Survey*, "Rapport Général," p. 68.
[46] Leon de Saint Moulin and Maurice Ducreux, "La phénomène Urbaine à Kinshasa," *Etudes Congolaises*, Kinshasa, XII, 4 (October–December, 1969), 125–27.
[7] *Ibid.*, p. 124.

[48] *Ibid.*, p. 125.
[49] *1967 Socio-Demographic Survey*, "Rapport Général," p. 33.
[50] See Etienne van de Walle, "Characteristics of African Demographic Data," in Brass et al., *Demography of Tropical Africa*, pp. 13–52.

TABLE 29.7

Sex ratios and proportions under 18 years of age by province, 1959 and 1970

| Province | Year | Population over 18 Years | | Population under 18 Years | | Sex Ratios (males per 100 females) | | | Percent under 18 Years | | |
|---|---|---|---|---|---|---|---|---|---|---|---|
| | | M | F | M | F | Over 18 | Under 18 | All ages | M | F | M & F |
| Kinshasa | 1959 | 108,483 | 83,606 | 92,788 | 95,904 | 129.8 | 96.8 | 112.1 | 46.1 | 53.4 | 49.6 |
| | 1970 | 358,864 | 261,429 | 354,134 | 348,612 | 137.3 | 101.6 | 116.9 | 49.7 | 57.1 | 53.1 |
| Bas-Zaïre | 1959 | 209,656 | 245,135 | 239,955 | 235,657 | 85.5 | 101.8 | 93.5 | 53.4 | 49.0 | 51.1 |
| | 1970 | 303,877 | 374,848 | 417,711 | 407,925 | 81.1 | 102.4 | 92.2 | 57.9 | 52.1 | 54.9 |
| Bandundu | 1959 | 438,731 | 572,220 | 503,666 | 475,339 | 76.7 | 106.0 | 90.0 | 53.4 | 45.4 | 49.2 |
| | 1970 | 545,343 | 686,104 | 698,232 | 670,877 | 79.5 | 104.1 | 91.6 | 56.1 | 49.4 | 52.6 |
| Equateur | 1959 | 508,277 | 580,363 | 391,268 | 356,630 | 87.6 | 109.7 | 96.0 | 43.5 | 38.1 | 40.7 |
| | 1970 | 602,920 | 699,554 | 576,264 | 553,074 | 86.2 | 104.2 | 94.1 | 48.9 | 44.2 | 46.4 |
| Haut-Zaïre | 1959 | 780,356 | 783,516 | 489,552 | 452,974 | 99.6 | 108.1 | 102.7 | 38.6 | 36.6 | 37.6 |
| | 1970 | 896,932 | 1,040,440 | 728,756 | 690,291 | 86.2 | 105.6 | 93.9 | 44.8 | 39.9 | 42.3 |
| Kivu | 1959 | 563,581 | 615,564 | 585,079 | 565,038 | 91.6 | 103.5 | 97.3 | 50.9 | 47.9 | 49.4 |
| | 1970 | 755,703 | 858,083 | 875,734 | 872,363 | 88.1 | 100.4 | 94.3 | 53.7 | 50.2 | 52.0 |
| Shaba | 1959 | 438,891 | 468,651 | 412,180 | 389,937 | 93.6 | 105.7 | 99.1 | 48.4 | 45.4 | 46.9 |
| | 1970 | 645,416 | 701,309 | 715,112 | 691,877 | 92.0 | 103.4 | 97.7 | 52.6 | 49.7 | 51.1 |
| Kasai Oriental | 1959 | 243,141 | 287,953 | 206,821 | 191,631 | 84.4 | 107.9 | 93.8 | 46.0 | 40.0 | 42.9 |
| | 1970 | 418,591 | 500,632 | 480,477 | 482,531 | 83.6 | 101.7 | 92.4 | 53.4 | 48.6 | 50.9 |
| Kasai Occidental | 1959 | 317,870 | 358,881 | 301,650 | 273,477 | 88.6 | 110.3 | 98.0 | 48.7 | 43.2 | 45.9 |
| | 1970 | 473,178 | 548,551 | 708,692 | 703,440 | 86.3 | 100.7 | 94.4 | 60.0 | 56.2 | 58.0 |
| Zaïre | 1959 | 3,608,986 | 3,995,889 | 3,222,959 | 3,036,587 | 90.3 | 106.1 | 97.1 | 47.2 | 43.2 | 45.1 |
| | 1970 | 5,000,824 | 5,670,950 | 5,555,112 | 5,410,990 | 88.2 | 102.7 | 95.3 | 52.6 | 48.8 | 50.7 |

SOURCES: 1959—Statistics relative to the year 1959, AIMO, Léopoldville (nationals + neighboring Africans). 1970—Administrative Census, July 31, 1970 (nationals + foreigners). (See appendix to this chapter.)

some women under 18 years of age into the adult classification was explicitly authorized in the 1970 census instructions.[51]

The proportion of young people in the population may well explain the part played by the "youths" in the different political parties since 1960 and in the social movements which appeared later on. Observers have been struck by the extreme youth of the *simba* rebels of the years 1963–1965. The increase in the proportion of children is occurring everywhere, as much in the interior

[51] *1970 Administrative Census*, April 31, 1968, p. 5: "The young woman, married, divorced, or widow, even if she has not reached the age of 18, is considered as having reached adulthood."

as in the cities. For large towns, the increase could be explained by greater immigration than in the past of already formed families. But this phenomenon is at the same time observed in the rural areas of emigration. One may see in this change, much more clearly than in the increase of the volume of the population, an indication, not only of declining child mortality, but of a rise in the birth rate in the last ten years.

## POPULATION AND THE SPREAD OF EDUCATION

The effort put into school education in Zaïre has always been considerable. Since independence, it has been more strongly oriented toward the development of secondary teaching and the reaching of equality between the sexes at all levels.

The results are encouraging. From 1961–1962 to 1968–1969 the number of pupils in elementary classes increased from 820,000 to 2,666,034 at an average annual growth rate of 5.6 percent; the students in secondary classes increased from 57,000 to 222,196 during the same period at an average annual growth rate of 21.5 percent. In 1961–1962, there were 38 girls per hundred boys in primary school and 14 in secondary school. In 1968–1969, these ratios were 54 and 19 respectively.[52]

In 1961–1962, 3 universities and 29 establishments for higher nonuniversity education contained a total of 1,379 students. In 1969–1970 the number of students increased to 10,212, exhibiting an average annual growth rate of 28.5 percent.[53]

These results were obtained because of an increasing budgetary share awarded to national education.[54] The share of education

expenditure "is set for 1970 at some 25 percent of total resources. If we add the private expenses of parents and those of the local authorities, as well as the cost paid for by foreign technical assistance, we note that the country allocates to education more than 5 percent of its gross national product."[55]

## PRACTICES INFLUENCING FERTILITY

The information existing on this subject is scattered in a whole series of anthropological and medical publications. We mainly use here the excellent summary prepared by Romaniuk.[56] For the very recent period, no systematic study has to our knowledge been made.[57]

TRADITIONAL PROCEDURES. The Zaïrien woman was traditionally subjected to numerous *sexual taboos*, for reasons of menstruation, pregnancy, nursing, and even for motives remote from sexual relations and childbearing such as a death, a collective hunt, a fishing expedition, and so on.

[52] Figures drawn from *Statistiques Scolaires* (annual since 1961–1962), Zaïre, National Education Ministry.
[53] The figures on the number of students are drawn from "Etudes Supérieures en République Démocratique du Congo," *Catholic Education Office* (Kinshasa, 1970), p. 76.
[54] *Bilan, 1965–1970*, complete edition, p. 250.

[55] Banque Nationale du Zaïre, *Rapport Annuel 1969–1970* p. 83.
[56] Romaniuk, *La Fécondité des Populations Congolaises*, chap. IX.
[57] Certain interesting information appears in the answers given to a pilot survey in Kinshasa, *Institut National de la Statistique*, working documents, end of 1968.

TABLE 29.8
Sex ratios and proportions under 18 years of age for the main cities (1970)[a]

| Cities | Population over 18 Years | | Population under 18 Years | | Sex Ratios (males per 100 females) | | | Percent under 18 Years, 1958 | | | |
|---|---|---|---|---|---|---|---|---|---|---|---|
| | M | F | M | F | Over 18 | Under 18 | All ages | M | F | M & F | M & F |
| Matadi | 24,169 | 20,716 | 33,416 | 32,135 | 116.7 | 104.0 | 109.0 | 58.0 | 60.8 | 59.4 | 49.6 |
| Bandundu | 17,946 | 15,978 | 20,051 | 20,492 | 112.3 | 97.8 | 104.2 | 52.8 | 56.2 | 54.4 | 53.3 |
| Kikwit | 28,338 | 21,452 | 33,033 | 29,137 | 132.1 | 113.4 | 121.3 | 53.8 | 57.6 | 55.5 | 50.0 |
| Mbandaka | 27,920 | 26,357 | 28,003 | 25,630 | 105.9 | 109.3 | 107.6 | 50.1 | 49.3 | 49.7 | 38.3 |
| Kisangani | 58,963 | 60,292 | 57,163 | 53,178 | 97.8 | 107.5 | 102.3 | 49.2 | 46.9 | 48.1 | 40.6 |
| Bukavu | 30,357 | 27,008 | 38,557 | 38,938 | 112.4 | 99.0 | 104.5 | 55.9 | 59.0 | 57.5 | 57.4 |
| Lubumbashi | 77,875 | 65,946 | 90,199 | 83,980 | 118.1 | 107.4 | 112.5 | 53.7 | 56.0 | 54.8 | 52.1 |
| Likasi | 33,353 | 30,514 | 41,661 | 40,866 | 109.3 | 101.9 | 105.1 | 55.5 | 57.3 | 56.4 | 50.2 |
| Mbuji Mayi | 59,750 | 57,312 | 69,629 | 69,463 | 104.3 | 100.2 | 102.1 | 53.8 | 54.8 | 54.3 | 48.2 |
| Luluabourg | 87,854 | 94,753 | 123,103 | 123,250 | 92.7 | 99.9 | 96.8 | 58.1 | 56.5 | 57.4 | 50.1 |

SOURCES: 1970—Administrative Census, July 31, 1970. (See appendix to this chapter.) 1958—Rapport aux Chambres Législatives.
[a] Kinshasa appears in Table 29.7.

The taboos related to sexual relations and childbearing, which exist to a different degree from tribe to tribe, are practically nonexistent among the breeders of cattle and the consumers of animal milk. The taboos are above all concerned with children's health. They certainly help to produce wider birth spacing, supplementing the effect of prolonged breast feeding. The comparison of the mean interval between successive live births among the Bashi (27.9 months) and the Bandibu (34.7) is significant in this respect. This difference, existing in spite of the similarity of procreative and other behavior patterns is explained apparently by the different attitudes adopted toward post-natal abstinence. In Kinshasa, the interval has been declining and was in 1960 already down to $26\frac{1}{2}$ months.[58]

The death of a father, a mother, a chief, a spouse, or a child entails substantial periods of compulsory abstinence. Even if this taboo continues to be observed to the same degree, it will be enforced on increasingly fewer occasions with the diminution of mortality.

*Abortion* is traditionally operated by the decoction of various plants and roots administered orally or internally in the vagina. Mechanical methods are less popular. Abortion has most often been the act of married women, usually in the spirit of reprisals against their husbands or husbands' families. It has also been practiced to avoid the severe social sanctions attached to pre-matrimonial or adulterous pregnancies in certain ethnic groups.

Traditional life also knew of *contraception*. It was practiced for example to avoid childbirth dreaded by very young girls.[59] Three types of techniques were particularly employed:

(1) The occlusion, already found among the Bapindi and the Bambunda before World War I[60] (achieved by the use of a plug made of fabric or cotton among the Budja, of a rolled leaf among the Azande, etc.)

(2) The expulsion of the sperm either by vaginal washing (decoction of leaves, plant juice, etc , although similar washings with an essentially hygienic aim, but capable of producing contraceptive or even abortive effects, sometimes unknown to the users, must be pointed out), or in certain regions, by mechanical maneuvers (striking in the back or nervo-muscular movements)

(3) *Coitus interruptus*

Generally speaking, the sexual taboos traditionally constituted the most potent and most widespread form of birth control in Zaïre. Abortion and especially contraception were used only occasionally, and their incidence on fertility cannot be measured in our present state of knowledge. When motivation is present, the means used are sometimes inefficient; on the other hand, certain practices are accompanied among certain unmotivated persons by restrictive but unsuspected effects on fertility.

RECENT CHANGES. New motivations for fertility restriction are appearing and new and more adequate means of regulation are being sought. The concern for the mother's health is appearing beside the older concern for that of the child. The latter continues to be strongly felt by women and is the main reason that two-year or more spacing between births is considered desirable.

The observance of postnatal abstinence tends to disappear in the cities, mainly because wives desire to keep their husbands within the limits of strictly monogamous unions. The loosening of the taboos certainly renders an increase in fertility possible. In Luluabourg, for instance, numerous cases of successive annual births have been pointed out. Because of this, women are becoming more interested in modern contraceptive methods (especially pills and IUDS) and in greater use of traditional methods. Men know of condoms, but the extent of their use has not been determined.

The diffusion of the knowledge and of means appropriate to rational birth control is

---

[58] See Romaniuk, *La Fécondité des Populations Congolaises,* pp. 284–285.

[59] See J. Vansina, "La Famille Nucléaire chez les Bashoong," *Africa,* XXVIII, 2 (April 1958), quoted by Romaniuk, *La Fécondité des Populations Congolaises*, p. 290.

[60] See N. E. Himes, *Medical History of Contraception* (New York: Gamut Press, 1963), p. 10.

still today the responsibility of individual doctors, members of the nursing personnel, social workers, or teachers, and the spread of modern contraception has depended on their initiative. It is certain that modern birth control has not yet reached the level where it would have a measurable impact on fertility, even for a specific social group.

Numerous data show the accelerating spread of the awareness of the disadvantages of a too large family with limited resources, especially for those aspiring to high levels of education for the children.

Abortion seems to become more general in urban centers, unless its existence is simply more visible than previously. It is not only the practice of unmarried women, but also of married women overburdened by too close pregnancies or oppressed by the scantiness of resources to satisfy the most basic needs of an already large family. The abortive techniques remain furtive and crafty; the women adopt recently introduced materials: quinine, dagenan, laundry blue, etc. Abortion remains legally prohibited.[61]

The government of Zaïre has not, up until now, taken any official position on the restriction of fertility, either favorable or unfavorable. The legislative measures prohibiting the propagation of abortion and contraception (treated on the same level) go back to 1933.[62] They are being neither pushed nor repealed. Also, although the abolition of the prohibitions is considered as a first condition for the widespread propagation of family planning,[63] contraceptives are being imported and sold, and individual efforts to publicize and assist family planning receive no interference. Public servants and doctors attend without objection meetings or conferences on the subject. Press articles periodically discuss the advantages and drawbacks of birth control. The RTNC[64]

itself broadcasts from time to time programs rather favorable to planned fertility. The absence of an official position is accompanied by the nonexistence of any governmental service specifically charged with family planning.

## CONCLUSION

The use of demographic information was hardly known during the first years of political independence, and the collection of fundamental population data progressed very slowly. The 1970 administrative census has just filled the gap.

The interest and the merits of this survey, which some people said was impossible to realize under the present conditions, must be underlined. For certain cities, districts and territories, the administrative census has confirmed past forecasts or estimates and the figures published have all the guarantees of probability. On the other hand, for others, the figures indicate a large increase, for which we do not always see the explanations in spite of the migratory movements which have occurred.[65]

The interest of the governing circles in demographic data was stimulated, during recent years, by the approach of the 1970 presidential and legislative elections. The last administrative census was taken with the major aim of determining the population of the electoral voting districts to decide on the number of representatives to send, for each region, to the National Assembly, and with the intention of revising the electoral lists.

The government of a country, with a population which has traditionally believed in a high fertility rate and which has so often suffered from almost random declines in the birth rate,[66] cannot but congratulate itself on an increasing volume of citizens which also seems to boost national prestige. The large population revealed in the results of

---

[61] *Penal Code*, Book II, Title VI, section 1, articles 165–166.
[62] *Ibid.*, section IV, article 178.
[63] Henry Levin, "Commercial Distribution of Contraception in Developing Countries," *Demography*, V, 2 (1968).
[64] Radio Télévision Nationale Congolaise.

[65] Banque Nationale du Zaïre, *Rapport Annuel 1969–1970*, p. 81.
[66] See Romaniuk, "L'Aspect Démographique"; "Fécondité et Stérilité"; "La Fécondité des Populations Congolaises," chaps. X and XI.

the census provoked enthusiasm, even if it is recognized that it poses certain problems. Officials generally see in the country's low density an asset for the future and a confirmation that the volume of the population is very low with regard to the potential capacity of the country.

In the more immediate future low density poses the problem of achieving an economic return on the creation of the needed infrastructure in rural regions. The present preoccupations of the authorities are the raising of per capita income, the constant necessity for creating new jobs, and the growing needs for social services (schools, hospitals, housing).[67]

Official optimism is sustained by the general improvement of the economy. The 1965–1970 period was marked by a transition from recession to boom. The comparative trend of economic and demographic growth does not create any worry. Even if it really does average 4.2 percent per annum, population growth is exceeded by the growth of the GDP, which, in real terms, has averaged 5 percent over the last few years.[68] The projected growth rate of the gross national income during the 1970–1980 decade is 6 percent.[69] However, economic development must profit first of all those already living according to the plan for social progress decided by President Mobutu; "It has been necessary, to repair the accumulated ruins, to put you at the service of the economy; during the decade which is beginning, the economy will be the one at the service of man."[70]

### Appendix: Official Demographic Statistics

1955–1957 DEMOGRAPHIC SURVEY

*Tableau général de la démographie congolaise: Enquête démographique par sondage, 1955–1957: Analyse générale des résultats statistiques.* Central Government, Ministry

[67] *Bilan, 1965–1970*, complete edition, p. 238.
[68] *Ibid.*, chap. IV.
[69] Press conference of the finance minister presenting the state's budget for 1971, *L'Etoile* newspaper, December 29, 1970.
[70] Policy speech of the head of state, December 5, 1970, *Le Progrès* newspaper, December 7, 1970.

of Planning and Economic Co-ordination, Statistical Services, Léopoldville, 1961.

Detailed Fascicules:

no. 1, City of Léopoldville, 1957
no. 2, Suburban Territory, 1957
nos. 3–4, Districts of Bas-Congo and Cataracts, 1957
no. 5, Tshuapa District, 1958
no. 7, Maniema District, 1959

(These first fascicules have been published under the heading: Congo Belge, 2ème Direction Générale, 1ère Direction, AIMO, *Enquêtes démographiques*.)

f. b, Equateur Province, 1959
f. e, Katanga Province, 1960
f. f, Kasai Province, 1959

(These fascicules have appeared under the heading: Congo Belge, Affaires Economiques, Direction de la Statistique, Bulletin mensuel des statistiques générales du Congo Belge et du Ruanda-Urundi, Série spéciale no. 3, *Enquête démographique 1956–57*.)

no. 11, Lac Léopold II—Kwilu—Kwango Districts, 1961
no. 12, Nord and Sud-Kivu Districts (no date)
f. e, followed: Katanga, 1961

(These fascicules have appeared under the heading: République du Congo, Ministère du plan et de la coordination économique, Service des statistiques, Démographie, *Résultats de l'enquête démographique*.)

1967 SOCIODEMOGRAPHIC SURVEY (KINSHASA)

—Codes des tableaux statistiques du recensement par sondage, May 1969.
—Résultats par commune du sondage au 1/10ème—July 1969.
—Etude sociodémographique de Kinshasa 1967, Rapport général, May 1969.

Kinshasa: National Office of Research and Development, National Institute of Statistics.)

1970 ADMINISTRATIVE CENSUS

1968, April 11—Ordonnance No. 68/181 du 11 avril 1968 relative au Recensement Général de la population de la République Démocratique du Congo (Ministère de l'Intérieur, 2ème Direction).

1968, April 30—Vade-mecum à l'usage des autorités administratives et agents chargés du recensement (Ministère de l'Intérieur, 2ème Direction).

1968, May 22—Arrété ministériel no. 68/102 du 22 mai 1968 portant mesure d'exécution de l'ordonnance no. 68/181 du 11 avril 1968 relative au recensement général de la population de la R.D.C. (Ministère de l'Intérieur, 2ème Direction).

1968, May 24—Introduction relative au recensement de la population de la République Démocratique du Congo, 1968 (Ministère de l'Intérieur, 2ème Direction).

1968, September 6—Arrêté ministériel no. 150 du 6 septembre 1968, portant mesure d'exécution de l'ordonnance no. 68/181 du 11 avril 1968 relative au recensement général de la population de la R.D.C. (Ministère de l'Intérieur, 2ème Direction).

1968, September 7—Lettre circulaire du Ministre de l'Intérieur aux Gouverneurs de Province—no. 252/01/5550/0624/68 du 7 septembre 1968, sur la révision périodique du recensement (Ministère de l'Intérieur, 2ème Direction).

1969, February 4—Circulaire du Ministère de l'Intérieur no. 252/01/0983/0217/69 du 4 février 1969 sur organisation du recensement et étude des populations de la République Démocratique du Congo (Ministère de l'Intérieur, 2ème Direction).

1969, March 8—Circulaire à MM. les Présidents des Sous-Commissions de recensement no. 252/01/4756/0480/69 du 8 mars 1969 sur l'organisation et le déroulement des opérations (Ministère de l'Intérieur, 2ème Direction).

1970, July 31—Arrêté ministériel no. 1236 du 31 juillet 1970, portant proclamation des résultats du recensement général 1970 de la République Démocratique du Congo. (The appendix gives the figures.)

RUFAST—Instructions pour la mise en application du système de recensement par fiches (circulaire du 18 septembre 1922)—in *Recueil à l'usage des fonctionnaires et des agents du service territorial au Congo Belge*. Brussels: Ministère des Colonies, 1930, p. 249–259.

ECONOMIC SITUATION—*La Situation Economique du Congo Belge et du Ruanda-Urundi, en 1950 . . . 1959*. Brussels: Belgian Ministry of Colonies, Department of Economic Studies.

ANNUAL STATISTICS . . . annexe statistique au Discours du Gouverneur Général, Léopoldville. (Exists for the years 1947–1959). (The 1959 figures have been published separately in *Bulletin Annuel des Statistiques du Congo Belge*).

# CHAPTER THIRTY

## Dahomey

ETIENNE VAN DE WALLE

⠿

THE ADMINISTRATIVE RECORDS. Dahomey, like other territories under French colonial rule, had administrative records of population, improperly called "censuses." These were lists of taxpayers and their families, routinely kept by the village headmen, and periodically checked and revised by an agent of the central administration on a rotating basis. Typically, the "census" had to be completely updated every five years. There was a built-in tendency to underestimate the population, since, at any time, a large proportion of the data would have been compiled several years ago. Furthermore, as the emphasis was on the administrative aims of the enumeration, and mainly on the enumeration of taxpayers, the tendency was to underreport women and children, while men would try to evade registration. Parts of the country were never enumerated at all, as for instance the Tchi county, a small marshy area near the Togolese border. The counts of the fast-changing population in the larger cities were known to be unreliable.

The early administrative estimates of the population of Dahomey, from 1910 to 1923, hover between 800,000 and 900,000 people.[1] The "census" became more systematic from 1924 on; Table 30.1 gives the evolution of the total population estimated between 1924 and 1960. Part of the apparent increase between these dates may perhaps be attributed to improving coverage.

It is generally accepted that, although this type of demographic source tends to underestimate the size of the population, the biases may be fairly constant through time, since they are the result of uniform administrative methods. Therefore these data may be used to evaluate population increase through time. Taking the record at face value, the population more than doubled between 1924 and 1960, averaging an annual rate of increase of

[1] The information on Dahomey's population until 1960 is drawn from an Appendix to the published results of the 1961 Demographic Inquiry: "Annexe III. Renseignements démographiques antérieurs à l'enquête 1961" in République du Dahomey, *Enquête Démographique au Dahomey, 1961: Résultats définitifs*, République Française, Ministère de la Coopération, INSEE, Service de Coopération (Paris, 1964), pp. 303–9.

TABLE 30.1

Administrative estimates of the population of Dahomey, 1924–1956

| Year | Number (in thousands) | Year | Number (in thousands) |
|------|------------------------|------|------------------------|
| 1924 | 924.3 | 1945 | 1,456.5 |
| 1925 | 968.0 | 1946 | 1,478.6 |
| 1926 | 1,016.3 | 1947 | 1,473.6 |
| 1927 | 1,056.0 | 1948 | 1,511.7 |
| 1928 | 1,083.0 | 1949 | 1,524.9 |
| 1929 | 1,079.2 | 1950 | 1,538.0 |
| 1930–35 | No estimates | 1951 | 1,548.9 |
| 1936 | 1,225.7 | 1952 | 1,560.4 |
| 1937 | No estimate | 1953 | 1,582.5 |
| 1938 | 1,324.8 | 1954 | 1,606.3 |
| 1939–41 | No estimates | 1955 | 1,664.3 |
| 1942 | 1,427.2 | 1956 | 1,730.6 |
| 1943 | No estimate | 1957–59 | No estimates |
| 1944 | 1,424.1 | 1960 | (1,896.1)[a] |

SOURCE: République du Dahomey, *Enquête Démographique au Dahomey, 1961: Résultats définitifs* (Paris, 1964), pp. 304 and 19–23.

[a] Estimated by multiplying the rural and urban population estimates given by the *Report* on the 1961 Demographic Inquiry, by 0.907 and 0.840 respectively, to eliminate the correction for under-enumeration of the "census" (see text).

2 percent a year. Even if the 1924 figure reflected an enumeration 20 percent less complete than the 1960 one, there was still in the meantime a very considerable rate of growth: 1.5 percent per annum on average, totaling 71 percent for the whole period. This occurred despite very high mortality and little immigration. It is important to stress this evidence of prolonged population growth during the whole period since the beginning of adequate administrative records, because a sustained rapid increase of this nature cannot fail to have had important social and economic consequences.

The extent to which the 1960 administrative estimate was itself an understatement can be assessed from the results of the 1961 demographic inquiry. The "census" results, as available in November 1960, were used as a sampling frame for the selection of villages for the demographic inquiry that took place from May to September 1961, and which we shall discuss presently. The number of people in the sample was compared with the administrative population of each of the villages surveyed. In the urban stratum, a 10 percent sample of town blocks was selected from maps and aerial photographs, and this surveyed population was used to estimate the total town population, which then was compared to the official estimate. These comparisons suggested that the administrative counts, compiled it is true several months earlier, underestimated the population at the time of the inquiry by 9.3 percent in the rural areas, and by 16 percent in the towns (excluding Abomey and Bohicon), a combined underestimate for the country of 10 percent.[2] The total population of Dahomey in 1961 was estimated at 2,106,000, with a margin of error due to random sampling of 5 percent.

The administrative "census" can be used to derive further information by region. Population growth in north Dahomey appears to have been slower than in the south: 1 percent against 2 percent a year between 1936 and 1956, the extreme dates for which regional data are available. The "census" data, adjusted for underenumeration, can serve to compute density by subareas, such as *départements* or *sous-préfectures* (see map in Figure 30.1). Unfortunately, the administrative "census" was not systematically kept up after 1960. At present, it is out of date, and could probably not be used even to establish a sampling frame for a new inquiry.

THE DEMOGRAPHIC INQUIRY. The 1961 sample inquiry remains the main source of information on the demography of Dahomey, and the only systematic investigation on such subjects as age distribution, nuptiality, fertility, mortality, tribal distribution, and religion. There have been other demographic surveys in small parts of the country,

[2] Unfortunately, the *Report* of the demographic inquiry fails to give the official "census" figure for 1960. The figure of a 9.3 percent underestimate of the rural areas is given in the *Report*, p. 19. The figure of 16 percent for the urban areas was derived from a table on p. 20 of the *Report*. These two percentages were then used to calculate the "census" figure for 1960, given in Table 28.1. Uncertainty originates in the fact that Abomey and Bohicon were not surveyed in 1961, and the *Report* gives only an estimate of their population, without mentioning the official figure for these towns.

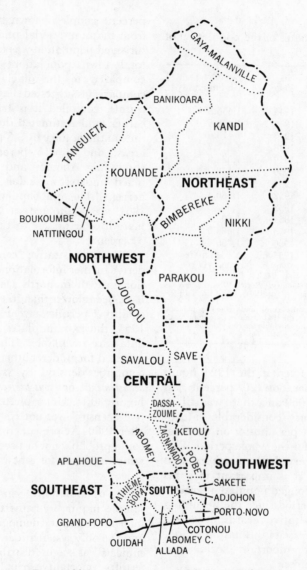

FIGURE 30.1.   *Administrative Subdivisions, Dahomey*

and there exists some independent evidence on subjects touched upon in the inquiry—professions, education, migratory movements, etc. The information on births and deaths in the inquiry is only an imperfect substitute for complete vital registration. But, as it is, the 1961 inquiry is unique, and, although badly outdated, it is still the main source of demographic data.

Because the Dahomey demographic in-quiry, and most of the inquiries conducted in French-speaking countries of Africa on the same pattern, were extremely successful in fulfilling their objectives, it is difficult to recognize their essential limitations. The first round of inquiries was essentially a pioneering effort, a probe, of which the results should have been confirmed (or invalidated) as soon as possible by new studies. Although the field methods had been tried elsewhere in other inquiries under INSEE sponsorship, there was still, when the Dahomey inquiry was taken, a great dearth of evaluation of the results. Some of the comparative work that was required before one could properly evaluate results has only been done since the round of inquiries was completed.[3] Further comparisons with data collected in the same area on the same subjects, but at a later date and with improved methods, are badly needed before the basic demographic situation in Dahomey can be assessed with any certainty. Otherwise, of course, almost nothing can be said about trends, and most of all about trends in mortality and the rate of population increase; while the study of differentials is almost impossible.

OTHER SOURCES. A few inquiries have been conducted in small areas of Dahomey since 1961. There was a demographic census of Cotonou in 1964, and several rural surveys were taken in conjunction with the planning or execution of rural development projects in the south.[4] On the whole, these studies constitute a technical regression from the standards of the 1961 inquiry, and add little to our demographic knowledge of the region.

[3] For instance, in William Brass et al., eds., *The Demography of Tropical Africa* (Princeton, N.J.: 1968), and in INSEE-INED, *Afrique Noire, Madagascar, Comores, Démographie Comparée* (Paris, 1967).

[4] The reports of these inquiries had only limited distribution, and the present writer may have missed some of them. He has seen the following ones: (a) République du Dahomey, Ministère des Finances, des Affaires Economiques et du Plan, Service Central de la Statistique, "Information Statistique: Coopérative de Houin-Agamé" (mimeographed), Cotonou, 1964. This is a study of 13,000 persons. (b) République du Dahomey, Ministère du Développement Rural et de la Coopération, "Projet d'Aménagement agro-Industriel de la Région d'Agonvy," Annexe 1, SO. NA. DER. (mimeographed), Porto-Novo, 1966 (28,000 persons). (c) République du Dahomey, Ministère des Affaires Etrangères, du Plan et du Tourisme, Direction de la Statistique, Recensement Démographique du Grand-Hinvi, 1966 (38,000 people). (d) The agricultural survey of the Région du Mono, containing some demographic information, was made available to the writer in a typed version without title page. The area covered by the survey contained 240,000 inhabitants, and a sample of 1 percent was interviewed.

Their organizers made no attempts to compare their results with the 1961 results, nor to innovate and try new techniques.

Vital registration is making slow progress. In principle, a birth certificate is a prerequisite for admission in the public school system. Births in maternity services (35,500 in 1967, or about one-quarter of all births) and deaths in hospitals are registered. Registration of births may approach completeness in Cotonou. It is hard to evaluate the extent of registration in the rest of the country because results are not centralized; but it is evident that only a small percentage of vital events are ever reported.

## POPULATION DISTRIBUTION

Table 30.2 gives population estimates by *départements* and overall densities at this level. The map in Figure 28.2 indicates densities by smaller administrative areas, the *sous-préfectures*.

TABLE 30.2
Population and density by département, Dahomey, 1961

| Département | Population (in thousands) | Density (persons per sq. mile) |
|---|---|---|
| Sud (South) | 309.4 | 249 |
| Sud-Est (Southeast) | 463.5 | 256 |
| Sud-Ouest (Southwest) | 289.9 | 197 |
| Center | 425.1 | 60 |
| Nord-Est (Northeast) | 304.6 | 16 |
| Nord-Ouest (Northwest) | 313.5 | 26 |
| Total | 2,106.0 | 48 |

SOURCE: *Enquête Démographique au Dahomey*, p. 22.

Figure 30.2 brings out one of the basic characteristics of population distribution in the region, shared by Dahomey and her neighbors. The highest population densities are encountered along the coast, and the hinterland is generally sparsely populated. Thus, 58 percent of the population inhabit about 12 percent of the territory, in a strip

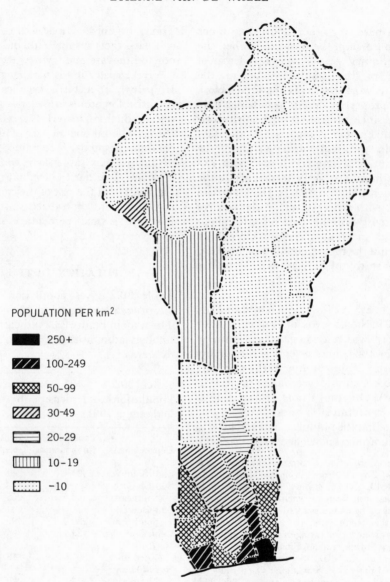

FIGURE 30.2. *Population Density, Dahomey*

situated within 125 miles of the sea. This concentration is partly the result of geography, and partly of history. The strip along the coast consists of the most fertile soil in the country, the alluvial coastal plain and the rich *terres de barre* (clay soils) with their natural palm forest; rainfall is fairly abundant. Various related tribes in the area were unified by the powerful Fon kings of Abomey, who acquired the monopoly of the slave trade. For several centuries, cultural contacts with the outside world, political unity, and military power ensured a degree of prosperity in the south. The slaves were obtained by armed forays to the interior, mainly to the center of the country inhabited by Yorubas. In part, this explains the lower densities of middle Dahomey. In the north, a Bariba kingdom (Borgu) was established at an early date, and it organized the slave traffic toward the coast. This, however, is rather poor savanna land and the inadequate rainfall does not favor dense occupation. Nomadic Fulani (Peuls) drive their cattle in the area, and live in association with the Baribas. In the northwest, remnants of palaeonigritic tribes of the area (known collectively as Sombas)

have protected themselves from slave raids by retreating to the mountain range of the Atakora. There they have developed a labor-intensive agriculture. Benefiting from relatively favorable climatic and hydrologic conditions, they have built up rather high population densities in the valleys and on the mountain slopes.

The map in Figure 30.3 indicates roughly

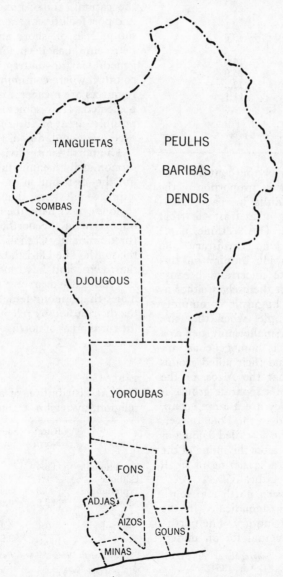

FIGURE 30.3.    *Groups of Tribes, Dahomey*

TABLE 30.3

Percent distribution of ethnic groups by numbers of adult population[a] according to the 1961 inquiry, Dahomey

| Groups | Percent |
|---|---|
| *Northern* | |
| Fulani | 2.5 |
| "Djougous" | 4.6 |
| Sombas | 3.3 |
| "Tanguiétas" | 4.1 |
| Dendis and related tribes | 2.1 |
| Baribas and related tribes | 12.6 |
| *Southern* | |
| Yorubas and related tribes | 14.0 |
| Fons and related tribes | 25.9 |
| Gouns, Setos, and Toris | 12.3 |
| Adjas and Ouatchis | 11.1 |
| Aizos | 4.6 |
| Minas, Plas, and Pedahs | 3.0 |

SOURCE: *Enquête Démographique au Dahomey*, p. 66.
[a] 15 years and over.

the tribal subdivisions of the country. The tribal categories (given in proportion of the total population of adults in Table 28.3) represent a regrouping of at least 46 tribal groups identified in the IFAN ethnic map.[5] Any regrouping of this kind is arbitrary. The returns of a demographic inquiry on this subject are often quite uncertain, because respondents may report themselves either as belonging to a larger linguistic community (as Yorubas, for example, when they are actually Hollis) or to a smaller unit such as a clan. South Dahomey is homogeneous culturally, and the Fon and their allied groups dominate. The fact that the Aizos, or the Adjas for instance, rate a separate group, is due to the fact that they are a large group, although closely related to the Fons proper. On the other hand, the so-called Djougous and Tanguiétas, called after the name of the *sous-préfectures*, regroup a scattering of small tribes, often unrelated culturally.[6]

The distinction between north and south Dahomey was made systematically in the tabulations of the 1961 inquiry. The north–south dichotomy is essential for an under-

[5] P. Mercier, *Cartes ethno-démographiques de l'Ouest africain*, Feuilles No. 5, IFAN (Dakar, 1954).
[6] République du Dahomey, *Plan de Développement économique et social, 1966–1970* (Cotonou, 1966).

standing of the economic, social, and political characteristics of the country. There is, however, an ill-defined transition region, inhabited by Yoruba groups, and combined with the south in the tabulations. The south is a region of cash crops, including the new agricultural development schemes where selected palm trees are cultivated. The important cities and above all Porto-Novo, the capital, and Cotonou, where industries and port facilities are concentrated, are in the south. It is off shore and in the south that petroleum has been found. The north, in general, is the underprivileged part of the country, where communications are difficult, resources are meager, and public services are neglected. It is sometimes considered as a possible area of future settlement for the excessive population of the south.

The north–south division is culturally and economically meaningful, and it is valid also for the distribution of religions. Although animist cults are dominant in the rural regions everywhere, the Moslem faith is more important in the north, and Christian sects (predominantly Catholicism) are dominant in the south. The Christians are the majority in the towns, and have more followers among the young than among the old, and among males than among females. Table 30.4 gives the distribution by religion among adults, for the rural areas of north and south, and for the towns.

TABLE 30.4

Percent distribution of adults[a] according to religion, by region, Dahomey, 1961 inquiry

| Religion | Rural North | Rural South | Urban Areas | All Areas |
|---|---|---|---|---|
| Traditional[b] | 68.4 | 77.9 | 24.5 | 70.6 |
| Catholic | 1.4 | 12.4 | 47.9 | 12.3 |
| Protestant | 0.3 | 3.5 | 3.2 | 2.6 |
| Moslem | 29.5 | 4.9 | 23.5 | 13.6 |
| Other and not stated | 0.4 | 1.2 | 0.9 | 1.0 |
| *Totals* | 100.0 | 99.9 | 100.0 | 100.1 |

SOURCE: *Enquête Démographique au Dahomey*, p. 121.

[a] 15 years and over.
[b] Includes "without religion," a surprisingly important category in the north.

## POPULATION GROWTH
## AND ITS COMPONENTS

Nowhere are the defects and uncertainties of the 1961 inquiry more apparent than in its use to evaluate the growth rate and its components, mortality, fertility, and migration. The question of migration will be examined later. The discussion here will concentrate on the evidence concerning the level of natural increase. Valuable information was obtained in 1961, but the difficulties in analyzing it are inherent in the inquiry method. A body of analytical methods is now available to cope with this type of information. The main information collected in the inquiry related to the following:

(1) The number of births and deaths during the previous 12 months, reported by the head of *concession* (compound) as having occurred in the *concession*
(2) The number of children born and surviving to women over 15 years of age at the time of the inquiry during their entire lives.

The first series of questions should provide enough information to compute a crude birth rate and a crude death rate if the reporting of vital events is complete, and if no bias exists in evaluating the reference period of 12 months. The official rates, computed directly from the reported data, and related to the total population, are given in Table 30.5. These rates were accepted by the authors of the *Report* on the demographic survey, and were

used, for instance, in economic planning to estimate the population growth rate in the country.

The raw findings of the inquiry, however, are suspect on several counts. The Report itself notes that the sex ratio at birth (male births per hundred female births) was suspiciously low: 95 for the whole country, whereas the sex ratio among children ever born over the reproductive life of women was 105, a figure more in line with expected values. In one *département*, the Sud-Ouest (Southwest), the sex ratio at birth was as low as 84, while the apparent birth rate was 69 per thousand, a figure that the authors of the report dismiss as "much too high . . . it should be reduced by approximately ten points."[7] This in turn would reduce the crude birth rate in the rural south by 2.3 points.[8] The report attributes the overestimate to a reference period error, more pronounced for girls, as their physical development is less rapid than that of boys, and as they are given less attention than boys.[9] In other words, some births (and more so among female children than among male) were reported as having occurred during the last 12 months, whereas the children were in fact older.

There are also reasons to suspect the reported mortality. The report comments that "in the cities, the extremely low level of mortality seems somewhat surprising . . . one may admit . . . that the inquiry has underestimated mortality [in Cotonou and Porto-Novo]."[10] Furthermore, the Report admits that infant mortality is obviously underestimated in the rural north where it is reported as 111 deaths of children under one year per thousand births, and in the cities, where it is reported as 45 per thousand. Despite this critical discussion of the evidence, the Report ends up accepting the reported levels of vital rates. But the conclusion is at least implicit that there must have been some underestimation of mortality, and perhaps an overestimation of fertility.

TABLE 30.5
Official crude birth and death rates and rates of natural increase, Dahomey, 1961 inquiry (per thousand)

| Region | Crude Birth Rate | Crude Death Rate | Rate of Natural Increase |
|---|---|---|---|
| Rural north | 47.8 | 30.3 | 17.5 |
| Rural south | 57.1 | 26.2 | 30.9 |
| Urban areas | 48.0 | 11.9 | 36.1 |
| Dahomey | 54.0 | 26.0 | 28.0 |

SOURCE: *Enquête Démographique au Dahomey*, p. 153.

[7] *Enquête Démographique au Dahomey, 1961.*
[8] *Ibid.*, p. 128.
[9] *Ibid.*, p. 14.
[10] *Ibid.*, p. 143.

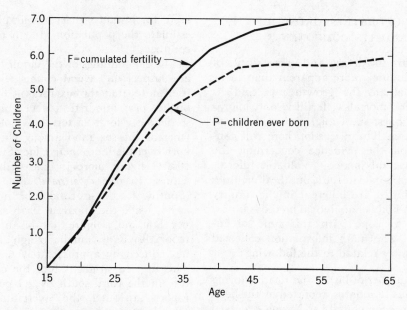

FIGURE 30.4. *Comparison of Number of Children Ever Born per Woman, and Cumulated Age-Specific Fertility Rates, Dahomey,* 1961 *Enquiry*

In the mortality section of a comparative treatment of the INSEE demographic inquiries, Blayo concludes that all inquiries probably underestimate mortality, that the results obtained by this method in the African context are questionable, and that they do not permit a conclusion on the actual level of the crude death rate.[11] In the section on fertility, Nadot ends up accepting the official crude birth rate, and his arguments are worth discussing.[12] Note that Nadot does not analyze Dahomey in great detail, and does not consider regions separately.

When one plots on the same graph the number of children born by age of the mothers, and the cumulated age-specific fertility rates of the year previous to the survey, the latter curve is constantly above the former in Dahomey (see Figure 30.4). If one assumes that fertility has been fairly constant in the past, then the discrepancy between the two curves needs explanation. Nadot argues that

the relation of the curves at age 50 proves that older women tend to omit children from their answers to the question on parity. The argument is questionable, since reported parity does not decrease after 50 with increasing age and there is no evidence of further "forgetting" after the end of reproductive life. Nadot decides in favor of the reliability of the cumulated fertility curve, instead of the parity curve, because of an argument drawn from the age distribution. With the mortality recorded in Dahomey, the number of children aged under ten years is compatible with the birth rate reported for the last 12 months.[13] Unfortunately, this does not clinch the argument, because: (1) recorded mortality is certainly underestimated, and (2) the age group under ten tends to be overestimated in most demographic surveys in Africa.[14] These two elements affect the estimate in opposite directions.

An alternative explanation of Figure 30.4 was given by Brass in his analysis of the

[11] INSEE, Service de Coopération, and INED, *Afrique Noire, Madagascar, Comores: Démographie Comparée* (Paris, 1967), section IV, p. 49.
[12] *Ibid.*, section III, pp. 55–56.

[13] *Ibid.* The method is explained in section III, pp. 68–69.
[14] Brass et al., *Demography of Tropical Africa*, pp. 45–46.

Dahomey inquiry.[15] Brass was using preliminary data, and restricted his discussion to the rural population of Dahomey. On the other hand, he analyzed north and south Dahomey separately. He accepted as approximately correct the number of births reported during the previous 12 months in north Dahomey, but concluded that births recorded in the rural south had actually taken place during a longer time span than 12 months. According to Brass, the fact that the cumulated fertility curve in Figure 30.4 is above the parity curve at all ages, reflects the overreporting of births in south Dahomey because of confusion on the reference period of 12 months. This can be corrected by deflating fertility by the ratio of parity over cumulated fertility at the ages 20–24 $(P_2/F_2)$.[16] The resulting fertility indices are as follows:

|  | Crude Birth Rate (per thousand) | Total Fertility |
|---|---|---|
| North rural | 51 | 6.36 |
| South rural | 51 | 6.56 |
| Dahomey | 51 | 6.49 |

The Brass method seems to offer the best estimate of fertility using only direct information on fertility, but its value could be jeopardized by extensive age misreporting. There exists, however, an alternative, indirect way of estimating the level of fertility, by using stable population theory. The age distribution is the reflect of past fertility and mortality.

The present level of fertility in Dahomey is probably close to that of the past, while mortality changes have only a small impact on age distribution, one that can be accounted for if need be. Therefore, provided we ascertain the mortality level at the time of the survey, and use an index of the age distribution that is free of bias, the level of the birth

rate can be read off from a stable population model. The results from an extensive study of African demographic material at the Office of Population Research in Princeton, have led to the tentative conclusion that this method in general gives the most reliable estimates of the crude birth rate under African conditions.[17] The best index of the age distribution often appears to be the proportion of the population of both sexes reported under age 15; the best index of mortality is generally the proportion of the children surviving to age 2 $(l_2)$ among children ever born. The methods used are explained in more detail by Page in Chapter 2 of this book.

The mortality index is given in Table 30.6.[18] The proportion surviving to age two,

TABLE 30.6

Mortality level estimated from the proportion children reported surviving to ages 2, 3, and 5 years, Dahomey, 1961

| Region | $l_2$ | $l_2$ Implied by $l_2$ and $l_5$ | Corresponding Female $\overset{\circ}{e}_0$ |
|---|---|---|---|
| North rural | 0.759 | 0.757 | 40 years |
| South rural | 0.712 | 0.707 | 35 years |
| Dahomey | 0.733 | 0.729 | 37.5 years |

NOTE: $l_2$ and $l_5$ are proportions surviving to exact ages 2 and 5 years respectively; $\overset{\circ}{e}_0$ is the expectation of life at birth.

as reported by the 1961 inquiry, is consistent with the proportion reported surviving to ages three and five respectively. Unfortunately, the method gives little indication of mortality at higher ages. Brass has attempted to reconstruct a life table for Dahomey by combining the childhood mortality from the data on surviving children, with the information on deaths during the last 12 months.[19] However, for the sake of the

[15] Ibid., chap. 7, in particular pp. 379–392.
[16] The method is explained in United Nations, Manual IV, Methods of Estimating Basic Demographic Measures from Incomplete Data (New York, 1967), chap. VII. Results given in the text are slightly different from those published in Brass et al., Demography of Tropical Africa, because Brass used provisional data and a slightly different method to match ages of F2 and P2.

[17] Hilary Page and Ansley J. Coale, "Estimates of Fertility and Child Mortality in Africa South of the Sahara," Seminar on Population Growth and Economic Development, Nairobi, December 1969, mimeographed.
[18] Infant mortality was computed according to the Sullivan method. Ibid., p. 5. All the computations in this section were made by H. Page, to whom I am indebted for their use.
[19] Brass et al., Demography of Tropical Africa, pp. 381 ff.

TABLE 30.7
Estimates of crude birth and death rates, natural increase and total fertility ratio by the stable population method, Dahomey, 1961

| Region | CBR | CDR | NI | TFR |
|---|---|---|---|---|
| North rural | 53.0 | 25.5 | 27.6 | 7.3 |
| South rural | 54.3 | 30.9 | 23.4 | 7.2 |
| Dahomey | 53.5 | 28.4 | 25.1 | 7.2 |

estimates of the crude rates in Table 30.7, it has been assumed that the general mortality pattern conformed to the Western model.[20] Table 30.7 presents estimates of vital characteristics for Dahomey by the stable population method. The estimates of mortality are higher than those produced directly by the inquiry, while the estimates of fertility are somewhat lower. Thus, the rate of natural increase is well below the one estimated directly.

No more than the previous estimates can the rates given in Table 30.7 be presented as definitive estimates of fertility and mortality in Dahomey. Indeed, they are based on uncertain data that have not been confirmed by other sources. There is no agreement among serious and competent analysts of these data. The possibility remains, for example, that mortality is actually higher in the north than in the south, as knowledge of the general conditions in Dahomey would lead us to suspect. The north in general is less developed, and has had less access to modern medicine. In neighboring countries, the mortality gradient goes from the coast to the more isolated and neglected north. The administrative population data discussed in the beginning of this chapter suggest that the population growth has been considerably higher in the south, a fact that can only in part be explained by migratory movements and must find its explanation in mortality and fertility differentials contrary to those suggested by Table 30.7.

[20] In Ansley J. Coale and Paul Demeny, *Regional Life Tables and Stable Populations* (Princeton, N.J.: Princeton University Press, 1968).

In view of these circumstances, the study of fertility and mortality differentials, and of factors affecting fertility and mortality, is difficult. The impact of errors of observation is probably larger than the differentials themselves. The uncertainty is inevitable under the circumstances: there has been only one single demographic inquiry, largely experimental in character, in a country where the very idea of population study was novel. The 1961 inquiry should be considered merely as a stepping-stone; there is great need for further investigation.

Not only are the results of the 1961 inquiry difficult to interpret, but the demographic situation has evolved since 1961 in ways that cannot be assessed. At least, it is probable that fertility has changed little in ten years. But the trend in mortality, and therefore of the rate of increase, cannot even be conjectured. There has been a total absence of quantitative information on this subject since 1961. There is little possible doubt that the course of mortality in the most developed parts of Dahomey, in the Cotonou region for example, is a decline. In many parts of the country, however, there is only limited access to modern medicine and it is not clear whether the balance of change since 1961 has resulted in improved public health. The number of government doctors has decreased from 78 in 1962 to 55 in 1968. In 1969, the network of rural dispensaries appeared to be neglected and poorly supplied with medical supplies. The long lines of patients that can be witnessed in many other countries of Africa were absent in Dahomey. But on the other hand, there were pharmacies even in remote villages, and medical supplies could be purchased commercially everywhere. A vaccination campaign against smallpox and measles, jointly sponsored by UNICEF and AID, was in progress. Plans were being made for the eradication of malaria. Any evaluation of the net result of these efforts will be frustrated as long as regular demographic investigation is not organized.

MIGRATION. There is, on the whole, in Africa, even less information on migration

TABLE 30.8

Absent residents and visitors by sex and region, in absolute numbers and as percentages of usual residents, Dahomey, 1961

| | Number (in thousands) | | | | Percent | | | |
| | Males | | Females | | Males | | Females | |
| Region | Absent residents | Visitors | Absent residents | Visitors | Absent residents | Visitors | Absent residents | Visitors |
|---|---|---|---|---|---|---|---|---|
| North rural | 17.4 | 8.6 | 21.9 | 18.9 | 6.0 | 3.0 | 8.0 | 6.9 |
| South rural | 22.7 | 11.4 | 23.0 | 23.9 | 3.9 | 1.9 | 3.6 | 3.8 |
| Urban | 2.0 | 3.1 | 2.4 | 5.0 | 2.2 | 3.5 | 2.5 | 5.3 |
| Dahomey | 42.1 | 23.1 | 47.4 | 47.9 | 4.4 | 2.4 | 4.7 | 4.8 |

SOURCE: *Enquête Démographique au Dahomey*, p. 171.

than on other components of population growth. In the Dahomey inquiry, two questions were addressed to the subject. First, the population was distributed into present and absent residents, and in addition, visitors. Second, all residents were asked a question about their place of birth.

Knowledge of the number of absentees and visitors provides some insight on in- and out-migration. The information, however, is not easy to interpret. In a closed population, the number of visitors and of absent residents should be equal. In the inquiry, a visitor was defined as a person who had spent the night prior to the inquiry in the sample area, but did not reside there habitually. An absent resident was one who had not spent the night there, and had been absent for less than five years. When there is migration to and from outside the country, the number of visitors and absent residents may not be equal. In Dahomey, there was in general a reasonable degree of consistency for females, but there were about twice as many absent male residents as there were male visitors (see Table 30.8). Part of the difference at least must be accounted for by international migration. According to the 1960 census of Ghana, there were 11,000 Dahomean-born adult men and 6,900 women reported in that country.[21] Some of them, of course, had been absent for more than five years. According to the Dahomey inquiry, there were 5,700 resident adult men and 2,400 resident adult women in Ghana. The total numbers

reported outside of Dahomey were 9,300 adult men and 4,400 adult women. Thus, it seems that international migration does not explain all of the discrepancy between the number of absent residents and visitors. As in many instances, the information collected is not sufficiently precise to elucidate the matter. This could be a result of imprecise definition, or of the attempt of some men to evade enumeration.

The question on place of birth, when tabulated by place of residence, provides information on the net outcome, at the time of the survey, of what may have been a long series of movements. The data are restricted to residents of the area where the inquiry took place, and provide information both on in- and out-migration inside the country, but only on in-migration from other countries (Table 30.9). The largest part of the movement appears to be of short range, and much can be attributed to the exogamy of women. Migration to cities has been moderate, and very similar for both sexes. A little over 50 percent of the adult population of cities was born outside of the place of residence; the proportion rises to 70 percent in Cotonou.

These figures are placed in perspective by Roussel in a review of migration data in the INSEE inquiries.[22] With respect to temporary movements and labor migrations, as well as to long-term changes of residence, the Dahomean population is among the least mobile in French-speaking Africa. Exogamy is not very frequent, perhaps because Dahomean

[21] *1960 Population Census of Ghana*, IV (Accra: Census Office, 1964), p. 175.

[22] Louis Roussel, "Déplacements temporaires et migratoires," *Démographie Comparée*, II, Section 7.

TABLE 30.9
Place of birth of residents, all ages, Dahomey, 1961

| Place Born | Males (thousands) | Percent | Females (thousands) | Percent |
|---|---|---|---|---|
| Place of residence | 913.8 | 89.5 | 810.6 | 76.4 |
| Same *département* | 56.6 | 5.6 | 185.6 | 17.4 |
| Other *département* | 34.8 | 3.4 | 44.6 | 4.2 |
| Other countries | 14.5 | 1.4 | 20.2 | 1.9 |
| Not specified | 0.8 | 0.1 | 0.9 | 0.1 |
| *Total* | 1,020.6 | 100.0 | 1,061.9 | 100.0 |

SOURCE: *Enquête Démographique au Dahomey*, pp. 276–277.

villages are large. The sex ratio of absentees is exceptionally low, because women seem to move at least as much as men. The urban population is exceptionally homogeneous, and to a larger degree than in most other West African countries, either born in the town or close by. There is great mobility of labor, and the visit of distant relatives is an accepted custom; but most movements are temporary. In a sample inquiry preparatory to the organization of an agricultural development scheme in the Mono region (*Département du Sud-Ouest*), the answers elicited by a question to heads of farms on their visits outside of the region, indicated that a great amount of movement takes place, and that there is little rural isolation.[23] (See Table 30.10.)

Since 1961, return movements of Dahomeans employed in neighboring countries have occurred. The most recent major movement was that from Ghana in late 1969. However catastrophic for the individuals involved, the impact of these movements must have been slight on the growth rate of the country, and on age distribution and other population characteristics. We shall assume in the following section that migration exerts no significant effect on population characteristics.

AGE DISTRIBUTION. If the population is not unduly influenced by migration the age dis-

tribution can be approximated by a stable population with the fertility and mortality estimated for Dahomey. Table 30.11 presents estimates of the age distribution in percentages, based on the vital characteristics presented in Table 30.7. Figure 30.5 compares the reported age distribution in the inquiry with the stable estimate. The comparison indicates what the defects in the reporting of age may be. They are typical of many African censuses and inquiries. The most striking features are the apparent shortage of males between 10 and 35 years, and of women between 10 and 20. It is plausible that at least some men and women in the ages where the shortages occur are reported as either older or younger. It would seem likely, however, that some escaped enumeration, either because they were outside the country at the time, or because they suspected hidden motives behind the enumeration.

TABLE 30.10
Percent of household heads having made at least one trip to a destination outside of the Mono region, Dahomey, 1964

| Destination | Percent |
|---|---|
| Abomey | 53 |
| Cotonou | 50 |
| Lomé | 53 |
| Ghana | 25 |
| Nigeria | 3 |
| Others | 30 |

SOURCE: République du Dahomey, *Programme d'action régionale pour le département du Sud-Ouest*, (Etudes Complémentaires), Enquête Psychosociologique, BDPA, 1 (1966), p. 88.

[23] République du Dahomey, *Programme d'action régionale pour le département du Sud-Ouest* (Etudes Complémentaires), Enquête Psychosociologique, BDPA, 1 (1966), p. 88.

TABLE 30.11

Percentage age distribution of Dahomey and of the major rural divisions, based on stable models,[a] and the rates (per thousand) on which the models are based

| Age Group | North Rural | | South Rural | | Dahomey | |
|---|---|---|---|---|---|---|
| | M | F | M | F | M | F |
| 0–4 | 19.32 | 19.11 | 18.86 | 18.64 | 19.01 | 18.78 |
| 5–9 | 15.14 | 15.00 | 14.70 | 14.54 | 14.88 | 14.73 |
| 10–14 | 12.79 | 12.64 | 12.61 | 12.43 | 12.69 | 12.51 |
| 15–19 | 10.83 | 10.65 | 10.81 | 10.61 | 10.82 | 10.63 |
| 20–24 | 9.04 | 8.89 | 9.15 | 8.96 | 9.12 | 8.94 |
| 25–29 | 7.48 | 7.36 | 7.64 | 7.49 | 7.58 | 7.46 |
| 30–34 | 6.14 | 6.06 | 6.32 | 6.23 | 6.25 | 6.16 |
| 35–39 | 4.99 | 4.95 | 5.18 | 5.12 | 5.11 | 5.06 |
| 40–44 | 3.99 | 4.02 | 4.16 | 4.19 | 4.10 | 4.12 |
| 45–49 | 3.16 | 3.24 | 3.28 | 3.40 | 3.23 | 3.34 |
| 50–54 | 2.43 | 2.57 | 2.53 | 2.71 | 2.48 | 2.65 |
| 55–59 | 1.80 | 1.99 | 1.86 | 2.09 | 1.83 | 2.04 |
| 60–64 | 1.27 | 1.46 | 1.30 | 1.53 | 1.29 | 1.50 |
| 65–69 | 0.82 | 1.00 | 0.83 | 1.02 | 0.83 | 1.02 |
| 70–74 | 0.47 | 0.60 | 0.47 | 0.61 | 0.47 | 0.61 |
| 75–79 | 0.23 | 0.31 | 0.21 | 0.30 | 0.22 | 0.31 |
| 80+ | 0.10 | 1.15 | 0.09 | 0.13 | 0.09 | 0.14 |
| Total | 100.00 | 100.00 | 100.00 | 100.00 | 100.00 | 100.00 |

| | | | | | |
|---|---|---|---|---|---|
| Level of mortality[b] | 8.37 | | | 6.36 | 7.22 |
| Crude birth rate | 53.03 | | | 54.34 | 53.52 |
| Crude death rate | 25.47 | | | 30.93 | 28.43 |
| Rate of natural increase | 27.56 | | | 23.41 | 25.09 |

[a] Stable populations of the Western set in Ansley J. Coale and Paul Demeny, *Regional Model Life Tables and Stable Population* (Princeton, N.J.: Princeton University Press, 1968), chosen to conform to the crude rates estimated in Table 30.7.
[b] That is, expressed as a fractional level between the published life table levels.

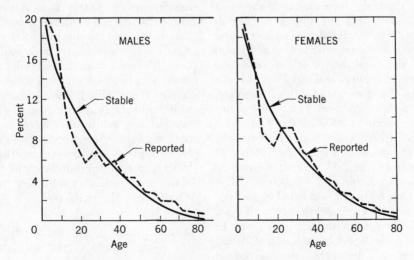

FIGURE 30.5.  *Comparison of the Reported Population with a Stable Estimate, Dahomey. 1961 Enquiry*

TABLE 30.12
Recorded and estimated sex ratios, by regions, Dahomey, 1961

| Region | Males per 100 Females | |
| | Recorded | Theoretical[a] |
| --- | --- | --- |
| Rural north | 105 | 98 |
| Rural south | 92 | 97 |
| Urban | 96 | — |
| Dahomey | 96 | 98 |

[a] In stable "West" model populations with fertility and mortality as in Table 30.11 and sex ratio at birth of 103.

An examination of the sex ratio of the population also suggests underenumeration. The sex ratio of the stable population that we have considered, with a sex ratio at birth of 103 males per hundred females, should be close to 98 for the whole population. Theoretical and enumerated sex ratios for the two large subdivisions of Dahomey appear in Table 30.12. The north has an abnormally high sex ratio, and this may perhaps be related to the Moslem custom of hiding women in purdah; in contrast, the south has an abnormally low sex ratio. It might be noted that the impact of migration remains unknown.

POPULATION PROJECTIONS. The preparation of population projections is largely an academic exercise, since any assignment of the trends of fertility and mortality even in the recent past, is clouded by uncertainty. The purpose of the exercise is to explore and illustrate the implications of an eventual decline of mortality and fertility on the population size, the rate of natural increase, and the age distribution. The projections cover the period 1970–2000. The base population in 1970 was obtained by assuming that the growth rate during the 1960s had been proceeding at 2.51 percent a year, to produce a population of 2,640,000 by 1970, that the crude birth rate was equal to 53.5 per thousand and the crude death rate to 28.4 per thousand (these rates are the ones given in Table 30.7). The age distribution in 1970 was assumed to be the stable one, given in Table 30.11.

Two sets of projections were prepared with the same mortality decline but different fertility trends. Mortality was assumed to decline, slowly first, to an expectation of life at birth of 40 years for females and 37.3 for males in 1980, and then faster, and linearly, to one of 60 for females and 56.5 for males in the year 2000. The acceleration corresponds to great, and expected, improvements in public health and preventive medicine, including eradication campaigns against malaria and other pandemics. The low and the high variants differ according to the hypotheses made about the course of fertility. In the high variant fertility was assumed to remain constant; in the low variant general fertility was reduced linearly by 50 percent in the coming 30 years. The latter course is improbable, and would only be brought about if the government was committed fully and immediately to a program of fertility reduction.

However, the purpose of the computation was to show what impact such a resolute program might have, and what will be likely to happen in its absence. Tables 30.13 and 30.14 present the results of the two projections, in terms of the evolution of the total population and of its growth rate. We shall come back to the results of these projections when we discuss school enrollment and labor force prospects. At this point, it is sufficient to draw attention to the large growth potential that is implicit in the present fertility, and which will come about from expected and desirable reductions in mortality. Furthermore, the most optimistic course of fertility decline foreseeable for the immediate future would still imply a high rate of growth: 2.3 percent a year if fertility were cut in half in the coming 30 years, yielding a total increase of 98 percent by the end of the century. Without any fertility decline, the population of Dahomey would be multiplied by two-and-a-half before the year 2000.

SOCIAL AND ECONOMIC IMPLICATIONS
OF POPULATION GROWTH

SCHOOL ENROLLMENT AND LITERACY. Among the most obvious effects of fast population

TABLE 30.13

The population of Dahomey between 1970 and 2000, according to two assumptions

| | High Projection | | Low Projection | |
| Date | Number (thousands) | 1970 = 100 | Number (thousands) | 1970 = 100 |
|---|---|---|---|---|
| 1970 | 2,640 | 100 | 2,640 | 100 |
| 1975 | 3,003 | 114 | 2,979 | 113 |
| 1980 | 3,435 | 130 | 3,333 | 126 |
| 1985 | 3,991 | 151 | 3,735 | 141 |
| 1990 | 4,714 | 179 | 4,194 | 159 |
| 1995 | 5,643 | 214 | 4,969 | 178 |
| 2000 | 6,828 | 259 | 5,221 | 198 |

TABLE 30.14

Percentage growth per year, by five-year periods and for the total period, under two sets of assumptions

| Period | High Projection | Low Projection |
|---|---|---|
| 1970–75 | 2.6 | 2.4 |
| 1975–80 | 2.7 | 2.2 |
| 1980–85 | 3.0 | 2.3 |
| 1985–90 | 3.3 | 2.3 |
| 1990–95 | 3.6 | 2.3 |
| 1995–2000 | 3.8 | 2.1 |
| Average 1970–2000 | 3.2 | 2.3 |

growth are the high cost of education, and the difficulty in providing employment to a rapidly growing labor force. Education is a particularly sensitive policy issue in Africa; and the very young age distribution caused by high fertility exacts a high price from any government committed to fight illiteracy.

TABLE 30.15

Percent literate above age 15, by age and sex, Dahomey, 1961

| Age | Males | Females |
|---|---|---|
| 15–24 | 14.5 | 3.9 |
| 25–34 | 7.1 | 1.5 |
| 35–44 | 6.4 | 1.1 |
| 45–54 | 5.0 | 0.4 |
| 55–64 | 3.5 | 0.2 |
| 65+ | 1.9 | 0.2 |
| Total | 7.7 | 1.9 |

SOURCE: *Enquête Démographique au Dahomey*, p. 118.

The 1961 demographic inquiry collected information on literacy, while school enrollment data are obtained directly from compilations made by the education ministry. The proportion literate by age and sex is given in Table 30.15. Since the ability to read and write is acquired mostly in schools, and since most of the schooling is completed by age 15, the age distribution of literacy gives a reliable indication of the past evolution of education. Those aged 15–24 years in 1961 had been educated roughly in the decade prior to the inquiry, between 1952 and 1962, during which they were aged 5–14 years. Similarly, those aged 25–34 in 1961 had gone to school between 1942 and 1951, and so on. Therefore, the decline of literacy with age reflects the expansion of the school system over time. It must be noted also that there are strong differentials by sex. Table 30.16 gives some indication of regional differences. The difference between north and south, and between the urban and rural segments, are noteworthy.

TABLE 30.16

Percent literate by region, ages 15 and over, Dahomey 1961

| Region | Males | Females |
|---|---|---|
| Rural north | 1.6 | 0.4 |
| Rural south | 4.5 | 0.8 |
| Cities | 46.5 | 14.2 |
| Dahomey | 7.7 | 1.9 |

SOURCE: *Enquête Démographique au Dahomey*, p. 118.

School enrollment data are last available for 1967–1968.[24] There were 96,600 boys and 43,100 girls in the six primary grades, and 4,600 boys and 2,400 girls in secondary schools. The primary enrollment represented about 37 percent of the population between 6 and 12, the school-going ages (although pupils are actually recruited over a much wider age span). About one-half of the boys of school-going age, and one-quarter of the girls, were attending classes.

Remote as they are from an ideal of universal education, these percentages already represent a heavy burden on the economy of Dahomey. Twenty-three percent of the national budget is devoted to education. It is accepted officially that the present share of education in public expenditures will not be exceeded in the near future. The government policy aims at maintaining the present quality of education. Assuming that a constant proportion of the school age population will continue to attend schools, it can be shown with the help of projections that, without fertility decline, there would be a large increase in the absolute number of illiterate children (Table 30.17). However, if fertility were declining (low variant of the projection), the same amount of money spent on education would rapidly permit the proportion attending school to increase, and the absolute number of illiterate children in the country would eventually decrease.

EMPLOYMENT. Employment statistics are one of the areas that are the most difficult to cover in an inquiry of the Dahomey type. No rigorous criteria are used to establish whether a person is employed or not. In particular, women engaged in agriculture often are reported as "inactive." On the other hand, no attempt is made to evaluate the extent of underemployment. The 1961 inquiry attempted to distinguish between large sectors of activity (80 percent of the males were reported in the primary sector, i.e., mainly agriculture and fishing), between the tradi-

TABLE 30.17
Projection of school age populations and future enrollments, with a constant share of the national budget devoted to education, according to two fertility hypotheses, Dahomey, 1970–2000.

| Year | School Age Population (thousands) | Number in Schools (thousands) | Percent in Schools | Unable to be Enrolled (thousands) |
|---|---|---|---|---|
| High projection: No fertility decline | | | | |
| 1970 | 434 | 149 | 34.3 | 285 |
| 1975 | 496 | 170 | 34.3 | 326 |
| 1980 | 565 | 194 | 34.3 | 371 |
| 1985 | 654 | 224 | 34.3 | 430 |
| 1990 | 785 | 269 | 34.3 | 516 |
| 1995 | 963 | 330 | 34.3 | 633 |
| 2000 | 1,188 | 407 | 34.3 | 781 |
| Low projection: Fertility decline | | | | |
| 1970 | 434 | 149 | 34.3 | 285 |
| 1975 | 496 | 170 | 34.3 | 326 |
| 1980 | 552 | 194 | 35.1 | 358 |
| 1985 | 597 | 224 | 37.5 | 373 |
| 1990 | 650 | 269 | 41.4 | 381 |
| 1995 | 716 | 330 | 46.1 | 386 |
| 2000 | 774 | 407 | 52.6 | 367 |

tional and the modern part of the economy (13 percent of the men were reported in the "modern" sector, but 51 percent of the women, because of the large number of self-employed petty traders reported in that category), and between salaried, unemployed, self-employed, and unpaid family helpers.

Perhaps the most interesting information, in this wealth of untested classifications, is the number of salaried men in the modern sector: 32,500. It is possible, however, that even this includes a large number of unemployed or partly employed men.[25] The interest of this grouping is that it gives a ready measure of employment in the capitalized sector of the economy and the public sector. This estimate can be compared with more direct statistics, derived from employers' reports to official agencies. In 1965, there were 35,800 salaried men, of whom 15,200 were in the public

[24] République du Dahomey, Ministère de l'éducation nationale, de la jeunesse et des sports, *Statistiques Scolaires 1967–68* (Porto-Novo, 1969).

[25] *Enquête Démographique au Dahomey*, p. 104.

TABLE 30.18

Projection of the male labor force according to two hypotheses of fertility change, Dahomey, 1970–2000

| Year | High Projection | Low Projection |
|------|-----------------|----------------|
| 1970 | 677 | 677 |
| 1975 | 771 | 771 |
| 1980 | 881 | 881 |
| 1985 | 1,015 | 1,015 |
| 1990 | 1,176 | 1,166 |
| 1995 | 1,380 | 1,334 |
| 2000 | 1,643 | 1,525 |

sector.[26] The continuous enlargement of the public sector has put great stress on Dahomey's budget. In recent years, two-thirds of the national expenditure has been spent on wages, other personnel costs, and social security. The expansion will encounter limits, and the plan foresaw only a moderate expansion of employment opportunities between 1966 and 1970. The capital investment it allocated, though quite large, would have created only about 5,000 new jobs. The ratio of new employment created per amount invested was one position per 7 million francs CFA (or approximately U.S. $26,000) invested.[27] Indeed, modern industry employs little untrained labor. It is too early to tell whether the plan's provision will eventuate. But meanwhile, the male labor force (i.e., the number of men in the age group 15–65) will have increased by more than 60,000. Most of those accrued to the traditional sector, although a substantial increase in the number of urban unemployed has been observed in recent years. Available statistics are too imprecise to document this, however. In the coming years, a large increase in the labor force must be expected, and it can be assumed safely that it will not be absorbed by the urban modern sector of the economy. Table 30.18 presents the projected labor force growth until the year 2000, under a high and low fertility variant. The effect of a fertility decline would not affect the labor force for a

[26] République du Dahomey, *Plan de Développement*, p. 408.

[27] *Ibid.*, p. 422.

considerable time, because the workers entering the labor force during the coming 15 years have already been born.

RURAL DENSITIES. Dahomey's population is a fast-growing one, and at least in the south, the land has reached an uncommonly high density of occupation. The plan notes that

as a consequence of population increase in the south, a shortage of land is being felt, and over-cultivated soils are being exhausted.[28]

It is difficult to evaluate the extent to which overcropping has had a detrimental effect on the fertility of the good clay soils of southern Dahomey. Writing, it is true in 1953, Brasseur, who intensively studied the Porto-Novo palm forest, came to the conclusion that, after years of abuse of the soils, and despite a substantial reduction of fallow periods, there were no signs of fertility exhaustion.[29] Since then land use in the area has intensified and the Porto-Novo area is quoted by agricultural specialists as the region of Dahomey where overpopulation is most evident.

In general, increases in population density give no cause for alarm where improved methods of husbandry, including fertilizers and labor-intensive techniques, are widely used. However, the most obvious result of population pressure appears to date to have been the transformation of the land tenure system in the south. There is increasing fragmentation of holdings, and in many areas a system of private property has taken the place of the old communal system.[30] In the Mono area, for example, a survey of cultivation rights on a sample of 464 lots showed that 51 percent had been obtained by inheritance, and 11 percent by purchase. Only 31 percent had been distributed by the tribal authority

[28] *Ibid.*, p. 25.

[29] P. Brasseur-Marion and G. Brasseur, *Porto-Novo et sa Palmeraie*, Mémoires de l'IFAN (IFAN-Dakar, 1953), p. 125.

[30] Alfred Mondjannagni, "Problèmes démographiques et développement économique du Dahomey Méridional" (Paper presented at the Seminar on Population Growth and Economic Development, Nairobi, 1969, mimeographed).

in the traditional fashion; while a few were cultivated under temporary rights, such as leases.[31]

Another visible consequence of population increase has been the decline of trade. "The acceleration of demographic growth explains the increase in local consumption and the decrease in the exportable surplus."[32] Exports of agricultural products have stagnated or even declined in recent years, either, as in the case of palm oil and peanuts, because they can be consumed locally rather than exported, or because they were in direct competition with food crops. The agricultural development policy of the country has therefore stressed both the land tenure aspects (i.e., the need for consolidation) and the need for exports. Large palm-oil producing areas have been reorganized on a cooperative basis. Previous land rights in the area of the cooperatives entitles the owner to a part in the profits, but so does work in the fields. The formula is conceived as a way of employing landless rural people and of perhaps relieving unemployment in the cities.

A POPULATION POLICY? The last five-year plan laid some emphasis on the population problems of Dahomey. It noted that "rapid population growth . . . neutralizes an important mass of investments of which the only effect is to prevent the reduction of living standards."[33] It discussed population pressure on the land and employment problems. The interest has subsequently remained alive. In 1969, the government requested the visit of a mission of the Population Council to advise on population policy. The word "policy" may appear somewhat ambitious; but the climate seems favorable for a gradual start in the provision of some of the family planning services that are becoming available in more and more developing countries.

There is certainly, as yet, no demonstrated

[31] République du Dahomey, *Programme d'action régionale*, p. 96.
[32] République du Dahomey, *Plan de Développement*, p. 25.
[33] *Ibid.*

interest in fertility control from the population at large; but in the larger cities of the south, family planning would probably elicit the same interest as in the cities of other African countries where clinics and family planning associations provide such services. There is some evidence that abortions are increasingly practiced in Cotonou; and patients in the maternity services are spontaneously beginning to request advice on birth control. Some private clinics quietly provide contraceptive advice, and, in 1968, over 4,000 monthly cycles of oral contraceptives were sold by pharmacies (probably mostly to the expatriate population). A family planning center is planned as an annex to the Maternal and Child Health Center in Cotonou. The practice of family planning is gaining a foothold.

The concept of a population policy, however, at present is not only opposed to the tradition of high fertility in the country, but also to the legislation and the philosophy inherited from the French colonial period. Furthermore, a large part of the country's elite is Catholic, and they would be vulnerable if the local episcopate were to take an official position on the subject. Nevertheless, the temptation to introduce family planning programs will increasingly be felt as population continues to grow, as the problems of educating and employing larger numbers are compounded, and as an increasing part of investment is used up for demographic nonproductive purposes.

CONCLUSION

The most urgent need in the population field in Dahomey is probably a better knowledge of basic data, such as the growth rate and its components, and the distribution of the population and its characteristics. The country should place high in its priorities a national population census (it would be the first in its history), and new demographic inquiries, as well as the slow but consistent expansion of the vital registration system. Dahomey has now announced that it will hold a census in March 1975 and that this census will be part of the African Census Program, thus assuring eligibility for United Nations technical assistance. This might help overcome the complete lack of resources and personnel for surveys and the neglect of training and field research that appeared, in common with much of French-speaking Africa, to exist at the time of writing. Even so, the uncertain knowledge provided by the 1961 demographic inquiry will have to be stretched even further, probably until the late 1970s.

# CHAPTER THIRTY-ONE

# *Gabon*[1]

MICHEL FRANÇOIS

By 1970, Gabon had been an independent republic for ten years. It differs from the other West African countries in many ways that have important population consequences.

It is the most heavily forested country in Africa, having been left completely alone for a long time, but in the last few years it has been expanding rapidly and its economic takeoff is assured. The population appears to have been stationary or declining until about 1950; since then it has grown slowly, averaging about 1½ percent per annum. The fundamental causes, often far removed in time, of its demographic development have been primarily the slave trade, epidemics, and endemic disease. There have also been famines, general malnutrition, and the scattering of large tribes through a dense forest. Colonization only accentuated the tendency for uncertain population growth by forcibly breaking up families in many areas through intensive recruitment of manual labor and by creating a market economy which too quickly replaced the former agricultural and craft economy. The clash of the two civilizations, the disintegration of customary institutions, and the equatorial forest and climate were also jointly responsible for the decline in population between 1930 and 1950.

Thus, under the pressure of natural conditions, disease, and a particular form of colonization, the Gabonese population reached a critical state, and was the subject of investigation by the Population Commission convened in Libreville in 1946. The consequences of this demographic history are still very important: a small population which has become the object of great concern,[2] low population densities with nevertheless very considerable variation,[3] a very low growth rate[4] with a relatively small margin of the birth rate over the death rate, high infant mortality and a great number of stillbirths,

[1] This chapter analyzes the population data available up to, but not including, the 1969–1970 census.
[2] Less than 500,000 inhabitants.
[3] 1.3–23 inhabitants per square mile depending on the district.
[4] Crude birth rate 35 per thousand, crude death rate 20 per thousand, infant mortality rate 229 per thousand.

and general population instability caused by large local migratory movements partly arising from the economic structure.[5]

## DESCRIPTION OF THE REGION

With an area of 106,000 square miles, Gabon is one of the smallest and least populated African countries. It is located astride the equator, and the equatorial conditions are very pronounced: consistently high temperatures, abundant rainfall, luxuriant vegetation, and day and night of practically equal length.[6] The humidity varies between 70 and 98 percent. Situated on the western coast of the continent, Gabon has 1,000 miles of forested borderland with Equatorial Guinea, Cameroon, and the People's Republic of the Congo, and 500 miles of coastline (see Figure 31.1). In relief, it is divided into three parts: a coastal strip, a series of plateaus, and two mountain ranges; the highest point is Mount Iboundji, 5,160 feet. The soil is generally too acid to be rich, but is able to support the cultivation of edible roots. The surface water flow after rain is very large over soils which are saturated with water nine months of the year and over subsoils with impermeable concretions. The basin of the Ogooué River (750 miles long) extends over 85,000 square miles (82 percent of the country) and the dense equatorial forest covers 72 percent of the land.

Superimposed on the traditional Gabonese landscape of forested countryside, shifting cultivation, and scattered villages is, in an increasing number of places, a modern landscape of factories, derricks, construction sites, and new buildings—irresistible poles of attraction for the people.

[5] The urban population has tripled in ten years (rural-urban migration).
[6] Average temperature: 79°F; rainfall: 80–120 inches, depending on the region. The principal products are now: okoumé wood (800,000 tons per year); crude oil (4.5 million tons per year); manganese ore (1.2 million tons per year); and uranium concentrate (1,300 tons per year). There are many industries (wood, food, chemical, metal, cement, textile, refineries, etc.). Much is expected from the rich iron deposits and the Trans-Gabon railway.

## CENSUS AND SURVEYS

The first national census of the population conducted by statisticians was taken in 1960–1961;[7] and the second, organized by the National Statistical and Economic Studies Service in 1969–1970, is now at the stage of data processing.[8] There was, however, a previous history of population data collection. The last quinquennial census of French Equatorial Africa was made in 1936; and since then, the local administration supposedly brought the census up to date annually, in order to establish lists of taxpayers, draftees, and voters. This was not in fact done regularly. Nor were any of these administrative censuses taken at the same time throughout the country, which makes it impossible to estimate the population for any one reference year. Moreover, it is certain that the methods of census taking varied from one area to another and that those used in every case underestimated the population size. In fact the censuses were an instrument of local administration, a simple headcount made by gathering the people together.

On the basis of published texts and various administrative reports, two hypotheses can be put forward about the development of the Gabonese population in the present century (see Figure 31.2): slow and continuous decline until 1950, or relative stagnation. Good but partial evidence has been found for both cases; and it is not possible, therefore, to give a formal proof or certain evidence of either hypothesis. On the other hand, it is certain that from 1930 to 1950 the indigenous population was in a state of decline.

The computation of projections of the Gabonese population from the 1960–1961 population sample survey is based on two series of data: the supposed known data, which refer to the situation in 1960–1961, and the unknown data, which are the probable trends of births and deaths estimated from those registered in 1960–1961. The first

[7] *Population Census, 1960–1961*, III *Census and Demographic Surveys*, SNSEE.
[8] E. Fausther, Head of the National Statistical and Economic Studies Service (SNSEE).

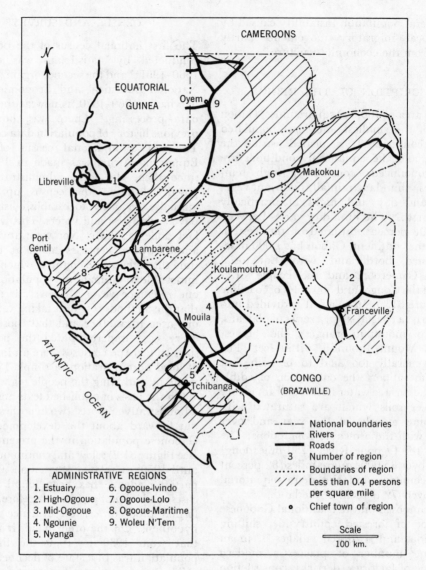

FIGURE 31.1.   *Gabon: Regions, Roads, and Population Density*

results of the second census (1969–1970) will be available in 1971 and the comparison between the two complete coverages will bring greater certainty.

THE NATIONAL POPULATION CENSUS 1960–1961. The census and the population sample survey, carried out at the same time, were the first statistical operations undertaken in the Gabon Republic. They benefited from the experience and methods of the INSEE-Cooperation[9] in close collaboration with the National Statistics Department,[10] but were not the subject of any special report on the methodology or any critical study of their validity.

[9] M. R. Blanc, INSEE administrator, prepared the operation, the questionnaires, and the manual and supervised the initial work.
[10] The Head of the Statistics Department in 1960 was M. J. Arnaud (INSEE).

The control proceedings (control list, sampling frame, village book, controller's book, recapitulative lists, extraction of some results) were complete and efficient. Censusing mistakes (omissions or double counts, which change the quantitative results, and also errors in declaration) have been very limited because of the methods used. Errors of processing were more numerous, but changes from one cell to another in the tables only concerned small numbers.

As a rule, the fact that a census and a sample survey are carried out at the same time should allow the results of the former to be controlled by the latter. Unfortunately, the determination of the total numbers by the survey suffered from several faults which prevent us from using it for verifying the census on this score. Because of the greater reliability of the census data, the results of the survey have been corrected with the help of census data.

THE POPULATION SAMPLE SURVEY, 1960–1961.[11] Even if the sample survey, which paralleled the census and which sought additional information, had been better than the census, it still could not have been used as a verification of total numbers. Because of the lack of supporting personnel, and contrary to what was originally intended, it included the inhabitants of villages, towns, and work

[11] Population Census and Surveys 1960–1961, INSEE-Cooperation-SNSEE; whole of Gabon.

camps not covered by the census; thus the check on the census exists only for population aggregates and not for individuals. Moreover, this check on aggregates has been reduced in value by the replacement of units and the choice of certain fractions of villages (or work camps or towns) in a manner which has not always been statistically correct.

In these conditions, therefore, it is of little value to inflate the results obtained by survey to total numbers, based only on the data of the original sampling frame. That is why we have concluded that it is preferable to correct these results (as well as all other data furnished by the survey) using the results obtained by census, or, more precisely, to extrapolate them from the sum of the crude results of the census and the survey. The main survey data of interest, therefore, are the proportional distributions of population characteristics and the information on vital rates.

The sample was formed in three different ways, according to whether it concerned villages in the bush, towns, or work camps. The sampling frame for the villages consisted of a list of population clusters. The drawing was systematic (one cluster in ten as a rule). The six parishes were surveyed by a systematic selection from a list of households (one in five as a rule). In the work camps the sampling fraction was one in ten.

For the villages and the work camps, the sampling fraction varied somewhat according to region but averaged for the whole

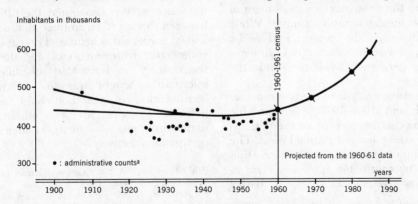

FIGURE 31.2. *Hypothesis of Development of the Gabonese Population in the Twentieth Century*

[a] According to the year, these counts were for the resident or indigenous population on the one hand, and part or all of the present territory on the other.

country 11.6. It also varied in the towns, but averaged for the whole country 5.5.

The survey brought out very clearly the main errors in enumeration in Gabon, and this observation was essential for the improvement and correction of future studies. Some examples are: the huge deficit of children under 1 month (voluntary omission); the significant excess of children of 11 months of age; the deficits in the 10–14 year age group; the inconsistency between stated current fertility (previous 12 months) and total fertility (due to omissions by the old women); and the inconsistencies in the mortality data (poor distribution of deaths by age). However, for most of these anomalies and inconsistencies, demographic statistical techniques allow adjustments to be made.

A comparison of certain results of the two operations indicate that individual data were better collected in the survey. The study of regularity indices, based on sex and age ratios, testify to this, and it is certain that the 1960–1961 survey remains the basic document for population studies in Gabon.

THE NATIONAL POPULATION CENSUS, 1969–1970.[12]    The 1969–1970 national census was the first undertaking of what is planned to be a permanent and continuous recording of demographic facts. The entire plan was for a 100 percent enumeration for relatively few questions, a standard demographic sample survey, a sociomedical survey focused on fertility, and the progressive establishment of special areas for demographic study.[13] While it was under way, this project had to be modified in view of the number and caliber of supporting personnel available and the budget granted.

A comparative analysis of the two censuses (1960–1961 and 1969–1970), will provide sufficient information to replace the population survey which has not justified itself. The establishment of special areas for observation will allow, by continuous interview (two to three survey rounds a year), a better knowledge of births, deaths, and migration. These special areas will provide our first real understanding of many aspects of fertility, stillbirth, and infant mortality (sociomedical survey).

The planned simultaneous census[14] could not be carried out because of the failure to achieve the necessary integration of the government services for the operation. However, each town was enumerated within a 24-hour period.[15] The information gathered was transferred to optical-mark cards (IBM = 1132) and collated by computer (IBM = 360).[16]

The quality of such census results depends in the first place on the quality of the questionnaire. The type of form, the presentation and the order of questions, the filling in of the answers, the coding and instructions were all studied. Special tests were carried out employing different criteria: number in order of the individuals by household; Christian names, surnames, and nicknames; age; ethnic group; place of birth; place where the person counted worked, studied, or resided; the number and periods of time at present residence; occupation and current work; and other aspects of employment and education. From the results of these tests, we studied the formulating of the questions and their positions, errors of interpretation and processing, the bias introduced, and the time necessary for carrying out the work according to two methods: village assembly or hut-by-hut canvass. We also tested the differences between the use of an enumeration notebook and a household schedule. The capital was enumerated with notebooks, and the rest of the country on household schedules. The information sought was the geographical identification of the household and—for individuals—name, sex, age, ethnic group/nationality, place of birth, residence, and occupational activity.

---

[12] "Methodology," *National Population Census, 1969–1970,* SNSEE.

[13] Special demographic areas, SNSEE, 1970.

[14] M. François, "A Simultaneous Census in Gabon, Methodological Test," 1969.

[15] Libreville: 73,000 inhabitants counted on June 1, 1969.

[16] *National Population Census 1969–1970,* machine-sorted punched cards, 1132/360, SNSEE.

The preliminary studies, the tests, and the census of the capital constituted a pilot operation of high standard during which the regional organization and logistic to be used were perfected, as were recruitment methods, the training of the enumerators, the publicity and other aspects of the preparation of the population, and the system of control cards.

The qualifications of the enumerators had been determined during the preparation of the questionnaire; they were mainly students attending school in each census zone (34 rural and work estate zones and 10 urban zones) who carried out the field work. Because of the simplicity of the questionnaire, the appointment of a head supervisor for each zone (specialized interviewers from the Statistics Department, accustomed to the difficulties of the field work) and the number of enumerators (about 4,000, employed for periods of 3–15 days), no manual was prepared, but explanatory notes were distributed. The relatively small supervisory staff had to be satisfied with the completeness of the census coverage and the quality of the entries, and thus the census lasted longer than the time originally allotted (12 months instead of 8).

The direct coding of information on optical mark cards is especially difficult despite controls. The optical reader rejects only omissions, double markings, and inconsistencies between different entries. It is necessary to wait for the listing by town, village, or work camp to appear in order to compare the number of residents with that of the manual count, and thus measure the relative error. But comparison with the 1960–1961 census will also provide many indications of the validity of the results, as will the continuing population count, which started with this census as a baseline estimate, and other statistical sources (especially the census of the Major Epidemics Department). Contrasting the original plans with what has been achieved, it is now clear that the effort demanded from the technical staff to create a suitable methodology for Gabon over a few months by modifying and adapting what was imported was too much. The supervisors in each zone could only meet the demands upon

them with the continuing support of regional and national organization. We have been able to confirm that a complete demographic operation does not work when it consists of a single, large ten-yearly effort, and that the continuous collection of demographic data at the regional level is necessary. This is one of the aims of the special areas being set up in Gabon.

CENSUSES IN THE CAPITAL, 1960, 1964, 1969.[17] The capital, Libreville, has benefited from a more continuous demographic observation than the rest of the country. The first demographic documents were the 1943 census and a municipal census in 1953. Libreville has also been the subject of a unique study by Lasserre.[18]

Simultaneous enumeration in all urban areas requires very elaborate preparation. In 1969 the census employed air-photos, schematic diagrams of small parcels of land, and very exact and well-defined divisions. The method which was perfected then should allow these operations to be repeated frequently, which will allow close observation of the very fast growth of the towns.

ESTIMATED CURRENT AND
PROJECTED VITAL RATES

The processing of the 1969–1970 complete enumeration is under way in Gabon, and the estimates of vital rates will be available in 1971. The comparison of the two 100 percent counts (1960–1961 and 1969–1970) will make it possible to estimate likely trends in population growth on sound data and to measure the accuracy of the projections made ten years ago.

We quote here from Chapter 7, "Projections" of the results published for 1960–1961,

[17] *Population Census and Surveys 1960–1961*, results for Libreville. Census of the population of the parish of Libreville, October 11, 1964 (SNSEE, Parish of Libreville); Census June 1, 1969, "Libreville, Its Demographic Expansion."
[18] G. Lasserre, *Libreville, the Town and Its Region* (Paris, 1958); "The Mechanisms of the Growth and Population Structures of Libreville 1953–1970," *Bordeaux-Talence Colloquy* (1970), CNRS, ORSTOM.

TABLE 31.1

Projected age-specific fertility rates (annual births per 1,000 females)

| Age (in years) | 1960–1964 | 1965–1969 | 1970–1974 | 1975–1979 | 1980–1985 |
|---|---|---|---|---|---|
| 15–19 | 160 | 162 | 164 | 166 | 169 |
| 20–24 | 193 | 199 | 205 | 211 | 216 |
| 25–29 | 173 | 178 | 183 | 188 | 194 |
| 30–34 | 134 | 138 | 142 | 146 | 150 |
| 35–39 | 101 | 104 | 107 | 110 | 114 |
| 40–44 | 42 | 43 | 44 | 45 | 47 |
| 45–49 | 26 | 27 | 28 | 29 | 30 |
| Total fertility ratio | 4.15 | 4.26 | 4.37 | 4.48 | 4.60 |

SOURCE: *Population Census and Surveys 1960–1961*. Whole of Gabon (INSEE-Cooperation-SNSEE), Table 113. p. 134.

and the rates indicated there (fertility, mortality, and natural increase):

The calculation of population projections involves the use of two series of data, the first known (at least theoretically), the second unknown, about which it will thus be necessary to form some hypotheses. The data supposed known are those which refer to the original situation (age and sex structure, rhythm of births and deaths); those unknown concern the probable changes in this rhythm. To be completely rigorous in our analysis, we would have to take equally into account external migratory movements and their probable changes. To simplify matters, we will neglect such movements here and consider the Gabonese population to be closed. Therefore, the following forecasts ought to be considered as a simple attempt to define a margin of greatest probability in a group of very diverse situations, each one of which has a nonnegligible probability of being realized.

This degree of probability will not and, moreover, cannot be specified.... The hypothesis which will be selected, then, must be considered to be only that which seems to be most likely to occur.... Population projections are nothing more than tools to be perfected as more and better data become available....[19]

FERTILITY. The increase in fertility between the present and 1985 has been estimated at 10 percent in the time series presented in Table 31.1.

MORTALITY. The basic rate of mortality decline used in the projections is that sug-

gested by the United Nations.[20] Taking into account the much higher rate of male mortality, we have used the basic rate for the female population and a rate of decline twice as great for males. (In Libreville in 1970 male mortality was still 50 percent greater than that of females.) Mortality conditions by sex and age would, therefore, be those given in Table 31.2 for each of the periods considered.

NATURAL INCREASE. The results of various calculations agree on an average annual growth of about 1 percent over the period 1960–1985, yielding a total indigenous population in 1970 of about 475,000 rising to 500,000 with the inclusion of resident foreigners. The results of the 1969–1970 census will show if this is correct. We are clearly dealing with a very modest increase compared to the rates observed in most third-world countries; indeed it is impossible to preclude a further population decline in Gabon.

This examination covers a period equal to about one generation, during which it was supposed that the rate of growth would increase from its 1960 level of 0.5 percent (birth rate, 35 per thousand and death rate, 30 per thousand) to 1.5 percent (birth rate, 35 per thousand and death rate, 20 per thousand). The birth rate does not change,

[19] *Census and Demographic Surveys 1960–1961*; whole of Gabon, final results.

[20] United Nations Department of Economic and Social Affairs, *Manuals on Methods of Estimating Population, Manual III: Methods for Population Projections by Sex and Age*, ST/SOA Series A, Population Studies No. 25 (New York, 1956).

TABLE 31.2
Projected age-specific death rates (deaths per 1,000 persons) and expectations of life at birth, 1960–1985

| Age | 1960–1964 | | 1965–1969 | | 1970–1974 | | 1975–1979 | | 1980–1985 | |
|---|---|---|---|---|---|---|---|---|---|---|
| | M | F | M | F | M | F | M | F | M | F |
| 0 | 371 | 168 | 316 | 152 | 270 | 136 | 229 | 122 | 194 | 108 |
| 1–4 | 58 | 21 | 45 | 19 | 35 | 16 | 28 | 14 | 21 | 12 |
| 5–9 | 14 | 5 | 11 | 5 | 9 | 4 | 7 | 3 | 5 | 3 |
| 10–14 | 9 | 4 | 7 | 3 | 6 | 3 | 4 | 3 | 3 | 2 |
| 15–19 | 12 | 6 | 10 | 5 | 8 | 4 | 7 | 4 | 5 | 3 |
| 20–24 | 15 | 8 | 13 | 7 | 11 | 6 | 9 | 5 | 8 | 4 |
| 25–29 | 18 | 8 | 15 | 7 | 12 | 6 | 10 | 6 | 8 | 5 |
| 30–34 | 21 | 9 | 17 | 8 | 13 | 7 | 11 | 6 | 9 | 5 |
| 35–39 | 25 | 10 | 20 | 8 | 16 | 7 | 12 | 6 | 10 | 5 |
| 40–44 | 31 | 11 | 25 | 9 | 19 | 8 | 15 | 7 | 12 | 6 |
| 45–49 | 39 | 13 | 31 | 11 | 24 | 10 | 19 | 9 | 15 | 8 |
| 50–54 | 47 | 16 | 38 | 15 | 30 | 13 | 25 | 12 | 20 | 11 |
| 55–59 | 58 | 22 | 48 | 20 | 40 | 18 | 33 | 16 | 28 | 15 |
| 60–64 | 72 | 32 | 62 | 29 | 52 | 27 | 45 | 25 | 39 | 23 |
| 65–69 | 94 | 47 | 83 | 44 | 72 | 41 | 64 | 38 | 56 | 36 |
| 70+ | 196 | 125 | 176 | 121 | 159 | 116 | 146 | 112 | 135 | 108 |
| All ages | 39 | 22 | 33 | 21 | 29 | 20 | 25 | 19 | 22 | 18 |
| Expectation of life at birth (years) | 25 | 45 | 30 | 47.5 | 35 | 50 | 40 | 52.5 | 45 | 55 |

SOURCE: *Population Census and Surveys 1960–1961*, Table 114, p. 135.

despite a predicted increase in the fertility rate, because of the relatively smaller groups of women of childbearing age (28 percent of the population in 1960–1964 compared to 26 percent in 1980–1984). Table 31.3 presents the growth of the Gabonese population as calculated in 1961.

Several very localized studies which cannot be taken as a measure of the national situation, done recently in Libreville, indicate that a measurable decrease in primary sterility is more likely to occur than an increase in the fertility rate of nonsterile women. The hypothesis advanced by some concerning the very limited growth of the population, that the "demographic problem" of Gabon is as much a result of sterility (30 percent of all women) as of stillbirths and infant mortality, might turn out to be true. It is equally likely that the projections somewhat underestimate the capacity for growth in urban populations. There is reasonably complete registration in Libreville; and the averages there in 1961–1970 were 45 per thousand for the birth rate and 12.5 per thousand for the death rate, yielding a rate of natural increase of 32.5 percent.

GROWTH FACTORS. The effect of social factors tending to reduce the number of births is usually much greater in an urban area than in a rural one. In Gabon, however, the growth rate is higher in the city than in the rest of the country (2 percent in contrast to 1 percent in 1960–1961, and an average of $3\frac{1}{4}$ percent in the capital since 1961). In the last ten years the urban population has tripled, at the expense of the rural population.

Under such conditions, the urban environment can be considered the most important general growth factor in the country. This is a result of better hygiene, better nutrition, a higher standard of living, more thorough health care[21] and a concentration of doctors, midwives, and nurses,

[21] The 1965 campaign to locate cases of disease and to provide vaccinations, for example, reached 95 percent of the population of Libreville.

TABLE 31.3
Population projections, 1960–1985 (in thousands)

| Age | 1960 | | 1965 | | 1970 | | 1975 | | 1980 | | 1985 | |
|---|---|---|---|---|---|---|---|---|---|---|---|---|
| | M | F | M | F | M | F | M | F | M | F | M | F |
| 0–4 | 32.5 | 33.8 | 25.8 | 30.8 | 27.0 | 30.8 | 30.9 | 33.9 | 36.0 | 38.4 | 40.8 | 44.5 |
| 5–9 | 27.1 | 25.8 | 26.6 | 31.5 | 22.2 | 28.9 | 24.0 | 29.1 | 28.1 | 32.4 | 33.4 | 36.9 |
| 10–14 | 20.0 | 16.5 | 25.6 | 25.2 | 25.5 | 30.8 | 21.4 | 28.4 | 23.3 | 28.7 | 27.5 | 32.0 |
| 15–19 | 12.9 | 15.6 | 19.0 | 16.1 | 24.6 | 24.7 | 24.6 | 30.3 | 20.8 | 28.0 | 22.8 | 28.3 |
| 20–24 | 14.2 | 19.6 | 12.1 | 15.1 | 18.0 | 15.6 | 23.4 | 24.1 | 23.7 | 29.6 | 20.2 | 27.4 |
| 25–29 | 15.1 | 21.4 | 13.1 | 18.8 | 11.3 | 14.5 | 16.9 | 15.1 | 22.3 | 23.5 | 22.8 | 28.9 |
| 30–34 | 13.8 | 20.0 | 13.8 | 20.5 | 12.1 | 18.1 | 10.6 | 14.1 | 16.1 | 14.7 | 21.4 | 22.9 |
| 35–39 | 15.1 | 21.4 | 12.3 | 19.2 | 12.6 | 19.7 | 11.3 | 17.5 | 10.0 | 13.6 | 15.3 | 14.3 |
| 40–44 | 13.8 | 16.9 | 13.1 | 20.3 | 11.0 | 18.4 | 11.5 | 18.9 | 10.5 | 16.9 | 9.4 | 13.2 |
| 45–49 | 13.4 | 14.3 | 11.6 | 16.0 | 11.5 | 19.3 | 9.9 | 17.5 | 10.6 | 18.2 | 9.8 | 16.3 |
| 50–54 | 8.5 | 10.2 | 10.8 | 13.3 | 9.8 | 15.0 | 10.0 | 18.2 | 8.9 | 16.6 | 9.6 | 17.3 |
| 55–59 | 6.7 | 8.0 | 6.5 | 9.3 | 8.7 | 12.2 | 8.2 | 13.8 | 8.7 | 17.0 | 7.9 | 15.6 |
| 60–64 | 4.9 | 6.7 | 4.8 | 7.0 | 5.0 | 8.3 | 6.9 | 10.9 | 6.8 | 12.5 | 7.4 | 15.4 |
| 65–69 | 3.1 | 4.0 | 3.2 | 5.5 | 3.4 | 5.9 | 3.7 | 7.0 | 5.3 | 9.3 | 5.4 | 10.8 |
| 70+ | 3.6 | 5.3 | 3.6 | 5.7 | 3 8 | 7.0 | 4.1 | 8.0 | 4.5 | 9.5 | 6.1 | 12.1 |
| All ages | 204.7 | 239.6 | 202.1 | 254.2 | 206.3 | 269.1 | 217.4 | 287.0 | 235.5 | 308.9 | 259.8 | 336.2 |
| Both sexes | 444.3 | | 456.3 | | 475.4 | | 504.4 | | 544.4 | | 596.1 | |

SOURCE: *Population Census and Surveys 1960–1961.*

with hospitals, dispensaries, and maternal and infant care centers (PMI).

Regular consultation and care by competent personnel is a normal part of urban life, and is readily adopted by new arrivals to the city. Overall, Gabon occupies a privileged position in regard to health care with one doctor for every 6,000 inhabitants. Among the African members of WHO, only South Africa and the island of Mauritius have a higher doctor-patient ratio. The effects of this situation are seen in a much lower urban mortality rate and a reduction of sterility. Health levels should now be well above the levels in rural areas too as a result of the campaigns against endemic diseases, conducted by the SGE (Epidemic Service of the Ministry of Health), which are increasingly reaching into the remote parts of the country.

## POPULATION DISTRIBUTION

PRESENT DISTRIBUTION OF THE POPULATION. The only resource formerly exploited in Gabon was its wood, *okoumé*. Colonization consisted mainly of more or less itinerant logging camps near the coast; this is one of

the reasons for the absence of cities and a reliable internal road system during the first half of the present century. It was not until 194ɔ that the capital, Libreville, had more than 10,000 inhabitants.

Since the early years of independence the entire country has been shaken by a rapidly expanding economy: prospecting for and exploiting of minerals; public works projects; logging camps; construction at civil engineering sites, dams, and factories; the planning of a railway; and the construction of the port of Owendo, etc. The distribution pattern has been radically altered by the rural exodus. However the geographic dispersion remains much the same for populations still outside the areas of new economic activity, which frequently brings about modifications in the pattern of villages (regrouping, breaking up, moving).

The distributions within administrative regions[22] are unstable: one canton becomes empty while another doubles its population; one region witnesses spectacular growth

[22] Gabon is at present divided into 9 administrative regions with 34 districts and 111 cantons.

while another sees its population decline; while at the same time, the towns have roughly tripled their population. In the midst of these regions in upheaval, efforts are being made to stabilize some areas with programs of rural development and other works. It has not yet been possible to measure their effectiveness.

According to estimates made at the end of the 1969–1970 census, there has been a decrease in the number of villages of the order of 30 percent compared with 1960, and an increase in the number of inhabitants per village of the order of 25 percent (1960: 80 persons per village; 1970: 100 persons per village). These changes, however, are certainly underestimated, since the lists available for 1969–1970 still include many small encampments.

Table 31.4 demonstrates the effect of these changes. The last column is very indicative of

TABLE 31.4
Comparison of regional distributions of villages

| Region | 1960–1961 | 1969–1970 | Difference (percent) |
|---|---|---|---|
| Estuaire | 233 | 211 | −10 |
| Haut-Ogooué | 251 | 366 | +46 |
| Moyen-Ogooué | 234 | 241 | +3 |
| Ngounié | 938 | 485 | −48 |
| Nyanga | 994 | 242 | −76 |
| Ogooué-Ivindo | 241 | 261 | +8 |
| Ogooué-Lolo | 456 | 348 | −24 |
| Ogooué-Maritime | 167 | 164 | −2 |
| Wolen-N'Tem | 714 | 697 | −2 |
| *Gabon* | 4,228 | 3,015 | −29 |

the great upheaval in the regional location of villages. For the work camps, of which the majority still are used for logging, the censuses recorded 20 percent fewer in 1969–1970. This decrease is not very significant. There has been a substantial decline in the number of foreign logging enterprises, to the benefit of the largest ones, as a result of the opening up of the second zone to logging; many small Gabonese logging enterprises were formerly located in the first zone.

POPULATION DENSITY. In ten years the population density in Gabon has increased from 4.4 to 4.7 persons per square mile.[23] Excluding the capital, only the Ngounié and Wolen-N'Tem regions have a density greater than 5 (even in these regions there are large unoccupied areas), and it does not seem possible that any other region will be found to have reached this density by 1970. In 1960–1961 the density within each district varied from 1.3 to 23 persons per square mile; and we expect to find many important modifications in 1970 in this pattern. The density in the capital district is currently about 47 persons per square mile; but in 1967–1968 it varied from one sector to another from 0.3 to 12.5 dwellings per acre, or 9 to 325 persons per square mile.[24]

In this country where two-thirds of the land has a density under 0.4 persons per square mile and where villages are usually established along the roads, it would also be possible to calculate a linear density. This would be significant only at the district or ethnic level.

These great differentials in density and the very small size of villages are not to be explained solely by the current rural exodus or gradual migratory movements. During the last century, there were some very large villages with 10–15 or more men in the guard corps; and it cannot be denied that epidemics, famines, and wars have wiped out many villages, as well as entire groups of the population.

ETHNIC GROUPS. The detailed ethnic distribution in Gabon is a veritable riddle. The National Statistical Service's list was compiled in collaboration with Biffot and Perrois.[25] It is difficult to make use of the distribution for 1960–1961, because it covers only that part of the population 14 years or older, and there are great differences in age structure between the

[23] G. Sautter has drawn up two very detailed maps of population density in Volume II of his *De l'Atlantique au fleuve Congo, une Géographie du Sous-peuplement* (Paris, La Haye, Mouton, 1966).
[24] Study on the standard of living in Libreville, 1967–1968, "Housing in Libreville," SNSEE (July 1969).
[25] Respectively, a sociologist and an ethnologist at ORSTOM.

TABLE 31.5
Ethnic distribution, 1960–1961 (Over 14 years of age)

| Ethnic Group | Percent | Ethnic Group | Percent |
|---|---|---|---|
| Apindji | 0.4 | Fang | 30.9 |
| Bakélé | 3.4 | Massango | 3.9 |
| Bakota | 6.6 | Mitsogo | 2.9 |
| Bakwélé[a] | — | Myéné | 4.2 |
| Balumbu | 2.9 | Obamba | 6.0 |
| Bandzabi | 13.2 | Okandé | 2.4 |
| Bapounu | 11.3 | Pygmé | 0.7 |
| Batéké | 2.7 | Seké | 0.2 |
| Bavoungou | 1.0 | Other ethnic | |
| Eshira | 5.7 | groups | 1.6 |
| | | Total | 100.0 |

[a] In 1960–1961 classified as Apindji, Bakélé, or Bakota.

various ethnic groups.[26] Table 31.5 presents the distribution for those 14 and over in 1960–1961, according to the ethnic groupings used in 1969–1970.

Certain ethnic groups, unable to withstand epidemics, famines, wars and the slave trade, have been eliminated in historical times. Others now exist in numbers very much smaller than those estimated for the nineteenth century or the beginning of the twentieth.

RELIGION.    No study appears to have been undertaken of the religions of Gabon; but two surveys (1966 and 1970) were conducted in the capital by the archbishopric of Libreville. The Catholic Church is estimated to account for 70 percent of the population (36 parishes, 268 schools and colleges) and the Protestant Church for 10 percent (31 parishes, 80 schools and colleges). Only the foreigners from West Africa are Moslem (3,000 at the most). There are many syncretic and traditional sects to which the great majority of the population belongs; but the proportion of Christians belonging to these sects is unknown.

[26] Depending on the ethnic group, the survival rate at age 1 year (among children of women aged 15–19 years) varied in 1960–1961 from 50 to 80 percent, and the infant mortality rate for children born to women from 15 to 49 varied from 80 to 200 per thousand.

## AGE AND SEX STRUCTURE

AGE DISTRIBUTION.    The detailed age distribution of the population in 1960–1961 (by month for the first year and by year thereafter) presents many anomalies. Such occurrences are not uncommon in populations where the adults have little or no education; and we know that these anomalies are essentially due to systematic errors.

In the distribution by month (0–11 months), the considerable deficit for those under a month (voluntary omissions in keeping with custom) and the great excess at 11 months (error around the important turning point of one year) can be eliminated by adjusting these two deviant age groups. We thus obtain an "ideal" shape, representing approximately the survival curve corresponding to an infant mortality rate of 150 per thousand, as hypothesized. For the older ages when distributed in single years, the customary attraction of certain numbers (0, 5, even numbers) considerably disturbs the pyramid. The age group, "1 year," likewise displays a considerable deficit, due in part to a bad interpretation around this important age. It seems more realistic under such conditions to analyze the pyramid by quinquennial groups (see Table 31.6).

For males, the number of those between 15–19 years covered by the census corresponds, in large part, to the number in school. Some of the children who are really 15 or 16 years old are declared to be less than 15 (those not initiated, in particular, and not in school) and others are declared to be over 19 (initiated young men who do not, or no longer, go to school). For females, the stated age is directly tied to marriage and motherhood. Young unmarried women are said to be under 15, those in the higher years of school and not married are said to be 15–19, married women are 20 or over, depending on the number of children they have, with a maximum total number 35–40 years. For men as well as women the most important systematic error in the noting of ages stems from the very sharp distinction between the child and the adult.

TABLE 31.6

Smoothing of the total population by sex and age (percentage distribution)

| Age (in years) | Age Statement at Census | | Smoothed Distribution | |
|---|---|---|---|---|
| | M | F | M | F |
| 0–4 | 5.9 | 6.1 | 7.3 | 7.6 |
| 5–9 | 5.2 | 4.9 | 6.1 | 5.8 |
| 10–14 | 4.1 | 3.3 | 4.5 | 3.7 |
| 15–19 | 2.3 | 2.9 | 2.9 | 3.5 |
| 20–24 | 3.1 | 4.0 | 3.2 | 4.4 |
| 25–29 | 3.5 | 4.6 | 3.4 | 4.8 |
| 30–34 | 3.2 | 4.8 | 3.1 | 4.5 |
| 35–39 | 3.9 | 5.7 | 3.4 | 4.8 |
| 40–44 | 3.6 | 4.5 | 3.1 | 3.8 |
| 45–49 | 3.8 | 3.9 | 3.0 | 3.2 |
| 50–54 | 2.4 | 2.7 | 1.9 | 2.3 |
| 55–59 | 1.8 | 2.1 | 1.5 | 1.8 |
| 60–64 | 1.3 | 1.7 | 1.1 | 1.5 |
| 65–69 | 0.8 | 1.1 | 0.7 | 0.9 |
| 70+ | 1.0 | 1.6 | 0.8 | 1.2 |
| All ages | 46.1 | 53.9 | 46.1 | 53.9 |

In addition to these systematic errors, there are other events known to introduce apparent anomalies in the age structure, deficits which are directly linked with the epidemics and famines that raged over almost all the regions of the interior in 1924–1927, and with the intensive recruitment of manual labor by loggers after 1928.

The distribution by sex in regions such as Nyanga, Ngounié, or Ogooué-Lolo in 1960–1961 gave a ratio of less than 70 males per hundred females for the group 15–19 years; and it varied from 45–52 in the 30–34 year group. We must obviously take into account the rural-urban migration after Gabon became independent, when many young men were drawn to the large towns.

A year-by-year comparative study of the 1960–1961 age groups with those of 1969–1970 makes it possible to deal with the age structure in Gabon much less hypothetically. Nevertheless, the problem of knowing ages is still, and will long remain, crucial, since the registration of vital statistics, although compulsory, is not practiced. Continuous observation seems to be the only solution until an effective registry is established.

The distribution by major age groups has changed. Those under 15 years, less than 30 percent in 1938, accounted for 35 percent of the population in 1960–1961. But the predictions made on the basis of the survey indicate a relative decline until 1980 for this group, and a figure of 36 percent in 1985. In Libreville in 1960–1961 this group formed 29 percent of the population; in 1964, 30.7 percent; and in 1969, 34.8 percent.

DISTRIBUTION BY SEX. Gabon is also unique in its sex ratio, nationally averaging only 85 males per hundred females. Figure 31.3 shows sex ratios by age group for four populations: the whole of Gabon (1960–1961); the Nyanga region (1960–1961); Libreville (1960–1961); and all the countries studied in *Comparative Demography*.[27]

The size and nature of the variations in sex ratios make it very difficult to attempt an analysis of the distribution by sex in Gabon as a function of age. We know from the beginning that there are systematic errors in age determination (the distinction between child and adult, for example); but we must also add to these an underestimation of the number of women between 10 and 14 years and of the number of men from 20–24 years, in accord with the deficits noted above. It is also certain that Gabon, like the rest of Central Africa, paid a heavy toll in the war efforts of its former colonizers. It is interesting to note the contrast in Figure 31.3 between the capital (enormous growth as a result of the rural migrants) and the Nyanga region, which was still losing its male population at this time (1960–1961).

On the regional level marked distortions are noticeable arising from the large migratory movements and the variations in mortality depending on the circumstances from one period to another. In 1938 the sex ratio was 75. The enormous decline in population from 1908–1930 in Upper Ogooué, due to sleeping sickness and the ensuing permanent exodus of adult males, has been noted. The sex ratio in the logging camps of

[27] "Afrique Noire, Madagascar, Comores," *Démographie Comparée*, INSEE, INED, DGRST (Paris 1967).

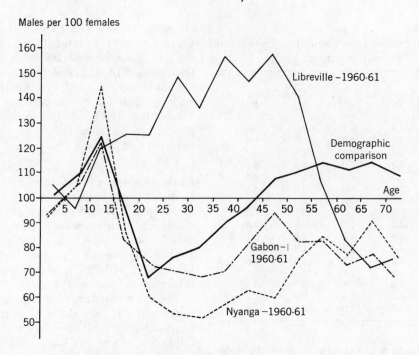

FIGURE 31.3.  *A Comparison of Sex Ratios, by Age*

Fougamou and Mimongo in 1938 was 358 for adults; and 60 percent of the men who had been recruited never returned home after their contracts ended. This explains the distortions in the distributions as well as the population decline up to 1959. Male mortality, much higher than female mortality, also adds imbalance to this distribution. Out of almost 6,000 observed births in 1970, 62 percent of those stillborn and 65 percent of those who died during the first week were boys. Three-fifths of the total number of deaths registered in Libreville in 1970 were males. The male mortality rate in 1960–1961 was 39 per thousand, as against 22 per thousand for females. It will certainly be a matter of years before there can be any lowering of the current male mortality rate, which seems to be a phenomenon peculiar to Gabon.

### EDUCATION

According to the 1960–1961 census, 53 percent of those 15 years and older spoke no French, the official language. The proportions were as follows: males, 24 percent; females 74

percent. There is no more recent data available for the whole of the country to compare with the 1960 figures; but a survey on illiteracy was conducted in Libreville in 1968.[28]

In 1960–1961 the illiterates made up the following proportions: males, 77 percent; females, 95 percent; population as a whole, 87 percent. For the past ten years, Gabon has been conducting an excellent education campaign, and the people's education office of the Ministry of National Education is very active. The current illiteracy rate is estimated to have fallen below 75 percent.

Education is compulsory for those 6–16 years old; however, the Ministry of Education at present considers it possible to provide schooling for only 80 percent of this group, given the average of eight school years necessary to complete the formal six years of primary education. In addition to those in primary school, there are the secondary school pupils who are also affected by the compulsory education requirements. Thus the

[28] "Illiteracy in Libreville 1968," Education Department, SNSEE.

rate of primary schooling in 1969 was said to be 96.4 percent.[29] The index of the numbers at school in 1969 compared with a base of 100 for 1958 was 223 for primary school and 1,003 for secondary school.

It is quite remarkable to note that in 1969 girls accounted for 47 percent of the primary level pupils, a rise from less than one-third to nearly one-half of all students in a decade. The following estimates were made at the beginning of the 1970 school year: 100,000 pupils; 2,500 classes; 2,700 teaching personnel (headmasters, directors, professors, teachers, supervisors, etc.). The Normal School and a university are under construction, and an Information Systems School (OCAM) is to be built in the near future. The University Institute of Technology has been functioning for several years and the university has begun giving courses.

The 1968 illiteracy survey in Libreville found that among the population over 12 years of age, two women out of three and two men out of five could neither read nor write; that almost three-quarters of the illiterates were 30 years old or more; that the illiteracy rate was inversely proportional to the number of people living together in households with fewer than 10 persons, although this result does not seem to hold for households with more than ten people. The illiterate population consisted mainly of recently arrived immigrants from the interior.

With the progressive reduction of illiteracy and a very high rate of schooling and specialized training in the university, the Gabonese should be able more and more to replace the foreign technicians and skilled workers (70 percent of all workers in these categories in 1960–1961) and, much more slowly, those in specialized professional fields. It is also important that they should train agriculturalists for the scientific production of foodstuffs.

## OCCUPATION

From the 1960–1961 census, we have available only a distribution by socio-

[29] It appears to have been 79 percent in 1970, which casts doubt on the 1969 statistic.

TABLE 31.7

Distribution of Gabonese by socioprofessional category, 1960–1961

| Categories | Number | Percent |
|---|---|---|
| Farmers, planters, salaried and nonsalaried agricultural laborers | 150,004 | 48.6 |
| Employers, liberal professions, artisans, tradesmen, self-employed | 14,210 | 4.6 |
| Managers, executives, engineers, etc. | 4,309 | 1.4 |
| Clerical and office workers (nonmanual workers) | 3,517 | 1.1 |
| Manual workers | 36,986 | 12.0 |
| Administrative staff | 4,699 | 1.5 |
| Miscellaneous, unoccupied, not stated | 94,877 | 30.8 |
| Whole of Gabon | 308,602 | 100.0 |

professional category of the population aged 14 or over (see Table 31.7). The 1969–1970 census will provide a series of data on trades and occupations.

Certainly it is very difficult to define precisely from the available information trade and professional activity; the socioprofessional categories in Table 31.7 are open to question. The agricultural survey of 1960–1961 indicated that for heads of households in farming areas, the activities termed secondary were, in fact, the main occupations.

Two groups in Table 31.7 are very large: almost half of the population covered gave an agricultural occupation; and one in three belonged to the nonemployed sector (students, the ill, the aged, and those out of work). These two categories will certainly be greatly modified when the 1969–70 census data are made available, with a sharp decline in the number of agricultural workers and a marked rise among salaried workers and the nonemployed (particularly students).

In 1960–1961, expatriates numbered 16 percent of all persons in the second category, 31 percent of those in the third category, and 32 percent of the nonmanual workers. These proportions should be currently undergoing important changes as a result of the government's active program of "Gabonization"— except among the managers and skilled employees, who cannot yet be replaced by Gabonese.

Occupational rates by sex and age group for residents have been calculated, but it is unknown to what extent each person was fully and continuously employed in the stated occupation. The activity rates for women are much lower than for men at all ages; but the rates for women were probably underestimated by the census. It would seem that men begin working very young and continue working until quite old (the activity rate for the age group 60–69 years is over 80 percent). The differences in the rates for the two sexes are particularly marked in the age range 20–29 (93 and 56 percent), but the rates are practically the same between 15–19 years (46 and 44 percent). The occupational rate for men was very high in the urban centers and in the work sites outside. There were great differences between the various regions in the activity rates recorded for the youngest and oldest ages. In the agricultural sector, manual labor is done mainly by women and the methods of cultivation are mostly traditional.

The Gabonese Office of Social Assistance has a data-processing center to handle information on employers and salaried workers. Every year it presents in its report a table using the ILO-Gabon nomenclature (see Table 31.8). Among the occupational sectors, certain undertakings are in a prominent

TABLE 31.8
Distribution of salaried workers by occupational sector, 1968

| Occupational Group | Number | Percent |
|---|---|---|
| Farming, fishing, hunting, stock raising, forestry | 9,484 | 15.3 |
| (Extractive) industries | 4,853 | 7.8 |
| Food industries, lumber processing | 4,308 | 6.9 |
| Chemical and metal industries, refining | 1,702 | 2.8 |
| Public works, building | 9,265 | 14.9 |
| Power industries | 439 | 0.7 |
| Commerce, supplies, banks, insurance | 5,843 | 9.4 |
| Transport | 3,795 | 6.1 |
| Services | 22,465 | 36.1 |
| Whole of salaried workers | 62,154 | 100.0 |

position; lumbering represents more than 80 percent of the first group; manganese, uranium, and oil make up 98 percent of the second group; sawmills and machine-processing of wood are 67 percent of the third group; construction companies and public works strictly defined represent 89 percent of the fifth group; maritime transport (excluding coasting) is 51 percent of the eighth group; and employees of government services and civil servants make up 65 percent of the final group.

To these salaried workers should be added about a thousand foreigners (technical assistants and diplomats). The current average annual growth rate among salaried workers seems to be about 7 percent. About one-tenth as many women as men appear to be salaried workers.

In 1960–1961, 63 percent of those employed were involved in traditional occupations: 31 percent of the men and 94 percent of the women. The traditional sector is very largely the domain of women. The modern sector of the economy employs 37 percent of the workers: 69 percent of the men but only 6 percent of the women. It should be noted that it is only in the coastal areas of Estuary (Libreville) and Ogooué-Maritime (Port Gentil) that a sizable percentage of women is found in the modern sector; in the other regions (except for Middle Ogooué), the percentage is negligible.

A detailed series of data on professions and status within a profession for Libreville in 1964 is found in a document published by the National Statistical Service.[30]

A memorandum was put out in 1968 on the use of time by the residents of Ngounié, based on data collected during a 1963 survey on the budget and living conditions.[31] It consists mainly of a distribution by sex of work time, varying from 2–25 percent of all time during the year for men and from 2–36 percent for women. For men 31 percent of their time is

[30] Census of the Population: Community of Libreville, National Statistical Service (August 1965).
[31] An experimental study of the use of time by the inhabitants of Ngounié in Gabon, based on statistical documents, etc.

devoted to traditional or modern products, 26 percent to rest, and 4 percent to agricultural production. Women spend 36 percent of their time on household tasks, more than 17 percent on agricultural work, and 13 percent at rest. For both groups, travel takes up 8 percent of the time. Men build and repair the huts, take charge of deforesting future farmland, fish, and hunt. Women do household and agricultural work. This division of labor is a fundamental characteristic of the village society. The author of the memorandum discussed the severe imbalance in working time between men and women. Men in rural areas seem to be largely idle, and this might accentuate the massive migration to the towns, which is important in Ngounié as in other regions.

## HOUSING, MARRIAGE, AND THE FAMILY

HOUSING. There are no reliable data on housing in Gabon except for the capital.[32] The responses on the subject in questionnaires used in 1963 in the rural areas have never been processed and this indicator of the standard of living is therefore not available for the whole of the country.

The villages are characterized by their smallness (an average of 80 inhabitants in 1960–1961, with half the villages having a population of less than 50) and their instability. In general they are rather poor. The quality of construction varies greatly from region to region: Those which are far from the roads and the centers of activity are often better built and better maintained. Construction materials vary according to availability: bark, bamboo, hewn logs, reinforced earth, etc.; with thatch roofs which often serve as a natural decoration.[33] Usually there is an individual dwelling place for each household unit of production and consumption. The furniture and tools are still produced by

artisans, often in the village itself. Virtually all the people own the huts they live in; but in the large towns some rental of traditional housing takes place.

Three types of dwelling can be defined: huts built of traditional materials; mixed huts (sawed logs, semihard); and modern buildings. There are also tenement houses and huts made of salvaged materials in the cities. One might equally well classify dwellings on other criteria: e.g., the traditional with an outdoor kitchen versus the modern with an interior one.

In the capital, excluding nondomestic buildings, there are an average of three rooms per dwelling and 1.4 dwellings per acre, with great variations depending on the part of the city. The rural-urban migration which brings more than 4,000 Gabonese to Libreville each year poses enormous economic problems; and the urban infrastructure (roads, water, electricity, sanitation, etc.) cannot keep up with the rate of expansion of the city. Scarcely 12 percent of the dwellings were supplied with water and electricity in 1968.

MARRIAGE. Marriage is, without exception, exogamous; and a knowledge of the genealogies makes it possible to recognize the members of a clan and to know to which women men can be married. However, one can speak of ethnic endogamy; and, considering the smallness of many ethnic groups, the question of consanguineous marriages could be posed. It should be possible to study this question when data are available from the 1971–72 sociomedical survey. The persistence of ethnic separation is still very clear.[34] Membership in a clan is passed on patrilineally or matrilineally, depending on the clan.[35] Marriage is concluded after payment to the father or the maternal uncle (depending on the type of kinship) of certain valuables constituting the bridewealth (officially forbidden since 1963). This is an obstacle to marriage for young men and facilitates the polygamy of

[32] "Study of Living Conditions in Libreville, 1961–1962"; *Study on the Standards of Living in Libreville, 1967–1968*, Part I, "Housing in Libreville" (to be published).

[33] M. François, "Notes on the Construction of Huts in Gabon" (to be published).

[34] In 1960–1961, 93 percent of marriages were ethnically homogeneous.

[35] H. Deschamps, Oral traditions and records of Gabon.

older ones, who often have young wives. In Gabon as a whole, more than 60 percent of men aged 20–24 and 35 percent of those aged 25–29 were unmarried in 1960–1961. The proportions are higher in the cities; and the proportion of men polygamously married increases consistently with age until 60–70 years. The Bureau of Vital Statistics in the capital registered 17 marriages by modern law and 577 by traditional law in 1968.

The customary classification of the matrimonial state is very complex, especially for women, and undoubtedly leads to confusion during census enumeration. Are engaged girls considered single or married? Is concubinage a precise concept among the people? What about young widows who, by custom, become wives in another household? What is the position of childless women, who are declared to be single although they are married?

The polygamy rate is relatively low in Gabon and reaches its maximum of 1.6 for the whole of the country for males over 60 years of age. The maximums vary from one area to another (1.7 in the rural zone; 1.3 in the town; 1.4 in the work camps) and also from one age or ethnic group to another (among the Myéné, a maximum of 1.5 from 30–39 years; among the Eshira, 1.9 from 60–69 years).

The proportion of widows is naturally much higher than that of widowers (16 percent: 3 percent). Polygamy accentuates this phenomenon.

THE FAMILY. The family structure reflects the predominantly matrilineal nature of the society, and it is usually the maternal uncle who is the head of the family. The basic unit consists of the husband, his wife or wives, and their children. Relatives or friends may be added to this core group.

In Gabon, communal living is little practiced compared with most of Africa, where it is on average almost ten times as common. The average size of a household in 1960–1961 was very low: 3.9 persons. It varied by region (3 in Estuary, 5 in Nyanga), by milieu (4.1 in the villages; 3.4 in the towns; 2.8 in the work camps), and by ethnic group

(3.5 among the Bakota and Mbédés; 4.1 among the Eshira and the Fang). The size was, however, highly correlated with socio-professional categories (2.9 for household employees; 6.2 for those in administration, teaching, and the liberal professions).

Monogamous households were in the majority making up 56 percent. Polygamous households accounted for 28 percent of the total, and 21 percent of the households were incomplete (one partner dead or absent).

The age difference between spouses is especially great for marriages where the woman married young (13 years for women under 20), and decreases for older women partly because of remarriage. Two tendencies were noted in 1960–1961: Couples were often jointly engaged in some sort of modern activity; and, on the other hand, the proportion of nonworking women was higher when the husband was in a modern occupation.

## FERTILITY AND STERILITY

All the information we have since the beginning of colonization indicates the importance of sterility as a factor in the low birth rate; and we shall see evidence of this in the high rates for spontaneous abortion and stillbirths (as well as the high infant mortality). However, certain ethnic groups found in the interior of the country in the nineteenth century were reported to be fertile (the Apindji, for example). Fertility levels differ very greatly between the different ethnic groups.

There are no regular or even reliable vital statistics available, except for such centers as Libreville, despite the fact that birth and death registration is legally compulsory. The only estimations of fertility are those from the 1960–1961 survey. The fertility rates, number of children, and fertility indices are given in Tables 31.9 and 31.10.

The adjusted cumulated fertility curve[36] coincides satisfactorily with the curve for number of children; and the latter two coincide fairly well at the beginning of the

[36] Final number of children born/total cumulated fertility.

TABLE 31.9
Fertility measures, 1960–1961

| Age (in years) | (1) Age Specific Birth Rates | (2) "Cumulated" Fertility | (3) Average Number of Live Births | Percentage by which (2) Exceeds (3) |
|---|---|---|---|---|
| 15–19 | 171 | | 0.46 | 9 |
| 20 | | 0.85 | | |
| 20–24 | 190 | | 1.19 | 29 |
| 25 | | 1.80 | | |
| 25–29 | 173 | | 1.76 | 39 |
| 30 | | 2.65 | | |
| 30–34 | 127 | | 2.13 | 46 |
| 35 | | 3.30 | | |
| 35–39 | 98 | | 2.47 | 53 |
| 40 | | 3.80 | | |
| 40–44 | 43 | | 2.50 | 51 |
| 45 | | 4.00 | | |
| 45–49 | 27 | | 2.78 | 48 |
| 50 | | 4.15 | | |
| 50+ | | | 3.20 | |

period considered, which indicates that the data for the 12 months prior to the survey were correct. The deformation of the number of children curve in relation to the cumulated fertility curve is due to errors in reporting of the total number of children; the failure to report births rises with the time that has elapsed since the births.

We have used 1960–1961 fertility to measure the most probable annual level of

TABLE 31.10
Fertility and child survival

| | | |
|---|---|---|
| Number per thousand surviving to exact age: | 0 | 1,000 |
| | 1 year | 771 |
| | 5 years | 657 |
| | 10 years | 626 |
| | 0 | 13.6 |
| Total numbers enumerated (in thousands) | 1–4 years | 40.0 |
| | 5–9 years | 45.0 |
| | All ages | 444.3 |
| Crude birth rate | 35 per thousand | |
| Rate of natural increase | 0.5 percent | |
| Total fertility ratio | 4.15 | |
| Completed fertility | 2.78 | |
| Estimates of | 0–4 | 3.91 |
| completed fertility | 5–9 | 3.90 |
| according to | 0–9 | 3.90 |
| proportions aged: | | |

Estimates have been made by employing Model Life Tables, level 10 for men, level 50 for women. United Nations, *Manuals on Methods of Estimating Population, Manual III: Methods for Population Projection by Sex and Age* (New York, 1956).

births. The crude birth rate was 35 per thousand; the corresponding general fertility rate was 116 per thousand females aged 15–49; and gross reproduction rate was 2.1. These are the lowest rates recorded in Africa. Of the women, 35 percent had had no live births; 17 percent had borne only one child; 12 percent had borne two; 9 percent three; 8 percent four; 6 percent five, and so on. We also noted a continued upward displacement of modal fertility as the mother's age increased. For women of 15–19 years, the greatest number have borne one child; for those 20–24, two children; 25–29, four children; 30–34, six; and 35–39, eight.

Contrary to what usually is observed in Africa, fertility is higher in the towns than in the rural areas (crude birth rates of 42 and 33 respectively; general fertility rates of 156 and 109). In the rural areas it is very low. This difference is now of great importance, because the urban population has more than tripled in ten years; and the population projections of 1960–1961 could thus be underestimates. The variations in these two fertility rates are also considerable from one region to another (Nyanga: 52 and 170; Ogooué-Lolo: 25 and 80), and from one ethnic group to another.

We can approach the question of biological factors affecting fertility by the index of total sterility (percentage of women never having had a live birth); and Gabon is particularly conspicuous in this respect, with 35 percent of all women in 1960–1961 in this category. For the 15–19 year age group, the figures are within the usual range for Africa; but in the older age groups they are almost double those found elsewhere (Table 31.11). Considering

TABLE 31.11
Index of primary sterility, 1960–1961

| Age of Females (in years) | Percent Who Have Never Borne a Live Child |
|---|---|
| 15–19 | 65 |
| 20–24 | 41 |
| 25–29 | 34 |
| 30–34 | 36 |
| 35–39 | 33 |
| 40–44 | 36 |
| 45–49 | 32 |
| 50+ | 30 |

this index as one of biological sterility for women over 30 years of age, Gabon's position is certainly the worst in Africa. Not the least important cause of this sterility is venereal disease.

Although the urban environment is considered more healthy in terms of most diseases, 31.9 percent of the women in Libreville in 1960–1961 had had no live births. Conjugal life is greatly disturbed by the mobility of the men and rural emigration, as well as by certain taboos which further increase the periods when there is no sexual intercourse. The effects of polygyny and the large number of unmarried men have also been pointed out. Fertility declines with an increase in the number of wives in polygynous households (general fertility rates of 128 in one-wife households, 111 in two-wife ones, 99 in three-or-more wife households). The general fertility rate in 1960–1961 varied from 103 to 218 by socioprofessional category of the husband. No study has been made of induced abortion; but it is thought that the problem is not negligible, especially among young girls in the cities; and the government has taken measures to try to prevent it.

## MORTALITY AND MORBIDITY

MORTALITY. A substantial body of information shows clearly that up to 1950 the population was declining: many large villages were wiped out by smallpox in 1840–1850, and a huge reduction of population was caused in High-Ogooué in 1923–1930 by sleeping sickness (18 percent of deaths among recruited workers in the area were attributed to it). Whole ethnic groups have disappeared including the Adyoumba, the Enenga, and many more now forgotten. Other ethnic groups are in the process of disappearing; the previously numerous Apindji numbered only 1,700 by 1960–1961. The population of whole regions was declining rapidly, for example, Ogooué-Ivindo (sex ratio 65 males per hundred females, 35–40 percent of women sterile, 5 deaths for each birth, infant mortality rates of 200–300 per thousand), Ogooué-Lolo, High-Ogooué, Ngounié, and Nyanga.

The country has known epidemics, famine, malnutrition, overindulgence in alcohol (local or imported),[37] intensive labor recruitment,[38] in past times the slave-trade, isolation of small groups in a huge hostile forest, and until 1925 rural areas with only one or two doctors (Doctor Albert Schweitzer among them). In these conditions, how could a people survive? It was not until around 1950 that this drainage of human beings could be stopped.

We still have mortality data only from the 1960–1961 survey and usable registration figures from parish registers only for inner Libreville. Two types of information were gathered in 1960–1961: deaths according to sex and age in each family during the previous 12 months, and the number of children dead or surviving per woman at the time of the survey.

The calculated crude death rate of 30 per thousand was very high, and it was much greater for males than females (39 as against

[37] Over 3 million gallons of wine and beer and over 20,000 gallons of spirits were imported each year ("Health Department Report" Plan, 1966).
[38] Only 50 percent of the men were considered fit for the work camps, and of those recruited 18 percent died and 30 percent never "returned to the village."

22 per thousand). The stillbirth rate is doubt-less very high, but we have no figures for the country. Abortions are only very incom-pletely reported, but nevertheless they repre-sent 15 percent of reported pregnancies. Of the 6,000 women registered in 1970 as entering hospitals to give birth,[39] 4.2 percent had stillbirths (3.5 percent in towns and 6 percent in rural areas) and 1.2 percent had babies who died within the first week (0.75 percent in towns and 1.5 percent in the rural areas).[40] Thus, 94 percent of women have children alive one week after completing a full-term pregnancy (95 percent in town and 92.6 percent in rural areas). Infant mortality in Gabon in 1960–1961 was the third highest in Africa (Zambia 259 per thousand births, Mali 250, Gabon 229).[41]

The crude death rate of 30 per thousand, regarded as being the most probable, corre-sponds with an expectation of life at birth in the United Nations model life tables of around 32 years, with a significant differential by sex (25 years for males, 45 for females). We have already mentioned the link, on the one hand, which may exist between this low expectation of life for men and the large proportion of bachelors, thus leading to low birth rate, and, on the other hand, the permanent imbalance of the distribution by sex, with a male mortal-ity exceeding that of females by 77 percent. According to the report on neonatal and post-neonatal mortality in 1970,[42] 61.4 percent of stillbirths are boys, and boys make up 65.2 percent of deaths of the first week. The Technical Office of the Ministry of Health is collecting information on fetal mortality by sex and time since conception from the medical centers. The information already

TABLE 31.12
Mortality differentials by region, ethnicity, and residence, 1960–1961: extreme levels (rates per thousand)

| Distribution | Crude Death Rates | Infant Mortality Rate |
|---|---|---|
| *By region* | | |
| Wolen-N'Tem | 23 | 54 |
| Ogooué-Ivindo | 20 | 47 |
| Haut-Ogooué | 59 | 236 |
| *By ethnic group* | | |
| Fang | 25 | 84 |
| Mbédé | 34 | 199 |
| Okandé | 36 | 102 |
| *By residence* | | |
| Rural | 31 | 133 |
| Urban | 21 | 78 |

collected indicates, on the one hand, twice as many premature boys as girls, and on the other, twice as many male as female fetuses spontaneously aborting. Table 31.12 demon-strates some mortality differentials.

The average number of surviving children was 1.39 in 1960–1961 and the infant mortality rate increased from 72 per thousand for the children of women 20–24 years of age, to 253 per thousand, with women 45–49 years of age.

MORBIDITY. Every year the Health Depart-ment[43] presents a series of tables of the incidence of disease. Over the last ten years there has always been the same classification of data by order of importance, and this corresponds also to the earlier information still.

For children under one year of age, 5.5 percent are recorded as having had chicken pox, measles, and mumps; 13 percent had intestinal worms; 13 percent had scabies; 15 percent had diseases of the digestive system; 24 percent had diseases of the respiratory passages; and 24 percent had malaria. For all people treated, 10 percent had respiratory diseases, 12 percent malaria, and 13 percent ankylostomiasis and other complaints caused by worms. Five percent of women are treated

[39] Statistics on neonatal and postneonatal mortality for confinements in areas covered by hospital in 1970 (Technical Office of the Ministry of Health, Dr. J. C. Gilles).

[40] Pregnancy abnormalities are more frequent in the rural areas and curative services and nursing facilities are better in the towns.

[41] Statistics on neonatal and postneonatal mortality for confinements in areas covered by hospital in 1970 (Technical Office of the Ministry of Health).

[42] It is probable that half of all children born in Gabon do not survive to the age of five years.

[43] *Annual Report*, Ministry of Public Health and Population.

for diseases of the genital organs. But all this information only concerns the people who come for treatment and in these conditions it is preferable to refer to the annual reports of the Major Endemic Diseases Department, whose mobile teams cover a very large proportion of the population. The 1969 report specifies that malaria is the most frequently occurring endemic disease and the major cause of mortality. In the second position we find all the diseases of the respiratory system. Bilharzia infects a fairly large part of the population and urethritis has been constantly increasing. Gonorrhea is the third most common disease reported, undoubtedly one of the explanations of the high level of sterility in Gabon.

Weight at birth is considered as an indicator of the nutritional state of a population, and in Gabon it averages the same level as reported for the rest of Africa. Breast feeding is satisfactory until six months, but subsequent mixed feeding and weaning are unsatisfactory. The vitamin deficiencies are mainly those of vitamin B2, and are connected more with the environment than lack of food. The basis of the common and serious multiple infections of the intestines is the frequent contamination of fruits and vegetables. Locally produced intoxicating drinks also cause ill health where their ingredients can be grown. The use of *Iboga*[44] has the advantages, but also the drawbacks of the amphetamines, and lessens resistance to infectious disease. The 15-year development plan (1966–1980) for the Health Services advocates the creation of special health areas, in order to fight the prolific parasite life efficiently (bilharzia, mosquitoes, leeches, flies, etc.), and shows that these improved conditions are essential for the improvement of everyone's condition. Such modern areas seem to be appearing spontaneously, wherever people turn from traditional agriculture.

The effort made in Gabon in recent years has been enormous. With fewer than 6,000 inhabitants per doctor and one hospital bed for each 11,000 inhabitants, Gabon has a density of medical coverage five times as high as the average for Africa, which partly explains the population growth since 1950. In the last three years of the 1960s more than a million vaccinations were given (smallpox, BCG, yellow fever, and measles). But several more years of effort will be necessary to reduce the individual, biological, and ecological factors tending to high mortality, all of which are much more pronounced in Gabon than elsewhere.

## MIGRATION

Sautter[45] thinks there are reasons to believe that the Gabonese population was more numerous at the end of the last century. All the research we have undertaken supports this.[46] However, we cannot deduce how numerous that population was. Soutter also believes that the forest has screened Gabon from the large intracontinental migratory movements. The country has therefore found itself with small isolated groups in a hostile forest, necessarily leading to enforced consanguinary marriages. The explorer, Du Chaillu,[47] was early struck by the isolation of these populations from the rest of the world. Generally speaking, it is almost certain that, except for the Fang, population movements toward the west (i.e., toward the coast) have had a very marked destructive effect.[48] The spectacular depopulation was not originally due to colonial intervention, which only accelerated it, but to the creation of real human drains,[49] by epidemics and famine and by the slave trade, and it is certain that regions such as High Ogooué, for example,

[44] Hallucinatory plant, of which the grated bark and the wood of the root are used. This sacred bush is credited with magical properties and is used by the initiated of the Cwiti to communicate with their ancestors; see André Raponda Walker and Roger Sillans, *Rites and Beliefs of the Gabonese Peoples* (Paris, 1962), pp. 46 and 48.

[45] Sautter, *De l'Atlantique au fleuve Congo*.
[46] See Figure 29.1.
[47] Paul Belloni du Chaillu, *Wild Africa* (Paris, 1868).
[48] Sautter, *De l'Atlantique au fleuve Congo*.
[49] The estimation of "nonreturn to village" 1938 was between 60 and 75 percent of the whole of those recruited.

have been suffering a passive and permanent exodus for many years.

Today, rural-urban migration accentuates more and more this depopulation of the inland, which was relatively stabilized when a colony, thanks to plantation crops (coffee, cocoa, and peanuts) and the absence of large urban centers (this excludes the effect of recruitment for work camps). However, in ten years of independence the urban population has tripled, and each year Libreville must absorb an extra 1 percent of the Gabonese population.[50] For 20 years, the interior of the country has been shaken by the departure of a population which could not resist the attraction of the economic centers.

This draining of the rural society is very serious, for one of the main roles of rural population is to meet the food needs of all the consumers wherever they are, and over the last few years it has no longer appeared capable of adequately supplying the main urban centers. The condition of the markets and the price of food prove it.

Foreigners living in Gabon only make up 5–6 percent of the population, and this proportion is unlikely to change. In 1960–1961 there were about 21,000 foreigners, of whom 16,000 were African; but the African foreigners have been changing for the last ten years in nationality and number, this being closely linked with the political history of the country. According to the 1960–1961 survey, the non-African foreigners (91 percent of whom were French) were concentrated in the 25–44 age group (54 percent of the whole). The French nationals, although continuing to increase, declined in proportion during the 1960s. The African foreign population has a predominance of males, there being one-third more men than women.

At the moment, the number of Gabonese living abroad (diplomatic and consular representatives, students, and professional probationers) is estimated at 1,500 and it is

certain that, with the new University, the number of Gabonese students living abroad will fall progressively from 1970 on.

The 1960–1961 survey presents two ways of measuring internal movements: the place of birth, which allows a determination of the number of people who have left their place of birth, but does not show whether they lived there at one time or another, or whether they lived elsewhere; and the place of former residence, which gives a much more objective idea of "definitive" moves. Temporary movements have been studied from the information on length of residence at the time of the census.

The analysis of the data on those "born in the place of census" and "born elsewhere" shows the very high mobility of the population as a whole, compared with other African countries: 48 percent of men and 59 percent of women do not live in their place of birth (see Figure 31.4).

The maximums are reached earlier for women (25–29 years) than for men (30–34 years). The villages are very small and there are consequently few marriages between inhabitants of the same village. There has also been a tendency for men to "return to the village" to end their days.

Differences according to environment are very clear and very logical. Apart from a certain number of children, all the inhabitants of a work camp come from elsewhere, and, except for the natives of a city, all the people who live in it are "foreigners." In the villages, on the other hand, there still remain 30–40 percent of those born there. On the regional scale, we can classify all the results and find that whatever the sex, there are two distinct groups: for the youngest age groups (a) fewer than 15 percent "born elsewhere" or (b) over 30 percent, accompanied by, for men of over 65 years of age (a) fewer than 35 percent and (b) over 65 percent. There are three regions of low male migration (see Figure 31.4): High Ogooué, Ogooué-Lolo, and Wolen N'Tem, and all the other regions except Ogooué-Ivindo are of the same type as "the whole of Gabon." For Ogooué-Ivindo the graph begins at 5 percent "born elsewhere" and

[50] The number of Gabonese arriving in Libreville from the interior between 1961 and 1970 has been estimated at 35,500 by G. Lasserre, *Mechanisms of Population Growth and Structures in Libreville, 1953–1970,* and at 28,500 by the SNSEE.

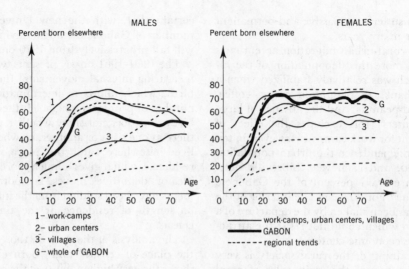

MALES

Percent born elsewhere

1 – work-camps
2 – urban centers
3 – villages
G – whole of GABON

FEMALES

Percent born elsewhere

———— work-camps, urban centers, villages
━━━━ GABON
------- regional trends

FIGURE 31.4.　*Proportion of Residents Born Outside Place of Enumeration of Census, by Sex and Age*

increases regularly with age to reach 80 percent for the 65–69 years group. For women the regions form two distinct groups at the beginning; beyond 20 years there is a series of steps graduating approximately from 15 percent "born elsewhere" to over 90 percent for the Wolen N'Tem. At 15 years the average proportion of women "born elsewhere" reaches 70 percent in the whole of Gabon, this being a consequence of exogamous marriages. There are large differences between the sexes in Wolen N'Tem (20 percent for men and 95 percent for women), which is very characteristic of the major ethnic group (97 percent are Fangs). For men, we find proportions "born in the village" of 93 percent, 88 percent, and 83 percent respectively for High-Ogooué, Ogooué-Lolo, and Wolen N'Tem.

By cross-tabulating the region of birth with the region of residence, we obtain tables of interregional movements. Three regions were the destination of the migrations: the Estuary, (45 percent of all residents being immigrants), Ogooué-Maritime (44 percent), and Mid-Ogooué (29 percent). For the last region, this 1960–1961 picture will be less marked in 1970, as the number of forest work camps, which were considerable, have declined despite the installation of new camps in

Ndjole. Thus it is evident that Libreville (Estuary) and Port Gentil (Ogooué-Maritime) were the destinations of most of the migrations. The mining centers of Haute-Ogooué must now be added to this. In the other regions the percentage of "born out of the region" varied from 3–7 percent. The three south Gabon regions, Nyanga, Ngounié, and Ogooué-Lolo, account for over 77 percent of the emigrants, with Ngounié alone having 39 percent. The differences we find between residents "born elsewhere," and natives of the territory living outside the region, correspond to the number of foreigners.

Even if the motivation is no longer the same, the east-west migration flow continues, and will be shown to have increased still further when the 1969–70 data are available, except in the case of Haute-Ogooué. There are three reasons: work, family, or collective move (the moving of a village or work camp). For men, the motives are obviously economic, but they are not the only ones. There is also the attraction of the town, and many motives are of a largely psychological type: hope of a better work and a higher standard of living, social rise, or need of education, especially for the young people, but also, as Lassere[51] has

[51] Lasserre, *Libreville*.

written, people come "without clearly conceived motives." The women move at the time of marriage, or to join their husbands, as the continuing decline in the sex ratios in Libreville proves: from 127 males per hundred females in 1964 to 113 in 1969.

The flow of arrivals into the towns, which was increasing more and more until 1955, and then declined, picked up again from 1962. The population of Libreville is now increasing by 6–7 percent per year because of immigration.[52]

The study of absentees and visitors in the 1960–1961 data led to the conclusion that about 10 percent of the population were on the move at any one time. Roussel[53] classes a certain number of African countries according to three indicators of the importance of migration for work: sex ratios of the absentees, the percentage of those of 15 years of age and over among the whole of the male absentees, and the percentage of absentees among the male residents of 15 years of age and over. For the first two indicators, Gabon is classed as the country with the lowest rates. Manual workers are resident where they work, there are no seasonal workers, and labor movement involves more and more whole households. If there is agreement between the first two indicators, there is none for the third, where Gabon scores highly, the very high rate of schooling in Gabon perhaps being a valid explanation of this.

From data collected with a questionnaire used during the budget survey of rural areas in 1963 (Ngounié and Wolen N'Tem), an observation on the migration of men of "14 years and over" provides interesting information[54]: The volume of migration is inversely related to the distance to be traveled to the work camps; a majority of first departures occur before 15 years of age (67 percent); most jobs secured were as unskilled workers on the first journey but status improved with the number of journeys, and the length of absence.

We must also stress the frequent absence from the village of a majority of adults working in the camps or on plantations or fishing and hunting.

ECONOMIC AND SOCIAL IMPLICATIONS OF LOW POPULATION GROWTH

The economic takeoff of Gabon is an undeniable fact. The GDP (gross domestic product) in 1967 was 37 percent greater than that of 1962, and the average annual increase of budgetary returns between 1964 and 1970 was 10.7 percent. But, if the annual rate of growth in the added value in such sectors as mining and the power industries (26 and 39 percent respectively) reflects this expansion, as does the soaring of the forestry sector in 1969 (the most profitable sector of the economy) after the opening up of the second zone, in contrast we can but turn to the "agriculture—stockbreeding—fishing—hunting" sector, which has been dropping by about 2 percent each year, and examine the stagnation of salaries in the private sector. The rise in household consumption (around U.S. $60 a year) means little for it includes money going to households outside the country.[55]

In the 1971 budget, 28.5 percent is allocated to development and capital expenditures and 71.5 percent to current expenses. In the budget for current expenses 1.5 percent is provided for agriculture and stock breeding, 12.8 percent for education, 6.2 percent for public health and 1.1 percent for the Ministry of Youth, Sports, Arts, and Civic Service and the Ministry of Work. In the budget for development there is 3.8 percent for agriculture, fishing, and forestry, 9.3 percent for social and community equipment, and 30 percent for building the infrastructure. It is obvious that, for the moment, we cannot speak of investment in the subsistence sector, and a few very localized actions are not

---

[52] Between 1961 and 1970, 28,500 Gabonese probably moved from the interior to the capital (SNSEE estimate).

[53] "Temporary Moves and Migration," *Démographie Comparée*.

[54] TyLong, *Ngounié, Migration of Men of Fourteen Years and Over*, INSEE-Cooperation (1969).

[55] Gross national product per capita was estimated by the World Bank to be U.S. $280 in 1965.

sufficient to stop the rural exodus. In 1960–1961, the agricultural survey estimates at 71,000 the number of farmers, whatever the type of crop (commercial or food) representing 63 percent of men over 20 years of age in Gabon. The remaining 37 percent were salaried workers or inactive. For 1970, the estimated number of men in the same group is perceptibly lower than that of 1960, and the average annual increase of salaried workers since 1961 is around 6–7 percent. In these conditions, how many food farmers, who accounted for 70 percent of the cultivated land in 1960–1961, with 53 percent of the farms under $2\frac{1}{2}$ acres (average size $3\frac{1}{2}$ acres), can be left now?

It is certain that the difficulty of penetrating into the interior of the country has not helped the food producing sector, and that the considerable effort made at the present moment to build the infrastructure will turn production further away from food farming. Meanwhile, the towns are spreading more and more, and there are ever fewer farmers. There is not yet any real problem of unemployment or underemployment, but the building of the railway (Transgabonese) will pose serious problems if many of the workers have to be found among the rural population of Gabon.

Concentrated industry is characterized by high mechanization using local nonskilled workers and exiled technicians, when they cannot be found on the spot. Gabon is, therefore, moving toward national affluence and much internal poverty,[56] a modern sector and a traditional sector on the decline.

Whatever the type of economy chosen, men are necessary, and Gabon has very few. A rural population is necessary to meet the food needs of the whole of the consumers, and it decreases each year.

It is by bringing the rural areas to life again, by giving rural development priority, and by the commercialization of food production that part of the solution to the problem of the rural-urban migration will be found. Whether we like it or not, a return to the land is necessary, but with money. It is by the development of intensive scientific farming that the country will arrive at a better distribution of national income.

## POPULATION POLICY AND PROSPECTS FOR DEMOGRAPHIC STUDIES

Officially there are, at the time of writing, 630,000 persons in Gabon (although we have no proof of this). We do not know why this exact number is chosen. The puzzle is the greater as the administrative "censuses" provide figures lower than those of the Statistics Department which are nevertheless used for economic or socioeconomic studies and for planning.

The French have introduced the practice of the "administrative census," a regular count and an instrument of local administration (including tax collecting). The system has as much value as the territorial one, and I think that on the whole it broke down with independence . . . . The population survey, which is usually complementary to the census, has played an important role in French-speaking countries, but it was an exceptional operation, depending on outside funds. And the French seem to have stopped believing in its effectiveness, before a tradition could be established . . . .[57]

Until 1964, the FAC[58] undertook all the statistical studies, but since 1965 Gabon has carried out this type of operation by itself with restricted technical aid. No special attention was given to the National Statistics Department until 1969, and the surveys and demography office, with about U.S. $5,400 dollars a year, obviously could not undertake anything serious. Because the United Nations named 1970 as population census year, $218,000[59] were granted in the 1969 development budget for the carrying out of a census,

---

[56] This poverty is relative only and cannot be compared with that in many other developing countries. In 1963 in Ngounié average annual household income varied from U.S. $8 to $468. Fifty percent of households had an income of less than $52.

[57] Etienne van de Walle, *Colloquy on African Demography*, INED, INSEE, ORSTOM (Paris, 1970).
[58] Aid and Cooperation Fund of the French Republic.
[59] The total amount allocated in this special budget is U.S. $270,000.

an operation considered necessary for the construction of the second five-year plan (1971–1975). For 1971, $36,000 were envisaged under the heading of the UDEAC-CHAD regional project[60] for the continuous collection of demographic data, a project which is to be submitted to the United Nations' Fund for Population Activities.

These budgetary problems, like the more serious ones of recruitment and organization, could be solved if a demographic division were developed, and the Gabonese government seems to intend to do this. After considering several demographic projects, the one put forward in Addis Ababa in 1968[61] raised a great deal of interest, but Gabon is still the only country which has gone ahead with it, and in 1970 even it had only carried out the first of the four envisaged operations (national census, population survey, fertility survey, creation of special study areas). The program for continuous collection of demographic data in the UDEAC-CHAD area, in the setting of the worldwide censuses recommended by the United Nations, decided upon at Bangui and subsequently Libreville in 1970, is taking over the Gabon project adapted to the needs of all these countries.[62]

Whatever the outcome of this project, the first pilot area will be in operation in Gabon in 1971. Its system is based on household registration set up from the 1969–1970 census household cards and kept up to date through periodic household-by-household visits to the villages. From the information gathered during these visits a child register (based on births) and a female register (recording pregnancies, confinements, and what eventuates from the pregnancy) will be created. Every village surveyed will also possess a book for recording births and deaths. Two or three rounds of visits a year are foreseen and a coverage of around 10,000 persons by each observer. It is from these different registers

opened and kept up to date that specific studies will be undertaken (on fertility, stillbirths, infant mortality, general mortality, ages, and so on, and also comparison with parish registers). A punched card system will eventually be undertaken.

The 1971–72 sociomedical survey on fertility studied fertility problems from three aspects: the measuring of fertility and its variations, the analysis of related social factors, and the analysis of biological and medical factors. This survey should be attached to the special survey areas. The Gabonese government has a well-defined population policy, with active implementation in the fields of health, labor, and education, although confined to certain domains that only concern the privileged classes. Social legislation is fairly far developed: the Gabonese State Insurance Fund (family allowances, maternity allowances, prenatal and bonuses at birth); the Work Survey (protecting the employment of young people and women); Social Services, as well as health legislation (major endemic diseases, endemo-epidemic diseases, maternal and infant protection, dispensary, school hygiene, etc.). Out of the 1971 budget, more than U.S. $4 million are allocated for the Ministry of Public Health and Population. The main objectives of the 15-year plan (1966–1980) for the development of the health services are to extend to the whole population the systems which the privileged groups (i.e., the socially insured) now benefit from, the prevention of epidemics (by vaccination, sanitary education, and improved sanitation), an increase in the birth rate, and the protection of child health and welfare which is regarded as threatened.

CONCLUSION

The improvement in the demographic situation since 1950 should not deceive us. Population growth is still seriously slowed down by many aftereffects of the past years. It is therefore absolutely necessary that the problems posed by the population for development should be attacked consistently. The special demographic observation areas

[60] Economic and Customs Union of Central Africa (Cameroon, People's Republic of the Congo, Central African Republic, and Gabon), UDEAC.

[61] Study group on the organization and conducting of censuses of population and housing, June 17–29, 1968, ECA, Addis Ababa.

[62] Special survey areas, June 1970, SNSEE.

advocated for some years by the Gabon Statistics Department could bring the elements which are now lacking, despite two national censuses (1960–1961 and 1969–1971), and could allow the sociomedical survey to be carried out.[63] The development of the Demographic Division would permit these aims to be realized.

The demographic factor plays an essential role in many aspects of the social and economic development, and the underpopulation of the country does not help this development. Rural-urban migration is expanding too rapidly a nonagricultural community whose needs for local food are not being adequately satisfied. Moreover, the

rapid development of education could play an important role in further swelling those internal migrations from the rural areas toward the towns and other economically developing areas. The rural areas which are being emptied have a clear tendency to economic stagnation, if not to decline.

Population growth is still in a precarious position. Primary sterility is far too high and completed family size fairly low. Despite an excellent medical coverage, stillbirths and infant mortality remain very high. Excessive male mortality at all ages (including the fetus) should be studied very seriously. The lack of males will soon be felt much more acutely, for the Gabonese will have to return to the land while at the same time providing manpower to continue the extraordinary economic expansion of the country.

[63] M. François, "Reflections on the Socio-Medical Survey in Gabon" (1969).

Occupying about 125,000 square miles, the Republic of the Ivory Coast faces the Atlantic Ocean along 400 miles of coast stretching from Ghana to Liberia. Its general form is one of an irregular square, bordering Mali and Upper Volta in the north, and Guinea in the northwest (see Figure 32.1).

Two zones, which are ecologically very different, constitute Ivory Coast, the savanna in the north, and dense forest in the south. The savanna, which in the far north is the Sudanese type, with small trees scattered sporadically, thickens out southward, especially in the huge triangle where the Baoulé district cuts into the forest zone. With no transitional vegetation, the forest suddenly begins and continues on to the lake system which stretches all along the coast. Agriculture in the savanna zone is still largely of the subsistence type, whereas in the forest zone the cultivation of crops for export, especially coffee and cocoa, has developed a substantial market economy. This ecological contrast explains much of the movement of the population within the country.

## GENERAL SKETCH OF THE POPULATION AND POSSIBLE TRENDS

STATISTICAL SOURCES. Ivory Coast has never had a full census. Population estimates were based until 1955 on counts carried out by French administrators. Closely connected with tax collection, these operations gave rise to much evasion and resulted in an undercount of the population. So in 1956 the total number of the population was estimated at about 2,660,000 inhabitants.[1]

An initial set of demographical surveys covered the whole country between 1957 and 1958 and allowed a more exact appraisal of the real position. The complete population then was estimated at 3,200,000 persons. Since then, a succession of counts and surveys has provided a statistical series which is satisfactorily consistent. Meanwhile, the administrative censuses have improved considerably following the abolition of the poll

[1] Service of Overseas Statistics, "Overseas, 1958" (Paris, 1959).

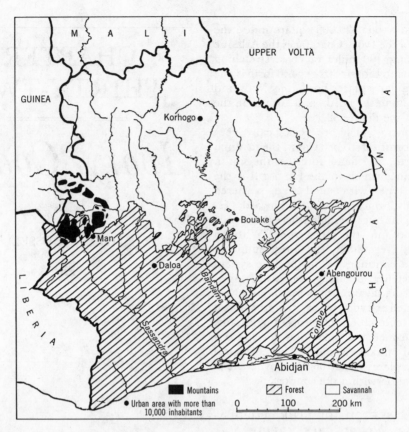

FIGURE 32.1.   *The Ivory Coast*

tax by the government on the second day of independence.

The massive campaign against smallpox during the years 1962 and 1963 occasioned a complete count of the population in terms of the number of vaccinations. In spite of local mistakes, which are always possible, this operation gave comparable data of the population by residential center. The results of this work have been recorded in the "List of localities of the Ivory Coast."[2] The general population was estimated at 3,700,000 inhabitants.

During the same period, the Minister of Planning decided to undertake, over almost all the territory, a series of regional studies, each one comprising a sample survey of the population. For the regional surveys dealing with rural districts the variance has been 1.8 percent. For the towns, the results are less certain. On the whole, the general estimate is doubtless correct to within about 5 percent. Thus, as the total population for 1965 has been estimated at 4,000,000 inhabitants,[3] we can be reasonably sure that the actual population at this date was between 3,800,000 and 4,200,000. On this basis, and taking into account an annual rate of increase of 3 percent, the estimated 1970 population is in the region of 4,600,000.[4]

[2] Ministry of Public Health and Ministry of Economic and Financial Affairs, Statistical Service, *List of Localities of the Ivory Coast*, Abidjan, 1965.

[3] See Ministry of Planning, *Ivory Coast, 1965: Population* (Abidjan, 1967). An overall bibliography of the demography of Ivory Coast is appended.

[4] It should be noted that, in 1965, 300,000 foreigners were temporarily employed in Ivory Coast, and this population is not included in the estimates of the total legal population given here.

TABLE 32.1

Hypotheses on which population projections are based,
Ivory Coast, 1965–1984 (annual rates and levels)

|  | 1965–69 | 1970–74 | 1975–79 | 1980–84 |
|---|---|---|---|---|
| Natural increase | | | | |
| Crude birth rate | | | | |
| (per thousand) | 50 | 50 | 46 | 44 |
| Crude death rate | | | | |
| (per thousand) | 27 | 25 | 20 | 18 |
| Rate of natural increase | | | | |
| (per thousand) | 23 | 25 | 26 | 26 |
| | | | | |
| Immigrational increase | | | | |
| Hypotheses about level of | | | | |
| net increase | | | | |
| (numbers in thousands) | | | | |
| high | 40 | 40 | 30 | 25 |
| medium | 30 | 30 | 20 | 15 |
| low | 20 | 20 | 10 | 10 |

COMPONENTS OF DEMOGRAPHIC GROWTH. The population surveys undertaken between 1962 and 1964 have allowed the approximate measuring of the different components of demographic growth. The birth rate was computed to be about 50 per thousand and the death rate slightly higher than 29 per thousand. The rate of natural increase was thus estimated at 2.1 percent. In order to construct projections, we employed the hypotheses in Table 32.1.

A fertility decline is projected starting in 1975. It is probable that around this date Ivory Coast will become one of the countries "in demographic transition," i.e., one with declining fertility. This change should occur first in the towns and secondary centers. It may well be that the decline has already started in Abidjan.[5] In terms of mortality change, the improvement in living conditions and the development of the health infrastructure should lead to a very perceptible lowering of the death rate and an even more noticeable drop in infant mortality.

As for the annual migratory balance, we know that its variations do not show the same degree of inertia as the components of natural growth. Indeed we have employed three hypotheses. We estimated that between 1960 and 1965 the positive migratory balance was in the region of 40,000 foreigners per year.[6] We consider that, henceforward, such a flow would constitute an upper limit. In fact, even if it is true that the difference in the standard of living between Ivory Coast and its northern neighbors will be maintained and will constantly encourage immigration, it seems that other factors must slow down this movement. In rural districts, the native population is more and more reluctant to give up for nothing the usufruct of a section of village land, while the practice of selling land freehold is still very rare. In urban areas, the employment market will doubtless become ever more competitive, even for laborers' jobs, which have been quite readily left to foreigners until recently.

It seems, therefore, that migrational change is most likely to follow either the medium hypothesis (i.e., the annual settlement of 30,000 foreigners) or the low one (i.e., the annual settlement of 20,000–30,000 foreigners). These hypotheses allow us to construct the population projections presented in Table 32.2.

In terms of residents only, we can thus,

[5] SEMA, in its survey, estimated the birth rate in Abidjan as 47 per thousand. Taking into account an age structure especially favorable to fertility, this index corresponds to a general fertility rate of 175 instead of 190 for Ivory Coast as a whole.

[6] See Ministry of Planning, *Ivory Coast, 1965: Population*, pp. 158–59.

TABLE 32.2

Population projections, Ivory Coast, 1965–1980 (in thousands)

| Population | 1965 | 1970 | 1975 | 1980 |
|---|---|---|---|---|
| Resident | | | | |
| Medium hypothesis of natural increase | 4,000 | 4,630 | 5,380 | 6,250 |
| Low hypothesis of natural increase | 4,000 | 4,580 | 5,280 | 6,130 |
| On temporary stay (foreign laborers & their families) | 300 | 350 | 420 | Not estimated |
| Total (actual population) | | | | |
| Medium projection | 4,300 | 4,980 | 5,800 | — |

proceeding from the 1965 estimate, reckon the population of Ivory Coast at around 5,300,000 inhabitants in 1975 and more than 6,100,000 in 1980. In roughly 25 years, from 1955–1980, this population will doubtless have more than doubled, from less than 3 million to more than 6 million inhabitants. This total growth corresponds to an annual rate of about 3 percent. In order to understand this growth, and to distinguish better the problems it poses, we must now study its distribution and its composition.

## POPULATION DISTRIBUTION AND STRUCTURE

Fishermen, foresters, farmers, tradesmen, combatants, craftsmen, artists, in kingdoms or anarchic gerontocracies, the many peoples of the Ivory Coast each led their own special existence behind the tightly closed partitions formed by the traditions of the forest, the family, mysticism or the crafts.[7]

It is in these terms that Rougerie describes the position of Ivory Coast as it appeared about a century ago. Since then, the partitioning of the groups has disappeared and their heterogeneity has diminished, but the cultural differences, the unequal richness of natural resources, and the creation of an urban network have maintained a large diversity between regions and human groups.

[7] C. Rougerie, *The Ivory Coast*, PUF (Paris, 1969), p. 5.

DISTRIBUTION OF THE POPULATION OVER ITS LAND AREA. Over the whole area of 125,000 square miles, Ivory Coast has a population density of a little more than 35 persons per square mile. The map (Figure 32.2) shows a very varied population distribution. Three population concentrations are particularly evident around Man, Korhogo, and, most of all, Bouaké. To this must be added the less conspicuous population grouping around the capital, Abidjan. In none of these cases is the explanation of these concentrations in terms of purely physical factors entirely satisfactory. The existence of suitable natural resources obviously forms a condition which is necessary, but it is insufficient explanation for the high concentrations actually found.

It is true that the savanna has long constituted an area more favorable to human settlement than the forest, but it is only around Korhogo and Bouaké that we find high to very high densities. We can see that in forest zones the population has often settled along the communication lines, leaving fairly wide empty spaces between the meshes of this network. We can also see zones which are almost completely deserted, especially the southwest of the country.

These irregularities suggest the importance of the historical factor in the geographical distribution of the population. The high density seen around Man can be explained by the mountainous nature of this zone; it provided an ideal refuge for the groups driven out of their territories. The Samory military campaigns also contributed by increasing the density of the two savanna zones spared by the war, the Korhogo district and the area situated to the northwest of Bouaké. The concentration of population around Abidjan is evidently due to the administrative and economic functions of the city.

ETHNIC DISTRIBUTION. Settled either in the savanna (the Baoulé) or the forest (the Agni and the Abron), the Akan tribe alone represents a quarter of the population of Ivory Coast. Moreover, the tribe has culturally affected profoundly all the lake

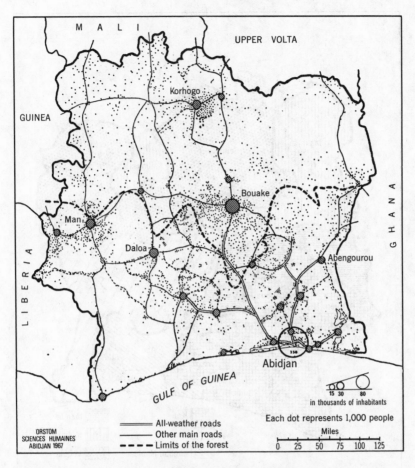

FIGURE 32.2. *Population Distribution, Ivory Coast,* 1963

peoples. Table 32.3 and Figure 32.3 give a fairly precise picture of the geographic distribution and numerical importance of these groups.

Internal and external migratory movements during half a century have led to substantial local modifications, but on the whole the distribution shown in Figure 32.3 is still valid. However, we must not forget that the ethnic composition of urban centers is often very complex.

Finally, it is important to note that nearly 700,000 foreigners are settled in Ivory Coast. Malian and Voltaic peoples alone account for more than half a million inhabitants, while Europeans, of whom the very large majority are French, number about 40,000.

AGE STRUCTURE. For the country as a whole, starting with data for 1965, and taking into account the factors of natural growth and migration, we can calculate, as in Table 32.4, the probable distribution of the population of Ivory Coast, by sex and age group, around 1970. With large age groups we obtain, for 1,000 inhabitants, the distribution shown in Table 32.5.

The youthfulness of the population is clearly shown, since out of every ten inhabitants of Ivory Coast, seven are under 30 years of age, and four are under 15 years. There are doubtless some errors in age statement and estimation, but they cannot change in any appreciable way the relationships between the age groups.

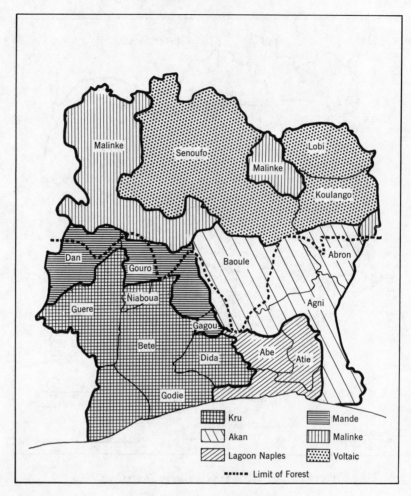

FIGURE 32.3.  *Ethnic Distribution*

LEVEL OF SCHOOLING. Since 1957 a considerable effort has been made in Ivory Coast to reduce illiteracy. It has been expressed above all by the very fast rise in the number of children at school. Thus, on January 1, 1958, there were 126,000 pupils in primary schools;[8] their number is now about 400,000. Now, one in every two children in Ivory Coast will attend school.[9] The difference between

boys and girls is still important. However, it is lessening, especially in the towns.

In the secondary schools, the 4,000 pupils of 1957–1958 have since been multiplied by 15. Finally, Abidjan now has its own university, attended in 1967 by more than 1,600 students.

These general data were needed in order to allow a more accurate appraisal of the population differences existing in Ivory Coast. We could obviously consider separately very many subpopulations presenting characteristics which, for one reason or another, are peculiar to them. It has seemed more advisable to keep to a division which, while remaining simple, allows us to explain the

[8] Service of Overseas Statistics, "Overseas, 1958," p. 769.
[9] UNESCO uses the following standard: On average the potential school population represents 20 percent of the total population, or about 920,000 children in Ivory Coast. Taking into account secondary and technical schools, the population of less than 15 years of age actually at school is almost 460,000 pupils.

TABLE 32.3

Approximate population distribution according to ethnic group, 1965 (In thousands)

| Ethnic Grouping | Total Number Resident in Territory of Origin | Total Number Resident Outside Territory of Origin | Total Number in Ivory Coast |
|---|---|---|---|
| Akan | | | |
| Abron | 45 | 5 | 50 |
| Agni | 165 | 20 | 185 |
| Baoulé | 620 | 145 | 765 |
| Krou | | | |
| Bété | 295 | 30 | 325 |
| Dida | 105 | 10 | 115 |
| Godié | 17 | 3 | 20 |
| Guéré-Ouobé | 180 | 30 | 210 |
| Others | 35 | 5 | 40 |
| Lake people | | | |
| Abé | 70 | 15 | 85 |
| Abouré | 18 | 7 | 25 |
| Atié | 135 | 25 | 160 |
| Others | 100 | 25 | 125 |
| Malinké | 400 | 265 | 665 |
| South Mandé | | | |
| Dan | 230 | 15 | 245 |
| Gouro-Gagou | 90 | 15 | 105 |
| Voltaic | | | |
| Lobi | 30 | 5 | 35 |
| Sénoufo | 425 | 40 | 465 |
| Others | | 200 | 200 |
| Others | | 180 | 180 |
| All groups | 2,960 | 1,040 | 4,000 |

major contemporary demographic trends. In the rural areas, we will distinguish the savanna and forest zones. On the other hand, the urban population will be considered as a whole.

## POPULATION DATA
## BY ECOLOGICAL REGION

None of the three groups which we are going to examine really forms a homogeneous whole. In the rural region, cultural and economic differences remain important even within the same ecological zone. As for the towns, their size and function give to each one a marked individuality. The proposed division is based above all on differences inherited from the past and on shared problems. The solution of these problems will determine their progress in the years immediately ahead.

RURAL AREAS IN THE SAVANNA ZONE. Within the boundaries marked on the map (Figure

TABLE 32.4

Projected distribution of population by sex and age group, 1970

| Age Group | Number (in thousands) | | Distribution (per 100 Persons) | |
|---|---|---|---|---|
| | M | F | M | F |
| 0–4 | 420 | 403 | 91 | 87 |
| 5–9 | 326 | 327 | 70 | 71 |
| 10–14 | 265 | 264 | 57 | 57 |
| 15–19 | 216 | 215 | 47 | 47 |
| 20–24 | 201 | 214 | 43 | 46 |
| 25–29 | 194 | 193 | 42 | 42 |
| 30–34 | 179 | 154 | 39 | 33 |
| 35–39 | 148 | 122 | 32 | 26 |
| 40–44 | 124 | 99 | 27 | 21 |
| 45–49 | 99 | 82 | 21 | 18 |
| 50–54 | 72 | 67 | 16 | 14 |
| 55–59 | 51 | 50 | 11 | 11 |
| 60+ | 75 | 70 | 16 | 15 |
| Total | 2,370 | 2,260 | 512 | 488 |

32.2) the savanna zone contains a little over 1,500,000 rural population. The factor common to the whole of this zone is the prevalence of a subsistence economy. The essential nourishment is still drawn from produce of the family's own cultivation. The level of income is, on average, less than U.S. $20 a year per person. In these conditions, we can easily imagine that the traditional structures have remained fairly decisive, as can be shown by even a brief analysis of some sociocultural characteristics.

Let us look first at the composition of the agricultural labor force according to the worker's status. Table 32.6 shows the status of males working in agriculture in different areas of the savanna rural zone and contrasts this with the forest.

TABLE 32.5

Projected population distribution per thousand persons by major age group, 1980

| Age Group | Male | Female | Total |
|---|---|---|---|
| 0–14 | 218 | 214 | 432 |
| 15–29 | 132 | 134 | 266 |
| 30–64 | 146 | 125 | 271 |
| 65+ | 16 | 15 | 31 |
| Total | 512 | 488 | 100 |

TABLE 32.6

Percentage distribution of male agricultural workers according to employment status

| Status | Savanna Rural Zone | | | | Forest Rural Zone |
| | Korhogo | Odienné | Bouaké | All Areas | |
|---|---|---|---|---|---|
| Cultivators | 38 | 33 | 56 | 44 | 57 |
| Family helpers | 62 | 65 | 38 | 54 | 15 |
| Wage earners | 0 | 2 | 6 | 2 | 28 |
| All statuses | 100 | 100 | 100 | 100 | 100 |

If we make a general comparison of the savanna and forest zones, we note a very different labor distribution. In the former, wage earners only form 2 percent of the work force, in contrast to 28 percent in the latter. In the forest zone, only one person in six or seven is a family help; in the savanna the proportion is over one in two. So, in one area we find mainly cultivation by families, with considerable participation of grown sons. In the other, wage earners are twice as numerous as family helpers. Note that the situation is a little different for Bouaké. We shall come across this relative exception again when examining other characteristics, and will find the explanation later.

Subsistence cultivation demands the continuation of the traditional, extended family. At Korhogo and Odienné, around 1962, the average family size was more than 12 people; at Bouaké it was only 7. Moreover, these quantitative data do not show the encompassing kind of solidarity, which, by many mutual loans, often joins together different segments of the same lineage.

Such a society still remains largely ruled by the law of custom. It has long put up a passive, but effective, resistance to the school which it considers a menace to social unity. The child who goes to school is lost to the agricultural labor force, and, at the end of his primary education, he leaves the village for good. The incompatibility between unchanged traditional values and the culture transmitted by the school amply explains the backwardness of schooling in this zone; the school attendance rate is scarcely 35 percent

in the Baoulé district and only 15 percent in the rest of the savanna.

Resistance to school has also arisen, at least locally, from a religious factor. The Moslem religion, practiced above all in the north of the savanna zone, considers the public school as a cultural threat, and its followers have refused to send their children there. The influence of this religion seems to be increasing, but at the same time its opposition to schooling is now declining.

Even in 1965 the savanna zone was obviously still largely controlled by traditional cultural systems. The young people remained bound to family cultivation for a very long time, and could only escape from it by leaving the village. The "old ones" controlled the "circulation" of the women and the distribution of land. In certain cases they did not hesitate to use traditional magic to maintain the gerontocracy against challenge. All in all, the rural exodus remained limited, except in the Bouaké district, which, from every point of view, occupies a very special position in the savanna.

This unusual position is to be explained above all by a special cultural factor: the traditional individualism of the Baoulé. This characteristic has, moreover, taken on new forms in the modern socioeconomic context. Among the women, this attitude is expressed by a rural exodus which is more pronounced than in any other ethnic group. Among the men, the nearness of available lands in the forest zone has led to the establishment of coffee plantations, or else, among the younger men, their seasonal hiring by a planter. Constant moving between Baoulé country and the place of work allowed them to reconcile traditional attachment to their village land and their desire for autonomy.

This "colonization" of part of the forest has naturally lessened the importance of the subsistence economy for them. More than all the other groups in the savanna, they participate in the contemporary changes in behavior exhibited by the forest populations.

RURAL AREAS IN THE FOREST ZONE. The legal population (i.e., persons of Ivory Coast residence) of this region is estimated at about 1,750,000 people. Over and above the characteristics peculiar to each group, the forest populations have a basic common denominator: Their way of life is ordered by an economy centered on the growth of crops for export, especially coffee and cocoa. The different ethnic groups have reacted more or less quickly and according to their traditions, to the introduction of industrial cultivation, but today this new economy imposes a certain number of common restraints on all of them.

In a forest still largely uncultivated, the only factor limiting production was for a long time the labor force. Subsequently, the recruiting of foreign laborers allowed a rapid extension of the area under plantations. The abundance of land and the relative scarcity of local labor was rapidly to bring about the following consequences: (1) a progressive widening of the ring of plantations around the village (thus it becomes more and more difficult to work them directly from the village center, and a huge camp system is set up, bringing with it a double existence for the inhabitants; home in the village on Sundays and everyday life at the camp); (2) the arrival of numerous foreigners, first of all as seasonal or permanent laborers, and then, when they obtained a plot of forest land, as planters; (3) a general rise in the level of aspirations (a desire for the advancement of their children and hence both the multiplication of schools and also a huge exodus of the youth toward urban centers).

Thus the relative importance of family labor dwindled rapidly. Table 32.7 allows us to compare this situation with that in the savanna zone. The Man region reveals a distribution very different from that of the two other regions. This is because its evolution has been slowed down by its remote geographical position, far from the port of Abidjan and at the same time far from the recruitment zones for the foreign labor force. Abengourou and Daloa-Gagnoa on the other hand show distributions of the labor force fairly similar to each other and very different from those noted in the savanna. In these typical forest areas, the proportion of labor supplied by wage earners is well over 30 percent, while the family helpers, mainly young people less than 21 years old, make in fact a minor, usually only part-time, contribution. Thus, the forest zone economy is dependent on the presence of about 200,000 laborers, usually living in camps, paid either a fixed wage or, more and more rarely, a fraction of the output.

This situation leads to a much smaller family size than is found in the savanna: 6 people on average per household instead of the 12 noted in the Korhogo and Odienné districts. Mutual work loans among segments of the same extended family have almost completely disappeared here. It is no longer the village or the large family which forms the basic unit, but a special type of nuclear family characterized in particular by a large degree of economic independence for wives.

The general desire for advancement has inevitably helped the development of schooling. In a radius of 125 miles around Abidjan, more than 70 percent of the children now attend school (about 90 percent of the boys and 50 percent of the girls). In the rest of the forest zone, the rates vary between 40 and 60 percent, but they are always very much

TABLE 32.7

Percentage distribution of male agricultural workers according to employment status

| Status | Abengourou | Forest Rural Zone Daloa-Gagnoa | Man | AllAreas | Savanna Rural Zone |
|---|---|---|---|---|---|
| Cultivators | 46 | 56 | 78 | 57 | 44 |
| Family helpers | 13 | 11 | 17 | 15 | 54 |
| Wage earners | 41 | 33 | 5 | 28 | 2 |
| All statuses | 100 | 100 | 100 | 100 | 100 |

higher than the usual rates found in the savanna.

With regard to schooling, another factor of cultural change which has played an important role is the spread of Christianity, whether it is Catholicism, Protestantism, or a local syncretic cult. Missions initially played the fundamental role in establishing schools and these tended to be in the non-Moslem areas of the south. Islam has hardly penetrated the forest, at least in the rural regions. Moreover, the traditional religious practices still have a certain importance even where Christianity is officially practiced by the great majority of the population.

With a monetary income, which by 1963 exceeded U.S.$50 per capita; the spread of instruction; the progressive modernization of cultural techniques; the intensity of economic and cultural exchange between town and country and the general yearning for modernity, the populations of the forest zone (and especially those of the southeast) already show characteristics close to those found in the urban areas.

THE URBAN AREAS.    The total number of the urban population depends on the definition of urban areas. If we only take as towns the centers of more than 10,000 inhabitants, only about 20 towns in Ivory Coast fit this description. Together, they add up to about a million inhabitants. The national capital alone accounts for half this figure. These centers are unequally spread out over the land. Half of them are within 125 miles of Abidjan. However, among the main towns of Ivory Coast we must also distinguish Bouaké, which, with its 100,000 inhabitants, forms a very active pole of development in the heart of the savanna.

This definition of urban area is perhaps a little narrow. There is, in fact, in each of the 100 subprefectures, at least one center filling certain urban functions (i.e., the administrative center of the subprefecture). Even if the inhabitants of these centers are few, and even if many of them are farmers, the town is, nevertheless, part of the network of administrative and commercial nodes which

TABLE 32.8
Distribution of the urban population by sex and age group, 1970

| Age Group | Number of Persons (in thousands) | | Percentage Distribution of Total Population | | |
|---|---|---|---|---|---|
| | M | F | M | F | M & F |
| 0–4 | 135 | 132 | 9.4 | 9.2 | 18.6 |
| 5–9 | 87 | 88 | 6.1 | 6.2 | 12.3 |
| 10–14 | 76 | 75 | 5.3 | 5.2 | 10.5 |
| 15–19 | 105 | 109 | 7.3 | 7.6 | 14.9 |
| 20–24 | 63 | 61 | 4.4 | 4.3 | 8.7 |
| 25–29 | 59 | 64 | 4.1 | 4.5 | 8.6 |
| 30–34 | 60 | 54 | 4.2 | 3.8 | 8.0 |
| 35–39 | 50 | 38 | 3.4 | 2.7 | 6.1 |
| 40–44 | 36 | 24 | 2.5 | 1.7 | 4.2 |
| 45–49 | 24 | 15 | 1.7 | 1.0 | 2.7 |
| 50–54 | 18 | 12 | 1.3 | 0.8 | 2.1 |
| 55–59 | 11 | 7 | 0.8 | 0.5 | 1.3 |
| 60+ | 16 | 11 | 1.2 | 0.8 | 2.0 |
| All ages | 740 | 690 | 51.7 | 48.3 | 100.0 |

checker and animate the rural region, thus playing an urban role. If we take these secondary centers into consideration, the total number of the urban population comes to about 1,400,000 people. Here we shall generally consider the urban population in this wider sense, while occasionally using a more restricted definition when drawing attention to the characteristics of Abidjan or of the few very large towns.

For 1970 we have only a general distribution of urban population. Summed up in Table 32.8, it can be compared, thanks to the graph (Figure 32.4) with the corresponding structure of the rural region.

The differences from one region to another are evident. In the towns, the percentage that men and women of 15–24 years form of the population of all ages is twice as great as in the country. Thus, despite the considerable difference in the total numbers of urban and rural population[10] in this age group there are as many townsfolk as rural people—about 220,000 of each. From 25–40 years, the two pyramids show a similar general form. On the other hand, their peaks are markedly different: Almost 4 percent of the rural population are over 60 years old in contrast to only 2 percent of the urban population.

[10] In the rural areas, 3,200,000; in the towns, 1,420,000.

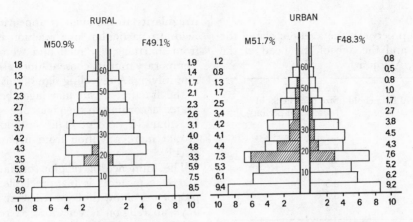

FIGURE 32.4. *Age Pyramids, Urban and Rural Population*, 1970

This age structure is a composite one. Certain towns, especially Abidjan, have a much younger structure still. Thus, in 1965, males 20–39 years of age alone made up 24 percent of the capital's population, while the combined figure for all the other urban centers was less than 17 percent. The causes and consequences of these structures will be discussed later. First we must define with more precision the other characteristics of the town population.

Between the traditional village family and the city household the rupture seems complete. For the former, labor force requirements, the number of children, and economic means fit together naturally. There are no worries about work or lodging. For the latter, income is measured by wage-paid work; available space is limited and hard to find; and the child is a burden and rarely an aid. It is easy to understand that in these conditions the average household size varies between four and five people.

If the *nuclear* type of household is the most prevalent, the extended family has, however, not disappeared. For example, in Abidjan in 1964, among 60,000 urban households, about a quarter had taken in, as a permanent guest, some connection of the husband or wife such as a nephew, a brother, a cousin, or simply a friend's son. The addition is often a child taken on for the duration of his studies, or a young relative who has arrived recently and has not yet found a job. All in all, these "guests" accounted for almost 50,000 people, or 15 percent of the total urban population. We can appreciate the role played by such a practice in the mechanics of the rural exodus to the towns.

Another type of household, which is very common in urban areas, is formed by single persons living alone or in groups of two or three. In all, they accounted for almost 10,000 households containing 10 percent of Abidjan's population.[11] Apart from the SEMA study, we only have some quantitative data[12] on the composition of urban households. They suffice to show that the situation in the capital is not exceptional.

The small size of urban households is doubtless related to the average age of the head of the household, which is relatively low. In Table 32.9 we can see that there is a relationship between the size of the household and the age of its head.

But the relationship is much closer if we compare the size of the household with the length of time since the head of the household took up his residence in the town (see Figure 32.5). Usually, within a few years the urban family will scarcely differ, at least in size, from the family in the forest villages. The traditional taking in of guests will, however,

[11] SEMA, *Socioeconomic Study of Abidjan*, CASHA-SEMA (Abidjan, 1965), pp. 185 and 186 and fn. 6.
[12] Especially on Daloa-Gagnoa and Toumodi.

TABLE 32.9
Relationship between the average size of the
household and the age of the head of the
household, Abidjan

| Age of Head of Household | Average Size of Household (number of persons) |
|---|---|
| 20–24 | 2.7 |
| 25–29 | 3.6 |
| 30–34 | 4.3 |
| 35–39 | 4.7 |
| 40–49 | 5.5 |
| 50–59 | 5.2 |
| 60+ | 4.8 |

often give it a less homogeneous composition
than that found in the rural forest region.

Finally, it should be noted that the urban
family is changing into something very different from the traditional Ivory Coast family,
a process with far-reaching implications. The
marriage institution itself is undergoing very
substantial change. Formerly, custom and
family rites governed the conditions of
marriage and assured its stability. Tomorrow,
modern legislation will doubtless be acknowledged as the general standard. But, today is a
period of transition, and if the young people
no longer give much credit to custom, that
does not mean that they have yet chosen a
new model. It is undeniable that a degree of

irregularity in behavior is appearing in this
field. In particular, one reaction is a flight
from marriage, by men and women alike.
Temporary mutual consent unions seem to be
multiplying. A revealing sign of this situation
is the fraction of all marriages being celebrated according to the civil code: generally
less than 15 percent. This situation should
attract more attention from urban sociologists.[13]

The influence of religion on family and
marriage patterns is inappreciable. Yet the
proportion of townsfolk who declare that they
have no religion is very low. It reaches its
maximum at Abidjan, and even there it does
not rise above 6 percent.

Christianity and Islam share nine-tenths of
the urban population in proportions which
vary locally, but, over the whole country, are
very close.[14] The traditional religion, contrary
to the position in the rural areas, is followed
by only about 5 percent of the population.

Another cultural characteristic of the urban
region is the relatively high proportion of
literate persons. In 1965, more than one-third

[13] Polygamy, forbidden in 1964, should henceforth
decline in incidence. From 1955–1963, change in this
direction was very slow, and it is likely that *de facto*
polygamy will continue for a considerable time in new
forms.
[14] Abidjan, for example, has 41 percent Catholics and
8 percent Protestants, and 39 percent Moslems.

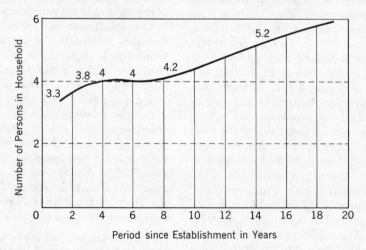

FIGURE 32.5.    *Average Size of Households by Period Since Establishment, Abidjan, 1964*

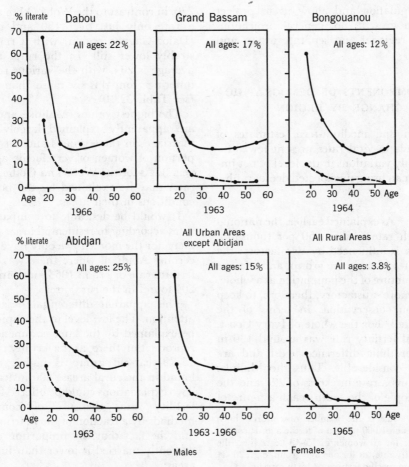

FIGURE 32.6. *Percentage of Population Able to Read and Write in Selected Urban Areas and in the Rural Area, by Age, Ivory Coast, 1963–1965*

of the male population in Abidjan knew how to read and write, compared with only 8 percent of the rural population. Figure 32.6 allows the comparison of different regions in the mid-1960s. It is certain that the percentages have since increased substantially in the urban centers, while it is impossible, because of the rural exodus of the educated, to affirm that the same thing is happening in the villages.

From the graphs in Figure 32.6 two essential facts stand out: (1) the substantial extent by which male literacy exceeds that of females; (2) the very high degree of literacy among the younger age groups. The pro-

portions noted in 1963 for the 15–19-year-old age group should today apply up to 25 years of age.

Thus in the towns there is a completely new situation coming about: The majority of the young male adults know how to read and write. Their adaptation to the urban region is obviously helped by this. It also leads to a rise in their level of aspiration. We shall see what influence this cultural change can have on the employment market when we deal with it thoroughly in the last part of the chapter. Before arriving at this point, we must examine more closely the strictly demographic factors which explain the current distribution of the population and allow us to project population growth, not general projections now, but regional and separate urban and rural ones.

## THE COMPONENTS OF DEMOGRAPHIC CHANGE BY REGION

Short-term and medium-term estimates of likely trends in vital rates present few difficulties. Only variations in the level of net immigration can bring unexpected demographic change.

FERTILITY.  As explained earlier, the national crude birth rate is about 50 per thousand. This index is influenced by two factors: the fertility rates of each age group, and the age and sex structure of the population as a whole. It will be more satisfactory, therefore, to keep most of our observations in terms of the fertility rate.[15] For the whole of Ivory Coast, the general fertility rate was around 190 in 1965. Interethnic differences exist and are sometimes considerable. Thus the Malinké tribe exhibits a rate in excess of 220 and the Voltaic people of the south reach a figure of

[15] *The fertility rate* is the number of children born annually to each 1,000 women of fertile age. It can be studied either for all women of 15–49 years (i.e., the general fertility rate) or for one age group, e.g., 20–24 years (i.e., age-specific fertility or birth rates).

270, in contrast to the Wobé (Man area) with a rate only just over 130 and the Godié (Daloa-Gagnoa region) with a rate demonstrably lower still. In the rural areas, the average is 204, with the various regions not differing from this by more than 20 points (see Table 32.10).

The highest values (Malinké and Voltaic) are apparently explained largely by early marriages in these groups and the high proportion of women of very fertile age (20–24 years). As for the Wobé and Godié, their low rates may be explained by the poor health conditions in their areas.

It would be desirable to compare fertility rates according to residential area. Unfortunately, for the moment we only have data concerning Abidjan, where there was a general fertility rate of 175 in 1963, in contrast to the 204 found in the rural areas.

This apparent differential deserves close attention. The low level in the capital cannot be explained by the later commencement of reproduction there, as the fertility rate for the 15–19-year-old group is higher than that found in the rural areas: 206 instead of 192. Two explanations could be offered for the low fertility rate: the use of contraceptive methods by a fraction of the married women, and the fact that the proportion of women currently married is lower than in the rural areas.

TABLE 32.10
Age-specific fertility rates by residential area and ethnic group (per 1,000 women)

| Age Group | Abengourou | Bouaké | Rural Areas, 1962–64 Daloa-Gagnoa | Korhogo | Man | Odienné | All Rural Areas 1962–4 | All Rural Areas 1958 | Abidjan 1963 |
|---|---|---|---|---|---|---|---|---|---|
| 15–19 | 207 | 207 | 181 | 196 | 138 | 214 | 192 | 217 | 206 |
| 20–24 | 310 | 281 | 293 | 286 | 242 | 310 | 289 | 319 | 230 |
| 25–29 | 289 | 286 | 255 | 235 | 220 | 270 | 264 | 289 | 215 |
| 30–34 | 251 | 221 | 241 | 203 | 183 | 235 | 226 | 209 | 196 |
| 35–39 | 184 | 163 | 153 | 130 | 115 | 180 | 158 | 167 | 125 |
| 40–44 | 93 | 131 | 100 | 75 | 88 | 110 | 102 | 66 | 67 |
| 45–49 | 31 | 52 | 40 | 25 | 61 | 50 | 44 | 36 | 29 |
| All ages (i.e., general fertility rate) | 228 | 208 | 196 | 184 | 170 | 222 | 204 | 220 | 175 |

SOURCES: All Rural Areas, 1958—Demographic Report, 1958, p. 72; Abidjan—report 8, p. 87.

TABLE 32.11
Mortality data for six urban centers (rates per thousand) 1960's

|  | Abengourou | Bouaké | Korhogo | Man | Odienné | Abidjan |
|---|---|---|---|---|---|---|
| Crude death rate | 27 | 26 | 30 | 30 | 35 | — |
| Infant mortality rate | 188 | 167 | 189 | 109 | 210 | 175 |

The first suggestion is improbable; reliable sources of information seem to confirm that the use of contraceptive methods is still exceptional. The second explanation is apparently more justifiable. In Abidjan only 78 percent of females over 15 years old are married, as against 83 percent in rural areas. Admittedly, the difference is less pronounced in the important age span, 15–40 years of age, in which the percentage is 82 in Abidjan compared with 86 in rural areas. The importance of this also is lessened by the fact that the fertility of the single women is not negligible.

We must admit that we do not know the reason for lower urban fertility and that our data on the subject are insufficient. Certain women, especially those single or living in mutual consent unions, probably leave the town at the end of their pregnancy to give birth in their native village. There, after the birth, they may leave the child with its grandparents. In any case, the problem of fertility, like that of nuptiality, in the urban region, is deserving of a thorough study in a country where the population living in the towns and secondary centers will account for about 40 percent of the total population by 1975.

With regard to fertility in the rural areas, surveys made around 1958 yielded a general fertility rate of 220 per thousand, and those made in 1962–1964 produced a slightly lower rate, 204 per thousand. Thus there would seem to have been a drop of 7 percent in fertility. However, the heterogeneous nature of the samples does not allow a reliable conclusion to be drawn from this comparison.

In conclusion, it seems that the fertility for the whole of Ivory Coast is either constant or dropping slightly. The youthful structure of the age pyramid will undoubtedly keep the birth rate more or less constant in the short run, but only a specialized study could give precise data on likely fertility trends.

MORTALITY. The study of mortality in tropical Africa is particularly difficult. Certain ethnic groups are reluctant to recall recent deaths or to declare children who lived only a few days. Table 32.11 assembles the only reasonably reliable data we have for Ivory Coast.

In order to obtain a table of mortality rates by age group, the only possible procedure, given the available data, is to choose a model life table from among those published by the United Nations,[16] with an infant mortality rate around 180 per thousand. The 1958 survey had employed level 25 of these tables. For 1965 it seemed possible to adopt level 30, which corresponds to an expectation of life at birth of 35 years. Table 32.12 gives the mortality rates by age group corresponding to this standard table, while Figure 32.7 shows, for 1,000 live births of each sex, the number of survivors at a given age.

The important investments foreseen by the government in the sphere of public health, especially in preventive medicine, should, along with the wiping out of smallpox, allow the mortality rate to drop along the lines predicted in Table 32.1, and so to fall below 20 per thousand by 1980.

MIGRATORY MOVEMENTS. Population movements within Ivory Coast are very important, whether rural exodus to the towns, movement from one rural zone to another, or finally the inflow of foreigners, either as temporary

[16] United Nations Department of Economic and Social Affairs, *Manuals on Methods of Estimating Population, Manual III: Methods for Population Projections by Sex and Age,* ST/SOA Series A, Population Studies No. 25 (New York, 1956), pp. 72–81.

TABLE 32.12

Postulated age-specific death rates, Ivory Coast, Mid-1960s

| Age in Years | Male | Female |
|---|---|---|
| 0 | 270.2 | 239.8 |
| 1–4 | 35.1 | 35.5 |
| 5–9 | 8.6 | 8.9 |
| 10–14 | 5.6 | 6.3 |
| 15–19 | 8.0 | 8.9 |
| 20–24 | 11.2 | 11.9 |
| 25–29 | 12.1 | 13.5 |
| 30–34 | 13.5 | 11.6 |
| 35–39 | 15.6 | 15.9 |
| 40–44 | 19.9 | 17.3 |
| 45–49 | 24.1 | 20.1 |
| 50–54 | 30.4 | 29.8 |
| 55–59 | 39.6 | 31.9 |
| 60–64 | 52.5 | 44.3 |
| 65–69 | 72.5 | 63.0 |
| 70–74 | 104.5 | 93.4 |
| 75–79 | 148.7 | 138.9 |
| 80–84 | 215.6 | 202.9 |
| 85+ | 344.6 | 310.6 |

SOURCE: United Nations, *Manual on Methods of Estimating Populations, Manual III: Methods for Population Projections by Sex and Age* (New York, 1956), p. 72. The table includes elements from several models.

workers or fixed immigrants. We shall look at these different types of movement in turn so as to take them into account for setting up population forecasts by geographical sector and region of dwelling (or habitat).

*Internal migration.* Migrations from one rural area within the country to another have so far, except for local exceptions, been of relatively low volume. Table 32.13 has been constructed for the mid-1960s using the figures from various regional surveys.

Since the mid-1960s, it is probable that the only noteworthy change has been the increase in the flow of Baoulé toward the Daloa-Gagnoa zone. In contrast, the years to come will no doubt see important movements of the population. On the one hand, the coming into service of the Kossou Dam (in the Central Department)[17] will require the moving of about 100,000 Baoulé. On the other hand, the development of the southwestern region, around San Pedro, cannot be carried out without the attraction of a large number of planters and wage earners into this practically

[17] The dam will be filled in stages beginning in 1971.

uninhabited zone (less than five persons per square mile).

But the most important internal movement nowadays is the rural exodus to the towns, a flow which above all concerns the 15–24-year-old population. A recent survey[18] has shown the importance of this movement and established the importance of the level of school attendance in determining the volume of the outward flow. Although restricted to four sample regions, the results of this study are highly suggestive. Of all 15–29-year-olds born in villages, one-third now live in urban areas. The corresponding proportion for girls is one-fifth. If we restrict our attention to the rural youth enrolled at school, the percentage of those who subsequently move to town is over 70, for boys and girls alike (see Figure 32.8).

*External migration.* The migration of foreigners into the rural areas is of two kinds. One is temporary, involving agricultural workers employed as laborers in the forest area plantations. The other involves those workers who have been able to obtain a plot of forest land, especially between 1950 and 1960, and have settled there permanently as planters. The Agni district in particular has thus taken in thousands of Voltaics and Malenké. But, as pointed out earlier, this type of settlement has become increasingly difficult. The total number of foreigners living in the rural areas was estimated at 270,000 in 1965[19] and must be over 300,000 today.

In the urban areas, the surveys and censuses made between 1960 and 1965 show that the "born abroad" residents formed 29 percent of the population.[20] If we added their direct descendants, more than 35 percent of the population should be considered foreign—in all about 400,000 people, to whom should be added 40,000–50,000 Europeans.

In total in 1965 there were about 700,000 foreigners permanently living in Ivory Coast.

[18] ILO-UNICEF Survey, Ministry of Planning, *The Rural Exodus of the Young People,* ILO, 1969; see also Louis Roussel, "Measuring Rural-Urban Drift in Developing Countries: A Suggested Method," *International Labor Review,* CI, 3 (March 1970), 229–246.
[19] That is, 150,000 born outside the country and 120,000 children born in Ivory Coast of foreigners.
[20] In Abidjan, the proportion was 33 percent.

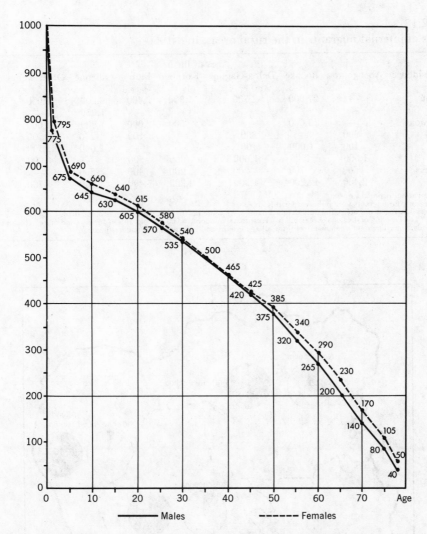

FIGURE 32.7. *Theoretical Number of Survivors by Age for Cohorts of* 1,000 *Births of Each Sex*

SOURCE: United Nations, *Manuals on Methods of Estimating Population.* Manual II: *Methods for Population Projections by Sex and Age* (New York, 1956), p. 76.

If we add temporary workers and their families, we arrive at the final figure of a million foreigners present by one right or another. The distribution of these foreigners by nationality can only be very approximate. Taking into account the temporary workers (i.e., those from Upper Volta) Voltaics alone are estimated to form 40 percent of the total. Of the more permanent residents, one-third are Malians, one-third Voltaics, and one-third are from other African countries.

Moreover, these figures only give a fairly crude idea of the importance of foreigners on Ivory Coast. The greatest proportion of foreigners is among the young adults. At Abidjan, in 1963, 45 percent of the 20–29-year-olds were born abroad. In towns such as Dabou and Anyama more than half of this age group was born abroad.

We must nevertheless qualify this observation by emphasizing the great mobility of the immigrant population. Table 32.14 illustrates

TABLE 32.13

Estimates of internal migrants in the rural areas, mid-1960s

| Area of Residence | Abengourou | Bouaké | Daloa-Gagnoa | Area of Birth Korhogo | Man | Odienné | Other Zones | Totals |
|---|---|---|---|---|---|---|---|---|
| Abengourou | — | 27,000 | 2,700 | 1,300 | 2,400 | 6,200 | 2,000 | 41,600 |
| Bouaké | — | — | — | — | — | 1,000 | — | 1,000 |
| Daloa-Gagnoa | — | 13,000 | — | 500 | 2,000 | 1,500 | 1,000 | 18,000 |
| Korhogo | 200 | — | 300 | — | 100 | 200 | 200 | 1,000 |
| Man | 100 | 1,000 | 100 | — | — | 2,000 | 500 | 3,700 |
| Odienné[a] | 1,500 | 500 | 1,000 | 800 | 500 | — | 1,000 | 5,300 |
| Other zones[b] | 600 | 700 | 200 | 200 | 400 | 300 | — | 2,400 |
| *Totals* | 2,400 | 42,200[c] | 4,300 | 2,800 | 5,400 | 11,200 | 4,700 | 73,000 |

SOURCES: The various regional surveys.
[a] Total figures only for migrants were published for this area.
[b] For these very heterogeneous areas, the only data available were those for the suburban districts of Abidjan.
[c] The report, "The Peopling of the Bouaké region," p. 61, estimates at about 36,000 the migrants of 15 years and more living in the rural area outside the study zone. The number shown here is for all age groups and is doubtless an underestimate.

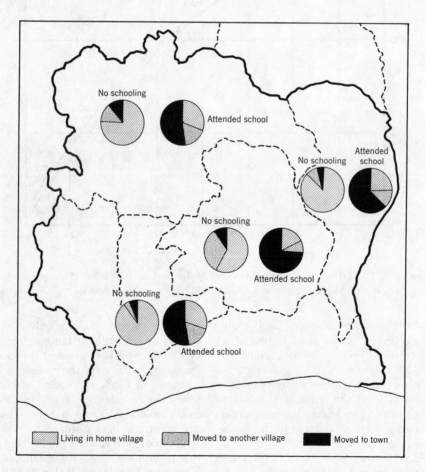

FIGURE 32.8.  *Present Residence by Region of Birth and Education of Young Persons, 1968*

TABLE 32.14
Stability of immigrant residence as a proportion over time of those remaining

| Duration of Residence of Cohort | Abidjan Survey M | F | Yaoundé Survey M & F |
|---|---|---|---|
| On arrival | 1,000 | 1,000 | 1,000 |
| After 7 months[a] | — | — | 795 |
| After 1 year | 800 | 830 | 710 |
| After 2 years | 660 | 640 | 590 |
| After 3 years | 630 | 630 | 540 |
| After 4 years | 620 | 600 | 500 |
| After 5 years | 590 | 590 | 450 |
| After 6 years | 530 | 540 | 420 |
| After 7 years | 450 | 500 | 390 |
| After 8 years | 360 | 450 | — |
| After 11 years | 240 | 360 | — |

SOURCE: Louis Roussel, François Turlot, and R. Vaurs, "La
Mobilité de la Population Urbaine en Afrique Noire: deux essais de
mesure, Abidjan et Yaoundé," *Population*, II (1968), 340.
[a] The total number present after 7 months, 1 year, etc., is the
number of those who have not left the town regardless of whether
they have changed houses within the town or not.

the mobility of those who had recently immigrated into Abidjan. It concerns foreigners
as well as the nationals, but there is every
reason to believe that the mobility of the first
group is at least equal to that of the second
(see Figure 32.9).

Of the 700,000 foreigners living in Ivory
Coast in 1965, only a fraction of them could
be described as residentially stable. In the
urban region it was often very difficult to distinguish the worker on temporary stay from
the permanently settled foreigner.

Immigration has continued since 1965.
Probably about 40,000 more foreigners have
come to join the 270,000 already in the rural
zone, while in the towns the number of
foreigners has no doubt gone up from 400,000
to around 500,000. On the whole, taking the
Europeans too into account, the total number
of foreign residents now amounts to about
850,000 people. There are in addition at any
given time about 350,000 foreign temporary
or seasonal agricultural laborers, giving a
total of 1,200,000 foreigners or about one-
quarter of all persons in the country. The total
data discussed above have been used to construct Table 32.15, which includes the
demographic forecasts by ecological areas.

POPULATION CHANGE
AND SOCIOECONOMIC PROBLEMS
THE LAND SITUATION.   With 39 inhabitants
per square mile, Ivory Coast is far from

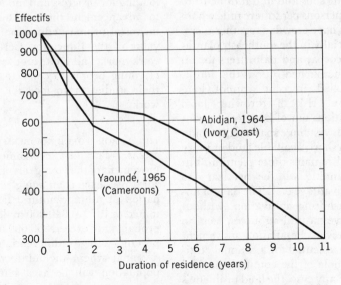

FIGURE 32.9.   *Population Remaining Resident in Town per 1,000
In-Migrant Arrivals by Duration of Residence*

SOURCE: Louis Roussel, Francois Turlot, and R. Vaurs, "La Mobilité de la Population Urbaine en Afrique Noire: Deux essais de Mesure
*Population*, 1968, II, 340.

TABLE 32.15

Projections of residential population, 1965–1980[a] (in thousands)

| Area | 1965 Total | Specified components | 1970 Total | Specified components | 1975 Total | Specified components | 1980 Total | Specified Components |
|---|---|---|---|---|---|---|---|---|
| Abidjan | 330 | | 500 | | 820 | | 1,100 | |
| Male workers[b] | | 114 | | 167 | | 250 | | 335 |
| Forest areas | 1,951 | | 2,296 | | 2,772 | | 3,253 | |
| Rural population | | 1,562 | | 1,751 | | 2,009 | | 2,163 |
| Urban population | | 389 | | 545 | | 763 | | 1,100 |
| Rural workers[c] | | 422 | | 455 | | 500 | | 538 |
| Urban workers[c] | | 109 | | 163 | | 229 | | 330 |
| Savanna areas | 1,719 | | 1,834 | | 1,788 | | 1,907 | |
| Rural population[c] | | 1,458 | | 1,514 | | 1,408 | | 1,467 |
| Urban population[c] | | 261 | | 320 | | 380 | | 440 |
| Rural workers[c] | | 393 | | 386 | | 338 | | 362 |
| Urban workers[c] | | 73 | | 96 | | 114 | | 132 |
| Total national population | 4,000 | | 4,630 | | 5,380 | | 6,260 | |

[a] The population considered is one of permanent residents. To this must be added people on temporary or seasonal stay for employment; they numbered about 300,000 in 1965, counting their families as well. The growth of this group will depend partly on the size of the deficit in the indigenous workforce offering for certain types of employment.
[b] Working population is defined here as population of working age, whatever the employment status.
[c] Male workers only.

reaching its demographic saturation point. Nevertheless, land problems do exist. Certain regions, such as the districts around Korhogo, have deteriorating soils and find it difficult to nourish the 200 persons per square mile whom historical factors have crowded together there. Elsewhere, especially in the southeast, plantations of coffee, cocoa, and palm trees for oil have largely encroached upon the forest. Their uncontrolled invasion cannot long continue without risk of throwing local ecological conditions out of balance. In contrast, in the southwest huge spaces still remain undeveloped. In short, available land in Ivory Coast in general remains quite plentiful, but increasingly planning will be necessary to make the best advantage of it. The days of uncontrolled and shifting cultivation, without action to conserve natural resources, seem to have passed forever. Population movement has proved to be essential for a rational cultivation of the whole of the country's natural resources. But in any case, the land problem is not yet severe, and the land of Ivory Coast could doubtless feed several million more inhabitants. The economic history of the country is in no way influenced by the threat of famine. The dominant feeling, especially among the young people, is an impatient longing for progress and modernity. This will for advancement, the rapid movement toward universal primary education, and the falling value of the Education Certificate[21] on the work market all incite an ever larger number of young people to come to town to pursue their studies or to look for nonagricultural work.

THE LABOR FORCE PROBLEM IN THE RURAL AREAS. The first economic result of the movement of the young out of agriculture and rural residence is an aging and relative stagnation of the agricultural labor force. Estimated in 1970 at 840,000 male workers, it will probably not exceed 900,000 by 1980. It is important also to differentiate between the savanna, where the numbers of the active population will be at a standstill, and the

[21] This education certificate is a diploma confirming the successful completion of six years of primary education.

forest, where a slow increase, explained solely by foreign immigration, is likely to occur. Two economic circumstances make this type of change alarming. On the one hand, the government has set under way a vast program of agricultural development and modernization, especially of export agriculture, in savanna and forest alike. The transition from extensive to intensive cultivation, whether of rice or coffee, usually can only be successfully undertaken by young farmers able to absorb and apply more modern methods of production and management. If nearly all the young people leave the rural region after their primary schooling, it is difficult to see how the replacement of traditional farmers by modern cultivators can be brought about. Besides this qualitative problem, it will still be necessary to find the extra labor-force numbers necessary for realizing these aims. Extra supplies of foreign laborers could be called upon, but this would pose increasingly difficult social problems. Moreover, this solution would only work in areas where the value of production is high enough to justify the use of paid labor. At the present moment, this condition is only fulfilled in the forest area.

THE EMPLOYMENT PROBLEM IN THE URBAN REGION. The labor force problems in the rural region can with some difficulties be solved for the immediate future, but the employment problem in the town promises to be much more urgent. Urban unemployment has not yet developed in a really alarming way in Ivory Coast. It is, in fact, the ease with which employment has hitherto been obtained which has encouraged the flow of foreign workers and young Ivory Coasters of rural origin toward Abidjan and the other urban centers. The economic expansion allowed all the candidates to obtain, if not the dreamed-of position, at least a paying job. What is more, African solidarity and hospitality allowed those who were for the moment without work to wait for an offer worth accepting.

By 1970 wage-paid jobs in the towns amounted to about 240,000 posts, of which around 190,000 were in the modern sector.[22] But from now on several factors will combine to make it very difficult to maintain full employment. (1) The age structure of urban male workers is extremely youthful. There are scarcely more than 20,000 over 50 years of age. Thus, during the decade from 1970, the number of posts made available by retirement will be no greater than this number, but during the same period, the number of young urban residents who will want work will be about ten times as many, as can be seen in Figure 30.4. Retirements will therefore bring only one-tenth of the new aspirants into jobs. The remainder can only be satisfied if new positions come into existence. (2) Because of the undeniable progress of the economy of Ivory Coast, as compared with most of its neighbors, some of the young people have developed an aversion to anything except permanent, middle-class positions. In the urban region, foreigners account for almost two-thirds of the manual laborers. Few Ivory Coasters are candidates for these jobs. Even if the Ivory Coast can continue to provide work for all its nationals, it is obvious that it is not in a position to make everyone a civil servant, office worker, or other highly qualified worker. (3) A large number of executive posts are occupied by Europeans, and the government is justly concerned with Africanizing these jobs. But this change over must be accompanied by the training of local technicians and executives, which takes a considerable time.

## CONCLUSION

At present, Ivory Coast is in a transitional state. The modernization of the rural sector is not advanced enough to retain the young people there. At the same time, industrialization is not sufficiently developed yet for the employment opportunities to be able to meet the needs of the increasing flow of new townsmen. In these conditions, the aspiration level of young people is ahead of the success, which

[22] Estimates based on Ministry of Planning, *Ivory Coast, 1965: Employment* (Abidjan, 1968), pp. 128–29.

is nonetheless noteworthy, of the Ivory Coast economy. In particular, it is not realistic to consider that the rural exodus can continue indefinitely at the present rate; in a country where the main part of the national income is drawn from agriculture, the demographic condition of the countryside must be a consideration of the highest priority.

Even if substantially reduced, the rural exodus would in the long run compromise the country's prosperity, especially if the townsfolk were too ready to refuse jobs as manual or semiskilled laborers.[23] The modernization of the rural areas and a modification of the young people's attitude toward suitable occupations will be two of the main variables which will determine economic and demographic change in Ivory Coast during the next ten years.

[23] See *ibid.*, pp. 149 ff.

*Appendix: Important Studies*

(Titles translated from French)

Ministry of Economic and Financial Affairs of the Ivory Coast Republic and INSEE, Cooperation Service. *Abidjan Census 1955.* Abidjan, 1965.

——*Demographic Survey 1957–1958.* Abidjan, 1965.

Ministry of Planning. *Ivory Coast 1965: Population.* Abidjan, 1967.

——*Ivory Coast 1965: Employment.* Abidjan, 1967.

——*Ten-Year Projections and Supplements to Ten-Year Projections.* Abidjan, 1967 and 1968.

——and SEMA (Society of Economics and Applied Mathematics.) *Socioeconomic Study of the Abidjan Urban Zone,* in particular reports 3, supplement to 3, 6, and 8. Abidjan, 1965.

Ministry of Public Health and Ministry of Economic and Financial Affairs, Statistical Service. *List of Localities of the Ivory Coast.* Abidjan, 1965.

*Regional Studies.* Each study contains a report dedicated to demographic problems.

## INTRODUCTION

Among the countries covered in this book, Niger has certain unique characteristics which influence its demographic structure. First, it is vast in size, but, for the most part, it is sparsely inhabited. There are two zones with higher density, in the Hausa (Hawsa) region along the frontier with Nigeria; and in the Djerma (Zarma)-Songhay region along the Niger River. The two principal population groups are the descendants of the Hausa kingdoms and the Songhay empire. Their areas of residence correspond respectively to the savanna zone and the more humid section of the sahelian zone, a zone intermediate between savanna and desert.

Second, Niger forms with Chad, Mali, and Senegal the "march land" between "black" West Africa and North Africa. The desert, which makes up a considerable proportion of Niger, is no barrier, but rather, throughout history and today, there has been constant movement across the Sahara. This is reflected, for example, in the heterogeneous origin of the population of Niamey, the capital: there are Djermas and Songhays; Hausas (Hawsas); Fulani (Peuls); Tuaregs from the desert; Moors, Arabs, and "Algerians"; Yorubas, Ewes, Minas, Fons, and other Dahomeyan and Togolese people; Wolofs, Bambaras, and Gourmantches; and, of course, Europeans, Lebanese, and Syrians.

Third, with Upper Volta, Mali, and eastern Senegal, Niger is a labor reservoir, and migration tempers the entire economic and social life of the country. Seasonality is a marked characteristic whether the migration is internal or international; whether it is to Nigeria to coincide with groundnut harvesting, or to Ghana in the off season for cultivation, or whether it is local for harvesting. These patterns have been broken recently by the expulsion of Nigériens from Ghana and Ivory Coast. They were among the groups first affected because they held jobs scheduled for Ghanaians, primarily as traders. Among the total numbers expelled from Ghana, the 20,000 or 30,000 from Niger is a small proportion, but in Niger the effect

# CHAPTER THIRTY-THREE

## *Niger*

ISSAKA DANKOUSSOU,
SOULEYMANE DIARRA,
DIOULDE LAYA,
AND
D. IAN POOL

on migration has been marked, particularly in certain cantons, as will be discussed.

Fourth, the population is overwhelmingly Moslem. This society has been exposed throughout its history to outside influences, east–west across the savanna and sahel and north–south over the desert, but has been less exposed to the expansion of European culture than have the societies along the coast of West Africa.

Finally, in common with much of West Africa, fertility levels are high nationally, for reasons which we shall endeavor to explain. However, the eastern section of the country adjacent to Chad, Cameroon, and north-eastern Nigeria has lower fertility, and is actually an extension of the Central African low fertility belt.

## SOURCES OF DATA

In the Republic of Niger, as in the major part of West Africa, numerical data remain incomplete and inexact. In lieu of full censuses many African countries have taken sample censuses. By extrapolation from the sample, it is possible to obtain estimates relating to the entire population. Thus, the one real census, that of 1960, was in fact a sample census.[1]

Before the 1960 census there were so-called administrative censuses, a system which is now being reestablished. Commencing in Zinder in 1968, the *Direction de la Statistique* has initiated an analysis of "village documents" giving the following information; the number of people, migration, fertility, infant mortality, and certain economic and geographical data. On January 14, 1970, this was extended to all of Niger, and was carried out for sedentary groups from January–March 1970, and for nomads from April–June.

In addition to the national census, there have been two "censuses" of Niamey, one in 1959–1960, the other in 1966. The 1966 census was not considered particularly ac-

curate, while Bernus, the researcher who has most carefully studied Niamey, stated that the results of the 1959 census were not satisfactory: "*Devant l'incohérence des chiffres et les multiples erreurs relevées, il a fallu y renoncer.*"[2]

## SPECIAL SURVEYS

There have been a number of special surveys, most notably the family budget study and the work of Bernus, both on Niamey[3] and Rouch's surveys on migration.[4] Another survey, carried out in July and August 1970 will be referred to frequently here, so that a fuller description is warranted.[5]

Using a vertical aerial photograph of Niamey taken in January 1969, the city was divided into more than 260 clusters of concessions of approximately equal size, other than in the residential zones, such as the plateau, where clusters were much larger. Industrial and commercial areas were excluded. At random 20 percent of the clusters were selected in each case so as to give a 10 percent random selection of blocks. Two blocks, almost entirely composed of European villas, were replaced by two others randomly selected on the same basis. Then a census was taken of each block and dwelling unit therein.

[1] INSEE, Service de la coopération, *Etude Démographique du Niger*, 2 vols. (Paris, 1963). Hereinafter referred to as *Census, 1960.*

[2] Suzanne Bernus, *Niamey: Population et Habitat*, République du Niger Etudes Nigeriennes, II: IFAN-CNRS (Niamey, 1967). A loose translation might be: "Because of the lack of comparability of the numerical results and the many errors in totals, it is necessary to disclaim it."

[3] Republic of Niger, Service de Statistiques, *Les Budgets familiaux Africains à Niamey, 1961–62* (Paris: Ministère de la Coopération, 1964); and Suzanne Bernus, *Particularismes Ethniques en Milieu Urbain: L'exemple de Niamey*, University of Paris, Mémoires de l'Institut d'Ethnologie, I (Paris, 1969).

[4] Jean Rouch's surveys; see footnotes 13 and 14.

[5] The survey was financed by the Population Council and carried out by a group from Cornell University under the direction of one of the authors of this chapter, and in collaboration with the Centre Nigérien des Recherches en Sciences Humaines (CNRSH) and the Service Central de la Statistique. The direction was, in addition to D. I. Pool, Judy Harrington, Garba Hima, Joel Gregory, Janet Pool, and Joseph Thomas. See D. I. Pool, *Enquête sur la Fécondité et la Famille au Niger*, Collection Méthodologique, No. 1, CNRSH (Niamey, 1970).

There was then a principal sample covering all women aged 15–49 in the sample concessions, followed by two subsamples interviewing in detail women drawn from the principal sample. We have included data in this chapter based on provisional tabulations taken from this survey, giving information on the population of Niamey. The cumulated fertility rates from this survey are the first ever for Niamey.

Additionally, the same questionnaire used for the principal survey in Niamey was employed in ten villages in the Djerma-Songhay region mainly in interviewing Djermas and Songhays, but including also Bellas, Fulani, Tuaregs, Wogo (related to Djermas), and Hausas. The villages were selected randomly. Certain provisional results from this sample will be included here. It approximates to stratum 6 in the 1960 census, so that we have cumulated fertility rates for two dates to compare. Finally, in January 1971 a comparable rural sample of eight Hausa and Hausa–Béribéri villages were interviewed employing the same sector-sampling method. This last survey zone corresponds approximately to stratum 2 in the 1960 census, but there is evidence to suggest that there were proportionately more Béribéri (Buduma) in the 1971 sample than in the 1960 census thus making certain direct comparisons difficult.[6]

## DISTRIBUTION AND DENSITY OF POPULATION IN NIGER

The Republic of Niger had, at the 1960 census, 2,876,000 inhabitants. According to official estimates, the population of Niger was 3,775,000 on January 1, 1969. With an area

of 460,000 square miles[7] the republic, as a whole, has a mean population density of eight persons per square mile. However, the population is distributed unequally, there being areas which have very low densities.

UNEQUAL SPATIAL DISTRIBUTION OF POPULATION. If one deducts from the total area of Niger the desert zones covering about 350,000 square miles, one is left with an average density of almost 35 per square mile. This section of the country, the arable zone, is the narrow band of territory situated to the south of the 12-inch rainfall line. As the arable zone contains more than 3 million people on only 110,000 square miles of land, more than nine-tenths of the people occupy less than one-quarter of the land surface. Moreover, the stark contrast between the empty north and the relatively densely settled south is merely one of many contrasts, some of which are found even within the arable zone.

REGIONS WITH HIGH DENSITIES. Two sections of the southern arable zone are relatively densely settled, with average population densities of over 40 persons per square mile. The first is the central Niger, the area limited in the south by the frontier with Nigeria, to the west by the Tahoua Road, and to the east by a line passing Zinder; in other words, the total area given over to agriculture in the departments of Tahoua, Maradi, and Zinder. In this section, almost empty plateaus parallel the fossil valleys (i.e., valleys made by bygone rivers) of Maggia and Gulbi where the density is in places 130–180 per square mile or higher.

The second densely settled sector extends along the Niger River between Say and Tillabéry. There, the density at times exceeds 180 persons per square mile in the alluvial valley and along the banks of the Niger where one finds fishing villages.

[6] D. I. Pool, and Victor L. Piché, *Enquête sur la Fécondité au Niger Central*, Collection Méthodologique No. 2, CNRSH (Niamey, 1971). The proportion of women sterile at 35–49 years for the sample (18 percent) was much higher than at the 1960 census (10 percent) and is similar to the level recorded for women 45–49 in stratum 1, at the census (16 percent). The 1971 sample was along the eastern or stratum 1 boundary area of stratum 2.

[7] Source: Service Central de la Statistique, Niamey. The figure for the area is taken from Commissariat Général du Développement, *Annuaire Statistique* (Niamey 1967), p. 3. But this figure conflicts with the area given in Pierre Donnaint, *Le Niger: Cours de Géographie* (Niamey: Ministère de l'Education Nationale, 1966), p. 4. This is the official geography textbook.

AREAS WITH LOW DENSITIES IN SOUTHERN NIGER. In the same region where one finds high densities, there are also densities as low as 15–40 persons per square mile, notably in the west of the country and in the northern part of the central region. Areas with densities as low as 2–15 persons per square mile are found in southwestern Niger in the region of Téra near the Malian and Voltaic borders. Similarly low densities are found in the east between Zinder and Lake Chad.

DESERT REGIONS WITH FEW PEOPLE. Four-fifths of Niger has a population density of less than 2 persons per square mile. However, even in the vast desert region, one occasionally finds densely settled oases although the eastern desert, called Téniré, is only an immense and absolutely uninhabited sea of sand. The Aïr Massif dominates the western limit of this, and, around the town of Agadez, there is a concentration of essentially nomadic population.

## FACTORS WHICH AFFECT THE DISTRIBUTION OF POPULATION

The unequal distribution of Niger's population results from a combination of many factors. Some are natural causes, others are socioeconomic.

NATURAL CAUSES. Most of Niger belongs to the desert zone and is characterized by extreme aridity. Thus, the presence of water in oases or in the fossil valleys is a determinant of settlement. This is the explanation of the low density of the nine-tenths of the country made up of sand dune deserts (*erg*) or stony deserts (*reg*).

In the sahelien zone the density of population correlates directly with the amount and regularity of rainfall. This is a region given over to nomadic pastoralism and to sporadic and precarious cultivation. The low density in certain regions is explained also by the impossibility of practicing diverse or abundant agriculture because the soils are infertile or are submitted to intense erosion by agents such as the sun, wind, and rain. Thus, the granitic formations of Liptako in the west, of Aïr to the north, and of Mounio to the east are lightly settled. In other regions, sandstones over extensive areas, leaching, or the presence of skeletal soils contribute to the low densities which are found above all on the plateaus.

SOCIOECONOMIC CAUSES. The process of settlement varies from region to region and is intimately related to the history of the societies which together make up the population of Niger. In spite of the importance of culture contact, these groups are differentiated, above all linguistically, and this differentiation gives a distinct personality to the area which each society has profoundly marked with its own imprint.

Niger has been throughout the centuries the scene for large-scale population movements which have not always favored the formation of dense settlement patterns. However, certain ethnic groups are closely attached to the land and, as they constitute strongly concentrated village communities, they have benefited from a compact social organization. The Hausa descendants of the inhabitants of former kingdoms make up one-half of the population of Niger. Actually, they are really not a single ethnic group, but rather they form a series of groups having a common language; one can distinguish in central Niger the Konnawa, the Aderawa, the Goberawa, the Karsinawa, the Tazarawa, and the Kanawa. Hard-working cultivators and traders, they are found along the more humid southern fringe of Niger. It is worth noting that the largest proportion of the Hausa ethnic group inhabits Nigeria, but even today some groups from Nigeria emigrate to central Niger to set up new zones of settlement.

The Djerma and the Songhay, who speak two related languages, represent the second most important social group. They live in the west of the country, but the Songhay properly speaking occupy the region along the Niger River from the Malian border to Tillabéry, with another enclave at Gaya. The Djerma, by contrast, occupy the "Djermaganda" region adjacent to the Songhay country. One finds Djermas all along the river as far as the frontiers with Dahomey and Nigeria, and even in the region of Dosso. Together the Djermas and Songhays, along with some minority groups such as the Kourtey pastoralists and the Wogo fisherfolk who inhabit islands on the river between Tillabéry and Ayerou, make up one-quarter of the population of Niger. Today these peoples, formerly renowned as warriors, have become cultivators and pastoralists.

The Kanuri, composed of diverse groups such as the Béribéri, the Manga, the Dagara, the Kanemba, and the Buduma, are dispersed across the Lake Chad basin, to the east of Zinder. They number 6 percent of the total population, and practice a mixed agri-cultural-pastoral economy.

The Fulani form about one-eighth of Niger's population. They are nomads found in every corner of the country. As pastoralists they occupy above all the regions in the sahelien zone where the agricultural density is lowest. But, for several decades, there has been a progressive conversion of Fulani nomads to sedentary occupations.

The Tuaregs, and their former servants, called the Bella by the Djerma or Buzu by the Hausa, make up about one-tenth of the population of Niger. Like the Fulani they are pastoral nomads, mainly in the region between Aïr in the north and the sedentary agricultural zone to the south. However, a tendency toward permanent settlement has been apparent for a long time, notably in the riverine region around Téra and in central Niger around Madaoua and Tahoua.

Foreigners constitute a negligible propor-tion of the population, perhaps numbering 20,000 people, among whom 6,000 are Europeans and Lebanese, living mainly in the capital, Niamey, and in three other large economic foci in the country: Zinder, Maradi, and Tahoua-Agadez.

## URBAN AND RURAL POPULATION

In Niger, perhaps more than any other West African country, the contrast between the rural and urban populations is very marked.

RURAL POPULATION. The Nigérien popula-tion is primarily rural, for more than nine-tenths of the inhabitants are distributed in some 8,000 villages and 1,000 tribes or nomadic groups. Nearly one-fifth of the population practices pastoral nomadism, but there has been a gradual movement among pastoralists to become sedentary. This results sometimes in conflicts over the rights to the occupation of land. In fact, in the sahel of Niger pastoralism and agriculture form two antagonistic forms of rural economy, because, on the one hand, good pasturage is rare, and, on the other hand, there is an insufficiency of land suitable for cultivation.

More than three-quarters of the villages have fewer than 500 inhabitants, and 5,000 of the 8,000 have fewer than 200. The large villages are found above all in Hausaland, where socioeconomic and geographic factors have favored their implantation. But for many years there has been a colonization movement to new areas in the sahelien zone. This has resulted from two factors: the con-temporary rural population explosion and the introduction of cash cropping of groundnuts for export. Numerous hamlets set up for cultivation have become, as they developed, small villages totally autonomous from the rural centers which gave them birth in the first place.[8]

URBAN GROWTH. Urbanization is a pheno-menon which was of little significance until recently in Niger. But, since independence, urbanization has accelerated.[9] According to estimates, four towns had more than 20,000 inhabitants in 1969.[10] By this date, the capital, Niamey, had almost 60,000 inhabi-tants, an official estimate lower than two others for the same date (Table 33.1); this was followed by Zinder with 29,000, Maradi

[8] Gerd Spittler, "Migrations et développement éco-nomique: Exemple du Canton de Tibiri (Département Maradi)" (Unpublished paper, Freiburg, West Germany, Institut für Soziologie, June 1970.
[9] Boubou Hama, L'exode Rural: Un Problème de Fond, Documents, Editions de la Croix-Rouge Nigérienne (Niamey, 1960).
[10] Source: Service Central de la Statistique, Niamey.

TABLE 33.1

Population of Niamey according to various estimates

| Date | Number | Source |
|------|--------|--------|
| 1959 | 29,950 | Census (see Bernus, fn. 2) |
| 1961 | 34,500 | *Enquête, budgets familiaux* (see fn. 3) |
| 1966 | 58,816 | Census, *Mairie, Annuaire Statistique 1967* |
| 1969 | 60,000 | Official estimate |
| 1969 | 70,000 | Survey, Ministry of Works[a] |
| 1970 | 82,000–87,000 | Based on 10% sample survey (see fn. 5) |

[a] République du Niger, Ministère des Travaux Publics, Transportation, Mines, et de l'urbanisme, *L'Habitat à Niamey* (Niamey, 1969).

(21,000), and Tahoua (20,000). One dozen administrative centers each have a population of less than 10,000. Thus, in all, fewer than 250,000 people live in urban areas. Although the functions of these centers are essentially administrative and commercial, their populations have often conserved a way of life, and even many occupational activities, which are rural. Nevertheless, the growth of Niamey has been rapid, regardless of which estimate one accepts. Urbanization will present an increasingly difficult problem, particularly if Niamey grows as predicted.[11]

## MIGRATION

INTERNAL MIGRATION. Colonization and rural-urban migration are not the only population movements in Niger. Among other internal migrations it is worth noting that of the nomads who practice transhumance with their animals searching for pasture and water. Nearly 600,000 Tuaregs and Fulani make this movement throughout the length of the year, across the region where they are dispersed between the semidesert and the arable zone.

[11] See the projection in République du Niger, *L'habitat à Niamey* (Niamey, 1969), for 1990 of 500,000 inhabitants, or almost one-twelfth of the total population of Niger by then. It is difficult to accept this projection. A very rapid growth rate of 6–8 percent per annum, for example, would give a population in 1990 of 250,000–300,000. But even this number would create difficult problems.

The sedentary agriculturalists often migrate also, but at fixed periods during the year. These seasonal movements of rural Nigériens are far from being negligible. The census (1960) showed that 130,000 persons were absent from their normal residence. Among these, 80,000 were in a different region of Niger, notably in the urban centers. During the dry season, from November to May, a large number of rural inhabitants go into the the towns in search of work or to live with relatives.

INTERNATIONAL MIGRATION. In 1960 about two-fifths of persons absent from their normal place of residence were outside the country. Thus, more than 50,000 Nigériens are absent each year seeking work in the coastal countries, notably Ghana, Chad, Cameroon, Nigeria, and Ivory Coast. This migration is largely of young men, with a mean age of about 29 years. The movement is essentially seasonal, as they leave Niger about September returning in March for the cultivation season.[12] Some emigrants had formed communities in Ghana over many decades, and these groups made up the bulk of the 20,000–30,000 Nigériens expelled from Ghana and Ivory Coast to return to a country they had not seen for many years. Nevertheless the more typical migrant stayed on average only 4–5 months. Permanent communities developed outside the country for all ethnic groups, but overall, in Ghana, for example, it was the Hausas who stayed the longest and were most likely to be married, whereas 59 percent of "Zabramas" (Djermis and Songhays) in Ghana stayed less than one year and 71 percent less than two years.[13] Hausas went typically to Nigeria, Ghana, and Ivory Coast (concentrating in Abidjan), while Djermis and Songhays went to Ghana and Ivory

[12] This is also shown by the statistics collected by the Ministry of the Interior on all entries and departures through border posts. At Makalondi and Gaya, the routes taken toward Ghana, there were, in 1966 for example, higher than usual numbers of arrivals or departures corresponding to these dates.

[13] Jean Rouch, *Migrations au Ghana* (Enquête 1953–1955), Société des Africanistes (Paris: Musée de l'Homme, 1956).

Coast. Nigériens from Dosso, Tahoua, and Niamey tended to go to Ivory Coast, whereas from Téra and Tillabéry the destination was Ghana.[14]

Their occupation outside Niger, a temporary one, frequently is petty trading, an occupation which was among the first to be reserved in Ghana for Ghanaians. In the past the migrants have often returned year after year to the same foreign region. Thus, among "Zabramas" interviewed in Ghana, 75 percent had made more than one stay, 55 percent more than two, and 40 percent more than three stays.[15]

The effect in Niger varies from area to area. In the Djerma region, according to returns by canton, 6 percent of the population had migrated to the coast each year, 4.8 percent to Ghana, with the proportion rising to 9.4 percent in the Tillabéry area, and to 25–45 percent for men aged 20–40 years in the same area.[16] Elsewhere, as in the area of Ader Doutchi, 18 percent of the men were reported to have migrated each year.[17]

The revenue acquired by migrants during their stay outside the country serves in their villages of origin to pay taxes and to procure consumer durables for their families. Moreover, the young men use the money to pay bridewealth. But these beneficial effects often do not compensate even for the temporary absences of those who go to the coast or to the towns. In fact, rural development is often held back for lack of manpower. This is the case in the Niger River valley above Niamey, where all persons of young and dynamic age are habitually absent. It appears, at least before the application recently of the new rules in Ghana, difficult to reduce the rural exodus

which persists by force of habit and above all by the need for cash and consumer durables.

## FERTILITY

Table 33.2 gives a range of crude birth rates and fertility rates for 1960, estimated by different methods from the census of that year. All of them present much the same picture: Fertility levels are very high, perhaps exceeded in West Africa only by certain coastal countries.

These data are, of course, affected by considerable errors. Among the most serious detected during the calculations were the following: (1) Contrary to general experience, ages 0–4 and 5–9 may be overenumerated (this affects calculations employing reverse survival ratios). (2) Females are underenumerated at 10–14 years but overenumerated at 15–44 and particularly at 25–29 years. (3) There is a deficit, by comparison with the stable population, of younger adult males, but this may be a factor of migration. (4) There may be underreporting of births in the long-term retrospective data (reducing the estimate of completed family size). (5) The sex ratios for "current" births (i.e., births in the last 12 months) are such that the quality of these data is in doubt. Moreover, as the census was taken throughout the dry season of 1959–1960, and given the marked seasonality of migration (see above) and births (see below), there is every possibility that the duration of 12 months was not accurately established by the respondent. (6) Data on survivorship of children born alive appear to have fewer defects than that for "current" live births, (i.e., those of the last 12 months).

In summary, Rele's method, although not the most sophisticated, may be the least affected by the defects noted above. Furthermore, Rele's own analyses have shown that his method is robust under varying conditions even when the assumptions are changed quite radically (i.e., $e_0^0 = 30$; $e_0^0 = 40$). His rate confirms that calculated from the stable model, and is fairly close to that derived from

---

[14] Jean Rouch, "Rapport sur les Migrations Nigériennes vers la Basse Côte d'Ivoire," mimeographed, Abidjan, August 6, 1957.

[15] Rouch, *Migrations au Ghana*.

[16] *Ibid.*

[17] Henri Raulin, *Rapport de Mission Ader-Doutchi*, CNRSH (Niamey, 1965). Ader Doutchi is in the Mauri region. Mauris speak either Djerma or Hausa and have adopted the way of life of either group. Their home region is in the fossil valley of Dallo Maouri and around Dogondoutchi which lies between central and western Niger. The majority speak Hausa.

TABLE 33.2

Estimated vital rates, various methods, Niger, 1960 census

| Method / Rate | Stable population models | Survivorship to two years of age $(l_2)$[a] | Rele[b] | Brass[c] | Current rates[d] | Cumulated rates[d] | Reverse survivorship[d] |
|---|---|---|---|---|---|---|---|
| Crude birth rate | 56.8 | 54.7 | 56.4 (61.1) | | 52 | | |
| Age-specific birth rates | | | | | | | |
| 15–19 | | | | 0.171 | 0.175 | | |
| 20–24 | | | | 0.333 | 0.341 | | |
| 25–29 | | | | 0.299 | 0.306 | | |
| 30–34 | | | | 0.253 | 0.259 | | |
| 35–39 | | | | 0.186 | 0.191 | | |
| 40–44 | | | | 0.097 | 0.099 | | |
| 45–49 | | | | 0.046 | 0.047 | | |
| Gross reproduction rate | 3.5 | | | 3.4 | 3.7 | | |
| Total fertility rate | 7.2 | | | 6.9 | 7.1 | | |
| Completed fertility | | | | | | 5.8 | 7.3(0–4) 8.6(5–9) 7.9(0–9) |
| Crude death rate | 31.8 | 25.2 | | | | | |
| Growth rate | 25.0 | 29.5 | | | | | |

SOURCE: Judy Harrington, Martha Little, and Elizabeth Wolniakowski, "Working Paper on Nigérien Vital Rates," unpublished paper Cornell University (June 1970).
[a] Assuming a growth rate of 3 percent and a mortality level of 9.527 ("West" family model); see United Nations, *Methods of Estimating Basic Demographic Measures from Incomplete Data, Manual IV* (New York, 1967).
[b] Using a child-woman ratio Co-4/W15–49 and assuming expectation of life at birth = 40 years. The figures in brackets assume $e_0{}^0 = 30$ years. See J. R. Rele, *Fertility Analysis through Extension of Stable Population Concepts*, Population Monograph Series, 2 (Berkeley: University of California Press, 1967).
[c] Using $P/F$ ratio at 20–24; see United Nations, *Manual IV*, and William Brass and Ansley J. Coale, "Methods of Analysis and Estimation," in William Brass et al., eds., *The Demography of Tropical Africa* (Princeton, N.J.: Princeton University Press, 1968).
[d] Taken from INSEE (Service de la Coopération) *Démographie Comparée*, I (Paris, 1968).

methods taking into account survivorship of live births. The latter method yields a birth rate at the upper limit of the range finally accepted by the census report (50–55 per thousand).[18]

Given that fertility was high in 1960, have

[18] The mean between the cumulated and the current levels.

there been changes over time? Are there differentials, and, if so, what factors contribute to the variations?

Table 33.3 gives data for each of the strata at the 1960 census. Niamey and the north were excluded from the census, so that essentially these are regional differences in the sedentary agricultural zone of Niger. One

TABLE 33.3

Crude birth rates and measures of fertility by stratum 1960 census

| | Stratum 1 | 2 | 3 | 4 | 5 | 6 |
|---|---|---|---|---|---|---|
| Crude birth rate | 44.6 | 62.3 | 62.4 | 72.1 | 60.2 | 48.9 |
| Gross fertility rate[a] | 122 | 253 | 290 | 208 | 261 | 214 |
| Mean number of infants ever born alive | | | | | | |
| To women 45–49 | 4.13 | 5.37 | 6.16 | 6.11 | 5.52 | 6.27 |
| To women 50+ | 4.11 | 5.02 | 5.93 | 5.64 | 5.88 | 5.96 |

SOURCES: Crude birth data—Harrington et al., "Nigérien Vital Rates," using stable methods; Gross fertility rate and Mean number of infants— Census, 1960.
[a] The gross fertility rate is "current" births to women aged 15–49 years (expressed per thousand women).

TABLE 33.4

Percentage of women aged 45–49 who have never given birth

| | | | Stratum | | | |
|---|---|---|---|---|---|---|
| All Niger | 1 | 2 | 3 | 4 | 5 | 6 |
| 6.3 | 16.0 | 8.9 | 7.2 | 5.3 | 7.0 | 5.2 |

Source: Census, 1960.

distinction is outstanding: that between stratum 1, peopled by Kanuris, and the rest of the country. There is no medical or socio-logical study of this group, so it is difficult to analyze this differential.

However, there are certain factors which can be noted: (1) This region abuts the central African low fertility belt.[19] (2) The Kanuri are pastoralists as well as agri-culturalists, and therefore the unsettled existence which affects nomadic pastoralists may operate among the Kanuri (for example, in a special census of nomads the crude birth rate for Tuaregs was shown to be 52 per thousand and for Fulani 41.).[20] (3) Levels of absolute sterility are higher (Table 33.4) in stratum 1 than elsewhere in Niger, possibly the product of medical factors.

The other major differential shown by the 1960 census was between women who had

been married once and those who had been married more than once. The higher the number of marriages the lower the completed family size.[21] It is difficult to know whether this factor affects fertility in stratum 1. The effect does not derive from marriage structure, for polygyny is slightly less frequent among the Kanuris than among the Hausas. However, it is possible that Kanuris marry later than other groups, but after an adolescence which is less closely supervised and hence during which extramarital sexual relations are more common and frequent. This may have the same effect as multiple marriage.

These were the major differentials in 1960, but have there been changes since then? The 1970 fertility survey in the rural section of the Djerma-Songhay region permits a comparison to be made between 1960 and 1970. The 1960 data are for stratum 6, which, of course, excluded Niamey. The data for cumulated fertility rates by age are given in Table 33.5 for the two dates. Allowing for the size of the 1970 sample, particularly at older ages, it is probable that there has been little change in rural stratum 6 between 1960 and 1970. Preliminary data for a survey of 737 women carried out in January 1971 in central Niger (Hausa region) also indicate that

[19] See William Brass et al., eds., *The Demography of Tropical Africa* (Princeton, N.J., 1968), pp. 166–67.
[20] INSEE, *Etude Démographique et Economique en Milieu Nomade* (Paris, 1966), p. 70.

[21] A similar differential has been shown for Ghana, see D. I. Pool, "Conjugal Patterns in Ghana," *Canadian Review of Anthropology and Sociology*, V, 4 (1968).

TABLE 33.5

Comparison between fertility levels, 1960 and 1970: average number of live births per woman and percent of women with no live births, Djerma-Songhay region

| | Age Group (in years) | | | | | | | |
|---|---|---|---|---|---|---|---|---|
| | 15–19 | 20–24 | 25–29 | 30–34 | 35–39 | 40–44 | 45–49 | (40–49) |
| Average number of live births: 1960 | 0.4 | 1.8 | 3.0 | 4.4 | 5.1 | 5.5 | 6.3 | — |
| 1970 | 0.5 | 2.1 | 3.3 | 3.9 | 4.6 | 5.3 | 5.0 | 5.1 |
| Percent with no live births: | | | | | | | | |
| 1960 | 73 | 19 | 9 | 8 | 8 | 9 | 5 | — |
| 1970 | 76 | 11 | 7 | 7 | 7 | 4 | 9 | — |
| 1970 sample | N = 176 | 157 | 191 | 118 | 83 | 57 | 82 | 139 |

Sources: 1960—Census, 1960. Their age groups were 14–19, 20–24, etc; 1970—Sample, 1970; see D. Ian Pool, "Résultats Provisoires," *Enquête sur la Fécondité et la Famille au Niger*, Collection Méthodologique, No. 1, CNRSH (Niamey, 1970), p. iv.

TABLE 33.6

Rural-urban fertility differential by age group: average number of live births per woman and percent of women with no live births, Niamey and Djerma-Songhay region

| Average number of live | | | | Age Group | | | | |
|---|---|---|---|---|---|---|---|---|
| births | 15–19 | 20–24 | 25–29 | 30–34 | 35–39 | 40–44 | 45–49 | (40–49) |
| Niamey | 0.5 | 1.7 | 2.6 | 3.3 | 4.1 | 4.0 | 4.0 | 4.0 |
| Rural region | 0.5 | 2.1 | 3.3 | 3.9 | 4.6 | 5.3 | 5.0 | 5.1 |
| Percentage of women with no live births: | | | | | | | | |
| Niamey | 71 | 23 | 15 | 13 | 12 | 18 | 29 | — |
| Rural region | 67 | 11 | 7 | 7 | 7 | 4 | 9 | — |
| Niamey            N = 347 | | 434 | 541 | 308 | 209 | 174 | 111 | 285 |

SOURCE: Pool, "Résultats Provisoires," p. iv.

changes between 1960 and 1971 were minimal there.[22]

From the 1970 sample, we have the first viable fertility data for Niamey. Table 33.6 compares Niamey at this date with the 1970 data for the surrounding rural region. The fertility of Niamey women was lower than that of rural women, particularly at older ages where it approximated one live birth, and, by comparison with the rural data for 1960, two live births. Moreover, the proportion of sterile women in Niamey was higher than in any rural region (see Table 33.4). We will offer an explanation of urban fertility in terms of changing patterns of urbanization, and particularly an explanation of the fact that younger urban women have much the same fertility as younger rural women. Furthermore, it is necessary to explain why current fertility in Niamey (vis à vis cumulated fertility rates shown in Table 31.6) is relatively high.

[22] There is apparently overrepresentation of women aged 25–29 years in the sample, the same defect as noted earlier for the census, and as has been reported almost invariably in West African population counts. The sample also contains more women, 45–49, than one would anticipate. Pool and Piché, *Enquête sur la Fécondité au Niger Central*, Table 3. Preliminary results in this survey were (see also footnote 6):

Fertility Central Niger 1960 and 1971 (live births per woman)

| Age group | 15–19 | 20–24 | 25–29 | 30–34 | 35+ |
|---|---|---|---|---|---|
| Census 1960 | | | | | |
| (stratum 2) | 0.5 | 1.8 | 2.9 | 3.6 | 5.7 |
| Survey 1971 | 0.6 | 1.7 | 2.5 | 3.6 | 4.3 |

Current fertility is based on crude birth rates (CBR) and general fertility rates (GFR) calculated from registration data for 1967 obtained from the *Mairie* (i.e., city administration). The data are presented in Table 33.7. The most reasonable crude birth rate would be that obtained with a base population from 80,000–85,000. This, in itself, is a confirmation of our earlier estimate of the size of Niamey.

A GFR of 207 per 1,000 and a CBR of 49 are close to the GFR of 214 and the CBR of 48.9 (Table 33.3) established for stratum 6 in the 1960 census. However, among women at reproductive ages those at the high risk ages (20–29 years) made up a higher proportion of the Niamey population than was true at the 1960 census for the rural Djerma-Songhay.

TABLE 33.7

Crude birth rate (1967) for Niamey under varying assumptions about the size of the city,[a] and general fertility rates (1967)

| | Assuming Population Was | | | |
|---|---|---|---|---|
| | 60,000 | 70,000 | 80,000 | 85,000 |
| Crude birth rate (per 1,000) | 70 | 60 | 52 | 49 |
| General fertility rate = 207 per 1,000 $\left(\dfrac{\text{births registered}}{\text{females 15–49}}\right)^{b}$ | | | | |

[a] See Table 33.1.

[b] $F\ 15\text{–}49 = 10 \times \left\{ \text{females } 15\text{–}49,\ 1970\ \text{survey} \times \dfrac{(100)^{3}}{(106)} \right\}$

TABLE 33.8

Percentage age distribution, females of reproductive age, Niamey and stratum 6

| | Age Group | | | | |
|---|---|---|---|---|---|
| | 15–19 | 20–29 | 30–39 | 40–49 | Total[a] |
| Niamey, 1970 | 16 | 46 | 24 | 13 | 99 |
| Stratum 6, 1960 | 27 | 34 | 25 | 15 | 101 |

SOURCES: Pool, "Résultats Provisoires," pp. iii and iv; Census, 1960.
[a] Totals vary from 100 because of rounding.

region surrounding Niamey, as is shown in Table 33.8.

Nevertheless, the GFR and CBR are higher than would be suggested by the data on Niamey for completed family size. At first there might appear to be a conflict here, but actually there is none. The bulk of the registered births came from younger women (less than 35 years), while, as already shown, this group is inflated by comparison with the surrounding rural region. Moreover, the fertility of younger women is closer to that of rural women than is the fertility of older women (Table 33.6). Finally, a high proportion of older women in Niamey are sterile.

All these facts taken together suggest that the pattern of urbanization is the factor responsible for this phenomenon. At first rural-urban migration of women must have been highly selective; women who had fewer children or who were sterile were proportionately more common among in-migrants than among women who remained in the rural areas. More recently the characteristics of the in-migrants have become more normal and

less selective.[23] However, at this stage, other factors operate among certain *évolué* groups, particularly the factor of modernization resulting from a wider range of experience in urban areas and from education. Thus, not surprisingly, the fertility at younger ages of women with some education is lower than that of women with no education. These data are given in Table 33.9.

Urban women live in an environment where new ideas are being discussed, including many aspects of family life; for example, topics such as bride price, polygyny, and the rights of women are debated publicly in the press by young *évolués*.[24] Many of these persons are government clerks who receive generous family allowances (2,500 West African francs, i.e., about U.S. $9, per month per child). Recently, a law was passed, for reasons of governmental financial economy, limiting this allowance to the first six children, a change which provoked much discussion among *évolués*.

This urban atmosphere of discussion and challenge does induce changes in the social

[23] A pattern of this type has emerged for Ouagadougou (see Chapter 37).
[24] One series of articles and letters in *Le Niger* terminated in July 1967 with the publication (July 17) of a report on a speech by Dr. S. Mwathi of the Kenyan FPA introduced by the statement: "*Nous publions ci-dessous, des propos tenus par le Dr. Mwathi . . . tout en espérant qu'ils feront réfléchir les familles nigériennes*" (i.e., "We publish below some considered observations by Dr. Mwathi . . . fully hoping that they will cause Nigérien families to reflect on these matters.") The debate was, of course, among a very limited group in the community.

TABLE 33.9

Fertility by education, Niamey, 1970: average number of live births per woman at each age group

| | Age Group | | | | | | | |
|---|---|---|---|---|---|---|---|---|
| | 15–19 | 20–24 | 25–29 | 30–34 | 35–39 | 40–44 | 45–49 | 49–49 |
| Women never educated | 0.5 | 1.8 | 2.7 | 3.2 | 4.1 | 4.1 | 4.0 | 4.0 |
| Women with some education[a] | 0.2 | 1.4 | 2.1 | 4.2 | 4.3 | 2.9 | 4.0 | 3.3 |
| Number of women ever educated[a] | 98 | 76 | 76 | 34 | 16 | 14 | 7 | 21 |
| Percentage at each age ever educated[a] | 28 | 18 | 14 | 11 | 8 | 8 | 6 | 7 |

SOURCE: Pool, "Résultats Provisoires," pp. iii and iv.
[a] Including Koranic, primary, and secondary schooling as well as education beyond schooling.

TABLE 33.10

Attitudes toward family size, Niamey and Djerma-Songhay rural region, 1970: (1) Desired family size; (2) discussion of number of children with husband; (3) consideration of family size; (4) desire for more children

| Question | Percent Answering: | | | | | |
|---|---|---|---|---|---|---|
| (1) "Do you believe that a woman should have a large family with many children or a small family with few children?" | Large | Small | What God gives | Don't know | Total | Number of Respondents |
| Niamey | 39 | 5 | 35 | 21 | 100 | 2,053 |
| Rural | 30 | 1 | 42 | 27 | 100 | 865 |
| Of those who answered "large": "Large, that is to say how many?" | Number given | Average number | Many | Don't know | Total | |
| Niamey | 74 | 9.1[a] | 7 | 19 | 100 | |
| Rural | 46 | 10.1[a] | 8 | 46 | 100 | |
| Of those who answered "small": "Small, that is to say how many?" | | | | | | |
| Niamey | 83 | 4.1 | — | 17 | 100 | |
| Rural | Insufficient | cases | | | | |
| Of those who answered "What God gives": "God, how many *does* he give?" | | | | | | |
| Niamey | 19 | 8.5[a] | 6 | 74 | 99 | |
| Rural | Insufficient cases | | | 9 | | |
| (2) "Have you ever discussed with your husband the number of children you want?" | Yes | No | Don't know | No response | Total | |
| Niamey | 7 | 84 | 2 | 6 | 99 | |
| Rural | 1 | 94 | 2 | 3 | 100 | |
| (3) "Have you ever thought about the number of children you want?" | | | | | | |
| Niamey | 22 | 64 | 7 | 8 | 101 | |
| Rural | 12 | 72 | 13 | 3 | 100 | |
| (4) "Do you want to have more children?" | Yes | No | What God gives | Don't know | No response | Total |
| Niamey | 76 | 8 | 7 | 5 | 4 | 100 |
| Rural | 74 | 8 | 8 | 8 | 3 | 101 |

SOURCES: Pool, "Résultats Provisoires," and unpublished data.
[a] These had a bimodal distribution, the modes being 10 and 12.

attitudes of women. Norms long accepted are reconsidered and new ideas adopted. Thus in Table 33.10 a comparison is made between rural and urban data to evaluate differential attitudes toward the size of families and decisions about family size.

Generally, urban women were more able to answer these questions than were rural ones, and were less likely to be fatalistic about their lives and future prospects. However, the differences were not extremely marked, while, in both cases, there was a strong tendency to accept "what God gives." It is notable that most of the women who replied to questions *Ça dépend de Dieu* (i.e., "It all depends on God") also were unable to go any further in relating what they had done or thought on these matters or in outlining their hopes.[25]

The factors influencing fertility levels in rural Niger appear to be those one would expect in a conservative rural population. Preliminary tabulations of the 1970 sample survey show a mean age at first marriage in the Djerma-Songhay region of 16 years. Lactation is prolonged there (17 months), and minimum abstention is governed by the Moslem proscription of 40 days, although abstinence is usually considerably longer (mean = 4 months; median between 1 and 2 months). On inspection the urban data show a similar trend, with, perhaps, an older age at first marriage. However divorce appears frequent among urban women, being often a reason for in-migration, either to escape an unhappy arranged marriage, or as a result of a sterile union where the man has divorced his spouse. These divorcees often take up prostitution, and, indeed, a number stated in the survey that this was the reason they had come to Niamey.[26]

As with many other aspects of Nigérien life, fertility is markedly seasonal, possibly as an outcome of seasonal migration. In Table 33.11 the monthly distribution of births registered for 1967 at the *Mairie* in Niamey is compared with that for Ouagadougou. In both cases fertility was lower earlier in the year, or nine months after the wet season, than later. The apparent lower conception rates in the wet season could result from the temporary migration of men to the farms. It is worth noting that Ghanaian cities have a similar minimum[27] (actually bimodal as related to the two coastal wet seasons). More importantly, it may well be Niamey rather than the rural areas which is affected by this

[25] See Fatoumata Agnes Diarra, "La Femme Zarma entre la Tradition et la Modernité" (Doctoral Thesis Faculté des Lettres et Sciences Humaines, Université de Paris, 1970), To be published Editions Anthropos (Paris 1971), pp. 154–58. Replying to questions posed to them in a survey directed by Dr. Diarra, herself a Djerma, on "Reasons for spacing of births," "Methods for spacing births," and "Desired Number of Children," the largest proportion of Djerma women respondents (respectively: 40, 50, and 33 percent) placed their "trust in God."

[26] See also, Bernus, *Particularismes Ethniques en Milieu Urbain*, pp. 152–64.

[27] J. Holzer, *The Seasonality of Vital Events in Ghana*, Institute of Statistics, University of Ghana (Legon, 1967); and J. Holzer, "Seasonality of Vital Events in Selected Cities of Ghana: An Analysis of Registration Data Relating to the Period, 1956–60," in John C. Caldwell and C. Okonjo, eds., *The Population of Tropical Africa* (London: Longmans, Green and Company, and New York: Columbia University Press, 1968), pp. 225–33.

TABLE 33.11
Monthly distribution of registered births, Niamey (1967) and Ouagadougou (1968)

| Month | Niamey | | | Ouagadougou | | |
|---|---|---|---|---|---|---|
| | Number | Percentage of annual births | Percentage deviation from monthly average | Number | Percentage of annual births | Percentage deviation from monthly average |
| January | 308 | 7.4 | −12 | 447 | 7.6 | −9 |
| February | 255 | 6.1 | −27 | 421 | 7.2 | −14 |
| March | 320 | 7.6 | −8 | 517 | 8.8 | +5 |
| April | 322 | 7.7 | −8 | 489 | 8.3 | 0 |
| May | 339 | 8.1 | −3 | 496 | 8.4 | +1 |
| June | 316 | 7.6 | −9 | 542 | 9.2 | +11 |
| July | 329 | 7.9 | −6 | 460 | 7.8 | −6 |
| August | 419 | 10.0 | +20 | 450 | 7.7 | −8 |
| September | 422 | 10.1 | +21 | 471 | 8.0 | −4 |
| October | 400 | 9.6 | +15 | 544 | 9.2 | +11 |
| November | 363 | 8.7 | +4 | 523 | 8.9 | +7 |
| December | 393 | 9.4 | +13 | 523 | 8.9 | +7 |
| Total | 4,186 | 100.2 | | 5,883 | 100.0 | |

SOURCES: Niamey—birth registrations at the *Mairie*, 1967. Ouagadougou—data collected by Guy Planès, Direction de la Statistique. For Ouagadougou the mean interval between birth and registration was 9.8 days for male babies and 12.1 for females, but the medians were 3 days (M), 4 days (F).

seasonality because Niamey residents have further to go to their farms than do rural cultivators. This may be yet another explanation of the rural-urban differential in fertility.

## MORTALITY

Crude death rates for Niger were given in Table 33.2. They indicate clearly that mortality is very high. Similarly, life expectation at birth must be very low, being perhaps around 37 years in 1960.[28] It is most important to seek possible factors which might produce a decline in mortality outside Niamey, for only two-fifths of the country's approximately 50 doctors work in areas outside the capital.

Perhaps the most hopeful developments for a country such as Niger, where budgetary priorities preclude for the time being the development of extensive health infrastructures, is the use of mass vaccination programs for certain critical diseases. The first program was against smallpox, and by 1969 70 percent of the population had been vaccinated, and, of these, 76 percent were classified immune from smallpox. No cases of the disease have been reported since April 1969. However, smallpox was, outside epidemic years, never a great killer. Rather it is the so-called childhood diseases which are critical. Among these the greatest advances have been made against measles once the problem of refrigerating live vaccine was overcome ingeniously by the use of styrofoam boxes and by return visits every ten days for new ice supplies by the vaccination teams to the few ice machines scattered through the country. So far all "susceptibles" in the cities have been covered, but rural coverage is fairly low to date. However, it is hoped that soon 80 percent of the population at risk will be vaccinated each year.[29] One would envisage, then, the same kind of

mortality declines as will be analyzed in Chapter 37, on Upper Volta.

Other attacks on disease include the public health measures undertaken by the dispensaries and the Ministry of Health, especially the spread of antibiotics, which are employed for diverse purposes, and the enforcement in some quarters of cities of general hygiene by the *chef de quartiers*.

## CONCLUSION

At the moment it is difficult to suggest future growth patterns in view of the various courses mortality declines might take, and the as yet unknown effect of a higher than normal return migration rate for 1970. Certainly there is every indication that, for the vast majority of rural Nigériens, fertility will remain at present levels for some time. This, unless mortality declines very steeply, would imply a growth rate of about 3 percent per annum or higher. The official projections given in Table 33.12 suggest growth rates of almost 15 percent per quinquennium during the 1970s.

TABLE 33.12
Projected total population of Niger

| Date[a] | Population | Population Index (1970 = 100) |
|---|---|---|
| 1970 | 3,873,413 | 100.0 |
| 1975 | 4,425,343 | 114.3 |
| 1980 | 5,055,906 | 130.5 |

SOURCE: Ministry of Education, based on projections by the Statistical Service.
[a] January 1 of each year.

Given a high growth rate such as this, there appear to be three major implications for Niger. First, and particularly if the rural work force is swollen by returned migrants, there will be pressure on rural resources, especially on farm land. Already, as shown above, there has been a marked colonization movement which has extended to the northern limits of the arable zone in central Niger.

[28] R. K. Som, "Some Demographic Indicators for Africa," in Caldwell and Okonjo, *Population of Tropical Africa*, p. 193.
[29] Data on smallpox and measles: Tony Masso, U.S. Public Health Service, and Administrative Aid *Lutte contre la variole et la rougeole*, Service des Grandes Endémies, Niamey, January 1970 (personal communication).

Second, education, a national priority, will be severely affected. Already it is difficult to increase the levels of education, even given an annual expenditure of 12 percent of the gross domestic product or more than 300 West African francs per person (i.e., over U.S. $1) on it, as was the budgetary estimate for 1970. It is hoped to increase enrollment from 81,454 pupils, as of January 1, 1970, to 162,000 by 1982, by doubling the number of classrooms.[30] Yet, high fertility and an increase in survivor-

[30] Personal communication from M. Moussa Doufaye, Ministère de l'Education Nationale.

ship could mean that most of the new classroom space will be taken up by expanding school populations in areas already served by schools rather than in opening up new schools.

Third, there may well be an increase in the rate of urbanization. Already there is much doubt about the size of Niamey's population, and we have suggested here that its size may be greater than is officially recognized. In any case, future growth is likely to be such that there will be severe problems both for rural and urban Niger.

# CHAPTER THIRTY-FOUR

# *The Nomads of Niger*

M. F. GANON

▦

THIS chapter describes a survey carried out from 1962 to 1964 among peoples with a pastoral, nomadic environment. It was the first statistical survey attempted in West Africa of a nonsedentary population.

If the survey methods for settled environments can now be considered developed, this is certainly not the case for the nomadic environment, where until recently the difficulties of employing the usual statistical methods have seemed insurmountable. This survey had therefore two very different main aims: (1) to gather the maximum of statistical information on nomadic populations in Niger, and (2) to adapt existing survey methods or to find new ones which could be used in the nomadic environment.

## SURVEY METHODS AND RESULTS

At the conclusion of the project, when the information considered unusable had been rejected, the results which were issued consisted of the following: (a) demographic estimates of the total nomadic population, and individual and collective data for this population; (b) family budgets, structure of family budgets, and estimates of expenditure and income; and (c) nutrition, nature, and adequacy of diet and estimates of average consumption.

Much of the survey was of an innovative nature. Several sampling and survey procedures were tried out using as sampling units households, water holes, tribes, and so on. It was found that none of them alone was fully satisfactory and that only a combination of methods made possible a large enough sample to yield an overview of all the nomadic people in the area distinguishing the various groups and describing sex and age patterns. A smaller subsample yielded data on nomadic movements.[1] As well as methodological and technical problems, the practical problems of organizing and carrying through the survey work are of considerable magnitude in Niger, even in the settled areas. These become predominant when work is being done in the

[1] M. F. Ganon and J. A. Ribet, *Demographic and Economic Study in Nomadic Environment*, I (Paris, 1966), 80 ff.

nomadic environment. There are problems of transport, difficulties in recruiting and training survey staff, sociological and ethnic problems, logistic difficulties (keeping up supplies of food, survey materials, and vehicle spares), climatic and health problems, and difficulties of making contacts and securing information.

To take as an example the Tahoua prefecture, the survey found a population of 92,500 people or 11.5 percent more Tuaregs and 9 percent more Fulani (Peuls) than the administrative censuses had claimed some years earlier. However, it appears certain that the survey resulted in an undercount especially of females, as can be seen in Table 34.1,

TABLE 34.1
Percentage distribution of ethnic groups by sex, nomad areas, 1962–1964

| Ethnic Group | Male | Female | Both Sexes |
|---|---|---|---|
| Tuaregs | 53 | 47 | 100 |
| Fulani | 54 | 46 | 100 |

which should be judged in light of the fact that all previous tropical African surveys have enumerated a majority of females.

Nomadic populations may of course be different, but it is more probable that the relatively small number of females is due to social attitudes leading to their concealment. There is also some tendency to conceal all population. The factors which appeared to play a role were the unwillingness of the men to present their wives, and of the wives to be interviewed; attempts to keep taxation down and the concealment of polygyny. It might be noted that, although all the "real" Tuaregs declare themselves to be monogamous, we have only to compare the ages of the children of the household head and divorced wives with the ages of the children of the present wife to calculate that many household heads must have been polygamists at certain periods.

If we assumed the number of women to be at least equal to that of men in each ethnic group, which is plausible since emigration of women is nonexistent, we should obtain the following total population figures: Tuaregs, 82,000; Fulani, 18,000; or a total of about 100,000 nomads of these two types in Tahoua prefecture.

By ethnic and subethnic groupings the proportional distribution would be the following: "real" Tuaregs—17 percent, Arabs—12 percent, Bouzous—53 percent, totaling for these three groups who are usually just called "Tuaregs" 82 percent; and Bororo—8 percent, Farfarou—10 percent, totaling for these two groups who are together called Fulani, 18 percent. The undercounting was probably greatest among the Bororo, because the kind of life they lead makes them very difficult to contact, and among the Arabs spread out over a very large surface area and living outside the borders of Niger, Mali, and Algeria.

The analysis of the survey data suggested the following vital rates: Fulani, birth rate of 41 per thousand and death rate of 22; Tuaregs, birth rate of 52 per thousand and death rate of 27. Thus the rate of natural increase was about 2 percent for Fulani and 2.5 percent for Tuaregs. It is possible that the Fulani rate is lower than the real one partly because of the failure to provide all information, especially by the bororos, and partly because the Fulani interviewers were usually less good than the Tuareg interviewers.

The average size of households was 4.2 persons among the Tuaregs, 4.1 among Bororos, and 5.3 among Farfarous (i.e., 4.6 among all Fulani).

## SEX AND AGE STRUCTURE

The predominance of males was less striking among Tuareg children (less than 15 years old) than among adults, but was more pronounced for Fulani children.

An examination of the population structure in 10-year age groups reveals a surprisingly large number of children enumerated as under 10 years of age among the Fulani and a reduction in the 10–19 years age group. This reduction is similar to that found in most African population counts, and is probably caused by the difficulty in determining precisely the age of adolescents and young adults. It appeared that the problem arose from the enumeration as 20–29 of those adolescents who looked more mature and the enumeration as under 10 of those adolescents who looked younger.

The Fulani population was apparently much younger than the Tuareg one. There have been no similar surveys of other nomadic populations to allow the further comparison of either.

It is clear that when dealing with nomads it would be more fitting to describe old age as beginning at 50 instead of 60, for the conditions of nomadic life are harsh and wearing, and after 50 years of age, the nomad regards his workload as no longer a full one.

The common features in the nomad marriage patterns are the paying of bridewealth to the wife's parents, and the relative ease of marriage and divorce. Polygyny is permitted but seems to be practiced only rarely except by persons of high standing. The proportion of unmarried adult males is extremely high, especially among the Tuaregs. This phenomenon is probably partly explained by the existence of Bouzou servants, who are generally unmarried. Among the Fulani the explanation is more likely to be found in the easier sexual relationships which make marriage less necessary. Moreover, the men generally marry later than the women. Most of the marriages contracted by the Fulani were around 30 years for men and 20 years for women, and by the Tuaregs around 40 years for men and 30 years for women. The number of widows is much higher than that of widowers because even an old widower is able to remarry a young woman provided he is rich enough to pay her bridewealth. However, among women the proportion of widows increases rapidly with age, and around 55 years there are almost as many widows as married women. Indeed for a woman in her fifties remarriage is very difficult.

No distinction was made in the survey between marriage and free union or concubinage as this distinction has little significance because of the fragility of conjugal ties.

The fairly low number of divorcees reflects the ease with which new unions can be formed, especially among the Fulani.

The distribution of the survey population by age, sex, and marital condition reveals the presence of unmarried people of both sexes at all ages among the Tuaregs, whereas among the Fulani there are practically no unmarried women after 20 years of age and few unmarried men after 30 years. The number of widows and divorcees increases with age, and among the Tuaregs reaches by old age 65 percent of females and 18 percent of males. Among the Fulani the figures reach 53 percent for women and 9 percent for men. The proportion of married women increases with age up to 40 years (about the end of the reproductive period) and then falls away fairly quickly, although less quickly among the Fulani than the Tuaregs. Among the Tuaregs 49 percent of women are blood relations of their husbands, who in 43 percent of cases are their cousins. The proportions are still higher among the Fulani: 63 percent of women are related to their husbands and 45 percent of these are cousins. An examination of women by age and relationship with their husbands indicates that previous generations had a stronger tendency still to marry someone "of the family." This excludes the very old women who, either by forgetfulness or by doubt about which husband the question applied to, provided conflicting answers. The young people seem to be turning toward more "free" marriages, without family ties.

## OCCUPATION

The occupation of the groups studied is essentially based on pastoralism. It is practiced by 95 percent of Fulani and 78 percent of Tuareg men. The difference is due to the presence among the Tuaregs of the sedentary Bouzous whose main activity is farming (11 percent) and the tent Bouzous (servants) who make up 7 percent of the whole. The women are in most cases housewives; 96 percent of Fulani and 84 percent of Tuareg women are thus occupied. If we add the "servants" to the latter, we reach 93 percent. The rest is divided among craftsmen, stock breeders, and farmers (5 percent).

## POPULATION GROWTH

The rates of increase of the groups studied are within the rates usually found in African environments, although the figure obtained for the Fulani is fairly low, i.e., 1.9 percent for Fulani and 2.5 percent for Tuaregs. Apart from the indications gathered on the Moors in the Senegal Valley, there are no comparable rates for the other African populations. Nevertheless, the figures obtained remain near to those computed for neighboring rural and sedentary populations.

## FERTILITY

AVERAGE NUMBER OF CHILDREN EVER BORNE BY AGE OF MOTHER AND COMPLETED FERTILITY. The average number of children ever borne by the women in the sample was 3.25 for the Fulani and 2.48 for the Tuaregs. This is a surprisingly large difference. If we calculate completed fertility by considering only the women of 50 years of age, that for Fulani women was about 4.8 live born children per women, and that for Tuareg women about 3.9. Part of the explanation for this differential is the much higher fertility among young Fulani women, doubtless due to their relatively earlier ages at marriage. Because of memory lapse, it is better to take completed fertility to be the average number ever borne by women 40–49 years of age, which is moreover the age group yielding the maximum values: 5.8 for Fulani and 4.3 for Tuaregs.

The Bororos reported average fertility lower than that of the whole Fulani group, and this was especially the case with the nomadic Bouzous, mainly because many of them are servants and single. This causes even lower fertility than that of the Tuaregs. On the other hand, the sedentary Bouzous report fertility equal to that of the Bororos.

The proportions of women definitely sterile (i.e., who have finished their reproductive period without having had any children) are high (15 percent for Fulani and 21 percent

for Tuaregs) compared with most African populations among whom rates generally vary from 6–12 percent. Exceptions are Gabon (32 percent) and the People's Republic of the Congo (17 percent).

The proportions of survivors from all births reported by mothers at the time of the survey was 81.4 percent for Fulani and 74.1 percent for Tuaregs.

The sex ratio at birth was reported to be 122 males per 100 females for Fulani and 110 for Tuaregs. The sex ratio among survivors was 125 for Fulani and 110 for Tuaregs. Mortality seems higher for girls than boys among Fulani while there appears to be no difference for Tuaregs.

CURRENT FERTILITY. Data on births during the previous 12 months suggest crude birth rates of 41 for Fulani and 52 for Tuaregs. General fertility rates were 189 for Fulani and 209 for Tuaregs. The rates are an astonishing reversal of the figures for completed fertility and suggest that the two groups had quite different concepts of 12 months.

COMPARISON OF CURRENT AND PAST FERTILITY. The cumulated rates of present fertility are consistently higher than past figures and could be interpreted as the sign of a relatively recent rise in fertility.[2] The high proportion of children already pointed out, especially among the Fulani, could offer support for this.

GROSS REPRODUCTION RATE. Gross reproduction rates were calculated from current fertility data as 3.2 for Tuaregs and 2.9 for Fulani.

## MORTALITY

SURVIVORSHIP BY AGE. Survivorship is determined by the number of living children among the total number of children born to each woman. By computing the proportions

[2] Hypothesis made in M. Lafarge, *Enquête Démographique en République Centrafricaine, 1959–60*, INSEE-Cooperation, Ministère de la Coopération, and Service de la Statistique Générale de la République Centrafricaine (Paris, 1966).

TABLE 34.2

Survivorship of children by sex and ethnic group according to mothers' age

| Mothers' Ages | Fulani M | F | M & F | Tuaregs M | F | M & F |
|---|---|---|---|---|---|---|
| 15–19 years | 0.83 | 0.95 | 0.89 | 0.79 | 0.90 | 0.85 |
| 20–29 | 0.86 | 0.84 | 0.85 | 0.77 | 0.81 | 0.79 |
| 30–39 | 0.82 | 0.82 | 0.82 | 0.76 | 0.74 | 0.75 |
| 40–49 | 0.80 | 0.75 | 0.78 | 0.69 | 0.72 | 0.70 |
| 50+ | 0.78 | 0.74 | 0.76 | 0.74 | 0.67 | 0.71 |

of survivors for each age group of mothers and the average age of the children born to these mothers, we can draw curves of child survival. Table 34.2 compares survivorship of children between Fulani and Tuaregs according to the age of the mother.

The average age of children ever born is around 20 years when the mother's fertile period ends (50 years). The survival rate corresponding to this age amounts to 70 percent for Tuaregs and 78 percent for Fulani, which, even taking into account a probable overestimate, is fairly high when compared with other African countries.

CRUDE DEATH RATES. Crude death rates were calculated from deaths reported during the previous 12 months as 22 per thousand for Fulani and 27 for Tuaregs. By sex, these rates yield slightly higher male mortality for Tuaregs, but for the Fulani there was substantially higher female mortality by a margin which seemed surprising (see Table 34.3).

The validity of all mortality data is limited to the year of survey, for mortality can vary greatly from year to year. Birth cohorts would be reduced by the reported current mortality to half by 15 years among the Tuaregs and by 35 years among the Fulani.

TABLE 34.3

Crude death rates by sex (per thousand)

|  | Male | Female | Both Sexes |
|---|---|---|---|
| Peuls | 20 | 27 | 23 |
| Tuaregs | 28 | 27 | 27 |

TABLE 34.4

Infant mortality rates by sex

|  | Male | Female | Both Sexes |
|---|---|---|---|
| Fulani | 145 | 184 | 164 |
| Tuaregs | 152 | 90 | 121 |

INFANT MORTALITY. Infant mortality rates calculated approximately from births and deaths reported for the previous 12 months were 164 per thousand live births for the Fulani and 121 for the Tuaregs. Table 34.4 shows surprising sex differentials.

Other methods can be used to estimate infant mortality. The computation of the proportion of deaths among the total number of children born to women from 15 to under 20 years of age yields rate of 113 for Fulani and 143 for Tuaregs and the methods developed by Brass would raise these to 141 for Fulani and 161 for Tuaregs.

NATURAL INCREASE. The difference between birth and death rates yields levels of natural increase of 1.9 percent for Fulani and 2.5 percent for Tuaregs, which is comparable with that of other African countries. It evidences a fairly rapid growth tending to a doubling of total numbers in under 30 years.

NET REPRODUCTION RATE. Another way of determining the natural increase of population is provided by the net reproduction rate. This rate is 1.5 for both ethnic groups and indicates that the present population should be replaced by total numbers 1.5 times more numerous at the end of one generation, and corresponds to a rate of natural increase of as low as 1.6 percent.

CAUSES OF DEATH ACCORDING TO DECLARED SYMPTOMS. Beside infirmities, the survey allows us to state, for a small subsample, the causes of death. This subsample was for about 1,000 deaths.

The method used in studying the causes of death (the easiest in the absence of doctors and qualified staff) consisted in drawing up a list, in the native tongue, of the major mortal diseases and their symptoms. The interviewers ticked off the corresponding answer on this list. Deaths due to accidents or confinements gave no problems, and certain endemic diseases such as cerebro-spinal meningitis and smallpox were well known to the populations regularly struck by them.

The study brought out the predominance of deaths due to "fever." In fact, this term covers several fever diseases of which malaria was the major one. These "fevers" represent 27 percent of deaths among the Tuaregs and 40 percent among the Fulani. Measles causes 18 percent of Tuareg deaths and 11 percent of Fulani deaths; neuro-toxicosis and dehydration strike young children (7 percent and 8 percent); tuberculosis and tetanus (occurring among young children) are followed in importance by a series of lesser diseases.

### COLLECTIVE DATA

For the nomadic survey, the household was defined as the husband (or head of household), his wife or wives, their children and, on occasion, other relatives or nonrelated persons living permanently with the head of the household and economically dependent on him. The average size of the households in the sample was 4.15 persons for the Tuaregs and 4.63 persons for the Fulani. It should be noted that the figure obtained for the Tuaregs applies in fact to complete Tuareg households (i.e., servants included). A figure for the Tuaregs alone would have no significance where collective data is concerned.

For both ethnic groups the distribution rises to a maximum for households of four persons and then decreases. Very large households (20 and over) are extremely rare and remain the prerogative of clan or tribal heads.

The age of the household head has an evident influence on the size of the household, which increases regularly to reach a maximum around 55 years of age for Tuaregs and 45 years for Fulani. The proportion of female heads of household is very small (4 percent or less by ethnic group). Pure nomadism does not seem to tolerate women as household heads, but their proportion increases in settled groups with less harsh conditions of life.

### DATA ON HOUSEHOLD BUDGETS

The following were the chief features noted about monetary matters: (1) Almost the sole source of income is from the sale of stock. (2) The level of monetary exchange is low. (3) There are, however, relatively rare but large expenditures (some associated with marriage). (4) There are frequent barter exchanges. (5) The barter operations are on a small scale and concern only a small range of goods, most of which are everyday essentials.

The sale of stock can be undertaken in three ways: at the market, to a broker who visits the group, or by the breeder himself taking them to the distant market. These sales of stock must cover all the large expenses. The animals sold are mainly cattle, together with, among the Farfarous, sheep and goats. On average, each household sells two or three head of cattle a year. The other returns (sale of milk, butter, and skins) cover extra expenses and are particularly the concern of women. The proportion of the money spent on food is about one-third. Among the Fulani, this food is almost exclusively based on milk, millet being consumed in much smaller quantity than among the Tuaregs. Consumption of meat is reserved for festivities and ceremonies and also happens from time to time when an animal dies. The diet is supplemented by things gathered; leaves and berries, condiments, kola nuts, and sometimes tea and sugar.

Besides food, the large expenses are taxes (25 percent) and clothing (21 percent). At the time of the survey, taxes in the Republic of Niger were of two kinds: (1) personal tax (called capital and only concerning adults); (2) tax on cattle (adult animals only).

Fulani clothing is very simple. It consists of indigo loin cloths for women, hide breeches for men, sandals of skin or old tires, some iron or copper jewelry and, exceptionally, *boubou* and *litham*.

Equipment expenses (8 percent of the whole) consist of axes, matting, pottery, gourds, sabers for men, harnesses for the riding and pack animals, farming tools of local make, water skins, and so on. Money also has to be spent on the installation and repair of shallow draining troughs.

Among the expenses of the Fulani household is the buying of cattle to renew the herd, of sheep and goats as food for festivities and ceremonies, and of camels for riding. These latter expenses are mainly undertaken by rich owners who wish to show their rank.

Finally there are expenses arising from damage caused by the animals. In the growing season the animals sometimes stray into fields near certain water sources, thus finding more fodder but causing damage. This usually leads to interminable discussions about the paying of a fine by the animals' owners. These compensations may be considered usual, if irregular expenses for the pastoralists.

The estimated cash value of barter transactions was surprisingly small although observers have assumed that most of the Fulani's economic exchanges were made in this way. In fact the estimated value of barter was about 13 percent of all exchanges.

Thus average annual household expenditure amounted to about U.S. $75. This was made up of monetary transaction and barter, to which should be added about $70 subsistence production consumed.

Among the Tuaregs, the sale of cattle also represents the main source of monetary income. These sales cover the large expenses (taxes, clothing, and millet) and they represent 89 percent of all cash income. The sources of income of this kind could be split up in the following way: sheep and goats, 27 percent; cattle, 33 percent; camels, 40 percent. Additional income is earned from crafts, especially that done by smiths who tend to have inherited their occupations. Under the general term of "smith" are grouped numerous craftsmen working in leather as well as iron and copper. Production consists mostly of wallets, sandals, sabers, agricultural tools, axes, jewelry, and wicker-work.

Where trade is concerned, besides the profession of caravaneer, certain Tuaregs are hawkers of tea, sugar, and tobacco while the Bouzous sell part of their millet production. The annual earnings of Tuareg households average U.S. $80.

Clothing is the highest item in expenditure at 26 percent, followed by taxes (24 percent), and food (20 percent). Food is largely made up of millet (80 percent) and tea and sugar (16 percent). The Tuareg diet is based on milk and millet, which are consumed in much larger quantities than among the Fulani; it is supplemented by things gathered, meat (when animals die or for ceremonies), condiments, tea, and sugar. Tobacco and natron, in quids, are also consumed in considerable quantities. Clothing expenses form the largest part of the money spent, for the Tuareg (or Arab) costume is more elaborate than the Fulani one: it comprises *boubous*, veils, dresses, trousers, sandals, *chèches*, leather wallets, and charms, as well as iron and copper jewelry, and often the Kano *litham*, a piece of material dyed bright blue, which is the origin of the "blue men" legend, and which is very expensive, costing about U.S. $40 each.

Equipment expenses make up 16 percent of the whole. The equipment of the Tuareg household is much more varied than that of the Fulani household and is composed largely of hide tents, beds, cooking utensils, gourds, matting, weapons, tools of local make, harnesses and saddles for camels and draught oxen.

Stock buying includes sheep and goats for festivities, and camels for bridewealth or for riding. Damage caused by the animals is also a major expense. However, Tuaregs, and especially Bouzous, are much more careful than the Fulani, and for a very good reason: the millet fields damaged usually belong to them. Finally, Tuaregs seem more given to barter than Fulani. Barter represents about 19 percent of their economic exchanges. The average Tuareg household budget amounts to about U.S. $100 of economic exchange (money and barter transactions) and about $125 of subsistence production (i.e., a total of $225).

# CHAPTER THIRTY-FIVE

## *Senegal*

B. LACOMBE, B. LAMY,
AND J. VAUGELADE

PARADOXICALLY, the total population of Senegal can only be estimated. The sole survey, carried out in 1960–1961, was practically fruitless apart from the publication of distribution data. Some aspects, however, are very thoroughly known, for recent regional surveys provide very accurate data on certain demographic variables.

The Senegalese economy, in which groundnuts now predominate, is based upon external trade. Historically, this colonial economy began with gum trading in the Senegal River valley, but since the 1920s, groundnut production has grown to supplant all other commercial agriculture. Even this began to decline in the 1960s, and as yet no other crop or new economic activity shows any real promise of providing a viable alternative. So called "useful" Senegal[1] is now limited to a belt comprising a quarter of the national area, 70 percent of the population and of the cultivated area, and almost all of the infrastructure and industrial plant.[2]

### DEMOGRAPHIC SOURCES

ENUMERATIONS FOR TAXATION PURPOSES. Ever since the colonial period the authorities have striven to follow population changes so as to estimate the anticipated taxation receipts at the village level. The population estimates made for this purpose were subdivided by age and sex. However, in the rural areas the estimated sex distribution is biased by the fact that the enumerations also are used for the allotment of groundnut seeds to taxpayers (225 lbs. per man and 112 per woman) and so in accordance with the local situation the farmers misstate the sex distribution of the total numbers for their own advantage. Also, seasonal workers are counted as residents, which results in considerable regional differences. In urban areas the constant coming and going of the population precludes any serious counting.

[1] Useful Senegal corresponds to areas in which the population density exceeds 80 persons per square mile.
[2] P. Metgé, *Le Peuplement du Sénégal*, 2 vols., Aménagement du Territoire (Dakar, October 1966).

TABLE 35.1
Percentage fiscal enumeration makeup

| Age (in years) | Niakhar M | Niakhar F | Paos-Koto M | Paos-Koto F |
|---|---|---|---|---|
| 0 –14 | 61 | 51 | 36 | 32 |
| 15–59 | 107 | 101 | 117 | 68 |
| 60+ | 45 | 29 | 31 | 23 |
| All ages | 80 | 77 | 76 | 50 |
| Total population according to the census | 33,464 | | 18,976 | |

SOURCE: Demographic survey, Sine-Saloum, 1963.

Fiscal enumerations can thus not be used as a basis for demographic analysis. Varying with age and social class, with temporary circumstances or special local conditions, the estimates overcount or undercount different sections of the population. The only constants are the persistent undercounting of non-taxpayers and, in groundnut producing areas, the overestimation of the adult male population, as shown in Table 35.1.

URBAN CENSUSES AND CENSUSES OF FOREIGN POPULATION. Urban censuses were carried out in five towns between 1951 and 1955, but the first enumerations date back to the beginning of this century. With the exception of the 1955 Dakar census, which has been thoroughly analyzed, these counts yielded little information.

Throughout French Western Africa, censuses of foreign (i.e., essentially French) population were taken in 1946, 1951, and 1956. These only aimed at a total count.

THE 1957 MIDDLE SENEGAL RIVER VALLEY (MISOES) SURVEY[3]

Carried out by the Social and Economic Mission for the River Senegal (MISOES), the multidisciplinary survey of the middle Senegal River valley was designed as part of a general project of land improvement for the River region (dam building, irrigation, etc.) and specifically as a study of the agri-

[3] J. L. Boutillier, P. Cantrelle, et al., *La Moyenne Vallée du Sénégal* (Paris, 1962).

cultural potential of an area with 300,000 inhabitants.

The demographic section of the survey included a sample census in which 42,000 persons, in clusters numbering about 300, were drawn as a one-in-five fraction in the towns and a one-in-ten fraction in the rural villages. In the course of a single visit a retrospective inquiry was made into the events of the preceding year. The basic record was one collective index card per family with one line for each individual. Another document recorded the fertility of female respondents.

This survey was of a highly satisfactory quality. Table 35.2 shows that if carried out carefully a retrospective survey will yield valuable data. But, as the crude data do not appear in the final publication, the latter cannot provide a basis for any further analyses.

THE 1960–1961 NATIONAL DEMOGRAPHIC SAMPLE SURVEY[4]. This sample survey also made use of retrospective schedules. For the sampling in the urban area (which included Dakar and the main cities), a list of the urban sectors was drawn up on the 1-in-20 scale for the purposes of random choice. The rural area was divided into strata according to the population of the villages (as estimated from the enumeration for taxation purposes).

The random choice within each stratum was made with unequal probabilities increasing with the size of the village. All persons in the villages chosen were included in the sample.

[4] See L. Verrière, *La Population du Sénégal (aspects quantitatifs)* (Dakar: University of Dakar, 1965), and Service de la Statistique, *Résultats de l'Enquête Démographique 1960–1961 (Résultats Régionaux)* (Dakar, 1964).

TABLE 35.2
Sampling quota in the rural area

| Size of Village | Sampling Quota |
|---|---|
| Under 99 inhabitants | 1 in 160 |
| 100–499 inhabitants | 1 in 60 |
| 500 inhabitants or more | 1 in 20 |

SOURCE: 1960–1961 National Demographic Survey.

THE DEMOGRAPHIC SURVEY IN THE SINE-SALOUM REGION[5]. For the survey carried out in 1962–1966 by the Senegal Statistics Department and ORSTOM under the direction of Pierre Cantrelle two sections were chosen in the Sine-Saloum region. One, the *arrondissement* of Niakhar, is an old area of settlement, with 95 percent of the population belonging to the Serer tribe, and a high density (220 persons per square mile); the other, the *arrondissement* of Paos-Koto, is of more recent settlement, ethnically heterogeneous and of lower density (101 persons per square mile).

The survey involved the creation of an up-to-date register of names based on the family schedules of the initial census, and the coverage of the entire population of both the selected areas by censuses held each year.

The purpose of the survey was twofold: (1) the study of natural increase and migration, and (2) the testing of the efficiency of the rural registration services with a view to their possible improvement.

This survey method, by providing a reference population at either end of the annual interval, allows for a much more accurate enumeration than is possible with simple retrospective data.

OTHER SURVEYS. One class of surveys employed periodic interviews as in the Sine-Saloum study. Among these were the surveys of infant mortality,[6] of fertility, and of the population of Pikine (a town on the outskirts of Dakar). In these surveys, to be discussed below, the basic record is the individual schedule.

Another class of survey includes two studies of a specialized nature. One was the processing of the Dakar death registers; the other was the comparison of the registers in the parish of Palmarin (a Fakao village) relating to 3,000 persons over a period of 20 years with a retrospective survey in the same area. This Palmarin methodological study made it possible to collect accurate data on mortality, births, and fertility over a long period of time.[7]

SETTLEMENT SURVEYS. Two other important surveys should be mentioned: Metgé's 1966 study[8] and Pelissier's rural study[9] which provided an historical account of the various settlement waves and showed the present distribution of the different social groups.

## SENEGAL AND ITS ECONOMY

GEOGRAPHIC CONDITIONS. Located at the extreme western limit of the African continent, Senegal forms a rough semicircle centered upon Dakar. The greater part of the country is the result of marine deposition, but in eastern Senegal the old continental shelf is responsible for a few hills which seldom exceed 650 feet. Volcanic activity produced Cape Verde, a group of basalt islands linked to the mainland by a stretch of sand. (See Figure 35.1.)

The river system is made up of four rivers: the Sénégal and its affluent, the Falémé; the Saloum which becomes a major river after its junction with the Sine; the Gambia, which is Senegalese in its upper reaches only; and the Casamance. All these rivers are navigable and formed the routes for the colonial penetration.

The climate is divided into two seasons: the rainy season (July to September) and the dry season. Passing from north to south, the local rainfall rises from 10 to 70 inches a year. The vegetation changes from the sahelian in the extreme north, through the savanna bush to the forests of the Casamance.

In the coastal region the climate is tempered by the proximity of the sea. This region is also characterized by a special geomorphology composed of dunes with underground

[5] P. Cantrelle, "Etude Démographique dans la Région du Sine-Saloum (Sénégal) Etat Civil et Observation Démographiques 1963–1965," *Travaux et Documents de l'ORSTOM*, 1 (Paris, 1969).

[6] P. Cantrelle, "Mortalité de l'enfant dans la Région de Khombole-Thiènaba 1964–68," *Cahiers de l'ORSTOM*, Série Sciences Humaines, VI, 4 (Paris, 1969).

[7] B. Lacombe, "Fakao (Sénégal) Dépouillement de Registres Paroissiaux et Enquête Démographique Rétrospective: Méthodologie et Résultats," Travaux et Documents de l'ORSTOM, 7 (Paris, 1970).

[8] Metgé, *Le Peuplement du Sénégal.*

[9] P. Pellissier, *Les Paysans du Sénégal* (St. Yrieix, 1966).

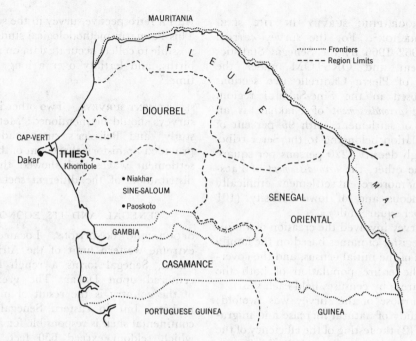

FIGURE 35.1.    *Senegal*

water appearing as ponds in the hollows but disappearing during the dry season. This area of fertile depressions, the Niayes, is used for market gardening during the dry season.

AGRICULTURE AND THE IMPORTANCE OF GROUNDNUTS. Introduced during the colonial period, groundnuts now provide the chief cash crop.[10] The cultivation of $2\frac{1}{2}$ acres of groundnuts requires approximately 85 day's work and 220 pounds of seeds for a crop of three-quarters of a ton representing an income of about U.S. $500. An active man using traditional farming equipment can cultivate $2\frac{1}{2}$ acres equally divided between millet and groundnuts (biennial rotation of crops interrupted by periods of fallow).

The crop depends particularly on the rainfall—that is, on its volume but even more on its distribution throughout the rainy season and especially on the amount of rain which falls after the sowing. When the rains following the sowing are insufficient, the crop

is threatened and the yield can fall to half its normal volume. A farmer never sows groundnuts twice in one year. But the possibility of a second sowing of millet makes it possible to compensate, partly at least, for unfavorable rainfall.

Most cultivable areas are equally divided between groundnuts and millet, other food crops playing only a very secondary part. It is true that in recent years the groundnut farming areas do not seem to have been increasing,[11] whereas food crops have been spreading. However it is a matter for conjecture whether or not this constitutes a trend. It may be no more than the result of several years of poor crops (for groundnuts have suffered badly from the poor climatic conditions of the last few years). Still it is more likely that the farmers' disinclination to grow groundnuts results from a drop in price of about U.S. 0.7 cents per pound in 1968 (the average price paid to the producer fell from about 3.4 cents per pound to about

[10] Seventy-six percent of the active male population were farmers in 1960–1961, see Verrière, *La Population du Sénégal*.

[11] The available statistics are too inexact to allow any certain conclusion.

2.7 cents). This fall in price has not been compensated by any improvement in yield, despite increased purchases of farming equipment which have burdened the farmers with new debts. If it were not for the need to pay off these additional debts, which takes up about a third of the farmers' cash incomes, it is likely that the movement away from groundnuts would have been more marked.

The economic importance of groundnuts has induced the government to take over the control of their sale. (1) A department of commercial agriculture has been given the monopoly of sales to oil mills and shelling works (for export); (2) a network of co-operative agencies serves as an intermediary between the department and the producers (with a monopoly established in 1967).

Groundnut products constitute more than 70 percent of the country's total exports. Before export, one-third of the groundnut crop is shelled and the remainder is ground into oil.

INDUSTRY.[12] The development of different industries was encouraged by the prevailing laissez-faire attitudes. In investing capital, the industrialists, most of them French, wanted: (1) to cut down freight charges by processing raw materials (especially groundnuts) locally; (2) to benefit from lighter taxes than in their own country.

Today, over 90 percent of the industries are concentrated in the Cape Verde region, a location which affords them maximum advantages (developed infrastructure, proximity to a port, the presence of the administrative authorities, and the concentration of population and industrial concerns).

The industry was originally designed to meet the needs of French West Africa. With the independence in 1960 of the different states of the Federation, the shrinking of the market resulted in the underemployment of production capacity. This underemployment has yet to disappear (50–80 percent capacity is believed to be currently employed).

Another consequence is the stagnation of employment throughout these last ten years (stationary at about 24,000 persons). Since the employment capacity of both government and private services is saturated, the number of unemployed inevitably increases: 35,000 were listed as applying for jobs in 1968 in Dakar alone.

Europeans hold most of the managerial positions. However, the proportion of Senegalese in such positions is rising constantly, as from 35 percent in 1962 to 39 percent in 1967.

Local products supply 80 percent of the domestic demand for farm and food products, 22 percent of the demand for manufactured goods other than food products (especially textiles and chemicals), but the engineering and electrical industries supply only 2 percent of local needs.

The total industrial contribution to the gross domestic product is relatively small—only 21 percent as compared with the 43 percent contribution of services, the 20 percent of commercial agriculture, and the 16 percent of subsistence farming.

TRADE. During the colonial period, trade was under the control of a few large European firms. These imposed complete vertical integration, from import-export to retail trade, using a system of subsidiaries in the market towns. These subsidiaries sold imported consumption goods locally and bought groundnuts for export. After the government had taken over control of groundnut sales the activities of the subsidiaries slackened until they finally closed down.

At present, the upper levels of trade (wholesale, import and wholesale, and the retail stores in Dakar) are controlled by Lebanese and European businessmen although there are a few Senegalese wholesalers on a smaller scale. The lower levels (market town retailers, itinerant and inland retailers) are the monopoly of Senegalese and Moorish merchants.[13]

[12] See Service de la Statistique, *Les Industries du Sénégal* (Dakar, 1965).

[13] See ISEA, *Commercialisation et Diffusion des Produits Alimentaires Importés* (Dakar, 1966).

Retail trade is characterized by the vast number of small retailers (1 for approximately every 100 persons). The level of consumption is still low; in rural areas, it does not exceed U.S. $35 per capita per annum. A considerable proportion of this expenditure is spent on festivities and other celebrations.

In order to meet the requirements of African customers living in the cities and market towns, whose purchasing power is rising, a new type of trade is now developing: a multiple store offering a choice of products (at a fixed price), corresponding to the needs of the average wage earner.

Commercialism in Senegal is not a simple matter of selling goods, but rather a complex one of providing goods and associated services, especially credit. In rural areas loans are essential to bridge the annual lack of income from August to October. An inquiry in Casamance showed that this break lasted for more than two months for more than half of the population. Few people except civil servants and their families (who have a constant income) can escape this break. During this period, loans are granted only to cover the purchase of essential food stuffs, mainly oils and cereals. It is at this time that rates of interest are at their highest.[14]

DISTRIBUTION OF THE NATIONAL INCOME. The national income per capita stood at U.S. $220 in 1968.[15] The aggregate national income is unequally divided between the following: (1) 130,000 wage earners whose average yearly income is over U.S. $1,800, and who, with their families, make up a quarter of the population and live on two-thirds of the national income; (2) farmers,

whose income is subject to important fluctuations, according to the current price and aggregate production of groundnuts, and who represent three-quarters of the population; (3) certain groups who stand apart because of their standards of living, for example, in urban areas, the parliamentary and business middle classes and the foreigners (in 1959, foreigners accounted for 25 percent of the consumption according to an estimate by the BCEAO, the central bank of French Western Africa) and, in rural areas, the rural middle classes (*marabouts* and big land owners).

Some redistribution of the national income takes place through two causes. (1) There is a seasonal migration of country people (most of them unmarried) seeking jobs for the duration of the dry season from November to May during which there is no farming to be done. These migrations account for a transfer of income in favor of rural areas although the importance and size of the transfer cannot be easily assessed. (2) There is also a transfer from wage earners to unemployed persons as a result of family obligations.

## POPULATION PATTERNS

AGE STRUCTURE. Of the estimated 3,109,000 persons enumerated in the 1960–1961 National Survey, 60,000 were non-Africans. For the purposes of demographic analysis, non-Africans will be omitted.[16] Table 35.3a and Figure 35.2 show the distribution of the populations by age and sex groups. The pyramid (Figure 35.2) clearly shows the age pattern to be in keeping with what is generally expected: a high proportion of young population (aged under 10), and an incorrect distribution of age groups between 10 and 29 as a result of an inaccurate assessment of ages. A glance at Figure 35.3, which sets forth the sex ratios, shows that an equilibrium between both sexes is never attained; between the ages

---

[14] The loan conditions make it impossible to estimate a true rate of interest, for loans are granted from before the harvest to after the harvest, the actual length of the period not being an important determinant. The loan is often in kind against repayment in kind with goods, the value of which fluctuates according to the season. Over a year the rate of interest, expressed in monetary terms, generally exceeds 100 percent.

[15] Service de la Statistique, *La Situation Economique en 1968* (Dakar, 1970).

[16] As non-Africans are mostly of importance in economic rather than demographic terms, they have not been dealt with here.

TABLE 35.3
African population by age groups (in thousands) (a) 1960–1961 National Demographic Survey

| Age Groups | Males | Females | Both Sexes | Sex Ratio[a] |
|---|---|---|---|---|
| 0–4 years | 282 | 290 | 572 | 97 |
| 5–9 | 245 | 231 | 476 | 106 |
| 10–14 | 136 | 115 | 251 | 118 |
| 15–19 | 102 | 129 | 231 | 79 |
| 0–24 | 102 | 140 | 242 | 73 |
| 25–29 | 119 | 162 | 281 | 73 |
| 30–34 | 102 | 110 | 212 | 93 |
| 35–39 | 89 | 94 | 183 | 95 |
| 40–44 | 69 | 65 | 134 | 106 |
| 45–49 | 70 | 60 | 130 | 117 |
| 50–54 | 51 | 42 | 93 | 121 |
| 55–59 | 43 | 31 | 74 | 139 |
| 60–64 | 31 | 25 | 56 | 124 |
| 65–69 | 20 | 16 | 36 | 125 |
| 70+ | 38 | 40 | 78 | 95 |
| Total | 1,499 | 1,550 | 3,049 | 97 |

[a] Sex ratio = number of males to 100 females of the same age group.

(b) 1966 Fakao Survey

| Age Groups | Males | Females | Both Sexes | Sex Ratio[a] |
|---|---|---|---|---|
| 0–4 | 184 | 192 | 376 | 96 |
| 5–9 | 173 | 167 | 340 | 104 |
| 10–14 | 135 | 140 | 275 | 96 |
| 15–19 | 145 | 138 | 283 | 105 |
| 20–24 | 126 | 137 | 263 | 92 |
| 25–29 | 139 | 128 | 267 | 109 |
| 30–34 | 139 | 127 | 266 | 110 |
| 35–39 | 95 | 85 | 180 | 112 |
| 40–44 | 70 | 78 | 148 | 90 |
| 45–49 | 60 | 75 | 135 | 80 |
| 50–54 | 70 | 67 | 137 | 104 |
| 55–59 | 46 | 49 | 95 | 94 |
| 60–64 | 34 | 32 | 66 | 106 |
| 65–69 | 33 | 66 | 99 | — |
| 70+ | 51 | 38 | 89 | 81 |
| Total | 1,500 | 1,519 | 3,019 | 99 |

[a] Sex ratio = number of males to 100 females of the same age group.

of 15 and 35, there are "too many" women, and over 40 "not enough."

The historical calendars given to the enumerators for their field work often turn out to be of very little use. The age of the subject interviewed is generally assessed according to his social status, marital situation, and number of children. Hence biases develop in the case of young adults, especially around the age of marriage.

One of the sample inquiries corroborates this analysis by providing a comparatively accurate pyramid for the village of Fakao (see Table 35.3b and Figure 35.4), which

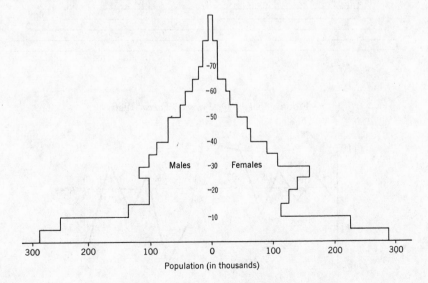

FIGURE 35.2. *Age Pyramid, Senegal,* 1960–1961

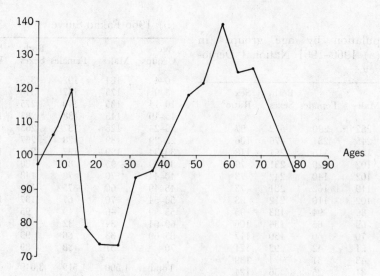

FIGURE 35.3.  *Sex Ratios, Senegal, 1960–1961*

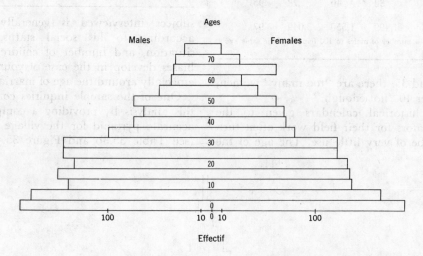

FIGURE 35.4.  *Age Pyramid, Fakao, 1966*

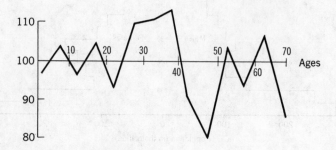

FIGURE 35.5.  *Sex Ratios, Fakao, 1966*

TABLE 35.4
Population distribution by region
Population (in thousands.)

| Region | African | Non-African | Total | Area (sq. miles) | Density (persons per sq. mile) |
|---|---|---|---|---|---|
| Cape Verde | 398.1 | 45.5 | 443.6 | 212 | 2,092 |
| Thiès | 405.6 | 4.1 | 409.7 | 2,549 | 1,607 |
| Diourbel | 502.1 | 0.9 | 503.0 | 12,953 | 39 |
| Sine-Saloum | 721.1 | 6.0 | 727.1 | 9,245 | 79 |
| River | 342.6 | 2.8 | 345.4 | 17,037 | 20 |
| Casamance | 528.9 | 0.9 | 529.8 | 10,946 | 48 |
| Eastern Senegal | 151.2 | — | 151.2 | 23,012 | 7 |
| All Senegal | 3,049.6 | 60.2 | 3,109.8 | 75,954 | 41 |

SOURCE: 1960–1961 National Demographic Survey.

shows a population unaffected by migration. It represents all *natives* of Fakao, wherever their residence may be. It does not show the typical gap around the age of 20, which systematically appears in other diagrams. The recorded sex ratio (see Figure 35.5), omitting the inaccuracies due to the preference for round figures, fluctuates around 100 up to the age of 30, which is in accordance with the fact that for persons aged under 30 in 1966 a fairly accurate registration of births has been ensured by the performance and recording of baptisms since the 1930s.

GEOGRAPHIC DISTRIBUTION. Table 35.4 shows the distribution of the population by administrative region. The marked disparity in the distribution appears at once, a disparity so great that the average density varies between 2,090 persons per square mile in Cape Verde

and 8 persons per square mile in Eastern Senegal.

The disparity between regions also is reflected in the age pattern (Table 35.5): The youngest population is that of Cape Verde (i.e., an essentially urban one) whereas the oldest population is to be found in the regions of Diourbel and Thiès, the traditional strongholds of groundnut production, and in the River region, three regions which are all subject to substantial emigration. The 22 urban or semiurban communities constitute 27 percent of the national population.

SOCIAL GROUPS. (Table 35.6) shows the distribution of Senegal by tribes. The members of the Wolof tribe dominate, not only numerically (they comprise 34 percent of the population) and by their language which is known to most of the population, but also by their propensity for migration: the eastward progress of the groundnut frontier and the settlement in the "new lands" were essentially their achievements. The Wolof tribe, which emerged during the fifteenth century, is further characterized by a remarkable gift for assimilating others, which the Tuculor alone have been able to resist.

TABLE 35.5
Age distribution by region (in percent)

| Region | Age Group (percent) | | | |
|---|---|---|---|---|
| | 0–14 | 15–59 | 60+ | Total |
| Cape Verde | 45 | 52 | 3 | 100 |
| Thiès | 44 | 50 | 6 | 100 |
| Diourbel | 40 | 52 | 8 | 100 |
| Sine-Saloum | 42 | 53 | 5 | 100 |
| River | 43 | 50 | 7 | 100 |
| Casamance | 44 | 52 | 4 | 100 |
| Eastern Senegal | 39 | 56 | 5 | 100 |
| All Senegal | 42.5 | 51.9 | 5.6 | 100.0 |

SOURCE: 1960–1961 National Demographic Survey.

LANGUAGES. The four main tribes, which together make up 80 percent of the population, speak three languages: Wolof, Serer, and Peul (the language of the Fulani). The Tuculor speak a language very close to Peul.

TABLE 35.6
Tribal distribution

| Tribe | Percent of Population |
|---|---|
| Wolof | 34.1 |
| Serer | 17.6 |
| Fulani | 15.7 |
| Tuculor | 12.5 |
| Tola | 6.2 |
| Mandinka | 3.3 |
| Sarakolé | 2.4 |
| Malinké | 1.0 |
| Moors | 1.0 |
| Socé | 0.7 |
| Bambara | 0.6 |
| Various Casamance tribes | 4.0 |
| Others | 0.9 |
| Total | 100.0 |

SOURCE: 1960–1961 National Demographic Survey.

French, the official language, is known to only 11 percent of the population, but this figure conceals important disparities: (a) between the sexes—21 percent of the male population as opposed to 2 percent of the female population understand French; and (b) between regions—in Cape Verde, 35 percent of the males and 5 percent of the females are literate in French.

A comparison of these percentages with the school attendance figures for the 6–13-year age group (Table 35.7) shows that the schooling of girls is increasing rapidly, without however approaching the level of literacy already attained by boys.

RELIGION. Senegal is an Islamic country; 91 percent of the population is Moslem. The dynamic Murid Brotherhood are largely responsible for this religious homogeneity, as well as for the national integration of the various groups in Senegal through "Wolofization." Table 35.8 shows the breakdown by religion.

## POPULATION CHANGE

VITAL STATISTICS. The rates given by the principal Senegalese surveys are shown in Table 35.9. However the indices given in Table 35.9 are not strictly comparable because of the different methods used to obtain them.

The results of certain of these surveys, such as the national and the Sine-Saloum studies, demonstrate differences between various types of area. Thus the death rate is lower and the fertility rate is higher in urban than in rural areas. In Niakhar, an area of old-established settlement and high density, the death rate is much higher than in Paos-Koto, an area of recent settlement and lower density.

Some of the surveys make it possible to analyze fertility differences between tribes (see Table 35.10). In each survey, the lowest rates are those of the nomadic tribes: the Moors and Fulani.

Only the Sine-Saloum and Fakao surveys give any indication of marked fluctuations from one year to the next (see Tables 35.11

TABLE 35.7
Literacy and school attendance

| | Cape Verde | Thiès | Diourbel | Sine-Saloum | River | Casamance | Eastern Senegal | All Senegal |
|---|---|---|---|---|---|---|---|---|
| Whole Population: percent literate in French | | | | | | | | |
| Males | 35 | 9 | 3 | 11 | 7 | 9 | 1 | 11 |
| Females | 5 | 1 | — | 1 | 1 | 1 | — | 1 |
| Population aged 6–13: percent undergoing schooling in French | | | | | | | | |
| Males | 63 | 20 | 6 | 26 | 14 | 21 | 6 | 23 |
| Females | 43 | 13 | 3 | 14 | 6 | 10 | 1 | 14 |

SOURCE: 1960–1961 National Demographic Survey.

TABLE 35.8
African population by religion

|  | Religion | | | |
| --- | --- | --- | --- | --- |
|  | Moslem | Christian | Other | Total |
| Population (thousands) | 2,781 | 126 | 142 | 3,049 |
| Percent | 91.2 | 4.1 | 4.7 | 100.0 |

SOURCE: 1960–1961 National Demographic Survey.

and 35.12). In the case of Fakao, it appeared upon analysis that, apart from the two years of exceptionally high mortality which affected the death rates of the period 1940–1944 and 1950–1954, the death rate remained at a constant level throughout the period considered.

The Sine-Saloum and Fakao surveys provide death rate tables, set forth in Table 35.13 and Figure 35.6. The Paos-Koto series, except for the youngest, have been presented in ten-year age groups so as to avoid the irregularities entailed by the division into five-year groups. For the same reason, the Fakao series is set forth in ten-year groups throughout.

MIGRATION. The geographic distribution of the Senegalese population is at present undergoing profound changes.

A significant rural exodus is shown in the increase in urban population, which is particularly noticeable in Dakar where the rate of growth was above 6 percent for 1923–1961 and above 9.6 percent for 1955–1961.

Between 1955 and 1964, the rate of growth of the urban population in Senegal was 7 percent, against an approximate 2 percent for the national population. The Tuculor region of the Senegal valley is one of those areas most seriously affected by this rural outflow.

Another movement drains the population of the older settlements (Cayor and Baol in the regions of Thiès and Diourbel respectively) into the "new lands" of the upper Saloum valley, Eastern Senegal, and the upper Casamance valley. New lands are thus peopled as the frontier of the groundnut belt moves eastward.

This migration is of an essentially economic nature. The eastward surges coincide with breakdowns in groundnut production. Unfavorable economic circumstances thus encourage the migratory flow toward the "new lands."

SPECIFIC STUDIES

Three surveys, all longitudinal, are particularly interesting for the specificity and

TABLE 35.9
Vital rates

| Geographical Area | Crude Birth Rate[a] | Crude Death Rate[a] | Natural Increase[d] | Infant Mortality Rate | Probability of Dying Between 1 & 5 Yrs. $(4q1)$ | Surviving Children Aged 5 (per 100 births) | Fertility Rate[a] | Final Descent |
| --- | --- | --- | --- | --- | --- | --- | --- | --- |
| All Senegal | 43.3 | 16.7 | 2.7 | 93 | 264 | 66 | 178 | 5.7 |
| Rural | 43.2 | 18.7 | 2.5 | 109 | — | — | 160 | — |
| Urban | 43.7 | 9.5[b] | 3.4 | 36[b] | — | — | 185 | — |
| River | 44.6 | 23.5 | 2.1 | 190 | 46 | 68 | 184 | 5.3 |
| Niakhar | 49.0 | 34.3 | 1.5 | 170 | 109 | 52 | 217 | 6.8 |
| Paos-Koto | 51.1 | 27.3 | 2.4 | 130 | 81 | 62 | 219 | 6.6 |
| Niakhar (corrected)[c] | 53.5 | 38.8 | 1.5 | 240 | 109 | 47 | 227 | — |
| Fakao | 37.7 | 19.7 | 1.8 | 196 | 67 | 61 | 280 | 7.7 |

SOURCES: All Senegal—1960–1961 National Demographic Survey; River—1957 Middle Senegal River Valley (MISOES) Survey; Niakhar and Paos-Koto—Demographic survey, Sine-Saloum, 1963–1965; Fakao survey, 1940–1966.

[a] per thousand.
[b] According to Dakar vital records, the death rate is 15.9 per thousand and the infant mortality rate is 89 per thousand.
[c] The Niakhar data have been corrected with the infant mortality rate computed from the outcome of pregnancies. The resulting 9 percent underestimation of births implied a correction of birth and fertility rates. Such a correction is not available for Paos-Koto where an underestimation similar to that of Niakhar would give a 185 per thousand probability of infant death.
[d] per hundred.

TABLE 35.10
Fertility rate (per thousand) by tribe

| Survey | Tribe Tuculor | Moors | Wolof | Fulani | Serer |
|--------|------|-------|-------|--------|-------|
| MISOES, 1957 | 204 | 132 | 173 | 172 | — |
| Sine-Saloum, 1963–1965 | 195 | — | 229 | 161 | 219 |

SOURCE: 1957 Middle Senegal River Valley (MISOES) Survey; Demographic survey, Sine-Saloum, 1963.

TABLE 35.12
Survivors aged 5, quinquennial fluctuation

| Period | Survivors Aged 5 (percent) |
|--------|------|
| 1940–44 | 56 |
| 1945–49 | 64 |
| 1950–54 | 61 |
| 1955–59 | 63 |

SOURCE: Fakao survey.

accuracy of some of their results: the Khombole, Sine-Saloum, and Fakao surveys.

MORTALITY. Contrary to the working hypotheses (based on non-African experience) assumed in the drawing up of standard mortality tables, the data collected in these surveys show that mortality falls little in the first years of life as age rises.

Thus in Khombole the probability of dying remains fairly constant up to the age of two, and appears even higher for one year of age than for less than one year. However, a possible underestimation of the probability at less than one year must be taken into account (Table 35.14).

In the two other surveys, which cover larger numbers, probability of death data are available for each month (Table 35.15). These three series of probability figures by month (see Figures 35.7 and 35.8) strongly suggest the existence of a mortality peak at the age of weaning (18 months) among Senegalese children living in the groundnut belt covered by these surveys. Certainly children in these regions pass very abruptly

TABLE 35.11
Annual fluctuations of births and deaths (per thousand)

| | Niakhar | | Paos-Koto | |
|------|------|------|------|------|
| Year | Fertility rate | Death rate | Fertility rate | Death rate |
| 1963 | 222 | 34.4 | 229 | 24.2 |
| 1964 | 198 | 35.3 | 197 | 27.2 |
| 1965 | 229 | 33.4 | 234 | 30.6 |
| Total | 217 | 34.4 | 219 | 27.3 |

SOURCE: Demographic survey, Sine-Saloum, 1963.

from a suckling to an adult diet, based upon cereals. The precipitousness of the change might well be the main cause of the excessive mortality observed around the eighteenth month of age.

The Niakhar data relating to children under one year old must be interpreted with caution, for the infant mortality rate centers at 240 per thousand according to the outcome of registered pregnancies instead of the 170 per thousand given by the survey, which implies that omissions amounted to about one-third. The distribution of these omissions cannot be known. The Paos-Koto data, collected by the same method, are subject to the same bias. (see notes to Table 35.9).

The Fakao data, if divided into two time series, qualify this interpretation,[17] for this mortality peak at the age of weaning only appears in the more recent period: The probability of death falls regularly for the generations born in 1945–1952, whereas those born in 1956–1963 show a higher mortality at 24 months than at 12 (see Figure 35.9). Upon a still finer analysis, this excess mortality will be found to affect essentially children weaned during the rainy season (July to October) which is also the food-gap season. The researchers noted that this phenomenon seems to be a compensation for the lower mortality at birth in the generations of the 1956–1963 period, who received regular medical assistance after the founding, in 1957, of a dispensary comprising outpatients' and maternity departments.

[17] See B. Lacombe and J. Vaugelade, "Mortalité au Sevrage, Mortalité Saisonnière. Un exemple: Fakao (Sénégal)," Population, XXV, 2 (March–April 1969), 339–43.

Mortality quotients
(annual level)

Qx ‰

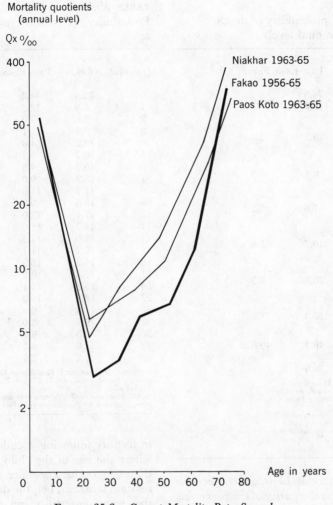

FIGURE 35.6.  *Current Mortality Rate, Senegal*

FERTILITY. The only currently available data on fertility are those of Fakao. A two-year repeated multiround survey of fertility, which lasted until the end of 1969, still is being processed.

The main advantage of the Fakao survey is that it provides precise data, as events have been registered continuously for a period of 30 years. The analysis proceeded and developed from the calculation of intervals between births.

The most interesting statistical series are the following: (1) The average interval between consecutive births by serial number in the 130 complete families (i.e., those in which the wife is aged over 45) is shown in Table 35.16. Compared with data of the same type, this series strongly reminds one of that observed for Japanese women in 1952.

(2) The increase with parity in the probability of families being complete (that is, the proportion of mothers of at least $N$ children, who have at least $N + 1$ children) is shown in Table 35.17.

(3) Light is thrown on the relationship between fertility and child mortality by the

TABLE 35.13

Mortality table: probability of death (per thousand, annual level)

| Age (years) | Niakhar | Paos-Koto | Fakao, |
|---|---|---|---|
| 0–4 | 91.0[a] | 76.5 | |
| 5–9 | 10.1 | 12.0 | 41.6 |
| 10–14 | 4.2 | | |
| 15–19 | 4.9 | 5.2 | 2.8 |
| 20–24 | 6.4 | | |
| 25–29 | 7.1 | 6.4 | 3.3 |
| 30–34 | 9.6 | | |
| 35–39 | 8.6 | 7.6 | 5.2 |
| 40–44 | 11.1 | | |
| 45–49 | 13.6 | 10.7 | 5.6 |
| 50–54 | 18.2 | | |
| 55–59 | 24.0 | 20.8 | 9.3 |
| 60–64 | 29.2 | | |
| 65–69 | 41.4 | 32.3 | 21.6 |
| 70–79 | 72.7 | 48.3 | 49.8 |
| 80+ | 136.9 | 78.9 | |

SOURCES: Niakhar and Paos-Koto—Demographic Survey, Sine-Saloum, 1963; Fakao—Fakao Survey, 1956–1965.
a If we take into account the corrected probability of death at the age of 0 year (see Table 35.9), the probability for the 0–4-year group is 104.3 per thousand.

study of the intervals between consecutive births according to the parity of the preceding birth.[18] Table 35.18 shows a strong increase

[18] See B. Lacombe and J. Vaugelade, "Fécondité Mortalité et Allaitement, Schema d'Analyse," *Population*, XXV, 2 (March–April 1969), 343–48.

TABLE 35.14

Probability of death (per thousand) Khombole, 1964–1968

| Age (years) | Town of Khombole | Rural Areas 1 | 2 |
|---|---|---|---|
| 0 | 82 | 200 | 200 |
| 1 | 93 | 192 | 222 |
| 2 | 76 | 160 | 195 |
| 3 | 10 | 56 | 69 |
| 4 | 10 | 19 | 25 |

TABLE 35.15

Probability of death (per thousand) by age

| Age (months) | Niakhar | Paos-Koto | Fakao |
|---|---|---|---|
| 0 | 42.5 | 44.8 | 83.6 |
| 1 | 8.9 | 12.3 | 11.3 |
| 2 | 9.8 | 7.0 | 10.7 |
| 3 | 9.3 | 5.1 | 9.3 |
| 4 | 10.2 | 4.8 | 11.4 |
| 5 | 10.7 | 5.2 | 12.1 |
| 6 | 10.0 | 4.5 | 12.2 |
| 7 | 15.3 | 9.0 | 12.7 |
| 8 | 17.1 | 11.0 | 11.6 |
| 9 | 18.6 | 9.9 | 12.4 |
| 10 | 17.1 | 12.0 | 10.7 |
| 11 | 14.3 | 11.0 | 11.7 |
| 12 | 15.6 | 11.3 | 11.1 |
| 15 | 15.2 | 11.1 | 9.6 |
| 18 | 16.2 | 10.9 | 7.9 |
| 21 | 16.5 | 10.3 | 6.7 |
| 24 | 15.8 | 10.1 | 7.0 |
| 27 | 13.9 | 10.0 | 7.1 |
| 30 | 11.8 | 9.4 | 6.6 |
| 33 | 9.7 | 8.0 | 5.7 |
| 36 | 8.0 | 6.7 | 4.5 |
| 42 | 5.8 | 4.5 | 3.5 |
| 48 | 4.2 | 2.9 | 2.9 |

SOURCES: Niakhar and Paos-Koto—Demographic survey, Sine-Saloum, 1963; Fakao—Fakao survey, 1943–1963.
NOTE: Most probability figures over one year of age were estimated by graphic interpolation.

in fertility following a child's death in cases where the age of the child at death was less than 18 months. For older children, this correlation weakens, i.e., the death-weaning and the weaning-fertility relationship weakens as the age of the first child increases. However, the conception-weaning-death relationship clearly exists and accounts for the probability figures indicated above.

(4) The pattern of interpregnancy intervals can also be used as a basis for the calculation of fertility probabilities. An increase in the conception rate can be observed at the age of weaning (18–20 months). See Table 35.19.

(5) The fertility of women under 20 years of age is lower than that of women aged 20 or more. (See Table 35.20). If we compare these series to the probability of fertility by duration of marriage, we see that fertility follows a non-Malthusian trend since it depends

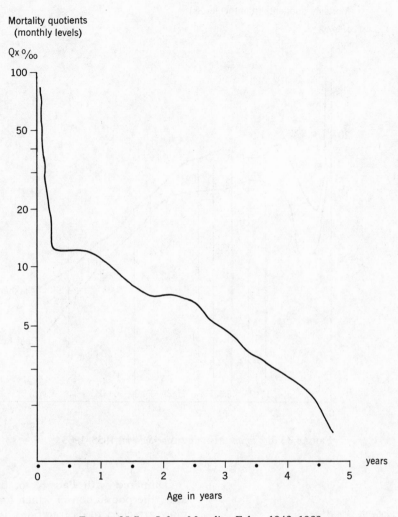

Mortality quotients
(monthly levels)

Qx ‰

Age in years

FIGURE 35.7.  *Infant Mortality, Fakao, 1943–1963*

essentially upon the age of the female, and little upon the duration of marriage.

MIGRATION. The Sine-Saloum survey provided the means for a special examination of population mobility data. Table 35.21 sets forth the main results. Despite important regional disparities the seasonal pattern of mobility is practically constant. The farmers' slack season, which is also the trading season (i.e., the season of groundnut sales) is the period of highest mobility.

At Paos-Koto, an area of Wolof and assimil-

ated populations, migration results from an essentially economic cause: a desire for fertile lands suited to groundnut farming. Settlement there is of recent date and the population is not yet entirely settled. Families settle for a trial period and readily move on if their hopes are frustrated, going further eastward. They are not bound by any feeling of attachment to the soil, and speculation on groundnuts strengthens this lack of stability. Thus the conditions created by the modern economy seem to be the chief cause of migration flows.

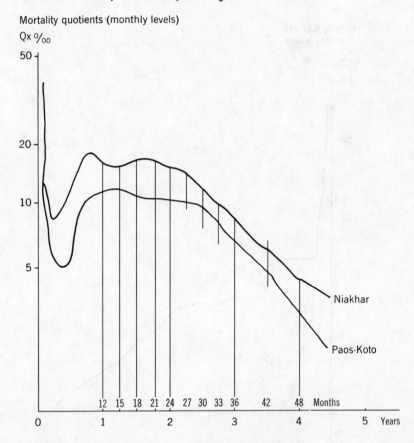

FIGURE 35.8.   *Infant Mortality, Sine-Saloum, 1953–1965*

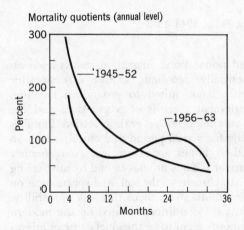

FIGURE 35.9.   *Mortality from Ages 0 to 3 Years*

Compared with Paos-Koto, the Niakhar area, the population of which has remained more attached to its traditions, is characterized by lower mobility. The size of migrant groups is also smaller and the ties of kinship there appear to be more compelling than among the Wolof. Relatives living outside the family compound are readily entrusted with the young and the children; and the importance of maternal lineage accounts for frequent long stays of women and their children away from their husbands' compounds. On the other hand, the cohesion of the Serer society compels young men to leave their fathers' or uncles' homes in order to go and try their luck elsewhere. Later on, they will come back to their home villages and marry. Their wives and children will not

TABLE 35.16
Average intervals between consecutive births

| Births: | 1–2 | 2–3 | 3–4 | 4–5 | 5–6 | 6–7 | 7–8 | 8–9 | 9–10 | 10–11 | 11–12 | Total |
|---------|-----|-----|-----|-----|-----|-----|-----|-----|------|-------|-------|-------|
| Months: | 32 | 35 | 37 | 36 | 34 | 33 | 36 | 32 | 31 | 28 | 34 | 34.5 |

SOURCE: Fakao survey.

TABLE 35.17
Probability of families increasing by parity

| 1 | 2 | 3 | 4 | 5 | 6 | 7 | 8 | 9 | 10 | 11 |
|---|---|---|---|---|---|---|---|---|----|----|
| 0.98 | 0.99 | 0.98 | 0.95 | 0.89 | 0.90 | 0.72 | 0.70 | 0.56 | 0.55 | 0.31 |

SOURCE: Fakao survey.

go and live with them until much later. All these traditions combine to increase the trend towards solitary migration. Where group migration occurs, a group generally excludes the head of the family.

### PROSPECTS

A FEW PROBLEMS. Considering the purpose of the present work, the construction of

TABLE 35.18
Probability of pregnancy by length of period since previous birth and age of death of this child[a]

| Interval between previous birth and beginning of next pregnancy (in months) | Age of Precedent Child at its Death (in months) | | | | |
|---|---|---|---|---|---|
| | 0–5 | 6–11 | 12–17 | 18–23 | 24–29 |
| 0–2 | — | | | | |
| 3–8 | 0.12 | 0.01 | 0.01 | | |
| 9–14 | 0.10 | 0.18 | 0.02 | 0.01 | 0.02 |
| 15–20 | 0.13 | 0.12 | 0.20 | 0.09 | 0.10 |
| 21–26 | 0.09 | 0.13 | 0.08 | 0.17 | 0.10 |
| 27–32 | 0.11 | 0.06 | 0.14 | 0.23 | 0.15 |

SOURCE: Fakao survey.
NOTE: The line divides between conceptions *preceding* the first child's death (above) and conceptions *following* its death (below).
[a] Confined to cases where previous birth was followed by a death.

projections should aim at establishing a parallel between the growth of production, especially agricultural production, and the increase in the population so as to assess their possible reciprocal influences. The complexity of economic change and the scarcity of data make it impossible to draw up producion projections.

There remains the possibility of assessing population prospects, but it is necessary to distinguish between urban and rural population. Owing to the growing relative importance of the urban population, the lower mortality in urban areas should normally result in a lower national death rate. This fall will be reinforced by the fall due to the improvement of living standards in both rural and urban areas.

As for fertility, it can be assumed that there will be no changes in rural areas In urban areas, several factors will probably interact with mutually contradictory effects: (1) A decrease in infant mortality, due to a longer period of breast feeding, will lengthen the average interval between consecutive births and cause lower fertility. (2) The emergence and development of bottle feeding should, with earlier weaning, shorten the interval between consecutive births and increase fertility. (3) The possible influence of laws encouraging birth control (a draft is currently under discussion) cannot be assessed beforehand. (4) The improvement of socioeconomic

TABLE 35.19

Pregnant women: pattern by interval between births where the preceding child has lived over 12 months

| Interval between Consecutive Births (in months) | Children Born | Female Population Exposed to Pregnancy[a] | Probability of Conception (monthly level) | Interval between Birth and Next Conception (in months) |
|---|---|---|---|---|
| less than 11 | 12 | 1,648 | 0.00 | 0–2 |
| 12–14 | 18 | 1,636 | 0.00 | 3–5 |
| 15–17 | 19 | 1,618 | 0.00 | 6–8 |
| 18–20 | 46 | 1,599 | 0.00 | 9–11 |
| 21–23 | 102 | 1,553 | 0.02 | 12–14 |
| 24–26 | 186 | 1,451 | 0.04 | 15–17 |
| 27–29 | 238 | 1,265 | 0.06 | 18–20 |
| 30–32 | 299 | 1,027 | 0.10 | 21–23 |
| 33–35 | 228 | 728 | 0.11 | 24–26 |
| 36–38 | 176 | 500 | 0.12 | 27–29 |
| 39–41 | 94 | 324 | 0.10 | 30–32 |
| 42–44 | 63 | 230 | 0.09 | 33–35 |
| 45–47 | 39 | 167 | 0.08 | 36–38 |
| 48+ | 128 | 128 | | 39+ |
| Total | 1,648 | 0 | — | — |

SOURCE: Fakao survey.
[a] The calculations concern 583 females; each female is counted as many times as accurate intervals have been found in her fertility schedule.

standards should result in lower fertility. It seems somewhat bold to forecast the resultant course of fertility, and therefore it will be assumed to remain constant in urban areas also.

As regards the internal migration balance, it cannot properly be assessed without data on the rate and pattern by age. Besides, economic hypotheses are, generally speaking, the one decisive element in the forecast of the possible evolution of geographic distribution. The unavailability of such hypotheses precludes the drawing up of any geographic prospects.

Metgé and Verrière tried to establish prospects on different bases, though both their studies are trend projections starting from corrected data.

PROJECTIONS BY AGE. Verrière's aim was to construct projections by age and sex. He first eliminated from the population pattern the biases due to mis-statement of age. Using the mortality table of Niakhar-Paos-Koto, he constructed a population pyramid with a total population equal to that yielded by the 1960–1961 national survey Projections then were calculated employing the following hypotheses: (1) a constant fertility of 215 births per thousand females aged 15–49; (2) a declining mortality

TABLE 35.20

Probability of legitimate conception

| Age when married | Age of the Female | | | | | | |
|---|---|---|---|---|---|---|---|
| | 15–19 | 20–24 | 25–29 | 30–34 | 35–39 | 40–44 | 45–49 |
| 15–19 | 0.33 | 0.39 | 0.35 | 0.33 | 0.32 | 0.13 | 0.05 |
| 20–24 | | 0.39 | 0.36 | 0.34 | 0.30 | 0.25 | 0.06 |

SOURCE: Fakao survey.

TABLE 35.21
Sine-Saloum: 1963–1965 migration

|  | Niakhar | Paos-Koto |
|---|---|---|
| Annual Mobility Rate (percent) | 16 | 25 |
| Percentage of migrants from January to May | 74 | 77 |
| Percentage of lone migrants | 69 | 51 |
| Average size of migrant groups[a] lone migrants not included | 3.3 | 4.2 |
| Distribution of 100 groups of migrants by composition of the groups — Unrelated | 14 | 17 |
| Relatives, *without* head of family | 50 | 25 |
| Relatives, *with* head of family | 36 | 58 |

SOURCE: B. Lacombe, *Mobilité et Migration. Quelques résultats de l'enquête de Sine-Saloum (Sénégal)*, ORSTOM (Paris, 1969).
[a] A group of migrants can be defined as a group of individuals moving together from the same compound to the same place.

resulting in a six months per year increase in life expectancy.

According to his calculations, the population should increase from 3,049,000 in 1960 to 4,731,000 in 1980 and up to 4,846,000 in 1985. This represents an annual rate of growth of 2.2 percent. Given the above hypotheses we may forecast an increasingly youthful age structure (see Table 35.22).

PROJECTIONS BY AREA. Metgé's research concerned the geographic distribution of the population. His computations do not take into account the age pattern, as this cannot be projected by area. He hypothesizes a 5 percent rate of growth for urban population and a 1 percent rate of growth for rural population. The reference population is that of 1964 estimated by bringing up to date the 1960–1961 figure, and whose

TABLE 35.22
Population prospects (in percent)

|  | Ages | | | | Population (in thousands) |
|---|---|---|---|---|---|
|  | 0–19 | 20–39 | 40–59 | 60+ |  |
| 1960–61 survey | 50 | 30 | 14 | 6 | 3,049 |
| Verrière correction 1960–61 | 50 | 28 | 15 | 7 | 3,049 |
| Projected for 1980 | 54 | 27 | 14 | 5 | 4,731 |
| Projected for 1985 | 50 | 30 | 14 | 6 | 4,846 |

SOURCE: 1960–1961 National Demographic Survey.

geographic distribution has also been estimated.

He thus found a 2.3 percent national rate of growth (see Table 35.23). The importance of the urban areas is expected to increase considerably. What makes these prospects interesting is not the aggregate population figure, but the pattern, by age in Verrière and by urban and rural areas in Metgé. Present data do not allow the construction of projections integrating both variables.

TABLE 35.23
Population prospects

|  | Rural Areas (percent) | Urban Areas (percent) | National Population (in thousands) |
|---|---|---|---|
| 1964 | 74 | 26 | 3,370 |
| 1980 | 59 | 41 | 4,870 |
| Rate of growth | 1 | 5 | 2.3% |

SOURCE: Metgé survey.

# CHAPTER THIRTY-SIX

## *Togo*

TOM K. KUMEKPOR

▦

THIS chapter examines a survey of rural women in southern Togo and their attitudes toward family planning, contraception, and abortion. The survey was undertaken to pretest the methods and questionnaires to be used in the planned countrywide KAP survey of the Republic of Togo by the Department of Sociology and the Department of Preventive and Social Medicine of the University of Ghana and the Department of Geography of the Institut de Bénin, Lomé, Togo.

One of the conditions of the agreement with the Institut de Bénin was that their students at Lomé should be utilized as interviewers as a means of introducing them to field work experience. This condition necessarily implied that the survey should take place at a time when the students were on holidays. The five-day Mardi Gras holiday in February 1969 was therefore set aside for the field work.

SAMPLING METHODS AND PROBLEMS. Because of linguistic, transport, and communication problems on the one hand and the relatively short time (five days) available for the field work on the other hand, it was decided to restrict the survey to the predominantly Ewe-speaking Maritime Region, excluding the "Commune" of Lomé.

(1) The Maritime Region was first of all divided into the existing three administrative districts (*circonscriptions*):

> Anecho
> Tsevie
> Tabligbo

(2) Each district was further divided (on the basis of the 1961 Demographic Sample Survey) into the following four locality size groups:

(a) Places with a population of 10,000 or more inhabitants
(b) Places with a population of 5,000–9,999 inhabitants
(c) Places with a population of 1,000–4,999 inhabitants
(d) Places with a population of under 1,000 inhabitants

(3) The proportion of the total population of the region residing in each of the three administrative districts was calculated to establish the proportion of the sample to be selected from each district.

(4) The proportion of the total regional population in 1961 residing in each of the four locality categories was calculated to estimate the proportion of the sample to be selected from each locality category.

(5) For each district the proportion of the total population living in each of the four locality categories was calculated to establish the proportion of the sample from the district to be selected from each category.

SELECTION OF ACTUAL SAMPLE TOWNS AND VILLAGES. (a) There were only two towns (Anecho and Tsevie) with 10,000 inhabitants or more and one town (Vogan) in the 5,000–9,999 range in the region. They were therefore automatically selected.

(b) For each administrative district, all the localities in each size-category were arranged according to the size of the population in 1961. Depending on the total number of villages and the number of sample villages allocated to the particular size category in a particular district, a sampling fraction was established for each size category in each district. Employing systematic sampling, the sampling fraction was used to select the predetermined number of sample villages from each locality size category for each district. For each sample town or village, depending upon size and the number of houses allotted to each category, the number of houses from which interviews were to be held in each center was determined.

RECRUITMENT AND TRAINING OF INTERVIEWERS. An interviewer's manual was prepared and distributed to each of the 60 student interviewers recruited by the Department of Geography of the Institut du Bénin, Lomé, to be used as a basis of the training program for the field work.

The first problem of the survey was met at the level of the training of interviewers. The only one of the six supervisors recruited by the

Institut du Bénin who reported at the training session disappeared after the first session. Of the 60 potential student interviewers, 34 did not understand Ewe, the predominant language of the region, and could not therefore take part in the interviewing. They could be used only as listers and were trained as such. Their training was, therefore, concerned basically with problems of preparing house lists and selecting sample houses for each sample town or village. The training of the remaining 26 interviewers excluded most of the problems of sampling and selection of sample houses but concentrated mainly on interviewing techniques and problems.

FIELD OPERATIONS. The Ministry of Interior and Local Administration advised all the district administrative officers in charge of the different districts to explain the purpose of the survey to people in their districts and ask for their cooperation. In addition, the radio carried a series of announcements on the survey both in French and in the local languages.

There were two groups of field workers (the listers and the interviewers) for each administrative district. The listers went ahead of the interviewers to make initial contacts with the local and traditional authorities and to select the sample houses. On arrival in each center, they went to the district administrative officer or village chief to discuss and arrange together a plan of work. The listers were given a predetermined number of houses to be selected. They were instructed to treat each traditional section (quarter) of a town or village as a separate unit for purposes of selecting the sample. Houses in each section of the town or village were listed and a separate sampling fraction established for each section depending upon the proportion of the total number of houses in the town or village located in each section (quarter) and the total number of houses assigned to the village or town as a whole.

The sampling fraction established for each sector of the town was used in selecting sample houses for that sector. The house numbers of all sample houses which were boldly written in white chalk on the conspicuous part of the house were encircled with colored chalk for easy identification by the interviewers. A map of the town showing the position and numbers of houses selected for the sample was deposited with the village chief or administrative officer before the listers left for the next sample village.

On arriving in each sample village, the interviewers went to see the chief to introduce themselves. Since the groundwork to establish rapport had already been done by the listers, they only collected the map of the town to study carefully. They spent some time familiarizing themselves with the town and locating the sample houses, using the map prepared by the listers. This was followed by the actual interview of the head of each household and of all women aged 15 years and over in each sample house.

In all 293 females, 15 years and over, were interviewed in the three administrative districts of the region under study. The following are the sociodemographic characteristics of the 293 respondents.

## SOCIODEMOGRAPHIC CHARACTERISTICS

ETHNIC DISTRIBUTION OF RESPONDENTS. The region, being a predominantly Ewe area, yielded a sample in which 74 percent of the women were Ewe, while 15 percent belonged to other tribes, and 11 percent did not state their ethnic origin (See Table 36.1.)

RELIGION. Traditional religion seems to be very strong in the area studied. This may explain the high illiteracy rate among the population studied since there is a strong

TABLE 36.1
Ethnic origin of 293 women of the Maritime Region

| Ethnic Origin | Percent |
| --- | --- |
| Ewe | 74 |
| Others | 15 |
| Not stated | 11 |
| Total | 100 |

TABLE 36.2
Age distribution of 293 women of the Maritime Region

| Age Group (in years) | Percent |
| --- | --- |
| Under 20 | 15 |
| 20–25 | 15 |
| 25–29 | 18 |
| 30–34 | 15 |
| 35–39 | 6 |
| 40–44 | 6 |
| 45–49 | 5 |
| 50+ | 11 |
| Not stated | 9 |
| Total | 100 |

correlation between illiteracy and adherence to traditional religion in Togo. Of the women interviewed 61 percent claimed to be adherents of traditional religion, 25 percent were Catholics, 12 percent were Protestants, 1 percent were Moslems, and another 1 percent were adherents of Apostolic and spiritual churches.

AGE DISTRIBUTION. The sample population was relatively young and consequently the great majority of the women were still within the active reproductive age groups. One-third were under 25 years of age, another third between 25 and 34 years, and 6 percent between 35 and 40 years, making a total of 72 percent under 40 years of age, while 11 percent were 50 years and over and 17 percent gave no indication of their age (see Table 36.2).

EDUCATION AND OCCUPATION. The educational status of the informants was very low. Over four-fifths were illiterate (i.e., they had never been to school), 6 percent had primary school education (i.e., 2–4 years of schooling), 4 percent had middle school education (5–7 years schooling), while only two women (under 1 percent) had any secondary schooling. Nine percent did not give any information on their education and were most probably also illiterate. We are therefore dealing with a predominantly illiterate female population, whose experiences are

TABLE 36.3

Education and occupation of 293 women in the Maritime Region

| Status | Percent |
|---|---|
| *Education* | |
| Illiterate/no schooling | 81 |
| Primary school, 2–4 years | 6 |
| Middle school, 5–7 years | 4 |
| Secondary school | — |
| No information | 9 |
| Total | 100 |
| *Occupation* | |
| Housewife-farmer | 66 |
| Trader | 25 |
| Student | 3 |
| Apprentice | 2 |
| Clerical + other | 4 |
| Total | 100 |

TABLE 36.4

Number of living children per woman

| Number of Living Children | Percent (N = 293) |
|---|---|
| None | 21 |
| 1 | 18 |
| 2 | 21 |
| 3 | 14 |
| 4 | 11 |
| 5 | 6 |
| 6 | 6 |
| 7 or more | 3 |
| Total | 100 |
| Average number of living children per woman | 2.34 |
| Average number of living children per mother | 3.0 |

most likely limited to the strong influences of their rural environment. As the area covered was very largely rural, it is not surprising that 66 percent of the women interviewed were housewife-farmers, while 25 percent were traders, 3 percent were students, 2 percent were apprentices, and the remaining 4 percent were in clerical and other miscellaneous occupations (see Table 36.3).

MARITAL STATUS AND CHILDBEARING EXPERIENCE. The level of marriage was high among the women interviewed. The majority of them were thus exposed to a high risk of becoming pregnant. Of the total, 11 percent were single, 75 percent were in a stable marital relation, and 2 percent were widowed. Another 12 percent did not provide sufficient information on their marital status.

With such a high marriage rate in a rural environment, where marriage necessarily implies childbearing, one would expect a higher number of children than the recorded 2.34 living children per woman. However, this relatively low number of children per woman can be accounted for by the fact that one-fifth had no children at all while almost one-third were under 25 years of age, a fact of importance since the peak of childbearing for the area under discussion is around 25–29 years (see Table 36.4).

AGE AT MARRIAGE. As might be expected from a predominantly rural, peasant-agricultural, illiterate West African group of women such as those under discussion, marriage took place quite early. While only 1 percent married under 15 years of age, 52 percent, or slightly more than half the women interviewed, married at 15–19 years, and another 22 percent married at 20–24 years. This brings the proportion married under 25 years to 75 percent. Of the remainder, 6 percent reported they were first married at 25–29 years and another 2 percent married at 30–35 years. As high a proportion as 17 percent either did not know or failed to state the age at which they were first married.

ATTITUDES TO FAMILY PLANNING

When dealing with a predominantly rural, illiterate group, among whom the institutionalized practice of limitation of pregnancies through widespread use of contraceptives has not become firmly entrenched in the general value system, direct questions on family planning or the use of contraceptives or even questions on the frequency of discussion among couples about family planning become meaningless and often misleading. Most surveys which have approached the question from this angle have obtained either meaningless answers or, at the best, disappointing results. A more realistic approach to the problem seems to be to attempt to find out whether the people examined: (1) have any ideas about the spacing of children; (2) are aware of the consequences of too frequent births at too short intervals; or (3) space their children at all, and, if they do, what difficulties they encounter.

Answers to these questions are the most likely to throw light on the group's attitudes to family planning and the limitation of births. Moreover, they indicate whether or not the people draw any distinction between spacing of children and limitation of pregnancy; and, if they do, what the distinctions are.

ATTITUDE TO SPACING. Nine-tenths of the respondents would like to have their children spaced out, while 8 percent would like theirs close together, and 2 percent could not say how they wanted their children spaced out. In terms of family planning, this finding is very significant whether or not the women studied did in fact have their children spaced out. The fact remains that the *desire* not to have children too close together exists among nine out of ten women interviewed. Any observed discrepancy between what these women say and what they practice may therefore be explained by the fact that the women did not know how to achieve the desired birth interval between their children or even where to obtain any information on the subject.

IDEAS ABOUT THE SPACE BETWEEN CHILDREN. The majority of the women did not only want their children spaced out but 98 percent had definite ideas about the approximate number of years they wanted between their children. Thus 8 percent would like a space of one year between their children, while 23 percent prefer two-year intervals, and 50 percent, or half the total number, prefer

three-year intervals. Another 17 percent would like to have their children at intervals of four or more years. Thus, the desire of 90 percent of the women to have their children spaced out is supported further by the fact that two-thirds would insist on an interval of at least three years and another quarter on a two-year interval. It can, therefore, be concluded that having children well spaced out at intervals not less than three years is the ideal form of childbearing that the majority of these women want (see Table 36.5).

TABLE 36.5
Desired interval between births

| Number of Years Desired Between Births | Spacing Preferred (in percent) | | |
|---|---|---|---|
| | Children Close Together (N = 23) | Children Spaced Out (N = 264) | Total (N = 293) |
| 1 | 8 | — | 8 |
| 2 | — | 23 | 23 |
| 3 | — | 50 | 50 |
| 4 or more | — | 17 | 17 |
| Not stated | — | — | 2 |
| Total | 8 | 90 | 100 |

PUTTING IDEAS OF SPACING CHILDREN INTO PRACTICE. In terms of family planning, it is not sufficient to know whether women would like their children spaced out or not. It is equally important to find out whether they attempt to achieve the goal and how they do it. One out of five women interviewed would "do nothing about it," "leave it to God or destiny," or "don't really know what to do." Here, therefore, is a group of women, numbering at least one-fifth of those interviewed, who, although they would like to space their children at definite birth intervals around three years, have no idea how to achieve this and therefore resign themselves to fate or destiny and rationalize the situation by saying "a child is a child and must be accepted as such" or "it is God or Destiny who decides on the interval between births." We thus have a group likely to become potential users of patent contraception (at least for spacing purposes) if they are taught to realize that although children are gifts of God or destiny, depending upon the individual's own resources, health, and ability to care for the children, a woman can decide when to have a child as well as when she has enough and wants to have no more.

However, 62 percent (i.e., more than three out of every five women in our sample) would either: (1) come to a definite agreement with their husbands or; (2) avoid their husband's sexual approaches; or (3) simply sleep elsewhere or move to their parents. This means that 62 percent of the women adopt some form of sexual abstinence to achieve the desired interval between their children (see Table 36.6). One form of this, "coming to definite terms with husband" involves getting the spouse to agree to the need for the wife not to have too many children at too close intervals. This pre-supposes the full cooperation, sympathy, and goodwill of the husband. But it is not always possible since it is hardly the case in traditional West African societies that both the husband and the wife have an equal say on matters of sex and children. In these circumstances, such agreements between husband and wife on sexual abstinence are usually feasible when it is in the interest of the husband or where the husband is the one who recognizes the need to space children and therefore is ready to impose some sexual discipline on himself. However, this is usually not so and the reason is to be found in this following common expression of the women interviewed: "The men don't have to carry a pregnancy for nine months." It is possible in some marriages to come to such an "entente" between husbands and wives, and some women (especially those of strong personality and those who are economically and psychologically independent) do achieve this.

Another form of sexual abstinence is for the woman simply to refuse or avoid her husband's sexual approaches. This in fact is a drastic measure in the society for a woman to take and she must be fully convinced about what she is doing to take such a decision since such an action may well lead to marital discord. Fortunately, such decisions are not taken in isolation but are usually combined with some sort of temporary physical separation of the spouses, usually in the form of the wife going to live with her own or the husband's parents. It is to be noted here that sexual abstinence in the form of avoiding a husband's sexual advances by moving away is in fact easier than it at first seems. This is because the practice of temporary physical separation of spouses is institutionally supported; Ewe women usually are encouraged to move away from their husbands either immediately after the birth of a young child (not returning till they are ready for another child) or when there is a dispute which the woman considers serious enough to justify temporary separation pending reconciliation.

Another method adopted to achieve the desired spacing between children, which is the choice of 9 percent of the sample, is sexual abstinence on the part of the woman while advising or condoning the husband's satisfaction of his sexual desires elsewhere or advising the husband to take another wife (i.e., keeping temporarily a sexual distance from the husband). This solution, and to some extent the one discussed just before it, throws some light on traditional Ewe wives' attitudes to polygyny. Keeping a sexual distance from the husband but allowing him to satisfy himself elsewhere rather than being the only sexual partner and being exposed to the risk of unlimited pregnancies is accepted as the lesser of two evils.

However, with the education of women, and both husbands and wives increasingly participating in wage labor, sexual abstinence on the part of the woman by moving away to her parents will become more difficult and less popular as a method of spacing births because the woman's obligations will be no longer to her husband only but also to her employer. Illiterate housewives who are not in wage labor employment are able to use this method because they do not have the same dual obligations. Thus, with increasing female education and participation in the labor force, the proportion of wives separating from their husbands in order to space births is likely to be greatly reduced. This is not due to education per se, but to the consequences of education. Conditions of employment will not allow them to go away to their parents for unlimited periods and the difficulty of obtaining housing in the urban areas is likely to compel this category of women to continue sharing their husbands' homes. Contraceptives are likely to appeal much more to this category of women rather than physical separation. This may account not only for the observed higher incidence of contraceptive use among educated women in West Africa but also for the reluctance of this category of women to approve of polygynous marital relations. Attempts to interpret observed relationships between educational status and contraceptive use rates must therefore take note of this point.

EXTENT OF PATENT CONTRACEPTIVE USAGE FOR SPACING CHILDREN. Only 8 percent (i.e., only 1 in 12) of those interviewed would consult a doctor or midwife about contraception or would use drugs for the purpose of achieving the better spacing of children (see Table 36.6). Patent contraceptives are therefore not likely to be used by most of the women interviewed for the spacing of children except, perhaps, for this 8 percent.

ABORTION FOR SPACING PURPOSES. It is worthy of note that at least 1 percent of the women had the courage to say that they would resort to induced abortion to achieve their desired spacing interval (Table 36.6). In this respect, it is important not to underestimate the important role of traditional medicine and the use of herbs and barks which are effective traditional abortifacients.

EFFECTS OF TOO MANY CHILDREN AT TOO SHORT INTERVALS. *On the mother*. Whether the women interviewed do space their children or have them too close together, one thing is clear from this survey. As many as 87 percent of those interviewed clearly recognize for various reasons the adverse effects of unlimited births on mothers. However, 9 percent felt there need not be any such effect, although even here they usually qualified their statement by saying "what matters is that the mothers should be in good health."

TABLE 36.6
Methods adopted to achieve desired spacing between births

| Method | Percent Using Method (N = 293) |
|---|---|
| Do nothing; leave it to God or destiny or don't know what to do | 20 |
| Would come to definite terms with husband, or would avoid husband's sexual approaches, or would sleep elsewhere or move to parents | 62 |
| Would advise husband to satisfy himself elsewhere, or find another woman for husband, or suggest polygyny | 9 |
| Would see doctor/midwife or would use drugs | 8 |
| Would resort to induced abortion | 1 |
| Total | 100 |

In fact, only 4 percent did not seem to know of the possibility of any effects or what such effects might be.

Concerning the specific nature of the effects of a rapid succession of births at too close intervals on mothers, more than five-sixths (84 percent) saw the ill effects in terms of the mother's health, 11 percent saw the effects in economic and financial terms with emphasis on the mother's inability to give adequate support to the children, and another 11 percent felt that such a situation often led to the psychological and emotional unhappiness of the mother (Table 36.7).

*On the children*. Such adverse consequences resulting from the lack of suitable spacing between children are equally seen to affect children as well. While only 3 percent of the women did not seem to know what the effects might be on their children and 6 percent claimed there would be no effects, the majority of them felt the effects were equally adverse on children as on mothers. While 19 percent saw the lack of suitable spacing between births as making it difficult for parents to provide adequate educational and financial support for the children, 72 percent

TABLE 36.7

Effects of lack of suitable spacing on mothers and children

| Type of Effect | Percent of Mothers (N = 293) | Percent of Children |
|---|---|---|
| None | 9 | 6 |
| Mother's health | 77 | — |
| Children's health | — | 72 |
| Economical & financial | 11 | 19 |
| Psychological & emotional | 11 | — |
| Don't know | 4 | 3 |
| Total | 112[a] | 100 |

[a] Some women mentioned more than one effect.

saw the effects in two highly related factors: (1) in terms of the health of the child (and the possible death of the previous child), and specifically (2) in terms of nutritional deficiency leading to kwashiorkor.

Although the women fully recognize the ill effects of lack of suitable birth intervals between their children, it is equally clear from the methods of spacing children described above (Table 36.7) that these women cannot really succeed in keeping the desired interval between their children without definite hardships and inconveniences in the form of self-imposed sexual abstinence by a physical break between spouses. The same ends could have been achieved (perhaps more efficiently) by using contraceptives.

How, then, are the women studied willing or able to impose such sexual hardships on themselves? The answer was sought through the question "How long should a woman wait after childbirth before having sexual relations with her husband?"

It has already been mentioned that women return to their husbands only when they are ready to risk having another child, a practice which is perfectly rational in a non-contracepting society where sexual relations are likely to be equated with pregnancy. In situations such as these, the extent to which women are willing to impose such hardships on themselves can be a reliable indication of not only their recognition of the need to space their births or even to limit the number of

their children, but also the extent to which they are willing to put this into practice. Thus 24 percent of the women would be ready for sexual activity in less than one year, 21 percent would prefer waiting for two years, while 26 percent would not resume marital relations before three or more years, and 4 percent insist that the period depends on the health of the mother. Only 2 percent did not know how long they should wait after childbirth before risking another pregnancy (see Table 36.8).

The women not only have clear-cut ideas of the effects of lack of suitable birth intervals on themselves and their children, but they also have, as is shown in Table 36.8, clear ideas as to when they would be willing to risk another pregnancy. This, to some extent, explains the observed regularity in birth intervals of most West African women and to some extent throws light on such usual answers from women to questions on spacing of children: "I have mine usually spaced out at $X$ year intervals" or "I have my children after every 2 or 3 years."

Most KAP studies have over-concentrated on women, with little or no concern for men. This is unfortunate because it requires the active participation of both a man and a women for a pregnancy to occur. Although it is the woman who experiences the pregnancy, much of the pressure for sexual activity or for another pregnancy may come from the man. Thus, although a woman may like to have her

TABLE 36.8

Period after a birth women would be willing to wait before resuming sexual relations with husbands

| Period (in years) | Percent (N = 293) |
|---|---|
| Less than 1 | 18 |
| 1 | 19 |
| 2 | 21 |
| 3 or more | 26 |
| Depends on health of mother | 4 |
| Don't know | 2 |
| Total | 100 |

children at desired spacing intervals, pressure from her sexual partner or lack or absence of a sexual partner may make it impossible for her to achieve this ideal. Thus the actual child-spacing habits of a woman are the result of a sort of compromise between the woman and her sexual partner in the interest of their marital stability. In most traditional West African societies, it can safely be assumed that this interval is influenced by (1) the circumstances of the marriage (e.g., whether monogamous or polygynous), as well as (2) the extent to which the woman is willing to insist on her "sexual freedom" even at the risk of marital disharmony.

It is from this angle that it was deemed necessary in this survey to follow the question on desired spacing interval by the question on the woman's own attitudes to her spouse's or sexual partner's views on the desired spacing interval. Thus, as to the question, "Would your husband or sexual partner agree to this period," 50 percent of the respondents felt their husbands or sexual partners would agree, 28 percent felt their husbands or sexual partners would not, while 10 percent insisted that, whether their husbands agreed to the specified period or not, they would not be prepared to yield to them. This is a clear indication of the strong determination on the part of at least one-tenth of our respondents to risk having children only when they want them or are ready for them. It is interesting to note that at least 12 percent of the respondents did not know what the feelings of their husbands or sexual partners would be on this issue. In this case, the 12 percent can express only their own feeling which might be modified by their husband's or sexual partner's sexual inclinations.

After discussing the question of spacing of children and the ideal spacing interval between births, the respondents were confronted directly with the question of whether they thought they would do something in the future to avoid having children too frequently. Twenty-six percent indicated that they would either consult a doctor or paramedical personnel or use drugs or herbs to avoid unwanted pregnancies. This is a positive sign of

interest in contraceptives by at least a quarter of the respondents. Still 13 percent insisted they would adopt the traditional method of physically moving away from their husbands or sexual partners, or refuse their sexual advances or simply condone a co-wife situation, while 9 percent feared their husbands would not like it or would punish them if they did anything to prevent pregnancy, and 5 percent would accept what God gives them or would do nothing for religious reasons. As high a proportion as 47 percent planned to do nothing in future to prevent unwanted pregnancies (see Table 36.9).

TABLE 36.9

Attitudes about preventing unwanted pregnancies in the future

| Intended Action | Percent (N = 293) |
|---|---|
| Would do nothing | 47 |
| Would consult a doctor/paramedical personnel or use drugs/herbs | 26 |
| Would move away from husband/keep sexual distance from husband/condone a co-wife situation | 13 |
| Husband would object | 9 |
| Would accept what God gives | 5 |
| Total | 100 |

EFFECT OF THE SOCIAL ENVIRONMENT ON ATTITUDES TO FAMILY PLANNING AND CONTRACEPTIVE PRACTICES.    In most African societies there exist taboos of different sorts surrounding sex and discussions involving sex. Thus, the social environment and what people estimate to be the likely public reaction to sexual matters would greatly influence their own expressed views on sex and practices pertaining to sex. When the question was put to the respondents as to whether they thought the people in their area felt free to discuss questions of spacing of children or regulation of pregnancies, 10 percent said they did not know what the situation was, 33 percent felt such a freedom of public expression on such matters existed, while 57 percent denied this. Thus, it could be concluded that, while the majority of the women might be inhibited by the social environment from freely expressing their views on regulation of pregnancies, at least one-third of the women felt they were not so inhibited.

THE HOSPITAL AND CLINIC IN RELATION TO FAMILY PLANNING. It is increasingly being recognized by most people, even in the rural areas of West Africa, that the hospital/clinic/health post can play a really crucial role in saving the life of people. What is not certain is whether people associate the hospital with the possibility of regulating pregnancies. The question was, therefore, asked as to whether the women knew the hospital could help them to space their children better and to have only the number they wanted. To this question 29 percent answered yes, a further 10 percent said it was possible the hospital might help, 48 percent (or a little under half) replied that the hospital could not do this, and another 7 percent, while replying no, still added that, although the hospitals do not do so at the moment it might be possible they could render such services. The important thing to stress here is that, if family planning is to be made an integral part of health services, then there is the need for more education on the potentialities and problems of hospitals and health centers in this area. The basis for this association between health, childbirth, and related values and practices already has strong foundations in traditional beliefs, attitudes, and behavior pertaining to antenatal and postnatal care. As demonstrated above (Table 36.9), the problem of too many and too frequent births is seen in its adverse health effects on the child (72 percent of the respondents) and on the mother (77 percent of the respondents) in addition to adverse psychological effects on the mother (11 percent of respondents).

PREGNANCY CONTROL AND REGULATION OF BIRTHS. Up to this point, most of the questions asked have been in one way or the other directed toward the spacing of children. The next set of questions were geared more specifically toward pregnancy control or the regulation of births. Instead of asking the

question about knowledge of contraceptives directly, it was thought better to approach the issue indirectly by asking respondents what they would do in order to avoid being pregnant too often or at a time when they do not want another child. As in the case of spacing, the most popular practice advocated was the traditional method of the woman imposing some amount of sexual deprivation on herself. Thus, over half of the informants (54 percent) would impose a sexual separation between themselves and their husbands, while 31 percent would do nothing, 9 percent would leave everything to God or destiny and accept the child as such, 3 percent would use available or existing methods or see the doctor, while another 3 percent would use herbs or resort to induced abortion (see Table 36.10).

TABLE 36.10
Attitudes about avoiding being pregnant too often or at a time another child is not wanted

| Intended Precautionary Measure | Percent (N = 293) |
|---|---|
| Would use available or existing methods/see the doctor | 3 |
| Would use herbs/resort to induced abortion | 3 |
| Would leave everything to God or destiny and accept the child as a child | 9 |
| Would do nothing | 31 |
| Would impose sexual separation between self and husband/sexual deprivation | 54 |
| Total | 100 |

APPROVAL OR DISAPPROVAL OF FAMILY PLANNING AND CONTRACEPTIVE PRACTICES. Although it may seem embarrassing to say what one would do in situations which are personal and controversial, especially those invoking public reaction, it is sometimes easier to get people to express their views much more freely if the question asks what they think others would do in similar situations. The question of attitudes to the regulation of pregnancies was therefore put indirectly thus: "Do you approve of women (not necessarily yourself) doing something not to have children too often?'' Over a quarter (26 percent) answered "yes" (i.e., they approved of the use of contraceptives as a means of regulating births). On the other hand, 70 percent answered "no," which appeared to mean that they disapproved of the practice, while 4 percent remained uncommitted. Purely on the basis of these answers, one might be tempted to conclude widespread disapproval of the use of contraceptives as a means of pregnancy control. However, an analysis of the follow-up question, "What are your reasons?" reveals that most of the "no" answers were in fact "conditional approval" or "qualified disapproval." The reasons are as follows: 5 percent could say nothing because they had no children; 8 percent insisted that a woman must accept all pregnancies because "a child is a child"; 29 percent argued that such a thing amounts to a criminal act or a destruction of life, especially in view of the fact that the methods employed usually are viewed with a strong religious bias; 6 percent felt that too frequent births might affect or weaken the mother's health; while 21 percent approved of the practice but felt the means or methods were not known to the women who usually found themselves in such situations. The most important, and by far the most interesting reason, was given by the 41 percent who insisted that the circumstances surrounding the pregnancy were the most important determining factor. Such circumstances as finance and ability to support existing children, education of children, and mother's health were stressed (see Table 36.11).

The most important points to emphasize here are: (1) the recognition by at least 41 percent of the women of some of the most important factors necessitating family planning in Togo today; (2) the recognition by 21 percent of the hazards involved (sometimes leading to loss of life), and (3) the need for wider family planning education especially as to the potential as well as the medical and health soundness of the methods as expressed by 21 percent of the informants.

The answers to this question throw light on

TABLE 36.11
Attitudes about the regulation of pregnancies

(a) Do You Approve of Women Doing Something To Avoid Having Too Many Children Too Often?

| Attitude to Use of Contraceptives | Percent (N = 293) |
|---|---|
| Yes | 26 |
| No | 70 |
| Uncommitted | 4 |
| Total | 100 |

(b) What Are Your Reasons for These Views?

| Reason for Expressed View | Percent (N = 293) | |
|---|---|---|
| I can say nothing because I have no children | 4 | uncommitted |
| All pregnancies must be accepted because "a child is a child" | 8 | 37 actual disapproval |
| It is destroying life; it is criminal; against religion and morals; the methods are dangerous | 29 | |
| Mother's health might be affected; mother becomes weak if she has too many children | 6 | approval |
| The women don't know; women are ignorant of family planning methods | 21 | |
| To avoid having too many children; ability to support children; circumstances surrounding the pregnancy | 41 | conditional approval |
| Total | 109[a] | |

[a] Some respondents gave more than one reason to support their views.

an interesting and important methodological point relating to similar questions requiring a "yes" or "no" answer. In this particular case, 26 percent of the respondents answered "yes" to the question (i.e., they approved of women doing something to avoid unnecessary pregnancies), 70 percent answered "no," which might be interpreted to mean the disapproval of the practice, while 4 percent remained uncommitted. Solely on the basis of these answers, one might be tempted to conclude that only one-quarter of the women approved of the use of contraceptives as a means of pregnancy control. However, an analysis of the follow-up question "What are your reasons?" reveals that most of the "no's" to the question were in fact "conditional approval/disapproval." The follow-up question shows that the actual instances of disapproval accounted for only 37 percent, not 70 percent. The methodological point illustrated here is that, when the concepts are not clear to, or not well understood by, the respondents, they are likely to answer "no" and "don't know" instead of committing themselves. Hence, a large proportion of "no's" or "don't knows" have been reported in some attitudinal surveys in West Africa. It is, therefore, advisable to follow such questions by asking the respondents to justify their answers. This allows respondents to express themselves more fully on the question as illustrated in Table 36.11.

PREVIOUS CONTRACEPTIVE PRACTICE AND USE. Despite the views expressed on approval or disapproval of pregnancy control methods, 88 percent of the respondents have never tried such methods before; 10 percent had done so, while 2 percent remain uncommitted. The different reasons given for approval or disapproval of pregnancy control methods apart, the important fact remains that the social environment which imposes taboos of different sorts on public and open discussions of sex constitutes an important inhibiting factor to the adoption of family planning techniques. Equally important is the fact that, even where people are favorably disposed to accepting such methods, in the majority of cases the women do not know where to go to seek reliable information or whom to consult; in the very rare cases where such information is available, there is the tendency to fear for health and medical hazards.

The following evidence supports the above arguments: (1) 68 percent of the women did not know whom to consult for family planning and contraceptive advice; (2) 64 percent were willing to receive information on family planning and contraceptive practice while a further 3 percent were willing to receive information but were somewhat apprehensive;

(3) 62 percent of the women, with 31 percent against and 7 percent undecided, were willing to utilize family planning facilities, if provided, to help them solve their pregnancy problems; (4) 57 percent in contrast to 37 percent against and 6 percent "don't knows," felt contraceptives were "good," would help them plan their families, solve their financial problems, improve the health of the mother and child, and finally help fight against induced abortion.

## ABORTION

ATTITUDES TOWARD ABORTION. At the time of the survey, 16 percent of the women were pregnant. Of the 84 percent who were not pregnant, 65 percent accounted for their situation with such reasons as "too many children," "still nursing a child," or absence or temporary separation from husband; 19 percent gave economic and financial reasons; 12 percent were either students or felt they were too young to have children; and 4 percent either did not know why they were not pregnant or had no reason to offer.

The question on attitudes to abortion was approached from two directions: (1) from the direction of an unwanted pregnancy or a pregnancy which occurs when the mother, for one reason or another, might not be ready for it, and (2) from a straightforward expression of views on abortion.

On the question, "What would you do if pregnancy occurs earlier than you expect or at a time you are not ready for it?" the following answers were obtained: 77 percent would do nothing, keep the pregnancy and accept the child "as a child"; 9 percent would consult the doctor; 8 percent were undecided; while 6 percent unambiguously stated that they would resort to induced abortion (see Table 36.12).

In a straightforward expression of views on abortion, 90 percent felt it to be dangerous, criminal and/or against religion, tradition, and morality; 9 percent believed it was good but dangerous, and, as such, it is better to remain pregnant. Only 1 percent remained

TABLE 36.12
Attitudes toward abortion

(a) *What Would You Do If Pregnancy Occurs Earlier than You Expect It?*

| Intended Action | Percent (N = 293) |
|---|---|
| Would do nothing/keep the pregnancy | 77 |
| Would consult a doctor | 9 |
| Undecided | 8 |
| Resort to induced abortion | 6 |
| Total | 100 |

(b) *Attitudes to Induced Abortion*

| Expressed Attitude | Percent (N = 293) |
|---|---|
| It is bad/dangerous, criminal/against religion | 90 |
| It is good but dangerous | 9 |
| Uncommitted | 1 |
| Total | 100 |

TABLE 36.13
Attitudes about tradition/custom and abortion

| Traditional/Customary View | Percent (N = 293) |
|---|---|
| Abortion is condemned by custom, tradition, or religion | 41 |
| Abortion is criminal | 37 |
| Traditional authorities have passed laws against abortion | 12 |
| People fear having abortion | 4 |
| Others | 6 |
| Total | 100 |

uncommitted or did not want to express their views on the issue (Table 36.12).

Although the attitudes toward induced abortion expressed above are supposedly personal, they were nevertheless influenced, to some extent, by the sociocultural atmosphere. The next stage in our analysis therefore attempts to find out not the *personal* or the *individual* attitude to abortion but what the custom or tradition of the particular area says on abortion, bearing in mind that the two, the individual and the customary or traditional views, are likely to be highly related.

One-eighth of the respondents believed that the traditional authorities have passed laws against abortion, the breaking of which carry very heavy penalties. To 41 percent of the respondents, abortion is condemned by custom or tradition while 37 percent emphasized that abortionists are considered criminals, evil doers, and enemies of the ancestors. It is interesting to note that 4 percent of the respondents felt that, although there were no traditional laws against abortion, people fear to commit abortion because of the dangers involved. Six percent of the respondents gave miscellaneous answers to the question (see Table 36.13).

If there are such heavy traditional or customary sanctions against abortion, why should people resort to it? Almost one-third of the answers emphasized circumstances surrounding particular pregnancies, or having more children than one's means could support, or becoming pregnant without a responsible husband to support the child. Almost one-quarter felt that young women resort to abortion simply to enable them to lead a carefree life or to enjoy sex without bearing the consequences. However, 11 percent pointed out that the decision to resort to abortion might be forced on the individual purely by certain embarrassing situations such as when a close member of the family was responsible for the pregnancy (see Table 36.14).

On what grounds (if any) then should abortion be justified? About three-quarters

TABLE 36.14
Attitudes about why women resort to abortion

| Reason for Abortion | Percent (N = 293) |
|---|---|
| Circumstances surrounding the pregnancy may compel women to resort to abortion | 37 |
| Young women resort to abortion to lead a loose sexual life | 22 |
| Certain embarrassing situations may force women to abort | 11 |
| Don't know/uncommitted | 30 |
| Total | 100 |

(74 percent) of the informants were of the opinion that abortion should not be justified under any condition whatsoever since it is criminal, disgraceful, against religion, tradition, or morality. However, just under one-fifth (18 percent) insisted that abortion should be justified on (1) health grounds; (2) when a woman, too young to have a child, becomes pregnant; (3) when a woman, already having more children than she can support, becomes pregnant; or (4) because of other circumstances surrounding the pregnancy. In addition to the 18 percent who would justify abortion on the grounds enumerated above, it is noteworthy that an additional 8 percent would advocate abortion on the grounds of the poor financial position of the parents with special emphasis on the parents' ability to adequately support, care for, and educate an additional child. Thus, at least 26 percent, or one in every four, of those interviewed would justify abortion under one condition or another (see Table 36.15).

TABLE 36.15
Attitudes about conditions justifying abortion

| Condition | Percent (N = 293) | |
|---|---|---|
| Under no condition should abortion be justified | 74 | |
| Depending upon circumstances surrounding the pregnancy | 18 | |
| Financial position of parents (in terms of ability to support and educate an additional child) | 8 | 26 |
| Total | 100 | |

TRENDS IN ABORTION RATES. There are certain things which go on in a society irrespective of any particular individual's views on the issue. One thing of this type is abortion. No matter how strongly a particular individual might oppose abortion, there still remains the fact that a certain amount of abortion goes on in the society every year. What is socially important, in addition to the actual trends in abortion rates, is that people are aware of the nature and direction of the trends. Thus, despite the strong conviction generally expressed that custom and tradition condemn abortion as immoral and despite the fact that local authorities usually passed laws carrying severe sanctions against abortion, the women were nevertheless aware of the fact that a substantial amount of induced abortion is going on in the society, even in the rural areas. They, therefore, clearly recognized the discrepancy between what "ought to be" and "what actually happens" in their society, so far at least as abortion was concerned. Thus, 52 percent of those interviewed felt abortion was on the increase in their area; 2 percent felt it was stationary; while 11 percent saw a decline in abortion trends. As large a proportion as 35 percent did not know anything about the supposed direction of abortion trends in their area. What then are the reasons for these expressed views on abortion trends? Just under half (49 percent) of the informants (i.e., 94 percent of those who felt abortion trends were on the increase) claimed that their expressed views were based on the facts that people (especially the young) do actually practice abortion and that "there is much talk about it nowadays." One-eighth argued that there are people who specialize in the art of abortion and emphasized that the practice must be prevalent enough to lead to the emergence of specialist abortionists. Another 13 percent pointed out that people no longer want a large number of children or that women without husbands do not want to have children with no one to support them. On the other hand, 10 percent saw a decline in abortion trends as a result of abortion laws passed by traditional authorities and the heavy penalties attached to such laws, or as a result of religious sanctions. However, 26 percent did not assign any reason to the views expressed by them. Although 52 percent said that abortion trends were on the increase, a larger proportion (74 percent) in justifying their views, gave reasons explaining why abortion trends were on the increase. Thus, a larger proportion (22 percent more) than the 52 percent who said "yes" to the question requiring a direct expression of views on abortion trends were aware of the increasing rise in abortion in their area (see Table 36.16).

TABLE 36.16

Views about trends in abortion rates

(a) *Is Abortion on the Increase, Declining, or Stationary?*

| Abortion Trends | Percent (N = 293) |
|---|---|
| On the increase | 52 positive trends |
| Declining | 11 negative trends |
| Stationary | 2 |
| Don't know | 35 |
| Total | 100 |

(b) *What Are Your Reasons for These Views?*

| Reasons for Views on Abortion Trends | Percent (N = 293) |
|---|---|
| People, especially the young, practice it/there is much talk about it nowadays | 49 |
| People no longer want a large number of children/women don't want to have children with no husband to support them | 13 |
| There are specialized abortionists | 12 |
| Abortion laws have reduced the incidence of abortion | 10 negative |
| No reason assigned/don't know | 16 |
| Total | 100 |

The first three reasons grouped together: 74 positive trend

In this respect it is significant to note that the proportion who felt abortion trends were on the decline remained relatively constant (10 percent as against 11 percent) while the proportion of "don't know" reduced from 35 to 26 percent. This is further supporting evidence for the need for follow-up questions to clarify straightforward "yes/no" answers to questions requiring expression of views on attitudes in KAP surveys in particular. In this particular case, the follow-up question has provided an opportunity to those who might not have properly understood the concepts used in the question, or who did not want to commit themselves on questions which might seem controversial, for further statement on the issue. Thus 22 percent more, who could not directly (for one reason or another) say abortion rates were on the increase, at least had the opportunity to indicate this or indirectly allude to it in the reasons given to support their answer. In the same way, a number of women (at least 9 percent), who did not want to commit themselves on the direct question but replied "don't know," had the opportunity at least to indicate their actual feeling.

SUMMARY

The information analyzed in this chapter has shown that very little or no family planning is practiced by the women concerned. However, the majority of them were clearly aware of the adverse effects of too many children at too short intervals, not only on themselves but on their children. They see such effects mainly in terms of health hazards to the mother and health and nutritional hazards to the children as well as in economic terms. It is also clear that the women are becoming increasingly aware of the associated economic burdens of a large number of children with the present high cost of living. This is shown by an appreciable proportion of respondents indicating that the decision to maintain a pregnancy should depend on the circumstances surrounding such a pregnancy.

The women interviewed may have had a large number of children at too short intervals. However, their answers show that if they had their own way, the bulk of them would have their children well spaced out at around three-year intervals. If they do not at present achieve this, it does not mean that they do not know the implications of having many children too close together but rather it is because they do not know *how* or they do not have the *means* to achieve this without too much physical, emotional, and matrimonial hardship to themselves. At present, most of them attempt to do this by imposing sexual restrictions on themselves by moving away from their husbands; but this seems to be highly unnecessary in these days of advanced contraceptive technology. They should be able to achieve the same ends without unnecessary and costly hardships. The most important factor, however, is that they are aware of the need to space their children; their only problem is a lack of knowledge of modern methods of regulating births.

The social environment within which reproduction takes place is very important in the formation of people's attitudes toward pregnancy regulation. It seems the effect of this factor is relatively strong on the population studied. Although 72 percent felt that people who have too many children at too short intervals would be publicly ridiculed, as many as 75 percent also felt that people do not feel free to talk about sex and the regulation of pregnancy publicly and easily. Much propaganda and educational activities need to be directed toward minimizing this influence of the social environment. The proportion of people who feel they can turn to the hospital for family planning help still remains relatively low (39 percent). This situation needs to be improved if family planning is to be integrated into health programs.

There still exists the unfortunate confusion of contraception with abortion. This is reflected in the large proportion of the women (70 percent) who disapproved of women doing something to avoid unwanted pregnancies. There is therefore a need for intensive and extensive family planning education to teach women not only of the possibilities and potentialities of contraceptives but also their safety and medical soundness as well as to eradicate from their minds, once and for all, the unfortunate confusion of contraceptive practice with abortion. Under the existing conditions of ignorance of the health and medical soundness of contraceptives, many women are likely not to have anything to do with any programs they feel advocate the taking away of life which is considered criminal and morally and religiously repugnant.

One of the encouraging findings of this survey, in terms of future family planning projects, is that, although the bulk of the women do not at present practice family planning or use commercial contraceptives, 57 percent felt contraceptives are good while 64 percent (or almost two out of every three) are willing to have access to information on family planning, the only reservation being the fear or the doubts and the social gloom surrounding the practice.

Although the majority of those interviewed would not publicly support induced abortion, there was strong evidence throughout the survey that a small but relatively important proportion was willing to resort to abortion and was ready to say this openly to interviewers. This may point to the increasing realization of the burdens of too many children in situations of absolute ignorance of modern means of pregnancy control methods.

Customary, traditional, moral, and religious institutions and practices strongly condemn abortion. However there is increasing awareness among the population that, despite these sanctions, people still practice abortion. This is reflected in such answers as "people do practice it," "there are people specializing in it," and "certain types of pregnancies can be embarrassing." This perhaps leads about a quarter of the respondents (26 percent) to endorse publicly abortion under certain conditions. These answers are an indication that under certain circumstances the social pressure on the individual to abort can be great indeed.

Another striking aspect of the findings is that as many as 52 percent of the women interviewed felt abortion rates were currently on the increase as against only 11 percent who felt they were decreasing. This proportion increased to 74 percent on further probing.

The results of this survey are still exploratory but they do throw doubts on many ideas held about attitudes of rural women to family planning. Our findings show that rural women are not as conservative as they are usually pictured; that the basic problem is that of *ignorance* of the means and possibilities, as well as safety or hazards of family planning methods and techniques. The rural woman is willing to have access to family planning techniques and may be willing to adopt these wholeheartedly provided she is approached in the right manner.

# CHAPTER THIRTY-SEVEN

# *Upper Volta*

ANDRÉ COUREL
AND D. IAN POOL[1]

▦

UPPER Volta provides probably the most extreme West African example of labor-force migration, for the country's twentieth-century role has been as a labor reservoir. The result is large-scale seasonal and semi-permanent migration to the focuses of development, located primarily in the two neighboring coastal countries of Ghana and Ivory Coast. This one demographic factor affects the way of life of a significant proportion of Upper Volta's inhabitants, while its recent economic and social history and even politics, have been strongly influenced by migrants and returnees.

History and environment together have fashioned this migration. One can include history because the colonial French governments not merely encouraged the recruitment of Voltaics to work in Ivory Coast or in the French armed forces, but effectively forced migration by introducing heavy head taxes on what was an essentially subsistence economy. The net effect, somewhat unintended, was to encourage migration to Ghana as well as Ivory Coast. Environmental factors operate because Upper Volta is located, for the most part, in the savanna zone. Its exploitable natural resources appear at present to be limited, while, in some areas, land of less than top arable quality supports a high rural density of population. This is particularly true in the central area, the region of the Mossis, the most important ethnic group.

Migration is not the sole force operating. The demographic structure of Upper Volta also is affected by the country's rich cultural

[1] The authors wish to acknowledge the help given by the Direction de la Statistique, and particularly by M. Georges Sanogho, the Director, and M. Guy Planès, Assistant Technique Français. The 1969 survey was carried out under the direction of D. I. Pool, who was aided by Sidiki Philippe Coulibaly, Marie Françoise Courel, Joel Gregory, Wilhelmina Leigh, Martha Little, Janet Pool, and Charles Thomas, and in collaboration with the Centre Voltaique de la Recherche Scientifique (CVRS). The authors wish to thank the staff of the CVRS, particularly its former Director and Assistant Directors M. Izard, Mme. Plattiel, and M. Catry, and the other collaborators in the fertility survey. We have drawn on manuscripts written by Joel Gregory and Martha Little.

heritage, which is extremely diverse. Overlaying a traditional diversity are the introduced traits of the Christian and Moslem religions and new patterns of economic behavior. This rich diversity is demonstrated, not only in Upper Volta's history, dances, and art, but also in culturally determined factors which might affect demographic trends, such as conjugal patterns, weaning, and postpartum abstention from intercourse.

## DATA SOURCES AND METHODS

SOURCES.[2] With only one general demographic sample census, carried out in 1960, Upper Volta's prime demographic need is for further official data. The most important source of data for Upper Volta was the 1960 census, designed and carried out by Rémy Clairin of INSEE's Service de la Coopération, who was also instrumental in analyzing and writing up the provisional results (with Pierre

Cantrelle) as well as the definitive results which covered all rural areas and secondary centers, but not Ouagadougou or Bobo-Dioulasso, the principal cities. A full census was made of Ouagadougou, the capital, in 1961, which was followed by a sample survey in 1968. By contrast, there are virtually no data for Bobo-Dioulasso the second city, other than the administrative "census" and a socioeconomic sample survey made in 1959.

Administrative "censuses" are taken at five yearly intervals for tax purposes. They are highly unreliable because there is poor enumeration of older men and children who are not taxable, while those persons who are taxable avoid enumeration. The 1960 sample census showed that the administrative "censuses" were 10–41 percent underenumerated, this varying from district to district and the average being 24 percent (rural) and 33 percent (secondary urban centers). Apart from these sources, one is restricted to special surveys and to secondary sources (e.g., the statistics of the *Direction de la Santé Rurale*; the statistics on *Le Traffic Voyageurs* for the railway to Abidjan, an important route for migrants). Finally, there is legislation for compulsory vital registration, but even in Ouagadougou this is not entirely effective.[3]

METHODS. *The sample survey of 1960*: The sampling fraction for this *sample census* was 1-in-10 in secondary centers and 1-in-50 in rural areas. But of an estimated 7,067 villages, 237 were censused.

The method followed was the same as that normally practiced for francophone African countries. There was a probability sample based on the administration's documentation of villages, with stratification according to the size of the villages and their geographic and ethnic distribution. The survey lasted

---

[2] The major sources for this chapter are the following: *Published:* (a) Ministère de la Coopération (France) INSEE, *Recensement Démographique de Ouagadougou 1961–1962: Résultats Définitifs* (Paris, 1962); (b) Pierre Cantrelle and Rémy Clairin, Service de la Statistique et Ministère de la Coopération (France) INSEE (Service de la Cooperation) *La Situation Démographique en Haute-Volta: Résultats Partiels de l'Enquête Démographique, 1960–1961* (Paris, 1962); (c) *Etudes Démographiques et Socio-Économiques du Centre Urbain de Bobo-Dioulasso et Enquête Détaillée sur Deux Quartiers de la Ville* (Rapport pour la Société d'Etudes pour le Développement Economique et Social, Paris); (d) Gérard Rémy, "Les Migrations de Travail dans la Région de Nobéré (Cercle de Manga)," *Cahiers de l'ORSTOM*, Séries Sciences Humains, V, 4 (1968); (e) Françoise Izard, "Bibliographie Générale de la Haute Volta: 1956–1965," *Recherches Voltaïques*, 7 (Ouagadougou, 1967); (f) D. Ian Pool et al., "L'Enquête sur la Fécondité en Haute-Volta," *Notes et Documents Voltaïques*, II, 4 (July–September 1969); (g) Ministère du Plan et des Travaux Publiques, Direction de la Statistique (Upper Volta) Bulletin Mensuel d'Information Statistique et Economique; *Supplement, Enquête Démographique de Ouagadougou, 1968*, Direction de la Statistique (Ouagadougou, 1969). *Unpublished at the time of writing:* The definitive report of the 1960 sample census was published by INSEE in 1971. In 1970 the Direction de la Statistique et de la Mécanographie (Ouagadougou) prepared a section of the manuscript for limited distribution for which the authors were given access [referred to here as census 1960 (D)].

[3] It has been estimated that the underregistration level in Ouagadougou is 30–40 percent. At the 1968 survey, there were 60,000 persons in the central area of the city (vis à vis the outskirts), with a crude birth rate of 50–60 per thousand. This gives 900–1,000 births, but only 600 were registered, and some of these were from the outskirts.

seven months from October 1960 to April 1961.

*The census of Ouagadougou, 1961*: A complete census of this city was carried out from May 1961 to January 1962, but the questionnaire was less detailed than that for the national sample census.[4]

*The sample survey of Ouagadougou, 1968*: This sample covered only the central city area. It was a cluster sample, with a short questionnaire and apparently with a sampling fraction of something less than 1-in-2 (it varied from quarter to quarter).

## ETHNIC AND GEOGRAPHICAL DISTRIBUTION OF THE POPULATION

Upper Volta is a complex ethnic mosaic. A detailed distribution has been established by IFAN, but, in order to have a general idea of a quantitative picture, it is useful to report data obtained in the census of 1960 for nine regions (strata) and nine "families" consisting of the principal ethnic groups. These are given in Table 37.1. A description of the strata of the survey will permit us to discuss the ethnic distribution.[5]

The Fulani (Peuls) are an ethnic group living in the northernmost stratum. They represent somewhere around 10.4 percent of the total Voltaic population, but they are very dispersed, for almost one-half of the group lives outside the northern stratum (Table 37.1). This northern region is sahelien and is characterized by the predominance of herding and by a low density of population. The density is 16 persons per square mile. Economic and social development, the improvement of agricultural techniques, and an increase in the number of watering points have tended to make a change in the habits of this population from nomadism toward a

[4] This census was taken during the wet and then dry seasons, and thus there would be tremendous diversity in the levels of underenumeration, for there is a pronounced wet season in the adjacent areas of cultivation.

[5] See also IFAN, *Cartes Ethno-Démographiques de la Haute-Volta*, 3 and 4 (North) (IFAN-Dakar, 1963).

TABLE 37.1

Ethnic and Geographical distribution, population of Upper Volta

(a) Density of the Population by Stratum 1960

| Stratum | Area (sq. miles) | Population (thousands) | Density (persons per sq. mile) |
|---|---|---|---|
| (A) North | 15,700 | 245 | 16 |
| (B) Yatenga | 4,600 | 540 | 117 |
| (C) Mossi | 20,000 | 715 | 36 |
| (D) Bissa | 2,800 | 238 | 85 |
| (E) Gourma | 18,600 | 215 | 12 |
| (F) Gourounsi | 9,200 | 287 | 31 |
| (G) West | 18,800 | 737 | 39 |
| (H) Sénoufo | 7,600 | 281 | 37 |
| (I) Lobi | 8,700 | 229 | 26 |
| Total[a] | 106,000 | 4,487 | 42 |

(b) Percentage Distribution of the Population by Major Ethnic Group, 1960[b]

| | | |
|---|---|---|
| (I) | Mossi (& related) | 48.0 |
| (II) | Bissa | 4.7 |
| (III) | Gourmantché | 4.5 |
| (IV) | Bobo | 6.7 |
| (V) | Mandé (e.g., Marka) | 6.9 |
| (VI) | Gourounsi | 5.3 |
| (VII) | Sénoufo | 5.5 |
| (VIII) | Lobi, Dagari | 7.0 |
| (IX) | Fulani (Peul) | 10.4 |
| (X) | Others | 1.0 |
| | Total[b] | 100.0 |

(c) Percentage Distribution of Major Ethnic Groups, by Religion

| Group | Animists | Moslems | Christians | Total |
|---|---|---|---|---|
| Mossi | 75.3 | 21.9 | 2.8 | 100.0 |
| Bissa | 76.5 | 19.0 | 4.5 | 100.0 |
| Gourmantché | 94.5 | 4.8 | 0.7 | 100.0 |
| Bobo | 84.6 | 5.0 | 10.4 | 100.0 |
| Mandé | 44.6 | 49.5 | 5.9 | 100.0 |
| Gourounsi | 91.8 | 5.8 | 2.4 | 100.0 |
| Sénoufo | 90.5 | 9.1 | 0.4 | 100.0 |
| Lobi, Dagari | 81.8 | 4.4 | 13.8 | 100.0 |
| Fulani (Peul) & Tuareg | 3.2 | 96.8 | 0.0 | 100.0 |
| Others | 1.3 | 95.1 | 3.6 | 100.0 |

SOURCE: 1960 census.
[a] The total includes Ouagadougou and Bobo-Dioulasso.
[b] Not including the cities of Ouagadougou and Bobo-Dioulasso.

simple transhumance régime. In the savanna zone proper, south of the sahelien zone, one finds Fulani encampments close to villages of the local ethnic groups, and the Fulani there look after the villagers' animals. The Fulani, as well as some other smaller groups in this region of Upper Volta (Tuaregs and Bella), are entirely Moslem in contrast to the other ethnic groups of the country who are, for the most part, animists.

The Mossi live in the central part of the country (strata B and C). They constitute the dominant ethnic group in the country with 48 percent of the population. The Yatanga Mossi (stratum B), who formerly made up a distinct kingdom, live in a zone with a very dense population averaging 119 persons per square mile. The central Mossi (stratum C) exhibit the same characteristic, but to a lesser degree, with an average density of 85 persons per square mile. The Mossi heartland is a typical savanna zone, where the cultivation of millet, often on exhausted soils, is the principal activity of the population.

The Mossi constitute a reservoir for emigration, as much for movement to foreign countries (Ivory Coast and Ghana) as to the interior of Upper Volta. But, over and above this factor, there are other cultural forces operating. For example, the traditional sociopolitical structure was strongly hierarchical, and is a factor which still plays an important role in socioeconomic development. Again Islam, which was a recent arrival, had attained by 1960 converts among only 21.9 percent of the Mossi population.

The Bissas (stratum D) are closely associated with the Mossi, for they have been under Mossi political influence for a long time. The Bissa language is different from Mossi but they have customs which are very similar.

The Gourmantchés, whom one finds in the eastern part of the country (stratum E), have also been under the political influence of the Mossis, but still retain different customs and a different language. The low density of population in the Gourmantché country (ten persons per square mile) contrasts sharply with the neighboring Mossi region. Along certain sections of the frontier between the two groups, Mossi pressure has been so strong that it has resulted in the occupation by Mossis of new areas.

In stratum F are found the Gourounsi, who for the most part are cultivators. They live in small independent groups and to this date ethnologists differ over whether they have a common descent. Political authority remains with patriarchs, while religion, both animist and ancestral worship, plays an important social role.

In spite of a diversity of origin and of language in the central western stratum D, there is a certain cultural unity between these western populations. Dioula is the lingua franca throughout this entire region, but one can distinguish three principal ethnic groups: Bobos, Markas (whose language is closely related to Dioula), and Samos. A little over half of the population of this region is Moslem.

A small section of the Sénoufo ethnic group are found in Upper Volta in stratum H. Far from central control and mistrusting the government, the Sénoufo had the highest rates of underenumeration (41 percent) in the administrative censuses. They are very independent, but they have developed the most advanced agricultural techniques in Upper Volta, in particular the cultivation of rice.

A zone which is virtually uninhabited separates the Sénoufo from their neighbors the Lobis. The Lobis, Birifors, Dagaris, and Wilés (stratum I) have come into Upper Volta from Ghana. This movement commenced during the sixteenth century and has continued almost until today. They recognize no authority, political or traditional, above the head of the family. Their way of life remains to this day perhaps the most traditional of all Voltaic groups.

## FERTILITY

Fertility was reported upon in detail for the 1960 nationwide and the 1962 Ouagadougou censuses. The task here is to determine if changes have occurred since then, and whether any fertility differentials are apparent.

The levels, and the major differentials, for 1960 are given in Table 37.2. Fertility levels

TABLE 37.2
Fertility levels, 1960

(a) Levels

|  | Census, 1960 | Princeton Project Adjustment[a] |
|---|---|---|
| Crude birth rate (per thousand) | 49 | 49 |
| Total fertility ratio | 6.1 | 6.5 |

(b) Differentials(1960 census)

| Tribe | Total fertility ratio |
|---|---|
| Mossi | 6.6 |
| Fulani (Peul) | 5.5 |
| Gourmantché | 5.5 |
| Gourounsi | 5.6 |
| Bobo, Samo | 5.5 |
| Marka | — |
| Sénoufo-Toussian | 5.8 |
| Lobi-Dagari | 6.1 |

[a] From William Brass et al., eds. *The Demography of Tropical Africa* (Princeton, N.J.: Princeton University Press, 1968) p. 158.

are high, and are at least comparable with those of the surrounding African countries. The major regional differential was that between the central region—the Mossi "heartland"—where fertility was very high, and other regions and tribes, particularly the Bobos, Markas, and Peuls.

Comparative data, taken from the fertility survey of 1969[6] (Tables 37.3 and 37.4), generally show little significant difference between fertility in various areas once account is taken of small numbers at older age groups. The 1969 data, the first for the city, suggest that Bobo-Dioulasso does not differ markedly from Ouagadougou; nor do the rural samples differ substantially from the urban. If there is any difference, it is, as is more clearly seen in Table 37.4, that Ouagadougou has a slightly lower fertility level than Bobo-Dioulasso or the rural Mossi areas. This is supported by data in an independent sample drawn from two of

[6] D. I. Pool et al., "L'Enquête sur la Fécondité en Haute-Volta," *Notes et Documents Voltaiques* (July–September 1969), reporting on a sample survey carried out by the author at that time in Ouagadougou and Bobo-Dioulasso.

Ouagadougou's rural-urban fringes: "Zogona," a new settlement of migrants and Mossis; and "Barrage" which is homogeneously Mossi.[7]

The results are supported by data showing a change in the proportions married at ages 15–19 between the 1962 and the 1968 official surveys of Ouagadougou. In 1962, 35 percent of women 15–19 were never married, but by 1968 this had risen to 56 percent.

Moreover, as might be expected for a capital, there is a growing class of educated people who fill civil service and similar appointments at executive and lower levels. Among urbanites, there are already some suggestions of the occurrence of differentials by education at younger ages as is shown in Table 37.5. Again, the Ouagadougou–Bobo-Dioulasso differential is maintained.

These differentials are very small and too much stress should not be put on them. Furthermore, they may not reflect attitudinal changes as much as an increase in the age at marriage resulting from the prolongation of schooling. Indeed, as is shown in Table 37.6, Voltaic women overwhelmingly accept large family norms. Yet, there are some differentials which may reflect incipient attitudinal changes among fringe and urban women, and particularly the better educated. Levels of "don't know" responses declined among these groups, while a majority of women with secondary and higher education in Ouagadougou favored "small" families. However, the proportions who have received this level of education are so small that differentials of this type will not affect the society as a

[7] The low fertility at older ages may be a result of migration selectivity. That is, older low-fertility women could migrate to Ouagadougou, while the highly fertile could not. One wonders whether this could be a partial explanation of the very low fertility at older ages in the 1962 survey of Ouagadougou. Generally the explanation given has been that the enumeration was poor. This subject is discussed in detail in a paper prepared by D. I. Pool and Sidiki P. Coulibaly, eds. (in press): *Quelques aspects de la démographie de la Haute Volta*, Monograph series C.V.R.S. Other chapters include those on culture and fertility, education and fertility, conjugal patterns, survivorship, and migration.

TABLE 37.3
Average number of live births per female, by age

| Survey | Age Group | | | | | | |
|---|---|---|---|---|---|---|---|
| | 15–19 | 20–24 | 25–29 | 30–34 | 35–39 | 40–44 | 45–49 |
| *Rural* | | | | | | | |
| Upper Volta (1960) | 0.3 | 1.7 | 3.1 | 4.1 | 4.8 | 5.1 | 5.3 |
| Rural Survey (1969) | 0.2 | 1.9 | 3.7 | 4.7 | 6.2 | 5.7[a] | 7.7[a] |
| Rural Mossi (1960) | 0.2 | 1.6 | 3.1 | 4.3 | 5.1 | 5.6 | 5.7 |
| Rural Mossi (1969) | 0.2 | 1.3[a] | 3.5 | 4.5 | 6.8 | 5.4[a] | 7.5[a] |
| *Urban* | | | | | | | |
| Ouagadougou | | | | | | | |
| (1962)[b] | 0.2 | 1.9 | 3.3 | 4.6 | 5.5 | 6.3 | 6.6 |
| (1969) | 0.4 | 1.9 | 2.7 | 4.4 | 5.3 | 5.0[a] | 6.2[a] |
| Bobo-Dioulasso | | | | | | | |
| (1969) | 0.8 | 1.9 | 3.8 | 5.1 | 6.0[a] | 5.9[a] | 6.0[a] |

[a] Fewer than 45 respondents.
[b] Estimated from République Voltaique, Service de la Statistique Générale *Recensement Demographique, Ouagadougou*, 1961–62 (Paris: Ministère de la Cooperation, 1964), Graph 21. The retrospective data in that survey have a most peculiar distribution, so the estimation has been made from cumulated rates based on births reported for the 12 months previous to the inquiry.

whole for some years to come. Any prognosis of fertility then, would clearly state that the present high levels will continue for a considerable period. Moreover, it is even doubtful whether there will be any widespread demand for family planning for some time to come. In fact, any suggestion of family planning could well be offensive to the majority of women who adhere to "large family" norms.

### MORTALITY

The data on mortality are given in Table 37.7. Unlike migration and fertility there are few data on mortality additional to those in the 1960 census report. In 1960, levels of

TABLE 37.4
Fertility differentials, 1969

| Region | Age Group | | | |
|---|---|---|---|---|
| | 15–19 | 20–24 | 25–29 | 35+ |
| Ouagadougou | 0.4 | 1.9 | 3.4 | 5.5 |
| Bobo-Dioulasso | 0.8 | 1.9 | 4.2 | 6.0 |
| Rural-urban fringe | 0.5 | 1.8 | 3.7 | 4.8 |
| Rural | 0.2 | 1.9 | 4.1 | 6.1 |
| Mossi country | 0.2 | 1.3 | 4.0 | 6.5 |

mortality were very high and life expectation was very low.

The most important observations are the following: (1) Estimates of mortality levels vary according to the method of estimation so that there is doubt as to the level of

TABLE 37.5
Education and fertility: average number of children born alive to women by level of education, 1969[a]

| | Age Group | | | |
|---|---|---|---|---|
| | 15–19 | 20–24 | 25–34 | 35+ |
| *Ouagadougou* | | | | |
| No schooling | 0.6 | 2.1 | 3.8 | 5.5 |
| Primary, rural, and Koranic schools | 0.3 | 2.0 | 3.7 | 5.7 |
| Secondary school and above | 0.1 | 0.6 | 3.0 | —[b] |
| *Bobo-Dioulasso* | | | | |
| No schooling | 1.0 | 2.0 | 4.3 | 5.9 |
| Primary, rural, and Koranic schools | 0.6 | 2.0 | 4.2 | 6.3 |
| Secondary school and above | 0.0 | 1.2 | 3.8 | —[b] |

[a] This table must be interpreted with care, for although the samples were quite large (Bobo-Dioulasso, $N = 370$; and Ouagadougou, $N = 773$), the respondents with higher levels of education were very few in number.
[b] One respondent.

TABLE 37.6
Percent of respondents favoring large or small families,
Upper Volta, 1969 survey

(a) By Residence

| | Don't Know | Large | Small | God's Will | Total | Large as Percent of Large and Small |
|---|---|---|---|---|---|---|
| *Rural villages* | | | | | | |
| Mossi—1 | 51 | 40 | 1 | 8 | 100 | 98 |
| Mossi—2 | 62 | 26 | 1 | 11 | 100 | 97 |
| Marka | 12 | 82 | 2 | 5 | 101 | 98 |
| Fulani (Peul) | 76 | 24 | — | — | 100 | 100 |
| *Rural-urban fringe* | | | | | | |
| Mossi | 45 | 36 | 9 | 11 | 101 | 80 |
| Mixed | 75 | 9 | 14 | 3 | 101 | 39 |
| *Urban* | | | | | | |
| Ouagadougou | 22 | 47 | 16 | 14 | 99 | 75 |
| Bobo-Dioulasso | 27 | 32 | 24 | 17 | 100 | 57 |

(b) By Education (urban women only)

| | Don't Know and God's Will | Large | Small | Total | Large as Percent of Large and Small |
|---|---|---|---|---|---|
| *Ouagadougou* | | | | | |
| None | 42 | 49 | 9 | 100 | 85 |
| Koranic & primary | 29 | 43 | 28 | 100 | 61 |
| Secondary plus | 22 | 20 | 57 | 99 | 26 |
| *Bobo-Dioulasso* | | | | | |
| None | 48 | 34 | 17 | 99 | 67 |
| Koranic & primary | 38 | 24 | 38 | 100 | 39 |
| Secondary plus | 32 | 24 | 44 | 100 | 35 |

mortality, although unquestionably it is high (2) Male expectation of life at birth equaled or slightly exceeded that of females, a pattern unlike that of some other African countries, but similar to many other non-African countries when their mortality levels were

TABLE 37.7
Indices of mortality, 1960

| | 1960 Census | Princeton Project Adjustment[a] |
|---|---|---|
| Male expectation of life at birth | 31 | — |
| Female expectation of life at birth | 31 | — |
| Crude death rate | 32 | 36 |
| Infant mortality rate | 182 | 263 |

[a] Brass et al., *Demography of Tropical Africa*, p. 158. These rates are calculated from 1960 census data by newly developed methods.

high. Thus, one does not know whether this male-female differential resulted from substantive or methodological factors. (3) There is a strong likelihood of changes in the levels of mortality occurring in the very near future. We will discuss this observation and the likely effects of such a trend further.

There is a possibility that the measles control campaign will be extended. The effect on the mortality of infants and young children of a vaccination campaign against measles which follows a triennial pattern is rather limited. However, if vaccination is repeated on a yearly basis, as is now contemplated in Upper Volta, this would significantly reduce the importance of measles as a cause of mortality for certain age groups which are highly exposed to the risk of measles mortality, those being ages at which possibly half the deaths are a direct or indirect consequence of measles. If the policy of annual vaccination were introduced, expectation of life at birth in 1975, Courel has calculated, would rise from 36 years to about 43 years. That is, between 10,000 and 15,000 deaths of children of less than 15 years would be avoided each year, and this one change would soon alter the age distribution of the population, creating a heavier burden on the schooling system for the country.

Indeed, preliminary analysis of gross survivorship data (deaths/live births) based on the 1969 survey show that survivorship is lowest in rural Upper Volta and highest in the urban areas. There were, moreover, differentials by education, with the offspring of educated women having highest levels of survival. These differentials suggest that life expectation among more favored groups may be well above the national average, and even that urban cohorts may now be experiencing life chances as high as all Ghanaians, or an expectation of life at birth of 40 years or more.[8]

### INTERNATIONAL MIGRATION[9]

International migration is a factor of overwhelming importance to Voltaic society. As will be shown, many aspects of Voltaic life are affected by the very considerable movements of population, particularly of men, that occur each year. Two simple facts will illustrate this. First, out of males aged 20–29 years, one in five is absent in a foreign country at any given time. Second, between one-quarter and one-fifth of the migrants have immigrated or will immigrate more than one time during the course of their lives.

[8] This work is being carried out by Judy Harrington. The implications about life chances are based on a comparison made with the survival data given in S. K. Gaisie, "Estimation of Vital Rates for Ghana," *Population Studies*, XXIII, 1 (March 1969), 21–42.

[9] Some of this section is drawn from the definitive report on the 1960 census to be published soon (see footnote 2). The rest (referred to here as census 1960 (Q.I.), is taken from a manuscript prepared by Rémy Clairin (INSEE) using the questionnaire on absent household members.

Fortunately, the 1960 sample census furnished two types of rather valuable information. First, a document was filled in for each absent resident, noting the place to which he had gone, the expected duration of the absence, and the principal demographic facts about him. Second, a detailed questionnaire was filled in by all men and women more than 14 years of age who had stayed more than six months outside Upper Volta at some time, but who were resident in Upper Volta at the time of the survey. It is thus possible to understand the history and the sociology of migration from the second set of data and at the same time to analyze the situation as it was in 1960. Let us start with the second set of data and look at the history of migration.

HISTORY. Table 37.8 gives the evolution of migration during the twentieth century up until 1960. The dates in this table correspond to some principal historical facts in the recent history of Upper Volta. These are (1) 1923, the date at which recruitment of Upper Voltaic laborers commenced; (2) 1932, when Upper Volta ceased to be a separate colony

TABLE 37.8
History of migration from Upper Volta: percentage of migrations reported in 1960 survey as having occurred during specified periods[a]

| Period | Departure | Return |
| --- | --- | --- |
| Up to 1923 | 2.9 | 1.8 |
| 1924–1932 | 7.7 | 5.4 |
| 1933–1940 | 10.0 | 6.5 |
| 1940–1945 | 12.6 | 12.9 |
| 1946–1950 | 13.0 | 11.4 |
| 1951–1955 | 21.8 | 18.7 |
| 1956–1960 | 31.4 | 42.1 |
| Unknown | 0.6 | 1.2 |
| Total | 100.0 | 100.0 |

SOURCE: 1960 census, D (Definitive Results).
[a] Clearly there would have been a large proportion of recent returnees alive to be enumerated, so these data are biased toward the latest migrations. However, they are presented here as they form the basis for two subsequent tables (37.9 and 37.10), in which one must assume that enumeration errors were the same for each time period.

TABLE 37.9
Reasons for migration, by period

| Years | Recruited for Labor | Reason Military & Police Service | Need for Money | Other | Total |
|---|---|---|---|---|---|
| Up to 1923 | 12.8 | 67.4 | 18.5 | 1.3 | 100.0 |
| 1924–1932 | 11.3 | 58.5 | 28.2 | 2.0 | 100.0 |
| 1933–1939 | 18.7 | 49.2 | 31.1 | 1.0 | 100.0 |
| 1940–1945 | 35.6 | 26.7 | 35.2 | 2.5 | 100.0 |
| 1945–1950 | 15.9 | 13.2 | 67.1 | 3.8 | 100.0 |
| 1950–1955 | 1.5 | 4.7 | 90.6 | 3.2 | 100.0 |
| 1955–1960 | 0.4 | 2.8 | 94.9 | 1.9 | 100.0 |
| All periods | 10.2 | 18.4 | 69.0 | 2.4 | 100.0 |

SOURCE: 1960 census (D).

and, for the most part, was incorporated in the colony of the Ivory Coast; (3) the period 1940–1945, during World War II; (4) the period at the end and immediately after the war which saw the return both of military men and of laborers who had been forced to work in Ivory Coast; and (5) the period since 1946–1950, which has been one of voluntary migration.

Table 37.9 indicates the reasons for migration at each period. At first, migration was primarily to join the army. From 1923, however, recruitment (i.e., forced labor) rose in importance, as did "voluntary" migration to earn money. Today, the need for money is the major reason for migration.

It should also be noted that, as forced labor officially ceased in 1945, the figures for 1945–1950 and 1950–1955 must have been due either to a mistake on the part of the interviewee about the date of his migration or else to his failure to distinguish between being recruited by an official organization and being recruited by a private recruiter to work in Ghana or Ivory Coast as a laborer.

Finally, it should be noted that Voltaics formed a sizable proportion of the so-called Senegalese French colonial troops, and to this day the *Anciens Combattants* are an important group socially among the middle-aged and elderly males.

Once military service diminished in importance the two principal countries of destination became Ivory Coast and Ghana. Recruitment of people to work on projects for the development of the Niger valley (*Office du Niger*) does not seem to have set in train a strong movement toward Mali. It is interesting to note the changes in balance in selecting between Ghana and Ivory Coast as the destinations of migration (Table 37.10).

The movement between Upper Volta and Ivory Coast on the one hand and Upper Volta and Ghana on the other hand varied according to economic and historical events occurring at various times. For example, the 1920s saw the cocoa boom in Ghana, a period which drew migrants to that country from all over West Africa. Then, in 1932 the frontier with Ghana was closed, while there

TABLE 37.10
Number of migrations to Ivory Coast per 100 migrations to Ghana, by period

| Period: | Up to 1923 | 1924–32 | 1933–9 | 1940–5 | 1946–50 | 1951–5 | 1956–60 | All periods |
|---|---|---|---|---|---|---|---|---|
| Ratio: | 33 | 43 | 105 | 168 | 128 | 168 | 220 | 160 |

SOURCE: 1960 census (D).

was an increase in requisitions for labor to go down to the Ivory Coast. During the war, of course, officially there was no movement between Ghana and the other two countries, but, with the end of the war, the borders were opened again and forced labor to Ivory Coast was stopped. Since 1950, the Ivorien economy has grown at a rapid rate, while the intervention of private organizations, which recruit laborers from Upper Volta for that country, has meant that the movement toward Ivory Coast has increased relative to the movement toward Ghana.

At the same time, all migration appears to have been increasing. Rémy Clairin, who directed the 1960 sample census of Upper Volta, estimated that the number of departures increased from 14,260 in 1956 to 27,640 in 1960, an annual rate of increase of 14 percent. These were temporary departures (see below).

SOCIOLOGICAL AND ECONOMIC FACTORS IN MIGRATION.[10] Utilizing the same data source, namely the forms filled in by returned mi-

[10] See also George Sanogho, "Les Migrations Voltaïques" (Paper presented at OECD meeting of Experts on Demographic Change in Tropical Africa, September 1970); and Joel Gregory (in press): "Migration vers la Région de Ouagadougou" in Pool & Coulibaly, eds., *Quelques aspects de la démographie de la Haute Volta*. In particular Gregory analyzed the high mobility and stepwise migration of Voltaics.

grants enumerated during the 1960 census, it is possible to make an analysis of a number of social and economic factors of importance. First, for the most part, the migrants had worked at low-status occupations. Fifty-two percent of the former migrants had worked at harvesting and cultivation, either in Ivory Coast or on cocoa farms of Ghana. A further 24 percent had been laborers in industry and commerce, but they were employed primarily as dock workers or stewards and in other lower status jobs. Another 18 percent of the migrants had been in the military or police in their country of destination, while 6 percent were in various other occupations. However, this distribution varied markedly by country of destination as is shown in Table 37.11.

Table 37.11 refers to all the returned migrants, but data for the period 1956–1960 show that the decline in military and police recruitment has continued. Thus 70.1 percent of migrants of this period went to work in cultivation and agriculture, 21.1 percent in industry and commerce, but only 2.8 percent in the military or the police. Furthermore, if one looks at the category of agriculture in more detail, one finds a high level of specialization. Thus, 68.8 percent of agricultural workers are employed in Ivory Coast in coffee plantations, whereas, for Ghana, 73.2 percent are employed in cocoa harvesting. Most of the workers in agriculture today organize their departures themselves. That is,

TABLE 37.11
Occupation, by country of destination

| Occupation | Country of Destination | | | | |
| | Ivory Coast | Ghana | Other African countries | Non-African countries | All Countries |
|---|---|---|---|---|---|
| Agricultural laborer | 65.9 | 61.7 | 4.0 | — | 51.8 |
| Laborer in industry & commerce | 27.2 | 30.1 | 10.8 | — | 23.9 |
| Army & police | 1.5 | 0.5 | 80.0 | 98.7 | 18.4 |
| Other occupations or no occupation | 5.4 | 7.7 | 5.2 | 1.3 | 5.9 |
| Totals | 100.0 | 100.0 | 100.0 | 100.0 | 100.0 |

SOURCE: 1960 census (D).

TABLE 37.12

Percentage distribution of emigrants by duration of employment separated by country of destination

| Country of Destination | Duration of Employment (years) | | | | |
|---|---|---|---|---|---|
| | Less than 1 | 1 | 2–4 | 5+ | Total |
| Ivory Coast | 21.5 | 51.1 | 22.8 | 4.6 | 100.0 |
| Ghana | 25.0 | 38.2 | 26.3 | 10.5 | 100.0 |
| Other | 3.2 | 12.5 | 65.9 | 18.4 | 100.0 |
| All countries | 18.8 | 39.3 | 32.7 | 9.2 | 100.0 |

SOURCE: 1960 census (D).

67.7 percent of the workers in the coffee plantations and 91.8 percent in cocoa farming have left by their own means which shows the reduced role of departures organized by the *Service de la main d'Oeuvre*.

Table 37.12 shows the proportion of immigrations by country of destination according to duration of employment. Typically, a migrant going to Ghana stayed less than one year or perhaps just one year. A migrant to Ivory Coast might have stayed longer, but then one-quarter to one-fifth of those who returned to Upper Volta made a second migration during their working life, and the interval between these two immigrations appears to have been, according to calculations made by Rémy Clairin, between two and three years.

The final economic point is the benefit to the migrant of his stay in a foreign country.

Again, Clairin has arrived at the estimates of total gain for each migrant in the period 1956–1960 according to country of destination, set out in Table 37.13. The large totals for returning migrants from other countries is a result, of course, of much longer durations of stay and the fact that people working in those countries were, generally speaking, in military and police service and thus had regular incomes.

THE SITUATION IN 1960. The demographic survey of 1960 also furnished a wide range of data on absent residents, that is to say, individuals who had remained sociologically part of the family or of the village, of which they were members before they had departed. Almost certainly, some of these absent residents had decided to stay permanently in foreign countries, but this would not have been known in the village.

Table 37.14 gives the persons absent in 1960 according to country of destination and the duration of residence in those foreign countries up to the time of the inquiry while Table 35.15 gives the mean duration of absence according to country of destination. These tables indicate clearly that the duration of absence is longer in Ivory Coast than in Ghana. The proportion of absentees remaining permanently there is likely to be higher than in Ghana; the movement to Ghana is more often seasonal and is well organized to coincide with cocoa harvesting.

TABLE 37.13

Estimated average gain per migrant from Upper Volta for each migration, 1956–1960

| Country of Employment | Gain (CFA francs) | | | Gain (U.S. dollars)[a] | | |
|---|---|---|---|---|---|---|
| | In cash | In goods | Total | In cash | In goods | Total |
| Ivory Coast | 9,300 | 4,800 | 14,100 | 38 | 19 | 57 |
| Ghana | 5,900 | 4,300 | 10,200 | 24 | 17 | 41 |
| Other countries | 45,100 | 12,000 | 57,100 | 182 | 49 | 231 |
| All countries | 9,600 | 5,000 | 14,600 | 39 | 20 | 59 |

SOURCE: Unpublished calculation by Rémy Clairin from 1960 sample survey data (Q.I.).
[a] These calculations are based on the exchange rates after the devaluation of December 28, 1958 (i.e., $1 = 247 CFA). For earning before that time the amount in U.S. dollars should be increased by 12 percent and for average gain over the whole five-year period by about 6 percent (see International Monetary Funds' Annual Schedules of Par Values).

TABLE 37.14

Absent household members, by country of destination, 1960

(a) As a Percentage of Local Population of Same Sex

| Sex of Absent Member | Ivory Coast | Ghana | Mali | Other African | Outside Africa | Total |
|---|---|---|---|---|---|---|
| Male | 3.5 | 2.0 | 0.2 | 0.4 | 0.1 | 6.2 |
| Female | 0.6 | 0.2 | 0.0 | 0.1 | 0.0 | 0.9 |

(b) By Duration of Absence

| Sex of Absent Member | Ivory Coast | Ghana | Other | Total |
|---|---|---|---|---|
| Males (in months) | | | | |
| Less than 1 | 6.0 | 11.3 | 6.9 | 7.7 |
| 1–5 | 12.6 | 39.2 | 11.9 | 25.2 |
| 6+ | 74.4 | 49.5 | 81.2 | 67.1 |
| Total | 100.0 | 100.0 | 100.0 | 100.0 |
| Females (in months) | | | | |
| Less than 1 | 5.0 | 14.2 | 1.2 | 6.6 |
| 1–5 | 7.4 | 27.3 | 22.1 | 14.3 |
| 6+ | 87.6 | 58.5 | 76.6 | 79.1 |
| Total | 100.0 | 100.0 | 100.0 | 100.0 |

SOURCE: 1960 census (Q.I.).

The selection of migrants is heavily weighted toward particular groups. This is illustrated by Table 37.16 which shows that 20 percent of men 20–29 years of age throughout the country are absent at any one time compared with 6.2 percent of the total male population of Upper Volta. Among women the overall percentage absent is 0.9 but this rises to 2.1 at 20–29 years of age, in itself a very significant proportion, but small by comparison with males at the same age. As these figures show, there is a heavily unbalanced sex ratio among both the absent and those left behind, and this observation is supported further by the data for each tribe given in Table 37.17. Of people absent it is only among the Sénoufo that the number of female migrants per hundred male migrants reaches 50. The lowest sex ratios are found in the two countries to which migrants go primarily for short-term laboring jobs, that is Ivory Coast and Ghana.

TABLE 37.15

Mean duration of absence, by country of destination (in months)

| Country | Males | Females |
|---|---|---|
| Ivory Coast | 24.5 | 29.0 |
| Ghana | 15.0 | 17.5 |
| Mali | 28.0 | 26.0 |
| Other countries | 29.0 | 24.0 |

SOURCE: 1960 census (Q.I.).

TABLE 37.16

Age of absent household members, 1960

| Age Groups (in years) | Percentage of Villagers of Same Sex | |
|---|---|---|
| | Males | Females |
| Under 10 | 0.8 | 0.6 |
| 10–19 | 9.8 | 1.6 |
| 20–29 | 20.1 | 2.1 |
| 30–39 | 7.7 | 0.5 |
| 40–49 | 2.0 | 0.1 |
| 50–59 | 0.5 | — |
| 60+ | 0.2 | — |
| Unknown | 13.6 | 3.8 |
| All ages | 6.2 | 0 9 |

SOURCE: 1960 census (Q.I.).

TABLE 37.17
Sex ratios of absent
household members
by tribe, 1960 (fe-
males per hundred
males)

| | |
|---|---|
| Fulani (Peul) | 7.4 |
| Mossi | 6.9 |
| Bissa | 29.3 |
| Gourmantché | 5.3 |
| Mandé | 21.9 |
| Bobo | 29.1 |
| Gourounsi | 22.9 |
| Sénoufo | 50.3 |
| Lobi | 16.9 |
| Other | 24.9 |
| Together | 15.5 |

SOURCE: 1960 census (Q.I.).

Table 37.17 also permits us to distinguish two types of migration. Among certain groups, the heaviest migration is into the country which neighbors their home region in Upper Volta. For these movements, such as that of the Lobis and the Dagaris into Ghana or the Fulani into Mali, it is probably safe to say that the people absent are following traditional migration patterns, or are merely in neighboring villages separated nationally as a result of comparatively recent political divisions. which have cut through tribal territories. By contrast, the Mossis tend to move to all destinations, but this is also true to a degree for certain of the other groups. The Mossis make up the majority of the absent people, at least among the men, for three out of four (and these are the three most important) of the destinations given in Table 37.18, and, in fact, there are relatively more Mossis absent than would be expected from their proportion of the total population.

Among female migrants the trends are less clear. However, there is ample evidence of women taking part in the "traditional"

TABLE 37.18
Percentage distribution by tribe of absent household members
subdivided by country of destination, 1960

| Sex and Ethnic Group | Ivory Coast | Ghana | Mali | Other Countries | All Countries | Distribution of Total Population of Upper Volta |
|---|---|---|---|---|---|---|
| **Males** | | | | | | |
| Mossi | 63.3 | 50.3 | 54.2 | 19.7 | 53.3 | 48.0 |
| Bissa | 3.0 | 10.3 | — | 8.6 | 5.7 | 4.7 |
| Gourmantché | 0.5 | 2.9 | — | 7.2 | 1.8 | 4.5 |
| Bobo | 5.5 | 1.0 | 6.0 | 17.6 | 5.0 | 6.7 |
| Mandé | 8.1 | 1.6 | 10.5 | 8.2 | 6.0 | 6.9 |
| Gourounsi | 4.9 | 11.3 | 1.9 | 4.6 | 6.9 | 5.3 |
| Sénoufo | 5.4 | — | 5.3 | 14.2 | 4.3 | 5.5 |
| Lobi-Dagani | 6.4 | 16.5 | 4.5 | 12.2 | 10.1 | 7.0 |
| Fulani | 2.4 | 3.5 | 16.5 | 4.8 | 3.3 | 10.4 |
| Others | 0.5 | 2.6 | 1.1 | 4.9 | 1.6 | 1.0 |
| Total | 100.0 | 100.0 | 100.0 | 100.0 | 100.0 | 100.0 |
| **Females** | | | | | | |
| Mossi | 40.6 | 13.5 | 18.9 | 18.9 | 31.0 | 47.8 |
| Bissa | 5.8 | 30.0 | 2.5 | 2.5 | 10.8 | 4.7 |
| Gourmantché | — | 0.9 | 3.0 | 3.0 | 0.7 | 4.4 |
| Bobo | 9.1 | — | 9.1 | 9.1 | 7.0 | 6.7 |
| Mandé | 16.3 | — | 8.7 | 8.7 | 11.3 | 7.0 |
| Gourounsi | 6.2 | 26.9 | 1.6 | 1.6 | 10.1 | 5.1 |
| Sénoufo | 13.2 | — | 36.6 | 36.6 | 13.9 | 5.7 |
| Lobi-Dagani | 7.6 | 25.4 | 3.3 | 3.3 | 11.0 | 7.1 |
| Fulani | 1.1 | — | 5.5 | 5.5 | 1.6 | 10.5 |
| Others | 0.1 | 3.3 | 10.8 | 10.8 | 2.6 | 1.0 |
| Total | 100.0 | 100.0 | 100.0 | 100.0 | 100.0 | 100.0 |

SOURCE: 1960 census (Q.I.).

migration to marry endogamously. In such cases, they would take up patrilocal residence and the migration would be short. Examples are, perhaps, the Bissa to Ghana, the Gourounsi to Ghana, the Lobis and Dagaris to Ghana, the Mandés to Ivory Coast, and the Sénoufo to Ivory Coast and Mali. It is interesting that comparatively few Fulani women migrate to Mali, in direct contrast to male Fulani which supports the notion that the movement of men is predominantly a transhumance or nomadic movement following their flocks and herds.

SOME GENERAL CONSIDERATIONS. Migration is clearly an important factor in Voltaic society. But what is the likely number of people absent in one time? Earlier we gave an estimate made by Clairin of 27,640 departures during 1960. These were temporary migrations of longer than six months by persons over 14 years of age. However the 1960 survey found when it obtained information about absentees, that, in the same year, there were 135,000 people away in foreign countries. The anticipated duration of absence also was obtained, showing that 33 percent of the men out of the country had been away for less than six months in contrast to 21 percent of the women. Thus, about 90,000 were expected to be absent for more than six months. As the mean duration of migrations of more than 6 months is about 30 months, there must be about 36,000 departures each year. The difference of 9,000 between the estimate of 27,640 departures in 1960 made by Clairin and the estimate of 36,000 made here is explained by the fact that Clairin's method did not permit him to take into account the migrants who remained in foreign countries. By these calculations, it would seem then that perhaps 9,000 of the people who depart each year stay away permanently; that is, about one-quarter of each year's group of migrants do not return to Upper Volta.

For the projections given in Table 37.19, which may be compared with those in Table 37.22, we have adopted the figure of 10,000 permanent departures each year. These might well be subdivided again as 6,600 men and 3,400 women. The projections in Table 37.19 are of movements which are more subject to sudden fluctuations than any

TABLE 37.19
Population projections taking account of international migration[a] (in thousands)

| Category[b] | Sex | 1960 | 1965 | 1970 | 1975 | 1980 | 1985 | 1990 |
|---|---|---|---|---|---|---|---|---|
| | Males | | | | | | | |
| 1 | | 2,171 | 2,395 | 2,654 | 2,957 | 3,303 | 3,706 | 4,169 |
| 2 | | 2,171 | 2,363 | 2,585 | 2,849 | 3,152 | 3,507 | 3,917 |
| 3 | | 2,041 | 2,220 | 2,430 | 2,678 | 2,963 | 3,297 | 3,682 |
| | Females | | | | | | | |
| 1 | | 2,201 | 2,412 | 2,654 | 2,939 | 3,265 | 3,641 | 4,078 |
| 2 | | 2,201 | 2,395 | 2,619 | 2,884 | 3,188 | 3,540 | 3,950 |
| 3 | | 2,179 | 2,371 | 2,593 | 2,855 | 3,156 | 3,505 | 3,910 |
| | Both sexes | | | | | | | |
| 1 | | 4,372 | 4,807 | 5,308 | 5,896 | 6,568 | 7,347 | 8,247 |
| 2 | | 4,372 | 4,757 | 5,204 | 5,733 | 6,340 | 7,047 | 7,867 |
| 3 | | 4,220 | 4,591 | 5,023 | 5,533 | 6,119 | 6,802 | 7,592 |

SOURCE: Calculated by André Courel for the next development plan of Upper Volta.
[a] Compare with Table 37.22.
[b] Categories: 1. Residents including persons absent temporarily plus persons absent permanently who departed after 1960.
2. Residents (including persons absent temporarily only).
3. Residents in Upper Volta.

other of the population phenomena projected in this chapter. Migration is obviously affected by sudden policy changes, a point vividly illustrated by the recent expulsion of migrants from Ghana and Ivory Coast.

It is difficult to obtain data on expulsions of Voltaics from Ivory Coast, or indeed from Ghana. In the case of Ghana, however, the Voltaics, by contrast with Nigerians, Togolese, and Nigériens, were in occupations at the end of 1969 and the beginning of 1970 which were not in demand for Ghanaians, and thus the expulsion of Voltaics, so far, has not been heavy. Nevertheless, if this were to occur, the effect on employment in Upper Volta would be very severe. In January 1970, it appeared that the number of returnees coming from Ghana as a result of the explusions was somewhere between 300 and 2,000; 300 was the figure provided by a Ghanaian embassy official, while 2,000, perhaps a maximum estimate, was the figure given by people who had been vaccinating returned migrants, among whom there had been an outbreak of yellow fever. Not only would a massive return, if and when it occurred, have a marked effect on the economy, but, in addition, many of the estimates of vital rates, which depend on the population being quasi-stable, would also be affected by a movement which would be highly age selective.

Apart from policy changes migration movements are still subject to considerable fluctuation. Thus, for example, statistics drawn from the data on third-class passengers traveling on the express from Upper Volta to Ivory Coast indicate marked fluctuations during the period 1964 and 1968 between a net gain of 15,400 for Upper Volta in 1966 and a net loss from Upper Volta of 34,800 in 1968.

These railway statistics also show that the mean number of departures per year by this route, which is not the only route, was about 10,000 during the period 1964–1968. This would clearly be an underestimate of the number of departures even to Ivory Coast alone. Indeed, there are other sources of data which suggest that the estimates of Voltaics in foreign countries used here, and drawn from Upper Volta data, may be far too low.

In the 1960 census of Ghana there were 100,050 males and 37,750 females born in Upper Volta of whom 97,290 males and 35,180 females were of Voltaic ethnic origin. Taking the latter figures, this gives a total of 132,470 Voltaics in Ghana alone in 1960. Using the earlier data, presented in Table 37.10, showing that the ratio of Voltaics going to Ivory Coast recently would be between 1.0 and 2.2 times the number going to Ghana, there would, under these circumstances, be between 132,000 and 291,000 Voltaics in Ivory Coast and a total number absent in the two countries alone of 424,000. Including other areas in which there are Voltaics, the total absent temporarily or permanently may thus have been as much as three to three-and-one-half times higher than the total reported by the Upper Volta census.

## URBANIZATION

In 1960, approximately 5 percent of the population lived in urban centers of any size (i.e., Ouagadougou, Bobo-Dioulasso, and Koudougou) and 12 secondary urban centers (see Table 37.20). The secondary centers were small, for even Koudougou had only 25,000 inhabitants, and, in total, the secondary centers added up to only 90,000 people.

A further 165,000 lived in settlements of more than 5,000 persons. Allowing 6 percent growth per annum as the average for Ouagadougou, Bobo-Dioulasso, and Koudougou, including their rural-urban fringes, 4 percent per annum for the secondary centers, and 3 percent per annum for the smaller centers, which for the most part, are merely large villages,[11] projections indicate that approximately 14 percent of the population will be living in centers of 5,000 and above by 1980, with 10 percent in Ouagadougou, Bobo-Dioulasso, Koudougou, and the 12 secondary centers. Thus this latter group will triple in number and double their proportion of the total population in the course of 20 years.

[11] These assumptions are based on rates of growth drawn from a comparison between the administrative censuses and the 1960 census, except that for the principal centers, which is derived from a comparison between the 1962 and 1968 censuses of Ouagadougou.

TABLE 37.20
Urban population (in thousands)

| Major Urban Centers | Numbers | | Percentage of Total Population[a] | | Percentage of Residential Population[b] | | Assumed Annual Percentage Rate of Growth |
|---|---|---|---|---|---|---|---|
| | 1960 | 1980 | 1960 | 1980 | 1960 | 1980 | |
| Ouagadougou | 60 | 190 | | | | | |
| Bobo-Dioulasso | 50 | 150 | | | | | |
| Koudougou | 25 | 75 | | | | | |
| First subtotal | 130 | 415 | 3.0 | 6.3 | 3.1 | 6.8 | 6 |
| Secondary urban centers | 90 | 195 | | | | | 4 |
| Second subtotal | 220 | 610 | 5.0 | 9.3 | 5.2 | 10.0 | |
| Villages with more than 5,000 inhabitants | 165 | 300 | | | | | 3 |
| Total urban | 385 | 910 | 8.8 | 13.6 | 9.1 | 14.9 | |

a As a percentage of category 1 in Table 37.19.
b As a percentage of category 3 in Table 37.19.

Clearly this rate of urbanization carries with it planning and other social and economic problems.

The data we have referred to merely cover total numbers of population which can be defined by residence as "urban." However, a notable characteristic of the towns of Upper Volta is the considerable proportion of their population who are agricultural rather than urban workers. This is shown in Table 37.21. Thus, 33 percent of the male working-age population of the major urban centers—Ouagadougou, Bobo-Dioulasso, and Koudougou—was engaged in agriculture in 1960, and a considerable number of the remainder were students.

## FUTURE GROWTH[12]

It is very hazardous to project demographic data in order to obtain estimates of the population until 1990. The fact that one has

[12] The source for this section is the projection made by the Direction de la Statistique for the next development plan.

access now only to one survey, that of 1960, renders all estimates very weak, particularly those which concern the phenomenon of migration, which although of great importance, is not easily measured. In the projections which follow, the 1960 survey has been employed. Since the data were not of high quality a number of assumptions have been made and have been confirmed, wherever possible, by further indices calculated from the 1960 survey.

Two sets of projections have been constructed in Table 37.22. Those in part (a) do not assume any decline in mortality due to measles while those in part (b) assume such a decline.

ASSUMPTIONS ON WHICH THE PROJECTIONS WERE BASED. *Age structure.* The age structure of the population was taken from the 1960 survey. It was necessary however to smooth the age pyramid by using a stable population model, as the raw data contained many irregularities.

TABLE 37.21
Percent distribution of the male labor force by sector, 1960

| Residential Area | Primary | Secondary | Sector Tertiary | Students | Unemployed |
|---|---|---|---|---|---|
| Rural | 92 | 2 | 2 | 1 | 3 |
| Villages with over 5,000 inhabitants | 80 | 7 | 5 | 3 | 5 |
| Secondary urban centers | 62 | 12 | 16 | 6 | 4 |
| Major urban centers | 33 | 22 | 22 | 13 | 10 |

TABLE 37.22
Population projections, 1960–1990 (in thousands)

(a) Median Assumption

|  | | | | Males | | | |
|---|---|---|---|---|---|---|---|
|  | 1960 | 1965 | 1970 | 1975 | 1980 | 1985 | 1990 |
| Births (preceding 5 years) |  | 583 | 645 | 712 | 785 | 868 | 964 |
| Age groups (years) |  |  |  |  |  |  |  |
| 0–4 | 371 | 429 | 477 | 533 | 595 | 665 | 747 |
| 5–9 | 284 | 312 | 364 | 407 | 459 | 516 | 582 |
| 10–14 | 250 | 269 | 298 | 348 | 390 | 441 | 495 |
| 15–19 | 220 | 242 | 261 | 290 | 338 | 380 | 430 |
| 20–24 | 193 | 210 | 232 | 252 | 280 | 326 | 368 |
| 25–29 | 169 | 184 | 200 | 221 | 241 | 266 | 313 |
| 30–34 | 143 | 159 | 173 | 189 | 210 | 231 | 254 |
| 35–39 | 124 | 134 | 148 | 162 | 178 | 198 | 219 |
| 40–44 | 104 | 114 | 124 | 138 | 151 | 167 | 186 |
| 45–49 | 85 | 95 | 104 | 114 | 127 | 139 | 154 |
| 50–54 | 72 | 75 | 84 | 93 | 102 | 114 | 126 |
| 55–59 | 54 | 61 | 64 | 72 | 81 | 89 | 100 |
| 60–64 | 39 | 44 | 50 | 52 | 60 | 68 | 75 |
| 65–69 | 28 | 30 | 34 | 39 | 41 | 48 | 54 |
| 70+ | 35 | 37 | 41 | 47 | 50 | 58 | 66 |
| Total | 2,171 | 2,395 | 2,654 | 2,957 | 3,303 | 3,706 | 4,169 |

|  | | | | Females | | | |
|---|---|---|---|---|---|---|---|
|  | 1960 | 1965 | 1970 | 1975 | 1980 | 1985 | 1990 |
| Births (preceding 5 years) |  | 563 | 620 | 684 | 754 | 833 | 926 |
| Age groups (years) |  |  |  |  |  |  |  |
| 0–4 | 385 | 411 | 459 | 512 | 572 | 639 | 718 |
| 5–9 | 297 | 324 | 349 | 392 | 441 | 496 | 559 |
| 10–14 | 255 | 283 | 309 | 334 | 375 | 423 | 476 |
| 15–19 | 227 | 247 | 275 | 301 | 325 | 365 | 413 |
| 20–24 | 196 | 218 | 238 | 264 | 290 | 313 | 353 |
| 25–29 | 170 | 187 | 207 | 227 | 253 | 276 | 300 |
| 30–34 | 145 | 159 | 175 | 196 | 215 | 243 | 263 |
| 35–39 | 123 | 135 | 148 | 164 | 184 | 203 | 230 |
| 40–44 | 103 | 114 | 125 | 138 | 153 | 173 | 191 |
| 45–49 | 86 | 94 | 104 | 114 | 127 | 142 | 160 |
| 50–54 | 71 | 76 | 83 | 93 | 103 | 114 | 128 |
| 55–59 | 53 | 60 | 65 | 72 | 80 | 89 | 100 |
| 60–64 | 40 | 42 | 49 | 53 | 60 | 67 | 75 |
| 65–69 | 24 | 30 | 33 | 38 | 42 | 47 | 54 |
| 70+ | 26 | 32 | 35 | 41 | 45 | 51 | 58 |
| Total | 2,201 | 2,412 | 2,654 | 2,939 | 3,265 | 3,641 | 4,078 |

|  | Both Sexes (total only) | | | | | | |
|---|---|---|---|---|---|---|---|
| All ages | 1960 | 1965 | 1970 | 1975 | 1980 | 1985 | 1990 |
|  | 4,372 | 4,807 | 5,308 | 5,896 | 6,568 | 7,347 | 8,247 |

TABLE 37.22 (*contd.*)

(b) High Assumption (assuming progressive eradication of measles after 1970)

| | | | Males | | | | |
|---|---|---|---|---|---|---|---|
| | 1960 | 1965 | 1970 | 1975 | 1980 | 1985 | 1990 |
| Births (preceding 5 years) | | 583 | 645 | 712 | 788 | 883 | 1,008 |
| Age groups (years) | | | | | | | |
| 0–4 | 371 | 429 | 477 | 575 | 641 | 725 | 835 |
| 5–9 | 284 | 312 | 364 | 438 | 531 | 594 | 674 |
| 10–14 | 250 | 269 | 298 | 354 | 426 | 518 | 579 |
| 15–19 | 220 | 242 | 261 | 290 | 346 | 417 | 506 |
| 20–24 | 193 | 210 | 232 | 252 | 280 | 334 | 403 |
| 25–29 | 169 | 184 | 200 | 221 | 241 | 266 | 321 |
| 30–34 | 143 | 159 | 173 | 189 | 210 | 231 | 254 |
| 35–39 | 124 | 134 | 148 | 162 | 178 | 198 | 219 |
| 40–44 | 104 | 114 | 124 | 138 | 151 | 167 | 186 |
| 45–49 | 85 | 95 | 104 | 114 | 127 | 139 | 154 |
| 50–54 | 72 | 75 | 84 | 93 | 102 | 114 | 126 |
| 55–59 | 54 | 61 | 64 | 72 | 81 | 89 | 100 |
| 60–64 | 39 | 44 | 50 | 52 | 60 | 68 | 75 |
| 65–69 | 28 | 30 | 34 | 39 | 41 | 48 | 54 |
| 70+ | 35 | 37 | 41 | 47 | 50 | 58 | 66 |
| Totals | 2,171 | 2,395 | 2,654 | 3,036 | 3,465 | 3,966 | 4,552 |

| | | | Females | | | | |
|---|---|---|---|---|---|---|---|
| | 1960 | 1965 | 1970 | 1975 | 1980 | 1985 | 1990 |
| Births (preceding 5 years) | | 563 | 620 | 684 | 757 | 848 | 968 |
| Age groups (years) | | | | | | | |
| 0–4 | 385 | 411 | 459 | 553 | 616 | 696 | 802 |
| 5–9 | 297 | 324 | 349 | 422 | 510 | 570 | 647 |
| 10–14 | 255 | 283 | 309 | 340 | 410 | 497 | 556 |
| 15–19 | 227 | 247 | 275 | 301 | 332 | 402 | 487 |
| 20–24 | 196 | 218 | 238 | 264 | 290 | 321 | 388 |
| 25–29 | 170 | 187 | 207 | 227 | 253 | 276 | 307 |
| 30–34 | 145 | 159 | 175 | 196 | 215 | 243 | 263 |
| 35–39 | 123 | 135 | 148 | 164 | 184 | 203 | 230 |
| 40–44 | 103 | 114 | 125 | 138 | 153 | 173 | 191 |
| 45–49 | 86 | 94 | 104 | 114 | 127 | 142 | 160 |
| 50–54 | 71 | 76 | 83 | 93 | 103 | 114 | 128 |
| 55–59 | 53 | 60 | 65 | 72 | 80 | 89 | 100 |
| 60–64 | 40 | 42 | 49 | 53 | 60 | 67 | 75 |
| 65–69 | 24 | 30 | 33 | 38 | 42 | 47 | 54 |
| 70+ | 26 | 32 | 35 | 41 | 45 | 51 | 58 |
| Total | 2,201 | 2,412 | 2,654 | 3,016 | 3,420 | 3,891 | 4,446 |

Both Sexes (totals only)

| | 1960 | 1965 | 1970 | 1975 | 1980 | 1985 | 1990 |
|---|---|---|---|---|---|---|---|
| All ages | 4,372 | 4,807 | 5,308 | 6,052 | 6,885 | 7,857 | 8,998 |

*Mortality*. The assumption on which mortality trends are based is that the mortality level in 1990 in rural areas will be the same as that in 1960 in the secondary urban centers. This is based on the fact that there were available in secondary urban centers health facilities which were not available to the great majority of the rural population living outside these centers. As no vaccination campaign, with the single exception of that against measles, has so far attacked the major causes of death, it seems probable that the decline in mortality between 1960 and 1990 will be the product of a slow improvement in health conditions and will not involve rapid changes in patterns of mortality. The major emphases so far in public health campaigns have been on yellow fever, smallpox, and similar diseases, which, under normal circumstances, make up a large proportion of the total number of deaths only during the increasingly rare epidemic years.

However, the discussion above of mortality did suggest the possibility of a steeper decline in the death rates if, and when, a three-year cycle of measles vaccination is introduced. In Table 37.22(b) projections which take this factor into account are presented.

*Fertility*. In view of the lack of change between the 1960 and 1969 surveys, except apparently for the widening of few minor differentials, it is unlikely that fertility will change appreciably for the next five to seven years at least. It must also be recalled that there is at present no policy for the limitation of births or the introduction of family planning in Upper Volta, while abortion is illegal. Laws relating to abortion and family planning follow the old French law (now repealed in France), but may be largely irrelevant because there is an extremely limited demand for family planning. Throughout these projections then, fertility rates have been held constant at the 1960 level.

*Migration*. The population used for the projections is the *de jure* population (i.e., it includes both the residents present and those temporarily absent). In 1960, the proportion absent was 11.8 percent among men and 6.1 percent among women, of whom nearly half were in foreign countries at the time of the survey. A proportion of those absent will never return to Upper Volta, but the exact number is actually impossible to determine. Moreover, if one looks at the data for the Abidjan railway, which are the only data giving any indication of yearly change, there are annual fluctuations in the rate of migration, and these appear, in fact, to coincide with the volume of the harvest in Upper Volta. Thus in 1965, there were 20,000 net persons lost to Upper Volta. This loss was only 15,000 in 1966, 3,000 in 1967, but 42,000 in 1968. The low net loss from 1966–1967 coincides with a record harvest. There is also considerable uncertainty about the future, because of the migration policies of both Ivory Coast and Upper Volta, which could change very rapidly, and indeed have done so recently. Because of all these problems and because the data are so limited, it has been decided to ignore migration in the projections presented.

METHOD OF CALCULATION. In keeping with the assumptions given above, quinquennial age groups have been projected using life tables to determine survivorship. Births have been calculated by the application of general fertility rates to all women aged 15–49.

## CONCLUSION

There is every likelihood of rapid population growth in the years immediately ahead. The current rate of population growth is 2.0 percent per annum, and there is every chance that the population will at least double between 1960 and 1990. The multiplication of population and its impact will be even more marked in urban centers. Ultimately, this process must give rise to concern about the fertility component of the growth rate, but, for the moment, migration still remains the crucial element of growth. This factor has been exacerbated by the recent changes of laws in Ivory Coast and Ghana.

# Index

Abortion, 14, 59, 64, 78, 82–83, 86–90 *passim; see also under countries, subhead* Family planning
Abstinence, 51–52, 59–60, 214; 217 *(table); see also under countries, subhead* Family planning
Accidents: as cause of death, 109–10
Acsadi, György, 65, 97
Addo, Nelson O., v, 137, 149, 360, 367–424
Adelman, Irma, 304
*Afrique Noire, Madagascar, Comores, Démographie Comparée,* 30
Age: distribution, 4; census errors, 5–8, 29–30, 31–32; of pregnancy, 94; of death, 114 *(table);* economic implications in distribution, 151–52; migrants, 158 *(table); see also under countries, subhead* Population
Agriculture: production, mortality and, 115–16; population and, 139–45; employment and unemployment in, 146–48; *see also under countries*
Allan, William, 143
Alldridge, Thomas J., 463
Ardener, E., 51, 341
Argentina, 341
Australia, 341, 416, 459, 538
Austria, 341

Bakare, C. G. M., 231
Belgium, 538
Benjamin, Eugene, v. 427–54
Berlin Conference (1884), 155
Bernus, Suzanne, 680
Birth control, *see under* Family planning, *subhead* Contraceptives, use of
Birth rate, 4, 5, 13, 14, 17–19 *(table),* 35–36, 166 *(table),* 194–97; estimates , 46–47; *see also* Family planning; Fertility
Blacker, J. G. C., 308, 309, 341, 526
Blake, J., 647
Blanc, R., 341
Blayo, Yves, 100, 102, 106, 618
Boateng, E. A., 140
Bohannon, Laura and Paul, 198, 240
Bolivia, 341
Boserup, E., 141
Bott, E., 474
Bouquet, Christian, v, 23, 565–81
Bourgeois-Pichat method, 107
Boute, Joseph M., v, 12, 592–609
Brass, William, 5, 7, 8, 33–35, 38–39, 46, 101–6 *passim,* 268, 269, 271, 494, 497, 613, 618–19, 686, 687, 740, 742
Brazil, 341
Brinton, Crane, 193
Buntjer, B. J., 326
Burgess, E. W., 282
Burundi, 44, 86 *(table),* 308

Busia, K. A., 363

Caldwell, John C., v, 3–28, 36, 53–55 *passim,* 58–97, 136, 151, 166, 174, 179, 215–20 *passim,* 302, 308, 309, 340, 341, 343, 352, 353, 356, 359, 360, 493–526
Callaway, A., 167
Cameroon, 543–64; fertility, 12, 32 *(table),* 37, 341, 548, 552–56; migration, 21, 558–60; marriage, 48, 51, 551–52, age at, 11, 511; agriculture, 142, 561–62; employment, 147; public health expenditures, 178 *(table);* subdivisions, 545–46 *(map);* economy, 546; religion, 546–48 *passim,* 564; education, 550–51; abortion, 556; contraceptives, use of, 556
——mortality, 10, 100–2 *passim,* 106, 108, 115, 548, 556–58; infant, 101–3 *passim,* 557–58; cause of death, 109
——population, 86 *(table),* 138, 144, 548–52; censuses, 7, 562–63; policy, 12, 173, 562–63; statistical sources, 56, 543–44; ethnic groups, 543, 546–47, 550–51, 556–57, 563–64; estimates, 543, 547 *(table);* surveys, 544, 563; growth, 544–46, 548, 552–56, 560–62, rates, 546–47; rural-urban, 547–48, 550, 561–62; density, 548–49 *(map);* distribution, 549–50; life expectancy, 558
Canada, 538
Cantrelle, Pierre, v, 7, 9, 98–118, 136, 737
Cassava, *see* Manioc
Catholics, 26, 75, 81, 204, 213, 436, 444, 447, 616, 628, 640, 666, 722
Censuses, 101; value of data, 5–7; *see also under countries, subhead* Population
Central African Republic: fertility, 29, 32 *(table),* 37, 341, estimates, 41, 42 *(table),* 4; rural-urban, 53 *(table)* survey, 31; statistical sources, 56; population, 86 *(table);* mortality, 101, 102, infant, 102; employment, 148; public health expenditures, 178
Ceylon, 341, 359
Chad, 565–91; economic development, 15, 568–73; fertility, 23, 24, 576–78, urban-rural, 11, 53 *(table),* estimates, 41, 42 *(table);* mortality, 101, 102, 577, 578, cause of death, 109; migration, 154, 577, *(table),* 579–80, 581; public health expenditures, 178 *(table);* family allowances, 181; environment, 565–66; history, 567–68; agriculture, 568–70; herding, 570–71; fisheries, 571; mining, 571; industrialization, 571–72; communications, 572; education, 573; religion, 573, 585, 589; government, 573–74; social change, 573–75; urbanization, 574, 584; marriage, 577–78; pronatalism, 588–91; child labor, 589–90
——family planning, 70 *(table),* 72 *(table),* 87, 586–89; family size, 70, 72 *(table),* 81, 583–86; contraceptives, use of, 587–88

755

**John C. Caldwell** is in the Department of Demography at the Australian National University. **Nelson O. Addo** is in the Population Dynamics Programme and **Samuel K. Gaisie** is in the United Nations Regional Institute for Population Studies at the University of Ghana. **Adenola A. Igun** is in the Institute of Population and Manpower Studies and **P. O. Olusanya** is in the Department of Sociology and Anthropology at the University of Ife.